The Law of Suretyship

SECOND EDITION

Edward G. Gallagher, *Editor*

TORT AND INSURANCE PRACTICE
AMERICAN BAR ASSOCIATION

Defending Liberty
Pursuing Justice

Cover design by Jim Colao.

Printed in the United States of America.

04 03 02 01 00 5 4 3 2 1

Library of Congress Cataloging-in-Publication Data

The law of suretyship / Edward G. Gallagher, editor.
p. cm.
Includes bibliographical references.
ISBN 1-57073-780-0
1. Suretyship and guaranty—United States. I. Gallagher, Edward G. (Edward Graham)
II. American Bar Association. Tort and Insurance Practice Section.

KF1223 .L39 2000 00-029305
346.7307'4--dc21

Discounts are available for books ordered in bulk. Special consideration is given to state bars, CLE programs, and other bar-related organizations. Inquire at Publications Planning & Marketing, American Bar Association, 750 North Lake Shore Drive, Chicago, Illinois 606ll.

www.abanet.org/abapubs

Preface

In 1992, the Law of Suretyship project was conceived to meet two needs of the surety industry. The first was for a modern legal treatise on suretyship and the second for a program designed to train younger or less experienced surety claims attorneys and others working on surety claims. The result was the first edition of *The Law of Suretyship*, published by the American Bar Association in 1993, which has sold over 1500 copies and become a standard reference in the industry. The Law of Suretyship program was presented four times, in New York, Los Angeles, Chicago and Atlanta, during 1993 to 1995, and had over 500 attendees.

Since 1995, the American Bar Association Tort and Insurance Practice Section's Fidelity and Surety Law Committee (FSLC) has presented a series of more sophisticated programs aimed at experienced surety attorneys, but there has been no update of the basic text for younger people. The surety industry has changed in many ways with new products and obligations, and many new people have started to work for surety companies and the law firms and consultants who support them.

This Second Edition of *The Law of Suretyship* has been substantially revised. It contains expanded discussions of commercial surety obligations and new topics of importance to the industry as a whole as well as complete updates of Chapters on contract bonds, indemnity rights, subrogation and bankruptcy. Fifteen of the topics or authors are new to the Second Edition, and all of us who worked on it believe that the Second Edition will be useful to anyone working in the surety industry including underwriters and producers as well as claims personnel, lawyers and consultants.

I want to thank the authors who gave generously of their time and talents to make this project a success. This and other books on fidelity and surety law topics published by the American Bar Association are written without any monetary return to the authors. Nevertheless, they are collectively the best source of secondary authority on fidelity and surety law and a tribute to the hard work and dedication of fidelity and surety professionals.

Edward G. Gallagher
Editor-in-Chief
Vienna, Virginia
January, 2000

Contributors

Mary Jeanne Anderson • Senior Vice President and Assistant Secretary of the Fidelity and Deposit Company of Maryland and Colonial American Casualty and Surety Company. She is a 22-year veteran of F&D and has been involved in underwriting contract surety risks at the Home Office level since 1977. She received her Bachelor of Arts, *magna cum laude*, from Providence College (1976) and her Juris Doctor degree, *with honors*, from the University of Maryland School of Law (1982) and was admitted to the Maryland Bar in 1982.

George J. Bachrach • Partner in the Baltimore, Maryland and Washington, D.C. law firm of Whiteford, Taylor & Preston, LLP, practicing primarily in the areas of surety law and bankruptcy. He received his Bachelor of Arts degree, *cum laude*, from Harvard University in 1971 and his Juris Doctor degree from Georgetown University Law Center in 1974. He is Chair-Elect-Elect of the ABA/TIPS Fidelity and Surety Law Committee.

John V. Burch • Partner in the Atlanta, Georgia law firm of Bovis, Kyle & Burch, LLC, practicing primarily in the areas of fidelity and surety law and construction litigation. He received his Bachelor of Arts degree from the University of Georgia in 1965 and his Juris Doctor degree from the University of Georgia in 1967 (Phi Delta Phi). He was a member of the Editorial Board of the Georgia Law Review from 1966-67.

Maureen D. Carman • Vice President and General Counsel for Cumberland Surety Insurance Company, Inc., and in prior years had served as a managing attorney for the Kentucky Natural Resources and Environmental Protection Cabinet, as well as a private practitioner. She is a 1974 graduate of the University of Kentucky, receiving a Bachelor of Arts degree with Distinction in the Honors Program and a Juris Doctor degree in 1979.

James A. Carpenter • Vice President - Claims Division with NAS Surety Group/Washington International Insurance Company. Mr. Carpenter graduated from Illinois State University in 1974, received his Juris Doctor degree from Loyola University School of Law in Chicago in 1977, and is licensed to practice law in the State of Illinois.

Thomas J. Casamassima • Senior Partner in the firm of Anderson, McPharlin & Conners, LLP. Before joining Anderson, McPharlin & Conners, he was Associate General Counsel for the California State University and College system. He is a graduate of the UCLA School of Law.

Allen N. David • Partner in the Boston law firm of Peabody & Arnold, Boston, Massachusetts. He specializes in civil litigation, focusing on the defense of professional liability and surety and fidelity matters. Mr. David received his Bachelor of Arts degree from the University of Massachusetts and his Juris Doctor degree from Boston University of Law.

M. Michael Egan • Partner at the law firm of Gleaton, Persons, Egan & Jones in Atlanta, Georgia. He received his B.A. and an M.A. from Duke University. He graduated *cum laude* from the University of Georgia Law School, where he was Notes Editor on the Georgia Law Review. Thereafter, he clerked for Honorable Wilbur D. Owens, Jr. of the United States District Court for the Middle District of Georgia.

Edward G. Gallagher • General Counsel of The Surety Association of America and practices law in Washington, D.C., Virginia and Maryland as a Shareholder in the Vienna, Virginia office of Wickwire Gavin, P.C. He is a graduate of Williams College and The George Washington University National Law Center. He is a past Chair of the ABA/TIPS Fidelity and Surety Law Committee.

L. Franklin Elmore • Shareholder in the firm of Ogletree, Deakins, Nash, Smoak & Stewart, P.C. in Greenville, South Carolina. He is a graduate of Francis Marion College and the received his Juris Doctor degree from the University of South Carolina in 1976.

Julia Blackwell Gelinas • Partner in the Indianapolis, Indiana law firm of Locke, Reynolds LLP. She graduated from St. Mary's College at Notre Dame, Indiana, and received her Juris Doctor degree from Indiana University Law School at Indianapolis. She is a Vice-Chair of the ABA/TIPS Fidelity & Surety Law Committee.

Patrick Q. Hustead • Member of The Hustead Law Firm, Denver, Colorado. He received his Bachelor of Science degree from the University of Colorado, and his D.E. degree from the University of Paris at the Sorbonne. He received his Juris Doctor degree from Boston College in 1987.

Kelly Allbritton Katzman • Partner in the Dallas, Texas law firm of Strasburger & Price, L.L.P. She received her Bachelor of Arts degree from the University of Texas, and her Juris Doctor degree from the Southern Methodist University.

Bruce C. King • Shareholder in the law firm of Carlton, Fields, Ward, Emmanuel, Smith & Cutler in Miami, Florida. He received his Bachelor of Arts degree from Allegheny College and his Juris Doctor degree from the University of Pittsburgh.

Marilyn Klinger • Partner in the Los Angeles, California office of Sedgwick, Detert, Moran & Arnold. She graduated with a B.S. degree from the University of Santa Clara, *cum laude*, and a Juris Doctor degree from the University of California, Hastings College of Law, Order of the Coif. She is a Vice-Chair of the ABA/TIPS Fidelity & Surety Law Committee.

James A. Knox, Jr. • Partner in the Chicago, Illinois law firm of Tressler, Soderstrom, Maloney & Priess. He graduated with a B.A. from Southern Methodist University, and received his Juris Doctor degree from the University of Texas School of Law.

L. Jay Labe • Member of Tilly & Graves, P.C., Denver, Colorado. He received his Bachelor of Arts and Juris Doctor degrees from the University of Colorado.

Kevin L. Lybeck • Senior Vice President and Secretary of Contractors Bonding and Insurance Company in Seattle, Washington. He received his Bachelor of Arts degree, with honors, from Montana State University, and received his Juris Doctor degree, *cum laude*, from Gonzaga University School of Law. He currently serves as a Vice-Chair of the ABA/TIPS Fidelity & Surety Law Committee.

Jay M. Mann • A founding Partner in the Phoenix law firm of Dyer, Mann, Berens & Wisner, LLP. He received his Bachelor of Arts degree from the University of Illinois in 1972, and his Juris Doctor degree from Loyola University (Chicago) School of Law in 1975. He is a Vice-Chair of the ABA/TIPS Fidelity & Surety Law Committee.

Theodore G. Martinez • Assistant Vice President, Commercial Surety in the home office of Reliance Surety Company. He holds a B.S. degree from Rochester Institute of Technology. Prior to joining Reliance Surety Company, he held various field management positions at SAFECO and Continental Surety.

Martha L. Perkins • Senior Counsel in charge of all fidelity and surety matters with the American Insurance Association in Washington, D.C. She joined the American Insurance Association in 1994. She received her Juris Doctor degree, with honors, from Mississippi College School of Law, where she was Editor-in-chief of the Law Review. She formerly practiced law with a Jackson, Mississippi, firm, specializing in fidelity, surety and construction litigation. Ms. Perkins is President of the Fidelity Law Association and an associate editor of the *Tort & Insurance Law Journal*.

Chad L. Schexnayder • Partner in the Phoenix, Arizona law firm of Jennings, Haug & Cunningham, LLP. He graduated with a Bachelor of Arts degree from Washington University in St. Louis, and received his Juris Doctor degree from Arizona State University. He is a Vice Chair of the ABA/TIPS Fidelity & Surety Law Committee.

Lynn M. Schubert • President of The Surety Association of America. She received her B.S. degree in Business Administration, *magna cum laude*, from East Carolina University and her Juris Doctor degree from the University of Notre Dame Law School. She is a past member of the Council of the American Bar Association Tort and Insurance Practice Section and a past chair of its Fidelity and Surety Law Committee.

Armen Shahinian • Member of the Roseland, New Jersey, firm of Wolff & Samson, P.A. He holds a Bachelor of Arts degree from Brown University (1971) and his Juris Doctor degree from New York University School of Law (1974). He is Chair-Elect of the ABA/TIPS Fidelity and Surety Law Committee.

H. Bruce Shreves • Partner in the New Orleans, Louisiana, law firm of Simon, Peragine, Smith & Redfearn, L.L.P. He received his Juris Doctor degree from Georgetown Law School. He is Chair of the ABA/TIPS Fidelity and Surety Law Committee.

Dean B. Thomson • Shareholder in the firm of Fabyanske, Westra & Hart, P.A., in Minneapolis, Minnesota. He holds a Bachelor of Arts degree from Carlton College and a Juris Doctor, *cum laude*, from the University of Minnesota. Mr. Thomson serves on the Board of Directors of the Minnesota Associated General Contractors.

David C. Veis • Member of Robins, Kaplan, Miller & Ciresi, L.L.P. in Los Angeles, California. He received his Bachelor of Arts degree from the University of California at Los Angeles, his M.A.

from the University of Southern California and his Juris Doctor degree from Southwestern University.

William H. Woods ● Partner in the Columbus, Ohio, law firm of McNamara and McNamara. He is a graduate of Ohio State University, B.S. 1968 and J.D. 1973. Mr. Woods serves as the Historian/Recorder of the ABA/TIPS Fidelity and Surety Law Committee.

TABLE OF CONTENTS

Chapter 1 - Introduction 1
Edward G. Gallagher

Chapter 2 - Historical Development of Suretyship From Prehistoric Custom to a Century's Experience with the Compensated Corporate Surety 3
William H. Woods

Chapter 3 - Why Obligees Buy Bonds 41
Lynn M. Schubert

Chapter 4 - How Contract Surety Bonds Are Underwritten 49
Stewart R. Duke and Mary Jeanne Anderson

Chapter 5 - Bid Bonds 63
Allen N. David

Chapter 6 - Contract Performance Bonds 81
Marilyn Klinger, James P. Dwik and Kevin L. Lybeck

Chapter 7 - Discharge of the Performance Bond Surety 119
M. Michael Egan and Marla Eastwood

Chapter 8 - Purpose of the Payment Bond and Who and What is Covered 147
Kelly Allbritton Katzman

Chapter 9 - Procedural Requirements 179
Julia Blackwell Gelinas

Chapter 10 - Fiduciary Bonds 191
James A. Knox, Jr.

Chapter 11 - Judicial Bonds 203
L. Franklin Elmore and Mason A. Goldsmith, Jr.

Chapter 12 - Subdivision Bonds 211
David C. Veis, Laura P. Nash and Edward D. Lodgen

Chapter 13 - Customs Bond Claims 225
Laura J. Maurer and James A. Carpenter

Chapter 14 - License and Permit Bonds 263
Patrick Q. Hustead and Duane E. Bolin

Chapter 15 - Workers' Compensation Self-Insurance Bonds 269
Theodore G. Martinez

Chapter 16 - Reclamation Bonds 279
Maureen D. Carman

Chapter 17 - Bail Bonds 289
L. Jay Labe

Chapter 18 - Financial Guaranty 303
Martha L. Perkins

Chapter 19 - Medicare and Medicaid Bonds 313
Edward G. Gallagher

Chapter 20 - Bankruptcy and the Surety 317
Chad L. Schexnayder

Chapter 21 - Arbitration of Performance Bond Disputes 375
H. Bruce Shreves and Kevin L. Lybeck

Chapter 22 - Extra-Contractual Damages 393
Thomas J. Casamassima, Mark E. Aronson and Frank E. Marchetti

Chapter 23 - The Surety's Subrogation Rights 419
George J. Bachrach and John V. Burch

Chapter 24 - Exoneration and Quia Timet 455
Jay M. Mann

Chapter 25 - The General Agreement of Indemnity 487
Armen Shahinian

Chapter 26 - The Surety's Right to Indemnity (Indemnitor's Defenses and Counterclaims) 527
Bruce C. King

Chapter 27 - Contractor Default Insurance and Directed Suretyship 539
Lynn M. Schubert, Dean B. Thomson and Edward G. Gallagher

1

Introduction

Edward G. Gallagher

A surety is traditionally defined as someone who contracts to answer for the debt or default of another.[1] The principal is the primary obligor, the obligee is the person to whom the principal and surety owe a duty, and the surety is the secondary obligor.[2] Under the statute of frauds, a suretyship contact must be in writing.[3]

Compensated sureties are almost invariably[4] insurance companies, and by statute in most states sureties are regulated by the insurance commissioner. It is important to understand, however, that surety is a unique type of insurance governed in many ways by very different principles. Several chapters in this book will address the differences between suretyship and other types of insurance. In brief, however, suretyship is a financial guarantee under which the surety suffers a loss only if the principal fails to perform its obligation and is financially unable to reimburse the surety. Surety underwriting is based on the financial and technical capability of the principal. The surety does not anticipate a loss, and if there is any appreciable likelihood of a default, the surety will not write the bond. The surety provides the obligee with prequalification of possible bidders and assurance that the project will be completed for the contract price.

An insurer, on the other hand, spreads the risk of fortuitous losses over the group exposed to them. The insurer expects that a certain percentage of its insureds will suffer a loss during the policy period and sets its premiums accordingly. If a covered loss is suffered, the insurer, in effect, has the primary obligation to pay and has no recourse against the insured. The insured has exchanged the possibility of a loss for the certainty of a, presumably smaller, "loss" (*i.e.*, the premium). The insurer pays for losses instead of avoiding them through prequalification, financing or other techniques available to a surety.

At one time, fidelity bonds were a type of suretyship in which the surety knew or investigated the proposed principal and satisfied itself of his or her honesty before writing the bond. Modern fidelity bonds, however, are really insurance against loss through certain types of dishonesty. The premiums are actuarially based on the insured's type of business, financial performance, internal controls and number of employees. The insurer almost never evaluates the integrity of the insured's individual employees. This book, therefore, does not include fidelity bonds

---

1. Stearns, *The Law of Suretyship*, § 1.1 (5th ed. W.H. Anderson Co., 1951); 74 *Am. Jur.* 2d *Suretyship* § 1.

2. 74 *Am. Jur.* 2d *Suretyship* § 1.

3. The first comprehensive statute of frauds was enacted in England in 1676 (29 Car. II § 4) and provided that no action could be brought on a promise to answer for the debt, default or miscarriage of another unless the promise or some memorandum thereof was in writing.

4. At one time, defaults by Individual Sureties were a significant problem for United States contracting agencies and, particularly, for unsuspecting subcontractors and suppliers who assumed they were protected by a solvent, Miller Act surety. In 1989 the applicable regulations were amended to make an individual surety provide a security interest in certain types of assets to guarantee performance of his or her bond obligations. See 48 C.F. R. § 28.203. Holding prospective individual sureties to financial standards has largely eliminated the problem.

which have, in any event, been extensively discussed in other American Bar Association publications.[5]

In order to understand the unique position of the surety and its obligations and rights, one must know the historical background and development of the law of suretyship. It is not enough to know a rule or result in a particular case if one does not understand why the case was decided as it was. Sureties, like virtually all other businesses, are faced with a constantly changing legal environment. In order to identify the proper response to each new issue, the surety or its attorneys and advisors must understand the past and reason from it. This book describes the law applicable to modern corporate sureties and the reasoning behind the law.

5. See, for example, Clore, ed. *Financial Institution Bonds*, Second Edition (American Bar Association, 1999); Keeley and Sukel, ed. *Handling Fidelity Bond Claims*, (American Bar Association, 1999); and Schroeder, ed. *Commercial Crime Policy* (American Bar Association, 1997).

2

Historical Development Of Suretyship From Prehistoric Custom To A Century's Experience With The Compensated Corporate Surety

William H. Woods

Introduction

A review of the development of the law that governs the contemporary corporate contract surety is, in fact, a review of the legal history of commercial transactions. Suretyship, in a generic sense, originated in prehistoric times as a three party arrangement intended to provide personal security for the payment of a debt or the performance of an obligation. Legal historians have traced the origins of the law of formal contracts, as well as the law of collateral security to these prehistoric three party arrangements that we now call suretyship.

The term "surety" derives from the Middle English and Old French term "seurte." The term "seurte" was, in turn, derived from the Latin term "securitas," which is also the root of the term "security." *Webster's New Universal Unabridged Dictionary* (2 ed. 1979) includes the following definitions of "security":

> 5. something given as a pledge of repayment, fulfillment of a promise, etc.; a guarantee.
> 6. a person who agrees to make good the failure of another to pay, perform a duty, etc.; surety.

Baldwin's Century Edition of *Bouvier's Law Dictionary* (1948) defines "surety" as: "A person who binds himself for the payment of a sum of money, or for the performance of something else, for another."

Suretyship is the oldest of the three principal forms of collateral security. The *Restatement of the Law of Security* states:

> *Scope Note:* Security is an interest in chattels, in land, or in the obligation of a third party. A security interest must be the result of a transaction that gives recourse against a particular chattel or land or against a third party on an obligation. The purpose of security is generally to secure the repayment of money, but it may also secure the performance of any duty.
> The obligation of a third party who acts as a surety is classified in this Restatement within the general category of Security. This classification is also found in the German and Austrian Codes. While not found specifically in the French Code, this classification is also often adopted by French commentators on the French Code.[1]

1. *Restatement of the Law of Security* at 1-2 (1941).

From ancient customs the law governing the American surety evolved in the Roman Codes, the reported decisions of the English Courts of Common Law and Equity and the commercial customs and practices that became known as the Law Merchant of London. The first contract surety bond written by a corporation in the United States was issued in 1887, approximately midway between the American Revolution that formally separated the law of this country from the law of England and the present.[2] The industrial, transportation and communications revolutions were underway and well established legal principles were being adapted to increasingly complex commercial transactions.

Consequently, the legal principles that govern today's compensated corporate surety began their evolution in the reported decisions of our courts at a time when: the traditionally separate courts of common law and equity were being combined into a single court; corporations were replacing proprietorships and partnerships as the predominate form of business entity; and administrative agencies were first being created by state legislatures as a means of regulating the growing economic power of railroad and insurance companies.

I. *Ancient Suretyship*

With this general outline of the development of the law of corporate suretyship in mind let us turn to the ancient origins of the contract surety bond. The customs of prehistoric civilization developed over thousands of years before they were recorded, therefore little is known of their origin.[3] The first known record of suretyship is a tablet from the Library of Sargon I, King of Accad and Sumer (*circa* 2750 B.C.). The tablet refers to an agreement between a farmer, who was entering the king's army, and a second farmer, who agreed to properly cultivate the soldier's farm and return half the produce to the soldier. The tablet states that a merchant from the city of Accad guaranteed the performance of the lessee.[4] The identification of the surety as a merchant from a nearby city suggests the inference that this first record describes suretyship for profit.

The Surety was apparently a well established part of ancient commerce, but surviving literature is replete with strong warnings against the dangers inherent in answering for the debts of another. C. W. Crist, Jr.'s 1939 first edition of *Corporate Suretyship* states:

---

2. Morgan, *The History and Economics of Suretyship*, 13 Cornell L. Q. 487, 492-493 (1927). The introduction dates of the six classes of corporate surety bonds were: 1) Fidelity (1865); 2) Executors, Administrators and Other Fiduciaries (pre-1879); 3) Court bonds, i.e. appeal, replevin, attachment (1881); 4) Contract (1887); 5) License and Permit (1890); and 6) Public Officials (1894).

3. The history of suretyship extends far longer than the first stone tablet found in the ruins of the library of Sargon I.

> The time that elapsed between the empire of Sargon I and the conquest of Babylon by Alexander the Great was as long, be it noted, at the least estimate, as the time from Alexander the Great to the present day. And before the time of Sargon, men had been settled in the Sumerian land, living in towns, worshipping in temples, following an orderly Neolithic agricultural life in an organized community for at least as long again. ...

One of the most difficult things for both the writer and student of History is to sustain the sense of these time-intervals and prevent the ages becoming shortened by the perspective in his imagination. Half the duration of human civilization and the keys to all its chief institutions are to be found *before* Sargon I. Wells, *The Outline of History*, 141 (1922).

4. Morgan, *The History and Economics of Suretyship*, 12 Cornell L. Q. 153 (1926). [For the curious: The Akkadians of Sargon I conquered the Sumerians. Sargon I's empire endured for two hundred years and covered the area from the Persian Gulf to the Mediterranean.]

> Suffice it to say that almost every reference now extant to early suretyship sounds also a note of warning to those who might, however reluctantly, be willing to act as surety for a friend. Thus from early Greece comes that sound bit of philosophical advice found inscribed on a tablet in the Delphian Temple, and attributed to Thales, the Greek sage and philosopher, that "suretyship is the precursor of ruin." Many similar warnings may be found in the Bible. Some nine centuries before the Christian Era, King Solomon, ... warned the citizenry of Israel, "My son, if thou be surety for thy friend, if thou hast stricken thy hand with a stranger, thou art ensnared with the words of thy mouth, thou art taken with the words of thy mouth." [Prov. 6:1-2][5] Further, "He that is surety for a stranger [the Hebrew word for another] shall smart for it; and he that hateth suretyship is sure." [Prov. 11: 15] Again, "A man void of understanding striketh hands and becometh surety in the presence of his friend." [Prov. 17: 18] Then follows a timely warning: "Take his garment that is surety for a stranger." [Prov. 20: 16] This is probably the earliest reference to the modern expression of "losing one's shirt" if one assumes a certain risk. Ecclesiasticus paints an even blacker picture: "Suretyship hath undone many of good estate, and shaken them as a wave of the sea; mighty men hath it driven from their homes, so that they had to wander in strange lands." [Eccles. (Wisdom of Sirach) 29: 18][6]

For those of us who regularly represent corporate sureties, it often seems that contemporary courts strive mightily to make these ancient warnings a reality for our clients. However, the history of the law of suretyship is the history of a search for the means of making this manifestly risky, but essential, form of security readily available in commercial transactions. The goal is to strike a balance that will provide the intended security without making the surety's risk so great that it is economically prohibitive.

The conclusion of William H. Lloyd's excellent 1916 law review article, *The Surety*, points out that the development of the compensated corporate surety is merely the latest stage in the continuing evolution of a system of security that has been essential to the expansion of commerce throughout history. Mr. Lloyd wrote:

> From dungeon of the kinsman hostage to the well-furnished office of the modern bonding company may appear too long and circuitous an excursion to be condensed into so brief a narrative; perhaps, to the romantically minded it may seem to result in an anti-climax. But the story has a unity of its own with a conclusion of general application, were epilogues the fashion. Here is displayed one small phase of the struggle for cooperation that has characterized human progress. For the liability that falls so heavily on the individual the ancient corrective is sacrifice, the foundation of generous instincts which have permanently influenced ideas of propriety, but amount to no more than a shifting of the burden from one individual to another. The joint pledge of faith marks an advance; taken in concert by the co-promisors, there is identity of risk, but it is coupled with a moral obligation, that in time becomes a legal duty, to equalize the loss or place it where it belongs. Larger enterprises call for greater alliances of adventurers and specialization in the calculation of the hazards; security is obtained through association; the *premium payer* is now the ultimate surety. As the knowledge acquired through these operations becomes more scientific and their management increasingly efficient, group indemnity on a more extended scale may be anticipated. The same tendency is reflected in other branches of the law. Such a result must lead to a revision of much that now seems of importance in the law of suretyship and guaranty, but, happily there will be no dearth of new

5. This may be the origin of the often applied doctrine of *contra proferentum* that will be mentioned later in this Chapter. For an in depth discussion of the doctrine and its history *see* Dingus & Haley, *The Doctrine of Contra Proferentum in Bankers Blanket Bond Litigation*, X Forum 75-80 (1974).

6. C. W. Crist, *Corporate Suretyship* 1-2 (2d ed. 1950).

problems. "The force which is evolving throughout the organized world is a limited force, which is always seeking to transcend itself and always remains inadequate to the work it would fain produce."[7]

III. *Suretyship in the Roman Civil Law*

Personal suretyship was the dominant form of security in early Rome. The Roman concept of suretyship, like the early English concept, was based on the theory that the surety was not compensated and was motivated by duty rather than profit. Roman civil law, like the later English common law, provided the surety with certain unique rights and defenses in order to encourage individuals to voluntarily undertake the risks inherent in this form of security. A Tulane Law Review article, *Roman Law Bases of Suretyship in Some Modern Civil Codes*, notes:

> The purpose of the suretyship obligation is to secure the performance of the principal obligation, and, as has been noted often, this form of personal security was the most popular and preferred form in the commercial life of classical Rome. Only during the later period of the Empire did real security become preferable and more commonly used. As the contract of suretyship emanated from the Roman concept of friendship, with its attendant duties, it was normally gratuitous in nature, and the rules governing suretyship reflected this fact.[8]

This article provides an excellent review of the principles of suretyship found in the Roman Codes.

The ancient Roman Codes are the basis of the civil law of suretyship followed in many countries and an important influence upon the civil law of the State of Louisiana. The extent to which Roman civil law was incorporated into the law of England has been the subject of substantial debate. Blackstone and other advocates of English common law rooted in the customs and practices of the inhabitants of England tend to down play the importance of Roman law.[9] While the

---

7. Lloyd, *The Surety*, 66 U. Pa. L. Rev. 40, 67 (1916). This article contains the best single source of citations to early authorities discussing fundamental principles of suretyship, including, from the common law of England: general development (pp. 47-58); right of indemnity (pp. 58-59); right of subrogation (pp. 59-61); right of contribution (pp. 61-62); Roman privilege of division, that has been rejected in England and America as inconsistent with joint and several liability (pp. 62-63); Roman privilege of discussion, recognized in most civil law jurisdictions -- requires creditor to execute against the property of principal debtor upon the demand of the surety (pp. 63-64); and exoneration (pp. 64-65).

8. Jones, *Roman Law Bases of Suretyship in Some Modern Civil Codes*, 52 Tul. L. Rev. 129 (1977).

9. Although many of the rules of law followed by American common law courts are similar to the rules found in civil codes, the rules have substantially different origins. *Blackstone's Commentaries*, state:

> Far be it from me to derogate from the study of the civil law, considered (apart from any abiding authority) as a collection of written reason. No man is more thoroughly persuaded of the general excellence of its rules and the usual equity of its decisions, nor is better convinced of its use as well as ornament to the scholar, the divine, the statesman, and even the common lawyer. But we must not carry our veneration so far as to sacrifice our Alfred and Edward to the names of Theodosius and Justinian; we must not prefer the edict of the praetor, or the rescript of the Roman emperor, to our own immemorial customs, or the sanctions of an English parliament; unless we can also prefer the despotic monarchy of Rome and Byzantium, for whose meridians the former were calculated, to the free constitution of Britain, which the latter are adapted to perpetuate.
>
> Without detracting, therefore, from the real merits which abound in the imperial law, I hope I may have leave to assert, that if an Englishman must be ignorant of either the one or the other, he had better be a stranger to the Roman than the English institutions. For I think it an undeniable position, that a competent knowledge of the laws of that society in which we live, is the proper accomplishment of every gentleman and scholar; a highly useful, I had almost said essential, part of liberal and polite education. T. Cooley, *Blackstone's Commentaries*

proponents of equity, which relied heavily upon the civil law of Rome, view the civil law as being of greater importance.[10] The resolution of this debate is beyond the scope of this paper, but later in this chapter we will see that equitable doctrines based upon Roman civil law were of great importance in this country.

IV. *Ancient English Suretyship*

The English law of suretyship has its origins in the very first contracts.[11] One theory of the development of the formal English contract is set forth in a 1910 Columbia Law Review article, which explains:

> In old Germanic law on the Continent the formal contract appears to have developed gradually out of the still earlier practice of presenting chattels of substantial value and living hostages as security. It became possible for the debtor to bind himself contractually by giving his creditor some chattel of trifling value as a formal pledge and by furnishing at the same time substantial personal security in the shape of sureties. By this transaction the debtor came under the obligation of redeeming the formal pledge -- the pledge of trifling value -- by the fulfillment of his promise. But, strangely enough, in the ancient law it was the surety, not the debtor himself, who was directly and primarily responsible to the creditor for the redemption of the formal pledge; the giver of the pledge, the debtor himself, was in turn directly answerable to his surety.[12] Later the formal contract was freed from this curious conception of suretyship: by delivering the pledge of trifling value to his creditor the debtor himself assumed a direct responsibility to his creditor.[13]

A similar practice was followed by Germanic immigrants to England. The article states:

> In its earliest history the Anglo-Saxon formal contract appears to have been concluded by the delivery of a chattel of no substantial value (*wed, vadium*) and the furnishing of sureties (*borh, plegium*). But other formal acts, in addition to the delivery of a *wed*, soon came to be viewed as sufficient to create a binding contractual obligation; and the formality might thus consist, for instance, in the handgrasp, the oath, the pledge of good faith.[14]

These ancient customs appear to be the origin of the most fundamental of the Surety's rights, the right of indemnity. The article states:

---

on the Laws of England 2 (2d ed. 1872).

10. I *Pomeroy's Equitable Jurisprudence and Equitable Remedies* 2 (1905) states:

> The researches of modern juridical scholars have exposed the falsity of much that has been written by English authors [the author and his father were Americans], such as Blackstone and Coke, with respect to the origin of their law, and have demonstrated the existence of the closest relations between the Roman jurisprudence and the early English common law. These relations with the growing common law were disturbed, and finally broken, from political motives and considerations; but with equity jurisprudence they became, for that very reason, even more intimate, and have continued until the present day.

11. Arnold, *The Compensated Surety*, 26 Colum. L. Rev. 171 (1926).

12. It can certainly be argued that this was the first contract of insurance and that it was coupled with a clear right of subrogation against a third party who ought to be legally responsible for payment. Thus, we can continue the academic debate: is suretyship a form of insurance or is insurance a form of suretyship?

13. Hazeltine, *The Formal Contract of Early English Law*, Selected Readings on the Law of Contracts 1 (1931). *See also* 10 Colum. L. Rev. 608 (1910).

14. Hazeltine, *supra* at 2.

> Two passages in the laws, one in Ine and one in Alfred, seem to indicate that in the earlier history of the formal contract -- in the period when the contract was still bound up with suretyship -- the surety was primarily and directly liable to the creditor and the debtor in turn to the surety. From these passages we may perhaps conclude that the *wed* -- the object of trifling value, the formal pledge -- was first delivered by the debtor to the creditor and then passed by the creditor over to the surety; and, although our Anglo-Saxon sources are silent upon the point, it is probable that the responsibility of the debtor to the surety signified that the surety, by means of his possession of the *wed*, was entitled to disdain upon the goods of the debtor in case he did not pay.[15]

V. *English Law of Suretyship (1189 TO 1776)*

From these prehistoric Anglo-Saxon customs, the evolution of the law of suretyship can be traced to three separate and distinct English legal traditions: the Common Law; Equity; and the Law Merchant of London. Each of these systems for dispute resolution developed its own unique substantive and procedural rules that were frequently in conflict with the rules applied in the other systems. These three separate and distinct sources of English rules of law developed independently of each other for over six hundred years, from the beginning of recorded English legal history in 1189 to well after the American Revolution in 1776.

As a result of this tripartite division of the English judicial system, it is futile to attempt to state universal principles of the law of English suretyship. A diligent researcher can find credible support for conflicting rules of decision regarding nearly every important issue of the law of suretyship. The principles applied in the courts of common law and equity are easier to find because the judges of the common law courts and the chancellors of the courts of equity issued written opinions. Consequently, the decisions of these courts of record remained available to be cited by future generations of litigants.

On the other hand, the Law Merchant developed from unrecorded customs and practices of the merchants. These more pragmatic, but less scholarly rules of commercial usage were not recorded and were apparently unknown to, or intentionally ignored by, the English courts. Even after the common law courts recognized the usages of trade as a source law, judges continued to prefer the more rigid, but familiar, rules of the traditional common law.

Unwritten English law is based upon the customs and usages of the various ethnic groups that inhabited England. Blackstone's *Commentaries on the Law of England*, that were first published in 1765, ten years before the American Revolution and at the time that Lord Mansfield was beginning to attempt to incorporate principles from the Law Merchant and Equity into English Common Law, explained the controlling law of England at that time in this manner:

> The municipal law of England, or the rule of civil conduct prescribed to the inhabitants of this kingdom, may with sufficient propriety be divided into two kinds: the *lex non scripta*, the unwritten, or common law; and the *lex scripta*, the written, or statute law.[16]

The basis of the unwritten or common law was established custom. Blackstone's *Commentaries* explain:

---

15. *Id.* at 4.
16. T. Cooley, *supra* note 9, at 37.

> Whence it is that in our law the goodness of a custom depends upon its having been used time out of mind; or, in the solemnity of our legal phrase, **time whereof the memory of man runneth not to the contrary**. This it is that gives it its weight and authority: and of this nature are the maxims and customs which compose the common law, or *lex non scripta*, of this kingdom.

This unwritten, or common, law is properly distinguishable into three kinds: 1. *General customs*; which are the universal rule of the whole kingdom, and form the common law, in its stricter and more usual signification. 2. *Particular customs*; which, for the most part, affect only the inhabitants of particular districts. 3. *Certain particular laws*; which, by custom, are adopted and used by some particular courts, of pretty general and extensive jurisdiction.[17]

The principles of suretyship that developed in written decisions of the King's courts up to the time of the American Revolution were based primarily upon Blackstone's first kind of common law -- rules of general or universal application. Such rules generally applied to personal, rather than to commercial transactions.

The rules that governed commercial transactions developed as part of the unrecorded Law Merchant of London. Commercial suretyship and insurance, which was unknown to the common law until the seventeenth century, developed primarily as part of the unwritten Law Merchant which was an important part of Blackstone's second kind of common law -- rules unique to the inhabitants of particular districts. With regard to these local customs, *Blackstone's Commentaries* state:

> To this head [local customs] may most properly be referred a particular system of customs used only among one set of the king's subjects, called the customs of merchants, or *lex mercatoria*: which, however different from the general rules of the common law, is yet ingrafted into it, and made a part of it; being allowed, for the benefit of trade, to be of the utmost validity in all commercial transactions: for it is a maxim of law, that "cuilibet in sua arte credendum est [Credence should be given to one skilled in his profession]."[18]

With this background we can turn to a discussion of each of these separate traditions that were only beginning to be combined at the time of the American Revolution.

A. THE ENGLISH COMMON LAW

The English Common Law Courts began their development during the 35 year reign of Henry II (1154 to 1189).[19] Henry established a system of royal courts to regain power that his

17. *Id.* at 40.
18. *Id.* at 45.
19. W. Churchill, *A History of the English Speaking People*, states:

> It is a maxim of English law that legal memory begins with the accession of Richard I in 1189. The date was for a technical reason by a statute of Edward I. It could scarcely have been more appropriately chosen however, for with the close of the reign of Henry II we are on the threshold of a new epoch in the history of English law. With the establishment of a system of royal courts, giving the same justice all over the country, the old diversity of local law was rapidly broken down, and a law common to the whole land and to all men soon took its place. A modern lawyer, transported to the England of Henry's predecessor, would find himself in strange surroundings; with the system that Henry bequeathed to his son he would feel almost at home. That is the measure of the great King's achievement. He had laid the foundations of the English Common Law, upon which succeeding generations would build. Changes in the design would arise, but its main outlines were not to be altered. *Id.* at

predecessor had lost to feudal barons, not to encourage commerce. The resolution of commercial disputes was apparently left to local courts. Henry attracted litigants to his royal courts by providing a uniform system of justice throughout his kingdom and by offering trial by jury.

Henry's common law system was based upon the King's prerogative to issue royal writs. Winston Churchill's *A History of the English Speaking People* explains:

> Henry also had to provide means whereby the litigant, eager for royal justice, could remove his case out of the court of his lord into the King's court. The device which Henry used was the royal writ. At all costs baronial rights must be formally respected; but by straining the traditional rights of the Crown it was possible to claim that particular types of cases fell within the King's province. Upon this principle Henry evolved a number of set formulae, or writs, each fitted to a certain type of case; and any man who could by some fiction fit his own case to the wording of one of the royal writs might claim the King's justice. The wording of the writs was rigid, but at this date new forms of writ might still be given. For about eighty years they increased in number, and with each new form a fresh blow was struck at the feudal courts. It was not until de Montfort's revolt against the third Henry in the thirteenth century that the multiplication of the writs was checked and the number fixed at something under two hundred. This system then endured for six hundred years. However the times might change, society had to adapt itself to that unbending framework. Inevitably English law became weighted with archaisms and legal fictions. The whole course of a case might depend on the writ with which it was begun, for every writ had its special procedure, mode of trial, and eventual remedy.[20]

The inflexibility of the royal writs and the rigid adherence to established precedent that was required to establish uniformity were important factors leading to the development of the more adaptable royal courts of equity. *Pomeroy's Equitable Jurisprudence*, explains the rigidity of the writ system:

> The precedents of all the writs which had been thus established were kept in an office connected with the chancery, called the **Registra Brevium**. Certain officers of the chancery were charged with the duty of issuing the writs to plaintiffs, and this they did by selecting and copying the one which agreed with the facts of the applicant's case. If no writ could be found in the collection which substantially corresponded with the facts constituting the ground of complaint, the plaintiff could have no action. The chancery clerks could not draw up entirely new writs, nor alter the existing ones in any substantial manner;...[21]

Our knowledge of early English common law comes from the Year Books, in which the decisions of the King's courts were reported, and treatises commenting on these decisions. Early treatises, including the first English treatise, Bracton's *A Tract on the Laws and Customs of England*, discusses principles of suretyship that were well established by 1250. The surety's right of indemnity was an important issue at this time.

The *Registra Brevium* contained a specific writ providing a surety with indemnity, but it could not be used unless the surety was specifically identified as a surety in a written instrument. Lloyd's law review article, *The Surety*, explains:

> There was in the register an ancient writ, expressly intended for the relief of sureties; the writ *de plegiis acquietandis*, by which, as Fitzherbert describes it, the surety who had paid could summon the debtor to acquit him of the sum whereof he had put himself in pledge. If this action had developed

221-222.

20. *Id.* at 220-21.

21. Pomeroy, *supra* note 10, at 28.

> further, at least one phase of the history of suretyship would have been different. But the spirit of the age was unfavorable. It was held that when two were jointly and severally bound for the debt of one and the surety was sued and paid the debt, he could not have *de plegiis acquietandis*. For the writ did not lie "without express naming as surety of fidejussor in the writing."[22]

Lloyd's article goes on to explain:

> Sureties who have discharged the debt, says Glanvill, may have recourse to the principal by action of debt, and this is borne out by Bracton's Note Book where it also appears, in a case reported from Exxex in 1223, that the defendant may wage his law.[23] If the surety is wise he obtains a counter-bond of indemnity, as in *Wroteham v. Canewold*[24], a practice still followed by prudent persons. A pledge, however, observes Glanvill, who has been amerced cannot recover from the principal. Indeed it required a clause in Magna Charta to give sureties of the king's debtors the benefit of process to compel reimbursement, ...[25]

With regard to the surety's right of indemnity, the Magna Charta states:

> Neither we nor our bailiffs will seize the lands or rents of a debtor for any debt so long as his goods are sufficient for payment of the debt. And if the principal debtor fail in payment of the debt, having nothing wherewith to pay, will not pay where he is able, the pledges shall answer for the debt. And if they will, they shall have the lands and rents of the debtor until they be satisfied of that which they before paid for him, except that the debtor can show himself to be acquitted against said sureties.[26]

The writs were divided into two classes of action: 1) *Real Actions*, that involved lands and estates and interests in lands; and 2) *Personal Actions*, that concerned persons, chattels, contracts and torts. The personal *ex contractu* actions of "Debt," a sum of money due by express agreement, and "Covenant," a contract under seal, were the actions of primary concern to the surety. Many of the principles of law applicable to the compensated corporate surety developed from the common law action of "Covenant." Some of the reasons for this development will be discussed at this point and some of the reasons will be mentioned later in this chapter in regard to the development of the law governing American corporations.

The action for "Debt" was often based upon a verbal agreement. Problems relating to the proof of verbal agreements to answer for the debt of another became a frequent source of difficult litigation. These problems were addressed by a section of the Statute of Frauds enacted by the English Parliament in 1676. Arnold's *Outlines of Suretyship and Guaranty* published in 1927 explains:

> Prior to 1676, to form a valid simple contract required only competent parties, meeting of minds, consideration, and legality of subject matter. Except contracts under seal, a writing was unnecessary,

22. Lloyd, *supra* note 7, at 52.

23. "Bracton's Note Book Vol. III, p. 499, pl 1641. Hugo de Lectona sues Robert de Suttona in debt because Radulfus Bacun loaned money to Robert upon Hugo's pledge and Hugo disdained to render the same to Radulfus for Robert. Robert comes and defends, denying that Hugo was his pledge or paid anything for him. Therefore it is considered that he defend himself twelve handed and come such a day with his law. *See also* case pl. 1969 in same volume." *Id.* at 51, n51.

24. "Y.B. 4 Edw. II (S.S.) 147 (1311)." *Id.* at 51, n52.

25. Lloyd, *supra* note 7, at 51.

26. "9 Hen. III, Chap. 8. See also: 2 Co. Inst. 20, *King v. Bennet*, Wightwick I (1810); Manning's Exchequer Practice, Chap. IX." as cited by Lloyd above. *Id.* at 51, n54.

and if a contract were in writing it added nothing to its effectiveness. During the reign of Charles II, the statute of frauds was enacted, which, so far as it affected contracts of guaranty, provided that:

> No action shall be brought whereby ... to charge the defendant upon any special promise to answer for the debt, default or miscarriages of another person; ... unless the agreement upon which such action shall be brought, or some memorandum or note thereof, shall be in writing, and signed by the party to be charged therewith, or some other person thereunto by him lawfully authorized.[27]

Arnold goes on to explain the historical circumstances of the enactment of the Statute of Frauds:

> A surety or guarantor makes himself liable solely because of his promise. It is difficult for him in every case to protect himself against perjury or inaccurate testimony if his promise is verbal. Fraudulent claims were presented to estates and perjured testimony given to bolster verbal agreements until the legislative branch of government enacted the statute to prevent such wrongs. Again, when the statute was passed, the parties to an action were incompetent to testify in court. In consequence, the facts could not be ascertained from those who would naturally know them. Large interests depended in some case on corrupt witnesses. This appealed to the enactors of the statute. Its purpose was "to secure defendants against unfounded and fraudulent claims." As an early American jurist expressed it:
>
> The object of the statute manifestly was, to secure the highest and most satisfactory species of evidence, in a case, where a party, without apparent benefit to himself, enters into stipulations of suretyship, and where there would be great temptation, on the part of a creditor, in danger of losing his debt by the insolvency of his debtor, to support a suit against the friends or relatives of a debtor, a father, son, or brother, by means of false evidence; by exaggerating words or recommendation, encouragement to forbearance, and requests for indulgence, into positive contracts." [*Nelson v. Boynton* (1841) 3 Met. (Mass.) 396, 37 Am. Dec. 148, 149. See *Crawford v. Edison* (1887) 47 Ohio St. 239, 13 N.E. 80, 82.][28]

An example of an early case of the kind that arose under the Statute of Frauds is the case of the "financially irresponsible horseman." A son borrowed a horse from a neighbor and rode it so hard that the horse died. The neighbor demanded indemnity for his loss, but the son could not pay. In order to satisfy the neighbor, the son's father promised to pay the damages, but later changed his mind. The issue presented to the court was whether the father's promise was a promise to answer for the debt of another within the meaning of the Statute of Frauds. The court held that it was and that the neighbor could not recover on the verbal promise.

The ancient concept of suretyship also played an incidental, but interesting, role in the development of the jurisdiction of the English Common Law Courts and the development of the common law of contracts. In addition to his struggle to regain power from his barons, Henry was also competing with the Roman Catholic Church and Thomas Becket, the Archbishop of Canterbury (1162-70). On December 29, 1170, Becket was slain by four of Henry's knights. In 1172, Henry made peace with the Papacy by entering into the Compromise of Avranches. Under the terms of the Compromise, the Church retained a system of ecclesiastical courts independent of royal authority. This system of ecclesiastical courts continued to exist until the Reformation of the Church.

---

27. E. Arnold, *Outlines of Suretyship and Guaranty* 61 (1927).
28. *Id.* at 62.

More than two hundred and fifty years before the reign of Henry II, human sureties had been replaced in certain agreements. A law review article, *The Formal Contract of Early English Law*, explains:

> ...; but in quite another place in his laws Alfred refers to Godsuretyship (*god-borh, Dei plegium*). Probably this mysterious *god-borh* is to be viewed as a particularly solemn kind of formal promise. The debtor, by his solemn promise, binds himself and he calls upon God to be his surety for the faithful performance of this contract with the creditor. In this form the contract is of course strikingly like the promissory oath and pledge of good faith.[29]

With regard to the effect of this concept upon the jurisdiction of the rival royal and church courts, the article states:

> Especially in the ecclesiastical courts the oath and the pledge of faith exercised a dominating influence; and partly owing to the church's claim of jurisdiction over these contracts there came the serious conflicts between the ecclesiastical and the temporal courts that mark the times of Becket and Henry. But with the gradual growth of the common law the line between the contract of the church and the contract of the state became clearly defined. The church courts recognized and enforced formal contracts concluded by oath and by pledge of faith. The state courts would have nothing to do with either of these formalities and they developed the formal contract along newer lines in harmony with the social growth of the times; they evolved in fact the formal contracts of the common law, the contract under seal and the contract of record.[30]

The common law of suretyship therefore developed within the jurisdiction of the royal courts, whose judges were appointed by the King and who shared the King's antipathy for the law of the church that was based in large part upon Roman principles of justice. *Pomeroy's Equity Jurisprudence* states:

> In the reign of Henry III the barons formally declared that they would not suffer the kingdom to be governed by the Roman law; and the common law judges prohibited it from being any longer cited in their courts. This action of the barons and judges was certainly a mistake, and it produced an opposite effect from the one intended. The Roman law, instead of being banished, was simply transferred to another court, which was not governed by common-law doctrines. As the law courts intentionally cut themselves off from all opportunity of borrowing equitable principles from this foreign source, the necessity arose for a separate tribunal, in which those principles could be recognized. It therefore followed, immediately upon this prohibition, that the hitherto narrow jurisdiction of the Court of Chancery was greatly increased, and extended over subject-matters which required an ample and constant use of Roman law doctrines. To the same cause was chiefly due the selection, which was really a necessity, of chancellors from among the ecclesiastic, during the period while the jurisdiction of this court was thus enlarged and established.[31]

B. ENGLISH EQUITY

The English Courts of Equity developed for a number of reasons discussed above, including: the inflexibility of the writ system; the rigid adherence to precedence; and the conflict between the

29. Hazeltine, *supra* note 13, at 5.
30. *Id.* at 9.
31. Pomeroy, *supra* note 10, at 24-25.

church and the feudal system of government. The Courts of Equity, like the Common Law Courts, were based upon the authority of the King, but the Courts of Equity were much more flexible in granting relief based on the unique facts of each case. The early chancellors of equity relied to a great degree upon principles of "natural justice" rooted in the civil law of Rome.

The jurisdiction of the courts of equity extended to providing a remedy where none was provided by law, as well as to correcting what the chancellors viewed as erroneous principles of law applied by the judges of the common law courts. *Pomeroy's Equity Jurisprudence* states:

> In the original delegation of general authority by the Crown to the Chancellor, over matters falling under the King's judicial prerogative of grace, such authority was to be exercised according to Conscience, Equity, Good Faith and Honesty. It was undoubtedly a maxim, even in the earliest times, that the equitable jurisdiction of chancery only extended to such matters as *were not remediable by the common law*. ... At the same time they exercised a jurisdiction which was *corrective* of the law, and this was undoubtedly the most important part of their functions. It is absolutely certain from all the existing records, and from the result itself of their work, that they did not refrain from deciding any particular case, according to their views of equity and good conscience, merely because the doctrine which they followed or established in making the decision was inconsistent with the rule of law applicable to the same facts, nor because the law had deliberately and intentionally refused to acknowledge the existence of a primary right, or to give a remedy under those facts and circumstances.[32]

The willingness of the Courts of Equity to avoid rules of law established by the Common Law Courts had important implications for sureties. *Pomeroy's Equity Jurisprudence* states:

> When an obligee, by reason of loss or other accident, could not produce the bond, he was prohibited by an express rule of the law from maintaining an action on it; but the Court of Chancery, upon proof of such facts, would grant him full relief, by enforcing the obligation. Conversely, if an obligor or other debtor upon a sealed instrument had paid the debt in full, but had neglected to take a release or a surrender of the bond, the law held him still liable, and gave him no defense in an action brought to recover payment of the debt a second time; but chancery admitted and enforced this conscientious defense by restraining the creditor from prosecuting his legal action.[33]

The surety's four fundamental rights of indemnity,[34] exoneration,[35] subrogation[36] and contribution[37] were recognized and applied in the courts of equity by the fifteenth century.

C. LAW MERCHANT OF LONDON

The final source of principles of English suretyship is the unwritten customs and practices of merchants known as the Law Merchant. Beginning in the mid-eighteenth century, principles of commercial suretyship and insurance were contemporaneously incorporated into English Common

---

32. *Id.* at 52.
33. *Id.* at 53.
34. Lloyd, *supra* note 7 at 58-59.
35. *Id.* at 59.
36. *Id.* at 59-61.
37. *Id.* at 61-62.

Law from the Law Merchant. The Law Merchant, like English Equity, developed because of deficiencies in the law as administered by the King's common law courts.

By the time of Elizabeth I, the traditional uncompensated personal suretyship of the Common Law was manifestly inadequate to meet the demands of expanding commerce. Sir Walter Raleigh wrote:

> If any desire thee to be his surety, give him a part of what thou hast to spare; if he press thee further, he is not thy friend at all, for friendship rather chooses harm to itself than offereth it. If thou be bound for a stranger, thou art a fool; if for a merchant, thou puttest thy estate to learn to swim; if for a churchman, he hath no inheritance; if for a lawyer, he will find an evasion by a syllable or word to abuse thee; if for a poor man, thou mayest pay it thyself; if for a rich man, he needs not; therefore, from suretyship, as from manslayer or enchanter, bless thyself ...[38]

Therefore, merchants developed their own rules of law for the conduct of their businesses that were independent of the law applied by the King's courts. An 1893 *Harvard Law Review* article written by Sir Frederick Pollock states:

> Even in the regular law-books we hear of customs in London and elsewhere to allow covenants to be proved by word of mouth, or, at any rate, to admit proof by tally[39] where the king's court would require a deed. Attempts were made to obtain a footing for these customs in the king's courts, but they seem to have uniformly failed. We still know very little of the procedure and rules of proof of the courts which administered the law merchant; and what the books describe as special customs may perhaps have been nothing but the application of general or at least English mercantile usage. There is nothing to show that such customs, general or special, had any effective influence on the development of the common law. Formalism prevailed in the superior courts, and in the fifteenth century the strongest and most acute-minded judges who had administered the king's justice since Edward I.'s time found themselves without any adequate means, in the way of either doctrine or practice, of keeping abreast of the needs of business and facing the competition of the ecclesiastical courts.[40]

Principles of the law of suretyship and the law of insurance developed as part of the Law Merchant long before any attempt was made to incorporate the Law Merchant into the Common Law of England.

1. Suretyship

38. Morgan, *The History and Economics of Suretyship*, 12 Cornell L. Q. 153, 162 (1926), citing 60 *Bankers' Magazine* 216.

39. *Bouvier's Law Dictionary* (1984) defines "tally" as:

> "A stick cut into two parts on each whereof is marked, with notches or otherwise, what is due between debtor and creditor. Hence, the tallier of the exchequer is now called the teller. ... One party must have one part, and the other the other, and they must match. Tallies in the exchequer were abolished by 23 Geo. III. c. 82, and were ordered destroyed in 1834. They were thereupon used in such quantities to heat the stoves in the house of lords that it is supposed they were the cause of the fire which destroyed both houses of parliament. There was the same usage in France."

40. Pollack, *Contracts in Early English Law*, Selected Readings on the Law of Contracts 21 (1931). *See also* 6 Harv. L. Rev. 389 (1893).

With regard to suretyship under the Law Merchant, Lloyd's article, *The Surety*, explains:

> No part of the history of English law is more obscure than that connected with the Law Merchant but it is only reasonable to suppose that a constantly increasing number of tradesmen were learning the value of credit and accustoming themselves to the use of the various forms of commercial paper introduced by the merchants who frequented the cosmopolitan markets and fairs. Gerard Malynes, *Merchant*, says: "If any merchant do passe his word for another, it maketh him, as *fidejussor*, to perform the same, and the act done before is a sufficient good consideration, and they all agree that *bond fides inter mercatores est servanda*, faith or trust is to be kept between merchants, and that also must be done without quillets or titles of the law, to avoid interruption of traffique."[41]

2. Insurance

English insurance law developed from the practices of Italian merchants that were incorporated into the Law Merchant of London long before the common law courts took any notice of insurance. A 1904 treatise on the law of insurance states:

> The first satisfactory evidence that we have of any extensive use of the contract of insurance is to be found in the history and records of the medieval maritime states of Italy. From the twelfth to the sixteenth centuries the Italian republics of Venice, Florence, and Genoa flourished greatly by reason of their extensive maritime commerce, and it was among these Italian merchants that the contract of insurance first received that attention which the manifest benefits to be derived from its use would justify. Insurances were certainly effected as early as the beginning of the thirteenth century, and probably in the tenth century. From Italy the custom of making mutual contracts of insurance spread rapidly over the whole of commercial Europe, and early came to be practiced extensively by the merchants in towns forming the Hanseatic League. As early as 1310 there was a chamber of assurance in Bruges, and there is record of a statutory form of policy in Florence as early as 1520. In fact, the word "policy" is a monument to the Italian origin of insurance, it being derived from the Italian word "politizia."[42]

With regard to the English law of insurance, the 1893 edition of Richards, *A Treatise on the Law of Insurance*, states:

> A recorded mention of insurance in England in 1548 indicates that the practice of insuring had been in vogue there for some time, and somewhat later, on opening Queen Elizabeth's first parliament, Lord Bacon saist, "Doth not the wise merchant in every adventure of danger give part to have the rest assured?" But for many years after its introduction into that country, the law of insurance was unknown to the courts of Westminister, and insurance disputes were as a rule settled by arbitration of mercantile men.

The first reported insurance case belongs to the year 1589, and is mentioned by Sir Edward Coke [Dowdale's case, Cokes Reports, part 6, p. 476], in which it was held, "where as well the contract as the performance of it is wholly made or to be done beyond sea, it is not triable by our law, but if the promise be made in England it shall be tried."

41. Lloyd, *supra* note 7, at 55.
42. W. Vance, *Handbook on the Law of Insurance* 4 (1904).

> In 1601, to provide for the growing practice of resorting to litigation, a special tribunal for trial of marine insurance cases was established in England, ...
>
> This informal tribunal -- which consisted of the Judge of the Admiralty, the Recorder of London, two doctors of civil law, two common lawyers, and eight grave and discreet merchants, or any five of them -- died a natural death within a century after its organization, and by degrees insurance disputes began to come within the jurisdiction of the common law courts of England.[43]

During the period between the collapse of this informal panel and Lord Mansfield's term as Chief Justice, the common law courts had little involvement with insurance issues. A 1908 Columbia Law Review article states:

> The failure of this special court seems to have discouraged any further attempts to better an almost intolerable situation, for the hundred and fifty years intervening between the enactment of 43 Eliz. and the appointment of Mansfield as Chief Justice of the Court of King's Bench are almost a barren waste as far as the history of the development of insurance law is concerned. The common law judges did not grow in wisdom or in the favor of those having insurance causes. The merchants and underwriters continued to submit their disputes to arbitrators and commissions, sedulously avoiding the common law courts. It is said that, all told, the reported insurance cases determined at law prior to Lord Mansfield's time did not exceed sixty in number, nor among these can there be found one that clearly establishes a great principle or that can be fairly considered a leading case. So slight was the grasp of the common law judges of this period upon the nature and true function of the contract of insurance that as late as 1746 it was uncertain whether an insurable interest was necessary to support a policy, although the fundamental principle requiring the presence of such an interest was perfectly well understood by the Continental authorities of an earlier time.[44]

D. INCORPORATION OF EQUITY AND THE LAW MERCHANT INTO THE COMMON LAW

Lord Mansfield, who was Chief Justice of the King's Bench from 1756 to 1788, began the process of incorporating Equity and the Law Merchant into the Common Law. Lord Mansfield's term as Chief Justice included the period of the American Revolution and ended at time that our Constitution was being framed to replace the Articles of Confederation. With regard to Lord Mansfield's contribution to the English law of contracts, a 1916 article in the *Harvard Law Review* states:

> The English Law of Contract, for example, is scientific and complete, it assumed scientific form at a happy time, just when the genius of Lord Mansfield had incorporated the Law of Merchant (surely a priceless adoption) into English Law. Had the structure been earlier framed, it might well have been cramped and inelastic; the archaic `special contracts' which survive alongside the innominate contracts of modern business, and stand in such puzzling relationship to general theory of contract, are warnings of what might have happened.[45]

---

43. Richards, *A Treatise on the Law of Insurance* 7-8 (2d ed. 1893).
44. Vance, *The Early History of Insurance Law*, 8 Colum. L. Rev. 1, 15-16 (1908).
45. Jenks, *English Civil Law*, 30 Harv. L. Rev. 1 (1916).

Lord Mansfield is also credited with bringing principles of insurance law from the Law Merchant to the Common Law. Richards, *A Treatise on the Law of Insurance*, published in 1893, shortly after the first corporate contract surety bond was written in this country, states:

> ..., and during his illustrious career he [Lord Mansfield] was conspicuous in making the policy of insurance the subject of careful study. From old sea laws, the foreign ordinances, the writings of jurists, and usages of trade, he drew and shaped those principles which formed the nucleus of the present system of insurance law.[46]

From the historical perspective of the Law Merchant of Lord Mansfield's time, the primary distinction between the three party surety bond and the two party insurance policy was that suretyship involved an identifiable human Principal who had a duty to indemnify the Surety. If the Surety was required to indemnify the Obligee for loss due to the default of the human Principal, the Principal had a duty to indemnify the Surety. Therefore, in theory, the surety should not suffer a loss from the risk assumed. However, the mere ability to avoid a loss obviously did not provide any incentive for a person to undertake the well known dangers inherent in suretyship. Consequently, a commercial surety charged a premium: 1) to cover operating expenses; 2) to cover losses caused by the inability of some Principals to provide indemnity; and 3) to earn a profit.

On the other hand, the insurance of Lord Mansfield's time provided indemnity for loss through the forces of nature, primarily the hazards of the sea. The Insurer obviously had no recourse against such forces. Therefore, if an Insurer was required to indemnify the Insured, the Insurer sustained a loss that could not be recovered. Consequently, the commercial insurer charged a premium: 1) to cover operating expenses; 2) to cover unavoidable losses caused by the risks of nature assumed; and 3) to earn a profit. The financial stability of the insurer therefore depended upon the pooling of risks and the actuarial principle of averages, rather than the financial ability of the Principal.

Over time, however, this historical distinction between insurance and suretyship became less clear. The types of risks assumed by insurers broadened to include loss from human conduct, both intentional and unintentional. Two party blanket fidelity insurance policies issued by incorporated insurers began to replace three party individual fidelity bonds written by individuals. Scientific knowledge increased to provide greater insights into the causes of losses. Once human responsibility for insured losses could be fixed, the courts applied the equitable principle of subrogation to insurers, as well as to sureties.

Lord Mansfield's attempt to incorporate principles from Equity and the Law Merchant into the Common Law was not universally appreciated by English common law judges or scholars. *Pomeroy's Equity Jurisprudence and Equitable Remedies*, published in 1905, states:

> Lord Mansfield was the first great English judge who consciously, and with systematic and persistent purpose, adopted the policy of the Roman praetors, endeavored to impart a new life and give a new direction to the growth of the common law, and by means of equitable principles in combination with its own methods to reform the law from within. As a reward for these innovations, Lord Mansfield was charged in his own day -- and the accusation has been handed down as a part of judicial history -- with ignorance of the English law.[47]

46. Richards, *supra* note 43, at 8.
47. Pomeroy, *supra* note 10, at 21.

The incorporation of the usages of trade from the Law Merchant into the common law administered by the King's courts involved consideration of three issues. *Blackstone's Commentaries* state: "The rules relating to particular customs regard either the *proof* of their existence; their *legality* when proved; or their usual method of *allowance*."[48] The first issue directed the court's attention to the factual existence of the custom. The second required a determination of whether the custom was a good custom that should be followed. Blackstone lists seven factors that were to be considered by the court in making this determination.[49] The third required a strict construction of a custom in derogation of the general or common law.

Lord Mansfield's successors used this rigid formula to resist incorporating the informal customs of the market place into the Common Law. In fact, the formal written policy of insurance developed, at least in part, because the common law courts were unwilling to enforce the less formal contracts commonly used by merchants. An 1867 treatise states:

> It is often desirable to conclude an agreement for insurance immediately, lest some intelligence should induce one of the parties to recede. Accordingly, *it is the practice with private English insurers, on agreeing upon a risk, to subscribe a "slip," or short memorandum of the proposed insurance*, which, according to the statement of one of a special jury, and so probably a man particularly acquainted with the course of business, is considered to be binding on parties; but Lord Kenyon held that it was not legally binding for want of a stamp, and Lord Ellenborough gave it, in effect the same opinion.[50]

Nevertheless, from the perspective of American insurance law, the work of Lord Mansfield is of paramount importance. W. R. Vance, a George Washington University Professor of Law, writing in 1908 concluded:

> Lord Mansfield became Chief Justice of the Court of King's Bench in 1756, which may rightly be considered as the date of the beginning of the development of the modern law of insurance as a part of the common law system. This great judge, thanks to his more liberal Scottish training, was not so slavishly attached to common law precedents as to be unable to perceive the necessity of recognizing merchants' customs in determining rights under merchants' contracts, not so bigoted as to be unwilling to seek light from foreign sources. In insurance causes, as with causes involving other branches of the law merchant, he impanelled juries of merchants and underwriters, to establish customs and usages current among those who made insurances, and diligently consulted the time-honored maritime laws of the Continent, and the treatises of English and Continental writers. Thus he not only gave prompt justice to litigants who appeared before him, and provided a fit tribunal for merchants, but he saw so clearly the fundamentals of the theory of insurance, and understood so well its practical

---

48. T. Cooley, *supra* note 9, at 75.

49. 1. That it have been used so long, that the memory of man runneth not to the contrary.
 2. It must have been *continued.*
 3. It must have been *peaceable*, and acquiesced in; not subject to contention and dispute.
 4. Customs must be *reasonable*; or rather, taken negatively, they must not be unreasonable.
 5. Customs ought to be certain.
 6. Custom, though established by consent, must be (when established) *compulsory;* and not left to option of every man, whether he will use them or no.
 7. Lastly, customs must be *consistent* with each other; one custom cannot be set up in opposition to another.

 Id. at 46-48.

50. 1 Phillips, *A Treatise on the Law of Insurance* 10 (5th ed. 1867). Lord Kenyon and Lord Ellenborough were successors of Lord Mansfield.

applications to the needs of business and commerce, that the numerous doctrines that he laid down have survived all of the many changes in commercial conditions and methods that have since taken place, and almost without exception they apply as well to the commercial transactions of today as to those of Mansfield's own time.[51]

The attempt to reconcile conflicting principles drawn from Common Law, Equity and the Law Merchant is the source of many of the issues of suretyship law that have been litigated in American courts since the American Revolution. Our contemporary courts continue the struggle to combine these three distinct pillars of English legal history into a single common foundation for American law governing the compensated corporate surety.

VI. *Early American Law and Suretyship*

A. CONFLICTING AND UNSETTLED RULES FROM THE LAW OF ENGLAND

At the time of the American Revolution, principles taken from the Law Merchant and Equity were just beginning to be incorporated into the Common Law. The tension between the rules of suretyship that emanated from these three separate and distinct legal traditions is illustrated by the treatment of the surety's right of indemnity in an early American edition of an English treatise on the law of suretyship. Fell's *A Treatise on the Law of Mercantile Guarantees and of Principal and Surety in General* published in 1825 states:

> 24. It seems that, "in ancient times, no action could have been maintained at law where a surety had paid the debt of his principal, except he had a counter security."
> 25. But, by custom of London, where the surety paid a debt, and had no counter-bond, he might maintain an action for money paid to the defendant's use, upon the implied contract.
> 26. So, in equity -- If the surety be damnified, he shall be relieved against the principal, although he have no counter security.
> 27. This principle has been since admitted, generally at law; [But without an express stipulation, a surety, who pays the debt of his principal, can only require his **money to be refunded** to him with interest, although he may have suffered by the sacrifice of his property to pay the debt. *Vance v. Lancaster,* 1 Hayward (Tenn.) Rep. 240.] and it is said, by Buller, J. in the case of *Toussaint* and others v. *Martinnant*, cited below, that, "the first case of the kind, in which the plaintiff succeeded, was before Gould, J., at Dochester."[52]

B. FACTORS EFFECTING THE DEVELOPMENT OF THE AMERICAN LAW OF SURETYSHIP

The principles of law governing English and American suretyship and insurance practice have common origins, but the development of the American law is substantially different than that of England. The newly independent American colonies were not important centers of international

51. Vance, *supra* note 44, at 16-17.
52. Fell, *A Treatise on the Law of Mercantile Guarantees and of Principal and Surety in General* 234 (1825).

trade with established mercantile customs. Commercial activity was largely local with a focus on the settlement of vast areas of land. This lead to greater concern with the development of personal insurance such as fire,[53] life and travel insurance, rather than commercial insurance. Even the benefit of these forms of insurance was viewed with some doubt by the general public.[54]

The law of the various states was largely independent and, naturally, focused on local concerns. Consequently, the adoption of the "common law of England" was not uniform. For example, in 1910 the Maine Supreme Court held that the common law of England was never in force in Maine, except so far as it was adopted in the usages and customs of the people of Maine.[55]

Moreover, the sovereignty of the several states with regard to domestic policy was highly prized and carefully protected. The regulation of insurance was left to state government, rather than to the common Federal government. Until 1944, the Supreme Court followed the rule that insurance was not interstate commerce and therefore was not subject to Federal regulation.[56] After the Court overturned earlier rulings and held that insurance was interstate commerce, Congress enacted legislation that left the regulation of insurance to the states.

In addition, the Revolution had severed the law of the newly created states from the law of England. While the independent colonies adopted the form of the English courts of law and equity, the revolt against the King had undermined the foundation of the law derived from the King's ancient prerogatives. A 1975 treatise on Equity explains:

> After the Revolution, most of the newly-constituted states established courts of chancery, but at first these for the most part administered only a rough layman's equity. There was no American equity jurisprudence; the English precedents were inaccessible and not well settled, and there was in any event a hostility to all things English; many of the judges were laymen. The history of equity in the United States as a system of law as distinguished from a system of lay magisterial discretion in hard cases dates from the second decade of the last century. Joseph Story became a justice of the Supreme Court of the United States and began to sit in equity cases in the Circuit of Massachusetts in 1814; James Kent became Chancellor of New York in 1814.[57]

Most early commercial disputes appear to have been resolved through the informal practices of merchants, rather than in the courts. The first reported opinion regarding life insurance was

53. The first fire insurance company in this country was founded in Philadelphia in 1752. Benjamin Franklin was one of its early directors. Richards, *supra* note 43, at 12.

54. Humble, *Law of Insurance*, 14 Modern American Law 4 (1915), states:

> A large proportion of murders and from fifteen to fifty per cent of our fire losses would not occur but for the fact that the life and fire insurance exists. Nevertheless, the advantages of those forms of insurance so completely outweigh the disadvantages that no sane person would argue in favor of their extinction.

55. *Conant v. Jordan*, 77 A. 938, 107 Me. 227 (1910).

56. *United States v. South-Eastern Underwriters Assn.*, 322 U.S. 533 (1944).

57. E.D. Re, *Cases and Material on Equity and Equitable Remedies* 15 (1975).

published in 1809.[58] With regard to insurance litigation in general, Friedman, *A History of American Law*, states:

> Even litigation about claims was not very frequent, it seems, until late in the century [19th]. There were perhaps as few as one hundred reported cases on life insurance down to 1870. These were of course all appellate cases, but they suggest that trial litigation was also less dense than in the next generation. Fire and marine insurance were the main subjects of these early cases. By the 1890's, appellate decisions on insurance law had mushroomed. In the *Century Digest* (1896), there were 2,808 pages densely packed with brief summaries of insurance cases.[59]

Statutes were drawn and enacted by popularly elected legislators who focused on the concerns of their local constituents, rather than on the traditional prerogatives of the King, or even the mercantile practices of Europe. In the late nineteenth century, these state legislatures turned to a new institution, regulatory agencies, to supervise the activities of insurers that operated in their states. Therefore, a great diversity developed in the law. Certainly, there was no "common law," in the sense of universal law, that was applicable to sureties.

With regard to suretyship, the various states' legislatures adopted inconsistent terminology. The *Restatement of Security* states:

> The possible convenience of having certain terms denote only particular types of surety obligations has resulted in some jurisdictions in the use of "suretyship" as a general term and "guaranty" as meaning some particular type of surety contract. In several states "guaranty" is used as the general term and "suretyship" with a restricted meaning. There has never been general agreement as to which term is to be broader and which the narrower. ...
>
> Suretyship obligations are contractual, and the important point of inquiry should be the precise undertaking of the surety and the duty of the principal. The recognition of the existence of different forms of contractual suretyship and the emphasis upon the obligation assumed in a particular case, are of greater significance than the distribution of labels to various types of contracts.[60]

C. EARLY AMERICAN INSURANCE PRACTICE

In the early years of our country's history, insurance contracts were not well developed. Lloyds was founded in a London coffee shop in the late seventeenth century and was not formed into a society with fixed rules until 1769. The first Lloyds' Policy was not adopted until 1779.[61]

58. *Lord v. Dall*, 12 Mass. 115 (1809). With regard to the opinion, Richard's treatise states:

> It was in that case contended by the defendant that no valid contract of life insurance could be made within the State of Massachusetts, in as much as the law of England in that regard, it was said, had never been adopted in this country; but the court sustained the contract on the ground that it was not repugnant to general policy of the law or to good morals, and that no reason had been given for condemning such contracts, except by the French Courts which considered "that it is indecorous to set a price upon the life of a freeman which is above all price" -- a reason pronounced insufficient by the court, especially as coming from France, "where" Chief Judge Parker remarked, "freedom had never been known." Richards, *supra* note 43, at 12-13.

59. L. Friedman, *A History of American Law* 545 (2d ed. 1985).

60. *Restatement of the Law of Security* §82 at 9 (1941).

61. Richards, *supra* note 43, at 9.

Consequently, early insurance policies were very informal. The fifth edition of Phillips, *A Treatise on the Law of Insurance*, published in 1867, states:

> "A policy of insurance has been considered as an obscure, incoherent, and a very strange instrument." [Per Mansfield, C.J. 4 Taunt. 380] But the obscurity and uncertainty complained of do not probably arise altogether from any imperfection in the policy which can be remedied. [Mr. Justice Lawrence says, "It is wonderful that policies should be drawn with so much laxity." *Marsden v. Reid*, 3 East, 579. Chief Justice Marshall, "Policies of Insurance are generally the most informal instruments which are brought into courts of justice." 5 Cranch, 342. And again, "The contract of insurance is very loosely drawn." 6 Cranch, 45. Lord Mansfield said, "The instrument is conceived in an inaccurate form of words." 1 Burr 347. But that "length of time and a variety of decisions have reduced it to a certainty." Dougl. 270.] *A contract embracing so many interests and parties, and liable to be affected by so many events, cannot but be subject to some difficulties of construction, however skillfully it may be drawn.*[62]

The informality of the early insurance contract is illustrated in an 1840 treatise. Hammond, *A Treatise on the Law of Fire Insurance,* states:

> In *Levy v. Merrill*, 4 Greenl.R. 180, where a marine policy contained the words -- "Touching the risks I am willing to bear, the same as contained in the regular policies of insurance, and should any difficulty arise in adjusting this policy, I am willing that the same should be adjusted according to rules established at Lloyd's or at the regular insurance offices in the United States."[63]

Even though early contracts of insurance were entered into by individuals or partnerships, the terms of the contract were construed most strongly against the insurer. The opinion of Chief Justice John Marshall in *Yeaton v. Fry* states:

> Policies of insurance are generally the most informal instruments which are brought into courts of justice; and there are no instruments which are more liberally construed, in order to effect the real intention of the parties, if that intention can be clearly ascertained.[64]

D. INSURANCE POLICIES ISSUED BY CORPORATIONS

Corporations were developing as the predominate form of business at the same time that the written contract of insurance was developing. Friedman, *A History of American Law*, states:

> Corporations were uncommon before 1800. And few of those which existed were business corporations. Almost all of the colonial corporations were churches, charities, or cities or boroughs. New York City was a chartered corporation. In all the 18th century, charters were issued to only 335 businesses. Only seven of those were during the colonial period: 181 were issued between 1796 and 1800. Banks, insurance companies, water companies, and companies organized to build or run canals, turnpikes, and bridges made up the overwhelming majority of those early corporations.[65]

---

62. 1 Phillips, *supra* note 50, at 4-5.
63. E. Hammond, *A Treatise on the Law of Fire Insurance* 59 (1840).
64. 5 Cr. 335-343, 3 L.Ed. 117, 120 (1809).
65. L. Friedman, *supra* note 59, at 188-89.

The corporate form of business was relatively new and, therefore, the controlling principles of law were largely developed in this country. The *Preface* to Theobald's 1836 treatise, *On Principal and Surety and Principal and Agent*, states:

> However simple and easy of application at first view may appear the principles of the Law of Principal and Agent, yet whoever under takes to digest and simplify the numerous questions, which the extension of modern commerce, and different forms in which mercantile business, and the subject of commercial agency, have brought under legal investigation, will soon find no easy task. The extent and variety also of incorporated companies and voluntary associations which daily spring into existence, in this country especially, give the subject an importance unknown to modern Europe. The decisions upon the numerous questions that have arisen in our courts in reference to those associations have not been overlooked; and it is hoped they may be found of some use. It certainly gives the whole subject an increasing importance, as the interests involved are commonly of vast magnitude affecting every relation in life.

Even though Theobald's treatise deals with suretyship and agency, it does not appear that he anticipated the development of the corporate surety a half century later.

At this time, basic principles of contract law were being adapted to the corporate form of business. Lawson's humorous view of leading cases, which was published in 1892, states:

> There was an old doctrine, that lingered in the courts for many years, to the effect that a corporation could make no contract except by its corporate seal, the reason given being, as expressed by an old time judge that they were "invisible, immortal, and had no souls" and therefore, were incapable of manifesting their intention by any personal or oral discourse.[66]

Prior to the Civil War, the corporate insurer was just beginning its development. The individual insurer was still an important factor in the market. Hammond, *A Treatise on the Law of Fire Insurance*, published in 1840, states:

> The policy of insurance, is a written contract, signed by the insurer, or an agent on his behalf; or, in the case of an insurance by a corporation, by the authorized agent of the company, who is usually the president.[67]

By the late nineteenth century however, corporate insurance was the rule, rather than the exception. Richards, *A Treatise on the Law of Insurance*, published in 1893, states:

> The bulk of the business of insurance is now transacted by corporations, which, on account of their exemption from liability to natural death, and their facility for raising capital and extending their operations over wide areas of territory, are peculiarly well adapted to serve in the capacity of insurers.[68]

Corporations were well suited to the essential function of pooling the risk of loss and spreading it over a large number of risks by charging a premium that was intended to be sufficient

66. Lawson, *Leading Cases Simplified* 53 (1892).
67. E. Hammond, *supra* note 63, at 59.
68. Richards, *supra* note 43, at 3.

to pay operating expenses, losses and earn a profit for shareholders. Dunham, *The Business of Insurance*, states:

> The primary requisite essential to a contract of insurance is assumption of Risk of Loss and undertaking to indemnify the insured against loss.
>
> It is characteristic of insurance that a number of risks are accepted, some of which will involve losses, and that such losses are spread over all the risks so as to enable the insurer to accept such risk at a slight fraction of the possible liability upon it.[69]

E. STATE INSURANCE COMMISSIONS

Regardless of their utility, the increasing power of corporations was a matter of substantial concern to the general public. With regard to the development of corporations, Friedman, *A History of American Law*, states:

> The word "soulless" constantly recurs in debates over corporations. Everyone knew that corporations were really run by human beings. Yet the metaphor was not entirely pointless. Corporations did not die, and had no ultimate limit to their size. There were no natural bounds to their life or to their greed. Corporations, it was feared, could concentrate the worst urges of whole groups of men; the economic power of a corporation would not be tempered by the mentality of any one person, or by considerations of family or morality. People hated and distrusted corporations, the way some fear computers today, which are also soulless, also capable of joining the wit, skill, and malevolence of many minds.[70]

Among the concerns of the general public was the use of carefully drawn policies that the public perceived as being unfairly enforced by the courts. In 1887, the same year that the first corporate contract surety bond was issued, a speech presented to the American Bar Association discussed the increasing state control over insurers that was being exercised through legislation enforced by state regulatory agencies. The speaker, who strongly opposed any governmental interference with private enterprise, stated:

> It will be further observed that prejudice against corporations generally, and insurance companies in particular, exists principally in small cities and towns, and in the rural districts. The business of insurance in such sections, *where it produces friction*, is, as a general rule, transacted by strangers to the people.[71]

The speaker noted the inability of insurance companies to defend themselves effectively in the legislatures of that period. He continued:

> It is useless to reply that this result is unjust and oppressive to the companies! The fact remains, and is incontrovertible. Imperative instruction from principals to be fair and liberal, the small percentage

69. H. Dunham, *The Business of Insurance* 6-7 (1912).

70. L. Friedman, *supra* note 59, at 194.

71. Jackson, *Indemnity the Essence of Insurance: Causes and Consequences of Legislative Qualifying this Principle*, 10 A.B.A. Reports 261, 275 (1887).

> of contested claims, etc., constitutes no satisfactory response. The public may be unreasonable, but as legislation depends at last upon the views of the voters, their prejudices must be removed, if possible, though based upon no just or tenable foundation.[72]

Finally, he warned that state regulation of insurance companies was coming. The speech states:

> What statesman, or political economist, forty, or even thirty, years ago, foresaw the establishment of the railroad commissions, State and National? Would not the leaders of thought in this country have promptly replied to the proposition, that the law of supply and demand, free competition, would regulate freights, etc., and protect people? And yet the commissions, whether, wisely or unwisely, have been established by law! Next to railroad companies, in the universality and intimacy of their relations with the public, we have insurance companies, and whilst in the nature of their franchises, they differ in many respects from the former, yet there is analogy sufficient to apprehend that causes which lead to the hostile legislation against the one may invoke it against the other.[73]

A History of American Law points out the growth of state regulation of the insurance industry.

> The urge to regulate, however, was cumulative and persistent. In 1873, twelve states had "some form of institutionalized insurance regulation"; in 1890, seventeen states; in 1905, twenty-two.[74]

VII. *Corporate Suretyship*

A. ORIGINS OF CORPORATE CONTRACT SURETYSHIP

While the concept of suretyship is of ancient origin, the history of corporate contract suretyship in this country is very short, spanning little more than 100 years. The development of corporate suretyship began in England, prior to the American Revolution. In 1720, a company was formed to "insure to all masters and mistresses whatever loss they shall sustain by Theft from any servant."[75] The fate of this first commercial enterprise intended to replace private suretyship is unknown, but it appears that more than one hundred years passed before corporate suretyship developed further.

In the August, 1840 issue of the *Dublin Review*, Professor DeMorgan of London University, proposed to apply the "principle of averages" to the underwriting of fidelity insurance. Professor DeMorgan contended that this principle ought to apply to dishonesty as well as to death or fire or any other hazard that was subject to insurance.[76] Willis D. Morgan's 1926 article, *The History and Economics of Suretyship*, states:

> This plan was an innovation, it embodied the first proposal to organize a fidelity insurance company, the operations of which would be in accordance with the established insurance principle, that of averages. But it contemplated only a fidelity business, the least important of modern surety lines.

72. *Id.*
73. *Id.* at 277.
74. L. Friedman, *supra* note 59, at 443.
75. Morgan, *supra* note 4, at 163.
76. *Id.* at 164.

Three years previously, an American, William L. Haskins, had published a pamphlet entitled, "Considerations on the Project and Institution of a Guarantee Company, on a New Plan, with some general views on Credit, Confidence and Currency," in which the organization of a company named, "The New York Guarantee Co." was proposed. ***

The proposed functions of this company are briefly stated in Section 10 of the plan. "The object and business of the Association will be to **guarantee** the payment of notes and **other written obligations or contracts**, whether of individuals, corporations, or private associations; to undertake the strict fulfillment and execution of trusts, escrows, wills, and endowments; to exercise other duties of Financial Mediation and Agency, and to do other things relative thereto."[77]

Based upon his careful research, Mr. Morgan concluded: "To this American, Haskins, is thus to go all credit for having first conceived of the corporate surety, in its broader and more significant aspects."[78] However, The New York Guarantee Co. was never formed.

The Guarantee Society of London, following Professor DeMorgan's plan for fidelity insurance based upon the "principle of averages," began operation in 1840. Less than two years later, Parliament passed an act entitled "An Act for regulating Legal Proceedings by or against `The Guarantee Society,' and for granting certain powers thereto."[79] In 1843, the Deputy Chairman of the Guarantee Society, published a pamphlet entitled, "Suretyship, The Dangers and Defects of Private Security and their Remedy."[80]

In 1852, corporate contract suretyship was proposed. The prospectus for the Contract Guarantee Co. stated: "The object for which this company is incorporated, is to supersede the necessity of individual security under commercial or trading contracts by providing that of an associated body."[81] The Contract Guarantee Co. was never formed.

In 1853, a prospectus for another company stated:

> The success of those companies which have been established to provide a substitute for personal guarantees for fidelity is well known; but no company at present exists securing the performance of contracts. *** One of the objects of this Society, therefore, will be to take the place of the surety in those instances, so that any contractor of known respectability and ascertained credit may be able immediately to offer to his principal an undoubted and unquestionable security for the due performance of this contract.[82]

American Surety Co. was incorporated in New York on April 14, 1884 and was the first United States company devoted exclusively to surety underwriting.[83] In 1887, the American Surety Co. became the first United States corporation to write a contract surety bond.

B. THE EARLY AMERICAN MARKET FOR CORPORATE SURETY BONDS

77. *Id.* at 164-65. A footnote states: "A copy of this pamphlet is to be found in the Library of Congress, Washington, D.C. It was published by D. Felt and Co., 245 Pearl St., New York City, in 1837."

78. *Id.* at 165.

79. *Id.* at 166.

80. *Id.* at 166-67.

81. *Id.* at 169.

82. *Id.*

83. Morgan, *supra* note 2, at 491-92.

Nearly fifty years ago, the United State Fidelity and Guaranty Company published a company history that included a brief description of the United States in the early years of compensated corporate suretyship. The company history states:

> In 1896 the population of the then forty-five states was about half of what the population of the nation is today. In that year Utah became a state; Oklahoma, Arizona and New Mexico still were territories. William McKinley, Civil War veteran, defeated William Jennings Bryan for the presidency of the United States, a country in which more than sixty per cent of the people lived on farms and in small towns. In all but two states, women were barred from voting. Ladies did not smoke - at least in public. Tightly corseted, with large puffed sleeves and with voluminous skirts that swept the ground, they represented the dignity and modesty of the then Victorian mode.
>
> There were perhaps 100 automobiles in 1896, but not a single filling station in all America. Telephones were few, and electricity cast but feeble light over a land where there were no movies, no radios, no electric refrigeration, no airplanes, no income tax, no World Series. The Baltimore Orioles became the champion baseball club, with such players as John McGraw, Willie Keeler, Hughie Jennings, and Wilbert Robinson. The first 18 hold golf course in America was three years old. Victoria had reigned fifty-nine years as England's queen, and Nicholas II, destined to be the last of the czars, was ascending the throne of his fathers. First-class passage to Europe cost $50.00.
>
> Much of America's frontier remained. Some free land was yet to be taken up by those who wanted to go West and start anew. Canada, in its northern reaches, was largely undeveloped. The industrial golden age of the new world was still to come.
>
> There were no huge industrial plants. Mass production lay in the future. Bicycles were the craze, but there were not a dozen miles of concrete road. Dirt roads in counties and cobblestone streets in cities were almost universal. Rural free delivery service was established only after the Act of 1896. It was, indeed, the horse and buggy age!
>
> It took courage to launch a new business, for the financial panic of 1893 had not been forgotten. At that time, however, the foundations of corporate suretyship in America were being laid, and its development was just ahead with the even more spectacular development of casualty insurance to follow not many years later. Both suretyship and casualty insurance came into being in response to a need; their functions had to be performed if there was to be that expansion of commerce and industry which now supports the American standard of living.[84]

Ten years after the founding of American Surety Co., Congress was faced with $35,000,000 in unpaid debts of private sureties.[85] Congress adopted the Heard Act, requiring that the performance of federal contracts be secured by corporate sureties. A 1926 law review article noted:

> Prior to 1894, all bonds of indemnity in favor of the United States were executed by individuals. Because of the insolvency of individual bondsmen, judgments obtained against them in many instances were worthless. At nearly every session of Congress, bills were introduced for the relief of debtors who had guaranteed the obligation of another to the United States. The federal government regards the corporate surety as preferable. The corporate surety never dies, and by close supervision the loss from insolvency is seldom experienced. The companies which may become sureties on bonds where the United States is obligee are required to make quarterly reports to the Secretary of the

84. C. Fitzpatrick & E. Buse, *Fifty Years of Suretyship and Insurance* 13-15 (1946).
85. *Id.* at 67.

> Treasury and submit to inspection, in addition to the supervision exercised by the state empowering them to engage in business. The most recent information of the Treasury Department shows it has approved forty-seven companies authorized to become sureties on federal bonds.[86]

Corporate suretyship was initiated with great enthusiasm. The Preface to C. W. Crist, Jr.'s 1939 first edition of *Corporate Suretyship* states:

> Corporate suretyship, to its earnest practitioners, is the most interesting, the most elusive, the most paradoxical, the most fascinating, of all gainful enterprises. In that it touches upon every type of responsibility, and secures the seasonable discharge of that responsibility, it deserves rank among the elect of businesses and professions. In that it seeks to overcome the frailty of human intentions and lend certainty to the real or implied promise, it is lifted to a plane above the bartering of goods or services.

However, before corporate suretyship could become a major form of commercial security, corporate sureties had to overcome the centuries old English tradition of the uncompensated personal surety. The history of U.S.F.& G. states:

> Personal suretyship was the enemy; unremitting attack must be made on it; and the public must be educated, John R. Bland [Founder of U.S.F.& G.] told his men. But that was a slow process. Personal suretyship persisted, and many looked on the corporate surety with suspicion. *** Neither was the public ready to relinquish suddenly the practice of personal suretyship and accept a new-fangled device, no matter how enthusiastic its converts were. A state treasurer went so far as to refuse to deposit public money in a bank, the deposits of which were guaranteed by a surety company, charging that "it isn't collateral or security of any sort."[87]

C. THE SURETY ASSOCIATION OF AMERICA AND THE TOWNER RATING BUREAU

Despite the enthusiasm of the pioneers of compensated corporate suretyship, heavy losses and the aggressive actions of state regulators lead to the formation of an association to promote the interests of compensated sureties. The history of United States Fidelity and Guaranty Company, published in 1946, explains the origin of the Surety Association of America:

> At the eventful convention of the insurance commissioners in 1908, the statement was made that nine out of fourteen companies had lost heavily in capital and surplus in the preceding four years, and that only five indicated an ability to make a profit under existing conditions. The commissioners' committee on surety companies concluded that it was "time that this most useful business had a system to safeguard the solvency of the companies, for the benefit of the public." Thereupon a resolution was adopted that "a special committee, consisting of nine members, to be known as the Fidelity and Surety Committee, shall be appointed. It shall formulate recommendations for uniform laws or regulations covering the following: capital required, character of assets, special deposits, salvage, indemnity, collateral, reserves for losses, expired bonds upon which claim may be made, adequate rates, unearned premiums, and agreements of indemnity holding reinsurers harmless."[88]

---

86. Arnold, *supra* note 11, at 172.
87. C. Fitzpatrick and E. Buse, *supra* note 84, at 37-38.
88. *Id.* at 68-9.

In response to the initiative of the state regulators, the Surety Association of America was formed in 1908 by fourteen underwriting companies to "devise and give effect to measures for the protection of their common interest and for the observance of the amenities that should exist among them."[89]

At the same time, the underwriters decided that a common rating bureau charged with computing and furnishing rates to subscribers should be formed. With regard to the formation of the Towner Rating Bureau, the history of U.S.F.& G. states:

> With respect to the rating situation, committees of underwriters were designated in 1908 to formulate premium rates for various classes of bonds. Alonzo G. Oakley, then an underwriter in the Company's New York office, was one of the group which calculated the first rates to be adopted. After the experience of a year, the companies decided in 1909 that the function of rate making should be carried on not by the companies themselves but by an independent rating bureau, and the Towner Rating Bureau, headed by Rutherford B. Towner, who had been an underwriter with American Surety Company, was established as an independent enterprise, computing and furnishing rates to subscribers.[90]

VIII. *American Law of Corporate Contract Suretyship*

As one would naturally suspect, interested parties had substantially different views regarding the rules of law that should be applied to compensated corporate sureties. These differences were exacerbated by the lack of any universally accepted principles of the law of suretyship. Stearns' 1903 edition of *The Law of Suretyship*, states:

> The same want of harmony that characterizes the decisions in respect to other questions relating to contracts of guaranty and suretyship is found among the decisions relating to the construction of these contracts. A learned jurist, in delivering the opinion of the court in a recent case in New York, says, "I have examined a great number of cases in the English as well as American reports, in which the construction of guaranties has been involved, hoping to deduce from them some principles which would enable us to decide the case at bar, without adding another to the multitude of cases which rest on their own facts, and are supported only by the adjudications in the cases themselves. I very much doubt whether it is possible to arrive at any principle which can be followed, except in now and then a case, for the reason that so much must always depend on the language of the guaranty, and still more on the intention of the parties, as derived from the guaranty and circumstances under which it is drawn, that rules become general in terms used to express them, and but few cases will occur to which they will apply."[91]

Starting, then, with the certainty that the principles of construction of this class of contracts cannot be reduced to general rules of universal application, it only remains to examine the cases themselves, and from them extract as far as may be such principles of construction as are reasonably well settled.[92]

---

89. *Id.*
90. *Id.* at 70.
91. *Crist v. Burlingame*, 62 Barb. 351, 354 (1862).
92. A. Stearns, *The Law of Suretyship* 108-109 (1st ed. 1903).

In the early editions of his treatise, Stearns argued that the same rules of construction should be applied to the contract of the compensated corporate surety as had been previously applied to the uncompensated individual accommodation surety. Stearns' 1903 first edition states:

> Corporate Suretyship as a business enterprise has been developed within very recent times. The earlier ventures in so called fidelity insurance were unsuited to the needs of the business of the country, and the advantage derived from the application of business methods in the making of a class of suretyship contracts that were hitherto loosely and hastily drawn has only recently become appreciated.
>
> The principles of law defining the rights of the parties to a suretyship contract must of necessity be the same, whether the surety is a private person or an incorporated company, except so far as the liabilities of the latter are controlled and limited by the doctrine of *ultra vires*.
>
> It would seem also to be a self-evident proposition that the contractual relation is the same whether the surety receives compensation for his undertaking, or enters into the contract for the accommodation of the principal.

The courts in some jurisdictions have met the question growing out of this class of business engagements as if Corporate Suretyship involved new and novel questions of law, to be treated experimentally like an invention in science or a discovery of a hitherto unknown force in nature, and the judgment of some of the courts appears to have been suspended until it could be more fully determined what effect this business innovation was to have upon the affairs of the people.[93]

However, the public officials that administered public contracts bonded by corporate sureties had a different view. The Preface to the 1922 edition of Donnelly's *A Treatise on the Law of Public Contracts* states:

> In the leisure hours which fell to my lot in the occupancy of public office, I undertook to gather notes upon the law of Public Contracts. As I proceeded with my work it occurred to me that no book had ever been written on the law of Public Contracts and so I entered upon the task of gathering together for the benefit of the profession all of the principles relating to the subject.[94]

With regard to the interpretation of the obligation of the compensated corporate surety, Mr. Donnelly concluded "[t]here should be no favoritism or tenderness shown to a company organized to act as surety for hire."[95]

A. INITIAL SUPREME COURT DECISIONS

The first opinion of the Supreme Court interpreting a bond issued by a compensated corporate surety involved a fidelity bond. The Court held that the rules of construction that apply to a contract of insurance were to be applied to the interpretation of the obligation of a corporate surety. The 1898 opinion in *American Surety Co. v. Pauly (No. 1)* stated:

---

93. *Id.* at 441-442.

94. J. Donnelly, *A Treatise on the Law of Public Contracts* (1922).

95. *Id.* at 466. In support of his conclusion, Mr. Donnelly cited *Richardson v. Steuben County*, 226 N.Y. 13, 122 N.E. 449; *Village of Argyle v. Plunkett*, 226 N.Y. 306, 124 N.E. 1; *Getchell v. Peterson*, 124 Iowa 599, 615, 100 N.W. 550; and *U.S.F. & G. v. United States*, 191 U.S. 416, 48 L.Ed. 242."

> If, looking at all its provisions, the bond is fairly and reasonably susceptible of two constructions, one favorable to the bank and the other favorable to the surety company, the former, if consistent with the objects for which the bond was given, must be adopted, and this for the reason that the instrument which the court is invited to interpret was drawn by the attorneys, officers or agents of the surety company. This is a well established rule in the law of insurance.[96]

The Supreme Court clarified this rule of interpretation in a companion case, *American Surety Co. v. Pauly (No. 2)*. The opinion states:

> It is, of course, unquestioned that many authorities hold that where there is an ambiguity in a contract of insurance a reasonable doubt as to its construction will be resolved in favor of the insured, because the policy is presumed to have been drawn by the officers or agents of the insurer. But granting *arguendo* that this rule applies to a contract of suretyship of the character of that under consideration, I know of no case which pushes the principle to the extent of holding that the express provisions of a contract must be destroyed and thereby a liability be enforced against the insurer, not in harmony with the contract, in conflict with its spirit, in violation of the manifest intention of the parties, and productive of great injustice.[97]

The first Supreme Court decision to interpret the obligation of a compensated surety on a bond provided pursuant to the Heard Act was *Guaranty Co. v. Pressed Brick Co.* in 1903.[98] The surety claimed that it was discharged by an alteration in the contract made without its consent. Counsel for the claimant materialman argued:

> We contend that the obligation assumed by these so-called guaranty and surety companies, in cases of this kind, is that of insurers and they should be and are being so treated by the courts, and that the law which governs those who for a premium paid assume a possible risk should be applied to them, rather than that they should be deemed "favorites of the law," a term used (somewhat unhappily perhaps) with respect to that social surety, who from motives of kindness and friendship, without interest in the profit and without consideration, voluntarily assume liability for the performance of contracts by, and possible faults of, neighbors and friends.[99]

The Court did not cite, but followed the earlier opinion in *American Surety Co. v. Pauly*. The opinion states:

> The facts of this case do not call for an expression of opinion as to whether, if an unusual credit were given, and in the meantime the principal obligor had become insolvent, or the surety were otherwise damnified by the delay, it might not be exonerated; since neither of these contingencies supervened in this case, we are remitted to the naked proposition whether the giving of a customary credit, with no evidence of loss thereby occasioned, is sufficient to discharge the surety. We find no difficulty whatever in answering this question in the negative. The rule of *strictissimi juris* is a stringent one, and is liable at times to work a practical injustice. It is one which ought not to be extended to contracts not within the reason of the rule, particularly when the bond is underwritten by a corporation, which has undertaken for a profit to insure the obligee against a failure of performance

96. 170 U.S. 133 (1898).
97. 170 U.S. 160, 181 (1898).
98. 191 U.S. 416 (1903).
99. *Id.* at 420.

on the part of the principal obligor. Such a contract should be interpreted liberally in favor of the sub-contractor, with a view of furthering the beneficent object of the statute.[100]

Two years later, in *Hill v. American Surety Co.*, the Supreme Court followed the decision in *Guaranty Co. v. Pressed Brick Co.* and held that the obligation of the compensated surety ought to be construed in light of the surrounding circumstances, including the purpose of any relevant statutes. The opinion states:

> The courts of this country have generally given to statutes intending to secure to those furnishing labor and supplies for the construction of buildings a liberal interpretation, with a view of effecting their purpose to require payment to those who have contributed by their labor or material to the erection of buildings to be owned and enjoyed by those who profit by the contribution of such labor or materials. *Mining Co. v. Cullens*, 104 U.S. 176, 177. And the rule which permits a surety to stand upon his strict legal rights, when applicable, does not prevent a construction of the bond with a view to determining the fair scope and meaning of the contract in the light of the language used and the circumstances surrounding the parties. *Ulster County Savings In. v. Young*, 161 N.Y. 23, 30.[101]

The rule of contract interpretation applied by the Supreme Court to the obligation of the compensated surety is not a rule of special application that is unique to the two party contract of insurance. The rule is one of general application to contracts of all types. Arant's *Handbook of the Law of Suretyship and Guaranty*, published in 1931, states:

> The compensated surety has never been regarded as a favorite of the law. Its promise is generally said to be in the nature of a contract of insurance, and the rules applicable to the construction of insurance policies applicable to it. Hence, where its language is ambiguous, that meaning is adopted which is most favorable to the promisee. This is generally justifiable because the contract is generally drawn by the surety's attorney's agents or officers.

However, it is not a rule of construction especially applicable to the promises of compensated sureties or insurers, but a rule that is applicable wherever the ambiguous language is chosen by the promisor.[102]

In applying this general rule of contract construction to the obligation of the compensated corporate surety a number of courts failed to consider the fundamental differences between a three party contract of suretyship and a two party contract of insurance.

B. EFFECTS OF APPLYING PRINCIPLES OF INSURANCE LAW TO SURETYSHIP

The failure of early court opinions to discuss this fundamental difference between a contract of insurance and a contract of suretyship lead to a number of problems that were apparently not anticipated until a number of courts began to treat surety bonds and insurance policies as being the same type of agreement. At first it appeared that the application of this rule of construction would provide greater security for the creditor without affecting the unique rights and defenses of the surety

100. *Id.* at 426.

101. 200 U.S. 197, 202-03 (1905).

102. H. Arant, *Handbook of the Law of Suretyship and Guaranty* 146 (1931).

that arise out of the three party surety relationship. The Preface to the 1903 edition of Stearns' *The Law of Suretyship*, states:

> It is also true that the rights of the creditor or beneficiary of the suretyship are now receiving a more favorable construction than that was accorded by earlier cases. This without doubt arises in part because of the advent of Corporate Suretyship.
>
> These corporations have challenged the attention of the courts to the more exact relations between the parties to a suretyship undertaking, and many of the later cases are in marked contrast to the earlier adjudications, which in many instances set down the law of suretyship as being merely a series of rules whereby a person bound to pay the debt of another is assisted in evading his liability. ...

The business of the great Commercial States in which the English Common Law is administered is today conducted upon a system of credit which involves the collateral obligations of third persons to an extent fully equal to the direct promise of the debtor to pay, or to perform the duty contracted for, and there is just demand for rules of universal application.

The failure of courts to consider the traditional rights and defenses of a surety that are not applicable to insurers has caused a substantial lack of uniformity and predictability in the law governing the compensated corporate surety. The proper resolution of controversies involving compensated corporate sureties requires the consideration of three interrelated issues. *Williston on Contracts*, states:

> Three categories of questions have arisen:
> 1. Interpretation and construction of the corporate compensated surety's contract with the creditor;
> 2. His rights of recourse against his principal;
> 3. The availability of the ordinary defenses of the uncompensated surety.[103]

The tendency of many courts to treat rights and defenses of a compensated surety as being the same as the rights and defenses of an insurer, ignores three generally recognized distinctions between a contract of insurance and a suretyship. Freedman's *Richards on the Law of Insurance* states:

> There are three fundamental differences between Insurance and Suretyship: (1) a surety obligation or bond is a three party agreement among the Principal who gives the bond, the Obligee in whose favor the bond is issued, and the Surety, an individual, partnership or corporation; whereas the insurance contract is merely a two-party agreement between the insurer and the insured and/or beneficiary; (2) the Surety should theoretically suffer no loss since the risk is within the control of the Principal, whereas the Insurer expects losses, due to fortuitous events over which it has no control, in accord with a table of averages or experience; and (3) the premium paid for a surety obligation or bond is comparable to a service charge or fee, although personal sureties usually do not exact compensation, whereas the insurance premium, even for a fidelity bond, is actuarily computed upon the assumption that certain losses will occur in accordance with the table of averages or experience.[104]

103. 10 *Williston on Contracts* §1213 at 707 (3d ed. 1967).
104. W. Freedman, *Richards on the Law of Insurance* 98-99 (6th ed. 1990).

The almost ritualistic equation of corporate suretyship with insurance has substantially increased the amount of litigation and increased the cost of commercial surety credit. *Williston on Contracts* states:

> Attempted equation of corporate compensated suretyship with insurance in a general way without distinguishing interpretation problems of suretyship rights and defenses must inevitably lead to unnecessary confusion and unfortunate misconceptions.
>
> This confusion may be avoided if suretyship intricacies are unravelled by the use of suretyship principles in light of the factual differences between the compensated surety and the accommodation surety. When the courts are not uniformly true to suretyship concepts, the surety may base his risk calculations on the prospect of having a surety's rights and remedies, only to find himself stripped of them at the crucial time.[105]

A second effect of the tendency of a number of courts to treat commercial suretyship as the equivalent of insurance, was to substantially reduce the study and teaching of the principles of suretyship. By the beginning of the twentieth century, the law of suretyship had developed into a major part of our common law. The Preface to the 1903 edition of Stearns' *The Law of Suretyship,* states:

> The case law involving questions of suretyship is one of the largest constituents of the common law. The equities arising out of a suretyship relationship are extended by analogy to many transactions which cannot be denominated as obligations to pay the debt of another, but come within the range of essential elements of a suretyship undertaking.

As a result of this widespread application of legal principles associated with suretyship prior to the advent of corporate surety bonds written by insurance companies, many scholarly treatises dealing with the law governing the surety were published in the nineteenth century and the first half of the twentieth century. Many of the treatises and law review articles cited in this paper were published by professors who specialized in teaching suretyship.

Suretyship was an important component of the curriculum of law schools throughout the country. The Ohio State University College of Law, taught "Mortgages and Suretyship" from 1923 to 1926 and then a separate course in "Suretyship" from 1926 to 1950.[106] In 1951, the last edition of Stearns' textbook on suretyship was published. That same year, Ohio State eliminated its course on suretyship. The security aspects of suretyship were taught as part of a course called "Commercial Law II" and a seminar entitled "Problems in Public Contracts" was initiated. The seminar included the study of contractor's bonds. The seminar was discontinued in 1961 and the study of suretyship as an identifiable part of the curriculum disappeared.

The tendency of courts to equate corporate commercial suretyship with insurance must surely be one of the major reasons that suretyship is no longer the subject of substantial scholarly attention. The Preface to the 1922, third edition, of Stearns' *The Law of Suretyship* states:

---

105. 10 *Williston on Contracts* §1213 at 708 (3d ed. 1967).

106. I was unable to locate the catalogs of course curriculum of The Ohio State University College of Law for the years prior to 1923.

> The revision shows that although the law of suretyship is not a closed subject, the rules applicable to corporate or compensated suretyship are essentially the same as those applicable to the law of insurance.

The tendency to treat commercial suretyship as part of the law of insurance seems to have added another complicating factor to an already unsettled area of the law and at the same time diminished the scholarly study of the law of suretyship.

C. CONFLICT BETWEEN THE COMMON LAW OF CONTRACTS AND EQUITY

Uncertainty in the law governing commercial suretyship has also been increased by the conflict between the application of principles drawn from equity and the common law of contracts. This conflict between the rules of the common law and equitable principles has been a focal point of litigation involving sureties. The Foreword to Arant's *Handbook of the Law of Suretyship and Guaranty*, published in 1931, explains the conflict:

> This volume represents an attempt to discuss in somewhat critical fashion the elementary principles of suretyship. The writer's efforts to teach the subject, extending over a number of years, have resulted in dissatisfaction with a good deal of the rather well settled law in this field, doubtless not an uncommon experience. *** Reflection has left him somewhat astonished at the extent to which the law in this field, particularly as it pertains to the surety's defenses, is mere corollary of the surety's equitable right of subrogation. Whether the defense set up be the creditor's extension of time to the principal, release of security, release of the principal debtor or failure to utilize security, not to mention others, the courts' conclusions are almost invariably made to depend upon the result of inquiry as to whether the right of subrogation has been impaired. *** The dissatisfaction referred to has led the writer to inquire whether there may not be other bases upon which more desirable conclusions could be rationalized.

Having been less a student of equity than of contracts, it was natural that his approach would be more from the contract point of view, and that he would be less impressed by the traditional view that impairment of the equitable right of subrogation must discharge the surety. Inquiry as to the scope of the risk assumed by the surety, rather than whether the right of subrogation has been impaired, appeared to be the initial inquiry, requiring always that the function of the surety in the ordinary business transaction be kept constantly in mind. When the risk assumed by the surety has been determined, conclusion as to whether particular matter should operate as a discharge is relatively easy. The surety must expect his obligation to have effect in the midst of business carried on according to common practice. If this is so, it would seem to follow that the creditor is not called upon to take any special steps to safeguard the interest of the surety. As long as his relations with the principal debtor accord with ordinary business practice, he should enjoy the security of his surety's undertaking. It must be admitted, however, that it is now often necessary to speculate as to what common practice is with respect to a particular matter, but speculation by courts and writers is a not uncommon phenomenon where a fact is obviously relevant, and no investigation or proof discloses what it is.[107]

Until 1848, the Courts of Law and Equity were separate. In 1848, New York consolidated its separate courts of law and equity into a single court. The opponents of the trend started by New

107. H. Arant, *supra* note 102, at vii-viii.

York were concerned that common law judges would look to the common law, rather than to equity, in resolving disputes before them. By 1887, twenty-two states and territories had adopted codes of procedure that abolished the distinction between courts of law and equity. In 1938, the Federal courts joined the trend.[108]

By the middle of this century, the study and teaching of Equity in the law schools of this country, like the study and teaching of suretyship, was declining. From 1923 to 1941, The Ohio State University College of Law offered three courses in equity. Beginning in 1942, the third course was dropped and in the 1950-51 academic year the separate courses in equity were eliminated. Equity continued to taught as part of courses on "Remedies" and "Restitution."

D. THE RISE OF THE "NEW LAW MERCHANT

In addition to the tension created by the consolidation of the courts of law and equity, the courts continued to struggle, as Arant noted above, with the incorporation of common business practices into the common law. An interesting 1916 Harvard Law Review Article entitled, *Suretyship at "Law Merchant"*, points out the continuing debate about the Law Merchant and its incorporation into the common law. The article states:

> In its report to the Conference of Commissioners on Uniform State Laws at the Washington meeting in 1914, the Committee on Uniformity of Judicial Decisions in Cases Arising Under Uniform Laws discusses at some length the failure of courts to make uniform application of the provisions of the Uniform Negotiable Instruments Act. It finds that this failure has been due principally to lack of knowledge of the "law merchant," quotes from a number of decisions giving judicial sanction to the purpose of the uniform statute, and summarizes:
>
> "With all due respect to the learning of the lawyers and the judges of our country candor calls upon us, in the performance of the duty of writing this report, to call attention to the evidence furnished by these decisions of cases under the Uniform Negotiable Instruments Law, that many of the counsel therein and many of the judges in their opinions are more imbued with the spirit of the common law than with the spirit of the `Law Merchant.' The word `surety' is not to be found even once in the uniform statute under consideration, yet counsel, in their briefs and arguments, as well as judges in their opinions, speak constantly of certain parties to the cases as being sureties. It is a common law term, unknown to the `Law Merchant.' This carrying over into the field of the `Law Merchant' the use of terms of the common law shows that the lawyers and judges have not learned to think in terms of the `Law Merchant' when dealing with questions under the `Law Merchant,' but think and therefore reason as if they were still dealing with questions under the common law. It is this obliteration or ignoring of the distinction between two different systems that leads the judges in many of these cases, including some above cited, to speak of `the common law of negotiable instruments,' meaning the `Law Merchant.' We do not speak of the common law of equity, nor of the common law of admiralty. The `Law Merchant,' like equity, is not a part of the common law; it is a separate system of law."[109]

Today's Uniform Commercial Code attempts to incorporate the substantive law tradition of the Law Merchant with the use of defined terms such as "Course of Dealing"; "Usage of Trade";

---

108. E.D. Re, supra note 57, at 16.
109. Raymond, *Suretyship at "Law Merchant"*, 30 Harv. L. Rev. 141 (1916).

"Merchant"; and "Between Merchants." It also defines the term "Surety" to include guarantor.[110]

The growing contemporary emphasis on Alternative Dispute Resolution (ADR), seems to lead us back to the traditional procedural practices of the merchants of London in the fourteenth, fifteenth, sixteenth and seventeenth centuries before Lord Mansfield began to attempt to incorporate the Law Merchant into the Common Law. Perhaps the wide variety of alternative means of avoiding and resolving commercial disputes should be called the "New Law Merchant."

Even our contemporary law courts cannot resist the tradition of the special jury of the Law Merchant. Under the headline *In Manhattan, New Court Cuts Business Cases*, the January 5, 1993 Wall Street Journal reported:

> In New York State and elsewhere, civil-court judges generally are expected to preside over a range of litigation, including business and non-business cases. But New York court officials, frustrated by a backlog of almost 50,000 civil cases, believe judges with a business specialty may be able to grasp more quickly the complex issues involved in many commercial cases. In addition, the judges will be permitted to develop their own procedures to streamline cases and encourage settlements of suits.

Lawyers in several states have been campaigning for specialized trial courts to handle business litigation, but Matthew Crosson, New York's top court administrator, said the Manhattan arrangement is the first in which a general trial court has implemented such a program.

The Pennsylvania Legislature has been considering a bill that would set up a specialized court system for business litigation but has not acted to date. Delaware already has a specialized business court, but it isn't part of the state's regular court system and deals only with matters of corporate governance and requests for court orders and injunctions, so-called equity matters.

While the New York experiment of dividing "business" and "non-business" cases may be unique, Federal and State courts throughout the country have developed a variety of alternative dispute resolution techniques that are being used to attempt to avoid the delays and expense associated with the resolution of disputes under the substantive and procedural law of their respective jurisdictions. Two of the chapters of this book will discuss arbitration of disputes involving the performance bond surety and the payment bond surety.

IX. *Conclusion*

Over the course of its historical development, Suretyship has assumed many forms -- formal, informal -- verbal, written, implied at law -- compensated, uncompensated -- individual, partnership, corporation. The obligation of the surety has been defined by statutes, courts of common law and equity, regulatory agencies and panels of arbitrators, both formal and informal. Principles of suretyship have been applied to a wide variety of circumstances. The rules of law that should properly be applied to the contemporary corporate contract bond surety are difficult to separate from the many diverse, and often conflicting, rules of law that have been applied over many centuries in resolving disputes involving "Sureties" or parties that have "Surety Status."

The January 29, 1993 Report of Daniel Mungall, Jr., Associated Reporter for the *Restatement of the Law -- Suretyship*, raises concern regarding whether the principles of law that

110. *See* U.C.C. 1-201(PP).

should be applied to sureties on construction contract bonds can be effectively isolated. Mr. Mungall concluded, in part:

> This is a fascinating experience. Having worked in the Fidelity and Surety field for about fifty years, it has been an eye-opener for me to find that there is this other world involving credit enhancement devices in financial transactions which can be broadly characterized as suretyship and in which the principles and the attitudes of the practitioners are somewhat different from ours. Additionally there are accommodation parties to negotiable instruments and the Uniform Commercial Code has provisions dealing with this "suretyship" situation. I am told that the current revision of the Code provides that a release of the principal will *never* release the Surety. The development of a project that will set forth reasonably consistent rules of these various worlds without trampling on the accepted principles in any one of them is challenging, to say the least.[111]

Perhaps the time has come to add a new chapter to the Uniform Commercial Code dealing exclusively with the rights, defenses and liabilities of the compensated corporate surety, rather than to attempt to state principles of law of universal application to all transactions that create "suretyship status."

111. Mungall, Status Report on the Restatement of the Law -- Suretyship 7-6 (unpublished paper presented at the 1993 Fidelity and Surety Law Committee Annual Mid-Winter Meeting).

3

Why Obligees Buy Bonds

Lynn M. Schubert

Introduction

Why do obligees spend the money to purchase surety bonds for their construction projects? Assurance. Assurance that their project will be completed in accordance with the contract documents, and assurance that the people who work on the project will be paid for their work. That certainly is the answer we in the surety world tell ourselves. Might it not be, instead, that obligees buy bonds because law requires them to do so? Both answers are true.

In 1894, Congress decided to protect itself and persons furnishing labor and materials from construction defaults by requiring contractors on federal public works projects to "execute the usual penal bond, with good and sufficient sureties, with the additional obligations that such contractor or contractors shall promptly make payments to all persons supplying him or them labor and materials in the prosecution of the work provided for in such contract ...." [1] This requirement, contained in the Heard Act, was amended in 1905 to give the United States the sole right to sue on the bond until six months from final settlement between the U.S. and the contractor.[2] This caused great difficulty for subcontractors and suppliers, and Congress in the early 1930s began holding hearings on this issue. On March 8, 1935, the U.S. House of Representatives Committee on the Judiciary, Subcommittee No. 1, chaired by the Honorable John E. Miller, held a hearing on various bills which had been introduced to amend the Heard Act.[3] In 1935, Congress superseded the Heard Act with the Miller Act[4], retaining first right of payment for the owner under the performance bond, but giving claimants a first right to payment under a separate payment bond. The Miller Act also added a threshold below which bonds were not required of $2,000. In 1978, the Miller Act was amended to increase the threshold to $25,000,[5] and in 1994 it was amended again to raise the threshold for performance bonds to $100,000, but it retained a requirement for "payment protection" for contracts of $25,000 or more.[6] One of the options for providing payment protection was a payment bond.

Clearly the U.S. government believes that the protection provided by a surety bond is valuable.

---

1. The Heard Act, H.R. 86, signed by the President August 13, 1894, Congressional Record – House, Fifty-third Congress, Second Session, page 8592.

2. Hearing of the United States House of Representatives, Committee on the Judiciary, Subcommittee No. 1, Friday March 8, 1935, Statement of Edward H. Cushman, Philadelphia, PA, p. 23.

3. At that hearing, Mr. Dockweiler spoke directly about the requirement for settlement with the government. "From the standpoint of laborers, subcontractors, and materialmen, they are compelled to wait unduly long; and should a contractor default, they are really denied substantial justice on account of this unreasonable delay. Hearing of the United States House of Representatives, Committee on the Judiciary, Subcomittee No. 1, Friday March 8, 1935, Statement of John F. Dockweiler, A Representative in Congress from the Senate of California, p. 14.

4. 40 U.S.C.A. §270 a-f.

5. Act Nov. 2, 1978, subsec. (a).

6. Oct. 13, 1994, P. L. 103-355, Title IV, Subtitle B, § 4104(a)(A) and (B), 108 Stat. 3341 and 3342.

All states and many local jurisdictions have followed suit and now require surety bonds for public works projects of various sizes. Thus, for public entity obligees, the decision to purchase bonds traditionally has not been a decision at all. Rather, it is a public mandate instituted after much discussion of the value of the product. However, as public bodies turn closer scrutiny on all expenditures, more public bodies are questioning the need for, effectiveness of, and cost of these bonds.

Detractors of surety bonds often assert that bonds no longer provide the protection they should. They claim that sureties no longer prequalify contractors, giving bonds to anyone just to get a premium, and that to recover on a bond claim you have to wait years and go to court. Disappointed payment bond claimants make these same claims. These assertions might not be true, but they clearly are the perception of some purchasers, former purchasers and beneficiaries of surety bonds.

To retain government mandates for surety products, the industry must become competent at articulating the true value of surety bonds and ensure that bonds continue to provide this value.

In addition to the critical audience of public owners, is the world of private construction owners and contractors who are not required to buy surety bonds, but must be convinced that they add value to the project. Potential claimants on the bonds, whether performance or payment bonds, also need to be convinced. So, this paper will discuss not only the true value of bonds, but also how that value can be communicated in the most effective fashion to increase the use of surety bonds in both the public and private sectors.

I. Prequalification

The hallmark of the surety underwriting process is prequalification of the contractor. The fundamental concept underlying contract surety bonds is that contractor default is a preventable event, not a fortuitous one. Therefore, sureties spend a great deal of money in the underwriting process in the belief that they can prevent greater expenditures for claims at the end of the day. This prequalification process benefits the obligee (the owner if it is a contractor bond and the contractor if it is a subcontractor bond) in many ways.

First, it allows the obligee to avoid the cost of attempting to prequalify every potential bidder. In fact, it would be close to impossible for an obligee to obtain and evaluate the detailed financial and other information each surety maintains for each of its contractors. Second, it avoids the opportunity for politics in the bid award. Third, it provides an independent third party evaluation of the bidders, and a solvent company to stand behind that evaluation. A contractor which has been evaluated by a third party and determined to be qualified to perform the work is less likely to cause delay and disruption on the project. Additionally, if an obligee is the only entity conducting prequalification, there is no place for a contractor to go for a "second opinion." The surety prequalification process allows a contractor which is rejected by one surety to go to another surety with its application. Since each surety has different underwriting guidelines and target markets, often contractors rejected by one surety will find bonding with another. This allows more contractors to bid on the work, increasing competition and often lowering prices.

Although it is true that contractors which would not receive bonding in a hard market are receiving bonds today, that does not mean sureties have abandoned prequalification altogether. Both sureties and contractors have become more sophisticated in their business analysis and planning. Contractors are finding ways to expand beyond their traditional expertise and geographic limitations. Sureties carefully review the contractor's ability and preparations to make these expansions and award bonding on a more individualized basis rather than by following cut and dried underwriting rules. This increases competition for the obligees, again resulting in better overall prices.

But the true beauty of this system is that while prequalification by a surety increases the odds of a trouble free project, if the surety does issue a bond for a contractor which ultimately does get into trouble and defaults on the contract, the surety is there to ensure that the contract can be completed.

II. Claims.

The second obvious benefit to obligees of a surety bond is contract completion. If the contractor defaults, the surety is there to ensure that the contract can be completed. In the U.S., when obligees require bonds they usually require both a performance and a payment bond, both in the full amount of the bonded contract. Thus, if a contractor defaults, the surety could be liable for up to two hundred percent of the contract price. One hundred percent of the contract price, over and above the balance remaining in the original contract funds, is available to the obligee to complete the work and another one hundred percent is available to subcontractors, suppliers and laborers to pay them for work performed on the project. Both of these obligations of the surety benefit the purchaser of the bond, the obligee.

The most immediately attractive benefit to the obligee is the obligation of contract completion. Most surety bonds give the surety the option to choose how to handle a default. The most recent version of the American Institute of Architects standard performance bond, for example, provides that in the event of default a surety

> … shall promptly and at the Surety's expense take one of the following actions:
>
> **4.1** Arrange for the Contractor, with consent of the Owner, to perform and complete the Construction Contract; or
>
> **4.2** Undertake to perform and complete the Construction Contract itself, through its agents or through independent contractors; or
>
> **4.3** Waive its right to perform and complete, arrange for completion, or obtain a new contractor and with reasonable promptness under the circumstances:
>
> **.1** After investigation, determine the amount for which it may be liable to the Owner and, as soon as practicable after the amount is determined, tender payment therefor to the Owner; or
>
> **.2** Deny liability in whole or in part and notify the Owner citing reasons therefor.
>
> **6** After the Owner has terminated the Contractor's right to complete the Construction

> Contract, and if the Surety elects to act under Subparagraph 4.1, 4.2 or 4.3 above, ...[7]

Certainly the obligee must cooperate with the surety to evaluate the current situation and attempt to keep the project moving as quickly as possible. But the obligee is not required to put the contract out for rebid under most public procurement rules (which would delay the project), is not required to seek additional funding from the taxpayers, is not required to evaluate the claims of subcontractors and suppliers, is not required to allocate the remaining contract balances between performance of the contract and payment of unpaid subs and suppliers, and essentially is protected from the difficulties these things would cause. The surety handles these matters.

Additionally, both the obligee and subcontractors, suppliers and laborers benefit from the surety's obligations under the payment bond. If there is no payment bond, unpaid subcontractors, suppliers and laborers will look to the owner for payment if the contractor defaults on the project. Both public and private owners will find themselves barraged by claimants wanting to be paid. These owners will have to determine the validity of each claim and how to keep these claimants working until their claim is evaluated and paid. They also may be required to pay for the same work twice. Although the owner might already have paid the contractor for the work, if the contractor did not pass on the payment to the party who performed the work, the owner may have to pay again to keep the work moving. This is even more likely on a private project since private owners will find liens placed on the construction project. To have those liens released the owner must litigate or pay the claims.

A payment bond also directly benefits the subcontractors, suppliers and laborers on the project. The bond allows a direct claim against the surety for work performed on the bonded contract. The surety is responsible to evaluate the claim independently and pay if warranted. This allows subcontractors and suppliers to bid for work with contractors with whom they do not have a personal history, relying on the surety's guarantee of payment. It also allows these subcontractors and suppliers to submit a bid that does not include a contingency for non-payment, reducing the bid price. This difference in bid price might be the factor which makes the subcontractor or supplier the bidder of choice to the contractor. Payment bonds can keep a subcontractor or supplier in business rather than facing bankruptcy. Small and emerging subcontractors particularly benefit from the protection of the payment bond as they are more likely to be adversely affected by non-payment on one project. This benefit to small and emerging contractors dovetails perfectly with the public policy of many public entities to encourage small, emerging, minority and women owned businesses.

It is clear that performance and payment bonds provide many obvious benefits to owners, contractors and claimants. What about other reasons obligees should buy bonds?

III. Unseen Services of a Surety

Surety services are not limited to prequalification and claims paying. In fact, much of what a surety does is for contractors either before or when they begin to have trouble on a project. Obligees, however, seldom hear about these valuable services of the surety. In fact, if everything goes right, the obligee never will know that there was trouble. Sureties frequently receive requests for financing from contractors. After all, if the contractor doesn't make payroll on Friday, you can be sure there will be no workers on Monday.

---

7. AIA Document A312 December 1984 Ed.

Sometimes a contractor in financial trouble, but otherwise qualified to perform the work, can avoid default and complete all its bonded and nonbonded work with short term financial assistance. Of course, contractors do not want the owners or developers to know that they are in any trouble, so neither the contractor nor the surety mentions this advance to the obligee. The needs of contractors in trouble range from something as simple as a loan to something as complex as the surety essentially taking over the contractor and assisting with completion of all projects. Avoiding a default is almost always better than cleaning up after one. Further, if you can keep your contractor solvent, you can recover the money you advance at some point when the situation improves. This is not always true when the contractor defaults and perhaps goes bankrupt. Even the best indemnity agreements cannot produce blood from a stone.

IV. What Does an Obligee Want?

The one thing every obligee wants, whether it is an owner or a contractor, is for the construction project to be completed on time, within budget, and with minimal trouble. Surety bonds can make that happen, but the entire industry: underwriters, brokers and agents, claims personnel and outside lawyers and consultants must have that as our first priority. If we do not, owners and contractors will continue the current trend of deciding that surety bonds are not "a product we want." That is just what the attorneys with the New York Department of Design and Construction said when they drafted a particularly onerous bond form a few years ago. The product being offered by the surety industry was not what they wanted to buy. They wanted to be able to call on the surety as soon as they believed there was a default and have the surety restart the project immediately. Yes, they were willing to allow the surety to reserve its rights, willing to discuss whether or not the declaration of default was correct, and even willing to repay the surety funds paid due to an improper declaration of default, all after the project was complete. What they wanted was the project moving! This is not unusual, or perhaps even unreasonable.

Many of the proposed onerous bond forms include that one requirement. In one fashion or another, the project must be kept moving. Many sureties understand this need of owners and contractors and have put in place systems which allow just that to happen. Proactive claims handling is not unusual in the surety world. However, other sureties still send each claim to outside counsel with instructions to investigate fully and carefully, and eventually provide a recommendation as to whether or not the default has been declared properly, the extent of the improper and incomplete work, all possible defenses the surety might have, and what option the surety should choose. While this detailed analysis is taking place the construction project sits dormant, perhaps deteriorating in the weather, clearly getting no closer to being completed on time. While the surety may be well within its contractual and legal rights to take this approach, it does nothing to encourage that obligee to buy another surety bond.

Sureties must understand just what it is they are selling and be sure that they deliver on that promise.

V. Why Obligees Should be Convinced – Contractor Failure

Often obligees claim they do not need the prequalification services of a surety because they only hire contractors they know, or perform their own prequalification process. Although this traditionally has not been possible for most public owners, more and more are putting in place qualification procedures for contractors to be allowed to bid on public work. Private owners, of course, always have evaluated who bids on their construction projects, and general contractors are limited in their choice of subcontractors and suppliers only by price, qualifications and minority and women business enterprise goals. These owners and contractors are typical construction industry people – forever optimists. "I know this contractor/subcontractor, I have worked with this company in the past, nothing could go wrong on this project." Yet we all know that the rate of contractor failure belies this belief.

From 1990 through 1998 91,096 contractors failed in the United States, leaving behind $23,039,782,868 in liabilities.[8] In 1998 specialty trade contractors experienced the most failure: 5,590, with 3,695 general building contractors and 283 heavy construction contractors failing.[9] These failures are not limited to new or small contractors. Five years ago, who would have thought that Morrison-Knudson, Holzman or Guy Atkinson would be in the trouble they are or cause the losses they have? According to Engineering News Record, "Daewoo, Holzman and Perini are among the largest, oldest and most sophisticated construction firms in the world. If they can get into trouble, anyone can.[10] The risk of contractor failure is real, and owners and contractors must face that fact. The impact on them, however can be minimized with good risk management. One of the best tools for risk management of a construction project is surety bonds.

VI. How to Convince an Obligee of the Value of Bonds

To convince an obligee of the value of bonds, they must understand the bond, believe that what it provides it valuable, and believe that the benefits in fact will be provided.

Obligees often do not understand just what a surety bond does, the relationships among all the parties, or how to work together with the surety to either prevent defaults or move most efficiently if a default occurs. A surety bond is not like an automobile insurance policy — you can't just have an accident and call your insurer to send you a check. Most owners, however, do not really understand this. Obligees, both owners and contractors, must be educated as to just what the surety bond guarantees. Certainly, they must be taught about the prequalification process and the benefits that provides, but they also must know just what the bonds guarantee in the event of a contractor default. They must understand the three party nature of the relationships among the obligee, the principal and the surety. They must understand why the surety must investigate the claim to ensure it was a proper default. They must understand that the surety is liable only if the contractor is liable, and that the contractor remains responsible to the surety if the surety makes payment on the bond. Yet, they also must be convinced that the surety bond does provide protection.

One of the best methods to convince obligees of the value of bonds is with real examples. The Surety Association of America, the National Association of Surety Bond Producers and the Surety Information Office ("SIO") all collect examples of these "success stories." When you can describe how a surety's intervention kept an $18.4 million roadway project moving despite the contractor's financial difficulties, completing the project ahead of schedule, and you can quote the owner as saying "[The surety] has proven its resourcefulness and dedication to efficient and smooth running operation" and that completion was a result of the surety's "quest for excellence and proven service," it goes a long way to combat

8. Engineering News Record, July 12, 1999 "Surety: Where the Industry is and Where it is Going," p.S-23.

9. Business Failure Record – Dun & Bradstreet

10. Engineering News Record, December 6, 1999, p.72.

unsubstantiated claims of bad experience with surety companies. Compilations of some of these success stories, along with various other materials, including a presentation designed specifically to address owners, are available from SIO.[11]

VII. Conclusion

Why is all this important? Isn't it true that value always wins and if surety bonds truly are the most valuable product, then owners and contractors will continue to purchase them? Maybe, maybe not. First, do surety bonds meet the needs of obligees? If so, then it is a matter of education. If not, then it is a matter of making sure we all; underwriters, brokers and agents, outside counsel and consultants, are doing our part to make the bonds work. Whether it is drafting balanced bond forms, being more creative in the types of bonds we are willing to write, being more proactive in our claims handing, or just being more communicative with the obligees, everyone should play a part. Second, do obligees know the real story? There is a phrase used in Washington, DC that applies in this situation: "perception is reality." If obligees perceive that bonds do not meet their needs, or that they will never recover on a surety bond claim short of litigation, they will move away from using bonds.

We all must take it upon ourselves to educate potential obligees about the value of bonds. Surety bonds are a product which serve a significant public policy purpose and well as business purpose, and the surety industry is one of integrity and excellence. It is up to us to be sure others know this and help us keep it alive and vital now and in the new millenium.

11. Surety Information Office, 5225 Wisconsin Avenue, NW, Suite 600, Washington, DC 20015-2014, phone (202) 686-7463, fax (202) 686-3656, www.sio@sio.org

4

How Contract Surety Bonds Are Underwritten

Stewart R. Duke
Mary Jeanne Anderson

Introduction

The construction industry in the United States is a vast, multifaceted industry that does projects ranging from paving your driveway for several thousand dollars to building huge airport, rail and highway jobs in the billion dollar range. These undertakings are performed by contractors who tell the owner, be that the federal, state or city government, the local county, the hospital district, the library district, the school district or the private owner, "I will build that project according to a set of plans and specifications you provide and I will see that all the bills are paid for all the material and labor that goes into that project. Further, I will build it for a firm price that I have "estimated" today, regardless of what it actually costs me to do it. I will sign a contract telling you that I will build this project within a given time for a pre-determined price even though the project may take one, two or three years longer to complete than anticipated. I will turn the project over to you just as the architect and/or engineer has designed it and all the bills for the labor and material going in to that job will be paid. I, the contractor, have faith that you, the owner, have the money and will pay me for my work throughout this project, and that if you request changes, you will pay me additionally for those changes."

This is basically what the contractor undertakes and what we, the bonding company, guarantee.

Our subject today is "How Contract Bonds are Underwritten". We will follow the process step by step from the time the contractor decides he wants to do bonded work through to the surety's decision to provide bonding credit. The process will be examined from the roles of the three key players in the process: the contractor, the bond producer and the surety.

I. What The Prospective Principal Should Do

A. Determination to Be a Bonded Contractor

A contractor must first decide if he wants to be a contractor who performs bonded work. In this process there are two major things that he should consider. The first consideration is that a contractor who can furnish bonds almost certainly guarantees that he will be able to obtain work denied nonbondable contractors. This greatly expands his opportunities to aquire work and make money. The second consideration is that bonding companies require a certain amount of ongoing information from the contractor. The contractor must be willing and able to provide a comprehensive package of information regarding his company's financial condition and capabilities. Some contractors simply do not have the desire or perhaps the ability to furnish the comprehensive information needed by the bonding company, thereby in effect shutting themselves off from a huge source of construction revenues.

There are two general areas of bonded work: public work and privately owned work.

Since shortly after the turn of the century when Edwin Warfield convinced the federal government that they should bond all federal construction projects, nearly all public bodies have been requiring surety bonds on public works. Most public bodies, including the federal government, the state government, cities, counties, hospital districts, school districts, library districts and so on, require that projects over a certain dollar threshold level and time duration be bonded. These are statutory requirements which generally cannot be waived. Bonding provides two important services to the owner: the prequalification of the contractor's ability to perform the work (underwriting) and the protection of the taxpayers' money by guaranteeing the project will be completed on time and the bills paid (claims handling).

For the most part, the contracting officers for the federal government or the school board or for that matter most public bodies simply do not have the time or expertise to prequalify every contractor that wants to bid on a project. By requiring a bid bond at the proposal stage and then a performance and payment bond when the contract is signed, the owner's representative is assured that the bonding company has put the contractor through a thorough prequalification process. This prequalification process is a hidden asset of the bondable contractor. It is a stamp of approval setting him apart from others who have not passed the rigorous prequalification standards of the bonding company.

On public work the contractor is almost always assured that the money is available to pay for the work and that the contractor will receive his earned estimates and retainage on a timely basis. Equally important to the contractor and surety is that on public work the contract terms and bonds are generally fair and have stood the test of time. On the negative side, public work often carries the bureaucracy common to government bodies, and the administrative work required can be quite burdensome to say the least.

Industry figures suggest that as much as 85% of all contract surety premium is derived from bonds written on public projects. Therefore, only 15% of the industry's premium source is from bonds written on private projects. While of less magnitude, bonded private work is still an important source of revenues for both the contractor and the surety. There are really no requirements by any governmental entities that privately owned jobs be bonded. Fortunately, we are seeing more and more private projects being bonded at the request of the lending institutions who are providing the owner with the financing for the work.

On private work, there is no guarantee that the owner has money available to pay for the work as there is on public projects. There have been some very successful contractors who do a lot of private work who have been left with slow or hung receivables from private owners who ran out of money. This can severely hamper the contractor's cash flow and ability to pay his bills which in turn will limit his ability to get additional bond credit.

A contractor is faced with less bureaucracy in doing private work, but on the other hand the contractor may be confronted with onerous contract terms and bond forms drafted by the private owner. If the terms are unfair or one sided, the surety will refuse to write the bonds.

Because of these differences in doing public versus private work, it is common for a contractor to specialize in either one or another. However, even a contractor doing exclusively private work may be required to provide bonding from time to time and will therefore need to go through the surety's underwriting process.

B. Financial Reporting.

Another major consideration a contractor faces in determining whether or not he wants to become a bondable contractor is the type of financial reporting and sophistication of cost records required. Too many times in the past, we have seen contractors apply for bonds who really did not know whether or not they were making money on a given job or for that matter on any of their jobs. They operated on the basis that if they had more cash at the end of the year than they had at the beginning of the year, then they had a successful year. That sort of record keeping is simply not sufficient for the bonding company who needs to know that the contractor has not only sufficient capital to finance his jobs through to completion but a financial buffer as well to absorb any unanticipated losses or slow receivables on his work. Therefore, good financial information is the backbone of the surety's underwriting process.

1. Selection of a CPA Firm

The first step in the actual prequalification process begins with the contractor's selection of a qualified, construction oriented CPA firm, a firm that fully understands the intricacies of construction accounting. There are CPA firms that are perfectly capable at what they do --- which is not always construction accounting. Construction accounting is like no other: for a widget manufacturer, inventory is the value of finished widgets on hand; for a contractor, inventory is the value of the work completed on jobs underway. Determining the value of that completed work is far more complicated than just counting widgets, particularly when actual costs and profits are never known until the job is complete.

The truly professional construction CPA concentrates on contractors and is closely allied with the contractor's bonding company and bank. When deciding on a CPA firm, the contractor should talk to other contractors and interview CPA firms to make certain they can handle his business. They should be able to set up a cost control system for the contractor, a system that can readily supply profit and cost information on each job not only for the bonding company and the banker but for the contractor himself. Spread sheet information on the jobs in progress should tell the contractor, bonding company and banker if the individual jobs are making money, if the projected bid profit is holding or fading and if the contractor will make enough money with this work to cover his overhead and show a bottom line profit. If the contractor sees profit fade on a job, he can immediately address the situation by more tightly controlling the costs, cutting overhead or doing whatever is necessary to return the job to profit. The CPA must be able to provide detailed and accurrate information on which the contractor can base management decisions.

The contractor's method of accounting and the quality of his cost records and financial statements are of primary importance to the underwriting of bonds by the surety company.

2. Financial Philosophies

When deciding to become a bondable contractor there are certain necessary steps that must be taken, steps that should not, cannot be passed or side stepped. The bonding company is looking for contractors with not only the technical ability to build a building, a bridge, a treatment plant or a road but with the financial strength to withstand reverses that frequently come in the construction business. These reverses most often are not of the contractor's own making: a subcontractor going broke, an owner who does not or cannot pay on time, unplanned labor disputes and a myriad of other things that can cause the contractor such problems that his bond must be called upon to respond.

A contractor must have a solid financial position to support bonding credit and a financial philosophy that will assure the bonding company that the financial position will continue to be strong. This requires the contractor to adequately capitalize his company and maintain sufficient net worth and working capital to finance his work and to provide a buffer to absorb any unforeseen financial set backs. There must be a commitment from the contractor to leave profits in the company as well so that the capital base continues to grow as the size jobs and programs do.

Bondable contractors always need working capital so for them to incur any unnecessary drain on working capital is counter productive. A number of contractors, particularly those in the heavy or highway arena, need tremendous amounts of equipment. From time to time we see contractors who feel compelled to purchase this equipment outright, thereby in some instances totally wiping out their working capital. We find in most instances that contractors who lease or buy equipment with long term financing are just as successful as those who pay cash for that equipment.

When a contractor in the heavy or highway business begins to consider being a bondable contractor, it is most important that he keep in mind the need for working capital and strongly consider leasing or at the very least stretching out payments as long as possible when purchasing or arranging for equipment. But at the same time, too much debt service can destroy a contractor if he is unable to keep up with the principal and interest payments. Therefore, equipment should be aquired on a "need to have" basis and not just so the contractor can have the biggest, newest, most exotic machinery or largest fleet in the state.

3. Credit Reports

An indirect financial consideration is the timely payment of bills to creditors and subcontractors. Since the payment bond guarantees that the bills for labor and material going into the job will be paid, the surety company is particularly interested in the bill paying habits of potential customers. The contractor wants to keep his subcontractors and suppliers happy so they will continue to work with him. In many instances it is even worth the contractor's borrowing money if necessary to pay bills on time. The discount a contractor can receive on prompt payment can go a long way toward the interest payments on a bank line, taking some of the sting out of the borrowing. The key is to keep the contractor's record clean thereby potentially giving a greater bonding capacity.

4. Banking

Not only will a good banking relationship make it possible for a contractor to finance equipment over several years, but also it gives a contractor the ability to set up and keep a line of credit or possibly a revolving line of credit to use to finance his day to day operations. With a normal or revolving line of credit the contractor will, as mentioned above, be able to have money available to take advantage of supplier discounts and be able to withstand a period of bad weather or other work stoppages when no estimates are coming in. It is vitally important that a contractor have a good relationship with his banker.

5. Continuity Plan

Another indirect financial consideration is planning for the future with a well funded and well thought out continuity plan. This is best done early in the overall consideration to become a bondable contractor because it is an item in which the bonding company will be very interested. The plan must be set up so the company will not be financially crippled in the event of the death or departure of a major stockholder or owner. The plan should leave the contractor with working capital and worth, so any pay outs under the plan should be funded over a number of years. Key man life insurance can oftentimes be the make or break factor when a principal of a construction company dies unexpectedly.

C. Other Considerations.

One thing the contractor who is applying for his first bond often does not understand is that the performance and payment bond obligations have few exceptions --- the bond does not say the bonding company will arrange for completion of the job except for bad weather, except when a subcontractor goes broke, except when an owner is paying slowly; it simply says the contractor will do the job according to the terms and conditions of the contract and if he cannot the bonding company will see that the job is completed and the bills are paid. The contractor should understand the legal obligations and rights of both the contractor and the bonding company as well as the potential ramifications of a claim under the bond. This can have a bearing on how or even if a contractor approaches a bonded project.

II. Role of the SuretyBond Producer

The discussion of the role of surety bond producer should most certainly be prefaced by a discussion of the **professional** surety bond producer vs. the surety bond producer. There was a time when a contractor could retain his brother-in-law, the local insurance agent, or his best golfing buddy who happened to be an insurance agent to help him secure a bonding line with a bonding company. Unfortunately, it is not wise to rely on other than the truly professional surety bond producer. As financial reporting has become more sophisticated and contract terms have become more onerous, it is vital to have an agent, a bond producer, who speaks the language of the construction company and the bonding company; who understands why the bonding company wants a copy of the 1120S; who wants to know about locked in capital of a Subchapter S company; and who understands over and underbillings, profit fades and all the things in which the bonding company is vitally interested.

In addition, the professional surety producer should be active in construction industry organizations and associations so he will be aware of information vital to the contractor and bonding company. He should be able to explain to the contractor the various bonding and insurance companies' concerns and to discuss industry issues and initiatives. If nothing else, the professional bond producer will become familiar with other contractors, subcontractors, suppliers, architects and public officials operating within the contractor's marketplace. These factors all go toward making the relationship between the producer, contractor and bonding company a more knowledgeable one. The selection of a professional bond producer is a must in the overall scenario of how contract bonds are underwritten.

The professional surety bond producer's actual role is one of lending support to both the contractor and the bonding company. It is the bond producer who meets with the contractor and gathers all the underwriting information. He is the initial underwriter of the account for the bonding company. As with most things, presentation has a great deal to do with the ultimate success of any endeavor. It is the role of the producer to make certain the contractor's experience, credit record and financial condition are presented in the most favorable manner, thus the need for someone who understands what the bonding company wants to see in order to consider an account for bond credit.

In addition to presenting the initial underwriting case to the bonding company, it is the producer's continuing role to gather annual financial information, bank line information, spread sheet information and all the other items needed by the bonding company. On an ongoing basis the producer must furnish interim job progress information obtained from the contractor, and he should be well aware of any problems the contractor is experiencing, any change in ownership, any major equipment purchases or any other changes in the contractor's operation. The agent should keep the surety informed of any new areas the contractor is considering, such as bidding work out of his normal operating territory or undertaking an entirely different category of work, all the things that go to make up surprises to the bonding company. Bonding companies don't like to find out by reading the daily newspaper that the stock in their contractor's company has been sold to someone else or that a building contractor has taken out plans on a highway job. The professional bond producer should be aware of these types of things and should pass them on to the bonding company.

The more day to day role of the producer is that of obtaining information for the actual bidding of the work. In many instances the surety company must review the bid bond form, the contract itself and the performance and payment bond forms before a risk can be approved. Therefore, the producer must be able to obtain and evaluate this information himself prior to passing it along to the bonding company. If the information raises an issue, a professional producer will address and resolve the issue before sending the information to the bonding company rather than wait for their analysis and request for more information. If the producer is not adding value, then he is only a middle man and not really supporting his client.

III. Role of the Company Underwriter

The initial role of the company underwriter is to evaluate the proposed contractor's account. This process normally begins with the bond producer's submission of the contract account to the local branch office of the bonding company. As mentioned earlier, the initial presentation is highly important. It is often the very first time the bonding company has seen this particular account; therefore the information and presentation by the bond producer must give the bonding company not only an overview of the entire construction operation but a feeling of comfort with the risk in order to proceed with the consideration of the account.

The bonding company will probably want a New Account Profile form completed, a form that will be 4 to 6 pages in length which gives a quick overview of the construction company. The New Account Profile will ask for the following information:

- ownership breakdown of the company;
- number of years in business;
- type of work performed;
- largest jobs completed, including descriptions of the work and final profit;
- method of reporting financial information;
- method of reporting taxes;
- continuity plans;
- bank arrangements;
- related companies;
- subcontractor policies;
- prior surety relationships; and so on.

In addition to this profile of the construction company itself, the bonding company will frequently require resumes on the owners and key employees. The success or failure of individuals in prior operations can, in some instances, be a major consideration by the bonding company. Many times when submitting a proposal to the bonding company, the contractor will include a comprehensive listing of prior projects bid by various individuals within his organization and the bidding results. In addition to this list of projects bid, we many times see a listing of recent jobs obtained and completed showing the gross profit on each job. This sort of information is invaluable to the prospective bonding company as it gives them a quick overview of strengths and weaknesses in the bidding process of the potential new contract account.

The bonding company normally asks about and wants copies of the construction firm's continuity plan, the plan that enables the firm itself to continue to operate, financially strong, in the event of the departure or death of a major owner. As mentioned earlier, the bond has few exceptions. There is no exception for a major stockholder dying unexpectedly, for example. If the bonding company is on a large, long term job and a major owner dies and the company is obligated to purchase back his interest in the company, there can be a major financial drain on the company at a time when the company cannot afford it. Even worse, there can be a major impact on the management of the organization if no one else has been groomed to handle the deceased's duties. Therefore, the bond underwriter is vitally interested in the prospective contractor's continuity plan.

The underwriter looks for both financial and managerial continuity in the Plan. Does it allow for a long term buy back of the departing owner's interest? Will this buy back destroy the contractor's working capital and worth? Is there life insurance to fund this buy back in the event of a death? Is there a mechanism in the continuity plan to extend the buy back of the departing owner's interest -- say 5 to 10 years? Who else can step into the shoes of each key member of the management team? In other words, can the bonding company feel secure in the knowledge that the construction company will continue to be a viable entity to complete that large, long term job in the event a major owner dies or departs the operation.

The bonding company will ask for copies of prior tax returns, particularly if they are looking at a Subchapter S corporation. Contractors can pay taxes on an accounting basis different than the one used in the financial statement. The tax filings are used to determine the adequacy of tax reserves set up against income in the statement. They are also useful to verify the items in the CPA statement and to determine the taxed portion of Subchapter S earnings, information not normally included in the CPA statement.

At least three prior fiscal year end financial statements are most frequently requested by the bonding company. Financial statements should be prepared on a percentage of completion basis and include spread sheets on jobs under way and those completed during that fiscal year. With these spread sheets, the bonding company can track jobs bid, see if the original bid profit is holding up, see if there is profit fade and see if there are overbillings or if there are underbillings. The bonding company can normally tell by looking at three fiscal year end statements if a prospective new account is growing too rapidly, is increasing debt at too rapid a pace or is not making money. Three statements give a quick comparison showing trends and fluctuations in working capital, net worth, current and debt ratios, dividend policies and all the other financial factors that go to the maintenance of bonding capacity.

Next the bonding company will check out the new client's credit record, his bill paying habits if you will. Inasmuch as the bonding company is guaranteeing the contractor will pay his subcontractors and suppliers on bonded jobs, they are vitally interested in this facet of a contractor's activities. Often suppliers and subcontractors are contacted directly to gather this information. Many times the bonding company will contact subcontractors who have done work for the prospective bond account. The opposite is true when the bonding company is considering a trade contractor; we contact various general contractors for whom the trade has worked to see what kind of reputation he, the trade contractor, has for doing his job and paying <u>his</u> subcontractors and suppliers.

In certain instances, prior owners and architects are contacted to give the bonding company a greater comfort level regarding the contractor's reputation and capabilities. Often in the New Account Profile there is a place to list architects and prior owners so the bonding company readily has this information to use at its discretion.

Following the branch office initial contact and review of the prospective new contract account, it is normally forwarded to the bonding company's home office. Various bonding companies have different levels at which the branch must send papers to the home office. For this discussion we are assuming the account is of a size that must be submitted to the home office.

In a great many instances the submission sent to the home office by the branch is thorough enough that few additional questions are asked. The size and complexity of the account determines the amount of home office involvement. Since many home office underwriters are attorneys and CPAs and in some instances both, they will often find things in the financial statements, continuity plan, bank notes or security agreements about which they would like greater information. That word information is one that is often discussed by the bond producer and contractor. When I say discussed, the discussion is usually: "Why does the bonding company want so much information?" It is pure and simply because the bond underwriter in the branch or home office many times finds information within a certain document that may cause a bond loss.

For example, we are frequently told that a bank loan is long term, therefore, the due date should not effect working capital. But in asking for and examining copies of the bank note and security agreement, we find that the note is due within 15 months. That is long term according to accounting rules as the due date falls beyond the current fiscal year. However, if the surety is bonding jobs that will last 2-3 years, the borrowed funds will come due before the work is completed, and if the note is not renewed, the working capital can be wiped out at a critical point. Other points may jump out at the underwriter as well. For example, we have found situations where the stock in the construction company has been held as collateral on a loan leaving the surety in a pretty bad position should there be a default.

In close examination of spreadsheets showing the progress of specific jobs, the underwriter might find major fades in the original profit estimate or a job being not completed timely, going into the penalty phase. Sometimes when looking at gross profit on all the contractor's jobs on hand, we find it is less than the contractor's historical overhead and determine that as long as he continues to get work and maintain cash flow, things will be okay; but if he goes for several months without getting a new job to generate more cash, it would not take long for major problems to occur.

The underwriter might find that the continuity plan is set up to pay out in one year, which could totally deplete the working capital and a large part of the contractor's worth. There are a myriad of items that can be gleaned from close examination of various pieces of information requested by the bonding company and these observations may not only circumvent a loss to the surety company but prevent the contractor from having a loss as well.

After the initial underwriting has been completed by the branch and home office underwriter, after all the questions have been answered satisfactorily and a contractor/bonding company relationship has been established, oftentimes come --- *more questions* on specific jobs, specific contract documents and specific bond forms. Bonding companies are frequently accused of wanting too much information, but in the overall scheme of surety underwriting, information supplied to the bonding company may not only prevent a bond loss but save the contractor from disaster. On larger jobs we normally review the construction contract and bond forms in the home office. To my surprise I have had contractors say things like, "You really read those contracts, don't you?" when we point out to them a particularly onerous contract or bond term, a long term warranty, a defeasance clause, a declared default provision in the bond or a totally unreasonable hold harmless and/or indemnity clause, any one of which could cause major repercussions to the contractor and possibly to the bonding company.

The system of first review by the branch followed by home office review is a system of checks and balances. The role of a company underwriter is not only to protect his company from a loss but also to help the contractor protect and preserve his company and his worth. The role of the company underwriter is not one of an order taker, not one of simply a bond writer, but as the name implies, an underwriter. The underwriter is a person who looks at all the financial figures, the credit experience, the bonding relationship and the technical expertise and makes an underwriting decision --- an educated, well thought out decision that will benefit both the surety company and the contractor client.

The underwriting of surety bonds is not an exact science; however, underwriting can be refined through the cooperation of the producer, the surety company and the contractor to a point where we can each prosper and hold losses to a minimum. In this process the role of the producer, the role of the company underwriter and of course the role of the contractor all mesh into this system, uniquely American, that enables our construction industry to be one of the largest, most diversified and innovative on the face of the earth.

IV. Indemnity and Collateral

A. Indemnity

Indemnity to the surety will be covered in greater depth in other parts of this program, so we will not get into the legal aspects at all. This discussion that follows is based on outside indemnity, not the normal indemnification of the surety by the construction firm itself.

Sureties prefer and for the most part obtain personal indemnity on most construction corporations and partnerships. Aside from the legal ramifications of the indemnity and indemnity agreement, we feel that it is a manifestation by the stockholders and/or partners of a construction firm that they are fully behind their company and have faith enough in their company to, as we say, "get on the line".

Since American construction companies are for the most part family owned, many times with the husband, wife and their children all involved in the construction company, devoting almost their entire life to the endeavor, it is normally not a difficult task to obtain personal indemnity of those involved. This is, of course, not the case in publicly held corporations which have huge net worths and make outside indemnity unnecessary.

Additional outside indemnity can increase bonding capacity. For the most part the bonding capacity is predicated upon the worth and working capital in the principal corporation itself but occasionally bonding credit can be increased by adding the worth and working capital of outside principals who give their personal indemnity.

Although we see relatively few construction companies which are limited partnerships, in those cases it is prudent to obtain the additional personal indemnity of the limited partners. This is done for basically the same reasons as outlined above, to indicate to us that they are willing to stand behind their construction operation and in some small measure lend financial strength to the working capital and worth of the front line construction company thereby giving potentially greater bonding capacity.

Finally, and perhaps most importantly, the principal and outside indemnitors must be instructed to read and acknowledge an understanding of what they are signing when they sign an indemnity agreement. It is important that they recognize their responsibilities and rights as well as those of the bonding company.

B. Collateral

From an underwriting standpoint, the use of collateral is normally <u>not</u> a consideration. In the first place, contract bonds must be written on the merits of the applicant, the financial strength, experience and credit worthiness of the applicant. If an applicant lacks any one of these features and we do not feel comfortable enough to write the bond, the use of collateral certainly does not enhance the risk.

Rather than confuse the issue on collateral for contract surety bond underwriting, it fair to say that collateral is not an underwriting tool used except by those bonding companies who service the infrequent bond users who are not set up for bonding credit in the standard markets. Collateral is often used as a normal underwriting tool for other types of surety bonds.

V. Reinsurance

The ability to spread risk through reinsurance is one of the most important facets of the surety industry, particularly today as the contract prices and bond penalties are larger than ever before.

Through the process of reinsurance, the primary company gains capacity to handle bonds that are larger than the surety's risk appetite on a single bond. Reinsurance also provides capacity for the surety on bonds that are larger than the single bond amount allowed by its authorized Treasury List capacity.

For example, a surety company that has a policyholders' surplus of $250,000,000 would be qualified by the U. S. Treasury Department to write a single bond with a penalty up to $25,000,000, which is 10% of its surplus. However, the surety may not want to expose its surplus to a single loss this large, so the surety would pass part of the risk of loss and the associated premium to another company, a reinsurer. The reinsurer would pay the surety a commission to reimburse the surety for the costs it incurred in aquiring and underwriting the bond. If there is a loss on the bond, the surety and the reinsurer will share in the loss proportionate to the amount of the risk each assumed on the bond.

Reinsurance is a critical tool in enabling a surety to write single bonds in amounts in excess of its Treasury limitation. As an example, let's use the same hypothetical surety mentioned above with a $25,000,000 Treasury limit. If one of the surety's contractor clients needs a $40,000,000 bond, the surety must get reinsurance to cover the amount in excess of its Treasury limit, which would be $15,000,000 in this example. Additionally, some owners, including the federal government, require that the surety signing a bond in an amount exceeding its Treaury limit have another surety or approved reinsurer also sign the bond as a co-surety. Together the companies must have a combined Treasury limit equal to or greater than the bond penalty.

A. Treaty Reinsurance

Any discussion of reinsurance must begin with an understanding of treaty or automatic reinsurance. This is a contract, or treaty, between the primary surety company and the reinsuring company that says basically that the reinsuring company will automatically accept a share of the risk on a defined part of the business that the surety writes. A few classes of business are specifically excluded, and these will be reinsured only by special exception. In all other cases the reinsurer will accept its share automatically. In reality, while the reinsurer does not underwrite each contractor or bond written by the surety, the reinsurer has underwritten the surety company itself and feels comfortable with its underwriting ability, its book of business, its expertise, its ethics and so on and is comfortable enough to, as we say in the surety business, "give them the pen" to commit the reinsurers' financial statement on bonds.

Since many of the professional reinsurers have similar arrangements with a number of primary bonding companies, it is evident that they can build up a huge book of business. Therefore to protect themselves and to give themselves additional capacity, the reinsurers also have treaties with other reinsurers under which they retrocede portions of their risk.

One common form of treaty reinsurance is the pro-rata or surplus share treaty under which the reinsurer participates on a pro-rata basis on all bonds over a certain threshhold amount written by the surety. This protects the surety from problems if there is a high frequency of losses as the reinsurer takes a piece of the loss on each bond under the treaty.

The other common form of treaty reinsurance is excess of loss coverage. This may take several forms such as excess cover over a given aggregate loss, a specific occurrence loss on a given account or even an excess cover over a specific loss on a given pre-set amount. This form of excess coverage, or catastrophe coverage, keeps the primary company from incurring loss over a given amount on their entire book of business. For example, the surety will take care of all losses on all accounts in a given year aggregating up to $50,000,000 and above that amount the reinsurer will pick up the losses. Excess of loss reinsurance protects against severity of losses. It prevents a catastrophic year from bankrupting the surety.

The subject of treaty reinsurance is a broad one, one that could be carried on ad infinitum, but suffice it to say it's a system that has worked well for the primary surety company, the construction industry, the owners and material suppliers. It is a system that has given our market capacity to handle some extremely large bonds.

B. Facultative Reinsurance.

Unlike treaty reinsurance where the reinsurer underwrites the primary company itself, facultative reinsurance is a system whereby each risk is specifically underwritten by both the surety and reinsuring company.

Facultative reinsurance most often comes into play when a primary company has a bond of a size that is greater than the aggregate amount which can be written within the limits of its own capacity and that of its treaty. Use the example of the surety with a $25,000,000 Treasury limit that needs to execute a $150,000,000 bond. The primary company within its appetite and within its treasury limit may keep up to $25,000,000 of the bond and reinsure with its treaty the next $50,000,000, but that leaves them short of coverage by $75,000,000. This remaining portion would have to be covered facultatively, which is really no more than going to other primary companies and offering them, with a special underwriting package, a portion of that $75,000,000 of coverage needed. The home office underwriter will typically send submissions to six or seven other primary companies asking them to participate on the bond and the other companies normally come back and accept varying amounts totaling up the $75,000,000 needed. The entire $150,000,000 bond is covered in a relatively short time with the risk being spread among the primary company who is actually writing the bond, possibly five to ten reinsurers who are on the primary company's treaty and possibly five to ten facultative reinsurers.

VI. Conclusion

This represents a very high level review of "How Contract Bonds Are Underwritten". It is a subject difficult to cover in a single paper due to a seemingly infinite number of factors which can influence a decision on a particular risk. The underwriting process is both an art form and a science relying heavily on accurrate information and common sense. It is a process that is uniquely American, a process that has served and will continue to serve the construction industry, public owners, private owners and the credit industry well.

It is a process that is understood by few, frequently under fire by many, but one that ultimately has prevailed and thrived.

5

Bid Bonds

Allen N. David

I. Introduction

A bid bond is a very limited form of performance bond. It guarantees that if the principal is the successful bidder, the principal will enter a contract with the obligee and will provide the appropriate security in the form of performance and payment bonds.[1] The purpose of a bid bond is to "afford protection against a change involving substantial damages, loss or detriment by the party soliciting the bids." [2] The penal sum of the bid bond is usually in the amount of 5% to 10% of the bid. In the event the principal does not enter into a contract, the extent of the surety's liability will depend upon the precise wording of the bond.

The most common form of bid bond used for private contracts is the so-called damage bond. Under this type of bond, the surety is liable to the obligee for the damages caused by the principal's failure to execute a contract. Usually, the measure of damages will be the difference between the principal's bid and the bid of the next highest bidder, but can also include delay damages.[3] The language of the American Institute of Architects bid bond is typical of damages-type bid bonds:

> NOW, THEREFORE, if the Obligee shall accept the bid of the Principal and the Principal shall enter into a Contract with the Obligee in accordance with the terms of such bid, and give such bond or bonds as may be specified in the bidding or Contract Documents with good and sufficient surety for the faithful performance of such Contract and for the prompt payment of labor and material furnished in the prosecution thereof, or in the event of the failure of the Principal to enter such Contract and give such bond or bonds, if the Principal shall pay to the Obligee the difference not to exceed the penalty hereof between the amount specified in said bid and such larger amount for which the Obligee may in good faith contract with another party to perform the Work covered by said bid, then the obligation shall be null and void, otherwise to remain in full force and effect.[4]

The second type of bid bond is a forfeiture-type bond. Though less common than the damage bond, it may be encountered on some public contracts. The main difference between the forfeiture and damage bonds is that the forfeiture bond treats the penal sum as liquidated damages. If the principal inexcusably fails to enter into a contract or provide

---

1. See generally *Chas. H. Tompkins Co. v. Lumberman's Mut. Cas. Co.*, 732 F. Supp. 1368, 1373 (E.D. Va. 1990); 13A Couch on Insurance Second §48:151 (rev. ed. 1982); 10 Appleman on Insurance §5831 (rev. ed. 1981).

2. *Peter Kiewit Sons' Co. v. Washington State Dep't of Transp.*, 30 Wash. App. 424, 428, 635 P.2d 740, 743 (1981).

3. See, e.g., *Peerless Ins. Co. v. United States*, 674 F. Supp. 1202, 1208 (E.D. Va. 1987) (surety liable for difference in bids plus reprocurement costs).

4. Bid Bond, AIA Document A310 (Feb., 1970 ed.)

bonds, the surety forfeits the penal sum, even though the obligee's actual damages may be less than the penal sum.[5]

Regardless of the type of bid bond used, the surety's liability is limited to the penal sum of the bond. From the surety's perspective, there is no liability, either on the bond or extracontractually, beyond the penal sum, nor is there any obligation to issue performance or payment bonds. The surety's right to refuse to issue performance and payment bonds is usually predicated on language in an indemnity agreement or bond application expressly reserving to the surety the right to refuse to issue any other bonds.[6] In general, the surety's right to refuse to issue bonds has been upheld.

Because of the surety's limited undertaking and financial exposure, bid bonds are issued for a nominal premium.[7] Cases involving bid bonds are relatively rare.[8] This chapter will examine the rights and liabilities of the parties to a bid bond in those cases in which the parties' obligations are in dispute. It will examine the circumstances under which a bid bond surety may be relieved of liability because of mistakes of the principal or because of the fault of the obligee. It will then examine the consequences of a principal's supplying a bid bond that does not conform to the requirements of the invitation to bid. Finally, it will discuss several developing theories under which parties have attempted to impose obligations on a bid bond surety in addition to those the surety expressly undertakes in the bond. These theories of extended liability include potential liability to the principal and indemnitors for refusing to issue payment and performance bonds, and efforts by principal and third parties to convert bid bonds into payment and performance bonds.

II. Relief From Liability - Bid Mistakes

A. PRINCIPAL'S ERROR - BID MISTAKES

By far the most frequently litigated bid bond issue is that of the circumstances under which a bidder can be relieved from liability because of errors in the bid. In most instances, the mistake will be unilateral in that it is solely the fault of the bidder. Contract law has typically disfavored efforts to rescind or reform a contract because of a unilateral mistake.[9] Nevertheless, courts have generally allowed bidders to rescind or reform a bid where it would be inequitable to require the bidder to adhere to the bid.[10]

Mistakes in bids can usually be attributed to four causes: clerical errors, mathematical errors, errors in interpreting plans and specifications, and errors in judgment. Only the first

---

5. See Palo & *Dodini v. Oakland*, 79 Cal. App. 2d 739, 747, 180 P.2d 764, 769 (1947); *Lake Geneva v. States Improvement Co.*, 45 Wis. 2d 50, 57, 172 N.W.2d 176, 180 (1969); *Merrill v. Wenzel Bros.*, Inc., 88 Wis. 2d 676, 277 N.W.2d 799 (1979).

6. See, e.g., *L&M Enterprises, Inc. v. Hartford Acc. & Indem. Co.*, 700 F. Supp. 517, 519 (General Indemnity Agreement provided: "The surety may decline to execute any bond for which request is made without measuring any liability . . . ."); Chas. H. Tompkins Co., 732 F. Supp. at 1372 (General Agreement of Indemnity provided that surety "is not required by reason of any application for a bond or by reason of having issued previous bond or bonds or otherwise," to execute any additional bonds).

7. See *Sheet Metal Employers Ass'n, Inc. v. Giordano*, 230 P.2d 25, 188 N.E.2d 329 (1963); *Chas. H. Tompkins Co. v. Lumberman's Mut. Cas. Co.*, 732 F. Supp. 1368, 1372-73 (E.D. Va. 1990).

8. *Bolivar Reorganized School Dist. v. American Sur. Co.*, 307 S.W.2d 405, 411 (Mo. 1957).

9. See generally Restatement (Second) of Contracts §§153, 154 (1981); Restatement of Restitution §12 (1937).

10. See generally Annotation, 70 A.L.R.2d 1370, 1375-77 (1960); Annotation, 2 A.L.R.4th 991 (1980); Grimes & Walker, Unilateral Mistakes in Construction Bids: Methods of Proof and Theories of Recovery, 5 B.C. Ind. & Comm. L. Rev. 213 (1964).

three can be the basis for rescission or reformation. Errors in judgment are generally held to be the responsibility of the bidder from which there is no relief.[11] In such cases, the contractor will usually choose to forfeit the bid bond if the amount of the forfeiture is less than the cost of signing and performing the contract.

In those cases in which there is a possibility for relief, courts will typically examine four criteria to determine whether the mistake is the kind for which rescission or reformation will be allowed: (1) whether the mistake relates to a basic assumption on which the contract is made, (2) whether enforcement of the bid would be inequitable, (3) whether the parties can be returned to the status quo, and (4) whether the mistake occurred regardless of the exercise of ordinary care.[12]

The first factor -- that the mistake must relate to a basic assumption of the contract -- means that the mistake must be one of fact and not an error in judgment. Most often, the mistake will be a clerical error in transposing numbers from worksheets to the bid form or a mistake in addition.[13] Mistakes can also be based on errors in reading plans and specifications.[14] It should be noted, however, that an error based on a misinterpretation of plans and specifications lacks the objective quality of clerical and mathematical errors and is more likely to be deemed an error of judgment.

The second factor -- unconscionability --is the most important. Unconscionability will be measured in terms of the magnitude of the mistake and its effect on the bidder. The mistaken bidder bears the burden of establishing the bid he would have made had he not been mistaken and the effect the mistake will have in terms of the loss he will sustain if he is not relieved of the consequences of the bid.[15] If the mistake will not have a serious effect on the bidder, or if the mistake resulted in a bid that was within the range of the other bids, a court may find that enforcement of the bid would not be unconscionable.[16]

The third factor -- the ability to return the parties to the status quo before the bid opening -- is closely related to the issue of prompt discovery of the mistake and prompt notification to the awarding authority. If the awarding authority is notified of the mistake immediately after the bid opening, it will usually be difficult for the awarding authority to argue

---

11. See *Osberg Const. Co. v. City of the Dalles*, 300 F. Supp. 442, 445 (D. Or. 1969); *Ruggiero v. United States*, 420 F.2d 709, 713 (Cl. Ct. 1970).

12. *M. J. McDonough Co. v. Jane Lamb Mem. Hosp.*, 302 F. Supp. 482, 485 (S.D. Iowa 1969); Dick Corp. v. Associated Elec. Coop., Inc., 475 F. Supp. 15, 20 (W.D. Mo. 1979); *Peerless Cas. Co. v. Housing Auth. of Hazelhurst*, 228 F.2d 376 (5th Cir. 1955); *Mount St. Mary's College v. Aetna Cas. & Sur. Co.*, 233 F. Supp. 787 (D. Md. 1964), aff'd, 344 F.2d 331 (4th Cir. 1965); *Puget Sound Painters, Inc. v. State*, 45 Wash. 2d 819, 278 P.2d 302 (1954); *M. F. Kemper Const. Co. v. Los Angeles*, 37 Cal. 2d 696, 235 P.2d 7 (1951), *Baltimore v. DeLuca-Davis Const. Co.*, 210 Md. 518, 124 A.2d 557 (1956); *Donaldson v. Abraham*, 68 Wash. 208, 122 P. 1003 (1912). See generally Annotation, 2 A.L.R. 4th 991 (1980).

13. See *Dick Corp. v. Associated Elec. Coop., Inc.*, 475 F. Supp. 15 (W.D. Mo. 1979) (error in transposition); *Wallace Indus. Const. v. Louisiana Elec. Coop.*, 348 F. Supp. 675 (M.D. La. 1972) (error in addition); *Osberg Const. Co. v. City of the Dalles*, 300 F. Supp. 442 (D. Or. 1969) (relief from bid mistakes usually based on clerical or mathematical errors).

14. *See Balban Gordon Co. v. Brighton Sewer Dist.*, 67 Misc. 2d 76, 323 N.Y.S.2d 724 (1971); *Brook Lea Country Club, Inc. v. Hanover Ins. Co.*, 61 Misc. 2d 896, 306 N.Y.S.2d 780 (1969); *Connecticut v. F.H. McGraw & Co.*, 41 F. Supp. 369 (D. Conn. 1941); *Union Tank Car Co. v. Wheat Bros.*, 15 Utah 2d 101, 387 P.2d 1000 (1964).

15. See *M. J. McDonough Co. v. Jane Lamb Mem. Hosp.*, 302 F. Supp 482 (S.D. Iowa 1969) (error of 10% of total bid*); Dick Corp. v. Associated Elec. Coop., Inc.*, 475 F. Supp. 15 (W.D. Mo. 1979) ($1,000,000 error); *National Fire Ins. Co. v. Brown & Martin Co.*, 726 F. Supp. 1036 (D.S.C. 1989), aff'd, 907 F.2d 1139 (4th Cir. 1990). See generally Restatement (Second) of Contracts §153 comment c (1981).

16. See *Crenshaw County Hosp. Bd. v. St. Paul Fire & Marine Ins. Co.*, 411 F.2d 213 (5th Cir. 1969). *Cf. O'Neill v. Broadview, Inc.*, 112 So.2d 280 (Fla. App. 1959).

that it has been prejudiced by the mistake.[17] If, however, the party inviting the bid has already relied on the mistaken bid, relief might be denied.[18] This will usually arise in the context of a general contractor soliciting bids from subcontractors for inclusion in the general contractor's own bid. If the general contractor uses a mistaken sub-bid in calculating its own bid, the mistaken subcontractor may not be able to rescind or reform its sub-bid if the general contractor has already submitted its bid to the awarding authority.[19]

The final factor -- absence of negligence -- could be more accurately described as an absence of gross negligence or bad faith. Most bid mistakes involve negligence to some degree, even if only an error in transposing numbers, and the cases allowing rescission or reformation implicitly acknowledge this fact. Indeed, some cases explicitly recognize that the bidder need not be free from negligence if the bidder acts in good faith and the other criteria for relief are satisfied.[20]

Although the majority rule is that a bidder can be relieved of the consequences of a mistaken bid under the appropriate circumstances, at least two jurisdictions -- Pennsylvania and Ohio -- appear to adhere to the "firm bid" rule under which bidders and sureties are strictly liable for bid mistakes. The rule is based on the need for certainty, which courts find embodied in bid bond statutes.[21] In Pennsylvania at least, there is the ability to ameliorate this rigid rule by resorting to the principle that conditions for a forfeiture of the bid security must be "fully ripe." If the awarding authority has not strictly complied with its obligations under the bidding statute, the conditions will not be "fully ripe" for a forfeiture and the bidder can rescind its bid.[22]

B. OWNER'S ERROR

In addition to bid errors, principals and sureties can be relieved of liability on bid bonds if the owner's or awarding authority's acceptance of the bid does not conform to the procedures established in the bid invitations. To be sure, most of the cases involving nonconforming acceptances also involve bid errors, which is not surprising because contractors would not ordinarily want to withdraw a bid unless there was a problem with it. A nonconforming acceptance by the owner, however, is an independently sufficient justification for the

17. *Baltimore v. DeLuca-Davis Const. Co.*, 210 Md. 518, 124 A.2d 557 (1956); *State ex rel. Arkansas State Highway Comm'n v. Ottinger*, 334 S.W.2d 694 (Ark. 1960); *Balban-Gordon Co. v. Brighton Sewer Dist.*, 67 Misc. 2d 76, 323 N.Y.S.2d 724 (1971); *La Conner v. American Const. Co.*, 21 Wash. App. 2d 336, 585 P.2d 162 (1978). *Contrast A&A Elec., Inc. v. King*, 54 Cal. App. 3d 457, 126 Cal. Rptr. 585 (1976) (no relief where evidence was insufficient to support finding that bidder had given city notice of mistake).

18. See generally Restatement (Second) of Contracts §153 comment d (1981). See *North Branford v. Fanelli*, 1997 Conn Super. LEXIS 2479 (Sept. 10, 1997) (no relief where awarding authority has accepted bid and bidder delays in notifying authority of mistake).

19. See *Drennan v. Star Paving Co.*, 51 Cal. 2d 409, 333 P.2d 757 (1958); *John J. Calnan v. Talsma Bldrs., Inc.*, 67 Ill. 3d 213, 367 N.E.2d 695 (1977).

20. See *Powder Horn Const. Co. v. Florence*, 754 P.2d 356 (Colo. 1988); *First Baptist Church v. Barber Contracting*, 189 Ga. App. 804, 377 S.E.2d 717 (1989); *Ruggiero v. United States*, 420 F.2d 709, 713 (Ct. Cl. 1970) ("the contractor need not be free from blame"). Contrast *Clinton County Dept. of Public Works v. American Bank & Trust Co.*, 406 Mich. 85, 267 N.W.2d 7 (1979).

21. *Colella v. Allegheny County*, 391 Pa. 103, 137 A.2d 265 (1958); *Hedden v. Northampton Area Joint School Auth.*, 396 Pa. 328, 152 A.2d 463 (1959); *Board of Ed. v. Sever-Williams Co.*, 22 Ohio St. 2d 107, 258 N.E.2d 605, cert. denied, 400 U.S. 916 (1970); *Columbus v. Independent Towel Supply Co.*, 51 Ohio App. 2d 250, 367 N.E.2d 915 (1977).

22. See *Hanover Area School Dist. v. Sarkisian Bros., Inc.* 514 F. Supp. 697 (M.D. Pa. 1981) (awarding authority delayed in awarding contract thus relieving bidder of its obligations); *Travelers Indem. Co. v. Susquehanna County Commissioners*, 17 Pa. Commw. 209, 331 A.2d 918 (1975).

withdrawal of a bid and is recognized even in those jurisdictions which adhere to the "firm bid" rule.[23]

Nonconforming acceptances fall into two general categories: (1) delay in awarding the contract and (2) conditional or ambiguous acceptances. In both types of cases, the defense proceeds from the basic contract principle that an acceptance must substantially correspond to the offer for a contract to be formed. If no contract is formed, the bidder is free to withdraw the bid.[24]

1. Delay. Most bid invitations specify the time within which the owner must award the contract, usually 30 to 90 days. The bidder is required to keep its bid open, sign a contract, and present payment and performance bonds during this time. If the owner fails to award the contract within the specified period, the bidder can withdraw its bid.[25] This appears to be the case even if the bidder has acknowledged a mistake in its bid and has requested permission to withdraw it. In Travelers Indem. Co. v. Susquehanna County Commissioners,[26] the invitation to bid provided that bidders could withdraw bids 30 days after the bid opening so long as the bidder had not been notified that its bid had been accepted. If the bid was accepted and the bidder failed to execute the contract and provide a performance bond within 10 days after receiving notice of the acceptance, the bidder would forfeit the bid bond. When the bids were opened, the awarding authority voted to award the contract to the low bidder, but never informed the low bidder in writing of its acceptance. The low bidder then discovered it had made an error in its bid and requested permission to withdraw it. The awarding authority concluded that the low bidder could not perform the contract, awarded the contract to the second lowest bidder, and brought suit against the low bidder's bid bond surety. The court noted that "[t]he conditions of forfeiture are included in the instruction to bidders, all of which form a material part of the contract between the parties. Compliance, therefore, is necessary for the enforcement of rights and obligations arising thereunder."[27] Because the awarding authority had never notified the low bidder of the acceptance in writing and had failed to present the low bidder with a contract for execution, it had not complied with the instructions to bidders. Notwithstanding that the low bidder had requested permission to withdraw its bid, because there was no actual withdrawal within the 30 days prescribed in the invitation to bid, the awarding authority could not recover on the bid bond.[28]

2. Conditional and Ambiguous Acceptances. Acceptances which state that they are subject to certain conditions or which do not clearly indicate which portions of a bid are

---

23. Id.

24. De minimis deviations in the acceptance will probably result in the formation of a contract. Cf. *Crenshaw County Hosp. Bd. v. St. Paul Fire & Marine Ins. Co.*, 411 F.2d 213 (5th Cir. 1969); *Hanover Area School Dist. v. Sarkisian Bros.*, 514 F. Supp. 697, 702 (M.D. Pa. 1981).

25. See, e.g., *Hanover Area School Dist. v. Sarkisian Bros.*, 514 F. Supp. 697 (M.D. Pa. 1981); *Travelers Indem. Co. v. Susquehanna County Commissioners*, 17 Pa. Commw. 209, 331 A.2d 918 (1975); *Hennepin Public Water Dist. v. Petersen Constr. Co.*, 54 Ill. 2d 327, 297 N.E.2d 131 (1973); *Hendrickson Bros. v. County of Suffolk*, 54 A.D.2d 602, 395 N.Y.S.2d 236 (1977).

26.. 17 Pa. Commw. 209, 331 A.2d 918 (1975).

27. Id. at 213; 331 A.2d at 920.

28. Id. See also *Hennepin Public Water Dist. v. Petersen Constr. Co.*, 54 Ill. App. 2d 327, 332, 297 N.E.2d 131, 134-35 (1973) (low bidder who would have been unable to obtain required payment and performance bonds allowed to withdraw bid where awarding authority failed to award contract within 60 day period).

being accepted may entitle a bidder to withdraw its bid.[29] Illustrative of this type of case is Board of Governors v. Building Systems Housing Corp.[30] in which the awarding authority accepted the low bid subject to approval of the Department of Housing and Urban Development and the sale of the bonds necessary to finance the construction. The court held that the bidder was entitled to withdraw its bid because the "conditional acceptance, since it was not identical to the offer, amounted to a counteroffer and had the effect of rejecting the bidder's offer."[31] Note, however, that courts are divided on whether an acceptance that is conditioned only on the approval of a government agency, diverges sufficiently from the offer so as to constitute a rejection and counteroffer.[32]

III. *Nonconforming Bid Bonds*

A nonconforming bid bond submitted with a bid makes the bid defective. Most invitations to bid say that the contract will be awarded to the lowest "responsive and responsible bidder." A nonconforming bid bond will probably result in a technically nonresponsive bid. Because of the relatively limited purpose of bid bonds, however, courts and awarding authorities have shown a greater willingness to accept nonconforming bid bonds than to overlook other deficiencies in the bid. In federal procurement cases. "[w]hen a bid bond is alleged to be defective ... the determinative issue is whether the surety has sufficiently manifested an intention to be bound under the [invitation for bid] so that the bid bond would be enforceable by the government in the event of a default by the contractor."[33]

Cases involving nonconforming bid bonds arise in two contexts: challenges by a low bidder whose bid was rejected because of a nonconforming bid bond, and challenges by a disappointed next lowest bidder where the low bidder has submitted a nonconforming bid bond. In the first category of cases -- challenges by a low bidder who supplied a nonconforming bid bond -- unless the deficiency in the bond was of an extremely formal nature, the awarding authority's decision to reject the bid will probably be upheld.[34]

In the second category of cases -- challenges by the next lowest bidder to have the low bidder's bid rejected as nonresponsive -- there is a greater likelihood that certain deficiencies will be deemed de minimis. The rationale for these decisions is that the bidding process is designed to obtain the lowest price. If the low bidder is responsible and has submitted an otherwise responsive bid, and if there is adequate security for the bid, awarding authorities are reluctant to forego the cost savings because of a technical defect in the bid bond. The issue in these cases is what types of defects are de minimis, and these have been held to range from minor typographical errors to a complete failure to submit a bid bond.

---

29. See, e.g., *Board of Governors v. Building Systems Housing Corp.*, 62 Mich. App. 77, 233 N.W.2d 195 (1975) (conditional acceptance); *Lexington Housing Authority v. Continental Cas. Co.*, 210 F. Supp. 732 (W.D. Tenn. 1962) (same); *Blue Mountain Constr. Co. v. Grant County School Dist.*, 49 Wash. 2d 685, 306 P.2d 209 (1957) (acceptance did not indicate which alternates were being accepted).

30 62 Mich. App. 77, 233 N.W.2d 195 (1975).

31. Id. at 81, 233 N.W.2d at 197.

32. Compare *Lexington Housing Authority v. Continental Cas. Co.*, 210 F. Supp. 732 (W.D. Tenn. 1962) (acceptance not effective where it was subject to approval by government agency) with *Crenshaw County Hosp. Bd. v. St. Paul Fire & Marine Ins. Co.*, 411 F.2d 213 (5th Cir. 1969) (approval by government agency is formality not affecting validity of acceptance).

33. *PCI/RCI, a Joint Venture v. United States*, 36 Fed. Cl. 761, 773 (Cl. Ct. 1996).

34. See *M&L Indus., Inc. v. Terrebone Parish Consolidated Gov't*, 602 So.2d 321 (La. App. 1992); *SMP Developers, Inc. v. Housing Auth. of Waterbury*, 1990 WL 271002 (Conn. Super. Ct., May 17, 1990); *Donald M. Clement Contractor, Inc. v. St. Charles Parish*, 424 So.2d 86 (La. App. 1988).

The simplest cases are those in which there is a minor error in the bond. For example, in Sullivan v. Baton Rouge,[35] the penal sum of the bond was not stated in dollars and cents but rather specified that it was for five per cent of the bid. The court held that this type of discrepancy would not invalidate the bid. Similarly, courts have held that where defects in bid bonds are cured before or immediately after the bids are opened, the defect can be waived. In R.W. Rhine, Inc. v. Tacoma,[36] the low bidder mixed up two bid bonds and sent the wrong bond to the awarding authority with its bid. The error was noted when the bids were opened and the low bidder allowed to substitute the correct bond. Noting that the correct bond existed on the date the bid was opened and that allowing the low bidder to substitute the bonds did not confer any benefit, the court held that the irregularity could be waived.[37] Likewise, in Marvec Allstate, Inc. v. Gray & Fear, Inc.,[38] the court held that an awarding authority could allow a low bidder to replace a bid bond that was $100,000 below the amount required where the mistake was due to the misapplication of the statutory formula for determining the penal sum of the bond and where the bidder provided a proper bond within 24 hours of the opening of the bids.[39] Other discrepancies that courts have deemed de minimis include: bonds issued by sureties not authorized to do business in the jurisdiction, [40] lack of original signatures, [41] and minor discrepancies in the penal sum.[42] It should be noted, however, that in each of these cases the bid was technically nonresponsible and probably could have been rejected by the awarding authority.

Decisions in cases dealing with discrepancies in the names of the parties to bid bonds are split. In Nationwide Roofing & Sheet Metal Co. v. United States,[43] the Claims Court held that a bid bond issued in connection with a federal contract that improperly identified the obligee as a state rather than as the United States was acceptable. Discrepancies in the name of the principal, however, may be treated differently. In In re A.D. Roe Co.,[44] the low bidder was A.D. Roe Co., but the bid bond identified the principal as a joint venture, A.D. Roe Co. and others. The comptroller general ruled that the bid was nonresponsive since "a bid bond which names a principal different from the nominal bidder is deficient and the defect may not be waived as a minor informality."[45]

Another class of cases involves those in which the bidder submits security other than a bid bond: for example, a letter of credit or a certified check. There is no doubt that the bid would be nonresponsive and the awarding authority justified in rejecting the bid if it chose to do so. In many ways, however, the security provided by, say, a letter of credit is superior to that of a bid bond. The issuer of a letter of credit has far fewer defenses available to it than does a bid bond surety. Thus, awarding authorities have shown some flexibility in dealing with alternative

35. 345 So.2d 912 (La. App. 1976).

36. 13 Wash. App. 597, 536 P.2d 677 (1975).

37. Id. at 660-601, 536 P.2d at 679.

38. 148 N.J. Super. 481, 372 A.2d 1156 (1977).

39. Id. at 491-92, 372 A.2d at 1161.

40. *George & Benjamin General Contractors v. Gov't of Virgin Islands*, 921 F.Supp. 304 (D.V.I. 1996).

41. *Firth Constr. Co. v. United States* 36 Fed. Ct. 268 (Cl. Ct. 1996); *PCI/RCI a Joint Venture v. United States* 36 Fed. Ct. 761 (Cl. Ct. 1996).

42. *Boh Bros. Constr. Co. v Dept. of Transp. & Devel.*, 698 So.20 675 (La. App. 1997) (discrepancy of less than 1%).

43. 14 Cl. Ct. 733 (1988).

44. 54 Comp. Gen. 271 (1974).

45. Id. at 273. See also *K-W Constr. Co. v. United States*, 671 F.2d 481 (Ct. Cl. 1982) (contracting officer could reject bid where name on bid was "K.W. Western Constructors" and name on bid bond was "K-W Construction, Inc.").

forms of bid security and have accepted letters of credit and cashiers checks.[46] Financial guarantees
providing less security than letters of credit and cashier's checks will probably not be deemed acceptable substitutes for bid bonds,[47] nor will substantial deviations in the penal sum. [48]

Finally, there are those cases in which the low bidder submits neither a bid bond nor any other type of bid security. In most cases, the bid will be rejected as nonresponsive. Indeed, this result is probably mandatory if the bidding statute requires bid bonds. If, however, the bidding statute makes bid bonds discretionary or allows the awarding authority to waive discrepancies in the bid, even the complete failure to provide a bid bond may not invalidate the bid.[49]

IV. *Liability Of Bid Bond Surety Beyond The Penal Sum Of The Bond*

Difficult economic times put extraordinary strain on some conventional legal relationships. Parties who, in more prosperous times, would not question the rights and obligations arising out of their legal relationship with another party, in hard times may be driven to take positions that not only modify the relationship, but radically redefine and extend it. Such attempts to extend a surety's liability have been made in the area of bid bonds, with limited success.

The issue arises when sureties who have issued bid bonds to a principal who is a successful bidder refuse to then issue performance or payment bonds. It generally occurs in three specific contexts: (1) indemnitors and principals resisting indemnity obligations arising under the bid bond; (2) indemnitors and principals seeking consequential damages from the surety's refusal to issue performance or payment bonds; and (3) third parties, usually obligees, attempting to convert the bid bond into a performance or payment bond.

A. THEORIES OF EXTENDED LIABILITY

On its face, the bid bond surety's claim to be free of any liability, beyond the penal sum of the bond appears invulnerable. The language of the bond expressly limits the surety's liability to the penal sum, and the language of the indemnity agreement absolves the surety from any obligation to issue performance and payment bonds. Indeed, in most cases, the combination of the bond language and the indemnity agreement will safely see the surety through any claim for damages in excess of the penal sum. There are, however, a number of cases in which claimants have been able to pierce the surety's rather formidable array of defenses. These cases generally rely on one or more of the following theories: (1) the surety is

46. See *McCord Contract Floors, Inc. v. Dothan*, 492 So.2d 996 (Fla. 1986) (letter of credit); *Vukelic v. Unibank*, 1992 WL 214470 (Ohio App., Sept. 1, 1992) (same); *Robinson Elec. Co. v. Dade County*, 417 So.2d 1032 (Fla. App. 1982) (cashiers check). See also *Township of River Vale v. R.J. Longo Const. Co.*, 127 N.J. Super. 207, 316 A.2d 737 (1974) (bid bond is acceptable alternative to invitation to bid calling for certified checks); *Boh Bros. Constr. Co. v. Dept. of Transp. & Devel.* 698 So.2d 675 (La. App. 1997) ("proposal guaranty").

47. See, e.g., *Kennedy Temporaries v. Comptroller of the Treasury*, 57 Md. App. 22, 468 A.2d 1026 (1984) (letter from bank that bank would provide collateral to be held as security for performances should bid be accepted does not satisfy statutory bid bond requirement).

48. *Bodine Elec. v. City of Champaign*, 305 Ill App. 3d 431, 238 Ill. Dec. 368, 711 N.E.2d 471 (1998) (penal sum of 5% of bid rather than 10% deemed material).

49. See, e.g., *F.H. Meyers Const. Co. v. New Orleans*, 570 So. 2d 84 (La. App. 1990); *L&M Demolition, Inc. v. New Orleans*, 534 So. 2d 27 (La. App. 1988); *Shannon H. Holloway Const. Co. v. Louisville & Jefferson County Metro. Sewer Dist.*, 674 S.W.2d 523 (Ky. Ct. App. 1983).

under an express contract to issue performance and payment bonds; (2) the surety is under an implied contract to issue performance and payment bonds based on custom and usage in the area; and (3) negligence. To a large extent, these theories converge, and it is often difficult to differentiate the way in which courts apply them. Because different consequences can flow from each theory, however, it is helpful to try to keep them separate.

1. Express Contract. Arguments that the surety is under an express contract to issue payment and performance bonds are usually based on two theories: first, the bid bond requires the surety to issue performance and payment bonds, and second, apart from the bid bond, the surety has otherwise expressly bound itself to issue bonds.

Arguments based on the language in the bid bond have not met with notable success. In one of the few cases to accept the argument, United States ex rel. Empire Plastics Corp. v, Western Cas. & Sur. Co., [50] the court relied upon the bid bond's condition -- which the court characterized as a "promise to give such good and sufficient bond or bonds as may be required . . .," -- and held that this language "necessarily obligated [the principal and the surety] to secure a statutory payment bond and that this obligation was necessarily intended for the benefit of third-party laborers and materialmen."[51]

The flaws in this analysis are readily apparent. First, there is no indication in the case that the surety had an indemnity agreement with the principal. Arguably, if there had been an indemnity agreement containing language excusing the surety from issuing additional bonds, the result might have been different. But, second, even assuming there was no indemnity agreement -- a large assumption given their near universal use -- the language of the bid bond simply does not support the court's holding. The court's analysis depends on its characterization of the condition in the bid bond that the principal give whatever bonds are required as a "promise" the principal and surety give to the obligee. This is a fundamental misunderstanding of the nature of surety bonds. The surety's only promise, in a bid bond, or most other types of bonds, is to pay money unless certain conditions are met. The surety does not ordinarily itself agree to perform the conditions.[52] That obligation rests with the principal. Thus, in the context of a bid bond, it is the principal's obligation to enter into a contract with the obligee, and it is the principal's obligation to provide performance and payment bonds. To claim that the surety has agreed to provide these bonds would be to claim also that the surety has agreed to enter into a contract with the obligee, since both obligations are conditions of the bond. The latter proposition is absurd, which underscores the error in the former proposition, i.e., that the surety has expressly agreed to provide payment and performance bonds.

A more coherent and rigorous analysis of a bid bond surety's express contractual obligation is seen in Chas. A. Tompkins Co. v. Lumberman's Mut. Cas. Co.,[53] in which a general contractor-obligee brought a claim against a subcontractor's bid bond surety on the ground that the bid bond obligated the surety to supply a performance bond. The obligee argued that the bid bond required the surety to issue payment and performance bonds to its principal, and that the obligee was a third party beneficiary of the agreement between the surety and the principal. The court disagreed on two grounds. First, the surety had introduced evidence of an indemnity agreement which contained language excusing the surety from issuing

50. 429 F.2d 905 (10th Cir. 1970).

51. Id. at 906.

52. An exception is where the surety expressly agrees to undertake certain obligations if the principal fails to do so, as in a completion bond.

53. 732 F. Supp. 1368 (E.D. Va. 1990).

other bonds. The court noted that the indemnity agreement was an "integral part of the contract" between the principal and the surety, and that the language of the indemnity agreement "flatly and fully negates any duty on Lumbermans to issue a payment and performance bond after issuing the bid bond."[54]

Second, the court rejected the argument that the language of the bid bond required the surety to issue payment and performance bonds. It noted that the bond language made

> clear that the obligation to furnish a payment and performance bond falls on the principal . . ., not the surety. . . . The bid bond explicitly states that: 'the Principal shall . . . enter into the contract in writing and give bond.' [The surety's] obligation arose only 'if the Principal shall fail' to perform. In that event, the bid bond only required [the surety] to 'pay to the Obligee the damages which the Obligee may suffer by reason of such failure, not exceeding the penalty of this bond.' Thus stated, [the surety's] sole duty was to pay any damages [the obligee] suffered, up to the penal sum of the bond, in the event [the principal] failed either to enter into the subcontract when awarded or to post an acceptable payment and performance bond. Accordingly, the bid bond did not expressly impose any duty on [the surety] to provide a payment and performance bond; that duty was [the principal's] alone.[55]

A similar case is L&M Enterprises, Inc. v. Hartford Acc. & Indem. Co.,[56] in which a principal sued its surety for refusing to issue performance and payment bonds. Although not entirely clear from the court's opinion, the principal seemed to base its argument on the language of the bid bond. The court noted that the express language of the indemnity agreement defined the rights and duties of the parties, including the surety's right to "decline to issue any bond for which request is made without being subject to liability for such a decision."[57] Accordingly, the court held that the surety was under no express contractual obligation to issue performance and payment bonds.[58]

Although the language of the bid bond is not a particularly secure foundation upon which to base an express contractual obligation to issue performance and payment bonds, other means by which a surety would expressly obligate itself to issue bonds are limited only by the ordinary rules of contract. In principle, there is no reason why a bid bond surety could not expressly agree to issue performance and payment bonds. Such an agreement, if supported by consideration, would be entirely consistent with the language in the indemnity agreement allowing the surety to decline to issue bonds.[59] To be enforceable however the agreement would probably have to be in writing in order to satisfy the Statute of Frauds.[60] There are several cases, however, in which courts have reorganized the existence of a contract to issue bonds notwithstanding the absence of a writing. In In re Outer Banks Contractors, Inc.[61] the court found that there was a contract, but held that the principal's misrepresentation relieved the surety of its obligation to issue bonds. In L.G. Defelice, Inc. v. Fireman's Ins. Co.,[62] the court

---

54. Id. at 1373.
55. Id. at 1374.
56. 700 F. Supp. 517 (D. Colo. 1988).
57. Id. at 519.
58. Id.
59. *Cf. Den-Mar Const. Co. v. American Ins. Co.*, 290 N.W.2d 737, 742 n.2 (Minn. 1979) ("under the proper fact situation, a surety on a bid bond may be bound by an implicit agreement to issue final bonding").
60. See Chas. H. Tompkins Co., 732 F. Supp. at 1377 (bid bond itself does not satisfy Statute of Frauds).
61. 1995 Bankr. LEXIS 1255 (E.D.N.C. Bankr. July 27, 1995).
62. 41 F. Supp.2d 152 (D. Conn. 1998).

held that the issue of whether there was a contract was a question of fact sufficient to withstand the surety's motion for summary judgment, but declined to reach the merits of the issue.

2. Implied Contract. A more common theory is breach of an implied contract to issue performance and payment bonds. Typically, the existence of the implied contract will be predicated upon some local "custom" that a surety who issues a bid bond will, as a matter of course, issue performance and payment bonds. To reach this conclusion, however, a court must first deal with the language in the indemnity agreement freeing the surety from the obligation to issue bonds. The argument based on an implied contract, then, usually has two facets: first, that the exoneration language in the indemnity agreement does not prevent the formation of an implied contract; and second, that there are sufficient facts upon which to base an implied contract.

Both of these facets figure prominently in the leading case in this area, L.F. Pace & Sons, Inc. v. Travelers Indem. Co.[63] In that case, a surety that had issued a bid bond to a principal who became the successful bidder refused to issue payment and performance bonds. The principal not only lost the contract, but ultimately went out of business completely. It attributed the failure of its business to the surety's refusal to issue the bonds and sought to hold the surety liable for all damages, including damages attributable to the loss of the business.[64] In affirming a judgment for the principal, the Appellate Court of Connecticut first rejected the surety's argument that the indemnity agreement freed it from any obligation to issue performance and payment bonds. Paragraph 9 of the General Agreement of Indemnity authorized the surety "at its option [to] decline to execute or participate in, or procure the execution of, any such bonds without impairing the validity of the General Agreement of Indemnity."[65] With virtually no discussion of the relationship between the indemnity agreement and the surety's obligation to issue bonds, the court held that "while the defendant was free to refuse to issue any bond, once it chose to issue a bid bond there arose an agreement, implied in fact, that Travelers would issue the necessary performance and payment bonds."[66] In the court's view, Paragraph 9 of the indemnity agreement

> does not insulate the [surety] from liability for refusing to issue a bond which it was otherwise obligated to issue. The indemnity agreement primarily lists the obligations owed by the plaintiff, as indemnitor, to the [surety]. By its terms, such obligations would mature if the defendant were required to pay on any bond which was issued on the plaintiff's behalf.[67]

The purpose of Paragraph 9, according to the court, is to preclude the indemnitor "from asserting the surety's failure to issue any bond as a defense to an action for indemnification for losses under any executed bonds."[68] Having concluded that the "indemnity agreement did not evidence the parties' intent as to the [surety's] obligation to issue performance and payment bonds after issuing a bid bond," the court then held that evidence of custom and usage in the industry could be used to establish that a surety who issues a bid bond impliedly agrees to issue

---

63. 9 Conn. App. 30, 514 A.2d 766, cert. denied, 210 Conn. 811, 516 A.2d 886 (1986).
64. Id. at 32-34; 514 A.2d at 768-69.
65. Id. at 35, 514 A.2d at 769.
66. Id. 514 A.2d at 770.
67. Id. at 36-37, 514 A.2d at 770.
68. Id. at 37, 514 A.2d at 770.

performance and payment bonds.[69] The Pace decision has been followed by the federal court in Connecticut. In L.G. Defelice, Inc. v. Fireman's Ins. Co.,[70] the court denied the principal's motion for summary judgment holding that there was a question of fact as to "whether it is customary within the surety industry to regard an extended relationship between such parties as a contractual commitment."[71]

A similar analysis is seen in Commercial Ins. Co. v. Hartwell Excavating Co.,[72] in which a principal invoked an implied contract to issue performance and payment bonds as a defense to a surety's indemnity action to recover losses sustained on a bid bond it had issued for the principal. The principal based its implied contract on the custom and usage in the area that a surety who issues a bid bond always issues performance and payment bonds. The surety objected to the introduction of the custom and usage evidence, relying on language in the "Application for Contract Bond," which the surety contended freed it from the obligation to issue any bonds. The court disagreed, holding that the Application was ambiguous because it was an application for bid, performance, and payment bonds. "The instrument did not contain any other language which would identify one specific bond as being applied for. Since said application was not on its face clear, as to just which bond or bonds were being applied for, the [trial] court was justified in considering it to be ambiguous in that respect."[73] Given the ambiguity, the court allowed the evidence of custom and usage, which included testimony from the surety's local agent that he usually issued performance and payment bonds after issuing a bid bond.[74]

It is only in the dissenting opinion that one learns that the Application for Contract Bond, which the court found ambiguous, contained the following additional clause:

> [T]he company reserves the right to decline to issue the bond for which application is hereby made, and that no claim may be made against the Company in consequence of its failure to execute such bond.[75]

This language does not specify which bond or bonds the surety can refuse to issue, and thus does not cure the court's perceived ambiguity in the Application regarding which bond the principal was applying for. It should, however, render the ambiguity irrelevant, because even if the Application was deemed an application for three separate bonds, this clause would seem to allow the surety to issue or refuse to issue any one of the bonds.

The Pace and Hartwell cases have not gone uncriticized. Indeed, the holding in Pace has been described as "nonsensical" and "inexplicable."[76] One of the most remarkable aspects of these cases, however, is that they are easily distinguishable on their facts. The holdings of both cases hinge on language -- in an indemnity agreement in Pace and a bond application in Hartwell -- that is arguably ambiguous as to the surety's obligation to issue additional bonds. In Pace, the indemnity agreement allowed the surety to "decline to execute . . . any such bonds without impairing the validity of this General Agreement of Indemnity." The court construed this language to mean that a surety could decline to issue a bid bond, but once it chose to issue a

69. Id. at 38, 514 A.2d at 771.
70. 41 F. Supp.2d 152 (D. Conn. 1998).
71. Id. at 161.
72. 89 Idaho 531, 407 P.2d 312 (1965).
73. Id. at 541, 407 P.2d at 317.
74. Id. at 539, 407 P.2d at 316.
75. Id. at 548, 407 P.2d at 322.
76. *Chas. H. Tompkins Co. v. Lumbermans Mut. Cas. Co.*, 732 F. Supp. 1368, 1373, (D. Va. 1990).

bid bond, it was obligated to issue payment and performance bonds.[77] In Hartwell, the court held that the bond application was ambiguous because it referred to three bonds.[78]

Given the Pace and Hartwell courts' treatment of the language in the indemnity agreement and bond application which apparently excused the surety from issuing performance and payment bonds, one may legitimately question whether any language, regardless of how explicit it might be, would have protected the surety in those cases. Nevertheless, the courts' holdings rest in part on the fact that the language excusing the surety was either inadequate or ambiguous. This suggests that language explicitly negating the surety's obligation to issue performance and payment bonds should protect the surety from a claim based on an implied contract to issue those bonds[79]. This result seems compelled by the principle that one cannot imply a contract from conduct where there is express language in a written contract dealing with the same matter.[80]

An additional defense to a claim based on an implied contract is the Statute of Frauds, which does not appear to have been raised in either the Pace or Hartwell cases. The requirement that a contract "to charge any person upon a promise to answer for the debt or default of another" be in writing and signed by the person to be charged has been a part of the Statute of Frauds since the eighteenth century and exists in some form in virtually every jurisdiction.[81] An implied contract based on custom and usage manifestly does not comply with the Statute of Frauds,[82] nor does an oral representation by a surety's agent that bonds would be available.[83] Moreover, the language in indemnity agreements excusing the surety from issuing additional bonds presents an additional hurdle to any attempt to circumvent the Statute of Frauds based on notions of reasonable reliance and estoppel.

3. Tort Theories. The least common theory asserted against bid bond sureties is that they are under an obligation to use reasonable care to provide payment and performance bonds for their principals. Although there is no reported case in which a principal has been successful with this argument, at least one court has recognized the viability of the theory. In L.G. Defilice, Inc. v. Fireman's Ins. Co.,[84] the court refused to grant the surety's motion for summary judgment holding that there was question of fact as to the nature and scope of the duty of care.[85] A more typical case is Den-Mar Const. Co. v. American Ins. Co.[86] In that case, a principal attempted to resist a bid bond surety's indemnification claim by arguing that the surety had breached a duty of care it owed to the principal. Specifically, the principal contended that "because of the peculiar relationship between it and [the surety], a duty in tort was imposed upon [the surety] to use reasonable efforts in furnishing a performance and payment bond."[87] The Minnesota Supreme Court rejected this argument noting that in general an insurer has no

77. 9 Conn. App. at 35, 514 A.2d at 769-70.

78. 89 Idaho at 541, 407 P.2d at 317.

79. See L&M Enterprises, 700 F. Supp. at 519; Chas. H. Tompkins Co., 732 F. Supp. at 1374-75.

80. See generally A. Corbin, 1 Contracts § 18 (1951). This might not, however, protect a surety against a claim that it waived the express contract in some fashion and that an implied contract obligating the surety to issue payment and performance bonds arose thereafter.

81. See generally Restatement (Second) of Contracts, 281-290 (1979).

82. See, e.g., Chas. H. Tompkins Co., 732 F. Supp. at 1376-77.

83. See, e.g., *Tudor Dev. Group, Inc. v. United States Fidelity & Guar. Corp.*, 692 F. Supp. 461, 463 (M.D. Pa. 1988).

84. 41 F. Supp.2d 152 (D. Conn. 1998).

85. Id. at 164.

86. 290 N.W. 737 (Minn. 1979).

87. Id. at 741.

obligation to accept an application for insurance, and that "[s]imilarly, no duty of care was imposed upon [the surety] to accept [the principal's] application for the performance bond or payment bond. Any duty must be based on contract. . . ."[88] Thus, the surety could not be liable for "negligent failure to issue the final bonding."[89]

Despite its current undeveloped state, this theory may prove to be a fertile source of litigation as principals attempt to impose fiduciary obligations on sureties. In the lender liability context, borrowers have had some "limited success in converting a debtor-creditor relationship into a more fiduciary relationship."[90] Although the analogy between the principal-surety and borrower-lender relationships is not perfect, it is sufficiently close that there may be more attempts to hold sureties liable based on various tort theories. These challenges may come not only from principals, but also from obligees who could argue that they too are parties to the tripartite surety arrangement, and that they too stand in a fiduciary relationship with the surety.

B. APPLICATION OF THE THEORIES

Any of the above theories can be used by any party seeking relief against a bid bond surety who has refused to issue performance and payment bonds. The relief sought typically falls into one of three categories.

1. Principal's Defense Against Surety's Indemnity Claim. The most common relief sought against a bid bond surety, apart from a claim on the bid bond itself, is the defense principals frequently raise when a surety seeks indemnification against them arising out of the surety's losses on the bid bond. If the principal's inability to enter into the contract is a result of the surety's refusal to issue performance and payment bonds, the principal might resist indemnifying the surety on the ground that the surety's losses were the result of its own refusal to issue final bonding. The success of this argument will depend on two things: (1) the manner in which the court treats the language in the indemnity agreement excusing the surety from issuing performance and payment bonds; and (2) the court's acceptance of some theory under which the surety was obligated to issue the bonds.

With respect to the first issue, courts have not been inclined to free principals of the language in their indemnity agreements whereby they acknowledge that the surety is free to refuse to issue bonds. This language, assuming it is sufficiently explicit, will ordinarily prevent a principal from escaping its indemnity obligation.[91] Even the Appellate Court of Connecticut in L.F. Pace & Sons, Inc. v. Travelers Indem. Co. acknowledges that such language precludes indemnitors "from asserting the surety's failure to issue any bond as a defense to an action for indemnification for losses under any executed bonds."[92] Indeed, one of the few cases in which a principal-indemnitor has surmounted the obstacle is Commercial Ins. Co. v. Hartwell Excavating Co. in which the Supreme Court of Idaho simply ignored language in the bond application that appeared to have freed the surety from any obligation to issue bonds.[93]

88. Id. at 742.

89. Id.

90. See generally E. Manneno, Lender Liability and Banking Litigation, §3.03 (1990).

91.. See *Travelers Indem. Co. v. Buffalo Motor & Generator Corp.*, 58 App. Div. 2d 978, 397 N.Y.S.2d 257 (1977); *Green River Gas Co. v. United States Fidelity & Guar. Co.*, 557 S.W.2d 428 (Ky. 1977).

92. 9 Conn. App. at 37, 514 A.2d at 771.

93. 89 Idaho at 548, 407 P.2d at 322.

2. Principal's Affirmative Claim For Damages. A principal may use the surety's refusal to issue performance and payment bonds offensively rather than purely defensively. Under this scenario, the principal sues the surety for lost profits on the project the principal had to forego, plus any other consequential damages the principal can attribute to the surety's refusal to issue the bonds. The surety thus faces open-ended liability. In what appears to be the sole reported case involving such a claim, L F. Pace & Sons, Inc. v Travelers Indem. Co.,[94] the principal claimed that the surety's refusal to issue the bonds drove the principal out of business. The principal sought, and recovered, lost profits on the contract the surety refused to bond, damages for the loss of the principal's business based on the fair market value of the business, and punitive damages. The court based its holding on a theory of implied contract arising out of custom and usage in the industry.[95] Having found the existence of an implied contract, the court then held that the damages were foreseeable.

> The defendant [i.e. the surety] was aware that the plaintiff's business consisted almost exclusively of public construction which required bid, performance and payment bonds. There was evidence that the plaintiff was in a weakened financial condition. The defendant knew or should have known that failure to act as the surety on the performance and payment bonds, after acting as surety on the bid bond, could have a severe impact on the ability of the plaintiff to obtain the necessary bonds from other sources. The defendant was also aware that the continued inability of the plaintiff to obtain bonding would result in the termination of the business.[96]

Paradoxically, the court held that the language in the indemnity agreement authorizing the surety to "decline to execute . . . any bonds . . ." meant that the principal could not raise the surety's failure to issue bonds as a defense to an indemnification action under an executed bond.[97] Under the Pace court's reasoning, one could have the anomalous situation of a surety being held liable for breach of an implied contract to issue performance and payment bonds and being able to successfully assert a set-off for the amount for which the principal is liable to it under the bid bond.[98] Moreover, the court never really attempts to reconcile the language of the indemnity agreement with its acknowledgement that "custom and usage would not be the basis for the defendant's obligation if the plaintiff knew or had reason to know that the defendant had an intention inconsistent with such usage."[99] An express, written reservation of the right to decline to issue bonds, acknowledged by the principal, is at the very least an intent inconsistent with the alleged custom and usage of issuing performance and payment bonds.

Finally, this type of claim raises serious issues of causation. Although one cannot rule out the possibility that a surety's refusal to issue performance and payment bonds might cause the principal's business to fail, it is not at all obvious that this is a proximate or even foreseeable result. A contractor's fortunes are more likely to rise and fall with the real estate market and the construction industry generally than with the decision of a particular surety to refuse to issue bonds. If a contractor's surety refuses to issue performance and payment bonds, an otherwise financially healthy contractor should be able to obtain bonds elsewhere. If the contractor is

---

94. 9 Conn. App. 30, 514 A.2d 766 (1986), cert. denied, 210 Conn. 811, 516 A.2d 886 (1986).

95. Id. at 38-39, 514 A.2d at 774.

96. Id. at 40, 514 A.2d at 772.

97. Id. at 36-37, 514 A.2d at 769-70.

98. In Pace, the surety apparently made demand on the indemnitors, but took no further action to enforce its indemnity rights. Id. at 33, 514 A.2d at 769.

99. Id. at 38-39, 514 A.2d at 771.

unable to do so, it is probably because of the contractor's poor financial prospects. Indeed, in Pace, the contractor was in a "weakened financial condition" and was under a restriction on the size of projects it could bid.[100] The surety's refusal may be in response to economic forces which neither the surety nor the principal control, but in such a case, a surety's refusal to bond a failing contractor can hardly be said to be the legal cause of the contractor's failure.

3. Claims By Third Parties. Once one posits the existence of an implied contract between the surety and principal to issue performance and payment bonds, it is difficult to confine the surety's obligations under such an implied contract solely to the principal. The suretyship arrangement is tripartite, and obligees have rights under bonds. If the surety has impliedly agreed with the principal to issue bonds, the putative obligee, usually an owner or general contractor, can claim to be a third party beneficiary of that implied contract. Consequently, the argument the obligee would raise is the same as the one the principal would raise: as a third-party beneficiary, the obligee's rights would rise no higher than the principal's rights.[101] One main difference, however, is that the surety's liability to the obligee would probably be limited to the penal sum of the bonds it had impliedly agreed to provide.

The leading case in this area is Chas. H. Tompkins Co. v. Lumberman's Mut. Cas. Co.,[102] in which a general contractor-obligee brought an action against a subcontractor's bid bond surety claiming that the surety had expressly or impliedly agreed to issue performance and payment bonds. The court rejected the claim, partly on the ground that no such agreements existed, and partly on policy grounds.

With respect to the claim that the bid bond constituted an express agreement to provide performance and payment bonds, the court pointed to the language in the indemnity agreement authorizing the surety to decline to issue bonds. This, the court held, was "an integral part of the contract between [the principal] and [the surety] governing the issuance of bonds."[103] The language of the indemnity agreement "flatly and fully negates any duty on [the surety] to issue a payment and performance bond after issuing the bid bond."[104] The obligee was "bound by this language, for it is axiomatic that a third party beneficiary, as a non-negotiating party, must take the contract as he finds it."[105]

The court rejected the argument that the language in the indemnity agreement served merely to preclude the principal from raising the surety's refusal to issue bonds as a defense to an indemnity claim. Calling the holding in Pace "nonsensical," the court observed that a bid bond is separate from a payment or a performance bond. A surety's liability under a bid bond is usually limited to 5% to 10% of the bid, as opposed to the much higher penal sums on performance and payment bonds, and the underwriting considerations that go into issuing bid bonds reflect the difference in risk. The court noted that it was commercially reasonable "to insert language in indemnity contracts with principals negating any duty to issue a performance and payment bond simply because a bid bond was issued. And it is commercially sensible, as well as legally correct, for courts to give effect to this plain language. To hold otherwise

100. Id. at 40, 33, 514 A.2d at 772, 768.
101. See Chas. H. Tompkins Co., 732 F. Supp. at 1373.
102. 732 F. Supp. 1368 (E.D. Va. 1990).
103. Id. at 1372.
104. Id.
105. Id. at 1373.

effectively imposes an additional liability on the bid bond issuer not contemplated by the bid bond and contrary to the plainly expressed intent of the parties."[106]

Turning to the argument based on implied contract, the court observed that "custom and usage cannot be invoked to create contract duties that did not previously exist or that are inconsistent with the contract."[107] The court viewed the "contract" as the bid bond under which the surety's sole duty was to pay damages as a result of the principal's failure to enter into a contract or to provide performance and payment bonds. "[I]ncorporation of custom and usage in this instance would contradict the express terms of the parties' agreement, a result not permitted under the most liberal interpretation of contract law."[108] Here, the obligee was invoking custom and usage not merely to explain the terms of the existing agreement or to supplement the agreement, but to create major new obligations.[109]

The court buttressed its holding by invoking policy reasons why a surety should not be under an implied duty to issue performance and payment bonds. A bid bond surety undertakes a limited risk based on very limited information. One may also add that the surety either issues bid bonds without a premium or charges a small premium, reflecting the degree of risk.[110] It is not until the bids are received that the surety is in a position to determine whether its principal is capable of performing the contract and whether the bid is reasonable. A large bid differential, for example, will alert the surety that its principal may have intentionally or negligently underbid the project.[111] "Depriving the surety of this information is commercially unreasonable and inconsistent with the existence of the bid bond and the performance and payment bonds as separate transactions."[112] The court concluded that requiring a bid bond surety to issue performance and payment bonds would make bid bonds more difficult and more expensive to obtain.[113]

A case reaching the same result but for slightly different reasons is Collum Mechanical Constr. Co. v. S.C. Baptist Hospital,[114] in which the court rejected a subcontractor's claim to be a third party beneficiary of the surety's obligation to provide a payment bond. Relying on the language in the bid bond, the court held that the principal had the obligation to provide a payment bond, not the surety. The surety, therefore, had no obligation as to which the subcontractor could be a beneficiary.[115]

---

106. Id. The court also makes the common-sensical observation that if the parties intended that the issuance of the bid bond required the surety to issue a performance bond, they would save time and expense by issuing a single bond covering bid and performance. The fact that they did not do so indicates that bid and erformance bonds "are separate and distinct transactions such that a surety contract may . . . make clear that the issuance of one does not warrant an implied obligation to issue the other." Id.

107. Id. at 1374.

108. Id. at 1375.

109. Id. at 1375, 1376.

110.See *Sheet Metal Employers' Ass'n v. Giordano*, 188 N.E.2d 329, 230 Ohio 2d 25 (Ohio Ct. Common Pleas 1963).

111. 732 F. Supp. at 1376. See, e.g., *L&M Enterprises, Inc. v. Hartford Acc. & Indem. Co.*, 700 F. Supp. 517, 518 (D. Colo. 1488) (bid bond surety refused to issue performance and payment bonds where principal's bid was more than 30% lower than next lowest bidders'.).

112. 732 F. Supp. at 1376.

113. Id.

114. 1999 WL 508533 (S.C. App. May 3, 1999)

115.. Id. at 4-5.

6

Contract Performance Bonds

Marilyn Klinger
James P. Diwik
Kevin L. Lybeck

I. *Performance Bonds Generally*

Suretyship is a contractual relationship, synonymous with guaranty, in which one party promises to be answerable for the debt, default, or miscarriage of another.[1] In the typical construction setting, performance bonds[2] provide protection to the project owner (the obligee) in the event the bonded contractor (the principal) defaults. The principal is the one primarily and ultimately obligated to build the project. The bond is issued on behalf of or for the principal who is usually the one who purchases the performance bond from the surety. However, it is often the obligee who requires the performance bond. In most states and under federal law, performance bonds are required of the prime or general contractor for the construction of public improvements. In addition, many sureties require their general contractor clients to obtain performance bonds from their subcontractors. Thus, the prime contractor has the role of both principal and obligee with the subcontractor as the principal in the latter situation.

The surety is obligated to the obligee pursuant to the terms of the performance bond, the underlying bonded contract, and any statutory provisions that may govern and is relieved of any duty to the obligee if the principal performs.[3] Thus, the bond, the underlying contract, and any statutes that may require the bond define the scope of the surety's obligation. Interestingly, to this day, many surety bonds continue to include the rather arcane language that was used hundreds of years ago to describe, in a seemingly negative fashion, the surety's obligation under the bond. The following is an example of that language:

> THE CONDITION OF THIS OBLIGATION IS SUCH that if the Contractor shall in all things stand to and abide by, and well and truly keep and perform the covenants, conditions and agreements in the foregoing contract on his part to be kept and performed, then this obligation shall be null and void; otherwise it shall remain in full force and effect.

---

1. RESTATEMENT THIRD, SURETYSHIP AND GUARANTY § 1 (1996); Ca. Civ. Code § 2787; *Madison County Farmer's Assn. v. American Employers' Ins. Co.*, 209 F.2d 581, 585 (8th Cir. 1954).

2. For a discussion of the creation of the suretyship relationship in the performance bond context, see, Sauer, *Creation of the Relationship*, Ch. 1, THE LAW OF PERFORMANCE BONDS (American Bar Association, 1999, Moelmann and Harris, ed.)

3. RESTATEMENT THIRD, SURETYSHIP AND GUARANTY § 39 and 48 (1996). See also, *Tri-State Ins. Co. v. U. S.*, 340 F.2d 542, 545 (8th Cir. 1965); *Sanitary Systems, Inc. v. Am. Surety Co. of New York*, 331 F.2d 438 (8th Cir. 1964); *Atterbury v. Carpenter*, 321 F.2d 921, 923 (9th Cir. 1963); *National Union Fire Ins. Co. of Pittsburgh, Pa. v. Alexander*, 728 F.Supp. 192, 198 (S.D.N.Y. 1989); *Tudor Dev. Group. Inc. v. United States Fidelity & Guaranty*, 692 F.Supp. 461, 463 (M.D. Pa. 1988).

If the principal on the project defaults on the underlying contract, the surety has a contractual obligation to the obligee with regard to completion of the project.[4] Where the surety arranges for the performance of the contract pursuant to its performance bond obligations, however, the principal and, if appropriate, third party indemnitors nonetheless bear the ultimate liability for the surety's loss because of the surety's contractual, statutory and/or equitable rights of indemnification and reimbursement.[5] In other words, the principal must indemnify and reimburse the surety for any losses and expenses it incurs as a result of having the issued the performance bond.[6]

Performance bonds are issued with monetary limits, sometimes called "penal sums," "bond penalties," or "bond amounts," which limit the surety's liability under the bond. Except under certain circumstances,[7] the performance bond surety is not liable to the obligee for completion costs to the extent that they exceed the penal sum of the bond.[8]

In most modern-day circumstances, the bonds giving rise to the surety's obligations are generic performance bonds, not specifically completion bonds or indemnity bonds. Completion bonds provide that the surety, upon default of the principal, has essentially a single option under the bond: To take over and effectuate completion the contract work. Indemnity bonds, on the other hand, define the surety's obligation as that of indemnifying the obligee for any losses the obligee may suffer as a result of the principal's failure to perform the underlying contract.

With respect to a generic performance bond, the surety generally has no absolute duty to effectuate the completion of the project. However, it may be bound to pay the costs of completion up to its bond limit if it does not effectuate completion by some other means. Put differently, the surety is not limited in its performance of its bond obligation to the payment of money, but rather it has the option of arranging for completion in some form or another, should it be in the surety's best interest to do so.

Typically, the terms and conditions of the underlying "bonded" construction contract must be construed together with the terms of the performance bond to determine the surety's liability.[9] Put differently, the obligee's right of recovery against the performance bond surety typically does

---

4. *Hays Livestock Comm'n. Co., Inc. v. Maly Livestock Comm'n Co., Inc.*, 498 F.2d 925, 932 (10th Cir. 1974).

5. RESTATEMENT THIRD, SURETY AND GUARANTY § 22 (1996); *U.S. v. Shimer*, 367 U.S. 374, 388, 81 S.Ct. 1554 (1961); *Fidelity & Deposit Co. of Maryland v. Bristol Steel & Iron Works, Inc.*, 722 F.2d 1160, 1163-65 (4th Cir.1983) ; *In re J.T. Moran Financial Corp.*, 124 B.R. 926, 930 (Bankr. S.D.N.Y. 1991).

6. For a thorough discussion of the surety's indemnity rights, see, Ruprecht, *Surety's Rights and Remedies Against Principals and Against Indemnitors Under The General Indemnity Agreement*, Ch. 5, THE LAW OF PERFORMANCE BONDS (American Bar Association, 1999, Moelmann and Harris, ed.).

7. *Burns v. Massachusetts Bonding and Insurance Company*. 62 Cal.App.2d 972 (1944); *Harris v. Northwestern National Ins. Co.*, 6 Cal.App.4th 1061 (1992) (noting that the liability arises not out of a condition of the bond but out of liability imposed by statute and is based upon the surety's status as a party litigant, not for breach of the condition of the bond); *Lawrence Tractor Co. v. Carlisle Ins. Co.*, 202 CA3d 949 (1988) (surety only liable for attorney fees beyond the penal sum of the bond if provided for by statute or if the bond provision regarding attorneys fees specifically obligated the surety to pay attorney fees in excess of the penal sum of the bond).

8. *Simmons, Inc. v. Pinkerton's, Inc.*, 762 F.2d 591, 608 (7th Cir. 1985); *Coyne-Delany Co., Inc. v. Capital Development Bd. of State of Ill.*, 717 F.2d 385, 393 (7th Cir. 1983); *Hartford Acc. and Indem. Co. v. Ind. Accident Comm.*, 216 Cal. 40 (1932). *But see, Caron v. Andrew*, 133 Cal.App.2d 402, 284 P.2d 544 (1955); *In re Technology for Energy, Corp.*, 123 B.R. 979 (Bankr. E.D. Tenn. 1991) (surety that takes over performance of contract has a duty to complete the contract without regard to penal sum of bond).

9. *H.H. Robertson Co. v. Lumberman's Mut. Cas. Co.*, 94 F.R.D. 578, 583 (W.D. Pa. 1982), *aff'd* 696 F.2d 982 (3rd Cir. 1982); *State of Florida v. Wesley Const. Co.*, 316 F.Supp. 490, 497 (S.D. Fla. 1970).

not extend beyond the right of recovery which the obligee has against the principal under the original construction contract.[10] In most performance bond forms, the underlying construction contract is expressly incorporated by reference. In some states, the construction contract is automatically, by operation of law, incorporated by reference.[11] Regardless, the underlying construction contract essentially defines the surety's liability in the event of its principal's default. In other words, courts interpret a surety's obligation by the terms of both the performance bond and the underlying contract, particularly if the bond incorporates the contract by reference.[12]

A. THE PERFORMANCE BOND SURETY'S OPTIONS

1. Before Principal's Default

The surety, not being a party to the construction contract, cannot itself declare a default and issue a default termination if the owner takes no action on this issue when the principal is clearly not performing. Arguably, the surety may raise the defense of failure to mitigate, or at least oppose any consequential damage claims, if the owner delays in declaring the default and terminating the contract. Some indemnity agreements may allow the surety to take over the project if it becomes aware of the principal's default although it is quite rare for a surety to utilize that provision. If the surety has cause, it may also demand that the obligee withhold payment of the contract funds for the surety's benefit, which may bring the principal and obligee "to the table" and, if the obligee refuses, cause the obligee to "pay twice" if its refusal to withhold funds causes loss to the surety. The most practical response is for the surety to take the lead, stimulate negotiations between the parties, and move toward an agreement for completing the project.

2. Upon Principal's Default[13]

Many obligees have a common misconception and/or engage in wishful thinking by expecting that when a performance bond surety is advised of its principal's default, failure to perform, or delay in performance, the surety will mobilize manpower and equipment to the project

10. *Madison County, supra* note 1, at 585; *National Union Fire Ins. Co. of Pittsburgh, Pa. v. D&L Const. Co.*, 353 F.2d 169, 175 (8th Cir. 1965), cert. *denied, 384* U.S. 941 (1966); *Trustees of Bricklayers Local No. 3 v. Reeco*, 747 F.Supp. 606, 614 (D. Nev. 1990).

11. *See e.g.*, ILL. REV. STAT. ch. 29, para. 15 (1990), which provides in relevant part:

> Each (State of Illinois public works bond) is deemed to contain the following provisions whether such provisions are inserted in such bond or not:
>
> > The principal and sureties on this bond agree that all the undertakings, covenants, terms, conditions and agreements of the contract or contracts entered into between the principal and the State or any political subdivision thereof will be performed and fulfilled . . . .

12. *See, e.g., Pacific Employers Ins. Co. v. City of Berkeley*, 158 Cal.App.3d 145 (1984); *Cates Constr., Inc. v. Talbot Partners*, 21 Cal.4th 28 (1999); *Pacific States Elec. Co. v. United States Fid. & Guar. Co.* (1930) 109 CA 691, 293 P 812 (contract attached to bond and incorporated by reference); *Callan v. Empire State Surety Co.*, 20 Cal.App. 483 (1912).

13. For an additional discussion on this subject, see, Mercier and Harris, *Rights of Surety In Event of Default*, Ch. 3, THE LAW OF PERFORMANCE BONDS (American Bar Association, 1999, Moelmann and Harris, ed.).

site and immediately go about completing the project.[14] Actually, where the principal is in default or has abandoned the project and the surety, the performance bond surety has a variety of options with respect to fulfilling its performance bond obligations.

In practice, the performance bond surety has five basic options from which to choose when called upon to perform: (1) Buy back the bond; (2) Finance the principal; (3) Tender a new contractor; (4) Take over and arrange completion; or (5) Have the obligee complete.[15]

Later on in this chapter there is a discussion about the situation where the principal disputes the validity of the obligee's default declaration. However, for purposes of outlining a surety's options under a performance bond, it is assumed that the obligee default terminated the principal for good cause.

a. Tendering a New Contractor.[16] A performance bond surety may obtain independent bids to complete the work or otherwise identify a completion contractor and tender that completion contractor to the obligee, usually with a performance and payment bond from another surety. In addition to tendering the completion contractor with new bonds in favor of the obligee, the surety with tender the difference in price between the original contract and the completion contract up to the performance bond penal sum. The completion contractor will thereafter enter into a separate contract directly with the obligee.

In order to keep the completion price down, the surety may also arrange for ratification agreements with acceptable subcontractors of the principal. Those ratification agreements may either be between the subcontractor and the surety, with the surety then assigning the subcontract to the completion contractor, or the surety may arrange that the ratification agreement is directly between the subcontractor and the completion contractor. In either situation, the surety usually assures that the subcontractor is paid any outstanding balances under the subcontract and the subcontractor reaffirms its performance obligation under the subcontract.

In exchange for the tender, as described above, the surety receives a release of its liability under the performance bond. Even if the obligee agrees to a tender situation, it may refuse, however, to provide a full release to the surety in that the release will not include the latent defects of the original contractor. At the same time, the completion contractor often refuses to take the risk of those latent defects. Accordingly, the tender agreement between the obligee and the surety will carve out an exception to the release and include a reservation with respect to the original contractor's latent defects. In addition, the surety and the completion contractor may enter into a side agreement whereby the completion contractor will be protected in the event latent defects are discovered that are clearly the fault of the original contractor and the completion contractor is called upon to repair and/or replace same.

Tendering a completing contractor has its obvious advantages.[17] In fact, this option is arguably the favored option of sureties if they are able to convince the obligees to agree to it. First,

---

14. CMA Consulting Group Technical Review, The Direct Completion Option . . . Pros and Cons (January 1990).

15. For an excellent discussion on a performance bond surety's options upon default of its principal, see generally Thompson, *Completion Options Available to a Performance Bond Surety Other Than Financing its Principal*, 17 THE FORUM 1215 (1982); Webster, *The Surety's Decision on What To Do*, 17 THE FORUM 1168 (1982); and Schroeder, *Providing Financial Support to the Contractor*, 17 THE FORUM 1190 (1982).

16. For a thorough review of the issue of tendering a new contractor to the obligee, see, Baumgartner, *Tender*, Ch. 6 BOND DEFAULT MANUAL (American Bar Association, 2d ed. 1995, Clore, ed.).

17. Wisner, *supra* note 20. See *also*, Frazier, *Takeover or Tender? Post Default Alternatives on Federal Contracts for the Performance Bond Surety* (American Bar Association 1992).

the surety's loss is fixed and certain, negating the surety's exposure to future unforeseen and uncontrollable events which may substantially increase its loss under the performance bond, in addition to potentially facilitating an early recovery from the indemnitors. Additionally, the surety avoids the financial responsibility for existing and/or future indebtedness which may not otherwise be an obligation under the performance bond.

Tendering halts the expense of attorneys and consultants as well as the surety's own administrative personnel. It removes the surety from the day to day rigors of contract administration. There is a whole new contract where the obligee and the completion contractor are in direct communication with each other as if there never was an original contractor and surety.

It is essentially a fresh start between the obligee and the completion contractor. It is this fresh start which is the most appealing from the standpoint of the obligee. Admittedly, some obligees would prefer to keep the original surety "on the hook" even if the original surety has offered a new surety with the completion contractor. Also, some public owners are reluctant to enter into a new contract with the completion contractor as they are concerned that they may be violating various competitive bidding laws and requirements. In order to overcome that objection, it is appropriate to enter into a three-party agreement involving the obligee, the surety, and the completion contractor.[18] The terms and conditions of the three-party agreement contain all of the elements of a tender, including a release of the surety, but for appearance's sake, it looks more like a takeover agreement, which many obligees are more familiar and comfortable with. Surety takeovers are discussed below. They involve the original surety staying involved until the completion contractor has finished the project.

The tender option, however, does have disadvantages.[19] Tendering is less desirable where the project is near completion, as the costs and time delay associated with obtaining bids from completion contractors may outweigh the risks associated with other surety options, such as financing which can be put into effect relatively seamlessly so that there is no interruption in physical construction. The process of preparing a bid package, obtaining bids, and awarding the completion contract can often be time consuming, thereby exposing the surety to the obligee's claim of delay damages.

Additionally, the cost of a completion contractor on a lump sum basis will probably include not only a full markup plus bond premium, but also a sizeable contingency fee included to protect against the unfamiliarity of the project and potentially defective work of the principal and its subcontractors prior to default.[20] As noted above, if the completion contractor is given assurances of additional compensation should it come across latent defects of the original contractor, the price of the completion contractor can be reduced accordingly.

As noted above, in the event that the performance bond language does not clearly provide the surety with the option to tender a new completion contractor, the surety must convince the obligee that entering into a new contract is in its best interests.[21] For example, the surety may point

---

18. See, Dickey and Burch, *Performance Bond Claims,* wherein the authors indicate that the public contracting officers hesitancy to accept the tender of a completing contractor is based upon their unfamiliarity with the Federal Acquisition Regulation System, 48 C.F.R. 1.000 *et seq.*

19. Frazier, *supra* note 22.

20. See generally, CMA Consulting Group Technical Quarterly, *Reletting: The* Manageable Option (Winter 1986).

21. 48 C.F.R. 49.405 provides that the contracting officer may arrange for completion of the work by awarding a new contract stating in relevant part: "The new contract may be the result of sealed bidding or any other appropriate contracting method or procedure." The AIA A312 Performance Bond form provides, as one of the options

out that the obligee will have direct, unfettered control over the project completion without having to communicate through the surety. Furthermore, the obligee will be able to enjoy the financial integrity and strength of a new contractor and the protection of a new performance and payment bond surety, while enjoying the additional financial security of a cash infusion from the original surety to secure the contract funds deficit.

b. Surety Takeover.[22] Pursuant to a takeover agreement with the obligee, the performance bond surety may step in and arrange for completion of the project itself, either through a qualified completion contractor or a consultant/construction manager.[23] Completion by the surety differs from tender of a new contractor directly to the obligee. In the tender situation, the surety offers a qualified completion contractor which contracts directly with the obligee. The surety also tenders the difference in the original contract and completion contract price, and obtains a release of its liability under the performance bond.

In the completion situation, on the other hand, the surety enters into a takeover agreement with the obligee to complete the project. The surety usually, but not always, obtains the obligee's agreement that the penal sum of the performance bond remains the limit of the surety's obligation. The surety also attempts to obtain the obligee's agreement to pay to the surety all remaining contract balances.[24] Thereafter, the surety will typically negotiate a completion contract with a new completion contractor who commits to complete the contract, oftentimes obtaining a performance bond from another surety with the original surety named as the obligee.

On occasion, the surety will contract with a construction manager and have that construction manager manage the subcontractors to completion. Also, sureties sometimes utilize their own consultants to complete the project functioning in the same manner as a construction manager.

The use of construction managers/consultants to complete is often more appropriate where the project is near completion, and the costs, delays and/or risks associated with reletting the project or financing the defaulted principal appear to be excessive. Specifically, a construction manager/consultant will enable the surety to take over the job with little or no project work stoppage, avoiding the costs and delay damages associated with a halted project.

By completing the project "itself," the surety obtains greater control than it would have had it elected to require the obligee to complete, discussed below, because the surety can select the completing contractor or construction managers/consultants to finish the project as well as control the costs of completion.[25] Moreover, the surety is able to require a 100% performance bond for the amount of the completion contract from the completion contractor, naming itself as obligee or naming its obligee and itself as co-obligees, allowing the surety to pass on the potential liability for unsuccessful completion of the project.[26]

---

available to the surety, tendering a completion contractor to the obligee including the difference in price between the original contract and the completion contract.

22. For a thorough review of the issue of taking over and completing, see, Kowalczyk and Kazlow, *Takeover and Completion*, Ch. 5 BOND DEFAULT MANUAL (American Bar Association, 2d ed. 1995, Clore, ed.).

23. A surety may condition its decision to complete upon the execution of a takeover agreement by the Government owner/obligee. F.A.R. 49.404(C).

24. For a thorough discussion of the surety's right to those contract balances, see, Gallagher, *Entitlement To Contract Proceeds*, Ch. 4, THE LAW OF PERFORMANCE BONDS (American Bar Association, 1999, Moelmann and Harris, ed.).

25. CMA Consulting Group Technical Review, *The Direct Completion Option* . . . Pros *and* Cons, (January 1990) ; Frazier, supra note 22.

26. Frazier, *supra* note 22.

As in the tender situation above, the surety may obtain ratification agreements from selected subcontractors in order to reduce the completion contract price. Such a procedure would be imperative if the surety used a construction manager/consultant to complete such that it would require additional effort on the part of the surety in arranging for ratification agreements with subcontractors.

In many default situations, there arises a debate as to whether a subcontractor/supplier is obligated to complete the contract for the surety at the original subcontract/purchase order prices. The surety argues that, by way of subrogation, it is subrogated to the rights of its principal in the subcontract/purchase order and, therefore, the subcontractor/supplier must perform for the surety. Hence, the reason for ratification agreements is to avoid a dispute over the issue. Ratification agreements can come in the form of assignments of the subcontracts/purchase orders or, alternatively, express ratification agreements wherein the subcontractors and suppliers agree to complete the work without an increase in cost.

The downside to surety takeovers occurs when there is no takeover agreement with specific contractual provisions within the takeover agreement both allowing the surety to reserve its bond defenses (if any) against the owner,[27] and limiting the scope of the surety's liability in connection with the takeover. In those cases where there is no express limitation as to the surety's liability, the surety arguably assumes full responsibility to complete the work.[28] Consequently, that surety may be responsible for the entire cost of completion plus other consequential damages for which the principal alone would have otherwise been liable even if that cost and those damages exceed the penal sum of the performance bond.[29] The concept is often called "waiving the bond penalty." The theory is that upon takeover, the surety stands in the shoes of the principal for all purposes. Of note, the cases which have found such a penalty waiver rely upon the terms of the surety's bond, which often do not describe the surety's options in remedying the principal's default. Essentially, the courts find that the surety proceeded "outside" the terms of the bond. The opposite result may be reached where the surety's bond terms expressly include, as an option to the surety, taking over and completing the project.[30]

Because of an inability to cap their losses, many sureties will not choose this option for this reason alone. That is the reason all sureties attempt to write into takeover agreements a provision whereby the surety's liability will not exceed the penal sum of the bond and any amounts paid in connection with completing the project will be credited against that penal sum. Some obligees reject such an attempt unless they are convinced that the cost to complete could never exceed the bond penalty. Other obligees understand that if they do not agree to the cap, the surety may not agree to

---

27. Mazzera v. Ramsey, 72 Cal.App. 601 (1925).

28. Wisner, Jensen & Leo, *Completion by the Surety: Assessing Risk & Limiting Loss*; Wisner, *supra* note 20.

29. *In Re Technology For Energy Corp.*, 123 B.R. 979 (Bankr. E.D. Tenn., 1991) [supplemented at 140 B.R. 214 (Bankr. E.D. Tenn., 1992) (surety that takes over performance of contract has a duty to complete the contract without regard to penal sum of bond); *Klien v. J.D. & J.M. Collins*, 159 La. 704, 106 So. 120 (1925); *McWalters & Barlett v. United States*, 272 F.2d 291 (10th Cir., 1959); *Beers v. Wolf*, 116 Mo. 179, 22 S.W. 620 (1893); *Howard v. Fisher*, 86 Colo. 493, 283 P. 1042 (1930); *Mazzera v. Ramsey*, 72 Cal.App. 601, 238 P. 101 (1925); *Griffith v. Rundle*, 23 Wash. 453, 63 P. 199 (1900); *Ausplund v. Aetna Indemnity Co.*, 47 Ore. 10, 81 P. 571 (1905); *Hunt v. Bankers & Shippers Ins. Co.*, 73 A.D.2d 797, 423 N.Y.S.2d 718 (1979), *aff'd at* 50 N.Y.2d 938; *Copeland Sand & Gravel v. Ins. Co. of North America*, 288 Ore. 325, 607 P.2d 718 (1980); *State of Oregon v. St. Paul*, 288 F.2d 32 (9th Cir., 1961); *Riva Ridge Apartments v. Fisher*, 745 P.2d 1034 (App. Colo. 1987).

30. See, Kowalczyk and Kazlow, *Takeover and Completion*, Ch. 5 BOND DEFAULT MANUAL (American Bar Association, 2d ed. 1995, Clore, ed.); AIA Bond Form A312.

take over and complete the project, refusing to risk an increase in their liability that was otherwise limited.

In sum, a surety should only choose to complete the project itself where the cost is less than other options, and the risks associated with completion appear manageable. Generally speaking, the farther along completion the project is, the more seriously the surety should consider completing the project itself. By the surety agreeing to complete the project, the obligee may be willing to grant the surety certain, important concessions. For example, the surety may be able to obtain a waiver of liquidated damages or extensions of time for completion of certain items of work.

c. Financing the Principal.[31] The performance bond surety may finance the principal to complete the project by advancing funds to pay its bills (including job related and possibly general overhead or other business expenses of the principal). This alternative may be attractive where the principal was unable to perform because of a lack of financial resources and/or cash flow difficulties but the principal's work was satisfactory and the percentage of completion is substantial. Financing eliminates the learning curve which occurs when a new contractor is brought onto a project. A surety's decision to finance its principal should only be made after careful consideration of the factors causing the financial problems and/or default, including the condition of the project and any other bonded or unbonded projects of the principal.[32]

One can imagine that once the surety becomes involved, the principal is full of good intentions to complete the work, pay creditors, stay in business, and eventually repay the surety for its cash outlay. However, the factors leading up to the principal's financial difficulties and/or default are frequently not the result of a temporary cash flow problem, but rather the result of the principal's own poor business judgment or lack of management skills. Consequently, the surety should conduct a thorough and complete investigation of the principal, its outstanding projects, and its business operations generally, in addition to its books and records, prior to making the decision to finance the principal.

For instance, the surety must have complete cooperation from the principal, in addition to confidence in the ability of the principal and its management to competently complete the project. Obviously, without such cooperation and competence, the surety will likely be unable to complete the project or, at a minimum, lessen the time and expense needed to complete. Additionally, the surety would be well advised to confirm that the principal has good relationships with its subcontractors, creditors, and the obligee. Without the support of these entities, the principal's completion of the project even with the surety's financial assistance may be met with skepticism and resistance, further retarding timely completion.

Often, financing is an appropriate option where the project is close to completion, particularly because it is difficult to obtain completion bids or completion contractors at a late stage in a project on anything other than a time and material basis. Potential completing contractors are fearful that they will be unable to discover all the necessary work for completion in addition to latent defects, thus sustaining a large loss if they commit themselves to a lump sum/fixed price or guaranteed maximum. Conversely, where a project is just getting underway, it is often much easier to obtain completing contractors on a fixed price basis because of the lesser concern of completing defective work or a project in trouble.

---

31. For a thorough review of the issue of financing the performance bond principal, see, Bachrach, *Financing The Principal*, Ch. 4 BOND DEFAULT MANUAL (American Bar Association, 2d ed. 1995, Clore, ed.).

32. See, *Lambert v. Maryland Casualty Co.*, 418 So.2d 553 (La. 1982), wherein the court held that a performance bond surety is under a duty to act "reasonably" when deciding whether to finance a defaulted contractor.

Financing the principal may also be particularly appropriate where a shutdown of the job may result in substantial liquidated damages. It eliminates the time it takes to demobilize and mobilize and provides job momentum and continuity. Moreover, financing may be the only viable option where there are no other qualified contractors to complete the work, particularly in those instances where the principal engages in a highly specialized area of construction, the work of the contractor is proprietary, or where the project is located in some remote area, resulting in an inability to bid the work to potential completing contractors.

A major disadvantage in financing the principal is that it offers no ceiling on the performance bond surety's liability. Essentially, the surety will be cast in the role of lender and not performance bond surety.[33] The surety potentially exposes itself to a loss in excess of the bond penal sum should the obligee default the principal, notwithstanding the surety's funding, and the surety is called upon to honor its bond obligations. Thus, if the performance bond surety is seriously considering the financing option, the surety should (1) be extremely comfortable with its cost to complete estimate, (2) monitor the project status and expenditures therefor extremely closely, and (3) if at all possible, obtain the obligee's agreement that the cost of financing, over and above the available contract funds, will reduce the penal sum of the bond. Because financing necessarily involves costs and expenses not within the scope of the performance bond, such an agreement by the obligee is critical to containing the surety's maximum potential liability.

Another problem with financing is that the contractor may delay completion of the project as the project draws to an end because that will cut off the flow of funds from the surety, including overhead. The surety, to avoid this predicament, should attempt to build into its financing agreement with the principal certain incentives to encourage the principal to complete the project as soon as possible such as obtaining collateral from the principal and/or indemnitors.

Further, financing can be a more expensive method of achieving project completion as it requires the surety to monitor both completion and the expenditure of the funds. Sureties typically arrange for construction consultants or funds control agents, at a cost, to monitor the projects and administer the joint control aspect of the vast majority of financing arrangements.

In deciding whether to finance the principal, the performance bond surety should expressly reserve the right to exercise absolute discretion and control over the decision to discontinue financing. This reservation may prove crucial in protecting the surety's interests if the principal is unable to complete or the initial projected financing budget is short of the actual cost. In this event, the best interests of the surety may lie in resorting to other alternatives.

When financing the principal, the surety may invite lawsuits by the defaulted contractors creditors alleging that the surety, by its involvement in the finances and business practice of the principal, has become the alter ego of the principal and, therefore, liable for its debts.[34] The surety

33. Wisner, BOND DEFAULT MANUAL (American Bar Association 1987), Bachrach, *Financing The Principal*, Ch. 4 BOND DEFAULT MANUAL (American Bar Association, 2d ed. 1995, Clore, ed.) *But see*, e.g., *Aetna Cas. & Sur. Co. v. United States*, 845 F.2d 971 (Fed. Cir. 1988) and *Indemnity Ins. Co. Of North Am. v. Lane Contracting Corp.*, 227 F. Supp. 143 (D. Neb. 1964) for argument that financing surety is acting in accordance with its legal obligations under its performance bond and is not a volunteer lending money outside the scope of its performance bond. *See also, Lacy v. Maryland Cas. Co.*, 32 F2d 48 (4th Cir. 1929); *Morgenthau v. Fidelity and Deposit Co. of Md.*, 94 F.2d 632 (D.C. Cir. 1937); and *Great American Ins. Co. v. U.S.*, 481 F2d 1298 (Ct. Cl. 1973) for proposition that the surety will receive a "credit" against competing creditors for the "loan" or financing amount when asserting its equitable subrogation rights.

34. *See, James E. McFadden, Inc. v. Baltimore Contractors, Inc.*, 609 F.Supp. 1102 (E.D. Pa. 1985); *John G. Lambros Co. v. Aetna Cas. & Surety Co.*, 468 F.Supp. 624 (S.D.N.Y. 1979); and *Irwin & Leighton, Inc. v. W.M. Anderson Co.*, 532 A.2d 983 (Del. 1987).

may also be accused of being an "insider" in connection with bankruptcy matters should the principal ultimately find itself seeking bankruptcy protection.[35] Thus, the surety should exercise care in exerting control over the principal's business efforts in order to escape such allegations.

Once the decision to finance is made, the surety is confronted with the choice of how to finance the principal. Financing of the principal can be achieved in a number of ways. First, the surety can advance its own funds directly to the principal through a joint control or trust account. Second, the surety can guarantee a bank loan to the principal, a favorable alternative only where the surety is relatively certain that the principal is capable of repaying the loan. Third, the surety can "back door" finance by paying certain bills, to wit, subcontractors and suppliers. Fourth, the surety can provide additional bonding to the principal.

d. Buy Back the Performance Bond. Where a review of the project indicates that the cost to complete minus the remaining contract balance is at or exceeds the penal limit of the performance bond, the surety should seriously consider tendering payment to the obligee equal to the cost to complete minus the remaining contract balance in exchange for a full and final release.

This option is often considered attractive to the obligee because it will provide an infusion of cash, oftentimes a matter of critical concern to the obligee at the time of the default. For the surety, it offers a quick resolution to what could otherwise prove to be an enormous undertaking, potentially exposing the surety to liability in excess of the bond penal limit.

However, this option potentially presents the risk of a claim from the principal and/or indemnitor(s) that the surety's decision to tender the penal sum of the bond, or some lesser negotiated amount, was premature or constitutes a failure to mitigate damages, thereby claiming forfeiture of the surety's right to indemnification. Consequently, the surety should carefully investigate the net cost to complete (minus the remaining contract balance) in relation to the bond penalty and the amount the obligee is willing to accept, prior to tendering the bond amount or a negotiated sum. It is also always appropriate and recommended to consult with and/or provide notice to the principal and indemnitor(s) in connection with any negotiations and payment to the obligee.

e. The Owner Complete Option.[36] The performance bond surety may choose to allow the obligee to complete or contract for completion itself. The surety would subsequently pay the difference between the cost of completion and the contract balance. Of course, the surety is well advised to review the bond in addition to applicable statutes to confirm that the decision to require completion of the contract by the owner is not in derogation of the surety's contractual, legal or statutory obligations.

For example, the American Institute of Architects' AIA Document A312, Performance Bond, expressly provides that the surety may waive its right to perform and complete, thereby causing the owner to complete the project.

By requiring the owner to complete, the surety can avoid involvement in and, thus, the risks associated with being between the project owner and the completion contractor. Practically, because sureties are not contractors, they do not have direct involvement with the construction itself, including dealing with workers, subcontractors, suppliers, and the obligee and the myriad of pitfalls associated with being unfamiliar with the local construction practices and regulations. Nonetheless,

---

35. For an excellent article discussing a surety's potential "insider" liability for pre-petition financing of the principal/debtor, see Mann and Schexnayder, *An Overview of Surety and Bankruptcy Law*, No. 2 Defense Research Institute Vol. 1990.

36. For a thorough review of completion by the bond obligee, see, Griffin, *Completion By The Bond Obligee*, Ch. 7, BOND DEFAULT MANUAL (American Bar Association, 2d ed. 1995, Clore, ed.).

as a takeover surety, with a takeover agreement with the obligee and a completion contract with the completion contractor, the surety does stay involved. Sureties are even more involved when, in proceeding with the takeover option, they do so with a construction manager/consulting dealing directly with subcontractors, rather than a completion contractor. Thus, by having the owner complete, all of those issues are completely avoided.

On the downside, allowing the owner to complete, which has, in the past, been referred to as the "do-nothing" option, leaves the surety without any control whatsoever on the costs incurred in the completion of the project and, ultimately the amount of damages the obligee will seek under the performance bond. Needless to say, the surety will always issue warnings to the obligee that it must do all that it can reasonably to mitigate its damages. However, such warnings are usually not very effective, and the surety often has an uphill battle to prove that the obligee incurred a greater cost in completing than it should have.

In addition, this option often tempts a lawsuit by the obligee for breach of the performance bond, with accompanying claims of "bad faith." The obligee will seek to hold the performance bond surety liable for extracontractual damages over and above the penal sum of the bond including punitive damages.[37] For these reasons, the "do-nothing" option is not particularly attractive to the surety.

B. POTENTIAL LIMITATIONS ON THE PERFORMANCE BOND SURETY'S OPTIONS

Now that the options are known and the benefits and pitfalls laid out, there are various factors which may influence whether and how a performance bond surety will proceed.

1. The Performance Bond

Most bond forms do not contain any enumeration of the surety's options under the performance bond. In those cases, the surety chooses those options set forth by surety scholars and created by the realities of surety practice.

In contrast, certain bond forms actually specify the surety's options upon default of the principal.[38] The AIA Document A312 Performance Bond, December 1984 Edition, specifically sets forth the various options available to the performance bond surety, stating in pertinent part:

> 4 When the owner has satisfied the conditions of Paragraph 3, the Surety shall promptly and at the Surety's expense take one of the following actions:
>
> 4.1 Arrange for the Contractor, with the consent of the owner, to perform and complete the Construction Contract; or
>
> 4.2 Undertake to perform and complete the Construction Contract itself, through its agents or through independent contractors; or

---

37. For a discussion of performance bond sureties' liability for extracontractual damages, see, Shields, *Extracontractual Liability of Performance Bond Sureties*, Ch. 7, THE LAW OF PERFORMANCE BONDS (American Bar Association, 1999, Moelmann and Harris, ed.).

38. See, AIA A311 Performance Bond, February 1970 Edition; AIA A312 Performance Bond, December 1984 Edition; Engineers' Joint Contract Documents Committee Form EJDC No. 1910-28A; and Miller Act Standard Form 25 (Rev. 1-90).

4.3 Obtain bids or negotiated proposals from qualified contractors acceptable to the Owner for a contract for performance and completion of the Construction Contract, arrange for a contract to be prepared for execution by the Owner and the contractor selected with the Owner's concurrence, to be secured with performance and payment bonds executed by a qualified surety equivalent to the bonds issued on the Construction Contract, and pay to the owner the amount of damages as described in Paragraph 6 in excess of the Balance of the Contract Price incurred by the Owner resulting from the Contractor's default; or

4.4 Waive its right to perform and complete, arrange for completion, or obtain a new contractor and with reasonable promptness under the circumstances:

.1 After investigation, determine the amount for which it may be liable to the Owner and, as soon as practicable after the amount is determined, tender payment therefor to the Owner; or

.2 Deny liability in whole or in part and notify the Owner citing reasons therefor.

As the above indicates, AIA A312 clearly sets forth a number of options available to a surety under its performance bond following the obligee's default of its principal.[39] It also specifically reserves the owner's right to concur in the selection of the new contractor (paragraphs 4.1 and 4.3). However, the owner's participation in the contractor selection process, in reality, is rarely significant.

2. Defenses under the Bond[40]

Sureties have certain defenses to an obligee's demand upon a performance bond which may discharge or reduce the surety's liability to the obligee. Any defenses available to its principal are available to the surety, including, for example, defective plans and specifications[41] impossibility of performance,[42] a material or cardinal alteration to the underlying contract without the surety's knowledge,[43] a substantial or cardinal extension of time by the obligee for the principal's performance of the contract,[44] misrepresentation or concealment,[45] overpayment and/or failure to mitigate by the obligee (although the discharge is likely to be only *pro tanto*, that is, only to the

39. AIA Document A311 Performance Bond provides that, upon default of the principal, the performance bond surety has two options: (1) complete the contract itself; or (2) obtain bids for completion from contractors and finance the project to completion, if necessary, over and above the remaining contract balance.

40. For a discussion of performance bond sureties' defenses, see, Gelinas, *Defenses Available to the Surety*, Ch. 9, THE LAW OF PERFORMANCE BONDS (American Bar Association, 1999, Moelmann and Harris, ed.).

41. 13 Am. Jur. 2d, Building and Construction Contracts § 28 (1964); *United States v. Spearin,* 248 U.S. 132 (1918); *Hercules, Inc. v. U.S.*, 516 U.S. 417 (1996); *USA Petroleum Corp. v. U.S.*, 821 F.2d 622 (Fed.Cir. 1987).

42. RESTATEMENT (2d) OF THE LAW OF CONTRACTS § 261 (1981).

43. *U.S. v. Freel,* 186 U.S. 309, 22 S.Ct. 875 (1902); *Texaco Refining & Marketing v. Aetna Cas. & Sur.*, 895 F.2d 637 (9th Cir. 1990); *United States v. Reliance Ins. Co.*, 799 F.2d 1382 (9th Cir. 1986) ; *Texaco Refining & Mktg., Inc. v. Aetna Cas. & Sur. Co.*, 895 F.2d 637 (9th Cir. 1990) (distinguishing and criticizing *Reliance Insurance Co., supra,* which required a showing of prejudice to the surety for there to be an exoneration); *Argonaut Ins. Co. v. Town of Cloverdale*, 699 F.2d 417 (7th Cir. 1983); *Bopst v. Columbia*, 37 F.Supp. 32 (MD 1940); V.I.P. Agency v. Duffy Elec., Inc., 92 Cal.App.3d 849 (1979); *ITT Diversified Credit Corp. v. Highlands Ins. Co.*, 191 Cal.App.3d 301 (1987).

44. *Keene Corp. v. International Fidelity Ins. Co.*, 736 F.2d 388 (7th Cir. 1984); *Bank of Nova Scotia v. St. Croix Drive-In Theater*, 728 F.2d 177 (3rd Cir. 1984).

45. *Sumitomo Bank v. Iwasaki,* 70 Cal.2d 81 (1968).

extent of the overpayment or over-expenditure),[46] statute of limitations, improper/inadequate notice of default which is prejudicial to the surety,[47] or failure to pursue other remedies when surety requests obligee to do so.[48]

3. Default Termination[49]

Before proceeding with any completion arrangements under a performance bond, sureties often first try to confirm that the principal is in default and unable or unwilling to cure the default.[50]

If there has been no default, some sureties respond to an obligee's demand for performance by advising that the surety is not in a position to take any action as there has been no declaration of default or formal default termination of the principal. The primary basis for a surety so responding is its fear of being accused of interfering in the contract between the obligee and the principal. It is the conventional wisdom in the industry that the surety runs such a risk.

A surety should be able to defeat a principal's claim of interference by demonstrating the surety's financial interest in the underlying contract.[51] When there is an economic interest to protect, the person is privileged to interfere in the contract of another that threatens that interest.[52] Suretyship is a tri-partite relationship involving the obligee, the principal, and the surety. It is difficult to find a better example of a situation where the "interfering" party, the surety, has a financial interest in the subject contract. Both the principal's and obligee's performance impacts that interest.[53] Accordingly, conventional wisdom notwithstanding, sureties have very good grounds for arguing that they should not and cannot be liable for claims of interference if they become involved in the dealings of the obligee and the principal. There is no doubt that principals will threaten and, in fact, do file lawsuits alleging such interference. Assuming, however, that the surety acts properly, taking into account to the extent possible the interests of *all* parties involved, the surety's exposure should be minimal.

There are also cases that hold that a performance bond surety is required to perform only when the obligee has properly declared the principal in default.[54] If a surety takes over a project

---

46. *Balboa Insurance Co. v. U.S.*, 775 F.2d 1158 (Fed. Cir. 1985); *Pacific Coast Eng'g Co. v. Detroit Fid. & Sur. Co.*, 214 Cal 384 (1931); *American Insurance v. Heritage Construction Corp.*, 268 F.Supp. 336 (ND Cal 1966)(as to overpayment).

47. 48 C.F.R. 49.402-3 provides default procedure to be followed by federal owner/obligee; *Union Indem. Co. v. Lang,* 71 F.2d 901 (9th Cir. 1934).

48. *Ca. Civ. Code* §2845*; Sukut-Coulson, Inc. v. Allied Canon Co.*, 85 Cal.App.3d 648 (1978); *Glickman v. Collins,* 13 Cal.3d 852 (1975); *United California Bank v. Maltzman,* 44 Cal.App.3d 41 (1974).

49. For an in-depth discussion of this issue, see, Lentz, *Default, Notice of Default, Impact Upon Surety's Obligations Where Notice is Not Given*, Ch. 2, THE LAW OF PERFORMANCE BONDS (American Bar Association, 1999, Moelmann and Harris, ed.).

50. For a discussion on verifying an obligee's default of the principal, see Collins, *Conducting an Effective Surety Investigation* (1988 National Conference on Surety Claims, San Francisco, CA).

51. See *Zoby v. American Fidelity Company*, 242 F.2d 76, 79 (4th Cir. 1957), finding no interference where the surety recommended to the obligee that it complete the contract with a new contractor: "Where the alleged interferer is a financially interest party, and such interest motivates its conduct, it cannot be said that [the interferer] is an officious or malicious meddler." See also, *Leo Spear Constr. Co. v. Fidelity & Casualty Co. of N.Y.*, 446 F.2d 439 (2d Cir. 1977) and *Gerstner Construction v. American Ins. Co.*, 520 F.2d 790 (8th Cir. 1975).

52. See, for example, *Richardson v. La Rancherita*, 98 Cal.App.3d 73 (1979).

53. *Seaboard Surety Co. v. Dale Construction Co.*, 230 F.2d 625 (1st Cir. 1956).

54. *Hays Livestock Comm'n. Co. v. Maly Livestock Comm'n. Co.*, 498 F.2d 925 (10th Cir. 1974); *Zager v. Columbia Casualty Co.*, 43 P.2d 949 (Wash. 1935).

when the principal is not in default or has not been properly declared in default, the principal will argue that the surety is nothing more than a volunteer and defend against an indemnity claim on that basis.[55] "The liability of the principal is the measure of the surety's liability, and should the surety pay where the principal has no actual liability it is not entitled to recover from the principal or the indemnitors because the payment is deemed to be voluntary."[56]

However, for the principal and indemnitors to defeat an indemnity claim, they must prove that but for the surety's performance, the principal would have been able to complete the project thereby avoiding a bond claim in its entirety. Alternatively, the principal and indemnitors must prove that the obligee was somehow able to recover a greater amount than it would have been able to recover if the surety had not performed. Moreover, most general indemnity agreements today provide that a surety is entitled to reimbursement for any payment made in good faith under the *belief*, correct or not, that it was liable or that it was necessary or expedient to make that payment.[57]

The AIA contract forms, as well as other standard contracts, contain specific provisions pertaining to default, notice to cure, and termination of the principal. When determining whether the principal is, in fact, in default, the surety would be wise to confirm that the obligee complied with the aforementioned contract provisions. In the absence of such contractual provisions, a declaration of default from the obligee terminating the principal is often sufficient. Likewise, a voluntary letter of default from the principal acknowledging its lack of funds to complete and/or inability to continue without the surety's assistance will suffice.

II. Dispute Between the Obligee and Principal

The following discussion focuses on the surety's response when the principal is adamant that the default was wrongful such that the obligee is in breach of contract. Nonetheless, the obligee typically asserts a claim against the performance bond surety to perform the contract in accordance with the performance bond and the contract documents.

A. THE "CLASSIC DILEMMA"[58]

Frequently, the performance bond surety finds itself in what has commonly been referred to as the "classic dilemma"[59] describing the situation wherein the obligee has declared the principal in default and demanded that the surety perform pursuant to its bond, while the principal asserts that it is not in default and that the default termination is wrongful.

---

55. *Terra Resources, Inc. v. Lake Charles Dredging & Towing, Inc.*, 695 F.2d 828 (5th Cir. 1983); *Fidelity and Deposit Co. of Maryland v. Bristol Steel & Iron Works*, 722 F.2d 1160 (4th Cir. 1983); *Comm'n. Ins. Co. of Newark, N.J. v. Pacific-Peru Constr. Corp.*, 558 F.2d 948 (9th Cir. 1977).

56. Bruce King, "Indemnitor's Defenses and Counterclaims," Chapter 30, *The Law of Suretyship* (Gallagher, ed. 1993), p. 30-2.

57. Lerner and Witten, *Salvage/Subrogation Considerations*, Ch. 13, BOND DEFAULT MANUAL (American Bar Association, 2d ed. 1995, Clore, ed.).

58. For an in-depth discussion of the surety's "classic dilemma," see, Bruner, O'Connor, and Hartnett, The Surety's Analysis of Investigative Results: "To Perform or Not to Perform–That is the Question," Ch. 3, BOND DEFAULT MANUAL (American Bar Association, 2d ed. 1995, Clore, ed.).

59. Hinchey, *Surety's Performance Over Protest of Principal: Considerations and Risks*, Fidelity and Surety Law Committee, Annual Meeting 1986.

In this situation, if the surety sides with the principal and does not arrange for completion based upon the principal's claim that there was no event of default, the obligee may contend that the surety has breached its bond obligations and file suit against the surety, including therein claims of bad faith seeking to recover extracontractual damages in excess of the bond penal sum.[60]

On the other hand, if the surety sides with the obligee and completes, in addition to an interference claim and a claim of breach of the covenant of good faith and fair dealing,[61] the principal and indemnitors may defend against any subsequent indemnity action that the surety brings on the grounds that the surety should not have arranged for completion and by doing so acted as a volunteer, impairing or forfeiting the surety's right to indemnification and reimbursement.[62] Of course, the ability of the principal to assert these defenses turns upon the terms of the bond and the indemnity agreement.

Typically, where there is no indemnity agreement, the surety that settles with the obligee must demonstrate that it was legally obligated to honor the principal's obligation in order to obtain reimbursement from the principal.[63] As noted above, however, some courts have held that any party who agrees to indemnify a surety on performance bond claims, is liable to the surety, regardless of whether the surety's determination that the principal is in default ultimately proves incorrect or not so long as the surety acted in good faith and did not abuse its discretion in making such payments.[64] Accordingly, the surety armed with a general indemnity agreement is usually free from the burden to prove that it was legally obligated to honor the principal's obligation. This freedom is particularly available where the general indemnity agreement expressly provides that the surety may perform under the performance bond, over protest of the principal, without regard to whether or not the principal was correctly declared in default by the obligee.[65] Even armed with this right, however, many jurisdictions require the surety to act reasonably and in good faith.[66]

Regardless of the existence of a general indemnity agreement, the surety may consider filing an action for declaratory relief against the principal, indemnitors, and obligee seeking a declaration of its rights and obligations under the bond. Also, a surety may file a *quia timet* and/or exoneration action seeking to compel the principal to secure the surety's potential damages or exonerate the

---

60. For a discussion of performance bond sureties' liability for extracontractual damages, see, Shields, *Extracontractual Liability of Performance Bond Sureties*, Ch. 7, THE LAW OF PERFORMANCE BONDS (American Bar Association, 1999, Moelmann and Harris, ed.).

61. *See, Transamerica Premier v. Brighton School*, 940 P.2d 348 (Colo. 1997); *Szarkowski v. Reliance Ins. Co.*, 404 N.W.2d 502 (N.D. 1987); *Loyal Order of Moose v. Intern Fidelity*, 797 P.2d 622 (Alaska 1990); *K-W Industries v. National Sur. Corp.*, 231 Mont. 461 (1988); *Dodge v. Fidelity & Deposit Co. of Md.*, 161 Ariz. 344, 778 P.2d 1240 (1989); *but see, Cates Constr. Inc. v. Talbot Partners*, 21 Cal.4th 28 (1999); *Great American Ins. v. N. Austin Utility*, 908 S.W.2d 415 (Tex. 1995).

62. *Terra Resources, Inc. v. Lake Charles Dredging & Towing, Inc.*, 695 F.2d 828 (5th Cir. 1983); *Fidelity and Deposit Co. of Maryland v. Bristol Steel & Iron Works*, 722 F. 2d 1160 (4th Cir. 1983); *Comm'n. Ins. Co. of Newark, N.J. v. Pacific-Peru Constr. Corp.*, 558 F.2d 948(9th Cir. 1977).

63. *Kigp v. Paul*, 103 P.2d 675 (Mont. 1940).

64. *Reliance Ins. Co. v. Romine*, 707 F.Supp. 550 (S.D.Ga. 1989), aff'd, 888 F.2d 1344 (11th Cir. 1989); *Boney v. Central Mut. Ins. Co. of Chicago*, 197 S.E. 122 (N.C. 1938).

65. *Safeco Ins. Co. v. Criterion Inv. Corp.*, 732 F. Supp. 834 (E.D. Tenn. 1989); *Ins. Co. of North America v. Bath*, 726 F.Supp. 1247 (D. Wyo. 1989); and *Continental Cas. Co. v. Guterman*, 708 F.Supp. 953 (N.D. Ill. 1989). *See generally*, Fields, *Some Aspects of Surety Indemnitor Relationships*, 39 Ins. Couns. J. 541 (1972).

66. *Fidelity and Deposit Co. of Maryland v. Bristol Steel & Iron Works*, 722 F.2d 1160 (4th Cir. 1983); *Transamerica Ins. Co. v. Bloomfield*, 401 F.2d 357 (6th Cir. 1968).

surety by requiring the principal to perform or satisfy the underlying obligation.[67] Unfortunately, this step is time-consuming and is, therefore, rarely employed, at least not in lieu of otherwise addressing the obligee's demand.

In sum, all default situations mandate that the surety be aware of its obligations to and the rights of its principal, the indemnitors, and the obligee under the performance bond.[68] Therefore, the surety should give immediate notification of the obligee's demand to the principal and indemnitors to provide them with not only an opportunity to discuss the demand among themselves and with the surety, but allow them to cure the default, where possible.

B. THE SURETY'S DUTY TO INVESTIGATE[69]

Generally, it is the duty of the performance bond surety to investigate a performance bond demand as rapidly as possible in an effort to determine available options in which to cure the default in addition to meeting its good faith obligations under the bond to avoid additional exposure and risk.[70] In fact, many state legislatures have enacted legislation imposing upon insurers the obligation to promptly investigate and evaluate the propriety of bond claims.[71]

In its investigation, the performance bond surety must evaluate not only the obligee's claims against the principal and the surety, but also (1) the principal's claims against others to which the surety will be subrogated, and (2) the surety's claims for exoneration or indemnification against the principal and the indemnitors.[72] Moreover, where the propriety of the obligee's termination of the principal is disputed, the surety's investigation is absolutely critical to prevent an assertion that the surety had a legal duty to investigate and failed to do so.[73] A surety's determination of the propriety

---

67. *See generally*, Mann, *Exoneration and Quia Timet*, Ch. 28 THE LAW OF SURETYSHIP (American Bar Association, 1993, Gallagher, ed.); Mann and Jennings, *Quia Timet: A Remedy for the Fearful Surety*, 20 Forum 685 (1985); Auerbacher, *Quia Timet: Relief by Summary Judgment on Indemnity Agreement*, 39 Ins. Couns. J. 536 (1972); Hinchey, *Surety's Performance over Principal Is Protest*, *supra* at note 45.

68. See, Clarke, Demski and Ziolkowski, *Rights and Remedies by Principals or Indemnitors Against the Surety*, Ch. 8, THE LAW OF PERFORMANCE BONDS (American Bar Association, 1999, Moelmann and Harris, ed.); Reinert, *The Duty of the Performing Surety to the Bond Principal and the Indemnitors: Good Faith*, 15 THE FORUM 1005 (1980).

69. For a thorough review of the surety's investigation in the performance bond context, see, Piper, *The Surety's Investigation*, Ch. 2, Section A, BOND DEFAULT MANUAL (American Bar Association, 2d ed. 1995, Clore, ed.)

70. For cases holding that a surety's failure to investigate a principal's default prior to denying liability under the performance bond constitutes bad faith on the surety's part and subjects it to tort liability, see *Tonking v. The Bob Eldridge Const. Co.*, 808 S.W.2d 849 (Mo. Ct. App. 1991); *Dodge v. Fidelity & Deposit Company of Maryland*, 778 P.2d 1240 (Ariz. 1989); *Loyal Order- of Moose v. International Fidelity*, 797 P.2d 622 (Alaska 1990). But cf. *Brinderson-Newberg Joint Venture v. Pacific Erectors, Inc.*, 971 F.2d 272 (9th Cir. 1992) (No duty to investigate where surety in good faith has reason to believe that genuine dispute concerning liability exists); *Farmers Union Central Exchange v. Reliance Ins. Co.*, 675 F.Supp. 1534 (D. N.D. 1987) (Surety had no duty to investigate where claims were inaccurate and not properly documented).

71. *See e.g.*, California Insurance Code § 790.03 and California Code of Regulations, Title 10, Chapter 5, § 2695.10.

72. Britt, *The Surety's Investigation*, 18 THE FORUM 1151 (1982).

73. An investigation of the default is never really a consideration vis a vis the obligee. However, most sureties consider it an absolute necessity to achieve three basic objectives: (1) Avoid liability for extracontractual damages and penalties in a subsequent bad faith claim; (2) Preservation of the surety's claim for indemnity against the principal and indemnitors; and (3) Accurately determine the correctness of the default termination. Hinchey, *supra* note 2.

of a default encompasses a single issue: Whether the principal has materially breached the underlying construction contract.[74]

Following receipt of a demand from the obligee, the surety should immediately commence an investigation of the default which includes reviewing records, interviewing the obligee and the principal and, often, a site inspection. It is common for the surety to utilize the services of a construction consultant knowledgeable in the area of construction.[75] Generally, the surety will conduct its investigation with three goals in mind: (1) To identify the obligations that the surety has undertaken by virtue of having issued the performance bond; (2) To recover as much of the surety's loss and expense as possible; and (3) To minimize the surety's expense and further exposure to loss.[76]

As a part of the surety's investigation, it looks into the physical status of the project, including (1) an estimate of the percentage of completion, (2) a description of any technical problems encountered or defective construction alleged, (3) a description of any construction or payment disputes with the owner or with subcontractors or suppliers, and (4) an estimate of the time of completion.

In addition, the surety needs a financial recapitulation of the project, indicating the payments made to date on the contract, the amounts paid to the subcontractors and suppliers, the amount remaining unpaid under the contract, accrued payables to subcontractors and suppliers, and the contractor's estimate of the amount that will be necessary to complete the project and pay all project-related obligations.

The surety also investigates the principal's financial condition, including other projects and all payables. This investigation should include a list of all assets that might be available to the surety and an analysis of any encumbrances against these assets. Important information to be obtained include unpaid taxes, state or federal, including the contractor's withholding taxes, a breakdown of the monthly overhead of the operation, the projected cash flow, and the extent of "front-loading," (i.e., inflation in price breakdown attributed to work performed early in construction). Most sureties also try to obtain a financial history of the projects currently in progress to ascertain whether contract funds have been diverted from one project to another. This information is often helpful in understanding why the principal is in financial difficulty, which is important to the surety in deciding which of its options it should exercise.

The result of the surety's investigation should confirm the validity of either: (1) The obligee's declaration of default; or (2) The principal's contention of improper termination. On occasion, the surety cannot determine who is right and who is wrong or it determines that both the obligee and principal are partially correct and partially incorrect. In those situations, where the principal disputes the termination, the surety normally considers one of two options. First, the surety can acknowledge the principal's default and perform under the performance bond, subjecting itself to a potential lawsuit by the principal and/or indemnitors and/or defenses to its attempt to obtain reimburse and indemnity. Second, the surety can do nothing, essentially siding with the principal, subjecting itself to the possibility of a claim, whether valid or not, by the obligee for not only the

---

74. For a discussion as to the "who"I "what" and "how" of the investigation, *see* Britt, *supra* note 15.

75. For a thorough review of the use of consultants to assist in the surety's investigation of bond defaults, see, Givens, *The Surety's Use of Consultants in Connection with Contract Bond Defaults*, Ch. 2, Section B, BOND DEFAULT MANUAL (American Bar Association, 2d ed. 1995, Clore, ed.).

76. Britt, *supra*.

costs of completion, but extracontractual damages for the surety's "bad faith" refusal to perform under its performance bond.

There is a third option available, depending upon the particular circumstances of the case. The surety can agree to perform, reserving any and all of the principal's rights to pursue the obligee for breach of contract based on the obligee's alleged improper termination.

III. *Scope of the Performance Bond Surety's Liability*[77]

As a general rule, the bond itself defines the scope of the performance bond surety's liability.[78] If the performance bond incorporates by reference the construction contract, the provisions of the construction contract are generally treated as provisions of the bond.[79]

If the bond is required by statute,[80] the statute will define the liability of the performance bond surety,[81] even when the bond is not literally in statutory form.[82] In a majority of jurisdictions, if the bond provides coverage in excess of the coverage required by the statute, the performance bond surety will be deemed to have agreed to provide that greater level of coverage.[83] Based on the theory that a surety issuing a statutory bond is a primary obligor rather than a secondary obligor, some courts have found that certain defenses usually available to the bond principal may not benefit

---

77. See also, Gregory and Rune, *Liability of the Performance Bond Surety*, Ch. 6, THE LAW OF PERFORMANCE BONDS (American Bar Association, 1999, Moelmann and Harris, ed.)

78. *L & A Contracting Co. v. Southern Concrete Servs.*, 17 F.3d 106, 109 (5th Cir.1994); *Marshall Contractors, Inc. v. Peerless Ins. Co.*, 827 F. Supp. 91, 94 (D.R.I. 1993); *Farmers Union Coop. Assn v. Mid-States Constr. Co.*, 322 NW.2d 373 (Neb. 1982); *General State Auth. v. Sutter Corp.*, 403 A.2d 1022 (Pa. Commw. Ct. 1979); *South Carolina Pub. Serv. Comm'n v. Colonial Constr. Co.*, 266 S.E.2d 76 (S.C. 1980); *New Amsterdam Casualty Co. v. Bettes*, 407 SW.2d 307 (Tex. 1966); *Waukesha Concrete Prods. Co. v. Capitol Indem. Corp.*, 379 N.W.2d 333 (Wis. Ct. App. 1985).

79. *Fayetteville Investors v. Commercial Builders, Inc.*, 936 F.2d 1462 (4th Cir. 1991); *Date Benz, Inc. v. American Casualty Co.*, 303 F.2d 80 (9th Cir. 1962); *Southern Roofing & Petroleum Co. v. Aetna Ins. Co.*, 293 F. Supp. 725 (E.D. Tenn. 1968); *Jen-Mar Constr. Co. v. Brown,* 55 Cal. Rptr. 832 (Ct. App. 1967); *Fisher v. Fidelity & Deposit Co.*, 466 N.E.2d 332 (Ill. App. Ct. 1984); *Mid-States Constr.*, 322 N.W.2d 373; *Colonial Constr.*,266 S.E.2d 76; *Waukesha,* 379 NW.2d 333.

80. See, for example, 40 U.S.C.A. § 270a (West Supp. 1986).

81. *Paul Schoonover, Inc. v. Ram Constr., Inc.*, 630 P.2d 27 (Ariz. 1981); *Colonial Constr.*, 266 S.E.2d 76; *City of San Antonio v. Argonaut Ins. Co.*, 644 SW.2d 90 (Tex. Ct. App. 1982); *City of Marshall v. American Gen. Ins. Co.*, 623 SW.2d 445 (Tex. Ct. App. 1981); Washington Int'l Ins. Co. v. Superior Court, 62 Cal.App.4th 981 (1998).

82. *Water Works, Gas & Sewer Bd. v. P.A. Buchanan Contracting Co.*, 318 So. 2d 267 (Ala. 1975).

83. *Florida Keys Community College v. Insurance Co. of N. Am.*, 456 So. 2d 1250 (Fla. Dist. Ct. App. 1984); *Fenetz v. Stine,* 407 So. 2d 1381 (La. Ct. App. 1981); *Bullard v. State*, 394 So. 2d 626 (La. Ct. App. 1980); *City of Marshall,* 623 SW.2d 445 (citing general rule but finding no excess coverage provided in bond). *But see* Tex. Gov't. Code Ann. § 2253.023(b) (West 1994); *W.S. Dickey Clay Mfg. Co. v. Ferguson Inv. Co.*, 388 P.2d 300 (Okla. 1963) (holding bond provisions outside scope of statute are invalid and cannot support cause of action); *Colonial Constr.,supra*, 266 S.E.2d 76 (holding public works surety not liable for expansion and improvements mandated by administrative regulations promulgated subsequent to execution of bond); *Hartford Accident & Indem. Co. v. Arizona Dept. of Transp.*, 838 P.2d 1325, 1327 (Ariz. Ct. App. 1992).

the surety.[84] Ambiguous language in a bond issued under a statute will often be interpreted according to the statutory intent.[85]

The performance bond usually incorporates the principal's contract such that the surety's liability is coextensive with that of its principal.[86] Accordingly, the surety is not liable if its principal is not liable.[87] In addition, many courts hold that the performance bond surety assumes no liability beyond that set forth in the bond.[88] Thus, the surety is usually not liable for an amount in excess of the penal sum of the performance bond.[89] The surety can limit its liability by disclaiming liability for certain damages,[90] although it is rarely done. Again, although it is rarely done, the surety can also expressly set forth that the surety's sole obligation is to guarantee completion of the construction contract and nothing more.[91] The surety generally has the right to assert any of the defenses available to its principal.[92] If the obligee waives or releases its claim against the principal,

---

84. See, *e.g., Powers Regulator Co. v Seaboard Sur. Co.,* 204 Cal.App.2d 338, 348 (1962) (construing law governing public works payment bonds). But see, *Golden Eagle Ins. Co. v. First Nationwide Fin. Corp.* 26 Cal.App.4 160 (1994) (surety's liability primary only in sense that claimant has direct right of action against surety).

85. *Weber v Pacific Indem. Co.*, 204 Cal.App.2d 334 (1962) (finding that performance bond issued under Subdivision Map Act did not include payment bond protecting contractor of subdivider-principal). *But see, Rexroth & Rexroth, Inc. v. General* Cas. Co., 242 Cal.App.2d 363 (1966) (finding that surety could provide enforceable common law payment bond, printed on back of statutory subdivision performance bond).

86. *Sorensen v. Ewing,* 448 P.2d 110 (Ariz. Ct. App. 1968); *Cates Construction v. Talbot Partners, 21 Cal.4th 28 (1999); Amerson v. Christman,* 68 Cal. Rptr. 378 (Ct. App. 1968); *Nicholson & Loup, Inc. v. Carl E. Woodward, Inc.*, 596 So. 2d 374, 390 (La. Ct. App. 1992); *Congregation of St. Peter's Roman Catholic Church v. Simon*, 497 So. 2d 409 (La. Ct. App. 1986); *In re Macdonald's Estate,* 67 N.W.2d 227 (Mich.1954); *Howard Constr. Co. v. Teddy Woods Constr. Co.*, 817 S.W.2d 556, 564 (Mo. Ct. App. 1991); *Babylon Assocs. v. Suffolk County*, 475 N.Y.S.2d 869 (App. Div. 1984); *Haywood County Consol. Sch. Sys. v. United States Fidelity & Guar. Co.,* 257 S.E.2d 670 (N.C. Ct. App. 1979); *Waukesha Concrete Prods. Co. v. Capitol Indem. Corp.,* 379 NW.2d 333 (Wis. Ct. App. 1985).

87. *Rockland County v. Aetna Casualty & Sur. Co.,* 514 N.Y.S.2d 102 (App. Div.1987); cf. *Westwood Corp. v. Bowen*, 815 P.2d 1282, 1287 (Or. Ct. App. 1991) (principal and surety entitled to offset remaining contract balances against obligee's damages, and as contract balances exceeded obligee's damages, surety had no liability under its bond).

88. *Tudor Dev. Group, Inc. v. United States Fidelity & Guar. Co.,* 692 F. Supp. 461 (M.D. Pa. 1988); *American Home Assur. Co. v. Larkin Gen. Hosp.*, 593 So. 2d 195 (Fla. 1992); *Alexander & Baldwin,* 532 P.2d 1007; *Farmers Union Coop. Assn. v. Mid-States Constr. Co.*, 322 NW.2d 373 (Neb. 1982); *General State Auth. v. Sutter Corp.,* 403 A.2d 1022 (Pa. Commw. Ct. 1979); *Colonial Constr.*, 266 S.E.2d 76; *Board of County Supervisors v. Sie-Gray Developers, Inc.*, 334 S.E.2d 542 (Va. 1985); *Waukesha,* 379 NW.2d 333.

89. *In re Technology for Energy Corp. (Public Serv. Elec. & Gas Co. v. Technology for Energy Corp.)*, 140 B.R. 214 (Bankr. E.D. Tenn. 1992) (holding that surety's liability is limited to the penal sum of the bond despite change orders significantly increasing the dollar amount of the bonded contract beyond the penal sum of the bond); *Aetna Casualty & Sur. Co. v. Butte-Meade Sanitary Water Dist.*, 500 F. Supp. 193 (D. S.D. 1980); *Amerson, supra*, 68 Cal. Rptr. 378; *Riva Ridge Apartments v. Robert G. Fisher Co.,* 745 P.2d 1034 (Colo. Ct. App. 1987); *Fisher v. Fidelity & Deposit Co.*, 466 N.E.2d 332 (Ill. App. Ct. 1984); *Hunt v. Bankers & Shippers Ins. Co.,* 423 N.Y.S.2d 718 (App. Div. 1979), *aff'd,* 409 N.E.2d 928 (N.Y. 1980); *General State Auth. v. Sutter Corp.*, 403 A.2d 1022 (Pa. Commw. Ct. 1979); *Board of County Supervisors v. Sie-Gray Developers, Inc.*, 334 S.E.2d 542 (Va. 1985); *Board of Supervisors v. Safeco Ins. Co. of Am.*, 310 S.E. 2d 445 (Va. 1983). *But see, Insurance Co. of North America. v. United States*, 951 F.2d 1244 (Fed. Cir. 1991) (allowing prejudgment interest even though it increased the surety's liability beyond the face amount of the bond).

90. *Alexander & Baldwin,* 532 P.2d 1007.

91. *Larkin Gen.*, 593 So. 2d 195. *But see Amerson,* 68 Cal, Rptr. 378 (holding exact same bond language was broad enough to allow for the recovery of consequential damages).

92. *Rhode Island Hosp. Trust Natl Bank v. Ohio Casualty Ins. Co.*, 789 F.2d 74 (1st Cir. 1986); *Commercial Standard Ins. Co. v. Alabama Surface Mining Reclamation Comm'n,* 443 So. 2d 1245, 1249 (Ala. Civ. App. 1983), *cert. denied,* 467 U.S. 1242 (1984); *In re* Macdonald's Estate, 67 NW.2d 227 (Mich. 1954); *Exton Drive-In, Inc. v. Home Indem. Co.,* 261 A.2d 319 (Pa. 1969), *cert. denied,* 400 U.S. 819 (1970); *Board of Supervisors v. Southern*

it also waives or releases its claim against the surety.[93] Furthermore, if the bonded contract is voided because it was induced by fraud, the bond will also be voided as it was only covering obligations under the contract.[94] If the bond incorporates the principal's construction contract, the terms of the construction contract must be read in conjunction with the terms of the bond to determine the surety's liability.

A. Claims by Someone Other than the Named Obligee

Claimants other than the obligee have employed at least three theories in an attempt to recover from the performance bond surety. Those theories are (1) that the claimant is a third-party beneficiary of the bond; (2) that the obligee has assigned its right to pursue the bond to the claimant; and (3) that the claimant is subrogated to the rights of the named obligee. The outcomes of cases decided under these three theories of recovery have turned upon the specific language found in the bond, the underlying contract, and the applicable statute, if the bond is required by a statute.

1. Third-Party Beneficiary Claims

The theory most often pursued when attempting to recover from a performance bond surety is the third-party beneficiary theory. There are no hard and fast rules as to the language needed in either the contract or the bond to support a claim under this theory, and consequently the cases construing this issue are inconsistent and conflicting.

a. Suppliers and Subcontractors. When a statute imposes an obligation upon the performance bond surety to pay for labor and/or materials, a majority of courts have allowed suppliers and subcontractors to recover from the performance bond surety regardless of the language contained in the bond.[95] Likewise, a majority of courts have held that where the performance bond is conditioned upon the contractor's faithful performance of all terms and conditions of the contract, and where the contract expressly requires the contractor to pay for all labor and materials used, suppliers and subcontractors have a right of action against the surety as third-party beneficiaries of the performance bond.[96]

Cross Coal Corp., 380 S.E.2d 636 (Va. 1989); *see also* sources cited *infra* note 54. *But see Smith Plumbing Co. v. Aetna Casualty & Sur. Co.*, 720 P.2d 499 (Ariz.) (holding surety was not allowed to assert the personal defenses of its principal*), cert. denied, 479 U.S. 987 (1986); Aaron* v. Bankers & Shippers Ins. Co., 475 So. 2d 3 79, 382 (La. Ct. App. 1985).

93. *Barr/Nelson, Inc. v. Tonto's, Inc.*, 336 NW.2d 46 (Minn. 1983).

94. *Taylor & Jennings, Inc. v. Bellino Bros. Constr. Co.*, 483 N.Y.S.2d 813 (App. Div. 1984).

95. *Houdaille Indus. v. United Bonding Ins. Co.*, 453 F.2d 1048 (5th Cir. 1972); *Higgins & Coufal v. Massachusetts Bonding & Ins. Co.*, 112 F. Supp. 390 (D. Neb. 1953); *State ex rel W.M. Carroll & Co. v. K.L. House Constr. Co.*, 656 P.2d 236 (N.M. 1982). *But see McQueen Contracting, Inc. v. Fidelity & Deposit Co.*, 863 F.2d 1216, *modified on other grounds*, 871 F.2d 32 (5th Cir. 1989) (The payment bond was exhausted. The Mississippi statute required that the performance bond contain a provision to pay for labor and material. The court, however, denied recovery against the performance bond. The court held that by providing the payment bond, the coverage required by the statute had been met.).

96. *Royal Indem. Co. v. Alexander Indus.*, 211 A.2d 919 (Del. 1965); *Neenah Foundry Co. v. National Sur. Corp.*, 197 N.E.2d 744 (Ill. App. Ct. 1964); *Ill-Mo Contractors, Inc. v. Aalcan Demolition & Contracting Co.*, 431 SW.2d 165 (Mo. 1968); *Acoustics, Inc. v. American Sur. Co.*, 320 P.2d 626 (Nev. 1958); *Amelco Window Corp. v. Federal Ins. Co.*, 317 A.2d 398 (N.J. Super. Ct. App. Div. 1974); *Gibbs v. Trinity Universal Ins. Co.*, 330 P.2d 1035 (Okla. 1958); *Engen v. Peerless Ins. Co.*, 382 SW.2d 541 (Tenn. Ct. App. 1964); *Bristol Steel & Iron Works v. Plank,*

If the contract does not impose an express obligation upon the contractor, and thus, by incorporation, upon the performance bond surety to pay suppliers and subcontractors, the courts are split regarding whether claimants can recover from the performance bond surety under a third-party beneficiary theory. Some courts require that the contract contain an express promise to pay before the performance bond surety will be obligated to pay for labor and/or materials.[97] Other courts go farther and refuse to allow recovery against the performance bond on a third-party beneficiary theory when the contract contains a promise to pay for labor and materials but the bond does not.[98]

Conversely, in other jurisdictions, subcontractors and suppliers have been allowed to recover when the contract incorporated into the bond does not expressly require the principal to pay suppliers or subcontractors, but contains other language that the courts have found sufficient to evidence an intent to benefit the claimants.[99] For example, one court allowed a subcontractor to recover from a performance bond surety when the contract obligated the principal to provide both a performance and a payment bond. In that case, only a performance bond was provided, but the performance bond was in twice the amount of the contract and was conditioned upon the principal's faithful performance of all terms and conditions of the contract.[100] Likewise, where a performance bond is conditioned upon faithful performance of the contract by the principal and the contract obligates the contractor to furnish all materials and labor necessary to construct a building, two courts have found an implied promise on the surety's part to pay for labor and materials so furnished.[101]

---

178 S.E. 58 (Va. 1935); RESTATEMENT THIRD, SURETY AND GUARANTY § 69 (1996).

97. *Johns-Manville Sales Corp. v. Reliance Ins. Co.*, 410 F.2d 277 (9th Cir. 1969); *Smith-Kelly Supply Co. v. General Constr. Corp.*, 399 F. Supp. 184 (S.D. Ala.), *aff'd*, 519 F.2d 1087 (5th Cir. 1975); *Crane Co. v. Borwick Trenching Corp.*, 32 P.2d 387 (Cal. Dist. Ct. App. 1934); *Garco Indus. Equip. Co. v. Mallory*, 485 N.E.2d 652 (Ind. Ct. App. 1985); *Cretex Cos. v. Construction Leaders, Inc.*, 342 NW.2d 135 (Minn. 1984); *Wilbur Waggoner Equip. Rental & Excavating Co. v. Bumiller*, 542 SW.2d 32 (Mo. Ct. App.1976); *Wyoming Mach. Co. v. United States Fidelity & Guar. Co.*, 614 P.2d 716 (Wyo.1980); RESTATEMENT THIRD, SURETY AND GUARANTY § 69 (1996).

98. *Treasure State Indus. v. Welch*, 567 P.2d 947 (Mont. 1977); *Pioneer Concrete & Fuel, Inc. v. Apex Constr., Inc.*, 664 P.2d 938 (Mont. 1983) (following *Welsch*, but finding the surety liable under a "theory of equitable responsibility" because the surety had required the principal to turnover its assets to the surety preventing the principal from paying the claimant). *But see, Weber v Pacific Indem. Co.* (1962) 204 Cal.App.2d 334, 22 Cal.Rptr. 366 (finding that performance bond issued under California Subdivision Map Act did not protect contractor of subdivider-principal even though bond included payment bond language because no legislative intent to protect contractors).

99. *Anchorage Sand & Gravel Co. v. Alaska Dock & Bridge Builders, Inc.*, 119 F. Supp. 943 (D. Alaska 1954) ("[A] bond guaranteeing faithful performance of a subcontract to furnish labor and materials implies a promise to pay therefor."); *Pacific States Elec. Co. v. United States Fidelity & Guar. Co.*, 293 P. 812 (Cal. Dist. Ct. App. 1930) ("A bond which undertakes to guarantee the faithful performance of a subcontract to furnish all necessary labor and materials for a specified portion of a structure implies a promise to pay for such labor and materials so furnished. It is unreasonable to hold the obligation is fulfilled by the mere supplying of the labor and materials."); *Westinghouse Elec. Corp. v. Mills & Elevator Co.*, 118 NW.2d 528 (Iowa 1962); *Algonite Stone Mfg. Co. v. Fidelity & Deposit Co.*, 163 P. 1076 (Kan. 1917) ("[T]he laborers and materialmen are sufficiently designated as a class for whose benefit the condition requiring the contractor to pay for labor and material was inserted in the contract, and that therefore they may maintain this action upon the bond."); *Dealers Elec. Supply v. United States Fidelity & Guar. Co.*, 258 NW.2d 131 (Neb. 1977); *Crowley v. United States Fidelity & Guar. Co.*, 69 P. 784 (Wash. 1902) ("[T]he true meaning and intent of the provision [of the contract] requiring the contractor to furnish materials was certainly that he should pay for them, and not that he should simply supply them. . . . If the contractor furnished materials under the contract for which he did not pay, and on account of which liens were filed against his property, it became the duty of the contractor, or in default thereof the surety, to pay these liens; and neglecting to do so, and thereby causing damages to respondent, the respondent was entitled to recover.").

100. *Anchorage Sand & Gravel*, *supra*, 119 F. Supp. 943.

101. *Pacific States Elec.*, *supra*, 293 P. 812; *Crowley*, *supra*, 69 P. 784.

Courts have uniformly denied recovery to claimants against indemnity bonds on a third-party beneficiary theory.[102] The courts find have reasoned that the indemnity provision in the performance bond evidences no intent to benefit anyone other than the named obligee. Likewise, courts have uniformly denied claims against subdivision performance bonds that developers provide to public entities to ensure that public improvements, such as streets, sewers, and sidewalks, are installed.[103] The courts have reasoned that the language in the bond evidences an intent to benefit only the public entity, and not third parties.

A majority of courts have also denied supplier and subcontractor claims against performance bonds that contain the following or similar language: "No right of action shall accrue on this bond to or for the use of any party other than the obligee herein."[104] The courts have held that this language clearly indicates the parties did not intend for the bond to benefit anyone other than the named obligee.

Furthermore, a majority of courts have held that a claimant is not entitled to recover against the performance bond when a payment bond was also provided or should have been, but the payment bond was unavailable to satisfy the claims because of the payment bond surety's insolvency,[105] the claimant's missing the time period within which to notify the surety,[106] exhaustion of the payment bond,[107] or failure to provide the required payment bond.[108] Under these circumstances, the suppliers and subcontractors were not intended to be third-party beneficiaries of the performance bond.

---

102. *Bevard v. New Amsterdam Casualty Co.*, 132 A.2d 157 (D.C. 1957); *Bourrett v. W.M. Bride Constr. Co.*, 84 N.W.2d 4 (Iowa 1957); *Board of Ed. ex rel. Breedon v. Victor N. Judson Inc.*, 126 A.2d 615 (Md. 1956); *Cleveland Window Glass & Door Co. v. National Sur. Co.*, 161 N.E. 280 (Ohio 1928).

103. *Corn Constr. Co. v. Aetna Casualty & Sur. Co.*, 295 F.2d 685 (10th Cir. 1961); *Evola v. Wendt Constr. Co.*, 338 P.2d 498 (Cal. Ct. App. 1959); *Marks & Masters Constr., Inc. v. Western Casualty & Sur. Co.*, 684 S.W.2d 863 (Mo. Ct. App. 1984); *Scales Douwes Corp. v. Paulaura Realty Corp.*, 249 N.E.2d 760 (N.Y. 1969); *Mineola Paving Co. v. Rowan Realty Corp.*, 225 N.Y.S.2d 637 Sup. Ct. 1962), *W.S. Dickey Clay Mfg. Co. v. Ferguson Inv. Co.*, 388 P.2d 300 (Okla. 1963); *Hewson Constr., Inc. v. Reintree Corp.*, 685 P.2d 1062 (Wash. 1984).

104. *American Radiator & Standard Sanitary Corp. v. Forbes*, 259 F.2d 147 (9th Cir.1958) (indemnity bond provided that "third parties are expressly denied the right to sue thereon"); *Luke v. Southern Sur. Co.*, 286 P. 490 (Cal. Dist. Ct. App. 1930) ("No right of action shall accrue under this bond to or for the use of any person other than the said ... (owner)."); *Aetna Ins. Co. v. Estero Mfg. & Builders Supply, Inc.*, 174 So. 2d 747 (Fla. Dist. Ct. App. 1965) ("[N]o right of action shall accrue upon or by reason hereof to or for the use or benefit of anyone other than the obligee(s) herein named."); *Houdaille Indus. v. United Bonding Ins. Co.*, 453 F.2d 1048 (5th Cir. 1972); *Tony & Leo, Inc. v. United States Fidelity & Guar. Co.*, 281 NW.2d 862 (Minn. 1979); *Stahlhut v. Sirloin Stockade, Inc.*, 568 SW.2d 269 (Mo. Ct. App. 1978) ("No right of action shall accrue on this bond to or for the use of any person or corporation other than the Owner."); *West Durham Lumber Co. v. Aetna Casualty & Sur. Co.*, 184 S. E. 2d 3 99 (N. C. Ct. App. 197 1), *cert. denied,* 185 S.E.2d 704 (N.C. 1972). *But see Pacific Ins. Co. v. Wilbanks*, 214 So. 2d 279 (Ala. 1968) ("The exclusionary clause is repugnant to and inconsistent with all the terms and conditions of the bond which precede it. . . . [T]he inconsistency in the bond, the exclusionary clause, which cannot be reconciled with prior or first-stated conditions in the contract guaranteed, must be resolved in favor of the prior or first-stated conditions in the contract." Court concluded that the bond was intended not only for the benefit of the owner-obligee, but also intended for the benefit of laborers and materialmen, and the claim was allowed.); *Haynes Hardware Co. v. Western Casualty & Sur. Co.*, 133 P.2d 574 (Kan. 1943) (holding that bond provision denying benefits to third-party claimants was inconsistent with contract provision (incorporated into the bond) protecting laborers and suppliers; general provisions prevail over conflicting specific provisions when determining the intent of the parties).

105. *Jimco, Inc. v. Gentilly Terrace Apartments, Inc.*, 230 So. 2d 281 (La. Ct. App. 1970).

106. *G.A. Mosites Co. v. Aetna Casualty & Sur. Co.*, 545 P.2d 746 (Okla. 1976).

107. *McQueen Contracting, Inc. v. Fidelity & Deposit Co.*, 863 F.2d 1216, *modified on other grounds,* 871 F.2d 32 (5th Cir, 1989); *Stahlhut v. Sirloin Stockade, Inc.*, 568 SW.2d 269 (Mo. Ct. App. 1978).

108. *United States ex rel Warren v. Kimrey*, 489 F.2d 339 (8th Cir. 1974).

Lastly, a majority of courts have denied subcontractors' and suppliers' claims against performance bonds provided pursuant to the Miller Act.[109] The courts have reasoned that the intent of Congress in enacting the Miller Act was to provide the performance bond for the protection of the government's interests, and not that of subcontractors, suppliers, and laborers.

b. Co-Prime Contractors. A majority of courts have held that a prime contractor is not a third-party beneficiary of the performance bond that the co-prime contractor's surety provided to the owner.[110] The courts have declined to hold that a prime contractor is a third-party beneficiary of the performance bond where there is a clause in the bond limiting the right to make claim on the bond to the named obligee.[111] Furthermore, where a payment bond has been required as well, the courts have refused to allow recovery against the performance bond, reasoning that the parties knew how to provide third-party beneficiary status when they wrote the bond and chose not to.[112] However, at least one court has allowed recovery against the performance bond surety on a third-party beneficiary theory where the bond guaranteed all terms and conditions of the contract and the contract imposed an obligation on the principal to settle with its co-primes for all loss occasioned by the principal's negligence.[113]

c. Owners' Claim Against Subcontractors' Performance Bonds. A majority of courts confronted with the owner of a construction project bringing claim against the subcontractor's performance bond surety have denied the owner's claim.[114] The courts have uniformly denied recovery against the performance bond surety when the bond contained a clause limiting the right

---

109. *United States ex rel. James E. Simon Co. v. Ardelt-Horn Constr. Co.*, 446 F.2d 820 (8th Cir. 197 1), *cert. denied,* 404 U.S. 1060 (1972); *Transamerica Premier Ins. Co. v. Ober*, 894 F.Supp. 471 (D.Me. 1995); *United States Fidelity & Guar. Co. v. A&A Mach. Shop*, 330 F. Supp. 1403 (S.D. Tex. 1971); *Sun Ins. Co. of N.Y. v. Diversified Eng'rs, Inc.*, 240 F. Supp. 606 (D. Mont. 1965), *United States ex rel. Lichter v. Henke Constr. Co.*, 35 F. Supp. 388 (W.D. Mo. 1940). *But see United States ex rel. Edward I-lines Lumber Co. v. Kalady Constr. Co.*, 227 F. Supp. 10 17 (N.D. Ill. 1964) (holding that wage claims would be covered by the Miller Act performance bond despite the existence of a payment bond, where the penal sum of the payment bond had been exhausted and the failure to pay 'wages was in violation of the contract terms; court relied upon cases decided under the Heard Act, which provided that only a performance bond was required and that same bond would cover such claim); *United States ex rel. Blount Fabricators, Inc. v. Pitt Gen. Contractors, Inc.*, 769 F. Supp. 1016 (E.D. Tenn. 1991) (relied on *Kalady* decision).

110. *J. Louis Crum Corp. v. Alfred Lindgren, Inc.*, 564 S.W.2d 544 (Mo. Ct. App. 1978); *M.G.M. Constr. Corp. v. New Jersey Educ. Facilities Auth.*, 532 A.2d 764 (N.J. Super Ct. Law Div. 1987); *Novak & Co. v. Travelers Indem. Co.*, 392 N.Y.S.2d 901 (App. Div.), *appeal denied,* 367 N.E.2d 660 (N.Y. 1977); *Van Cor, Inc. v. American Casualty Co.*, 208 A.2d 267 (Pa. 1965); *Moore Constr. Co. v. Clarksville Dep't of Elec.*, 707 S.W.2d I (Tenn. Ct. App. 1985). *But see Aetna Casualty & Sur. Co. v. Doleac Elec. Co.*, 471 So. 2d 325 (Miss. 1985) (companion case to the *Hanberry* decision cited next and arose out of the same construction project and involved the same contract and performance bond); *Hanberry Corp. v. State Bldg. Comm'n*, 390 So. 2d 277 (Miss. 1980) (Contract imposed an obligation on the co-prime to settle with other prime contractors for any loss or damage on the work caused by the negligent acts of the co-prime. The bond guaranteed "all the undertakings, covenants, terms, conditions, and agreements of said contract." The court allowed the prime to recover against the co-prime's performance bond surety because the surety "issued its performance-payment bond knowing that [the co-prime] had the obligation to [the prime].").

111. *Moore Constr., supra,* 707 S.W.2d 1.

112. *Novak & Co., supra,* 392 N.Y.S.2d 901; Van *Cor, Inc., supra,* 208 A.2d 267.

113. *Doleac Elec., supra,* 471 So. 2d 325; *Hanberry Corp., supra,* 390 So. 2d 277.

114. *Pierce Assocs. v. Nemours Found.*, 865 F.2d 530 (3d Cir. 1988), *cert. denied,* 492 U.S. 907 (1989); *Rush Presbyterian St. Luke's Medical Ctr. v. Safeco Ins. Co. of Am.*, 825 F.2d 1204 (7th Cir. 1987); *Augusta Court Co-owners Ass'n. v. Levin, Roth & Kasner*, 971 S.W.2d 119 (Tx.App. 1998); *Southern Patrician Assocs. v. International Fidelity Ins. Co.*, 381 S.E.2d 98 (Ga. Ct. App. 1989); *Board of Educ. v. Fred L. Ockerlund, Jr. & Assocs.*, 519 N.E.2d 95 (Ill. App. Ct. 1988); *Young v. General Ins. Co. of Am.*, 337 N.E.2d 739 (Ill. App. Ct. 1975). *But see Crabtree v. Aetna Casualty & Sur. Co.*, 438 So. 2d 102 (Fla. Dist. Ct. App. 1983).

to make claim thereon to the named obligee or its successor.[115] One court even denied the claim of an owner who had been assigned all of the prime contractor's rights against the subcontractor and the performance bond surety because the owner was an assignee, not a successor of the obligee, and the bond limited the right to make claim thereon to the named obligee or its successor.[116]

d. Adjacent Property and/or Business Owners. The courts have consistently denied claims brought against performance bond sureties by owners of property and/or businesses adjacent to the construction site that have been injured by the negligent acts of the surety's principal.[117] The courts have developed at least three theories to deny these claims. First, courts have held that the bond does not operate as an all-risk insurance policy.[118] Second, courts have reasoned that if tort claimants were allowed to recover, there would be no protection for the intended beneficiaries of the bond.[119] Third, courts have held that they could find no language in either the bond or the contract imposing an obligation upon the surety to pay tort claimants.[120] However, one court allowed an adjoining landowner to sue the surety for damages when the bond contained a provision under which the surety agreed to indemnify all parties against damages and related hazards in relation to the performance of the principal's work.[121]

e. Successor Owners. Successor owners have had mixed success making claims against the performance bond surety of the previous owner's prime contractor. Claimants have been unsuccessful when the language in the bond limited those who could make claim against the bond to the named obligee,[122] and when the claimant was not in existence when the contract and bond were executed (the parties could not have intended for a nonexistent entity to be a beneficiary of the contract).[123] Conversely, one court allowed the successor owner to recover, reasoning that the bond

---

115. *Pierce Assocs., supra,* 865 F.2d 530; *Rush Presbyterian, supra,* 825 F.2d 1204; *Southern Patrician, supra,* 381 S.E.2d 98, *Ockerlund, supra,* 519 N.E.2d 95; *Young, supra,* 337 N.E.2d 739.

116. *Southern Patrician, supra,* 381 S.E.2d 98.

117. *Tri-State Ins. Co. v. United States*, 340 F.2d 542 (8th Cir. 1965); *Bona v. Peoples Gas Sys.*, 557 So. 2d 581 (Fla. Dist. Ct. App. 1989); *Long v. City of Midway*, 311 S.E.2d 508 (Ga. Ct. App. 1983); *State ex rel Hay v. United States Fidelity & Guar. Co.*, 172 N.E. 656 (Ind. 1930); *City of Univ. City ex rel Mackey v. Frank Miceli & Sons Realty & Bldg. Co.*, 347 SW.2d 131 (Mo. 1961); *John L. Roper Lumber Co. v. Lawson*, 143 S.E. 847 (N.C. 1928); *Anthony v. Construction Prods.*, 677 SW.2d 4 (Tenn. Ct. App. 1984); *Richmond Shopping Ctr. v. Wiley N. Jackson Co.*, 255 S.E.2d 518 (Va. 1979); *Kniess v. American Sur. Co.*, 300 N.W. 913 (Wis. 1941).

118. *Tri-State Ins., supra,* 340 F.2d 542 (holding that the performance bond did not "operate as an all risks policy of public liability insurance for the benefit of tort claimants"), *City of Midway, supra,* 311 S.E.2d 508; *City of Univ. City, supra,* 347 SW.2d 131 (stating that the bond was not "a substitute for public liability insurance").

119. *City of Midway, supra,* 311 S.E.2d 508 (holding that a performance bond should not be a substitute for public liability insurance; if it allowed tort claimants to proceed against the bond, it would exhaust funds designed to guarantee the payment for labor and materials arising out of a public contract).

120. *State ex rel. Hay, supra,* 172 N.E. 656; *City of Univ. City, supra,* 347 SW.2d 13 1; *Roper Lumber, supra,* 143 S.E. 847 (N.C. 1928); *Anthony, supra,* 677 SW.2d 4; *Richmond Shopping Or., supra,* 255 S.E.2d 518; *Kniess, supra,* 300 N.W. 913.

121. *Cooper v. Massachusetts Bonding & Ins. Co.*, 186 SW.2d 549 (Mo. Ct. App. 1944). *See also Hardware Dealers Mut. Ins. Co. v. R.H. Hidey, Inc.*, 84 NW.2d 795, 798 (Mich. 1957), in which the court stated:

> It will be noted that the performance bond, in terms, is not restricted to cover possible failure on the part of the contractor to construct the pumping station in accordance with the plans and specifications, but extends to and includes all obligations assumed by said contractor under its agreement. The language used is sufficiently broad to cover the undertaking with reference to the assumption of liability resulting from property damage to certain third parties.

122. *Board of Educ. v. Fred L. Ockerlund, Jr. & Assocs.*, 519 N.E.2d 95 (Ill. App. Ct. 1988).

123. *Beach Point Condominium Assn. v. Beach Point Corp.*, 480 So. 2d 239 (Fla. Dist. Ct. App. 1985).

did not prohibit the transfer of title, and that the contract, which was incorporated into the bond, bound the principal not only to the original owner, but also to its successor.[124]

f. Personal Injury/Wrongful Death Claimants. Courts have routinely denied personal injury and wrongful death claims asserted against the performance bond surety arising out of the negligent acts of the principal and/or the principal's employees.[125] The claims have been denied on the basis that the bond, contract, and statute, if applicable, did not contain language evidencing the parties' intent for these types of claims to be allowed. As one court reasoned, if tort claimants were allowed to recover, there would be no protection for the intended beneficiaries of the bond.[126]

2. Assignees of Performance Bond Obligees

As a general rule, absent prejudice to the surety[127] or language in the bond limiting the surety's liability to the named obligee or its successors,[128] the obligee can assign its right to make claim against the performance bond surety to a third party without the surety's consent,[129] and the surety will be obligated to the third-party assignee to the same extent that it was obligated to the assignor. The courts have universally held that the assignee takes the assignment subject to the defenses of the surety's principal.[130] Thus, except for personal defenses,[131] the surety has the right to assert all other defenses of its principal.[132]

3. Claimants Alleging That They Are Subrogated to the Rights of the Obligee

---

124. *Balboa Ins. Co. v. Snyder Consol. Indep. Sch. Dist.*, 574 S.W.2d 879 (Tex. Civ. App. 1978). *But see Fleck v. National Property Management, Inc.*, 590 P.2d 1254 (Utah 1979) (holding that purchaser at foreclosure sale was not allowed to recover against performance bond surety because it was not foreseeable that the principal's failure to construct the improvements would bring about the foreclosure of the trust deed and resulting loss of title).

125. *Foshee v. Daoust Constr. Co.*, 185 F.2d 23 (7th Cir. 1950); *National Sur. Co. v. Ulmen*, 68 F.2d 330 (9th Cir. 1933), *cert. denied*, 292 U.S. 624 (1934); *United States ex rel Spencer v. Massachusetts Bonding & Ins. Co.*, 18 F.2d 203 (6th Cir. 1927); *United States Fidelity & Guar. Co. v. Eubanks*, 87 S.W.2d 248 (Tex. 1935).

126. *Eubanks, supra*, 87 S.W.2d 248.

127. *Hunters Pointe Partners Ltd. Partnership v. United States Fidelity & Guar. Co.*, 442 N.W.2d 778 (Mich. Ct. App. 1989).

128. *Southern Patrician Assocs. v. International Fidelity Ins. Co.*, 381 S.E.2d 98 (Ga. Ct. App. 1989); *Young v. General Ins. Co. of Am.*, 337 N.E.2d 739 (Ill. App. Ct.1975).

129. *Transdulles Centre Ltd. Partnership v. USX Corp.*, 761 F. Supp. 430 (E.D. Va. 1991); *Chris Nelson & Son, Inc. v. Michigan Corp.*, 269 N.W.2d 295 (Mich. Ct. App. 1978).

130. *National Am. Bank v. Southcoast Contractors*, 276 So. 2d 777 (La. Ct. App. 1973); *Standard Sur. & Casualty Co. v. Kelley*, 170 P.2d 251 (Okla. 1946).

131. *Smith Plumbing Co. v. Aetna Casualty & Sur. Co.*, 720 P.2d 499 (Ariz.), *cert. denied*, 479 U.S. 987 (1986); *Aaron v. Bankers & Shippers Ins. Co.*, 475 So. 2d 379, 382 (La. Ct. App. 1985).

132. *Granite Computer Leasing Corp. v. Travelers Indem. Corp.*, 894 F.2d 547 (2d Cir. 1990); *Rhode Island Hosp. Trust Natl Bank v. Ohio Casualty Ins. Co.*, 789 F.2d 74 (1st Cir. 1986); *Asociacion de Azucareros de Guatemala v. United States Nat'l Bank*, 423 F.2d 638 (9th Cir. 1970) (Not a suretyship case, but in rejecting defendant's comparison between its status as issuer of a letter of credit with a surety's obligation under a bond, the court stated: "A surety is generally not liable on his undertaking unless his principal is liable and in default on the underlying debt. The defenses of the principal are available to the surety and, if the underlying debt is canceled, the surety's obligation ceases."); *Commercial Standard Ins. Co. v. Alabama Surface Mining Reclamation Comm'n.*, 443 So. 2d 1245 (Ala. Civ. App. 1983), *cert. denied*, 467 U.S. 1242 (1984); *State Athletic Comm'n v. Massachusetts Bonding & Ins. Co.*, 117 P.2d 75 (Cal. Dist. Ct. App. 1941); *Southcoasl Contractors*, 276 So. 2d 777. *See generally Village of Rosemont v. Lentin Lumber Co.*, 494 N.E.2d 592 (Ill, App. Ct. 1986); *Stephens v. First Bank & Trust*, 540 SW.2d 572 (Tex. Civ. App. 1976); *see also* sources cited *supra* note 14.

Claimants pursuing performance bond sureties on an equitable subrogation theory have had mixed success depending upon their identities and the nature of their claims. A defaulted prime contractor's performance bond surety is generally subrogated to its principal's right to pursue a subcontractor's performance bond surety.[133] Similarly, one court held that the liability insurance carrier was subrogated to the rights of the owner/insured against the contractor's performance bond surety for the contractor's negligence.[134] On the other hand, banks that have loaned money used to pay for labor and materials are not subrogated to the rights, if any, of those laborers and suppliers against the principal/borrower's performance bond surety.[135] Also, unpaid suppliers and subcontractors have been unable to recover against a Miller Act performance bond surety on the theory that they are equitably subrogated to the rights of the United States government.[136]

B. Claims by the Obligee

When a bonded contractor defaults on its obligations under its contract with an obligee, the obligee may incur a variety of damages for which the contractor may be liable. Those damages include costs incurred in completing and/or remedying defects in the contractor's work, damages associated with the delayed completion of the project, lost profit or lost business opportunity damages, attorneys' fees, damages associated with the contractor's negligence and/or failure to obtain liability insurance, and damages incurred due to the contractor's failure to honor its warranty and/or correct latent defects in its work.

The success or failure of obligees in recovering from the performance bond surety turns upon the damages for which the surety has agreed to be responsible as defined by the performance bond and the construction contract, if it is incorporated into the bond. Absent language of limitation in either the bond or the contract, the surety's liability has been found to be coextensive with that of its principal. Thus, the surety may be liable for all direct and consequential damages for which its principal is responsible due to the principal's breach of the bonded contract.[137] There is another line of authority that holds that a surety cannot be held liable for consequential damages, specifically delay damages, unless the bond and/or the contract explicitly so provided because the usual purpose

---

133. *Continental Casualty Co. v. Hartford Accident & Indem. Co.*, 52 Cal. Rptr. 533 (Dist. Ct. App. 1966) ("As a general rule, if a subcontractor's bond is put up in order to indemnify the prime contractor for any claim for which the latter may be held liable and for the payment of which the subcontractor is primarily liable, the subcontractor's surety is required to indemnify the principal contractor (or the latter's surety) for any liability imposed upon him for labor and materials furnished to the subcontractor."); *Argonaut Ins. Co. v. Commercial Standard Ins. Co.*, 380 So. 2d 1066 (Fla. Dist. Ct. App. 1980) (treating performance bond surety of defaulted prime contractor as "successor" within the meaning of language in the bond limiting "right of action" to, among others, prime contractor's if successors"); *Menorah Nursing Home v. Zukov*, 548 N.Y.S.2d 702 (App, Div. 1989).

134. *Hartford Fire Ins. Co. v. Riefolo Constr. Co.*, 410 A.2d 658 (N.J. 1980) (under the terms of the contract, the risk of loss remained with the contractor until the project was accepted and by failing to repair damages caused by a fire during construction, the contractor breached its contract; performance bond surety liable for the cost of repair); *But see, National Union Fire Ins. Co. v. Riggs Nat'l Bank of Wash.*, 646 A.2d 966 (D.C.App. 1994).

135. *United States ex rel. First Continental Nat'l Bank & Trust Co. v. Western Contracting Corp.*, 341 F.2d 383 (8th Cir. 1965); *American State Bank v. United States Fidelity & Guar. Co.*, 331 F.2d 479 (7th Cir. 1964).

136. *United States ex rel. James E. Simon Co. v. Ardelt-Horn Constr. Co.*, 446 F.2d 820 (8th Cir. 1971), *cert. denied,* 404 U.S. 1060 (1972); *United States Fidelity & Guar. Co. v. A&A Machine Shop*, 330 F. Supp. 1403 (S.D. Tex. 1971).

137. *See, e.g., Cates Construction v. Talbot Partners*, 21 Cal.4th 28 (1999).

of a performance bond is to ensure the completion of the construction contract upon the contractor's default.[138]

1. Incomplete or Defective Work (Not Including Delay Damages)

When the principal and surety fail to perform as contractually agreed, the normal measure of damages is the reasonable amount it would cost over and above the remaining contract balance, to complete the construction and/or remedy the defective work.[139] The obligee has an obligation to mitigate its damages.[140] The surety is not liable for any additional costs incurred because of work performed that was not covered by the principal's construction contract.[141] Furthermore, if completion of the work or correction of the defective work would result in economic waste, one measure of the obligee's damages may be the difference in value of the structure as constructed and its value had it been constructed according to the contract, not the cost to complete the project.[142]

In addition to the surety's obligation to pay the obligee for the additional expense it incurs in completing the principal's contractual obligations, the surety may be liable for other damages the principal caused if the bond language is broad enough. For example, an obligee was successful in recovering overhead and profit where the bonded construction contract provided for such recovery and where the bond was conditioned upon the principal's indemnifying the obligee against loss or damage directly caused by the failure of the principal to faithfully perform the subcontract.[143] Furthermore, one court allowed an obligee to recover additional "costs" from the surety when the construction contract, which was incorporated into the bond, contained a provision allowing the obligee a percentage mark-up on the funds expended by the obligee to complete the construction contract.[144] However, absent a provision in the bond or contract that allows for recovery of overhead as a percentage of the cost to complete, the obligee may need to prove that the principal's default caused the obligee to incur additional overhead that it would not otherwise have incurred.[145]

Additionally, if the obligee completes the construction contract with its own forces, it will be entitled to recover the payroll taxes, additional insurance premiums, payroll processing expenses,

---

138. *American Home Assur. Co. v. Larkin Gen. Hosp.* 593 So.2d 195 (Fla. 1992) (delay damages); *L&A Contracting Co. v. Southern Concrete Services, Inc.* 17 F.3d 106 (5th Cir. 1994) (delay damages); *United States Leasing Corp. v duPont*, 69 Cal.2d 275 (1968); *Bloom v Bender*, 48 Cal2d 793 (1959).

139. *American Sur. Co. v. United States*, 317 F.2d 652 (8th Cir. 1963); *Miracle Mile Shopping Ctr. v. National Union Indem. Co.*, 299 F.2d 780 (7th Cir. 1962); *McGovney & McKee, Inc. v. City of Berea*, 448 F. Supp. 1049 (E.D. Ky. 1978); *Sorensen v. Ewing*, 448 P.2d 110 (Ariz. Ct. App. 1968); *Amerson v. Christman*, 68 Cal. Rptr. 3 78 (Ct. App. 1968); *Urbanowicz v. Rayon-Beau Constr. Co., Inc.*, 43 3 A. 2d 10 17 (Conn. Super. Ct. 198 1); *Robinhorne Constr. Corp. v. Snyder*, 251 N.E.2d 641 (Ill. App. Ct. 1969), *aff'd*, 265 N.E.2d 670 (Ill. 1970); *Calandro Dev., Inc. v. R.M. Butler Contractors*, 249 So. 2d 254 (La. Ct. App. 1971); *Louise Caroline Nursing Home v. Dix Constr. Corp.*, 285 N.E.2d 904 (Mass. 1972); *New Amsterdam Casualty Co. v. Bettes*, 407 SW.2d 307 (Tex. 1966); *J & J Elec., Inc. v. Gilbert H. Moen Co.*, 516 P.2d 217 (Wash. Ct. App 1973).

140. *Town of Newington v. General Sanitation Serv. Co.*, 491 A.2d 363 (Conn. 1985); *Fisher, supra*, 466 N.E.2d 332; *Tynan Incinerator Co. v. International Fidelity Ins. Co.*, 499 N.Y.S.2d 118 (App. Div. 1986).

141. *Southern Roofing & Petroleum Co. v. Aetna Ins. Co.*, 293 F. Supp. 725 (E.D. Tenn. 1968).

142. *Forsythe v. Starnes*, 554 S.W.2d 100 (Mo. Ct. App. 1977); *Fidelity & Deposit Co. v. Stool*, 607 S.W.2d 17 (Tex. Civ. App. 1980); *American Employers' Ins. Co. v. Huddleston*, 39 S.W.2d 952 (Tex. Civ. App. 1931), *aff'd*, 70 S.W.2d 696 (Tex. 1934).

143. *Jen-Mar Constr. Co. v. Brown*, 55 Cal. Rptr. 832 (Ct. App. 1967); *see also Interstate Markings, Inc. v. Mingus Constructors, Inc.*, 941 F. 2d 1010, 1014 (9th Cir. 1991); *Dale Benz, Inc. v. American Casualty Co.*, 303 F.2d 80 (9th Cir. 1962).

144. *Southern Roofing, supra*, 293 F. Supp. 725.

145. *Asphalt Paving Co. v. United States Fidelity & Guar. Co.*, 671 P.2d 10 13 (Colo. Ct. App. 1983).

and other costs associated with the labor it supplied.[146] If the surety elects not to complete the work of its principal but to reimburse the obligee for those sums expended in excess of the remaining contract balance, the obligee may be allowed to recover prejudgment interest on the funds expended in excess of the remaining contract balance in completing the defaulted principal's work.[147] However, if the surety has an offsetting claim, the obligee's claim must be offset against the surety's claim and only the balance will bear interest.[148] The obligee may be able to recover for the cost of additional supervision that becomes necessary as a result of the principal's default.[149] Furthermore, if authorized by contract, statute or equitable basis, attorneys' fees may be recoverable as well.[150]

2. Unexcused Delays

Time is usually of the essence in a construction contract. If the principal, without excuse, delays the completion of the project, the obligee is entitled to be compensated for the damages it sustains. Due to the difficulty and expense associated with proving damages, obligees often insert liquidated damage clauses into their construction contracts. In the absence of an enforceable liquidated damage clause, the obligee will have to prove its actual delay damages.

a. Liquidated Damages. The parties to a construction contract may agree in advance to liquidate the damages recoverable by the obligee if the contractor, without excuse, delays the completion of the project. Such clauses, commonly referred to as liquidated damage clauses, are regularly incorporated into construction contracts. Generally, liquidated damage clauses provide that a specified amount of damages are recoverable by the obligee from the contractor for each day the contractor delays the completion of the project beyond the contractually agreed upon date. If a contract contains a liquidated damage clause, the obligee's recovery for delay damages is limited to the amount specified,[151] unless the contract provides otherwise.[152] The date the liquidated damages will cease to accrue depends upon the intent of the parties as expressed by the language used in the

146. *Id.*

147. *Interstate Markings, Inc. v. Mingus Constructors, Inc.*, 941 F.2d 1010, 1015 (9th Cir. 1991); *United States v. American Mfgs. Mut. Casualty Co.*, 901 F.2d 370, 373 (4th Cir.), *cert. denied,* 111 S. Ct. 143 (1990); *United States v. Seaboard Surety Co.*, 817 F.2d 956, 966 (2d Cir. 1987); *National Union Fire Ins. Co. v. D & L Constr. Co.*, 353 F.2d 169 (8th Cir. 1965), *cert. denied,* 3 84 U. S. 941 (1966); *Asphalt Paving, supra,* 671 P.2d 10 13; *Fisher v. Fidelity & Deposit Co.*, 466 N.E.2d 332 (Ill.. App. Ct. 1984); *Tynan Incinerator Co. v. International Fidelity Ins. Co.*, 499 N.Y. S.2d 118 (App. Div. 1986); *Village of Newark v. James F. Leary Constr. Co.*, 194 N.Y. S. 212 (Sup. Ct. 1922); *cf.* JR. Kemper, Annotation, *Allowance of Prejudgment Interest on Builder's Recovery in Action for Breach of Construction Contract,* 60 A.L.R.3d 487 (1974). *But see Church of the Holy Spirit v. Bevco, Inc.*, 338 N.W.2d 601 (Neb. 1983).

148. *Burnett & Doty Dev. Co. v. Phillips*, 148 Cal. Rptr. 569, 573 (Ct. App. 1978) (standing for the general proposition, but holding that the performance bond surety's principal was not entitled to prejudgment interest on the remaining contract balance held by the obligee where the damages sustained by the obligee as a result of the principal's breach of its contractual obligations exceeded the remaining contract balance).

149. *Donlan v. American Bonding & Trust Co.*, 51 S.E. 924 (N.C. 1905); *State v. Service Elec. & Supply, Inc.*, 3 10 NW.2d 626 (Wis. Ct. App. 198 1), *aff'd,* 316 NW.2d 390 (Wis. 1982).

150. See *infra* part 3 for a detailed discussion of the recovery of attorneys' fees.

151. *County of Dauphin v. Fidelity & Deposit Co.*, 770 F. Supp. 248 (M.D. Pa.), *aff'd,* 937 F.2d 596 (3d Cir. 1991); *Bums v. Hanover Ins. Co.*, 454 A.2d 325 (D.C. 1982); *Waters v. Key Colony East, Inc.*, 345 So. 2d 367 (Fla. Dist. Ct. App. 1977).

152. *Burns, supra,* 454 A.2d 325.

construction contract. In most cases, liquidated damages cease to accrue upon substantial completion of the project.[153]

If the construction contract is incorporated into the performance bond and contains an enforceable liquidated damage clause, the general rule is that the performance bond surety will be liable for liquidated damages in the event that its principal, without excuse, delays the completion of the project.[154] Furthermore, if the bonded subcontract contains a flowdown or conduit clause, and the prime contract contains a liquidated damage provision, the surety may be deemed to have agreed to pay liquidated damages in the amount specified in the prime contract.[155]

Other factors affect the ability of the obligee to recover liquidated damages as well. For example, if the obligee contributes to the delay or terminates the contractor's rights to proceed, or if the contractor itself abandons the project, questions arise regarding the enforceability of liquidated damage clauses. Furthermore, the obligee, by its actions, may be deemed to have waived its rights to recover liquidated damages.

If the contractor abandons performance on the project or the obligee terminates the contractor's right to proceed, there is a split of authority regarding the recoverability of liquidated damages.[156] Some courts have determined that the parties did not contemplate the imposition of liquidated damages when obligee terminates the contractor or the principal abandons the project and, therefore, the courts do not allow them to be recovered.[157] In other words, what occurred was not late performance but rather no performance. In jurisdictions allowing for the recovery of liquidated

153. *Toombs & Co.*, 91-1 B.C.A. (CCH) $ 23,403 (Sept. 18,1990); *Wickham Contracting Co.*, 86-2 B.C.A. (CCH) 118,887 (Mar. 31, 1986); *Electrical Enters.*, 74-1 B.C.A. (CCH) 110,400 (Dec. 28, 1973); *Stone v. City of Arcola*, 536 N.E.2d 1329 (Ill. App. Ct. 1989) (holding that owner had to stop assessing liquidated damages once contractor achieved substantial completion of the project). *But see Ledbetter Bros. v. North Carolina Dep't of Transp.*, 314 S.E.2d 761 (N.C. Ct. App. 1984) (holding that liquidated damages accrued until project was completed).

154. *Aetna Casualty & Sur. Co. v. Butte-Meade Sanitary Water Dist.*, 500 F. Supp. 193 (D. S.D. 1980); *Southern Roofing & Petroleum Co. v. Aetna Ins. Co.*, 293 F. Supp. 725 (E.D. Tenn. 1968); *Mason v. City of Albertville*, 158 So. 2d 924 (Ala. 1963); *Pacific Employers Ins. Co. v. City of Berkeley*, 204 Cal. Rptr. 387 (Ct. App. 1984).

155. *Industrial Indem. Co. v. Wick Constr. Co.*, 680 P.2d 1100 (Alaska 1984).

156. Jurisdictions not allowing liquidated damages to be assessed: *United States v. American Sur. Co.*, 322 U.S. 96 (1944) (construing an "unambiguous contract that clearly limits the right to liquidated damages to situations where the Government does not at any time terminate the contractor's right to proceed"); *United States v. Marietta Mfg. Co.*, 53 F.R.D. 390 (S.D. W. Va. 1971); *McGovney & McKee, Inc. v. City of Berea*, 448 F. Supp. 1049 (E.D. Ky. 1978) ("[W]here the completion date is no longer within the power of the contractor to control and where the actual damages can be ascertained as in this case, then recovery for liquidated damages in addition to actual damages is not allowable."), *aff'd mem.*, 627 F.2d 1091 (6th Cir. 1980); *Continental Reality Corp. v. Andrew J. Crevolin Co.*, 380 F. Supp. 246 (S.D. W. Va. 1974) ("[A]bandonment is a breach, voiding the liquidated damage clause."); *Manart Textile Co. v. United States*, 77 F. Supp. 924 (Ct. Cl. 1948); *Arctic Contractors, Inc. v. State*, 564 P.2d 30 (Alaska 1977); *East Larimer County Water Dist. v. Centric Corp.*, 693 P.2d 1019 (Colo. Ct. App. 1984); *Twin River Constr. Co. v. Public Water Dist. No. 6*, 653 SW.2d 682, 693 (Mo. Ct. App. 1983); *City of Elmira v. Larry Walter, Inc.*, 564 N.E.2d 655 (N.Y. 1990); *Subsurfco, Inc. v. B-Y Water Dist.*, 337 NW.2d 448 (S.D. 1983). Jurisdictions allowing, liquidated damages to be assessed: *United States v. Continental Casualty Co.*, 210 F. Supp. 433 (S.D.N.Y. 1962) (express contract provision allowing liquidated damages if government terminated contractor's right to proceed); *United States v. American Employers Ins. Co.*, 141 F. Supp. 281 (E.D. Pa. 1956) (express contract provision allowing liquidated damages if government terminated contractor's right to proceed); *City of Boston v. New England Sales & Mfg Corp.*, 438 N.E.2d 68 (Mass. 1982) (holding that city's right to daily liquidated damages did not end when contractor abandoned the work; liquidated damages were payable until the project reasonably should have been completed).

157. *See generally McGovney & McKee*, 448 F. Supp. 1049; *East Larimer County*, 693 P.2d 1019 ("When an owner terminates a contract, the cost of completion is recoverable; the liquidated damages are not recoverable."); *City of Elmira supra*, 564 N.E.2d 655; *Subsurfco, supra*, 337 N.W.2d 448.

damages in the event of termination or abandonment, the rationale is that by not awarding liquidated damages, the courts would be denying the aggrieved party the remedy that was contractually agreed upon.[158]

In conclusion, if the performance bond incorporates the underlying contract and the underlying contract contains an enforceable liquidated damage clause, the surety will likely be held liable for those liquidated damages that are properly assessed against its principal. However, one must carefully examine the language of the bond itself and the law of the jurisdiction in which the dispute has arisen to determine if the imposition of liquidated damages is appropriate under the circumstances.

b. Actual Delay Damages. In the event that the contractor delays, without excuse, the completion of a contract where time is of the essence, and the bonded contract does not contain an enforceable liquidated damage clause, whether the performance bond surety will be responsible for actual delay damages will depend upon the damages for which the surety has agreed to be responsible as set forth in the bond form.[159] Damages that obligees seek to recover from the performance bond surety due to unexcused delays in the completion of the project most commonly include increased interest costs, loss of profits, loss of rents, increased home office and field overhead costs, and other increased costs due to delays in the construction. Set forth below are various types of delay damages that obligees have either recovered or sought to recover from the performance bond surety.

(1) Increased Interest Expense. Typically, an obligee will obtain loans to enable it to finance a project. If the project is delayed, the obligee will incur additional interest expense that it may be able to recover from the contractor and its performance bond surety. The type of additional interest expense an obligee may incur will vary from case to case. However, in all instances, the obligee will seek to recover interest for the additional period of time and/or higher interest rates on its loan.

The surety's responsibility for the obligee's additional costs will depend upon two factors. First, it must be determined whether the language in the performance bond, the contract (if it is incorporated into the bond) and/or the statute (if the bond is a public works bond) allows for such interest to be recovered against the performance bond surety. Second, it must be determined whether the interest expense is considered a direct damage or a consequential damage of the contractor's breach. Direct damages are those damages that naturally flow from the contractor's breach of contract.[160] Consequential damages are those damages that arise because of the intervention of "special circumstances" that are not ordinarily predictable.[161] Some courts have found that the obligee is not entitled to recover consequential damages unless it is determined that the special

158. *See for example, New England Sales, supra,* 438 N.E.2d 68.

159. For example, section 6.3 of the AIA Document A312 performance bond, December 1984 edition, provides that the surety shall be responsible for delay damages. Furthermore, section 4.2 of the AGC Document No. 606 subcontract performance bond, 1988 edition, provides that the surety shall be responsible for delay damages. There is a split of authority, however, regarding whether delay damages are recoverable from the performance bond surety under the AIA Document A311 performance bond. *See, e.g., Amerson v. Christman,* 68 Cal. Rptr. 378 (Ct. App. 1968) (interpreting language in AIA Document A311, held it was broad enough to allow for the recovery of delay damages). *But see American Home Assur. Co. v. Larkin Gen. Hosp.*, 593 So. 2d 195 (Fla. 1992) (interpreting language in AIA Document A311 performance bond, held that the language was not broad enough to allow for the recovery of delay damages).

160. *Roanoke Hosp. Assn v. Doyle & Russell, Inc.*, 214 S.E.2d 155 (Va. 1975).

161. *Id.*

circumstances were within the contemplation of the contracting parties at the time the contract was formed.[162]

Typically, absent language of limitation in either the performance bond or contract, the performance bond surety will be responsible for the additional interest expense incurred by the obligee on its construction loan for the period of time of the delay.[163] Courts have freely allowed for the recovery of this type of interest expense as it flows directly from the contractor's breach of the construction contract.[164] However, the more difficult type of interest expense to recover is that incurred due to an increase in the interest rate. As a general rule, these damages are classified as consequential.[165] Thus, the obligee will not be entitled to recover unless the obligee can prove that the damages were foreseeable at the time the construction contract was formed.[166]

(2) Loss of Use Damages. The failure of a contractor to timely complete the project can result in the obligee's sustaining loss of use damages. Loss of use damages include lost profits, loss of rental income, interest on the value of the project for the period of time that completion is delayed, and additional rental expense on existing facilities. Absent a limitation in the bond itself, the obligee will generally be able to recover from the performance bond surety loss of use damages occasioned by the bonded contractor's unexcused delays.[167]

If the project is one from which the obligee would have derived profit, the obligee will be entitled to recoup its damages for lost profits during the period of delay.[168] However, lost profit damages can only be recovered if they were foreseeable at the time the parties entered into the contract and can be proven with reasonable certainty.[169]

In the event that the obligee cannot recover lost profit damages, the courts have allowed two other theories of recovery. The first is the fair rental value of the property during the period of the delay.[170] However, the obligee will not be allowed to recover for loss of rental income if the obligee fails to mitigate the impact of the contractor's default[171] or fails to show a reasonable rental value

---

162. *Id.*

163. *New Amsterdam Casualty Co. v. Mitchell*, 325 F.2d 474 (5th Cir. 1963); *Roanoke Hosp., supra,* 214 S.E.2d 155; *Hemenway Co. v. Bartex, Inc.*, 373 So. 2d 1356 (La. Ct. App. 1979); *Continental Reality Corp. v. Andrew J. Crevolin Co.*, 380 F. Supp. 246 (S.D. W. Va. 1974); *Safeway Stores, Inc. v. Massachusetts Bonding & Ins. Co.*, 20 Cal. Rptr. 820 (1962); *but see, Brewhouse Ltd. v. New Orleans Public Service, Inc.*, 614 So.2d 118 (La.Ct.App. 1993).

164. *Roanoke Hosp., supra,* 214 S.E.2d 155.

165. *Id.*

166. *Id.*

167. *Andrew J. Crevolin Co., supra,* 380 F. Supp. 246 (loss of profits); Burnett & Doty Dev. Co. v. Phillips, 148 Cal. Rptr. 569 (Ct. App. 1978) (loss of profits); Bossier Medical Properties v. Abbott & Williams Constr. Co., 557 So. 2d 1131 (La. Ct. App. 1990) (loss of rental income); Donlan v. American Bonding & Trust Co., 51 S.E. 924 (N.C. 1905) (loss of rental income); Smart v. United States Fidelity & Guar. Co., 513 SW.2d 291 (Tex. Civ. App. 1974) (loss of profits); State Sur. Co. v. Lamb Constr. Co., 625 P.2d 184 (Wyo. 1981) (loss of rental income).

168. *Burnett & Doty, supra,* 148 Cal. Rptr. 569; *South Carolina Fed. Sav. Bank v. Thornton Crosby Dev. Co.*, 399 S.E.2d 8,11-12 (S.C. Ct. App. 1990), aff'd, 1992 WL 236668 (S.C. Sept. 21, 1992); *Smart, supra,* 513 SW.2d 291.

169. *Gurney Indus. v. St. Paul Fire & Marine Ins. Co.*, 467 F.2d 588 (4th Cir. 1972) ("[A]nticipated profits of a new and untried business which were attributable solely to the unfinished condition of the business premises were too speculative to provide a basis for an award of damages."); *Thornion-Crosby Dev., supra,* 399 S. E. 2d at 11; *Exton Drive-In, Inc. v. Home Indem. Co.*, 261 A.2d 319 (Pa. 1969), *cert. denied,* 400 U.S. 819 (1970).

170. *Bossier Medical, supra,* 557 So. 2d 113 1; *Donlan, supra,* 51 S.E. 924; *Lamb Constr., supra,* 625 P.2d 184. *But see New Amsterdam Casualty Co. v. Mitchell*, 325 F.2d 474 (5th Cir. 1963) (denying recovery of rent as a windfall to the developer where the developer had not contemplated renting the house and where there was not evidence that the houses were not built for resale and sold for the same price, though at a later date).

171. *Fisher v. Fidelity & Deposit Co.*, 466 N.E.2d 332 (Ill. App. Ct. 1984).

for the premises and fails to provide proof as to the reasonable length of time required to have the building completed and a tenant secured therefor.[172] Furthermore, if the project is for sale and the obligee is forced to sell the project for a reduced price, the obligee will not be entitled to recover for loss of rents during the period of delay; its recovery will be limited to its loss on the sale of the project.[173] The other possible basis for recovery is interest on the value of the property during the period of delay.[174]

If the obligee intends to occupy the structure that is being constructed, and the contractor's unexcused delay obligates the obligee to pay additional rent on its existing facilities, courts have allowed the obligee to recover for the additional rental expense.[175]

(3) Overhead and Other Miscellaneous Expenses. In the event that the general contractor or a subcontractor delays the completion of the project without excuse, the owner or general contractor, absent a limitation in the bond itself, may be able to recover from the performance bond surety all other recoverable damages occasioned by the bonded contractor's default. For example, the general contractor and/or owner have been able to recover from the defaulted contractor's performance bond surety for extended home office overhead,[176] increased equipment costs,[177] premium or overtime pay,[178] increased labor costs due to labor inefficiencies and/or changes in the mode of construction occasioned by the contractor's default,[179] additional job site costs for supervision,[180] costs of winterizing the project,[181] costs of maintenance of security guards and facility,[182] utility costs,[183] storage costs,[184] additional insurance premiums,[185] additional architectural fees,[186] and material costs escalation.[187]

3. Attorneys' Fees

---

172. *New Amsterdam Casualty Co. v. Bettes*, 407 SW.2d 307 (Tex. 1966).

173. *Hunt v. Bankers & Shippers Ins. Co.*, 423 N.Y. S.2d 718 (App. Div. 1979), aff'd, 409 N.E.2d 928 (N.Y. 1980).

174. *Miracle Mile Shopping Ctr. v. National Union Indem. Co.*, 299 F.2d 780 (7th Cir. 1962).

175. *Amerson v. Christman*, 68 Cal. Rptr. 378 (Ct. App. 1968); *Hemenway Co. v. Bartex, Inc.*, 373 So. 2d 1356 (La. App. 1979); *Maryland Casualty Co. v. Cunningham*, 173 So. 506, 509 (Ala. 1937).

176. *General Ins. Co. of Am. v. Hercules Constr. Co.*, 385 F.2d 13 (8th Cir. 1967); *Aetna Casualty & Sur. Co. v. Doleac Elec. Co.*, 471 So. 2d 325 (Miss. 1985) (allowing co prime contractor to recover from another co-prime contractor's performance bond surety for extended home office overhead).

177. *Hercules Constr., supra*, 385 F.2d 13.

178. *Id.*

179. *Id. But see Asphalt Paving Co. v. United States Fidelity & Guar. Co.*, 671 P.2d 10 13 (Colo. Ct. App. 1983) (disallowing damages attributable to wage increase during delay).

180. *Hercules Constr., supra*, 385 F.2d 13; *Donlan v. American Bonding & Trust Co.*, 51 S.E. 924 (N.C. 1905).

181. *Continental Reality Corp. v. Andrew J. Crevolin Co.*, 380 F. Supp. 246 (S.D. W.Va. 1974); *McLeod v. National Sur. Co.*, 158 N.W. 619 (Minn. 1916).

182. *Andrew J Crevolin Co., supra*, 3 80 F. Supp. 246.

183. *Roanoke Hosp. Assn. v. Doyle & Russell, Inc.*, 214 S.E.2d 155 (Va. 1975).

184. *Id.*

185. *Safeway Stores, Inc. v. Massachusetts Bonding & Ins. Co.*, 20 Cal. Rptr. 820 (1962); *Roanoke Hosp., supra*, 214 S.E.2d 155.

186. *Safeway Stores, supra*, 20 Cal. Rptr. 820.

187. *Costanza v. Cannata*, 36 So. 2d 627 (La. 1948).

In a majority of jurisdictions the obligee, if the prevailing party, is entitled to recover its attorneys' fees from the performance bond surety only where such recovery is authorized by statute, contract, or a recognized equitable basis.[188]

Many jurisdictions have enacted statutes that allow for the recovery of attorneys' fees from the performance bond surety.[189] For example, in Nebraska[190]and Florida,[191] the obligee is entitled to recover its reasonable attorneys' fees simply by being the prevailing party. Conversely, in Illinois,[192] Missouri,[193] and South Dakota[194] the obligee is entitled to recover its attorneys' fees only if it can prove that the surety acted vexatiously in refusing to pay its claim.

Attorneys' fees may also be awarded if provided for by the contract. Obviously, if the bond form itself contains an attorneys' fees clause, the obligee will be able to recover attorneys' fees from the performance bond surety.[195] Likewise, where the bonded contract contains an attorneys' fee clause it is likely that the obligee can recover same.[196] Where the language in the bond obligates the surety to indemnify the obligee for all damage occasioned by the principal's default,[197] attorneys' fees may be recovered. Also, if the bonded subcontract is incorporated into the bond and contains a flowdown clause in which the subcontractor assumes all of the general contractor's obligations to the owner, including the obligation to hold the owner harmless from all costs and attorneys' fees regarding the issue in dispute, the subcontractor's performance bond surety may be obligated to the obligee for attorneys' fees incurred in resolving that dispute.[198]

Obligees seeking to recover attorneys' fees have had mixed success where neither the bond nor the bonded contract contained an attorneys' fee clause, but the bond contained broad indemnity language. Some jurisdictions refuse to award attorneys' fees in the absence of an express provision

---

188. *Ranger Constr. Co. v. Prince William County Sch. Bd.*, 605 F.2d 1298 (4th Cir.1979); *Cincinnati Ins. Co. v. City of Talladega*, 342 So. 2d 331 (Ala. 1977); *Walters Air Conditioning Co. v. Firemen's Fund Ins. Co.*, 252 So. 2d 919 (La. Ct. App. 1971); *National Sur. Co. v. Trustees of Runnelstown Consol. Sch.*, 111 So. 445 (Miss. 1927). *But see* Alaska Civ. R. 82 (making it mandatory for the prevailing party to be awarded attorneys' fees based upon a percentage of the amount recovered and whether the matter was contested, contested without trial, or noncontested).

189. Ark. Code Ann. § 23-79-208 (Michie 1987); Fla. Stat. Ann. § 627.756 (West 1984); Ga. Code Ann. § 10-7-30 (1990) (Ga. Code Ann. § 103-210 (Harrison 1989)); Idaho Code § 41-1839 (1991); 111. Ann. Stat. ch. 73, para. 767 (Smith-Hurd 1965); Kan. Stat. Ann. § 40-256 (1986); La. Rev. Stat. Ann. §§ 9:3902 (West 1991), 22:658 (West 1978); Mo. Ann. Stat. § 375.420 (Vernon 1991); Mont. Code Ann. § 33-1-616 (1991); Neb. Rev. Stat. § 44-359 (1988); Or. Rev. Stat. § 742.061 (1991); S.D. Codified Laws Ann. § 58-12-3 (1990); Va. Code Ann. § 38.2-209 (Michie 1990).

190. Neb. Rev. Stat. § 44-359.

191. Fla. Stat. Ann. § 627.756.

192. Ill. Ann. Stat. ch. 73, para. 767.

193. Mo. Ann. Stat. § 375.420.

194. S.D. Codified Laws Ann. § 58-12-3.

195. *City of Sacramento v. Trans Pac. Indus.*, 159 Cal. Rptr. 514 (Ct. App. 1979); *Klein v. Collins*, 106 So. 120 (La. 1925); *Town of Winnsboro v. Barnard & Burk, Inc.*, 294 So. 2d 867 (La. Ct. App. 1974); *Commonwealth v. Manor Mines, Inc.*, 544 A. 2d 53 8 (Pa. Commw. Ct. 1988) (allowing 5% of amount of bond as attorneys' fees pursuant to express provision in the bond), aff'd, 565 A.2d 428 (Pa. 1989); *Whitten v. Alling & Cory Co.*, 526 S.W.2d 245 (Tex. Civ. App. 1975).

196. *Austin v. Parker*, 672 F.2d 508 (5th Cir. 1982)(superseded by statute, *Serigne v Magnolia Fire and Cas. Co.*, 650 So.2d 422 (La.App.Ct. 1995); *Dale Benz, Inc. v. American Casualty Co.*, 303 F.2d 80 (9th Cir. 1962); *but see, D&O Contractors, Inc. v. Terrebonne Parish School Bd.*, 545 So.2d 588 (La.Ct.App. 1989).

197. *Maryland Casualty Co. v. Cunningham*, 173 So. 506 (Ala. 1937).

198. *Iowa Concrete Breaking Corp. v. Jewat Trucking, Inc.*, 444 NW.2d 865 (Minn. Ct. App. 1989).

allowing for their recovery, following the American rule.[199] Other jurisdictions have allowed the obligee to recover its attorneys' fees where the bond contains language obligating the surety to indemnify and hold the obligee harmless from all losses, damages, costs and expenses occasioned by the principal's default.[200]

Absent a contractual or statutory basis for the imposition of attorneys' fees, the obligee will typically not be able to recover its attorneys' fees from the surety unless an equitable basis for such recovery exists.

4. Negligence and Lack of Liability Insurance

Almost every construction contract has a requirement that the contractor obtain liability insurance. One of the purposes of this requirement is to protect the obligee against negligent acts of the contractor. Unfortunately, for a variety of reasons, including oversight, the financial condition of the contractor, or a hardening of the insurance market, the obligee may find that the insurance protection it required the contractor to provide is not available. It is at this juncture, often times, that the obligee will seek to recover the damages it sustains as a result of a contractor's negligence from the contractor's performance bond surety.

In many jurisdictions, public works obligees have been unsuccessful in recovering from the performance bond surety for personal injury and property damage caused by its principal's negligence.[201] However, one court imposed liability upon the public works performance bond surety where the bond contained a broad indemnity clause obligating the surety to indemnify the obligee for all damages occasioned by the principal's negligence.[202] The applicable statute did not require the coverage; the court enforced the indemnity provision in any event, finding that the surety knowingly agreed to provide the additional protection.[203]

---

199. *Tomlinson v. Sentry Eng'g. & Constr., Inc.*, 777 F.2d 918 (4th Cir. 1985); *Martin v. Hartford Acc. & Ins. Co.*, 316 S.E.2d 126 (N.C.App. 1984); *Fausett Builders, Inc. v. Globe Indem. Co.*, 247 SW.2d 469 (Ark. 1952); *Federal Sur. Co. v. Basin Constr. Co.*, 5 P.2d 775 (Mont. 1931); *Robbins v. Melbrook Realty Co.*, 213 N.Y.S.2d 403 (Sup. Ct. 1961).

200. *City of Grandview v. Hudson*, 377 F.2d 694 (8th Cir. 1967); *National Union Fire Ins. Co. v. Denver Brick & Pipe Co.*, 427 P.2d 861 (Colo. 1967); *Robinhorne Constr. Corp. v. Snyder*, 251 N.E.2d 641 (Ill. App. Ct. 1969), *aff'd*, 265 N.E.2d 670 (Ill. 1970); *Mundy v. Knutson Constr. Co.*, 294 SW.2d 371 (Tex. 1956).

201. *Water Works, Gas & Sewer Bd. v. P.A. Buchanan Contracting Co.*, 318 So. 2d 267, 271 (Ala. 1975) ("The common practice of referencing in the surety bond the construction contract between the Board and the contractor does not change a ... statutory performance and completion bond into either a common-law bond or a liability insurance policy for the payment of tort claims."); *State Highway Admin. v. Tranamerica Ins. Co.*, 367 A.2d 509 (Md. 1976); *De Vries v. City of Austin*, 110 NW.2d 529, 538-39 (Minn.1961) ("It is clear from the provisions of [the applicable statute] as well as from the language of the bond and the contract that the purpose of the bond was not to protect the obligee therein against liability for damages arising because of negligence in the contractor's performance of the work. . . . Further, it is obvious that, if the bond here was intended to cover the obligee's liability for the contractor's negligence in the performance of the work, the contract provisions requiring him to furnish liability insurance covering such negligence for the city's protection would not have been added."); *Township of Wyckoff v. Sarna*, 347 A.2d 16, 19 (N.J. Super. Ct. App. Div. 1975) ("Nothing in the statute [requiring the performance bond] suggests that it was designed to insure the municipality against liability for its negligence in connection with the installation of such improvements or to indemnify it against negligence claims by third parties against it or the developer. Nor is there anything in the bond which lends itself to the interpretation that such was its purpose."); *City of Marshall v. American Gen. Ins. Co.*, 623 SW.2d 445 (Tex. Ct. App. 1981).

202. *Bullard v. State*, 394 So. 2d 626 (La. Ct. App. 1980).

203. *Id.* at 629.

On non-public works projects where the bonded contract imposes an obligation upon the contractor to indemnify the obligee for damages occasioned by the contractor's negligence, and the performance bond incorporates the contract and is conditioned upon the contractor's performing all terms and conditions of the contract, a number of courts have imposed an obligation upon the surety to be answerable for the damages sustained due to the contractor's negligence.[204] However, one court, despite a broad indemnity provision in the bonded contract, found otherwise.[205] The court held that the surety had "fulfilled its obligation by completing the work covered by the subcontract."[206]

The performance bond surety may also have liability for risks that the contractor's liability insurance policy would normally cover but did not because liability insurance was never obtained or lapsed. In at least two cases, the courts imposed liability upon the surety for damages that the liability insurance policy would have otherwise covered.[207] The courts found that the surety was liable for all damages occasioned by the contractor's failure to provide insurance coverage.[208]

Courts have also imposed liability upon the performance bond surety when the performance bond itself contained a broad indemnity clause obligating the performance bond surety to indemnify the obligee for those damages sustained as a result of its principal's negligence.[209]

To combat obligees' attempts to turn the performance bond into an all-risk liability policy, the legislatures in some states have enacted statutes that prohibit obligees from imposing liability for personal injury and/or property damage sustained as a result of the principal's negligence upon the performance bond surety.[210] The statutes in New Jersey and Louisiana apply only to public works projects. The statute enacted by the Washington state legislature, however, applies to both public and private projects.

5. Breach of Warranty and Latent Defects

The language of the bond and the bonded contract, if it is incorporated into the bond, controls the performance bond surety's liability for claims occurring after the contractor has

---

204. *Sorensen v. Ewing*, 448 P.2d 110 (Ariz. Ct. App. 1968); *Safeway Stores, Inc. v. Massachusetts Bonding & Ins. Co., supra*, 20 Cal. Rptr. 820, 822 (1962) (contract contained broad indemnity provision and surety stipulated that its liability was coextensive with that of its principal; thus, there was no analysis by the court addressing why the surety would be responsible for these types of damages); *Sanitary District v. United States Fidelity & Guar. Co.*, 65 N.E.2d 364, 368 (Ill. 1946) ("The contractor having assumed and agreed to pay all damages to real or personal property resulting from the use of explosives, or from blasting, in the prosecution of the work, and the bond by its terms specifically guaranteeing the performance of that obligation, the liability of the surety under the bond to pay such damages and to indemnify the district against the payment of the same is clear."); *Haywood County Consol. Sch. Sys. v. United States Fidelity & Guar. Co.*, 257 S.E.2d 670, 671 (N.C. Ct. App. 1979) ("Contractor's responsibility to carry liability insurance did not remove his liability under [provision of the contract requiring contractor to indemnify owner against damages caused by contractor's negligence]. And Contractor's liability is the measure of [surety]'s liability.").

205. *National Sur. Corp. v. Charles Carter & Co.*, 539 F.2d 450 (5th Cir. 1976).

206. *Id.* at 457.

207. *Carroll-Boone Water Dist. v. M. & P. Equip. Co.*, 661 S.W.2d 345 (Ark. 1983); *Hartford Fire Ins. Co. v. Riefolo Constr. Co.*, 410 A.2d 658 (N.J. 1980).

208. *Carroll-Boone, supra,* 661 SW.2d at 350-5 1; *Riefolo Constr., supra,* 410 A.2d at 663-64.

209. *Capua v. W.E. ONeil Constr. Co.*, 367 N.E.2d 669, 670-71 (Ill. 1977); *Bullard v. State*, 394 So. 2d 626, 628 (La. Ct. App. 1980); *People v. Westchester Colprovia Corp.*, 147 N.Y.S.2d 185, 187 (App. Div. 1955) ("We construe the disputed portion of the performance bond as a contract to indemnity the State against its own negligence. Such an agreement is not illegal.").

210. La. Rev. Stat. Ann. § 38:2241 (West 1989) (public works)- N.J. Stat. Ann. § 2A:44 143 (West Supp. 1992) (public works); Wash. Rev. Code Ann. § 19.72.107 (West Supp. 1993) (public and private works).

completed the project and the owner has accepted the project regarding warranty claims and/or damages incurred in remedying latent defects in the contractor's work.

a. Warranty. Virtually every construction contract contains a warranty or guaranty provision under which the contractor is obligated to warrant or guarantee its work for a period of time (typically one year) after the completion of the project. Where the bond itself provides that it will cover warranty claims, the surety will be liable for the obligee's damages resulting from the principal's breach of the warranty provision. The surety may also be liable where the contract contains a warranty provision and the bond expressly incorporates the underlying contract.[211]

However, if the terms of the performance bond speak only to finishing the work in the event that the principal fails to do so, the surety might have an argument that it is not responsible for warranty claims.[212]

b. Latent Defects. The liability of the surety, like the contractor, for latent defects in the contractor's work that are not discovered until after the warranty or guaranty period has expired depends upon whether the parties intended for the warranty or guaranty to be the owner's exclusive remedy. If not, one must determine whether the defect is one for which the surety has agreed to be responsible as defined by the bond. In that regard, one must examine the bond, the contract (if it is incorporated into the bond), and the statute (if the bond is required by the statute) to determine whether the performance bond surety is responsible for latent defects in the contractor's work. If the surety is responsible for latent defects in its principal's work, one must then determine whether the applicable statute of limitations and/or statute of repose has expired.

In the event that the contractor fails to perform its work in accordance with the plans and specifications as it is contractually obligated to do, and the bond is conditioned upon the contractor's faithful performance of all of its obligations under the contract, a majority of courts have held the performance bond surety liable for latent defects in its principal's work, whether those defects are discovered before or after the applicable warranty period, if any, has run.[213]

---

211. *Tudor Dev. Group, Inc. v. United States Fidelity & Guar. Co.*, 692 F. Supp. 461, 465 (M.D. Pa. 1988); *Turner Constr., Inc. v. American States Ins. Co.*, 579 A.2d 915, 918 (Pa. Super. Ct. 1990); *cf. Trustees of Ind. Univ. v. Aetna Casualty & Surety Co.*, 920 F.2d 429, 436 (7th Cir. 1990), overruled on other grounds, *Watson v. Amedco Steel, Inc.*, 29 F.3d 274 (7th Cir. 1994) (when a warranty claim arises regarding the failure of materials that were specified by the owner but warranted by the contractor, the contractor's surety may or may not be liable; if the materials specified by the owner were not suitable for the purpose for which they were specified (as opposed to being defectively manufactured), the surety will not be responsible to remedy the defect).

212. *Kiva Constr. & Eng'g, Inc. v. International Fidelity Ins. Co.*, 749 F. Supp. 753, 756 (W.D. La. 1990) (finding that ten-year contractual warranty was not and never had been supported by the performance bond; surety's liability "was limited solely to the instance where [the contractor] failed to meet its construction obligation"), *aff'd*, 961 F.2d 213 (5th Cir. 1992). *But see Sorensen v. Ewing*, 448 P.2d 110, 112-13 (Ariz. Ct. App. 1968) (holding without analysis that the performance bond surety's liability was coextensive with that of its principal under the AIA Document A311 performance bond and that the surety was liable for damages incurred when the contractor breached the guaranty provision of the contract).

213. *School Bd. v. St. Paul Fire & Marine Ins. Co.*, 449 So. 2d 872, 874 (Fla. Dist. Ct. App. 1984); *McDevitt & Street Co. v. K-C Air Conditioning Serv.*, 418 S.E.2d 87, 93 (Ga. Ct. App. 1992); *Board of Regents v. Wilson*, 326 N.E.2d 216, 221 (Ill. App. Ct. 1975); *City of Osceola v. Gjellefald Constr. Co.*, 279 N.W. 590, 594 (Iowa 1938); *Congregation of St. Peter's Roman Catholic Church v. Simon*, 497 So. 2d 409, 414 (La. Ct. App. 1986); *Newton Housing Auth. v. Cumberland Constr. Co.*, 358 N.E.2d 474, 479 (Mass. App. Ct. 1977); *Hunters Pointe Partners Ltd. Partnership v. United States Fidelity & Guar. Co.*, 486 NW.2d 136, 138 (Mich. Ct. App. 1992); *Carrols Equities Corp. v. Villnave*, 395 N.Y.S.2d 800, 803 (App. Div. 1977); *Town of Tonawanda v. Stapell, Mumm & Beals Corp.*, 270 N.Y.S. 377, 380 (App. Div.), *aff'd*, 193 N.E. 419 (N.Y. 1934); *Salem Realty Co. v. Batson*, 123 S.E.2d 744, 751-52 (N.C. 1962); *Houston Fire & Casualty Ins. Co. v. Riesel Indep. Sch. Dist.*, 375 SW.2d 323, 327 (Tex. Civ.

The period of time within which the obligee must commence its action against the contractor may differ from that against the surety. For example, if the performance bond is required by a public works statute, and the public works statute contains a statute of limitations, the period of time within which the obligee must pursue the surety will be controlled by the statute.[214] Likewise, in the absence of a statutory prohibition,[215] if the bond itself contains a limitation of actions clause, and the period of time within which the obligee is required to institute its suit is deemed reasonable, a majority of jurisdictions will require that the obligee institute its cause of action within the period specified in the bond.[216] However, in the absence of a statute of limitations in a public works statute or a limitation of actions clause in the bond itself, the obligee will be required to institute its cause of action against the surety before the expiration of the applicable statute of limitations or statute of repose.

Whether the statute of repose will control the time period within which the obligee must institute its action against the performance bond surety will vary from jurisdiction to jurisdiction. In some jurisdictions, the legislatures have specifically included the surety within the class of parties intended to be protected by the statute.[217] Thus, in those jurisdictions, the surety is clearly protected by the statute. However, when the statute of repose does not specifically include the surety, there is a split of authority regarding whether the surety is entitled to rely upon the statute.[218] The Superior

---

App. 1964). *But see, Florida Bd. of Regents v. Fidelity & Deposit Co.*, 416 So. 2d 30, 32 (Fla. Dist. Ct. App. 1982)(holding that purpose of performance bond is to insure physical completion of the work upon default and to insure against any losses which the owner may suffer if performance default occurs; once building is accepted, surety cannot be held responsible for latent defects), rejected by *Federal Insurance Co. v. The Southwest Florida Retirement Center, Inc.*, 707 So.2d 1119 (Fla. 1998).

214. *Transamerica Ins. Co. v. Housing Auth.*, 669 SW.2d 818, 822 (Tex. Ct. App. 1984), *District Sch. Bd. v. Safeco Ins. Co.*, 434 So. 2d 38 (Fla. Dist. Ct. App. 1983) (*per curiam*).

215. Ala. Code § 6-2-15 (1975); Ariz. Rev'. Stat. Ann. § 20-1115 (1990) (limitation period can be no shorter than two years); Fla. Stat. Ann. § 95.03 (West 1982); Me. Rev. Stat. Ann. tit. 24-A, § 2433 (West 1964) (limitation period can be no shorter than two years); Md. Ann. Code art. 48A, § 377B (1991), Neb. Rev. Stat. § 44-357 (1988); Okla. Stat. Ann. tit. 15, § 216 (1966); S.C. Code Ann. § 15-3-140 (Law. Co-op. 1977); S.D. Codified Laws Ann. § 53-9-6 (1990); Tex. Civ. Prac. & Rem. Code Ann. § 16.070 (West 1992) (limitation period can be no shorter than two years); Utah Code Ann. § 3 1 A-21-3 13 (1991).

216. *In re 1616 Reminc Ltd. Partnership (United States Elevator Corp. v. 1616 Reminc Ltd. Partnership)*, 9 B.R. 679 (Bankr. E.D. Va. 1981); *Board of Educ. v. Hartford Accident & Indem. Co.*, 504 N.E.2d 1000 (Ill. App. Ct. 1987); *Webb v. Kentucky Farm Bureau Ins. Co.*, 577 SW.2d 17 (Ky. Ct. App. 1978); *Con-Plex, Div. of U.S. Indus. v. Vicon, Inc.*, 448 So. 2d 191 (La. Ct. App. 1984); *General Elec. Co. v. Lexington Contracting Corp.*, 292 N.E.2d 874 (Mass. 1973) (payment bond); *Camelot Excavating Co. v. St. Paul Fire & Marine Ins. Co.*, 301 NW.2d 275 (Mich. 1981) (payment bond); *Yeshiva Univ. v. Fidelity & Deposit Co.*, 500 N.Y.S.2d 241 (App. Div. 1986); *City of Midland v. Waller*, 430 SW.2d 473 (Tex. 1968); *Quin Blair Enters. v. Julien Constr. Co.*, 597 P.2d 945 (Wyo. 1979). *Bul see Alaska Energy Auth. v. Fairmont Ins. Co.*, 845 P.2d 420 (Alaska 1993) (holding "contractual time limitations to bring suit will not be enforced without some showing of prejudice" to the surety); *Rechtsteiner v. National Sur, Co.*, 187 P. 34 (Cal. Dist. Ct. App. 1919); *Sheard v. United States Fidelity & Guar. Co.*, 107 P. 1024 (Wash. 1910).

217. See, e.g., Cal. Civ. Proc. Code § 377.15 (West 1973); Haw. Rev. Stat. § 657-8 (1988); Ill. Rev. Stat. ch. 110, para. 13-214 (1984); N.C. Gen. Stat. § 1-50 (1983); S.C. Code Ann. § 15-3-640 (Law. Co-op. Supp. 1991).

218. *Travelers Indem. Co. v. Hennepin County*, 918 F.2d 66, 68 (8th Cir. 1990) (allowing surety to assert statute of repose as a defense); *County of Hudson v. Terminal Constr. Corp.*, 381 A.2d 355, 358 (N.J. Super. Ct. App. Div. 1977) (allowing surety to assert statute of repose as a defense). *But see President of Georgetown College v. Madden*, 505 F.Supp. 557, 591 (D. Md. 1980) (allowing owner to recover from contractor's surety although statute of repose had expired against contractor where statute did not specifically extend protection to surety), *aff'd in part, appeal dismissed in part,* 660 F. 2d 91 (4th Cir. 1981); *Regents of the Univ. v. Hartford Accident & Indem. Co.*, 581 P.2d 197, 201-05 (Cal. 1978) (holding statute of repose does not protect surety; California statute of repose was subsequently amended to include sureties.); *People ex rel, Skinner v. Hellmuth, Obata & Kassabaum, Inc.*, 500 N.E.2d 34, 38-39 (Ill. 1986) (holding statute of repose does not protect surety; Illinois statute of repose was subsequently

Court of New Jersey held that the statute of repose was available as a defense for the performance bond surety.[219] The court stated: "It is a long settled principle that the existence of a subsisting debt of the principal is essential to a suit against the surety. . . . Therefore, since plaintiff did not have a cause of action against [the principal], they had no cause of action against [the performance bond surety]."[220] By contrast, in Illinois,[221] California,[222] and Maryland,[223] courts held that the performance bond surety was not protected by the statute of repose as the statute did not specifically provide for the protection of the surety. Given the contractor's obligation to indemnify the surety pursuant to the terms of the general indemnity agreement, these courts circumvented the protection the legislatures intended to afford the contractor in enacting the statutes of repose. To correct this problem, the legislatures in both Illinois and California subsequently amended the statutes of repose specifically to include sureties within the protected class.

amended to include sureties).

219. *Terminal Constr., supra,* 381 A.2d at 358.

220. *Id.*

221. *People ex rel. Skinner, supra,* 500 N.E.2d at 38-39.

222. *Regents of the Univ., supra,* 581 P.2d at 201-05.

223. *President of Georgetown College v. Madden,* 505 F. Supp. 557, 591 (D. Md. 1980), aff'd in part, appeal dismissed in part, 660 F.2d 91 (4th Cir. 198 1).

7

Discharge of the Performance Bond Surety

M. Michael Egan
Marla Eastwood

Discharge under the law of contracts is the release or cancellation of the obligation of the contract even if the contract has not been carried out in full.[1] Discharge can also be the result of full performance. In either case, the binding force of the contract is terminated. Discharge of the surety occurs when through some act of the obligee, the surety is liberated from its contractual obligation.[2] The traditional grounds for discharge based on an act of the obligee are: (1) giving of time to the principal, (2) alteration of the bonded contract, (3) misrepresentation, concealment, or fraud, (4) relinquishing or losing security, and (5) release of the principal.[3] As one would expect, consent of the surety to any of these acts, whether given at the time of the act or in the contract of suretyship, prevents a discharge.[4] In addition, a compensated surety is usually required to demonstrate affirmatively actual prejudice arising from the act of the obligee.[5] In the absence of actual prejudice, the compensated surety usually remains bound.[6] Finally, even if the surety demonstrates prejudice, in some circumstances the discharge will be limited to the extent of the demonstrated prejudice.[7] In these circumstances the surety is said to be discharged pro tanto, a Latin phrase meaning "for as much as may be".

The surety may also, of course, obtain a discharge through performance, either by itself or by its principal. Because of the joint and several nature of the suretyship liability, it is frequently said that the surety is not liable if the principal is not liable.[8] Accordingly, discharge of the surety can also occur in those instances in which the obligee so materially and substantially breaches its obligation on the underlying bonded contract that the principal is discharged.[9]

---

1. *Black's Law Dictionary*, (Rev. 4th ed. 1968).
2. Stearns, *Law of Suretyship* 105 (Elder 5th ed. 1951).
3. G. Brandt, *The Law of Suretyship and Guaranty* 607 (1905).
4. 17 Am.Jur. 2d. *Contractor's Bonds* § 28 (1990).
5. 10 *Williston on Contracts, Contracts of Suretyship and Guaranty* § 1240 (Jaeger 3d ed. 1967).
6. Stearns, *The Law of Suretyship* 120 (Elder 5th ed. 1951).
7. *Ling Electric, Inc. v. Federal Ins. Co.*, 406 F.2d 561 (4th Cir. 1973)
8. *National Sur. Co. v. George E. Breece Lumber Co.*, 60 F.2d 847 (10th Cir. 1932); 74 Am.Jur. 2d *Suretyship* § 98 (1974); 72 C.J.S. *Principal and Surety* § 94 (1987); *Continental Bank & Trust Co. v. Am. Bonding Co.*, 605 F.2d 1049 (8th Cir. 1979).
9. *Chicago College of Osteopathic Medicine v. George A. Fuller Co.*, 719 F.2d 1335 (7th Cir. 1983). This payment process is as generally outlined in the A201-1987 General Conditions promulgated by the American Institute of Architects. The first reported case recognizing the surety is entitled to a discharge on account of overpayment is *Calvert v. London Dock Co.*, 2 Keen 639 (1838). Other cases in the United States readily followed this lead. *See Prairie State Bank v. United States*, 164 U.S. 227, 17 S.Ct. 142, 41 L.Ed. 412 (1896); *Village of Chester v. Leonard*, 68 Conn. 495, 37 A. 397 (1897); *Finney v. Condon*, 86 Ill. 78 (1877); *Taylor v. Jeter*, 23 Mo. 244 (1856); *Evans v. Graden*, 126 Mo. 72, 28 S.W. 439 (1894).

Finally, the surety is likewise no longer obligated if the applicable statute of limitations has run, nor if the bond was procured through fraud, concealment, or misrepresentation.

I. *Discharge Through Overpayments Or Premature Payments*

A. INTRODUCTION

In building contracts, the obligation of a bonded principal is to provide, in a timely fashion, labor and materials in accordance with the requirements of the construction contract. The obligation of the owner-obligee is to make periodic payments, usually monthly, based on the percentage of completion of work in place and materials stored. Timely and appropriate payment to the principal is the chief obligation of the obligee owner in a construction contract. The payment terms frequently call for the hold back of a percentage of the earned contract funds as retainage. Finally, the payment process involves a periodic review by an architect or engineer of the actual work in place in order to determine if the amount claimed by the contractor in the monthly pay request is a proper reflection of the work and materials in place at the jobsite. This has two aspects. The first is the amount of work in place. The second is whether the work is in accordance with the plans and specifications. The failure of the work to comply with the plans and specifications may take many forms. The most significant non-compliance occurs when the work, although in place, is shoddy and unworkmanlike. After the architect has reviewed the work in order to determine the quality and quantity of the labor and materials present, the architect will then certify to the owner the amount which should be paid to the contractor. This certification in turn commences a contractual time within which payment by the owner must occur.[10]

From the perspective of the surety, the unearned, unpaid contract balances represent security for the performance of the work called for in the contract. When the performance bond is executed by the surety, the surety undertakes the obligation with the valid contractual expectation that the contract price of the underlying bonded contract shall, during the course of the work, be available for the completion of the work. Furthermore, whether implied by law or by virtue of language in the bond itself, the owner obligee remains bound to expend all the contract balances in order to complete the work.

Most performance bonds contain an incorporation clause which has great legal significance. The incorporation clause adopts by reference the entire, underlying bonded contract into the text of the bond itself. Thus the surety is entitled, either by operation of law or by the incorporation of the contract itself into the bond, to rely upon the payment terms of the contract with respect to the timing and amount of payment to the bonded principal, including provisions with respect to retainage. In this sense, the contract balances, both earned and unearned, are deemed collateral for the performance of the principal.

10. American Institute of Architects A201-1987 General Conditions.

B. CONTRACT BALANCES AS COLLATERAL

Beginning in the early nineteenth century, courts readily recognized that the risk of the surety is directly related to the owner's compliance with these payment terms.[11] For example, if the owner is required contractually to withhold a specific percentage of the earned contract balance as retainage, the courts have had little difficulty in recognizing that the contractual purpose of the retainage provision is to provide financial inducement to the contractor to complete the bonded contract.[12] While retainage provisions vary in the amount and timing of ultimate release, the logic remains the same: because the retainage can only be obtained by the contractor upon completion of the work, the contractor's financial motivation is to achieve completion, thereby simultaneously discharging the surety through performance.[13] Premature payment occurs under the contract when the retainage, which represents earned, but unpaid, contract balances, is paid to the contractor prior to the time called for in the underlying contract. While this might benefit the principal, it seldom benefits the surety. The premature payment of the retainage is thus seen as a release by the obligee of collateral for the performance of the underlying contract and the consequence, at common law, was a complete discharge for the surety.[14]

In addition to premature payment, the courts also recognize that the underlying risk of the surety is directly related to overpayment of the contract balances.[15] For example, if the owner were to pay the contractor eighty percent of the contract balances when only forty percent of the work is present and when the owner's obligation under the contract was to pay only for work and materials in place, then the harm to the surety is obvious and demonstrable.[16] Similarly, if the owner pays the contractor for work which is not in accordance with the plans and specifications, then the collateral, the contract balances, has been wrongfully dissipated by virtue of its having been paid to the contractor for shoddy workmanship. Under these circumstances a surety is discharged because the

---

11. *Kiessig v. Allspaugh*, 91 Cal. 231, 27 P. 662 (1891).

12. In *Calvert v. London Dock Co.*, 2 Keen 639 (1838), the court noted that "the effect of this stipulation [retainage] was, at the same time, to urge Streather [the principal] to perform the work, and to leave in the hands of the company a fund wherewith to complete the work if he did not... ."; *Globe Indem. Co. v. Unity Rys. Co.*, 272 F. 607 (3rd Cir. 1921); *Elfinwild Volunteer Fire Dep't. v. Int'l Fidelity Ins. Co.*, 530 F.Supp. 111 (W.D.Pa. 1982); *Phoenix Indem. Co. v. Nicholas*, 121 F.Supp. 168 (N.D.Cal. 1954).

13. Herschel W. Arrant, *Handbook of the Law of Suretyship and Guaranty* 244 (1931); *but cf. Corporation of President of Church of Jesus Christ of Latter Day Saints v. Hartford Accident & Indem. Co.*, 98 Utah 297, 95 P.2d 736 (1939) (dissent recognizing discharge for premature payment); *but see Leila Hosp. & Health Center v. Xonics Med. Sys. Inc.*, 948 F.2d 271 (6th Cir. 1991) (no discharge because the surety did not obtain an express agreement on reserves).

14. *Gato v. Warrington*, 37 Fla. 542, 19 So. 883 (1896); *City Council of Greenville v. Ormond*, 51 S.C. 121, 28 S.E. 147 (1897); *Glenn County v. Jones*, 146 Cal. 518, 80 P. 695 (1905); *Reliance Ins. Co. v. Colbert*, 365 F.2d 530 (D.C.Cir. 1966).

15. *See* Town of Melville v. Safeco Ins. Co., 651 So.2d 404 (La.App. 1995); G. Brandt, *The Law of Suretyship and Guaranty* 939 (1905); Glassman Constr. Co., Inc. v. Fidelity and Casualty Co., 356 F.2d 340 (D.C.Cir. 1966). The method of payment can be in kind. Continental Illinois Bank & Trust Co. v. Indem. Ins. Co. of North Am., 1990 W.L. 133216 (N.D. Ill. 1990).

16. Airtrol Eng'g Co., Inc. v. United States Fidelity and Guar. Co., 345 So.2d 1271 (La.App. 1977); Walters Air Conditioning Co. v. Fireman's Fund Ins. Co., 252 So.2d 919 (La.App. 1971); Central Towers Apartments, Inc. v. Martin, 61 Tenn.App. 244, 453 S.W.2d 789 (1969); Sandusky Grain Co. v. Borden's Condensed Milk Co., 214 Mich. 306, 183 N.W. 218 (1921).

courts recognize that the payment clause in the underlying bonded contract, which requires payment only for good work, is for the benefit of the surety as well as the obligee.[17]

The legal basis of the discharge for premature payment or overpayment varies. Some courts have viewed the act of the obligee as a material alteration to the contract.[18] Other courts have utilized the impairment-of-the-right-of-subrogation theory as the decisional basis for discharge.[19] Under the equitable doctrine of subrogation, a surety which performs is equitably subrogated to the owner's rights to withhold the contract balances for improper or untimely performance. If the owner has wasted the contract balances in contravention of the contract's terms and its own rights, then the surety's right of subrogation is impaired. While in some instances the basis of the decision has little practical impact, the legal theory of discharge relates closely to whether the discharge of the surety will be total or only pro tanto. If the contract has been materially altered, a complete discharge is more likely, whereas if the court views the matter as only an impairment of the surety's right of subrogation, the logical result is to discharge the surety only to the amount of the actual impairment. By far the most common result is to permit only a pro tanto discharge for the compensated surety.[20]

A modern development has been the Third Restatement of Suretyship and Guaranty which expressly recognizes the defense. In essence, three separate sections combine to recognize that the proper performance by the owner of its obligations of payment is security to the surety and that the loss of this security causes a discharge of the surety to the extent of loss. The operative provisions are as follows:

---

17. *See* Annot., *Payments or advancements to the building contractor by the obligee as affecting rights as between the obligee and the surety on contractor's bond,* 121 A.L.R. 10 (1936); Randall I. Marimor and Gilbert J. Schroeder, *Overpayment of the Principal As A Defense to the Surety*, (Fidelity and Surety Law Committee Mid-Year Meeting, 1997); James A. Knox, Jr., *Quid without the Quo: The Surety's Overpayment Defense*, 13 Constr. Lawyer 3 (Oct. 93).

18. Stearns, *Law of Suretyship* 123 (Elder 5th ed. 1951); *Anthony P. Miller, Inc. v. Needham*, 35 F.Supp. 332 (E.D.Pa. 1940); *Cowdery v. Hahn*, 105 Wis. 455, 81 N.W. 882 (1900); *see Southwood Builders, Inc. v. Peerless Ins. Co.*, 235 Va. 164, 366 S.E.2d 104 (1988). A provision in the bond that alterations will not release the surety has been held not to apply to premature payment. *Fort Worth Indep. School Dist. v. Aetna Casualty & Sur. Co.*, 48 F.2d 1 (5th Cir. 1942); *Aetna Casualty & Sur. Co. v. Robertson Lumber Co.*, 3 S.W.2d 895 (Tex.Civ.App. 1928); *Blackburn v. Morel*, 13 Ga.App. 516, 79 S.E. 492 (1913).

19. *United States v. Continental Cas. Co.*, 512 F.2d 475 (5th Cir., 1975); *Glassman Constr. Co., Inc. v. Fidelity and Casualty Co.*, 356 F.2d 340 (D.C. Cir. 1966); *Fort Worth Indep. School Dist. v. Aetna Casualty & Sur. Co.*, 48 F.2d 1 (5th Cir. 1931); *Globe Indem. Co. v. Southern Pac. Co.*, 30 F.2d 580 (2d Cir. 1929); *Inland-Ryerson Const. Prods. Co., Inc. v. Brazier Constr. Co., Inc.*, 500 P.2d 1014 (Wash. App. 1972).

20. *National Union Indem. Co. v. G.E. Bass and Company, Inc.*, 369 F.2d 75 (5th Cir. 1966); *National Union Fire Ins. Co. v. D&L Constr. Co.*, 353 F.2d 169, 175 (8th Cir. 1965); *see also* Restatement of Security, § 132 (1941); *State of Louisiana v. Wilco Constr. Co., Inc.*, 393 So.2d 885 (La.App. 4th Cir. 1981); *see also United States v. Continental Casualty Co.*, 512 F.2d 475 (5th Cir. 1975); Arant, *Rationale of the Rule That an Obligee's Premature Payment Discharges His Surety*, 80 *U.Pa.L.Rev.* 842 (1932); *United States v. Continental Casualty Co.*, 512 F.2d 475 (5th Cir. 1975) (any act of the creditor depriving the surety of subrogation rights discharges the surety pro tanto); *Town of Melville v. Safeco Ins. Co. of America,* 589 So.2d 625 (La.App. 1991). Some courts have refused to recognize even a pro tanto discharge, finding, in essence, that the terms of the contract with regard to payment are only for the protection of the owner. *Ramada Dev. Co. v. United States Fidelity & Guar. Co.*, 626 F.2d 517 (6th Cir. 1980); *American Casualty Co. v. Board of Educ.*, 228 F.Supp. 843 (W.D.Okla. 1964) (failure to ascertain whether the contractor had paid its bills).

§28. Rights Obtained Through Subrogation.

(1) To the extent that the [surety] is subrogated to the rights of the obligee, the [surety] may enforce, for its benefit, the rights of the obligee as though the underlying obligation had not been satisfied: ...

> (C) against any interest in property securing ... the obligation of the principal obligor ... against whom the rights of the obligee may be enforced.... .

§31. Secondary Obligor's Right to Return Performance; Obligee's Right of Setoff.

(1) For purposes of a subrogated [surety's] right to enforce for its benefit the obligee's rights against property securing the underlying obligation (§28(1)(c)), performance owed by the obligee to the principal obligor pursuant to the contract creating the underlying obligation ("return performance") is security for the underlying obligation.

§42. Impairment of Collateral

(1) If the underlying obligation is secured by a security interest in collateral and the obligee impairs the value of that interest, the [surety] is discharged to the extent that such impairment would otherwise increase the difference between the maximum amount recoverable by the [surety] pursuant to its subrogation rights [§28] and the value of the [surety's] interest in the collateral.

(2) Impairing the value of a security interest in collateral includes: ...

> (B) release of collateral without ... equivalent reduction of the underlying obligation.[21]

Importantly, these sections are explained in the accompanying illustration and comments. Illustration 3 to Section 42 is the classic defense of prepayment of unearned contract balances to the principal as an impairment of the surety's collateral. This interpretation is buttressed by Comment C of Section 31 which explains that if an obligee pays a principal before payment is owed under the bonded contract, then the surety may be impaired in the event it is called upon to perform. In other words, a premature payment under a construction contract would harm a performance bond surety because its collateral in the form of contract balances has been wrongfully diminished.

21. Restatement Third, Suretyship and Guaranty §§28(a)(c), 42 and 31.

C. APPLICATION OF THE OVERPAYMENT DEFENSES

The effectiveness of the overpayment or prepayment defense for the surety depends heavily upon the factual circumstances of each case. For example, if the owner has used reasonable prudence in dealing with the payment of the contract balances, the mere fact that an excess payment has occurred will not discharge the surety.[22] In this respect, the periodic pay requests are often called "estimates," and both industry custom and the usual contract documents do not intend that the payment process for percentage of completion is to be exact. Stated in slightly different terms, the normal construction contract obligation is to pay a stated percentage at a particular time or upon the occurrence of contractually defined conditions. A covenant of this nature is entirely different from a promise not to pay more than a stated percentage or not to pay unless the condition has occurred.[23] Accordingly, reasonable leeway is given owners in the payment process.[24] The courts examine the owner's good faith in making the overpayment and take into account whether the owner had a reasonable basis to believe the bonded principal would complete.[25]

In addition, for a commercial surety issuing a normal performance bond, the courts will look closely at the question of whether a payment which is not in accordance with the contract documents caused actual harm to the surety.[26] This is a matter of close examination of the facts in each case.

---

22. *Ramada Dev. Co. v. United States Fid. & Guar. Co.*, 626 F.2d 517 (6th Cir. 1980); *Verdugo Highlands, Inc. v. Security Ins. Co. of New Haven*, 49 Ca.Rptr. 736 (Cal.App. 1966); *Veneto v. McClosky*, 128 N.E.2d 337 (Mass. 1955); *Salem v. W.K. Batson Co.*, 123 S.E.2d 744 (N.C. 1962); *Town of East Long Meadow v. Maryland Cas. Co.*, 206 N.E.2d 54 (Mass. 1965); *Martin v. Robinson*, 127 Kan. 100, 272 P. 149 (1928); *American Sur. Co. v. Scott & Co.*, 18 Okla. 264, 90 P. 7 (1907); *see Leghorn v. Nydell*, 39 Wash. 17, 80 P. 833 (1905); *Hochevar v. Maryland Casualty Co.*, 114 F.2d 948 (6th Cir. 1940).

23. Herschel W. Arant, *Handbook of the Law on Suretyship and Guaranty* 248 (1931); *Ruckman and Hansen, Inc. v. Contracting & Material Co.*, 328 F.2d 744 (7th Cir. 1964); *Argonaut Ins. Co. v. Town of Cloverdale*, 699 F.2d 417 (7th Cir. 1983).

24. *Argonaut Ins. Co. v. Town of Cloverdale*, 699 F.2d 417 (7th Cir. 1983); *Ruckman & Hansen, Inc. v. Contracting & Material Co.* 328 F.2d 744 (7th Cir. 1964); Robert B. Wedge, *The Surety's Discharge Defense, How Viable is it to the Claims of Owner and Lenders?*, (Fidelity & Surety Law Committee Annual Meeting, July 1985).

25. *Ramada Dev. Co. v. United States Fidelity & Guar. Co.*, 626 F.2d 517 (6th Cir. 1980); *American Fidelity Fire Ins. Co. v. Pavia-Byrne Eng'g Corp.*, 393 So.2d 830 (La.App. 1981); *J&J Elec., Inc. v. Gilbert H. Moen Co.*, 9 Wash.App. 954, 516 P.2d 217, 223 (1973); *Town of Wakefield v. Am. Sur. Co.*, 209 Mass. 173, 95 N.E. 350 (1911); *City of New Haven v. National Steam Economizer Co.*, 79 Conn. 482, 65 A. 959 (1907). Similarly, it has been held that when the owner pays on forged or fraudulent pay requests in honest belief of their correctness, the surety is not thereby discharged. *New Amsterdam Casualty Co. v. Betts*, 407 S.W.2d 307 (Tex.App. 1966); *see also Van Buren County v. American Sur. Co.*, 137 Iowa 490, 115 N.W. 24 (1908). However, the good faith defense is unavailable to an owner who acts with a callous failure to inquire into the status of materials not on site. *United Pacific Ins. Co. v. United States*, 16 Cl.Ct. 555 (1989). Where the obligee acts with negligence or with bad faith, a discharge will be allowed. *Continental Ins. Co. v. City of Virginia Beach*, 908 F. Supp. 341 (E.D. Va. 1995); *Transamerica Ins. Co. v. United States*, 6 Cl. Ct. 367 (1984).

26. *Fireman's Fund Ins. Corp. v. United States*, 15 Cl.Ct. 225 (1988); *Argonaut Ins. Co. v. Town of Cloverdale*, 699 F.2d 417 (7th Cir. 1983); *Development Corp. of Am. v. United Bonding Ins. Co.*, 413 F.2d 823 (5th Cir. 1969); *Ruckman & Hansen, Inc. v. Contracting & Mats. Co.*, 328 F.2d 744, 746-747 (7th Cir. 1964); *Mergentime Corp. v. Washington Metro. Area Transit Auth.*, 775 F.Supp. 14 (D.D.C. 1991); *Lippert Bros., Inc. v. National Union Fire Ins. Co.*, 247 F.Supp. 874, 867 (W.D.Okla. 1965); *Gibbs v. Hartford Accident & Indem. Co.*, 62 So.2d 599 (Fla. 1952); *United Bonding Ins. Co. v. Southeast Regional Builders, Inc.*, 236 So.2d 460, 464 (Fla.App. 1970); *Equitable Fire & Marine Ins. Co. v. Tiernan Bldg. Corp.*, 190 So.2d 197 (Fla.App. 1966); *United Bonding Ins. Co. v. W.S. Newell, Inc.*, 285 Ala. 371, 232 So.2d 616 (1969); *Park Presbyterian Church v. Cameron & Co.*, 38 S.W.2d 901 (Tex.App. 1931). Kramer, *Effect of Premature Payments on Surety Bond, 7 Miami Law Quarterly* 590 (1953). For an example of the court distinguishing between two unauthorized advance payments, one prejudicial and the other not, *see Transamerica Ins. Co. v. City of Kennewick*, 785 F.2d 660 (9th Cir. 1986).

For example, a premature release of retainage does not discharge the surety if the payments were made by joint check to the general contractor and its materialmen and subcontractors.[27] The logic of such a holding is that the security in the form of the retainage was expended to discharge the surety's obligations under the payment bond, thereby assuring that the surety's overall obligations were reduced because payment went to those who had provided labor and material. Under this analysis, a payment by joint check, even if not expressly permitted in the general contract, would be unlikely to discharge the surety as a departure from the terms of payment.[28] An example of this approach appears in *Ramada Development Company v. United States Fidelity & Guaranty Company*.[29] Contrary to the contract's terms, the general contractor-obligee knowingly made payments which were not due to the subcontractor-principal. The surety claimed discharge because of departure from the contract's payment terms. However, the payments went to pay the principal's employees. The court found, therefore, that the payments were for the overall benefit of the project and had not materially increased the surety's risk. Accordingly, the surety was held not to be discharged. Some obligees have been permitted to avert the surety's discharge by showing that the funds, although not paid in accordance with the contract, went directly for the completion of the work and hence were for the surety's ultimate benefit as well as the principal's.[30] In essence, the obligee is permitted to trace the funds themselves in order to show what became of the prematurely released collateral. A demonstration that the funds went into completion costs negates the surety's claim that it has been harmed through dissipation of its collateral.

D. OVERPAYMENT IN FEDERAL CONTRACTS

In federal contracts, overpayment by the government may result in a pro tanto discharge of the surety.[31] However, the government must have acted in an arbitrary and capricious manner.[32] The Federal Circuit Court of Appeals established an eight-point test to determine whether the government acted reasonably in making payments to a contractor in default.[33] These criteria focus on many of the same factors other courts have used in the context of private bonds to determine whether the surety has been harmed.[34] The process is one of balancing the obligee's conduct against the surety's

27. Advancements to pay laborers and materialmen for which the surety would have been liable in any event do not release the surety. *American Sur. Co. v. Noe*, 245 Ky. 42, 53 S.W.2d 178 (1932); *United Bonding Ins. Co. v. W.S. Newell, Inc.*, 285 Ala. 371, 232 So.2d 616 (1969); *St. John's College v. Aetna Indem. Co.*, 201 N.Y. 335, 94 N.E. 994 (N.Y.App. 1911).

28. *See, e.g. Transamerica Ins. Co. v. Kennewick*, 785 F.2d 660 (9th Cir. 1986) (pro tanto discharge allowed in part); *Empire State Sur. Co. v. City of Des Moines*, 152 Iowa 531, 131 N.W. 870 (1911) (premature payment made to prevent laborers and materialmen from asserting liens, therefore surety not discharged); *Manhattan Co. v. United States Fidelity & Guar. Co.*, 77 Wash. 405, 137 P. 1003 (1914) (overpayments to prevent liens do not discharge a compensated surety).

29. 626 F.2d 517 (6th Cir. 1980).

30. *United Bonding Ins. Co. v. W. S. Newell, Inc.* , 232 So.2d 616 (Ala. 1969); *Ferguson Contracting Co. v. Charles E. Storey Constr. Co.*, 417 S.W.2d 228, 231 (1967); *Steck v. Home Indem. Co.*, 74 N.M. 419, 394 P.2d 267 (1964); *Gibbs v. Hartford Acc. & Indem. Co*, 62 So.2d 599 (Fla. 1952); *Andsley Inc. v. United Pacific Ins. Co.* 332 P.2d 1000 (Nev. 1958); *Y.M.C.A.'s Assignee of Paducah v. Indem. Ins. Co. of North America*, 244 Ky. 473, 51 S.W.2d 463 (1932).

31. *National Surety Corp. v. United States,* 31 Fed. Cl. 565(1994).

32. *Reliance Ins. Co. v. United States*, 27 Fed. Cir. 815 (1993); *United States Fidelity & Guar. Co. v. United States,* 676 F.2d 622 (Cl.Ct. 1982).

33. *Balboa Ins. Co. v. United States*, 775 F.2d 1158, 1164-65 (Fed. Cir. 1985).

34. Id.

harm. These cases require, however, that the surety must notify the government of the principal's default.[35]

E. CERTIFICATION OF PAY REQUESTS AND THE OVERPAYMENT DEFENSE

The role of the architect in the payment process also has a significant effect upon the overpayment defense of the surety. The A.I.A.'s general conditions require the owner to make payment in accordance with the certification of the architect. Accordingly, some courts have held that because the owner became obligated to pay upon the certificate of the architect, the surety is not entitled to a discharge for overpayment by the owner.[36] The surety's claim, if any, under these circumstances is against the architect, but the surety is deprived of the performance bond defense.[37] Other courts have appropriately viewed the architect as the owner's representative, as is clearly set out in the A.I.A. documents.[38] Hence, as a question of agency, the acts of the architect are attributed to the owner, and thus, over-certification by the architect results in discharge. This is a particularly appropriate outcome when the over-certification occurs because the work paid for is shoddy and defective. The loss to the surety, if it were required to perform, is undeniable. Yet the loss occurred through the owner's representatives' failure to guard the collateral.

Finally, there have been circumstances in which, despite the contract's terms, an architect has not been used in the payment process. If the failure to use an architect as required by the contract documents has resulted in overpayment, it has been held that this worked a discharge of the surety to the extent of overpayment.[39] An example of this outcome is *Southwood Builders, Inc. v. Peerless Insurance Company*, which involved a performance bond given by a subcontractor, which named the general contractor as obligee.[40] While the court recognized that the old rule of "strict construction" no longer applied to a compensated surety in Virginia, the court examined the subcontract's requirement that an architect certify the amounts due to the subcontractor, and found that a departure from this requirement by the obligee was a material variation from the original contract's terms, thereby establishing prejudice to the surety. Because the general contractor had made substantial payments to the subcontractor before they were due, the court found that the surety was discharged.

---

35. *Firemen's Fund Ins. Co. v. United States*, 909 F.2d 495 (Fed. Cir. 1990); *Reliance Ins. Co. v. United States*, 27 Fed. Cl. 815 (1993).

36. *City of Houma v. Mun. & Indus. Pipe Serv., Inc.*, 884 F.2d 886 (5th Cir. 1989); *National Am. Bank v. South Coast Contractors, Inc.*, 226 So.2d 777 (La.App. 1973); *Balboa Ins. Co. v. Fulton County*, 148 Ga.App. 328, 251 S.E.2d 123 (1978); *see also J&J Elec., Inc. v. Gilbert H. Moen Co.*, 9 Wash.App. 954, 516 P.2d 217, 223 (1973).

37. *City of Houma v. Municipal and Indus. Pipe Serv. Inc.*, 884 F.2d 886 (5th Cir. 1989); *see Continental Ins. Co. v. City of Virginia Beach*, 908 F.Supp. 341, 342 (E.D.Va. 1995).

38. *Transamerica Ins. Co. v. Kennewick*, 785 F.2d 660 (9th Cir. 1986); *Transamerica Ins. Co. v. Housing Auth. of City of Victoria*, 669 S.W.2d 818, 822 (Tex.Civ.App. 1984) (imposing upon the owner the legal effect of the architect having issued a certificate of completion).

39. *Verdugo Highlands, Inc. v. Security Ins. Co.*, 240 Cal.App.2d 527, 49 Cal.Rep. 736, 742 (1966); *see Baldwin v. Becker*, 277 F. 930 (8th Cir. 1921) (failure to use the architect as a material alteration in the contract). With regard to the pro tanto nature of the discharge, *see Crouse v. Stanley*, 199 N.C. 186, 154 S.E. 40 (1930).

40. *Southwood Builders, Inc. v. Peerless Ins. Co.*, 235 Va. 164, 366 S.E.2d 104 (1988). Some courts have refused to permit a discharge, even though an architect's certificate was not obtained when it is shown that the payments were, in fact, used to complete the bonded contract. *Maryland Casualty Co. v. Eagle River Union Free High School Dist.*, 188 Wis. 520, 205 N.W. 926 (1925); *St. John's College v. Aetna Indem. Co.*, 201 N.Y. 335, 94 N.E. 994 (N.Y.App. 1911).

Under some construction contracts, such as local government improvements, one will find a contractual requirement that not only must the architect certify the work, but also the owner must certify the work in order to qualify for state or federal funding from yet another public agency. In these situations, the owner's direct participation in the overpayment process clearly strengthens the surety's hand in asserting a defense of this nature.[41]

F. BURDEN OF PROOF FOR THE DEFENSE

An important point is the procedural posture of the case itself and the placement of the burden with regard to the defense. Discharge through overpayment or premature payment is normally a defense on which the surety bears the burden of proof.[42] This applies not only to proving the fact of overpayment, but also, for a compensated surety, to proving the harm occasioned by overpayment. However, a significant line of authority has held that if the premature payment is a material alteration in the contract terms, then the discharge will be total unless the obligee can show the extent of harm.[43] The burden thus shifts back to the obligee to demonstrate that despite a material deviation from the payment terms, actual harm either did not ensue, or that the harm is only to a certain amount. It has been held, for example, that if there is a subsequent material written change to the payment process between the principal and the owner, then it is the obligee who must show that the discharge should only be pro tanto, as opposed to total.[44] Absent an ability by the obligee to measure the extent of prejudice, a complete discharge would be permitted.[45] Other courts have required the surety alone to demonstrate the extent and amount of material prejudice arising from an overpayment. A natural concomitant of these cases is that a payment by the owner in excess of the amount approved by the architect will result in discharge.[46]

An example of a pro tanto discharge is found in *Airtrol Engineering Company, Inc. v. United States Fidelity and Guaranty Company* in which $24,400.00 in advance payments to a subcontractor were made in violation of the express terms of the contract.[47] The Louisiana Court of Appeals relieved the surety of its obligation by permitting a pro tanto discharge arising from the overpayment. Importantly, premature payment is a defense only for the surety. The principal cannot complain that the owner violated a term which was for the owner's benefit. On the other hand, the courts recognize that the term is also for the surety's benefit and thus, under appropriate circumstances, permit a discharge.[48] There is no duty, however, on the part of the obligee to withhold payment from a

---

41. *See Talbert v. Bounds & Allen*, 123 So.2d 815 (La.App. 1960).

42. *Firemen's Fund Ins. Co. v. United States*, 909 F.2d 495 (9th Cir. 1990); *De Luxe Glass Co. v. Martin*, 116 Utah 144, 208 P.2d 1127 (1949) (prejudice will not be presumed from release of retainage).

43. *National Union Indem. Co. v. G.E. Bass & Co., Inc.*, 369 F.2d 75 (5th Cir. 1966); *Mergentime Corp. v. Washington Metro. Area Transit Auth.*, 775 F.Supp. 14 (D.D.C. 1951) (surety discharged entirely if there has been a material alteration which has increased the risk of loss and caused prejudice that cannot be measured); *see also Reliance Ins. Co. v. Colbert*, 365 F.2d 530, 535 (D.C. Cir. 1966). This principle is also set forth in the Restatement of Security § 128(b).

44. *National Union Indem. Co. v. G.E. Bass & Co., Inc.*, 369 F.2d 75 (5th Cir. 1966).

45. Id.

46. Id.; *see* Meyer *The Surety's Liability as Affected by Contract Alterations and Unauthorized Payments: How Much is Too Much?*, 15 *The Forum* 982 (1979).

47. 345 So.2d 1271 (La.Ct.App. 1977).

48. *Continental Ins. Co. v. City of Virginia Beach*, 908 F. Supp. 341 (E.D. Va. 1995); *Anthony P. Miller, Inc. v. Neadum*, 35 F.Supp. 332 (1940); *see* Stearns, *Law of Suretyship*, 123 (Elder 5th ed. 1951).

principal who is financially strapped.[49] So long as the payment process itself is followed with reasonable prudence, the surety cannot claim that the owner's representative should have withheld a progress payment only because the contractor was in trouble financially.

Occasionally, the overpayment to the principal is characterized by the obligee as a loan.[50] This is sometimes formalized through the execution of promissory notes and the like. The courts examine closely the form of the transaction in order to determine whether it was, in fact, a legitimate loan. Others look to the substance of what is occurring and recognize that the obligee is not in the business of making loans, but rather is, as a matter of substance, paying contract balances early with the hope of completion. Accordingly, under these circumstances, the surety is still discharged.[51]

II. *MATERIAL ALTERATIONS OR CHANGES AS A DISCHARGE OF THE SURETY*

A material alteration or change in the underlying contract has long been a grounds for discharge of the surety. The historical origin of this doctrine is important background for understanding its application in case law. The common law doctrine of suretyship was developed for the accommodation surety who agreed to be bound without pay or other benefit. The uncompensated, accommodation surety was entitled to have its obligations measured by the legal principle of *strictissimi juris*, a Latin phrase meaning, "of the strictest right or law". In practice, the slightest change in the underlying obligation agreed to between the principal and the obligee resulted in a complete discharge of the surety, because the surety, absent consent, was deemed to be bound only to the extent of the original agreement. Thus a material alteration in the underlying contract resulted in a discharge. Further, any increase in the risk of the surety, however slight, worked a discharge.

Beginning in the nineteenth century, commercial suretyship became an industry in itself. Requiring bonds from financially sound sureties became common. For example, the Heard Act in 1894 required surety bonds for all federal building contracts.[52] This commercial need was filled by insurance companies. Accordingly, with regard to the interpretation of the surety's contract or the application of the surety's defenses, the courts quickly distinguished between the corporate insurer and the private, uncompensated surety.[53] However, the doctrine that a material alteration in the contract will discharge even a compensated surety continued in its legal vitality because of the fundamental nature of suretyship.[54] As observed by Williston, notwithstanding that the corporate

---

49. *United States Fidelity & Guar. Co. v. United States*, 676 F.2d 622 (Cl.Ct. 1982); *see also Argonaut Ins. Co. v. United States*, 434 F.2d 1362 (Cl.Ct. 1970); *Royal Indem. Co. v. United States*, 529 F.2d 1312 (Cl.Ct. 1976); *United States Fidelity & Guar. Co. v. United States*, 475 F.2d 1377 (Cl.Ct. 1973).

50. Some cases have refused to find that the loan is a prepayment, and therefore, the surety is not discharged. *Union Oil Co. v. Pacific Sur. Co.*, 182 Cal. 69, 187 P. 14 (1920); *but cf. St. John's College v. Aetna Indem. Co.*, 201 N.Y. 335, 94 N.E. 994 (N.Y.App. 1911).

51. *Hamilton v. Republic Casualty Co.*, 102 W.Va. 32, 135 S.E. 259 (1926).

52. Earl C. Arnold, *Outlines of Suretyship and Guaranty*, 360-61 (1927). In 1894 the Heard Act, c.280, 28 Stat. 278, was passed and provided for a combined payment and performance bond on federal construction projects.

53. G. Brandt, *The Law of Suretyship and Guaranty* 152 (1905); 10 *Williston on Contracts*, § 1213 (Jaeger 3d ed. 1967).

54. *Compare* Employers Ins. of Wausau v. Constr. Management Eng'rs of Fla., Inc., 297 S.C. 354, 377 S.E.2d 119 (1989) *with* Young v. Am. Bonding Co. of Baltimore, 228 Pa. 373, 77 A. 623, 626 (1910).

surety and the corporate insurer both charge a premium, investigate the risk, and usually prepare their own contracts, insurance and suretyship also have, from a legal perspective, fundamental differences.[55] The chief difference arises in the tripartite relationship in which the principal is jointly and severally bound with the surety and the surety, if required to pay, is entitled by operation of law to exoneration by its principal.[56] Accordingly, the principle remains vibrant that the surety, even if compensated, is entitled to measure its obligations by the scope of its original undertaking. A material change in the undertaking without the surety's consent will cause a discharge.[57]

A. A CHANGE IN THE OBLIGEE OR THE PRINCIPAL

Performance bonds name a specific entity as obligee and sometimes, with a dual obligee rider, name additional, specific obligees. A change in the named obligee by virtue of an assignment of the construction contract, along with the duties owed under the performance bond, does not discharge the surety.[58] As a usual matter, the underlying contract binds not only the parties, but also their successors and assigns. It is unusual that either the bond or the contract prohibit a formal assignment by the owner-obligee, but the AIA A311 performance bond does not permit suit by an assignee. Hence, a mere change in the obligee is usually not a defense, particularly where the terms of the contract have been otherwise performed by the successor.[59] Some courts have required that the assignment must be express.[60] However, even absent an express assignment, the successor obligee is permitted to enforce the bond when the successor is, for all practical purposes, the same entity as the original obligee, or where no demonstrable harm to the surety has arisen by virtue of the change in obligees.[61]

A change in the principal is obviously more likely to cause an increase in the risk of the surety than a change in the obligee. The logic behind the discharge of the surety when the principal changes is that the bond is issued for a specific principal whose financial attributes, character and capacity to perform were all investigated by the surety as a prerequisite to issuing the bond. Bonds are not written on the basis of a "risk pool," but rather more closely resemble a credit transaction, such as a bank loan. From this it follows that a change in the entity performing the construction work can amount to a material increase in the risk of the surety and thereby become a proper reason

---

55. 10 *Williston on Contracts, Contracts of Suretyship and Guaranty* § 1213 (Jaeger 3d ed. 1967).

56. *See A.J. Kellos Constr. Co., Inc. v. Balboa Ins. Co.*, 495 F.Supp. 408 (S.D.Ga. 1980).

57. Employer's Ins. of Wausau v. Constr. Management Eng'rs of Fla., Inc., 377 S.E.2d 119 (1989); *United States v. Reliance Ins. Co.*, 799 F.2d 1382 (9th Cir. 1986); *see also* §37 of the Restatement of the Law (Third) of Suretyship and Guaranty.

58. *Hunters Pointe Partners Ltd. Partnership v. United States Fidelity & Guar. Co.*, 177 Mich.App. 45, 442 N.W.2d 778 (1989); *but see Southern Patrician Assoc. v. Int'l Fid. Ins. Co.*, 191 Ga. App. 106, 381 S.E.2d 98 (1989) (right of action clause precludes an assignee on an A311 bond form).

59. *State v. Int'l Fidelity Ins. Co.*, 152 A.D. 77, 547 N.Y.S. 2d 466 (1989); *Travelers Indem. Co. v. Dahlen*, 734 S.W.2d 729 (Tex.Civ.App. 1987); *Anstalt v. F.I.A. Ins. Co.*, 749 F.2d 175 (3rd Cir. 1984).

60. *Southern Patrician Assoc. v. Int'l Fidelity Ins. Co.*, 191 Ga.App. 106, 381 S.E.2d 98 (1989); *Cotton States Mut. Ins. Co. v. Conner*, 387 So.2d 125 (Ala.S.Ct. 1980).

61. *State v. Int'l Fidelity Ins. Co.*, 152 A.D.2d 77, 547 N.Y.S.2d 466 (1989); *see however General State Auth. v. Sutter Corp.*, 403 A.2d 1022 (Pa. 1979) (holding that on a roof warranty and a bond supporting it, only owner of the roof, the sole obligee on the bond, could recover).

for discharge.[62] However, the circumstances of the change and the result of the change must be closely examined in each instance in order to determine whether a discharge defense is applicable. Finally, some case law in this area cannot be harmonized because, in essence, some courts have been unwilling to permit the defense.[63]

Older decisions tended to look only at the question of whether the bonded entity had changed.[64] If, after the issuance of the bond, the membership of a partnership had changed, if a partnership had become a corporation, or if an individual had changed by forming a corporation, some courts held that the surety was thereby discharged.[65] However, as discussed above, the courts began to distinguish between compensated sureties and accommodation sureties, with the consequence that courts began to review closely the nature of the change in principal in order to determine whether any real harm had flowed to the surety.[66] If the individual who was bonded simply changed its name or the form of doing business, the court would refuse to find harm of any kind to a compensated surety.[67] Thus, there would be no discharge. Likewise adding partners to a partnership or changing from a sole proprietorship to a corporation would not work a discharge, particularly where the individuals involved and their financial resources did not change.[68] In addition, most performance bonds contain language that the principal and surety, along with their successors and assigns, are bound under the bond. Some courts have found in this standard language an implied consent by the surety to remain bound even if the principal should assign the underlying bonded contract, either expressly or impliedly, to a third party.[69]

Determining whether the change in principal will result in a discharge requires close examination of the transaction. On the one hand, because novation releases the original obligor, it is also a complete discharge of even a compensated surety.[70] On the other hand, in an assignment, the assignor remains bound and becomes a surety by operation of law for the performance of the

62. *Mead Samuel & Co., Inc. v. United States Fidelity & Guar. Co.*, 125 Ariz. 525, 611 P.2d 112 (Ariz.App. 1980); *but see Armstrong Transfer & Storage v. Marissa Constr. Co.*, 458 S.E.2d 481 (Ga. App. 1995) (no discharge from adding an additional joint general contractor).

63. An example of a court being apparently unwilling to recognize the underlying validity of the fundamental concept of suretyship is *Leila Hosp. and Health Center v. Xonics Medical Sys., Inc.*, 948 F.2d 271 (6th Cir. 1991).

64. *Friendly v. Nat'l Sur. Co.*, 46 Wash. 71, 89 P. 177 (1907).

65. Annot., *Change in name, location, composition or structure of obligor commercial enterprise subsequent to execution of guaranty or suretyship agreement as affecting the liability of guarantor or surety to the obligee,* 69 A.L.R. 3rd 567 (1976); *Bianco v. Firemen's Fund Indem.*, 232 P.2d 386 (Ariz. 1951); *Spokane Union Stockyards Co. v. Maryland Casualty Co.*, 178 P. 3 (Wash. 1919).

66. *See generally* Annot., *supra*, n. 65.

67. *Coken Co., Inc. v. Dep't of Public Works*, 402 N.E.2d 1110 (Mass.App. 1980).

68. *Adams v. Haigler*, 123 Ga. 659 (1905); *United States Fidelity & Guar. Co. v. Burton Lumber Co.*, 221 S.W. 699 (Tex.Civ.App. 1920); *National Sur. Co. v. George E. Breece Lumber,* 60 F.2d 847 (10th Cir. 1932); *Wisconsin Mirror & Plate Co. v. Fidelity & Deposit Co.*, 190 Wis. 105, 208 N.W. 933 (1926); *see also Armstrong Transfer & Storage Co. v. Mann Constr. Inc.*, 217 Ga.App. 538, 458 S.E.2d 481 (1995) (holding that addition of job superintendent to contract as "joint general contractor" did not constitute a change in principal, as superintendent was merely an agent in general contractor).

69. *Illinois Sur. Co. v. John Davis Co.*, 244 U.S. 376, 37 S.Ct. 614, 617, 61 L.Ed. 1206 (1917); *see, e.g., James Miles & Son Co. v. Aetna Casualty and Sur. Co.*, 1 F.Supp. 295 (1927) (D.C.Mass. 1932); *United Bonding Ins. Co. v. Southeast Regional Builders, Inc.*, 236 So.2d 460, 463 (Fla.App. 1970); *Beco, Inc. v. Am. Fidelity Fire & Marine Ins. Co.*, 370 So.2d 1343 (Miss. 1979).

70. *Zuni Constr. Co. v. Great American Ins. Co.*, 86 Nev. 364, 468 P.2d 980 (1970); *MacKenzie Laboratories, Inc. v. Lawrence,* 80 F.Supp. 710 (D.C.Md. 1948).

assignee.[71] The courts are thus left with the task of determining the nature of the transaction. If the owner obligee agrees that the original principal may substitute performance through a new party and that the original principal is discharged, then a novation occurred and discharge of the surety follows.[72] But, if the obligee simply consents to an assignment in which the original principal remains bound, then whether the surety is discharged depends upon a number of factors.[73] The proper analysis should be that the surety who has not consented to the assignment has an opportunity to demonstrate whether this change represents a material increase in its risk from which should flow a discharge.[74]

Only the obligee on a performance bond can "assign" the bond. For the principal and the surety, the bond, once issued, contains only duties of performance on their part. There is no performance under the bond itself by the obligee which can be, in any sense, "assigned" to the new contractor who undertakes performance of the underlying construction contract. The principal may delegate its duties to another, but may not "assign" them.[75] The principal and the surety hence remain bound on the bond. The discharge for the surety will arise, if at all, from a demonstration of actual prejudice.[76] In the end, the analysis depends on whether the surety has been placed in a significantly different position than it occupied before the change was made.[77] One can readily imagine that changing who is performing the underlying construction contract could result in a significant increase in the risk to the surety. Thus the substitution of a new party with the consent of the owner, but without the consent of the surety, may result in a discharge of the surety.[78]

B. MATERIAL ALTERATIONS IN THE BONDED CONTRACT

1. The Nature of the Defense and the Surety's Consent

Occasionally, following a default, the surety's investigation of the dealings between the obligee and the principal reveals that the original bonded contract has been changed in some fashion which required greater performance by the principal than was originally required in the bonded contract. A compensated surety can obtain a discharge upon these facts if the change in the work

71. *Hart v. DeLowe Partners, Ltd.*, 147 Ga.App. 715, 250 S.E.2d 169 (1978); *Oellerich v. First Fed. Savings & Loan Assn.*, 552 F.2d 1109, 1111 (5th Cir. 1977); *see* Stearns, *Law of Suretyship*, 10 (Elder 5th ed. 1951); *see also Westinghouse Credit Corp. v. Wolfer*, 88 Cal.Rep. 654, 657 (1970) (assignor becomes surety by operation of law); *Walin v. Young*, 180 P.2d 535, 537 (Ore. 1947) (assignor of mortgage becomes surety by operation of law); *see also In re Liquidation of Union Indemnity Ins. Co.*, 234 A.D.2d 120, 651 N.Y.S.2d 436 (1996).

72. Novation is the substitution by mutual agreement of one debtor for another whereby the old debt is discharged. *Randall v. Norton*, 192 Ga.App. 734, 386 S.E.2d 518, 520 (1989) (no novation without a release of the original debtor). Therefore, since the principal, as the original debtor, is released from liability, the surety is likewise released.

73. *Leila Hosp. and Health Center v. Xonics Medical Sys., Inc.*, 948 F.2d 271 (6th Cir. 1991); *Los Angeles Stone Co. v. Nat'l Sur. Co.*, 178 Cal. 247, 173 P. 79 (1918); *First Baptist Church of Oxford v. Hendricks*, 107 Miss. 267, 65 So. 244 (1914).

74. A possible example of such prejudice would be that the substituted party performing has less financial capacity than the original principal and less ability to perform the specific kind of work presented by the bonded project.

75. *Tony and Leo, Inc. v. United States Fidelity and Guar. Co.*, 281 N.W.2d 862 (Minn.S.Ct. 1979).

76. A case to the contrary is *Stahlhut v. Sirloin Stockade, Inc.*, 568 S.W.2d 269 (Mo.App. 1978) (payment bond claim).

77. Stearns, *Law of Suretyship* 109 (Elder 5th ed. 1951).

78. *Glenn Falls Ins. Co. v. Wright Contracting Co.*, 276 F.Supp. 122 (D.C.Md. 1965).

represents a material, substantial departure from the original risk, so that a reasonable person would either have not undertaken the risk at all, or would have charged a greater premium.[79] However, as in other areas, it must be demonstrated by the surety that there was no consent to the change.[80]

In the construction contract context, consent of the surety to the change is often found in two sources. First construction work by its nature frequently results in changes. Some courts have viewed this proclivity toward change as being within the contemplation of the parties when the bond was issued as a necessary outgrowth of customary industry practice.[81] Other courts have looked at the construction contract itself which usually contains a provision for ordering changes in the work.[82] The change order provisions in the underlying contract, which are often incorporated by reference into the performance bond itself, are seen as implied consent by the surety at the outset to changes in the contract. Finally, performance bonds themselves occasionally contain a provision that alterations in the underlying contract are consented to by the surety.[83] Accordingly, in the majority of situations, even significant changes in the work undertaken by the principal will be deemed to have been consented to at the outset by the surety.

There is an important exception to this proposition. Even when the bond or the underlying contract suggests consent of the surety to changes in the work, a "cardinal change" which is beyond the scope of the original contract, will nonetheless discharge the surety.[84] Although courts do not

---

79. *See e.g., Varlotta Constr. Corp. v. Sette-Juliano Constr. Corp*, 234 A.D.2d 183, 651 N.Y.S.2d 484 (1996). *In re Liquidation of Union Indem. Ins. Co. of New York*, 220 A.D.2d 339, 632 N.Y.S.2d 788 (1995). However, if the alteration, even though material, is one that was contemplated by the terms of the agreement, no discharge will be permitted. *Graham v. United States*, 231 U.S. 474, 34 S.Ct. 148, 58 L.Ed. 319 (1913); *see also Honolulu Roofing Co. v. Felix*, 49 Hawaii 578, 426 P.2d 298 (1967); *Miller-Jones Furniture Co. v. Smith Ice & Cold-Storage Co.*, 66 Ark. 287, 50 S.W. 508 (1899); *In re Liquidation of Union Indem. Ins. Co. Of NY*, 234 A.D.2d 120, 651 N.Y.S.2d 436 (1996); *H&S Corp. v. United States Fidelity & Guar. Co.*, 667 So.2d 393 (Fla.App. 1995); *United Bonding Ins. Co. v. Atlantic Roofing & Sheet Metal*, 221 So.2d 461 (Fla.Ct.App. 1969).

80. *See Am-Haul Carting v. Contractors Casualty & Sur. Co.*, 33 F.Supp. 2d 235 (S.D.N.Y. 1998) (testimony of bonding agent established consent to change orders). It has been the practice for many years by obligees to attempt to ward off this defense by putting in the bond what amounts to consent on the part of the surety. The A311 bond, for example, states that, "The surety hereby waives notice of any alteration or extension of time made by the owner." One "form" Little Miller Act performance bond in Georgia contains the following wavier: "The said surety to this bond, for value received, hereby stipulates and agrees that no change or changes, extension of time or extensions of time, alteration or alterations, addition or additions to the terms of the contract or to the work to be performed thereunder, or the specifications or drawings accompanying the same shall in any way affect its obligation under this bond, and it does hereby waive notice of any such change or changes, extension of time or extensions of time, alteration or alterations, or addition or additions to the terms of the contract, to the work, or to the specifications or drawings." Such provision was necessary because up until 1978, any change in the underlying contract, no matter how minor, would discharge even a compensated surety. *Palmes v. Southern Mechanical Co.*, 117 Ga.App. 672, 161 S.E.2d 413 (1968) (discharge of the surety for $150.00 change order). All of this changed with *Houston Gen. Ins. Co. v. Brock Constr. Co., Inc.*, 241 Ga. 460 (1978) in which it was held that compensated sureties will only be discharged for a material increase in their risk.

81. *Wagner v. Frazier*, 712 S.W.2d 109 (Tenn. App. 1986); *Massachusetts Bonding & Ins. Co. v. John R. Thompson*, 88 F.2d 825 (8th Cir. 1937); *George A. Hormel & Co. v. American Bonding Co.*, 112 Minn. 288, 128 N.W.12 (1910); *see also* Diane P. Chapman, *Preserving the Principal's Contract Claims and Defenses* (Fidelity & Surety Midyear Meeting, 1995).

82. For an example of the surety consenting as a part of the original transaction to change, *see Samuelson v. Promontory Inv. Corp.*, 85 Ore.App. 315, 736 P.2d 207 (1987); *see, e.g., Honolulu Roofing Co. v. Felix*, 49 Hawaii 578, 426 P.2d 298 (1967) (contract price change); *Glades County v. Detroit Fidelity & Sur. Co.*, 57 F.2d 449 (5th Cir. 1932).

83. *See* the AIA A312 bond, Paragraph 8.

84. *J.D. Hedin Constr. Co. v. United States*, 347 F.2d 235 (Ct.Cl. 1965); *see* Meyer, *The Surety's Liability as Affected by Contract Alterations and Unauthorized Payments: How Much is Too Much?*, 15 *The Forum* 982 (1979); Gallagher, *What Constitutes a Material Alteration in a Bonded Contract Sufficient to Discharge the Surety?*, (1966) A.B.A. Section of Insurance, Negligence, and Compensation Law Proceedings 350; *Edward R. Marden Corp. v. United States*,

generally use the phrase "cardinal change," courts have applied the "cardinal change" concept to find a discharge under these circumstances in which the parties could not have reasonably anticipated the change in question as being within the scope of the work when the contract was commenced.[85] For example, in *Employer's Insurance of Wausau v. Construction Management Engineers* the bonded subcontractor executed, on March 6th, a subcontract in the amount of $2.3 million.[86] A subcontract performance bond was issued in that amount. On March 7th, without the surety's knowledge, the subcontractor executed an additional agreement by which it took over all of the work of the general contractor for a total contract price of $6.2 million, which encompassed within it the work of the original $2.3 million subcontract. The court found that this represented a substantial modification in the contract and went well beyond the intent of the parties with regard to the surety's original obligation. Accordingly, at least as between the obligee and the surety, the surety was deemed to be discharged from any obligation under its bond. The phrase "cardinal change" does not appear in the case, but the fundamental concept is the same.

2. Examples of Material Alteration; Burden of Proof

Whether a change will cause a discharge of the surety is a factually intense question in which the terms of the underlying contract must be weighed against the specific circumstances.[87] For example, a slight increase in the building height, along with a change in a window size and the omission of a window, clearly do not amount to a material alteration sufficient for a discharge (even though the entire construction project was quite small).[88] Changing the location of the building from one lot to another also has been held not to discharge a surety.[89] In one case, adding an entire floor to a building was deemed to discharge the surety[90], while in another case, adding a basement was not

---

94 Ct.Cl. 799, 442 F.2d 364 (1971); *see, e.g., Freund v. United States*, 260 U.S. 60, 63 (1922); *Roberts v. Security Trust & Savings Bank*, 196 Cal. 575, 238 P. 673 (1925). The change must not only be material, but also must be one that was "not fairly within the contemplation of the parties at the time the contract was made." Massachusetts Bonding & Ins. Co. v. John R. Thompson Co., 88 F.2d 825, 829 (8th Cir. 1937); *see also* King, "Who *Will Pay? Surety Coverage Issues" A.B.A. Fidelity & Surety* Law Committee Mid-year Meeting (1998).

85. The "cardinal change" analysis is drawn from case law developed in federal procurement law by the U.S. Court of Claims; *see, e.g. Air-A-Plane Corp. v. United States*, 187 Cl.Ct. 269, 408 F.2d 1030 (1969). A "cardinal change" is one which is outside the scope of the original contract. *See, e.g. Fidelity Bond & Mortgage Co. v. Am. Sur. Co.*, 14 Tenn.App. 211 (1931); *Southern Constr. Co. v. Southern Sur. Co.*, 10 Tenn.App. 506 (1926); *Altman v. Sproles*, 161 Ark. 128, 255 S.W. 573 (1923); *see also Hensler v. City of Los Angeles*, 268 P.2d 12 (Cal.App. 1954) (owner not permitted to abandon original contract by deleting major portions of it); *United States Fidelity & Guar. Co. v. United States ex. rel.* Smoot, 298 F. 365 (D.C. Cir. 1924); *see also* Bruner, O'Conner and Hartnett, "The Surety's Analysis of Investigative Results: To Perform or Not to Perform, That is the Question," *Bond Default Manual* (Second Edition, 1995).

86. *Employers Ins. of Wausau v. Constr. Management Eng'rs of Fla., Inc.*, 297 S.C. 354, 377 S.E.2d 119 (S.C.App. 1989).

87. *See, e.g., Board of Supervisors of Fairfax County v. Southern Cross Coal Corp.*, 238 Va. 91, 380 S.E.2d 636 (1989) (change from the original plans and specifications not a material alteration).

88. *Fisher v. Fidelity & Deposit Co. of Maryland*, 125 Ill.App. 3rd 632, 466 N.E.2d 332 (1984); *Guy T. Williams Realty, Inc. v. Shamrock Constr. Co.*, 564 So.2d 689 (La.App. 1990) (change in plans and specifications does not result in discharge).

89. *Segari v. Mazzei*, 116 La. 1026, 41 So. 245 (1906). Another example of a change in location and in specifications not discharging the surety is *Massachusetts Bonding and Ins. Co. v. John R. Thompson Co.*, 88 F.2d 825 (8th Cir. 1937).

90. *Miller-Jones Furniture Co. v. T. Smith Ice & Cold Storage Co.*, 66 Ark. 287, 50 S.W. 508 (1899); *Zimmerman v. Judah*, 13 Ind. 286 (1959) (one additional story discharges the surety); *but see Lamsen v. Maryland Cas. Co.*, 196 Iowa 1185, 194 N.W. 70 (1923).

sufficient to work a discharge. A fundamental change in the nature of the project from, for example, a warehouse to a hospital is illustrative of the kind of qualitative change which would result in a discharge.[91] Furthermore a vast number of change orders radically increasing the scope of the work and materially increasing the risk upon the surety can work a discharge even though the principal has agreed to these changes.[92] One does not, however, measure the degree of risk increase merely in the dollar amount of change.[93]

As with the question of premature payment, the general rule is that the burden of proving this defense rests upon the surety.[94] In this area, the focus is upon whether there has been a material alteration in the overall undertaking of the surety. If there has been a material change which causes actual prejudice to the surety, then the tendency of the courts is to give a complete discharge or, in the alternative, to permit the obligee to go forward with a showing that the discharge can be measured and hence limited.[95] But, as a practical matter, the claim on the surety is usually made because the principal is unable to perform and frequently the question of prejudice is related to whether the material alteration was part of the reason for the principal's financial demise. Finally, even if the material alteration did not result in the principal's financial demise, the surety is nonetheless entitled to a discharge if its fundamental undertaking has been altered in a significant, material way. As described by one court, a material change is "one that a careful and prudent person

91. *American Druggists Ins. v. Thompson Lumber Co.*, 349 N.W.2d 569 (Minn.App. 1984); *Fisher v. Fidelity and Deposit Co. of Maryland*, 125 Ill.App.3d 632, 466 N.E.2d 332 (1984).

92. When the changes bear a reasonable relationship in extent and value to the original project, the surety is not discharged. *Prestigiacomo v. Phoenix Ins. Co.*, 231 So.2d 431 (La.App. 1970); *see also Aetna Casualty & Surety Co. v. LFO Constr. Corp.*, 207 A.D.2d 274, 615 N.Y.S.2d 389 (1994) (issue of fact on material alteration and change orders). The number of changes is not necessarily determinative because a single change may be sufficient, depending upon its nature and quality. *P.L. Saddler v. United States*, 287 F.2d 411 (Cl.Ct. 1961) (not a suretyship case). Slight deviations in the plans and specifications will certainly not discharge the surety. *Schreiber v. Worm*, 164 Ind. 7, 72 N.E. 852, 854 (1904).

93. A disturbing decision is *Carroll-Boone Water Dist. v. M. & P. Equip. Co.*, 280 Ark. 560, 661 S.W.2d 345 (1983) in which the court held that the owner's failure to insist upon the obtaining of builders' risk insurance was not a material alteration to the contract which would discharge the surety. The case is distinguishable from those situations in which the general contractor breaches the contract by failing to procure the builders' risk insurance as required; *see, e.g., Hartford Fire Ins. Co. v. Riefolo Constr. Co., Inc.*, 81 N.J. 514, 410 A.2d 658 (1980). As with all material alteration cases, it can be characterized as a "breach of contract" by the principal, but the essence of these decisions is that the principal and obligee have agreed together, without the consent of the surety. This would certainly seem applicable to a decision on the part of the obligee not to insist upon a certificate of insurance showing builders' risk. In form, it is no different from the failure of the owner to insist upon lien releases as required by the contract for the release of retainage. The latter has been held many times to result in a discharge to the surety. 17 Am.Jur.2d *Contractors' Bonds* § 44 (1990). *See, e.g., L.B. Gilmore v. Royal Indem. Co.*, 240 F.2d 101 (5th Cir. 1956). A mere change in the contract price alone will certainly not discharge the surety. *Burdette v. Laescola*, 40 Md.App. 720, 395 A.2d 169 (1978); *Maryland Casualty Co. v. First Nat'l Bank of Eufaula*, 165 So.2d 359 (Ala. 1964) (bid bond); *see generally Wunderlich Contracting Co. v. United States*, 351 F.2d 956 (Cl.Ct. 1965).

94. *See, e.g. Reliance Ins. Co. v. Dahlstrom Corp.*, 568 S.W.2d 733 (1978).

95. The obligee has the burden of proving that it can be limited to the extent of prejudice. *See Mergentime Corp. v. Washington Metropolitan Area Transit Auth.*, 775 F.Supp. 14, 21 (D.D.C. 1991). This case relied upon the Restatement of Security, § 128(b), and *Reliance Ins. Co. v. Colbert*, 365 F.2d 530, 535 (D.C.Cir. 1966), which stands for the proposition that if the creditor and the principal have so modified the contract as to impose on the surety a risk of loss which is substantially different, and this risk of loss cannot be measured, then the discharge shall be total unless the obligee can meet the burden of proving the extent of loss. *See also St. Petersburg Bank & Trust Co. v. Boutin*, 445 F.2d 1028 (5th Cir. 1971).

undertaking the risk would regard as substantially increasing the chance of loss."[96] Whether the chance of loss has been increased is viewed from the perspective of when the bond was issued. Thus, the mere fact that no specifications were ever written for a contract will not discharge the surety because this condition existed at the outset.[97] In the end these questions present a jury issue as to the nature of the change and whether it suffices for a discharge.[98]

An example of the application of the material alteration doctrine can be found in *United States v. Reliance Insurance Company* in which the surety was exonerated from its performance bond obligations because of a change in allocation of revenues without the surety's consent.[99] The court observed as follows:

> A surety company is not a public utility. It may, for any or no reason, conclude not to furnish its bond with respect to a particular contract. When it has committed itself with respect to one contract, amendments which convert that agreement into a significantly different one should be brought to the attention of the surety so that it may exercise its own business judgment as to whether it wishes to continue its commitment. It is not for the parties to the contract to decide among themselves that their amendments are of no interest to the surety, at least when, as here, those amendments go beyond mere matter of form.[100]

In the end, whether the change is conceived of as a cardinal change or a material change, the surety must satisfy its burden of proof that on the facts of the specific case at hand either the quality or the magnitude of the changes resulted in a modification which took the work outside the scope of the original bargain and also resulted in demonstrable prejudice to the surety.[101] If all that is proven is that a material change occurred, this will not, without more, meet the surety's burden.

3. Material Alteration Distinguished From Obligee Breach of Contract and Obligee Failure to Mitigate

A material alteration in the contract should be distinguished from a failure to meet contract conditions which will be discussed below. In some decisions, the courts tend to blur the distinction between a material alteration and the failure on the obligee, in subsequent performance, to abide by the conditions of the underlying contract. For example, it has been held that the owner's failure to insist upon the general contractor procuring builder's risk insurance as required by the contract is simply a failure to abide by a contract term, rather than a material alteration in the agreement.[102] Similarly, the owner's failure to pay when required is not a "material alteration" in the contract.

---

96. *Samuelson v. Promontory Inv. Corp.*, 85 Ore.App. 315, 736 P.2d 207 (Ore.App. 1987); *Carols Equities Corp. v. Villnave*, 57 Ad.2d 1044, 395 N.Y.S.2d 800 (1977) (without a material change there is no discharge); *Fidelity & Deposit Co. of Maryland v. Olney Assoc., Inc.*, 72 Md.App. 367, 530 A.2d 1 (1987) (must be a material alteration which increases the surety's risk).

97. *Wagner v. Frazier*, 712 S.W.2d 109 (Tenn.App. 1986).

98. *Fireman's Fund Ins. Co. v. United States*, 15 Cl.Ct. 225 (1988); *Reliance Ins. Co. v. Colbert*, 365 F.2d 530 (D.C. Cir. 1966); *United States Fidelity & Guar. Co. v. United States ex. rel. Smoot*, 298 F. 365 (1924).

99. *United States v. Reliance Ins. Co.*, 799 F.2d 1382 (9th Cir. 1986).

100. Id. at 1386 (quoting *Reliance Ins. Co. v. Colbert*, 365 F.2d 530, 534 (D.C.Cir. 1966).

101. *See Anstalt v. F.I.A. Ins. Co.*, 749 F.2d 175 (3rd Cir. 1984); *Ramada Dev. Co. v. United States Fidelity & Guar. Co.*, 626 F.2d 517 (6th Cir. 1980); *Continental Bank & Trust Co. v. American Bonding Co.*, 605 F.2d 1049 (8th Cir. 1979); 17 Am.Jur.2d *Contractors' Bonds* §§ 31, 32 (1990).

102. *Compare* the result in *Hohn v. Shideler*, 164 Ind. 242, 72 N.E. 575 (1904).

Rather, it is simply the owner's failure to meet all the owner's obligations under the bonded agreement. In a technical sense, a material alteration in the underlying contract arises only when the principal and the obligee together agree to modify the underlying contract without the surety's consent, thereby changing the nature of what was originally bonded. Similarly, if the obligee is not directly involved in the modification, the courts are unlikely to give a discharge to the surety.[103]

Occasionally, one will find courts referring to a material alteration in the contract when the underlying facts actually involve only the manner in which the obligee itself has completed the bonded contract.[104] In other words, if a completing obligee performs work which is different than the work called for under the original contract, some courts have analyzed this change as a "material alteration" which may discharge the surety.[105] In fact, it is really a matter of mitigation of damages. Deviations in the completion contract from the original contract clearly are the source of a defense to the surety, but only the rare case goes so far as to discharge the surety when the question is really one of appropriate damages.

III. *DISCHARGE OF THE SURETY BY AN EXTENSION OF TIME OR BY FAILURE TO GIVE NOTICE*

The modern rule is that extensions of time for performance by the obligee do not discharge the surety.[106] Under traditional principles of suretyship, an unauthorized extension of time for contract performance would exonerate the surety.[107] The rationale for the traditional rule was based upon the logic that a time extension would increase the risk of the principal's non-performance or impair the surety's rights of subrogation. However, demonstrating actual prejudice to the compensated surety arising from an unauthorized time extension is extremely difficult.[108] A time extension for performance of a construction contract is normally to the clear benefit of the principal without a corresponding obvious detriment to the surety. Furthermore, as with other material alterations, some performance bonds contain a waiver of defense to reasonable time modifications, either expressly in the bond or by implication through terms of the underlying contract, permitting extensions of the contract time. Accordingly, it has been observed that, "this defense appears to be all but extinct."[109]

---

103. The logic behind discharge is that the obligee and principal have, themselves, altered the agreement as undertaken by the original contract of suretyship. If the obligee does not agree to the "alteration", there is no discharge.

104. *United States Fidelity & Guar. Co. v. United States,* 194 F. 611 (1912); *Empson v. Aetna Casualty & Sur. Co.*, 71 Colo. 282, 206 P. 378 (1922).

105. *See* Carnaghan, *Deviations in Relet Contract, Pro Tanto Discharge of the Surety to the Extent Prejudicial,* 10 *The Forum* 63 (1974).

106. Earl C. Arnold, *Outlines of Suretyship and Guaranty* 152 (1927).

107. G. Brandt, *The Law of Suretyship and Guaranty* 719 (1905); Uniontown Bank v. Mackey, 140 U.S. 220, 11 S.Ct. 844, 35 L.Ed. 45 (1891); Schwartz v. American Sur. Co., 231 Mass. 490, 121 N.E. 424 (1919).

108. *Guaranty Co. v. Pressed Brick Co.*, 191 U.S. 416, 24 S.Ct. 142, 48 L.Ed. 242 (1903); *Basic Asphalt & Constr. Corp. v. Parliament Ins. Co.*, 531 F.2d 702 (5th Cir. 1976); *Goeke v. Merchants Nat'l Bank & Trust Co.*, 467 N.E.2d 760 (Ind.App. 1984) (bond itself contained a consent to extensions of time); *West v. Detroit Fidelity & Surety Co.*, 118 Neb. 544, 225 N.W. 673 (1929); *see, e.g. Keene Corp. v. Int'l Fidelity Ins. Co.*, 736 F.2d 388 (7th Cir. 1984); *A/C Elec. Co. v. Aetna Ins. Co.*, 247 A.2d 708 (Md. 1968).

109. Kaplan, *Performance Bond Claims: The Surety's Defenses, An Update* (Fidelity and Surety Law Committee Annual Meeting, 1991); *see generally* King, *Notice Provisions in Payment and Performance Bonds: What Effect Does Non-Compliance Have on the Surety's Liability*, 5 *Construction Lawyer No. 3* at 7 (Summer, 1984).

However, as with all discharge defenses, the facts must be closely examined in order to determine if the giving of time can be shown to have worked directly to the detriment of the surety.[110] An example would be an attempt to impose liquidated damages upon the surety as a result of the failure of the principal to perform on time. If the obligee has granted unwarranted extensions of time to the principal, the surety may be able to show that, through the liquidated damages clause, its risk was thereby increased. While this falls within the purview of failure on the part of the obligee to mitigate damages, there are still those circumstances in which it can be characterized by the surety as a defense arising from a material, unauthorized alteration in the contract's basic terms as to time of performance, with the consequence of clear and demonstrable injury to the surety.[111] Nonetheless, the circumstances under which such a discharge would be allowed are rare.

As to notice, this likewise is a discharge defense which rarely is meaningful for the surety.[112] First, even under the common law, failure to give notice was seldom viewed as a reason to discharge the surety.[113] Second, performance bonds historically have not had strict notice requirements in them. Although the new A.I.A. A312 performance bond requires notice to the surety in order to provide an opportunity to meet with the obligee owner before an actual declaration of default, it is unlikely that the failure to give such notice will result in a discharge to the surety. The A201 General Conditions have long required that the surety be given notice of default. This has not, however, resulted in a discharge of the surety when the default notice provisions are not met.[114]

Notice should be distinguished from an entirely viable defense, the failure of the obligee to declare a default to the surety.[115] If a performance bond requires a declaration of default, then the surety may, under appropriate circumstances, be discharged by the failure of the obligee to declare a default. The purpose of such a provision in the bond is to give the surety a clear demarcation in which the principal's right to perform the underlying contract has been formally terminated and the surety is now called upon to perform through a claim by the obligee. The surety can indeed be harmed if the obligee simply takes over all the principal's work without declaring a default to the surety. The surety would be deprived by such conduct from an opportunity to mitigate its loss.

The declaration of default provision also addresses another problem for the performance bond surety, which is the tendency of the parties to copy the surety on job correspondence when a serious dispute arises. In essence, until there is a formal, contractual declaration of default, the surety is not required to become involved in these on-going disputes. The parties themselves are not truly looking to the surety to perform; rather, it is a form of "sword rattling." In fact, while such letters might plainly demonstrate the surety had actual notice of ongoing disputes, it is not, under a bond requiring a declaration, a trigger of the surety's duty to either mitigate or perform. Hence, the failure to give a declaration of default is a serious omission on the part of the obligee.

---

110. *See, e.g., Blackhawk Heating & Plumbing Co., Inc. v. Seaboard Sur. Co.*, 534 F.Supp. 309 (N.D.Ill. 1982).

111. Id.

112. A case in which the surety did avoid liability because of failure to give notice involved delay claims which potentially could have been avoided with proper notice. *Blackhawk Heating & Plumbing Co., Inc. v. Seaboard Sur. Co.*, 534 F.Supp. 309 (N.D.Ill. 1982).

113. 10 *Williston on Contracts, Contracts of Suretyship and Guaranty* § 1237 (Jaeger 3d ed. 1967).

114. *Winston Corp. v. Continental Casualty Co.*, 508 F.2d 1298, 1304 (6th Cir. 1975).

115. *L&A Contracting Co. v. Southern Concrete Servs., Inc.*, 17 F.3d 106 (5th Cir. 1994).

The surety can, in some jurisdictions, obtain a discharge in those circumstances in which the notice of default is stated as a strict condition precedent for legal action on the bond.[116] But even if the notice requirement is a contractual condition precedent, some courts, in essence, read the notice out of the bond if there has been no showing by the surety of actual prejudice.[117] The courts likewise have ignored bond notice requirements where it has been shown that the surety had actual knowledge of the claim or some other ambiguity in the contract relieved the obligee of giving proper notice.[118] As one commentator observed concerning notice provisions: "The contracts of compensated sureties frequently contain such a condition, but some courts are reluctant to give the condition its ordinary meaning; and hold that the surety is discharged only to the extent of the loss suffered."[119]

In conclusion, only in the most egregious of circumstances will failure to give notice result in a discharge.[120] Absent language in the bond making notice of default a strict condition precedent to bring suit on the bond, no notice defense will free the compensated surety of its bond obligation.

IV. *DISCHARGE BY VIRTUE OF THE OBLIGEE'S FAILURE TO MEET ITS OBLIGATIONS*

One of the fundamental tenets of suretyship is that the surety is not liable if the principal is not liable.[121] In other words, if the principal is not liable to the owner under the underlying general contract, then likewise the surety is not liable on the performance bond. In most instances, the surety will be discharged by virtue of the underlying contract having been discharged through some breach on the part of the obligee.

The most important obligation on the part of the obligee is timely payment in an appropriate amount pursuant to the terms of the bonded contract. If the principal lawfully ceases performance under the contract because of nonpayment, then the principal has been released from performance by virtue of the obligee's material breach of contract. Under these circumstances, the surety is also not liable.[122] The typical performance bond requires that the owner have performed the owner's obligations under the bonded contract in order for there to be an obligation to perform on the part

116. *See New Amsterdam Casualty Co. v. Central Nat'l Fire Ins. Co.*, 4 F.2d 203 (8th Cir. 1925); *American Ind. Constr. Co., Inc. v. Travelers Indem. Co.*, 54 A.D.2d 679, 387 N.Y.S.2d 260, *aff'd* 42 N.Y.2d 1041, 399 N.Y.S.2d 206, 369 N.E.2d 762 (1977); R.C. *Walters Co., Inc. v. DeBower*, 191 Neb. 544, 216 N.W.2d 515 (1974); *Ulster Elec. Supply Co. v. Maryland Casualty Co.*, 35 A.D.2d 309, 316 N.Y.2d 159, *aff'd* 30 N.Y.2d 712, 332 N.Y.S.2d 648, 283 N.E.2d 622 (1972).

117. 10 *Williston on Contracts, Contracts of Suretyship and Guaranty* § 1237 (Jaeger 3d ed. 1967).

118. *See Winston Corp. v. Continental Casualty Co.*, 508 F.2d 1293 (6th Cir. 1975); *see also Jack v. Craighead Rice Milling Co.*, 167 F.2d 96 (6th Cir. 1948); *R.C. Walters Co., Inc. v. DeBower*, 191 Neb. 544, 216 N.W.2d 515 (1974); *Bayer & Mingolia Constr. Co. v. Deschenes*, 348 Mass. 594, 205 N.E.2d 208 (1965); *Ireland's Lumber Yard v. Progressive Contractors, Inc.*, 122 N.W.2d 554 (N.D. 1963); *Paisner v. Renaud*, 102 N.H. 27, 149 A.2d 867 (1959).

119. 10 *Williston on Contracts, Contracts of Suretyship and Guaranty* § 1237 (Jaeger 3d ed. 1967).

120. *United States Fidelity & Guar. Co. v. Orlando Utils. Comm'n*, 564 F.Supp. 962 (M.D.Fla. 1983); *Menorah Nursing Home, Inc. v. Zukoff*, 548 N.Y.S.2d 702, 708 (App.Div. 1989).

121. Restatement (Third) of Suretyship and Guaranty § 34(1)(a) and (b) (1996); Stearns, *The Law of Suretyship* 200 (Elder 5th ed. 1951); 74 Am.Jur. 2d, *Suretyship* § 165 (1974).

122. 74 Am.Jur. 2d, *Suretyship* § 94 (1974).

of the surety.[123] Such language in the bond is a restatement of the law, namely that the obligee must have appropriately performed its contract obligations in order for the principal and the surety to be liable.[124] There are countless examples of cases in which the surety is made a party along with the principal, but it is obvious from a reading of the cases that the main controversy is a dispute between the principal and the obligee. If the principal wins the dispute, then the surety is not liable. In addition, if the obligee breaches other important duties, such as providing contractually required information, then the principal and the surety are discharged together.[125]

Whether the principal is freed from an obligation to perform under the bonded contract is a topic unto itself. The obligee, in order to have rights against its principal, and in order to have rights against its performance bond, need not comply punctiliously with every single contract provision.[126] A substantial compliance with the underlying contract will normally suffice.[127] But where there is a substantial, material default on the part of the owner-obligee, there is no liability on the part of the surety.[128] For example, in *Chicago College of Osteopathic Medicine v. George A. Fuller Company*, the court found that the owner had failed to provide proper information to the general contractor, and had breached its duty of timely payment.[129] Thus, not only was the principal, the general contractor, found to be discharged, but so also its surety. In effect, whenever the principal would be contractually justified in rescinding the contract and in refusing to perform further, the surety is not liable for completion.[130] By contrast, a *de minimis* departure of the obligee from its contractual duties as owner do not discharge the surety.[131]

V. *STATUTE OF LIMITATIONS FOR A PERFORMANCE BOND SURETY*

Determining the appropriate statute of limitations for a performance bond is a difficult task which is best accomplished by carefully weighing and examining a number of factors. First, one

---

123. *Delta Paving Co. v. Woolridge*, 209 So.2d 581 (La.App. 1967); *see, e.g.*, the AIA A311 bond, which states as a condition to the surety's performance the following: "...the owner having performed owner's obligations thereunder...". In the AIA A312 bond, the surety's obligations are contingent upon there being no "owner default."

124. *Farrell Heating, Plumbing, Air Conditioning Contractors, Inc. v. Facility Dev. and Improvement Corp.*, 68 A.D.2d 958, 414 N.Y.S.2d 767 (1979); *see, e.g., Texas Bank & Trust Co. v. Campbell Bros., Inc.*, 569 S.W.2d 35 (Tex.Civ.App. 1978); *United States Fidelity and Guar. Co. v. N.J.B. Prime Investors*, 6 Mass.App. 455, 377 N.E.2d 440 (1978); *see also Birnant v. Aetna Casualty & Sur. Co.*, 28 A.D. 978, 283 N.Y.S.2d 393 (1967); *Standard Accident Ins. Co. v. Copper Hills Motor Hotels, Inc.*, 2 Ariz.App. 46, 406 P.2d 248 (1965), *vac'd* 102 Ariz. 26, 424 P.2d 154 (1967).

125. *Chicago College of Osteopathic Medicine v. George A. Fuller Co.*, 719 F.2d 1335 (7th Cir. 1983); *Ling Elec., Inc. v. Federal Ins. Co.*, 406 F.2d 561 (4th Cir. 1969), *cert. denied, sub nom. Alpha Continental v. United States*, 395 U.S. 922, 89 S.Ct. 774, 23 L.Ed.2d 239 (1969).

126. G. Brandt, *The Law of Suretyship and Guaranty* 179 (1905).

127. See, e.g., *Granite Computer Leasing Corp. v. Travelers Indem. Co.*, 894 F.2d 547 (2d Cir. 1990) (holding government's design approval delays were not a material breach which justified the bonded subcontractor's abandonment).

128. *See, e.g., Knutson v. Metallic Slab Form Co.*, 128 F.2d 408 (5th Cir. 1942). A wrongful termination is a material breach by the obligee. *See* Village of Fox Lake, *supra*, n. 5.

129. *Chicago College of Osteopathic Medicine v. George A. Fuller Co., supra*, n. 1.

130. *East Crossroads Center, Inc. v. Mellon-Stewart Co.*, 416 Pa. 229, 205 A.2d 865 (1965); *see also Roel Partnership v. Amwest Sur. Ins. Co.*, 258 A.D.2d 780, 685 N.Y.S.2d 832 (1999) (holding owner's failure to make progress payments to general contractor after certification by the architect relieved the surety of its obligations under performance bond).

131. *Massachusetts Bonding & Ins. Co. v. John R. Thompson Co.*, 88 F.2d 825 (8th Cir. 1937).

must determine whether the performance bond is given pursuant to a statute or is a private bond. Second, one must determine the triggering date for commencement of the applicable period. This may be set by agreement in the bond itself, or it may be determined by reference to statute. Third, one must examine the nature of the claim itself. For example, one must consider whether the claim arises from failure to perform in the first instance, from a failure to perform a warranty, or from harm arising from a latent defect. Fourth, one must determine whether the bond itself contains a statute of limitations which is, by agreement, shorter or longer than the applicable statute of limitations. This bond language must be measured against the law of the specific jurisdiction in which the claim is being made because many states have a general statute of limitations which does not permit the parties, by agreement, to shorten the time within which to bring suit by less than a certain minimum time.[132]

A. CLAIMS ON PUBLIC PERFORMANCE BONDS.

In determining the appropriate statute of limitations applicable to a public performance bond, the starting point is the public statute pursuant to which the bond is given. It is a common principle in the interpretation of public bonds that the statute pursuant to which the bond is given will normally be read into the bond.[133] The typical result is that if the bond itself contains a shorter time limit than that set out in the statute, the parties will be deemed to have intended that the bond follow the statute. Hence, a shorter, agreed-upon time will be read out of the bond.[134] On the other hand, some courts have held that if the bond contains an agreement for a longer statute of limitations than that which is set forth in the applicable statute, then the more liberal provision will apply because the parties are deemed to have agreed to extend the statute of limitations beyond the requirements of the statute which required the bond in the first instance.[135] Finally, there are some courts which have taken the position that the language of the public performance bond statute in all cases prevails, such that, even if the term in the bond would give a longer time within which to file, this longer agreed-upon time is a nullity because it is contrary to the statute pursuant to which the bond was given.[136]

---

132. *See, e.g. Safeway Stores, Inc. v. Certainteed Corp.*, 687 S.W.2d 22 (Tex.App. 1984).

133. *City of San Antonio v. Argonaut Ins. Co.*, 644 S.W.2d 90 (Tex.App. 1982) (one year public performance bond statute of limitations read into the bond); *Florida Board of Regents v. Fidelity & Deposit Co. of Maryland,* 416 So.2d 30 (Fla.App. 1982). One interesting case is *Village of Fox Lake v. Aetna Casualty & Sur. Co.*, 534 N.E.2d 133 (Ill. App. 1989), wherein the court found that the principal had not materially breached the underlying contract, but that the obligee's termination of the principal was nonetheless proper in light of contract language permitting termination in the event of "any" violation of a contract term, including, in this case, the failure to make prompt payment to suppliers and subcontractors. Thus, the court reversed summary judgment which had been granted to the surety because of a determination that the principal had been wrongfully terminated and held that materiality of the breach was not relevant.

134. The bonds chosen for construction projects are often the choice of architects or engineers who put together the project manual. Hence, the AIA bonds, which are readily available to architects, frequently are used. The AIA A312 performance bond states in Paragraph 11 that the bond is to be deemed a statutory bond and any excess language contrary to the statute is to be read out of the bond. In a state such as Florida, language of this nature would have a very considerable effect where the courts are willing to lengthen the statute of limitations by finding the statutory bond is, in essence, a common law bond.

135. *Board of Educ. v. Hartford Accident and Indem. Co.*, 504 N.E.2d 1000 (Ill.App. 1987); *National Sur. Corp. v. Fischer Steel Corp.*, 213 Tenn. 396, 374 S.W.2d 372 (1964) (payment bond case).

136. *Denny & Assocs., Inc. v. Southern Aggregates Co.*, 184 Ga.App. 832, 363 S.E.2d 50 (1987) (payment bond case).

Because the date on which the statute of limitations begins to run is normally defined by the statute, such as, for example, the date of a certificate of substantial completion, the courts have a tendency to not extend the statute of limitations merely because a defect is latent. For example, *School Board of DeSoto County v. Safeco Insurance Company* involved latent defect claims against a performance bond given to a public owner pursuant to Florida's public bond statute.[137] The statute of limitations commenced under that statute with the completion of the "performance of the labor". The court held that this phrase, "performance of the labor" meant the same thing as the certification of substantial completion and acceptance by the owner. Accordingly, the fact that the defects were latent and could not be discovered did not toll the running of the statute of limitations. On the other hand, the cause of action for defective work does not accrue until there has been an acceptance of the work.[138]

The statute requiring a public bond will often contain within its body the statute of limitations for the bringing of an action on the bond. The length of time for bringing such claims tends to be much shorter than the typical statute of limitations.[139] For example, in Georgia, the public owner has one year within which to bring an action on the performance bond. As discussed above, the start date for the limitation period usually runs from a statutorily defined date, such as the completion of the contract or acceptance of the work by the public owner. This, in essence, becomes almost a statute of repose, and generally defeats latent defect claims.[140]

B. CLAIMS ON PRIVATE PERFORMANCE BONDS

On the other hand, if the bond is a private instrument, or is given with respect to a private project, then the general rule is that the courts are willing to enforce an agreed upon statute of limitations.[141] The AIA A311 performance bond requires that suit must be brought within two years from the date that final payment fell due to the principal. This provision becomes very significant because, much like the public performance bond statutes, it identifies a start date for the running of the statute of limitations. It has been held that suit must be brought within two years from the date last payment fell due, even when there are latent defects in the work which are not discovered until

---

137. *District School Bd. of DeSoto County v. Safeco Ins. Co.*, 434 So.2d 38 (Fla.App. 1983).

138. *Farrell Heating, Plumbing, Air Conditioning Contractors, Inc. v. Facility Dev. and Improvement Corp.*, 68 A.D.2d 958, 414 N.Y.S.2d 767 (1979).

139. *See, e.g.* the Florida statute, F.S. §255.05, discussed in *School Dist. of DeSoto County v. Safeco Ins. Co.*, 434 So.2d 38 (Fla.App. 1983).

140. *See, e.g. School Bd. of DeSoto County v. Safeco Ins. Co., supra*, n. 20.

141. *Elliott Constr. Co. v. United States Fidelity and Guar. Co.*, 424 So.2d 1202 (La.App. 1982) (private subcontractor bond on a public project); *In re* 616 Reminc Ltd. Partnership, 9 Bankr.Rep. 679 (E.D.Va. 1981) (bond contained a one year statute of limitations). Not all states, however, are willing to enforce an agreed upon statute of limitations such as the AIA A311 bond's requirement that suit be brought within two years from when the final payment fell due. *See Alaska Energy Auth. v. Fairmont Ins. Co.*, 845 P.2d 420 (Alaska 1993); *Sheehan v. Morris Irrigation*, 410 N.W.2d 569 (S.D. 1987). The statute of limitations on a subcontractor's bond on a public project is not controlled by the public payment bond or performance bond statute. *Barbero v. Equitable Gen. Ins. Co.*, 607 P.2d 670 (Okl. 1980). Accordingly, the agreed upon statute of limitations in a subcontractor's bond will be enforced; *see generally Thomas, Validity of a Limitation on a Claimant's Right to Sue Contained in a Construction Surety Bond*, 32 *Fed.Ins.Counsel Quarterly* 21 (1980); *Con-Plex, Div. of U.S. Indus., Inc. v. Vicon, Inc.*, 448 So.2d 191 (La.App. 1984); Annot. *Validity of Contractual Time Period Shorter Than the Statute of Limitations for Bringing Actions*, 6 A.L.R.3rd 1197.

after the two year period has passed.[142] In addition, this agreed upon start date makes important the architect's certificate of completion which the courts deem as an important line of demarcation.[143]

In applying the agreed upon statute of limitations, the courts normally deem the bond to be the instrument of the surety, and hence, look very closely at the facts surrounding the claim that the statute of limitations has run.[144] It is not uncommon for the courts to find either an ambiguity in the limiting language itself, or an uncertainty in the underlying facts which preclude the granting of summary judgment to the surety.[145]

There are limitations upon the general principle that an agreed upon statute of limitations will be enforced. First, in some states, there are general statutes which impose a limit upon the ability of parties to contract for a shorter statute of limitations than that provided for by law.[146] These statutes in essence, abrogate the freedom of contract in order to protect the public from contracts of adhesion, and hence, they are sometimes applied with considerable rigidness in order to annul the shorter statute of limitations set forth in the bond.[147] Second, there is often a judicially imposed limitation that the shortened period must be "reasonable."

C. THE SURETY'S RIGHT TO ASSERT THE PRINCIPAL'S STATUTE OF LIMITATIONS

The black letter principle of suretyship is that the surety's liability is coextensive with that of its principal. Therefore, if the statute of limitations has run against the principal so that it cannot be found liable, then the surety is likewise not subject to suit.[148] However, in the instance of a separate statute which is specifically applicable to the surety, it has been held that the surety may still be subject to suit even though the statute of limitations has run with respect to the principal.[149]

---

142. *Yeshiva Univ. v. Fidelity & Deposit Co. of Maryland*, 116 A.D.2d 49, 500 N.Y.S.2d 24 (1986) (interpreting the AIA two year bond limit).

143. *See Transamerica Ins. Co. v. Victoria Hous. Auth.*, 669 S.W.2d 818 (Tex.Civ.App. 1984).

144. *Merritt Elec., Inc. v. J. Boyle, Inc.*, 258 N.W.2d 539 (Wash. App. 1977); *Grady-Gould Watershed Improvement Dist. v. Transamerica Ins. Co.*, 570 F.2d 720 (8th Cir. 1978) (bond's shorter statute limitations will be liberally construed against the surety).

145. *Peter M. Trapolin & Assocs., Architects v. Twin City Fed.*, 488 So.2d 1191 (La.App. 1986); *Pardue Constr. Co. v. City of Toccoa*, 147 Ga.App. 132, 248 S.E.2d 199 (Ga.App. 1978).

146. *United States Fidelity and Guar. Co. v. Eastern Hills Methodist Church*, 609 S.W.2d 298 (Tex.Civ.App. 1980). In addition, there are judicially enforced limitations that a contractual limitation of actions must be reasonable. *Camelot Excavating Co. v. St. Paul Fire and Marine Ins. Co.*, 410 Mich. 118, 301 N.W. 275 (1981); *General Elec. Co. v. Lexington Contracting Corp.*, 363 Mass. 122, 292 N.E.2d 874 (1973).

147. *Safeway Stores, Inc. v. Certainteed Corp.*, 687 S.W.2d 22 (Tex.App. 1984) (nullifying the AIA two year performance bond statute of limitations); *Sheehan v. Morris Irrigation*, 410 N.W.2d 569 (S.D. 1987).

148. *State v. Bi-States Constr. Co., Inc.*, 269 N.W.2d 455 (Iowa 1978) (statute of limitations ran against the principal, therefore, surety also not liable); see also Restatement (Third) of Suretyship and Guaranty § 37(3)(e) (1996) ("failing to institute an action before expiration of the statute of limitations governing the underlying obligation" may discharge surety); Restatement (Third) of Suretyship and Guaranty § 43 (1996) (the expiration of the statute of limitations as to the underlying obligation operates the same as a release of the principal on the date of the expiration).

149. Regents of the *Univ. of California v. Hartford Accident and Indem. Co.*, 147 Cal.Rep. 486, 581 P.2d 197 (Cal. 1978).

Finally, in general, sureties have been permitted to raise the same statutes of repose as would be applicable to their principal.[150]

D. LATENT DEFECTS AND WARRANTY

The AIA general conditions contain a one year warranty against defects in material and workmanship. Although this warranty is generally viewed as a sword for the owner, and not a shield for the contractor, it has been held that latent defects which are discovered outside of this one year warranty period, if they are the result of a noncompliance with the original plans and specifications, result in liability for the principal, and therefore, also liability for the surety.[151] The obligee who discovers a latent defect in the construction work many years after substantial completion bears the burden of demonstrating that the defect was latent and could not have been discovered.[152] Furthermore, the obligee must demonstrate that the general statute of limitations has not run, an analysis which usually requires a review of whether the particular state in question has a discovery rule or a rule which runs from the original breach of contract. The breach of contract will be deemed in some jurisdictions to have occurred upon acceptance of work and not upon discovery of the defect.[153]

Finally, many construction contracts contain long term warranties, such as, for example, a twenty year warranty with regard to a roof bond. In the absence of a provision limiting the time within which to bring suit on the bond, and because the underlying bonded contract is normally incorporated by reference into the bond, the courts will find that it was the intention of the surety and the principal in issuing the performance bond to be bound by the contract's terms with regard to warranties.[154] Accordingly, in the absence of a provision in the bond limiting the time within which to bring suit, a claim may be made on a bond several years after the contract is complete, when a long term warranty obligation has been breached.

---

150. *County of Hudson v. Terminal Constr. Corp.*, 381 A.2d 355 (N.J. 1977); however, to the contrary, involving a public body is *Bellevue School Dist. v. Brazier Constr. Co.*, 103 Wash.2d 111, 691 P.2d 178 (1984); *see also* Thomas & Leo, *Application of Statutes of Limitation Governing Construction Activity to Construction Bond Sureties,* 10 *The Construction Lawyer* (Jan. 1990).

151. *NorAir Eng'g Corp. v. St. Joseph's Hosp., Inc.*, 147 Ga.App. 595, 249 S.E.2d 642, 647 (1978); *see also Burton Dixie Corp. v. Timothy McCarthy Constr. Co.*, 436 F.2d 405 (5th Cir. 1971); *Federal Ins. Co. v. Southwest Fla. Retirement Center, Inc.*, 707 So.2d 1119 (Fla. 1998); *Houston Fire & Ins. Co. v. Riesel Ind. School Dist.*, 375 S.W.2d 323, 325 (Tex.Civ.App. 1964).

152. *Grand Island School Dist. v. Celotex Corp.*, 279 N.W.2d 603 (Neb. 1979); *School Bd. of Pinnellas County v. St. Paul Fire and Marine Ins. Co.*, 449 So.2d 872 (Fla.App. 1984).

153. *School Bd. of Volusia County v. Fidelity Co. of Maryland*, 468 So.2d 431 (Fla.App. 1985); *see, e.g., President and Directors of Georgetown College v. Madden*, 505 F.Supp. 557 (D.C.Md. 1980).

154. *Lebco, Inc. v. MacGregor Park Nat'l Bank,* 500 S.W.2d 698 (Tex.App. 1973); *C&B Constr. Co. v. Nashville School Dist.*, 484 S.W.2d 519 (Ark. 1972); *Bd. of Regents v. Wilson*, 27 Ill.App. 3d 26, 326 N.E.2d 216 (1975); *Baker-Crowe Constr. Co. v. Hames Elec., Inc.*, 566 P.2d 153 (Okla.App. 1976); *contra Indep. Consol. School Dist. v. Carlstrom,* 151 N.W.2d 784 (Minn. 1967).

VI. *MISREPRESENTATION, CONCEALMENT OR FRAUD BY THE OBLIGEE*

If the obligee withholds from the surety information which it has reason to know to be critical to the determination of the surety as to whether to undertake the risk, then the suretyship obligation is void *ab initio* by virtue of the concealment.[155] The surety is thereby discharged. Although instances of such fraud are rare, they oftentimes involve the obligee's knowledge that the principal is in deep financial difficulty or is already in default on other obligations.[156] Occasionally they relate to the question of bonding line. The obligee, attracted by the low price which has been offered by the principal, wants to have this low price protected by a performance bond. However, when the principal is unable to procure a bond due to limitations in its bonding line (either for a single contract or for a total line), the obligee and principal work up a "solution." The "solution" is that the bond is written for a lesser amount for a separate contract which will include either all of the work or some portion of the work carved out in order to meet the surety's previously imposed lower bonding limit. However, neither the principal nor the obligee informs the surety that the total work is in fact greater in scope. This appears to be what occurred, for example, in *Employer's of Wausau v. Construction Managers of Florida.*[157]

Although the decision rests upon the basis of a material alteration of the contract, the substance of the transaction is the procurement of a bond, apparently, without full disclosure to the surety. In these instances, the obligee and the principal do not inform the surety of the fact which would be critical to its undertaking of the risk, namely that the contract is a much larger undertaking than is being represented. Concealment of this nature clearly permits a discharge of the surety.[158]

In order for a misrepresentation or concealment defense to be successful, if the misrepresentation or concealment is by someone other than the obligee, the obligee must know or have reason to know of the fraud and that such facts are unknown to the surety.[159] Even then, however, courts have shown an unwillingness to discharge the surety unless the surety made inquiry or the obligee had an affirmative duty to disclose the information at issue.[160] An affirmative duty to disclose may arise when the obligee deals directly with the surety in obtaining the bond, when the obligee's silence would amount to an affirmative misrepresentation (such as creating a

155. Restatement (Second) of Contracts § 164 (1981), comment e; Restatement (Second) of Security § 119 (1941), comment a; Restatement (Third) of Suretyship and Guaranty § 47 (1996); G. Brandt, *The Law of Suretyship and Guaranty* 843 (1905).

156. *St. Paul Fire & Marine Ins. Co. v. Commodity Credit Corp.*, 646 F.2d 1064 (5th Cir. 1981).

157. *Employer's Ins. of Wausau v. Construction Management Eng'rs of Florida, Inc.*, 297 S.C. 354, 377 S.E.2d 119 (S.C.App. 1989).

158. *See, e.g., Plant Process Equip. v. Continental Carbonic Prods.*, 1994 WL 201218 (N.D. Ill. May 17, 1994), 1994 LEXIS 6459 (N.D. Ill. May 17, 1994).

159. *Rocky Mountain Tool & Mach. Co. v. Tecon Corp.*, 371 F.2d 589 (10th Cir. 1966); *see also G&S Foods, Inc. v. Vavaroutsos*, 438 F. Supp. 122 (N.D. Ill. 1977) (regarding claim against guarantor of SBA loan). However, the surety may have duties of its own to discover alleged fraud. *See Armstrong Transfer and Storage Co. v. Mann Constr., Inc.*, 217 Ga. App. 538, 458 S.E.2d 481 (1995) (holding that alleged changes to underlying contract did not constitute fraud or misrepresentation, when surety could not reasonably rely upon unsigned, initial draft of a contract as a true representation of the relationship of the parties); *but see Pinkerton & Laws, Inc. v. Macro Constr., Inc.*, 226 Ga. App. 169, 485 S.E.2d 797 (1997) (holding that surety reasonably relied upon terms of unexecuted contract, when those terms were confirmed by the obligee, and thus, surety was discharged by obligee's misrepresentations).

160. *See., e.g., Rachman Bag Co. v. Liberty Mut. Ins. Co.*, 46 F.3d 230 (2d Cir. 1995); *Cam-Ful Indus., Inc. v. Fidelity & Deposit Co. of Maryland*, 922 F.2d 156 (2d Cir. 1991); *Iowa Concrete Breaking Corp. v. Jewat Trucking, Inc.*, 444 N.W.2d 865 (Minn. Ct. App. 1989).

misimpression), if the obligee colluded in the principal's deception, or if the obligee has unique access to material information.[161]

161. *See Rachman Bag Co.*, 46 F.3d at 236-237; *see also Damon v. Empire State Sur. Co.*, 161 A.D. 875, 146 N.Y.S. 996 (1914) (obligee signed contract stating principal had possession of certain notes which had been discounted to a third party, when principal had transferred notes at obligee's behest); *First Citizens Bank & Trust Co. v. Sherman's Estate*, 250 A.D. 339, 294 N.Y.S. 131 (1937) (obligee provided surety a list of collateral without disclosing that a large portion had been released).

8

Purpose of The Payment Bond and Who and What Is Covered

Kelly Allbritton Katzman

I. *Purpose of the Payment Bond*

A payment bond provides the remedy of payment to unpaid claimants who supply labor or materials to a construction project. By requiring that a contractor provide a payment bond, the obligee, usually the owner, is assured of obtaining a lien-free project in the case of a privately owned project, and of providing a source of payment in the case of a publicly owned project. Depending upon the type of project, various statutory provisions may govern the payment bond, as well as the claims made against it. The Miller Act[1] is applicable to most contracts for construction exceeding $100,000 on federally owned projects. Additionally, most states have statutes pertaining to construction projects owned by state or local governmental entities.[2] Many states also have statutes which govern or affect payment bond claims on privately owned construction projects.[3] Finally, in the absence of any applicable state or federal statute, payment bonds will generally be governed by the terms of the bond, and the applicable common law.

On private projects, a payment bond protects the owner's property from liens, by providing a source of payment to subcontractors and suppliers should the general contractor fail to make such payment. The owner will be the named obligee on the bond and the general contractor will be the bond principal. It is up to the owner to impose the contractual requirement that the contractor provide a payment bond, the cost of which will usually be included in the contractor's bid. Many states have statutes governing payment bonds issued for privately owned projects. Often, statutes pertaining to the perfection and filing of mechanic's liens will also include provisions governing private works payment bonds, and the requirements for perfecting claims against them. Generally the statutes will protect the owner by limiting a claimant's right to a mechanic's lien on the owner's property where an appropriate payment bond is in place.[4] Because the general contractor is usually responsible for keeping the owner's property free from liens, the general contractor may require that payment bonds be provided by its major subcontractors, to protect against liens by sub-

---

1. 40 U.S.C. § 270a, *et. seq.*

2. *See generally*, *Payment Bond Manual* (Edward Gallagher ed., 2nd ed. 1995), for a compilation of the various states' statutes.

3. *See, e.g.*, Cal. Civ. Code § 32325 *et seq.*; Col. Rev. Stat. § 38-22-129; Fla. Stat. § 713.33 *et seq.*; La. Rev. Stat. Ann. § 4802 *et. seq.*; Tex. Prop. Code Ann. § 53.201 *et. seq.*

4. *See, e.g.*, Tex. Prop. Code Ann. § 53.201(b).

subcontractors or suppliers. In such case, the general contractor will be the named obligee on the bond, and the subcontractor procuring the bond will be the bond principal.

Liens typically cannot be imposed upon publicly owned property. Therefore, on public projects a payment bond acts as a substitute for the property, and thus a remedy for unpaid subcontractors and suppliers who supply labor or material for the public benefit.[5] Most states' statutes governing publicly owned construction projects require the general contractor to provide a payment bond. These statutes will also often govern the requirements for perfecting claims against the bond. The public owner of the construction project, whether a federal, state, or local governmental entity, will be the named obligee on the bond. As with private projects, the contractor on a public project may also require certain subcontractors to provide payment bonds. These lower tier bonds on both private and public projects, known as "common law bonds," are private contracts, and the claims against them will not typically be governed by the statutes pertaining to the prime contractor's payment bond.

II. *Who May Make Payment Bond Claims*

The individuals or entities likely to make claims against the prime contractor's payment bond potentially include most all participants in the construction project, such as subcontractors; laborers; suppliers; materialmen; sub-subcontractors; tool and equipment supply or rental companies; repair service companies; utility companies providing water, electricity, fuel, telephone, or other services; consultants; engineers; and others who could claim to have contributed to the construction process. Although numerous parties may attempt to claim against the contractor's payment bond, parties actually entitled to assert a claim are limited, most often by statute, and in other instances, by the terms of the bond itself.

A. Public Projects -- Federal (The Miller Act)

The Miller Act provides that a payment bond issued on a Miller Act project is for the protection of all persons supplying labor and materials in the prosecution of the work provided for in the prime contract.[6] Claimants afforded coverage under a Miller Act bond, however, are limited to those persons who have furnished labor or material in the prosecution of the work, *and* who have an express or implied contractual relationship with the prime contractor, *or* who have a direct contractual relationship with a subcontractor.[7] Claimants having an express or implied contractual relationship with the prime contractor are known as first-tier claimants; claimants having a direct contractual relationship with a subcontractor are known as second-tier claimants. The Miller Act does not provide protection for any claimant more remote than a second-tier claimant. Because Miller Act payment bond coverage is limited to first- and second-tier claimants, and because the

5. *F.D. Rich Co., Inc. v. United States ex rel. Indus. Lumber Co., Inc.*, 417 U.S. 116, 122 (1974); *United States ex rel. Eastern Gulf*, Inc. v. Metzger Towing, Inc.., 910 F.2d 775, 780 (11th Cir. 1990); *United States ex rel. Ehmcke Sheet Metal Works v. Wausau Ins. Co.*, 755 F. Supp. 906, 908-909 (E.D. Ca. 1991).

6. 40 U.S.C. § 270a(A)(2)(1986).

7. 40 U.S.C. § 270b(a).

notification requirements vary for first- and second-tier claimants, the classification of claimants is important to the validity of a claim, and is frequently the subject of litigation.

1. First-Tier Claimant

Claimants who have either an express or implied contract with the prime contractor, are not required to give notice prior to making a claim or filing suit against a Miller Act payment bond,[8] whereas second-tier claimants are required to give written notice of their claims to the prime contractor in order to have a valid payment bond claim.[9] Parties having express contracts with the prime contractor are generally identifiable. However, a party without an express contract will often attempt to establish the existence of an implied contract with the prime contractor, in order to qualify as a first-tier claimant, avoid the Miller Act notice requirement, and come within the coverage of the payment bond.

a. Implied Contractual Relationship. The general rule appears to be that in order for a claimant to have an implied contractual relationship with a prime contractor, the prime contractor must in some way have assumed responsibility to the claimant to pay for the labor or materials upon which the claim is based.[10] For example, where a prime contractor agreed in writing with its subcontractor to pay for all materials, equipment rental, payroll, and other incidental charges directly, and deduct same from the amount due the subcontractor, and where the prime contractor in fact did so, a direct obligation on the part of the prime contractor to pay the claimant who was a materialman to the subcontractor was found to exist.[11] A "direct" obligation to pay, and thus an implied contractual relationship, has also been found where a prime contractor guarantees its subcontractor's accounts payable to material suppliers.[12] However, the existence of a joint check agreement between a prime contractor, its subcontractor, and the subcontractor's laborers or materialmen, generally does not create an obligation on the part of the prime contractor to pay the laborers and materialmen, such as to imply the contractual relationship necessary to exempt the claimant from the Miller Act notice requirements.[13] An assignment of contract proceeds by a

---

8. 40 U.S.C. § 270b(a); *Continental Casualty Co. v. United States ex rel. Robertson Lumber Co.*, 305 F.2d 794, 797 (8th Cir. 1962), *cert. denied*, 371 U.S. 922 (1962); *United States ex rel. Monroe-Langstroth, Inc. v. Praught*, 270 F.2d 235, 238 (1st Cir. 1959).

9. *Id.*; *See also United States ex rel. Tonawanda Tank Transport Service, Inc. v. Hartford Casualty Ins. Co.*, 738 F. Supp. 44, 45 (D. Mass. 1990)(supplier's later direct contractual relationship with prime contractor did not exempt it from notice requirement for monies owed to it by another subcontractor).

10. *United States ex rel. Blount Fabricators, Inc. v. Pitt. General Contractors, Inc.*, 769 F. Supp. 1016, 1019 (E.D. Tenn. 1991); *United States ex rel. Metal Mfg. v. Federal Ins. Co.*, 656 F. Supp. 1194, 1197 (D. Ariz. 1987).

11. *United States ex rel. Hargis v. Maryland Casualty Co.*, 64 F. Supp. 522, 528 (S.D. Cal. 1946).

12. *United States ex rel. W.E. Foley & Bros. v. United States Fidelity & Guar. Co.*, 113 F.2d 888, 890 (2nd Cir. 1940)(where express guarantee was found to create implied contractual relationship). *Cf. American Casualty Co. v. Southern Materials Co.*, 261 F.2d 197 (4th Cir. 1958) (contractor verbally agreed to pay materialmen of subcontractor after nonpayment by subcontractor); *United States ex rel. Greenwald-Supon, Inc. v. Gramercy Contractors, Inc.*, 433 F. Supp. 156, 160 (S.D. N.Y. 1977) (prime contractor agreed not to make final payment to subcontractor without obtaining a release from sub-subcontractor). *But cf. Fidelity & Deposit Co. of Md. v. Harris*, 360 F.2d 402, 410 (9th Cir. 1966) (direct purchase by prime contractor of materials did not imply direct contractual relationship with materialman for materials previously supplied by materialman to subcontractor).

13. *United States ex rel. Light & Power Util. Corp. v. Liles Constr. Co.*, 440 F.2d 474, 478 (5th Cir. 1971); *United States ex rel. State Elec. Supply v. Hesselden Constr. Co.*, 404 F.2d 774, 777 (10th Cir. 1968); *United States ex rel. Metal Mfg. v. Federal Ins. Co.*, 656 F. Supp. at 1198; *United States ex rel. Fordham v. P.W. Parker*, Inc., 504 F. Supp. 1066, 1072 (D. Md. 1980).

subcontractor to its materialman, even if approved by the prime contractor, likewise does not appear sufficient to establish an implied contractual relationship between the prime contractor and the materialman.[14]

2. Second-Tier Claimants

Just as claimants at the first-tier level will attempt to imply a contractual relationship with a prime contractor, other more remote claimants will attempt to establish a direct contractual relationship with a "subcontractor" in order to fall within the potential second-tier coverage of the Miller Act payment bond. A contract with a party other than a "subcontractor", even if that party has a contract directly with the prime contractor, is not sufficient to fall within the coverage of the Miller Act. Therefore, a frequently litigated issue at the second-tier level is whether or not a particular party is a "subcontractor" within the meaning of the Miller Act.

The Miller Act does not define its use of the word "subcontractor". However, the U.S. Supreme Court has defined a "subcontractor" under the Miller Act as one who performs for and takes from the prime contractor a specific part of the labor or material requirements of the original contract.[15] At least one prerequisite to qualifying as a subcontractor appears to be the existence of a contract with the prime contractor.[16] Furthermore, courts often apply what is referred to as the "substantial relationship test" which is generally based upon the substantiality and importance of the purported subcontractor's relationship with the prime contractor.[17]

Courts apply a balancing test with certain factors weighing in favor of or against a subcontractor relationship.[18] Factors which have been considered by courts in determining whether or not a party's relationship with the prime contractor is that of a subcontractor include whether materials provided by a purported subcontractor are custom items or part of inventory;[19] whether the material supplied is an integral part of the prime contract;[20] whether the items provided were

---

14. *United States ex rel. Henry Walke Co. v. Van De Riet*, 316 F.2d 912, 915 (4th Cir. 1963).

15. *Clifford F. MacEvoy Co. v. United States ex rel. Calvin Tomkins Co.*, 322 U.S. 102, 109 (1944). *See also J.W. Bateson Co. v. United States ex rel. Board of Trustees*, 434 U.S. at 590; *F.D. Rich Co. v. United States ex rel. Indus. Lumber Co.*, 417 U.S. at 123; *United States ex rel. Gulf States Enterprises, Inc. v. R.R. Tway, Inc.*, 938 F.2d 583, 587 (5th Cir. 1991).

16. *J.W. Bateson Co. v. United States ex rel. Board of Trustees*, 434 U.S. 586, 590 (1978); *United States ex rel. Morris Constr., Inc. v. Aetna Casualty Ins. Co.*, 908 F.2d 375, 377 (8th Cir. 1990); *United States ex rel. Gibson Equip. Co. v. Leon Perlin Co.*, 680 F.2d 340, 341 (4th Cir. 1982).

17. *F.D. Rich Co. v. United States ex rel. Indus. Lumber Co.*, 417 U.S. at 123. *See also United States ex rel. Morris Constr., Inc. v. Aetna Casualty Ins. Co.*, 908 F.2d at 377; *United States ex rel. Parker-Hannifin Corp. v. Lane Constr. Corp.*, 477 F. Supp. 400, 410-411 (M.D. Pa. 1979) (citing Rich and stating that "the test set forth in *MacEvoy* was a functional one and that a key to the test is the substantiality of the alleged subcontractor's performance and its importance in relationship to the entire project").

18. *United States ex rel. Conveyor Rental & Sales Co. v. Aetna Casualty & Surety Co.*, 981 F.2d 448, 451-52.

19. *See United States ex rel. Bryant v. Lembke Constr. Co.*, 370 F.2d 293, 295-296 (10th Cir. 1966); *United States ex rel. Wellman Engineering Co. v. MSI Corp.*, 350 F.2d 285, 287 (2nd Cir. 1965); *United States ex rel. Parker-Hannifin Corp. v. Lane Constr. Corp.*, 477 F. Supp. at 411.

20. *United States ex rel. Gibson Equipment Co, Inc. v. Leon Perlin Co., Inc.*, 680 F.2d at 341; *Basich Bros. Constr. Co. v. United States ex rel. Turner*, 159 F.2d 182, 183 (9th Cir. 1946).

fabricated according to a particular specification or shop drawing;[21] whether a party actually performs work at the project, or merely delivers materials or other items to the job site[22]; whether or not the purported subcontractor furnishes a performance bond covering the performance of work under its subcontract;[23] whether or not the purported subcontractor receives progress payments;[24] whether or not the purported subcontractor charges sales tax on equipment or materials provided to the prime contractor;[25] and the amount of the purported subcontract, or the value of the work thereunder in relation to the prime contract.[26]

A claimant who is more remote than a second-tier claimant is not entitled to recover under a Miller Act payment bond.[27] Accordingly, a claimant hired to perform work for a company hired by a subcontractor is too remote and not entitled to recover against a Miller Act payment bond.[28]

3. Other Potential Claimants

Parties other than subcontractors, or suppliers, laborers and materialmen to subcontractors, often attempt to assert standing to claim against a payment bond issued pursuant to the Miller Act. These claims are closely examined by the courts because, although the Miller Act is highly remedial in nature and is to be liberally construed, its main purpose is to protect those who furnish labor and

---

21. *United States ex rel. Parker-Hannifin Corp. v. Lane Constr. Corp.*, 477 F. Supp. at 411-413. *See also Miller Equip. Co. v. Colonial Steel & Iron Co.*, 383 F.2d 669, 674 (4th Cir. 1967), *cert. denied*, 390 U.S. 955 (1968); *Travelers Indem. Co. v. United States ex rel. Western Steel Co.*, 362 F.2d 896, 898 (9th Cir. 1966); *United States ex rel. Wellman Eng'g Co. v. MSI Corp.*, 350 F.2d at 286.

22. *United States ex rel Clark v. Lloyd T. Moon*, Inc., 698 F. Supp. 665, 667 (S.D. Miss. 1988); *United States ex rel Potomac Rigging Co. v. Wright Contracting Co.*, 194 F. Supp. 444, 450 (D. Md. 1961).

23. *See Aetna Cas. & Sur. Co. v. United States ex rel. Gibson Steel Co.*, 382 F.2d at 618; *United States ex rel. Clark v. Lloyd T. Moon, Inc.*, 698 F. Supp. at 667; *United States ex rel. Pioneer Steel Co. v. Ellis Constr. Co.*, 398 F. Supp. at 721-722 (wherein the courts considered the fact that no performance bond was given in determining that the companies providing the labor or materials were not subcontractors).

24. *United States ex rel. Wellman Eng'g Co. v. MSI Corp.*, 350 F.2d at 287; *Aetna Casualty & Sur. Co. v. United States ex rel. Gibson Steel*, 382 F.2d at 618; *United States ex rel. Clark v. Lloyd T. Moon*, Inc., 698 F. Supp. at 667.

25. *See United States ex rel. Pioneer Steel Co. v. Ellis Constr. Co.*, 398 F. Supp. at 721; *United States ex rel. Clark v. Lloyd T. Moon, Inc.*, 698 F. Supp. at 667.

26. *See Miller Equip. Co. v. Colonial Steel & Iron Co.*, 383 F.2d at 674 (wherein one of the factors considered by the court in finding a company to be a subcontractor was that the subcontract amount was more than fifteen percent (15%) of the prime contract amount), *cert. denied*, 390 U.S. 955 (1968); *Aetna Casualty & Sur. Co. v. United States ex rel. Gibson Steel*, 382 F.2d 615, 618 (5th Cir. 1967); *United States ex rel. Pioneer Steel Co. v. Ellis Constr. Co.*, 398 F. Supp. 719 (E.D. Tenn 1975) (where in each case the court considered the small percentage of purported subcontracts in determinating the companies were not subcontractors under the Miller Act).

27. *In The Matter of Garden State Erectors, Inc.*, 599 F.2d 1279, 1280-1281 (3rd Cir. 1979); *United States ex rel. Powers Regulator Co. v. Hartford Accident and Indem. Co.*, 376 F.2d 811 (1st Cir. 1967); *United States ex rel. Hasco Elec. Corp. v. Reliance Ins. Co.*, 390 F. Supp. 158, 160 (E.D. N.Y. 1975).

28. *Elmer v. United States Fidelity & Guar. Co.*, 275 F.2d 89, 90 (5th Cir. 1960), *cert. denied*, 363 U.S. 843 (1960). *Accord In The Matter of Garden State Erectors*, Inc., 599 F.2d at 1280-1281; *United States ex rel. Hasco Elec. Corp. v. Reliance Ins. Co.*, 390 F. Supp. at 160.

materials to public projects.[29] Furthermore, the Miller Act by its terms contains clear language of limitation which is not to be ignored in its construction and application.[30]

One type of claimant clearly outside the class entitled to protection under the Miller Act is a partner or joint venturer of the prime contractor.[31] Therefore, even where a party provides labor and materials to a government project, if that party is a partner, joint venturer, or another under the common control of the bond principal, such party will generally not be entitled to claim against a Miller Act bond.[32]

Another group which often attempts to make claims against a Miller Act payment bond consists of lenders or creditors of subcontractors, suppliers, laborers, or materialmen. The general rule is that a lender or creditor who loans or advances money to a subcontractor or supplier, even where such funds go to pay for labor or materials provided to the project, is not entitled to protection under a Miller Act payment bond.[33] An exception to this general rule is where a lender or creditor receives a valid assignment from the subcontractor or supplier of its claim to contract balances and therefore against the payment bond.[34] However, the assignee will still be bound by the applicable Miller Act notice requirements.[35]

B. Public Projects -- State (Little Miller Acts)

As with federal projects, there is no right to a mechanic's lien on public projects in most states. Protection of parties supplying labor or materials for construction of improvements owned by state or local governmental entities is therefore provided by statute, and the payment bond required by such statute. Many states' public works statutes are patterned after the federal Miller

29. *United States ex rel. Martin Steel Constructors, Inc. v. Avanti Constructors, Inc.*, 750 F.2d 759, 761 (9th Cir. 1984), *cert. denied*, 474 U.S. 817 (1985); *United States ex rel. Clark-Fontana Paint Co. v. Glassman Constr. Co.*, 397 F.2d 8, 10 (4th Cir. 1968), *aff'd*, 421 F.2d 212 (4th Cir. 1970).

30. *United States ex rel. Austin v. Western Elec. Co.*, 337 F.2d 568, 572 (9th Cir. 1964); *Sun Ins. Co. v. Diversified Eng'rs, Inc.*, 240 F. Supp. 606, 609 (D. Mont. 1965).

31. *United States ex rel. Briggs v. Grubb*, 358 F.2d 508, 512 (9th Cir. 1966); *St. Paul-Mercury Indem. Co. v. United States ex rel. Jones*, 238 F.2d 917, 921 (10th Cir. 1956); *American Casualty Co. v. Assiran*, 289 F. Supp. 645, 647 (D. Mass. 1968).

32. *United States ex rel. Briggs v. Grubb*, 358 F.2d at 512; *United States ex rel. Woodington Electric Co.*, Inc. v. United Pacific Ins. Co., 545 F.2d 1381, 1383 (4th Cir. 1976)(second subcontractor not a joint venturer for Miller Act purposes because parties not in equal control of work); *American Casualty Co. v. Assiran*, 289 F. Supp. at 647.

33. *United States ex rel. First Continental Nat'l. Bank & Trust Co. v. Western Contracting Corp.*, 341 F.2d 383, 387 (8th Cir. 1965); *United States ex rel. Allied Building Products Corp. v. Fed. Ins. Co.*, 729 F. Supp. 477, 479 (D. Md. 1990); *United States ex rel. Owens-Corning Fiberglass Corp. v. Brandt Constr. Co.*, 595 F. Supp. 1117, 1119 (C.D. Ill. 1984), *vacated*, 826 F.2d 643 (7th Cir. 1987), *cert. denied*, 484 U.S. 1026 (1988); *United States ex rel. Dorfman v. Standard Sur. & Casualty Co.*, 37 F. Supp. 323, 326 (S.D. N.Y. 1941).

34. *United States Fidelity & Guar. Co. v. United States ex rel. Bartlett*, 231 U.S. 237, 242-243 (1913); *Title Guar. & Trust Co. v. Crane Co.*, 219 U.S. 24, 35 (1911); *Nickell v. United States ex rel. D.W. Falls*, Inc., 355 F.2d 73, 76 (10th Cir. 1966); *United States ex rel. Wolther v. New Hampshire Fire Ins. Co.*, 173 F. Supp. 529, 535 (E.D. N.Y. 1959); *Cf. Psychiatric Institute of Washington*, D.C. v. Connecticut Gen. Life Ins. Co., 780 F. Supp. 24, 30 (D.D.C. 1992)(court cites *Bartlett to support proposition that under federal common law*, an assignee has the right to bring the claims of his assignor).

35. *Nickell v. United States ex rel. D.W. Falls*, 355 F.2d at 76; *Cf. Noblett v. General Electric Credit Corp.*, 400 F.2d 442, 447 (10th Cir. 1968), *cert. denied*, 393 U.S. 935 (1968) (assignee stands in the shoes of its assignor in regard to the right to recover, as well as the duty to undertake obligation).

Act, and are commonly referred to as "little Miller Acts".[36] State courts often look to federal case law developed under the Miller Act in determining claims against the little Miller Act payment bonds.[37] Like the federal Miller Act, many states' statutes specifically limit the type or class of claimant entitled to relief under the payment bond.[38] Other states have coverage more expansive than that of the federal Miller Act.[39] As a practical matter, each state's statute pertaining to public works projects, and the case law promulgated thereunder, should be carefully reviewed to determine not only whether a claimant has standing to assert a claim against the payment bond, but also what specific notice, limitations, or other requirements pertain to that class of claimant.

C. PRIVATE PROJECTS

In addition to statutes pertaining to payment bonds on public works projects, many states have enacted statutes governing payment bonds procured by general contractors on privately owned projects.[40] These private works statutes generally provide that where a general contractor furnishes a bond, in accordance with the statutory requirements (often pertaining to penal amount), then claimants ordinarily entitled to liens against the owner's property shall look instead to the contractor's payment bond.[41] Therefore, by requiring a general contractor to provide a valid payment bond, the owner can protect its property against liens of unpaid subcontractors and suppliers.

Many states' requirements for perfection of a claim against a private works payment bond are the same as, or are similar to, the requirements for perfecting a mechanic's lien.[42] Most lien or private works bond statutes are more liberal than public works statutes (both federal and state) in their limitations, if any, on who can make a claim against the bond. However, each state's statute pertaining to lien and bond claims on privately owned projects must be closely examined for applicable limitations, if any, on the allowable class of payment bond claimants.

D. COMMON LAW BONDS

In addition to public or private statutory payment bonds, other payment bonds exist which are not governed by any particular state or federal statute, and are referred to as "common law payment bonds." Common law payment bonds will generally be found at the second-tier level where

---

36. *See, e.g., Coast Elec. Co. v. Industrial Indem. Co.*, 144 Cal. App. 3d 879, 883, 193 Cal. Rptr. 74, 77 (1983); *Waterworks Gas & Sewer Bd. of Oneonta*, Inc. v. P.A. Buchanan Contracting Co., 294 Ala. 402, 318 So.2d 267, 269 (1975).

37. *See, e.g., LaGrand Steel v. A.S.C. Constructors*, Inc., 108 Idaho 817, 702 P.2d 855, 856 (Id. App. 1985); *Coast Elect. Co. v. Industrial Indem. Co.*, 193 Cal. Rptr. at 77; *Solite Masonry Units Corp. v. Piland Constr. Co.*, 217 Va. 727, 232 S.E.2d 759, 761 (1977); *Delduca v. United States Fidelity & Guar. Co.*, 357 F.2d 204-205 (5th Cir. 1966).

38. *See, e.g.*, § 255.5 Fla. Stat. Ann.; Cal. Civ. Code § 3267; *See also Payment Bond Manual* (Edward Gallagher ed., 2nd ed. 1995), for a compilation of excerpts of states' public works statutes.

39. *See, e.g.*, Art. 5160 Tex. Rev. Civ. Stat. Ann.; Mo. Rev. Stat. § 522.300; W. Va. Code § 38-2-39; Tenn. Code Ann. § 12-4-201 *et. seq.*

40. *See, e.g.*, Cal. Civ. Code § 3235 *et seq.*; Col. Rev. Stat. § 38-22-129; Fla. Stat. § 713.23 *et seq.*; La. Rev. Stat. Ann. § 4802 *et seq.*; Tex. Prop. Code § 53.201 *et seq.*; Utah Code Ann. § 14-2-1 *et seq.*; Miss. Code Ann. § 85-7-185.

41. *See* Tex. Prop. Code § 53.201(b); Utah Code Ann. § 14-2-1; Cal. Civ. Code §§ 3235-3237.

42. *See* Miss. Code Ann. § 85-7-185; Tex. Prop. Code § 53.206.

a subcontractor has obtained a payment bond for the benefit of its suppliers, laborers, and materialmen;[43] at the first tier level in the absence of any applicable state statute;[44] and on projects where governing statutes are found to be inapplicable.[45] Common law payment bonds are private contracts. Therefore, absent a state or federal statute specifically defining who can make a claim against a payment bond, the language of the particular bond must be examined to determine whether or not a party has standing to make a claim.[46]

Where separate performance and payment bonds are obtained, encompassing separate performance and payment obligations, it is generally recognized that the intended beneficiaries of the payment bond will be unpaid subcontractors, suppliers, laborers, and materialmen.[47] Often, however, a single bond instrument includes or is conditioned upon performance as well as payment of claims for labor and/or materials, and is stated to be for the benefit of a named obligee. In such case, the general rule is that for a claimant other than the named obligee to have standing to recover against the bond, such claimant must be a third-party beneficiary intended by the parties to the bond to benefit.[48] The intent of the parties, and therefore the class of intended claimants, is usually determined by examining the language of the particular bond.[49] As a general rule, if a common law payment bond expressly provides that no right of action shall accrue under the bond for the benefit of anyone other than the named obligee, claims by third-party laborers and materialmen will generally not be allowed.[50]

---

43. *See, e.g., Barbero v. Equitable Gen. Ins. Co.*, 607 P.2d 670, 673 (Okla. 1980).

44. *See, e.g., Barge & Co. v. Oakwood Steel Co.*, 128 Ga.App. 597, 197 S.E.2d 405, 406 (Ga. Ct. App. 1973); *Firemen's Fund Am. Ins. Cos. v. Milstid*, 253 So.2d 571, 574 (La. Ct. App. 1971), *cert. denied*, 260 La. 131, 255 So.2d 355 (1971).

45. *James D. Shea Co. v. Perini Corp.*, 2 Mass. App. Ct. 912, 321 N.E.2d 831, 832 (Mass. App. Ct. 1975); *Sherwin-Williams Co. v. American Indem. Co.*, 504 S.W.2d 400, 402 (Tex. 1973).

46. *Socar, Inc. v. St. Paul Fire & Marine Ins. Co.*, 288 S.C. 287, 341 S.E.2d 822, 823 (S.C. Ct. App. 1986); *Barbero v. Equitable Gen. Ins. Co.*, 607 P.2d at 672; *James D. Shea Co. v. Perini Corp.*, 321 N.E.2d at 832; *Robinson Explosives, Inc. v. Dalon Contracting Co.*, 132 Ga. App. 849, 209 S.E.2d 264, 266 (Ga. Ct. App. 1974).

47. *See Davis Wallbridge, Inc. v. Aetna Casualty & Sur. Co.*, 103 A.D.2d 1010, 478 N.Y.S.2d 389, 390 (N.Y. App. Div. 1984). *Cf. McQueen Contracting, Inc. v. Fidelity & Deposit Co. of Maryland*, 863 F.2d 1216, 1220 (5th Cir. 1989) *modified*, 871 F.2d 32 (5th Cir. 1989); *Stahlhut v. Sirloin Stockade*, Inc., 568 S.W.2d 269, 274 (Mo. Ct. App. 1978)(where in each case the courts found that where separate bonds were issued covering payment and performance obligations, no cause of action was contemplated against the performance bond by subcontractors or materialmen).

48. *CECO Corp. v. Plaza Point*, Inc., 573 S.W.2d 92, 94 (Mo. Ct. App. 1978); *See Wehr Constructors, Inc. v. Steel Fabricators, Inc.*, 769 S.W.2d 51, 56 (Ky. Ct. App. 1988); *Autocon Indus., Inc. v. Western States Constr. Co.*, 728 P.2d 374, 375 (Colo. Ct. App. 1986); *Frost v. Williams Mobile Offices*, Inc., 288 S.C. 444, 343 S.E.2d 441, 442 (S.C. 1986); *Jacobs Assoc. v. Argonaut Ins. Co.*, 282 Or. 551, 580 P.2d 529, 530-532 (Or. 1978); *Wilbur Waggoner Equip. Rental & Excavating Co. v. Bumiller*, 542 S.W.2d 32, 35 (Mo. Ct. App. 1976); *Certified Indus. Inc. v. Royal Indem. Co.*, 43 Misc.2d 761, 252 N.Y.S.2d 345, 346 (N.Y. Sup. Ct. 1964); *C. O. Sparks, Inc. v. Pacific Coast Paving Co.*,159 Cal. App. 2d 513, 324 P.2d 293, 295 (Cal. Dist. Ct. App. 1958).

49. *See, e.g., Kansas City N.O. Nelson Co. v. Mid-western Constr. Co.*, 782 S.W.2d 672, 679 (Mo. Ct. App. 1989); *Wehr Constructors, Inc. v. Steel Fabricators, Inc.*, 769 S.W.2d at 55-56; *Autocon Indus. Inc. v. Western States Constr. Co.*, 728 P.2d at 375-376; *Davis Wallbridge, Inc. v. Aetna Casualty Sur. Co.*, 478 N.Y.S.2d at 390; *Socar, Inc. v. St. Paul Fire and Marine Ins. Co.*, 341 S.E.2d at 823; *CECO Corp. v. Plaza Point, Inc.*, 573 S.W.2d at 94; *Robinson Explosives, Inc. v. Dalon Contracting Co.*, 209 S.E.2d at 266-267; *Barge & Co. v. Oakwood Steel Co.*, 128 Ga. App. 597, 197 S.E.2d 405, 407 (Ga. Ct. App. 1973); *Gordy v. United Pac. Ins. Group*, 243 Cal. App. 2d 445, 52 Cal. Rptr. 438, 439-440 (Cal. Dist. Ct. App. 1966); *Certified Indus., Inc. v. Royal Indem. Co.*, 252 N.Y.S.2d at 346.

50. *Tony & Leo, Inc. v. United States Fidelity & Guar. Co.*, 281 N.W.2d 862, 864 (Minn. 1979); *Sentry Indem. Co. v. Central Elec. Co.*, 136 Ga. App. 557, 222 S.E.2d 40, 41 (Ga. Ct. App. 1975); *Aetna Ins. Co. v Estero Mfg. & Bldrs. Supply*, 174 So.2d 747, 749 (Fla. Dist. Ct. App. 1965). *But cf. Carl Weissman & Sons v. St. Paul Fire &*

In addition to relying upon express language in the bond instrument, where the bond incorporates the underlying construction contract by reference, courts will often look to the terms and obligations of the contract to determine whether a party is a proper claimant under the bond.[51]

III. *What Is Covered by the Payment Bond*

In order to determine what type of claim is covered by a particular payment bond, the governing statute, if any, must be identified. The applicable statute and case law interpreting the statute, may dictate what is covered and what it not. The language of the bond may also provide specific coverage or limitations on the type of claims allowed under the bond. Finally, where the underlying construction contract is incorporated into the bond, then the terms and conditions of the contract may affect what type of claims are allowed under the payment bond.

Although a claimant must always consider the facts of its particular claim, some general principles can be applied to payment bond claims. First, the surety generally has the same defenses to payment of the claim that its principal has. For example, the claimant must not be in breach of its own contract.[52] The labor and materials supplied, for which payment is being claimed, must have been supplied in conformance with the claimant's contract or purchase order (which will typically require conformance with plans and specifications).[53] Additionally, the surety may avail itself of standard surety defenses, such as noncompliance with applicable notice or procedural requirements, or discharge in the case of a material alteration of the bonded contract.[54]

The Miller Act, governing federal projects, expressly provides coverage for labor and material used in the prosecution of the work.[55] However, for guidance as to what constitutes labor and material under the Miller Act, claimants must look to case law interpreting the federal statute. Many states' public works statutes are patterned after the Miller Act, and therefore also look to case law interpreting Miller Act coverage to determine what is covered by the state's public works payment bond.[56] Some states' public or private works statutes specify the type of claims allowed

---

Marine Ins. Co., 152 Mont 291, 448 P.2d 740, 743 (Mont. 1968) (where although the bond contained language providing no right of action by anyone other than named obligee, claim by supplier was allowed where underlying contract imposed obligation upon principal to pay for all labor and material used in connection with the contract).

51. *Barbero v. Equitable Gen. Ins. Co.*, 607 P.2d at 673; *Dealers Elec. Supply v. United States Fidelity & Guar. Co.*, 199 Neb. 269, 258 N.W.2d 131, 134 (Neb. 1977); *Wilbur Waggoner Equip. Rental & Excavating Co. v. Bumiller*, 542 S.W.2d at 36 (wherein claimant was not third-party beneficiary of bond where underlying contract, even though incorporated into bond, did not expressly impose obligation upon principal to pay third-parties for labor and materials); *C. O. Sparks*, Inc. v. Pacific Coast Paving Co., 324 P.2d at 295-296; *Acoustics, Inc. v. American Sur. Co.*, 74 Nev. 6, 320 P.2d 626, 627 (Nev. 1958).

52. *See, e.g.*, *United States ex rel. Soby v. Johnson*, 147 F. Supp. 523, 531 (D. Alaska 1957).

53. *See, e.g.*, *United States v. United States Fidelity & Guar. Co.*, 82 Vt. 103, 71 A. 1109, 1111 (Vt. 1909).

54. *See, e.g.*, *United States ex rel. Army Athletic Assoc. v. Reliance Ins. Co.*, 799 F.2d 1382, 1385 (9th Cir. 1986); *Continental Bank & Trust Co. v. American Bonding Co.*, 605 F.2d 1049, 1056 (8th Cir. 1979); *United States Fidelity & Guar. v. United States ex rel. Smoot*, 298 F. 365, 368 (D.C. Cir. 1924).

55. 40 U.S.C. § 270a(a)(2).

56. *See, e.g.*, *W.S.A., Inc. v. Stratton*, 680 F. Supp. 375 (S.D. Fla. 1988); *Hartford Accident & Indem. Co. v. District of Columbia*, 441 A.2d 969 (D.C. Cir. 1982); *United States Fidelity & Guar. Co. v. Miller*, 549 S.W.2d 316 (Ky. App. 1977); *City of Weipee ex rel. Les Schwab Tire Centers of Idaho, Inc. v. Yarno*, 96 Idaho 319, 528 P.2d 201 (Idaho 1974).

under payment bonds issued pursuant to those statutes. Where no statute applies, the terms of the bond, as well as common law principles, generally control.

Although it is difficult to discuss the various items or types of claims allowed under each states' public or private works statutes, the following discussion will attempt to review the various types of claims made, and allowed or rejected under the Miller Act, and by way of example under certain states' public or private works statutes or common law.

A. MILLER ACT

1. Labor

Claims for labor are covered by the express terms of the Miller Act.[57] Few claims for wages are actually made however, since laborers are usually employees of the subcontractor or contractor, and are paid concurrently with the performance of their work. However, if a bond principal defaults owing wages, then the wages will be covered by a Miller Act payment bond.[58]

Labor may also include architectural and other professional or supervisory services, where such work is provided at the job site, and for the bond principal or its subcontractor.[59]

a. Withholding Taxes. Where a surety makes payment under a payment bond of wages to a contractor's employees, the Internal Revenue Service (I.R.S.) may attempt to claim against the payment bond for federal withholding taxes. Historically, sureties have not been liable to the I.R.S. for withholding taxes, since payment of taxes to the government is an obligation of the contractor, separate and distinct from its contractual obligation to pay for labor or material used on the bonded project.[60] However, in 1966, the Miller Act was amended, making performance bonds on federal projects liable for federal withholding taxes.[61] Specific notice is required by the government to the surety for liability to be effective.[62] Also, the Internal Revenue Code, 26 U.S.C. § 3505, may impose liability for withholding taxes where the surety finances the contractor, thus providing funds to pay wages.[63]

---

57. 40 U.S.C. § 270a(a)(2); *See also United States ex rel. Olson v. W.H. Cates Constr. Co., Inc.*, 972 F.2d 987 (8th Cir. 1992); *United States ex rel. Morris Constr., Inc. v. Aetna Cas. Ins. Co.*, 908 F.2d 375, 376-77 (8th Cir. 1990); *United States ex rel. Briggs v. Grubb*, 358 F.2d 508, 512 (9th Cir. 1966).

58. *United States ex rel. Edward Hines Lumber Co. v. Kalady Constr. Co.*, 227 F.Supp. 1017, 1021 (N.D. Ill. 1964).

59. *See, e.g., United States ex rel. Olson v. W.H. Cates Constr. Co., Inc.*, 972 F.2d at 990; *United States ex rel. Naberhaus-Burke, Inc. v. Butt & Head, Inc.*, 535 F.Supp. 1155, 1158 (S.D. Ohio 1982); *United States ex rel. Thayer v. Metro Constr. Corp.*, 330 F.Supp. 386, 387 (E.D. Va. 1971).

60. *Nickell v. United States ex rel. Texas Vitrified Pipe Co.*, 340 F.2d 117, 119 (10th Cir. 1965); *United States v. Zschach Constr. Co.*, 110 F.Supp. 551 (E.D. Okla. 1953), *aff'd*, 209 F.2d 347 (10th Cir. 1954).

61. 40 U.S.C. § 270(a)(d); *United States v. Fidelity & Deposit Co. of Maryland*, 690 F.Supp. 905 (D. Haw. 1988); *United States v. American Mfrs. Mut. Cas. Co.*, 901 F.2d 370 (4th Cir. 1990).

62. 40 U.S.C. § 270(a)(d); *United States v. Fidelity & Deposit Co. of Maryland*, 690 F.Supp. at 907-09; *cf. United States v. American Mfrs. Mut. Cas. Co.*, 901 F.2d at 373-74.

63. 26 U.S.C. § 3505; *United States v. Falino*, 441 F.Supp. 153, 156-57 (E.D. N.Y. 1977); *See also Bellus v. United States*, 198 B.R. 792, 797-98 (N.D. Cal. 1995), *aff'd in part, rev'd in part*, 1997 U.S.Dist. LEXIS 25583 (9th Cir. Sept. 22, 1997); *Anderson v. United States*, 561 F.2d 162, 165 (8th Cir. 1977); *Pacific Nat'l Ins. Co. v. United States*, 422 F.2d 26 (9th Cir. 1970); *Kadah v. United States*, 600 F.Supp. 1302, 1308 (N.D. N.Y. 1985).

b. Union Contributions. Coverage will also typically be found under payment bonds for union contributions, and contributions to employee funds, such as health and welfare funds.[64] The basis for recovery of these items is that such payments are required in order for the employees to be paid in full for their labor.[65]

2. Materials

The early view of recovery for materials under a bond issued pursuant to the Miller Act or its predecessor was that recovery would be allowed only if the materials were actually incorporated into the permanent improvement being constructed.[66] This view therefore often excluded materials or other items necessary to the construction process such as fuel, oil, parts and tires for equipment used in construction; lumber and nails used in form work; transportation necessary for the construction process; and food and lodging required by the construction process. Eventually, the right of recovery was broadened to the more modern view which is to allow recovery for materials, if they were furnished with the reasonable expectation that they would be substantially consumed or used on the bonded project.[67]

Therefore, in addition to materials which are obviously incorporated into the final structure, items for which claimants have been allowed recovery under Miller Act payment bonds include

---

64. *United States ex rel. Sherman v. Carter*, 353 U.S. 210, 218-20 (1957); *Trustees of Colorado Carpenters & Millwrights Health Benefits Trust Fund v. Pinkard Constr. Co.*, 604 P.2d 683 (Colo. 1979); *Laborers' Dist. Council Trust Fund No. 2 v. General Concrete Constr. Corp.*, 90 Lab. Cas. (CCH) ¶ 33,954 (D.D.C. 1980) ; Cf. *Hilyer v. Morrison-Knudsen Constr. Co.*, 670 F.2d 208, 212 (D.C. Cir. 1981), *rev'd on other grounds*, 461 U.S. 624 (1983). *But see United States ex rel. United Bhd. of Carpenters & Joiners Local Union No. 2028 v. Woerfel Corp.*, 545 F.2d 1148 (8th Cir. 1976) (which denied claim by Union for unpaid wages of its members in absence of an assignment).

65. *United States ex rel. Sherman v. Carter*, 353 U.S. at 218-20; *Cf. Duncanson-Harrelson Co. v. Director, Office of Workers' Compensation Programs, United States Dept. of Labor*, 686 F.2d 1336, 1345 (9th Cir. 1982) *cert. granted, jmt. vacated*, 462 U.S. 1101 (1983), *rev'd on other grounds*, (1983). *But see Duncanson-Harrelson Co. v. Director, Office of Workers' Compensation Programs*, 713 F.2d 462 (1983); *Hilyer v. Morrison-Knudson Constr. Co.*, 670 F.2d at 212.

66. *See United States ex rel. Port Blakely Mill Co. v. Massachusetts Bonding & Ins. Co.*, 198 F. 923, 927 (W.D. Wash. 1912); *United States ex rel. Westinghouse Elec. Supply Co. v. Robbins*, 125 F.Supp. 25, 27 (D. Mass. 1954).

67. *United States Dept. of Navy ex rel. Andrews v. Delta Contractors Corp.*, 893 F.Supp. 125,130 (D.P.R. 1995); *United States ex rel. Dragone Bros., Inc. v. Moniaros Constr. Corp.*, 882 F.Supp. 1267 (E.D.N.Y. 1995); *United States ex rel. Krupp Steel Products, Inc. v. Aetna Ins. Co.*, 831 F.2d 978, 980 (11th Cir. 1987), *rev'd on other grounds*, 923 F.2d 1521 (1991); *United States ex rel. Canion v. Randall & Blake*, 817 F.2d 1188, 1191 (5th Cir. 1987); *United States ex rel. Carlson v. Continental Cas. Co.*, 414 F.2d 431, 433 (5th Cir. 1969); *United States ex rel. Westinghouse Elec. Supply Co. v. Endebrock-White Co.*, 275 F.2d 57, 60-62 (4th Cir. 1960); *United States ex rel. J.P. Byrne & Co. v. Fire Ass'n of Phila.*, 260 F.2d 541, 544 (2nd Cir. 1958); *cf. Commercial Standard Ins. Co. v. United States ex rel. Crane Co.*, 213 F.2d 106 (10th Cir. 1954).

fuel,[68] tires,[69] parts,[70] materials used in form work,[71] groceries or food,[72] lodging,[73] and transportation.[74]

Another issue often arising in payment bond claims for materials concerns diversion of materials. At times, materials will be ordered for use on a bonded project, but diverted to a different or non-bonded project. The general rule for a Miller Act claim is, where the claimant in good faith believed that the material was intended for the bonded project, the claimant will be entitled to recovery.[75] This holds true even where the materials are not delivered to the job site.[76]

a. Specially Fabricated Materials. Claims by suppliers of specially fabricated materials are subject to the same treatment as claims for materials generally. In other words, the materials must have been supplied in prosecution of the work under the prime contract, and the claimant must have a contractual relationship with either the prime contractor or a subcontractor. The fact that a product supplied by a lower tier party is custom fabricated for the project weighs strongly in favor of the existence of the necessary subcontractor relationship.[77] However, the fact that materials are specially

---

68. *United States ex rel. T.M.S. Mechanical Contractors, Inc. v. Millers Mut. Fire Ins. Co. of Texas*, 942 F.2d 946, 950 (5th Cir. 1991); *Glassell-Taylor Co. v. Magnolia Petroleum Co.*, 153 F.2d 527, 529 (5th Cir. 1946); *United States ex rel. Tom P. McDermott, Inc. v. Woods Constr. Co.*, 224 F.Supp. 406 (N.D. Okla. 1963); *United States ex rel. Harrington v. Trione*, 97 F.Supp. 522 (D. Colo. 1951); *United States ex rel. United States Rubber Co. v. Ambursen Dam Co.*, 3 F.Supp. 548, 552 (N.D. Cal. 1933).

69. *United States ex rel. J. P. Byrne & Co. v. Fire Assoc. of Philadelphia*, 260 F.2d at 544; *United States ex rel. Tom P. McDermott, Inc. v. Woods Constr. Co.*, 224 F.Supp. at 409; *United States ex rel. United States Rubber Co. v. Ambursen Dam Co.*, 3 F.Supp. at 552.

70. *United States ex rel. Mississippi Road Supply Co. v. H.R. Morgan, Inc.*, 542 F.2d 262, 267 (5th Cir. 1976); *United States ex rel. Skip Kirchdorfer, Inc. v. Aegis/Zublin Joint Venture*, 869 F.Supp. 387, 394-95 (E.D. Va. 1994); *United States ex rel. Malpass Constr. Co. v. Scotland Concrete Co.*, 294 F.Supp. 1299, 1301-1302 (E.D. N.C. 1968).

71. *United States ex rel. Dragone Bros. v. Moniaros Constr. Corp.*, 882 F.Supp. at 1270; *United States ex rel. Betts v. Continental Cas. Co.*, 230 F.Supp. 557, 559 (W.D. Pa. 1964).

72. *Brogan v. National Sur. Co.*, 246 U.S. 257, 263 (1918); *Equitable Cas. & Sur. Co. v. Helena Wholesale Grocery Co.*, 60 F.2d 380, 382-83 (8th Cir. 1932); *United States ex rel. J. E. Sadler & Co. v. W. H. French Dredging & Wrecking Co.*, 52 F.2d 235, 239 (D. Del. 1931); *United States ex rel. Belmont v. Mittry Bros. Constr. Co.*, 4 F.Supp. 216 (D. Idaho 1933), *aff'd*, 75 F.2d 79 (9th Cir. 1934). *But see Delaware Dredging Co. v. Tucker Stevedoring Co.*, 25 F.2d 44, 46 (3rd Cir. 1928).

73. *United States ex rel. T.M.S. Mechanical Contractors, Inc. v. Millers Mut. Fire Ins. Co. of Texas*, 942 F.2d at 950; *Massachusetts Bonding & Ins. Co. v. United States ex rel. Clarksdale Machinery Co.*, 88 F.2d 388, 389 (5th Cir. 1937); *United States ex rel. Taylor v. Fidelity & Deposit Co. of Maryland*, 4 F.Supp. 211, 213-14 (D. Idaho 1930).

74. *Standard Acc. Ins. Co. v. United States ex rel. Powell*, 302 U.S. 442 (1938); *United States ex rel. Mid Seven Transp. v. Blinderman Constr. Co., Inc.*, 735 F.Supp. 272, 273-74 (N.D. Ill. 1990); *United States ex rel. Carlisle Constr. Co., Inc. v. Coastal Structures, Inc.*, 689 F.Supp. 1092, 1098 (M.D. Fla. 1988).

75. *United States ex rel. Krupp Steel Products, Inc. v. Aetna Ins. Co.*, 831 F.2d at 980; *United States ex rel. Sunbelt Pipe Corp. v. United States Fid. & Guar. Co.*, 785 F.2d 468 (4th Cir. 1986); *United States ex rel. Carlson v. Continental Cas. Co.*, 414 F.2d at 433; *United States ex rel. Westinghouse Elec. Supply Co. v. Endebrock-White Co.*, 275 F.2d. at 60; *Glassell-Taylor Co. v. Magnolia Petroleum Co.*, 153 F.2d at 529; *United States ex rel. Dragone Bros., Inc. v. Moniaros Contracting Corp.*, 882 F.Supp. at 1272.

76. *See United States ex rel. Carlson v. Continental Casualty Co.*, 414 F.2d at 433; *United States ex rel. Dragone Bros., Inc. v. Moniaros Contracting Corp.*, 882 F. Supp. at 1272; *Ibex Industries, Inc. v. Coast Line Waterproofing*, 563 F.Supp 1142 (D.D.C. 1983); *United States ex rel. Lanahan Lumber Co., Inc. v. Spearin, Preston & Burrows, Inc.*, 496 F.Supp. 816, 817-18 (M.D. Fla. 1980).

77. *See Miller Equip. Co. v. Colonial Steel & Iron Co.*, 383 F.2d 669, 674 (4th Cir. 1967), (since lower tier claimant custom fabricated massive girders and accessories which were a key and integral part of the federal project, supplier to subcontractor was deemed a subcontractor and thus covered by the Miller Act payment bond); *United States*

fabricated is not in itself generally dispositive. The specially fabricated goods must typically be an integral and substantial of the project.[78]

3. Equipment

a. Capital Purchase. Payment bond claims relating to equipment will generally take one of two forms. The claim may arise out of nonpayment of the purchase price for the equipment, or nonpayment of the rental charges for the equipment. Where the claimant seeks recovery of the purchase price for equipment purchased and owned by the contractor or subcontractor, such claim will generally not be allowed under a Miller Act payment bond because the purchase is viewed as a capital expenditure for use on projects in addition to the bonded project.[79] As with claims for materials, when considering claims for the purchase price of equipment, courts will generally determine whether the equipment is substantially consumed on the bonded project.[80] If a claimant can show that the equipment was substantially consumed on the bonded project, then the claim may be allowed.[81]

b. Rental. Claims for unpaid rental charges for equipment are generally allowed under a Miller Act payment bond.[82] Another type of claim arising in connection with equipment rental is a

---

for the use of Wellman Eng'g Co. v. MSI Corp., 350 F.2d 285, 287 (2d Cir. 1965) (mechanism built to prime contract specifications for unique task weighed in favor of subcontractor relationship, and thus coverage under the Miller Act payment bond); *United States ex rel. Consolidated Pipe & Supply Co. v. Morrison-Knudsen Co., Inc.*, 687 F.2d 129 (6th Cir. 1982) (firm supplying specially fabricated pipe that could not be bought off the shelf and constituted 40% of the pipe used in the construction was deemed subcontractor for the purposes of protection under the Miller Act).

78. *See, e.g., United States ex rel. Conveyor Rental & Sales Co. v. Aetna Cas. & Sur. Co.*, 981 F.2d 448 (9th Cir. 1992) (wherein the court found that custom specifications for crushing rock at a certain plasticity index was not enough to find subcontractor relationship where specifications were merely descriptive of what was to be furnished); *Aetna Cas. & Sur. Co. v. United States ex rel. Gibson Steel Co.*, 382 F.2d 615, 617 (5th Cir. 1967) (uncomplicated custom manufacturing was not enough to establish a relationship of responsibility and importance, when claimant's contribution was only 2% of the final project); *Brown & Root, Inc. v. Gifford-Hill & Co.*, 319 F.2d 65, 66 (5th Cir. 1963) (specifications for sand and gravel deemed uncomplicated and thus claimant was not a subcontractor); *United States ex rel. Bryant v. Lembke Constr. Co.*, 370 F.2d 293, 296 (10th Cir. 1966); *United States ex rel. Pioneer Steel Co. v. Ellis Constr. Co., Inc.*, 398 F.Supp. 719, 721 (E.D. Tenn. 1975).

79. *United States ex rel. Eddies Sales & Leasing, Inc. v. Federal Ins. Co.*, 634 F.2d 1050, 1051 (10th Cir. 1980); *Transamerica Premier Ins. Co. v.* Ober, 894 F.Supp. 471 (D. Me. 1995); *United States ex rel. Skip Kirchdorfer, Inc. v. Aegis/Zublin Joint Venture*, 869 F.Supp. at 394-95; *United States ex rel. Bros. Builders Supply Co. v. Old World Artisans, Inc.*, 702 F. Supp. 1561, 1565 (N.D. Ga. 1988); *Ibex Indus. v. Coast Line Waterproofing*, 563 F.Supp. at 1145.

80. *United States ex rel. Eddies Sales & Leasing, Inc. v. Federal Ins. Co.*, 634 F.2d at 1051; *Transamerica Premier Ins. Co. v.* Ober, 894 F.Supp. at 483-84; *United States ex rel. Skip Kirchdorfer, Inc. v. Aegis/Zublin Joint Venture*, 869 F.Supp. at 394-95; *United States ex rel. Bros. Builders Supply Co. v. Old World Artisans, Inc.*, 702 F. Supp. at 1565; *Ibex Indus. v. Coast Line Waterproofing*, 563 F.Supp. at 1145; *see also, United States ex rel. Balzer Pac. Equip. Co. v. Fidelity & Deposit Co. of Maryland*, 895 F.2d at 550; *United States ex rel. Sunbelt Pipe Corp. v. United States Fid. & Guar. Co.*, 785 F.2d at 470.

81. *See, e.g., United States ex rel. Sunbelt Pipe Corp. v. United States Fid. & Guar. Co.*, 785 F.2d at 470; *United States ex rel. Bros. Builders Supply Co. v. Old World Artisans, Inc.*, 702 F.Supp. at 1565-1566; *Ibex Indus. v. Coastline Waterproofing*, 563 F.Supp. at 1145-1146.

82. *Illinois Sur. Co. v. John Davis Co.*, 244 U.S. 376, 383 (1917); *United States ex rel. Rent It Co., Inc. v. Aetna Cas. & Sur. Co.*, 988 F.2d 88 (10th Cir. 1993); *United States ex rel. Eddies Sales & Leasing, Inc. v. Federal Ins. Co.*, 634 F.2d at 1052; *United States ex rel. Carter-Schneider-Nelson, Inc. v. Campbell*, 293 F.2d 816, 818 (9th Cir. 1961); *United States ex rel. Moseley v. Mann*, 197 F.2d 39, 41 (10th Cir. 1952); *Continental Cas. Co. v. Clarence L. Boyd Co.*, 140 F.2d 115, 116 (10th Cir. 1944); *United States Dept. of Navy ex rel. Andrews v. Delta Contractors*

claim for idle time when equipment is located on a project, but not used. Such claims will typically be allowed if the reason the equipment remains on the project unused is reasonable, for example, for the purpose of mitigating damages, and is not the fault of the equipment supplier.[83] A related issue is when the rental period ends for purposes of timing of a claim under the Miller Act, when equipment has ceased being used, but remains on a project. This determination also depends for the most part on why the equipment remained on the project. If the fault is beyond the control of the equipment supplier, then the rental period will usually be deemed to end at the time of the actual return of the equipment.[84]

Claims have also been asserted against Miller Act payment bonds by equipment suppliers, whose equipment was lost or damaged to such an extent it was deemed a loss. In such instances, courts are hesitant to turn a Miller Act payment bond into an insurance policy and thus will not typically hold a surety liable for its principal's negligence.[85] However, where the loss (*i.e.*, consumption) was an expected result of the use of the equipment, then the Miller Act bond may be liable.[86] Also, where the contractor expressly assumes the risk of loss or damage to the equipment, the Miller Act payment bond may be liable.[87]

*c. **Repairs.*** As with bond claims for materials or equipment, the focus of a claim for repairs will generally be substantial consumption. In other words, did the repairs result from the normal and expected consumption of the equipment or tools used on the particular project, or are the repairs in the nature of capital improvements to the contractor's equipment or necessary to render the equipment available for other work.[88] Courts have found Miller Act payment bond coverage for repairs or maintenance to equipment and other items substantially consumed in the construction.[89] However, the specific contract provisions, if any, governing the extent of the principal's repair

---

Corp., 893 F.Supp. at 130; *Transamerica Premier Ins. Co. v. Ober*, 894 F.Supp. at 483; *United States ex rel. Skip Kirchdorfer, Inc. v. Aegis/Zublin Joint Venture*, 869 F.Supp. at 394-95; *United States ex rel. SGB Universal Builders Supply, Inc. v. Fidelity & Deposit Co. of Maryland*, 475 F.Supp. 672, 674 (E.D.N.Y. 1979); see also, *United States ex rel. Mississippi Road Supply Co. v. H. R. Morgan, Inc.*, 542 F.2d at 267 (wherein the court also relies on the rule regarding consumption of the product's useful life on the bonded project).

83. *United States Dept. of Navy ex rel. Andrews v. Delta Contractors Corp.*, 893 F.Supp. at 130-31; *United States ex rel. Carlisle Constr. Co., Inc. v. Coastal Structures, Inc.*, 689 F.Supp. at 1099-1100; *but see United States ex rel. Eastern Gulf, Inc. v. Metzger Towing, Inc.*, 910 F.2d 775 (11th Cir. 1990).

84. *United States Dept. of Navy ex rel. Andrews v. Delta Contractors Corp.*, 893 F.Supp. at 130; *United States ex rel. Carlisle Constr. Co., Inc. v. Coastal Structures, Inc.*, 689 F.Supp. at 1100; *United States ex rel. SGB Universal Builders Supply, Inc. v. Fidelity & Deposit Co. of Maryland*, 475 F.Supp. at 674.

85. *United States ex rel. Rent It Co. v. Aetna Cas. & Sur. Co.*, 988 F.2d at 90; *Transamerica Premier Ins. Co. v. Ober*, 894 F.Supp. at 483-84.

86. *Moran Towing Corp. v. M.A. Gammino Constr. Co.*, 363 F.2d 108, 115-16 (1st Cir. 1966).

87. *United States ex rel. Llewellyn Machinery Corp. v. National Sur. Corp.*, 268 F.2d 610 (5th Cir. 1959); *United States ex rel. Wyatt & Kipper Engineers, Inc. v. Ramstad Constr. Co.*, 194 F.Supp. 379, 382-83 (D. Alaska 1961).

88. *See, e.g., United States ex rel. Rent It Co., Inc. v. Aetna Cas. & Sur.* Co., 988 F.2d at 90; *Moran Towing Corp. v. M.A. Gammino Constr. Co.*, 363 F.2d at 115; *Continental Cas. Co. v. Clarence L. Boyd Co.*, 140 F.2d at 116; *United States ex rel. Skip Kirchdorfer, Inc. v. Aegis/Zublin Joint Venture*, 869 F.Supp. at 394-95; *United States ex rel. E&R Constr. Co., Inc. v. Guy H. James Constr. Co.*, 390 F.Supp. 1193, 1245 (M.D. Tenn. 1972), *aff'd*, 489 F.2d 756 (6th Cir. 1974).

89. *See United States ex rel. Mississippi Road Supply Co. v. H. R. Morgan, Inc.*, 542 F.2d at 267; *United States ex rel. Skip Kirchdorfer, Inc. v. Aegis/Zublin Joint* Venture, 869 F.Supp. at 394; *United States ex rel. Gorski Assoc., Inc. v. Chemical Waste Mgmt., Inc.*, 1994, U.S. Dist. LEXIS 1457 at *33 (E.D. Pa. Feb. 14, 1994); *United States ex rel. Chemetron Corp. v. George A. Fuller Co.*, 250 F.Supp. 649, 661 (D. Mont. 1965).

obligations will probably be considered,[90] as will the nature of the work and the damage which can be expected by the performance of such work.[91]

4. Services

A variety of services may be provided to a typical construction project. Payment bond claims for services are often simply classified as claims for labor or materials. Likewise, the analysis for determining whether a claim for certain services will be allowed under a payment bond is similar to the analysis of claims for labor or materials.

Skilled professional work involving actual superintending, supervision, or inspection at the job site, as distinguished from physical labor, is one type of services covered by the Miller Act.[92] Claims for architectural and engineering services have also been made the subject of payment bond claims. For the most part, services of architects, engineers, surveyors, or others performing similar consulting or design work on site will be entitled to claims under the Miller Act payment bond.[93]

Freight charges, or costs of transporting materials or equipment to the bonded job site are other services which have been the subject of payment bond claims. Cases construing such claims under Miller Act payment bonds have been decided both in favor of and against allowing such charges.[94] It generally appears as though freight and transportation charges will be allowed under a Miller Act payment bond if the charges are for transporting materials consumed or incorporated in the construction project.[95] This is true even if the claimant is the common carrier or shipper, rather than the Subcontractor or supplier actually providing the materials.[96] However, there is some question as to whether the charges for transporting or delivering the contractor's capital equipment will be covered by a Miller Act bond.[97]

---

90. *United States ex rel. Mississippi Road Supply Co. v. H.R. Morgan, Inc.*, 542 F.2d at 267; *Moran Towing Corp. v. M.A. Gammino Constr. Co.*, 363 F.2d at 115.

91. *Moran Towing Corp. v. M.A. Gammino Constr. Co.*, 363 F.2d at 115, *citing Massachusetts Bonding & Ins. Co. v. United States ex rel. Clarksdale Machinery Co.*, 88 F.2d 388 (5th Cir. 1937); *Transamerica Premier Ins. Co. v. Ober*, 894 F.Supp. at 482-83; *United States ex rel. Gorski Assoc., Inc. v. Chemical Waste Mgmt., Inc.*, 1994, U.S. Dist. LEXIS 1457 at *33.

92. *United States ex rel. Olson v. W.H. Cates Constr. Co., Inc.*, 972 F.2d at 990. *But see Trustees of Bricklayers and Allied Craftsmen, Local No. 3 Health & Welfare Trust v. Reynolds Elec. & Eng'g Co., Inc.*, 747 F.Supp. 606 (D. Nev. 1990), *aff'd* 958 F.2d 378 (Th Cir. 1992) (wherein manager of a federal project was not entitled to Miller Act coverage in that manager's employer was the bond obligee).

93. *See, e.g., United States ex rel. Naberhaus-Burke, Inc. v. Butt & Head, Inc.*, 535 F.Supp. at 1158; *United States ex rel. Thayer v. Metro Constr. Corp.*, 330 F.Supp. at 387; *National State Bank of Newark v. Terminal Constr. Corp.*, 217 F.Supp. 341, 360 (D.N.J. 1963), *aff'd per curiam* 328 F.2d 315 (3rd Cir. 1964).

94. *See United States ex rel. Carlisle Construction Co., Inc. v. Coastal Structures, Inc.*, 689 F.Supp. at 1098; *United States ex rel. Chemetron Corp. v. George A. Fuller Co.*, 250 F.Supp. at 661 (citing cases decided in favor of: *Title Guaranty & Trust Co. of Scranton, Pa. v. Crane Co.*, 219 U.S. 24 (1910); *United States ex rel. United States Rubber Co. v. Ambursen Dam Co.*, 3 F.Supp. 548; *Standard Accident Ins. Co. v. United States ex rel. Powell*, 89 F.2d 658 (5th Cir. 1937), *aff'd*, 302 U.S. 442 (1938) and against allowing costs of transporting material and equipment): *Mandel v. United States ex rel. Wharton & N.R. Co.*, 4 F.2d 629 (3rd Cir. 1925); *United States ex rel. Robert S. Green, Inc. v. C&W Constr. Co.*, 20 F.Supp. 879 (D. Md. 1937).

95. *Standard Accident Ins. Co. v. United States ex rel. L.R. Powell*, 302 U.S. at 443-44; *United States ex rel. Chemetron Corp. v. George A. Fuller Co.*, 250 F.Supp. at 661; *United States ex rel. Mid Seven Transp. v. Blinderman Constr. Co., Inc.*, 735 F.Supp. 272.

96. *Standard Accident Ins. Co. v. United States ex rel. L.B. Powell*, 302 U.S. 442; *United States ex rel. Mid Seven Transp. v. Blinderman Constr. Co.*, 735 F.Supp. at 273-74.

97. *See, e.g., United States v. Hercules Co.*, 52 F.2d 451, 452 (S.D. Miss. 1931).

5. Insurance Premiums

Claims against Miller Act payment bonds, seeking payment of premiums for liability and workers compensation insurance are typically not allowed, based upon the reasoning that insurance constitutes neither labor nor material.[98]

6. Loans

Another group which often attempts to make claims against a Miller Act payment bond consists of lenders or creditors of contractors or subcontractors. The general rule is that a lender or creditor who loans or advances money to one of such parties, even where the funds go to pay for labor or materials provided to the project, is not entitled to protection under a Miller Act payment bond.[99] An exception to this general rule is where a lender or creditor receives a valid assignment from the subcontractor of its claim under the bond.[100] However, the assignee will be bound by the applicable Miller Act notice requirements.[101]

7. Contract Damages

A Miller Act Surety will not generally be liable for damages resulting from the contractor's breach of contract (other than nonpayment for labor or materials).[102] However, the claimant should

98. *United States. ex rel. Cobb-Strecker-Dunphy & Zimmerman, Inc. v. M.A. Mortensen Co.*, 706 F.Supp. 685, 689-91 (D. Minn. 1989); *aff'd* , 894 F.2d 311 (8th Cir. 1990); *United States ex rel. Bordallo Consol. Inc. v. Markowitz Bros., Inc.*, 249 F.Supp. 610 (D. Guam 1966); *United States ex rel. West v. Peter Kiewit & Sons' Co.*, 235 F.Supp. 500, 502 (D. Alaska 1964); *United States ex rel. General Acc. Fire & Life Assur. Corp. v. Maguire Homes, Inc.*, 186 F.Supp. 659, 660 (D. Mass. 1959); *United States ex rel. New York Cas. Co. v. Standard Sur. & Cas. Co.*, 32 F. Supp. 836 (S.D. N.Y. 1940). *But see United States ex rel. Watsabaugh & Co. v. Seaboard Sur. Co.*, 26 F.Supp 681, 692 (D. Mont. 1938), *aff'd* 106 F.2d 355 (9th Cir. 1939).

99. *United States ex rel. First Continental Nat'l Bank & Trust Co. v. Western Contracting Corp.*, 341 F.2d 383, 387 (8th Cir. 1965); *Bill Curphy Co. v. Elliott*, 207 F.2d 103, 109 (5th Cir. 1953); *United States ex rel. Allied Bldg. Products Corp. v. Federal Ins. Co.*, 729 F.Supp. 477, 479 (D.Md. 1990); *United States ex rel. Owens-Corning Fiberglass Corp. v. Brandt Constr. Co.*, 595 F.Supp. 1117, 1119 (C.D. Ill. 1984), *vacated*, 826 F.2d 643 (7th Cir. 1987); *United States ex rel. Dorfman v. Standard Sur. & Cas. Co.*, 37 F.Supp. 323, 326 (S.D.N.Y. 1941).

100. *United States Fid. & Guar. Co. v. United States ex rel. Bartlett*, 231 U.S. 237, 242-243 (1913); *Title Guar. & Trust Co. v. Crane Co.*, 219 U.S. 24, 35 (1910); *Nickell v. United States ex rel. D.W. Falls, Inc.*, 355 F.2d 73, 76 (10th Cir. 1966); *United States ex rel. Wolther v. New Hampshire Fire Ins. Co.*, 173 F.Supp. 529, 535 (E.D.N.Y. 1959); *cf. Psychiatric Institute of Washington, D.C., Inc. v. Connecticut Gen. Life Ins. Co.*, 780 F.Supp. 24, 30 (D.D.C. 1992) (court cites *Bartlett* to support proposition that under federal common law, an assignee has the right to bring the claims of his assignor).

101. *Nickell v. United States ex rel. D.W. Falls, Inc.*, 355 F.2d at 76; *Cf. Noblett v. General Elec. Credit Corp.*, 400 F.2d 442, 447 (10th Cir. 1968), (assignee stands in the shoes of its assignor in regard to the right to recover, as well as the duty to undertake obligation).

102. *United States ex rel. Edward E. Morgan Co., Inc. v. Maryland Cas. Co.*, 147 F.2d 423 (5th Cir. 1945); *see also*, *United States ex rel. T.M.S. Mechanical Contractors, Inc. v. Miller Mut. Ins. Co. of Texas*, 942 F.2d at 953, *Arthur N. Olive Co., Inc .v. United States ex rel. Marino*, 297 F.2d 70 (1st Cir. 1961); *United States ex rel. Skip Kirchdorfer, Inc. v. Aegis/Zublin Joint Venture*, 869 F.Supp. at 394; *United States ex rel. Moran Towing Corp. v. Hartford Acc. & Indem. Co.*, 204 F.Supp. 353 (D.R.I. 1962); *United States ex rel. Wyatt & Kipper Engineers, Inc. v. Ramstad Constr. Co.*, 194 F.Supp. at 382.

be able to assert such contract claim against the contractor. Specific types of damages resulting from breach of contract have been addressed under the Miller Act.

a. Delay Damages. Until recently, most jurisdictions consistently denied claims for delay damages against a Miller Act payment bond reasoning that delay damages do not constitute labor performed or materials furnished in the prosecution of the work.[103] The District of Columbia Circuit was the first jurisdiction to significantly depart from the general rule denying delay damages under a Miller Act payment bond.[104] The reasons given by the District of Columbia Courts in their decisions allowing delay damages were first, delay damages would place subcontractors on government projects on equal footing with subcontractors on private projects where liens were available, and second, delay damages would compensate the subcontractor for the actual value of materials and services at the time they were furnished.[105]

More recently, jurisdictions other than the District of Columbia have ruled that a Miller Act surety can be liable for a claimant's increased labor and material costs incurred by reason of delay caused by the general contractor,[106] and even where the contractor is not at fault for such delay.[107] The reasoning of the courts in these more recent cases allowing delay damages appears to be similar to that of the District of Columbia Courts. That is, allowing delay damages would compensate a subcontractor for the additional out-of-pocket cost of labor and material furnished in the performance of the contract.[108] These courts also emphasize that the delay damages are not for breach of contract, but for "sums justly due" the subcontractor within the provisions of the Miller Act.[109]

b. Lost Profits. Although claims for increased out-of-pocket costs due to delay are typically allowed under a Miller Act payment bond, claims for lost profits caused by delay are not generally

---

103. *L.P. Friestedt Co. v. United States Fireproofing Co.,* 125 F.2d 1010 (10th Cir. 1942) ; *United States ex rel. Mobile Premix Concrete, Inc. v. Santa Fe Engineers, Inc.,* 515 F.Supp. 512, 516-17 (D. Colo. 1981); *United States ex rel. E & R Constr. Co., Inc. v. Guy H. James Constr. Co.,* 390 F.Supp. 1193, 1244-45 (M.D. Tenn. 1972), *aff'd,* 489 F.2d 756 (6th Cir. 1974); *United States ex rel. Pittsburgh-Des Moines Steel Co. v. MacDonald Constr. Co.,* 281 F.Supp. 1010, 1013 (E.D. Mo. 1968); *United States ex rel. Gutman v. P.J. Carlin Constr. Co.,* 254 F.Supp. 1001 (E.D. N.Y. 1965).

104. *See United States ex rel. Heller Elec. Co., Inc. v. William F. Klingensmith, Inc.,* 670 F.2d 1227, 1232 (D.C. Cir. 1982); *United States ex rel. Otis Elevator Co. v. Piracci Constr. Co., Inc.,* 405 F. Supp. 908, 909 (D.D.C. 1975); *United States ex rel. Mariana v. Piracci Constr. Co., Inc.,* 405 F.Supp. 904, 906-07 (D.D.C. 1975).

105. *United States ex rel. Heller Elec. Co., Inc. v. William F. Klingensmith, Inc.,* 670 F.2d at 1232; *United States ex rel. Otis Elevator Co. v. Piracci Constr. Co.,* 405 F. Supp. at 909; *United States ex rel. Mariana v. Piracci Constr. Co., Inc.,* 405 F.Supp. at 906-07.

106. *United States ex rel. Lochridge-Priest, Inc. v. Con-Real Support Group, Inc.,* 950 F.2d 284 (5th Cir. 1992); *Mai Steel Service, Inc. v. Blake Constr. Co.,* 981 F.2d 414 (9th Cir. 1992); *United States ex rel. T.M.S. Mechanical Contractors, Inc. v. Millers Mut. Fire Ins. Co. of Texas,* 942 F.2d at 952; *United States ex rel. Pertun Constr. Co. v. Harvesters Group, Inc.,* 918 F.2d 915, 918-19 (11th Cir. 1990); *United States ex rel. D&P Corp. v. Transamerica Ins. Co.,* 881 F.Supp. 1505 (D. Kan. 1995); *United States ex rel. Skip Kirchdorfer, Inc. v. Aegis/Zublin Joint Venture,* 869 F.Supp. at 395; *United States ex rel. Superior Insulation Co., Inc. v. Robert E. McKee, Inc.,* 702 F.Supp. 1298 (N.D. Tex. 1988).

107. *United States ex rel. Consolidated Electrical & Mechanicals, Inc. v. Biggs General Contracting,* Inc., 167 F.3d 432, 435 (8th Cir. 1999); *Mai Steel Service, Inc. v. Blake Constr. Co.,* 981 F.2d at 418-19; *United States ex rel. Superior Insulation Co., Inc. v. Robert E. McKee, Inc.,* 702 F.Supp. at 1301-02.

108. *See United States ex rel. T.M.S. Mechanical Contractors, Inc. v. Millers Mutual Fire Ins. Co. of Texas,* 942 F.2d at 952; *United States ex rel. Pertun Constr. Co. v. Harvesters Group, Inc.,* 918 F.2d at 918.

109. *See United States ex rel. T.M.S. Mechanical Contractors, Inc. v. Millers Mutual Fire Ins. Co. of Texas,* 942 F.2d at 952; *United States ex rel. Pertun Constr. Co. v. Harvesters Group, Inc.,* 918 F.2d at 918.

allowed.[110] The reasoning behind such denial is that a claim for lost profits does not involve an actual outlay by the claimant for labor or material, and therefore, is beyond the intent of the Miller Act.[111] An exception to this position is currently found in the Tenth Circuit, which allows a Miller Act payment bond claimant to recover for overhead and profit resulting from delay.[112] However, the lost profits must be established with reasonable certainty.[113]

Claims for lost profit have also been made in connection with non-delay related claims for breach of contract brought by payment bond claimants against bond principals and their sureties. Claims for lost profits arising out of such a breach have also generally been denied against Miller Act payment bond sureties,[114] although such claims can be pursued against the contractor bond principals.[115] Where a claim is for labor or materials already performed, the claimant will be entitled to his normal profit included in the agreed upon price for such work.[116]

c. Termination Damages. Miller Act payment bond claimants have also attempted to claim damages attributable to termination of their contracts.[117] However, where the amounts claimed are for items other than labor or materials furnished in prosecution of the work, such claims have generally been denied.[118]

8. Extra Contractual Damages

a. Quantum Meruit/Extras. A claim in quantum meruit, for the reasonable value of labor and materials furnished in the prosecution of the work of the prime contract, will generally be allowed under the Miller Act.[119] However as with any quantum meruit recovery, the claim must be

---

110. *United States ex rel. Consolidated Electrical & Mechanicals, Inc. v. Biggs General Contracting, Inc.*, 167 F.3d at 436; *Mai Steel Service, Inc. v. Blake Constr. Co.*, 981 F.2d at 418; *United States ex rel. T.M.S. Mechanical Contractors, Inc. v. Millers Mutual Fire Ins. Co. of Texas*, 942 F.2d at 953; *United States ex rel. Skip Kirchdorfer, Inc. v. Aegis/Zubin Joint Venture*, 869 F.Supp. at 394; *United States ex rel. Otis Elevator Co. v. Piracci Constr. Co., Inc.*, 405 F.Supp at 910.

111. *Mai Steel Service, Inc. v. Blake Constr. Co.*, 981 F.2d at 418; *United States ex rel. T.M.S. Mechanical Contractors, Inc. v. Millers Mutual Fire Ins. Co. of Texas*, 942 F.2d at 953.

112. *United States ex rel. D&P Corp. v. Transamerica Ins. Co.*, 881 F. Supp. at 1509; *Hensel Phelps Constr. Co. v. United States ex rel. Reynolds Elec. and Eng'g Co., Inc.*, 413 F.2d 701 (10th Cir. 1969); *Wynne v. United States ex rel. Mid-States Waterproofing Co., Inc.*, 382 F.2d 699 (10th Cir. 1967); *Wunderlich Contracting Co. v. United States ex rel. Reischel & Cottrell*, 240 F.2d 201 (10th Cir. 1957).

113. *United States ex rel. D&P Corp. v. Transamerica Ins. Co.*, 881 F. Supp. at 1509.

114. *Arthur N. Olive Co., Inc. v. United States ex rel. Marino*, 297 F.2d at 72; *United States ex rel. Moran Towing Corp. v. Hartford Acc. & Indem. Co.*, 204 F.Supp at 356. *But see United States ex rel. Morgan & Son Earth Moving, Inc. v. Timberland Paving & Constr. Co.*, 745 F.2d 595, 600 (9th Cir. 1984).

115. *Arthur N. Olive Co., Inc. v. United States ex rel. Marino*, 297 F.2d at 72; *United States ex rel. Moran Towing Corp. v. Hartford Acc. & Indem. Co.*, 204 F.Supp. at 356.

116. *United States ex rel. Morgan & Son Earth Moving, Inc. v. Timberland Paving & Constr. Co.*, 745 F.2d at 599.

117. *United States ex rel. T.M.S. Mechanical Contractors, Inc. v. Millers Mutual Fire Ins. Co. of Texas*, 942 F.2d at 953; *see also, Arthur N. Olive Co., Inc. v. United States ex rel. Marino*, 297 F.2d at 72.

118. *United States ex rel. T.M.S. Mechanical Contractors, Inc. v. Millers Mutual Fire Ins. Co. of Texas*, 942 F.2d at 953; *see also, Arthur N. Olive Co., Inc. v. United States ex rel. Marino*, 297 F.2d at 72.

119. *United States ex rel. C.J.C., Inc. v. Western States Mechanical Contractors, Inc.*, 834 F.2d 1533, 1539-40, 1550-1552 (10th Cir. 1987); *United States ex rel. B&M Roofing of Colo., Inc. v. AKM Assoc., Inc.*, 961 F.Supp. 1441, 1445-46 (D. Colo. 1997); *United States ex rel. D&P Corp. v. Transamerica Ins. Co.*, 881 F.Supp. at 1508; *United States ex rel. E&R Constr. Co., Inc. v. Guy H. James Constr. Co.*, 390 F.Supp. at 1210-1211; *United States ex rel. F.E. Robinson Co. of N.C., Inc. v. Alpha-Continental*, 273 F.Supp. 758, 774-78 (E.D.N.C. 1967), *aff'd*, 404 F.2d

outside any contract the claimant has on the project.[120] Therefore, where the claimant elects to continue to perform and receive payment under its contract, rather than to declare a breach and seek the reasonable value of his services, the quantum meruit claim may not be allowed.[121]

A claimant will also likely be entitled to recover under the Miller Act bond where it has provided extra work, labor or materials beyond or outside the terms of its contract.[122] The claimant will also typically be entitled to reasonable profit on such extra work.[123]

b. Penalties/Punitive Damages. Punitive damages are typically not allowed against a Miller Act surety.[124] Neither the terms of the Miller Act, nor other federal law, provides for punitive damages.[125] However, although attorneys' fees are not generally recoverable in Miller Act cases, where the surety is found to have acted vexatiously or in bad faith, a court may award attorneys fees as a punitive measure.[126]

c. Negligence. Damages resulting from a contractor's negligence are not generally recoverable against a Miller Act payment bond surety.[127] Courts are hesitant to turn a Miller Act payment bond into broader insurance coverage.[128] However, payment bond coverage may exist for the value of materials or equipment damaged, if the damage was an expected result of its use on the

---

343 (4th Cir. 1968); *United States ex rel. Moran Towing Corp. v. Hartford Acc. & Indem. Co.*, 204 F.Supp. at 356; *see also* Joseph E. Edward, LL.B., Annotation, *Quantum Meruit Recovery by Subcontractor Under Miller Act*, 26 A.L.R. Fed. 746 (1976).

120. *United States ex rel. Eastern Gulf, Inc. v. Metzger Towing, Inc.*, 910 F.2d at 780-81; *United States ex rel. Morgan & Son Earth Moving, Inc. v. Timberland Paving & Constr. Co.*, 745 F.2d at 598-99; *United States ex rel. D&P Corp. v. Transamerica Ins. Co.*, 881 F.Supp. at 1508; *United States ex rel. F.E. Robinson Co. of N.C., Inc. v. Alpha-Continental*, 273 F.Supp. at 776.

121. *United States ex rel. Eastern Gulf, Inc. v. Metzger Towing, Inc.*, 910 F.2d at 780-81; *United States ex rel. D&P Corp. v. Transamerica Ins. Co.*, 881 F.Supp. at 1508; *United States ex rel. Harkol, Inc. v. Americo Constr. Co., Inc.*, 168 F.Supp. 760, 761-62 (D. Mass. 1958).

122. *United States ex rel. Taylor & Polk Constr. Inc. v. Mill Valley Constr. Inc.*, 29 F.3d 154 (4th Cir. 1994); *Arthur N. Olive Co., Inc. v. United States ex rel. Marino*, 297 F.2d at 73; *Continental Cas. Co. v. Schaefer*, 173 F.2d 5 (9th Cir. 1949); *United States ex rel. D&P Corp. v. Transamerica Ins. Co.*, 881 F.Supp. at 1508; *United States ex rel. E&R Constr. Co., Inc. v. Guy H. James Constr. Co.*, 390 F.Supp. at 1245. *But see United States ex rel. Perosi Elec. Corp. v. Manshul Constr. Corp.*, 940 F.Supp. 492, 503-11 (E.D.N.Y. 1996) (wherein court refused claim by subcontractor for extra work absent explicit agreement by contractor to compensate subcontractor outside the contract).

123. *Arthur N. Olive Co., Inc. v. United States ex rel. Marino*, 297 F.2d at 73; *Continental Cas. Co. v. Schaefer*, 173 F.2d at 7.

124. *United States ex rel. Harbor Clean Corp. v. Zanis Contracting Corp.*, No. 95-CV-2318, 1996 U.S. Dist. LEXIS 21122, at *4 (E.D.N.Y. Aug. 28, 1996); *United States ex rel. Capps v. Fidelity & Deposit Co. of Maryland*, 875 F. Supp. 803, 810-11 (M.D. Ala. 1995); *United States ex rel. Pensacola Constr. Co. v. St. Paul Fire & Marine Ins. Co.*, 710 F. Supp. 638, 640 (W.D. La. 1989); *see also United States v. Seaboard Sur. Co.*, 817 F.2d 956, 963-64 (2d Cir. 1987). *But see United States ex rel. Cal's A/C & Electric v. The Famous Construction* Corp., 34 F. Supp. 2d 1042 (W.D.La. 1999); *K-W Industries v. National Surety Corp.*, 855 F.2d 640, 641-43 (9th Cir. 1988).

125. *United States ex rel. Harbor Clean Corp. v. Zanis Contracting Corp.*, 1996 U.S. Dist. LEXIS 21122, at *4; *United States ex rel. Capps v. Fidelity & Deposit Co. of Maryland*, 875 F. Supp. at 810-11; *United States ex rel. Pensacola Constr. Co. v. St. Paul Fire & Marine Ins. Co.*, 710 F. Supp. at 640.

126. *F.D. Rich Co., Inc. v. United States ex rel. Indus. Lumber Co., Inc.*, 417 U.S. 116 (1974); *United States ex rel. Yonkers Constr. Co. v. Western Contracting Corp.*, 935 F.2d 936 (8th Cir. 1991); *United States ex rel. General Elec. Supply Co. v. Minority Elec. Co.*, 537 F.Supp. 1018 (S.D. Ga. 1982).

127. *United States ex rel. Rent It Co. v. Aetna Cas. & Sur. Co.*, 988 F.2d at 90; *Transamerica Premier Ins. Co. v. Ober*, 894 F. Supp. at 483-84; *United States ex rel. E&R Constr. Co., Inc. v. Guy H. James Constr. Co.*, 390 F. Supp. at 1246; *United States ex rel. Moran Towing Corp. v. Hartford Acc. & Indem. Co.*, 204 F.Supp. at 355-56; *United States ex rel. Wyatt & Kipper Engineers, Inc. v. Ramstad Constr. Co.*, 194 F.Supp. at 382.

128. *Transamerican Premier Ins. Co. v. Ober*, 894 F.Supp. at 484.

project,[129] or if the contractor assumed the risk of loss or damage to the equipment or other items at issue.[130]

9. Attorneys' Fees

Historically, courts awarded attorneys' fees in connection with Miller Act bond claims pursuant to state statutes providing for recovery of attorneys' fees.[131] Courts reasoned that since the Miller Act was silent as to recovery of attorneys' fees, then state statutes providing for the recovery of attorneys' fees could be relied on to support such awards.[132]

However, in 1974, the U.S. Supreme Court in *F.D. Rich Co., Inc. v. United States ex rel. Industrial Lumber Co.*[133] changed courts' previous reliance on states' attorneys' fees statutes. The Supreme Court held that attorneys' fees are not recoverable under the Miller Act absent a federal statute, or an enforceable contract provision providing for the award of attorneys' fees.[134] The Supreme Court noted that federal courts followed the American Rule, whereby attorneys' fees are not recoverable in the absence of certain recognized exceptions. Such exceptions include the existence of a statute, or an enforceable contract provision, providing for the recovery of attorneys' fees, or the existence of conduct so egregious as to justify an award of attorneys' fees as a punitive measure.

Therefore, where a contract exists between the principal and the claimant which expressly provides for attorneys' fees, then the fees will generally be recoverable under the Miller Act payment bond.[135] However, an attorneys' fee provision in a contract between a claimant and a subcontractor (as distinguished from the prime contractor bond principal) will not be sufficient to support an award

129. *Moran Towing Corp. v. M.A. Gammino Constr. Co.*, 363 F.2d at 115-16, *citing, Massachusetts Bonding & Ins. Co. v. United States ex rel. Clarksdale Machinery Co.*, 88 F.2d 388 (5th Cir. 1937).

130. *United States ex rel. Wyatt & Kipper Engineers, Inc. v. Ramstad Constr. Co.*, 194 F.Supp. at 382-83; *United States ex rel. Llewellyn Machinery Corp. v. National Sur. Corp.*, 268 F.2d at 611-12.

131. *United States Fid. & Guar. Co. v. Hendry Corp.*, 391 F. 2d 13, 20 (5th Cir. 1968); *Boyd Callan, Inc. v. United States ex rel. Steves Indus., Inc.*, 328 F.2d 505, 511-12 (5th Cir. 1964); *United States ex rel. Western Steel Co. v. Travelers Indem. Co.*, 37 F.R.D. 322, 324 (D. Or. 1965), *aff'd*, 362 F.2d 896; *cf. United States ex rel. E&R Constr. Co., Inc. v. Guy H. James Constr. Co.*, 390 F.Supp. at 1246.

132. *United States Fid. & Guar. Co. v. Hendry Corp.*, 391 F. 2d at 20; *Boyd Callan, Inc. v. United States ex rel. Steves Indus., Inc.*, 328 F.2d at 511-12; *United States ex rel. Western Steel Co. v. Travelers Indem. Co.*, 37 F.R.D. at 324; *cf. United States ex rel. E&R Constr. Co., Inc. v. Guy H. James Constr. Co.*, 390 F.Supp. at 1246.

133. 417 U.S. 116 (1974).

134. *F.D. Rich Co., Inc. v. United States ex rel. Indus. Lumber Co., Inc.*, 417 U.S. at 126.

135. *United States ex rel. Maddux Supply Co. v. St. Paul Fire & Marine Ins. Co.*, 86 F.3d 332, 336 (4th Cir. 1996); *United States ex rel. Southeastern Mun. Supply Co., Inc. v. National Union Fire Ins. Co. of Pittsburgh*, 876 F.2d 92, 93 (11th Cir. 1989); *United States ex rel. Reed v. Callahan*, 884 F.2d 1180, 1185-86 (9th Cir. 1989); *United States ex rel. C.J.C., Inc. v. Western States Mechanical Contractors, Inc.*, 834 F.2d at 1548; *United States ex rel. Carter Equip. Co. v. H.R. Morgan, Inc.*, 544 F.2d 1271 (5th Cir. 1977), *reh'g granted*, 554 F.2d 164 (5th Cir. 1977); *Travelers Indem. Co. v. United States ex rel. Western Steel Co.*, 362 F.2d 896, 899 (9th Cir. 1966); *cf. United States ex rel. A.V. De Blasio Constr., Inc. v. Mountain States Constr. Co.*, 588 F.2d 259, 263 (9th Cir. 1978) (where court refused to enforce contract provision awarding attorney's fees because both parties acted improperly); *United States ex rel. Big 4 Rents, Inc. v. Ogamba*, No. C-96-4301-VRW, 1997 U.S. Dist. LEXIS 10455, at *4 (N.D. Cal. July 14, 1997); *United States ex rel. McAmis Ind. of Oregon, Inc. v. M. Cutter Co.*, No. 95-446-FR, 1996 U.S. Dist. LEXIS 11269, at *3-4 (D. Or. July 24, 1996); *United States ex rel. D&P Corp. v. Transamerica Ins. Co.*, 881 F.Supp. at 1510; *Transamerica Premier Ins. Co. v. Ober*, 894 F.Supp. at 484-486.

of attorneys' fees against the Miller Act Surety.[136] Further, a state statute providing for recovery of attorneys' fees in a contract action, without more, is not sufficient to support such award.[137]

Attorneys' fees have been awarded in situations where the surety's conduct is such as to justify an award of fees as a punitive measure.[138] However, an award of fees against the surety must be based, at least in part, on the surety's "bad faith" conduct occurring during the litigation process, and will not be supported by prelitigation conduct alone.[139] To a great extent, since the *F.D. Rich* case, attorneys' fees are not commonly awarded in connection with a Miller Act payment bond claim.[140]

A very recent case, *United States ex rel. Cal's A/C & Electric v. The Famous Construction Corp.*,[141] considered the issue of whether the 1988 amendments to the Prompt Payment Act, particularly 31 U.S.C.A. § 3905(j), served as an amendment or addendum to the Miller Act, thereby overruling *F.D. Rich*, and other similar cases which hold that the Miller Act in effect preempts state attorneys' fee statutes. The court in *The Famous Construction Corp.* held that the Prompt Payment Act, 31 U.S.C.A. § 3905(j), in fact overruled *F. D. Rich* and its progeny, in that the Prompt Payment Act expressly allows for subcontractors on federal projects to sue for an award of attorneys' fees and penalties for late payment or non-payment under the payment bond, in the event state law provided for such a cause of action. Although the Louisiana statute at issue in fact expressly provided for penalties and attorneys' fees for late payment,[142] § 3905(j) does not support the court's interpretation.

10. Interest

The United States Supreme Court in *F.D. Rich* ruled that a cause of action under the Miller Act is a matter of federal law, and therefore the remedy, as well as the right, is a matter of federal law. Following that reasoning, courts deciding Miller Act payment bond claims find that an award

---

136. *United States ex rel. Krupp Steel Products, Inc. v. Aetna Ins. Co.*, 831 F.2d at 983-84; *United States ex rel. L.K.L. Assoc. v. Crockett & Wells Constr., Inc.*, 730 F.Supp. 1066 (D. Utah 1990) (although agreement between claimant and subcontractor contained attorney fee provision, court refused to award attorneys fees against Miller Act Surety where no attorney fee provision was contained in the general contract or the bond).

137. *F.D. Rich Co., Inc. v. United States ex rel. Indus. Lumber Co., Inc., 417 U.S. at 127; United States ex rel. Howell Crane Serv. v. United States Fid. & Guar. Co.*, 861 F.2d. 110, 112-14 (5th Cir. 1988)*; United States ex rel. D&P Corp. v. Transamerica Ins. Co.*, 881 F.Supp. at 1510; *Transamerica Premier Ins. Co. v. Ober*, 894 F.Supp. at 484-86; *United States ex rel. Cool Temp, Inc. v. All American Bldg. Systems, Inc.*, 857 F.Supp. 69, 70 (N.D. Ga. 1994).

138. *F.D. Rich Co., Inc. v. United States ex rel. Indus. Lumber Co., Inc.*, 417 U.S. at 129*; United States ex rel. Yonkers Constr. Co. v. Western Contracting Corp.*, 935 F.2d at 942. *United States ex rel. General Elec. Supply Co. v. Minority Elec. Co.*, 537 F.Supp. at 1092.

139. *United States ex rel. Ascher Bros. Co. v. American Home Assurance Co.*, No. 98-C-0995, 1999 WL 618216 (N.D. Ill. Aug. 9, 1999); *Towerridge, Inc. v. T.A.O., Inc.*, 111 F.3d 758 (10th Cir. 1997), *relying on Chambers v. NASCO, Inc.*, 501 U.S. 32 (1991); *see also Lamb Eng'g & Constr. Co. v. Nebraska Public Power Dist.*, 103 F.3d 1422, 1435-36 (8th Cir. 1997); *Galveston County Navigation Dist. No. 1 v. Hopson Towing Co., Inc.*, 92 F.3d 353, 357-60 (5th Cir. 1996); *McLarty v. United States*, 6 F.3d 545, 549 (8th Cir. 1993).

140. *See, e.g., United States ex rel. Leno v. Summit Constr. Co.*, 892 F.2d 788, 791 (9th Cir. 1989); *United States ex rel. Pensacola Constr. Co. v. St. Paul Fire & Marine Ins. Co.*, 710 F. Supp. at 639-40; *United States ex rel. D&P Corp. v. Transamerica Ins. Co.*, 881 F.Supp. at 1510; *Transamerica Premier Ins. Co. v. Ober*, 894 F.Supp. at 484-86.

141. 34 F. Supp. 2d 1042 (W.D.La. 1999).

142. La. Rev. Stat. Ann. § 9:2784.

of prejudgment interest is a matter of federal law, within the discretion of the court.[143] However, the Miller Act does not provide a standard for the award of pre-judgment interest. Therefore, most claims decided under the Miller Act look to state law to determine issues relating to prejudgment interest.[144] A contract provision providing for the payment of interest on past due sums will also typically support an award of interest.[145]

Although state law or contract provisions will generally result in an award of interest, a question remains as to when the interest begins to run. Some courts have ruled that interest will not begin to run until demand is made under the bond.[146] Other courts have held that interest begins to accrue at the time payment should have been made.[147]

B. Little Miller and Other Statutory and Common Law Payment Bonds

1. Labor

Claims for labor are covered by the express terms of most Little Miller Acts as well as most statutes governing private works payment bonds. If a bond principal defaults owing wages, then the

143. *Towerridge, Inc. v. TAO, Inc.*, 111 F.3d at 763-64; *United States ex rel. Bartec Industries, Inc. v. United Pacific Co.*, 976 F.2d 1274, 1279 (9th Cir. 1992); *United States ex rel. Lochridge-Priest, Inc. v. Con-Real Support Group, Inc.*, 950 F.2d at 289; *United States ex rel. Yonkers Constr. Co. v. Western Contracting Corp.*, 935 F.2d at 941-42; *United States v. American Mfrs. Mut. Cas. Co.*, 901 F.2d at 372-73; *United States ex rel. C.J.C., Inc. v. Western States Mechanical Contractors, Inc.*, 834 F.2d at 1541-42; *United States ex rel. Canion v. Randall & Blake*, 817 F.2d at 1193; *United States ex rel. Georgia Elec. Supply Co. v. United States Fid. & Guar. Co.*, 656 F.2d 993, 997 (5th Cir. 1981); *United States ex rel. Confederate Constr. Co. v. United States Fid. & Guar. Co.*,644 F.2d 747, 749 (8th Cir. 1981); *United States ex rel. A.V. DeBlasio Constr. Inc. v. Mountain States Constr. Co.*, 588 F.2d at 263; *United States ex rel. National Roofing Services, Inc. v. Lovering-Johnson, Inc.*, 53 F. Supp. 2d 1142, 1148 (D. Kan. 1999); *United States ex rel. Spight v. Dominique*, No. 95-3683, 1996 U.S. Dist. LEXIS 18096, at *7-8 (E.D. La. Nov. 25, 1996); *United States ex rel. Balf Co. v. Casle Corp.*, 895 F. Supp. 420, 429 (D. Conn. 1995); *United States ex rel. Delta Metals, Inc. v. R. M. Wells Co.*, 497 F. Supp. 541, 545 (S.D. Ga. 1980).

144. *Towerridge, Inc. v. TAO, Inc.*, 111 F.3d at 763-64; *United States ex rel. Bartec Industries, Inc. v. United Pacific Co.*, 976 F.2d at 1279; *United States ex rel. Lochridge-Priest, Inc. v. Con-Real Support Group, Inc.*, 950 F.2d at 289; *United States ex rel. Yonkers Constr. Co. v. Western Contracting Corp.*, 935 F.2d at 941-42; *United States v. American Mfrs. Mut. Cas. Co.*, 901 F.2d at 372-73; *United States ex rel. C.J.C., Inc. v. Western States Mechanical Contractors, Inc.*, 834 F.2d at 1541-42; *United States ex rel. Canion v. Randall & Blake*, 817 F.2d at 1193; *United States ex rel. Georgia Elec. Supply Co. v. United States Fid. & Guar. Co.*, 656 F.2d at 997; *United States ex rel. Confederate Constr. Co. v. United States Fid. & Guar. Co.*,644 F.2d at 749; *United States ex rel. A.V. DeBlasio Constr. Inc. v. Mountain States Constr. Co.*, 588 F.2d at 263; *United States ex rel. Spight v. Dominique*, 1996 U.S. Dist. LEXIS 18096, at *7-8; *United States ex rel. Balf Co. v. Casle Corp.*, 895 F. Supp. at 429; *United States ex rel. Delta Metals, Inc. v. R.M. Wells Co.*, 497 F. Supp. at 545.

145. *United States ex rel. Maddux Supply Co. v. St. Paul Fire & Marine Ins. Co.*, 86 F.3d at 336; *D&L Constr. Co. v. Triangle Elec. Supply Co.*, 332 F.2d 1009, 1013 (8th Cir. 1964); *United States ex rel. Big 4 Rents, Inc. v. Ogamba*, 1997 U.S. Dist. LEXIS 10455, at *4; *United States ex rel. Billows Elec. Supply Co., Inc. v. E.J.T. Constr. Co., Inc.*, 517 F.Supp. 1178, 1183 (E.D. Pa. 1981), *aff'd*, 688 F.2d 827 (3rd Cir. 1982).

146. *Golden West Constr. Co. v. United States ex rel. Bernadot*, 304 F.2d 753, 757 (l0th Cir. 1962); *American Auto Ins. Co. v. United States ex rel. Luce*, 269 F.2d 406, 412 (1st Cir. 1959) *vacated*, 269 F.2d 406 (1st Cir. 1959); *United States ex rel. Caldwell Foundry & Mach. Co. v. Texas Constr. Co.*, 237 F.2d 705, 707 (5th Cir. 1955); *United States ex rel. Groisser & Shlager Iron Works, Inc. v. Walsh*, 240 F.Supp. 1019, 1021 (N.D. N.Y. 1965).

147. *See, e.g.*, *United States ex rel. Astro Cleaning & Packaging Corp. v. Jamison Co.*, 425 F.2d 1281, 1284 (6th Cir. 1970); *Baker & Ford Co. v. United States ex rel. Urban Plumbing & Heating Co.*, 363 F.2d 605, 607 (9th Cir. 1966) ; *J.F. White Eng'g Corp. v. United States ex rel. Pittsburgh Plate Glass Co.*, 311 F.2d 410, 413 (10th Cir. 1962); *DPC General Contractors, Inc. v. Cobo Co., Inc.*, 715 F.Supp. 367, 370 (S.D. Fla. 1989).

wages will be covered by most statutory and common law payment bonds.[148] At least one court has held that a claim by a store which cashed payroll checks of a subcontractor's laborers was allowed under a public works payment bond, where the checks were returned for insufficient funds.[149] At least one court has also allowed a Little Miller payment bond claim for standby labor, even though the laborers had not actually performed work in furtherance of the project.[150]

A payment bond surety has also been found liable for acceleration costs incurred in meeting the project completion schedule.[151] Likewise, liability has been found under a payment bond for early completion bonuses, under the reasoning that labor and materials were included in the bonus work.[152]

Labor may also include architectural, surveying, and other professional services, where such work is provided at the job site, and for the bond principal or its subcontractor.[153] Claims by entities which furnish labor forces for the job site may also be allowed.[154] However, mere administrative personnel, who do not provide actual labor on the job site, may not be permitted to recover under the public works payment bond.[155]

a. Withholding Taxes. Where a surety makes payment under a payment bond of wages to a contractor's employees, the Internal Revenue Service (I.R.S.) may attempt to claim against the payment bond for federal withholding taxes. The surety will not typically be liable for withholding taxes, unless the terms of the bond or an applicable statute provide otherwise.[156]

b. Union Contributions. Coverage will also typically be found under public works and common law payment bonds for union contributions, and contributions to employee funds, such as

---

148. *J.W.D., Inc. v. Federal Ins. Co.*, 806 S.W.2d 327, 329 (Tex. App. 1991); *Employers Mut. Cas. Co. v. Walker*, 811 S.W.2d 270, 271 (Tex. App. 1991); *Myers v. Alta Constr. Co.*, 235 P.2d 1 (Cal. 1951); *cf. Greaig v. Park West Constr. Co.*, 637 P.2d 1079, 1081 (Ariz. Ct. App. 1981) (wherein court acknowledged wages were covered but denied claim because of untimely notice).

149. *J.W.D., Inc. v. Federal Ins. Co.*, 806 S.W.2d at 329. *But see Dysart Corp. v. Seaboard Sur. Co.*, 688 A.2d 306 (Conn. 1997) (pub which cashed payroll checks of subcontractor's employees was not entitled to claim under public works payment bond upon checks being dishonored. Negotiation of check by pub was not sufficient to assign employees' rights under the public works bond).

150. *Blakeslee Arpaia Chapman, Inc. v. EI Constructors, Inc.*, 687 A.2d 506, 519 (Conn. 1997).

151. *Tremack Co. v. Homestead Paving Co.*, 582 So.2d 26 (Fla. Dist. Ct. App. 3d Dist. 1991).

152. *Moore Bros. Constr. Co. v. Brown & Root, Inc.*, 962 F. Supp. 838 (E.D.Va. 1997).

153. *See, e.g., Peerless Ins. Co. v. Board of County Comm'rs for Prince George's County ex rel. Ben Dyer Assoc., Inc.*, 237 A.2d 15, 17-18 (Md. 1968); *Myers v. Alta Constr. Co.*, 235 P.2d at 3.

154. *Contractors Labor Pool, Inc. v. Westway Contractors, Inc.*, 53 Cal. App. 4th 152 (Cal. Ct. App. 1997); *Myers v. Alta Constr. Co.*, 235 P.2d at 3.

155. *See R.E. Monks Constr. Co. v. Aetna Cas. & Sur. Co.*, No. 1 CA-CV-96-0477, 1997 U.S. Dist. LEXIS 150, at *10 (Ariz. Ct. App. Aug. 26, 1997); *Primo Team, Inc. v. Blake Constr. Co., Inc.*, 4 Cal. Rptr. 2d 701, 706 (Cal. Ct. App. 1992).

156. *Trinity Universal Ins. Co. v. United States*, 382 F.2d 317, 319 (5th Cir. 1967); *United States v. Hill*, 368 F.2d 617, 624 (5th Cir. 1966) ; *United States v. Maryland Cas. Co.*, 323 F.2d 473, 474-76 (5th Cir. 1963); *United States v. Crosland Constr. Co.*, 217 F.2d 275, 277 (4th Cir. 1954); *United States v. Commonwealth of Pa.*, 349 F.Supp. 1370, 1388 (E.D. Pa. 1972); *Miller v. Housing Auth. of New Orleans*, 190 So.2d 75, 79 (La. 1966).

health and welfare funds.[157] The basis for recovery of these items is that such payments are required in order for the employees to be paid in full for their labor.[158]

An issue which commonly arises in connection with claims for union contributions under state public works statutes (and states' mechanic's lien laws) is ERISA preemption. Payment bond sureties have taken the position that claims made under state public works statutes are preempted by ERISA. The trend in most states (with regard to most generally applicable state statutes as well as public works statutes) is to deny preemption, on the grounds that such statutes have only a tenuous or remote connection to ERISA plans, and do not result in the situation ERISA preemption was intended to guard against.[159]

Where sureties have recently attempted to assert an ERISA preemption defense to public works or other payment bond claims, such defenses have in most instances been rejected.[160] In denying the preemption defense, courts generally rely on the fact that lawsuits to enforce payment bond claims are common-law actions on contracts, and the public works bond statutes under which the claims are brought function without reference to ERISA, do not conflict with ERISA or affect any of the rights or duties relating to ERISA plans.[161]

2. Materials

Court decisions interpreting coverage of state public works payment bonds (as well as many states' public works and other statutes) have followed the trend in allowing a more expansive right

157. *Trustees for Michigan Laborers' Health Care Fund v. Warranty Builders, Inc.*, 921 F.Supp. 471, 473-75 (E.D. Mich. 1996), *aff'd*, 137 F.3d 427 (6th Cir. 1998); *Williams v. Ashland Eng'g Co., Inc.*, 863 F.Supp. 46, 48 (D. Mass. 1994), *aff'd*, 45 F.3d 588 (1st Cir. 1995); *Indiana Carpenters Cen. & W. Indiana Pension Fund v. Seaboard Sur. Co.*, 601 N.E. 2d 352, 354-56 (Ind. Ct. App. 1992); *Arizona Laborers, Teamsters & Cement Masons Local 395 Health & Welfare Trust Fund v. New Pueblo Constructors, Inc.*, 640 P.2d 209, 210 (Ariz. Ct. App. 1982); *Newark Laborers' Pension-Welfare Funds v. Commercial Union Ins. Co. of N.Y.*, 312 A.2d 649 (N.J. Super. Ct. App. Div. 1973); *see also*, Mass. Gen. Laws Ch. 149 § 29, N.Y. State Fin Law § 137-5(b). *But see State ex rel. Lawrence v. The American. Ins. Co.*, 559 A.2d 1247, 1250 (Del. 1989) (holding that fringe benefits are not wages and thus not within coverage of the public works payment bond).

158. *Trustees for Michigan Laborers' Health Care Fund v. Warranty Builders, Inc.*, 921 F.Supp. at 474; *Indiana Carpenters Cent. & W. Indiana Pension Fund v. Seaboard* Sur. Co., 601 N.E.2d at 354-56.

159. *See Board of Trustees of Operating Eng'rs Local 825 Fund Service Facilities v. L.B.S. Constr. Co., Inc.*, 691 A.2d 339 (N.J. 1997) for detailed historical analysis and development of ERISA preemption issues.

160. *Ragan v. Tri-County Excavating, Inc.*, 62 F.3d 501, 509-12 (3rd Cir. 1995); *Cement and Concrete Workers District Council Welfare Fund v. Frascone,* 68 F. Supp. 2d 166 (E.D.N.Y. 1999); *Trustees for Michigan Laborers' Health Care Fund v. Warranty Builders, Inc.*, 921 F.Supp. at 479; *International Union of Operating Eng'rs Local 57 v. Seaboard Sur. Co.*, 946 F.Supp. 141, 145-47 (D.R.I. 1996); *Board of Trustees of Operating Eng'rs Local 825 Fund Service Facilities v. L.B.S. Constr. Co., Inc.*, 691 A.2d at 347; *Eacott v. Insurance Co. of No. America*, 673 A.2d 587 (Conn. App. Ct. 1996); *Carpenters Local 261 Health & Welfare Fund v. National Union Fire Ins.*, 686 A.2d 1373 (Pa. Commw. Ct. 1996) *appeal denied*, 694 A.2d. 623 (Pa. 1997); *Hawaii Laborers' Trust Funds v. Maui Prince Hotel*, 918 P.2d 1143 (Hawaii 1996) (Hawaii mechanic's and materialman's lien law was not preempted by ERISA). *But see Operating Engineers Pension Trust v. Insurance Co. of the West*, 42 Cal. Rptr. 2d 1 (Cal. Ct. App. 1995) (holding that employee benefit trusts' claim against California public works payment bond for fringe benefit payments to trusts was preempted by ERISA); *Williams v. Ashland Eng'g Co., Inc.*, 863 F.Supp. at 48-50 (claim by Trustee of employee benefit plan for employer contributions, against public works payment bond, specifically securing payment for employer contributions to health and welfare funds among other things, was preempted by ERISA); *Puget Sound Elec. Workers Health & Welfare Trust Fund v. Merit Co.*, 870 P.2d 960, 962-64 (Wash. 1994).

161. *Board of Trustees of Operating Eng'rs Local 825 Fund Service Facilities v. L.B.S. Constr. Co., Inc.*, 691 A.2d at 346; *Trustees for Michigan Laborers' Health Care Fund v. Warranty Builders, Inc.*, 921 F.Supp. at 477.

of recovery for materials consumed or used in the construction process.[162] These courts and their decisions recognize that although certain items may never be incorporated into the final structure, they are nonetheless necessary for the accomplishment of the construction, and the performance of the contract.[163]

Therefore, in addition to materials which are obviously incorporated into the final structure, items for which claimants have been allowed recovery under Little Miller Act or other statutory and common law payment bonds, include fuel,[164] tires,[165] parts,[166] landscape materials and plants,[167] materials used in form work,[168] groceries or food,[169] and transportation.[170]

Another issue often arising in payment bond claims for materials concerns diversion of materials or claims for materials not actually used on the project. The general rule is where the claimant in good faith believed that the material was intended for the bonded project, the claimant will be entitled to recovery, even where the materials are not delivered to or incorporated into the job site.[171]

---

162. *See, e.g.*, *Webb Elec. Co. of Florida, Inc. v. New Thought Finishing, Inc.*, No. 92-2563, 1995 U.S. Dist. LEXIS 6663 at *11-13 (E.D. La. May 4, 1995); *Key Constructors, Inc. v. H&M Gas Co*, 537 So. 2d 1318, 1323 (Miss. 1989); *Houston General Ins. Co. v. Maples*, 375 So. 2d 1012, 1015 (Miss. 1979); *Slagle-Johnson Lumber Co., Inc. v. Landis Constr. Co.*, 379 So.2d 479, 482 (La. 1979) (overruling *H.R. Hayes Lumber Co. v. McConnell*, 146 So. 14 (La. 1932) which denied coverage for materials indirectly used in construction); *United States Fid. & Guar. Co. v. Miller*, 549 S.W.2d 316, 319 (Ky. Ct. App. 1977); *City of Weippe ex rel. Les Schwab Tire Centers, Inc. v. Yarno*, 528 P.2d 201 (Idaho 1974); *Commonwealth ex rel. Walters Tire Service, Inc. v. National Union Fire Ins. Co.*, 252 A.2d 593, 594-95 (Pa. 1969); *Dial v. Freeto Constr. Co.*, 381 P.2d 363, 365 (Kan. 1963).

163. *Western Cas. & Sur. Co. v. Stribling Bros. Mach. Co.*, 139 So. 2d 838 (Miss. 1962); *Seaboard Sur. Co. v. Bosarge*, 84 So.2d 517, 519 (Miss. 1956); *George T. Miller Constr. Co. v. Standard Oil Co.*, 185 N.E. 639 (Ind. 1933).

164. *Key Constructors, Inc. v. H&M Gas Co.*, 537 So.2d at 1321; *Houston General Ins. Co. v. Maples*, 375 So. 2d at 1015; *Dial v. Freeto Constr. Co.*, 381 P.2d at 365; *Western Cas. & Sur. Co. v. Stribling Bros. Mach. Co.*, 139 So.2d at 841; *George T. Miller Constr. Co. v. Standard Oil Co.*, 185 N.E. at 640; *see also* Ark. Stat. Ann. § 22-9-401, Iowa Code § 573.1; La. R.S. 38.2242.A.(1); Mo. Rev. Stat. § 107.170 (1993); N.Y. State Fin-Law § 137-5(a); N.C. Gen. Stat. § 44A-25(5).

165. *Houston General Ins. Co. v. Maples*, 375 So. 2d at 1015 (court indicated claim for tires would be allowed if they were substantially consumed on the project); *City of Weippe ex rel. Les Schwab Tire Centers, Inc. v. Yarno*, 528 P.2d at 204; *Commonwealth ex. rel. Walters Tire Serv., Inc. v. National Union Fire Ins. Co.*, 252 A.2d at 594-95.

166. *Mountaineer Euclid, Inc. v. Western Cas. & Sur. Co.*, 250 N.E.2d 768, 772 (Ohio Ct. App. 1969).

167. *A.G. Gaston Constr. Co., Inc. v. Hicks*, 674 So. 2d at 547.

168. *Webb Elec. Co. of Florida, Inc. v. New Thought Finishing, Inc.*, 1995 U.S. Dist. LEXIS 6663 at *12-13; *Slagle-Johnson Lumber Co., Inc. v. Landis Constr. Co.*, 379 So.2d at 482-483; *Empire State Sur. Co. v. City of Des Moines*, 132 N.W. 837 (Iowa 1911); *see also* Iowa Code § 573.1.

169. *Federal Paving Co. v. Raschka*, 141 N.E. 644 (Ind. App. 1923) (claim for feed for horses used in construction work allowed); *see also* Ark. Stat. Ann. § 22-9-401; Mo. Rev. Stat § 107.170 (1993).

170. *Metropolitan Cas. Ins. Co. of N.Y. v. Natural Rock Asphalt Corp.*, 6 N.E.2d 739 (Ind. App. 1937); *Indemnity Ins. Co. of No. America v. Portsmouth Ice, Coal & Bldg. Material Co.*, 172 N.E. 152, 153 (Ohio 1930).

171. *See Syro Steel Co. v. Eagle Constr. Co., Inc.*, 460 S.E.2d 371 (S.C. 1995); *Moore Elec. Supply, Inc. v. Ward*, 450 S.E.2d 96 (S.C. Ct. App. 1994); *Key Constructors, Inc. v. H&M Gas Co.*, 537 So.2d at 1323-24; *C.C.&T. Constr. Co., Inc. v. Coleman Bros. Corp.*, 391 N.E.2d 1256, 1258-59 (Mass. App. Ct. 1979); *Solite Masonry Units Corp. v. Piland Constr. Co., Inc.*, 232 S.E.2d 759, 761-62 (Va. 1977); *cf. American Masons' Supply Co. v. F.W. Brown Co.*, 384 A.2d 378 (Conn. 1978); *See also supra* Chapter 4.

a. Specially Fabricated Materials. There is no indication that claims by suppliers of specially fabricated materials will be treated differently from claims for materials generally.[172] Some states' public works and private works statutes specifically reference specially fabricated materials,[173] often to make clear that where materials are specially fabricated for a particular project, they need not be delivered or incorporated into the work in order to have a right to payment.[174]

3. Equipment

a. Capital Purchase. Payment bond claims relating to equipment may arise out of nonpayment of the purchase price for the equipment, or nonpayment of the rental charges for the equipment. Where the claimant seeks recovery of the purchase price for equipment purchased and owned by the contractor or subcontractor, such claim will generally not be allowed under most public works and other statutory and common law payment bonds, since the equipment purchased will be viewed as a capital investment by the contractor, to be used on projects in addition to the bonded project.[175] When considering claims for the purchase price of equipment, courts will generally determine whether the equipment is substantially consumed on the bonded project.[176]

b. Rental. Claims for unpaid rental charges for equipment are generally allowed under state public works bonds,[177] as well as under private works and common law bonds.[178] However, courts in some states have declined to follow the general rule allowing recovery of rentals.[179] Some states'

---

172. *See, e.g., Webb Elec. Co. of Florida, Inc. v. New Thought Finishing, Inc.*, 1995 U.S. Dist. LEXIS 6663 at *8-13.

173. *See, e.g.*, Haw. Rev. St. § 507-41; Mass. Gen. Laws Ch. 149 § 29; Tex. Govt. Code Ch. 2253.

174. *See, e.g., C.C.&T. Constr. Co., Inc. v. Coleman Bros. Corp.*, 391 N.E.2d at 1259. *But see Hope's Arch. Products, Inc. v. Lundy's Constr., Inc.*, 762 F.Supp. 1430, 1433-34 (D. Kan. 1991), *aff'd* 1 F.3d 1249 (10th Cir. 1993).

175. *Public Water Supply Dist. No. 3 ex rel. Victor L. Phillips Co., Inc. v. Reliance Ins. Co.*, 708 S.W.2d 190, 193 (Mo. Ct. App. 1986); *Montgomery v. Southern Sur.*, 162 N.E. 31 (Ind. App. 1928). *But see Illinois State Toll Hwy. Comm'n ex rel. Patten Tractor & Equip. Co.*, 186 N.E.2d 390 (Ill. Ct. App. 1962) (wherein court held public works payment bond surety liable for purchase price of equipment where language of bond was broader than statute and expressly guaranteed payment for machinery furnished for work).

176. *Public Water Supply Dist. No. 3 ex rel. Victor L. Phillips Co., Inc. v. Reliance Ins. Co.*, 708 S.W.2d at 193; *Montgomery v. Southern Sur.*, 162 N.E. at 33; *see also, Commonwealth ex rel. Walters Tire Serv., Inc. v. National Union Fire Ins. Co.*, 252 A.2d at 594-595; *Illinois State Toll Hwy. Comm'n ex rel. Patten Tractor & Equip. Co.*, 186 N.E.2d at 397.

177. *See, e.g., Blinne Contracting Co., Inc. v. Bobby Goins Enter., Inc.*, 715 F. Supp. 1044, 1046 (D. Kan. 1989); *Public Water Supply Dist. No. 3 ex rel. Victor L. Phillips Co., Inc. v. Reliance Ins. Co.*, 708 S.W.2d at 191-192; *McGee Steel Co. v. State ex rel. McDonald Indust. Alaska, Inc.*, 723 P.2d 611, 616-17 (Alaska 1986); *Houston General Ins. Co. v, Maples*, 375 So.2d at 1016; *Arizona Gunite Builders, Inc. v. Continental Cas. Co.*, 459 P.2d 724, 727 (Ariz. 1969); *Seldon v. S&S Aggregates Co.*, 441 S.W.2d 950, 953 (Tex. Civ. App. 1969); *McElhose v. Universal Sur. Co.*, 158 N.W.2d 228, 233 (Neb. 1968); *Mississippi Road Supply Co. v. Western Cas. & Sur. Co.*, 150 So.2d 847 (Miss. 1963); *Bower v. Tebbs*, 314 P.2d 731, 739 (Mont. 1957).

178. *See, e.g., Symons Corp. v. Insurance Co. of No. America*, 380 S.E.2d 550, 552 (N.C. Ct. App. 1989); *Forest Services, Inc. v. Fid. & Cas. Co. of N.Y.*, 171 S.E.2d 743, 745 (Ga. Ct. App. 1969); *United Bonding Ins. Co. v. M.D. Moody & Sons, Inc.*, 213 So.2d 263, 264 (Fla. Dist. Ct. App. 1968). *But see Western Cas. & Sur. Co. v. Stribling Bros. Mach. Co.*, 139 So.2d at 841 (where court held that equipment rental was not covered by terms of bond).

179. *See, e.g., Dow-Par, Inc. v. Lee Corp.*, 644 N.E.2d 150, 154 (Ind. Ct. App. 1994); *Rish v. Theo Bros. Constr. Co.*, 237 S.E.2d 61, 63 (S.C. 1977); *Williams Constr. Co. v. Construction Equip., Inc.*, 251 A.2d 864, 868-69 (Md. 1969).

statutes expressly include equipment rentals within the scope of the bond's coverage.[180] In addition to the governing statute, courts will also usually look to the express language of the bond in making a determination of coverage.[181]

Claims have also been allowed for rental payments where equipment is on the job site, but sitting idle, through no fault of the equipment supplier.[182]

*c. **Repairs.*** As with bond claims for materials or equipment, the focus in a claim for repairs will generally be one of "substantial consumption." In other words, did the repairs result from the normal and expected wear and tear and consumption of the equipment or tools used on the particular project, or are the repairs in the nature of capital improvements to the contractor's equipment.[183] Courts construing claims for repairs under state public works and other payment bonds generally allow repair costs if the equipment or other item was "consumed" in the bonded construction work.[184] However, the provisions of the governing statute will usually be controlling.[185] Where the rental contract provides for reimbursement of costs to repair rented equipment, payment bond coverage may exist for such repair costs.[186]

4. Services

The analysis for determining whether a claim for certain services will be allowed under a payment bond is similar to the analysis of claims for labor or materials. Freight charges, or costs of transporting materials or equipment to the bonded job site have been the subject of payment bond claims for services. Whether claims for transportation charges will be allowed under various states' public works or other payment bonds depends on the provisions of the underlying contract, as well as the terms of the bond and any applicable statutes.[187] Claims for the cost of transporting materials

---

180. *See, e.g.*, Neb. Rev. Stat. § 52-118.02; Ariz. Rev. Stat. § 32-1152(d); Mass. Gen. Laws Ch. 149, § 29; Cal. Civ. Code § 3110; Ark. Code Ann. § 22-9-401; Colo. Rev. Stat. §§ 38-26-105, 38-26-106; Haw. Rev. Stat. § 507-41; La. Rev. Stat. Ann. 38: 2242.A.(1); Me. Rev. Stat. Ann. tit. 14 § 871.3.B; N.Y. State Fin. Law § 137-5(a); N.C. Gen. Stat. § 44A-25(5).

181. *See, e.g., Owsley v. Henderson,* 45 S.E.2d 263, 265 (N.C. 1947); *United States Fid. & Guar. Co. v. Feenaughty Mach. Co.,* 85 P.2d 1085, 1090 (Wash. 1939).

182. *Blakeslee Arpaia Chapman, Inc. v. EI Constructors, Inc.*, 687 A.2d at 519; *Symons Corp. v. Insurance Co. of No. America*, 380 S.E.2d at 552 (equipment was on the job and ready to be used when needed).

183. *See, e.g., McGee Steel Co. v. State ex rel. McDonald Indus. Alaska, Inc.*, 723 P.2d at 618; *Sim's Crane Serv., Inc. v. Reliance Ins. Co.,* 514 F.Supp. 1033, 1045 (S.D. Ga. 1981), *aff'd,* 667 F.2d 30 (11th Cir. 1982); *Cecil I. Walker Mach. Co. v. Stauben, Inc.*, 230 S.E.2d 818, 821 (W. Va. 1976); *Clifton v. Norden,* 226 N.W. 940, 941-942 (Minn. 1929).

184. *Sim's Crane Serv., Inc. v. Reliance Ins. Co.,* 514 F.Supp. at 1044-1045; *Cecil I. Walker Mach. Co. v. Stauben, Inc.*, 230 S.E. 2d at 821; *Nelson v. Hagen,* 146 N.W. 2d 873 (N.D. 1966); *McGee Steel Co. v. State ex rel. McDonald Indus. Alaska, Inc.*, 723 P.2d at 618 (repairs to equipment covered by public works bond if there was a reasonable expectation that equipment would be substantially consumed on project).

185. *See, e.g., Mountaineer Euclid, Inc. v. Western Cas. & Sur. Co.,* 250 N.E. 2d at 772.

186. *R. J. Russo Trucking & Excavating, Inc. v. Pennsylvania Resourse Systems, Inc.*, 573 N.Y.S.2d 95, 99 (N.Y. App. Div. 1991); *See also Norquip Rental Corp. v. Sky Steel Erectors, Inc.,*, 854 P.2d 1185 (Ariz. Ct. App. 1993).

187. *See, e.g., State ex rel. George J. Shaw Hauling Co. v. Bob Eldridge Constr. Co.,* 397 S.W.2d 7, 9 (Mo. Ct. App. 1965); *Thompson Transport Co. v. Middlestates Constr. Co.,* 397 P. 2d 368 (Kan. 1964) *rev'd on other grounds,* 403 P.2d 999 (Kan. 1965); *Indemnity Ins. Co. of No. America v. Portsmouth Ice, Coal & Bldg. Material Co.,*,172 N.E. at 153.

to the job site have been allowed under state public works bonds.[188] Claims for transporting equipment have been both allowed[189] and disallowed.[190] Claims for the cost of storage of materials have been allowed.[191]

Design and engineering services have also been the subject of payment bond claims. For the most part, services of engineers, surveyors, or others performing similar consulting or design work for the prime contractor or a subcontractor will be entitled to claims under the relevant payment bond.[192]

5. Insurance Premiums

Claims against state public works and other bonds for recovery of liability or workers' compensation insurance premiums often will not be allowed since insurance constitutes neither labor nor material.[193] However, some states public works statutes expressly provide coverage for unpaid insurance premiums.[194]

6. Loans

Claims by lenders or creditors who loan or advance money to a contractor or subcontractor will typically not be allowed, even where such funds are used to pay for labor or materials, under most state public works payment bonds,[195] and most other payment bonds.[196]

---

188. *See, e.g.*, *Metropolitan Cas. Ins. Co. of N.Y. v. Natural Rock Asphalt Corp.*, 6 N.E.2d at 740; *Indemnity Ins. Co. of No. America v. Portsmouth Ice, Coal & Bldg. Material Co.*, 172 N.E. at 153; *Franzen v. Southern Sur. Co.*, 246 P. 30 (Wyo. 1926). *But see City of Alpena v. Murray Co.*, 123 N.W. 1128 (Mich. 1909).

189. *State ex rel. Don's Heavy Hauling, Inc. v. Frank D. Malone Constr. Co.*, 129 N.W.2d 900, 902 (S.D. 1964); *National Auto. & Cas. Ins. Co. of Los Angeles v. Wick Adair Trucks*, 292 P.2d 403, 405 (Okla. 1955); *cf. State ex rel. George J. Shaw Hauling Co. v. Bob Eldridge Constr. Co.*, 397 S.W.2d at 9.

190. *Hamilton v. Whittaker*, 186 P.2d 609, 610-11 (Wash. 1947).

191. *Hartford Acc. & Indem. Co. v. District of Columbia*, 441 A.2d 969, 973 (D.C. 1982).

192. *See, e.g.*, *Herbert S. Newman & Partners v. CFC Constr.*, 674 A.2d 1313, 1317 (Conn. 1996); *Peerless Ins. Co. v. Board of County Comm'rs for Prince George's County ex. rel. Ben Dyer Assoc., Inc.*, 237 A.2d at 17-18; *Kline v. Federal Ins. Co.*, 152 N.E.2d 911, 912-14 (Ohio Com. Pl. 1958); *Myers v. Alta Constr. Co.*, 235 P.2d at 3.

193. *See, e.g.*, *Trinity Universal Ins. Co. v. Patterson*, 570 S.W.2d 475, 477 (Tex. Civ. App. 1978) ; *Santa Rosa County ex rel. J.E. Daniels, Inc. v. Raymond Blanton Constr. Co.*, 138 So.2d 518, 520 (Fla. Dist. Ct. App. 1962); *Maryland Cas. Co. v. City of Seattle*, 118 P.2d 416, 417-18 (Wash. 1941); *Anderson v. United States Fid. & Guar. Co.*, 104 P.2d 906, 907 (N.M. 1940). *But see State ex rel. Fager & Friesen Ins. Agency v. Storms-Green Constr. Co.*, 382 S.W. 2d 812 (Mo. Ct. App. 1964); *Phoenix Indem. Co. v. Board of Pub. Instruction of Alachua County*, 114 So.2d 478 (Fla. Dist. Ct. App. 1959); *cf. CIT Group/Equip. Fin., Inc. v. Horizon Potash Corp.*, 884 P.2d 821 (N.M. Ct. App. 1994).

194. Ark. Code Ann. § 22-9-401; Iowa Code § 573.1; Minn. Stat. § 574.26, sub d.1(b); Mo. Rev. Stat. § 107.176; *See also, State ex rel. Mountain States Mut. Cas. Co. v. KNC, Inc.*, 740 P.2d 690 (N.M. 1987).

195. *Primo Team, Inc. v. Blake Constr. Co., Inc.*, 4 Cal. Rptr. 2d at 707-08; *Integon Indem. Corp. v. Bull*, 842 S.W.2d 1, 4 (Ark. 1992), *citing Ayres & Graves v. Ellis*, 49 S.W.2d 1056 (Ark. 1932); *Newport Trust Co. v. Susi*, 134 A.2d 543, 547-48 (Me. 1957); *see also, State ex rel. Fager & Friesen Ins. Agency v. Storms-Green Constr. Co.*, 382 S.W.2d at 815-17; *Bower v. Tebbs*, 314 P.2d at 736.

196. *Wasatch Bank of Pleasant Grove v. Surety Ins. Co. of Cal.*, 703 P.2d 298, 299-300 (Utah 1985); *United States ex rel. First Continental Nat'l Bank & Trust Co. v. Western Contracting Corp.*, 341 F.2d 383, 387-88 (8th Cir. 1965); *Bank of Auburn v. United States Fid. & Guar. Co.*, 295 F.2d 641 (5th Cir. 1961).

7. Contract Damages

a. Delay Damages. As with other bond claim issues, courts interpreting coverage for delay damages under public works and other payment bonds often look to case law interpreting the Miller Act for guidance. Therefore, many court decisions regarding coverage of state public works payment bonds have followed the holdings under the Miller Act denying claims for delay damages, reasoning that delay damages are not part of the cost of the materials and labor furnished.[197] Other courts follow the more recent Miller Act case holdings, allowing claims for increased labor and material costs incurred as a result of delays.[198]

b. Lost Profits. As claims for lost profits under the Miller Act are generally denied, claims against most states' Little Miller Act payment bonds are also denied.[199] However, where the profits claimed are part of the contract price of work actually performed by the claimant, they will likely be allowed against the payment bond.[200]

8. Extra Contractual Damages

a. Quantum Meruit/Extras. Although claims for extra work, falling outside the claimant's contract, are permitted under the liberal interpretation of public works statutes,[201] and even include profits on such extra work,[202] at least one court has held that the surety is not liable for work falling outside a claimant's subcontract, where the claimant failed to obtain written authorization for such work or a written change order as required by its subcontract.[203]

b. Punitive Damages. The payment bond surety will not generally be liable for statutory or other punitive damages imposed against its bond principal, or on the basis of the bond principal's conduct.[204]

---

197. *W.S.A., Inc. v. Stratton,* 680 F.Supp. 375, 377 (S.D. Fla. 1988); *Lite-Air Products, Inc. v. Fidelity & Deposit Co. of Maryland,* 437 F.Supp. 801 (E.D. Pa. 1977); *American Home Assur. Co. v. Larkin Gen. Hosp'l, Ltd.*, 593 So.2d 195 (Fla. 1992); *Salvino Steel & Iron Works, Inc. v. Fletcher & Sons, Inc.*, 580 A.2d 853, 856 (Pa. Super. Ct. 1990).

198. *Mai Steel Service, Inc. v. Blake Constr. Co.*, 981 F.2d at 420-421; *Hartford Acc. & Indem. Co. v. District of Columbia*, 441 A.2d at 972-73; *General Fed. Constr., Inc. v. D.R. Thomas, Inc.*, 451 A.2d 1250, 1256-58 (Md. 1982).

199. *Blakeslee Arpaia Chapman, Inc. v. EI Constructors, Inc.*, 687 A.2d at 517-18; *Herzog Contracting Corp. v. A&S Constr. Co.*, 751 P.2d 690, 692 (N.M. 1988); *Blinne Contracting Co., Inc. v. Bobby Goins Enter., Inc.*, 715 F.Supp. at 1047; *General Fed. Constr., Inc. v. D.R. Thomas, Inc.*, 451 A.2d at 1258; *Lite-Air Products, Inc. v. Fidelity & Deposit Co. of Maryland*, 437 F.Supp. at 803. *But see Downey, Inc. v. Bradley Center Corp.*, 524 N.W.2d 915 (Wis. Ct. App. 1994) (wherein court found that common law payment bond claimant was entitled to recover lost profits suffered on unrelated projects being performed by claimant as a result of delay by the contractor, on grounds that such consequential damages were sufficiently foreseeable).

200. *R. J. Russo Trucking & Excavating, Inc. v. Pennsylvania Resourse Systems, Inc.*, 573 N.Y.S.2d at 97-98.

201. *Blakeslee Arpaia Chapman, Inc. v. EI Constructors, Inc.*, 687 A.2d at 517-18; *O'Neil-Dunham, Inc. v. Pearson*, 137 S.E.2d 556, 557 (Ga. Ct. App. 1964).

202. *Blakeslee Arpaia Chapman, Inc. v. EI Constructors, Inc.*, 687 A.2d at 517-18.

203. *Dawson Corp. v. National Union Fire Ins. Co. of Pittsburgh, Pa.*, 666 A.2d 604 (N.J. Sup. Ct. App. Div. 1995).

204. *Strong v. C.I.R., Inc.*, 516 N.W.2d 719, 723 (Wis. 1994); *Ferris v. Haymore*, 967 F.2d 946, 953-54 (4th Cir. 1992); *Dean v. Seco Elec. Co.*, 519 N.E.2d 837, 804-41 (Ohio 1988); *State ex rel. Nichols v. Safeco Ins. Co. of America*, 671 P.2d 1151, 1156 (N.M. Ct. App. 1983); *Rogers v. Speros Constr. Co.*, 580 P.2d 750, 754 (Ariz. Ct. App.

*c. **Negligence.*** Damage resulting from a contractor's negligence will generally not be allowed against a payment bond.[205] However, such damages may be allowed if they are expected.[206] Damage resulting from a contractor's negligence may also be allowed against the surety if the payment bond expressly secures against damage resulting from negligence.[207]

9. Attorneys' Fees

Many states' public works statutes expressly provide for the recovery of attorneys' fees by a prevailing claimant and/or a prevailing party.[208] Where the controlling statute does not authorize an award of attorneys' fees, unless the conditions required by a particular state for an award of attorneys' fees are met, attorneys' fees will typically not be awarded.[209] Each state's statutes and case law governing public works payment bonds, as well as case law and statutes pertaining to attorneys' fee awards, must be reviewed in order to determine whether or not attorneys' fees are recoverable by the claimant or other prevailing party.[210]

Claims for attorneys' fees under other statutory or common law payment bonds are generally governed by the terms of the bond, or by the particular state's statute or common law pertaining to recovery of attorneys' fees in contract actions.[211]

10. Interest

Some state's public works and private works statutes expressly provide for pre-judgment interest.[212] Contract provisions requiring payment of interest on past due sums will typically be

1978); *Coates v. United States Fid. & Guar. Co.*, 525 S.W.2d 654, 657 (Mo. Ct. App. 1975).

205. *McGee Steel Co. v. State ex rel. McDonald Indus. Alaska, Inc.*, 723 P.2d at 618; *General Fed. Constr., Inc. v. D.R. Thomas, Inc.*, 451 A.2d at 1256-57.

206. *McGee Steel Co. v. State ex rel. McDonald Indus. Alaska, Inc.*, 723 P.2d at 618.

207. *Travelers Indem. Co. v. Hous. Auth. of City of Miami*, 256 So. 2d 230, 234 (Fla. Dist. Ct. App. 1972); *American Radiator & Standard Sanitary Corp. v. Albany Mun. Hous. Comm'n*, 441 S.W.2d 433, 434-35 (Ky. 1969).

208. *See, e.g.*, Ariz. Rev. Stat. § 34-222-F; Cal. Civ. Code §§ 3248(b), 3250; Conn. Gen. Stat. § 49-42(a); Fla. Stat. Ann. §§ 255.05, 627.756; Idaho Code § 54-1929; La. Rev. Stat. Ann. § 38: 2246; Mass. Gen. Laws Ch. 149, § 29; Minn. Stat. § 574.26, Subd.2; Miss. Code Ann. § 31-5-57; Mont. Code Ann. § 18-2-207; Neb. Rev. Stat. § 44-359; N.Y. State Fin. Law § 137.4(c); N.C. Gen. Stat. § 44A-35; Or. Rev. Stat. § 742.061; Tex. Gov. Code Ch. 2253.074; Utah Code Ann. § 63-56-38(5).

209. *See, e.g., Chadwick-BaRoss, Inc. v. T. Buck Constr., Inc.*, 627 A.2d 532 (Me. 1993).

210. *See, e.g., Newark Laborers' Pension-Welfare Funds v. Commercial Union Ins. Co. of N.Y.*, 312 A.2d at 653-54 (in which court held that costs and attorneys fees incurred in enforcement of bond claim would fall within public works payment bond coverage in order to provide workmen relief intended by the statute); *Liton Gen. Eng'g Contractor, Inc. v. United Pac. Ins.*, 20 Cal. Rptr. 2d 200 (Cal. Ct. App. 1993) (in which court held surety liable for claimant's attorneys fees incurred in arbitration between claimant and principal to which surety was not a party, on grounds that the arbitration proceeding was integral part of action on the bond and public works statute awarded fees to prevailing party in suit on a payment bond).

211. *See, e.g., T&R Painting Constr., Inc. v. St. Paul Fire & Marine Ins. Co.*, 29 Cal. Rptr. 2d 199 (Cal. Ct. App. 1994); *Martin v. Hartford Acc. & Indem. Co.*, 316 S.E.2d 126 (N.C. Ct. App. 1984); *Faulkner Concrete Pipe Co. v. United States Fid. & Guar. Co.*, 218 So.2d 1 (Miss. 1968).

212. *See, e.g.* Cal. Civ. Code § 3250; Colo. Rev. Stat. § 38-26-106; Conn. Gen. Stat. § 49-42(a); Or. Rev. Stat. 742.061.

enforceable against a payment bond surety.[213] Likewise, the bond provisions may include coverage for interest.[214] Where the contract and bond are silent, each state's case law and statutes governing awards of interest on, for example, contract actions or liquidated/unliquidated amounts, must be examined.[215] If interest is allowed against the bond, each state's governing law must also be examined to determine when the interest begins to run.[216]

IV. *Conclusion*

When determining whether various types of claims are covered by payment bonds, the critical issue is usually whether the subject claim is for labor or material furnished in the prosecution of the work under the bonded contract. However, as seen from the above discussion, what constitutes labor or material can vary widely depending on the governing statute and the jurisdiction in which the claim is being asserted. Therefore, the terms of the bond, as well as any governing statutes and applicable case law, must always be examined in the context of any given claim.

---

213. *State ex rel. Bob Davis Masonry, Inc. v. Safeco Ins. Co. of America*, 883 P.2d 144, 148 (N.M. 1994); *Price Bros. Co. v. Olin Constr. Co., Inc.*, 528 F.Supp. 716, 722 (W.D.N.Y. 1981); *Price Bros. Constr. Co., v. Charles J. Rogers Constr. Co.*, 304 N.W.2d 584, 588 (Mich. Ct. App. 1981); *Clow Corp. v. Metro Pipeline Co., Inc.*, 442 F.Supp. 583, 592-93 (N.D. Ga. 1977) (interest allowed on grounds that the interest was included in sums justly due the claimant). *But see Reliance Universal, Inc. of Ohio v. Ernest Renda Contracting Co., Inc.*, 454 A.2d 39, 44-46 (Pa. Super. Ct. 1982) (public works statute which did not demonstrate intent to cover interest controlled over terms of subcontract providing for payment of finance charges).

214. *State ex rel. Bob Davis Masonry, Inc. v. Safeco Ins. Co. of America*, 883 P.2d at 148 (where court found bond and public works statute called for coverage of sums justly due claimant, which thus included interest awarded against bond principal in prior judgment against principal).

215. *See, e.g., McQueen Contracting, Inc. v. Fidelity & Deposit Co. of Maryland*, 871 F.2d 32, 33 (5th Cir. 1989); *Hartford Acc. & Indem. Co. v. District of Columbia*, 441 A.2d at 974); *R.T. Woodfield, Inc. v. Montgomery County Bd. of Educ. ex rel. Int'l Tel. & Telegraph Corp.*, 248 A.2d 895, 898 (Md. 1969).

216. *See, e.g., R.T. Woodfield, Inc. v. Montgomery County Bd. of Educ. ex rel. Int'l Tel. & Telegraph Corp.*, 248 A.2d at 898 (in which court states that interest is due either from the date of the demand on the surety for payment and the refusal to pay, or from the date of filing suit), *citing Peerless Ins. Co. v. Board of County Comm'rs of Prince George's County ex. rel Ben Dyer Asso., Inc.*, 237 A.2d 15 (Md. 1968).

9

Procedural Requirements

Julia Blackwell Gelinas

Introduction

A payment bond is designed to protect subcontractors and suppliers by guaranteeing payment in the event that the principal defaults on its contractual obligation to these entities. To be eligible to make a claim for payment under the bond, there are several procedural requirements with which a claimant must comply. The nature and extent of the procedural requirements will vary depending upon the type of project involved. This chapter will discuss the standard procedural requirements for making a claim on the various type of payment bonds with an emphasis on the requirements for federal public works projects under the Miller Act.[1]

I. Notice

The first procedural requirement with which certain claimants must comply is the notice requirement. Under the Miller Act, timely notice is a condition precedent for any person having a direct contractual relationship with a subcontractor but no contractual relationship with the contractor, to recover under the payment bond.[2] This section will discuss several issues relating to the notice requirements of the Miller Act, and payment bonds in general, including the following: (a) the purpose of the notice; (b) to whom and from whom notice is required; (c) contents and form of the notice; and (d) the time period for giving notice.

PURPOSE OF THE NOTICE REQUIREMENT

There are two main purposes of the notice requirement under the Miller Act. One reason for the requirement is to set a definite period after which the general contractor can make payment to the subcontractors without fear that it will later face claims from those who supplied labor and materials to the subcontractors.[3] The second purpose of the act goes hand in hand with the first in that it affords the general contractor the opportunity to protect itself. The general contractor is liable to the subcontractors, and, under the Miller Act, it may also be directly liable to those with direct contractual relationships with its subcontractors. The Miller Act, therefore, requires that a supplier seeking payment from the general contractor must notify the general contractor promptly so that it may withhold payment from the subcontractor.[4] This enables the general contractor to avoid incurring double liability for the same obligation (paying

---

1. 40 U.S.C. § 270a *et seq.* The Miller Act "was intended to protect from non-payment those who furnish labor and materials in federal construction projects." *Pepper Burns Insulation, Inc. v. Artco Corp.*, 970 F.2d 1340, 1343 (4th Cir. 1992), *cert. denied.* 506 U.S. 1053 (1993). For a summary of the various state laws governing state and local public projects, see PAYMENT BOND MANUAL (Edward G. Gallagher et al. eds., 2d ed. 1995).

2. 40 U.S.C. § 270b(a); *Pepper Burns*, 970 F.2d at 1342.

3. *United States ex rel. Blue Circle West, Inc. v. Tucson Mechanical Contracting, Inc.*, 921 F.2d 911, 914 (9th Cir. 1990).

4. *Id.*

a subcontractor in full and later being forced to reimburse its surety for payment made to the unpaid supplier of its subcontractor.) By withholding payment until a date beyond the ninety-day limitation period or until proof is provided that all subcontractors and suppliers have been paid, the general contractor is able to limit the extent of its liability to those with whom it did not directly contract.[5]

B. To Whom and From Whom Notice Is Required

The Miller Act, and virtually all payment bonds, require a claimant to provide written notice of its claim for payment to the principal (for purposes of this discussion, the general contractor). Some private contracts, however, also require notice to be given to the surety and the owner when the claimant has a direct contract with the principal.[6]

Under the Miller Act, not all claimants must provide notice to the general contractor. The Miller Act states in pertinent part:

> Section 270b. Rights of Persons Furnishing Labor or Material.
>
> (a) . . . That any person having direct contractual relationship with a subcontractor but no contractual relationship express or implied with the contractor furnishing said payment bond shall have a right of action upon the said payment bond upon giving written notice to said contractor within ninety days from the date on which such person did or performed the last of the labor or furnished or supplied the last of the material for which such claim is made, . . .[7]

Since the general contractor is in the best position to know the status of its obligations to those with whom it has contracted, notice is only required from those claimants who do not have a direct contractual relationship with the general contractor.

A similar notice requirement is often found in bonds issued on private projects. For example, the notice provision found in AIA Document A312, Payment Bond, has virtually identical language to the Miller Act provision regarding notice to the general contractor when the claimant does not have a direct contract with the general contractor. The main distinction between the provisions is that under the AIA form, notice must also be given to the owner within the time requirement. Further, if the general contractor fails to remedy the situation within 30 days of the notice, the claimant must send written notice to the surety and the owner. AIA Document 311, on the other hand, makes notice to the contractor optional by requiring that notice be given to two of the following three entities: the principal, the owner, or the surety.[8] If a claimant encounters such a provision in practice, he or she should always give notice to the general contractor so that it may take whatever steps are necessary to protect itself against incurring liability under the bond as the result of the actions of its subcontractor or supplier. Upon receiving notice, the general contractor may take various steps to protect itself such as withholding payment from its subcontractor or issuing all further checks to the subcontractor as jointly payable to the subcontractor and the claimant. The general contractor's motivation to

5. A general contractor may also limit its liability by requiring its subcontractors to obtain payment bonds which inure to the benefit of the general contractor just as the general contractor's payment bond protects the owner/obligee of the project.

6. For instance, see AIA Document 312. The American Institute of Architects (AIA) is a private, non-profit organization headquartered in Washington, D.C. that publishes a variety of forms tailored to accommodate the various contracting entities and formats.

7. 40 U.S.C. § 270b(a).

8. AIA Document 311 seems to have been largely replaced by AIA Document 312.

ensure that the claimants are paid, stems from the very nature of the notice requirement - namely to alert the general contractor that the claimant will look to its surety for payment in the event that the subcontractor with whom the claimant contracted, fails to pay.

Not all suppliers are protected by the Miller Act or similar provisions. Under the Miller Act, as well as under the various "Little Miller Acts" found at the state level and on most private projects, the only entities covered by the payment bond are those subcontractors and suppliers who have a direct contractual relationship with the general contractor furnishing the bond or with one of the general contractor's subcontractors. The suppliers "in more remote relationships," such as persons who supply labor or material to a "mere materialman," are not protected by the Miller Act.[9] These more remote relationships are excluded from the protection of the Miller Act because it is difficult for the general contractor to identify and protect itself from such remote claims as opposed to claims against its subcontractors.

> The relatively few subcontractors who perform part of the original contract represent in a sense the prime contractor and are well known to him. It is easy for the prime contractor to secure himself against loss by requiring the subcontractors to give security by bond, or otherwise, for the payment of those who contract directly with the subcontractors. . . . But this method of protection is generally inadequate to cope with remote and undeterminable liabilities incurred by an ordinary materialman, who may be a manufacturer, a wholesaler or a retailer.[10]

The substantiality and importance of the relationship with the prime or general contractor determines whether one is a subcontractor or a mere materialman.[11] If the claimant is a supplier to a subcontractor, he or she is eligible to recover under the payment bond. However, if the claimant is a supplier to a materialman, no protection is afforded by the Miller Act.

C. Required Content and Form of the Notice

In order to preserve a claim against the general contractor and its payment bond surety, sub-subcontractors and suppliers must also pay careful attention to the form and content requirements of the applicable notice provisions. The first requirement is that notice must be in writing.[12] Written notice prevents misunderstandings and affords evidence of the communication of the claim to the general contractor.[13] While it is clear that a writing is required and that actual notice of a claim is not sufficient, the courts have generally accepted alternative methods of providing written notice. If a claimant is able to produce a receipt or other evidence to document that written notice was received by the general contractor, the fact that the claimant failed to send written notice in the prescribed manner probably will not be fatal to the claim.[14] Further, notice may be sufficient when given through a combination of documents even though the individual writings may not satisfy all the statutory requirements.[15]

---

9. *F.D. Rich Co., Inc. v. United States ex rel. Industrial Lumber Co., Inc.*, 417 U.S. 116, 122 (1974).
10. *Id.* at 123 (quoting *MacEvoy Co. v. United States ex rel. Tompkins Co.*, 322 U.S. 102, 110 (1944)).
11. *F.D. Rich Co.*, 417 U.S. at 123.
12. 40 U.S.C. § 270b(a).
13. *United States ex rel. Consolidated Electrical Distributors, Inc. v. Altech, Inc.*, 929 F.2d 1089, 1092 (5th Cir. 1991).
14. *United States ex rel. Kelly - Mohrhusen Co. v. Merle A. Patnode Co.*, 457 F.2d 116 (7th Cir. 1972); *United States ex rel. Moody v. American Ins. Co.*, 835 F.2d 745 (10th Cir. 1987).
15. *Moody*, 835 F.2d at 748; *United States ex rel. San Joaquin Blocklite v. Lloyd E. Tull, Inc.*, 770 F.2d 862 (9th Cir. 1985).

Oral notice by telephone or in person, however, has been found insufficient to satisfy the statutory requirement of the Miller Act.[16]

In addition to being in written form, the notice must contain the appropriate information to be considered sufficient notice. The written notice must alert the general contractor that the claimant is looking to the contractor for payment since the subcontractor has refused to meet its obligation.[17] The notice does not have to demand payment from the general contractor, but it must plainly appear "that the nature and the state of the indebtedness was brought home to the general contractor."[18] The general contractor, when notified generally that one of its subcontractors has failed to pay its bill, does not have a duty to inquire whether the supplier might look to it for payment. Rather, the duty is upon the supplier to notify the general contractor that it is looking to the contractor for payment of the debt.[19] This duty is not satisfied by the claimant sending the general contractor a copy of a collection letter, by a joint check arrangement between the general contractor and the subcontractor, or by the general contractor's preparation of a monthly payment estimate.[20]

The notice must also identify, with substantial accuracy, the amount claimed and the name of the party to whom the material was supplied or for whom the work was performed.[21] Notice has been considered sufficient, however, where the name of the subcontractor is missing when the name was supplied orally and the general contractor had knowledge of the identity of the subcontractor.[22] Also, notice which fails to specify the amount claimed may be sufficient when combined with another writing given to the contractor, even if the second writing is given to the contractor after the expiration of the ninety day time limit.[23]

Finally, to be sufficient, the notice must be sent or delivered in the appropriate manner. Prior to its amendment in 1999, the Miller Act required that notice be sent by certified or registered mail.[24] This provision was liberally construed, however, where the general contractor had actual notice of the claim. The courts reasoned that the purpose of this requirement was to assure receipt of the notice rather than to make the described method of notice mandatory.[25] In 1999, Congress amended the Miller Act to permit the notice to be sent by any means which provides written, third party verification of receipt. If the general contractor receives the required written notice within the specified time, the claimant's right to obtain payment from the general contractor will not be extinguished.

Although claimants must adhere to these notice requirements of the Miller Act, courts allow some informality in compliance with the statutory terms, especially where the general contractor has actual knowledge of the claim.[26] Courts are more rigid, however, in their interpretation of the requirements for the contents of the notice.[27] Adequate notice must "bring home" to the general contractor the fact that the supplier is looking to it for payment.

---

16. *United States ex rel. Brothers Builders Supply Company v. Old World Artisans, Inc.*, 702 F.Supp. 1561 (N.D. Ga. 1988).
17. *Tucson Mechanical Contracting*, 921 F.2d at 914.
18. *United States ex rel. Water Works Supply Corp. v George Hyman Constr. Co.*, 131 F.3d 28, 32 (1st Cir. 1997).
19. *Id.*
20. *Maccaferri Gabions, Inc. v. Dynateria*, 91 F.3d 1431 (11th Cir. 1996), *cert. denied* 520 U.S. 1167 (1997).
21. 40 U.S.C. § 270b(a).
22. *United States ex rel. Kelly - Mohrhusen Co. v. Merle A. Patnode Co.*, 457 F.2d 116 (7th Cir. 1972).
23. *United States ex rel. San Joaquin Blocklite v. Lloyd E. Tull, Inc.*, 770 F.2d 862 (9th Cir. 1985).
24. 40 U.S.C. § 270b(a).
25. *Moody*, 835 F.2d at 747.
26. *Id.* at 748; *George Hyman*, 131 F.3d at 32.
27. *Maccaferri Gabions*, 91 F.3d at 1437.

On private projects, the parties are free to negotiate their own provisions with respect to the acceptable means of providing notice of the existence of a claim. For instance, AIA Document A312 contains the following provision:

> Notice to the Surety, the Owner or the Contractor shall be mailed or delivered to the address shown on the signature page. Actual receipt of notice by Surety, the Owner or the Contractor, however accomplished, shall be sufficient compliance as of the date received at the address shown on the signature page.[28]

Since parties can negotiate their own notice provisions, it is important to carefully read the contract and comply with the notice requirements specified therein rather than merely relying on the statutory provisions or the courts previous decisions as to what constitutes sufficient notice.

D. Time Period for Giving Notice

Under the Miller Act and most private contracts, such as AIA document 312, written notice to the general contractor is required within ninety days from the date the claimant last performed labor or supplied materials.[29] Although courts have liberally construed some of the notice provisions, the time period within which notice must be provided has been strictly enforced by the courts.[30] This strict enforcement furthers the purpose of the notice requirement that general contractors have a date certain after which they are no longer at risk of liability to suppliers.[31]

The ninety-day time period commences on the day after the last day upon which a claimant furnished labor or materials. The determination as to the last day upon which the claimant furnished labor or materials is critical to the claim in two respects. First, this date determines when the ninety-day deadline expires. The written notice must be given on or before ninety days after that date. This notice is perfected when it is received rather than when it is mailed.[32] Second, it determines when the one-year time period for bringing suit against the surety begins to run.

One issue which arises in determining the last day upon which labor or supplies were furnished is whether the last labor or material supplied was part of the original contract or whether it was simply provided to correct defects and make repairs following the inspection of the project. Materials or labor supplied to correct defective items or to replace previously supplied material will not be considered in computing the ninety-day period.[33] However, if materials are not supplied with the claimant's final delivery of materials, but are supplied for the first time thereafter, the ninety day period is computed from the date upon which the materials were actually supplied, *i.e.,* the actual delivery date as opposed to the final scheduled delivery date.[34]

Disputes also can arise as to the date on which the ninety days commenced where there have been multiple deliveries made to a project. The issue becomes whether written notice must be provided within ninety days of each delivery or within ninety days from the date of the final delivery. It would appear that the courts when confronted with this issue focus on whether

28. AIA Document 312, Paragraph 12.
29. 40 U.S.C. § 270b(a); AIA Document 312, Paragraph 4.2.1.
30. *Pepper Burns,* 970 F.2d at 1343.
31. *Id.*
32. *Id.*
33. *Johnson Serv. Co. v. Trans American Ins. Co.,* 485 F.2d 164 (5th Cir. 1973).
34. *United States ex rel. Raymond Bergen, Inc. v. DeMatteo Constr. Co.,* 467 F.Supp. 22 (D.Conn. 1979).

there was a single contract or multiple contracts involved, as well as the reason for the gap in time between deliveries. For instance, the Fifth Circuit Court of Appeals in *United States ex rel. A & M Petroleum, Inc. v. Santa Fe Engineers, Inc.*,[35] held that a supplier who made 15 deliveries of diesel fuel over an eight-month span and gave written notice within ninety days from the date of the last delivery, provided sufficient notice for the entire claim. Notice was not required to be given within ninety days of *each* unpaid claim.[36] Similarly, in *United States ex rel. Water Works Supply Corp. v. George Hyman Construction Company,*[37] the court held that where the claims were based on an "open account theory," the notice period for all the deliveries began to run on the date of the last delivery to the project. On the other hand, the Second Circuit Court of Appeals in *United States ex rel. J.A. Edwards & Company v. Peter Reiss Construction Company*,[38] found that a gap of more than ninety days between the first and second series of material deliveries vitiated the notice provided within ninety days following the second set of deliveries, with respect to the first set of deliveries. Generally speaking, if the claimant has a single contract pursuant to which the deliveries are made, a ninety-day gap between deliveries will not prevent a claimant from making a claim for the entire obligation.[39] However, if there are multiple contracts or a series of deliveries followed by another definite and distinct series of deliveries, a claimant would be wise to put the general contractor on written notice within ninety days from the date of the last delivery within each series or within the completion of each contract in order to guarantee that the claim has been perfected.[40]

Another disputed issue with regard to the ninety day notice requirement is whether written notice may be given prior to the date the claimant last furnished labor or material on a project. There is some authority for the proposition that notice prior to the completion of the job is insufficient notice as it is premature.[41] More recent cases, however, tend to consider premature notice as timely and sufficient.[42] Since there is no danger of stale claims when notice is given prematurely, finding premature notice insufficient would defeat the purpose of the statute, which is to protect general contractors from stale claims by providing a definite the time period after which it will not be liable for claims of suppliers.[43]

Most states in their "Little Miller Acts" also require notice to be given to the general contractor within ninety days. States vary, however, in the manner in which they determine the beginning of the notice period. For instance, some statutory language mirrors the Miller Act language of ninety days from the last provision of labor or supplies. Other states, however, begin the notice period upon completion or final acceptance of the project.[44]

---

35. 822 F.2d 547 (5th Cir. 1987).
36. *Id.* at 548.
37. 131 F.3d 28 (1st Cir. 1997).
38. 273 F.2d 880 (2nd Cir. 1959), *cert. denied*, 362 U.S. 951 (1960).
39. *National Sur. Corp. v. United States ex rel. Way Panama, S.A.*, 378 F.2d 294 (5th Cir. 1967), *cert. denied*, 389 U.S. 1004 (1967); *United States ex rel. Edwards v. Peter Reiss Constr. Co.*, 273 F.2d 880 (2nd Cir., 1959).
40. *United States ex rel. I. Burack, Inc. v. Sovereign Constr. Co.*, 338 F.Supp. 657 (S.D.N.Y. 1972).
41. *United States ex rel. Kinlau Sheet Metal Works, Inc. v. Great American Ins. Co.*, 537 F.2d 222 (5th Cir. 1976).
42. *Moody,* 835 F.2d 745; *United States ex rel. Honeywell, Inc. v. A & L Mechanical Contractors, Inc.*, 677 F.2d 383 (4th Cir. 1982).
43. *Honeywell,* 677 F.2d at 386.
44. For a review of each state's requirement, see Michael I. Less, *Notice Requirements for Bond Claims, in* THE LAW OF PAYMENT BONDS 81, 93-108 (Kevin L. Lybeck & H. Bruce Shreves, eds., 1998).

II. Limitations

The Miller Act, as well as various state public works statutes and private payment bonds, generally require that a claimant commence suit on the payment bond within one year from the date upon which the claimant last performed labor or supplied material to the project. The Miller Act reads in pertinent part:

Section 270b. Rights of Persons Furnishing Labor or Material.

(b) Every suit instituted under this section shall be brought in the name of the United States for the use of the person suing, in the United States District Court for any district in which the contract was to be performed and executed and not elsewhere, irrespective of the amount in controversy in such suit, but no such suit shall be commenced after the expiration of one year after the day on which the last of the labor was performed or material was supplied by him. . . .[45]

It is important to note that, unlike the notice provision, this one-year limitation applies to all claimants rather than just to those without a direct contract with the general contractor. Under the Miller Act, the one-year deadline for commencing suit, like the ninety day written notice deadline, is a prerequisite to making a recovery on the bond.

As previously discussed, the date upon which the one-year time period begins to run is the same date used to compute the ninety day limitation period for providing written notice. A claimant must file suit within one year from the date on which the last of the labor was performed or the material supplied. As with the notice provision, the last day is difficult to determine when the labor performed might be considered repair work. Generally, the test used to determine whether the work performed is labor or merely repair work is whether the work performed and the material supplied was part of the original contract or is for the purpose of correcting defects or making repairs after the inspection of the project.[46] Factors to consider in this analysis include "the value of the materials, the original contract specifications, the unexpected nature of the work, and the importance of the materials to the operation of the system in which they are used."[47] The limitation period is not tolled by the furnishing of materials for the purpose of correcting or repairing the claimant's defective work.[48]

The last day on which material is supplied is also more difficult to determine when the material supplied is leased equipment, such as a crane. For leased equipment, the limitation period begins on the date on which the equipment was last available for the use of the project rather than when the equipment is delivered.[49] When material is furnished, the claimant's obligation is completed upon delivery. For leased equipment, however, the claimant's obligation does not terminate until the equipment is no longer available for use by the subcontractor.[50] The equipment is considered no longer available if the subcontractor abandons the project or if the general contractor terminates its contract with the subcontractor.[51] The

45. 40 U.S.C. § 270b(b).

46. *United States ex rel. Magna Masonry, Inc. v. R.T. Woodfield, Inc.*, 709 F.2d 249 (4th Cir. 1983).

47. *United States ex rel. Georgia Electric Supply Co., Inc. v. United States Fidelity and Guar. Co.*, 656 F.2d 993, 996 (5th Cir. 1981).

48. *United States ex rel. Mod-Form, Inc. v. Barton & Barton Co.*, 769 F.Supp. 235, 238 (E.D. Mich. 1991).

49. *United States ex rel. Pippin v. Youngdale Constr. Co., Inc.*, 923 F.2d 146, 149 (9th Cir. 1991).

50. *Id.* at 149-50.

51. *Id.* at 150.

supplier cannot toll the running of the limitation period by failing to remove the leased equipment from the project site.[52]

Suit may not be commenced against the surety until after the expiration of ninety days from the date that the last labor was done or material furnished. If the claimant is not paid within the ninety-day period, it may then file suit against the general contractor and surety. If suit is commenced during this ninety-day period, it is deemed premature and may be dismissed by the court.[53] If the dismissal does not occur until the one-year period expires, however, the claimant may be barred from pursuing the claim. If a claimant is confronted with this situation, there is case law suggesting that the court should not dismiss the action and forfeit the claimant's rights under the bond due to premature filing, but instead should permit a supplemental or amended complaint that will relate back to the time when suit could have been properly filed.[54]

Although the courts may be somewhat lenient with a premature filing, such is not the case with filings made after the limitation period has expired. The claimant must file suit within the one-year limitation period or the cause of action will be lost.[55] The one-year limitation period has been held to be binding on the claimant regardless of whether the construction contract contains a "pay when paid" clause or an arbitration clause which might otherwise be construed as extending this period.[56]

It should be noted that the ninety-day and one-year limitation periods and the strict adherence to the deadlines discussed above, primarily apply to public projects under the Miller Act and the state public works statutes. On a private project, the parties are free to negotiate whatever limitation periods they choose to impose.[57] The reader is advised to carefully review any applicable state statutes, local requirements, and the terms of the contract and payment bond to determine the applicable deadlines for filing a claim.[58]

Regardless of the type of project involved, the payment bond surety may be equitably estopped from raising a time limitation defense by virtue of its actions or representations. Asserting equitable estoppel does not necessarily require an allegation of actual fraud or deception.[59] If the payment bond surety presents the appearance of taking an active role in resolving a claim by corresponding with the parties or making payments thereon, the surety may not be permitted to later argue that the claimant failed to file suit within the one-year statute of limitations.[60] The claimant may also be able to argue that the surety is equitably estopped from asserting a statute of limitations defense if there is evidence which suggests that the surety made representations or engaged in conduct upon which the claimant justifiably relied in failing to timely file its claim.[61]

52. *United States ex rel. Gulf States Enterprises, Inc. v. R.R. Tway, Inc.*, 938 F.2d 583 (5th Cir. 1991).

53. *Marmet Corporation v. Frank Briscoe Co.*, 382 F.2d 906, 909 (6th Cir. 1962).

54. *See United States ex rel. Capital Elec. Supply Company, Inc. v. C.J. Elec. Contractors, Inc.*, 535 F.2d 1326 (1st Cir. 1976).

55. *4-Star Constr. Corp. v. United States*, 6 Cl. Ct. 271 (1984).

56. *United States ex rel. Scarborough v. C & M Contractors, Inc.*, 444 F.Supp 23 (D.Miss. 1977) (pay when paid clause); *United States ex rel. Portland Constr. Co. v. Weiss Pollution Control Corp.*, 532 F.2d 1009 (5th Cir. 1976) (arbitration).

57. *Krugman v. Elite Assoc.*, 562 N.Y.S.2d 188 (N.Y. App. 1990); *Camelot Excavating Co., Inc. v. St. Paul Fire & Marine Ins. Co.*, 301 N.W.2d 275 (Mich. 1981).

58. For a summary of suit limitations under "Little Miller Acts," see Robert F. Carney, *Suit Limitation, in* THE LAW OF PAYMENT BONDS 113, 121-132 (Kevin L. Lybeck & H. Bruce Shreves, eds., 1998).

59. *United States ex rel. Bernard Lumber Co., Inc. v. Lanier-Gervais Corp.*, 896 F.2d 162 (5th Cir. 1990).

60. *United States ex rel. Humble Oil & Refining Co. v. Fidelity & Cas. Co. of N.Y.*, 402 F.2d 893 (4th Cir. 1968).

61. *United States ex rel. Nelson v. Reliance Ins. Co.*, 436 F.2d 1366 (10th Cir. 1971).

III. Jurisdiction

The United States District Courts have subject matter jurisdiction over all Miller Act cases.[62] The parties cannot waive the exclusive jurisdiction of the federal court. Any contract provision requiring that suit be brought in state court is void.[63] Further, the amount in controversy and the citizenship of the parties is irrelevant as federal jurisdiction is based on a federal question for Miller Act cases.

For federal courts to have jurisdiction over Miller Act cases, the contract must be "for the construction, alteration, or repair of any public building or public work of the United States."[64] "Public work" is not defined in the statute. Typically, any claim on a project where the government owns the land and contracts for its improvement is covered by the Miller Act.[65] These factors are not controlling, however, and a project may be classified as a public work even though the government does not own the land and does not directly contract for the improvement.[66] Courts look to such factors as whether the government provides the funding and whether the project will serve the interests of the general public to determine whether a project is a public work.[67] Governmental funding of a project, while a factor to be considered, is not sufficient by itself to warrant Miller Act jurisdiction.[68]

If a claimant should mistakenly file in state court, the mistake could be fatal to the claim since the state court filing will not toll the one-year statute of limitations.[69] However, it should be noted that these jurisdictional limitations only apply to a suit on the payment bond against the surety. A claimant who has a direct contractual relationship with the principal is always free to bring a state court cause of action against the principal alone.[70]

The various "Little Miller Acts" and other state public works statutes generally require that suit be commenced in state court. The reader is cautioned to review a particular state's statutes carefully, for each state varies to some degree in how it handles the matter of jurisdiction. For example, some statutes require that suit be commenced in a particular court,[71] while other statutes may establish a procedure by which the amount of the claim will dictate in which court suit should be commenced.[72] In fact, there are some states where, by statute or case precedent, there is authority for the proposition that federal courts may also have jurisdiction over these matters.[73]

The jurisdictional provisions of public payment bond statutes, whether federal or state, ordinarily cannot be waived.[74] However, on a private project, the parties to the construction contract may always agree to modify the terms of the contract to change the jurisdictional

---

62. 40 U.S.C. § 270b and 28 U.S.C. § 1352.

63. *United States ex rel. B & D Mechanical Contractors, Inc. v. St. Paul Mercury Ins. Co.*, 70 F.3d 1115 (10th Cir. 1995), *cert. denied* 517 U.S. 1167 (1996).

64. 40 U.S.C. § 270a.

65. *United States ex rel. General Electric Supply v. USF&G*, 11 F.3d 577 (6th Cir. 1993).

66. *Sullivan v. Faras-RLS Group, Ltd.*, 795 F.Supp. 305, 307 (D.Ariz. 1992).

67. *Id.*; *United States Stephen B. Owens v. Olympic Marine Services, Inc.*, 827 F.Supp. 1232, 1234 (E.D.Va. 1993); .

68. *TIJ Materials Corp. v. Green Island Constr. Co., Inc.*, 131 F.R.D. 31 (D.R.I. 1990); *United States ex rel. General Electric Supply v. USF&G*, 11 F.3d 577 (6th Cir. 1993).

69. *United States ex rel. Harvey Gulf Int'l. Marine v. Maryland Cas. Co.*, 573 F.2d 245, 247 (5th Cir. 1978).

70. *United States ex rel. Gigliello v. Sovereign Constr. Co.*, 311 F.Supp. 371 (D.Mass. 1970).

71. *See* UTAH CODE ANN., 63-56-38(4); VT. STAT. ANN. tit. 19, § 10.

72. *See* IND. CODE § 5-16-5-2(e); MICH. COMP. LAWS § 129.209; NEV. REV. STAT. § 339.055.

73. *See* OR. REV. STAT. § 279.536(1).

74. *United States ex rel. Gigliello v. Sovereign Constr. Co.*, 311 F.Supp. 371, 373 (D.Mass. 1970).

provision. As an example, AIA Document A312 contains the following jurisdictional provision:

> 11. No suit or action shall be commenced by a Claimant under this Bond other than in a court of competent jurisdiction in the location in which the work or part of the work is located . .

Unless the surety asserts the original jurisdictional provision as a defense, suit may be commenced anywhere jurisdiction would otherwise be appropriate.

IV. Venue

Pursuant to the provisions of the Miller Act, a claimant must bring suit "in the United States District Court for any district in which the contract was to be performed and executed and not elsewhere. . ."[75] Courts have interpreted this language as a venue requirement.[76] Like jurisdiction, it applies regardless of the amount in controversy or the citizenship of the parties. Unlike subject matter jurisdiction, venue is waivable. While the venue provision is intended to benefit the surety, unless the surety affirmatively raises improper venue as a defense, the matter may be deemed waived.[77] Thus, if a claim is not brought in the proper district court, that court, since it has jurisdiction, may proceed to resolve the matter unless the surety timely raises its venue defense. If the surety does raise its venue defense, the district court may either dismiss the case or transfer the case to the proper district court. Since this is not a matter of jurisdiction, dismissals are rare and the most common course of action is for the district court to transfer the case.[78] Dismissal may be granted, however, where the plaintiff has failed to request transfer to the proper venue, even though the one-year statute of limitations under the Miller Act had expired.[79]

As discussed above, if a claimant files his or her claim in a court which lacks proper jurisdiction, the statute of limitations is not tolled and the claim may be barred. If the claimant files his or her claim in a court in which venue is not proper, however, the statute of limitations period may be tolled under the doctrine of equitable tolling.[80] In *United States v. M.J. Kelley Corp.*, the court found that the case was "particularly deserving" of the doctrine of equitable tolling as the venue and jurisdictional requirements governing overseas construction contracts under the Miller Act are ill-defined and unsettled.[81] Further, the court found that the claimant "zealously pursued its claim" and its actions were "taken in good faith."[82]

Since venue is waivable, contracts governed by the Miller Act may include a forum selection clause. Basically, a forum selection clause allows the parties to agree upon a court in which to resolve any disputes which may arise. A forum selection clause which is valid overrides the venue provision of the Miller Act.[83] The clause will be held valid and enforceable unless enforcement of the clause is shown by the resisting party to be unreasonable under the

---

75. 40 U.S.C. § 270b(b).

76. *United States ex rel. Pittsburgh Tank & Tower v. G & C Enterprises*, 62 F.3d 35 (1st Cir. 1995); *F.D. Rich*, 417 U.S. 116.

77. *United States ex rel. Bailey-Lewis-Williams of Fla. v. Peter Kiewit Sons Co.*, 195 F.Supp. 752 (D.D.C. 1961) *aff'd* 299 F.2d 930 (D.C. Cir. 1962).

78. *United States ex rel. Essex Machine Works v. Bondout Marine*, 312 F.Supp. 846 (S.D.N.Y. 1970).

79. *G & C Enterprises*, 62 F.3d at 36 (court looked at the fact that the claimant could pursue state law claims against the contractor and that there was no indication that the contractor was insolvent).

80. *United States ex rel. Skip Kirchdorfer, Inc. v. M.J. Kelley Corp.*, 995 F.2d 656, 659 (6th Cir. 1993).

81. *Id.* at 660.

82. *Id.*

83. *B & D Mechanical Contractors*, 70 F.3d 1117.

circumstances.[84] The forum selection clause should be given its full effect absent fraud, undue influence, or overweening bargaining power.[85] A forum selection clause may alter the venue provisions of the Miller Act, however, it will be void and unenforceable if it attempts to change the jurisdictional requirements by choosing a state court forum.[86]

With respect to state public projects and private projects, the reader is once again encouraged to carefully review the applicable statutes and the provisions of the payment bond and contract to determine the venue requirements for a particular project. Many states have venue requirements that are similar to the Miller Act, but this varies from state to state. Parties on private projects can usually select where a suit should be filed in the contract.

V. *Conclusion*

To obtain the protection afforded by the payment bond, it is extremely important for a claimant to follow all of the procedural requirements of the applicable statutes and contractual provisions. Failing to provide adequate and timely notice to the general contractor or other required parties will bar the claimant's ability to recover under the payment bond. Likewise, failing to file suit within the specified limitations period or filing suit in the wrong court will extinguish the claim. A claimant, therefore, must carefully examine the appropriate statutes and the bond itself to guarantee that it has satisfied all of the requirements and to protect its claim.

84. *The Bremen v. Zapata Offshore Company*, 407 U.S. 1 (1972).
85. *Carnival Cruise Lines, Inc. v. Shute*, 499 U.S.585, 591 (1991).
86. *B & D Mechanical Contractors,* 70 F.3d 1117.

10

Fiduciary Bonds

James A. Knox, Jr.

Introduction

Dickens and Trollope portrayed the Victorian chancery and probate courts as a haven for unsavory characters—a *Bleak House* of pettifoggers and graft. Fast forward to the 21st century. Widows, orphans and sureties may find the system still is treacherous. Sureties will never get as much sympathy as widows and orphans, but they can help themselves a great deal by learning something about what they're in for.

I. The Fiduciary

To understand fiduciary bonds, one must understand fiduciaries. Fiduciary is a term derived from Roman law. It means a person holding the character of a trustee, in whom trust and confidence has been placed.[1] A fiduciary has a duty to act primarily for another's benefit, with scrupulous good faith and candor.[2] The fiduciary bond is simply a guarantee of this. The types of fiduciaries who may need bonding include trustees (such as testamentary trustees, ERISA trustees and bankruptcy trustees), receivers, executors, administrators and guardians. A trustee is empowered to hold property in trust for the benefit of another.[3] A receiver is an officer appointed by the court to manage the affairs of a distressed business.[4] An executor is appointed by a testator to carry out the testator's will after his or her death, including the disposition of his or her estate.[5] An administrator is appointed by the court to administer the estate of an intestate decedent.[6] A guardian is invested with the duty of taking care of and managing the property and rights of another person, known as a ward, who for want of age, understanding or self-control, is deemed incapable of managing his or her own affairs.[7]

The administration of a decedent's estate under the Uniform Probate Code provides a good example of the duties of a fiduciary. Only fourteen states have adopted the code, but the rules elsewhere are similar. A probate proceeding is commenced by a petition with notice to heirs and other interested parties, pursuant to a will or as an intestate succession.[8] Administration is by a personal representative who must seek appointment by the court.[9] If

1. Black's Law Dictionary (6th ed. West 1990) 625.
2. *Id.*
3. *Id.* at 1514.
4. *Presto v. Coppice*, 296 A.2d 150 (Md. App. 1972).
5. Black's Law Dictionary at 570.
6. *Id.* at 46.
7. *Id.* at 706.
8. Uniform Probate Code ("UPC") §§ 3-301, 3-402.
9. UPC § 3-414.

appointed, letters of office are issued. Generally the representative may then proceed without court order to settle and distribute the estate but he or she may apply to the court for resolution of any issues.[10] He or she must (1) promptly advise heirs and devisees of his appointment;[11] (2) prepare and file an inventory and valuation of the decedent's property;[12] (3) take possession of the estate or leave it with person(s) presumably entitled to it; and (4) "take all steps reasonably necessary for the management, protection and preservation of the estate in his possession."[13]

To carry out these duties, the representative is authorized to receive, retain, manage, pay taxes on, insure, sell and borrow against estate assets. He may perform the decedent's contracts, continue or liquidate any business, prudently invest funds not needed to meet debts or expenses, prosecute and settle claims, and reasonably compensate himself for his services.[14] He may employ attorneys, accountants, and other agents to assist him in performance of his duties.[15] The propriety of such employment may be reviewed.[16]

Before the estate may be distributed to the heirs or devisees, creditors must be notified and the statutory procedure followed for presentment, prioritization and resolution of their claims.[17] The representative's work is completed by a petition for approval of a final accounting and distribution, termination of the appointment and closure of the estate. Termination also occurs upon resignation,[18] removal for cause,[19] or death. Grounds for removal include misrepresentation of facts leading to the appointment, disregard of court orders, incompetence, and mismanagement of the estate.

As a fiduciary, the representative must observe the standards of care applicable to a trustee.[20] He must "settle and distribute the estate of the decedent in accordance with the terms of any probated and effective will and this Code" and use his authority "for the best interest of successors to the estate."[21] He may not be surcharged for an act of administration or distribution if it was authorized at the time,[22] but he must "observe the standard in dealing with the trust assets that would be observed by a prudent man dealing with the property of another." If he has special skills, and was appointed on that basis, he must use them. [23] If he breaches his duties, he is liable to interested persons for any resulting damage or loss.[24] Any self-dealing, including any dealing with insiders, is voidable unless disclosed and approved by the court.[25]

Upon termination of his authority, a representative remains liable for any acts or omissions causing harm to the estate and must preserve the assets subject to his control,

---

10. UPC § 3-704.
11. UPC § 3-705.
12. UPC § 3-706.
13. UPC § 3-709.
14. UPC § 3-715.
15. UPC § 3-719.
16. UPC § 3-721.
17. UPC Part 8.
18. UPC § 3-610.
19. UPC § 3-611.
20. UPC §§ 3-703; 7-302.
21. UPC § 3-703(a).
22. UPC § 3-703(b).
23. UPC § 7-302.
24. UPC § 3-712.
25. UPC § 3-713.

account for them and deliver them.[26] Absent fraudulent concealment, an action for breach of fiduciary duty is barred unless commenced within six months of the closing order. [27]

II. The Fiduciary Bond

A. Parties and Construction

Like other surety bonds, a fiduciary bond arises only by express contract of the parties.[28] There are three parties to the bond: (1) the principal/fiduciary, whose debt or obligation is the subject of the transaction; (2) the obligee/beneficiary, to whom the debt or obligation runs; and (3) the surety, who undertakes to perform the debt or obligation if the principal defaults.[29]

As stated in *Chisholm v. House*,[30] an action on a trustee's bond:

> The liability of the trustees arises out of the trust agreement, and is based upon the faithful performance of the trust. The liability of Martin as surety arises by contract, and is governed by its terms and conditions. Its terms are to be interpreted by the same rules observed in other contracts. [Citations omitted]. But, having guaranteed the faithful performance of the trust, Martin's liability as surety is measured precisely by the liability of the trustees—whatever discharged the trustees discharged Martin. [Citations omitted]. And, conversely, whatever binds the trustees binds Martin, for as surety he can make no defense which the trustees waived, or by their conduct precluded themselves from making. [Citations omitted]. Any act of the principal which estops him from setting up a defense personal to himself, operates equally against his surety.

The terms of the bond are given their ordinary meaning, but if it is a statutory bond (as most fiduciary bonds are), the statute controls over any conflicting terms in the bond itself.[31] Even though a bond may not be executed or approved in the prescribed manner, the surety may be estopped from contending the statute does not apply.[32] Similarly, the surety may be estopped to deny the bond's recitals that the principal's appointment was valid.[33] That the surety was fraudulently induced to issue a fiduciary bond is no defense, absent participation in the fraud by the beneficiary or party seeking to recover on the bond.[34]

B. Terms and Conditions

---

26 UPC § 3-608.

27 UPC § 3-1005.

28 *Lawyers Surety Corp. v. Whitehead*, 719 So.2d 833 (Ala. 1998); *Estate of Camarda*, 425 N.Y.S.2d 1012 (Surr. Ct. 1980).

29 *Camarda*.

30 183 F.2d 698, 707 (10th Cir. 1950),

31 *Id.*

32 *Guardianship of Hampton*, 374 N.W.2d 264 (Minn. 1985).

33 *State ex rel. Stone v. United States Fidelity & Guaranty Co.*, 78 N.E.2d 881 (Ind. App. 1948).

34 *Estate of Polevski*, 452 A.2d 469 (App. Div. N.J. 1982); *Judge of Probate v. Nudd*, 199 A.2d 296 (N.H. 1964).

Under the Uniform Probate Code, a bond may be required by the will or by the court on its own or upon request by a party in interest or creditor.[35] The amount of the bond is generally set at twice the representative's sworn estimate of the value of the personal estate and the income expected from the personal and real estate over the next year.[36] The court must approve the bond and can require a different amount on petition.[37] The bond names the state as obligee for benefit of persons interested in the estate.[38] It "shall be conditioned upon the faithful discharge by the fiduciary of all duties according to law."[39] The surety is jointly and severally liable with the personal representative and consents to the jurisdiction of the court.[40] The surety is entitled to notice of any proceedings pertaining to the fiduciary duties of the representative and naming the surety as a party. Usually a proceeding against the surety is commenced on the petition of a successor personal representative or a co-representative but any party in interest has standing to sue for breach of the bond.[41] The bond is not void after the first recovery but may be proceeded against from time to time until the whole penalty is exhausted.[42]

Whether the Uniform Probate Code applies or not, the liability of the surety generally is coextensive with the principal's liability for losses caused by official acts or omissions.[43] The surety guarantees the fiduciary will faithfully perform his trust.[44] As one court put it, the bond protects against mismanagement, waste, and fraud.[45] The fiduciary must properly marshal, administer and account for all of the estate assets coming into his possession or control.[46] Reasonable care and diligence must be employed[47] to maximize the ultimate distribution to the beneficiaries of the estate, whether creditors, or heirs.[48] This is a continuing duty and any misappropriated or imprudently invested funds must be reimbursed.[49] The fiduciary is presumed to possess any funds traced to him and it is his burden to prove otherwise.[50].

In particular, claims against the estate must not be concealed.[51] Accurate records must be kept and court orders obeyed.[52] Estate assets must be appropriately insured.[53] Inappropriate

---

35 UPC §§ 3-601, 3-603, 3-605.

36 UPC § 3-604.

37 *Id.*

38 UPC § 3-606(1).

39 UPC § 3-606(2).

40 UPC § 3-606(3).

41 UPC § 3-606(3).

42 UPC § 3-606(4).

43 *Martin v. Hanschu*, 738 P.2d 96 (Kan. 1987).

44 *In re Foodsource, Inc.*, 130 B.R. 549 (N.D. Cal. 1991).

45 *Gabriella v. Sneer*, 613 S.W.2d 810 (Tex. App. 1981) (guardian's bond).

46 *Estate of Camarda*, 425 N.Y.S.2d 1012 (Surr. Ct. 1980)(executor); *State v. Steward*, 77 Cal. Rptr. 418 (Cal. App. 1969) (receiver's bond); *Strickland v. Jackson*, 130 S.E.2d 22 (N.C. 1963) (executor).

47 *In re Melenyzer*, 140 B.R. 143 (W.D. Tex. 1992).

48 *Id.*

49 *Estate of Dyniewicz*, 648 N.E.2d 1076 (Ill. App. 1995).

50 *Cross v. Old Republic Surety Co.*, 983 S.W.2d 771 (Tex. App. 1998) (administrator's bond); *Presto v. Coppice*, 296 A.2d 150 (Md. App. 1972).

51 *Cross*; *Estate of Sample v. Travelers Indem. Co.*, 603 S.W.2d 942 (Mo. 1980).

52 *Presto.*

53 *In re Kinross Manufacturing Corp.*, 174 B.R. 702 (W.D. Mich. 1994).

loans must not be made.[54] If estate assets need to be sold, the sale must be conducted so as to get the highest obtainable price, with no suppression of bidding.[55]

The fiduciary must keep trust property separate from his individual property and designate it as such. If he does, then he and his surety are not necessarily liable for a loss in the trust property's value. That loss must have been caused by a breach of duty on his part. But if he fails to segregate the trust property, he and his surety are strictly liable. This rule is intended to deter the trustee from speculating with trust property and claiming it as his own if it goes up in value but as trustee if it goes down. However, a merely technical failure to earmark may be forgiven, absent a corresponding loss.[56]

If the representative of a decedent's estate fails to identify and notify all heirs readily ascertainable by reasonable inquiry, he and his surety are liable to the omitted heirs in the amount of their share.[57] Similarly, a receiver's surety is liable if the receiver is obligated to convey trust property to a beneficiary but instead conveys it to another without authorization.[58]

The fiduciary forfeits any right to compensation if he breaches his duties.[59] Professionals such as attorneys or accountants may be retained but the fiduciary and his surety must answer if their retention or compensation is inappropriate or excessive.[60]

If the fiduciary neglects or fails to perform his duties, the fiduciary bond covers any resulting loss.[61] Ordinarily the surety is not liable absent negligence or wrongdoing by the fiduciary.[62] But proof of dishonest intent is unnecessary,[63] and good faith is not a defense.[64] However, the fiduciary should not be punished after the fact for decisions which at the time made seemed reasonable

Special rules apply to fiduciaries for insolvent estates. A bankruptcy trustee's bonded duties are not limited to tending to the undisputed property of the estate, but include secured property coming into his hands, and the duty of turning over such collateral or its proceeds to secured creditors.[65] Thus a priority creditor could recover on a receiver's bond when the receiver improperly distributed assets to lower priority creditors.[66]

An extreme example of this is *In re Reich*.[67] The surety for a bankruptcy trustee was held liable to the debtor for the collapse of a vacant building's roof. The trustee knew or

54 *Gabriella v. Sneer*, 613 S.W.2d 810 (Tex. App. 1981) (guardian's bond)

55 *In re Traffic Safety Co.*, 21 B.R. 669 (E.D. Pa. 1982).

56 *Lawyers Surety Corp. v. Whitehead*, 719 So.2d 833 (Ala. 1998) (conservator's bond).

57 *In re Estate of Kapelsohn*, 182 N.Y.S.2d 472 (Surr. Ct. 1958); *Stofft v. O'Shaughnessy*, 107 N.E.2d 643 (Ohio Prob. Ct., Franklin Cty. 1952); *Westhagen v. Harby*, 481 P.2d 438 (Wash. 1971).

58 *Presto*.

59 *Dyniewicz*; *In re Ferrante*, 51 F.3d 1473 (9th Cir. 1995); *American Fidelity Co. v. Barnard*, 181 A.2d 628 (N.H. 1962).

60 *Drake v. Trinity Universal Ins. Co.*, 600 S.W.2d 768 (1980).

61 *Dyniewicz*; *United States v. Associated Developers of Florida, Inc.*, 400 So.2d 17 (Fla. App. 1981) (receiver's bond).

62 *In re Shaefitz' Will*,62 160 N.Y.S.2d 698 (Surr. Ct. 1957).

63 *In re Kinross Manufacturing Corp.*, 174 B.R. 702 (W.D. Mich. 1994).

64 *Estate of Camarda*, 425 N.Y.S.2d 1012 (Surr. Ct. 1980).

65 *In re Louis Rosenberg Auto Parts, Inc.*, 209 B.R. 668 (W.D. Pa. 1997); *In re Ferrante*, 51 F.3d 1473 (9th Cir. 1995).

66 *Presto v. Coppice*, 296 A.2d 150 (Md. App. 1972) (secured creditor could recover on bond for receiver of thrift who distributed assets to depositors); *State v. Steward*, 77 Cal. Rptr. 418 (Cal. App. 1969) (state could recover on bond for receiver's failure to pay sales taxes withheld as priority over ordinary debts).

67 54 B.R. 995 (E.D. Mich. 1985).

should have known to remove the snow and had just enough funds in the estate to pay for it, but failed to do so. But in *In re James E. O'Connell Co., Inc.*, [68] a prospective purchaser of the debtor's business could not recover on the trustee's bond when the deal fell through. The trustee had not violated any court order or failed to faithfully account for the assets of estate.

III. Recurring Issues

A. STANDING

Typically the plaintiff in a fiduciary bond action will be a successor fiduciary, or one appointed ad litem. This follows from a general rule that only the estate through such representative has standing to sue on the bond for injury to the estate.[69] However, a third party owner of non-estate property has standing too, if the principal took that property into the estate and refused to make restitution.[70] Creditors of the estate have standing to sue on the fiduciary bond directly in some jurisdictions[71] but not in others.[72] On default by a bankruptcy trustee, relief is allowed against the surety either as a surcharge for the benefit of the estate, or as damages for the benefit of an injured party in interest.[73] Likewise, an omitted heir has standing to sue an estate representative's surety.[74]

B. RIPENESS

Generally it is a condition to an action on a fiduciary bond that there have been a final accounting and surcharge order determining the fiduciary's liability.[75] Thus if a statute requires that a claim be presented against an estate before its termination, failure to do that will bar relief against the surety.[76] Even a fiduciary's evasion of process may not excuse the beneficiary from obtaining a surcharge against the fiduciary before proceeding against the surety.[77] But some courts disagree.[78] In *Cross v. Old Republic Surety Co.*,[79] the court held that the creditor had no duty to join an insolvent principal as a party to an action on the bond even though the statute required the creditor obtain judgment against the principal. And an accounting to establish the principal's liability is not required if the amount of that liability can be ascertained without the accounting and the fiduciary has died, been removed, absconded

---

68 82 B.R. 118 (N.D. Cal. 1988).

69 *Scott v. State Farm Fire & Casualty Co.*, 947 S.W.2d 530 (Mo. App. 1997).

70 *Id.*

71 *In re Grant*, 381 N.E.2d 1348 (Ohio App. 1978) (creditor could sue administrator and surety directly).

72 *Matter of Vitale*, 414 N.Y.S.2d 370 (App. Div. 1979).

73 *In re George Schumann Tire and Battery Co., Inc.*, 145 B.R. 104 (M.D. Fla. 1992).

74 *Stofft v. O'Shaughnessy*, 107 N.E.2d 643 (Ohio Prob. Ct., Franklin Cty. 1952).

75 *United States v. Westchester Fire Ins. Co.*, 478 F.2d 133 (2d Cir. 1973); *State ex rel. Community Heating and Air Conditioning Co. v. Schwartz*, 452 S.W.2d 243 (Mo. App. 1970); *Griffith v. Western Surety Co.*, 432 P.2d 1019 (Ore. 1967); *Werner v. American Surety Co.*, 423 P.2d 86 (Wyo. 1967); *Howard v. Jeffrey*, 268 P.2d 897 (Okla. 1954); *Estate of Dwyer*, 335 P.2d 718 (Cal. App. 1959); *Guardianship of Petersen v. Universal Surety Co.*, 277 N.W.2d 428 (Neb. 1979).

76 *Cuda v. Safeco Ins. Co.*, 882 F. Supp. 967 (D. Ore. 1995).

77 *Price v. Price*, 239 Cal. Rptr. 158 (Cal. App. 1987).

78 *In re Grant*, 381 N.E.2d 1348 (Ohio App. 1978).

79 983 S.W.2d 771 (Tex. App. 1998).

with the funds, or is beyond the jurisdiction of the court.[80] Another exception is if the fiduciary procured his discharge by fraud.[81]

By the same token, absent fraud or collusion, the surety is considered a privy of its principal and is prima facie bound by a judgment against its principal.[82] However, the surety must be given notice and an opportunity to defend.[83] In effect, although a beneficiary or creditor may not be entitled to join a fiduciary's surety until the fiduciary's liability has been determined, that does not preclude the surety from intervening. The surety with notice may do this because it is bound by the outcome; it cannot relitigate the amount of the surcharge.[84]

C. Prior Loss

The surety is not liable for a preexisting debt of the fiduciary to the estate if the fiduciary was insolvent and unable to pay the debt throughout his term.[85] Similarly, the surety is not liable to a creditor if there was no money legally available in the estate to pay that creditor until after the bond term expired.[86] Further, some courts hold that the surety is not liable for loss or damage incurred prior to execution of bond.[87] Absent bond terms to the contrary, the surety is liable only for assets possessed by the principal during the bond period.[88] The bond guarantees against future, not past improprieties.[89] Thus the surety is not liable for a diminution in the value of an investment occurring before the bond was executed.[90] Nor is the surety responsible for a conversion by the fiduciary prior to his appointment and the filing of his bond. The principal had no duties of trust until his appointment; if he faithfully discharged those duties, the surety is not liable.[91] "[S]ureties do not agree to stand good for a failure to discharge a duty that was impossible at and before the time the bond was executed."[92]

But one must consider whether the principal breached a continuing duty to manage and account for estate assets. Thus if the principal wasted or converted estate property before the bond period, but could have reimbursed the estate from his own assets during the bond period, then the surety is liable.[93] Other courts have simply held that unless the bond expressly excludes liability for prior defaults, the surety will be liable for breaches of trust occurring

---

80 *Price v. Price*, 239 Cal. Rptr. 158 (Cal. App. 1987).

81 *Alexandrou v. Alexander*, 112 Cal. Rptr. 307 (Cal. App. 1974).

82 *Presto v. Coppice*, 296 A.2d 150 (Md. App. 1972); *In re Geraerdt's Estate*, 231 N.Y.S.2d 692 (Surr. Ct. 1962).

83 *Estate of Camarda*, 425 N.Y.S.2d 1012 (Surr. Ct. 1980); *Cross v. Old Republic Surety Co.*, 983 S.W.2d 771 (Tex. App. 1998); *Estate of Dyniewicz*, 648 N.E.2d 1076 (Ill. App. 1995).

84 *Estate of Davis*, 268 Cal. Rptr. 663 (Cal. App. 1990).

85 *Christ v. Aetna Cas. & Surety*, 667 P.2d 665 (Wyo. 1983); *Maryland Cas. Co. v. McCormack*, 488 S.W.2d 347 (Ky. App. 1972); *In re Shaefitz' Will*, 160 N.Y.S.2d 698 (Surr. Ct. 1957).

86 *Judge of Probate v. Nudd*, 219 A.2d 454 (N.H. 1966).

87 *Christ v. Aetna Cas. & Surety*, 667 P.2d 665 (Wyo. 1983).

88 *King v. Jones*, 971 S.W.2d 916 (Mo. App. 1998) (conservator's bond).

89 *Estate of Slack*, 509 N.W.2d 861 (Mich. 1994) (but see dissent); *Martin v. Hanschu*, 738 P.2d 96 (Kan. 1987).

90 *Slack.*

91 *Martin v. Hanschu*, 738 P.2d 96 (Kan. 1987).

92 *King v. Jones*, 971 S.W.2d 916, 922 (Mo. App. 1998), citing *State ex rel. Short v. Hardy*, 206 S.W. 904, 907 (Mo. App. 1918).

93 *Id.*

before the bond was executed.[94] But there still is no liability for losses occurring prior to the fiduciary's appointment.[95]

According to *In re Foodsource, Inc.*,[96] when a surety comes on the risk some period of time after the fiduciary's appointment, as a second bond, the majority rule is that such a bond is cumulative and liable for a prior default, the same as the initial bond. Unlike public official bonds, "later-filed, additional court-fiduciary bonds cover defalcations during the trustee's entire term, which, as the term is continuous, may have occurred prior to the bond's issuance."[97] But the court admitted, on closer analysis, that the fiduciary had to breach a duty during the later bond period, either to restore assets, if solvent, or to account for assets. Nonetheless, it is presumed as the later bond is issued that the fiduciary possesses all the assets of the estate received to that date. If he cannot account for those assets, it is a fresh breach of duty that the surety must mend.[98]

D. MULTIPLE CAPACITIES

A perplexing problem is the fiduciary bonded in multiple capacities. While in theory the termination of one capacity and commencement of the next ought to discharge the prior surety, in practice such allocation is difficult. In *American Fidelity Co. v. Barnard*,[99] the principal served first as a conservator and then as an executor and testamentary trustee, giving bond for all three roles. With the books and records in a haphazard state, it was "difficult to find where the embezzlement of one estate ended and the other began."[100] Was there a failure to account for assets in one capacity, a failure to obtain those assets in the next, or both? The court held:

> It was the duty of Barnard as trustee to demand from Barnard as executor the amount due the trust estate, and where the trustee has failed to receive the sum due and the executor has likewise failed to account for the sum due the trust estate, it is no answer on the part of the surety in an attempt to escape liability to say that the default occurred in Barnard's capacity as executor.[101]

Yet if the fiduciary properly transfers property to himself in another capacity, the surety for the prior capacity is not liable for subsequent defalcations.[102] In any event a fiduciary bond does not cover an action against a fiduciary in an individual capacity.[103]

E. COLOR OF OFFICE

To borrow the reasoning of a well-known fidelity case,[104] what is the rule when a fiduciary abuses his position not to steal from the estate, but to steal for it? Such malfeasance

94 *Estate of Camarda*, 425 N.Y.S.2d 1012 (Surr. Ct. 1980)
95 *Estate of Tomoschuk*, 381 N.Y.S.2d 911 (App. Div. 1976).
96 30 B.R. 549 (N.D. Cal. 1991).
97 *Id.* at 561.
98 *In re Foodsource, Inc.*, 130 B.R. 549 (N.D. Cal. 1991).
99 181 A.2d 628 (N.H. 1962).
100 *Id.* at 632
101 *Id.*
102 *Schilt v. Duvall*, 479 F.2d 1228 (DC Cir. 1973).
103 *State of Illinois v. Schechter*, 195 B.R. 380 (N.D. Ill. 1996).

is referred to as acting under color of office. The fiduciary of course will be liable to the third party victim. But the fiduciary's surety ordinarily is liable only for proper assets of the estate; the surety must answer for property received under color of office only if the bond or statute so provides.[105] To put it another way, non-estate property does not become an asset of the estate merely through commingling with estate property. As put in *Greenwich Savings Bank v. United States Fidelity & Guaranty Co.*:[106] "The machinations of the widow parading as an Administratrix were of her individual doing and did not come within the coverage of the estate fidelity bond." Even when a surety is accountable for property received under color of office, the surety is not liable for fraudulently procured life insurance proceeds, where the policy was void from its inception and thus the proceeds of the policy never entered the insured's estate.[107]

F. DISCHARGE

If the fiduciary's accounting is approved, the court will enter an order discharging him and his surety, and closing the estate. But this is no defense to prior wrongdoing discovered later—the estate can be reopened.[108] Limitations or laches should not run against a beneficiary who through legal incompetence or otherwise is justifiably ignorant of a fiduciary's fraud. Yet a creditor cannot stand by without objection to a receiver's final accounting that distributes assets to others, and then recover on the bond, absent fraud or "culpable negligence."[109]

A surety can also petition to be discharged in advance of its principal's discharge. In some states this may be done as of right,[110], while elsewhere it is at the discretion of the court.[111] A replacement bond or other security must be posted for the protection of the estate.[112] The surety need not show malfeasance by its principal.[113] The discharge is only from liability for subsequent misconduct.[114]

The validity of a beneficiary's release can be an issue. *In re Carpenter's Will*[115] involved a trust fund in favor of a widow and her three children. The widow and one of the sons, Henry, were bonded as the fund's trustees from 1912 to 1923, during which period they invaded and dissipated most of it. When the widow died in 1940, a second son, Theodore, sought relief against the surety. The surety pleaded that back in 1917, Theodore, upon

---

104 *Drexel Burnham Lambert Group v. Vigilant Ins. Co.*, 595 N.Y.S.2d 999, (Sup. Ct. 1993).

105 Cf. *Maryland Cas. Co. v. McCormack*, 488 S.W.2d 347 (Ky. App. 1972) (surety not liable under statute); *Federal Kemper Life Assur. Co. v. Old Republic Surety Co.*, 561 N.E.2d 1208 (Ill. App. 1990) (surety potentially liable under statute); *Gillium v. Hopkins*, 472 S.W.2d 436 (Mo. App. 1971) (surety liable*); Bank One of Ohio v. Brown*, 488 N.E.2d 939 (Ohio App. 1985) (surety liable).

106 345 N.E.2d 290, 292 (N.Y. 1976).

107 *Federal Kemper Life Assur. Co. v. Eichwedel*, 639 N.E.2d 246 (Ill. App. 1994).

108 *Estate of Dandier*, 847 P.2d 249 (Colo. App. 1993); *Gabriella v. Sneer*, 613 S.W.2d 810 (Tex. App. 1981) (guardian's bond); *Administrative Management Services, Inc. v. Fidelity and Deposit Co. of Maryland*, 152 Cal. Rptr. 620 (Cal. App. 1979) (receiver's bond); *Maryland Cas. Co. v. Ownes*, 74 So.2d 608 (Ala. 1954).

109 *College Club Dairy Inc. v. Amass*, 311 S.W.2d 532 (Ark. 1958).

110 *Estate of Rowell*, 156 So.2d 812 (Miss. 1963)

111 *Spradley v. St. Paul Fire & Marine Ins. Co.*, 134 S.E.2d 850 (Ga. App. 1964).

112 *Gabriella v. Sneer*, 613 S.W.2d 810 (Tex. App. 1981).

113 *Spradley*.

114 *Osborne Bonding & Surety Co. v. Glaze*, 497 S.E.2d 612 (Ga. App. 1998).

115 63 N.Y.S.2d 736 (NY App. Div. 1946).

obtaining his majority, had released the surety with knowledge of his mother and brother's misconduct. The court held this a valid defense.

However, in *Snyder v. United States Fidelity & Guaranty Co.*,[116], the court emphasized the need for court supervision to insure the integrity of the bonding process. The court orders the bond, approves it, and approves the discharge of principal. It follows that the court must approve any discharge of the surety as well, and not until it determines whether there has or may have been any harm to the beneficiary. The parties to the bond cannot divest the court of this duty. Thus a release signed by a ward upon reaching majority is invalid. The surety can seek its own release only by noticed motion. But there can be a hybrid situation. In *Sawyer v. State Surety Co.*,[117] the court held that a ward's stipulation in bankruptcy court that he would not enforce a judgment against the guardian, upon approval and acceptance by the county court, barred the ward from pursuing the surety.

A ward or infant cannot be estopped from recovering on the bond by that fact that he benefits from a wrongful dissipation of assets by the guardian. To permit such an estoppel would defeat the purpose of the bond, which is to prevent improvident spending of the ward's estate by court control through the guardian of that property.[118]

G. The Penal Sum, Attorney Fees and Interest

Multiple claims may be made on a fiduciary bond but the surety's aggregate liability cannot exceed the bond's penal sum.[119] That historically has included any liability for attorney fees.[120] But in *Nichols v. Preferred Nat. Ins. Co.*,[121] the Florida Supreme Court nixed both this rule and the rule that payment on a bond is not due until the principal's liability is established by court order. The court held that attorney fees may be awarded against a fiduciary's surety in excess of the penal sum under a statute allowing attorney fees against an insurer who fails to diligently investigate and pay a claim. In *Old Republic Surety Co. v. Reischmann*,[122] a lower court followed Nichols, but expressed concern over its "long-range impact." A surety may be faced with an uncooperative fiduciary and thus a costly and time-consuming investigation before it can reasonably determine its liability.[123] A rule requiring the surety to pay before the principal's liability was established could also interfere with the surety's indemnity rights against the principal.

Apart from the penal sum issue, some courts have held that attorney fees are not recoverable against a fiduciary's surety, absent fraud, bad faith or dishonesty.[124] Other courts have allowed a successor fiduciary to recover attorney's fees incurred both in removing the original representative and in compelling that representative to perform neglected duties or in

116 70 Cal. Rptr.2d 498 (Cal. App. 1997).

117 558 N.W.2d 43 (Neb. 1997).

118 *Estate of O'Leary*, 506 N.Y.S.2d 330 (N.Y. App. Div. 1986); *later opinion*, 521 N.Y.S.2d 138 (N.Y. App. Div. 1987).

119 *Campbell v. Employers' Liability Assur. Corp.*, 67 N.E.2d 230 (Mass. 1946); *Estate of Spinner*, 717 A.2d 362 (D.C. App. 1998).

120 *Guardianship of Davison*, 642 P.2d 1259 (Wash. App. 1982).

121 704 So.2d 1371 (1998).

122 713 So.2d 434 (Fla. App. 1998).

123 *Id.*

124 *Guardianship and Estate of P.A.H.*, 340 N.W.2d 577 (Wis. 1983).

performing the duties herself.[125] Interest may be allowed on the penal sum from the date the surety is notified of a breach or demand.[126]

H. Indemnity and Subrogation

The surety is subrogated to the rights of the estate or creditor against the principal or anyone else responsible for the loss.[127] But if the surety pays a bond claim without the court having found the fiduciary in default, the surety may be considered a volunteer and barred from recovering against the fiduciary.[128] However, the surety may also recover on its indemnity agreement against the principal,[129] and that agreement may preclude any volunteer defense. Nor can the fiduciary necessarily escape by filing bankruptcy. If there was fraud, the surety may be able to establish nondischargeability.[130] Subrogation against a fraudulent transferee is permitted.[131] And fraud or no fraud, upon satisfying an omitted distributee, the surety can obtain reimbursement from those who received in excess of their share.[132]

The surety may have remedies against accountants, attorneys, banks and others who facilitated the loss as well.[133] Thus a receiver's surety could recover against banks that the receiver used to embezzle from the estate as they had notice of his representative capacity and were liable as constructive trustees.[134] A guardian's surety could recover against the guardian's bank if it proved negligence, willful misconduct, or breach of contract by the bank.[135] Another guardian's surety could recover against financial institutions on notice they were dealing with a fiduciary.[136] But in a third case brought by a guardian's surety no relief was permitted against a title company which had issued a check to the guardian, nor against an attorney who had procured the bond. The defendants were not negligent, and the loss was unforeseeable; there was no proximate cause.[137]

Conclusion

The populist solution to probate woes is "Avoid Probate!" Populists are too simplistic. Many situations require court supervision through a bonded fiduciary. Many situations demand the entrusting or surrendering of one's affairs to another. Required or not, the bonding

---

125 *Lawyers Surety Corp. v. Larson*, 869 S.W.2d 649 (Tex. App. 1994).

126 *Guardianship of Davison*, 642 P.2d 1259 (Wash. App. 1982).

127 *United States Fidelity and Guaranty Co. v. Harper*, 561 S.W.2d 630 (Tex. App. 1978).

128 *Fengya v. Fengya*, 383 A.2d 1170 (N.J. App. Div. 1978).

129 See, e.g., *McGreevy v. Bremers*, 288 N.W.2d 490 (Neb. 1980) (surety was entitled to a setoff against any distribution to the principal); *In re Booker's Estate*, 91 N.Y.S.2d 16 (Surr. Ct. 1949).

130 *In re Yanke*, 230 B.R. 374 (8th Cir. BAP 1999); *In re Richardson*, 193 B.R. 378 (D.D.C. 1995).

131 *Akers v. Gillentine*, 231 S.W.2d 369 (Tenn. 1948) (guardian's surety was subrogated to right of ward to set aside a fraudulent conveyance to the guardian's wife).

132 *In re Estate of Kapelsohn*, 182 N.Y.S.2d 472 (Surr. Ct. 1958).

133 See *In re Conservatorship of W.L.*, 552 N.W.2d 734. (Minn. App. 1996) (surety allowed relief against bank that allowed conservator to withdraw funds without inquiring as to his authority).

134 *Matter of Quantum Dev. Co.*, 534 F.2d 532 (3rd Cir. 1976).

135 *Western Sur. Co. v. First Bank of South Dakota*, 427 N.W.2d 840 (S.D. 1988).

136 *State ex rel. Paden v. Carrel*, 597 S.W.2d 167 (Mo. App. 1979).

137 *Hartford Accident & Indem. Co.*, 395 So.2d 296 (Fla. App. 1981).

of that other is a wise precaution. Fiduciary bond sureties can best demonstrate their value by knowing and following the applicable law.

11

Judicial Bonds

L. Franklin Elmore
Mason A. Goldsmith, Jr.[1]

Introduction

"Judicial bonds" include those bonds which either a plaintiff or a defendant may be required to post in civil litigation. These bonds are typically required by a specific rule or statute, or by practice. Generally speaking, the purpose of a judicial bond is to ensure that the party required to post the bond will fulfill a particular obligation resulting from the litigation. Such obligations include the payment of court costs, the payment of monetary damages to the prevailing party, or the return of the seized property.[2]

This chapter will identify the most common types of judicial bonds and examine the prevailing litigant's method of enforcing its rights under such bonds, as well as the surety's scope of liability.

As a state-by-state review of judicial bonds is beyond the scope of this chapter, judicial bonds will be examined here primarily in the context of federal court proceedings. It is therefore important to consult local rules, statutes, and bond forms in each case.

I. *Types*

A. Appeal Bond

When a District Court renders a final judgment in a civil action, a losing party has the right to appeal. The Federal Rules of Appellate Procedure require the appellant to post an appeal bond to ensure the payment of the opposing party's court costs in the event the appeal is unsuccessful.[3] Only specific types of court costs are covered by a federal appeal bond, including: the cost of the preparation and transmission of the record; the reporter's transcript (if needed to determine the appeal); premiums paid for a supersedeas bond or other bond to preserve rights pending appeal; and, the fee for filing the notice of appeal.[4] Since state local rules or statutes determine which costs are recoverable under an appeal bond, these costs may vary from state to state.

---

1. L. Franklin Elmore is the managing shareholder, and Mason A. Goldsmith, Jr. is an associate, in the Construction and Surety Practice Group of the national law firm of Ogletree, Deakins, Nash, Smoak & Stewart, P.C. in its Greenville, South Carolina offices.

2. *See* Frank B. Keech, G. Price Hayden, and Mark S. Rhodes, *Miscellaneous Bonds*, in *Handling Fidelity, Surety and Financial Risk Claims* § 10.27, at 231 (Robert F. Cushman et al. eds., 2d ed. 1990); Dan L. Kirby, *Court Bonds*, in *The Law of Suretyship*, at 20-1 to 20-7 (Edward G. Gallagher ed. 1993).

3. *See F. R.. App. Proc., Rule 7.*

4. *F. R. App. Proc., Rule 39(e).*

The amount of an appeal bond is generally determined by the District Court[5], but can be considered by the appellate court if the appellee raises a challenge to the sufficiency of its amount.[6] Appeal bonds do not cover damages owed to the appellee or the appellee's attorneys' fees[7], but rather are limited only to those court costs which the applicable rule or statute specifically allows the prevailing party to recover.

The failure to timely file an appeal bond can result in dismissal of the appeal, depending upon such factors as the prejudice to the other party, the reason for the failure to file an appeal bond, and whether the appellant made an effort to cure the defect.[8] In some instances, appellees have been known to waive the appeal bond requirement in order to secure a decision on the merits.[9]

B. SUPERSEDEAS BOND

Although the same language is found in appeal and supersedeas bonds, these bonds are separate and distinct. A surety's obligations under these bonds should not be confused. Whereas an appeal bond ensures the payment of court costs, a supersedeas bond guarantees the successful trial court litigant that it will have a source of collection after the appeal. In the absence of a supersedeas bond, the filing of an appeal does not in and of itself prevent the winning party from taking steps to collect its judgment. To suspend such collection efforts during the appeal process, the appellant must obtain a stay of execution, also called a "writ of supersedeas," by filing a motion with the trial court and posting a supersedeas bond equal to or greater than the judgment.[10]

In federal court, the application for a stay of judgment or writ of supersedeas is generally made to the District Court, but can be made to the Court of Appeals or to an appellate judge if application to the District Court is impractical, is denied, or has not been promptly determined.[11] The party seeking to have the judgment stayed must file a bond sufficient to protect the prevailing trial court litigant. The amount of the supersedeas bond will normally take into account the amount needed to satisfy the judgment appealed from, as well as costs, interest, and other damages which might result from the staying of the judgment pending appeal.

It should be remembered that a supersedeas bond is not an absolute requirement for filing an appeal. If the appellant is unable to obtain a supersedeas bond[12] or simply chooses not to seek a stay of the judgment, it may go forward with the appeal and the prevailing litigant shall have the right to enforce its judgment during the appeal process. In such instances the appellant assumes the risk of being able to recover assets which are executed against if his appeal is subsequently successful.

If, on the other hand, an appeal is taken by the party prevailing at trial, the losing party may not be required to file a bond to stay collection efforts during its own appeal. Some circuits have held that the prevailing party's appeal operates as an automatic supersedeas.[13]

---

5. *See F. R.. App. Proc., Rule 7.*
6. *Speed* v. *Transamerica*, 18 F.R.D. 492 (D.Del. 1995).
7. *In re American President Lines, Inc.*, 779 F.2d 714 (US App. D.C. 1985).
8. *See Powers v. Citizens Union Nat'l Bank & Trust Co.*, 329 F.2d 507 (6th Cir. 1964).
9. *De Lourett v. Kerlin,* 182 F.2d 750 (5th Cir. 1950).
10. F. R. App. Proc., Rule 8(a).
11. F. R. App. Proc., Rule 8(a),(b).
[illegible] *Bank of Nova Scotia v. Pemberton*, 964 F.Supp. 189 (D.V.I. 1997)(appeal proceeded even though appellant [illegible]ost full supersedeas bond or to provide other security).
[illegible] *v. Atlas Machine & Iron Works*, 803 F.2d 794 (4th Cir. 1986) (noting that if the prevailing party appeals [illegible] favor, its appeal suspends execution of the judgment).

C. Injunction Bond/Bond For Dissolution Of Injunction

1. Injunction Bond

An injunction is an equitable remedy through which a court may order a person to refrain from doing a particular thing or taking a particular course of action. Its principal purpose is to preserve the status quo and to prevent acts which would cause irreparable harm or injury to one of the parties. In some instances a court may issue a "temporary injunction" or "preliminary injunction" after notice to the adverse party and a hearing, but prior to a final trial on the merits. When issuing such injunctions, the court may require the party seeking the injunction to furnish a bond to hold the enjoined party harmless should it eventually be determined the temporary injunction should not have been granted.

In federal court, the bond required for an injunction is governed by Rule 65 of the Federal Rules of Civil Procedure. Rule 65 provides that "[n]o restraining order or preliminary injunction shall issue except upon the giving of security by the applicant, in such sum as the court deems proper, for the payment of such costs and damages as may be incurred or suffered by any party who is found to have been wrongfully enjoined or restrained."[14]

Although the conditions of an injunction bond and the damages recoverable under an injunction bond differ among jurisdictions and are dependent on the facts of a particular case, their general purpose is the same - to ensure the defendant a source of recovery should the injunction subsequently be determined to have been granted in error. An injunction bond may obligate a surety to pay for costs, damages, and sometimes even attorneys' fees sustained as a result of a wrongful injunction.

2. Bond For Dissolution Of Injunction

An enjoined party may move the court to dissolve an injunction. At least one recognized treatise has asserted that in appropriate circumstances the court may require the party to post a bond to cover any damages which result from dissolution of the injunction.[15]

D. Attachment Bond/Bond For Release Or Dissolution Of Attachment

1. Attachment Bond

Attachment is a summary process whereby a plaintiff, without a full trial on the merits, may obtain a court order directing seizure of a defendant's property pending resolution of a civil suit in progress. The primary purpose of attachment is to early on obtain a source for satisfying a judgment which may later be obtained against a defendant who is likely to attempt to evade collection efforts. Because attachment allows for pre-judgment seizure of property it is considered to be an extraordinary remedy. While the requirements for attachment vary from jurisdiction to jurisdiction,

---

14. F. R. Civ. Proc., Rule 65(c).

15. *See* Frank B. Keech, G. Price Hayden, and Mark S. Rhodes, *Miscellaneous Bonds*, in *Handling Fidelity, Surety and Financial Risk Claims* § 10.27, at 231 (Robert F. Cushman et al. eds., 2d ed. 1990).

the typical grounds are that the defendant is a non-resident or foreign corporation; that the defendant has absconded with property or has concealed himself; that the defendant has or is about to remove property from the state; or, that the defendant has secreted or assigned property with the intent to defraud creditors.

A plaintiff seeking a writ of attachment is generally required to provide an attachment bond to protect the defendant from damages resulting from an erroneous deprivation of property and to minimize the risk of attachment claims made in bad faith. The purpose of an attachment bond is to provide a source of payment for the defendant's costs and damages resulting from the deprivation of property should the attachment later be set aside by the court.

Some state statutes expressly state the amount of the attachment bond[16], whereas other statutes leave the decision to require a bond and the amount of the bond to the discretion of the court.[17] Even though an attachment bond may satisfy the strict requirements of the attachment statute, a defendant may allege that it is insufficient to protect his interests and seek to increase the amount of the bond. In such instances the court has the discretion to consider such factors as the likelihood of the plaintiff's success on the merits and the potential damages to the defendant in deciding whether or not to order that the attachment bond be increased under threat of dismissal.[18]

2. Bond For Release Or Dissolution Of Attachment

A defendant seeking to regain possession of the property prior to a full trial on the merits may do so by filing a bond for release or dissolution of attachment. Depending on the law of the particular jurisdiction, the bond must be equal to or greater than the value of the attached property. The names and purposes of attachment, dissolution or release bonds vary from state to state.

In some states, the bonds serve only to release the attached property from the custody of the public official and are known as "release bonds," "delivery bonds," or "forthcoming bonds." Under this type of bond the surety essentially guarantees that if the judgment is rendered against the defendant, the property shall be forthcoming to satisfy the judgment or else the surety will be bound to the extent of the value of the property. Under this type of bond the lien of attachment remains against the property.

In other states, the bonds are known as "dissolution bonds" and actually dissolve the attachment in its entirety. The plaintiff's sole source of recovery becomes the bond, which is in effect substituted for the property.

E. REPLEVIN BOND/BOND FOR REDELIVERY OF PROPERTY REPLEVIED

1. Replevin Bond

Replevin, also known as claim and delivery, is an action through which a plaintiff can regain ssession of goods and chattels from a defendant who has unlawfully taken them from him and r damages resulting from the unlawful taking. The primary relief sought is the return of the the recovery of damages is generally incidental.[19] The procedure for pursuing a replevin

v. *Co. v. F.D.I.C.*, 916 P.2d 680 (Haw. 1996).
ore, 629 A.2d 357 (Conn. 1993).
Development Corp., 177 S.E.2d 328 (N.C. Ct. App. 1970).
tords v. Petrie, 39 F.2d 512 (1930).

action is prescribed by statute, but generally requires the plaintiff to (1) file an affidavit identifying the property and stating the plaintiff is its lawful owner and (2) post a replevin bond.

The purpose of a replevin bond is to protect the defendant from losses which may result from the plaintiff's seizure of the personal property. The bond is typically conditioned for the return of the property if it is ordered to be returned, as well as for the payment of damages proximately caused by the seizure.

2. Bond For Redelivery Of Property Replevied

Replevin statutes generally provide a procedure through which a defendant may post a redelivery bond and have the property returned to him. The right to file such a bond is oftentimes absolute. Such bonds act not only as a substitute for the property at issue, but also as security for any money judgment which the plaintiff recovers through his replevin action.

F. Miscellaneous Judicial Bonds

In addition to appeal, supersedeas, injunction, attachment and replevin bonds, there are other judicial bonds which some jurisdictions may require. In some instances, a sheriffs' indemnity bond may be required to protect the sheriff against liability resulting from the seizure of property if it is later determined that the seizure was wrongful.[20] Also, some courts require non-resident plaintiffs to post bond or undertaking to secure court costs and attorneys' fees that may be awarded to a defendant in a civil action.[21] Although the exact requirements of miscellaneous judicial bonds may vary, like other judicial bonds, the overall purpose is to ensure that the parties involved in litigation will fulfill their obligations.

II. *Enforcement of Judicial Bonds*

The filing or submission of a judicial bond constitutes a surety's submission to the jurisdiction of a court.[22] Since such bonds are deposited in place of cash, courts will typically treat them the same and deal with them summarily.

In federal court, the extent of a surety's liability under a judicial bond may be determined through an expedited summary hearing, without the necessity of an independent action.[23] The federal rules do not prohibit an independent action in state or federal court, but few parties choose to forego this expedited process. A court's refusal to allow a timely motion for such an expedited hearing is an abuse of discretion.[24] A bond claimant's decision to use the summary procedure or to initiate an independent action can have significant consequences. For example, the parties would have the right to a jury trial in an independent action, but not in a summary hearing.[25]

20. *See* Frank B. Keech, G. Price Hayden, and Mark S. Rhodes, *Miscellaneous Bonds*, in *Handling Fidelity, Surety and Financial Risk Claims* § 10.27, at 231 (Robert F. Cushman et al. eds., 2d ed. 1990).

21. Dan L. Kirby, *Court Bonds*, in *The Law of Suretyship*, at 20-1 to 20-7 (Edward G. Gallagher ed. 1993).

22. F. R. App. P., Rules 8(b); F. R. Civ. P., Rule 65.1.

23. F. R. App. P., Rules 8(b); F. R. Civ. P., Rule 65.1.

24. *Public Serv. Comm'n of Missouri v. Brashear Freight Lines, Inc.*, 312 U.S. 621 (1941) (holding that trial court's refusal to entertain enjoined parties, motion to assess damages under an injunction bond was improper).

25. Wright, Miller & Kane, *Federal Practice and Procedure: Civil 2d § 2972.*

The party seeking to recover under the bond is required to give the surety notice, and the failure to give notice will result in a judgment against the surety being vacated.[26] The surety must respond quickly after receiving notice of a hearing on the bond. Where it appears that a valid claim exists against the bond, the surety should prepare to contest the amount of liability or make arrangements to satisfy the obligations of the bond by either having its principal pay the judgment or by paying the judgment itself and seeking recovery from the principal's collateral and the indemnitors on the bond.

Regardless of whether a summary procedure or an independent action is pursued, a bond claimant cannot proceed against the bond until there has been a final determination on the merits. A determination is not final on an appeal or supersedeas bond until the trial court's judgment has been affirmed or the appellant's appeal has been dismissed. There must be a final determination that the plaintiff was not entitled to the temporary injunction, such as through a dismissal of the entire injunction[27] or a dissolution of only part of the injunction before a determination on an injunction bond is final.[28] Likewise, a party's voluntarily dismissal or abandonment of its appeal or request for injunctive relief constitutes a final determination on the merits and triggers liability on the bond.[29] However, if the opposing party consents to dismissal of the action, it is precluded from proceeding against the bond.[30]

III. *Scope of Liability*

A. Terms Of The Bond

As a general rule, a surety's liability on a judicial bond is governed by the court order which required the bond to be posted and the terms of the particular bond in question. It is extremely important that the language in a judicial bond address not only the conditions under which the surety may become liable (i.e. dismissal of appeal, adverse decision in an attachment or replevin action, reversal of injunction), but also the monetary limit of the surety's liability in the form of a penal sum.

An "injunction bond" enjoining a plaintiff from executing on a judgment cannot be treated as a "supersedeas bond." In *Virginia Plastics Co. v. Biostim, Inc..*[31] *A* surety appealed from a district court order requiring it to pay the face amount of an injunction bond to a plaintiff. On appeal the surety pointed out that since the bond was an injunction bond posted pursuant to Rule 65(c) of the Federal Rules of Civil Procedure, the plaintiff could not simply recover its judgment from the proceeds of the bond (as though it were a supersedeas bond), but instead had to show damages resulting from the injunction itself. At the time the injunction bond was posted the defendant was in poor financial condition and after the injunction was lifted the defendant filed for bankruptcy. Adopting the surety's argument, the Court found that in order to recover under the injunction bond

26. *City of New York v. Slayne,* 1 F.R.D. 742 (D.N.Y. 1941).

27. *Madison Shipping Corp. v. National Maritime Union,* 204 F.Supp. 22,23 (D.Pa. 1962)("We think the Court of Appeals direction 'to dismiss that portion of the complaint which seeks injunctive relief' must be regarded as equivalent to 'final judgment after trial,' for present purposes.")

28. *Atomic Oil Co. of Oklahoma, Inc. v. Bardahl Oil Co.,* 419 F.2d 1097 (10th Cir. 1969)(reduction of territorial application of injunction from thirty states to three states triggered preliminary injunction bond).

29. *United Motors Serv., Inc. v. Tropic-Aire, Inc.,* 57 F.2d 479 (8th Cir. 1932) (voluntary dismissal of request for injunctive relief).

30. *Golden Gate Mechanical Contractor's Ass'n v. Seaboard Sur. Co.,* 389 F.2d 892 (9th Cir. 1968).

31. 820 F.2d 76 (3rd Cir. 1987).

the plaintiff had to prove that the defendant's ability to satisfy the judgment had diminished during the injunction period, a difficult task in light of the defendant's earlier poor financial condition.

Similarly, an "appeal bond" which only covers the costs in appellate court cannot be treated as a "supersedeas bond" to assure payment of damages awarded in district court.[32]

B. Amount Of Damages

Generally speaking, a surety's liability cannot exceed the penal sum stated in a judicial bond.[33] The principal is not protected by the penal sum and may be liable for a greater amount than the surety. The measure of damages for a party intended to be covered by a judicial bond is either the losses which the unjustly restrained party has sustained during the period of restraint, or the principal's unjust enrichment during this time. The wrongfully restrained party bears the burden of proving the amount of his damages which were proximately caused by the wrongful action and cannot hold the surety liable for unrelated damages. This does not require the bond claimant to prove its damages to a mathematical certainty, a showing by the preponderance of the evidence is the standard used.

C. Defenses

Most judicial bonds are subject to the same general defenses relating to a surety's defenses against claims by an obligee. Additional defenses personal to the surety may also be asserted. In *Carriage Town, Inc. v. LandCo., Inc.*,[34] the Court considered a unilateral attempt by a plaintiff and defendant to apply a $250,000 preliminary injunction bond to a permanent injunction containing a $100,000 liquidated damages clause. The surety objected to the defendant's attempt to recover against the bond on two grounds. First, the surety claimed that there had been a material change in risk. A liquidated damages clause had been created and a ninety day cure period in the original contract for which the injunction bond had been issued had been shortened to only ten days. Second, the surety argued that the damages which the defendant sought to recover were a result of the subsequent permanent injunction, not the initial preliminary injunction which the surety had bonded. The District Court agreed and discharged the surety's obligations under the bond. According to the Court, the plaintiff and defendant lacked the power to unilaterally increase the risk under the bond and, in any event, the defendant's damages were the result of a different injunction than the surety had bonded.

In *Werbungs Und Commerz Union Austalt v. Collectors Guild, Ltd.*,[35] the Court recognized that a surety may be discharged from its obligations under a supersedeas bond by the collusive acts of a plaintiff and defendant. The surety alleged that its principal, the defendant, had colluded with the plaintiff by agreeing to accept $10,000 from the plaintiff in exchange for not retrying the damage portion of the case. Although the Court found insufficient evidence in the record to make a determination of the parties' rights in this particular case, it did remand the case to the bankruptcy court for findings of fact and conclusion of law in light of the surety's argument.

---

32. *City of New York v. Slayne*, 1 F.R.D. 742 (D.N.Y. 1941).

33. *Coyne-Delany Co. v. Capital Development Board of Illinois*, 717 F.2d 385 (7th Cir. 1983) (finding that surety could not be required to pay more than face amount of injunction bond).

34. 998 F.Supp. 646 (D.S.C. 1998).

35. 782 F.Supp. 870 (D.N.Y. 1991).

IV. *Conclusion*

Although the characteristics of particular judicial bonds may vary, their general purpose is clearly to ensure that parties involved in civil litigation will fulfill their respective obligations. Given the fact that judicial bonds are essentially financial guaranty bonds on which the surety may be called upon to act with relatively short notice, sureties are well advised to secure adequate collateral and strong indemnitors before issuing a judicial bond. Although certain defenses may be available to a surety, in most instances determinations of liability will be beyond the control of the surety and even its principal.

12

Subdivision Bonds

David C. Veis
Laura P. Nash
Edward D. Lodgen

Introduction

Although Subdivision Performance and Payment Bonds (Subdivision Bonds) are somewhat similar to traditional Public Works Performance and Payment Bonds (Public Works Bonds), there are many differences and distinctions which require a separate review, description and analysis. The unique aspects of Subdivision Bonds as compared with Public Works Bonds include:

(1) The governmental control mandated by the statutory scheme requiring a developer to enter into a Subdivision Agreement secured by Subdivision Bonds.
(2) The differing roles, positions and obligations of the principal and obligee on Subdivision Bonds.
(3) The shift of the funding responsibility for the placement of the improvements from the obligee to the principal.
(4) The distinctions in coverages and limitation periods.
(5) The special claims handling procedures and methodologies in avoiding and responding to claims from the obligee and/or third parties.

Each of the above distinctions will be discussed to highlight and focus upon special claims handling issues raised by Subdivision Bonds.

I. Governmental Control

A. THE POWER TO CONTROL SUBDIVISION GROWTH

Many states, counties, cities and other local governmental entities (hereinafter collectively referred to as Public Agency) have enacted statutes, codes or ordinances (hereinafter collectively referred to as Statutory Scheme) for regulating land use and subdivision growth. Obtaining approval from the Public Agency, whether through a subdivision map, permit or otherwise, is often the initial step a developer must take in developing a parcel of real property. The Statutory Scheme enacted by the Public Agency establishes its authority to regulate and control the design and improvements of subdivision developments within their jurisdiction. In the course of regulating the design and improvements within a subdivision, the Public Agency may impose conditions on the issuance of a subdivision map or other standards for the improvements. This power provides a means for the

Public Agency to require compliance with certain conditions by a developer in exchange for the right to subdivide.[1]

B. THE GOALS AND PURPOSES OF THE STATUTORY SCHEME

A primary goal of the Statutory Scheme is to encourage orderly community development by providing for the regulation and control of the design and improvement of a subdivision with proper consideration to its relation to adjoining areas.[2] The Statutory Scheme is intended to facilitate the coordination of subdivision planning (lot size, configuration, street patterns and utility easements) with the overall community planning shown on general and specific plans adopted by the Public Agency. A related purpose of the Statutory Scheme is to assure consistency of subdivision design and improvements with local standards for development, (type and density), public health and other environmental concerns. Another critical function of the Statutory Scheme is to insure that the developer properly installs streets, sewers and drains prior to their dedication to the Public Agency and its taking over their maintenance.[3] These goals and purposes will prevent the subdivision from becoming an undue burden on the community and local taxpayers.[4]

C. THE SUBDIVISION AGREEMENT AND THE SUBDIVISION BONDS

When public improvements required by the Public Agency as part of the Statutory Scheme have not been completed, the Public Agency often requires the developer to enter into an improvement agreement (Subdivision Agreement) as a condition to beginning any work of improvement on the property.[5] In the typical Subdivision Agreement entered into between a developer and a Public Agency, the developer agrees to construct the improvements required by the Public Agency at the developer's expense in accordance with the Statutory Scheme.

---

1. See, *Associated Home Builders, Inc. v. City of Walnut Creek*, 4 Cal.3d 633, 94 Cal.Rptr. 630 (Cal., 1971); *The Pines v. City of Santa Monica*, 29 Cal.3d 656, 175 Cal.Rptr. 336 (Cal., 1981); *Benny v. City of Alameda*, 105 Cal.App.3d 1006, 164 Cal.Rptr. 776 (Cal.App., 1980); *Bank of Southeastern Connecticut v. Nazarko Realty Group*, 49 Conn.App. 452, 714 A.2d 722 (Conn.App., 1998); and *City of Bellafontaine Neighbors v. J.J. Kelley Realty and Building Co.*, 460 S.W.2d 298, (Mo.App., 1970).

2. The basic purpose of a subdivision performance bond is to "assure those who purchase homes in a new subdivision that they will receive the public improvements that were a large part of the inducement to purchase lots and/or homes in that development." *Town of Southington v. Commercial Union Insurance Company*, 54 Conn.App. 328, 334, 735 A.2d 835 (Conn.App., 1999), certification granted in part by *Town of Southington v. Commercial Insurance Company*, 251 Conn. 906, 738 A.2d 1093 (Conn., 1999).

3. See, e.g. *Evola v. Wendt Construction Company*, 170 Cal.App.2d 21, 338 P.2d 498 (Cal.App., 1959) (the Subdivision. Map Act discussed in this case has since been amended).

4. "The reason for requiring the subdivider to install street improvements is directly related to the public health, safety and welfare. Such a requirement assures suitable access routes, advances the objectives of the community plan, and protects the municipality and its taxpayers from the burden of constructing additional streets to accommodate new developments." *General Insurance Company of America v. City of Colorado Springs*, 638 P.2d 752, 757 (Colo., 1982).

5. See, e.g., *South Central Coast Regional Comm. v. Charles A. Pratt Construction Company*, 128 Cal.App.3d 830, 180 Cal.Rptr.555 (Cal.App., 1982), called into doubt by *Lakeview Development Corp. v. City of South Lake Tahoe*, 915 F.2d 1290 (9th Cir. (Cal.) 1990).

Most Statutory Schemes require the developer's obligations under a Subdivision Agreement to be guaranteed by the posting of security acceptable to the Public Agency.[6] In addition to assuring faithful performance of the work covered by the Subdivision Agreement, security may be required to cover liability for changes or alterations in the work and cost and reasonable fees, including attorneys' fees.[7] Often, the Public Agency may require that the security warrant the work for one (1) year following completion and acceptance of the improvements, including liability for defective work, labor and materials.[8]

The form of security most commonly required of a developer is a faithful performance bond executed by a corporate surety.[9] Many Public Agencies also require a labor and material bond to accompany the performance bond.

The amount of security required to secure performance of the obligation under a Subdivision Agreement is determined by the Public Agency, generally within a prescribed monetary range. The portion of the security which guarantees faithful performance of the completion of the improvements or agreement (i.e. the performance bond) is generally in an amount not less than fifty percent (50%) or more than one hundred percent (100%) of the total estimated cost of the improvements (or the acts to be performed). The labor and material bond secures payment to the contractor, subcontractors, laborers, materialmen and persons furnishing equipment. Generally, the payment bond is not less than fifty percent (50%) or more than one hundred percent (100%) of the total estimated cost of the improvements. In addition to the base cost of the improvements, the security also can cover costs and reasonable expenses and fees, including attorneys' fees, that the Public Agency may incur in successfully enforcing the secured obligation.[10]

Once the improvement work commences, the developer and the Subdivision Performance Bond surety may be held liable until all subdivision improvements are completed and accepted.[11] In this regard, the developer and its surety would also be obligated to maintain and repair any completed improvements until all subdivision improvements guaranteed by the security are completed and accepted.[12] Even modifications to a Subdivision Agreement, such as extensions of time for completion of the work granted by the local agency without notice to the surety, may not exonerate the surety, as the Subdivision Agreement may incorporate a waiver of any notice requirements by the surety.[13]

---

6. See, e.g., 11 O.S. 1951 §1425; Connecticut General Statutes §8-25; RCW §58.17.130.

7. See e.g.,, *California Government Code*, §66499.9.

8. See, e.g., *California Government Code*, §66499.9(c).

9. An example of another form of security is found in *Vale Dean Canyon Homeowners Association v. Dean*, 100 Or.App. 158, 785 P.2d 772 (Or.App., 1990) wherein the Public Agency required a certificate of deposit as security to assure performance of the Subdivision Agreement.

10. See, e.g., *California Government Code*, §66499.

11. See, e.g., *Kern County v. Edgemont Development Corp.*, 222 Cal.App.2d 874, 879, 35 Cal.Rptr. 629 (Cal.App., 1963), and *Mount Florence Group v. City of Peekskill*, 652 N.Y.S.2d 814, 235 A.2d 787, (N.Y.A.D., 1997). See however, *Town of Southington v. Commercial Union Insurance Company*, 54 Conn.App. 328, 333-34, 735 A.2d 835 (Conn.App., 1999), certification granted in part by *Town of Southington v. Commercial Insurance Company*, 251 Conn. 906, 738 A.2d 1093 (Conn., 1999) interpreting a Connecticut statute to require the surety's completion of the improvements only to the extent necessary to serve conveyed lots.

12. *County of Kern* and *Mount Florence Group*, supra.

13. See, e.g., *City of Sacramento v. Trans Pacific Industries*, 98 Cal.App.3d 389, 400, 159 Cal.Rptr. 514 (Cal.App., 1979).

II. The Differing Roles, Positions And Obligations Of the Principal and Obligee

A. THE PRINCIPAL

Although Subdivision Bonds are somewhat similar to Public Works Bonds, the developer's role, position and obligation under a Subdivision Agreement as secured by the Subdivision Bonds is quite different from those of a contractor entering into a public works contract secured by Public Works Bonds. In a Public Works Bond, the surety secures the performance of the contractor. In a Subdivision Bond, the surety secures the obligations of the developer under the Subdivision Agreement. The Developer may or may not be the contractor. Where the developer is not the actual builder of the subdivision improvements and has separately contracted with a builder, there is no privity of contract between the surety and the builder of the subdivision improvements. If the builder defaults, the Public Agency has a claim against the developer under the Subdivision Agreement and its surety under the Subdivision Performance Bond. If the Public Agency makes demand on the Subdivision Performance Bond, the surety may communicate with the builder in an attempt to address the Public Agency's claim. The surety will, however, deal primarily with the developer as its principal to assure performance. As a result of the unique interplay between the parties, it is incumbent upon the surety to monitor the progress of the builder and communicate with the developer and Public Agency to assure the orderly completion of the obligations secured by the Subdivision Bonds.

B. THE OBLIGEE

The Subdivision Bonds secure the obligations of the developer under the Subdivision Agreement and name the Public Agency as the obligee.[14] The primary distinction in the role of the Public Agency as an obligee on Subdivision Bonds, as opposed to Public Works Bonds, is that the Public Agency has no obligation to pay the developer for the cost of the subdivision improvements. The consideration given by the Public Agency for the protections afforded under the Subdivision Bonds is the right to develop the subdivision. By accepting and acting upon this right, the developer assumes the obligation to pay for the subdivision improvements required under the Subdivision Agreement.

A secondary distinction between the role of the obligee on Subdivision Bonds as opposed to Public Works Bonds is that the obligee generally takes a far more active role in determining and dictating the scope, method and operation of the work to be performed on a public works contract as opposed to a Subdivision Agreement. Whereas, in a typical public works contract there are often detailed plans, specifications and subcontractor requirements, a typical Subdivision Agreement, by

14. In *Weber v. Pacific Indemnity Company*, 204 Cal.App.2d 334, 22 Cal.Rptr. 366 (Cal.App., 1962), in ruling the Public Agency was the sole obligee on a Subdivision Bond, the court denied a contractor's claim against the bond, even though the bond expressly covered all costs and expenses incurred in the performance of the subdivision agreement. But see, *City of University City v. Frank Miceli & Sons Realty & Building*, 347 S.W.2d 131 (Mo., 1961) in which the court acknowledged the homeowners as third party beneficiaries of a Subdivision Performance Bond and therefore proper claimants on the bond, but denied recovery on other grounds.

comparison, incorporates rather simple plans and limited engineer's estimates allowing the developer to utilize its own method and operation for completion, with no subcontractor designation requirements. The distinctions between a public works contract and a Subdivision Agreement are also demonstrated by contrasting the time requirements and damage exposures. Public works contracts generally include a detailed schedule of performance with a fixed date for completion which includes exposure for delay, liquidated and consequential damages. A Subdivision Agreement, by comparison, identifies a date generally one or two years in the future for completion. Within this broad time frame, which is relatively easily extended, the developer can schedule its work as it wants with no delay, liquidated or consequential damage exposure.

III. Shift in Funding

As noted, the developer assumes the responsibility to fund the costs of constructing or placing the subdivision improvements required by the Public Agency. From the surety's perspective, this shift in funding responsibility should be a critical part of its underwriting evaluation and if the Subdivision Bonds are written, funding of the improvements must be closely monitored. In this regard, the key areas of inquiry for the surety underwriters include:

(1) Has the developer properly estimated the costs necessary to complete the improvements? The Public Agency generally provides engineer's estimates for these expenses. The surety underwriter should attempt to ascertain the propriety of the engineer's estimates and any major deviation between the engineer's estimates and the amount the developer has budgeted for completion.

(2) Has the developer set aside sufficient funds to complete the subdivision improvements? If a project is to be self-funded by the developer, the surety must be assured that the developer has separately committed sufficient funds to complete the subdivision improvements. If a project is to be financed through a bank (hereinafter Set Aside Bank), it is normal procedure for the Set Aside Bank to provide the surety with an agreement which provides that the Set Aside Bank, as part of its commitment to fund the entire project, has segregated sufficient funds to be used solely for the completion of the subdivision improvements (Set Aside Agreement).[15] Ascertaining the precise source of payment and procedure to be followed in funding the subdivision improvements is an essential underwriting consideration.

(3) Has the developer or Set Aside Bank complied with its obligations by using the funds set aside to pay for the completion of the improvements and payment to the contractor, subcontractors and suppliers completing the improvements? Monitoring the activities of developer and the distribution from the Set Aside Bank are critical to avoid exposure to loss on the Subdivision Bonds.

15. See, e.g., *City of Los Angeles v. Anchor Casualty Company*, 204 Cal.App.2d 175, 22 Cal.Rptr. 278 (Cal.App., 1962).

IV. Distinction in Coverage and Limitation Periods

Although similar in some respects, a primary distinction between a Public Works Performance Bond and a Subdivision Performance Bond is in the scope of coverage. Both types of bonds incorporate the underlying contracts (public works contract and Subdivision Agreement) by reference.[16] However, while a Public Works Performance Bond provides security for the performance of all of the principal's contract work, a Subdivision Performance Bond guarantees only the public improvement portion of the overall development.[17] By way of example, a developer with a project to build a hundred single family residences may be required to enter into a Subdivision Agreement which includes completion of the subdivision improvements. The Subdivision Performance Bond guarantees only the developer's completion of the streets, curbs and gutters, storm drains, sewers and any grading necessary to accomplish these public improvements.[18] The Subdivision Performance Bond does not guarantee or involve any grading for individual lots or driveways, or the development or construction of the individual homes. The Public Agency's claim is limited to the improvements specifically included within the Subdivision Agreement. Therefore, if a developer fails to complete any portion of the actual homes, the Public Agency has no claim against the surety on the Subdivision Performance Bond for the completion of the homes, but is limited to the subdivision improvements set forth in the Subdivision Agreement.[19]

Another distinction in coverage is that a public works contract secured by a Public Works Performance Bond generally includes significant contract obligations including performance guarantees, warranties, and specific damage exposures (delay, consequential and liquidated damages). Although Subdivision Agreements often require the posting of a separate Warranty Bond or the subsequent reduction of the Subdivision Performance Bond to cover certain warranty obligations once the improvements are completed, Subdivision Performance Bonds generally do not include coverage for performance guarantees, delay, consequential or liquidated damages.[20]

As noted above, while Public Works Performance Bonds generally include broader coverage, the limitation period for making a claim on a Public Works Performance Bond is often

---

16. See, e.g., *City of Sacramento v. Trans Pacific Industries, Inc.*, 98 Cal.App.3d 389, 400, 159 Cal.Rptr. 514 (Cal.App., 1979) citing *Bloom v. Bender*, 48 Cal.2d 793, 313 P.2d 568 (Cal., 1957). See also, *City of O'Fallon v. Bank of Belleville*, 171 Ill.App.3d 584, 586, 525 N.E.2d 1162 (Ill.App., 1988) (an underlying agreement may be incorporated in bond where "alluded to," even if not specifically referred to in bond.) Further, an oral contract may in some jurisdictions constitute a valid basis for a contract of suretyship. See, *East Baton Rouge Parish v. Travelers Insurance Company*, 342 So.2d 226, (La.App., 1977).

17. *Township of Wyckoff v. Sarna*, 136 N.J.Super. 512, 347 A.2d 16 (N.J.Super.A.D., 1975).

18. Courts will construe a Subdivision Performance Bond in a fair and reasonable manner based upon a consideration of its language and provisions. In *City of O'Fallon v. Bank of Belleville*, 171 Ill.App.3d 584, 586, 525 N.E.2d 1162 (Ill.App., 1988), the surety argued that the portion of the development not completed by the developer -- the culvert -- was not covered by the Subdivision Bond which by its terms included streets and sidewalks. Interpreting the Subdivision Performance Bond as incorporating the Subdivision Agreement, the court held the surety bound to complete the improvements prescribed and required by the Public Agency. Thus, the court held that the definition of "street" in the Public Agency's ordinance encompassed the culvert. See also *Town of Brookfield v. Greenridge, Inc.*, 177 Conn. 527, 418 A.2d 907 (Conn., 1979) (implicit obligation to include underdrain in construction of road improvements based upon good road-building practice although underdrain was not specifically indicated on filed map nor spelled out in road specifications).

19. *Id.*

20. See, e.g., *Bd. of Supervisors of Stafford County v. Safeco Insurance Co. of America*, 226 Va. 329, 339, 310 S.E.2d 445 (Va., 1983) (Supreme Court of Virginia rejected County's claim for consequential damages other than interest, limiting recovery to the principal amount of the bond).

reduced by the terms of the bond to a period of time less than that which may be provided in statute. Excluding latent defects and certain warranty claims, most Public Work Performance Bonds have a limitation period included within the bond of one or two years from the date of acceptance or completion.

In sharp contrast, the limitation period on a Subdivision Performance Bond usually runs from the agreed upon completion date of the required improvements,[21] or as may be modified by any extensions granted by the Public Agency. The nature of subdivision development and the changes in the housing marketplace often require the developer to seek extensions on the time period afforded in the Subdivision Agreement for the completion of the improvements. Unless there is a dangerous condition or some other health hazard, the Public Agency regularly grants a developer's request for time extensions.

Most Subdivision Bond forms and the Statutory Scheme preclude the necessity of the Public Agency or the developer to notify the Surety of the extension.[22] Thus, whereas in most cases, the surety can determine its exposure on a Public Works Performance Bond within a couple of years of completion, the surety's exposure on a Subdivision Bond may regularly be extended out for six to ten years, or more. It is therefore very important for the surety to maintain open lines of communication with both the Public Agency and developer, and take appropriate action to monitor the financial status of the developer and the progress of the required improvements.

A particularly difficult issue involving the limitation period on Subdivision Bonds and the normal extensions afforded by the Public Agency involves the Set Aside Bank. Often, the Set Aside Agreement delivered to the surety to assure that there are sufficient funds for completion of the subdivision improvements include time limitations of their own. If the project is extended, it is incumbent upon the developer and the surety to make sure that the Set Aside Agreement is also extended. Therefore, not only should the surety monitor the completion of the project, it must also ensure that its security, i.e. the Set Aside Agreement, is in place. If the project is self-funded by the developer, the surety must be vigilant in assessing the developer's continuing ability to place the improvements, and where necessary or appropriate, request the furnishing of collateral to the surety.

Assuming that the surety is able to properly monitor the situation and protect against exposure, the limitation extensions common in the Subdivision Bond context often assist in negating exposure on the Subdivision Bonds. Subdivision development is often delayed when the economy or housing market is slow. When the market turns, in many cases it is possible for the developer to obtain new sources of revenue to complete the subdivision improvements so that it can sell the units. From the surety's perspective, it is important to understand and appreciate these issues and to work with the developer and Public Agency to mitigate its exposure to loss.

---

21. See, however, *Commercial Standard Insurance Company v. Tab Construction, Inc.*, 94 Nev. 536, 583 P.2d 449 (Nev., 1978) , wherein Subdivision Payment Bond contained six-month limitations period from the date of completion of improvements. However, the Supreme Court of Oklahoma rejected a limitations period set forth in the bond as void by a local statute, and further held a two year limitations period set forth in a sidewalk ordinance to be void as a violation of the State's Constitution. Instead, the Court applied a five (5) year limitations period for breach of contract. (*Sherwood Forest No. 2 Corp. v. City of Norman*, 1980 OK 191, 632 P.2d 368 (Okla., 1980), citing *City of Norman v. Liddell*, 596 P.2d 879 (Okla., 1979).)

22. See, e.g., *City of Sacramento v. Trans Pacific Industries*, 98 Cal.App.3d 389, 400, 159 Cal.Rptr. 514 (Cal.App., 1979).

V. Subdivision Bond Claim Handling

If a principal is declared in default on a Public Works Performance Bond, the surety must evaluate the default in the context of the terms and conditions of the construction contract. As a matter of practice, the Public Works Bond surety should always contact the principal to determine if there are any legitimate defenses to the default. Based upon its investigation, and assuming that the default is determined to be proper, the surety will exercise a variety of options, including, inter alia, financing the principal, tendering a completion contractor, providing a completion contractor or paying the bond penalty. The surety will evaluate a complicated set of factors including the availability and amount of remaining contract funds, the status of the completed work, the percentage of the completed work, whether the remaining work is to be performed by subcontractors and whether the subcontractors' contracts can be ratified and completed by the subcontractors.

If a principal is declared in default on a Subdivision Performance Bond, the initial investigation relative to the default is rather straightforward. If the time frame for completing the subdivision improvements has expired, it is within the limitation period for making a claim, and the improvements are not complete, generally the principal will have no defense to a demand on a Subdivision Performance Bond. As compared to a Public Works Performance Bond default, the traditional completion options of the Subdivision Performance Bond surety are also less complicated. In most cases, if no other approaches are available to the surety, it will either complete the work with a completion contractor or pay the obligee an amount necessary for the construction and installation of the required improvements, often the full penal sum of the bond.[23]

Recognizing that the completion options are somewhat limited, special pre-claim and post-claim handling procedures and methodologies may be established to limit or eliminate exposure on Subdivision Bonds. Avoiding exposure to loss on Subdivision Bonds requires vigilant and consistent monitoring and communication with the Public Agency, developer, principal, builder, indemnitors and Set Aside Bank well before any claim is made. After Subdivision Bonds are issued, key suggested pre-claim investigations and contacts include:

(1) The surety should obtain a projected schedule of completion of the subdivision improvements from the developer. The surety should monitor the progress of the subdivision improvement work. It should obtain periodic status reports from the Public Agency to be compared with the actual completion of the work within the developer's projected schedule. The surety should determine the reasons for any delay from the developer, and obtain assurances that the project will be completed on a timely schedule.

(2) If the developer is self-funding, it is essential for the surety to closely monitor the developer's financial ability to complete the subdivision improvements. If the developer has bank financing, it is incumbent upon the surety to communicate often with the Set Aside Bank to assure that the Set Aside Bank is properly disbursing funds as subdivision improvements are completed and that set aside funds are used solely for their intended purpose.

---

23. In *General Insurance Company of America v. City of Colorado Springs*, 638 P.2d 752, 757 (Colo., 1981), the Supreme Court of Colorado rejected the City's contention that the subdivision bond was a "penalty bond," liable in the full amount for the Principal's failure to perform, but rather deemed the bond an "indemnity bond," liable only for the actual cost of completing the required improvements.

(3) The surety must monitor the work performed by the builder and be sure that the developer and indemnitor(s) are properly reviewing and/or supervising the completion of the work.

(4) The surety must communicate with the developer to determine if there are any major changes in its development plans or financial condition which could impact its ability to timely complete the subdivision improvements. If a developer's financial condition changes or economic or marketplace conditions change, the developer must work with the Public Agency to make sure that appropriate extensions are applied for and obtained, and that the Set Aside Bank understands and agrees to maintain its financing and/or Set Aside Agreement during the extended time frame.

(5) The surety must communicate with the developer and the Set Aside Bank to assure that if the Set Aside Bank forecloses on the property, it will require any third party purchaser to assume or take title to the property subject to the developer's subdivision improvement obligations. These negotiations should also deal with the Set Aside Bank's obligations under the Set Aside Agreement. Although a Set Aside Bank may not have a legal obligation to work with the surety, if properly presented as an option, a Set Aside Bank will often work with the parties to deal fairly with the property.

(6) The surety must notify and communicate with the developer and all indemnitors relating to any potential problem relative to the completion of the subdivision improvements. Often, in the complicated interactions between the parties in a potential subdivision loss situation, the indemnitors are not given proper attention. Not only should the indemnitors be made aware of any potential claim, if provided for under the terms of the indemnity agreement, demand for collateral and other enforcement techniques under the indemnity agreement should be employed to maximize the involvement of the indemnitors to mitigate the ultimate exposure to loss. Often indemnitors have the ability to, and if properly communicated with will, take the necessary action to solve a developer's problems before a loss is suffered on the Subdivision Bonds.

Assuming that the foregoing preventative actions taken by the surety cannot avoid a claim, the following should be considered as part of a comprehensive investigation of the claim:

(1) Who is making the claim? Most Subdivision Performance Bonds identify the Public Agency as the sole obligee on the Subdivision Performance Bond and therefore any claim brought by any other party may be subject to denial.[24]

---

24. See, e.g., *Hewson Construction, Inc. v. Reintree Corporation*, 101 Wash.2d 819, 685 P.2d 1062 (Wash., 1984), and *W.S. Dickey Clay Mfg. Co. v. Ferguson Investment Company*, 1963 OK 298, 388 P.2d 300 (Okla., 1963). In *Hewson*, the court denied the subcontractor who installed the sidewalks on a subdivision improvement a right of action to enforce a Subdivision *Performance* Bond. The court rejected the subcontractor's argument that it was a third-party beneficiary of the Subdivision Performance Bond holding that such bonds run solely to the obligee-Public Agency. In *W.S. Dickey*, the court denied a material supplier a right of action against a Subdivision Bond despite the fact that the bond contained language binding the surety to laborers and materialmen. Finding that the subdivision law did not require the developer to guarantee payment for labor and materials the court held that the surety was confined to the measure of liability as contemplated by the law requiring the Subdivision Bond. See also, *Evola v. Wendt Construction Company*, 170 Cal.App.2d 21, 388 P.2d 498 (Cal.App., 1959) and *Norton v. First Federal Savings*, 128 Ariz. 176, 624 P.2d 854 (Ariz., 1981), called into doubt by *Hartford Accident and Indemnity Company v. Arizona Department of Transportation*, 172 Ariz. 564, 838 P.2d 1325 (Ariz.App., 1992). But see, *Vale Dean Canyon Homeowners Association v. Dean*, 100 Or.App. 158, 785 P.2d 772 (Or.App., 1990). In *Vale Dean*, an Oregon court permitted lot owners, as third party beneficiaries of the Subdivision Agreement, to enforce the terms of the Subdivision Agreement. The court based its decision on the finding that, in entering into the Subdivision Agreement, the Public Agency intended to benefit the lot owners. Interestingly, the court refused to give much credence to testimony by the Public Agency to the effect that its intent was to assure that the improvements would be placed at no cost to itself. This case may be limited to the particular

(2) Has the claim been timely presented? To make this determination, the Subdivision Agreement must be reviewed for the completion date and the appropriate statute of limitations must be applied. If it appears that the claim is time barred, that should not be the end of the surety's investigation. Most Statutory Schemes and most Subdivision Bonds, allow extensions of the completion dates without the surety's consent. Therefore, the surety must determine if any extensions have been granted. It should also seek information on what extension procedures were available to the Public Agency and whether it complied with its rules in extending the time for completion.

(3) Has the developer commenced any subdivision improvements? As noted in the previous sections, the Public Agency requires the issuance of Subdivision Bonds to assure that the development has no adverse effect on its overall development plan and to assure the improvements are installed at no cost to the Public Agency. If the developer decides not to move forward with the development and no work on the subdivision improvements has been commenced, a relatively strong argument can be made that the Public Agency should not be able to enforce the Subdivision Agreement or recover on the Subdivision Performance Bond.

For example, one California Court held that the surety's obligation on a subdivision bond commenced only after the principal had begun construction of the improvements.[25] "The language of the instrument of credit executed by [the bank] indicates that the parties intended to provide security for full completion of improvements whose construction had already begun."[26] As no work had been commenced and the Public Agency had no intention of completing the project, the court determined that no purpose would be served by imposing an obligation on the surety to complete the improvements or otherwise pay out on the bond. Similarly, the Appellate Court of Connecticut refused to hold the surety on a subdivision bond liable where "no lots in the subdivision had been conveyed." "[B]ecause no lots in the subdivision were conveyed, no improvements were required.[27]

(4) Who owns the property on which the subdivision improvements were to be completed? If the developer owns the property, it is likely that he will work with the Public Agency to obtain an extension. Generally, developers have signed indemnity agreements with the surety. Thus, any demand made by the Public Agency will be tendered to the developer. If the developer has lost the property in foreclosure, the foreclosing bank or a subsequent third-party purchaser may pressure the Public Agency to require completion of the subdivision improvements. As neither the foreclosing bank nor the third-party purchaser are obligees and have no direct right to make claim on the Subdivision Bonds, they often attempt to

---

circumstances of the case and the language of the particular Subdivision Agreement.

25. *County of Yuba v. Central Valley National Bank, Inc.*, 20 Cal.App.3d 109, 97 Cal.Rptr. 369 (Cal.App., 1971); holding limited by *City of Los Angeles v. Amwest Surety Insurance Co.*, 63 Cal.App.4th 378, 73 Cal.Rptr.729 (Cal.App., 1998).

26. *County of Yuba, supra,* at 112.

27. "The basic purpose of performance bonds is not to punish the developer for failure to make the required improvements, or to unduly benefit a local government, but to assure those who purchase homes in a new subdivision that they will receive the public improvements that were a large part of the inducement to purchase lots and/or homes in that development." *Town of Southington v. Commercial Union Insurance Co.*, 54 Conn.App. 328, 334, 735 A.2d 835 (Conn.App., 1999), certification granted in part by *Town of Southington v.Commercial Insurance Company*, 251 Conn. 906, 738 A.2d 1093 (Conn., 1999). See also, *Town of New Windsor v. Inbro Development Corp.*, 112 Misc.2d 983, 448 N.Y.S.2d 99 (N.Y.Supp., 1982), wherein the Statutory Scheme limited collection on the Subdivision Performance Bond to an amount commensurate with the extent of building development that had taken place in the subdivision. When the Public Agency filed suit to enforce payment on a Subdivision Performance Bond prior to any construction by the developer/principal the court held that condition of the Subdivision Performance Bond had not occurred.

> persuade the Public Agency to require the placement of the improvements. While the Public Agency arguably has no legal obligation to act on behalf of the bank or the third party purchasers, the Public Agency often finds it in its best interest to require the improvements. Communicating with the Public Agency early and explaining that these parties are receiving a windfall or an unjust benefit by the placement of the improvements may be helpful in persuading the Public Agency not to require the surety to place the improvements.

For example, in *City of Sacramento v. Trans Pacific Industries, Inc.*,[28] a subsequent purchaser of the property was able to persuade the Public Agency to pursue placement of the subdivision improvements for its benefit. In order to get certain improvements in place at no cost to the subsequent purchaser, the subsequent purchaser entered into an agreement with the Public Agency whereby he agreed to construct all the improvements on the parcels he purchased in exchange for the Public Agency's promise to reimburse him from any judgment the Public Agency was successful in recovering against the developer/principal and its surety in the lawsuit the Public Agency had already filed against the developer and surety.[29]

In order to preempt this situation, it is advisable to contact the Public Agency as soon as the surety learns of any property transfer. The surety should request that the Public Agency require any subsequent purchaser who is actually developing the property to execute a new Subdivision Agreement secured by appropriate bonds as a condition of any issuance of permits to commence work on the project in order to avoid an unjust resolution as between the surety and original developer. The unjust resolution is the result of the fact that the surety would have no indemnity rights against the subsequent purchaser. Such course of action by the Public Agency is supported by the general rules of suretyship and the covenant of good faith and fair dealing implied in all contracts which may be summarized as follows:

> The contract of suretyship imports entire good faith and confidence between the parties as to the whole transaction. The creditor is bound to observe good faith with the surety. He must withhold nothing, conceal nothing, release nothing which will possibly benefit the surety. He must not do any act injurious to the surety or inconsistent with its rights. He must not omit any act required by the surety which duty enjoins him to do, if such omission injures the surety.[30]

The Public Agency, as creditor, is therefore duty bound not to do any act injurious to the interests of the surety. Additionally, in every contract, including bonds which a surety executes for the benefit of the Public Agency, there is an implied covenant of good faith and fair dealing that neither

---

28. 98 Cal.App.3d 389, 159 Cal.Rptr. 514 (Cal.App., 1979).

29. See also, *Board of County Supervisors of Prince William County v. Sie-Gray Developers, Inc.*, 230 Va. 24, 334 S.E.2d 542 (Va., 1985), wherein the Court upheld an assignment of the County's rights under the Subdivision Performance Bond to a subsequent developer of the improvements, and *Will County v. Woodhill Enterprises, Inc.*, 4 Ill.App.3d 68, 274 N.E.2d 476 (Ill.App., 1971), in which the court allowed an assignee of Public Agency to pursue claim against Performance Bond. But see, *Morro Palisades Co. v. Hartford Acc. & Indem. Co.*, 52 Cal.2d 397, 340 P.2d 628 (Cal., 1959), in which the court denied an assignee's recovery against the bond, where the assignee did not seek to compel the subdivision improvements, but rather sought to recover a money judgment on its own behalf.

30. *Massachusetts Bonding & Ins. Co. v. Osborne*, 233 Cal.App.2d 648, 662, 43 Cal.Rptr. 761 (Cal.App., 1965), quoting *County of Glen v. Jones,* 146 Cal. 518, 520, 80 P. 695 (Cal., 1905).

party shall do anything which will have the effect of destroying or injuring the rights of the other to receive the fruits of the contract.[31]

(5) Has the public agency incurred any damage as a result of the developer's failure to complete the improvements? Once a determination has been made as to the surety's liability, the surety must also consider whether the Subdivision Performance Bond is a "penalty bond" or an "indemnity bond." A "penalty bond" may be treated by the courts as a liquidated damage should the developer fail to complete the improvements. Upon the default of the principal and timely notice of claim, the surety will be required to pay the full penal sum of the bond, regardless of whether or not the Public Agency has incurred any damage, or intends to complete the improvements.[32]

An "indemnity bond," however, will be liable only for the actual cost of completing the required improvements.[33] The purpose of such a bond is to provide funds necessary to cover the costs of completing the improvements. Recovery is limited to the reasonable completion costs, and may not exceed the face amount of the bond.[34] Some courts however, have held that the Public Agency may recover from the bond even if no loss has been incurred, or where the Public Agency failed to establish any intent or need to complete the bonded improvements.[35]

VI. Conclusion

Subdivision Bonds secure the obligations of the developer under the Subdivision Agreement. Basic handling of a claim against a Subdivision Bond should necessarily comply with the applicable statutory regulations and the surety's established claims handling procedures. Additionally, understanding and appreciating the unique aspects of Subdivision Bonds should assist the surety in establishing a monitoring program and developing special preventative procedures to avoid claims. Further, where claims are made against a surety on a Subdivision Bond, recognition of the roles, responsibilities and unique interplay between the principal, Public Agency, builder, indemnitors, and Set Aside Bank must be employed to establish alternative approaches or options to satisfy, reduce

31. See, e.g., *Kendall v. Ernest Pestana, Inc.*, 40 Cal.3d 488, 500, 220 Cal.Rptr 818 (Cal., 1985), superceded by statute on other grounds as stated in *Ranco Santa Paula Mobilehome Park, Ltd. v. Evans*, 26 Cal.App.4th 1139, 32 Cal.Rptr.2d 464 (Cal.App., 1994).

32. See, e.g., *Clark v. Barnard*, 108 U.S. 436, 2 S.Ct. 878 (U.S. Mass., 1883); *City of Los Angeles v. Amwest Surety Insurance Company*, 76 Cal.Rptr.2d 903 (Cal.App., 1998), ordered not to be officially published (Oct. 1998).

33. In *General Insurance Company of America v. City of Colorado Springs*, 638 P.2d 752, 757 (Colo., 1981), the Court rejected the City's contention that the subdivision bond was a "penalty bond," but rather deemed the bond an "indemnity bond," liable only for the actual cost of completing the required improvements. Relying upon, *United States v. Zerbey*, 271 U.S. 332, 46 S.Ct. 532 (U.S., 1926); *Morro Palisade Co. v. Hartford Accident & Indemnity Co.*, 52 Cal.2d 397, 340 P.2d 628 (Cal., 1959); *County of Los Angeles v. Margulis*, 6 Cal.App.2d 57, 44 P.2d 608, (Cal.App., 1935).

34. *Bd. of Supervisors of Stafford v. Safeco Insurance Company of America*, 226 Va. 329, 335, 310 S.E.2d 445 (Va.,1983). *Bd. of County Supervisors of Prince William County v. Sie-Gray Developers, Inc.*, 230 Va. 24, 334 S.E.2d 542 (Va., 1985). *Town of Poughkeepsie v. Holden Construction Co., Inc.*, 71 A.D.2d 886, 419 N.Y.S.2d 531 (N.Y.A.D., 1979), case remanded to assess Public Agency's damages resulting from developer's breach.

35. *Bd. of Supervisors of Stafford v. Safeco Insurance Company of America*, 226 Va. 329, 337-38, 310 S.E.2d 445 (Va., 1983). A surety stands in the shoes of its principal and may not assert defenses not available to the principal. The surety had conceded that the County's lack of intent to complete the improvements was not a viable defense to the principal's failure to complete the improvements. (Citing *Cohen v. Mayflower Corp.*, 196 Va. 1153, 1164, 86 S.E.2d 860 (Va., 1955).)

or eliminate the exposure of the surety. Consistent monitoring, communication and creativity, both before and after a claim is made, are the keys to superior Subdivision Bond claims handling.

13

Customs Bond Claims

Laura J. Maurer
James A. Carpenter

Introduction

A Customs Bond Claim Guidelines pamphlet was prepared by members of the Claims Advisory Committee of the Surety Association of America back in 1992. The stated purpose was to assist claims personnel handling customs bond claims in a non-electronic environment to recognize documents generated by the United States Customs Service and to be aware of the reason each document exists. It was and still is a pretty good guide, so few substantive changes were necessary. The authors have used the 1992 pamphlet as a starting point, made some changes in the organization of the material, and revised and updated the text and exhibits. We have also added some information about the realities of the electronic processes currently used. The U.S. Customs Service and sureties communicate much more electronically today than we did eight years ago, though the paper is still generated by the Customs Service, and therefore the explanation regarding the forms is still valid and useful. Electronic data is available to all sureties by way of monthly, weekly or nightly downloads from Customs.

I. Liquidated Damage Claims

A. Form 5955A - Addressed to Principal

Form 5955A (Exhibit 1) is entitled Notice of Penalty or Liquidated Damages Incurred and Demand for Payment" and bears the form number in the lower right hand corner. It is the first notification statement received in a U.S. Customs demand. It is addressed to the principal with a copy to the surety. It serves as a twofold notification device, advising both principal and surety of a Customs demand. It provides specific information concerning both the entry in question and the port where the alleged infraction occurred. One of the most important details of the 5955A is the case number located at the top right hand corner. This is the 5955A's identification number and it must be used when referring to this individual claim on any and all correspondence and/or payments made to Customs for settlement of this claim.

Sometimes a courtesy letter (similar to Exhibit 2) is included with the 5955A. The courtesy letter is addressed to the surety.

If the surety receives many of these documents on a daily or weekly basis, it may be advisable to develop guidelines for purposes of urgency of handling. Placing each Customs' correspondence into a category based on urgency can make handling much easier. Those 5955A forms addressed to the principal may be separated into those addressed to viable entities and those who are no longer in business, the later of which make surety involvement essential. If the surety receives relatively few notices, it may wish to treat each demand the same.

It is usually advisable to set up physical and/or electronic files to be used to retain all correspondence associated with a particular principal. The claims person will want to notify the principal by letter and telephone, to inform the principal of the demand and to advise the principal that it has the responsibility to resolve the matter.

B. FORM 5955A - ADDRESSED TO SURETY FORMAL DEMAND ON SURETY

This notice (Exhibit 3) is similar to the notice described above, except that now it is addressed to the surety, rather than the principal, and represents a Formal Demand on the surety. Upon receipt of such a notice, a check should be made to see if the principal has recently resolved the matter. If not, a letter should be sent to the principal advising of the demand on the surety and informing the principal of its responsibility to resolve the claim. If a file was not opened when the first 5955A, addressed to the Principal, was received, one should be opened at this point.

It is not uncommon that the information received by the surety from Customs is inadequate to identify the principal. Or, the wrong surety sometimes receives the demand. In the event that the claims person believes that some error has been made by Customs, further information may be obtained by calling or writing the Fines, Penalties & Forfeitures Office at the issuing port (see list following exhibits). The address is located on the bottom of the 5955A. The request for additional information should be directed to the port from which the demand originates. The surety should send a stamped, self-addressed envelope. If it is necessary, further information may be requested through the Freedom of Information Act. It may also be a good idea to contact the Customs Broker that was involved in the entry for additional information.

C. MITIGATION OF AMOUNT DEMANDED IN FORM 5955A

Within 60 days of Customs' issuance of the 5955A to the importer/principal, the principal has the right to file a petition requesting cancellation or mitigation of the amount assessed by Customs. A petition for relief need not be in any particular form. It should contain the facts relied upon by the principal to justify mitigation or cancellation of the claim. The petition should be filed in triplicate and be addressed to the appropriate port office listed on the 5955A. In some instances, depending on the type of violation, the importer/principal is also given the opportunity to pay an Option 1" amount. That amount is stated on the 5955A. If the Option 1 amount is paid, the principal forfeits its right to file a petition for cancellation or for further mitigation.

Within ten days after the expiration of the principal's petitioning period, or as soon thereafter as possible, Customs will make a formal demand on the surety by issuing a 5955A to the surety. The surety will then have an additional 60 days to make payment or file a petition for mitigation or cancellation. According to Customs' Regulations, the surety may raise any defense or issue that the principal could have raised. The surety's petition must also be filed in triplicate and be addressed to the appropriate port office. If the case is mitigated, the surety will receive the same mitigation that would have been due to the principal.

If an Option 1" amount was offered to the principal, the surety has the same right to submit payment of this amount, but as in the case of the principal, the surety also forfeits its right to file a petition.

If the principal filed a petition with Customs and was granted relief, but failed to make payment of the mitigated amount within the specified time, Customs will then make a demand on the surety, and the surety will be granted the right to pay the mitigated amount. This amount must be paid within 30 days. The 5955A will contain the information regarding the relief offered to the principal.

D. Form 6084 - Billing Notices To The Surety

If a penalty or liquidated damages claimed in the Form 5955A have not been settled or mitigated after the surety's 60 days expires, the next document the surety will receive is a Form 6084 (Exhibit 4). If the surety receives information electronically from Customs, then Customs' tapes will reflect that the claim has automatically entered the billing cycle after the surety's 60 days expires without a payment or petition being filed. The surety will probably want to investigate the cases that enter the billing cycle as soon as they receive information from Customs on tapes.

Customs Form 6084 is a computer-generated bill forwarded directly to the surety by the Port offices of the U.S. Customs Service. It is Customs' bill to the surety for fines, penalties or liquidated damages unpaid or unresolved by the principal or surety. It is not simply a notice to the surety of the principal's unpaid obligation. Rather, it is a bill, a demand upon the surety to pay money to the Customs Service. Once this has been received the claim has entered Customs final billing stage, and must be resolved.

As Customs regulations dictate that all claim notices and related correspondence be forwarded to the surety at its principal place of business, the Form 6084 is generally directed to the surety's home office.

The Form 6084 arrives in a snap-out type envelope. This original Form 6084 is pink and is accompanied by a white copy. Customs requests that the pink original be returned with payment to the appropriate District Office of the Customs Service. The white copy of the bill is the "Payer's copy".

The first Form 6084 is normally sent to the surety approximately 65 to 75 days after Customs has made its formal demand upon the surety. The form 6084 is titled "U.S. Customs Service Bill", and will generally offer the following information:

- the identity of the violator, which should be the same name as your bond principal;
- a fines, penalties or forfeiture case number, which should help you match the bill to earlier, related correspondence and documents from Customs;
- a bill number which will differ from the fines, penalties or forfeitures case number but which may be important in corresponding with the Customs Service;
- the address of the District Office of Customs presenting the bill;
- the type of charge assessed and the amount of the bill.

The bill might also include language similar to the following:

> Appropriate action was not taken on the assessed claim. The claim is due and payable within ten (10) days from the date of this demand. Only an offer in compromise or full payment of the demand will be accepted.

The affected surety should communicate with its principal, encouraging the principal to resolve the claim with the Customs Service or to provide documentation of any claim defenses.

Barring resolution of the claim following issuance of the initial Form 6084, the computer in the district office of Customs will produce a second billing (another Form 6084), some 14 days after the first one. The second 6084 will contain all of the information appearing in the first bill. It might also include language advising that the claim is delinquent, and if it is not satisfied immediately, sanctions may be proposed and the claim referred for legal action.

Again, the surety receiving the Customs bill will want to determine the position of its principal and remind the principal of its obligation to resolve the claim without a loss to the surety. Absent a prompt resolution of the claim, the computer in Customs' district office will produce a third billing (Form 6084). It will be mailed to the surety approximately 14 days after the second bill.

Most of the data appearing in the third Form 6084 will be identical to data shown in the preceding two bills. The third Form 6084 will also include the following language:

> FINAL DEMAND - DELINQUENT ACCOUNT. Claim will be referred for sanctions and legal action ten (10) days from the date of this demand.

It is critical for a surety to respond appropriately to formal demands by Customs or to the subsequent series of Form 6084 bills. A suit against the bond, a pre-show cause demand, a show cause demand, and sanctions are all tools used by the Customs Service against the unresponsive surety. The surety wishing to avoid this sort of conflict will see that it or its principal responds fully and promptly when the Forms 6084 begin to arrive.

The degree to which a surety will rely upon its principal to resolve claims by the Customs Service is as varied as the number of sureties writing customs bonds. Some sureties offer written responses directly to Customs in all cases in which a Form 6084 is issued. Other sureties rely upon their principals to correspond with Customs regarding the claims which generated the 6084. But all should be cognizant of the fact that the principal's failure to resolve a dispute is hardly a defense to the surety that has received formal demands and bills from the Customs Service.

E. Offer In Compromise Or Untimely Petition Of Amount Demanded In Form 6084

The options available once the case has gone into billing include:

- full payment;
- an Offer in Compromise;
- submission of documentation proving the violation never occurred; or
- an untimely petition for mitigation or cancellation.

A principal or surety is permitted to submit late petitions for relief at any time prior to issuance of a notice to show cause. However, any mitigation that may be granted as a result of the petition will be significantly higher than if the petition had been filed timely.

The amount of the Offer in Compromise must fall within Customs guidelines in order to be accepted by Customs. These guidelines vary according to the violation but in all cases the offer must be greater then the Option 1 amount, if offered, or the mitigated amount that was or would have been granted to the principal or surety. Customs will not recommend an acceptable amount, but in most ports they will advise you of the guidelines for a particular violation. Offers in Compromise may be presented at any time during the administrative process and at any time prior to the issuance of a notice to show cause.

F. Pre-Show Cause Letters

If the principal and surety fail to appropriately respond to either Form 5955A or a Form 6084 within the time frames set forth, the cases enter the Sanction Eligibility status. The National Seizure and Penalty Officers (NSPO's) will review the cases in this status to confirm that all documents are in their file, and all notices have been sent. After this review the NSPO will issue the surety a warning letter, the pre-show cause letter (Exhibit 5), indicating the numbers of the cases and the dollar amounts owed to Customs. The surety will be advised that a show cause letter will be issued if the cases are not resolved within 30 business days from the date of the letter. As a courtesy, the NSPO will fax a copy of the pre-show cause letter to the surety on the date that it is signed.

G. Show Cause Letters

If the principal and surety fail to respond to the pre-show cause letter or respond in a manner which Customs determines does not raise a significant legal issue justifying further delay in payment of the delinquent claims, the NSPO will issue a show cause letter to the surety (Exhibit 6). The show cause letter will demand full payment of the delinquent claims within 15 business days of the date of the letter.

The Customs Service's proposed guidelines for sanctioning sureties suggest that the threshold for imposing sanctions is either 30 claims without regard to dollar value or liability, or $250,000 in total assessed claim liability. Multiple claims against one continuous bond in a single bond year cannot be aggregated to exceed the value of that bond in order to meet the $250,000 claim liability amount. For example, if a $50,000 continuous bond is charged in the same effective year with 5 separate claims for liquidated damages claims issued for the full value of the bond, those claims cannot be aggregated to reach the $250,000 threshold.

The Customs Service realizes that these minimums may not meet the regulatory requirements for sureties to be significantly delinquent in all cases, and may therefore apply these guidelines on a company by company basis. Customs may determine that a surety is significantly delinquent upon lesser thresholds if circumstances indicate that such a determination would not be arbitrary, or would not be otherwise in violation of law or regulation.

If the surety or its principal make a bona fide offer to settle an outstanding case at any time prior to actual issuance, chances are good that no show cause or sanction action will be taken. If it is issued, the show cause letter will:

- Have an attachment identifying each delinquent case.

demonstrate the existence of a significant legal issue which justifies further delay in payment.

- Identify the person at Customs with whom the surety must deal.
- Describe the sanctions to be taken.

Customs is no longer required to negotiate. Once a show cause letter is issued, mitigation formulas no longer apply and no petitions for mitigation will be entertained. Any settlement less than the full bond amount or amount of penalty will be the exception rather than the rule.

The surety can still make an offer in compromise within the 15 business day period, but this has its dangers. Any reduction of the full claim must be reviewed by the Assistant Chief Counsel, and this takes time. In the meantime, an offer in compromise is neither a payment nor a substantive legal justification for non-payment within the meaning of the show cause notice.

While Customs may consider an offer in compromise and may ultimately accept it, the offer might not stop progress toward sanction action. Only full payment or substantive justification for non-payment in writing can assure the surety of that.

If Customs decides to go forward with sanctions they will send a written notification to the surety. No payment or offer thereafter on the cases included will serve to forestall, shorten, or eliminate the minimum sanction period of five (5) days. Even if the surety pays the cases in full after receiving the sanction notice, there will be at least five (5) days where its bonds will not be accepted. The proposed guidelines state that although regulation allows it as a matter of policy, until further notice U.S. Customs will not take any action of non-acceptance of bonds at a port level for delinquent sureties. Any action regarding non-acceptance of bonds from sureties shall be initiated on a national basis only. If the surety doesn't pay, the refusal to accept its bonds will continue until it does pay.

H. Customs Service Handbook

The Customs Service has published a Handbook, titled U.S. Customs Service, Office of Commercial Operations, Fines, Penalties and Forfeitures Handbook to assist Customs personnel. Although it is designed for Customs personnel, it is a valuable tool for surety personnel handling Customs claims. It is approximately 500 pages long and is updated periodically. The Table of Contents is attached as Exhibit 7.

A copy of the book, including six supplements, is $18.25. This price includes shipping and handling. To order a copy, contact: U.S. Customs Service, Office of Regulations and Rulings, 1300 Pennsylvania Avenue, Washington, D.C. 20229 or call 202-927-2257.

II. Increased Duty Claims

A. The 612 Report

On a monthly basis the Customs Service in Indianapolis produces a print-out or a "612 " report for each surety with a listing of delinquent amounts due for all bills other than fines, penalties or liquidated damages (billed by means of Forms 5955A and 6084). The bills reflected on the print-outs almost always represent claims for additional duties. These claims arise after liquidation of an entry where the Customs Service contends the value of the imported merchandise was understated or a higher duty rate should apply due to a change in the classification of the merchandise imported. Customs also provides surety with this information on monthly tapes. Weekly tapes can be received which update the status of the bills, and the amount of interest due.

The first page of each print-out contains a summary of all outstanding claims for the surety (Exhibit 8). The claims are broken down by the age of the bills (60 days to over 120 days) and a total is given for the number of outstanding bills in each category. The total amount due for each category is also shown. That amount is further broken down between principal and interest. Finally, a date will be shown through which any payments received will be reflected on the list.

After the first page, the print-out goes on to provide detailed information on all open bills. They are listed alphabetically by the name of the delinquent debtor (usually the principal) (Exhibit 9). If there are multiple bills for a single principal, they will be listed on the same page according to bill number.

At the top of each page there is descriptive information naming the principal and surety along with their respective company identification numbers. For each claim there will be information showing the bill and entry numbers, the billing location, and the document and bill dates. These dates generally correspond with the entry and liquidation dates, respectively. Identification by the surety of the correct bond under which the claim is made can be difficult where it has issued multiple bonds for a principal, or when it has no record of bonds written for the principal.

Once a bill listed on a print-out has been paid or otherwise resolved, it is simply not included on the next month's listing. If a surety receives weekly tapes from Customs, the Customs status is updated to reflect if a bill was paid or voided and the date that occurred. If, however, a surety doesn't receive the tapes, there is no other notice given to the surety that a bill has been resolved. Consequently, the latest print-out received from the Customs Service should reflect an accurate listing of what it views as open bills for that surety. Files can be obtained, if necessary, only at the port.

B. Protests Of Increased Duty Claims

If the principal elects to challenge the determination by the Customs Service that additional duties are owed, it can do so by filing a protest within 90 days after the date of the notice of liquidation. The surety is also able to file a protest on its own behalf. It must do so within 90 days after the date of demand for payment (90 days after receiving the initial 612 report with the bill appearing for the first time). A surety can not file a protest on behalf of a principal to extend their time for filing. If a surety does file a protest for that purpose, it can be construed as collusion by the Customs Service. After a protest has been filed, the print-out will indicate that a protest has been filed, the protest number, its status and, eventually, the date on which it is approved or denied.

While a protest is pending, the Customs Service will not take further action toward collection of the claimed amounts, but interest will continue to accrue. However, if a bill is not protested within 90 days and not paid after 120 days, the principal is eligible to be placed on sanction by the Customs Service in Indianapolis.

A surety should regularly review the status of bills under protest. Upon denial of the protest it will be necessary for the surety to confer with its principal to determine what action the principal intends to take. Three options are usually available to the principal: 1) pay the amount claimed including accrued interest; 2) seek further review under the procedures and criteria set forth in 19 CFR § 174.21 - 25, (Exhibit 10); or 3) seek a judicial determination of the matter by filing an action in the Court of International Trade. However, before filing such an action in the Court, the payment, including all accrued interest, must be made to the Customs Service.

If the principal does none of the above, the surety will have little choice but to satisfy the obligation. It should be noted that when additional duty claims are paid, the entire amount claimed must be tendered. These claims are not subject to mitigation, and they are not candidates for offers in compromise.

C. DELINQUENT INCREASED DUTY CLAIMS

Once a bill is over 120 days old and not under protest, the Customs Service in Indianapolis will issue the surety a Formal Demand for payment (Exhibit 11). They allow the surety 30 days to pay the claim or provide a substantial legal reason supporting non-payment. Customs may include the bond and entry documents with this notice. If the surety does not provide either payment or a substantial legal reason for non-payment, the bills will be referred to the Assistant Chief Counsel's office for collection. A notice will be sent by the Assistant Chief Counsel's office giving the surety 14 days to pay (Exhibit 12). If there is no response from the surety or an unacceptable one, the Assistant Chief Counsel's office will prepare a lawsuit against the surety for collection action. At this point the Customs Service can also consider placing the surety on sanction.

In handling additional duty claims a surety should develop its own standards and procedures consistent with its internal policies and commensurate with good claim handling practices. Correspondence and telephone contact with the principal, customs broker and agent are often advisable. The surety should be especially diligent with claims that are more than 120 days overdue and are not under protest.

III. *Conclusion*

As stated earlier, this material deals with the very basic procedures and the time frames which apply to claims made by U.S. Customs Service. It does not deal with the many technical defenses principals and sureties may have to claims.

The U.S. Customs Regulations are about as complex as the U.S. Tax Code. For the larger and/or more complicated U.S. Customs Service claims, it will often be advisable for the principal and the surety to seek customs and international trade advice, including retaining attorneys whose practice concentrates on that specialty.

EXHIBIT 1

Form 5955A - Addressed to Principal

Liquidated Damages Notice to Violater

DEPARTMENT OF THE TREASURY
UNITED STATES CUSTOMS SERVICE

F03

NOTICE OF PENALTY OR LIQUIDATED DAMAGES INCURRED AND DEMAND FOR PAYMENT

19 CFR 18.6, 172.31

Case Number: [redacted]

Port Name and Code: 0901 BUFFALO, NEW YORK

Investigation File No.

TO: [redacted]

ID: [redacted]

TEAM NUMBER: [redacted]

PAGE 1 OF 2

DEMAND IS HEREBY MADE FOR PAYMENT OF $ 2,141.09 representing ☐ Penalties or ☒ Liquidated Damages assessed against you for violation or law or regulation, or breach of bond, as set forth below:

TIB NUMBER: [redacted]
TIB ENTERED: 08/15/1997 IMPORTED: 08/15/1997
EXPORT/DESTRUCTION REQUIRED BY: 08/14/2000
MERCHANDISE DESCRIPTION:
SYSTEM AMPLIFIERS
LIQUIDATED DAMAGES HAVE BEEN COMPUTED AT TWICE THE DUTY DUE
FAILURE TO EXPORT OR DESTROY MERCHANDISE IN ACCORDANCE WITH THE TERMS AND CONDITIONS OF THE TEMPORARY IMPORTATION BOND.

LAW OR REGULATION VIOLATED	BOND BREACHED
19CFR10.39(D)(1)	BOND TYPE: IMPORTER BROKER BOND # [redacted]

DESCRIPTION OF BOND (if any)	Form Number	Amount	Date
		$ [redacted]	[redacted]

Name and Address of Principal on Bond: [redacted]

Name and Address of Surety on Bond: [redacted]

Surety Identification No.: [redacted]

If you feel there are extenuating circumstances, you have the right to object to the above action. Your petition should explain why you should not be penalized for the cited violation. Write the petition as a letter or in legal form; submit in (duplicate) (triplicate), addressed to the Commissioner of Customs, and forward to the FP&F Officer at

U.S. CUSTOMS SERVICE/FP&F, 111 W. HURON ST., ROOM 603, BUFFALO, NY 14202

Unless the amount herein demanded is paid or a petition for relief is filed with the FP&F Officer within the indicated time limit, further action will be taken in connection with your bond or the matter will be referred to the United States Attorney.

TIME LIMIT FOR PAYMENT OR FILING PETITION FOR RELIEF (Days from the date of this Notice): 60

Signature	Title	Date
MAUREEN OCONNOR	FP&F OFFICER	11/29/1999

EXHIBIT 2
"Courtesy Letter" to Surety
(The exact format and content may vary)

DEPARTMENT OF THE TREASURY
U.S. CUSTOMS SERVICE
BUFFALO, NEW YORK

Dear Gentlemen:

A principle for which you are a surety has been notified of a violation of Customs law or regulation. A copy of the Notice of penalty is enclosed for your information. The principle has sixty (60) day from the issuance date to file a petition, which could result in a reduction or cancellation of the total amount of the liquidated damages. You also have the right to file a petition with the due date referred to in the notice.

If the principle or you do not file a petition within the time specified, the full amount of the liquidated damages becomes due and payable, and an immediate demand will be made on you as the surety to pay the total amount due. You will be given sixty (60) days in which to file a petition or make payment before being considered a delinquent surety. Please return a copy of the Notice of penalty or Liquidated Damages incurred, CF5955a, with any payment or communications.

You are advised to contact your principle now in order to insure that a petition or settlement is made by the due date shown in the Notice of Penalty.

If you wish further information concerning this case, contact the Port Director or the Fines, Penalties and Forfeitures Officer, telephone number (716)646-3400.

Sincerely,

Maureen O'Connor
Fines, Penalties and
Forfeitures Officer

Enclosure(s)

EXHIBIT 3
Form 5955A - Addressed to the Surety
Formal Demand on Surety

DEPARTMENT OF THE TREASURY
UNITED STATES CUSTOMS SERVICE

F01

NOTICE OF PENALTY OR LIQUIDATED DAMAGES INCURRED AND DEMAND FOR PAYMENT

19 CFR 18.6, 172.31

Case Number: [redacted]

Port Name and Code: 3901 CHICAGO

Investigation File No.

TO: [redacted]

ID: [redacted]

TEAM NUMBER: [redacted]

PAGE 1 OF 1

DEMAND IS HEREBY MADE FOR PAYMENT OF $ 9,134.00 representing ☐ Penalties or ☒ Liquidated Damages assessed against you for violation or law or regulation, or breach of bond, as set forth below:

ENTRY NUMBER: [redacted] ENTRY DATE: 11/09/1999
SUMMARY DUE: 11/24/1999 (E/ES) FILED: 11/24/1999 NBR DAYS LATE: 0000
AMOUNT DUE: $4,566.93 (DUTY + ADD/CVD + TAXES + FEES)
ENTRY SUMMARY FILED TIMELY. ESTIMATED DUTIES, FEES, TAXES AND CHARGES NOT PAID.
MITIGATION WILL NOT BE CONSIDERED UNTIL THE ESTIMATED DUTIES, FEES, TAXES AND CHARGES ARE PAID.
OPTION 1 NOT OFFERED.

LAW OR REGULATION VIOLATED	BOND BREACHED
19CFR113.62(L)(4 19CFR113.62(A)(1	BOND TYPE: IMPORTER BROKER BOND # [redacted]

DESCRIPTION OF BOND (if any)	Form Number	Amount	Date
		$ [redacted]	[redacted]

ame and Address of Principal on Bond: [redacted]

ame and Address of Surety on Bond: [redacted] — Surety Identification No.: [redacted]

If you feel there are extenuating circumstances, you have the right to object to the above action. Your petition should explain why you should not be penalized for the cited violation. Write the petition as a letter or in legal form; submit in (duplicate) (triplicate), addressed to the Commissioner of Customs, and forward to the FP&F Officer at

U.S. CUSTOMS SERVICE/FP&F, 610 SOUTH CANAL ST, CHICAGO, IL 60607

Unless the amount herein demanded is paid or a petition for relief is filed with the FP&F Officer within the indicated time limit, further action will be taken in connection with your bond or the matter will be referred to the United States Attorney.

TIME LIMIT FOR PAYMENT OR FILING PETITION FOR RELIEF (Days from the date of this Notice): 60

gnature	Title	Date
BONITA HOOKS	FP&F OFFICER	11/30/1999

Customs Form 5955A (110195)

EXHIBIT 4

Form 6084

U.S. Customs Service Bill

SVCP - 2604

SEND CHECK MADE PAYABLE TO:
U.S. CUSTOMS SERVICE

U.S. CUSTOMS SERVICE/ATTN:
9 NORTH GRAND AVE
NOGALES AZ 85621

FOR SERVICE/CHARGE AT:

2604
NOGALES, AZ

REFER INQUIRIES TO:

U.S. CUSTOMS SERVICE/ATTN:
9 NORTH GRAND AVE
NOGALES AZ 85621

PLEASE ADVISE OF ANY CHANGE OF ADDRESS

U.S. CUSTOMS SERVICE BILL

ON THIS DATE	REFERENCE NAME	ASSIGN/ENTRY NO.	TYPE OF CHARGE	AMOUNT
05-13-99	FPF CASE ENTRY NO BOND NO		LIQ DAMAGES	100000.00

FINAL DEMAND - DELINQUENT ACCOUNT. CLAIM WILL BE REFERRED FOR SANCTIONS AND LEGAL ACTION TEN (10) DAYS FROM THE DATE OF THIS DEMAND.

BROKER: K76 VALENCIA INTL

VIOLATOR:
VIOLATION(S): 19CFR161.113 19CFR132.14 7USC1854
VIOLATION DATE: 05-13-1999
REFERENCE NUMBER: 02.011998

FILE COPY

PINK COPY OF BILL MUST BE MAILED WITH YOUR PAYMENT

THIRD NOTICE ISSUED: 12/04/1999
B SURETY 891

0371

FOR PROPER CREDIT TO YOUR ACCOUNT PAY FULL AMOUNT DUE UPON RECEIPT ▶	100000.00
AMOUNT DUE AFTER (INCLUDING INTEREST) ▶	

YOUR CUSTOMS IMPORTER NO	BILL DATE	BILL NUMBER
	12-04-99	3

DEPARTMENT OF THE TREASURY
U.S. CUSTOMS SERVICE
CUSTOMS FORM 6084 (040593)

EXHIBIT 5
Pre-Show Cause/Sanction Letter
Issued to Surety
Warning Notice may vary by Port

DEPARTMENT OF THE TREASURY
U.S. CUSTOMS SERVICE
PACIFIC REGION

DEC 23 1994

ENF 4 SD:F JGG

PRE-SANCTION NOTICE

Dear Sir:

According to our records, the penalty or liquidated damages cases shown on the attached list are significantly past due, and eligible for sanction. As the surety, your company is responsible for these cases. Title 19, Code of Federal Regulations, section 113.38, grants Customs the authority to refuse to accept bonds issued by delinquent sureties.

We are providing this list in order to give you the opportunity to resolve these cases prior to the commencement of formal sanction action under the above referenced provision. Please contact, or submit payment to, the appropriate district Fines, Penalties, and Forfeitures (FP&F) office to arrange settlement as soon as possible. If you fail to arrange settlement within thirty (30) days from the date of this letter, this office will proceed toward formal sanction.

If you have any questions regarding these cases, please contact the FP&F officers identified on the attachment. Please submit payments directly to the appropriate district FP&F office with a confirmation copy of your correspondence to: U.S. Customs Service, Fines, Penalties, and Forfeitures, 610 West Ash Street, Suite 1200, San Diego, CA 92101, Attention: Diane Harvey.

Sincerely,

RUDY M. CAMACHO
Regional Commissioner

RECEIVED

Attachments

cc: District Directors, Pacific Region
Director, Seizures & Penalties Division, Headquarters

REPLY TO: REGIONAL COMMISSIONER OF CUSTOMS
ONE WORLD TRADE CENTER, SUITE 705, LONG BEACH, CA 90831-0700

EXHIBIT 6
Show Cause Letter

DEPARTMENT OF THE TREASURY
U.S. CUSTOMS SERVICE
MIAMI, FLA.

REFER TO

August 2, 1990 ENF-1-0:I JS

Show Cause Letter

Gentlemen:

This is notice pursuant to 19 C.F.R. 113.38 (c)(4) for your company to pay or show just cause why it is delinquent in payment on outstanding debts incurred by your firm as surety under the terms of your Customs Bond(s). Specifically, the enclosed list reflects the relevant Customs case number(s), bond number(s), principal/importer and amount due for each case. Previously, you have been sent demands for payment and bills for all of these cases.

Within ten (10) days of receipt of this notice, payment must be made, or justification provided for failure to pay, or you must demonstrate the existence of a significant legal issue which justifies further delay in payment. The payment or other correspondence must be mailed to:

Regional Commissioner
c/o FP&F Program Manager
909 SE 1st Ave., RM 710
Miami, Florida 33131

If payment or justification for non-payment is not received within ten (10) days, I will issue instructions advising District Director(s) that no entries or other transactions secured by new single transaction or continuous bonds written by your company will be accepted. Written notice of my final decision to issue such sanctions will be provided to your company at least five days before their effective date. Pursuant to 19 C.F.R. 113.38 (c)(5), a copy of that decision will be posted in the Customhouse and forwarded to Customs Headquarters for publication in the Customs Bulletin. If sanctioned, 19 C.F.R. 113.38 (c)(6) provides that the sanction shall remain in effect for a minimum of five days or until all outstanding delinquencies are resolved, whichever is later. Furthermore, the failure to satisfy this demand for payment or justification may result in a recommendation to the appropriate Customs officer for national sanctions; and/or a recommendation to the Secretary of the Treasury that your company be removed from Treasury Department Circular 570 pursuant to 19 C.F.R. 113.39 and 31 C.F.R. 223.18(a).

REPLY TO: REGIONAL COMMISSIONER OF CUSTOMS, MIAMI, FLORIDA 33131

-2-

Any questions concerning this matter may be referred to Jack Silverman, FP&F Program Officer, at (305) 536-5283.

Sincerely,

George C. Corcoran, Jr.
Regional Commissioner

Enclosures

EXHIBIT 7

FINES, PENALTIES AND FORFEITURES HANDBOOK TABLE OF CONTENTS

INTRODUCTION TO FINES, PENALTIES AND FORFEITURES HANDBOOK....INT

Handbook Format....INT-1
A Special Note About Guidelines....INT-1
Updating of Materials....INT-1
Chapter Organization....INT-2
Chapter Key....INT-3

SEIZURE CASE PROCESSING....SCP

Seizure/Appraisal....SCP-1
Statute of Limitations....SCP-2
Issuance of Notices....SCP-3
Cancellation of Cases....SCP-6
Release of Seized Property....SCP-7
Constructive Seizure....SCP-9
Immediate Sale....SCP-10
Substitution of Collateral; Payment of Penalty to Effect Release....SCP-11
Responses to Seizure Notice....SCP-11
Issuance of Decision Letter....SCP-16
Compliance....SCP-18
Claims Against Proceeds of Sale....SCP-20
Letters of Credit....SCP-20
APPENDIX A: Notices of Seizure and Information for Claimants; Election of Proceedings....SCP-23
Form AFCS....SCP-25
Form AF....SCP-29
Election of Proceedings, Form AF....SCP-33
Form AF - Post....SCP-35
Election of Proceedings, Form AF - Post....SCP-39
Form JF....SCP-41
Election of Proceedings, Form JF....SCP-44
Acknowledgment of Early Release of Seized Merchandise....SCP-45
APPENDIX B: Notices of Seizure....SCP-47
19 U.S.C. 1595a(a)....SCP-49
49 U.S.C. 782....SCP-50
21 U.S.C. 881....SCP-51
19 U.S.C. 1703....SCP-52
19 U.S.C. 1497....SCP-53
19 U.S.C. 1459/1460....SCP-54
31 U.S.C. 5316/5317....SCP-55
18 U.S.C. 545....SCP-56
22 U.S.C. 401....SCP-57

APPENDIX C..SCP-59
Constructive Seizure Agreement..............................SCP-61
Sample Constructive Seizure Agreement.......................SCP-65
APPENDIX D..SCP-67
Treasury Rules..SCP-69
APPENDIX E..SCP-83
Hold Harmless Agreements....................................SCP-85

CONTRABAND RELATED CONVEYANCE SEIZURES AND FORFEITURES [19 U.S.C. 1595a(a); 21 U.S.C. 881; 49 U.S.C. 781/782; 19 U.S.C. 1703]......................................CON
Statutory Authority for Seizure and Forfeiture........CON-1
Common Carriers.......................................CON-3
Immediate Administrative Forfeiture Proceedings.......CON-5
General Considerations When Immediate Forfeiture is Not Appropriate..................................CON-6
Mitigation Guidelines: 19 U.S.C. 1595a(a), 21 U.S.C. 881, 49 U.S.C. 781/782...............................CON-8
Mitigation Guidelines: 19 U.S.C. 1703...............CON-10
Mitigation Guidelines - Petitioning for Proceeds of Sale Following Immediate Forfeiture.................CON-11

FAILURE TO DECLARE MERCHANDISE (19 U.S.C. 1497; 19 U.S.C. 1459/1460)..DEC
Declaration Requirements..............................DEC-1
Amendment of Declarations Permitted (19 CFR 148.16)...DEC-1
Elements of the Violation.............................DEC-2
Violator's Liability..................................DEC-2
Petty Violations......................................DEC-2
Serious Violations....................................DEC-2
Mitigation Guidelines.................................DEC-3
Civil Administrative Penalties for Failure to Declare Small Amounts of Controlled Substances...........DEC-8
APPENDIX...DEC-11
Administrative Penalty/Remission Chart..............DEC-13
Agreement to Pay Monetary Penalty...................DEC-15

FAILURE TO REPORT MONETARY INSTRUMENTS (31 U.S.C. 5316)......MON
Reporting Requirements................................MON-1
Amendment of Monetary Instrument Report Permitted.....MON-4
Violation Has Occurred If:............................MON-4
Criminal Liability Incurred...........................MON-5
Civil Liability Incurred..............................MON-5
Procedures for Deposit of Seized Monetary Instruments Into Interest Bearing Accounts.....................MON-6
Mitigation Guidelines.................................MON-7
APPENDIX A...MON-11
Stipulation and Power of Attorney...................MON-13
Directions for Completion of Stipulation............MON-15
Sample Cases..MON-17

APPENDIX B..MON-21
Definitions and Examples of Reportable Monetary Instruments................................MON-23

SMUGGLING: IMPORTATION CONTRARY TO LAW (18 U.S.C. 545)......SMU
History...SMU-1
Use...SMU-2
Violation...SMU-2
Mitigation..SMU-3

IMPORTATION AND EXPORTATION OF SELF-PROPELLED VEHICLES (19 U.S.C. 1627)....................................VEH
Violation - Knowing Importation, Exportation, or Attempted Importation or Exportation of Stolen Vehicles..VEH-1
Liabilities Incurred................................VEH-1
Mitigation Guidelines...............................VEH-1
Violation - Knowing Importation, Exportation, or Attempted Importation of Exportation of Vehicle With Altered VIN #..............................VEH-2
Liabilities Incurred................................VEH-2
Mitigation Guidelines...............................VEH-2
Violation - Failure to Present Documents Upon Exportation of Used Vehicle........................VEH-3

EXPORT CONTROL CASES...................................EXP
The Underlying Violation............................EXP-1
Matters Concerning the Department of State, Office of Munitions Control..............................EXP-1
Matters Concerning the Department of Commerce, Office of Export Administration and Office of Export Enforcement...........................EXP-2
Matters Concerning the Bureau of Census - Foreign Trade Statistics.................................EXP-5
The Sanction..EXP-5
22 U.S.C. 401.......................................EXP-5
Property or Assets of NATO..........................EXP-6
Merchandise Sold by U.S. to a Foreign Government..EXP-6
Constructive Seizure of Merchandise.................EXP-6
Mitigation Process - Handling of Petitions..........EXP-7
Matters Concerning the Department of State, Office of Munitions Control..............................EXP-7
Matters Concerning the Department of Commerce, Office of Export Administration and Office of Export Enforcement...........................EXP-7
Matters Concerning the Bureau of Census - Foreign Trade Statistics.................................EXP-7
Factors to Be Considered in Mitigation..............EXP-8
Seizure History.....................................EXP-8
Recommendations From State and Commerce Departments...EXP-8

Mitigation Guidelines....................................EXP-9
- Substantive Violations...............................EXP-9
- Technical Violations.................................EXP-9
- Bureau of Census Cases...............................EXP-10

VEHICLE SEIZURES, PENALTIES AND LIQUIDATED DAMAGES CLAIMS RELATED TO NON-COMPLIANCE WITH EPA AND DOT STANDARDS....EPA

Seizure and Penalty Cases................................EPA-1
- Failure to Manifest or Declare Automobiles Which Do Not Comply With EPA/DOT Standards........EPA-1
- Failure to Manifest or Declare Trucks Which Do Not Comply With EPA/DOT Standards...........EPA-3
- Non-Resident Imports Non-Conforming EPA-3
- Third Party Purchasers...............................EPA-3

Mitigation Guidelines, Seizure and Penalty Cases - Non-1592 Violations..................................EPA-4
- Special Note - Computing Domestic Value..........EPA-4
- Commercial Importations of Automobiles...........EPA-4
- Non-Commercial Importations of Automobiles.......EPA-5
- Commercial Importations of Trucks................EPA-6
- Non-Commercial Importations of Trucks............EPA-7
- Seizures Pursuant to 18 USC 545..................EPA-8

Mitigation Guidelines - Violations of 19 USC 1592.....EPA-8

Claims for Liquidated Damages.........................EPA-9

APPENDIX..EPA-11
- Importations of Non-Conforming Vehicles Subject to EPA and DOT Requirements - Other Agency Compliance Circular No. 169...............EPA-13

PENALTIES FOR ILLEGAL IMPORTATIONS [19 U.S.C. 1595a(b)]......IMP

Statutory Authority...................................IMP-1

Use of Statute (Examples).............................IMP-2

Mitigation Guidelines.................................IMP-2

VESSELS IN FOREIGN AND DOMESTIC TRADE........................VES

ARRIVAL AND ENTRY OF VESSELS..........................VES-1
- Failure to Report Arrival (19 USC 1433, 1436) or to Make Entry (19 USC 1434, 1435, 1436)..VES-1

MANIFEST RELATED VIOLATIONS...........................VES-2
- Failure to Deliver Manifest (19 USC 1439)........VES-2
- Failure to Correct Manifest (19 USC 1440)........VES-2
- Failure to Produce Manifest on Demand (19 USC 1584)...............................VES-2
- False Manifest - Overages of Merchandise Other Than Controlled Substances (19 USC 1584)....VES-3
- False Manifest - Shortages (19 USC 1584).........VES-4
- False Manifest - Controlled Substances in Commercial Quantities on Board Common Carriers.........VES-5

LANDING AND DELIVERY OF CARGO.........................VES-8
- Unlading Without Permit (19 USC 1448, 1453)......VES-8

Failure to Retain Merchandise at Place of Unlading [19 USC 1448, 1595a(b)]....................VES-10
Delivery Without Inspection [19 USC 1499, 1595a(b)]..VES-10
Unlading Passenger Without Permit (19 USC 1448, 1454)..VES-10
DEPARTURE OF VESSELS..VES-11
Failure to Comply With Procedures Upon Departure to a Foreign Port..........................VES-11
COASTWISE TRANSPORTATION..VES-12
Coastwise Transportation of Passengers (46 USC 289)................................VES-12
Coastwise Transportation of Merchandise (46 USC 883)................................VES-13
-39

PROCEDURES FOR ASSESSING AND PROCESSING VESSEL REPAIR PENALTIES..VRP
Requirements of Statute and Regulations...............VRP-1
Elements of Violation; Determination of Liability.....VRP-2
Penalty Assessment Procedures........................VRP-2
Mitigation Guidelines................................VRP-4
APPENDIX...VRP-7
Vessel Repairs - Declaration, Entry, and Liquidation Procedures......................VRP-9
- 17

AIR COMMERCE REGULATIONS..AIR
AIR COMMERCE STATUTES................................AIR-1
Entry and Clearance of Aircraft and Ports of Entry [19 USC 1509(b) and (c)]...................AIR-1
Entry and Clearance of Aircraft and Administration of Customs Laws (19 USC 1644)..............AIR-1
Liability and Penalties (19 USC 1474)............AIR-2
AIR COMMERCE REGULATIONS.............................AIR-2
Failure to Report Arrival (19 USC 1433, 1436) or to Make Entry (19 USC 1434, 1435, 1436).....AIR_2
MANIFEST RELATED VIOLATIONS..........................AIR-3
Failure to Deliver Manifest (19 USC 1439)........AIR-3
Failure to Correct Manifest (19 USC 1440)........AIR-3
Failure to Produce Manifest on Demand (19 USC 1584).................................AIR-3
False Manifest - Overages of Merchandise Other Than Controlled Substances (19 USC 1584).........AIR-3
False Manifest - Shortages (19 USC 1584).........AIR-5
False Manifest - Controlled Substances in Commercial Quantities on Board Common Carriers.........AIR-5
LANDING AND DELIVERY OF CARGO........................AIR-5
Unlading Without Permit (19 USC 1448, 1453)......AIR-5
Failure to Retain Merchandise at Place of Unlading [19 USC 1448, 1595a(b)]..................AIR-7
Delivery Without Inspection [19 USC 1499, 1595a(b)]..AIR-7

Unlading Passengers Without Permit (19 USC 1448, 1454)....AIR-7
DEPARTURE OF AIRCRAFT....AIR-8
Failure to Comply With Procedures Upon Departure to a Foreign Port (46 USC 91)....AIR-8
COASTWISE TRANSPORTATION....AIR-9
Coastwise Transportation of Passengers (46 USC 289)....AIR-9
Coastwise Transportation of Merchandise (46 USC 883)....AIR-10

LIQUIDATED DAMAGES....LDS
GENERAL INFORMATION....LDS-1
Liquidated Damages Involves a Breach of Contract.LDS-1
Statute of Limitations for Bond Violations....LDS-1
District Director's Authority....LDS-1
Offers in Compromise....LDS-2
LATE FILING OF ENTRY SUMMARIES (19 CFR 142.15)....LDS-3
Entry Summary Includes....LDS-3
Time of Filing....LDS-3
Determination of Liability....LDS-4
Issuance of Claim....LDS-5
Mitigation....LDS-5
FAILURE TO PROVIDE MISSING DOCUMENTS (19 USC 113.42)..LDS-7
Bond Requirements....LDS-7
Imposition/Cancellation of Claims....LDS-7
Mitigation Guidelines....LDS-8
FAILURE TO REDELIVER MERCHANDISE INTO CUSTOMS CUSTODY (19 CFR 141.113)....LDS-13
Merchandise Subject to Redelivery....LDS-13
Procedures: Demands for Redelivery and Claims for Liquidated Damages....LDS-14
Guidelines for Cancellation of Liquidated Damages Claims (Mitigation) When Petition Has Been Submitted....LDS-16
SHORTAGES, IRREGULAR DELIVERY, NON-DELIVERY (19 CFR 18.8)....LDS-19
Definition of Violations....LDS-19
Transportation and Exportation Bonds....LDS-19
Immediate Transportation Bond....LDS-21
Liabilities Incurred by Carriers....LDS-22
Degrees of Culpability for the Violation....LDS-22
Mitigation Guidelines....LDS-23
TEMPORARY IMPORTATION OF ARTICLES (19 CFR 10.39)....LDS-25
Terms of Temporary Importation Bond....LDS-25
Grounds for Breach of Temporary Importation Bonds....LDS-25
Mitigation Authority....LDS-26
Mitigation Guidelines....LDS-27

APPENDIX A.....................................LDS-29
Examples, Late Filing of Entries...........LDS-31
APPENDIX B.....................................LDS-33
Notice - Failure to File Entry Summary Timely.................................LDS-35
APPENDIX C.....................................LDS-37
Mitigation Guidelines for Late Filing of Entry Summary Claims.................LDS-39
APPENDIX D.....................................LDS-45
Notice - Failure to Timely File Missing Documents.............................LDS-47
APPENDIX E.....................................LDS-49
Notice to Redeliver or of Liquidated Damages Incurred and Demand for Payment.......LDS-51
APPENDIX F.....................................LDS-53
Identification of In-Bond Entry Types.....LDS-55

CARNETS (PART 114, SECTION 10.39, CUSTOMS REGULATIONS........CTS 79
General Considerations.............................CTS-1
A.T.A. Carnets.....................................CTS-1-3

19 U.S.C. 1592...FRD
Elements of the Violation...........................FRD-1
Definitions...FRD-2
Maximum Penalty Amounts.............................FRD-4
Penalty Dispositions Under Mitigation Guidelines......FRD-5
Procedures for Establishing Penalty Claim.............FRD-8
Seizures Under 19 USC 1592..........................FRD-14
Prior Disclosure....................................FRD-17
Burdens of Proof in Judicial Enforcement.............FRD-22
APPENDIX A..FRD-23
Statute of Limitations Waiver Form.............FRD-25
T.D. 76-33......................................FRD-27
APPENDIX B..FRD-31
Prepenalty Notice...............................FRD-33
APPENDIX C..FRD-37
Waiver of Right to Prepenalty Notice Under Section 1592.............................FRD-39
APPENDIX D..FRD-41
Notice of Penalty...............................FRD-43
APPENDIX E..FRD-45
Part 171 (Amended), Appendix B..................FRD-47-49

CLAIMS FOR AND AWARDS OF COMPENSATION........................INF
Statutory Provisions..................................INF-1
Entitlement...INF-2
Amount of Award.......................................INF-3
Authority to Approve Award............................INF-5
Handling of Information by Receiving Officers.........INF-6
Name of Informer Confidential.........................INF-6
Filing of Claim.......................................INF-7
Action of Receiving Officer...........................INF-7
Certification of Information..........................INF-9
Certification of Net Recoveries.......................INF-9
Partial Payment for Information......................INF-11
Payments to Federal Employees........................INF-12
Transmittal to the Miscellaneous Penalties Branch....INF-13
Headquarters Action..................................INF-13
Treasury Cases.......................................INF-17
Payment to the Informant.............................INF-17
APPENDIX...INF-19
Disclaimer of Interest in Award......................INF-21

COPYRIGHTS, TRADEMARKS AND PATENTS............................CTP
Copyright Violations..................................CTP-1
Regulations...CTP-1
Elements of Copyright Violations......................CTP-1
Genuine Copies..CTP-6
Options Upon Importation..............................CTP-7
Disposition of Articles Subject to Seizure............CTP-8
Trademark Violations..................................CTP-9
Applicable Laws......................................CTP-10
Elements of Trademark Violations.....................CTP-10
Disposition of Articles Subject to Seizure and Forfeiture...CTP-16
Patent Enforcement...................................CTP-18
Definition...CTP-18
Law..CTP-18
Regulations..CTP-22 -23

INDEX...IND
Index of Topics.......................................IND-1
Index of Statutes and Regulations....................IND-11
Index of Mitigation Guidelines by Statute............IND-15
Index of Forms.......................................IND-17

EXHIBIT 8

612 Report - to Surety
Summary of all outstanding bills for a specific surety.

ACSR-CL-612

FICHE INDEX: [redacted]

UNITED STATES CUSTOMS SERVICE

FORMAL DEMAND ON SURETY

FOR PAYMENT OF DELINQUENT AMOUNTS DUE

ALL BILLS OTHER THAN FINE, PENALTY AND LIQUIDATED DAMAGE BILLS

GENTLEMEN,

THIS IS A FORMAL DEMAND UPON YOU FOR PAYMENT OF THE AMOUNT(S) NOTED ON THE ENCLOSURE(S) HERETO. ENCLOSED HEREWITH IS A LISTING OF [redacted] BILL(S) TOTALING $ [redacted] ($ [redacted] PRINCIPAL AND $ [redacted] INTEREST) DUE TO THE UNITED STATES CUSTOMS SERVICE BY PRINCIPAL(S) FOR WHOM YOU ARE SURETY AND WHICH WERE DUE AND PAYABLE ON THE DATES INDICATED IN THE ENCLOSURE(S). FORMAL DEMANDS WERE MADE ON THE PRINCIPAL(S) INVOLVED BUT THE BILL(S) REMAIN UNPAID AS OF OCTOBER 31, 1999. UNDER THE TERMS OF YOUR BOND YOU ARE AN ORIGINAL PROMISOR AND DEBTOR WITH EACH OF YOUR PRINCIPALS

THE AMOUNT(S) IDENTIFIED ON THE ENCLOSURE(S) ARE SUMMARIZED BY AGE CATEGORY AS FOLLOWS:

[redacted] BILL(S) TOTALING $ [redacted] ($ [redacted] PRINCIPAL AND $ [redacted] INTEREST) ARE 60 OR MORE DAYS OLD.

[redacted] BILL(S) TOTALING $ [redacted] ($ [redacted] PRINCIPAL AND $ [redacted] INTEREST) ARE 90 OR MORE DAYS OLD.

[redacted] BILL(S) TOTALING $ [redacted] ($ [redacted] PRINCIPAL AND $ [redacted] INTEREST) ARE 120 OR MORE DAYS OLD AND APPEAR IN THIS CATEGORY FOR THE FIRST TIME.

[redacted] BILL(S) TOTALING $ [redacted] ($ [redacted] PRINCIPAL AND $ [redacted] INTEREST) ARE 120 OR MORE DAYS OLD AND HAVE APPEARED IN THIS CATEGORY ON PREVIOUS REPORTS.

IF ANY CLAIM TO WHICH THIS LETTER RELATES HAS BEEN PAID IN FULL SINCE OCTOBER 31, 1999. NO FURTHER ACTION WITH RESPECT TO THAT CLAIM IS REQUIRED OF YOU.

WE WISH TO CALL YOUR ATTENTION TO THE FACT THAT THE CLAIMS TO WHICH THIS LETTER RELATES ARE NOT NECESSARILY THE ONLY OUTSTANDING CLAIMS AGAINST YOUR COMPANY.

SINCERELY YOURS,

Pamela A. Miller

DIRECTOR, NATIONAL FINANCE CENTER

PLEASE DIRECT YOUR REPLIES TO THE DIRECTOR, NATIONAL FINANCE CENTER, U.S. CUSTOMS SERVICE, P.O. BOX 68911, 6026 LAKESIDE BLVD, INDIANAPOLIS, INDIANA 46268

EXHIBIT 9

"612 Report" Notice of Outstanding Bills for a prinicpal/debtor

ACSR-CL-612

FICHE INDEX: 891
RUN DATE: 12/02/99
RUN TIME: 00:44:19
SURETY PAGE: 02513

UNITED STATES CUSTOMS SERVICE
AUTOMATED COMMERCIAL SYSTEM

FORMAL DEMAND ON SURETY
FOR PAYMENT OF DELINQUENT AMOUNTS DUE
ALL BILLS OTHER THAN FINE, PENALTY AND LIQUIDATED DAMAGE BILLS
NOVEMBER 1999

SURETY	SURETY NUMBER	DELINQUENT DEBTOR	IMPORTER NUMBER	BANKRUPT

BILL N''MBER	BOND NUMBER	BILLING LOCATION	DOCUMENT DATE	ENTRY NUMBER	BILL DATE	AMOUNT DUE	PRINCIPAL AMT	INTEREST AMT	AGE CATEGORY 60	90	120	OVR
		LOS ANGELES INT	01/30/98		07/30/99	2587.83	2520.66	67.17			X	
NUMBER OF BILLS - 1				IMPORTER TOTALS		2587.83	2520.66	67.17				

PART 174—PROTESTS

Sec.
174.0 Scope.

Subpart A—General Provisions

174.1 Definitions.
174.2 Applicability of provisions.
174.3 Power of attorney to file protest.

Subpart B—Protests

174.11 Matters subject to protest.
174.12 Filing of protests.
174.13 Content of protest.
174.14 Amendment of protests.
174.15 Consolidation of protests filed by different parties.
174.16 Limitation on protests after reliquidation.

Subpart C—Review and Disposition of Protests

174.21 Time for review of protests.
174.22 Accelerated disposition of protest.
174.23 Further review of protests.
174.24 Criteria for further review.
174.25 Application for further review.
174.26 Review of protest after application for further review.
174.27 Disposition after further review.
174.28 Consideration of additional arguments.
174.29 Allowance or denial of protests.
174.30 Notice of denial of protest.
174.31 Judicial review of denial of protest.
174.32 Publication.

Authority: 19 U.S.C. 66, 1514, 1515, 1624.

Source: T.D. 70–181, 35 FR 13429, Aug. 22, 1970, unless otherwise noted.

§ 174.0 Scope.

This part deals with the administrative review of decisions of the port director, including the requirements for the filing of protests against such decisions, amendment of protests, review and accelerated disposition, and provisions dealing with further administrative review. Provisions applicable to Canadian and Mexican exporters and producers regarding administrative review and appeal of adverse marking decisions under the North American Free Trade Agreement are contained in part 181 of this chapter.

[T.D. 70–181, 35 FR 13429, Aug. 22, 1970, as amended by T.D. 94–1, 58 FR 69472, Dec. 30, 1993; T.D. 95–78, 60 FR 50038, Sept. 27, 1995]

Subpart A—General Provisions

§ 174.1 Definitions.

When used in this part, the following term shall have the meaning indicated:

Further review. "Further review" means review of the decision which is the subject of the protest by Customs officers on a level higher than the district, and in Region II by Customs officers who did not participate directly in the decision which is the subject of the protest.

[T.D. 95–77, 60 FR 50020, Sept. 27, 1995; T.D. 95–78, 60 FR 50038, Sept. 27, 1995]

§ 174.2 Applicability of provisions.

(a) *In general.* The provisions of this part shall be applicable to protests against decisions involving:

(1) Articles excluded from entry or entered or withdrawn from warehouse for consumption on or after October 1, 1970;

(2) Articles entered or withdrawn from warehouse for consumption prior to October 1, 1970, for which appraisement has not become final by October 1, 1970;

(3) Articles entered or withdrawn from warehouse for consumption prior to October 1, 1970, for which the appraisement has become final but with respect to which the entry has not been liquidated prior to October 1, 1970;

(4) Articles entered or withdrawn from warehouse for consumption with respect to which the entry has been liquidated prior to October 1, 1970, if

(i) The time for filing a protest has not expired and a protest has not been filed prior to October 1, 1970; or

(ii) A protest has been filed and has not been disallowed in whole or in part before October 1, 1970; or

(5) Articles excluded from entry before October 1, 1970, with respect to which

(i) The time for filing a protest has not expired and a protest has not been filed prior to October 1, 1970; or

(ii) A protest has been filed and has not been disallowed in whole or in part before October 1, 1970.

(b) *Limitation*—(1) *Appraisement not final.* When the appraisement of articles entered or withdrawn from warehouse for consumption prior to October 1, 1970, is not final by October 1, 1970, because an appeal for reappraisement was timely filed prior to such date, the provisions of this part relating to protests shall be applicable to a protest filed after the court's decision on the appeal to reappraisement has become final. Such protest shall not include issues which were raised or could have been raised on the appeal for reappraisement.

(2) *Appraisement final.* When the appraisement of articles entered or withdrawn from warehouse for consumption prior to October 1, 1970, has become final prior to October 1, 1970, but the entry has not been liquidated by such date, a protest filed in accordance with the provisions of this part after such liquidation shall not include issues which were raised or could have been raised on an appeal to reappraisement before the appraisement became final.

(3) *Protest not disallowed.* When a protest filed prior to October 1, 1970, has not been disallowed in whole or in part before such date, the provisions of this part shall be applicable to such protests. The time within which any action must be taken under the provisions of this part with respect to such a protest shall commence on the date the protest was in fact filed.

[T.D. 70–181, 35 FR, 13429, Aug. 22, 1970, as amended by T.D. 71–60, 36 FR 3116, Feb. 18, 1971]

§ 174.3 Power of attorney to file protest.

(a) *When required.* When a protest is filed by a person acting as agent or attorney in fact for the principal, other than an attorney at law or a customhouse broker or his authorized employee acting in his behalf, there shall have been filed or shall be filed with the protest a power of attorney which either specifically authorizes such agent to make, sign, and file the protest or grants unlimited authority to such agent. No power of attorney to file a protest shall be required in the following cases:

(1) *Attorney at law.* When the protest is filed by an attorney at law as agent or attorney for the principal, the signing of the protest as agent or attorney for the principal by the attorney at law shall be considered a declaration by him that he is currently a member in good standing of the highest court of a State, possession, territory, commonwealth, or the District of Columbia, and has been authorized to sign and file the protest for the principal.

(2) *Customhouse broker or his employee.* When a protest is filed by a customhouse broker, or an authorized employee acting in his behalf, as agent or attorney in fact for the principal, the signing of the protest by the customhouse broker or an authorized employee in his behalf shall be considered a declaration by the broker that he or the employee signing in his behalf, is authorized to sign and file the protest for the principal. The customhouse broker shall have, however, a general power of attorney to transact Customs business for the principal on Customs Form 5291.

(b) *Execution of power of attorney*—(1) *Corporation.* A corporate power of attorney to file protests shall be signed by a duly authorized officer or employee of the corporation. If the port director is otherwise satisfied as to the authority of such corporate officer or employee to grant such power of attorney, compliance with the requirements of § 141.37 of this chapter may be waived with respect to such power.

(2) *Partnership.* A partnership power of attorney to file protests may be signed by one member in the name of the partnership, provided the power recites the name of all the members.

(c) *Duration.* Powers of attorney issued by a partnership shall be limited to a period not to exceed 2 years from the date of receipt thereof by the port director. All other powers of attorney may be granted for an unlimited period.

(d) *Revocation.* Any power of attorney shall be subject to revocation at any time by written notice given to and received by the port director.

(Secs. 514, 515, 46 Stat. 734, as amended; 19 U.S.C. 1514, 1515)

[T.D. 70–181, 35 FR 13429, Aug. 22, 1970, as amended by T.D. 70–224, 35 FR 16243, Oct. 16, 1970; T.D. 73–175, 38 FR 17487, July 2, 1973; T.D. 95–78, 60 FR 50038, Sept. 27, 1995]

Subpart B—Protests

§ 174.11 Matters subject to protest.

The following decisions of the port director, including the legality of all orders and findings entering into the same, may be protested under the provisions of section 514, Tariff Act of 1930, as amended (19 U.S.C. 1514):

(a) The appraised value of merchandise;

(b) The classification and rate and amount of duties chargeable;

(c) All charges or exactions of whatever character within the jurisdiction of the Secretary of the Treasury;

(d) The exclusion of merchandise from entry or delivery under any provision of the Customs laws;

(e) The liquidation or reliquidation of an entry, or any modification thereof;

(f) The refusal to pay a claim for drawback; and

(g) The refusal to reliquidate an entry under section 520(c), Tariff Act of 1930, as amended (19 U.S.C. 1520(c)).

[T.D. 95–78, 60 FR 50038, Sept. 27, 1995]

§ 174.12 Filing of protests.

(a) *By whom filed.* Protests may be filed by:

(1) The importer or consignee shown on the entry papers, or their sureties;

(2) Any person paying any charge or exaction;

(3) Any person seeking entry or delivery;

(4) Any person filing a claim for drawback;

(5) With respect to a determination of origin under subpart G of part 181 of this chapter, any exporter or producer of the merchandise subject to that determination, if the exporter or producer completed and signed a Certificate of Origin covering the merchandise as provided for in § 181.11(a) of this chapter; or

(6) Any authorized agent of any of the persons described in paragraphs (a) (1) through (5) of this section, subject to the provisions of § 174.3.

(b) *Form and number of copies.* Protests against decisions of a port director shall be filed in quadruplicate on Customs Form 19 or a form of the same size clearly labeled "Protest" and setting forth the same content in its entirety, in the same order, addressed to the port director. All schedules or other attachments to a protest (other than samples or similar exhibits) shall also be filed in quadruplicate.

(c) *Identity of filer.* The identity of the person filing the protest or his agent, or attorney shall be noted on the protest. This may be accomplished through a signature which is handwritten in ink, stamped, typed, facsimile, telefax, or by electronic certification in ACS. If the person filing the protest is not the importer of record or consignee, the filer shall include his address and importer number, if any.

(d) *Place of filing.* Protests shall be filed with the port director whose decision is protested.

(e) *Time of filing.* Protests shall be filed, in accordance with section 514, Tariff Act of 1930, as amended (19 U.S.C. 1514), within 90 days after either:

(1) The date of notice of liquidation or reliquidation in accordance with §§ 159.9 or 159.10 of this chapter;

(2) The date of the decision, involving neither a liquidation nor reliquidation, as to which the protest is made (e.g., the date of an exaction, the date of written notice excluding merchandise from entry or delivery under any provision of the Customs laws or the date of a refusal to reliquidate under section 520(c)(1) of the Tariff Act of 1930, as amended, or the date of written notice of a denial of a claim filed under section 520(d) of the Tariff Act of 1930, as amended); or

(3) The date of mailing of notice of demand for payment against a bond in the case of a surety which has an unsatisfied legal claim under a bond written by the surety.

(f) *Date of filing.* The date on which a protest is received by the Customs officer with whom it is required to be filed shall be deemed the date on which it is filed.

(g) *Return of fifth copy.* If a fifth copy of the protest is presented for the purpose of having recorded thereon the date of its receipt and the protest number assigned thereto, such information shall be recorded thereon and the fifth copy shall be returned to the person filing the protest.

[T.D. 70–181, 35 FR 13429, Aug. 22, 1970, as amended by T.D. 71–15, 36 FR 778, Jan. 16, 1971; 36 FR 1058, Jan. 22, 1971; T.D. 73–175, 38 FR 17488, July 2, 1973; T.D. 80–271, 45 FR 75642, Nov. 17, 1980; T.D. 94–1, 58 FR 69472, Dec. 30, 1993; T.D. 94–55, 59 FR 34971, July 8, 1994; T.D. 95–68, 60 FR 46363, Sept. 6, 1995; T.D. 95–78, 60 FR 50038, Sept. 27, 1995]

§174.13 Contents of protest.

(a) *Contents, in general.* A protest shall contain the following information:

(1) The name and address of the protestant, i.e., the importer of record or consignee, and the name and address of his agent or attorney if signed by one of these;

(2) The importer number of the protestant. If the protestant is represented by an agent having power of attorney, the importer number of the agent shall also be shown;

(3) The number and date of the entry;

(4) The date of liquidation of the entry, or the date of a decision not involving a liquidation or reliquidation;

(5) A specific description of the merchandise affected by the decision as to which protest is made;

(6) The nature of, and justification for the objection set forth distinctly and specifically with respect to each category, payment, claim, decision, or refusal;

(7) The date of receipt and protest number of any protest previously filed that is the subject of a pending application for further review pursuant to subpart C of this part and that is alleged to involve the same merchandise and the same issues, if the protesting party requests disposition in accordance with the action taken on such previously filed protest; and

(8) If another party has not filed a timely protest, the surety's protest shall certify that the protest is not being filed collusively to extend another authorized person's time to protest.

(9) A declaration, to the best of the protestant's knowledge, as to whether the entry is the subject of drawback, or whether the entry has been referenced on a certificate of delivery or certificate of manufacture and delivery so as to enable a party to make such entry the subject of drawback (see §§ 181.50(b) and § 191.81(b) of this chapter).

(b) *Multiple entries.* A single protest may be filed with respect to more than one entry at any port if all such entries involve the same protesting party, and if the same category of merchandise and a decision or decisions common to all entries are the subject of the protest. In such circumstances, the entry numbers, dates of entry, and dates of liquidation of all such entries should be set forth as an attachment to the protest.

(c) *Optional designation for refunds.* If desired by the importer/consignee the statement "any refunds with respect to the entry under protest shall be mailed to the importer/consignee in care of ______________________"
(Name and Address of Agent)
may be appended to the protest. This designation supersedes any existing designation previously authorized on Customs Form 4811.

[T.D. 70–181, 35 FR 13429, Aug. 22, 1970, as amended by T.D. 80–271, 45 FR 75642, Nov. 17, 1980; T.D. 95–78, 60 FR 50038, Sept. 27, 1995; T.D. 98–16, 63 FR 10970, Mar. 5, 1998]

§174.14 Amendment of protests.

(a) *Time for filing.* A protest may be amended at any time prior to the expiration of the 90–day period within which such protest may be filed determined in accordance with §174.12(e). The amendment may assert additional claims pertaining to the administrative decision which is the subject of the protest, or may challenge an additional administrative decision relating to the same category of merchandise which is the subject of the protest. For the presentation of additional grounds or arguments in support of a valid protest after the 90-day period has expired see §174.28.

(b) *Form and number of copies of amendment.* An amendment to a protest shall be filed in quadruplicate on Customs Form 19 or on a form of the same size, clearly labeled "Amendment to Protest" at the top of the form. Schedules or other attachments (other than samples or similar exhibits) shall also be filed in quadruplicate.

(c) *Contents.* An amendment to a protest shall contain the following information:

(1) The name, address, and importer number of the protesting party, i.e., the importer of record or consignee, and the name and address of his agent or attorney if filed by one of these;

(2) The number and date of filing of the original protest;

(3) A specific description of the merchandise affected by the decision as to which the amendment to the protest is filed;

(4) The nature of and justification for the objection raised by the amendment set forth distinctly and specifically with respect to each category, payment, claim, decision, or refusal; and

(5) The date of receipt and protest number of any protest previously filed that is the subject of a pending application for further review and that is alleged to involve the same merchandise and the same issues involved in the amendment.

(d) *Identification of filer.* An amendment to a protest may be filed only by the person who originally filed such protest or his agent or attorney subject to the provisions of §174.3. The identity of the filer shall be noted on the amendment to a protest. Any acceptable method used to identify the filer described in §174.12(c) as being acceptable on a protest will be acceptable on an amendment to a protest.

(e) *Place and date of filing.* An amendment to a protest shall be filed with the port director with whom the protest was filed. The amendment shall be deemed filed on the date it is received by the Customs officer with whom it is required to be filed.

(f) *Return of fifth copy.* If a fifth copy of the amendment is presented for the purpose of having recorded thereon the date of its receipt, such information shall be recorded thereon and the fifth copy shall be returned to the person filing the amendment.

[T.D. 70–181, 35 FR 13429, Aug. 22, 1970, as amended by T.D. 94–55, 59 FR 34971, July 8, 1994; T.D. 95–78, 60 FR 50038, Sept. 27, 1995]

§174.15 Consolidation of protests filed by different parties.

(a) *General.* Subject to paragraph (b) of this section, separate protests relating to one category of merchandise covered by an entry shall be considered as a single protest whether filed as a single protest or filed as separate protests relating to the same category by one or more parties in interest or an authorized agent.

(b) *NAFTA transactions.* The following rules shall apply to a consolidation of multiple protests concerning a determination of origin under subpart G of part 181 of this chapter if one of the protests is filed by or on behalf of an exporter or producer described in §174.12(a)(5) of this part:

(1) If consolidation under paragraph (a) of this section is pursuant to specific written requests for consolidation received from all interested parties who filed protests under this part, those interested parties shall be deemed to have waived their rights to confidentiality as regards business information within the meaning of §181.121 of this chapter. In

such cases, a separate notice of the decision will be issued to each interested party under this part but without regard to whether the notice reflects confidential business information obtained from one but not all of those interested parties.

(2) If consolidation under paragraph (a) of this section is done by the port director in the absence of specific written requests for consolidation from all interested parties who filed protests under this part, no waiver of confidentiality by those interested parties shall be deemed to have taken place. In such cases, a separate notice of the decision will be issued to each interested party and each such notice shall adhere to the principle of confidentiality set forth in §181.121 of this chapter.

[T.D. 94–1, 58 FR 69472, Dec. 30, 1993; T.D. 95–78, 60 FR 50038, Sept. 27, 1995]

§174.16 Limitation on protests after reliquidation.

A protest shall not be filed against the decision of the port director on reliquidation upon any question not involved in the reliquidation.

[T.D. 95–78, 60 FR 50038, Sept. 27, 1995]

Subpart C—Review and Disposition of Protests

§174.21 Time for review of protests.

(a) *In general.* Except as provided in paragraph (b) of this section, the port director shall review and act on a protest filed in accordance with section 514, Tariff Act of 1930, as amended (19 U.S.C. 1514), within 2 years from the date the protest was filed. If several timely filed protests are treated as part of a single protest pursuant to §174.15, the 2-year period shall be deemed to run from the date the last such protest was filed in accordance with section 514, Tariff Act of 1930, as amended (19 U.S.C. 1514).

(b) *Protests relating to exclusion of merchandise.* If the protest relates to an administrative action involving exclusion of merchandise from entry or delivery under any provision of the Customs laws, the port director shall review and act on a protest filed in accordance with section 514, Tariff Act of 1930, as amended (19 U.S.C. 1514), within 30 days from the date the protest was filed, unless the person filing the protest shall request an additional delay for the purpose of presenting evidence or argument with respect to the matters involved in the protest. In no event shall the port director (or the Commissioner of Customs or his designee if the protest is the subject of further review as provided for in §§174.25 and 174.26) delay action on the protest beyond 30 days, or such additional time period as may be agreed to by the person filing the protest. Any protest filed pursuant to this paragraph shall clearly so state on its face.

[T.D. 74–37, 39 FR 2470, Jan. 22, 1974; T.D. 95–78, 60 FR 50038, Sept. 27, 1995]

§174.22 Accelerated disposition of protest.

(a) *Request for accelerated disposition.* Accelerated disposition of a protest filed in accordance with section 514, Tariff Act of 1930, as amended (19 U.S.C. 1514) may be obtained at any time after 90 days from the filing of such protest, by filing by registered or certified mail a written request for accelerated disposition with the port director to whom the protest was addressed.

(b) *Contents of request.* A request for accelerated disposition of protest shall contain the following information:

(1) The name, address, and importer number of the protestant, i.e., the importer of record or consignee, and the name and address of his agent or attorney if filed by one of these; and

(2) The date of filing and number of the protest for which accelerated disposition is requested.

(c) *Review following request.* The port director shall review the protest which is the subject of the request within 30 days from the date of mailing of a request for accelerated disposition filed in accordance with the provisions of this section, and may allow or deny the protest in whole or in part.

(d) *Failure to allow or deny protest within 30-day period.* If the port director fails to allow or deny a protest which is the subject of a request for accelerated disposition within 30 days from the date of mailing of such request, the protest shall be deemed to have been denied at the close of the 30th day following such date of mailing.

(e) *Multiple protests.* If several protests by different persons are timely filed and treated as part of a single protest pursuant to §174.15, a request for accelerated disposition filed by any one of the protesting parties shall be treated as a request for accelerated disposition by all the parties.

[T.D. 95–78, 60 FR 50038, Sept. 27, 1995]

§174.23 Further review of protests.

A protesting party may seek further review of a protest in lieu of review by the port director by filing, on the form prescribed in §174.25, an application for such review within the time allowed and in the manner prescribed by §174.12 for the filing of a protest. The filing of an application for further review shall not preclude a preliminary examination by the port director whose decision is the subject of the protest for the purpose of determining whether the protest may be allowed in full. If such preliminary examination indicates that the protest would be denied in whole or in part by the port director in the absence of an application for further review, however, he shall forward the protest and application for consideration in accordance with §174.26.

[T.D. 95–78, 60 FR 50038, Sept. 27, 1995]

§174.24 Criteria for further review.

Further review of a protest which would otherwise be denied by the port director shall be accorded a party filing an application for further review which meets the requirements of §174.25 when the decision against which the protest was filed:

(a) Is alleged to be inconsistent with a ruling of the Commissioner of Customs or his designee, or with a decision made at any port with respect to the same or substantially similar merchandise;

(b) Is alleged to involve questions of law or fact which have not been ruled upon by the Commissioner of Customs or his designee or by the Customs courts;

(c) Involves matters previously ruled upon by the Commissioner of Customs or his designee or by the Customs courts but facts are alleged or legal arguments presented which were not considered at the time of the original ruling; or

(d) Is alleged to involve questions which the Headquarters Office, United States Customs Service, refused to consider in the form of a request for internal advice pursuant to §177.11(b)(5) of this chapter.

[T.D. 70–181, 35 FR 13429, Aug. 22, 1970, as amended by T.D. 71–133, 36 FR 8732, May 12, 1971; T.D. 75–186, 40 FR 31928, July 30, 1975; T.D. 95–78, 60 FR 50038, Sept. 27, 1995]

§174.25 Application for further review.

(a) *Form and number of copies.* An application for further review may be filed on the same Customs Form 19 used for filing the protest for which further review is requested, or on a separate Customs Form 19. In either case, the Customs Form 19 shall be filed in quadruplicate. If a fifth copy of the application is presented for the purpose of having recorded thereon the date of its receipt, such information shall be recorded thereon and the fifth copy shall be returned to the person filing the application.

(b) *Contents.* An application for further review shall contain the following information:

(1) Information identifying the protest to which it applies and the protesting party and his importer number;

(2) Allegations that the protesting party:

(i) Has not previously received an adverse administrative decision from the Commissioner of Customs or his designee nor has presently pending an application for an administrative decision on the same claim with respect to the same category of merchandise; and

(ii) Has not received a final adverse decision from the Customs courts on the same claim with respect to the same category of merchandise and does not have an action involving such a claim pending before the Customs courts.

(3) A statement of any facts or additional legal arguments, not part of the record, upon which the protesting party relies, including the criterion set forth in §174.24 which justifies further review. A showing of facts that support the allegation of a criterion set forth in §174.24(c) will constitute a ground for the granting of further review in circumstances where the applicant's inability to affirmatively make the allegations described in paragraph (b)(2) of this section would otherwise result in its denial.

[T.D. 70–81, 35 FR 13429, Aug. 22, 1970, as amended by T.D. 78–99, 43 FR 13062, Mar. 29, 1978]

§174.26 Review of protest after application for further review.

(a) *Protest allowed.* If upon examination of a protest for which an application for further review was filed the port director is satisfied that the claim is valid, he shall allow the protest.

(b) *Other protests.* If upon examination of a protest for which an application for further review was filed the port director decides that the protest in his judgment should be denied in whole or in part, he shall forward the application together with the protest and appropriate documents to be reviewed as follows:

(1) A protest shall be reviewed by the Commissioner of Customs or his designee under Customs Delegation Order No. 1 (Revision 1), T.D. 69–126 (34 FR 8208), as amended from time to time, if the protest and application for review raise an issue involving either:

(i) Lack of uniformity of treatment;

(ii) The existence of an established and uniform practice;

(iii) The interpretation of a court decision or ruling of the Commissioner of Customs or his designee; or

(iv) Questions which have not been the subject of a Headquarters, U.S. Customs Service ruling or court decision.

(2) All other protests shall be reviewed by a designee of the port director who did not participate directly in the decision which is the subject of the protest.

[T.D. 95–78, 60 FR 50038, Sept. 27, 1995]

§174.27 Disposition after further review.

Upon completion of further review, the protest and appropriate documents forwarded for review shall be returned to the port director together with directions for the disposition of the protest.

[T.D. 95–78, 60 FR 50038, Sept. 27, 1995]

§174.28 Consideration of additional arguments.

In determining whether to allow or deny a protest filed within the time allowed, a reviewing officer may consider alternative claims and additional grounds or arguments submitted in writing by the protesting party with respect to any decision which is the subject of a valid protest at any time prior to disposition of the protest. In any case in which alternative claims or additional grounds or arguments are submitted orally, they shall be considered in the allowance or denial of the protest only if submitted in writing in conjunction with, or no later than 60 days after, such oral submission.

(R.S. 251, as amended, secs. 514, 624, 46 Stat. 734, as amended, 759; 19 U.S.C. 66, 1514, 1624)

[T.D. 71–15, 36 FR 778, Jan. 16, 1971]

§174.29 Allowance or denial of protests.

The port director shall allow or deny in whole or in part a protest filed in accordance with section 514, Tariff Act of 1930, as amended, 19 U.S.C. 1514) within 2 years from the date the protest was filed. If the protest is allowed in whole or in part the port director shall remit or refund any duties, charge, or exaction found to have been collected in excess, or pay any drawback found due. If a protest of an exporter or producer under §174.12(a)(5) of this part is allowed in whole or in part, any monies found to have been collected in excess shall be refunded to the party who paid the monies even if such party did not file an appropriate and timely protest under this part. If the protest is denied in whole or in part the port director shall give notice of the denial in the form and manner prescribed in §174.30.

[T.D. 70–181, 35 FR 13429, Aug. 22, 1970, as amended by T.D. 94–1, 58 FR 69472, Dec. 30, 1993; T.D. 95–78, 60 FR 50038, Sept. 27, 1995]

§174.30 Notice of denial of protest.

(a) *Issuance of notice.* Notice of denial of a protest shall be mailed to any person filing a protest or his agent in all cases other than those in which accelerated disposition was requested and in which no action has been taken within 30 days after the date of mailing of the request. The notice shall include a statement of the reasons for the denial, as well as a statement informing the protesting party of the right to file a civil action contesting the denial of the protest under section 514, Tariff Act of 1930, as amended (19 U.S.C. 1514). For purposes of section 515(a), Tariff Act of 1930, as amended (19 U.S.C. 1515(a)), the date appearing on such notice shall be deemed the date on which such notice was mailed.

(b) *Substitution of persons designated to receive notice.* The importer of record or consignee may give notice to the port director instructing that notice of denial of any protest involving merchandise imported in his name or on his behalf shall be mailed to a person other than the person filing such protest or the designee of such person. Such notice of substitution shall be filed in quadruplicate and shall identify the protest by number and date of receipt. Notice of denial of a protest shall be mailed to the substituted person so designated only if the notice of substitution is received by the port director prior to a denial by him of such protest.

(c) *Notification of payment of increased duties.* The port director shall note on the notice of denial of a protest the payment of all liquidated duties, charges, or exactions, if he has actual knowledge of such payment at the time that the protest is denied.

[T.D. 70–181, 35 FR 13429, Aug. 22, 1970, as amended by T.D. 80–271, 45 FR 75642, Nov. 17, 1980; T.D. 95–78, 60 FR 50038, Sept. 27, 1995]

§174.31 Judicial review of denial of protest.

Any person whose protest has been denied, in whole or in part, may contest the denial by filing a civil action in the United States Court of International Trade in accordance with 28 U.S.C. 2632 within 180 days after—

(a) The date of mailing of notice of denial, in whole or in part, of a protest, or

(b) The date a protest, for which accelerated disposition was requested, is deemed to have been denied in accordance with §174.22(d).

[T.D. 78–17, 43 FR 1938, Jan. 13, 1978, as amended by T.D. 85–90, 50 FR 21430, May 24, 1985]

§174.32 Publication.

Within 120 days after issuing a protest review decision, the Customs Service shall publish the decision in the Customs Bulletin or otherwise make it available for public inspection. Disclosure is governed by 31 CFR part 1 and 19 CFR part 103.

[T.D. 78–394, 43 FR 49791, Oct. 25, 1978]

EXHIBIT 11
Formal Demand on Surety for payment of Delinquent outstanding bills for a principal/debtor

DEPARTMENT OF THE TREASURY

U.S. CUSTOMS SERVICE

INDIANAPOLIS, INDIANA

FILE: [redacted]

Dear Sir:

This is a formal demand upon your company for immediate payment of the attached listing of [redacted] delinquent supplemental duty bills owed to the U.S. Customs Service by [redacted] for [redacted]

The U.S. Customs Service does not normally provide copies of entry and bond documents when initiating surety collection action for delinquent debts. However, in order to assist in resolving the referenced bills in a timely manner, a sampling of the respective documents are enclosed.

Payment for each of these bills should be made within 30 days of the date of this notice. To ensure that payments are properly credited, check(s) together with a copy of this demand and attachment should be addressed to:

U.S. Customs Service
Accounting Services Division
Accounts Receivable
Attn: Mary Anne Berry
P. O. Box 68911
Indianapolis, Indiana 46268

Any questions concerning this matter may be directed to me at at (317) 298-1200, extension 1387, or in writing at the above address.

Sincerely,

Mary Anne Berry

Mary Anne Berry
Accounts Technician
Accounts Receivable
Accounting Services Division

Enclosures

EXHIBIT 12

Letter to Surety from Asst. Chief Counsel giving final 14 days to pay

DEPARTMENT OF THE TREASURY

U.S. CUSTOMS SERVICE

INDIANAPOLIS, INDIANA

September 26, 1994

Refer to:
ACC DMS

Re: Delinquent [redacted]
Totaling $[redacted]
Principal: [redacted]

Dear Sir/Madam:

The Government's claim for duties past due and owing for the above-referenced entries has been forwarded to the Assistant Chief Counsel's Office for litigation. [redacted] As surety on a continuous entry bond effective for these entries, Customs mailed demand to you; however, we have been advised by Customs that you have failed and refused to pay the amount owed to the Government.

We would like to extend to you an opportunity to settle this matter before litigation, to save both you and the Federal government the burden and expense of court action. Please remit payment of the delinquent duties owed in the amount of [redacted] within **14 days** from receipt of this letter to:

Office of Assistant Chief Counsel
U.S. Customs Service
Reference 94-2611/DMS
P.O. Box 68914
Indianapolis, IN 46268-0914

A surety has derivative liability with its principal, United States v. Ataka America, Inc., 826 F. Supp. 495 (Ct. Int'l Trade 1993), [redacted]. Thus, you should be aware that if a lawsuit is required to collect these [redacted] we will be seeking interest from the due date.

REPLY TO: ASSISTANT CHIEF COUNSEL, 6026 LAKESIDE BOULEVARD, INDIANAPOLIS, INDIANA 46278
/09/22/94/T 94-2611

If you have any questions or wish to communicate an explanation for nonpayment, please contact Darlene M. Stephens, the attorney responsible for the matter, by telephone at 317-298-1233, or write to the above address. Thank you for your prompt attention to this important matter.

Sincerely,

ORIGINAL SIGNED BY
JOHN R. deROMOET

John R. deRomoet
Assistant Chief Counsel

Enclosure

PORT DIRECTORS

Port Director	Region	Phone #
	Northeast	
Portland, ME	Jeffrey Walgreen	207-771-3605
St. Albans, VT	Timothy Moran	802-524-6527 ext 207
Boston, MA	Victor Weeren	617-565-6144
Provodence, RI	Richard Barrette	401-941-6326 ext 112
Ogdensburg, NY	Douglas Ahrens	315-393-0660
Buffalo, NY	Joseph Wilson	716-646-3400
Philadelphia, PA	Allan Martocci	215-597-5593
Baltimore, MD	Carole Graves	410-962-2666
	New York	
NY Seaport Area	Kathleen Haage	201-443-0190
JFK Airport	Susan T. Mitchell	718-553-1542
Newark, NJ	Kathleen Haage	201-443-0190
	North Central	
Chicago, IL	Robyn Dessaure	312-983-1100
Cleveland, OH	John Regan	440-891-3804
Detroit, MI	Paul Schwartz	313-442-0369
Duluth, MN	Barbara Lambus	218-720-5682
Great Falls, MT	Mary Lou Nisttahuz	406-453-7631
Milwaukee, WI	Michael King	414-571-2860 ext 123
Minneapolis, MN	William Knoblauch	612-348-1692
Pembina, ND	Lowell Williams	701-825-6201
St. Louis, MO	John Porter	314-428-2662 ext 201
	Southeast	
Miami, FL	Thomas Winkowski	305-869-2800
Charleston, SC	Julian Miller	843-579-6500
Charlotte Amalie, VI	Louis Harrigan	340-774-2510 ext 223
Norfolk, VA	Jorge Flores	757-441-3400
San Juan, PR	Bonnie Lemert	787-729-6850
Savannah, GA	Angela Downey	912-447-3400
Tampa, FL	Vann Capps	813-228-2385
Washington, DC	Robert Jacksta	703-318-5901
Wilmington, NC	Patricia Molett	910-815-4601

South Central

New Orleans, LA	Leticia Moran	504-670-2391
Mobile, AL	Marylin Havens	334-441-5106

South West

Houston, TX	Paul Rimmer	281-985-6712
Dallas, TX	Mike Perron	972-574-2157
El Paso, TX	Eugene Kerven	915-872-3407
Laredo, TX	Eugenio Garza Jr.	956-726-2267
Nogales, AZ	P.T. Wright	520-287-1410 ext 210
Port Arthur, TX	Becky Parks	409-724-6309

Pacific

Los Angeles, CA	Irene Jancov	310-514-6001
Anchorage, AK	Daniel C. Holland	907-271-2687
Honolulu, HI	Nat Aycox	808-522-8063 ext 0
Portland, OR	Lewellyn Robison	503-326-2868
San Diego, CA	Rudy Camacho	619-557-5455
San Francisco, CA	Alice Rigdon	415-782-9200
Seattle, WA	Artis Moran	206-553-0770

Updated 12/3/99

BILLING PROCESS
LIQUIDATED DAMAGES

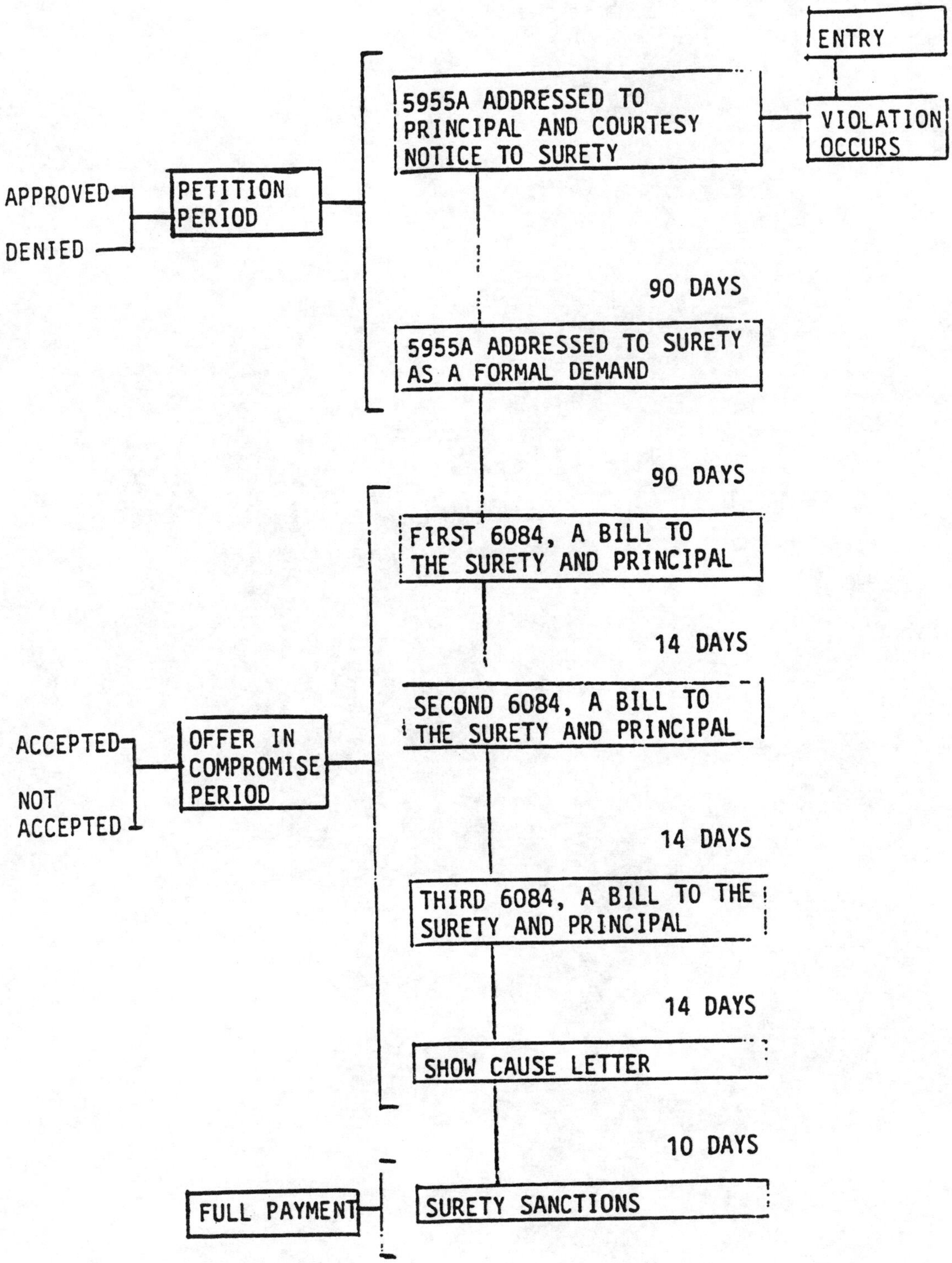

NOTE: Time Frames may vary from Port to Port

14

License and Permit Bonds

Patrick Q. Hustead
Duane E. Bolin

I. *The Basics*

License and permit bonds are non-glamorous workhorses within the surety realm. As their names suggest, license and permit bonds are bonds required as a prerequisite to the procurement of licenses or permits for various occupations and professions. As a result, license and permit bonds are an evolving breed of bond which reflect the ever-changing regulatory schemes throughout the states and various localities.

Born of various regulatory schemes, the language and structure of license and permit bonds have historically developed from state statutes, local ordinances, or other regulations. Thus, examination of license and permit bonds and their obligations requires a thorough examination of the regulation, statute, or ordinance from which the bond originates, as well as the bond's language. In general, however, license and permit bonds set forth that the surety shall indemnify the listed Obligee against all loss, costs, expenses, damage, etc. it suffers as a result of the listed Principal's non-compliance with or breach of any laws, statutes, ordinances, or regulations applicable to the particular license or permit issued to the Principal.

If the contemplated license or permit is not actually issued to the principal for some reason, the surety's obligation under the bond, in general, will not arise.[1] If the license or permit is issued and the bond takes effect, the license or permit bond will usually run concurrently with the license or permit period and any renewals of such periods. If a principal's license or permit is revoked or suspended for any reason, the bond will be considered ineffective as of the end of the license or permit period.

Given their regulatory/statutory origins, license and permit bonds are sometimes viewed as simplistic, harmless afterthoughts. As will be discussed in greater detail below, however, license and permit bonds take many forms, some of which have proved to be far from simple and far from harmless.

II. *Shapes And Sizes*

As one would expect from their regulatory/statutory origins, license and permit bonds come in a myriad of shapes and sizes. The most common license and permit bonds are those required of businesses particularly prone to dishonest conduct and those which protect citizens against loss of

1. *Massachusetts Bonding & Insurance Co. v. Bank of Aurora*, 238 P.2d 872 (Colo. 1951).

property entrusted to the principal. Examples of these most common types of license and permit bonds include motor vehicle dealer bonds and real estate broker bonds.

License and permit bonds also take the shape of those intended to protect public health and safety, including those required when a public privilege is involved which could potentially become a harm to the general public. Examples of these types of license and permit bonds include certain types of bonds issued to public works contractors. Finally, license and permit bonds also include those bonds which assure payment of taxes collected by the principal. Such tax–related license and permit bonds are commonly issued in the form of sales tax and gasoline tax bonds.

III. *Scope Of Coverage*

As noted above, the purpose of license and permit bonds is to ensure compliance with any laws, statutes, ordinances, or regulations applicable to the particular license or permit issued to the Principal. Thus, in contrast to other types of common surety bonds, license and permit bonds – per the language of the bonds themselves and the language of applicable statutes, ordinances, and regulations – do not require the surety to complete the contract (as would a performance bond) or pay for labor and material (as would a payment bond).

License and permit bonds, like all surety bonds, are to be interpreted according to the standards which govern the construction of contracts in general.[2] Unlike many other surety bonds, however, license and permit bonds also have a close connection to statutes, regulations, or ordinances which must be considered when interpreting such bonds.[3] Thus, when asked to determine the scope of a license or permit bond, a court will consider the language and purpose of the bond in conjunction with the terms of the statute, regulation, or ordinance upon which the bond is based.[4] In many cases, it will be key for a court to consider not only the plain language of the statute, regulation, or ordinance, but also the intent of the enacting body.[5]

The scope of coverage of license and permit bonds will generally be interpreted consistently with the intent of the regulation, statute, or ordinance upon which the particular bond is based.[6] Thus, the provisions of the statute are generally controlling and bond language which attempts to lessen a surety's liability will be disregarded.[7] Of course, a surety may choose to assume greater liability than required by regulation, statute, or ordinance, and such an undertaking by a surety will usually be enforced, as long as it was voluntarily assumed.[8]

2. *Western Surety Company v. Smith*, 914 P.2d 451 (Colo. Ct. App. 1995); *Edmonds v. Western Surety Company*, 962 P.2d 323 (Colo. Ct. App. 1998).

3. *Western Surety Company v. Smith*, 914 P.2d 451 (Colo. Ct. App. 1995).

4. *Id.*

5. *Id.; see also General Electric Credit Corp. v. Wolverine Ins. Co.*, 420 Mich. 176, 362 N.W.2d 595 (1984).

6. *U.S. Fidelity & Guaranty Co. v. Bross*, 118 Ariz. 599, 578 P.2d 1028 (1978).

7. *State v. Easley*, 207 Neb. 443, 299 N.W.2d 439 (1980); *Aetna Casualty & Surety Co. v. Woods*, 565 S.W.2d 861 (Tenn. 1978).

8. *Dennis Dillon Oldsmobile, GMC, Inc. v. Zdunich*, 668 P.2d 557 (Utah 1983).

IV. *Far From Simple, Far From Harmless*

As discussed above, license and permit bonds, given their regulatory/statutory origins, are often given little consideration in the overall surety bond scheme. Seen as simple and usually involving smaller bond penalties, license and permit bonds have gotten comparatively little attention from courts and sureties compared to more mainstream performance and payment bonds.

By way of illustration, the remainder of this paper will focus on several interesting cases and the license and permit bond issues highlighted in each. As these cases will show, the simple, harmless license and permit bond has created some potentially-large, interesting problems for sureties which expected such problems to arise only in conjunction with larger bonds.

A. THE (ALMOST) $1.5 MILLION MOTOR VEHICLE DEALER BOND

In Colorado, state statute requires motor vehicle dealers to post a $30,000 motor vehicle dealer bond (or a cash equivalent).[9] The $30,000 bond (or cash equivalent) is intended to serve as a reserve fund for reimbursement "for any loss or damage suffered by any retail consumer caused by violation of [this statute] by a motor vehicle dealer."[10] One can thus easily imagine the surety's surprise when it faced liability of $1.5 million on a simple, run-of-the-mill $30,000 motor vehicle dealer bond it issued to a Colorado dealer.

In *Western Surety Co. v. Smith*,[11] the surety challenged a grant of summary judgment against it made by the trial court, which found that the language of the motor vehicle dealer bond at issue was more expansive than the provisions of Colorado's motor vehicle dealer bond statute. Interpreting the bond's "to indemnify any and all persons . . . for any loss suffered . . . in the penal sum of $30,000" language, the trial court concluded that Western Surety Company was liable to pay up to the face amount of the bond ($30,000) to each of the approximately fifty claimants who had made a claim against the bond — an aggregate liability of up to $1.5 million on a $30,000 face value motor vehicle dealer bond.[12]

The Colorado Court of Appeals overturned the decision of the trial court, however, finding that, notwithstanding the bond's arguably more expansive language, the bond's language tracked the statutory language closely enough that it should be interpreted consistently with the intent of its originating statute which, in this case, intended a surety's obligation to be limited to the face amount of the bond — regardless of the number of claimants.[13] Thus, the surety's liability was limited to the face amount of the bond and the specter of a potential $1.5 million liability was avoided.

One might think the *Smith* case an anomaly, given the general rule that a surety's liability is generally limited to the penal sum of the bond.[14] At least one state supreme court, however, has made the *Smith* scenario a reality for a surety. In *Dennis Dillon Oldsmobile, GMC, Inc. v. Zdunich*,[15]

9. C.R.S.A. § 12-6-111 (1999).

10. *Id.*

11. 914 P.2d 451 (Colo. Ct. App. 1995).

12. *Id.*

13. *Id.*

14. *E.g., Rolen v. Ravnuff*, 315 F.Supp. 935 (D.C. Tenn. 1970); *Leggitt v. Humphreys*, 50 U.S. 297, 13 L.Ed. 145 (1850); *Maryland Cas. Co. v. Alford*, 111 F.2d 388 (10th Cir. 1940); *Bill Curphy Company v. Elliott*, 207 F.2d 103 (5th Cir. 1953).

15. 668 P.2d 557 (Utah 1983).

the Utah Supreme Court interpreted similarly broad bond language and found it to be broader than that required by statute. Consequently, the *Zdunich* Court upheld the lower court's holding that there was no aggregate limitation on the surety's liability on the bond, resulting in a potential liability of the full face value of the bond ($20,000) per claim.[16]

The lesson of *Smith* and *Zdunich* is thus an important one for sureties. When drafting bond language for license and permit bonds, it is crucial to track precisely the language of the originating regulation, statute, or ordinance. Tracking statutory language is the only sure way to constrict a surety's obligation to that contemplated by the statute. Thus, the statute itself should be incorporated into the bond by specific reference. To fail to do so can mean increasing potential maximum liability into the stratosphere, should a court interpret bond language, and consequently the surety's obligation, as broader than that dictated by statute.

A related consideration highlighted by these cases is the importance of the surety's use of an interpleader action to resolve all claims in one action, if possible, in order to obtain a discharge from further liability. Although a surety is not a trustee for all claimants and is under no general affirmative duty to discover all possible claimants to guarantee that a pro rata distribution is made, it could be held liable to remaining claimants even though it has already paid the full penalty of the bond if it is aware that other claims exist.[17] As a result, a surety should always consider the option of an interpleader action to resolve all known claims and obtain an express discharge from liability.

B. THE POTENTIALLY-EXPANSIVE DEFINITION OF "LOSS SUFFERED"

The issue of what exactly constitutes "loss suffered" by a claimant on a motor vehicle dealer bond arose in *Edmonds v. Western Surety Co.*[18] In *Edmonds*, the surety faced a claimant who had failed to collect $10,400 from the principal. Although the surety conceded liability on the $10,400 claim, the claimant sought to recover the entire amount of its judgment against the principal, which included treble damages pursuant to Colorado deceptive trade practices law, as well as attorneys' fees and prejudgment interest — the total of which exceeded the $30,000 bond limit.[19]

Interpreting the bond language and that of its originating statute, the Colorado Court of Appeals held that the obligation imposed upon the surety by the bond and the statute was one of indemnification.[20] Consequently, the *Edmonds* Court held that the award of treble damages in the instant case represented a penalty in excess of loss actually suffered by the claimant and was therefore not recoverable under the bond against the surety.[21]

On the other hand, the *Edmonds* Court found that attorneys' fees were properly recoverable under the bond against the surety. Attorneys' fees, while not ordinarily recoverable in a contract action pursuant to the American rule,[22] were characterized as losses suffered by the claimant in light

---

16. *Id.*

17. *Transamerica v. C.B. Concrete Company*, 669 P.2d 246 (Nev. 1983); *Fidelity & Deposit Co. v. Stephenson*, 79 P.2d 115 (Calif. Ct. App. 1938).

18. 962 P.2d 323 (Colo. Ct. App. 1998).

19. *Id.*

20. *Id.*

21. *Id; see also Darr v. Long*, 313 N.W.2d 215 (Neb. 1981) (minimum statutory recovery represented a reward for bringing a successful action and not actual damages and was therefore not recoverable).

22. *Globe and Republic Insurance Company of America v. Independent Trucking Co.*, 387 P.2d 644 (Okla. 1963).

of specific statutory authorization of recovery of such fees in the instant case. The *Edmonds* court was careful, however, to restrict its basis for its award of attorneys' fees to those cases in which a claimant recovers a judgment under a statute which expressly provides for such a recovery.[23]

Finally, the *Edmonds* Court also awarded the claimant prejudgment interest, noting that such interest was also a creature of statute and Colorado law expressly provides for recovery of interest on claims made against motor vehicle dealer bonds. Interestingly, the *Edmonds* Court hinted that a possible defense to a claim of interest might be made by a surety who could provide proof that it had "stood ready" to pay an amount the surety considered the claimant's "actual loss."[24]

As the *Edmonds* decisions reveals, the originating regulation, statute, or ordinance must be examined to determine what fees, costs, etc. a claimant may be able to recover. In addition, if a statutory recovery is the source of the claimant's "loss," attorneys' fees may be recoverable as well. Finally, sureties may ultimately face challenges based upon claimants seeking to recover excess damages — and a claimant may eventually win such a claim to the extent such excess damages can be characterized as "loss" as opposed to "penalty."[25]

C. THE BOND THAT CROSSED STATE LINES

One might assume that, given the regulatory/statutory origin of license and permit bonds, their reach would not extend beyond state lines, e.g. a particular motor vehicle dealer bond would have no extra-territorial effect beyond the state in which it was issued. As the case discussed below shows, however, such an assumption will not always hold true.

In *Mawyer v. Lumbermens Mutual Casualty Co.*,[26] the surety issued a motor vehicle dealer bond pursuant to the North Carolina Motor Vehicle Dealers and Manufacturers Licensing Law. A representative of the principal was subsequently sued in federal court for fraud for tampering with the odometer of a car which was sold to a wholesaler and ultimately to the plaintiff, a purchaser in Virginia. The plaintiff obtained a judgment of $5,767.50 which he in turn attempted to collect from the surety.[27]

The trial court granted summary judgment in favor of the surety, holding that the bond, issued under North Carolina's motor vehicle dealer bond statute, had no extra-territorial effect and thus could not be a source of relief for plaintiff, a resident of Virginia. The Supreme Court of Virginia, however, reversed the trial court's finding.[28]

Noting a split of authority on the issue, the *Mawyer* Court held that there was no language in either the North Carolina motor vehicle dealer bond statute or the surety's bond explicitly limiting the bond's application to North Carolina's borders. Admitting that neither the North Carolina statute nor the bond language expressly gave the bond extra-territorial effect, the Court nonetheless gave

23. *Edmonds v. Western Surety Co.*, 962 P.2d 323 (Colo. Ct. App. 1998); *see also Maryland Casualty Co. v. Cunningham*, 234 Ala. 80, 173 So. 506 (1937); *State Surety Co. v. Lamb Construction Co.*, 625 P.2d 184 (1981).

24. *Id.*

25. *Geters v. Eagle Ins. Co.*, 834 S.W.2d 49 (Tex. 1992) (holding surety liable for damages awarded pursuant to a Deceptive Trade Practices Act).

26. 377 S.E.2d 401 (Va. 1989).

27. *Id.*

28. *Id.*

the bond a broad interpretation "in favor of protecting the consumer and strictly against the fraudulent dealer and his surety."[29]

Other courts have agreed with the *Mawyer* Court's analysis, holding that, absent statutory or bond language explicitly limiting a bond's application to intrastate transactions, a bond will be given extra-territorial effect.[30] Evidencing the split to which the *Mawyer* Court refers, however, some courts have held that, when a regulation, statute, or ordinance conditions issuance of a license or permit upon the execution of a surety bond, a presumption exists that the bond's application does not extend beyond the borders of the issuing state.[31]

Thus, there remains a split of authority on whether license and permit bonds have extra-territorial effect. Consult the Idaho Supreme Court's reasoning in *Ore-Ida Potato Products, Inc. v. United Pacific Insurance Co.*[32] for a persuasive argument that the evolving general rule should be one of no extra-territorial application. The important lesson for a surety, however, is to study the law of the states in which license and permit bonds are being written to determine the likely extent of its obligation on those bonds.

V. *Conclusion*

License and permit bonds are far from simple, harmless creatures of statute. To the contrary, they can become quite complicated and potentially explosive because of either their language or their regulatory/statutory origins. While certain issues unique to license and permit bonds have been examined herein, one should remember that license and permit bonds also face a number of other issues, common to bonds of all types, which are discussed throughout this publication.

---

29. *Id.* at 402.

30. *E.g., South Seattle Auto Auction, Inc. v. Western Casualty and Surety Co.*, 598 P.2d 1269 (Ore. Ct. App. 1979); *United States Fidelity & Guaranty Co. v. Colonial Baking Co.*, 247 S.W.2d 997 (Ark. 1952).

31. *E.g., State Surety Co. v. Lensing*, 249 N.W.2d 608 (Iowa 1977); *Peerless Ins. v. Clark*, 487 P.2d 574 (Colo. Ct. App. 1971); *Ore-Ida Potato Products, Inc. v. United Pacific Ins. Co.*, 392 P.2d 191 (Idaho 1964).

32. 392 P.2d 191 (Idaho 1964).

15

Workers' Compensation Self-Insurance Bonds

Theodore G. Martinez

Introduction

Workers Compensation laws were created to enact a "no fault" system intended to provide injured workers with medical care and benefits, while protecting employers against injury-related lawsuits. By law, all business entities meeting certain requirements in terms of size and number of employees, are required to provide workers' compensation coverage for their employees.

There are different methods available to an employer for providing workers compensation benefits to employees: (1) Purchasing commercial insurance coverage in the open market from traditional carriers has been, by far, the most prevalent; (2) Contributing to a state run workers' compensation fund (i.e. state of Ohio); or (3) Qualifying as a self-insured. Some states allow a combination of these methods.

Workers' compensation coverage actually consists of five different types of benefits:

- Medical benefits are provided to workers injured on the job.
- Temporary total disability benefits are paid to workers who can't work at all for a limited time but who are expected to fully recover. The amount is a fraction of previous earnings; the proportion depends on the state.
- Permanent total disability benefits are paid when a person is unable to work at all because of injuries sustained.
- Permanent partial disability benefits are paid to workers who are permanently limited in the work they can do because of injuries sustained. In some states, benefits depend on actual earnings loss.
- Burial and survival benefits are paid on death claims.

All except medical benefits are considered indemnity costs and premiums are paid by employers as part of total payroll.

I. *Self-Insurance*

Historically, Workers' Compensation insurance has been an expensive form of coverage for most employers due to ever-increasing medical costs and overall expenses associated with employee indemnity benefits. Consequently, many employers choose to self-insure in an effort to contain costs. Oddly enough, the current "soft insurance market" has prompted many employers to revert back to a fully insured workers' comp program due to attractive insurance rates. Inevitably, the pendulum will swing in the opposite direction once losses increase and rates begin to climb.

When an employer elects to self-insure, there is no third party insurance company available to handle and pay claims - only the employer's (self) guarantee that funds from their own capital will be available to compensate all injured workers. In the near term, employers who qualify as a self-insured will enjoy substantial cash flow advantages because benefits are paid as they become due rather than when the loss is incurred.

Every company seeking self-insurance must first qualify to become a self-insured. Each state has its own guidelines (primarily financially oriented) to determine whether an employer may exercise the self-insurance option. When an employer does qualify, most states require that collateral security be posted to the state guaranteeing the employer's self-insured level. Acceptable forms of collateral typically consist of cash, certificates of deposit, letters of credit, treasury securities, or surety bonds. Often, a combination of these is allowed.

Normally, employers self-insure up to a certain level. The essence of self- insurance is to allow the employer to finance their own claims up to a per-occurrence limit. This limit , or SIR (self-insured retention), is established on the basis of a number of variables unique to each company:

- Overall financial capabilities of the self-insured.
- Claims experience based upon frequency and severity.
- "Risk" mentality of the self-insured.
- Maximum benefits legislation in the states where the self-insured conducts their business.

Above the SIR level, a self-insured will purchase an excess layer which is a workers' comp policy that responds to single and/or aggregate claims which exceed the self-insured level. Generally, this coverage is written on an "occurrence" basis, covering losses which occurred during the policy period. Usually, there are several layers of excess insurance coverage in place, culminating with an overall "umbrella" policy intended to cover catastrophic losses.

II. SURETY BOND

A workers' compensation self-insurance (WCSI) bond guarantees that workers comp benefits will be paid to injured workers or surviving spouses in accordance with state law. Since the exact obligation may vary by state it is important to understand the interpretation of each state's laws relating to WCSI bonds. The Surety Association of America (SAA) conducts a Workers' Compensation Self-Insurers Bond Survey on a periodic basis and an updated version is scheduled for release in the first half of 2000. Essentially, the survey provides an overview, by state, of key characteristics that pertain to their WCSI bond.

While each state defines its own WCSI regulations and bond requirements, there are some recurring issues which represent underwriting concerns to a surety:

A. LONG TERM LIABILITY

State laws vary, but the most onerous type of exposure is a WCSI obligation which may conceivably last the lifetime of an injured party (or sometimes beyond, extending to heirs). An example would be a construction worker struck by falling debris on a construction site. While the worker was not fatally injured, he may have received serious brain damage and is no longer capable of caring for himself. His long-term care will be funded by workers' comp insurance. If the employer is self-insured and the security to the state is in the form of a surety bond, then the bond obligation would technically cover the care for the life of the employee; a potentially long-term and very hazardous obligation.

A significant underwriting concern is the surety's **"tail"** exposure under the bond. Once again, the definition of "tail" exposure varies by state but essentially they may be classified into two broad categories:

1. Last Surety On: The current surety is obligated for **all** liability of the principal, dating back to the inception date of the employer's self-insurance status. Approximately one half of all states employ a form of Last Surety On coverage. The following language contained in paragraph # 2 of the state of California WCSI bond form (copy attached) is typical for a Last Surety On obligation: "The surety does, by these presents, undertake and agree that the obligation of this bond shall cover and extend to *all past, present, existing, and potential liability* of said principal, as a self-insurer, to the extent of the penal sum herein named, without regard to specific injuries, date or dates of injuries, happenings or events."

In true "last surety on" states, the surety may be relieved of **all** liability when a new bond or other acceptable security is posted to replace the existing bond. However, there are exceptions to this exoneration procedure. For instance, some states will employ a Last Surety On bond form only if a replacement security is in the form of another surety bond. If the replacement is a Letter of Credit, a state may require the original surety bond to be posted until all liability is fully extinguished. Clearly, this suggests that an underwriter must be familiar with how each state treats a prior surety bond when Last Surety On language is employed.

2. Occurrence: The surety remains liable for **any** liability that occurred while the bond was in-force. Theoretically, the liability continues until all injured employees covered under the bond are fully recovered or until all covered injuries are known and settled. The state of New Hampshire bond form (copy attached) is typical of an occurrence format: "...the condition of this bond is such that it shall remain in full force and effect until another bond and/or other guarantees have been substituted by the Principal...", further, "...this bond may be terminated by the Surety by written notice of its intention to do so...however, *such termination shall not relieve the Surety of its continual liability under this bond for obligations that occurred prior to the effective date of such termination.*"

The earlier example of the construction worker highlights how an occurrence bond could result in potentially long term liability to a surety.

As previously mentioned, many employers have converted back to a fully insured Workers' Comp insurance program because of lower insurance rates so they have relinquished their self insurance status. Consequently, many sureties with bonds in Last Surety On states are now faced with liability which technically converts to an Occurrence-like exposure since their bond is the last form of security. In these cases, a surety may be faced with long term exposure in states where they had underwritten the risk as a much shorter term liability.

B. Stacking Provisions:

Some states have stacking provisions in their statutes, which means that every year the bond liability stacks on top of the prior year. Typically, this is accomplished by making the surety bond an annual term obligation. A classic example is the language contained in paragraph # 2 of the WCSI bond to the Department of Labor under the Longshoreman's Act (copy attached). The bond reads "The liability of the Surety is...*during the period* beginning _______, 19__ and ending June 30, 19__." Consequently, the amount of the bond liability may not reflect actual loss history in all cases. Regardless of what the actual loss history is, the surety must assume its aggregate exposure is the sum of all bonds written over successive periods.

As a result, in those cases where an employer has a large number of employees in a self-insured program, the bond amount can become quite large over a short period of time.

C. Responsibility to Administer Claims:

Some states require the surety to administer all WCSI claims at their own expense should the employer fail to perform their duties. In these cases, the surety's true exposure is the bond penalty plus any potential claim administration costs.

D. Difficulty in Obtaining Release:

Clearly, most states will never release a surety from WCSI bond liability. This is of particular concern in cases where a surety takes collateral when issuing a bond. There have been cases where the surety may have relied on the interpretation of a state law and released collateral after a "replacement" surety was posted with the obligee. Later, when the "replacement" surety was found to be inadequate, the obligee proceeded against the prior surety for payment.

Even when the prior surety was found not liable, the legal fees to defend their position were considerable.

III. ACCOUNTING FOR SELF-INSURED LIABILITY

An understanding of how a self-insured accounts for its workers' compensation liabilities is important. Claims for workers compensation benefits may obligate an employer to a stream of annuity payments for five years, ten years, or beyond. The compounded effect of inflation over time, plus general aging factors that influence an injured party's health in later years tend to increase the degree of claim severity on long-term disability cases. Likewise, claim development for any single policy year may continue to accrue for three years or more, before the final aggregate for that policy year can be determined. Studies have shown that, on average, only 60% of policy year claims are reported after five years, though these generally involve the larger severity cases.

Known, and unknown, obligations under self-insured programs are direct liabilities of an employer and should be accrued as liabilities in their financial statements. Because of the uncertainty of the unknown claims yet to be reported, a surety may inquire about how accrued liabilities are developed.

IV. QUESTIONNAIRE

A tool utilized by several surety companies when underwriting a particular employer is what is commonly referred to as a WCSI questionnaire (sample attached). The form typically includes information on the Excess Insurance coverage; Plan Administrator; and most importantly, Claims Experience. The section on Claims Experience highlights a self-insured's history during the previous four years and beyond. Trends such as increasing & decreasing reserves; number of claims vs. remaining open claims; and the reasons for these changes are just some of the issues that are evaluated.

Some employers may provide copies of their actual loss runs (usually provided by a third party administrator) which focus on the nature, extent, and frequency of injuries and whether they are short or long term disabilities. The longer the term of the disabilities, the greater risk and exposure to a surety.

V. SUMMARY

The very nature of Workers' Comp self-insured coverage suggests a potentially long term level of exposure to both an employer and/or surety. While there are many underwriting tools available to assess such liability, the key to proper evaluation is to understand each of the elements that make up an employer's self-insurance program.

In addition to financial capacity, there should be an overall assessment of an employer's appetite for risk followed by a review of the steps taken to mitigate long term risk. Examining areas such as loss prevention programs; ongoing evaluation of a third party administrator; and follow-up audits are additional tools which may be utilized as part of a risk management program. But, clearly, the ideal form of risk mitigation is to employ a comprehensive plan that responds to the inherent risks of the Workers' Comp product line.

SURETY BOND

KNOWN ALL MEN BY THESE PRESENTS:

That we,
as Principal, and
as Surety, are holden and stand firmly bound and obliged unto the State of New Hampshire in the full and just sum of
Dollars ($) to the true payment whereof we bind ourselves, our heirs, and administrators, executors, successors and assigns, jointly and severally.

WHEREAS the Principal intends to pay direct the benefits in the amounts and manner and when due as provided by the Workers' Compensation law pursuant to RSA 281-A, thereby being a self-insurer for an indefinite period.

NOW THEREFORE, the condition of this bond is such that it shall remain in full force and effect until another bond and/or other guarantees have been substituted by the Principal in amounts to be approved by the Labor Commissioner, except if the Principal ceases to be an employer subject to the said statute or insures with an insurance carrier pursuant to RSA 281-A, in which events the liability of the Principal and of the Surety shall cease and determine, except as to such liability which has accrued during the life of this obligation, it being understood that the Surety shall be liable to the full extent of the penal sum herein stipulated for the default of the Principal in fully discharging any liability on his part accruing during the life of this obligation.

This bond may be terminated by the Surety by written notice of its intention to do so filed in the office of the Labor Commissioner, and by giving written notice thereof to the Principal in which event the Surety's liability shall terminate at the expiration of ninety (90) days from the date of such filing and not earlier. However, such termination shall not relieve the Surety of its continual liability under this bond for obligations that occurred prior the effective date of such termination.

This bond shall remain in the possession of the said Commissioner, even subsequent to its termination, except that the date of which this obligation ceases and determines shall be acknowledged in writing by the said Commissioner, as to both the Principal and the Surety.

The liability of the Surety hereunder shall not exceed in the aggregate the penal sum of Dollars ($)

The effective date of this bond is 19

IN WITNESS WHEREOF the said Principal and Surety have caused these presents to be executed in their names and behalf and their seals to be here affixed this day of A.D. 19

____
For Principal

____
Title

____
For Surety

____
Title

WCSI-2 (8/30/94)

Mailing Address:
Self-Insurance Plans
2848 Arden Way, Suite 105
Sacramento, California 95825

STATE OF CALIFORNIA

DEPARTMENT OF INDUSTRIAL RELATIONS
SELF-INSURANCE PLANS
SURETY BOND OF SELF INSURER OF WORKERS' COMPENSATION

(LABOR CODE SECTION 3701)

IN THE MATTER OF THE CERTIFICATE OF

Employer, Certificate No.

SURETY BOND
NO.

KNOW ALL PERSONS BY THESE PRESENTS:

THAT ______________________________
(Employer)

____

whose address for service is ______________________________

as PRINCIPAL, and ______________________________
(Surety)

whose address for service is, ______________________________

a corporation organized under the laws of ______________________________ and authorized to transact a general surety business in the State of California, as Surety, are held and firmly bound to the State of California in the penal sum of ______________________________ dollars ($) for which payment we bind ourselves, our heirs, executors, administrators, successors and assigns, jointly and severally, firmly by these presents.

WHEREAS, in accordance with the provisions of Sections 3700 to 3705 of the Labor Code of California, the Principal elected to self-insure, and made application for, or received from the Director of Industrial Relations of the State of California, a Certificate of Consent to Self-Insure, upon a furnishing of proof satisfactory to the Director of Industrial Relations of ability to self-insure and to compensate any or all employees of said principal for injury or disability, and their dependents for death incurred or sustained by said employees, pursuant to the terms, provisions and limitations of said Labor Code.

NOW THEREFORE, the conditions of this bond or obligation are such that if Principal shall pay and furnish compensation, pursuant to the terms, provisions and limitations of said Labor Code to its employees for injury or disability, and to the dependents of its employees for death incurred or sustained by said employees, then this bond or obligation shall be null and void; otherwise to remain in full force and effect.

FURTHERMORE, it is understood and agreed that:

1. This bond may be amended, by agreement between the parties hereto and the Director of Industrial Relations, as to the identity of the principal herein named and, by agreement of the parties hereto, as to the premium or rate of premium. Such amendment must be by endorsement upon, or rider to, this bond, executed by the surety and delivered to or filed with the Director.

2. The surety does, by these presents, undertake and agree that the obligation of this bond shall cover and extend to all past, present, existing, and potential liability of said principal, as a self-insurer, to the extent of the penal sum herein named, without regard to specific injuries, date or dates of injuries, happenings or events.

3. The penal sum of this bond may be increased or decreased, by agreement between the parties hereto and the Director of Industrial Relations, without impairing the obligation incurred under this bond for the overall coverage of the said principal, for all past, present, and existing and potential liability, as a self-insurer, without regard to specific injuries, date or dates of injuries, happenings or events, to the extent, in the aggregate, of the penal sum as increased or decreased. Such amendment must be by endorsement.

4. This bond shall be continuous in form and shall remain in full force and effect unless terminated in the manner provided by law.

5. The aggregate liability of the Surety hereunder on all claims whatsoever shall not exceed the penal sum of this bond in any event.

(Continued on Reverse Side)

6. Where the principal posts with the Director of Industrial Relations a replacement security deposit, in the form of a surety bond, irrevocable letter of credit, cash, securities or any combination thereof, in the full amount as may be required by the Director to secure all incurred liabilities for the payment of compensation of said principal under Labor Code Section 3701, the surety is released from the obligations under this surety bond upon the date of acceptance by the Director of said replacement security deposit.

7. In the event of a change in the proprietorship of the principal or the appointment of a receiver or trustee for said principal and thirty (30) days after the receipt of notice by the Director of Industrial Relations, State of California, given by registered or certified mail, by the principal or surety, herein named, the obligation of this bond shall terminate, save and except as to all past, present, existing and potential liability of the principal incurred as a self-insurer. This bond shall also terminate upon the revocation of the Certificate of Consent to Self-insure, save and except as to all past, present, existing and potential liability of the principal, incurred as a self-insurer; and the principal and the surety, herein named, shall be notified in writing, by said Director, in the event of such revocation.

8. If the said principal shall suspend payment of workers' compensation benefits or shall become insolvent or a receiver shall be appointed for its business, the undersigned surety will become liable for the workers' compensation obligations of the principal on the date benefits are suspended and the surety shall begin payments within thirty (30) days after receipt of written notification by the Director of Industrial Relations of California to begin payments under the terms of this bond.

9. When the surety excercises its obligation to pay claims, it shall pay benefits due to the principal's injured workers without a formal award of the Workers' Compensation Appeals Board and such payment will be a credit against the penal sum of the bond. Administrative and legal costs incurred by the surety in discharging its obligations shall also be a charge against the penal sum of the bond, however, the total amount of this surety bond set aside for the payment of said administrative and legal expenses shall be limited to a maximum of ten percent (10%) of the total penal sum of the bond pursuant to Labor Code Section 3701(b). Payment by the surety of the principal's obligation for administrative and legal expenses under Section 3701(b) in an amount not to exceed 10% of the penal sum of the bond shall satisfy in full the surety's obligation to pay said administrative and legal expenses of the principal.

10. If any part or provision of this bond shall be declared unenforceable or held to be invalid by a court of proper jurisdiction, such determination shall not affect the validity or enforceability of the other provisions or parts of this bond.

11. If the Director of Industrial Relations of California directs the Self Insurer Security Fund to assume the payment of the workers' compensation obligations of the principal pursuant to Labor Code Section 3701.5, the surety shall pay upon written demand by the Director and within thirty (30) days of receipt of such demand to the Self Insurer Security Fund the entire penal sum of the bond that remains unpaid.

12. Disputes concerning the posting, renewal, termination, exoneration, or return of all or any portion of the principal's security deposit or any liability arising out of the posting or failure to post security, or the adequacy of the security or the reasonableness of administrative costs, including legal costs, arising between or among a surety, the issuer of an agreement of assumption and guarantee of workers' compensation liabilities, the issuer of a letter of credit, any custodian of the security deposit, the principal, or the Self Insurer Security Fund shall be resolved by the Director of Industrial Relations of California pursuant to Labor Code Section 3701.5(g).

13. This bond is executed by the Surety to comply with the provisions of Chapter 2, Title 14, Part 2 of the Code of Civil Procedure and the provisions of Article 1, Chapter 4, Part 1, Division 4 of the Labor Code and said bond shall be subject to all terms and provisions thereof.

____
Name of Surety

____
Address

____
City, State, Zip

THIS bond is executed under an unrevoked appointment or power of attorney.

I certify (or declare) under penalty of perjury under the laws of the State of California that I have executed the foregoing surety bond under an unrevoked power of attorney.

Executed in ____________________ on _______________
(City/State) (Date)

____
Signature of Attorney-in-Fact

____
Printed or Typed name of Attorney-in-Fact

A copy of the transcript or record of the unrevoked appointment, power of attorney, bylaws, or other instrument, duly certified by the proper authority and attested by the seal of the insurer entitling or authorizing the person who executed the bond to do so for and in behalf of the insurer, must be filed in the office of the clerk of the county of Sacramento or must be included with this bond for such filing.

Form No. A4-20(4/92)

U.S. Department of Labor

Employment Standards Administration
Office of Workers' Compensation Programs

INDEMNITY BOND GIVEN BY SELF-INSURER UNDER THE PROVISIONS OF THE LONGSHORE AND HARBOR WORKERS' COMPENSATION ACT

Know all Men by these Presents:

That ____

______________________________________ of ______________

______________ (hereinafter called the Principal), as Principal, and ______________

____

a corporation organized under the laws of the State of ______________________

having its principal office at ______________________________ (hereinafter called the Surety), as Surety, are held and firmly bound unto the **United States of America** for the use and benefit of the employees of the Principal, in the sum of ______________ dollars, for the payment of which, well and truly to be made, we bind ourselves, jointly and severally, our joint and several heirs, executors and administrators, successors and assigns, firmly by these presents.

Whereas, in accordance with the provisions of Section 32 of the Longshore and Harbor Workers' Compensation Act enacted by Congress and approved March 4, 1927, the Principal has elected to pay compensation directly to its employees under the provisions of said Act and to likewise pay and discharge all the obligations resting upon it under any and all of the provisions of said Act so far as they relate to its employees.

Now, therefore, if the said Principal shall fully perform all the duties in this regard imposed upon it by said Act or any amendments thereto that may become effective during the life of this obligation, then this obligation shall be null and void, otherwise to remain in full force and effect, subject, however, to the following express conditions:

1. That the **Office of Workers' Compensation Programs** shall be, and hereby is, authorized to bring suit upon this obligation to procure prompt payment of compensation and benefits under the provisions of the said Longshore and Harbor Workers' Compensation Act, it being the intention that said Office in its discretion shall determine when recourse to suit shall be necessary in order to secure prompt payment.

2. The liability of the Surety is limited to the payments provided in the Longshore and Harbor Workers' Compensation Act, for and on account of injury or death occurring to the employees of the Principal during the

period beginning ______________________, 19____ and ending June 30, 19____.

In witness whereof, said Principal and said Surety have caused this instrument to be signed by their duly authorized officers, and their corporate seals to be hereunto affixed this ________ day of____________, 19____

Attest: ______________________ ______________________

______________________ ______________________

Attest: ______________________ ______________________

______________________ ______________________

Form LS-405
Rev. Sept. 1989

WORKERS' COMPENSATION SELF-INSURER'S BOND QUESTIONNAIRE

BASIC INFORMATION

PRINCIPAL		
OBLIGEE State of		
BOND NO.	BOND AMOUNT	EFFECTIVE DATE

EXCESS INSURANCE COVERAGE

1st LAYER - NAME OF CARRIER	AMOUNT OF LAYER $ OVER $
2nd LAYER - NAME OF CARRIER	AMOUNT OF LAYER $ OVER $
3rd LAYER - NAME OF CARRIER	AMOUNT OF LAYER $ OVER $
4th LAYER - NAME OF CARRIER	AMOUNT OF LAYER $ OVER $
5th LAYER - NAME OF CARRIER	AMOUNT OF LAYER $ OVER $
TOTAL AMOUNT OF COVERAGE $	AMOUNT OF DEDUCTIBLE/SELF-INSURED RETENTION $
DOES THE POLICY CONTAIN AN AGGREGATE STOP LOSS PROVISION?	HOW MUCH? $
POLICY PERIOD	

PLAN ADMINISTRATOR

NAME OF ADMINISTRATOR
ADDRESS (IF OUTSIDE FIRM)
DATE SELF-INSURANCE PROGRAM STARTED

CLAIMS EXPERIENCE

VALUED AS OF

YEAR	NO. OF CLAIMS	NO. OF OPEN CLAIMS	TOTAL INDEMNITY PAID	TOTAL MEDICAL PAID	TOTAL INDEMNITY RESERVED	TOTAL MEDICAL RESERVED
19			$	$	$	$
19			$	$	$	$
19			$	$	$	$
19			$	$	$	$
19 & Prior Years			$	$	$	$
TOTAL			$	$	$	$
TOTAL PAID/RESERVED (INDEMNITY + MEDICAL)			$		$ *	
TOTAL INCURRED (PAID + RESERVED)			$			
*AMOUNT OF RESERVES APPLICABLE TO LONG-TERM DISABILITY CASES			$			

16

Reclamation Bonds

Maureen D. Carman

Introduction

Reclamation bonds are required by state and federal regulatory authorities ("RA")and underwritten by surety and insurance companies to guarantee performance of reclamation on different types of mining and waste disposal operations. Unless otherwise noted, the term "reclamation bond" as used in this paper refers to the statutory bonds required by the Surface Mining Control and Reclamation Act of 1977, and the related state statutes which control the operation and reclamation of surface coal mining operations in the major coal producing states and territories.[1] While this article does not address other kinds of bonds guaranteeing reclamation, other federal and state statutes regulations govern reclamation which requires bonding for matters including hazardous waste, landfill closure and post-closure, hardrock mining, sand and gravel pits, fluorspar, gold , clay, and oil shale, to name a few other kinds of operations. However, this paper will address the statutory and regulatory requirements, underwriting criteria and relevant claims issues which arise from the issuance of coal mining reclamation bonds. This paper serves as a compendium with the article written on the subject in the First Edition of the Law of Suretyship, Chapter 24.[2] Part I of this paper

---

1. Alabama Surface Mining Control and Reclamation Act of 1981, Title I - IV, Ala. Code §9-16; Alaska - Alaska Surface Coal Mining Coal Mining Control and Reclamation Act, Alaska Stat. (AS) 27.21; Arizona - See Navaho Tribe below; Arkansas - Arkansas Surface and Coal Mining and Reclamation Code, Ark. Code Ann., Title 15-58; Colorado - Colorado Surface Coal Mining Act (1979), §34-33-101, Col. Rev. Stat. Ann. C.R.S. 1973 as amended; Georgia - Georgia Surface Mining Act of 1968, Title 12, Ga. Code Ann. (O.C.G.A.); Idaho - Idaho Code I.C. Title 47, Chap. 15; Illinois - Surface Coal Mining Land Conservation and Reclamation Act, 225 Ill. Rev. Stat. 720; Indiana - Ind. Code (IC) 13-4.1; Iowa - Iowa Code, Chapter 208; Kansas - Kansas Mined Land Conservation and Reclamation Act, Kan. Stat. Ann. (K.S.A.P.) 49-401 *et seq*.; Kentucky - Ky. Rev. Stat. Ann., Chapter 350; Louisiana - La. Rev. Stat. Ann., Title 43; Maryland - Environmental Article, Md. Code Ann., Title 15; Massachusetts - Mass. Gen. L. (M.G.L.), Chapter 21B; Mississippi - Miss. Code Ann., §53-9-1; Missouri - Mo. Rev. Stat. (RSMo), §444; Montana - Mont. Code Ann. (MCA), Title 82, Chapter 4, Part 2; Nevada - Nev. Rev. Stat. (NRS), Title 46; New Mexico- N.M. Stat. Ann. (NMSA) 1978, Chapter 69, Article 4; North Dakota - N.D. Cent. Code, Chapter 38-14.; Ohio - Ohio Rev. Code Ann., Chapter 1513; Oklahoma - Coal Reclamation Act of 1979, 45 Okal. Stat. Supp. 1980 §742-1 *et seq*.; Oregon - Or. Rev. Stat. (ORS), 517; Pennsylvania - Pa. Code, Title 25, Chapter 86-90; South Dakota - S.D. Codified Laws Ann., Chapter 6B, §45-6B-1 et seq.; Tennessee - (A federal jurisdiction), but *See* Tenn. Code Ann., §58 T.C.A.; Texas - Tex. Code Ann.., Title 4, Ch. 134; Utah - Utah Coal Mining Reclamation Act (1979), Utah Code Ann., Title 40, Chapter 10; Virginia - Va. Code Ann., Title 45; Washington - Wash. Rev. Code (RCW), Chapter 78.44; West Virginia - W. Va. Code, 1931 as amended, Chapter 22 - Article 3; Wyoming - Wyoming Environmental Quality Act, Wyo. Stat. (W.S.), §35-11-101 *et seq*.; Other Federal Lands Program Addresses: Crow Tribe, Crow Coal Regulatory Program, P.O. Box 460, Crow Agency, Montana 59022; Hopi Tribe, Office of Mining and Minerals Resources, Department of Natural Resources, The Hopi Tribe, P.O. Box 123, Kykotsmovi, Arizona 86039; Navaho Nation, Minerals Department, Division of Natural Resources, P.O. Box 1910, Window Rock, Arizona 86515; and Northern Cheyenne Department of Natural Resources, P.O. Box 128, Lame Deer, Montana 59043.

2. See Anne M. Walker "Reclamation Bonds," Edward G. Gallagher, ed., *The Law of Suretyship* (American Bar Association).

will address the statutory and regulatory requirements. Part II sets forth some of the underwriting criteria which are critical to an understanding of how reclamation bonds can be issued. Part III analyzes how claims on reclamation bonds arise and the considerations inherent in handling these claims.

I. *Statutory and Regulatory Requirements*

All regulations of surface coal mine reclamation spring from the Surface Mining Control and Reclamation Act of 1977 ("SMCRA").[3] For purposes of illustration throughout this paper, SMCRA and the Code of Federal Regulations ("C.F.R."), and Kentucky counterparts to SMCRA and C.F.R., will be used as references for examples of the regulatory scheme.[4]

Reclamation bonds are required under SMCRA.[5] Performance bonds are also required for contractors performing work under contracts administered under the Abandoned Mine Lands program pursuant to federal law, but are not governed by SMCRA. The regulatory scheme also provides for methods of extraction,[6] permitting of operations[7], plan of remediation[8], enforcement mechanisms[9], performance standards[10], bonds[11], and provisions of release and discharge of bonds.[12] Section 519(c) of SMCRA allows the RA authority to release an operator's bond in whole or in part, if the agency is satisfied that the reclamation required by law for that phase is accomplished.

A. PROCEDURES FOR RELEASE

The Office of Surface Mining ("OSM") issues regulations pertaining to the release of an operator's bond which are found at 30 C.F.R. §800.40. These regulations require that a permittee may file an application with the RA for the release of all or part of the performance bond liability applicable to a particular permit after all the required reclamation or a phase of reclamation covered by the bond has been accomplished.[13]

Prior to filing the bond release application, the permittee must notify adjoining property owners, surface owners, local governmental bodies, and other specified personnel by letter,[14] as well as advertising in a local newspaper the specifics of the release.[15]

---

3. Pub. L. 95-87, 30 U.S.C. 1201 *et seq.*
4. Kentucky Revised Statutes ("KRS"), Chapter 350; and Kentucky Administrative Regulations ("KAR").
5. 30 U.S.C. §1201 - 1328, 30 C.F.R. §800.
6. *See* the definition of "surface coal mining operations" at 30 U.S.C. 1291, SMCRA §701 28(A).
7. *See* 30 U.S.C. 1256, SMCRA §506; 30 U.S.C. §1260, SMCRA §510; 30 U.S.C. §1261, and SMCRA §511.
8. *See* 30 U.S.C. §1258, SMCRA §508.
9. *See* 30 U.S.C. §1267, SMCRA §517; 30 U.S.C. §1271, SMCRA §521.
10. *See* 30 U.S.C. §1265, SMCRA §515.
11. *See* 30 U.S.C. §1259, SMCRA §509.
12. *See* 30 U.S.C. §1269, SMCRA §519.
13. 30 C.F.R. §800.40(a), §800.40(c).
14. SMCRA §519(a); 30 U.S.C. §1269(a); 30 C.F.R. §800.40(a) - (2) (letters must be sent to adjoining property owners, local governmental bodies, planning agencies, sewage and water treatment authorities, and water companies in the locality of the surface mining and reclamation operation).
15. *Id.* SMCRA §519(a); 30 U.S.C. §1269(a); 30 C.F.R. §800.40-(a). Advertisement must be run once a week during four consecutive weeks and must include the permittee's name, permit number, approval date, precise location and size of the permit area involved, a summary of the reclamation, restoration and abatement work completed, description of

Weather permitting, the RA must inspect the reclamation work within thirty days of receipt of the complete bond release application to evaluate whether the criteria for the release of the bond have been successfully met.[16] The evaluation must consider such factors as the level of difficulty required to complete any remaining reclamation, the presence of surface and subsurface water pollution, the probability of continuance or future occurrence of such pollution, and an estimation of abating such pollution.[17] The surface owner, agent, or lessee must be given notice of the inspection and may participate with the RA in the bond release inspection.[18]

Affected persons have thirty days from the publication of the last newspaper advertisement to file written objections and request a hearing.[19] If requested, the RA must hold a hearing in the locality of the permit area, at the agency, or in the state capital. Public notice of the hearing must be given in a newspaper of general circulation at least two weeks before the date of the hearing, which must be held within thirty days of the date of the notice.[20]

In lieu of a hearing, but without prejudice to the right of an objector or the applicant, the RA may hold an informal conference to resolve written objections.[21] The RA must make a record of the informal conference, as well as furnish all parties with a written finding based on the informal conference and the reasons for that finding.[22]

Finally, the authority is required to notify the permittee and any interested parties within sixty days from the receipt of the completed application, or within thirty days after a public hearing held pursuant to §800.40(f) of its decision to release or not to release all or part of the bond.[23]

B. SCHEDULE FOR RELEASE

The schedule for a bond release is based on completion of each stage of a three-phase reclamation process. The completion of each phase allows the release of a certain percentage of the original bond amount.[24]

At the completion of the first phase, up to sixty percent (60%) of the total bond liability on the increment or on the permit area may be released.[25] This provision was included in every major version of SMCRA.[26] In the 1975 version, the House committee noted that the decision to release sixty percent (60%) of the bond "should be based on the regulatory authority's inspection and assessment of: (a) conformance with the requirements of the Act; and (b) an assessment of the

---

the results achieved, and the name and address of regulatory authority to which written comments or objections or requests for public hearings and informal conferences may be submitted.

16. SMCRA §519(b); 30 U.S.C. §1269(b); 30 C.F.R. §800.40(b).
17. 30 C.F.R. §800.40(b).
18. *Id.*, SMCRA §519(b); 30 U.S.C. §1269(b).
19. 30 C.F.R. §800.40(f). Under this section of the permit regulations "affected persons" are defined as those with valid legal interests which would be adversely affected by bond release, government officers with responsibility for developing and enforcing surface coal mining environmental standards, and government officers with jurisdiction or special expertise concerning related environment, social, or economic impacts.
20. 30 C.F.R. §800.40(f).
21. 30 C.F.R. §800.40(g).
22. *Id.*
23. C.F.R. §800.40(b).
24. For the criteria and schedule of bond release, See SMCRA §519(c); 30 U.S.C. §1269(c); 30 C.F.R. §800.40(c).
25. SMCRA §519(c).
26. COALEX State Inquiry Report - 61, 1 (1985).

significance of residual problems of surface and ground water pollution, and the cost of completing reclamation and abating pollution."[27]

The regulatory language essentially mirrors that of the SMCRA provision, but also notes parenthetically that the first phase may include the replacement of top soil.[28] Prior to 1983, OSM required topsoil replacement as part of its Phase I bond release; however, this requirement was removed to make the rules more closely reflect the wording of the Act.[29] In the preamble to its 1983 regulations, OSM noted that the Act did not necessarily include topsoil replacement in Phase I operations. Thus, the RA has the discretion to include or not include top soil replacement in Phase I reclamation.[30]

In the 1980 preamble to its final rules, OSM defined backfilling and regrading, topsoil replacement, and drainage control as follows:

(a) Backfilling and regrading: return of over burdened material to achieve rough contour as set forth in the reclamation plan.

(b) Topsoil replacement: return of the soil horizons which are capable of supporting vegetation and fine grading of this stratum to finished contours.

(c) Drainage control: construction of diversion ditches, swells, erosion-control structures, sediment control, and other aspects of fine grading, required before initial planting.[31]

An additional amount of the total original bond amount may be released at the conclusion of the second stage of the reclamation process.[32] However, sufficient bond liability must be retained to provide for the reestablishment of vegetation and the reconstruction of any drainage structures. Reclamation Phase II calls for the establishment of vegetation and the successful curtailment of any contribution of suspended soils to stream flow or run-off outside the permit area in excess of the law.[33] Based on a soil survey, the soil productivity of prime farmlands must have been returned to the equivalent levels of yield as non-mined land of the same soil type in surrounding area under equivalent management practices.[34] Reclamation Phase II also requires that necessary steps be successfully implemented to insure the future management of any silt dams retained as permanent impoundments.[35]

The final stage, reclamation Phase III, allows release of the remaining portion of the total performance bond if three separate criteria are successfully met. First, all surface coal mining and reclamation operations must have been successfully completed.[36] Second, the extended five to ten

---

27. H.R. Rep. No. 45, 94th Cong., 1st Sess. 203 (1975).
28. COALEX State Inquiry Report - 61, at 2.
29. *Id.*
30. 48 Fed. Reg. 32932, 32953 (1983).
31. 45 Fed. Reg. 52306, 52315 (1980).
32. 30 C.F.R. §800.40(c) (2). "When determining the amount of bond to be released after successful revegeitation has been established, the regulatory authority shall retain that amount of bond which would be sufficient to cover the cost of reestablishing vegetation if completed by a third party and for the period specified for operation responsibility in Section 515 of the Act for reestablishing vegetation."
33. *See* SMCRA §515(b) (10).
34. *Id.*
35. §800.40(c).
36. 30 C.F.R. §800.40(c) (3).

year liability period for operator responsibility must have expired.[37] Finally, the permittee must have adequately fulfilled the provisions of SMCRA and the permit.[38]

A relatively new hybrid reclamation performance bond is the Supplemental Assurance now required by the Commonwealth of Kentucky to further assure that contemporaneous reclamation will be completed. Specifically, if alternative distance limits or additional pits are approved, either upon or after issuance of a permit, the amounts specified in the regulation shall be posted with the RA.[39] While this assurance is not subject to the reclamation bond release requirement of 405 KAR 10:040, the assurance is released upon application filed by the permittee, and satisfactory backfilling and grading or highwall elimination, depending upon the method of mining for which the assurance was provided. 405 KAR 16:020 §6(1)-(5) provides as follows:

(a) The supplemental assurance shall not be subject to the bond releases of 405 KAR 10:040, but shall be returned in accordance with the requirements of this section.

(b) However, the requirements of 405 KAR 10:030, 405 KAR 10:035, and 405 KAR 10:050 shall apply to supplemental assurance.

(2) Contour mining (single seam). The amount required shall be $50,000 per 1500 feet, or any portion thereof, of additional distance approved for the first pit under Section 2 of this administrative regulation. If an additional pit or pits are approved, the amount shall be $50,000 per 1500 feet, or any portion thereof, including the first 1500 feet of each additional pit.

(3) Contour mining (multiple seam). For multiple seam contour mining operations subject to Section 2(4) of this administrative regulation, the amount required shall be $50,000 per 1500 feet, or any portion thereof, of additional distance approved for the first multiple seam operation under Section 2 of this administrative regulation. If any additional multiple seam operations are approved, the amount shall be $50,000 per 1500 feet, or any portion thereof, including the first 1500 feet of each additional multiple seam operation.

(4) Mountaintop removal. If a mountaintop removal operation begins by mining a contour cut around all or a portion of the mountaintop, that contour portion shall require the same supplemental assurance set forth in subsection (2) of this section.

(5) Area mining. The amount required shall be $50,000 for any four (4) spoil ridges, or any portion thereof, of additional distance approved for the first pit under Section 2 of this administrative regulation. If an additional pit or pits are approved, the amount shall be $50,000 for any four (4) spoil ridges, or any portion thereof, including the first four (4) spoil ridges of each additional pit.

In general, however, the essential elements of typical, non-hybrid statutory performance bonds for minerals include a method of extraction; plan of remediation or reclamation; specified enforcement mechanisms; notices of violation of state or federal law; provisions for the release and discharge of the bond, and payment of the bond proceeds upon forfeiture.

---

37. *Id., See also* 30 C.F.R. §816.116 and §817.116.

38. 30 C.F.R. §800.40(c) (3).

39. *See* 405 KAR 16:020. Upon application, inspection, and a determination that the area has been backfilled and graded or that the highwall has been eliminated, the supplemental assurance can be returned. See 405 KAR 16:020 §6(6).

II. *The Underwriter's Interest*

Most surety bonds find their genesis in a telephone call from the principal to an agent. The agent's commission is paid by the surety company for executing the bond.[40]

Most updated case law and treatises deal with the rights and obligations of the principal, surety and RA once the bond has been forfeited. Importantly, however, many rights and responsibilities of the parties have already been determined during the *underwriting* process. As in all other business transactions where credit is extended, the underwriter evaluates the credit worthiness of the principal/permittee and indemnitors who will provide the assurance that upon default of its reclamation obligations and loss to the surety, the principal/permittee will reimburse the surety.

The principal/permittee has the primary obligation of providing accurate financial and business data to the surety. Criminal liability can exist for the principal/indemnitor if false information is provided. In Kentucky, for example, KRS 517.090 provides as follows:

> (1) A person is guilty of issuing false financial statement when, with intent to defraud, he:
>
> (a) Knowingly makes or utters a written instrument which purports to describe the financial condition or ability to pay of himself or of some other person and which is inaccurate in some material respect; or
>
> (b) Represents in writing that a written instrument purporting to describe a person's financial condition or ability to pay as of prior date is accurate with respect to that person's financial condition or ability to pay, knowing the instrument to be materially inaccurate in that respect.
>
> (2) Issuing a false financial statement is a Class A misdemeanor.[41] Civil liability attaches to any person who violates KRS 517.090: Any person who violates KRS 517.090 shall be personally liable to any person damaged by the violation for the amount of the damage. This section shall not release the principal for whom the person may have acted from any liability, but the person liable and the principal for whom he acted in violating this section shall be jointly and severally liable. (1213b-2: amend. Acts 1974, ch. 406, § 314.)

Therefore, it is incumbent on the underwriter of reclamation bonds to evaluate the principal/permittee's information as thoroughly as possible. The data needed to underwrite a reclamation bond is different from any other kind of bond.

Leading companies in the reclamation bond market have become successful because of experienced staff who are knowledgeable about both the mining industry as well as the regulations, policies and practices governing the industry. First, a thorough underwriting process includes inspection of the mine sites to be bonded. The underwriter should examine any videotapes or photographs of the site, carefully comparing the regulatory reports on inspection to the actual on-ground risk at the time bonding is requested. This "snap-shot" aids the underwriter in evaluating the risk on the ground. A really astute underwriter realizes that cost to reclaim during an on-going

40. For other discussions of the agency responsibilities, *See*, Restatement (Second) of Agency §376, *et seq.* (1958); and 3 C.J.S. Agency, 390 *et seq.* (1973).

41. Enact. Acts 1974, ch. 406 § 153.

mining operation is usually different from the risk *after* a principal/permittee has defaulted and has headed for other realms.

There are five basic considerations for the underwriter:

(1) Financial Reports
(2) On-ground evaluation
  a. Coal quality
  b. Coal quantity
  c. Geological stability
  d. Accessibility to transportation
  e. History of violations, including current violations, if any
(3) Coal market
  a. Purchase order
  b. Short-term contract
  c. Long-term contract
(4) Marketability of reserve base
  a. Market for the permitted coal
  b. Adequate transportation
  c. Permit accessability to larger coal reserves
(5) Miscellaneous
  a. Equipment condition
  b. References
  c. History of company and individuals
  d. State and federal reports on company and individuals

A company's bond capacity is typically determined by its financial ability. However, a common problem with reclamation bonding in the past is that this standard surety approach of relying substantially on financial statements provided by the applicant, has failed. While primary dependence on financials has been the industry standard for some time, this writer suggests that on-ground conditions may weigh more heavily in the risk/creditworthiness equation.

The mining business is capital-intensive and requires enormous initial expenditure for leases, permitting requirements, equipment and bonding. Given the "long tail" of the bonded obligation, a surety should be ready for changes in the surface mining laws (there is no cardinal change defense!).[42] The underwriter is well-served to appreciate the unforgiving nature of the mining laws and the reality of mining business practices.

The failure of the permittee/principal to reclaim can result in the owners and controllers of the permittee/principal being placed on OSM's Applicant Violator System ("AVS"). A bond forfeiture can place these persons, as defined in the federal and state acts, in jeopardy for owing Abandoned Mine Land fees, civil penalties, reclamation costs in excess of the penal sum of the bond and even federal debarment.[43] Of course, the most serious consequence of being placed on the AVS is that no further permits will be issued until violations are addressed by the person affected.

42. KRS 350.230.

43. The purpose of 40 C.F.R. Part 32 (not a part of SMCRA) is to implement the intent of Executive Order No. 12549 and exclude enumerated persons from participating in federal financial and non-financial assistance and benefits of federal programs. A willful failure to abide by a statutory or regulatory requirement applicable to a public agreement or transaction could be applied to flagrant violators.

III. *Claims Considerations*

The best approach in controlling claims on reclamation bonds is to handle the claim *before* one is made by the RA. The normal triggering event in a reclamation bond forfeiture is an order signed by the top official of the state or federal agency. In Kentucky, for example, the surety must pay the penal bond sum "within seven (7) business days from the effective date" of the Secretary's Order forfeiting the bond.[44] However, there are many "flash points" before the order arrives on the claims desk ... and even a few salvage mechanisms after the money is paid by the surety.

First, the surety has the right to pay the penal sum; assist its principal; find a transferee; or reclaim.[45] Therefore, as soon as the surety discovers a violation which continues to be unabated on the ground (sometimes before the state and federal inspector cites a violation), the investigation can begin. Most indemnity agreements allow the surety to audit records and inspect, so a discreet inquiry about the operation, and perhaps the company's other operations, may be in order. Many things can temporarily disrupt an operation: weather, labor, cash flow problems, unyielding enforcement, or loss of a coal supply contract.

If a violation goes unabated for more than thirty (30) days after issuance of a Cessation Order, the bond associated with the permit (or increment of the permit under a Cessation Order), is ripe for forfeiture. The surety may face two situations: if the permittee continues to mine, one option is to enjoin it from any more mining until the violation is abated; or if the permittee has abandoned the site, the surety can utilize a limited power of attorney or its common law rights to begin the reclamation process. Most commonly, the permittee has left the site and the surety must effect reclamation itself.

In Kentucky, a formal procedure exists for notifying the surety and requesting the surety to declare what action it will take to cure. A letter, commonly called a "thirty day letter," is sent out to give the surety and permittee official notice that a bond will be forfeited. If the surety does not take "measures to secure bond release," the bond will be forfeited.[46] If the surety responds affirmatively, the state RA sends a reclamation agreement to be signed, stating specifically that the bond can be paid by the surety at any time in lieu of completing reclamation. If the surety will not be taking measures to secure release of its bond, then an administrative forfeiture action is initiated by the Division of Hearings which, if uncontested, results in the Order of Forfeiture.

Even if an Order of Forfeiture has been entered and monies paid to the obligee by the surety, there may be provisions in some states, like Kentucky, whereby the funds may be recouped. If the reclamation is accomplished after forfeiture, but before the state expends any funds, the surety can request the money to be returned.[47]

Interestingly, Kentucky is the only jurisdiction known to this writer which has such a formal system to achieve reclamation upon default of the permittee. Other jurisdictions appear to welcome reclamation by the surety and make the performance of reclamation in lieu of forfeiture a less cumbersome and desired outcome upon default of a permittee. These jurisdictions are in harmony with the federal directives and policy that bond forfeiture should be the remedy of last resort.

---

44. KRS 350.032.

45. *See Natural Resources and Environmental Protection Cabinet v. Whitley Development Corp.*, 940 S.W.2d 904 (Ky. App. 1997), at 907.

46. KRS 350.130.

47. KRS 350.131.

Other cures for the surety involve procuring a successor permittee to the site; assisting the permittee to find alternative operators; or assisting the permittee with financial and equipment resources. For a surety whose claims personnel are distant from the mine site in question, these undertakings can be daunting. Unlike typical construction contract surety work, this work is subject to strict regulation by *numerous* state regulatory authorities as well as federal oversight.[48] For example, inspectors from the federal Mine Safety and Health District office have attempted to cite sureties with violations of the Federal Mine Safety and Health Act of 1977 (MSHA) on sites where only surety sponsored reclamation was being accomplished. Once a violation is written, it is difficult to correct the mistake and most costly if it must be litigated. Knowing the local regulatory personnel is helpful and, in most cases, the resolution can be achieved. However, MSHA as well as OSM and state regulatory authorities have the ability to shut down a mining or reclamation operation pending final outcome of a dispute.

Underwriting and adjusting claims for reclamation bonds are fraught with pitfalls for the unwary. The key considerations for reclamation bonding are familiarity with the industry; knowledge of regulations governing the permitee/principals; and meticulous evaluation and oversight as the permittee/principal progresses to bond release.

48. Other federal acts which may impact a mine site consist of, but are not limited to, the following: Clean Air Act, 42 U.S.C. §7401 *et seq.*; Clean Water Act 33 U.S.C. §1251 *et seq.*; Resource Conservation and Recovery Action of 1976 (RCRA), 42 U.S.C. §6901 *et seq.*; Comprehensive Environmental Response Compensation and Liability Action (Superfund) 42 U.S.C. §9601 *et seq.*; Toxic Substance Control Act (TSCA) 15 U.S.C. §2601 *et seq.*; Safe Drinking Water Act (SDWA) 42 U.S.C. 300f *et seq.*; and Federal Mine Safety and Health Act of 1977 44 U.S.C. 3501 *et seq.*

17

Bail Bonds

L. Jay Labe

I. Overview

A. INTRODUCTION

Bail is the means through which our criminal justice system permits the release of an accused from custody, while ensuring his or her appearance at all required court proceedings. This paper focuses on commercial bail, which involves the release of the defendant into the custody of a professional bail bonding agent who has posted an appearance bond.[1] Approximately twenty insurance companies are currently writing bail on a national or multi-state basis. This paper addresses legal issues and concepts important to an understanding of the commercial bail industry, focusing primarily upon pre-trial bail bonding. Post-conviction and appeal bonds are not addressed. Property bonds and unsecured releases, such as personal recognizance bonds, are also beyond the scope of this paper.

Commercial bail is typically written through licensed and authorized bail bonding agents who underwrite the risk, obtain collateral, and post appearance bonds with a court. Because the operative concepts involved in bail are significantly different than those involved in the civil arena, bail is often misunderstood. Unlike other forms of suretyship, bail operates within the criminal court system and is adapted to meet its special needs. Another significant contrast arises from the unique relationship between the bail insurance company and its agent: The agent, rather than the insurance company, retains the largest share of both the premium and the risk.

An unfortunate common theme in the commercial bail industry is lack of uniformity. Some states regulate commercial bail through proactive departments of insurance, while others leave the administration of bail to the discretion of individual courts and judges. Significant statutory variation, involving bail forfeiture, exoneration, remission and fugitive recovery procedures, exist from state to state, within political subdivisions of states, and between the federal and state criminal justice systems. In addition to these statutory variations, there are a myriad of differences in local court rules, practices, forms and procedures. This diverse administrative system presents a monumental challenge to bail insurance companies writing in multiple jurisdictions.

B. THE OBJECTIVE OF BAIL

1. Commercial bail is authorized throughout the United States. The only exceptions are Illinois, Kentucky, Maine and Oregon.

The primary objective of a bail bond is to assure the defendant's appearance at all required court proceedings and trial.[2] Historically, the right to freedom before conviction is intertwined with the Anglo-Saxon doctrine that an accused is innocent until proven guilty.[3] The accused's right to freedom before conviction "permits unhampered preparation of a defense and serves to prevent the infliction of punishment prior to conviction."[4] Accordingly, the right to bail is a fundamental underpinning of our criminal justice system[5] and is an essential guardian of the presumption of innocence.[6] Bail should never be used as a means of punishing a defendant before conviction[7] or as a mechanism for public funding. When considering issues of bail forfeiture or remission, it is improper for a court to weigh the impact of its decision upon the public treasury.[8]

C. Basic Definitions

The defendant is the "principal" of a bail bond. A commercial bail bond, commonly referred to as an "appearance bond" or "recognizance bond," is executed by a "bail bonding agent" or "professional bail agent" who posts the bond using a power of attorney supplied by a "bail insurance company," also known as a "bail surety company." The "surety" on the bail bond is the bail insurance company. The surety, along with the principal, are the "obligors" of the bond. The "obligee" of the bail bond is commonly a public entity, most probably the state from whose detention facility the accused seeks release pending trial. A "forfeiture" is ordered by the court, when a defendant fails to appear as required. When all of the conditions of the bond have been met, the sureties are entitled to be "exonerated," "discharged" or released from further liability on bond. A surety who has previously paid the forfeiture, and subsequently returns the bond principal to custody, may be entitled to "remission," meaning that all or part of the forfeiture judgment will be reimbursed by the court.

II. Contractual Structure

Commercial bail involves a series of interrelated agreements. Primary among these is the appearance bond itself, which is a tripartite agreement binding the sureties and the accused bond principal to the state.[9] Before the appearance bond is executed, however, the bail bonding

---

2. *United States v. Diaz,* 811 F.2d 1412, 1415 (11th Cir. 1987).

3. *See generally Ray v. State,* 679 N.E.2d 1364 (Ind. Ct. App. 1997).

4. *Stack v. Boyle,* 342 U.S. 1, 4, 72 S. Ct. 1, 3 (1951) (citing *Hudson v. Parker*, 156 U.S. 277, 285, 15 S. Ct. 450, 453 (1895)).

5. *Sistrunk v. Lyons*, 646 F.2d 64, 70 (3d Cir. 1981).

6. *Stack*, 342 U.S. at 4, 72 S. Ct. at 3.

7. *See, e.g., People v. Benmore, et al.,* 298 Mich. 701, 702, 299 N.W. 773, 775 (1941); *Lucero v. District Ct.,* 188 Colo. 67, 71, 532 P.2d 955, 957 (1975); *McConathy v. State,* 528 S.W.2d 594, 596 (Tex. Ct. App. 1975) (holding that the forfeiture of bail can not be used as a means of imposing a fine).

8. *United States v. Velez,* 693 F.2d 1081 (11th Cir. 1982) ("Enrichment of the government is not the relevant purpose of a [bail] bond"); *In re Forfeiture of Bail Bond,* 209 Mich. App. 540, 544, 531 N.W.2d 806, 808 (1995) ("It is well settled that the purpose of a bond is to assure the appearance of a defendant and not to collect revenue."); *People v. Wilcox Ins. Co.,* 53 Cal.2d 651, 657, 2 Cal. Rptr. 754, 757, 349 P.2d 522 (1960) ("In matters [relating to bail bonds] there should be no element of revenue to the state nor punishment to the surety").

9. A bail bond agreement is a suretyship contract between the state on one side and an accused and his or her surety on the other side, whereby the surety guarantees the appearance of an accused. *See, e.g., United States v.*

agent and the accused will have entered into a contract for the bond to be posted by the surety in return for a premium, the defendant's agreement to indemnify the surety from loss and the principal's agreement to comply with the terms and conditions of the bond. This agreement may also involve third party indemnitors who, among other things, may provide collateral security to the surety.

In addition to agreements between the sureties and the principal, important agreements also exist between agents and insurance companies that make it possible for appearance bonds to be posted by the agent on behalf of the company. Although the terms of these contractual relationships may vary, there are a number of common themes and concepts that traditionally govern the manner in which commercial bonds are underwritten, posted, reported and secured.

A. Indemnity and Allocation of Risk

In the civil surety arena the term "indemnity" generally refers to a bond principal's obligation to the surety under a general indemnity agreement or at common law. Although a bail bond principal has the same indemnity obligations as a principal on a civil bond, in the world of commercial bail the principal is a fugitive when liability arises. As a result, bail insurance companies heavily rely upon indemnity agreements from their bonding agents. The bail bonding agent, in turn, looks to the principal and third-party indemnitors for reimbursement.

Commercial bail insurance companies tend to write bail through bail bonding agents who are liable for 100% of any losses sustained by the bail insurance company. To fully appreciate this unique feature of the bail industry, it is important to understand an agent receives a far greater share of the premium for each bail bond than that received by the insurance company. Although the exact percentages may vary, from company to company and from region to region, the premium split is generally in the neighborhood of 80% to the agent and 20% to the company.

The bonding agent's indemnity obligations are set forth in an agreement between the agent and the insurance company. There is no uniform nomenclature for this agreement. When the agreement is directly between an agent and an insurance company it is commonly called an "executing agent's agreement."

A common feature of executing agent agreements is the "build up fund;" known in the industry as the "BUF account." Bonding agents are generally required to pay an amount equal to 1% of the face amount of each bond into an account administered by the insurance company. If the bonding agent fails to pay a forfeiture judgment, leaving the insurance company exposed to liability, the company has the power to use the agent's BUF account to discharge the liability.

Executing agent agreements do not typically authorize bonding agents to engage in any activity on behalf of the insurance company other than writing appearance bonds and receiving premium. It would be unusual for such an agreement to authorize an agent to retain a bail recovery agent for apprehension of a non-appearing defendant.

Instead of entering into direct contracts with individual bonding agents, a bail insurance company may elect to operate through a general agent or a managing general agent. Central to this type of agreement is a provision requiring the general agent to fully indemnify the bail insurance company from loss. These agreements also contemplate that the general agent will

Vaccaro, 51 F.3d 189, 193 (9th Cir. 1995); *State v. Ericksons,* 106 N.M. 567, 567, 746 P.2d 1099, 1099 (1987); *see also* 8 C.J.S. *Bail* § 4 (1988); 8 AM. JUR. 2d *Bail and Recognizance* § 1 (1980).

contract with qualified and licensed individual bail bonding agents. These agents and subagents are engaged on a "liable" or "non-liable" basis. Non-liable agents[10] are not responsible to the general agent for losses. Liable agents, on the other hand, are contractually obligated to indemnify the general agent and the bail insurance company.

B. POWERS OF ATTORNEY

Most surety attorneys are familiar with powers of attorney that are commonly attached to commercial bonds in the civil arena. These authorize an "attorney-in-fact" to execute a surety bond in the name of the issuing company and can only be used by the individual (or individuals) whose name appears on the face of the power. Although civil powers of attorney may be sequentially numbered, the assigned number has no meaning outside of the issuing company's accounting department. The bond number established during the underwriting process uniformly takes precedence over the power number.

The term "power of attorney" has a vastly different meaning in the commercial bail industry. Bail "powers," as they are called, are issued by bail insurance companies on forms that can be executed by any licensed, and properly authorized, bail bonding agent. Bail powers are not restricted to a single "attorney in fact," or even a list of agents. Blanks are provided for insertion of the name of the executing agent. Powers are not effective unless attached to bonds with penal sums that are equal to or less than the face amount of the power.[11]

Agents affix these powers to appearance bonds that are posted with courts and detention facilities. As the powers are used, they are reported to the bail insurance company along with the required payment to the agent's BUF account and the company's share of the bond premium. Bail insurance companies issue powers to bonding agents in a variety of denominations or "face amounts." In order to obtain an additional inventory of powers, the agent may be asked to account for a prior inventory and to report on liability for active bonds. Executing agent agreements and general agency agreements typically place the responsibility for the administration and safekeeping of powers on the agent, who is liable to the insurance company for powers that are lost or misused.

Bail insurance companies almost universally rely upon power numbers to control and administer the stock of unused powers in the hands of bonding agents. They are also used to track liability on posted appearance bonds. Specialized numbering systems facilitate the process. These numbering systems also allow commercial sureties to approximate the extent of liability based solely on the power number. For example, the number XX500-0000000 may indicate that the power can be used to post an appearance bond with a face value of up to $500.00. When the bond is actually posted, however, the agent may report to the company, for example, that the power was used to post an appearance bond with a face amount of only $400.00.

10. The term "non-liable" agent relates only to the obligation of the agent to the general agent or bail insurance company, and does not mean the agent has no liability to the obligee.

11. Powers may also contain express restrictions that prevent their use with civil bonds, appeal bonds, immigration bonds or in combination with powers from the same company or other companies ("stacking").

C. UNDERWRITING

Underwriting a bail bond risk is the primary responsibility of a bail bonding agent. Underwriting involves the agent's assessment of the severity of the charges against the defendant and the agent's understanding of the accused's ties to the community. In a nutshell, the bail bonding agent must be cognizant of the risk of flight and must take reasonable steps to assure that the defendant makes all required appearances. Bail bonding agents understand that they are financially at risk from the moment they bond. They have a strong incentive to manage this risk by: (a) monitoring the whereabouts of the defendant; (b) reminding the defendant of scheduled court appearances; (c) making sure the defendant knows exactly where to appear and (d) remaining alert for any information that would reduce the likelihood that the defendant will appear. Although this vigilance may be driven by a profit motive, the justice system is the ultimate beneficiary when the accused appears at all required hearings.

A primary underwriting tool of a bail agent is collateralization of the risk. The bail bonding agent's agreement with the accused may involve the taking of cash collateral, property or other security that will facilitate the agent's payment of a forfeiture. A bail bonding agent may also obtain collateral security from third-party indemnitors, who are likely to be friends or family of the accused.

When a bail bonding agent takes collateral, the agent is acting in a fiduciary capacity.[12] The specific manner in which the collateral is held may be governed by a specific state statute as well as provisions in the agent's contract with the insurance company.[13] Once the terms and conditions of the bond have been met, the agent must return the collateral to the defendant or third-party indemnitors. Procedural requirements and the exact time frames within which collateral security must be returned, and real property reconveyed, are entirely dependent upon the statutes, rules and regulations of the individual jurisdiction.[14]

Executing agent agreements typically give agents wide latitude in underwriting and posting bail bonds. Agents are supplied with powers in a variety of denominations so that appearance bonds can be efficiently posted up to a predetermined level of authority. Appearance bonds in excess of the predetermined authority can be written with the express approval of the general agent or bail insurance company.

III. Regulation of Commercial Bail Sureties

Commercial bail is regulated in most states as a form of insurance. A bail insurance company must qualify for admission in each state under the same standards that apply to any

12. In California, the bail bonding agent is a fiduciary with respect to all funds received by the agent. *Saee* CAL. INS. CODE § 1733. Similarly, in Florida, all collateral and security is held in a fiduciary capacity by the bail bonding agent, and must be kept separate and apart from the bail bonding agent's other funds or assets. *See* FLA. STAT. ch. 648.442(3).

13. *See, e.g.*, UTAH CODE ANN. § 31A-35-605 (requiring that guaranty agreements be in writing). Bail insurance companies have reason to be concerned about the manner in which collateral is held by an agent. Regulatory authorities may be authorized to require the insurance company to make good on losses sustained by a consumer when an agents fails to return collateral. *See, e.g.* FLA. STAT. ch. 648.45(2)(n).

14. *See, e.g.*, CAL. INS. CODE § 1276.5; COLO. REV. STAT. § 16-4-104 (concerning real property taken as collateral); FLA. STAT. ch. 648.442(3) (collateral over $5,000 must be held by the insurer or managing general agent); UTAH CODE ANN. § 31A-35-603 (requiring a ten day return policy) and § 31A-35-605 (requiring that guaranty agreements be in writing).

other insurance company.[15] Bail agents are typically licensed and regulated in the same manner as any other insurance producer.[16] Prelicensure and continuing education requirements for bonding agents are common.[17]

Formal appointment of an agent by a bail insurance company with the state commissioner of insurance is required in most states.[18] Some jurisdictions go one step further and require that a current and certified "qualification power of attorney" be filed with every court or county where the bonding agent seeks to do business.[19] These qualification powers are provided by the bail insurance company and certify that the agent has authority to post appearance bonds up to a specified amount.

Many states require bail agents to meet specific financial criteria or deposit of cash or other security to guarantee their ability to pay forfeiture judgments.[20] In some jurisdictions, however, collateral deposit requirements are imposed upon agents at the local level.[21] Arizona, California and Nevada require bonding agents to provide a qualification bond, termed a "bond of bail agent," naming the state as obligee and conditioned upon the bail agent's performance of statutory obligations.[22] Qualified "cash" or "property" bonding agents are permitted to write a specified amount of bail liability, without the backing of an insurance company, in a limited number of jurisdictions.[23]

States use a variety of methods to ensure that bail bond forfeitures are paid. Forfeiture enforcement may be the responsibility of a state's department of insurance, its court system, or an independent regulatory entity.[24] A bail bonding agent who fails to pay a forfeiture judgment

---

15. Some jurisdictions require that bail insurance companies deposit collateral security. For example, the deposit requirements are $75,000 in Indiana and $50,000 in Louisiana. IND. CODE § 27-10-3-15, LA. REV. STAT. § 22:1025 ("Insurance Code").

16. Compare with New Jersey, which allows "limited insurance representatives" to write bail. *See* N.J. STAT. § 17:22A-16.1.

17. *See, e.g.* COLO. REV. STAT. § 12-7-102.5 (requiring only prelicensure education). Florida, Nevada and Tennesee require continuing education. *See* FLA. STAT. ch. 648.385; NEV. REV. STAT. § 697.230(1)(a); TENN. CODE ANN. § 40-11-401.

18. Colorado and Arizona are the only non-appointment states. Colorado requires each insurance company to maintain a list of producers for inspection upon reasonable notice. COLO. REV. STAT. § 10-2-416.5. Arizona requires bail insurance companies to file agent lists with the director of insurance on a yearly basis. ARIZ. REV. STAT. § 20-297.

19. *See, e.g.* Indiana, IND. CODE § 27-10-3-17, Nevada, NEV. REV. STAT. § 697.270, and North Carolina, N.C. GEN. STAT § 58-71-140.

20. *See, e.g.* N.C. GEN. STAT. § 58-71-145. In the federal system, a judicial officer must determine that the bail bond was executed by a solvent surety. *See* 18 U.S.C.A. § 3242(c)(xii). Typically, federal courts will require that a bail insurance company be listed on the Department of the Treasury, Fiscal Service, List Of Companies Holding Certificates Of Authority As Acceptable Sureties On Federal Bonds (Dept. Circular 570).

21. County Bail Boards in Texas are authorized to require an agent to deposit up to $50,000 in cash or property as security. *See* TEX. OCC. CODE ANN. art. 1704.160. Collateral security in excess of $150,000 per agent may be required in some Pennsylvania courts. ALLEGHENY COUNTY, PA. LOCAL RULES § 4008.1.

22. For example, Arizona requires a $10,000 bond of bail agent. *See* ARIZ. REV. STAT. § 20-320. California requires a $1,000 bond. *See* CAL. INS. CODE §§ 1802, 1803.5. A $25,000 bond is required in Nevada. *See* NEV. REV. STAT. § 697.190.

23. Cash or Property bonding agents are permitted in Mississippi (MISS. CODE ANN. § 83-39-7), North Carolina (N.C. GEN. STAT. §§ 58-71-1, -145), Ohio (OHIO REV. CODE ANN. § 4.03), South Carolina (S.C. CODE ANN. § 38-53-10), Tennessee (TENN. CODE ANN. § 40-11-122), Texas (TEX. CODE CRIM. P. ANN. § 17.01-.02) and Washington (WASH. REV. CODE § 18.185.010) up to specified limits based upon either financial qualifications or personal security posted. Colorado allows cash agents to write an unlimited amount of aggregate liability without the backing of an insurance company based only upon the filing of a single $50,000 qualification bond with the insurance commissioner. *See* COLO. REV. STAT. § 12-7-103(8)(a).

24. *See, e.g.*, FLA. STAT. ch. 648.45 (placing the responsibility of forfeiture enforcement on Florida's state department of insurance). In Texas counties with populations of 110,000 or more, "Bail Boards," rather than the

will risk license revocation, along with significant fines and penalties.[25] Some jurisdictions refuse to accept any further bonds from an agent who has failed to pay a forfeiture judgment.[26] Under this type of forfeiture enforcement system, courts and detention facilities place defaulting commercial sureties "on the board," meaning that their names appear on a list of sureties whose bonds are unacceptable to courts and detention facilities within that jurisdiction.[27] When an insurance company is placed "on the board," it generally means that appearance bonds will not be accepted from any agent using a power supplied by that company. The surety remains on the board until all unpaid forfeiture judgments are satisfied, exonerated or otherwise resolved.

IV. Setting Bail

The Eighth Amendment's excessive bail provision is integral to our concept of ordered liberty and is binding upon the states under the Fourteenth Amendment.[28] Excessive bail or denial of bail violates the Equal Protection Clause.[29] Because the practical effect of excessive bail is the denial of bail, logic compels the conclusion that the harm the Eighth Amendment aims to prevent the unnecessary deprivation of pretrial liberty.[30]

The Bail Reform Act of 1984,[31] state constitutions and statutes guarantee entitlement to bail in virtually all criminal cases, with the exception of capital offenses. Courts consider several factors when evaluating the amount of bail and the conditions of release that will reasonably assure both the appearance of a defendant and the safety of the community. These factors include: (a) the nature and seriousness of the charges; (b) the weight of the evidence; (c) the defendant's character; (d) the defendant's family and community ties; (e) flight risk; (f) the defendant's mental and physical condition; (g) the defendant's criminal history and involvement with drugs and alcohol; (h) the danger posed by the defendant to the community.[32] The Bail Reform Act requires the release of an accused under the least restrictive conditions, or combination of conditions that will reasonably assure appearance.[33] Only under rare circumstances will an accused in a federal matter be denied bail.

state department of insurance, are responsible for all commercial bail surety licensure and forfeiture issues. *See* TEXAS REV. CIV. STAT. ANN. art. § 2372p-3.

25. *See, e.g.*, CAL PENAL CODE § 1308; MO. REV. STAT. § 374.763(1); N.C. GEN. STAT. § 58-71-80.

26. *See, e.g.*, FLA. STAT. ch. 648.44(l); NEB. REV. STAT. § 11-124.

27. Both the bail bonding agent and the bail insurance company can be placed "on the board" in Colorado if forfeiture judgments are not paid when due. *See* COLO. REV. STAT. § 16-4-112. While on the board, the agent is prohibited from writing bonds anywhere in the State. *See* COLO. REV. STAT. § 12-7-109(1)(g).

28. *Meechaicum v. Fountain*, 696 F.2d 790, 791 (10th Cir. 1983).

29. *Pugh v. Rainwater*, 572 F.2d 1053, 1057 (5th Cir. 1978).

30. *See, e.g., Sistrunk v. Lyons*, 646 F.2d 64, 70 n.23 (3d Cir. 1981); *United States ex rel. Goodman v. Kehl*, 456 F.2d 863, 868 (2d Cir. 1972).

31. *See* Comprehensive Crime Control Act of 1984, Pub. L. No. 98-473, 98 Stat. 1976 (codified as amended in scattered sections of 18 U.S.C.).

32. *See, e.g., United States v. Orena*, 986 F.2d 623, 631 (2d Cir 1993) (danger to the community as a basis for refusing to grant bail); *United States v. Gebro*, 948 F.2d 1118, 1121 (9th Cir. 1991) (discussing "flight risk"); *United States v. Bosquez-Villarreal*, 868 F.2d 1388, 1389 (5th Cir. 1989) (refusal of bail based upon drug offenses); *Ray v. State*, 679 N.E.2d 1364, 1367 (Ind. Ct. App. 1997) ("[B]oth insuring a defendant's presence at trial and community safety may be considered in setting bail for defendants . . . ."). *See also* 18 U.S.C. § 3142(g).

33. *Gebro*, 948 F.2d at 1121; *see also* 18 U.S.C. § 3141.

V. Bond Forms

An appearance bond executed by both the bonding agent and the defendant, must be delivered to the court or detention facility with an attached power of attorney. A bail bonding agent generally uses an appearance bond form that is required by the jurisdiction holding the accused. State law, court rules and local practice result in a total lack of appearance bond form standardization. If there is no required form, the bonding agent will use a generic form that has a history of acceptance in the jurisdiction.

The bond or undertaking may be called an "appearance bond," "bail bond," "recognizance bond," or something similar. The following elements are likely to be present, in one form or another, in almost all appearance bond forms: (a) a face amount or "penal sum" payable to the state; (b) a statement of the primary condition; that the accused appear as required; (c) a blank for insertion of the general nature of the charges; (d) the name and address of the accused and the sureties; (e) the date, time and place of the next court appearance; and (f) a statement of applicable supplemental conditions, which are likely to involve prohibitions on criminal activity; prohibitions on the use or possession of firearms, drugs or alcohol; travel restrictions; reporting requirements and restrictions on personal associations or contacts.

VI. Revocation

A court can order revocation of a bail bond and the re-arrest of the accused for a variety of reasons. Prior to forfeiture, revocation can be ordered when the accused violates any condition of the release.[34] For example, bail will probably be revoked if the accused is charged with another criminal offense while released on bail.[35] Revocation is also likely if the court determines that there is a reasonable probability the accused will not appear or may cause harm to the community.[36]

The term "revocation" is sometimes used to refer to the right of the bail bonding agent to return the defendant to custody, with or without cause, in an effort to remove himself from further liability before forfeiture occurs.[37] Although an agent may be required to return all or part of the premium that was paid for the bond, courts do not require an agent to involuntarily remain on a risk.[38] If an agent becomes aware of circumstances giving rise to an increased risk of flight, the agent may find it necessary to return the defendant to custody.[39]

34. The sole exception to this rule is violation of the primary condition of the bond, namely failure to appear. In that event, the bond will be forfeited, not revoked.

35. *See, e.g.*, VIR. CODE ANN. § 19.2.135 ("A court may, in its discretion, in the event of a violation of any condition of a recognizance taken pursuant to this section, remand the principal to jail until the case is finally disposed of, and if the principal is remanded to jail, the surety is discharged from liability"); *see also United States v. Wilson*, 820 F. Supp. 1031, 1033 (N.D. Tex. 1993) (discussing revocation when the accused violates conditions of his or her release).

36. *See, e.g.*, MICH. COMP. LAWS ANN. § 765.26; *United States v. Maack*, 25 F. Supp. 2d 586, 586 (E.D. Penn. 1998) (upholding revocation of defendant's bail because there was probable cause he would pose danger to the community); *United States v. McNeal*, 960 F. Supp. 245, 246-47 (D. Kan. 1997) (discussing the types of factors a judicial officer must consider before revoking a defendant's pretrial release, including the issue of whether the defendant will pose danger to the community).

37. *See, e.g.*, *State v. Nugent*, 199 Conn. 537, 548, 508 A.2d, 728, 734 (1986).

38. *See, e.g.*, *Jordan v. Knight*, 250 Ala. 109, 111-12, 35 So. 2d 178, 179-81 (1984); *State v. Pelley*, 222 N.C. 684, 687, 24 S.E.2d 635, 637 (1943).

39. *See Johnson v. Hicks*, 288 Ark. 158, 160, 702 S.W.2d 797, 798 (1986) (concluding the agent had probable cause to believe the defendant committed a felony while released on bond).

VII. Bond Forfeiture

Under virtually all federal and state statutes a bail bond will be forfeited when the defendant fails to appear, thus violating the primary condition of the bail bond.[40] The specific procedure through which the bond is declared forfeited, and judgment entered, varies from jurisdiction to jurisdiction. The most common framework for this process begins at the non-appearance of the defendant with the declaration of a bond forfeiture and the issuance of a warrant for the arrest of the defendant. If the defendant fails to appear or be surrendered after a specific number of days, judgment is entered on the bond. The agent then has an additional window of opportunity to apprehend and surrender the defendant before the forfeiture judgment must be paid.

Specific forfeiture procedures depend upon the statutes and court rules of individual jurisdictions. Some jurisdictions enter judgment very promptly upon the declaration of a forfeiture. Other jurisdictions may issue a citation for a hearing at which the bonding agent will have an opportunity to "show cause" why the bond should not be forfeited, or judgment should not enter. Some jurisdictions leave procedures entirely within the discretion of the court. Procedures also vary, depending upon the court, as to when the agent must pay the forfeiture. Some systems may require immediate payment of the face amount of the bond. Most systems allow the agent some time to pay the judgment, although the time period can be as short as 10 days[41] or as long as one year.[42]

Notice of the forfeiture, the show cause hearing and the entry of judgment is generally served upon the bail bonding agent. Under the Federal System, notice to the surety is required when the government moves for entry of judgment.[43] Most states' procedures require that the court give a bail insurance company notice of the entry of judgment. In practice, however, some jurisdictions consider service of notice upon the agent to be "constructive notice" to the bail insurance company. When a defaulting agent ceases business or changes insurance companies, however, "constructive notice" effectively means that the insurance company will not receive actual notice of the entry of judgment and its efforts to timely resolve the forfeiture will be impeded.

Courts have wide discretion in setting aside forfeiture judgments.[44] If the defendant is promptly surrendered or if the court is satisfied that appearance and surrender by the defendant is impossible and without his fault, the forfeiture is likely to be set aside. A court may evaluate

---

40. *See* FED. R. CRIM. P. 46(e)(1). For further discussion on this issue also see Nancy M. King, Annotation, *Forfeiture of Bail for Breach of Conditions of Release Other Than That of Appearance*, 68 A.L.R.4th 1082 (1989).

41. For example, New Mexico only allows 10 days. *See* N.M. STAT. ANN. § 31-3-2.

42. Indiana allows the bonding agent 365 days to pay a forfeiture. *See* IND. CODE ANN. § 27-10-2-12. Hawaii and Nebraska allow 30 days. *See* HAWAII REV. STAT. § 804-51; NEB. REV. STAT. § 14-227. Alabama (ALA. CODE § 15-13-136), Idaho (IDAHO CODE § 19-2927), Minnesota (MINN. STAT. ANN. § 609.907), Mississippi (MISS. CODE ANN. § 99-5-25), and Oklahoma (OKL. STAT. tit. 59, § 1332) allow 90 days. Other states allow 180 days. *See, e.g.*, LA. REV. STAT. ANN. § 15:85; NEV. REV. STAT. § 178.509; TENN. CODE ANN. § 40-11-139. California allows up to 185 days. CAL. PENAL CODE § 1305.

43. *See* FED. R. CRIM. P. 46(e)(3); *see also U. S. v. Lacey*, 778 F.Supp. 1137, 1140 (D. Kan. 1991) (setting aside the judgment against a bail insurance company when the government conceded that actual notice had not been given). *But see, United States v. Navarrete-Martinez*, 776 F.2d 887 (10th Cir. 1985) (concluding that lack of notice was harmless error when the agent had actual knowledge).

44. *United States v. Amwest Sur. Ins. Co.*, 54 F.3d 601, 602 (9th Cir. 1995). *See also* FED. R. CRIM. P. 46(e)(2) & (4).

several factors when considering whether an injustice has been done by the forfeiture, including: (1) the willfulness of the breach of the bond conditions; (2) the cost, inconvenience and prejudice suffered by the government as a result of the breach; (3) explanatory or mitigating factors; (4) the appropriateness of the amount of the bond; and (5) the nature and extent of participation by the surety in apprehending and surrendering the defendant.

In the real world, the failure of a defendant to appear does not necessarily mean the defendant has fled. More likely than not, the defendant will subsequently appear and voice one of the time-honored excuses involving: (1) clerical errors about the time and place of the hearing; (2) oversleeping; or (3) traffic problems. Once a forfeiture has been ordered, however, the appearance bond should not be reinstated without the consent of the surety.

VIII. Exoneration and Remission

A bail surety is exonerated from liability under the terms and conditions of an appearance bond when the terms and conditions of the bond have been met. In the majority of criminal proceedings, the defendant appears at all court proceedings and the bond is discharged and exonerated when the defendant is convicted, acquitted, pleads guilty or nolo, or the charges are dropped.[45] If the bond is to be continued until sentencing, the surety must consent.[46] When a disposition of the case has been reached, the bond may be exonerated automatically by statute. On the other hand, some states may require that either the defendant or the bonding agent make application for the exoneration or for documentation that the bond has been discharged.

In the normal course of business, the discharge and exoneration of bonds is important. It is important bond principals and indemnitors who want their collateral security returned. It may be equally important to bonding agents who must show general agents and insurance companies that liability on issued powers has been resolved before new powers will be issued. Bail insurance companies commonly require agents to document that liability on existing powers has been extinguished in order to insure that agents are not writing liability in excess of their financial capacity to indemnify.

The defendant's compliance with the terms and conditions of a bond are not the only grounds for exoneration. If the accused dies prior to the date of the scheduled appearance the surety is exonerated.[47] A surety is entitled to be exonerated upon payment of a forfeiture judgment.[48] A surety may also be entitled to exoneration where the bond is canceled by the court[49] or if the bond is void because it was improperly taken by the court in the first instance.[50]

45. *See, e.g., People v. Henry,* 308 N.Y.S.2d 245, 33 A.D.2d 1031 (1970) (reversing lower court's order to reinstate released bail bond where the surety had performed all necessary contractual obligations and was exonerated from liability even though the judgment of conviction was reversed). *Cf. Commonwealth v. Hill,* 180 Pa. Super. 430, 119 A.2d 572, 573 (1956) (reversing the lower court's decision to release the surety because the defendant appeared as required and "[u]nder the terms of the recognizance the condition had therefore been fulfilled and the subsequent forfeiture was unwarranted").

46. *Rodriguez v. People,* 554 P.2d 291, 292 (Colo. 1976) (holding that the consent of the surety is required after a guilty plea because the risk of the surety has materially increased). Events that materially increase the risk of the surety have the effect of terminating the obligation. *See* RESTATEMENT (SECOND) OF SECURITY § 128(b) (1941).

47. *Taylor v. Taintor,* 83 U.S. (16 Wall.) 366, 21 L.Ed. 287 (1872). *See also* J. P. Ludington, Annotation, *Death of a Principal As Exoneration, Defense, Or Ground For Relief, Of Sureties On Bail Or Appearance Bond,* 63 A.L.R.2d 830, § 7[a] (1956).

48. *See, e.g.,* COLO. REV. STAT. § 16-4-108.

49. *See, e.g., State v. Gutierrez Barajas,* 153 Ariz. 511, 738 P.2d 786 (Ct. App. 1987); State v. Johnson, 92 N.E.2d 24, 27 (Ohio Ct. App. 1949).

Exoneration becomes significantly more complex after a forfeiture has occurred. The rules and procedures relating to exoneration vary widely between jurisdictions. They are greatly affected by the stage of the proceeding at which exoneration is being requested. For example, an agent will find that it is much easier to get a bond exonerated if the defendant is promptly apprehended and surrendered before the court enters judgment on the forfeiture. The difficulty in obtaining exoneration is likely to increase if the defendant is surrendered after a forfeiture judgment is entered. Once a forfeiture judgment is paid, the surety's entitlement to exoneration becomes entwined with the issue of "remission", which is the question of whether surrender of the defendant qualifies the surety for return of all or part of the payment.

A surety's entitlement to remission depends upon each jurisdiction's statutory scheme. For example, in Florida a surety's entitlement to remission is preserved only if there was no "breach of the bond," meaning that the forfeiture was paid before judgment entered.[51] Entitlement to remission may also require direct involvement by the surety in the apprehension and surrender of the defendant.[52] Entitlement to remission may also depend upon the time that has expired between the date of forfeiture or payment of judgment and the date the defendant is surrendered. New Jersey allows a bonding agent to apply for remission if the defendant is surrendered up to 4 years after the forfeiture.[53] Shorter time periods are more common. In Colorado, Connecticut and Florida, for example, the limit is one year.[54] In Oklahoma, on the other hand, the defendant must be surrendered within 90 days to qualify for remission.[55] The issue is left entirely to the discretion of the court in some states, including Delaware, Louisiana, Ohio and Tennessee.[56] California allows a bonding agent 180 days to produce the defendant or pay the forfeiture judgment, but after the forfeiture judgment is paid, no remission is allowed.[57]

Appearance bond defaults and forfeitures often occur if the defendant is incarcerated on other charges when a court appearance date arrives. If the defendant is incarcerated by the bailing state, the majority rule is that the forfeiture must be set aside because the state is in a position to produce the defendant in court, while the bonding agent cannot.[58] The law is less favorable to the surety when the defendant is incarcerated in a state other than the bailing state.[59] Although some states refuse to grant relief, the majority of states will grant a bail surety relief from the forfeiture depending upon the voluntary nature of the circumstances of the defendant's departure from the bailing state, the nature of the charges pending against the defendant and whether the bailing state has sought extradition.[60]

Entitlement to remission may also be affected by the Uniform Criminal Extradition Act which interjects a mandatory series of court proceedings that a foreign bondsman must follow to

50. *See* Francis M. Dougherty, J.D., Annotation, *Liability Of Surety On Bail Bond Taken Without Authority,* 27 A.L.R.4th 246, § 3 (1984).

51. FLA. STAT. ch. 903.28(1).

52. *See, e.g.,* FLA. STAT. ch. 903.28(2). *See also, e.g., People v. Johnson,* 395 P.2d 19, 23 (Colo. 1964); *State v. Hernandez,* 511 N.W.2d 535, 539 (Neb. Ct. App. 1993).

53. N. J. STAT. 2A:162-8.

54. *See* COLO. REV. STAT. § 16-4-112 (5)(j); CONN. GEN. STAT. § 54-65a; FLA. STAT. ch. 903.28(2).

55. OKLA. STAT. §59-1332 D(2).

56. *See* OHIO REV. CODE § 2937.39; TENN. CODE ANN § 40-11-204(a).

57. CAL. PENAL CODE § 1305.

58. *See* Lee R. Russ, J.D., Annotation, *Bail: Effect On Surety's Liability Under Bail Bond Of Principal's Subsequent Incarceration In Same Jurisdiction,* 35 A.L.R. 4th 1192 (1981).

59. *See, e.g., State v. Fields,* 137 N.J. Super. 76, 347 A.2d 810, 811 (1975).

60. *See generally* Russ, *supra* note 58.

obtain a warrant to arrest and remove a fugitive from bail from another jurisdiction.[61] In Hawaii, for example, the Court of Appeals determined that a bonding agent did not show sufficient good cause to set aside a forfeiture judgment where the agent failed to exercise any of the options available under American Samoa's UCEA to secure the defendant's arrest as a fugitive.[62]

IX. The Recovery Process and the Bail Agents Right to Arrest

A bonding agent has the right and authority to take the defendant into custody for the purpose of exonerating liability on the bail bond. This authority is founded upon common law, contract and statute. The common law basis for this authority is enunciated by the United States Supreme Court in *Taylor v. Taintor,*[63]

> When bail is given, the principal is regarded as delivered to the custody of his sureties. Their dominion is a continuance of the original imprisonment. Whenever they choose to do so, they may seize him and deliver him up in their discharge; and if that cannot be done at once, they may imprison him until it can be done. They may exercise their rights in person or by agent. They may pursue him into another State; may arrest him on the Sabbath; and, if necessary, may break and enter his house for that purpose. The seizure is not made by virtue of new process. None is needed. It is likened to the rearrest by the sheriff of an escaping prisoner.

The extensive powers of the bondsman recognized in *Taintor* to recapture the principal also derive from the contractual relationship between the surety and the defendant.[64] The bond agreement provides that the surety posts the bail, and in return, the principal agrees that the surety can retake him at any time, even before forfeiture of the bond.[65] By entering into this contract, not only does the principal voluntarily consent to the custody of the surety, but under common law, he also implicitly agrees that the surety or the surety's agent may use reasonable force in apprehending him.[66] Further, the contract establishes that the surety's right of recapture is private in nature, with the understanding that the government will not interfere.[67] Thus, this common law right of recapture establishes that the seizure of the principal by the surety is not

61. *See State v. Lopez,* 105 N.M. 538, 734 P.2d 778 (N.M. Ct. App. 1986), *cert. denied,* 499 U.S. 1092, 107 S. Ct. 1305 (1987) (addressing the New Mexico version of the Uniform Criminal Extradition Act found at N.M. STAT. ANN. §§ 31-4-1 to -30).

62. *See State v. Flores,* 962 P.2d 1008, 1015-17 (Hawaii Ct. App. 1998).

63. *Taylor v. Taintor,* 83 U.S. (16 Wall.) 366, 373, 21 L.Ed. 287, 295 (1872).

64. *Ouzts v. Maryland Nat'l Ins. Co.,* 505 F.2d 547 (9th Cir. 1974) (holding that California's version of the UCEA abrogated a foreign bonding agent's common law right to pursue, apprehend and remove his principal from California without resort to process); *State v. Mathis,* 349 N.C. 503, 509 S.E.2d 155 (1998); *State v. Tapia,* 468 N.W.2d 342 (Minn. Ct. App. 1991), *rev. denied,* (May 23, 1991).

65. *See, e.g., State v. Nugent,* 199 Conn. 537, 543, 508 A.2d 728, 731 (1986). Indiana's specimen form of agreement between the surety and principal provides that the surety has "control and jurisdiction over the principal during the term for which the bond is executed and shall have the right to apprehend, arrest, and surrender the principal to the proper officials at any time as provided by law." IND. ADMIN. CODE tit. 1-6.2-10.

66. *Fitzpatrick v. Williams,* 46 F.2d 40, 42 (5th Cir. 1931) (holding that the surety's right to arrest is "an original right that arises from the relationship between the principal and his bail, and not one derived through the state"); *Nugent,* 199 Conn. at 543, 508 A.2d at 731; *Livingston v. Browder,* 51 Ala. App. 366, 368, 285 So. 2d 923, 925 (1973); *In re Von Der Ahe,* 85 F. 959, 960 (W.D. Pa. 1898).

67. *Reese v. United States,* 76 U.S. (13 Wall.) 22, 25, 19 L. Ed. 541, 544 (1869).

technically an "arrest" and may be accomplished without process of law. State[68] and federal[69] statutes have supplemented the traditional common law rights of the bail surety to apprehend and return a bail jumper to custody. In some jurisdictions, breach of the condition of an appearance bond may also give rise to a separate criminal offense and additional charges.[70]

An agent may use reasonable means to ensure that the principal appears in court.[71] If the principal is apprehended in the state where the bond was taken, and there are no statutes to the contrary, the defendant can clearly be apprehended without any judicial or administrative process.[72] In many states an agent must follow specific procedures in affecting the apprehension of the defendant. For example, in Colorado, a bonding agent surrendering a defendant to a sheriff must supply the sheriff a certified copy of the bond.[73] A statute may also require that an apprehended defendant be brought before a court within a specific period of time.[74] Failure to follow statutory procedures can expose the arresting agent to civil liability.[75]

Although a state cannot arrest a defendant in another state without utilizing formal extradition proceedings,[76] it has been held that bail bondsmen have the right to cross state lines to apprehend defendants and it is not necessary for a bondsman to utilize the extradition process.[77] Bail bondsmen and "bounty hunters" are actors within the private sector, rather than state actors.[78] Forty states have enacted the 1936 revision of the Uniform Criminal Extradition Act ("UCEA").[79] Under the UCEA, a foreign bonding agent must seek a warrant from a court, or if the fugitive is arrested without a warrant, produce the fugitive in a court of the state where the defendant is arrested so that proceedings can be initiated to determine if the arrestee was the wanted person and whether the charges are extraditable.[80]

---

68. *See, e.g.,* ALA. CODE § 15-13-162; N.C. GEN. STAT. § 58-71-30. *See Livingson*, 51 Ala. App. at 369, 285 S.2d at 926.

69. 18 U.S.C.A. § 3149.

70. *People v. Lynn,* 89 Ill. App. 3 712, 44 Ill. Dec. 939, 412 N.E.2d 15 (2d Dist. 1980); *People v. Allen,* 28 Cal. App. 4th 575, 33 Ca. Rptr 2d 669 (1994); *McGee v. State,* 438 So. 2d 127 (Fla. Dist. Ct. App. 1983). *See also* COLO. REV. STAT. § 18-8-212.

71. *See generally State v. Nugent,* 199 Conn. 537, 508 A.2d 728, 732 (1986).

72. *Kear v. Hilton,* 699 F.2d 181 (4th Cir. 1983).

73. *See* COLO. REV. STAT § 16-4-108(1)(c).

74. *See* CAL. PENAL CODE § 1301 (stating that the defendant is required to be delivered to the court without undue delay, within 48 hours).

75. *See generally O.K. Bonding Co. Inc. v Milton,* 579 S.2d 602 (Ala. 1991).

76. *See, e.g., California v. Superior Ct,* 482 U.S. 400, 407 (1987). The extradition process is also required in federal cases pursuant to 18 U.S.C. § 3182 (1994).

77. *See Lopez v. McCotter,* 875 F.2d 273, 277 (10th Cir. 1989); *Ouzts v. Maryland Nat'l. Ins. Co.,* 505 F.2d 547, 554 (9th Cir. 1974); *U.S. v. Goodwin,* 440 F.2d 1152, 1156 (3d Cir. 1971); *Fitzpatrick v. Williams,* 46 F.2d 40, 41 (5th Cir. 1931).

78. *See Hunt v. Steve Dement Bail Bonds, Inc.,* 914 F.Supp. 1390 (W.D. La. 1996). If a bail bondsman receives support form a police officer in apprehending the defendant, the bondsman may be said to have acted under color of state law. *See, e.g., Bailey v. Kenney,* 791 F. Supp. 1511, 1521 (D. Kan. 1992).

79. 11 Uniform Crim. Extrad. Act 36 (1936 & Supp. 1993).

80. *See generally State v. Epps,* 585 P.2d 425,428 (Or. 1978).

The few cases that have directly addressed the impact of the UCEA in the context of bail fugitive recovery have diluted the common law and contractual recovery rights of the bail surety.[81] The extent to which an express waiver executed by a bond principal will be enforced remains to be decided.[82]

Commercial bail bonding agents commonly hire bounty hunters to locate and retrieve defendants on forfeited bonds. Bounty hunters act as representatives of the bail surety and they enjoy the bail surety's broad rights to pursue and arrest suspects.[83] The use of bail recovery agents, however, may be subject to a variety of state imposed restrictions.[84]

Conclusion

Bail is the least understood and most under-appreciated form of suretyship. This paper is written in an effort to promote a better understanding of the commercial bail industry and the invaluable community services that it provides. For example, as opposed to other forms of pretrial release, defendants in the custody of commercial bonding agents are much more likely to make required court appearances,[85] thereby enhancing the efficiency of our criminal courts.[86] Another significant benefit of commercial bail is that it is "user funded." The same financial incentives that drive the commercial bail industry also keep the responsibility for recovering fugitives within the private sector, placing no additional burden on the taxpayer. A more comprehensive understanding of commercial bail will facilitate the enactment of reasonable and more uniform laws that will enhance the efficiency of the industry and augment its long record of accomplishment.

---

81. *See, e.g., Landry v. A-Able Bonding, Inc.,* 75 F.3d 200, 206 (5th Cir. 1996) (holding that the Texas UCEA required the surrender of a Louisiana fugitive to Texas court); *McCotter,* 875 F.2d at 277 (holding that a commercial surety could not reasonably anticipate that the common law rights of a bail agent were proscribed and was thus deprived of due process); *Ouzts,* 505 F.2d at 552-53 (holding that the California UCEA abrogates common law rights of bail surety); *Commonwealth v. Wilkinson,* 613 N.E.2d 914, 917 (Mass. 1993) (Common law rights of bail surety abrogated by UCEA in Massachusetts); *Epps,* 585 P.2d at 429 (recognizing that Oregon abrogates a foreign bonding agent's common law right to pursue, apprehend and remove principal from state without resort to process); *State v. Lopez,* 105 N.M. 538, 542, 734 P.2d 778, 782 (N.M. Ct. App. 1986), *cert. denied,* 499 U.S. 1092, 107 S. Ct. 1305 (1987) (holding that the UCEA must be followed in the absence of the consent of bond principal).

82. *See Lopez,* 105 N.M. at 542, 734 P.2d at 782 (holding that the UCEA must be followed in the absence of the consent of bond principal). *But see Epps,* 585 P.2d at 427 (holding that the use of force obviates "consent" as the term is used in the UCEA).

83. Jonathan Drimmer, *When Man Hunts Man: The Rights and Duties of Bounty Hunters in the American Criminal Justice System*, 33 HOUS. L. REV. 731 (1996).

84 For example, bail enforcement licenses are required in California, Georgia, Nevada and Louisiana. *See* CAL. PENAL CODE §1299.06; GA. CODE ANN. §§ 16-11-129 and 17-6-56 to 58; NEV. REV. STAT. § 648.30, 697.173; LA. ADMIN. CODE §§ 4905 to 4907. A recovery agent cannot be employed in Colorado without a background investigation. COLO. REV. STAT. § 12-7-105.5. When a bail enforcement agent is used in Arizona, the department of insurance must be promptly notified. Annual reports are also required. *See* ARIZ. REV. STAT. § 13-3885C, D. In Florida, it is unlawful to represent oneself as a "bounty hunter" or "bail enforcement agent." No one other than a certified law enforcement officer is authorized to apprehend, detain, or arrest a principal on a bond in Florida, unless that person is qualified, licensed, and appointed as a bail bond agent in Florida, or by the state where the bond was written. FLA. STAT. ch 648.30(2) & (3).

85. BUREAU OF JUSTICE STATISTICS, U.S. DEPT. OF JUSTICE, PUB. NO. NCJ-148818, PRETRIAL RELEASE OF FELONY DEFENDANTS, at 9-12 (Nov. 1994).

86. Holly J. Joiner, *Private Police: Defending the Power of Professional Bail Bondsmen*, 32 INDIANA LAW REVIEW 1413, 1424 (1999).

18

Financial Guaranty

Martha L. Perkins

Introduction

Financial guaranty insurance is a type of insurance that provides an unconditional and irrevocable guaranty that indemnifies the insured against the nonpayment of principal and interest when due by an obligor on an insured debt obligation. Currently regulated as a separate and distinct line of insurance, financial guaranty insurance was once treated as a type of surety insurance and was regulated as such. Financial guaranty insurance is, in essence, a highly refined kind of surety bond.

Like surety insurance, financial guaranty insurance expects "no loss" underwriting. And, like surety insurance, financial guaranty insurance guarantees a contract of indebtedness or other monetary obligation. Unlike suretyship, however, financial guaranty insurance is used to improve the investment grade of an underlying obligation to pay principle and interest on a fixed schedule. By lending its claims-paying ability to its customers, such as municipal bond issuers, a financial guaranty insurer lowers the costs of the bond issuance.[1] This is the unique characteristic of financial guaranty insurance that distinguishes it, conceptually, from surety bonds.

Because of the statutory and regulatory environment that has evolved in response to the explosive growth of the financial guaranty industry, an understanding of the history of this product and its distinctive treatment is essential for those involved in both the surety industry and the financial guaranty industry. Statutory definitions do not necessarily provide a model of clarity for guidance in determining whether a specific product constitutes financial guaranty insurance or surety insurance. Therefore, a cloud of uncertainty often hangs over whether a specific product is a financial guaranty insurance product or a surety product.

This paper will set forth a brief history of the development of financial guaranty insurance and will examine the regulatory response to the growth of this industry and the complex issues emanating from its intensely regulated environment.

1. Financial guaranty insurers are both regulated and rated. They are regulated by state insurance departments and specific state legislation. They are rated by private rating agencies, such as Standard and Poor's, Moody's, Fitch, and Duff & Phelps.

I. The Rapid Development of the Financial Guaranty Insurance Industry and Its Potential Risks Raised Regulatory Concerns

The United States financial guaranty insurance industry began to emerge in 1971 when a single policy was written to guarantee a general obligation issue for the city of Juneau, Alaska.[2] From the early 1970s until the late 1980s, financial guaranty insurance was subject to regulation as property/casualty insurance generally and tended to be governed by the same statutes that applied to surety. Financial guaranty insurance experienced significant growth in the early to mid-1980s as a number of large property and casualty insurance companies entered the business. And the demand for financial guaranty insurance was fueled by highly publicized failures of issuers.[3]

A series of defaults with large losses in the financial guaranty line caused concern among state insurance regulators about the potential exposures. Indeed, the significant exposures ultimately led to insolvencies, as a financial guaranty insurer could suffer a single catastrophic loss through the failure of just one bond issuer to meet its obligation. In addition, numerous failures of one financial guarantee product could provide inordinate risk to the business. For example, the limited partnership financial guarantee bond was a product that flourished until a declining economy and tax reform legislation in 1986 combined to contribute to the failures of many limited partnerships, entrapping the companies that issued the financial guarantee bonds, and to the concerns of insurance regulators.[4]

Seeking to expand their opportunities in the financial services arena, surety companies issued financial guarantee bonds to finance limited partnerships. The limited partnerships, formed to take advantage of then-permitted tax shelters, purchased and operated real estate projects. In such a transaction, the limited partnership required its limited partners to make their capital contributions in the form of an amount of cash, usually small, and the balance with a promissory note in favor of the partnership. The partnership would then seek financing for the business from a lending institution and agreed to pledge the limited partners' promissory notes to the lender as collateral for the loan. The lender often required further security for the limited partners' promissory notes, which were initially stand-by letters of credit.

Letters of credit created administrative burdens, and in the late 1970s and early 1980s, property-casualty companies began writing financial guarantees to secure the limited partners' installment payments. Shocked with a sudden declining economy and tax reform legislation, many limited partnerships failed in the mid- and late 1980s; and the companies that issued the financial guarantee bonds felt the shock waves. The regulators took note. The issue of regulating this line of business became critical in the mid-80s, with regulators concerned that the current mode of regulating financial guaranty insurance as surety insurance was inadequate.

Accordingly, in the mid-1980s, insurance regulators began to craft and draft special regulations and statutes for insurers writing financial guaranty insurance. The National Association of Insurance Commissioners[5] appointed the Financial Guaranty Insurance Study Group in 1985 to develop regulations for this line of business. A first draft was released in

---

2. CONNING & COMPANY, FINANCIAL GUARANTY INSURANCE: FROM AN ACORN TO AN OAK TREE 57 (1998).

3. The 1983 default by the Washington Public Power Supply System (referred to, appropriately, as "WHOOPS,") on over $2 billion of revenue bonds encouraged investors to look for ways to protect their investments through financial guarantees.

4. For an excellent discussion of financial guarantee bonds, see Bruce Shreves, *Financial Guarantee Bonds*, *in* THE LAW OF SURETYSHIP 18-1 (Edward G. Gallagher ed. 1993).

5. Hereinafter NAIC.

December 1985, and the Financial Guaranty Insurance Model Act was adopted in June 1986,[6] with several amendments to it in 1987.[7] The Model Act sets out financial guaranty insurance as a separate and distinct line of insurance. In addition, in 1986, the NAIC began requiring insurance companies to report their financial guaranty business separately from surety.[8] Impatient with the NAIC process, several states, most notably New York, began the process of enacting legislation to regulate financial guaranty insurance as a separate line of business.

Since the 1980s, the financial guaranty insurance market has evolved into a complex and diverse business. Today, the primary financial guaranty insurance market consists of three main areas: (1) the municipal bond market; (2) the asset-backed market; and (3) the international market.[9] Insurance of municipal bond obligations comprises the largest portion of the financial guaranty insurance business. Municipal bond insurers lend their credit rating to bonds, notes, and other evidences of indebtedness issued by states and their political subdivisions, utility districts, public universities and hospitals, and other public entities. And while insurance provided to the municipal bond market has traditionally been the major source of revenue for the financial guaranty insurance industry, the market is saturated, spurring financial guaranty insurers to seek new markets.[10]

The first new market formed was the asset-backed market. Asset-backed transactions or securitizations are a form of structured financing that is secured by a specific pool of assets held by the issuing entity. These asset pools are typically comprised of mortgage-backed securities, home equity loans, credit card and auto loan receivables, or other assets.[11] This non-municipal financial guaranty insurance market is more diverse than the municipal bond insurance market and represents a significant growth opportunity for financial guaranty insurers.

Additionally, the international market represents another major growth opportunity.[12] Since 1971, the industry has evolved from purely municipal insurance to insurance for more complex financial instruments. The product mix of the industry has shifted from 100 percent municipal bonds in 1976 to 58 percent municipal bonds, 29 percent asset-backed securities, and 13 percent international bonds by 1996.[13] The financial guaranty insurance business is poised to expand dramatically.

II. The New York Insurance Law Was Amended in 1989 to Regulate "Financial Guaranty Insurance" Separately

The NAIC Model Act became the prototype for the financial guaranty insurance legislation enacted in the state of New York in 1989.[14] The New York Insurance Law was amended in 1989 to create Article 69 to regulate "financial guaranty insurance" as a separate

---

6. 1986 Proceedings of the NAIC II 12, 17, 206-07, 216-19, 219-27.

7. 1987 Proceedings of the NAIC I 11, 18, 161, 163-74.

8. See CONNING, supra note 2, at 46-47.

9. Robert D. Hogue, *Financial Perspectives and Overviews: The Changing Financial Guaranty Insurance Industry*, INSURANCE ADVOCATE, June 12, 1999, at 38.

10. *Id.* at 39.

11. *Id.*

12. *Id.* at 41.

13. CONNING, *supra* note 2, at 27.

14. Since 1970, municipal bond insurance had been regulated in New York under Regulation 61, which prescribed capital and reserve requirements and limitations on single risk and aggregate exposure. No other law addressed financial guaranty insurance other than Regulation 61, which was limited to municipal bonds.

type of insurance. The major effect of this legislation was to require any insurer issuing financial guaranty insurance to be a "financial guaranty insurance corporation." The new law provided that financial guaranty insurance could only be written (after a transition period) by monoline insurers. Thus, multiline insurers could not issue surety bonds if such bonds fell within the definition of financial guaranty insurance and outside the definition of delineated and permissible surety bonds.

With the passage of L.1989, chapter 48, Article 69, "Financial Guaranty Insurance Corporations," was added to the New York Insurance Law. An executive memorandum is instructive regarding the purpose of the legislation. The "Purpose" of the legislation was, in part:

> – To define "financial guaranty insurance" as a separate kind of insurance.
>
> – To authorize the formation and licensing of financial guaranty insurance corporations which would essentially be monoline insurers but would also be permitted to write surety, residual value and credit insurance.
>
> – To provide a transition period for multiline property/casualty insurers to convert to monoline insurers.
>
> – To specify the types of obligations for which financial guaranties may be written by a financial guaranty insurance corporation which would include municipal and corporate bonds.
>
> . . . .
>
> – To unlink fidelity insurance and surety insurance and treat them as separate kinds of insurance so as to permit a financial guaranty insurance corporation to write surety coverage but not fidelity, and *to redefine surety insurance by eliminating the kinds of transactions which become financial guaranty insurance subject to the provisions of new Article 69 (Financial Guaranty Insurance Corporations).*[15]

Thus, in 1989, a new kind of insurance, financial guaranty, was added to the New York Insurance Law; and multiline insurers were no longer permitted to write products that met the definition of "financial guaranty insurance." After the transition period, only monoline financial guaranty insurance corporations would be permitted to do so. The New York Insurance Law had been amended in order to regulate a line of business that with a single loss, the failure of a bond issue to meet its obligation, could result in a catastrophic loss causing the insolvency of the insurer. In section 1113(a)(25): "'Financial guaranty insurance,' means the

15. 2 McKinney's 1989 Session Laws of New York, *Memorandum of the State Executive Department*, at 2045-46 (McKinney 1990) (emphasis added).

kind of insurance defined in paragraph one of subsection (a) of section six thousand nine hundred one of this chapter."[16]

Article 69 of the New York Insurance Law governs Financial Guaranty Insurance Corporations, with section 6901 defining "financial guaranty insurance":

> (a)(1) "Financial guaranty insurance" means a surety bond, insurance policy or, when issued by an insurer or any person doing an insurance business as defined in paragraph one of subsection (b) of section one thousand one hundred one of this chapter, an indemnity contract, and any guaranty similar to the foregoing types, under which loss is payable, upon proof of occurrence of financial loss, to an insured claimant, obligee or indemnitee as a result of any of the following events:
>
> (A) failure of any obligor on or issuer of any debt instrument or other monetary obligation (including equity securities guarantied under a surety bond, insurance policy or indemnity contract) to pay when due to be paid by the obligor or scheduled at the time insured to be received by the holder of the obligation, principal, interest, premium, dividend or purchase price of or on, or other amounts due or payable with respect to, such instrument or obligation, when such failure is the result of a financial default or insolvency or, provided that such payment source is investment grade, any other failure to make payment, regardless of whether such obligation is incurred directly or as guarantor by or on behalf of another obligor that has also defaulted;
>
> (B) changes in the levels of interest rates, whether short or long term or the differential in interest rates between various markets or products;
>
> (C) changes in the rate of exchange of currency;
>
> (D) changes in the value of specific assets or commodities, financial or commodity indices, or price levels in general; or
>
> (E) other events which the superintendent determines are substantially similar to any of the foregoing.
>
> (2) Notwithstanding paragraph one of this subsection, "financial guaranty insurance" shall not include:
>
> . . . .

16. N.Y. INS. LAW § 1113(a)(25) (McKinney 1996).

> (B) fidelity and surety insurance as defined in paragraph sixteen of subsection (a) of section one thousand one hundred thirteen of this chapter; . . . .[17]

Section 6901(a)(1) lists the types of transactions that are specifically included in the definition of "financial guaranty insurance": (1) guaranty of indebtedness; (2) interest rate guaranty; (3) currency rate guaranty; (4) guaranty of financial or commodity indices; and (5) guaranty of other events determined by the superintendent to be "substantially similar to the foregoing."[18]

Section 6901(a)(2), however, excludes, fidelity and surety insurance as defined in section 1113(a)(16). Section 1113(a)(16) provides as follows:

> (16) "Fidelity and surety insurance," means:
>
> (A) Guaranteeing the fidelity of persons holding positions of public or private trust; and indemnifying banks, thrifts, brokers and other financial institutions against loss of money, securities, negotiable instruments, other specified valuable papers and tangible items of personal property caused by larceny, misplacement, destruction or other stated perils including loss while being transported in an armored motor vehicle or by messenger; and insurance for loss caused by the forgery of signatures on, or alteration of, specified document and valuable papers;
>
> (B) Insurance against losses that financial institutions become legally obligated to pay by reason of loss of customers' property from safe deposit boxes;
>
> (C) Any contract bond; including a bid, payment or maintenance bond or a performance bond where the bond is guaranteeing the execution of any contract other than a contract of indebtedness or other monetary obligation;
>
> (D) An indemnity bond for the benefit of a public body, railroad or charitable organization; a lost security or utility payment bond;
>
> (E) *Becoming surety on, or guaranteeing the performance of, any lawful contract*, not specifically provided for in this paragraph, *except* (i) mortgage guaranty insurance, which may only be written by an insurer authorized to write such insurance pursuant to article sixty-five of this chapter, (ii) *a contract that falls within the definition of financial guaranty insurance as set forth in paragraph one of subsection (a) of section six thousand nine hundred one of this chapter*, (iii) any insurance contract

17. N.Y. INS. LAW §§ 6901(a)(1) and (a)(2) (McKinney 1996).
18. 2 McKinney's 1989 Session Laws of New York, *Memorandum of the State Executive Department*, at 2048.

> unless such guaranty is authorized pursuant to subsection (c) of section one thousand one hundred fourteen of this article; or (iv) service contract reimbursement insurance as specified in paragraph twenty-eight of this subsection;
>
> (F) Becoming surety on, or guaranteeing the performance of, bonds and undertakings required or permitted in all judicial proceedings or otherwise by law allowed, including surety bonds accepted by states and municipal authorities in lieu of deposits as security for the performance of insurance contracts; and
>
> (G) Becoming surety on, or guaranteeing the performance of, a bond, which shall not exceed a period greater than five years, that guarantees the payment of a premium, deductible, or self-insured retention to an insurer issuing a workers' compensation or liability policy.[19]

Thus, subparagraph (E)(ii) of section 1113(a)(16) excludes from the definition of "surety insurance" a contract that falls within the definition of "financial guaranty insurance" in section 6901(a)(1).

To complicate matters further, pursuant to section 6902(a)(1)(B), a corporation organized to write financial guaranty insurance may also write certain other enumerated types of insurance, including surety insurance as defined in subparagraphs (C), (D), (E), and (F) of section 1113(a)(16).[20]

Simplified, as much as that might be possible, the statutory scheme for financial guaranty insurance provides as follows: section 6901, defining "financial guaranty insurance," excludes "fidelity and surety insurance" as defined in section 1113(a)(16); section 6902(a)(1)(B), however, provides that financial guaranty insurers are permitted to write surety insurance as defined in subparagraphs (C), (D), (E), and (F) only of section 1113(a)(16). On the other hand, surety insurers, pursuant to section 1113(a)(16)(E), are expressly precluded from writing a bond that falls within the definition of "financial guaranty insurance" as set forth in section 6901(a)(1). In sum, the statutes provide that monoline financial guaranty insurers are permitted to write many products defined as "surety," but multiline companies are generally precluded from writing financial guaranty insurance.

III. Whether a Product Is, Pursuant to New York Insurance Law, Surety Insurance or Financial Guaranty Insurance

19. N.Y. INS. LAW § 1113(a)(16) (McKinney Supp. 1999-2000) (emphasis added). Section 1113(a)(16) was amended in 1996, adding paragraph (G), to expand the definition of "surety insurance" to include cash-flow premium payment retro bonds.

20. When the definition of surety insurance was amended in 1996 to add subparagraph (G) to section 1113(a)(16), section 6902(a)(1)(B) was not similarly amended to include subparagraph (G) as a permissible type of surety insurance that a financial guaranty insurer could write.

The confusion created by this complex statutory scheme is reflected in informal legal opinions issued by the Office of General Counsel[21] of the New York Insurance Department.[22] Such confusion is particularly observed in the opinions expressed on whether a bank depository bond constitutes "fidelity and surety insurance" as authorized under section 1113(a)(16) or "financial guaranty insurance" pursuant to section 6901(a).

In a New York OGC, dated August 11, 1994, the General Counsel opined that bank depository bonds issued to satisfy the requirements of section 135.18 of the Ohio Revised Code fell within the ambit of section 1113(16)(F) and, therefore, were not subject to the section 6901(a) prohibition.[23] The OGC concluded that such bonds constitute "surety insurance" and not "financial guaranty insurance." It is worth noting that in an earlier opinion, dated June 1, 1990, the OGC had determined that a bank depository bond "fits squarely within the definition of a financial guaranty" as defined in section 6901(a)(1) and could not, therefore, fall within one of the exceptions listed in section 6901(a)(2)(B).[24]

In its 1994 opinion, however, the OGC retreated from that determination and concluded that a particular bank depository bond did indeed fall within the 6901(a)(2) exclusion pursuant to section 1113(a)(16)(F). The OGC observed that its earlier opinion was overbroad:

> [W]e have in the past opined that to the extent that a product comes within the definitions of both surety and financial guaranty insurance, it was the intent of the legislation to require that the product be considered financial guaranty insurance. *However, we now conclude that such a reading of the exclusion in [section 1113(a)(16)(E)] is overbroad.* Since the exclusion for financial guaranty insurance is contained only in subparagraph (E), it ought not be interpreted to apply to products written under subparagraphs (C), (D), or (F). . . . To the extent that a product overlaps subparagraph (E) and Section 6901(a)(1), it must be treated as financial guaranty insurance. *However, if the product comes within one of the other subparagraphs of paragraph (16), then the Section 6901(a)(2)(B) exclusion takes it out of financial guaranty insurance and places it squarely under surety insurance, even though it would otherwise come within the meaning of Section 6901(a)(1).*[25]

The OGC concluded that a multiline insurer would be permitted to issue a bond that met the definition of "financial guaranty insurance" pursuant to section 6901(a)(1) if that bond also met the definition of "surety insurance" pursuant to subparagraphs (C), (D), or (F) of section 1113(a)(16).

21. Hereinafter OGC.

22. While such opinions are informal and advisory in nature and are not binding on the courts or hearing officers in any administrative proceeding before the Insurance Department, such opinions should be noted with care. In the absence of case law on this issue, the OGC opinions provide some general guidance in interpreting the statutory provisions.

23. N.Y. OGC Opinion, Aug. 11, 1994.

24. N.Y. OGC Opinion, June 1, 1990. In this opinion the OGC noted that, prior to passage of the financial guaranty legislation, a bank depository bond would have been authorized as fidelity and surety insurance.

25. N.Y. OGC Opinion, Aug. 11, 1994 (emphasis added).

The facts as stated in the opinion were that a multiline property/casualty insurer wanted to issue a bank depository bond to guarantee public deposits made by a municipality in a bank. The bond would be issued pursuant to an Ohio statute that required security for repayment of public deposits made with the bank in excess of amounts insured by the Federal Deposit Insurance Corporation. The Ohio law did not require a bond, but it expressly allowed a bond as an alternative to satisfying the security requirement.

The multiline insurer argued, and the OGC agreed, that this bank depository bond, allowed by law to satisfy a security requirement, can be issued pursuant to section 1113(a)(16)(F). The salient language in section 1113(a)(16)(F) was "or otherwise by law allowed," interpreted as bonds that are allowed to satisfy a statutory security requirement, as the Ohio law permitted bonds as an alternative security. Without this statutory security requirement, the bond would have been deemed financial guaranty insurance under the exclusion in section 1113(a)(16)(E). In order to meet this requirement, "the bond must provide a benefit to the public that has been identified by an appropriate legislative body as being necessary for the public good."[26]

The OGC declined to "address at this time a law that expressly permits a bond as security for a purely private obligation, not affecting the public interest."[27] The inference, however, is that, to the extent that a bond promotes a private interest rather than the public good, it will not fall under the section 1113(a)(16)(F) definition of "surety insurance."

IV. The "Appleton Rule" Prohibits a Foreign or Alien Multiline Insurer Licensed in New York from Writing Financial Guaranty Insurance in New York or in Any Other State

A foreign (or an alien) insurer, licensed to do business in New York, is included in the New York prohibition against multiline insurers issuing those products that fall within the definition of financial guaranty insurance. Under New York insurance law, a "foreign insurer" is defined as "any insurer incorporated or organized under the laws of any state . . . other than this state."[28] A "foreign insurer" is subject to the provisions of section 1106(f), the so-called "Appleton Rule,"[29] which provides as follows:

> *No foreign insurer* and no United States branch of an alien insurer *which does outside of this state* any kind of combination of kinds of insurance business not permitted to be done in this state by similar domestic insurers hereafter organized, shall be or continue to be authorized to do an insurance business in this state, unless in the judgment of the superintendent the doing of such kind or combination of kinds of insurance business will not be prejudicial to the best interest of the people of this state.[30]

26. *Id.*
27. *Id.*
28. N.Y. INS. LAW § 107(a)(21) (McKinney 1985).
29. The Appleton Rule was named for the deputy superintendent of the New York Department of Insurance who formulated the ruling. The rule, which was adopted originally in the early 1900s as an administrative regulation, was enacted as part of the New York Insurance Law in 1939.
30. N.Y. INS. LAW § 1106(f) (McKinney 1985) (emphasis added).

This law provides that no foreign or alien insurer may be licensed by New York to write a type of insurance in New York, **or in any other state**, that is not permitted a domestic New York company.

The effect of this extraterritorial law is that a foreign company that might otherwise be permitted to write a product that falls within the definition of "financial guaranty insurance" under the New York statute is precluded from writing such a product anywhere, if it wants to be licensed in New York. There is strong incentive to accept the limitations of the rule because of the size of the potential premium volume in New York. Accordingly, pursuant to section 1106, a foreign multiline insurer is prohibited from writing financial guaranty insurance anywhere in the United States or in other countries; and it would stand to lose its license to do business in New York were it to write a product that fell under the New York definition of "financial guaranty insurance."[31]

V. Financial Guaranty Insurance Statutes Have Been Enacted in Several Other States

Sweeping legislation regulating the financial guaranty insurance industry has been enacted in only a few states. In addition to New York, the most notable legislation is in California,[32] Connecticut,[33] and Florida.[34] While there are similarities between the financial guaranty insurance statutes in New York and the other states, they are not identical; and insurers should not only consult the applicable law in New York but also those in other relevant jurisdictions.

VI. *Conclusion*

The insurance industry, including financial guaranty insurers and surety insurers, seeks to develop innovative new products. The intense competition in both industries generates new challenges and a quest for new growth opportunities. The passage of the Financial Services Modernization Act in 1999[35] reflects the rapid evolution of the financial services industry. The purpose of this sweeping legislation is to modernize the laws governing the insurance, banking, and securities industries, thereby bringing keener competition to the marketplace and enhancing the international competitiveness of the U.S. financial services community. How this legislation will impact financial guaranty insurers and surety insurers can be predicted, at this point, only with an educated guess. And what is the bright line between financial guaranty insurance and a financial guarantee bond? There are simply no generally accepted definitions that clarify the distinction. But, for certain, a thorough understanding of a specific jurisdiction's statutes, regulations, case law, and attorneys general opinions, if any, is essential in order to make informed, judicious decisions.

31. No case law or OGC opinion exists on this issue.
32. CAL. INS. CODE §§ 12100 TO 12122 (West 1994).
33. CONN. GEN. STAT. ANN. §§ 38a-92a to 38a-92n (West 1995).
34. FLA. STAT. ANN. §§ 627.971 to 627.975 (West 1995).
35. Pub. L. No. 106-102, 113 Stat. 1338 (1999). This law is also known as the Gramm-Leach-Bliley Act.

19

Medicare and Medicaid Bonds

Edward G. Gallagher

Health care expenditures consume a large and growing portion of the federal budget. In the Balanced Budget Act of 1997, Congress enacted a series of reforms designed to control the growth of Medicare and Medicaid spending. One area of concern was fraud and abuse, and one of the reforms was a requirement that providers of home health care, rehabilitation services and durable medical equipment furnish a bond as a condition of participation in Medicare or Medicaid programs.

In 1997 the Home Health Care benefit alone cost the federal government $17.8 billion. In 1996, approximately 6% of payments to Home Health Agencies (HHAs) were "overpayments" and approximately 1% of total payments were never recovered.[1]

The Balanced Budget Act left virtually everything about the bonds up to the Secretary of the Department of Health and Human Services (HHS) with two exceptions. The statute specified that the minimum amount of the bonds was to be $50,000 and that the bonding requirement would take effect on January 1, 1998. The HHS Health Care Financing Administration (HCFA) was charged with drafting regulations to define the rest of the bonding requirements.

On January 5, 1998, the Government published regulations[2] for the HHA bonding requirement. Separate bonds were required for Medicare and Medicaid in the amount of 15% of the prior year's program revenues but with a minimum of $50,000. The bonds were to guarantee the repayment of any overpayments made during the term of the bond as well as any civil money penalties or assessments arising out of such overpayments. The bond was not limited to overpayments resulting form fraud or abuse by the HHA.

There was no deadline for a claim to be made on the bonds, and the method by which HCFA pays and audits HHAs virtually guaranteed that any claims would be made years after the bond expired. This long, in fact at least theoretically unlimited, liability tail made the bonds an unattractive proposition for the surety and for the HHA, or the owners of the HHA who would very likely have to personally indemnify the surety for any losses on the bond or post collateral to secure the bond. The surety would have no way to know whether it had losses on a bond for one year before it was asked to write another bond for the next year. The surety's exposure if the HHA had overpayments could be several years of bond penalties before the first claim was made.

On June 1, 1998, HCFA published revised regulations[3] for the HHA bonds which addressed some of the problems with the January 5 regulations. The bond amount remained 15% of prior year's billings with a minimum amount of $50,000, but the condition of the bond was changed to payment of overpayments, civil money penalties and assessments discovered during the bond period

1. General Accounting Office, "*Medicare Home Health Agencies: Role of Surety Bonds in Increasing Scrutiny and Reducing Overpayments*" (B-280717, January 29, 1999), at page 3.

2. 63 Fed. Reg. 292.

3. 63 Fed. Reg. 29648. An interim notice of intent to amend the January 5 regulations had been published at 63 Fed. Reg. 10730 and 10732 on March 4, 1998.

and claimed against the surety during the bond period or within 3 months after the bond terminated. The new regulations also permitted a single continuous bond rather than a series of annual bonds. If the HHA provided a new bond, the liability of the old bond was at an end except for claims already made. The trigger for bond liability was changed from when the overpayments were made to when they were discovered. The surety could effectively limit its exposure to losses caused by an HHA to one bond penalty, and there was no longer a tail of potential liability after the termination of the bond. The June 1 regulations gave HHAs until July 31, 1998, to file the Medicare bonds (the date for filing the Medicaid bonds was to be set by each state but not later than September 29, 1998) but required that the bond terms start on January 1, 1998.

Some members of Congress believed that the bond regulations placed an excessively onerous burden on HHAs. Congress pressured HCFA to extend the filing deadline of July 31 even though approximately 40% of HHAs had already secured bonds. HCFA agreed to an extension until after the General Accounting Office ("GAO") reviewed the bond requirement and reported to Congress.

The GAO Report[4] was issued on January 29, 1999, and reaffirmed the value of a surety bond requirement in reducing fraud and abuse. GAO believed that HCFA made a "prudent choice in specifying the surety bond as a financial guarantee"[5] against overpayments as opposed to an anti-fraud bond. It recommended, however, that the bond amount be a flat $50,000 for all providers and that a single bond satisfy the Medicare and Medicaid requirements.[6] GAO believed that the scrutiny of the surety, and consequent exclusion of providers likely to defraud the program, could be achieved with the lower bond amount and that HCFA had not documented the need for a 15% bond in light of the fact that unrecovered overpayments were only 1% of annual expenditures. GAO also recommended that Congress consider exempting HHAs that had demonstrated fiscal responsibility such as those which had maintained a bond for a specified period and successfully returned any overpayments.

Following publication of the GAO Report, HCFA started work on new regulations for HHAs and for the other two categories of providers covered by the BBA bond requirement, suppliers of Durable Medical Equipment ("DMEs") and Rehabilitation agencies ("CORFs"). It was generally thought that HCFA intended to issue very similar regulations for the three categories with a flat $50,000 bond covering return of overpayments and civil money penalties and assessments. The condition of the bonds were expected to be very similar to the June 1, 1998, HHA regulations with the surety's exposure limited to claims asserted during the bond term or within a very short period thereafter.

Before HCFA published proposed regulations, however, Congress changed the bond requirements for HHAs only. As part of the Consolidated Appropriations Act[7], Congress amended the BBA requirement to provide that HHAs need provide a bond for only four years, that a single bond would satisfy both the Medicare and Medicaid requirement, and that the amount of the bond would be the lesser of $50,000 or 10% of the HHA's anticipated combined revenues from Medicare and Medicaid.

---

4. Footnote 2., *supra*.

5. *Id.*, page 21.

6. HCFA had issued instructions to the same affect allowing "small" HHAs to provide a single bond. The size threshold for this partial dispensation was to be $334,000 of annual program revenues.

7. P.L. 106-113 signed by the President on November 29, 1999.

Although this amendment applied only to HHAs, it delayed HCFA's issuance of proposed regulations for all three categories of providers. As this Chapter is written in January, 2000, HCFA has not published regulations for any of the three types of providers.

The best estimate of the date by which bonds will actually have to be filed is October 1, 2000. For DMEs and CORFs, the original BBA requirement of $50,000 still applies, and in the absence of further legislation the regulations will presumably require all such entities to file a $50,000 bond. HHAs presumably will be required to provide a bond in the amount of 10% of their Medicare and Medicaid revenues but not more than $50,000.

There is no reason to expect HCFA to abandon its desire for a bond to guarantee the return of overpayments (as opposed to payment of damages from fraud and abuse) or to vary the approach of the June 1, 1998, regulations requiring that the bond cover overpayments, civil money penalties and assessments claimed during the bond period. It is unclear how HCFA will rationalize a statute (the BBA) requiring bonds by January 1, 1998, with a regulation requiring that the bonds be filed almost three years later.

Conclusion

A surety bond requirement can be a very effective weapon in fighting fraud and abuse in government entitlements programs. A bond requirement provides a solvent guarantor, but more importantly, it helps exclude providers who will abuse the system.

20

Bankruptcy and the Surety

Chad L. Schexnayder

Introduction

When the surety receives voluminous payment claims or a notice of default, the spectre of bankruptcy is already present. A financially troubled principal is a likely candidate for a bankruptcy filing. Accordingly, the impact of bankruptcy law on the rights of the surety should be factored into all of the surety's decisions, both before and after any bankruptcy petition is filed.

The problem is that bankruptcy law is not a user-friendly body of law. Sitting down to read the Bankruptcy Code is more likely to induce slumber than to reveal the path to enlightenment. The purpose of this Chapter is to extract and focus on some of the more significant bankruptcy principles to a surety.

Several fundamental bankruptcy law concepts are introduced and discussed. This chapter will look at the effect of bankruptcy stays on claims against the payment bond and on the surety's claim for indemnification. Tolling of notice periods and statutes of limitations is discussed. This chapter will then address the payment bond surety's claims to a priority to bonded contract funds in the bankruptcy court and the actions the surety may take to protect that priority. The impact of the principal's bankruptcy filing on the surety's efforts to complete the bonded work is reviewed, followed by the impact of bankruptcy on the surety's ability to finance the completion of the bonded work by the principal.

Subsequently, the chapter reviews the potential liability of bond claimants and the surety to the debtor for preferential payments received prior to the bankruptcy, as well as defenses to preference claims. Finally, the chapter looks at the rights of the surety when the principal blindly pursues its own improbable agenda of reorganization, to the detriment of the surety's interests.

I. *Key Bankruptcy Concepts*

A. PROPERTY OF THE ESTATE

Upon the filing of a bankruptcy petition, an "estate" is created consisting of all property and property interests of the principal/debtor. All of the "property of the estate" becomes a part of the bankruptcy case, and subject to restrictions and protections imposed by bankruptcy law. 11 U.S.C. § 541 defines "property of the estate." Section 541[1] is so broad as to include within its scope almost

1. Unless otherwise indicated, all citations to "section ___," "§___," or "Code § ___" are to Title 11 of the United States Code, as amended, popularly known as the "Bankruptcy Code."

every conceivable interest of the debtor in property.[2] The statute's legislative history supports a broad interpretation of its scope.[3] Thus, the "estate" will ordinarily include all of the principal/debtor's property of any interest to the surety, such as subcontracts, equipment, contract proceeds, and claims against the project owners.

B. THE AUTOMATIC STAY

11 U.S.C. § 362(a) is the "automatic stay" provision of the Bankruptcy Code. Upon the filing of a petition under the Bankruptcy Code, this section imposes a stay, applicable to all entities, against virtually all collection activities or other acts that would improve a creditor's position against the debtor or the debtor's property. Section 362(a) lists acts that violate the automatic stay:

> (1) commencement or continuation of any legal proceedings against the debtor to enforce the surety's indemnification rights under the indemnity agreement [§ 362(a)(1)];
> (2) enforcement against the debtor or any property of the estate of a judgment for reimbursement and indemnification obtained before the commencement of the debtor's case [§ 362(a)(2)];
> (3) any act to obtain possession of or to exercise control over property of the debtor's estate [§ 362(a)(3)];
> (4) any act to create, perfect, or enforce any lien against property of the estate [§ 362(a)(4)];
> (5) any act to create, perfect, or enforce any lien against property of the estate to the extent such lien secures a claim that arose before the commencement of debtor's case [§ 362(a)(5)];
> (6) any act to collect, assess, or recover a claim against the debtor that arose before the commencement of the debtor's case [§ 362(a)(6)];
> (7) any act to setoff any debt under § 553 [§ 362(a)(7)].[4]

---

2. (a) The commencement of a case under section 301, 302, or 303 of this title creates an estate. Such estate is comprised of all the following property, wherever located and by whomever held:

> (1) Except as provided in subsections (b) and (c)(2) of this section, all legal or equitable interests of the debtor in property as of the commencement of the case.
> (2) All interests of the debtor and the debtor's spouse in community property . . .
> (3) Any interest in property that the trustee recovers under section 329(b), 363(n), 543, 550, 553, or 723 of this title.
> (4) Any interest in property preserved for the benefit of or order transferred to the estate under section 510(c) or 551 of this title.
> (5) Any interest in property that would have been property of the estate if such interest had been an interest of the debtor on the date of the filing of the petition, and that the debtor acquires or becomes entitled to acquire within 180 days after such date
>> (A) by bequest, devise, or inheritance;
>> (B) as a result of a property settlement agreement with debtor's spouse, or of an interlocutory or final divorce decree; or
>> (C) as a beneficiary of a life insurance policy or of a death benefit plan.
>
> (6) Proceeds, product, offspring, rents, or profits of or from property of the estate, except such as are earnings from services performed by an individual debtor after the commencement of the case.
> (7) Any interest in property that the estate acquires after the commencement of the case.

11 U.S.C.A. § 541(a) (1993 & Supp. 1998).

3. H.R. Rep. No. 95-595, 95th Cong., 1st Sess. 367-8 (1977); S. Rep. No. 95-989, 95th Cong. 2d Sess. 82-3 (1978).

4. Except as provided in subsection (b) of this section, a petition filed under section 301, 302, or 303 of this title, or an application filed under section 5(a)(3) of the Securities Investor Protection Act of 1970 (15 U.S.C. 78(a)(3)), operates as a stay, applicable to all entities, of -

The surety will find that most of the actions that it contemplates taking are likely to violate the stay, such as accepting voluntary letters of default from the principal, taking possession of the principal's projects, accepting payment of the bonded contract proceeds from the obligee, taking collateral, or enforcing an assignment of rights from the principal.

1. The Need for Information - Bankruptcy Rule 2004 Examination

In the early days and weeks of any bond default, the need for information is critical to the surety. The initial information concerning bonded contract status, unpaid suppliers and subcontractors, job progress, etc. is normally obtained from the principal. However, when a principal files bankruptcy with little or no advance warning to the surety, it may be difficult to obtain that information, notwithstanding the surety's contractual right to the records.[5] Without such information, the surety cannot make proper strategic decisions.

A principal that has just filed bankruptcy is faced with a myriad of conflicting demands and administrative obligations.[6] Faced with these burdens and deadlines, it is not unusual for the debtor to view the surety's information demands as being of secondary importance. This is particularly true if the principal views the surety as an adversary who wishes to "steal" the bonded projects.

Because of the automatic stay, the surety cannot simply demand and seize information from the principal. Fortunately, the Federal Rules of Bankruptcy Procedure provide an avenue of relief to the surety under these circumstances. Federal Rule of Bankruptcy Procedure, Rule 2004 authorizes an examination, not unlike a deposition, where the principal or its agents may be compelled to appear, produce and explain documentation.[7] One advantage of this Rule is that it does

---

(1) the commencement or continuation, including the issuance or employment of process, of a judicial, administrative, or other action or proceeding against the debtor that was or could have been commenced before the commencement of the case under this title, or to recover a claim against the debtor that arose before the commencement of the case under this title;

(2) the enforcement, against the debtor or against property of the estate, of a judgment obtained before the commencement of a case under this title;

(3) any act to obtain possession of property of the estate or of property from the estate, or to exercise control over property of the estate;

(4) any act to create, perfect, or enforce any lien against property of the estate;

(5) any act to create, perfect, or enforce against property of the debtor any lien to the extent that such lien secures a claim that arose before the commencement of the case under this title;

(6) any act to collect, assess, or recover a claim against the debtor that arose before the commencement of the case under this title;

(7) the setoff of any debt owing to the debtor that arose before the commencement of the case under this title against any claim against the debtor; and

(8) the commencement or continuation of a proceeding before the United States Tax Court concerning the debtor. 11 U.S.C. § 362(a).

5. "At any time and until such time as the liability of the Surety under any and all bonds or undertakings executed for or on the application of the undersigned is terminated, the Surety shall have the right to free access to the books, records and accounts of the undersigned. . . ." *Indemnity Agreement Update*, 52 Ins. Counsel J. 118, 144.

6. These bankruptcy obligations may include the preparation and filing of extensive schedules of assets and liabilities, a statement of financial affairs, interim operating reports, assembling documentation required by the United States Trustee's office, and preparation for the first meeting of creditors, to name a few.

7. Federal Rule of Bankruptcy Procedure 2004 provides:

> (a) Examination on Motion. On motion of any party in interest, the court may order the examination of any entity.
>
> (b) Scope of Examination. The examination of an entity under this Rule . . . may relate to the acts, conduct, or property or to the liabilities and financial condition of the debtor, or to any manner which

not require the surety to commence litigation against the principal before it may be used. The Rule does not incorporate an extended waiting period before the inspection is allowed or the documents must be produced, unlike ordinary discovery procedures under the Federal Rules of Civil Procedure.

Rule 2004 requires only that a motion or application be filed by the surety with the Bankruptcy Court, requesting the issuance of an order for examination. Pursuant to the advisory committee note to the Rule, it is contemplated that the motion may be heard ex parte and granted as a matter of course. In most districts, this is the practice, although local district rules should be consulted and observed in the filing of such a motion.

The scope of the Rule 2004 examination is very broad, as the language of the Rule would suggest.[8] Thus, the surety can use this rule to examine the debtor with respect to many aspects of bonded job performance, subrogation issues, and other particular matters of interest to the surety.

Attention should be given to the identification of the individual to be examined. Where a specific key project manager or principal of the debtor is known to possess the knowledge needed by the surety, that individual can be designated. However, the Rule 2004 procedure may be combined with the provisions of Federal Rule of Civil Procedure 30(b)(6), allowing the surety to impose upon the debtor/principal the duty to designate a spokesperson(s) with knowledge of the identified subject matters.[9] Thus, the surety need only identify the project or records on which testimony will be required, shifting to the principal the duty to produce knowledgeable individuals.

The order of the Court under Rule 2004 is sufficient to compel the attendance of the debtor at the examination. No subpoena is required.[10] If the debtor does not appear in response to the court's order, Federal Rule of Bankruptcy Procedure, Rule 2005 provides an additional procedure whereby an order to apprehend the debtor and bring the debtor before the court can be obtained.

2. Notice of Default/Termination of Bonded Contracts

When the performance bond surety receives a notice from the obligee or is contacted for assistance by the principal, the principal is likely to be in default in the performance of the bonded contract work. However, many contracts require a formal notice procedure with a cure period (a condition found in American Institute of Architects (AIA), Association of General Contractors (AGC) and many pre-printed form documents). It is not uncommon that such notice and opportunity to cure time periods have not expired prior to the principal's bankruptcy filing.

> may effect the administration of the debtor's estate, or to the debtor's right to a discharge. In . . . a reorganization case under Chapter 11 of the Code, . . . the examination may also relate to the operation of any business and the desirability of its continuance, the source of any money or property acquired or to be acquired by the debtor for purposes of consummating a plan and the consideration given or offered therefore, and any other matter relevant to the case or to the formulation of a plan.
>
> (c) Compelling Attendance and Production of Documentary Evidence. The attendance of an entity for examination and the production of documentary evidence may be compelled in the manner provided in Rule 9016 for the attendance of witnesses at a hearing or trial.
>
> (d) Time and Place of Examination of Debtor. The court may for cause shown and on terms as it may impose order the debtor to be examined under this Rule at any time or place it designates, whether within or without the district wherein the case is pending.

8. Courts have stated the scope of the Rule 2004 examination to be "so all encompassing as semantically to include and encourage harassment on every human subject." *In re Georgetown of Kettering,* 17 Bankr. 73, 75 (Bankr. S.D.Ohio 1981).

9. *In re Analytical Systems, Inc.*, 71 Bankr. 408 (Bankr. N.D.Ga. 1987).

10. *In re Fulton*, 52 Bankr. 627, 631 (Bankr. D.Utah 1985); Advisory Committee Note to Fed. R. Bankr. P. 2004.

The Bankruptcy Code recognizes the interest of a party to a contract to be property of the estate, protected by the automatic stay. Upon the filing of bankruptcy by the principal, the section 362 automatic stay precludes any act or notice to terminate the contract by the owner or surety. The Code thus requires that the surety file for stay relief before attempting to take over or re-let any uncompleted project not yet formally rejected by the principal.[11] Stay relief is required, no matter how hopeless the debtor's financial condition may be and no matter how improbable the debtor's ability to assume and complete the contract may be.[12]

Stay relief must be obtained before the obligee terminates the debtor/principal or the surety takes over the debtor/principal's work, even if the principal voluntarily concedes the default or abandons the project. Even where the affected parties all agree not to rely upon or invoke the provisions of the automatic stay, the court can insist that the Code requirements relative to the stay be met.[13] Consensual agreements between parties concerning the application of the automatic stay are permitted under the Bankruptcy Code, but only pursuant to the applicable rules and procedures and only as specifically authorized by court order after appropriate notice and opportunity for hearing.[14] Actions taken without observance of the procedures can be held "invalid, void and of no force and effect."[15] Thus, even the obliging principal who abandons the job the day after the petition is filed and acquiesces in the re-letting of the contract work should be required to execute a stipulation for stay relief and the same should be presented to the court immediately for approval. The Rules allow normal notice periods to be shortened under appropriate circumstances.

3. The Automatic Stay - Will It Stay a Lawsuit by a Claimant Against the Payment Bond?

Will the principal's bankruptcy stay a claimant from proceeding against the payment bond surety, or put another way, does a claimant need relief from the automatic stay to pursue its payment bond claim?

The automatic stay prohibits an unpaid subcontractor or supplier from filing suit against the contractor/principal. 11 U.S.C. § 362 (a)(3). However, the automatic stay will not ordinarily protect co-defendants in a payment bond collection suit, such as a surety or guarantor.[16]

The automatic stay not only protects the debtor, but also any property in which the debtor has any interest. If the debtor's payment bond is "property of the estate," then Section 362 (a)(3) will stay a claimant's suit against the payment bond surety.

---

11. 11 U.S.C.A. §§ 362, 541 (1979 & Supp. 1989). *In re Computer Communications, Inc.*, 824 F.2d 725, 728 (9th Cir. 1987); *In re Edwards Mobile Home Sales, Inc.*, 119 Bankr. 857, 860 (Bankr. M.D. Fla. 1990).

12. *In re Edwards Mobile Home Sales, Inc.*, 119 Bankr. 857, 860 (Bankr. M.D. Fla. 1990) (although surety bond was not assumable by the debtor under the provisions of 11 U.S.C. § 365(c)(2), relief from the automatic stay must still be sought to terminate.)

13. *In re Randall Enters., Inc.*, 115 Bankr. 292 (Bankr. D. Colo. 1990).

14. *Id.* at 295.

15. *Id. See also*, Colliers On Bankruptcy, ¶ 362.11[1], p. 362-115 (15th ed. rev.)

16. Collier on Bankruptcy (15th ed. Rev.) Vol. 3, ¶362.03 [3][d], p. 362-17; *Lynch v. Johns-Manville Sales Corp.*, 710 F.2d 1194, 1196-97 (6th Cir. 1983); *Wedgeworth v. Fibreboard Corp.*, 706 F.2d 541, 544 (5th Cir. 1983); *Pitts v. Unarco Industries, Inc.*, 698 F.2d 313, 314 (7th Cir. 1983) (per curiam); *In re Casgul of Nevada, Inc.*, 22 B.R. 65, 66 (Bankr. 9th Cir. 1982).

A number of reported decisions hold that surety bonds are not "property of the estate."[17] The courts typically recognize that a bond is not for the benefit of the principal/contractor/debtor, and that the principal has no right to recover on the bond.[18] For these reasons, the debtor has no property interest in the bond.[19]

Thus, if the automatic stay does not protect third parties, and if the payment bond is not property of the contractor's bankruptcy estate, the principal/contractor's bankruptcy should have no effect on the claimant's lawsuit against the surety. However, under certain circumstances, the principal or surety may seek and obtain a stay of the lawsuit against a payment bond.

a. *Expansion of the Automatic Stay*. The surety or the bankrupt contractor may argue that the automatic stay under 11 U.S.C. § 362 should be expanded under the general authority of *A.H. Robbins Co., Inc. v. Piccinin*[20] to protect the bond. In that decision, the 4th Circuit recognized that under unusual circumstances, the automatic stay may be expanded to protect non-debtor co-defendants. However, attempts to obtain a stay of actions against the bond or the surety pursuant to this specific rationale have been largely unsuccessful.[21]

In *U.S. For the Use and Benefit of Central Bldg. Supply, Inc. v. William F. Wilke, Inc.*,[22] the surety moved for a temporary stay of a claim against the payment bond. The court declined to expand the scope of the automatic stay under Section 362. However, the court did exercise its general equitable powers under Section 105 of the Bankruptcy Code[23] to stay the payment bond suit.[24]

b. *Stay Pursuant to the Bankruptcy Court's Equitable Powers*. The argument that a Section 105 injunction may be used to protect a surety or a bond has now been approved by the Supreme Court of the United States.[25] The Court affirmed that the jurisdiction of the bankruptcy courts[26] gives Section 105 the breadth necessary to create an enforceable injunction protecting the bond from creditors. However, the *Celotex* Court did not specifically review the correctness of the injunction issued by the bankruptcy court under the factual situation presented by that case.

Thus, it is clear that bankruptcy courts possess the power to enjoin actions against a surety bond. However, the courts do not often have the willingness to provide such protection to the surety.

---

17. *In re Lockard* 884 F.2d 1171, 1177 (9th Cir. 1989) (and the cases cited therein at page 1177); *McLean Trucking Company v. Department of Industrial Relations,* 74 B.R. 820, 826-28 (Bankr. W.D. N.C. 1987); *In re Capitol York Constr. Corp.*, 43 B.R. 52, 56 (Bankr. S.D.N.Y. 1984) (payment bond); *In re Jay Forni*, 33 B.R. 538, 541 (Bankr. N.D. Cal. 1983) (payment bond); *In re Buna Painting & Drywall Co., Inc.*, 503 F.2d 618 (9th Cir. 1974); *In re Apache Constr., Inc.*, 34 B.R. 415 (Bankr. D. Or. 1983); *In re Fintel*, 10 B.R. 50 (Bankr. D. Or. 1981).

18. Collier on Bankruptcy (15th ed. Rev.) Vol. 3, ¶362.03 [5][b] (distinguishing an insurance policy, which is generally held to be property of the estate, from claims against a guarantor or surety, which would not be stayed.)

19. Interestingly, bankruptcy courts have also held surety bonds to be "property of the estate." *See, e.g., In re Wegner Farms Co.*, 49 B.R. 440 (Bankr. N.D. Iowa 1985). Where a surety has attempted to cancel its bond when the principal was in bankruptcy, courts have held such a cancellation to be ineffective, because the bond is property of the estate and therefore protected by the provisions of the automatic stay. However, where the payment bond is sought to be protected by the stay, the courts reach exactly the opposite result, as the cases in note 17 demonstrate.

20. 788 F.2d 994 (4th Cir.). *cert denied* 479 U.S. 876, 107 S.Ct. 251, 93 L.Ed.2d 177 (1986).

21. *See infra* note 27. In a rare case, the court adopted an admittedly minority position to expand the automatic stay to delay a performance bond suit against the surety. *Trimec Inc. v. Zale Corp.*, 150 B.R. 685 (N.D. Ill. 1993).

22. 685 F. Supp. 936 (D. Md. 1988).

23. 11 U.S.C.A. § 105 (1993 & Supp. 1997).

24. 685 F. Supp. 936, 939 (D. Md. 1988).

25. *Celotex Corp. v. Edwards*, 514 U.S. 300, 115 S.Ct. 1493, 131 L.Ed.2d 403 (1995).

26. 11 U.S.C. § 1334 (b) and 157 (a) are the applicable jurisdictional statutes. *Celotex* overrules case law holding that a bankruptcy court is without jurisdiction to enjoin a suit against the surety on its bonds. *Globe Const. Co. v. Oklahoma City Housing*, 571 F.2d 1140 (10th Cir. 1978) (and cases cited therein on page 1143).

Arguments for stay of actions against a bond under the Section 362 "expanded automatic stay," or the Court's Section 105 injunctive powers, generally fail.[27] Bankruptcy Courts will analyze the request for a stay of suits against the bond under the standards for issuance of a temporary restraining order.[28]

Four elements have been derived from Rule 65, Federal Rules of Civil Procedure, as grounds for extending protection to third-party non-debtors under Section 105. These elements are:

1) Substantial likelihood that the movant will eventually prevail on the merits;
2) Irreparable harm to the bankruptcy estate if the injunction does not issue;
3) Proof that the threatened injury to the movant outweighs whatever damage the proposed injunction may cause the creditor; and
4) A showing that the injunction would not be adverse to the public interest.[29]

Some courts may be persuaded by a strong showing of the hardship to the surety that will be caused by the unavailability of the debtor's personnel to support and develop factually complex defenses. A court may be moved by the argument that the surety's secured indemnification claim will deprive the debtor of property essential to its reorganization. The choice of arguments in support of a stay will vary substantially on a case by case basis. "Rote" arguments, that would be available in every similar case, are the least likely to be persuasive.

Thus, case authority exists to support a request to enjoin the bond claimant's action against the surety. However, such a request is infrequently granted, and only upon a showing of injunction standards of substantial likelihood of success on the merits, irreparable harm to the movant, balancing of hardships, and the lack of adverse effect on the public interest.

4. The Automatic Stay - Will It Stay The Surety's Indemnity Claims Against Non-Debtor Indemnitors?

Often, the surety has obtained from its principal and selected third parties (parent corporations, key stockholders, general partners, etc.) an agreement that they will indemnify the surety for any losses suffered on bonds written for the principal. When losses are incurred, the surety will demand that these "indemnitors" reimburse the surety. The principal who has filed for bankruptcy protection will be insulated from the surety's demands by the automatic stay. The effect of the automatic stay upon a surety's action against indemnitors other than the principal/debtor is subject to the same legal analysis applicable to a stay of actions against the surety, discussed above.

---

27. *In re Duplitronics, Inc.*, 183 B.R. 1010 (Bankr. N.D. Ill. 1995). The judgment debtor sought to prevent payment by its supersedeas bond surety after the judgment had been affirmed on appeal. The Court rejected the request made pursuant to Section 105. *Accord, In re Keene Corp.*, 162 B.R. 935 (Bankr. S.D.N.Y. 1994). *In re Lockard*, 884 F.2d 1171, 1179; *In re Kora & Williams Corp.*, 97 B.R. 258 (Bankr. D. Md. 1988) (11 U.S.C. § 362(A)(1) and (3) stay extension rejected at page 259; §105 injunction request rejected at page 261); *McLean Trucking* Co., 74 B.R. 820, 829; *In re S. & M. Constructors, Inc.*, 144 B.R. 855, 862 (Bankr. W.D. Mo. 1992) (See note 6 at page 863 of the opinion, listing other cases rejecting application of stay to protect the surety.); *In re Capitol York Constr. Corp.*, 43 B.R. 52, 55-56 (Bankr. S.D.N.Y. 1984) (Court declines to extend automatic stay to protect Miller Act surety).

28. *American Imaging Servs., Inc. v. Eagle-Pitcher Indus., Inc.*, 963 F.2d 855, 858 (6th Cir. 1992). Not all courts have accepted the temporary restraining order standards as the appropriate burden of proof. *In re Keene Corp.*, 162 B.R. 935, 944 (Bankr. S.D.N.Y. 1994); *Accord In re Chateaugay Corp.*, 93 B.R. 26, 29 (S.D.N.Y. 1988).

29. *Mahaffey v. E-C-P of Arizona, Inc.*, 40 B.R. 469 (Bankr. D. Colo. 1984); *In Re Otero Mills, Inc.*, 25 B.R. 1018, 1021 (Bankr. D. N.M. 1982).

In recent years, actions against non-debtor guarantors have, on occasion, been enjoined. Requests to stay or enjoin surety suits against the indemnitors of a bankrupt principal are being asserted with increasing frequency.

Most courts are reluctant to extend the protection of Code section 362(a) to guarantors.[30] They have found nothing "unusual" about a guaranty agreement that would justify extending the automatic stay under section 362(a). "The very purpose of a guaranty is to assure the [creditor] that in the event the [debtor] defaults, the [creditor] will have someone to look to for reimbursement."[31]

a. *Application of Section 362(A) To Non-Debtor Indemnitors.* Section 362(a)(1) is generally said to be applicable only to the debtor, not third-party non-debtors.[32] Moreover, nothing in section 362 indicates that Congress intended to extend the statutory protection of section 362(a) beyond the debtor to non-debtor third-parties.[33] Yet, courts have acknowledged that there may be "unusual circumstances" such that the automatic stay may be extended to include proceedings against non-debtor third-parties.[34] "Unusual circumstances" which justify this extension of the automatic stay have been found to exist:

1) "[W]hen there is such identity between the debtor and third-party defendant that the debtor may be said to be the real party defendant and that a judgment against the third-party defendant will in effect be a judgment or a finding against the debtor;"[35] or
2) where proceedings against the non-debtor co-defendant(s) "would reduce or diminish the property of the debtor to the detriment of the debtor's creditors as a whole."[36]

---

30. *Credit Alliance Corp. v. Williams*, 851 F.2d 119 (4th Cir. 1988); *Williford v. Armstrong World Indus., Inc.*, 715 F.2d 124 (4th Cir. 1983).

31. *Credit Alliance*, 851 F.2d at 122 (quoting Rojas v. First Bank Nat'l Ass'n., 613 F. Supp. 968, 971 (E.D.N.Y. 1985)).

32. *Williford v. Armstrong World Indus., Inc.*, 715 F.2d 124 (4th Cir. 1983); *In re Anje Jewelry Co., Inc.*, 47 B.R. 485 (Bankr. E.D.N.Y. 1983); *Otoe County Nat'l Bank v. W&P Trucking, Inc.*, 754 F.2d 881, 883 (10th Cir. 1985); *In re Philadelphia Gold Corp.*, 56 B.R. 87 (Bankr. E.D. Pa. 1985); *Duffie v. Gorgan Enerserv Corp.*, 708 P.2d 809 (Colo. Ct. App. 1985).

33. Congress was well aware of the mechanism for extending the automatic stay to non-bankrupt parties when it intended to so, as exemplified by 11 U.S.C. 1301, which contains a narrowly drawn provision extending the automatic stay to individual co-signers of consumer debts. Nowhere else in the Bankruptcy Code is there a similar provision extending the automatic stay to non-debtor third-parties. *Credit Alliance*, 851 F.2d at 121.

34. *Credit Alliance*, 851 F.2d at 119; *A.H. Robins Co., Inc. v. Piccinin*, 788 F.2d 994 (4th Cir.), *cert. denied*, 479 U.S. 876 (1986); *W&P Trucking*, 754 F.2d at 883; *Fortier v. Dona Anna Plaza Partners*, 747 F.2d 1324, 1330 (10th Cir. 1984); *Globe Constr. Co. v. Oklahoma City Housing Auth.*, 571 F.2d 1140 (10th Cir.), *cert. denied*, 474 U.S. 818 (1978); *Wedgeworth v. Fibreboard Corp.*, 706 F.2d 541, 544 (5th Cir. 1983); *Williford*, 715 F.2d at 126-27; *Pitts v. Unarco Indus., Inc.*, 698 F.2d 313, 314 (7th Cir.), *cert. denied*, 464 U.S. 1003 (1983); *In re Magnus Harmonica Corp.*, 233 F.2d 803, 804 (3d Cir. 1956); *In re Arrow Huss, Inc.*, 51 B.R. 853 (Bankr. D. Utah 1985); *Stoller v. Baldwin-United Corp.*, 41 B.R. 884, 890 (Bankr. S.D. Ohio 1984); *Neubauer v. Owens-Corning Fiberglass Corp.*, 26 B.R. 644, 646 (Bankr. E.D. Wis.), *cert. denied*, 459 U.S. 1226 (1983); *In re Related Asbestos Cases*, 23 B.R. 523, 528-29 (Bankr. N.D. Cal. 1982); *Lynch v. Johns-Manville Sales Corp.*, 23 B.R. 750, 751 (Bankr. S.D. Ohio 1982), *aff'd*, 710 F.2d 1194, 1196-97 (6th Cir. 1983); *In re Aboussie Bros. Constr. Co.*, 8 B.R. 302, 303 (Bankr. E.D. Mo. 1981); *Royal Truck & Trailer, Inc. v. Armadora Maritima Salvadorena, S.A.*, 10 B.R. 488, 491 (Bankr. N.D. Ill. 1981); *McGinnis Lumber Co., Inc. v. Belser*, 385 F. Supp. 390 (D. S.C. 1974); *Teledyne Indus., Inc. v. Eon Corp.*, 373 F. Supp. 191, 203 (S.D.N.Y. 1974).

35. *A.H. Robins Co., Inc. v. Piccinin*, 788 F.2d 994, 999 (4th Cir.), *cert. denied*, 479 U.S. 876 (1986).

36. *Id.* at 1008.

To illustrate, the Fourth Circuit Court of Appeals in *A.H. Robins v. Piccinin*[37] referred to the situation of a third-party who would be entitled, by operation of law, to absolute indemnity by the debtor on account of any judgment that might result against the third-party in a pending lawsuit. "To refuse application of the statutory stay in that case would defeat the very purpose and intent" of section 362(a).[38]

Third parties who are liable to the surety may in some situations be indemnified by the debtor, either by contractual agreement or corporate formalities (*i.e.*, indemnity clause in corporate bylaws). In such cases, the *Piccinin* decision implies that the automatic stay under section 362(a) could be extended to these guarantors, thereby staying all further proceedings in the surety's action.

A review of the case law since *Piccinin* indicates that bankruptcy courts have been generally unwilling to extend the automatic stay to third-party non-debtors in those cases in which property of the estate is not involved.[39] In surety indemnity actions against third parties, property of the debtor's estate is not generally involved. Thus, absent unusual circumstances, it is doubtful that the automatic stay under section 362(a) would be extended to protect these guarantors. Nevertheless, as explained below, bankruptcy courts have certain equitable authority which may also be used to enjoin actions against non-debtor third-parties including insider guarantors.[40]

b. *Equitable Authority of Bankruptcy Court to Stay Surety Actions.* The statutory power of the Bankruptcy Court to stay actions involving non-debtor third-parties is not limited to sections 362(a)(1) or 362(a)(3).[41] The automatic stay under section 362(a) is available to third-party non-debtors under the court's equitable powers pursuant to section 105.[42] Section 105 does not specify the requirements for granting injunctive relief to non-debtor third-parties. Instead, bankruptcy courts have relied upon the traditional requirements set forth in Rule 65 of the Federal Rules of Civil Procedure.[43]

If the Rule 65 factors are present, actions against non-bankrupt third-parties may be enjoined. For example in *In re Otero Mills, Inc.*,[44] the debtor requested an injunction to prevent a creditor from proceeding on a judgment against one of the debtor's officers. The officer intended to sell certain personal property and apply the proceeds to the debts of the corporation. The creditor, on the other hand, wanted to foreclose on the property. Finding that the creditor would not be harmed by the issuance of an injunction, the court proceeded to enjoin the creditor's enforcement of its judgment against the officer under section 105. Critical to the court's decision was the possible effect of the continued proceeding on the debtor's reorganization. "[F]ailure to enjoin would effect

---

37. *Id.* at 999.

38. *Id.* at 999; *see also In re S.I. Acquisition, Inc.*, 817 F.2d 1142, 1147 (5th Cir. 1987); *Teachers Ins. & Annuity Ass'n of America v. Butler*, 58 B.R. 1019 (Bankr. S.D.N.Y.), *motion granted in part,* 803 F.2d 61 (2d Cir. 1986); *In re Meyerland Co.*, 82 B.R. 831 (Bankr. S.D. Tex. 1988); *In re Johns-Manville Corp.*, 33 B.R. 254, 263-64 (Bankr. S.D.N.Y. 1983); *In re Old Orchard Inv. Co.*, 31 B.R. 599, 603 (Bankr. W.D. Mich. 1983); *In re Otero Mills, Inc.*, 25 B.R. 1018, 1020-1021 (Bankr. D.N.M. 1982); *In re Metal Center, Inc.*, 31 B.R. 458, 462 (Bankr. D. Conn. 1983).

39. *Meyerland*, 82 B.R. at 832; *S.I. Acquisition*, 817 F.2d at 1142; *All Seasons Resorts*, 79 B.R. at 901 (indemnification of non-debtor third parties, who are officers of the debtor corporation, pursuant to the corporate debtor's bylaws, was not analogous to insurance policy of the corporate debtor and therefore did not constitute property of the bankruptcy estate); *see also Venegas Munoz*, 73 B.R. at 283.

40. *Piccinin*, 788 F.2d at 1002, 1003.

41. *Id.* at 1002.

42. *In re Otero Mills, Inc.*, 25 B.R. 1018, 1020-21 (Bankr. D. N.M. 1982).

43. *In re* Monroe Well Service, Inc., 67 B.R. 746 (Bankr. E.D. Pa. 1986); *Green v. Drexler*, 760 F.2d 406 (2d Cir. 1985).

44. 25 B.R. 1018 (Bankr. D. N.M. 1982).

[sic] the bankruptcy estate and would adversely or detrimentally influence and pressure the debtor through that third-party."[45]

Beyond the statutory powers under sections 105 and 362(a) to enjoin actions against third-party non-debtors, a Bankruptcy Court, under its comprehensive jurisdiction conferred by 28 U.S.C. section 1334, has the "inherent power of courts under their general equity powers and in the efficient management of the dockets to grant relief" in the form of an automatic stay.[46] In exercising this power, the Bankruptcy Court must (1) "weigh competing interests and maintain an even balance" and (2) justify the stay "by clear and convincing circumstances outweighing potential harm" to the party against whom it is operative.[47]

The non-debtor defendants in surety indemnity actions are generally liable independently of the debtor, with the result that an indemnity action will not harm the Chapter 7 debtor nor affect its property. Less clear is the situation whereby the insider guarantor, as owner, officer or director of a Chapter 11 debtor, is involved in the debtor's day-to-day management. In those cases, a Bankruptcy Court may consider enjoining the indemnity proceeding until a plan is confirmed, or the case dismissed or converted to Chapter 7.[48]

C. DOES BANKRUPTCY TOLL THE STATUTE OF LIMITATIONS FOR CLAIMS AGAINST THE BOND?

The automatic stay prevents the commencement or continuation of lawsuits against the debtor. The automatic stay is not intended to create a substantive defense in favor of the debtor. For this reason, the Bankruptcy Code contains a tolling statute, which is designed to protect the stayed creditor from loss of its claim due to expiration of the statute of limitations during the period actions are stayed.[49] Section 108(c) provides that when applicable non-bankruptcy law (ex. state little miller act, Miller Act) requires that a lawsuit be commenced against the debtor within a certain time period,

45. *Id.* at 1020. *See also In re Johns-Manville Corp.*, 26 B.R. 420 (Bankr. S.D.N.Y. 1983) (section 105 should be utilized to issue or extend stays to enjoin a variety of proceedings which will have an adverse impact on the debtor's ability to formulate a Chapter 11 plan).

46. *A.H. Robins Co., Inc. v. Piccinin*, 788 F.2d 994, 1003 (4th Cir.), *cert. denied,* 479 U.S. 876 (1986) (quoting *Williford v. Armstrong World Indus., Inc.*, 715 F.2d 124, 127 (4th Cir. 1983); *see also Austin v. Unarco Indus., Inc.*, 705 F.2d 1, 5 (1st Cir.), *cert. denied,* 463 U.S. 1247 (1983).

47. *Piccinin*, 788 F.2d at 1003.

48. *Piccinin*, 788 F.2d at 1008 (injunctive relief is appropriate under section 105 to restrain actions against the principal of the debtor upon his showing that the non-debtor's time, energy and commitment to the debtor are necessary for the formulation of a reorganization plan). *But cf. In re Philadelphia Gold Corp.*, 56 B.R. 87 (Bankr. E.D. Pa. 1985) (injunctive relief is not available even though the debtor's principal contended that he would be so diverted by litigation against him that he would be unable to devote his entire attention to the reorganization of the debtor corporation and obtain financing to fund the debtor corporation's plan of reorganization).

49. Except as provided in § 524 of this Title, if applicable non-bankruptcy law, an order entered in a non-bankruptcy proceeding, or an agreement fixed as a period for commencing or continuing a civil action in a court other than a bankruptcy court on a claim against the debtor, or against an individual with respect to which such individual is protected under § 1201 or 1301 of this Title, and such period has not expired before the date of the filing of the petition, then such period does not expire until the later of -

(1) The end of such period including any suspension of such period occurring on or after commencement of the case; or

(2) Thirty days after notice of the termination or expiration of the stay under § 362, 922, 1201, or 1301 of this Title, as the case may be, with respect to such claim.

11 U.S.C.A. § 108(c) (1993 & Supp. 1997).

and the bankruptcy petition is filed before that statutory period has run, the statutory period for the filing of suit is extended until 30 days after the stay is lifted.

1. Bankruptcy Filing by the Bond Principal

The statute of limitations for institution of suit against the surety will not be tolled (or extended) by the principal's filing of a bankruptcy petition.[50]

2. Bankruptcy Filing by the Claimant

Will applicable notice periods or the statute of limitations for filing suit against the surety be tolled (or extended) if the claimant has filed a bankruptcy petition? As discussed above, Section 108(c) will sometimes toll a statute of limitations for actions to be brought <u>against</u> the debtor. Subsections (a) and (b) of Section 108 serve a different purpose. These subsections extend the time for the debtor to serve notice or file suit, where such time period has not expired prior to the filing of the bankruptcy petition.[51]

Examples of notice periods would be the 90 day notice required under the Miller Act and some state little miller acts, or other notice requirement that may be established by the terms of a private payment bond. Section 108(b) extends the time for the debtor to give notice until as much as 60 days after the filing of a voluntary bankruptcy petition. Thus, the 90 day time period may be extended to as much as a 149 day notice period.

The extension of the notice period could be substantially longer, if an involuntary bankruptcy petition was filed against a claimant/debtor. If the notice period has not expired before the filing of the involuntary petition, the notice period is extended until 60 days after the claimant has been adjudicated to be a "debtor." In some cases, the litigation over the propriety of the involuntary bankruptcy petition may go on for a year or more. Thus, for a claimant whose

---

50. *See, Cumberland Metals, Inc. v. Kentucky Insurance Guaranty Association*, 801 S.W.2d 339 (Ky. App. 1990) (bond claim against surety not tolled by principal/contractor's bankruptcy filing); *United States ex rel. American Bank v. C.I.T. Construction, Inc.*, 944 F.2d 253 (5th Cir. 1991) (court rejects bond claimant's attempt to invoke 108(a) to extend statute of limitations).

51. § 108. Extension of Time

(a) If applicable nonbankruptcy law, an order entered in a nonbankruptcy proceeding, or an agreement fixes a period within which the debtor may commence an action, and such period has not expired before the date of the filing of the petition, the trustee may commence such action only before the later of:

(1) the end of such period, including any suspension of such period occurring on or after the commencement of the case; or

(2)two years after the order for relief.

(b) Except as provided in subsection (a) of this section, if applicable nonbankruptcy law, an order entered in a nonbankruptcy proceeding, or an agreement fixes a period within which the debtor or an individual protected under section 1201 or 1301 of this title may file any pleading, demand, notice, or proof of claim or loss, cure a default, or perform any other similar act, and such period has not expired before the date of the filing of the petition, the trustee may only file, cure, or perform, as the case may be, before the later of - -

(1) the end of such period, including any suspension of such period occurring on or after the commencement of the case; or

(2) 60 days after the order for relief.

11 U.S.C.A. §108(a) & (b) (1993 & Supp. 1997).

bankruptcy case began by the filing of an involuntary petition, the notice period extension could become quite lengthy.

The extension/tolling of the statute of limitations is more generous. Section 108(a) tolls the limitations period, whether statutory or contractual, for as much as two years after the filing of the voluntary bankruptcy. Like Section 108(b), an involuntary bankruptcy petition may result in an even longer extension, because the two years is measured from the "order for relief," which may be significantly later than the date of filing of the involuntary bankruptcy petition.

Thus, a claimant who files a bankruptcy petition just before the expiration of time to file suit on a Miller Act payment bond could have an additional two years in which to bring that suit. This potential of trailing claims must be investigated before decisions regarding final disbursement of bonded contract proceeds or release of collateral held by a surety can be made with confidence.

II. *The Surety's Rights in Bonded Contract Proceeds*

The surety's first concern in the bankruptcy context has traditionally been to obtain control of the balance of contract funds from the bonded construction contracts. Based upon longstanding authority, the surety assumes and believes that its priority to these funds is paramount. However, the principal/debtor, the principal's lenders and others may be quick to argue that the broad definition of "property of the estate" under the Bankruptcy Code limits the surety's rights.[52]

A. Are Bonded Contract Proceeds Property of the Estate?

The performance bond surety acquires rights of "equitable subrogation" to the balance of funds payable from the owner on the contract for which the bond was written. A surety's priority to bonded contract proceeds was firmly developed through a line of United States Supreme Court cases.[53]

In *Pearlman v. Reliance Insurance Company*,[54] the Supreme Court held that as between a surety and a trustee in bankruptcy, the surety is entitled to receive the contract proceeds to the extent necessary to reimburse it for its losses.[55] Because *Pearlman* dealt with bankruptcy law, it might be assumed that the surety's superior right to contract proceeds is equally clear inside and outside of the bankruptcy forum. However, some bankruptcy courts have been unwilling to embrace *Pearlman*, because the 1962 case was decided under the 1898 Bankruptcy Act,[56] and in 1978, Congress adopted

52. See generally, on this same topic; George F. Bachrach and Cynthia E. Rodgers-Waire, *The Surety's Rights to the Contract Funds in the Principal's Chapter 11 Bankrutpcy Case,* 35 Tort & Ins. L.J. 1 (1999).

53. *Prairie State Bank v. United States*, 164 U.S. 227, 17 S.Ct. 142, 41 L.Ed. 412 (1896); *Henningson v. United States Fidelity & Guaranty Co.*, 208 U.S. 404, 28 S.Ct. 389, 52 L.Ed. 547 (1908); *United States v. Munsey Trust Co.*, 332 U.S. 234, 67 S.Ct. 1599, 91 L.Ed. 2022 (1947).

54. 371 U.S. 132, 83 S.Ct. 232, 9 L.Ed.2d 190 (1962).

55. "The Bankruptcy Act simply does not authorize a trustee to distribute other people's property among a bankrupt's creditors." *Id.* at 135.

56. Act of July 1, 1898, Ch. 541, 30 Stat. 544 (amended 1938), *repealed by* Pub.L.No. 95-598, Title IV, § 401(a), Nov. 6, 1978, 92 Stat. 2682.

the Bankruptcy Code.[57] A post-Code analysis of the surety's claim to contract proceeds involves different statutes and principles than were considered by the *Pearlman* court.

The older Supreme Court decisions establishing the surety's priority interest in bonded contract proceeds appear to conflict with broad definition of "property of the estate" contained in Section 541 of the Bankruptcy Code.[58] The statute's legislative history supports a broad interpretation of its scope.[59]

Whether or not bonded contract proceeds are "property of the estate" under the Bankruptcy Code is a crucial issue to the surety. If the bonded contract proceeds are not "property of the estate," then the surety may immediately make demand upon the obligee to pay over those funds, may receive those funds, and apply them to reduce its loss. If the bonded contract funds are property of the estate, then these same actions would be a violation of the automatic bankruptcy stay, possibly subjecting the surety to damages and sanctions. Additionally, the bankrupt principal may lay claim to the bonded contract proceeds to be used in its reorganization, if those funds are "property of the estate."

1. Contract Funds Are Not Property of the Estate.

Some post Bankruptcy Code enactment decisions have simply adopted the *Pearlman* holding, finding that the equitable subrogation rights of the surety are superior to those of the debtor, and that the bonded contract proceeds are not property of the estate under Section 541.[60] Other courts have also held that bonded contract proceeds are not property of the estate, but have employed different rationales in order to resolve the apparent conflict between the broad scope of Section 541 and the precedent of *Pearlman v. Reliance.*

a. *Unsatisfied Conditions Precedent to the Debtor's Right to Payment.* Some courts have concluded that the debtor has no interest in contract proceeds, where the debtor's failure to pay for labor and materials would excuse the duty to pay the principal under the construction contract. In *In re Pacific Marine Dredging and Construction,*[61] a surety was required to pay the debtor/contractor's laborers and materialmen as a result of having issued a payment bond on the debtor's behalf. The issue was whether the surety or the debtor-in-possession had the superior claim to the retained contract funds. The court held that the funds were not property of the estate, and stated:

> This court agrees with other courts that have found that the contractor's failure to pay for labor and materials is just as much a failure to perform and carry out the terms of the contract as an abandonment of work. [Citations omitted.] *In short, plaintiff is not contractually obligated to pay the fund to debtor*. Due to debtor's breach of contract, the debtor does not have any legal or equitable interest in the fund. *Accordingly, the fund is not property of the estate.*[62] [Emphasis added.]

57. 11 U.S.C.A. §§ 101-1330 (1993 & Supp. 1998).

58. See note 2 for the text of 11 U.S.C § 541(a).

59. H.R. Rep. No. 95-595, 95th Cong., 1st Sess. 367-8 (1977); S. Rep. No. 95-989, 95th Cong. 2d Sess. 82-3 (1978).

60. *In re Massart Co.*, 105 Bankr. 610, 613 (W.D. Wash. 1989). *See also, In re QC Piping Installation, Inc.*, 225 Bankr. 553 (Bankr. E.D.N.Y. 1998); *In re Four Star Construction Co.*, 151 Bankr. 817 (Bankr. N.D. Ohio 1993).

61. 79 Bankr. 924 (Bankr. D. Or. 1987).

62. *Id.* at 929.

Several subsequent decisions have focused on contractual clauses that make payment of subcontractors and suppliers a precondition to the principal's right to be paid by the owner. The Third Circuit Court of Appeals has held that such a clause prevented the balance of contract funds from being paid to the bankruptcy court.[63] The principal had not paid the project bills, and the general conditions of the contract (American Institute of Architects, Document A201, 1987 Edition) provided that payment did not become due until the condition precedent was satisfied.

An Arizona court confronted the same issue and held that the principal's failure to provide lien waivers required by the contract documents caused the contract payment not to be due. The funds were therefore never a part of the contractor's bankruptcy estate.[64]

Where the law imposes the duty to see that the subcontractors and suppliers are paid, the owner's right to pay project bills, and the owner's concomitant right of recoupment against the contract proceeds for the amounts it has paid, furnish the basis for the surety to keep the funds away from the bankruptcy of the principal. Because the surety is subrogated to the rights of the owner, and because the owner could retain funds to recover payments it has made to subcontractors and suppliers, the surety can also reimburse itself.[65]

The ability of the surety to rely upon these decisions likely depends upon the fortuitous presence of a contract clause or state law that establishes a precondition to the payment obligation. However, these cases strongly support the surety's claim to the bonded contract proceeds in the principal's bankruptcy.

b. *The Bonded Contract Funds Are Held In "Trust" For The Benefit of Another.* Some courts have found bonded contract proceeds not to be property of the estate, relying not upon contractual conditions precedent, but upon trusts imposed upon the contract funds, under the provisions of state law or pursuant to contractual clauses. It is bankruptcy "black letter law" that property held in trust by the debtor does not become a part of the bankruptcy estate.[66] The existence of a valid trust is a question determined by reference to state law.[67]

---

63. *In re Modular Structures, Inc.*, 27 F.3d 72 (3rd Cir. 1994). *But see, In re Construction Alternatives, Inc.*, 2 F.3d 670 (6th Cir. 1993). (The surety argued that the principal had contractual duties to see that the subcontractors and materials suppliers were paid. However, the court focused on the absence of a right to withhold funds or an express condition precedent. The court refused to find that the fund was not due and payable to the debtor. While the decision held that the bonded contract proceeds were property of the estate, the court recognized the surety's interest in the funds.)

64. *Merchants Bonding Company v. Pima County, Arizona*, 860 P.2d 510, 512 (App. 1993).

65. *See Transamerica Ins. Co. v. United States*, 989 F.2d 1188 (Fed. Cir. 1993). In this case, the court acknowledges the surety's right of subrogation to set-offs the owner could have asserted. Interestingly, the court distinguished a case decided under Ohio law, noting that the applicable state law did not give the relevant rights of setoff to the state. Thus, the strength of this subrogation argument will vary from state to state.

66. "The United States Supreme Court has stated that Congress had plainly excluded from the estate the property of others held by the debtor in trust at the time of the filing of the petition. We stated in *In re Gurs*, 34 Bankr. 755, 757 (9th Cir. BAP 1983), that where the debtor possesses only a legal and not an equitable interest in property, the equitable interest does not become part of the bankrupt estate. Other sections of the Code, such as Sections 548 and 547, cannot be used to allow a bankrupt estate to benefit from property that the debtor did not own." *In re Torez*, 63 Bankr. 751, 753-54 (Bankr. 9th Cir. 1986), *aff'd*, 827 F.2d 1299 (9th Cir. 1987). *See Begier v. International Revenue Service*, 110 S.Ct. 2258 (1990) ("A 'debtor' does not own an equitable interest in property he holds in trust for another, that interest is not 'property of the estate,' nor is such an equitable interest 'property of the debtor' for purposes of § 547(b)."); *United States v. Whiting Pools, Inc.*, 462 U.S. 198, 205 nt. 10, 103 S.Ct. 2309, 2314 nt. 10, 76 L.Ed.2d 515, 522 nt. 10 (1983) ("Congress plainly excluded property of others held by the debtor in trust at the time of the filing of the petition."); *In re California Trade Technical Schools, Inc.*, 923 F.2d 641 (9th Cir. 1991) (funds held "in trust" were not property of the debtor for preferential transfer purposes).

67. *In re California Trade Technical Schools, Inc.*, 923 F.2d 641 (9th Cir. 1991).

Some state laws impose a trust on money owed to a contractor where subcontractors and materialmen remain unpaid. Courts have utilized these state trust fund statutes to find the funds belong to the unpaid suppliers and subcontractors, not the debtor.[68] In *In re D&B Electric, Inc.*[69] materialmen claimed uncashed checks made jointly payable to the materialmen and the debtor. Since the materialmen's equitable lien rights had expired, they contended that the funds held by the general contractor were held in trust for their benefit. Relying in part upon on a Kentucky statute, the court concluded that the funds were held in trust and were therefore not property of the estate. The court awarded the funds to the materialmen.[70]

Even in the absence of an express statute creating a trust, the court may find a trust to exist in favor of unpaid subcontractors and suppliers based on prior decisional law.[71] The *Universal Bonding Ins. Co. v. Gittens and Sprinkle Enterprises, Inc.* decision demonstrates the possible breadth of these holdings, finding a trust to exist both under New Jersey's state law trust fund statute, and on federal jobs under the authority of *Pearlman v. Reliance Ins. Co.*[72]

Valid trusts can be created by agreement, as well as by statute.[73] The bonded construction contract may contain provisions impressing a trust on contract proceeds. General Agreements of Indemnity commonly contain a pledge by the principal to hold bonded contract funds in trust for the surety and the benefit of subcontractors and suppliers. Less frequently, sureties have special collateral agreements or "fund control" agreements which may create a trust.

Generally, more than a contractual recitation of intent is required to establish a valid trust.[74] The formalities of a trust must be present and observed. The parties must have treated the contract proceeds like a trust fund before the bankruptcy. For example, courts may look to see if the fund has been segregated.[75] A failure to observe the trust formalities ordinarily required by state law may cause the surety's contractual "trust fund" claim to the bonded contract proceeds to fail.

2. Bonded Contract Proceeds Held to be Property of the Estate.

A number of bankruptcy courts have concluded that the bonded contract proceeds are "property of the estate" in the principal's bankruptcy.[76] However, these courts have also

---

68. *Selby v. Ford Motor Co. et al.* 590 F.2d 642 (6th Cir. 1979); *Parker v. Klochko Equipment Rental Co. Inc. et al.*, 590 F.2d 649 (6th Cir. 1979), *cert. denied*, 444 U.S. 831, 100 S.Ct. 60, 62 L.Ed.2d 40 (1979); See also, *In re Dunwell Hearing & Air Conditioning Contr. Corp.*, 78 Bankr. 667 (Bankr. E.D.N.Y. 1987).

69. 4 Bankr. 263 (Bankr. W.D. Ky. 1980).

70. *Id.* at 270.

71. *Universal Bonding Ins. Co. v. Gittens and Sprinkle Enterprises, Inc.*, 960 F.2d 366, 371 (3rd Cir. 1992). *See also USF&G v. United States*, 475 F.2d 1377 (Ct. Cl. 1973) (*en banc*); *United Elec. Corp. v. United States*, 647 F.2d 1082 (Fed. Cir. 1981).

72. *Universal Bonding Ins. Co. v. Gittens and Sprinkle Enterprises, Inc.*, 960 F.2d 366, 375-376.

73. *In re Alcon Demolition, Inc.*, 204 Bankr. 440, 448-49 (Bankr. D. N.J. 1997) (Court found elements of trust established by terms of indemnity agreement.); *Federal Ins. Co. v. Fifth Third Bank*, 867 F.2d 330 (6th Cir. 1989) (Court found funds held in trust from provision in bonded construction contract); *In re Gonzales*, 22 Bankr. 58 (Bankr. 9th Cir. 1982) (contractual provision validly created trust of contract funds).

74. *In re H&A Construction Co.*, 65 Bankr. 213 (Bankr. D. Mass. 1986).

75. *In re Construction Alternatives, Inc.*, 2 F.3d 670, 677 (6th Cir. 1993) (General Indemnity Agreement trust provision found insufficient to award fund to the surety, where principal had not segregated fund.)

76. *See e.g., In re Glover Const. Co., Inc.*, 30 Bankr. 873, 378 (Bankr. W.D. Ky. 1983) (Court concluded that progress payments were "property of the estate" noting the "remarkably broadened definition" of this phrase in 11 U.S.C. § 541). *In re Alliance Properties, Inc.*, 104 Bankr. 306 (Bankr. S.D. Cal. 1989); *In re Universal Builders, Inc.*, 53 Bankr. 183 (Bankr. M.D. Tenn. 1985); *In re Ram Constr. Co. Inc.*, 32 Bankr. 758 (Bankr. W.D. Pa. 1983).

acknowledged the surety's "interest" in these funds, under the doctrine of equitable subrogation. Under some decisions, the debtor/principal has obtained limited use of contract progress payments earned prior to bankruptcy. However, the bankruptcy courts have typically stopped short of allowing the debtor unrestricted use of the funds.

In *In re Alliance Properties, Inc.*,[77] the court concluded that the proceeds were property of the estate, noting the expansive definition of this phrase in Section 541. The court also concluded that once the surety paid various subcontractors' claims the surety obtained an equitable lien on the contract proceeds which was superior to any rights of the defaulting contractor and/or the estate. Thus, even though the *Alliance Properties* Court concluded that the bonded contract funds were property of the estate, the court awarded the funds to the surety because the funds were subject to the surety's equitable lien, a lien that related back to the time the bonds were written.

In two bankruptcy court decisions, *In re Glover Const. Co., Inc.*,[78] and *In re Ram Constr. Co. Inc.*,[79] the surety's lack of involvement in completing the construction projects was pivotal in the court's determination relating to unpaid progress payments.[80] The Chapter 11 debtors in both *Glover* and *Ram* were permitted to use the progress payments, but only with limitations designed to protect the surety's interests.

The *Glover* and *Ram* decisions recognize the surety's right of equitable subrogation, but reflect judicial attempts to assist a struggling completing contractor in litigation with a non-performing surety. Unfortunately, the courts' chosen method was to create an unwarranted distinction between contract progress payments and retention, and to use this distinction to limit the surety's rights under *Pearlman*.[81] This distinction has been roundly criticized in commentary, and rejected by better reasoned decisions.[82]

III. *Actions to Protect the Surety's Rights in Bonded Contract Proceeds*

Because the salient facts of each bond loss will vary, it cannot be said with certainty whether the bankruptcy court in any given case will find bonded contract proceeds to be or not to be "property of the estate." A surety's actions to gain control of bonded contract proceeds, if these fund are later held to be property of the estate, would be a violation of the automatic stay.

---

77. 104 Bankr. 306 (Bankr. S.D. Cal. 1989).

78. 30 Bankr. 873 (Bankr. W.D. Ky. 1983).

79. 32 Bankr. 758 (Bankr. W.D. Pa. 1983).

80. "[The surety] seeks unlimited authority over the construction funds but treats the duty of performance with patrician disdain. At no point has it sought to exercise its contractual option to step in and take over the jobs in question, although we have suggested in Court that the surety's most practical method of analyzing its potential exposure would be to periodically determine from one progress payment to the next, whether Glover can complete the work cheaper than a replacement contractor." *In re Glover Const. Co., Inc.*, 30 Bankr. at 882.. "Under the present circumstances, the Court believes that RAM is acting as a contractor for [the surety] in order to complete these contracts. The surety conducts an interesting dance to avoid this explicit statement. The Court has no inhibitions about stating it explicitly. The Court believes that this arrangement permits the Debtor to operate and to complete these contracts at a lower cost than the introduction of a new contractor. If that is not the case, [the surety] would or could easily replace RAM, in order to reduce their losses." *In re Ram Constr. Co. Inc.*, 32 Bankr. at 761.

81. *In re Universal Builders, Inc.*, 53 Bankr. 183 (Bankr. M.D. Tenn. 1985). (Decision follows *Glover*, recognizing distinction between retention and progress payments.)

82. *In re Fegert*, 88 Bankr. 258, 261 (Bankr. 9th Cir. 1988), *aff'd* 887 F.2d 955 (9th Cir 1989); *In re Alliance Properties, Inc.* 104 Bankr. 306 (Bankr. S.D. Cal. 1989).

Upon learning that its principal has filed for bankruptcy, a surety should act promptly to protect its interests in bonded contract proceeds and to limit the surety's liability under its bonds. The surety may consider sending carefully worded notices to the bond obligees, advising of the surety's priority claim to contract proceeds notwithstanding the bankruptcy. The surety should strongly consider filing motions with the Bankruptcy Court: (1) to lift the automatic stay, (2) for sequestration of the surety's cash collateral (the contract proceeds), (3) for adequate protection, if the court permits the principal to use the surety's cash collateral, and less frequently, (4) to compel the principal to assume or reject executory contracts. The surety may also be successful in compelling the obligee to exercise setoff rights against contract proceeds, thereby benefiting the surety.

A. Giving Notice to the Obligee

When a bond default has occurred, and the principal has not filed bankruptcy, one of the first items on the surety's "things to do" list will be to send a letter to the bond obligees, typically the project owner. This letter will typically advise the obligee of the default, but its fundamental purpose will be to place a demand upon the obligee to disburse no further contract funds to the principal. This letter is such a basic part of the surety's response to a bond default, that the letter appears in the published literature as a practice form.[83]

However, what if the principal has filed bankruptcy before the surety has an opportunity to send such notices to the bond obligees? Can the surety still send the notice to the obligee demanding that further contract proceeds be withheld from the principal? To answer these questions requires an analysis of Sections 362 and 541 of the Bankruptcy Code. As will be explained in more detail below, there is authority to support the argument that a limited notice may be sent by the surety to the obligee without violating the bankruptcy stay. The likely interpretation of the applicable bankruptcy statutes is that a declaration of default or a demand to withhold contract proceeds would violate the automatic stay. However, a more limited communication from the surety, coupled with the obligee's self-interest, may suffice to prevent the dissipation of bonded contract proceeds until bankruptcy court attention can be brought to bear.

As described above, 11 U.S.C. § 362(a) imposes a stay, applicable to all entities, against virtually all collection activities or other acts that would improve a creditor's position against the debtor or the debtor's property, effective upon the filing of a petition under the Bankruptcy Code.[84] Specifically, the inquiry is whether, under 11 U.S.C. § 362(a)(3), any communication with the obligee that results in the withholding of contract funds is an act to exercise control over "property of the estate."

As discussed previously, there is conflicting case law on the issue of whether bonded contract proceeds are "property of the estate." The surety can contend that because the bonded contract funds are not "property of the estate" under one line of authority, a letter from the surety to the obligee demanding that the funds be withheld from the debtor does not constitute a violation of the automatic stay (i.e., is not an act to exercise control over "property of the estate").

---

83. Charles A. Meeker and John W. Dondanville, *Construction Forms for Sureties*, CONSTRUCTION INDUSTRY FORMS, p. 329, ll. 13-8; Robert F. Cushman and George L. Blick, Editors. (1988); Bond Default Manual, (2d ed.) Clore, Duncan L., Editor, published by the Fidelity & Surety Law Committee, Tort and Insurance Practice Section, American Bar Association, Exhibit 13.7.

84. *See supra* note 4 for text of 11 U.S.C. § 362(a).

However, proceeding with a direct demand to the obligee may not succeed. If the bankruptcy court subsequently determines that the automatic stay was applicable, then the notice to the bond obligee will have been "invalid, void and of no force and effect."[85] A bond obligee paying funds to the principal over the surety's objection might be subject to an affirmative claim by the surety for the prejudice caused. However, if the condition precedent of notice to the bond obligee by the surety is held by the bankruptcy court to have been "void" because it violated the automatic stay of 11 U.S.C. § 362(a), then the surety will lose this valuable claim, and there may be no consequence to the obligee for ignoring the demand. If the bankruptcy court finds that the stay has been violated by the surety's demand, it may award damages to the debtors against the surety, if it finds the stay violation was willful.[86]

Several reported decisions from the United States Bankruptcy Court for the Southern District of Ohio furnish a possible solution to the surety's "notice" dilemma. These decisions, issued by two different judges in that court, both hold that it is not a violation of the automatic stay to send a notice to a third party advising them of their rights to withhold funds from the debtor.[87] In the *Hughes-Bechtol* decision, the party who sent the notice was a construction surety, who wrote the bond obligees. The debtor complained that the surety had violated the automatic stay. The court found that the surety's correspondence was predominantly informational in character, represented an isolated contact, and would therefore not be a violation of the automatic stay.[88] In the *Hughes-Bechtol* case, the surety sent letters advising the obligees that the principal had failed to pay certain claims and that those claimants had asserted claims against the bond written by the surety. The surety advised that it had paid claims and that it believed it had a direct right to the contract proceeds held by the obligee. In non-demanding language, the surety went on to state that it believed its claim to the contract fund was superior, and that the surety might continue to have a claim against the obligee if the contract funds were disbursed or any other action were taken by the bond obligee that prejudiced the surety's position.

What distinguishes the letters in *Hughes-Bechtol* from the normal surety form "notice to obligee" is that the *Hughes-Bechtol* letters contains no demand for the funds nor do they direct how the fund should be paid. Instead, they advise the bond obligee of certain facts and state the surety's position with respect to the bonded contract funds. The *Hughes-Bechtol* letters also avoid any statement that there is a legal default, or that the letter constitutes a declaration of default by the surety against the principal under the indemnity agreement or otherwise. Such a declaration would be a violation of the stay.[89]

Thus, the surety may choose to send an informational letter to the bond obligee, closely tracking the language approved by the court in the *Hughes-Bechto*l decision.[90] Clearly, demands, directions and default language should be avoided. If the surety's communication is attacked as a

---

85. *In re Schwartz*, 954 F.2d 569 (9th Cir. 1992); *In re Randall Enterprises, Inc.*, 115 Bankr. 292, 295 (Bankr. D.Colo. 1990); *In re Advent Corp.*, 24 Bankr. 612 (Bankr. 1st Cir. 1982); Collier on Bankruptcy, ¶ 362.11 [1], p. 362-111 (15th ed Rev. 1997) and cases cited at note 1.

86. 11 U.S.C. § 362(h).

87. *In re U.S. Electric, Inc.*, 123 Bankr. 262 (Bankr. S.D. Ohio 1990); *Matter of Hughes-Bechtol, Inc.*, 117 Bankr. 890 (Bankr. S.D. Ohio 1990).

88. *Hughes-Bechtol*, 117 Bankr. 890, 906.

89. *In re Computer Communications, Inc.*, 824 F.2d 725 (9th Cir. 1987); *Matter of Edwards Mobile Home Sales, Inc.*, 119 Bankr. 857 (Bankr. M.D. Fla. 1990).

90. It appears the *Hughes-Bechtol* Court knew the importance that would be placed upon its holding. The court attached copies of the letters as an appendix to the reported decision, removing any doubt as to the exact phraseology it found did not violate the automatic stay.

violation of the automatic stay, it can be persuasively argued that an "informational notice" is not the type of conduct the automatic stay was meant to prohibit. The use of the language previously approved by a reported bankruptcy court decision may help the surety defend a claim that the violation of the stay was "willful," a predicate finding before most courts would assess any sanction or penalties against the surety.

B. MOTION FOR RELIEF FROM THE AUTOMATIC STAY REGARDING BONDED CONTRACT PROCEEDS.

When the principal files for bankruptcy, the automatic stay provisions of the Bankruptcy Code operate to prevent any actions that may have a detrimental effect on the debtor, its property, or any interest of the debtor in any property.[91] Given this exhaustive list of potential acts proscribed by Code section 362(a), the surety must be extremely cautious to avoid running afoul of the automatic stay provisions. In many cases, this is difficult task for the surety.

The surety should be aware that knowledge of the bankruptcy filing is the legal equivalent of knowledge of the automatic stay.[92] Some bankruptcy courts hold that violations of the stay must be intentional and deliberate to be sanctionable.[93] However, some courts have held that monetary sanctions may be imposed for inadvertent violations of the automatic stay.[94] The sanctions available for a wilful violation are the actual damages incurred by the debtor, court costs, attorneys' fees, and in appropriate circumstances, punitive damages.[95]

The surety should promptly make a motion for relief from the automatic stay under Section 362(d).[96] The purpose of the motion will be to take control of the bonded contract funds. In appropriate circumstances, the surety may also seek to terminate the debtor-in-possession from controlling the work on the bonded projects.

There would be no need to lift the automatic stay if the subject contract funds are not property of the estate. For example, when there is a pre-petition default by a debtor who later files a petition under Chapter 7, the contract funds are likely outside the purview of the bankruptcy estate.

---

91. 11 U.S.C.A. §ù362(a) (1993 & Supp. 1997).

92. *See, e.g., In re NWFX, Inc.*, 81 Bankr. 500 (Bankr. W.D. Ark. 1987).

93. *See, e.g., In re Withrow*, 93 Bankr. 436 (Bankr. W.D.N.C. 1988).

94. *See, e.g., In re Inslaw, Inc.*, 76 Bankr. 224 (D.D.C. 1987).

95. 11 U.S.C.A. § 362(h) (1993 & Supp. 1997); *see also In re Computer Communications, Inc.*, 824 F.2d 725 (9th Cir. 1987). The threat to the surety of paying sanctions or actual damages to the bankrupt principal will be greatly reduced where the principal is a corporation. Better reasoned decisions have held that corporate debtors may not recover sanctions under § 362(h) because only an "individual" injured by a willful violation of the stay may recover damages under this section. *In re Manlon*, 168 Bankr. 594, 597 (Bankr. E. D. Ky. 1994); *In re Goodman*, 991 F.2d 613, 620 (9th Cir. 1993); *In re Pace*, 67 F.3d 187, 193 (9th Cir. 1995); *In re Cascade Roads, Inc.*, 34 F.3d 756, 766 (9th Cir. 1994); *In re Chateaugay Corp.* 920 F.2d 183, 187 (2d Cir. 1990); But see *In re Atlantic Bus. and Community Corp.*, 901 F.2d 325 (3rd Cir. 1990); *Budget Service Co. v. Better Homes of Virginia*, 804 F.2d 289 (4th Cir. 1986). A debtor may still seek sanctions under the Bankruptcy Court's contempt powers, but such an award is discretionary.

96. (d) On request of a party in interest and after notice and a hearing, the court shall grant relief from the stay provided under subsection (a) of this section, such as by terminating, annulling, modifying, or conditioning such stay---

(1) for cause, including the lack of adequate protection of an interest in property of such party in interest; or

(2) with respect to a stay of an act against property under subsection (a) of this section, if--

(A) the debtor does not have an equity in such property; and

(B) such property is not necessary to an effective reorganization.

11 U.S.C.A. § 362(d) (1993 & Supp. 1997).

In addition, the debtor loses all legal and equitable interests in the contract funds when it rejects an executory contract.[97] In most circumstances, actions taken by the surety to obtain contract funds without seeking relief from the automatic stay have a significant element of risk. It is always possible that a court may later find that the bonded contract funds are property of the estate. In the interests of prudence and to avoid sanctions, a surety can file a precautionary motion for relief from the stay under Section 362(d)(2). Such a motion is not an admission that the automatic stay applies to the surety's contract proceeds. The surety is merely seeking a court determination that the debtor has no interest in the bonded contract proceeds, due to the surety's superior rights of equitable subrogation.

In opposition to the surety's stay relief motion, the principal will often argue that the contract funds are essential to its effective reorganization. Especially at the inception of a case, such considerations may persuade the court to permit the debtor to use progress payments. It is often true that a debtor-in-possession will have little hope of successfully reorganizing without use of the bonded contract proceeds. To prevail upon a Section 362(d)(2) motion for relief from stay, the surety must show both that the debtor has no interest in the contract funds and that the funds are not necessary to an effective reorganization.[98]

Because of the broad scope of the automatic stay, there are a fairly large number of circumstances where the surety may need to file stay relief motions. The surety will seek relief from the stay when the surety has been completing a bonded project for a debtor/principal who was not properly defaulted pre-petition. the surety may not be able to collect progress draws until the stay is lifted. Another common situation is when an owner is holding retainage that is the subject of competing claims by the debtor, its financing bank, and the surety. Promptly, the surety must move for stay relief asking the court to determine the surety's priority rights under equitable subrogation and to lift the stay so as to allow the surety to collect the funds from the owner. In yet another situation, the surety may have been financing its principal by utilizing a trust fund account in which the principal holds legal title but the surety holds the equitable interest to the account. The debtor-in-possession may claim the funds in the trust account to be property of the estate because the account bears the principal's name. The debtor may wish to use those funds to finance its reorganization or a bankruptcy trustee may claim the funds to be used for distribution to the unsecured creditors. The surety must move for stay relief to have the court determine its priority in the funds and lift the stay to allow collection of those funds.

C. MOTION TO SEQUESTER CASH COLLATERAL AND, ALTERNATIVELY, FOR ADEQUATE PROTECTION.

When the surety has an interest in bonded contract funds that have been held to be property of the bankrupt estate, those funds are referred to as the surety's "cash collateral."[99] The trustee or debtor-in-possession is required to segregate and account for any cash collateral in its possession,

97. *In re Pacific Marine Dredging*, 79 Bankr. 924 (Bankr. D. Or. 1987).

98. 11 U.S.C.A. § 362(d)(2) (1993 & Supp. 1997).

99. 11 U.S.C. § 363(a) provides: "'[C]ash collateral' means cash, negotiable instruments, documents of title, securities, deposit accounts, or other cash equivalents whenever acquired in which the estate and an entity other than the estate have an interest and includes the proceeds, products, offspring, rents, or profits of property subject to a security interest as provided in section 552(b) of this title, whether existing before or after the commencement of a case under this title."

custody or control.[100] The trustee or debtor-in-possession is not permitted to use any cash collateral unless (a) the surety consents or (b) the court, after notice and a hearing, authorizes such use.[101]

Although the provisions of the Bankruptcy Court severely restrict a trustee's or debtor-in-possession's use of cash collateral, it is not uncommon for the surety to learn that its cash collateral has been dissipated.[102] The surety should promptly put its principal and the court on notice, by a brief court filing, that it does not consent to the use of bonded contract funds. Additionally, the surety should file a motion pursuant to Section 363(e) to prohibit or condition the principal's use of cash collateral. The motion should request that the principal be prohibited from using the surety's cash collateral. As a fall back position, the motion should alternately request that the cash collateral be segregated and the surety be provided adequate protection for any use of the funds by the principal.[103]

If the court will not prohibit the Chapter 11 debtor/principal's use of cash collateral, then the surety should be prepared to suggest the form of adequate protection.[104] A debtor-in-possession completing a bonded contract can be required to (1) limit its disbursement of funds to only those expenses required to keep the bonded contracts going, (2) permit the surety to control the debtor's payment of expenditures to assure the bonded monies are dedicated to the ongoing expenses of the bonded contracts, (3) provide an accounting for each project, so that income and expenses can be

---

100. 11 U.S.C.A. § 363(c)(4) (1993 & Supp. 1997).

101. 11 U.S.C.A. § 363(c)(2) (1993 & Supp. 1997).

102. Although the Bankruptcy Code specifically prohibits the debtor's use of cash collateral without consent of all interested parties or court order upon notice and a hearing, the Code does not specify any sanctions for the unapproved use of cash collateral. Therefore, in practice, a debtor-in-possession will tend to use the surety's cash collateral, *i.e.*, contract proceeds, until the surety moves the Bankruptcy Court for an order restricting such use. The surety is not without recourse, however, for the misuse by the debtor of contract proceeds. One bankruptcy court, while recognizing the absence of any express sanctions in the Bankruptcy Code, used section 105 to impose sanctions on a debtor-in-possession for its use of cash collateral without consent or court order. The court granted the secured creditor a replacement lien on the debtor-in-possession's post-petition accounts receivable and, to the extent that was not sufficient, a priority administrative claim. *In re Aerosmith Denton Corp.*, 36 Bankr. 116 (Bankr. N.D. Tex. 1983); *see also In re Rankin*, 49 Bankr. 565 (Bankr. W.D. Mo. 1985) (creditor allowed administrative priority claim to extent debtor-in-possession misused cash collateral where no other property available). In another case, where the debtor-in-possession and the secured party had stipulated to the use of cash collateral but the debtor-in-possession violated the terms of the stipulation, the court refused the debtor-in-possession's subsequent motion for court-approved use of cash collateral over the creditor's objections. *In re Oxford Royal Mushroom Prods., Inc.*, 19 Bankr. 974 (Bankr. E.D. Pa. 1982).

103. Adequate Protection. When adequate protection is required under section 362, 363 or 364 of this title of an interest of an entity in property, such adequate protection may be provided by--

(1) requiring the trustee to make a cash payment or periodic cash payments to such entity, to the extent that the stay under section 362 of this title, use, sale, or lease under section 363 of this title, or any grant of a lien under section 364 of this title results in a decrease in the value of such entity's interest in such property.

(2) providing to such entity an additional or replacement lien to the extent that such stay, use, sale, lease, or grant results in a decrease in the value of such entity's interest in such property; or

(3) granting such other relief, other than entitling such entity to compensation allowable under section 503(b)(1) of this title as an administrative expense, as will result in the realization by such entity of the indubitable equivalent of such entity's interest in such property.

11 U.S.C.A. § 361 (1993 & Supp. 1997).

104. The courts have fashioned adequate protection in a variety of ways to meet the needs of individual cases. *In re Anchorage Boat Sales, Inc.*, 4 Bankr. 635 (Bankr. E.D.N.Y. 1980) (debtor enjoined from taking any action to transfer, sell, or dispose of cash collateral subject to interest of creditor); *In re Earth Lite, Inc.*, 9 Bankr. 440 (Bankr. M.D. Fla. 1981) (equity cushion and personal guarantee of principals not sufficient; debtor allowed use of cash collateral if it cures default and make monthly contractual payments); *In re Certified Corp.*, 51 Bankr. 154 (D. Hawaii 1985) (debtor authorized to use cash collateral where creditor granted replacement liens and authority to inspect inventory while debtor required to file detailed daily reports with creditor and court and place all amounts collected in special account).

reviewed, (4) limit any salary payments to the debtor's stockholders, officers or their relatives,[105] and (5) not pay for equipment or expenses not necessary on the ongoing projects.[106]

D. Compelling The Obligee To Exercise Setoff Rights Against Other Contract Proceeds.

The principal will sometimes have multiple construction contracts with the same obligee, for example, a local municipality. While a default on one project may result in a claim against the surety, another project may be completed, with retention funds payable to the debtor. When the principal files for bankruptcy protection, the principal will claim the retention money should be paid into its bankruptcy, leaving the surety to pay the full claim of the obligee on the other project. The surety will want to require the obligee to use the contract proceeds in its possession to reduce the performance bond claim.

In a case decided under the Bankruptcy Code, the Fourth Circuit Court of Appeals relied upon the rationale of earlier precedents[107] to allow the surety to compel the obligee to setoff.[108] The surety had issued performance bonds regarding residential projects. The principal defaulted, and the surety would have liability to the obligee county for more that $60,000. The County held $40,850.00 in the principal/debtor's escrowed funds from other development agreements. The debtor's bankruptcy trustee and the County proposed to reach a compromise whereby a significant portion of that fund would be released to the debtor. The surety intervened and opposed that settlement, claiming it had the right to compel the County to assert a setoff to reduce any claims against the surety, equal to the $40,850.00. The Court held that the surety had a right to compel the County to assert its setoff rights against the insolvent debtor and thereby reduce the surety's liability.

IV. *Motion to Compel Assumption or Rejection of Executory Contracts*

The surety may need to move the Bankruptcy Court for an order requiring the principal to "move it or lose it." The Principal may be stalled in job progress, exposing the surety to dramatic delay demanges. Or, the principal may be battling the surety regarding contract proceeds or indemnification rights, foreclosing a cooperative effort to timely finish the bonded work. The surety may then need to file and prosecute a Motion to Compel Rejection of Executory Contract.

---

105. *See Ram Const.*, 32 Bankr. at 759. The *Glover Constr.* Court required progress payments to be used first to pay all bona fide claims against the bonded projects that the surety may become liable, and any surpluses could be used for the debtor's job-related operating and overhead expenses "most stringently viewed." 30 Bankr. at 882.

106. *But see In re Kuhn Constr. Co., Inc.*, 11 Bankr. 746 (Bankr. S.D. W.Va. 1981) (Court concluded that surety's equitable right of subrogation was subject to requirements of Article 9 of the UCC; the court held that the surety was not entitled to adequate protection and allowed the debtor to use the cash without the surety's consent); *In re Universal Builders, Inc.*, 53 Bankr. 183 (Bankr. M.D. Tenn. 1985) (Court denied surety's action for adequate protection as concerns unpaid progress payments finding that the surety had not perfected its interest in the funds. Further, the court improperly stated that even if the surety had perfected its interest, it would have been avoided under Section 552).

107. *U. S. ex rel. Johnson v. Morley Const. Co.*, 98 F.2d 781 (2d Cir. 1938), *cert. den. sub nom, Maryland Casualty Co. v. U. S. ex rel. Harrington*, 305 U.S. 651, 59 S.Ct. 244, 83 L.Ed. 421 (1938); *In re Yale Express System, Inc.*, 362 F.2d 111 (2d Cir. 1966).

108. *Merritt Commercial Savings & Loan, Inc. v. Guinee* (*In re James R. Corbitt Co.*), 766 F.2d 850 (4th Cir. 1985).

The Bankruptcy Code does not define "executory contract" but the legislative history identifies it as a contract "on which performance remains due to some extent on both sides."[109] Under this definition, construction contracts in various stages of completion will generally be considered executory contracts.[110] However, a contract is not considered executory if the debtor has defaulted and the contract has been terminated by the owner prior to the petition being filed.[111] The pre-petition termination must be complete and not subject to cure or reversal under either the terms of the contract or under state law.[112] The principal's interest in an executory contract is property of the estate under the Bankruptcy Code, and is protected by the automatic stay.[113]

Under section 365, the trustee or debtor-in-possession has three options: (1) assume the contract under section 365(b)(1(A)-(C); (2) assign the underlying contract under section 365(f)(1)-(3); or (3) reject the contract. If the principal has filed under Chapter 7, the trustee has 60 days from the date of filing to accept or reject the contract or it is deemed rejected.[114] If the petition has been filed under Chapter 11, the debtor-in-possession can assume or reject executory contracts at any time before confirmation of a plan of reorganization.[115]

---

109. The House and Senate Reports discuss section 365 as follows:

> Though there is no precise definition of what contracts are executory, it generally includes contracts on which performance remains due to some extent on both sides. A note is not usually an executory contract if the only performance that remains is repayment. Performance on one side of the contract would have been completed and the contract is no longer executory.

H.R. REP. NO. 595, *supra* note 47 at 347-48; S. REP. NO. 989, 95th Cong., 2d Sess. 58 (1978), *reprinted in* 1978 U.S. CODE CONG. & ADMIN. NEWS 5787, 5844.

Many courts rely on the following definition:

> [A] contract under which the obligation of both the bankrupt and the other party to the contract are so far unperformed that the failure of either to complete the performance would constitute a material breach excusing the performance of the other.

Countryman *Executory Contracts in Bankruptcy, Part I*, 57 MINN. L. REV. 439, 460 (1973); *see also* Countryman, *Executory Contracts in Bankruptcy, Part II*, 58 MINN. L. REV. 479 (1974).

Some courts have questioned the Countryman definition of executory contracts and held contracts to be executory as long as substantial performance is left on the part of the debtor (or estate). *In re Oxford Royal Mushroom Prods., Inc.*, 45 Bankr. 792 (Bankr. E.D. Pa. 1985) (unrecorded easement is executory contract); *In re Narquist*, 43 Bankr. 224 (Bankr. E.D. Wash. 1984) (covenant not to compete is executory contract).

110. Surety bonds and surety indemnity agreements have even been held to be executory contracts. *In re Padula*, 118 Bankr. 143 (Bankr. S.D. Fla. 1990); *In re Evans*, 91 Bankr. 1003 (Bankr. S.D. Fla. 1988).

111. *See, e.g., Moody v. Amoco Oil Co.*, 734 F.2d 1200 (7th Cir. 1984); Collier on Bankruptcy ¶ 365.02[2], p.365-20 (15th ed. Rev. 1997).

112. *Moody*, 734 F.2d at 1212; Collier on Bankruptcy ¶ 365.02[2], p.365-20-21 (15th ed. Rev. 1997); *cf. In re Waterkist Corp.*, 775 F.2d 1089 (9th Cir. 1985) (bare possessory interest in leasehold premises may be enough to allow debtor to assume lease).

113. *In re Computer Communications, Inc.*, 824 F.2d 725 (9th Cir. 1987).

114. 11 U.S.C.A. § 365(d)(1) (1993 & Supp. 1997).

115. 11 U.S.C.A. § 365(d)(2) (1993 & Supp. 1997).

A. Standards for Assumption

To assume an executory contract, the debtor must show that the contract is executory in nature, i.e., that it has not been completely terminated prior to the date of the bankruptcy filing. If there has been any default, the debtor must promptly cure the defaults,[116] and must demonstrate the ability to provide adequate assurances of future performance under the executory contract.[117] Where there has been no default by the debtor, the debtor may assume an executory contract without satisfying the above tests, so long as the assumption appears to be in the best interests of the estate.[118]

The courts have applied two different tests in ruling on a debtor's motion to assume or reject: the "burdensome property" test and the "business judgment" test.[119] The business judgment test is used by the majority of jurisdictions.[120] Under the business judgment test, the trustee or debtor-in-possession need only demonstrate that assumption or rejection of the executory contract will benefit the estate.[121] The court, in approving the application to assume or reject, must balance the benefits and burdens of assuming or rejecting a given contract.[122]

B. Opposing the Assumption

The surety has two options to oppose assumption of the bonded executory construction contract. First, the surety may seek, under Section 362(d)(1),[123] to have the debtor-in-possession terminated from controlling the work on the bonded projects. The "cause" as required under 362(d)(1) for the automatic stay to be lifted is that the construction contract is an executory contract that is not assumable by the principal. The construction contract is not assumable because the debtor-in-possession cannot cure the existing defaults and cannot provide adequate assurance of its future performance.[124] Typically, the debtor-in-possession has not paid numerous subcontractors, laborers and materialmen. This failure will be a default under most construction contracts. If the debtor-in-possession has no ability to cure these defaults, the court may give the surety relief from stay to complete the bonded projects. It will be incumbent upon the surety to advise the court of the amount of bonded contract funds remaining, the amount of unpaid subcontractors, laborers and materialman, and the estimated cost to complete the bonded project.

The second option of the surety is to file a motion under 11 U.S.C. § 365(d)(2), requesting the court to set a date by which the debtor/principal must assume or reject the contract. Because the order that will result from this motion does not compel a rejection, but only imposes a future deadline for the decision, this procedure is ordinarily too slow and unwieldy to be an effective tool

---

116. 11 U.S.C.A. § 365(b)(1)(A) (1993 & Supp. 1997).

117. 11 U.S.C.A. § 365(b)(1)(B), (C) (1993 & Supp. 1997).

118. *See In re Westview 74th Street Drug Corp.*, 59 Bankr. 747, 754 (Bankr. S.D.N.Y. 1986); *In re Great Northwest Recreation Center, Inc.*, 74 Bankr. 846, 856 (Bankr. D. Mont. 1987) and cases cited therein.

119. *In re Huff*, 81 Bankr. 531 (Bankr. D. Minn. 1988).

120. *Id.* at 537.

121. *Id.*

122. *See, e.g., In re Food City, Inc.*, 94 Bankr. 91 (Bankr. W.D. Tex. 1988) (court analyzed sixteen separate items in denying debtor-in-possession's request to assume executory labor contract).

123. The two subsections in Section 362(d) are in the disjunctive. Therefore, subsections 362(d)(1) and 362(d)(2) provide separate bases for relief from stay. *In re Sedona San Carlos Development Co.*, 59 Bankr. 113 (Bankr. D. Ariz. 1986).

124. 11 U.S.C.A. § 365(b)(1) (1993 & Supp. 1997).

for the surety.[125] The surety is not a direct party to the construction contract to be rejected, so the surety may not have standing to bring the motion. It is necessary to persuade the obligee to bring this motion, which may be difficult.[126]

If the contract contains a clause requiring that the contractor pay all materialmen and subcontractors, the owner and surety can argue that to cure the default, the debtor-in-possession must bring current the unpaid subcontractors and materialmen. If a court is persuaded that all unpaid materialmen and subcontractors must be brought current by the debtor who wants to assume the contract, the performance bond surety is obviously benefitted. Further, if the creditors are alerted to the fact that any losses on assumed contracts will entitle the surety to a priority claim, those creditors will be more apt to support a rejection which will permit the surety to step in and complete.

At the hearing on a motion to compel assumption or rejection, the surety's goal will be to prove that the debtor/principal cannot meet the requirements to assume an executory contract. The surety should request the court to set an immediate deadline. A good example of how this process should work can be found in the reported decision of *CM Systems, Inc.*[127] In that case, the debtor-in-possession had not been declared in default under the subject contract when the debtor filed its Chapter 11 petition. The Florida bankruptcy court analyzed the information about the project presented by the surety and the obligee and determined that the debtor-in-possession was behind schedule and that the project would lose money. Based upon these factors and this analysis, the court denied the debtor's motion to assume the contract, notwithstanding the fact it was not technically in default. The court noted that the rejection would benefit the estate by reducing claims. "Moreover, in the case of a large construction project where there is a payment and performance bond posted, an early takeover of the project by the bonding company may minimize, if not completely eliminate, damage claims."[128] In the *CM Systems* case, the surety had the good fortune to have the debtor promptly file a motion to assume the contract, thereby placing the issue in front of the court on a prompt basis. A wiser debtor might simply have chosen to defer the assumption/rejection issue and to continue to perform, thereby depriving the surety of this quick and easy method to place the performance issues in front of the court.

V. *Does the Surety have the Right to Use Debtor's Subcontractors*

Often the performance bond surety will require or desire the continued performance of the principal's subcontractors. These subcontractors may have already obtained long lead time materials or have access to personnel and equipment necessary to timely completion of the bonded contract. In a default not involving bankruptcy, the surety will attempt to obtain agreements from these parties to deliver their performance to the completing surety or a replacement contractor. Some of these subcontractors will view this as an opportunity to obtain additional incentives for their previously agreed upon performance.

---

125. The courts construing this section have generally required that the debtor be given a reasonable time in which to assume or reject. *See Matter of Dunes Casino Hotel*, 63 Bankr. 939, 948 (D. N.J. 1986).

126. The bond obligee is often a public entity who will be resistant to, or seemingly incapable of, prompt and decisive action. The surety often accompanies the request with an offer to bear the cost of preparing the necessary court filings.

127. 64 Bankr. 363 (Bankr. M.D. Fla. 1986).

128. *Id.* at 365.

In this unique instance, the bankruptcy of the principal may actually help the performance bond surety. After automatic stay issues have been dealt with and it is clear that the surety will complete the work, the Bankruptcy Code provides a mechanism whereby the subcontractors will be legally obligated to deliver their agreed performance to the surety. The debtor/principal may move to assume the executory subcontract agreements, and to assign those subcontracts to the surety.[129] The same standards for assumption of an executory contract discussed in the preceding section apply. However, it is a simple matter for the surety to establish to the court that it will cure existing defaults (pay the payment bond claims of the subcontractors) and provide adequate assurance of future performance (pay the subcontractors for the balance of their work). The assumption and assignment procedure permits the surety, working with the debtor, to obtain full performance of subcontractors, and grants a measure of immunity from opportunistic profiteering.

VI. *Does the Surety have the Right to Use Debtor's Equipment and Tools in Completion of Bonded Projects*

A. Surety's Right to Use Debtor's Equipment Under General Indemnity Agreement

Typically, the principal has executed an agreement of indemnity containing a provision that permits the surety to take possession of and to use the principal's equipment to complete the bonded work.[130] Such provisions have been enforced in favor of the surety.[131] The surety's right to use the principal's equipment after the principal has filed its bankruptcy petition is dubious and is complicated by the interplay of the doctrines of executory contracts, the automatic stay, and setoff or recoupment defenses.[132]

1. The Surety as a Creditor With an Interest in the Equipment

If the surety's claim to the right to use the principal's equipment arises from the indemnity agreement, it must be determined "what is the nature of the surety's claim under that agreement?" Where the agreement of indemnity has not been filed as a financing statement under the Uniform Commercial Code, the indemnity provision will not assist the surety competing against prior perfected security interests.[133] The surety's only recourse would be to make appropriate arrangements with the lienholder in order that the equipment can be utilized to complete the bonded project. An unperfected claim of security interest will not be successful as against the principal/debtor.[134]

---

129. 11 U.S.C.A. § 365(f)(2) (1993 & Supp. 1997).

130. A typical indemnity agreement provision is: "Upon the happening of an Event of Default, the Surety shall have the right to take immediate possession of the supplies, tools, plant, equipment and materials and to use, and consume if necessary, the same in the performance of the contracts by itself or by others."

131. *Travelers Indemnity Co. v. West Georgia National Bank,* 387 F. Supp. 1090 (N.D. Ga. 1974) (the court held that the surety's right to equipment and materials were greater than that of a general creditor claiming under an attachment or judgment).

132. *See* 11 U.S.C.A. §§ 365, 362, 542 and 553 (1979 & Supp. 1989), respectively.

133. *See Aetna Casualty & Surety Co. v. J.F. Brunken & Son, Inc.*, 357 F. Supp. 290 (D.S.D. 1973).

134. 11 U.S.C. § 544 (1979 & Supp. 1989).

If the agreement of indemnity has been filed as a financing statement under the Uniform Commercial Code, sufficiently in advance of the bankruptcy to avoid attack as a preferential transfer, the surety may be a secured creditor, pursuant to assignment clauses traditionally found in such agreements. The enforceability of assignment provisions in the agreement of indemnity as a grant of a security interest is beyond the scope of this chapter. The creditor body will likely oppose the surety's claimed security interest. The surety will need to file for relief from the automatic stay to take possession and use the equipment.

The grounds for stay relief found in sections 362(d)(1) and 362(d)(2) are alternative methods to obtain relief from the automatic stay. Relief may be granted for "cause" under section 362(d)(1) despite the debtor having equity in property.[135] Conversely, where there is no equity in the property and it is not necessary for an effective reorganization, stay relief may be granted even though the debtor claims it can adequately protect the moving party's interest in the property.[136]

The "necessary for an effective reorganization" requirement in section 362(d)(2)(B) is not applicable in a Chapter 7 case.[137] In a Chapter 11 case, however, the equity standard is modified by the addition of the "effective reorganization" requirement. In order for the debtor's equipment to be "necessary to an effective reorganization," the Supreme Court has recently held that the debtor has the burden of proving that there exists "a reasonable possibility of a successful reorganization within a reasonable time."[138] Many courts have concluded that the property's indispensability to the debtor's survival is insufficient to justify continuation of the stay.[139] On the other hand, it has also been held that property in a Chapter 11 case is always necessary to an effective reorganization.[140]

2. The Indemnity Agreement as an Executory Contract Permitting the Surety to Use the Equipment

Section 365 of the Bankruptcy Code addresses the rights of the principal/debtor in its executory contracts and leases. As explained above, section 365(a) empowers a debtor to assume or reject executory contracts, subject to court approval.[141] The agreement of indemnity will ordinarily not be viewed as an executory contract, and the surety would not be entitled to exercise rights thereunder, pending assumption or rejection of the contract by the debtor. This is because the surety has few or no affirmative obligations to the principal under the agreement of indemnity. In a pre-Bankruptcy Code case, *In re THL Financial Corp*,[142] an indemnity agreement executed by a corporation to its officers and directors was held not to be executory because no obligations remained except the corporation's obligation to indemnify.

---

135. *See In re Paradise Boat Leasing Corp.*, 5 Bankr. 822 (D.Virgin Islands 1980); *In re Certified Mortgage Corp.*, 19 Bankr. 369 (Bankr. M.D. Fla. 1982).

136. *See In re Sun Valley Ranches, Inc.*, 823 F.2d 1373 (9th Cir. 1987).

137. *See In re Preuss*, 15 Bankr. 896 (9th Cir. 1981) (Chapter 7).

138. *United Savings Ass'n v. Timbers of Inwood Forest Assoc. Ltd.*, 484 U.S. 365 (1988).

139. *See In re Clark Tech. Assocs., Ltd.*, 9 Bankr. 738 (Bankr. D. Conn. 1981) (debtor's high hopes, without any reasonable prospects for reorganization, are insufficient).

140. *See In re Sunstone Ridge Assocs.*, 51 Bankr. 560 (D. Utah 1985).

141. 11 U.S.C. § 365(d)(1). Bankruptcy Rule 6006 governs the procedure to seek court approval for assumption or rejection of an executory contract.

142. 446 F. Supp. 1329 (D. Hawaii 1977). *See also In re Van Dyk Research Corp.*, 13 Bankr. 487 (Bankr.D.N.J. 1981).

3. Surety's Right to Use Debtor's Equipment Obtained by Subrogation to Obligee's Position

An obligee may have contractual rights to use the debtor's equipment after the debtor defaults. Under the doctrine of equitable subrogation, the surety stands in the shoes of the obligee and is subrogated to the obligee's right to use the debtor's equipment once the surety becomes liable to the obligee under its performance bond.[143] However, the claim of the obligee is ordinarily that of an unsecured creditor, and for the reasons discussed above, will not be of great assistance to the surety.

Even though the construction contract between the obligee and the principal will likely be an executory contract,[144] the obligee will not be entitled to enforce the contract, including the right to use equipment, prior to debtors assumption of the executory contract. [145]

If the surety does maintain possession of the debtor's equipment and uses it in completion of bonded projects, then the debtor may claim that the party using its equipment should pay rent for such use. The debtor, under section 542(b), may demand that the party using its equipment turn over equipment rental to the estate. An exception to section 542(b) liability exists if the entity allegedly owing equipment rental has a valid right of setoff as provided in section 553.[146] For setoff to be successfully asserted, a creditor must demonstrate "mutuality of obligation." Mutuality requires that both obligations be held by the same parties, in the same right or capacity, and arise from pre-petition obligations.[147] Before a creditor can assert setoff it must seek relief from the automatic stay.[148] In *In re Flanagan Bros., Inc.*,[149] the court found that a general contractor, who made post-petition payments to suppliers of the debtor/subcontractor, could offset the amount paid against retainage owed to debtor and granted the general contractor relief from the stay to assert its setoff defense. It may be argued by the surety that the obligee has a claim against the debtor for its defaults, and that claim may be setoff by the obligee (and the surety by subrogation) against the claim for rents. For setoff to be allowed, the requirement of "mutuality" must be met. In shorthand, this requires the parties to stand in the same position to one another (arguably precluding subrogation) and have the same character of debt, i.e. both pre-petition or both post-petition. Mutuality presents hurdles to the setoff argument, because the debtor will argue that its defaults are pre-petition and the use of the equipment is post-petition. The counter argument would be that the right to use the equipment arose pursuant to a pre-petition construction contract as well.

Although not listed by name in section 542(b), recoupment may be a valid defense to the debtor's demands for turnover of equipment rental. To successfully assert a recoupment defense to the debtor's claim for equipment rental the claim against the debtor must arise from the same transaction.[150] The major distinction between recoupment and setoff is that recoupment does not

---

143. *See, e.g., United States v. Munsey Trust Co.*, 332 U.S. 234 (1947); Pearlman v. Reliance Ins. Co., 371 U.S. 132 (1962).

144. See note 109. But see, *In re Murtishi,* 55 Bankr. 564 (Bankr. N.D. Ill. 1985) (Court found that a debtor's pre-petition breach of contract rendered the contract non-executory because the non-breaching party no longer had a duty to perform under the contract.)

145. *In re Wilson*, 69 Bankr. 960, 956-66 (Bankr. N.D. Tex. 1987).

146. 11 U.S.C. § 542(b).

147. *See In re Denby Stores, Inc.*, 86 Bankr. 768 (Bankr. S.D.N.Y. 1988).

148. 11 U.S.C. § 362(a)(7).

149. 47 Bankr. 299 (Bankr. D.N.J. 1985).

150. *See In re B&L Oil Co.*, 782 F.2d 155 (10th Cir. 1986).

require mutuality of obligation.[151] *In re Clowards, Inc.*,[152] involved a debtor that failed to complete several construction subcontracts. The bankruptcy trustee sought to recover the contract proceeds remaining on each of the projects. The *Clowards* court held that the general contractors could assert claims in recoupment because both the trustee's and contractors' claims arose out of the same transaction. Therefore, the court allowed the trustee to recover against the contractor, subject to the contractors' claims in recoupment. Under the doctrine of recoupment, a surety's liability for equipment rental might be reduced to the extent of its loss on the project where the equipment was used or the extent of the obligee's damages from the debtor's default, without regard to whether the claims were post-petition or pre-petition.

VII. *Impact of Bankruptcy Upon the Surety's Ability to Finance the Principal's Completion of Bonded Work*

One of the performance bond surety's options in a default is to finance the principal's completion of the bonded work. As with any option, a bankruptcy filing or the potential of a bankruptcy filing will be an important consideration in both the decision to finance or not to finance and the terms that must be incorporated into a financing agreement.

A. Pre-Petition Financing of the Principal

1. Introduction

Under certain circumstances, the surety may elect to provide the contractor with the money necessary to complete projects. This chapter does not attempt to discuss the advisability or hazards of this particular surety option. Other authors have addressed this topic.[153] Assuming the decision to finance has been made, how may the surety and its financing agreement be affected by the subsequent bankruptcy filing by the principal?

By far the most important bankruptcy principle affecting any agreement with a financially distressed principal is the law of "avoidable preferences." The law of bankruptcy preferences examines past transactions against standards not necessarily contemplated at that time. This examination is triggered by the filing of a petition under the Bankruptcy Code. By way of example, in an avoidance action the bankrupt principal may argue that any assignments of the bonded contract proceeds to the surety were a preference and/or that any security interests given to the surety were a preference. The principal may also claim sole ownership of the funds present in joint control trust accounts at the time of the bankruptcy filing.

151. *See In re Hiler*, 99 Bankr. 238 (Bankr. D.N.J. 1989).

152. 42 Bankr. 627 (Bankr. D. Idaho 1984).

153. Joyce & Haug, *Financing the Contractor*, Bond Default Manual (R. Wisner. Ed. 1987); Schroeder, *Providing Financial Support to the Contractor*, 17 FORUM 1190 (1982); Schroeder, *Procedures and Instruments Utilized to Protect the Surety who Finances the Contractors*, 14 FORUM 830 (1979); Leo, *The Financing Surety and the Chapter 11 Principal* 26 Tort & Ins. L.J. 45 (1990).

2. The Law of Preference Liability

Once the principal files for bankruptcy, all transfers of property by the principal to the surety or other creditors within 90 days of bankruptcy may be avoided or undone under the preference provision of the Bankruptcy Code.[154] The financing agreement between the surety and its principal may be the target of a preference attack. Whether the agreement and the surety's benefits thereunder survive the attack may be affected by certain provisions in the financing agreement and the surety's actions under the agreement.

a. *Elements of Preference.* The Bankruptcy Code allows a trustee or debtor in possession to avoid[155] a pre-bankruptcy transfer[156] of the debtor's property[157] if certain conditions are met. There are six necessary elements to a preference action. They are:

(1) a transfer of property of the debtor,

(2) the transfer must be to or for the benefit of a creditor,

(3) the transfer must be for or on account of an antecedent debt owed by the debtor before the transfer was made,

(4) the transfer must have been made when the debtor was insolvent,

(5) the transfer must have been made during the ninety days immediately preceding the commencement of the case. If the transfer was made to an insider,[158] the transfer may be avoided

---

154. 11 U.S.C. § 547(b).

155. 11 U.S.C. § 547(b) (1979 & Supp. 1989).

156. "Transfer" is a broadly defined term, including every mode, voluntary and involuntary of disposing of property, including the granting of security interests in property. 11 U.S.C. § 101(54).

157. The Code does not define property as it is used in 11 U.S.C. § 547(b) but items constituting the debtor's estate are listed at 11 U.S.C. § 541: Section 541's definition of property of the estate is helpful in determining what constitutes property of the debtor under section 547 because (1) property of the debtor is property of the estate (except for statutory exemptions); and (2) the goal of section 547 is to avoid only those preferential transfers that result in depletion of the estate. *In re General Office Furniture Wholesalers, Inc.*, 42 Bankr. 232 (Bankr. E.D. Va. 1984).

158. 11 U.S.C. § 101(31) defines "insider" as follows:

"Insider" includes -

(A) if the debtor is an individual -
- (i) relative of the debtor or of a general partner of the debtor;
- (ii) partnership in which the debtor is a general partner;
- (iii) general partner of the debtor; or
- (iv) corporation of which the debtor is a director, officer, or person in control;

(B) if the debtor is a corporation -
- (i) director of the debtor;
- (ii) officer of the debtor;
- (iii) person in control of the debtor;
- (iv) partnership in which the debtor is a general partner;
- (v) general partner of the debtor; or
- (vi) relative of a general partner, director, officer, or person in control of the debtor;

(C) if the debtor is a partnership -
- (i) general partner of the debtor
- (ii) relative of a general partner in, general partner of, or person in control of the debtor;
- (iii) partnership in which the debtor is a general partner;
- (iv) general partner of the debtor; or
- (v) person in control of the debtor;

(D) if the debtor is a municipality, elected official of the debtor or relative of an elected official of the debtor;

(E) affiliate or insider of an affiliate as if such affiliate were the debtor; and

(F) managing agent of the debtor;

if it occurred during the period that begins one year before the filing of the petition and ends ninety days before the filing, if the insider to whom the transfer was made had reasonable cause to believe the debtor was insolvent at the time the transfer was made, and

(6) The transfer must enable the creditor, to or for whose benefit it was made, to receive a greater percentage of his claim than he would receive under the distributive provisions of the Bankruptcy Code. Specifically, the creditor must receive more than he would if the case were a liquidation case, if the transfer had not been made, and if the creditor received payment of the debt to the extent provided by the Bankruptcy Code.[159]

All six of the elements of preference must be present before the court will order the transfer avoided. A closer examination of the elements of the preference action brought against the surety and its financing agreement will often reveal that an allegedly preferential transfer does not satisfy all elements. For example, the debtor may attack a payment made just days before the bankruptcy from a trust account established under the financing agreement with the surety.

Financing agreements commonly provide for the establishment of joint control trust accounts. The joint control trust accounts will likely receive all of the deposits for project completion, including all the principal's accounts receivable, the principal's current funds and the surety's advances. The agreement will ordinarily make clear that the funds are held in trust for the benefit of the surety.

Bankruptcy courts look to state law to determine whether a valid trust was created. [160] In most states, the essential elements of a trust are: competent settler and a trustee, an intent to create a trust, an ascertainable trust res (i.e. property), and identifiable beneficiaries. For a surety/principal joint control trust account, the trust res is the funds in the joint control trust accounts, the settler is both the surety and the principal and the trustees are the various banks where the joint control trust accounts are located. The surety will be the beneficiary if the financing agreement has been properly worded. The element of trust that must be given special attention is the intent of the parties to create a trust. The surety's defense of a preference action will be made much easier if the financing agreement has very specific provisions that leave no doubt that an express trust is being created for the benefit of the surety.

The intent to create a trust may be further supported by explicit procedures for funding the completion of the bonded projects in the financing agreement. If the latitude granted to the principal to use the surety's funds is broad, it may indicate the funds are not "in trust," but were merely loaned to the principal. However, if specific procedures are observed during the financing period, the surety can effectively argue that it had no intention of giving the beneficial interest to the funds in the joint

---

11 U.S.C. § 101(31).

159. H.R. REP NO. 95-595, 95th Cong., 1st Sess. 372 (1977); S. REP NO. 95-989, 95th Cong., 2d Sess. 87 (1978); 11 U.S.C. § 547b.

160. *Matter of Torrez*, 63 Bankr. 751 (9th Cir. Bankr. 1986), affd. 827 F2d 1299 (9th Cir. 1987).

control trust account to its principal.[161] The ownership of the beneficial interest will be the owner of any monies left in accounts held in trust if the principal files for bankruptcy.[162]

Thus, the principal's preference attack on a payment under the financing agreement might be defeated by demonstrating that the monies were not "property of the debtor,"[163] but were instead funds held in trust for the surety and/or completion creditors.

In addition, not every transfer is made while the principal is insolvent. Increasingly, companies are advised by bankruptcy counsel to strategically time their bankruptcy filing, often before the financial situation becomes irreparable. It is an essential element of a preference action that the debtor must have been insolvent[164] when the transfer was made. Defaulting principals are often brought down by a cash flow crunch, and may not exhibit traditional balance sheet insolvency. As transfers subject to attack become increasingly distant in time from the bankruptcy filing, investigation may reveal that the principal was not insolvent, thereby providing grounds to defeat the preference claim.

The surety's defense may be aided by a financing agreement containing a recitation by the principal concerning it's present balance sheet solvency. Such a representation may also offer some measure of protection against later fraudulent conveyance claims, whether brought by the principal in his bankruptcy or by third parties.

b. *Exceptions To Preference.* There are seven statutory exceptions to the Code's preference avoiding power.[165] Even if a surety has received a transfer that satisfies the six elements of preference, if a surety can qualify under any one of the exceptions, then it is protected from avoidance of the preference. If it can qualify under several exceptions, it is protected by each to the extent it qualifies under each. Two sections provide exceptions of particular use in defending a financing agreement from preference attack, Sections 547(c)(1) and (4).[166] Both of these exceptions

---

161. In *Askew v. Resource Funding, Ltd.*, Cal.App.3d 402, 156 Cal.Rptr. 208 (1979), an agreement created a project account and contemplated that the funds would be spent on a specific project. The court held that a trust relationship was created because the agreement, between the transferor and the transferee of funds, provided for various safeguards and restrictions on the use of those funds by creating a committee which oversaw and approved expenditures before permitted withdrawals from the project account. The *Askew* Court stated:

> We thus conclude that the language of the Agreement makes it clear that the transferor, NCPA, did not intend the transferee, RGL, to have the beneficial interest in the property transferred, i.e., The $837,500, much less the "ownership" thereof. Seemingly, it would be difficult to draw a document with terminology more manifest as to the purpose of the funds in question than the Agreement before us.

94 Cal.App.3d at 409, 156 Cal.Rptr. At 211. (Emphasis added). *See also* Restatement (Second) of Trusts, § 12 cmt. g (1959).

162. *See* 11 U.S.C. § 541(d).

163. *See Begler v. International Revenue Service*, 110 S.Ct. 2258 (1990) ("A 'debtor' does not own an equitable interest in property he holds in trust for another, that interest is not 'property of the estate,' nor is such an equitable interest 'property of the debtor' for purposes of § 547(b)"); *United States v. Whiting Pools, Inc.*, 462 U.S. 198, 205 nt. 10, 103 S.Ct. 2309, 2314 nt. 10, 76 L.Ed.2d 515, 522 nt. 10 (1983) ("Congress plainly excluded property of others held by the debtor in trust at the time of the filing of the petition."); *In re California Trade Technical Schools, Inc.*, 923 F.2d 641 (9th Cir. 1991) (funds held "in trust" were not property of the debtor for preferential transfer purposes).

164. 11 U.S.C.A. § 101(32) (Supp. 1989).

165. 11 U.S.C.A. § 547(c) (1979 & Supp. 1989).

166. (C) The trustee may not avoid under this section a transfer -

(1) to the extent that such transfer was -

(A) intended by the debtor and the creditor to or for whose benefit such transfer was made to be a contemporaneous exchange for new value given to the debtor; and

(B) in fact a substantially contemporaneous exchange;

. . .

to preference incorporate the concept of "value" received by the debtor from the creditor who would otherwise have received a transfer considered preferential. Because the execution of a financing agreement and transfers occurring pursuant to a financing agreement involve benefit flowing to the debtor from the surety, these exceptions should offer defenses to preference attack in the principal's bankruptcy.

To use the Section 547(c)(1) exception, the surety must give "new value", as defined in Section 547(a)(2),[167] contemporaneously with the receipt of the debtor's transfer. The surety could defend the principal's preference action by showing that any transfers of assets or security by the principal to the surety were a contemporaneous exchange for the surety's new value (i.e. the surety's financing).

A creditor may obtain additional collateral from the debtor within the preference period, so long as some new value is given to the debtor. The new value may simply be a modification of debt terms, or some other substantial concession by the creditor. For example, in *In Re Spada,*[168] a preference action was brought against a bank alleging that the giving of a mortgage was preferential. Before the mortgage was given, the debtor was obligated to the bank on three separate unsecured loans. The debtor requested the bank to consolidate the loans and reduce the interest payments. In return for the mortgage, the bank reduced the interest rate, agreed to accept interest only payments during the first year of the loan, and agreed to subordinate its secured position if the debtor could obtain financing to build a shopping center. The *Spada* Court concluded that the bank's modification of the existing agreement and the giving of the mortgage by the debtor was a "contemporaneous exchange for new value" under Section 547(c)(1).

The financing agreement may be saved by its acknowledgement or modification of the surety's equitable lien on bonded contract funds. These valuable rights may aid the surety's defense of a preference action relating to the debtor's payment of bills that would be covered by the surety's bond obligations.[169]

If a court were to conclude that the principal's transfer of its property interests to the surety and the surety's commitment to finance were not a "substantially contemporaneous," exchange of new value, then the "subsequent advance" exception in Section 547(c)(4) may apply. Illustrative of the exception is the decision of *In Re Amarex, Inc.*[170] The debtor entered into an agreement with a group of creditors, under which the debtor made payments within 90 days of filing bankruptcy. The *Amarex* Court concluded that the creditors' payments to third party vendors, made on behalf of the

---

(4) To or for the benefit of a creditor, to the extent that, after such transfer, such creditor gave new value to or for the benefit of the debtor – (A) not secured by an otherwise unavoidable security interest; and (B) on account of which new value the debtor did not make an otherwise unavoidable transfer to or for the benefit of such creditor.

11 U.S.C. § 547(c)(1) and (c)(4), respectively.

167. 11 U.S.C. § 547(a)(2) provides: "'New Value' means money or money's worth in goods, services, or new credit, or release by a transferee of property previously transferred to such transferee in a transaction that is neither void nor voidable by the debtor or the trustee under any applicable law, including proceeds of such property, but does not include an obligation substituted for an existing obligation."

168. 91 Bankr. 668 (Bankr. M.D.Pa. 1988), *aff'd in part. rev'd in part.* 903 F.2d 971 (3rd Cir. 1990). On appeal, the Third Circuit held that new value was given, but remanded to determine the amount of new value given.

169. *See In re E.R. Fegert, Inc.*, 88 Bankr. 258 (9th Cir. bankr. 1988), *aff'd*, 887 F.2d 955 (9th Cir. 1989). The Chapter 7 trustee brought a preference clam seeking to recover from the surety for pre-petition payments made by a debtor/contractor to two subcontractors. The court held that the release of the subcontractors' rights against the surety, because the surety could have exercised its lien rights under the doctrine of equitable subrogation against the contract proceeds if the subcontractors had not been paid, constituted "new value" given to the debtor in a substantially contemporaneous exchange.

170. 88 bankr. 362 (W.D.Okla. 1988).

debtor, were a "subsequent advance" of new value each time the creditors paid the debtor's vendors.[171] Therefore, the surety's commitment to finance and its cash advances can be "new value" under Section 547(a)(2). Thus, whether the surety's new value is perceived as "contemporaneous" or "subsequent" to the debtor's transfer of property to the surety, the exceptions to preference in Sections 547(c)(1) or 547(c)(4) should apply to defeat the avoidance action.

The bankrupt principal may argue that the surety's finance money, to be used to pay expenses on the bonded projects, is not "new value" because the surety had a pre-existing duty under its bond to pay these expenses. The court must be made to understand that financing the principal goes significantly beyond the surety's bond obligations. A performing surety is not required to finance its principal to complete the bonded projects.[172] A surety is entitled to decide how to best complete bonded projects upon the principal's default.[173] Furthermore, the surety's financing may protect the principal's reputation, preserve favorable credit terms and relationships with suppliers and subcontractors, and provide other benefits to the principal. It will be helpful if the principal has considered and acknowledged these types of benefits in written financing agreement. The financing agreement may also require the surety to cover a portion of the principal's overhead or other expenses not covered by the surety's bonds. These benefits also constitute new value.

3. Other Financing Clauses That May Assist the Surety in Bankruptcy

The surety's exercise of its rights may be assisted by clauses found in the financing agreement which contemplate the potential bankruptcy filing. A clause attempting to prohibit the principal or indemnitors from filing a bankruptcy petition will be void as against public policy.[174]

However, some courts will dismiss a bankruptcy petition, in order to enforce the provisions of a pre-bankruptcy workout agreement.[175] A comprehensive financing or default agreement between the surety and principal would be very similar to the "workout agreements" that the courts have favored in the reported decisions dismissing bankruptcies. Such a clause will typically provide that the parties understood and intended the agreement to be an alternative to bankruptcy.

The financing agreement may also include clauses that entitle the surety to immediate relief from the automatic stay if the financing agreement is unsuccessful and the principal later files a

171. *See also Matter of Global Intern. Airways Corp.*, 80 Bankr. 983 (Bankr. W.D.Mo. 1987) (Debtor's payment of prior purchases was not a voidable preference because creditor's subsequent transfer of goods was "subsequent value" under 11 U.S.C. § 547(c)(4); *Matter of Marin Aviation, Inc.*, 53 Bankr. 497 (Bankr. D.N.J. 1984) (Debtor's transfer of security interest in helicopter was not a voidable preference because bank gave new value to debtor after transfer occurred).

172. *Fischer Construction Co. v. Fireman's Fund Insurance Co.*, 420 F.2d 271 (10th Cir. 1969).

173. *Aetna Cas. and Sur. Co. v. U.S.*, 845 F.2d 971, 975 (Fed. Cir. 1988); Thompson, *Completion Options Available to a Performance Bond Surety Other than Financing its Principal*, 17 FORUM 1215 (1982).

174. *In re Joshua Slocum Ltd.*, 922 F.2d 1081 (3d Cir. 1990); In re Club Tower L.P., 138 Bankr. 307 (Bankr. N.D.Ga. 1991).

175. *In re Colonial Ford, Inc.*, 24 Bankr. 1014, 1020 (Bankr. D. Utah 1982) (in order to encourage non-judicial workouts that are expeditious, economic, and sensible, "[w]here . . . the workout is comprehensive, and designed to end, not perpetuate, the creditor-company relations, dismissal under Section 305(a)(1) is appropriate."); *In re Pengo Industr.*, 962 F.2d 543, 549 (5th Cir. 1992), *cert. den.*, 506 U.S. 1000 ("[w]e strongly disfavor a judicial interpretation of the Bankruptcy Code that contravenes the substantial congressional policy favoring out-of-court consensual workouts."); *see also, In re Chateaugay Corp.*, 961 F.2d 378, 383 (2d Cir. 1992) (the court "will not attribute to Congress an intent to place a stumbling block in front of debtors seeking to avoid bankruptcy with the cooperation of their creditors [r]ather . . . Congress inten[ded] to encourage consensual workouts and . . . minimiz[e] bankruptcy filings. . . ").

bankruptcy petition. Some bankruptcy courts have upheld such clauses, interpreting the pre-petition agreement to be "cause" for relief from the automatic stay under 11 U.S.C. § 362 (d) (1).[176]

Even where such a clause is found in the financing agreement, and surety's bankruptcy counsel believes the bankruptcy court will likely enforce the stipulated stay relief, it would be advisable to first file a motion with the court and await the court ruling, rather than relying upon language stating that the stay is not applicable to the surety's actions at all.[177]

Financing or default agreements may provide a release to indemnitors or may reduce or "cap" the amount of the indemnity obligation owed to the surety. This concession may be given in exchange for cooperation, collateral or some other consideration. A "claw-back" clause is intended to take away the benefits granted by the agreement, if the principal later files bankruptcy. The clawback may occur if there is any subsequent bankruptcy or only if the bankruptcy filing occurs within the preference period. The clawback clause may be activated only by the principal's bankruptcy, or by the bankruptcy filing of the principal or any single indemnitor.

A clawback clause has two positive effects. First, it prevents the principal or indemnitors from unfairly claiming the benefits of the agreement, when their bankruptcy filing has destroyed or delayed benefits that should have flowed to the surety. Second, it creates incentives for the indemnitors and principal to stay out of bankruptcy, at least for the preference period. This purpose is particularly important where the surety has obtained new collateral under the terms of the agreement. The security interests will be avoidable if a bankruptcy is filed within the preference period, generally ninety (90) days.

A financing agreement that states that financial statements from the indemnitors and the principal have been requested, received and relied upon by the surety in entering into the agreement can be helpful in a practical sense to the surety. The clause often also recites that the principal and indemnitors understand and intend for the surety to rely upon the statements, and that this reliance is reasonable. If the information in the financial statements turns out to be inaccurate, the amounts loaned or losses incurred under the agreement may be non-dischargeable in a subsequent bankruptcy of the principal or the indemnitors. 11 U.S.C. § 523. A non-dischargeable claim benefits the surety in two ways. First, the debt can be pursued post-bankruptcy. Second, the principal or indemnitors may resist or avoid a bankruptcy filing altogether, because of the inability to discharge the debt owed to the surety.

B. POST-PETITION FINANCING OF THE PRINCIPAL

1. Introduction

A surety's decision to finance its debtor/principal after bankruptcy begins with the same considerations that apply outside of bankruptcy. The obvious goals are to minimize the surety's

176. *In re Powers*, 170 Bankr. 480 (Bankr. D. Mass. 1994); *In re Cheeks*, 167 Bankr. 817 (Bankr. D.SC. 1994); *In re Wheaton Oaks Office Partners,* 1992 WL 381047 (N.D. Ill.), (a provision regarding stay relief could constitute "cause" under 11 U.S.C. § 362(d)(1)); *In re Club Tower L.P.*, 138 Bankr. 307 (Bankr. N.D. Ga. 1991) (stay relief clause enforceable); *Contra, Farm Credit of Cent. Fla. v. Polk*, 160 Bankr. 870 (D. M.D. Fla. 1993); *Sky Group Int'l, Inc.*, 108 Bankr. 86 (Bankr. W.D. Pa. 1989); *Best Finance Corp.*, 74 Bankr. 243 (Bankr. P.R. 1987); *In re Jenkins Court Assoc. Ltd. Partnership*, 181 Bankr. 33 (Bankr. E.D. Pa. 1995) (Court declined to enforce waiver, but consider representations in pre-petition settlement agreement with hearing evidence to determine whether to grant stay relief.)

177. *In re Powers*, 170 Bankr. 480, 483 (Bankr. D. Mass. 1994).

losses by enabling the debtor/principal to complete the work and possibly obtain collateral to offset potential losses. In addition to the ordinary considerations surrounding a decision to finance, the surety contemplating Chapter 11 financing should weigh the code's inducements to provide financing to a debtor-in-possession. The extension of credit may entitle the surety to collateral either in a first priority or junior position, may be combined with cross-collateralization clauses, and may be conditioned upon a waiver of actions an antagonistic debtor/principal or indemnitors may threaten to bring against the surety.[178]

2. The Four Types of Post-Petition Credit.

The four different types of credit permissible under the Bankruptcy Code are set forth in Section 364(a), (b), (c) and (d).[179] Section 364(a) provides that if the "trustee" (which term also includes the debtor-in-possession)[180] is authorized to operate the debtor's business, the trustee may obtain unsecured credit and incur unsecured debt in the ordinary course of business, unless the court orders otherwise. Any such debt, usually trade debt, which is not paid will be given an administrative expense priority pursuant to Section 503(b)(1). This priority receives first distribution of unsecured funds under the plan or in liquidation. The risk of this type of financing is that a court may later determine it was incurred outside the ordinary course of business.[181] If prior court approval was not obtained, the creditor may lose its claim against the estate for the amount of

---

178. *In re Ellingsen MacLean Oil Co., Inc.*, 834 F.2d 599 (6th Cir. 1987), *cert. denied*, 488 U.S. 817 (1987) (Sixth Circuit affirmed bankruptcy court's financing order that provided for a waiver by the debtor of any possible fraudulent transfer claims against a lender).

179. Obtaining Credit.

(a) If the trustee is authorized to operate the business of the debtor under section 721, 1108, 1304, 1203, or 1204 of this title, unless the court orders otherwise, the trustee may obtain unsecured credit and incur unsecured debt in the ordinary course of business allowable under section 503(b)(1) of this title as an administrative expense.

(b) The court, after notice and a hearing, may authorize the trustee to obtain unsecured credit or to incur unsecured debt other than under subsection (a) of this section, allowable under section 503(b)(1) of this title as an administrative expense.

(c) If the trustee is unable to obtain unsecured credit allowable under section 503(b)(1) of this title as an administrative expense, the court, after notice and a hearing, may authorize the obtaining of credit or the incurring of debt–

(1) with priority over any or all administrative expenses of the kind specified in section 503(b) or 507(b) of this title;

(2) secured by a lien on property of the estate that is not otherwise subject to a lien; or

(3) secured by a junior lien on property of the estate that is subject to a lien.

(d) (1) The court, after notice and a hearing, may authorize the obtaining of credit or the incurring of debt secured by a senior or equal lien on property of the estate that is subject to a lien only if –

(A) the trustee is unable to obtain such credit otherwise; and

(B) there is adequate protection of the interest of the holder of the lien on the property of the estate on which such senior or equal lien is proposed to be granted.

. . . .

11 U.S.C. § 364.

180. 11 U.S.C. § 1107 (Debtor-in-Possession has the rights and duties of a trustee).

181. *In re Media Cent., Inc.*, 115 Bankr. 119 (Bankr. E.D.Tenn. 1990); *In re Lockwood Enterprises, Inc.*, 52 Bankr. 871 (Bankr. S.D.N.Y. 1985) (there was no proof that the debtor normally or customarily borrowed funds to meet payroll and operating expenses). Additionally, credit under Section 364(a) or (b) must be extended for "the actual, necessary costs and expenses of preserving the estate" to be given Section 503(b)(1) priority.

the credit extended.[182] A surety who will finance post-petition or who may execute bonds post-petition, should avoid the risk of financing under Section 364(a) and obtain court approval.

Credit incurred outside the ordinary course of business may also be given an administrative expense priority under Section 364(b). A court order approving this credit is required.

While Sections 364(a) and (b) provide administrative expense priority, inducements available under Sections 364(c) and (d) can provide the surety with much better protections for its post-petition financing. Section 364(c) offers three possible protections to the potential surety: (1) super priority status over all administrative expenses, (2) lien(s) on unencumbered property of the debtor, and/or (3) junior lien(s) on already encumbered property.[183]

To obtain protections under Section 364(c), the debtor must demonstrate that credit is unavailable on more favorable terms.[184] The debtor's burden includes establishing that credit under Section 364(b) is unavailable, that the credit is necessary for preservation of the estate, and that the "terms of the transaction are fair, reasonable, and adequate, given the circumstances of the debtor-borrower and the proposed lender."[185] In *Crouse Group*, the debtor/principal sought a financing order that gave the surety a super priority claim under Section 364(c)(1). In return, the surety would provide financing for another payroll period, but not for the completion of the bonded projects. Evidence suggested that the surety desired to keep the debtors/principals on the project only until the surety could find replacements for its principals. Thus, the *Crouse Group* Court denied the motion to approve the financing order.

Conversely, in *In Re Ames Dept. Stores, Inc.*,[186] the court granted a lending arrangement which gave Chemical Bank a super priority claim under Section 364(c)(1). The court found that the proposed financing would benefit the estate.

The differing results of these two cases highlights the requirement that the surety's financing must benefit the estate for a court to grant the protections of Section 364(c). This benefit is more likely to be proven where the financing order contains a commitment by the surety to fund the projects to completion, subject to various default provisions. Lesser financing commitments may be approved by the court, but the risk of rejection is increased.

A surety may be granted extraordinary protections under section 364(d), if the debtor has no other recourse for financing. This section permits the post-petition financier to "prime" an existing secured creditor on encumbered property as a condition to granting new or continued financing to the debtor. Similar to Section 364(c) financing, Section 364(d) financing requires that other financing on more favorable terms be unavailable.[187] Existing lienholders who will be primed must be adequately protected.[188] The debtor/principal has the burden of proving that the requirements of Section 364(d) are met.[189] In *In Re Snowshoe Co., Inc.*,[190] the court affirmed the

---

182. *In re Photo Promotion Associates, Inc.*, 881 F.2d 6 (2d Cir. 1989); *In re J.L. Graphics, Inc.*, 62 Bankr. 750 (Bankr. D.N.H. 1986).

183. 11 U.S.C. §364(c)(1), (2) and (3) respectively.

184. *In re Ames Dept. Stores, Inc.*, 115 Bankr. 34 (Bankr. S.D.N.Y. 1990) (Court concluded that the debtors met their burden of showing the unavailability of alternative unsecured financing by approaching four lending institutions with the capability of loaning the large sums necessary to sustain the debtors' operations).

185. *In re The Crouse Group, Inc.*, 71 Bankr. 544, 549 (Bankr. E.D.Pa. 1987).

186. 115 Bankr. 34 (Bankr. S.D.N.Y. 1990)

187. 11 U.S.C. § 364(d)(1)(A).

188. 11 U.S.C. § 364(d)(1)(B).

189. *In re 495 Cent. Park Ave. Corp.* 136 Bankr. 626 (Bankr. S.D.N.Y. 1992) (Debtor presented evidence that demonstrated that both prongs of 11 U.S.C. § 364(d) were met).

190. 789 F.2d 1085 (4th Cir. 1986).

district court's holding that an equity cushion in the primed property and the trustee's financial projection of repayment of the super priority loan were adequate to approve Section 364(d) financing.[191]

3. Cross-Collateralization

One of the most significant benefits that the surety may obtain for financing the debtor/principal is the opportunity to cross-collateralize. For example, the surety may gain security in contract proceeds from profitable bonded projects and unbonded projects to secure losses on other bonded jobs.

Some courts have held that cross-collateralization of a pre-petition debt with post-petition assets may never be approved.[192] Other courts examine cross-collateralization on a case-by-case basis to determine if the financing is in the best interests of the estate, rather than principally the pre-petition creditor.[193] For example, in *In Re Vanguard Diversified, Inc.*,[194] the court approved a financing agreement with a cross-collateralization clause because without the lender's continued financing, the debtor would probably cease business and be forced to liquidate.

Cross-collateralization should be sought by a surety providing financing for its principal to complete bonded projects. The court will rigorously scrutinize a cross-collateralization provision to determine the preferential treatment the surety's pre-petition claim will receive, as compared with the benefit the financing will bring to the estate. The debtor and the surety will be required to demonstrate how the financing benefits the estate.

4. The Safe-Harbor for the Post-Petition Financier

It is often necessary to put bankruptcy financing in place on an expedited basis. Even where the bankruptcy court approved financing, if a lender withheld funds until the appeal period passed, or until all appeals were concluded, the patient would die waiting for the medicine. Section 364(e) provides lenders with protection from the possibility that an appeal will unwind the transactions[195]. This section provides that if an appellate court reverses or modifies the financing order it will not affect the validity of the debt or any priority or loan granted to secure the debt, even though the

---

191. *In re Beker Industries Corp.* 58 Bankr. 725 (Bankr. S.D.N.Y. 1986) (Court authorized Section 364(d) borrowing that primed existing liens; case contains good discussion of adequate protection, valuation and cross-collateralization). Contra *In re Chevy Devco*, 78 Bankr. 585 (Bankr. C.D.Cal. 1987) (Section 364(d) motion denied where existing lien or was not granted adequate protection). Most courts have recognized that an equity cushion may constitute adequate protection. *In re Mellor*, 734 F.2d 1396 (9th Cir. 1984); *In re McCombs Properties VI, Ltd.*, 88 Bankr. 261 (Bankr. C.D.Cal. 1988). But see *In re Alyucan Interstate Corp.*, 12 Bankr. 803 (Bankr. D.Utah 1981) (Court rejects equity cushion as means of providing adequate protection, but contains list of cases at note 14 supporting the contrary view).

192. *Shapiro v. Saybrook Manuf. Co.*, 963 F.2d 1490 (11th Cir. 1992); *In re Monach Circuit Indus., Inc.*, 41 Bankr. 859 (Bankr. E.D.Pa. 1984) (Cross-collateralization amounts to impermissible preference and is not authorized by 11 U.S.C. § 364).

193. *In re Keystone Camera Prods. Corp.*, 126 Bankr. 177 (Bankr. D.N.J. 1991); *In re Baker Indus., Inc.*, 58 Bankr. 725 (Bankr. S.D.N.Y. 1986); *In re Robin Indus. Inc.*, 52 Bankr. 241 (Bankr. W.D.N.Y. 1985).

194. 31 Bankr. 364 (Bankr. E.D.N.Y. 1983).

195. 11 U.S.C. § 364(e) provides: "The reversal or modification on appeal of an authorization under this section to obtain credit or incur debt, or of a grant under this section of a priority or a lien, does not affect the validity of any debt so incurred, or any priority or lien so granted, to an entity that extended such credit in good faith, whether or not such entity knew of the pendency of the appeal, unless such authorization and the incurring of such debt, or the granting of such priority or lien, were stayed pending appeal."

lender knew of the pendency of the appeal, provided: (1) the appeal was not stayed under Federal Rule of Bankruptcy Procedure 8005,[196] and (2) the lender extended the credit in good faith. These two requirements for the safe harbor provided in Section 364(e) are addressed serially.

There is no automatic ten-day supersedeas or stay of a financing order under Federal Rule of Bankruptcy Procedure 7062. Thus, credit extended during the ten-day period after entry of the financing order should be protected.[197] Additionally, if no stay of the financing order is obtained, an appeal of the order may be dismissed because of mootness. A lender should be aware that if a financing order is affirmed on appeal by the district court or bankruptcy appellate panel, then an automatic ten-day stay of the financing order will be in place.[198]

Good faith is not defined in the Bankruptcy Code or Bankruptcy Rules. Therefore, courts have looked to standards employed in other areas of law for guidance (i.e. the Uniform Commercial Code).[199] As long as the loan serves the purpose of the Bankruptcy Code the lender will be deemed to have extended the credit in good faith and will be entitled to the protection of Section 364(e).[200]

The finding that the lender extended credit in good faith must be an explicit finding.[201] To avail itself of this safe harbor provision, the surety should require that any financing order explicitly contain a court finding that the surety is providing credit in good faith.

5. Implementing the Post-Petition Financing Agreement and Order

Similar to a pre-petition financing agreement, identification of the parties, bonds, bonded projects, and indemnity agreements, and acknowledgments of the principal's default and that the surety has an equitable lien on bonded contract funds should be set forth in the post-petition financing agreement. A statement of the specific purposes for which the surety's financing is intended should be included in the agreement.

Most importantly, the post-petition financing agreement should enumerate the protections the surety will receive under the various provisions of Section 364 (i.e. Super priority, lien on unencumbered property and/or a priming lien). The extent and nature of cross-collateralization given to the surety should be detailed. If a surety will receive any security interests in property of the estate, the financing order should specifically provide that the automatic stay is lifted for the surety to perfect the security interests under non-bankruptcy law.

The agreement may also provide that the debtor/principal has no objection to the surety's claim in the bankruptcy proceeding and no objection to the validity, extent and priority of the surety's equitable rights of subrogation to the bonded contract proceeds.

---

196. *In re Adams Apple, Inc.* 829 F.2d 1484 (9th Cir. 1987) (An order granting a lender a secured lien is a final order for purposes of appeal under 28 U.S.C. § 158(d)).

197. *Id.*

198. Fed. R. Bankr. P. 8017.

199. *Adams Apple,* 829 F.2d at 1489 (Court looked to good faith standard applied in foreclosure sales, i.e. misconduct defeating good faith includes fraud, collusion, or an attempt to take grossly unfair advantage of others).

200. *Adams Apple,* 829 F.2d at 1485 (Knowledge of illegality of a transaction destroys good faith); *Ellingsen MacLean Oil,* 834 F.2d 599 (Loan by existing secured lenders was not improper because it involved the settlement of a pre-existing dispute as well as the extension of post-petition credit). But *see In re EDC Holding Co.*, 676 F.2d 945 (7th Cir. 1982) (Lender's priority was revoked where the loan proceeds were used to fund a settlement between the debtor and a labor union involving payment of the union's legal expenses as a wage priority where they were not entitled to payment from the estate at all – effect was improper under the Bankruptcy Code).

201. *In re Revco D.S., Inc.*, 901 F.2d 1359 (6th Cir. 1990).

The indemnitors to the surety should be required to reaffirm their guarantees to the surety. The financing agreement and order should provide that they are binding on the debtor's successors and assigns. Moreover, the terms of the agreement and order should explicitly state that they survive the confirmation of a plan of reorganization, a subsequent bankruptcy filing, or a dismissal of the bankruptcy case.

The surety's obligation to finance must be terminable upon a default. The events of default suggested for inclusion in a financing agreement are: (1) conversion of the case to Chapter 7, (2) appointment of a trustee (or examiner with wide discretion), (3) debtor's filing of a plan of reorganization unacceptable to the surety, (4) an attack by a creditor on the surety's claim or the post-petition financing order, (5) debtor's failure to assume executory bonded construction contracts, and (6) if applicable, debtor's noncompliance with a budget included as a part of the financing order.

Finally, the surety should require that affirmative evidence be put in the record regarding the surety's good faith at the hearing to approve the financing. The financing order must make explicit and specific findings of the surety's good faith so as to provide the surety with the safe harbor protection of Section 364(e).

A surety should confirm that proper notice of the motion to approve financing was given. Notice of post-petition lending must be given to the creditors' committee, if appointed, or else to the twenty largest unsecured creditors, to any creditors with security interests or liens on post-petition assets, and to the U.S. Trustee.[202] Lack of sufficient notice may invalidate any financing agreement between the surety and the debtor-in-possession.[203]

VII. *Defense of Preference Actions by the Trustee/Debtor Seeking to Recover Money Paid to Project Subcontractors and Suppliers*

A. The Law Of Preference Liability

If certain characteristics are present in a transaction, it may be "avoided" under bankruptcy preference law. The "avoidance" of a transfer means that the trustee or debtor-in-possession can force the creditor who received a payment from the debtor before bankruptcy to repay the money to the bankruptcy estate. This repayment may be compelled notwithstanding the fact that the creditor was fully entitled to have its debt paid by the debtor at the time the creditor received the funds. The purpose of the preference power is to eliminate any incentive for creditors to race one another in an attempt to dismember the debtor on the eve of bankruptcy.[204] It also is said by courts that the preference doctrine furthers the purpose of "ratable distribution" by recapturing sums paid to only a few before bankruptcy, for general distribution to creditors under the Bankruptcy Code.[205]

Section 547(b) of the Bankruptcy Code gives a trustee or a debtor in possession the ability to avoid pre-bankruptcy transfers of the debtor's property that result in preferential treatment of a creditor. This is a very powerful tool to recover assets for the bankruptcy estate. As explained previously in this chapter, the necessary elements of a preference action are:

---

202. Fed. R. Bankr. P. 4001(c).
203. *In re Monarch Circuit Indus., Inc.*, 41 Bankr. 859 (Bankr. E.D.Pa. 1984).
204. *In re Balducci Oil Co., Inc.*, 33 B.R. 799, 805 (Bankr. N.D. Ga. 1983).
205. *Matter of Kennesaw Mint, Inc.*, 32 B.R. 799, 805 (Bankr. N.D. Ga. 1983).

1) A transfer must be made.

2) The transfer must be property of the debtor.

3) The transfer must be to or for the benefit of a creditor.

4) The transfer must be for or on account of an antecedent debt owed by the debtor before the transfer was made.

5) The transfer must have been made while the debtor was insolvent.

6) The transfer must have been during the 90 days immediately preceding the commencement of the case. If the transfer was made to an insider, the transfer may be avoided for the additional period that begins one year before the filing of the petition and ends 90 days before the filing.

7) The transfer must enable the creditor, to or for whose benefit it was made, to receive a greater percentage of its claim than it would receive under the distributive provisions of the Bankruptcy Code. In other words, the creditor must receive more than it would have received if the payments had not been made and the creditor received what it would in a Chapter 7 liquidation.

B. THE PREFERENCE COMPLAINT AGAINST A PROJECT SUPPLIER OR SUBCONTRACTOR - CAUSE FOR CONCERN TO THE SURETY

A preference action by the principal can have serious consequences to the payment bond surety as well as the payment bond claimant. The bond principal will likely have paid some project suppliers and subcontractors during the 90 days prior to its bankruptcy filing. The unpaid suppliers and subcontractors will likely assert claims against the surety's payment bond. If the debtor/principal recovers pre-petition payments from project suppliers and subcontractors by prosecuting preference actions, the debtor/principal may increase the payment bond surety's loss. If the pre-petition payments are recovered from the project suppliers and subcontractors, they will seek recovery from the payment bond. Although previously paid by the principal, the payment which was set aside as a preference will not discharge the surety.[206] The claimant may sue the surety directly following the principal's recovery of the preferential payment.

When confronted with the prospect of losing its pre-petition payment, the alert bond claimant will promptly act to preserve its contingent claim against the payment bond surety. The danger to the bond claimant is that the limitations period for suit on the payment bond could expire before the preference action is brought. For example, the action on the payment bond may have a one year statute of limitation, whereas the principal has two years from the bankruptcy filing to commence a preference action.[207] To protect against the possible loss of a payment bond claim, the claimant may join the surety in the pending preference action.[208] Claimants may seek an order of the bankruptcy court compelling the principal to file its preference action, if any, before the payment bond statute of limitations expires. Such a request has the effect of encouraging or hastening the principal's filing of a preference action, which will increase the surety's loss, if successful.

---

206. *In re Herman Cantor Corp.*, 15 B.R. 747, 750 (Bankr. E.D. Va. 1981), citing to Annot., 56 A.L.R. 1363 (1928); *Horner et al. v. First Nat. Bank of St. Mary's of Leonardtown, Md.*, 141 S.E. 767 (App. Va. 1928); *Swans v. Fourt Nat. Bank of St. Louis*, 117 Fed. 1 (8th Cir. 1902).

207. 11 U.S.C.A. §546(a) (1993 & Supp 1997).

208. *In re E.R. Fegert, Inc.*, 88 B.R. 258 (Bankr. 9th Cir. 1988), *aff'd,*, 887 F.2d 955 (9th Cir. 1989) (Surety brought in as third party in preference action brought against two subcontractors).

The immediate prosecution of a claim against the payment bond surety creates an interesting anomaly. The claimant has been paid, and the surety would have the defense of payment, until the preference is adjudicated and the claimant has returned the payment to the principal/debtor. Is a contingent claim against the bond ripe for adjudication? What if the limitations period expires before the bond claimant brings suit to recover the payment it lost to the preference action? Can the surety successfully assert the statute of limitations defense, thereby leaving the claimant unpaid and without a remedy? No reported decision has yet addressed these difficult questions, but such cases are currently pending before the courts.

C. THE PREFERENCE COMPLAINT AGAINST THE SURETY

A principal in bankruptcy may file a preference action against its surety to recover pre-bankruptcy payments made by the principal to laborers, subcontractors, materialmen and other trade creditors on a project bonded by the surety. In most cases, preference actions are brought against a party that received money from the debtor. However, the principal can assert a preference action against the surety even though the surety does not receive any payments directly. Such an action is based on the theory that the principal's payments to project laborers, materialmen, subcontractors and other trade creditors benefitted the surety, because the surety is absolved from paying debts covered under the surety's bonds.[209] The debtor's action against the surety is sometimes referred to as an "indirect preference action" because the surety receives the benefit of the principal's payments indirectly, by being relieved of bond obligations.

In *Newbery Corp. v. Fireman's Fund Ins. Co.*,[210] the theory of the indirect preference action is explained as follows:

> [The principal's] theory is based on a bankruptcy maxim that the estate may proceed directly against a surety, instead of circuitously recouping the preference from the creditor, forcing the creditor to proceed against the surety and then waiting for the surety to assert a claim against the estate for reimbursement.[211]

While the issue of a payment bond surety's preference liability is just beginning to receive attention in reported decisions, it is well-established in case law that payment by the debtor of a guaranteed debt is a payment "to or for the benefit of" the guarantor creditor under Section 547.[212] The legislative history of section 101(9)(A) further supports this finding.

> A guarantor of or surety for a claim against the debtor will also be a creditor, because he will hold a contingent claim against the debtor that will become fixed when he pays the creditor whose claim he has guaranteed or insured.[213]

209. *See, e.g.*, *Newbery Corp. v. Fireman's Fund Ins. Co.*, 106 B.R. 186 (D. Ariz. 1989).

210. 106 B.R. 186 (D. Ariz. 1989).

211. *Id.* at 187.

212. *See In re Robinson Brothers Drilling, Inc.*, 97 B.R. 77 (W.D. Okla. 1988); *In re V. N. Deprizio Constr. Co.*, 86 B.R. 545 (N.D. Ill. 1988), *aff'd,* 874 F.2d 1186 (7th Cir. 1989); *In re Mercon Indus., Inc.*, 37 B.R. 549 (Bankr. E.D. Pa. 1984); *In re R.A. Beck Builder, Inc.*, 34 B.R. 888 (Bankr. W.D. Pa. 1983).

213. H.R. REP. NO. 95-595, 95th Cong., 1st Sess. 309-10 (1977); S. REP. NO. 95-989, 95th Cong., 2nd Sess. 22 (1978); 1978 U.S. CODE CONG. & ADMIN. NEWS 5787, 5808, 6266-6267.

"Creditor" is defined in the Bankruptcy Code at section 101(9)(A) to mean an"entity that has a claim against the debtor that arose at the time of or before the order for relief concerning the debtor." Section 101(4)(A) defines "claim." A claim is a "right to payment, whether or not such right is . . . liquidated, unliquidated, fixed, contingent [or] matured . . . ."

When the surety issues its bond, it becomes contingently liable for its principal's debts on the bonded contract. At the same time, the surety acquires a contingent claim for indemnification from the principal. It is, therefore, a "creditor" for the purposes of section 547(b)(1).

By its payment to the subcontractors and materialmen on the bonded contract, the debtor discharges the surety of its contingent obligation to pay the guaranteed debt. "A payment to the creditor [obligee] discharges [the guarantor/surety], therefore, precisely as though made directly to him."[214] Therefore, a debtor's payment of bonded project debts is "for the benefit of" the surety who is a "creditor" for purposes of section 547(b)(1). Assuming the other elements of a preference under section 547 are satisfied, these payments are preferences to the surety which may be recovered from the surety just as if the payment had been made directly to the surety.[215]

D. Defenses Available to the Surety

1. Attacking the Preference Case in Chief

The debtor has the burden to establish each element of preference under Code § 547(b). If any element of a preference is not proven, then the preference action must fail.[216] The payment bond surety's successful defense of an indirect preference action may be shown by demonstrating the absence of one or more of the elements of Section 547(b).

2. Were the Transfers Property of the Debtor?

Code § 547(b) requires that the debtor demonstrate that any transfer be of an "interest of the debtor in property." The Bankruptcy Code does not define the phrase "property of the debtor" as it is used in § 547(b). "Generally, property belongs to the debtor for purposes of § 547 if its transfer will deprive the bankruptcy estate of something which could otherwise be used to satisfy the claims of creditors."[217]

a. *Funds Held In Trust.* The surety may utilize a trust theory to demonstrate that the debtor's payments to trade creditors were not transfers of the debtor's property. Under this theory, the contract funds assume a "trust nature" until the job is complete and laborers, materialmen, subcontractors and other trade creditors are paid.[218] In *Cooper v. Grisofe Electric Corp. (In re Building Dynamics, Inc.)*[219] the New York Bankruptcy Court addressed the issue of a debtor/contractor's claim that a payment to its subcontractor to pay in full all persons who furnished

214. *Smith v. Tostevin*, 247 F. 102, 103 (2d Cir. 1917).

215. *Newbery Corp. v. Fireman's Fund Ins. Co.*, 106 B.R. 186, 187 (D. Ariz. 1989).

216. 11 U.S.C.A. §ù547(g) (1993 & Supp. 1997); *In re Bullion Reserve of North America*, 836 F.2d 1214, 1217 (9th Cir. 1988), *cert. denied sub nom., Bozeck v. Danning*, 486 U.S. 1056 (1988).

217. *In re Bullion Reserve of North America*, 836 F.2d at 1217.

218. *Am. States Ins. Co. v. Ram Constr. Co. (In re Ram Constr. Co., Inc.)*, 32 B.R. 758 (Bankr. W.D. Pa. 1983).

219. 134 B.R. 715 (Bankr. W.D.N.Y. 1992).

material or performed labor on the property was a preference. Pursuant to a New York Lien law, funds received by a general contractor for the improvement of real property were held in trust prior to bankruptcy.[220] Based upon this New York Lien law the subcontractor contended that the payment to it was from trust funds that were not the debtor's property. The *Building Dynamics* Court agreed and held that the pre-petition payment to the subcontractor was not preferential because the funds paid to the subcontractor were not property of the debtor.

Payments made by a debtor may have been from monies held in trust pursuant to a state's trust fund statute. In states with this type of statute, the surety may defend a preference action because the monies used to pay those debts were held in trust. Thus, the funds would not be property of the debtor and the payments would not be preferential.[221]

Contractual provisions establishing the trust character of the funds the debtor used to pay project supplier and subcontractors will also provide the basis for a defense to the preference action.[222]

b. *Earmarked Funds*. Another defense the surety may assert to the claim that payments of funds to suppliers and subcontractors were preferential to the surety is the "earmarking doctrine." This doctrine applies where funds become available to the debtor that are intended and directed by the party providing the funds for the express purpose of paying the debtor's obligation to a specific creditor. The rule originated where the new "lender" was a guarantor or a surety of the debtor's obligation to the "old creditor." The equities of the doctrine protect a surety against the risk of his having to pay twice if the first payment is held to be an avoidable preference.[223]

If the earmarking doctrine is to apply, certain characteristics must be present in the transaction. There must be an agreement that the new funds will be used to pay a specified past debt. The agreement must be performed according to its terms. The transaction viewed as a whole (including the transfer in of the new funds and the transfer out to the old creditor) does not result in any diminution of the estate.[224]

---

220. N.Y. Lien Law, § 71(2) (1966 & Supp 1993). Other states have similar trust fund statutes, including Kentucky, Michigan, New Jersey, and Oklahoma.

221. *See, e.g., Begier v. Internal Revenue Service*, 110 S.Ct. 2258 (1990) ("A 'debtor' does not own an equitable interest in property he holds in trust for another, that interest is not 'property of the estate,' nor is such an equitable interest 'property of the debtor' for purposes of § 547(b)."); *Kupetz v. United States (In re California Trade Technical Schs., Inc.)* 923 F.2d 641 (9th Cir. 1991) (funds held "in trust" were not property of the debtor for preferential transfer purposes). See also the earlier discussion in this Chapter regarding whether bonded contract funds are property of the estate and subject to the automatic stay.

222. *Federal Ins. Co. v. Fifth Third Bank*, 867 F.2d 330 (6th Cir. 1989) (Court found funds held in trust from provision in bonded construction contract); *In re Gonzales*, 22 B.R. 58 (Bankr. 9th Cir. 1982) (contractual provision validly created trust of contract funds); *See In re Western Urethanes, Inc.*, 61 B.R. 243 (Bankr. D. Colo. 1986) (Court found no trust created by statute, and held against surety's position, after examining general agreement for indemnity and noting the absence of a trust provision).

223. *McCuskey v. Nat'l. Bank of Waterloo (In re Bohlen Enter., Ltd.)*, 859 F.2d 561, 566 (8th Cir. 1988) ("When new funds are provided by the new creditor to or for the benefit of the debtor for the purpose of paying the obligation owed to the old creditor, the funds are said to be 'earmarked' and the payment is held not to be a voidable preference."); *Mandross v. Peoples Banking Co. (In re Hartley)*, 825 F.2d 1067, 1070 (6th Cir. 1987) (When a third person loans money to a debtor specifically to enable him to satisfy the claim of a designated creditor, the general rule is that the proceeds are not the property of the debtor, and therefore the transfer of the proceeds to the creditor is not preferential); *Sierra Steel, Inc. v. S&S Steel Fabrication (In re Sierra Steel, Inc.)*, 96 B.R. 271, 274 (Bankr. 9th Cir. 1989) ("Under the earmarking doctrine, when a third party advances or loans funds to the debtor with instructions to use the funds to pay off another creditor, the funds are said to be earmarked for payment to a specific creditor or creditors and do not become property of the debtor.").

224. *In re Bohlen Enter., Ltd.* 859 F.2d at 566; *Coral Petroleum, Inc. v. Banque Paribas-London*, 797 F.2d 1351, *reh'g denied* 801 F.2d 398 (5th Cir. 1986).

For example, payments made to a bonded contractor by joint check may result in a defense under the earmarking doctrine. It is a fairly common practice in the construction industry for payments to be made to a contractor by check made jointly payable to the contractor and his supplier or subcontractor. If the contractor obtains the suppliers endorsement on the joint check, in exchange for the contractor's own check for the portion of the joint check due to the supplier, the elements of the earmarking doctrine are established. The funds were given to the contractor with the express agreement that the supplier's claim be satisfied therefrom. The estate has not been diminished, because but for the payment to the supplier, the estate could not have negotiated the joint check.

Another example can be found in payment or financing arrangements pursuant to which the contractor must request payment to be funded from a control account, established at the behest of an owner, a lender, or a surety. The contractor receives the funds expressly to pay enumerated project bills. These payments are "earmarked" for the supplier or subcontractor.

Where a court can conclude that the payments of funds from an account were held in trust or were "earmarked" funds, then the debtor will not be able to demonstrate that the payments were property of the debtor. Accordingly, the debtor's preference action to recover payments made from the account must fail.

3. 547(c) Affirmative Defenses

Under the case law, the potential liability of a payment bond surety for pre-petition payments to suppliers and subcontractors is established and known to bankruptcy practitioners.[225] Accordingly, these claims are being asserted against sureties more frequently.

However, not all preferential transfers are avoidable. Even if the debtor/principal has met its burden of proving the elements of a preference action, under section 547(b), the surety should be able to assert various affirmative defenses under section 547(c). There are seven statutory exceptions to the Bankruptcy Code's preference-avoiding power.[226] If a creditor can qualify under any one of the exceptions, then it is protected to the extent of the applicable exception. If a creditor can qualify under several exceptions, then it is protected by each to the extent it qualifies under each exception. The exceptions to preference of most interest to the surety are:

1) A payment that was intended by all parties to be a contemporaneous exchange for "new value,"[227] and was, in fact, substantially contemporaneous.[228]
2) Payment of a debt made and incurred in the ordinary course of both the debtor's and the transferee's business, and made according to ordinary business terms.[229]
3) An advance of new unsecured credit to the debtor after the allegedly preferential payment is made by the debtor.[230]

225. *See e.g., Newbery Corp. v. Fireman's Fund Ins. Co.*, 106 B.R. 186 (D. Ariz. 1989).

226. 11 U.S.C.A. § 547(c) (1993 and Supp. 1997).

227. "New value" is defined in 11 U.S.C.A. § 547(a)(2) as follows: "money or money's worth in goods, services, or new credit, or release by a transferee of property previously transferred to such transferee in a transaction that is neither void nor voidable by the debtor or the trustee under any applicable law, including proceeds of such property, but does not substitute for an existing obligation."

228. 11 U.S.C.A. § 547(c)(1) (1993 & Supp. 1997).

229. 11 U.S.C.A. § 547(c)(2) (1993 & Supp. 1997).

230. 11 U.S.C.A. § 547(c)(4) (1993 & Supp. 1997).

4) The fixing of a statutory lien that is not avoidable under section 545.[231] Payment in satisfaction of a statutory lien that is fully secured may not be a preferential transfer.

a. *Payments For the Benefit of a Payment Bond Surety May Fall Within the Contemporaneous Exchange For New Value Exception.* Section 547(c)(1) provides that the trustee may not avoid a transfer to the extent that such transfer was:

> (A) intended by the debtor and the creditor to or for whose benefit such transfer was made to be a contemporaneous exchange for new value given to the debtor; and
> (B) in fact a substantially contemporaneous exchange.

The Ninth Circuit Bankruptcy Appellate Panel in *In re Fegert*[232] addressed the issue of whether a payment bond surety is liable for preferential transfers paid by the debtor principal to creditors on a completed bonded project. In this case, the debtor/principal paid more than $80,000.00 to two subcontractors in settlement of a lawsuit against the debtor and its payment bond surety. Within 90 days thereafter, the debtor filed a petition for relief under Chapter 11 of the Bankruptcy Code.

The case was subsequently converted to Chapter 7 and a trustee was appointed. The trustee brought an action to avoid the payments to the subcontractors as preferential transfers. The subcontractors stipulated that the payments satisfied the elements of a preference as set out in section 547(b) but argued that the transfers fell within the contemporaneous exchange for new value exception of section 547(c)(1).

The *Fegert* court agreed that the payments fell within the contemporaneous exchange for new value exception and refused to avoid the preferential payments. The court's analysis was based entirely upon the payment bond surety's equitable subrogation rights and the effect those rights had upon the debtor.

The *Fegert* court found that the payment bond surety held a contingent claim for indemnification against the debtor. The court, following *Pearlman*, explained that if the surety had been required to complete the contract or pay the bond obligees the surety would have been subrogated to the obligee's right to be paid out of the contract balances. The surety's claim to the contract balances would have been superior to that of the bankruptcy estate.

If the debtor had not made the payments to the subcontractors, then the surety would have been required to advance funds to satisfy the bonded obligations. The surety would then have exercised its equitable lien rights to receive the contract proceeds which otherwise would have been paid to the debtor. When the debtor paid the subcontractors, the subcontractors released the surety from its contingent obligation to pay their claims. Contemporaneously therewith, the surety released its equitable lien on the contract funds thereby allowing the debtor to receive the contract funds. The release of this lien constituted a contemporaneous exchange of new value to the debtor.

The Ninth Circuit affirmed the BAP's *Fegert* decision.[233] It agreed with the BAP's analysis of the surety's equitable lien rights and followed the Fifth and Tenth Circuits' analysis of the "contemporaneous exchange for new value" exception:

231. 11 U.S.C.A. § 547(c)(6) (1993 & Supp. 1997).
232. 88 B.R. 258 (Bankr. 9th Cir. 1988), *aff'd*, 887 F.2d 955 (9th Cir. 1989).
233. 887 F.2d 955 (9th Cir. 1989).

> We agree with the Fifth and Tenth Circuits. By paying the subcontractors, Fegert avoided [the surety's] automatic and equitable lien. This constituted "new value" and placed the payments within section 546(c)(1).[234]

The issue in *Fegert* was whether the trustee could recover from the recipient of the preferential payments, *i.e.,* the subcontractors. However, the *Fegert* decision applies with equal force to the issue whether the surety receives an avoidable preference when the debtor makes preferential payments to its subcontractors and materialmen. Therefore, while the surety may receive a preference when the debtor pays its creditors, the preference falls within the safe harbor provisions of section 547(c)(1).

Based upon the analysis established in *Fegert*, the surety can move to dismiss the debtor's indirect preference action based upon the contemporaneous exchange for new value defense. The debtor may oppose the surety's motion on the basis that the debtor's payments were greater than the surety's release of its equitable lien on bonded contract proceeds.[235] In other words, the debtor will argue that the court must measure the amount of the "new value" the surety gives to the debtor to determine whether it is equivalent to the alleged preferential transfers. In *Newbery*[236] the district court held that the surety was required to show the amount of new value actually given to the debtor.[237]

Must the surety show that the new value released to the debtor was equivalent to the preferential payments? If so, the contemporaneous exchange for new value exception may not protect the surety in every instance. Section 547(c)(1) provides that the trustee may not avoid a preferential transfer "*to the extent* that such transfer was . . . a contemporaneous exchange for new value given to the debtor . . . ." (Emphasis added.) Thus, section 547 may require that the new value given to the debtor be measured to determine the "money's worth" of new value received by the debtor.

One Circuit has held that there is no valuation requirement in section 547(c)(1).[238] In *Rodman*, the debtor made otherwise preferential payments to a subcontractor in exchange for the release of a lien against the debtor's oil well. The parties later discovered that the well was dry and entirely worthless. The Tenth Circuit held that there is no *quid pro quo* valuation requirement in section 547, stating that "[t]he plain language of the definition does not require the valuation of the property transferred."[239]

Several bankruptcy court decisions have held that the release of lien rights alone is new value, without assessing the value of the lien released, or whether the lien released freed up an equal

---

234. 887 F.2d at 959.

235. *See, e.g., Milchem, Inc. v. Fredman* (*In re* Nucorp Energy, Inc.), 902 F.2d 729 (9th Cir. 1990) (To the extent that a preferential payment exceeds the amount of new value given by the creditor the exception to preference, under section 547(c)(1), provides no defense); *Lowrey v. U.P.G., Inc. (In re Robinson Bros. Drilling, Inc.*), 877 F.2d 32 (10th Cir. 1989) (court imposed same valuation requirement, and stated that the time to value the release of a lien is the time when the lien is released). *Cf., Kenan v. Fort Worth Pipe Co. (In re George Rodman, Inc.*), 792 F.2d 125, 128 (10th Cir. 1986) (court stated that "[t]he plain language of the definition [of section 547(c)(1)] does not require the valuation of the property transferred.").

236. *Newbery Corp. v. Fireman's Fund Ins. Co.*, 106 B.R. 186 (D. Ariz. 1989).

237. In the *Newbery* case, Fireman's Fund Insurance Company's motion to dismiss was granted by the Bankruptcy Court. The District Court reversed the Bankruptcy Court's dismissal of Newbery's indirect preference action, and remanded the action for the Bankruptcy Court to determine whether the new value given by Fireman's Fund Insurance Company as a result of its release of its equitable liens was equivalent to the amount of the alleged preferential payments.

238. *In re George Rodman, Inc.*, 792 F.2d 125 (10th Cir. 1986).

239. *Id.* at 128.

or greater amount of contract proceeds to the debtor. Judge Steen of the Bankruptcy Court for the Middle District of Louisiana found that the release of a lien by the creditor, which released the debtor from an indemnity obligation to the owner regarding this lien, was new value for purposes of section 547(c)(1).[240] The decision rejected the argument that the finding of "new value" to the debtor required a showing of contract funds in the hands of the owner sufficient to pay lien claimants, that would be released to the debtor by the preferential payment. This interpretation appears to conflict with the Ninth Circuit opinion in *Fegert*, and the District Court opinion in *Newbery v. Fireman's Fund*.

Based largely on the reasoning of Judge Steen's opinion in *In re Dick Henley*, other bankruptcy courts have held that the release by a paid subcontractor or materialman of claims against statutory lien bonds constitutes new value to the debtor.[241] Following the logic of these cases, the mere release of a payment bond claim that automatically occurs when a payment is made to the supplier or subcontractor is new value under section 547(c)(1).

Other Circuits, however, have taken a different stand on the issue and have required that the amount of new value be determined and that the portion of the preference which is protected by the contemporaneous exchange exception of section 547(c)(1) be limited to the amount of new value received by the debtor. Some courts have expressly held that section 547(c)(1) requires that the creditor prove the specific value of the "money or money's worth" that the debtor received.[242] Other courts which have addressed the contemporaneous exchange exception have strongly inferred that a valuation requirement exists.[243]

In *Fuel Oil Supply and Terminaling, Inc.*, the Fifth Circuit explained that the contemporaneous exchange defense "is grounded in the principle that the transfer of new value to the debtor will offset the payments, and the debtor's estate will not be depleted to the detriment of other creditors."[244]

The opinion in *Fegert* appears to imply a valuation requirement. In *Fegert*, the BAP explained that the contemporaneous exchange exception protected certain transfers because

240. *In re Dick Henley, Inc.*, 38 B.R. 210 (Bankr. M.D. La. 1984). In *Henley*, the debtor was a general contractor who made preferential payments to a subcontractor for services rendered. By applicable statute, the subcontractor held a lien on the owner's property to secure payment and for the services. The owner, in turn, held a statutory right of indemnification against the debtor. The court held that when the debtor paid its subcontractor, the subcontractor released its lien and the owner released its indemnity claim against the debtor. The court held that the release from the indemnity obligation was new value to the debtor for purposes of section 547(c)(1).

The *Henley* decision is particularly applicable to the payment bond surety case. A bond principal is generally contractually obligated to indemnify its surety and, in any event, is equitably obligated to do so. *Pearlman v. Reliance Ins. Co.*, 371 U.S. 132, 136 (1962). Therefore, to the extent the debtor relieves its surety of bonded obligations, the debtor is released from its indemnity obligations. Under *Henley*, this release is sufficient new value to protect the surety from preference liability. *Henley* has been criticized. *See, e.g., In re Fuel Oil Supply & Terminaling, Inc.*, 837 F.2d 224, 230 (5th Cir. 1988); *Fegert*, 88 B.R. 259.

241. *In re Anderson Plumbing Co.*, 71 B.R. 19 (Bankr. E.D. Cal. 1986); *In re Advanced Contractors*, 44 B.R. 239 (Bankr. M.D. Fla. 1984). *Anderson Plumbing* and *Advanced Contractors*, like *Henley*, have come under substantial criticism. *In re Cocolat, Inc.*, 176 B.R. 540, 548 (Bankr. N.D. Cal. 1995); *In re Bownic Insul. Contr. Inc.*, 134 B.R. 261, 264 (Bankr. S.D. Ohio 1991).

242. *In re Robinson Bros. Drilling, Inc.*, 877 F.2d 32 (10th Cir. 1989); *In re Jet Florida Sys., Inc.*, 861 F.2d 1555, 1558-1559 (11th Cir. 1988); *In re Nucorp Energy, Inc.*, 80 B.R. 517 (Bankr. S.D. Ca. 1987).

243. *In re Fuel Oil Supply & Terminaling, Inc.*, 837 F.2d 224 (5th Cir. 1988); *In re E.R. Fegert, Inc.*, 88 B.R. 258 (9th Cir. 1988), *aff'd*, 887 F.2d 955 (9th Cir. 1989).

244. *Fuel Oil*, 837 F.2d at 228.

"they do not affect the equality of distribution of estate assets."[245] This implies that the lien released must equal or exceed the allegedly preferential payments. The court noted:

> The Trustee does not dispute that the estate received post-petition more than the total paid to both subcontractors. [T]here was no diminution of the estate. Under these facts, the release of the subcontractors' rights against the surety, which in turn could have exercised its lien rights, constituted 'new value' being in a substantially contemporaneous exchange."[246]

The better reasoned authority interprets Section 547(c)(1) to require that the value of the equitable lien released by the payment bond surety will be the limit of the preference defense. Nonetheless, there is authority supporting a complete defense to the surety under Section 547(c)(1), simply because the surety's equitable lien on the contract balances has been released by the debtor's payments to suppliers and subcontractors.

b. *Trade Creditors May Have Made Subsequent Advances of New Value.* Another defense to the debtor's indirect preference action is the "subsequent advance"preference exception.[247] The purpose of this preference exception is to protect creditors who, after receiving a preferential payment, extend new unsecured credit to the debtor.

> A subsequent advance is excepted because it is reasoned that a creditor who contributes new value in return for payments from the incipient bankrupt, should not later be deemed to have depleted the bankruptcy estate to the disadvantage of others.[248]

In some situations, trade creditors extended unsecured credit to the debtor within the 90 days before bankruptcy by supplying materials or services to the debtor. If a trade creditor extended unsecured credit after a preferential payment was made to the trade creditor, then the subsequent advance defense may be applicable.

The debtor may argue that this affirmative defense can only be asserted by the transferees (i.e., the trade creditors) and not by the surety. Courts have supported the right of the indirect preference defendant to assert the preference defenses of the transferee.[249]

---

245. *Fegert*, 88 B.R. at 259.

246. *Id.* at 260.

247. The "subsequent advance" preference exception is provided for in section 547(c)(4), as follows:

"(c) The trustee may not avoid under this section a transfer. . .

(4) To or for the benefit of a creditor, to the extent that, after such transfer, such creditor gave new value to or for the benefit of the debtor–

(A) not secured by an otherwise unavoidable security interest; and

(B) on account of which new value the debtor did not make an otherwise unavoidable transfer to or for the benefit of such creditor;"

11 U.S.C.A. § 547(c)(4) (1993 & Supp. 1997).

248. *In re Jet Florida Sys., Inc.*, 841 F.2d 1082, 1083 (11 Cir. 1988).

249. *Newbery Corp.*, 106 B.R. at 187 n.2. Similarly, in *Harrison v. Brent Towing Co., Inc.* (*In re H & S Transportation Co., Inc.*), 939 F.2d 355 (6th Cir. 1991), a trustee brought a preference action against a boat owner for the debtor/boat operator's payments to fuel suppliers within 90 days before bankruptcy. The trustee argued that the debtor's payments indirectly benefitted the boat owner because the fuel suppliers liens against the boat were satisfied. Subsequently, the fuel suppliers sold additional fuel to the debtor on credit. The boat owner argued that it became subrogated to the rights of the fuel suppliers that had valid subsequent advance defenses. The *H & S Transportation* Court held that the boat owner, as subrogee to the rights of the fuel suppliers, was entitled to assert a defense based upon the fuel suppliers' subsequent advance defense. The surety should similarly be entitled to assert the subsequent advance defense that is available to trade creditors that extended credit to the debtor.

The debtor may argue that the subsequent advance defense requires that the creditors' advances of unsecured credit must remain unpaid. Some courts have interpreted § 547(c)(4)(B) to support this argument.[250] However, nothing in the language of § 547(c)(4) or the statute's legislative history requires that the new value remain unpaid. A split of authority exists, with other courts holding that the creditors had valid subsequent advance defenses even though their earlier extensions of new credit were repaid by the debtor.[251]

c. *The Payments May Fall Within the Ordinary Course of Business Exception.* Another section 547(c) safe harbor that may protect a payment bond surety is the "ordinary course of business" exception set forth at section 547(c)(2).[252] The payment of a debt made and incurred in the ordinary course of both the debtor's and the transferee's business, and made according to ordinary business terms, will not be a voidable preference. The purpose of this exception is to leave normal financial relations undisturbed. This exception exists because such transactions do not detract from the general policy of the preference section which is to discourage unusual activity by either the debtor or his creditors during the debtor's descent into bankruptcy.[253] "Thus, payments made by a debtor to employees, suppliers, for utilities and rent, and other similar operating expenses or trade credit transactions, were intended by Congress to be exempt from recovery as preferences."[254]

The courts have adopted two interpretations of section 547(c)(2).[255] The phrase "ordinary" can reasonably refer to the course of dealings between the debtor and the creditor, the course of dealings standard to the industry in which the debtor and creditor operate, or both. Some decisions hold that the court should:

> [C]onfine its inquiry to whether the manner and timing of the payments at issue were consistent with the manner and timing of previous payments by the debtor in its course of dealing with the creditor. . . .[256]

---

250. *In re Kroh Bros. Development Company*, 930 F.2d 648, 653 (8th Cir. 1991); *Valley Candle Mfg. Co. v. Stonitsch (In re Isis Foods, Inc.)* 39 B.R. 645 (W.D. Mo. 1984); *Matter of Bishop*, 17 B.R. 180 (Bankr. N.D. Ga. 1982). *Accord* Collier on Bankruptcy, (15th ed. Rev. 1997) ¶ 547.04[4] p. 547-58.

251. *In re IRFM, Inc.*, 52 F.3d 228, 231 (9th Cir 1995); *In the Matter of Toyota of Jefferson, Inc.*, 14 F.3d 1088, 1093 n.2 (5th Cir. 1994); *In re PNP Holdings Corp.*, 167 B.R. 619, 629 (Bankr. W.D. Wash. 1994); *Crichton v. Wheeling Nat'l Bank (In re Meredith Manor, Inc.)* 902 F.2d 257 (4th Cir. 1990); *Boyd v. The Water Doctor (In re Check Reporting Serv., Inc.)*, 140 B.R. 425, 431-34 (Bankr. W.D. Mich. 1992).

252. The "ordinary course of business" preference exception is provided for in section 547(c)(2), as follows:

"(c) The trustee may not avoid under this section a transfer. . .

(2) to the extent that such transfer was–

(A) in payment of a debt incurred by the debtor in the ordinary course of business or financial affairs of the debtor and the transferee;

(B) made in the ordinary course of business or financial affairs of the debtor and the transferee; and

(C) made according to ordinary business terms;"

11 U.S.C.A. § 547(c)(2) (1979 & Supp. 1993).

253. H.R. REP. NO. 95-595, 95th Cong., 1st Sess. 373-74 (1977); S. REP. NO. 95-989, 95th Cong., 2d Sess. 88 (1978); 11 U.S.C. § 547(c).

254. *Aguillard v. Bank of Lafayette* (*In re* Bourgeois), 58 B.R. 657, 659 (Bankr. W.D. La. 1986).

255. *See generally In re* Unimet Corp., 85 B.R. 450 (Bankr. M.D. Ohio 1988).

256. *Id.* at 453.

However, the majority of courts now expand the inquiry to include the additional requirement that the manner and timing of the payments at issue have been consistent with the ordinary course of business in the parties' industry.[257]

The classic example of an "ordinary course" payment would be the debtor's pre-petition payroll payments. In most situations in the construction industry, laborers receive payroll on the same day each week for the work performed during the preceding work week. This practice of making weekly payroll payments is consistent with the prior course of dealing between the employee and the debtor, and is consistent with the ordinary course of business in the construction industry. These type of payroll payments to a debtor's laborers are precisely the type of payments that are intended to be protected by the ordinary course of business exception to preference. Because payroll obligations are incurred and paid by the debtor in the ordinary course of its business, the payroll payments should be insulated from the debtor's preference attack under section 547(c)(2).[258]

When a payment bond surety faces a preference action, it should investigate the debtor's payment history with the paid creditors. As a matter of commercial reality, many contractors are frequently late to one degree or another in the payment of their subcontractors and materialmen.[259] If the surety can show that the payments, while on account of an antecedent debt, were made in the ordinary course of business as between the debtor and the transferee, then the transfers should be protected from the trustee's avoidance powers.[260] In the majority of jurisdictions, the surety would also be required to show that the payments were made within the ordinary course of business in the industry.

d. *The Debtor's Payments May be in Satisfaction of Perfected Statutory Liens.* Some of the debtor's preference claims may be for payments made to parties that held perfected statutory liens[261] prior to receiving payment. Code § 547(c)(6)[262] provides a preference exception if the transfer is the

257. *In re Fred Hawes Organization, Inc.*, 957 F.2d 239, 244 (6th Cir. 1992); *In re Loretto Winery Ltd.*, 107 B.R. 707, 709-10 (Bankr. 9th Cir. 1989).

258. The debtor's payroll payments are not recoverable for another reason. The debtor's laborers continued to work each week after receiving their weekly payroll. In all likelihood the laborers would have left the project if the debtor stopped paying its weekly payroll. The laborer's continued services after being paid were subsequent advances of new value. *See Apache Coal Co., Inc. v. U.M.W.A.* (*In re Apache Coal Co., Inc.*), 68 B.R. 314 (Bankr. W.D. Va. 1986). Thus, payroll payments may be further protected from the debtor's preference attack under section 547(c)(4).

259. Late payments are not *per se* excluded from being considered payments made in the ordinary course of business. Section 547(c)(2) has been found applicable to late payments when these type of payments are the standard practice between the parties and are not outside industry standards. *See Yurika Foods Corp. v. United Parcel Serv.* (*In re Yurika Foods Corp.*) 888 F.2d 42 (6th Cir. 1989); *Lovett v. St. Johnsbury Trucking*, 931 F.2d 494 (8th Cir. 1991). However, if payments are so late as to be inconsistent with prior transactions between the parties, the ordinary course of business exception will not provide a defense.

260. *In re Jerry-Sue Fashions, Inc.*, 89 B.R. 995 (Bankr. S.D. Fla. 1988); *In re Sunup/Sundown, Inc.*, 66 B.R. 1021 (Bankr. S.D. Fla. 1986); *In re Agency Refrigeration & Air Conditioning, Inc.*, 58 B.R. 877 (Bankr. D. N.H. 1986); *In re Ewald Bros., Inc.*, 45 B.R. 52 (Bankr. D. Minn. 1984).

261. A "lien" is defined as a "charge against or interest in property to secure payment of a debt or performance of an obligation." 11 U.S.C.A. § 101(37) (1993 & Supp. 1997). A "statutory lien" is defined as a lien that arises by force of statute, without prior consent between the parties and not obtainable through judicial means by other creditors. 11 U.S.C.A. § 101(53) (1993 & Supp. 1997). For a list of cases in which courts have considered various liens to be "statutory" for purposes of section 547(c)(6), *see Countryman*, at 804.

262. The "statutory lien" preference exception is provided for in section 547(c)(6), as follows:

> "(c) The trustee may not avoid under this section a transfer. . .
>
> (6) that is the fixing of a statutory lien that is not avoidable under section 545 of this title;"

11 U.S.C.A. § 547(c)(6) (1993 & Supp. 1997).

"fixing" of a statutory lien that is not avoidable under Code § 545.[263] While language of §ù 547(c)(6) does not appear to protect preferential transfers of money, at least one court has applied this section to protect payments made to a creditor with unperfected lien rights.[264]

4. The Surety May Not Be a Party From Whom Preferential Payments May Be Recovered

To determine preference liability, the following two-step analysis must be made: (1) has there been an avoidable transfer (Section 547) and; (2) from whom may the transfer be recovered (Section 550)?[265]

> The Code specifically 'separates the identification of avoidable transfers (§ 547) from the identification of those who must pay (§ 550).' . . . If it is determined that the transfer is a preference under 11 U.S.C. § 547(b) and none of the exceptions under 11 U.S.C. § 547(c) apply, we then look to section 550(a) to determine to whom the trustee may look for recovery of the property.[266]

Under § 550(a)(1) the debtor can recover a preferential transfer from the surety only if the debtor can prove that the surety was either: (1) the initial transferee of the preference or (2) the entity for whose benefit the initial transfer was made. Alternatively, under § 550(a)(2) the debtor can recover from the surety only if the surety was a subsequent transferee of the initial transfer.[267] In an indirect preference action, the allegation is that the debtor's payments to trade creditors were preferential to the surety, not because the surety receives the payments, but because the payments relieve the surety of obligations under its bond(s). Thus, the surety is neither an initial transferee nor a subsequent transferee, under sections 550(a)(1) or 550(a)(2), respectively.

---

263. The portion of section 545 that is relevant to an indirect preference action is section 545(2), which provides that a statutory lien on the debtor's property is subject to avoidance if it would be unenforceable against a bona fide purchaser of the property on which the lien is asserted as of the petition date. *See Saslow v. Andrew* (*In re Loretto Winery, Ltd.*), 898 F.2d 715 (9th Cir. 1990).

264. In *Cimmaron Oil Co., Inc. v. Cameron Consultants, Inc.*, 71 B.R. 1005 (N.D. Tex. 1987), *aff'd* 39 F.3d 320 (5th Cir. 1994), the court extended the statutory lien exception to the debtor's payments to a lienholder that did not perfect its statutory lien. The District court found that release of an inchoate lien right was not "new value" under Section 547(c)(1). The district court did hold, however, that the payments to the consultant were excepted from avoidance under § 547(c)(6). The court stated that the legislative history reflects Congress' intent that this statute also exempt "transfers in satisfaction of such liens," as follows:

> This interpretation of § 547(c)(6), while faithful to congressional intent, obviates the commercially unreasonable consequences that could result if the trustee were permitted to pay for a lienor's services, thereby precluding the perfecting of the lien, and later avoid the payments as preferences. *Id.* at 1011.

265. Liability of transferee of avoided transfer

(a) Except as otherwise provided in this section, to the extent that a transfer is avoided under section 544, 545, 547, 548, 549, 553(b), or 724(a) of this title, the trustee may recover, for the benefit of the estate, the property transferred, or, if the court so orders, the value of such property, from--

(1) the initial transferee of such transfer or the entity for whose benefit such transfer was made; or

(2) any immediate or mediate transferee of such initial transferee.

11 U.S.C.A. § 550(a) (1993 & Supp. 1997).

266. *In re H & S Trans. Co., Inc.*, 939 F.2d at 358.

267. *Nordberg v. Societe Generale (In re Chase & Sanborn Corp.)*, 848 F.2d 1196 (11th Cir. 1988); *Lippi. v. City Bank*, 955 F.2d 599 (9th Cir. 1992).

If the surety is not a "transferee" of the indirect preferences, the only way the surety can be held liable for the preferential payments, under section 550(a)(1), is if the surety is held to be an "entity for whose benefit [the initial] transfer was made." This phrase of section 550(a)(1) was analyzed in *Danning v. Miller* (*In re Bullion Reserve of North America*).[268] In this case, the sole issue was whether a fraudulent conveyance could be recovered from Miller, a party to an avoided transaction. Miller was not an initial or subsequent transferee of the funds, because he never had dominion over the funds. The *Bullion Reserve* Court held that for Miller to be an "entity for whose benefit such transfer was made" the initial transfer must have been made with an intent to benefit Miller. Because the initial transfer was not *made* for Miller's benefit, the court held that the Chapter 7 trustee could not recover the fraudulent conveyance from Miller.

Prior to bankruptcy, common sense suggests that the principal's intent in paying its trade creditors was to keep the business "afloat," to reduce officer's personal guaranty liability, or otherwise benefit itself, rather than because of any actual intent to benefit the payment bond surety. In these situations, *Danning v. Miller* may support a defense to a section 550 claim against the surety in an indirect preference action.

IX. *Opposing the Principal's Control of the Reorganization*

A. MOTION TO CONVERT CHAPTER 11 REORGANIZATION TO CHAPTER 7 LIQUIDATION

Under certain circumstances a surety can request that a Chapter 11 case be converted to a Chapter 7 proceeding under Section 1112(b). Often times a motion to convert will also request the appointment of a trustee in the alternative. If either of these requests is granted, then the debtor/principal's management will be displaced by an independent trustee. Mismanagement by the principal's officers and directors, the absence of any reorganization prospects, threats by management of groundless suits against the surety, or any number of other circumstances suggesting the bankruptcy process is not working may indicate that the surety should seek a conversion of the reorganization case to a liquidation.

Federal Rule of Bankruptcy Procedure 1017(d) provides the procedure for a voluntary conversion and the procedure for a creditor to seek conversion. Proceedings to convert a case are commenced by motion.[269] In general, in a Chapter 11 case, the court will take into consideration the best interests of both the creditors and the estate to determine whether conversion is appropriate. Section 1112(b) lists ten circumstances that constitute "cause" to convert or dismiss a case.[270] The

---

268. 922 F.2d 544 (9th Cir. 1991).
269. Fed. R. Bankr. P. 9014.
270. 11 U.S.C. § 1112(b) provides:

"[O]n request of a party in interest or the United States trustee, and after notice and a hearing, the court may convert a case under this chapter to a case under chapter 7 of this title or may dismiss a case under this chapter, whichever is in the best interest of creditors and the estate, for cause including–

(1) continuing loss to or diminution of the estate and absence of a reasonably likelihood of rehabilitation;

(2) inability to effectuate a plan;
(3) unreasonable delay by the debtor that is prejudicial to creditors;
(4) failure to propose a plan under section 1121 of this title within any time fixed by the court;
(5) denial of confirmation of every proposed plan and denial of a request made for additional time for

listed causes are not exclusive or exhaustive. Other "cause" may support conversion.[271] Whether "cause" for conversion has been proven lies in the sound discretion of the court.[272]

The surety should look first to Section 1112(B)(1) as a basis to convert a case to Chapter 7. The general deterioration of the debtor/principal's business since filing for bankruptcy may be the requisite "cause" to support conversion of the case.[273] Deterioration of the debtor/principal's business is not uncommon because the debtor generally loses his ability to obtain new bonds either prior to or after filing for bankruptcy. Without bonding, the debtor will probably be unable to bid and obtain new work necessary to generate cash flow. Absence of new work generally exacerbates the financial problems that were the original cause of the bankruptcy filing.

In addition to showing a "continuing loss or diminution of the estate," Section 1112(b)(1) requires a showing of an "absence of a reasonable likelihood of rehabilitation." Language in the U.S. Supreme Court Case of *United Savings v. Timbers of Inwood Forest, Ltd.*,[274] suggests that the debtor must have some "realistic" possibility of reorganizing, rather than a mere subjective belief that the debtor can reorganize. Although the *Timbers* case dealt with relief from the automatic stay under Section 362(d)(2), the court stated that for property to be necessary for an effective reorganization the debtor must demonstrate an effective reorganization is in "prospect" and that the debtor has "a reasonable probability of a successful reorganization within a reasonable time."[275] The surety can argue that the analogous standard in Section 1112(b) also requires that the debtor demonstrate more than a hope of reorganization. The continuing diminution of the estate, coupled with other negative financial factors, (i.e. lack of bonding support and inability to bid or obtain new work) makes Section 1112(b)(1) a viable basis for the surety to move to convert the case.

Section 1112(b)(2) and (b)(3) may also be grounds for conversion after a case has been pending for a significant period of time.[276] In most cases, a motion should not be made under either of these sections at the beginning of the case because they would probably not be well received by the court. However, if the debtor has been unable to bid or obtain new work and the debtor has been consuming assets of the estate for officers' salary and overhead for some time, the surety should be able to demonstrate "cause" under Section 1112(b)(2) ("inability to effectuate a plan") and/or (b)(3) ("unreasonable delay by the debtor that is prejudicial to creditors").

If the Chapter 11 case is converted to Chapter 7, then an independent trustee will be appointed to manage all the assets in the estate. The debtor/principal is required to turnover all

---

filing another plan or a modification of a plan;

(6) revocation of an order of confirmation under section 1144 of this title, and denial of confirmation of another plan or a modified plan under section 1129 of this title;

(7) inability to effectuate substantial consummation of a confirmed plan;

(8) material default by the debtor with respect to a confirmed plan;

(9) termination of a plan by reason of the occurrence of a condition specified in the plan; or

(10) nonpayment of any fees or charges required under chapter 123 of title 28."

271. 11 U.S.C. § 102(3); *In re C.J. Corp.*, 78 Bankr. 273 (Bankr. D.Haw 1987).

272. *In re Heatly*, 51 Bankr. 518 (Bankr. E.D.Pa. 1985).

273. *In re Photo Promotion Associates, Inc.*, 47 Bankr. 454 (Bankr. S.D.N.Y. 1985) (Court converted Chapter 11 case to Chapter 7 because the debtor's business generally deteriorated over five months after filing for bankruptcy).

274. 484 U.S. 365, 108 S.Ct. 626, 98 L.Ed.2d 740 (1988).

275. 484 U.S. at 376. *See also In re Oklahoma P.A.C. First Ltd. Partnership*, 122 Bankr. 394 (Bankr. D.Ariz. 1990) (Court follows *Timbers* and states, "*In essence, a mini-feasibility analysis of the Debtor's Plan is required.*"). *Id.* at 400.

276. *In re Belcher,* 65 Bankr. 47 (Bankr. S.D.Fla. 1986); *In re Eden Associates,* 13 Bankr. 578 (Bankr. S.D.N.Y. 1981); *Matter of Bock*, 58 Bankr. 374 (Bankr. M.D.Fla. 1986).

assets and records of the estate to the Chapter 7 trustee.[277] Additionally, a new time period for filing proofs of claim and objections to discharge commences after the conversion of the case.[278]

B. Motion to Appoint Trustee or Examiner

In most cases the debtor/principal will remain in possession of the estate in a Chapter 11 case.[279] The surety may move to appoint a Chapter 11 trustee or an examiner under Section 1104. A lesser standard of "cause" is applied to the request to appoint an examiner than would be applicable to a motion to appoint a trustee, because the examiner's appointment will not entirely displace debtor's current management.

1. Trustee

A motion to appoint a Chapter 11 trustee is brought under Section 1104(a).[280] When the circumstances of a case suggest something seriously wrong with management of the debtor's affairs, or some form of fraud is suspected, the surety should not hesitate to move to have a trustee appointed. Essentially, Section 1104 allows for appointment of a trustee if "fraud, dishonesty, incompetence or gross mismanagement" by the debtor can be demonstrated, or if such appointment is in the best interests of creditors.[281]

Evidence of embezzlement or intentional fraud will clearly support appointment of a trustee. Other behavior that will permit the appointment of a trustee include failure to pay post-petition taxes, failure to maintain insurance, commingling of personal and business assets, gross mismanagement or an inability to reorganize the debtor. The surety may also seek to appoint a trustee under the "best interests" test of Section 1104(a)(2). Under this alternative ground, the court will balance the equities to the creditors, the estate and the debtor. If possible, the surety should move under both grounds.

---

277. Fed. R. Bankr. P. 1019(5).

278. Fed. R. Bankr. P. 1019(3).

279. *See e.g., In re Colorado - Ute Elec. Ass'n, Inc.*, 120 Bankr. 164 (Bankr. D.Colo. 1990) (Appointment of a Chapter 11 trustee is an extraordinary remedy because there is a strong presumption that the debtor should remain in possession of the estate); *In re TS Industries, Inc.*, 125 Bankr. 638 (Bankr. D.Utah 1991) (same).

280. 11 U.S.C. § 1104(a) provides: "At any time after the commencement of the case but before confirmation of a plan, on request of a party in interest or the United States trustee, and after notice and a hearing, the court shall order the appointment of a trustee--

(1) for cause, including fraud, dishonesty, incompetence, or gross mismanagement of the affairs of the debtor by current management, either before or after the commencement of the case, or similar cause, but not including the number of holders of securities of the debtor or the amount of assets or liabilities of the debtor; or

(2) if such appointment is in the interests of creditors, any equity security holders, and other interests of the estate, without regard to the number of holders of securities of the debtor or the amount of assets or liabilities of the debtor."

281. *In re Sharon Steel Corp.*, 871 F.2d 1217 (3rd Cir. 1989). (Standards for appointment of a trustee are flexible and subject to the discretion of the bankruptcy court). It should be noted that a trustee may be appointed by the court for reasons not explicitly enumerated in Section 1104(a). *See* 11 U.S.C. § 102(3); *In re Oklahoma Refining Corp.*, 838 F.2d 1133 (10th Cir. 1988); *In re v. Savino Oil & Heating Co., Inc.*, 99 Bankr. 518 (Bankr. E.D.N.Y. 1989).

There are a large number of reported cases discussing the conduct and standards that will be considered in a motion to appoint a trustee. Other sources provide a thorough discussion of these cases and the many fact patterns justifying the appointment of a trustee.[282]

2. Examiner

The surety may also move to appoint an examiner. An examiner is essentially a trustee with limited powers. The grounds for appointment of an examiner under Section 1104(c), are (1) that the appointment is in the best interests of the estate and creditors, or (2) that the debtor's fixed, liquidated, unsecured debts exceed $5,000,000.[283] The "best interest" test will generally be met where the surety demonstrates allegations of fraud, misconduct and/or mismanagement. The alternative provision to appoint an examiner (i.e. When non-trade debt of the debtor exceeds $5,000,000) will come into play in rarer cases.

A lesser standard of "cause" is required to appoint an examiner, as opposed to having a trustee appointed, because an examiner only displaces the debtor from possessing designated assets of the estate or from performing certain functions. From a timing perspective, a motion to appointment an examiner will generally be better received at the beginning of a case than motions to appoint a trustee or to convert the case.

From the surety's perspective, an examiner can serve a number of useful functions. An examiner can review the debtor's financial condition and controls. Such actions can lead to conservation of assets of the estate, and possibly to additional discoveries that will support appointment of a trustee. Examiners may be appointed for the purpose of investigating and reviewing litigation the debtor has commenced or proposes to commence.[284] A debtor may be threatening preference, subordination and/or surety/lender liability suits. Having an examiner appointed will displace the debtor/principal with an impartial third party to review the alleged action(s) threatened against the surety to determine whether it is in the best interests of the estate to pursue the action(s) or not.[285]

---

282. Berdan and Arnold, *Displacing the Debtor in Possession: The Requests for and Advantages of the Appointment of a Trustee in Chapter 11 Proceedings*, 67 Marq. L. Rev. 457 (1984); Comment, *When the Bank Wants its Borrowers in Bankruptcy: Benefits of Bankruptcy for Lenders and Lender Liability Defendants*, 40 Me. L. Rev. 375, 399 (1988).

283. 11 U.S.C. § 1104(c) provides: "If the court does not order the appointment of a trustee under this section, then at any time before the confirmation of a plan, on request of a party in interest or the United States trustee, and after notice and a hearing, the court shall order the appointment of an examiner to conduct such an investigation of the debtor as is appropriate, including an investigation of any allegations of fraud, dishonesty, incompetence, misconduct, mismanagement, or irregularity in the management of the affairs of the debtor of or by current or former management of the debtor, if--

(1) such appointment is in the interests of creditors, any equity security holders, and other interests of the estate; or

(2) the debtor's fixed, liquidated, unsecured debts, other than debts for goods, services, or taxes, or owing to an insider, exceed $5,000,000."

284. 11 U.S.C. § 1106(b) requires an examiner to perform the duty of investigating causes of action available to the estate, as required under 11 U.S.C. § 1106(a)(4). *In re Carnegie Intern. Corp.*, 51 Bankr. 252 (Bankr. S.D.Ind. 1984) (Examiner appointed to investigate and, if warranted, pursue causes of action available to the estate); *Williamson v. Roppollo*, 114 Bankr. 127 (W.D.La. 1990) (same).

285. *See Meyer v. Fleming*, 327 U.S. 161, 165-167, 66 S.Ct. 382, 385-386, 90 L.Ed. 595 (1946) (The trustee should "make the choice which is most advantageous to the estate.") *In re Independent Clearing House Co.*, 41 Bankr. 985, 992 (D. Utah 1984) ("A bankruptcy trustee is not bound to pursue every cause of action, and may properly decide that the speculative nature of the suit and the expense do not warrant prosecution."); *In re Jefferson*, 59 Bankr. 707, 711

VIII. *Conclusion*

Knowledge of Bankruptcy law is invaluable to the surety. There is a relatively high likelihood of a financially distressed principal paying a visit to the bankruptcy court at some point. The Bankruptcy Code's effect on the respective rights of parties under a bond can be dramatic. Lawsuits and claims may be stayed from proceeding, filing and notice deadlines may be tolled, and the surety's ability to complete the bonded work may be delayed. The surety's claim to bonded contract proceeds is often challenged in the bankruptcy court. Various forms of bankruptcy court litigation may be necessary to protect the surety's rights, including the right of equitable subrogation.

However, it is not possible to accurately predict which principals will file a bankruptcy petition. Accordingly, all bond losses must be assessed with the thought of how a bankruptcy filing may delay the project completion, imperil the contract proceeds, or increase the payment bond claims. This chapter does not cover all of the law of bankruptcy that might be invoked by or against the surety. It is offered for what assistance it may give to those assigned to discharge the surety's obligations in a bankruptcy and pre-bankruptcy environment.

(S.D.Miss. 1986) ("Furthermore, the trustee is not bound to bring every possible suit . . . it was prudent for him to refrain here when considering the interest of the estate as a whole.").

21

Arbitration Of Performance Bond Disputes

H. Bruce Shreves
Kevin L. Lybeck[1]

Introduction

There was a time when the issue of whether to arbitrate or litigate would have been an easy one for surety companies: you simply would not agree to arbitrate any disputes involving the surety, even if your principal was bound by an arbitration clause. Well, times change. Arbitration of construction disputes has boomed over the last 10-15 years; it appears that the vast majority of complex construction disputes are arbitrated rather than litigated in state or federal courts.

It is also rare for the contractor in a major construction case not to have a performance bond which runs in favor of the owner, and payment bond in favor of subcontractors and suppliers. Therefore, the surety is often faced with a very difficult decision: does it voluntarily agree to subject itself to the jurisdiction of an arbitration tribunal, or does it insist that the issues involving the surety can be litigated only in court? Years ago the answer to that question was simple; today it is not for a variety of reasons, including, but not limited to, the expedited nature of arbitration proceedings; the more sophisticated arbitration panels, which include a number of construction/surety attorneys as part of the select panels; the cost and efficiency of arbitration; and the ability of parties in arbitration to shape their arbitration clauses to greatly limit the scope of the arbitration, and the ability of the arbitration panel to assess damages that would be considered beyond the scope of the contract and/or bond, such as consequential damages, penalties, punitive damages, etc.

This paper assumes the reader's familiarity with basic principals of arbitration, suretyship, and construction contract law. Accordingly, this Introduction is limited to that necessary to set the stage for the discussion of: (1) the arbitrability of the surety's disputes with the obligee and the principal, (2) the preclusive effect on the surety's rights of an arbitration in which the surety does not participate, and (3) the appeal procedures contained in the now proposed revision of the Uniform Arbitration Act.

The Federal Arbitration Act[2] was enacted to make any written agreement to submit an existing or future controversy to arbitration "valid, irrevocable, and enforceable, save upon such grounds as exist at law or in equity for the revocation of any contract."[3] The Federal Arbitration Act applies to "any maritime transaction or a contract evidencing a transaction involving commerce."[4]

---

1. The authors thank Charles C. Coffee of Simon, Peragine, Smith & Redfearn, L.L.P. for assistance in the research and drafting of this paper.

2. 9 U.S.C. §§1-16.

3. 9 U.S.C. §2.

4. *Id.*

Commerce is defined as interstate or foreign commerce, but excluding the employment contracts of seamen, railroad workers, or other workers engaged in foreign or interstate commerce.[5]

The Federal Arbitration Act is not merely procedural, but constitutes a body of substantive federal law.[6] This body of federal law is characterized by a very strong preference for arbitration.[7] Given the existence of a valid, written arbitration agreement, the question of whether a particular dispute is arbitrable under that agreement may be arbitrable.[8] In maritime transactions and transactions involving commerce, the Federal Arbitration Act preempts all contrary state law. Moreover, Congress intended to preempt the field to the full extent of its constitutional authority.[9] Accordingly, the Federal Arbitration Act applies to almost all construction contracts. In *Lost Creek Municipal Utility District v. Travis Industrial Painters, Inc.*,[10] the Federal Arbitration Act was held to preempt state law when the construction contract's only out-of-state connections were the domicile of the surety and the location of the plant that manufactured the paint.[11] In any event, State arbitration acts, to the extent not preempted, also often involve a strong preference for arbitration.[12]

The disadvantages of arbitration relative to litigation from the surety's standpoint were discussed by the U.S. District Court in *Pensacola Construction Co. v St. Paul Fire & Marine Insurance Co.*[13] In that case, the court recognized that the surety faced the "unhappy choice" of participating in the arbitration between its principal and a claimant, with consequent loss of procedural protections, or of not participating in the arbitration and risking the uncertain preclusive effect of an arbitrator's award.[14] Accordingly, the court held that St. Paul stated a valid claim for a declaratory judgment as to the preclusive effect of any ultimate arbitration award.[15] With respect to the disadvantages of participating in an arbitration, the court stated:

> Perhaps the most important substantive right that a party to arbitration loses is the right to have a decision rendered according to law. An arbiter need not explain his decision and there is little or no review for errors of fact or law. See *United Paper Workers v Misco*, 484 U.S. 29, 108 S.Ct. 364, 98 L. Ed. 2d 286 (1987) (arbitral decisions are largely insulated from judicial review); Motomura, *Arbitration and Collateral Estoppel: Using Preclusion to Shape Procedural Choices*, 63 Tul. L. Rev. 29, 37-45 (1983); and Shell, *Res Judicata and Collateral Estoppel Effects of Commercial Arbitration*, 35 U.C.L.A.L. Rev. 623, 633-635 (1988).
>
> The lack of procedural safeguards was discussed in *Alexander v. Gardner-Denver Co.*, 415 U.S. 36, 57-58, 94 S.Ct. 1011, 1024, 30 L. Ed. 2d 147 (1974):

---

5. 9 U.S.C. §1.

6. *Moses H. Cone Memorial Hospital v. Mercury Construction Corp.*, 460 U.S. 1, 25 n. 32, 103 S.Ct. 927, 925, n. 32 (U.S.N.C. 1983).

7. 460 U.S. at 24, 103 S.Ct. at 941.

8. E.g. *Acevedo Maldonado v. PPG Indus., Inc.*, 514 F.2d 614, 617 (1st Cir. (Puerto Rico) 1975).

9. *Foster v. Turley*, 808 F.2d 38, 40 (10th Cir. (N.M.) 1986); see, also, e.g., *Gautreaux v. Prudential Insurance Company of America*, 98-0286 at 5 (La. App. 1 Cir. 2/19/99), 728 So.2d 921, 924 (recognizing "the obvious preemption of the field by Congress"), *writ denied*, 99-0767 (La. 4/30/99) 734 So. 2d 205.

10. 827 S.W. 2d 103 (Tex. App. - Austin 1992).

11. *Id.* at 105.

12. E.g., *Jay Caldarera & Co. v. Louisiana Stadium and Exposition District*, 98-294 (La. App. 5 Cir. 12/16/98), 725 So. 2d 549.

13. 705 F. Supp. 306 (W.D. La. 1988).

14. 705 F. Supp. at 310.

15. 705 F. Supp. at 311. The preclusive effect of arbitration awards generally is discussed *infra* at 11.

> [T]he fact finding process in arbitration usually is not equivalent to judicial factfinding. The record of the arbitration proceedings is not as complete; the usual rules of evidence do not apply; and rights and procedures common to civil trials, such as discovery, compulsory process, cross examination, and testimony under oath, are severely limited or unavailable.[16]

This lack of procedural safeguards is rendered more intimidating by the circumstance that the limited provisions in the federal act for judicial review result in arbitration awards that usually are nonappealable as a practical matter.[17]

Nevertheless, arbitration does have advantages that may inure to the benefit of a construction surety, most notably the prospect of having complex issues turning on construction industry practices or technical matters decided by professionals in the field concerned, rather than by judges or juries.[18] It is, in any event, clear that the possibility of being compelled to arbitrate is of great importance to an unwilling surety.

I. *Compulsory Arbitration/Incorporation By Reference*

A nonsignatory to an arbitration agreement may be compelled nevertheless to arbitrate under several theories, all supposedly stemming from ordinary principles of agency and contract. The Second Circuit has recognized at least five such theories:

> 1) incorporation by reference; 2) assumption [implied conduct]; 3) agency; 4) veil piercing/alter ego; and 5) estoppel.[19]

This paper will consider those theories that seem potentially most applicable to a performance bond surety.

A construction contract surety that, on its principal's default, assumes the completion of the principal's contract will be bound by the terms of that contract, including any arbitration provision, at least absent an agreement to avoid arbitration. In *United States Fidelity & Guaranty Co. v. Bangor Area Joint School Authority*,[20] the defaulting contractor assigned the construction contract to the surety, which completed the project. Thereafter, the owner was able to compel the surety to arbitrate its claim to the remaining contract balance.[21] The same result was obtained in *Buck Run Baptist Church, Inc. v. Cumberland Surety Ins. Co.*[22] In *Buck Run Baptist*, it was the surety that sought successfully to compel arbitration. The *Buck Run Baptist* court noted that the surety, having

---

16. 705 F. Supp. at 310, n. 1 (bracketed material substituted by the court).

17. 9 U.S.C. §§10-11.

18. Michael J. Franks & John W. Heacock, *The Contract Surety's Involvement in and Preclusion by Arbitration Proceedings Involving its Principal: an Update With Drafting Documents*, presented at ABA Tort and Insurance Practice System 1999 Annual Meeting, (American Bar Association, 1999).

19. *Petitions of Laitasalo*, 196 B.R. 913, 918 (Bankr. S.D.N.Y. 1996) [quoting from *Thomson-CSF, S.A. v. American Arbitration Ass'n.*, 64 F.3d 773, 776 (2nd Cir. 1995) (bracketed material by *Laitasalo*)].

20. 355 F. Supp. 913 (E.D. Pa. 1973).

21. *Id.*

22. 983 S.W. 2d 501 (Ky. 1998).

caused a relet contractor to complete the work, "in effect, stood in the shoes of Z&J and became the contractor on the project. Consequently, [the surety] is entitled to enforce the construction contract arbitration agreement." (Bracketed material substituted.)[23] The *Buck Run Baptist* court also relied on the circumstance that the performance bond incorporated the terms of the construction contract, which included an arbitration provision.[24]

Incorporation by reference is the primary vehicle by which sureties may be compelled to arbitrate. The majority of courts applying incorporation analysis deem the arbitration clause of a construction contract incorporated by reference into a performance bond to apply even to disputes as to the bond's coverage, that is, to the surety's personal defenses. A minority of courts, however, applying a more limited incorporation analysis would exempt the surety's personal defenses from the operation of a construction contract arbitration clause incorporated by reference in a performance bond.

A. MAJORITY VIEW OF INCORPORATION

It is well established that incorporation by reference into a contract of the content of an extrinsic document generally is effective to achieve its intended purpose.[25] In *United States Fidelity & Guaranty Company v. West Point Construction Co.*,[26] a subcontractor's performance bond incorporated by reference the terms of the subcontract, which in turn contained an arbitration provision, in turn modified by reference to the arbitration provision contained in the prime contract.[27] After the default of the subcontractor, the general contractor sought to compel arbitration of its claim against the subcontractor's surety. Noting the incorporation of the subcontract into the bond, the court stated:

> We conclude that the incorporation of the subcontract into the bond expresses an intention of the parties, including USF&G, to arbitrate disputes. Our conclusion is supported by the strong policy favoring arbitration expressed by Congress in the Federal Arbitration Act.[28]

The *West Point* court nowhere explained the basis for its application of the federal preference in favor of enforcing arbitration agreements to the preliminary question of whether the surety had agreed to arbitrate. Section 2 of the FAA merely declares that written arbitration agreements "shall be valid, irrevocable, and enforceable, save upon such grounds as exist at law or in equity for the revocation of any contract."[29] Moreover, the Supreme Court has recognized that the question of whether parties agreed to arbitrate a matter should be determined by "ordinary state-law principles that govern the formation of contracts."[30] Accordingly, in affirming a district court order staying arbitration, because the event specified by the contracting parties as a predicate to arbitration of the commercial dispute had not occurred, the Second Circuit stated in 1989:

23. 983 S.W. 2d at 503.
24. *Id.*
25. E.g., *JS & H Construction Co. v. Richmond County Hospital Authority*, 473 F.2d 212, 215 (5th Cir. (Ga.) 1973).
26. 837 F.2d 1507 (11th Cir. (Ala.) 1988).
27. *Id.*
28. 837 F.2d at 1508 (footnote omitted).
29. 9 U.S.C. §2.
30. *First Options of Chicago, Inc. v. Kaplan*, 514 U.S. 938, 944, 115 S.Ct. 1920, 1924, (U.S. Pa. 1995).

> [T]hough even a narrow arbitration clause must be construed in light of the presumption in favor of arbitration, the court is not free to disregard the explicit boundaries set by the agreement between the parties.[31]

It should be noted that none of these cases appears to involve an incorporation clause that purported to avoid or limit incorporation of any arbitration clause contained in the underlying contract. Presumably such a specific limitation would be honored under ordinary principles of contract interpretation. Nevertheless, whether or not explicitly relying on a statutory preference for arbitration, many courts have applied the expansive view of incorporation expressed in *West Point*.[32] Other courts, while not ordering a surety to arbitrate, have applied the expansive view of the effect of a bond's incorporating a contract containing an arbitration provision to hold that the surety had agreed to arbitrate all issues, including its personal defenses.

In *Rashid v. Schenck Construction Co., Inc.*,[33] the West Virginia Supreme Court held that where the performance bond incorporated by reference a construction contract containing an arbitration provision, the surety had "agreed to arbitrate all aspects of disputes related to the contract ***and bond***." (Emphasis added.)[34] Applying the Federal Arbitration Act as having preempted state law, the West Virginia Court stated:

> Under the Federal Arbitration Act and federal case law, an arbitration agreement can be incorporated into a subcontract by reference in a general contract. Likewise, an agreement to arbitrate, where it is part of a general contract, can be incorporated into a bond by reference to the general contract. . . .
>
> In the case now before us, the contract between Schenck and the Rashids contains such an arbitration agreement, incorporated by reference into the bond. Consequently, we concur with the federal district court that USF&G agreed to arbitrate and thus, the arbitration award is final and binding, and should be given collateral estoppel effect.[35]

(Footnote omitted). Other cases have reached generally the same result.[36]

---

31. *Chevron USA, Inc., By And Through Chevron Resources Co. v. Consolidated Edison Co. of N.Y. Inc.*, 872 F.2d 534, 537-38 (2nd Cir. (N.Y.) 1989) (bracketed material substituted; citations omitted); *Gelco Corp. v. Baker Industries, Inc.*, 779 F.2d 26, 28 (8th Cir. (Minn.) 1985) (broad presumption in favor of arbitrability no longer applies when an arbitration clause contains specific limitations.

32. *Exchange Mutual Insurance Co. v. Haskell Co.*, 742 F.2d 274, 276 (6th Cir. (Tenn.) 1984); *Compania Espanola De Petroleos, S.A. v. Nereus Shipping, U.S.A.*, 527 F.2d 966, 971 (2d Cir. (N.Y.) 1975), *cert denied*, 426 U.S. 936, 96 S.Ct. 2650, (U.S.N.Y.) (1976); *Transamerica Premier Insurance Co. v. Collins & Co., General Contractors, Inc.*, 735 F. Supp. 1050, 1051 (N.D. Ga. 1990); *Hoffman v. Fidelity & Deposit Co. of M.D.*, 734 F. Supp. 192, 193 (D. N.J. 1990); *Cianbro Corp. v. Empresa Nacional De Ingenieria y Technologia, S.A.*, 697 F. Supp. 15 (D. Me. 1988); *Boys Club of San Fernando Valley, Inc. v. Fidelity & Deposit Co.*, 6 Cal. App. 4 1266, 8 Cal. Rptr. 2d 587, 589 (Cal. App. 2 Dist. 1992); *St. Paul Fire & Marine Insurance Company v. Woolley/Sweeney Hotel #5*, 545 So.2d 958, 958-59 (Fla. App. 4 Dist. 1989), *review denied*, 553 So. 2d 1166 (Fla. 1989); *Piqua v. Ohio Farmers Insurance Co.*, 617 N.E. 2d 780, 781 (Ohio App. 2 Dist. 1992).

33. 190 W. Va. 363, 438 S.E. 2d 543 (W. Va. 1993).

34. 190 W. Va. at 367, 438 S.E. 2d at 547 (emphasis added).

35. *Id.*

36. *Sue Klau Enterprises, Inc. v. American Fidelity Fire Insurance Company*, 551 F.2d 882 (1st Cir. (Puerto Rico) 1977), *cert denied*, 434 U.S. 854, 98 S.Ct. 172 (U.S. Puerto Rico 1977); *Thomas O'Connor & Co. v. Insurance Company of North America*, 697 F. Supp. 563 (D. Mass. 1998); *Henderson Investment Corp. v. International Fidelity Insurance Co.*, 575 So. 2d 770 (Fla. App. 5th Dist. 1991); *Bolingbrook Park District v. National-Ben Franklin Insurance Co. of Illinois*, 420 N.E. 2d 741 (Ill. App. 3 Dist. 1981); *Powers Regulator Co. v. United States Fidelity & Guaranty Co.*,

Under this expansive view of incorporation by reference, a surety can be compelled to arbitrate its personal defenses. *Hoffmann v. Fidelity & Deposit Co. of Maryland*,[37] was a case in which the surety, in response to the bond obligee's suit to enforce its demand for arbitration, moved for declaratory judgment that the obligee's claims against the surety were not arbitrable.[38]

The surety in *Hoffmann* argued first that the incorporation of the construction contract and the bond was intended only to define the scope of the work, and second that the incorporated language of the construction contract, applying by its terms only "between the parties to this agreement" did not bind the surety to arbitrate claims against it.[39] Rejecting these arguments, the court granted the obligee's cross motion for summary judgment and ordered arbitration.[40]

> Fidelity reads the arbitration clause too narrowly. . . . The courts have not construed such references to the parties as limiting the applicability of the arbitration clause to the parties to the main contract.
>
> The court concludes that the Third Circuit would follow the Eleventh, Sixth, Fifth, Second, and First Circuits and would require Fidelity to arbitrate its defenses to liability on the Bond. Federal policy favors arbitration and dictates liberal construction of arbitration clauses: . . . [41]

Sauce for the goose is, however, sauce for the gander. The surety also may be able to compel arbitration under the expansive view of arbitration cases.[42]

Although the parameters of the expansive view of incorporation by reference may be fairly apparent, some further illustration may be appropriate. In *Seaboard Surety Company v. Board of Chosen Freeholders Of The County Of Warren*,[43] a New Jersey appellate court was presented with a situation where, two general contractors having gone bankrupt, the obligee sought to compel the sureties to arbitrate the obligee's claims. The sureties sought a declaratory judgment that they could not be compelled to arbitrate and would not be bound by any arbitration in which they did not

---

388 N.E. 2d 1205 (Mass. App. Ct. 1979); *Sheffield Assembly of God Church, Inc. v. American Insurance Co.*, 870 S.W. 2d 926 (Mo. App. W.D. 1994).

37. 734 F. Supp. 192 (D.N.J. 1990).

38. 734 F. Supp. at 193.

39. 734 F. Supp. at 193-94.

40. 734 F. Supp. at 195.

41. 734 F. Supp. at 194-95. *United States Fidelity & Guaranty Co. v. West Point Construction Co.*, 837 F. 2d 1507, 1508 (11th Cir. 1988); *Exchange Mutual Insurance Co. v. Haskell Co.*, 742 F.2d 274, 276 (6th Cir. (Tenn.) 1984); *Compania Espanola de Petroleos v. Neraus Shipping*, 527 F. 2d 966, 973-74 (2d Cir. (N.Y.) 1975), *cert denied*, 426 U.S. 936, 96 S.Ct. 2650 (U.S.N.Y. 1976); *Cianbro Corp v. Empresa Nacional De Ingenieria*, 697 F. Supp. 15 (D. Me. 1988); see *J&S Construction Co., Inc. v. Travelers Indemnity Co.*, 520 F.2d 809, 810 (1st Cir. (Mass.) 1975) (surety permitted to stay litigation pending arbitration pursuant to incorporated clause); *Thomas O'Connor and Co. v. Insurance Co. of North America*, 697 F. Supp. 563 (D. Mass. 1988) (surety permitted to stay litigation pending arbitration); *Cost Brothers v. Travelers Indemnity Co.*, 760 F. 2d 58 (3d Cir. (Pa.) 1985) (surety not required to arbitrate because bond did not incorporate construction contract containing arbitration clause).

42. *Fireman's Insurance Co. of Newark, New Jersey v. Edgewater Beach Owner's Association, Inc.*, 1996 WL 509720 (N.D. Fla. 1996). See also, *Loyal Order of Moose v. Int'l Fidelity Ins.* Co., 797 P.2d 622, 629 (Alaska 1990); *J&S Construction Co. v. Travelers Indemnity Co.*, 520 F. 2d 809 (1st Cir. (Mass.) 1975); *Henderson Investment Corp. v. International Fidelity Insurance Co.*, 575 So. 2d 770 (Fla. Dist. Ct. App. 1991).

43. 222 N.J. Super. 409, 537 A. 2d 310 (N.J. Super. A. D. 1988); *cert denied*, 111 N.J. 630, 546 A.2d 545 (N.J. 1988).

participate. The New Jersey court held to the contrary on both points.[44] Noting that the sureties had had adequate notice of the arbitration proceeding to satisfy due process requirements, the court held that the sureties were obligated to arbitrate and if they did not do so, they would be bound by the result.[45]

In *Exchange Mutual Insurance Co. v. Haskell Co.*,[46] the court found that the surety's duty to arbitrate arose from a series of contracts. The general contract called for arbitration of all disputes "arising out of, or relating to, this contract or the breach thereof."[47] A subcontract provided that the subcontractor assumed, with respect to the general contractor, the same responsibilities of contractual performance that the general contractor owed to the owner pursuant to the general contract. The subcontractor obtained a performance bond which incorporated by reference the subcontract.[48] Holding that the surety was obligated to arbitrate the obligee's claim, the court stated:

> Although Mutual Exchange was not a signatory to the primary construction contract, the performance bond incorporated by reference the terms of the underlying subcontract. The subcontract, in turn, incorporated by reference the terms of the primary construction contract which imposed an obligation to submit all unresolved disputes to arbitration.[49]

Under similar analysis, a surety has been held to benefit from a provision in an incorporated arbitration clause that required as a prerequisite to arbitration the consent of a party into whose shoes the surety had moved.[50]

B. MINORITY VIEW OF INCORPORATION

A minority of courts have held that, when a performance bond incorporates by reference a contract containing an arbitration provision, the incorporation evidences the surety's intent to be bound by the outcome of an arbitration between its principal and the obligee only to the extent that the arbitration determines the merit of the obligee's claim against the principal. This view preserves the surety's personal (or coverage) defenses to be decided in a subsequent proceeding. The leading case for this is *Fidelity & Deposit Co. of Md. v. Parsons and Whittemore Contractors Corp.*[51]

Drawing a distinction between claims on the contract and claims on the bond, and noting that the arbitration provision contained in the contract did not refer to the bond, the *Parson and Whittemore* court stated:

> As to disputes between the general contractor and the subcontractor concerning failure of performance by the latter, those two parties expressly agree that their defenses should be submitted to arbitration for resolution. By contrast, there was no agreement on

44. 222 N.J. Super. at 419, 537 A. 2d at 314-15; *cert denied*, 111 N.J. 630, 546 A.2d 545 (N.J. 1988).
45. *Id.*
46. 742 F. 2d 274 (6th Cir. (Tenn.) 1984).
47. 742 F. 2d at 275 (emphasis deleted).
48. 742 F. 2d at 275-76).
49. 742 F. 2d at 276.
50. *Travelers Indemnity Corp. v. Hager Contractors, Inc.*, 389 N. W. 2d 257, 259-60 (Minn. App. 1986).
51. 48 N.Y. 2d 127, 397 N.E. 2d 380, 421 N.Y.S. 2d 869 (N.Y. 1979).

> the part of any party that controversies arising as to rights and obligations under the terms of the performance bond would be submitted to arbitration.[52]

The court buttressed its conclusion that the surety would be bound with respect to the merit of the obligee's claims against the principal by reference to suretyship law.

> The liability of the surety on a performance bond customarily follows the liability of the principal on the bond. By express provision of both the subcontract and performance bond, the liability of Central as principal and Fidelity as surety was joint and several; all reason argues against adjudication of such joint and several liability of the two obligors in separate forums.[53]

Similarly, in *Grundstad v. Ritt,*[54] the court held that a guarantor of an agreement containing an arbitration clause was bound to the result, because he had assumed that risk. Other cases recently following the *Parsons* and *Whittemore* analysis are *Hartford Accident and Indemnity Co. v. Scarlett Harbor Associates, Ltd.,*[55] and *Matson, Inc. v. Lamb & Associates Packaging, Inc.,*[56] In *Matson, Inc.*, the court held that arbitration with the principal was a prerequisite to the obligee suing the surety.[57] Additionally, the Supreme Court of Alaska has held that where the bond incorporates the construction contract, the surety may compel arbitration of the dispute between principal and obligee, the outcome of which will bind the surety, while nevertheless preserving its bond defenses.[58] It may be that the more restrained view of incorporation expressed in *Parsons* and *Whittemore* will gain acceptance in the future.

Of course, when the bond contains no incorporation clause at all, and the surety has not taken any action (such as letting a completion contract) that could be deemed an adoption of the underlying contract, the surety may escape compulsory arbitration in any event.[59] However, in that situation, the surety declines to participate in the arbitration at the risk of being bound to one degree or another by its result.[60]

II. *Preclusive Effect On The Surety Of An Arbitration Award As To Its Principal*

The Federal Arbitration Act, which controls the application of arbitration agreements in almost all construction contracts,[61] does not address the preclusive effect of arbitration awards. However, it does provide that where the parties are so agreed an award may be judicially confirmed and made the judgment of the confirming court.[62] In such cases, general concepts of res judicata and collateral estoppel may be applied. Indeed, such concepts may be applied even to unconfirmed

52. 48 N.Y. 2d at 131, 397 N.E. 2d at 382, 421 N.Y.S. 2d at 871.
53. 48 N.Y. 2d at 132, 397 N.E. 2d at 383, 421 N.Y.S. 2d at 872.
54. 166 F. 3d 867 (7th Cir. (Ill.) 1999).
55. 695 A. 2d 153 (Md. 1997).
56. 947 S. W. 2d 324 (Ark. 1997).
57. *Id.*
58. *Loyal Order of Moose v. Int'l Fidelity Ins. Co.*, 797 P.2d 622, 629 (Alaska 1990).
59. *E.g., WindowMaster Corp. v. B. G. Danis Co.*, 511 F. Supp. 157 (S.D. Ohio 1981).
60. *Id.*
61. See, Discussion, *supra* at n.n. 9-10 and text.
62. 9 U.S.C. §9.

arbitration awards. A surety, however, is not clearly in the shoes of its principal, in that it may have coverage defenses, or the principal may have been unable to present an effective defense.[63] Accordingly, the principles of res judicata and collateral estoppel should be, and often are, impacted by suretyship law.[64]

Judgments (and arbitration awards) ***in favor*** of the principal are conclusive in favor of the surety. In addition to res judicata and collateral estoppel,[65] the bedrock suretyship principle that the surety's liability cannot be greater than that of its principal compels this result.[66]

Judgments or arbitration awards ***against the principal*** may have three levels of preclusive effect. The judgment or award may establish the surety's liability (i.e., dispose of its personal defenses as well as the principal's). The judgment or award may have no preclusive effect on the surety. Or the judgment or award may constitute *prima facia* evidence of surety liability, or a rebuttable presumption of the principal's liability.[67]

Leaving aside bonds in which the surety specifically undertakes to pay judgments, cases conclusively binding a non-arbitrating surety to an arbitration award against its principal are relatively rare and usually involve some factor beyond rendition of the judgment or award, such as failure to take advantage of an opportunity to defend, or control of the principal's defense.[68]

Cases holding that an award or judgment against the principal has no preclusive effect at all on the surety also are not common.[69] The absence of any preclusive effect may arise by statute,[70] or by jurisprudence.[71]

Gearhart v. Pierce Enterprises, Inc.,[72] is of interest because the surety was a co-defendant and actively participated in the litigation where a default judgment was rendered against the principal. In holding that the surety was not bound by the default judgment, the court relied on the circumstances that the surety was defending against its own liability, and was not defending the principal, and was not responsible for events leading to the principal's default.[73]

Most cases fall into the middle ground and at least preserve the surety's coverage or personal defenses from the preclusive effect of an arbitration award against the principal. In *Von Engineering Co. v. R.W. Roberts Construction Co., Inc.*,[74] which apparently did not involve an incorporated

63. See, generally, James D. Ferrucci, "Effect Of An Arbitration Provision In The Principal's Contract With The Obligee," The Law Of Performance Bonds, 274-75, 280 (Moelmann, Lawrence R. & Harris, John T. eds., American Bar Association, 1999).

64. See, *Id.*

65. *Dimacopoulos v. Consort Development Corp.*, 158 A.D. 2d 658, 552 N.Y.S. 2d 124 (N.Y.A.D. 2d Depart. 1990).

66. Louisiana Civil Code article 3035 (suretyship is an accessory contract to fulfill the obligation of another) and 3059 (extinction of suretyship by extinction of principal obligation); *Rhode Island Hospital Trust National Bank v. Ohio Casualty Insurance Co., 789 F.2d 74 (1st Cir. (R.I.) 1986); Burdick Associates Owners Corp. v. Indemnity Insurance Co. of North America*, 166 A.D. 2d 402, 560 N.Y.S. 2d 481 (N.Y.A.D. 1990).

67. See, generally, *Ferrucci, supra*, at 276.

68. See, generally, *Ferrucci, supra*, at 277. See also, discussion of incorporation cases, *supra* at n.n. 24-57 and text.

69. See, Kevin L. Lybeck, "Arbitration And The Performance Bond Surety," The Law of Suretyship, 11-31 (Edward G. Gallagher, ed., American Bar Association, 1993).

70. California Civil Code §2855 (West 2000).

71. *Vigilanti v. Pfeiffer-Neumeyer Const. Corporation*, 25 F. Supp. 403 (E.D.N.Y. 1938) (involving a default judgment).

72. 105 Nev. 517, 779 P.2d 93 (Nev., 1989).

73. 105 Nev. At 520, 779 P.2d at 95.

74. 457 So. 2d 1080 (Fla. App. 5 Dist., 1984).

arbitration agreement, the Court of Appeal, reversing a judgment of dismissal in favor of the surety, held that an arbitration award against the surety would be conclusive if the surety had notice and an opportunity to defend, but otherwise would be only *prima facia* evidence of the surety's liability.[75] The court stated:

> The common law nevertheless recognizes that in certain situations such as where indemnity agreements are involved, a judgment against the indemnitee or principal may be conclusive (or even *prima facia* evidence) against the indemnitor or surety even though the latter did not participate in the earlier proceedings. American proffers no argument as to why such common law principles comport with due process in a judicial setting but would violate due process if applied to an arbitration award and we can think of none.[76]

In *Rouse Construction, Inc. v. Transamerica Insurance Company*,[77] the Court of Appeals was confronted with the issue of the preclusive effect on the surety of a default judgment rendered in Mississippi, confirming an arbitration award against the principal on a construction subcontract performance bond. The court noted that under Mississippi law, the surety would be bound by the default judgment. However, the court determined that the law of Georgia (where the district court sat) was applicable to the question of the preclusive effect of the judgment. Under Georgia law, the default judgment established only a rebuttable presumption of the principal's liability to the obligee.[78]

Somewhat differently, other courts deem a judgment or arbitration award against the principal to be *prima facia* evidence of the surety's liability.[79] In any event, in the broad middle ground, the surety generally should be allowed to assert its personal or surety defenses.[80] This view of preclusion is supported not only by suretyship law but by reference to fundamental principles of collateral estoppel. Surety defenses normally would not be decided in an arbitration involving only the principal and obligee. However, a surety that is obligated to arbitrate all issues, including its personal defenses,[81] but nevertheless ignores an invitation to arbitrate, should be bound conclusively by the arbitrator's decision.[82]

Of course, the situation in any state may be less than pellucid, and may be downright confusing. This is illustrated nicely by the Louisiana case of *Town of Melville v. Safeco Insurance Company of America*.[83] On the first appeal, the Louisiana Third Circuit affirmed the trial court

---

75. 457 So. 2d at 1082.

76. 457 So. 2d at 1082. See, also, *Parsons v. Whittemore & Associates*, 397 N.E. 2d 380 (N.Y. 1979) (discussed, *supra* at n. 50 and text).

77. 750 F. 2d 1492 (11th Cir. (Ga.) 1985).

78. 750 F. 2d at 1494.

79. *Heritage Insurance Company of America v. Foster Electric Co. Inc.*, 393 So. 2d 28 (Fla. App. 3 Dist. 1981); *P.R. Post Corp. v. Maryland Casualty Company*, 403 Mich. 543, 271 N.W. 2d 521, 525 (Mich. 1978); see, also, Restatement of Security §139 (1941) (judgment obtained other than by default or confession).

80. Lybeck, *supra*, at 11-3; see, *American Home Assurance Company v. Larkin General Hospital, Ltd.*, 593 So. 2d 195, 198 (Fla. 1992) (coverage defense raised in response to arbitration award), except where, under cases following *Von Engineering*, the surety has passed up an adequate opportunity to defend. 457 So. 2d 1080 (Fla. App. 5 Dist. 1984).

81. This obligation may arise pursuant to incorporation in the bond of an arbitration provision, discussed, *supra*, at n.n. 24-57 and text, or by statute, as in *Rhode Island*. R.I. General Law §10-3-21.

82. E.g., *Kearsarge Metallurgical Corp. v. Peerless Insurance Co.*, 383 Mass. 162, 418 N.E. 2d 580 (Mass. 1981).

83. 589 So. 2d 625 (La. App. 3 Cir. 1991), *reversed*, 593 So. 2d 376 (La. 1992), appeal after remand, 94-1039 (La. App. 3 Cir. 3/1/95), 651 So. 2d 404; *writ denied*, 95-0836 (La. 5/5/95) 654 So. 2d 333.

judgment that the surety on a construction contract was conclusively bound by an arbitration award against its principal. The court acknowledged that the surety was entitled to a *pro tanto* release if the obligee had made overpayments to the surety's prejudice, but found that the record contained no evidence of such payments. Accordingly, the court affirmed the judgment against the surety, reasoning that the surety had no standing collaterally to attack the arbitration award.[84]

The Supreme Court reversed, and remanded so that the surety might present evidence of its personal defenses. The three-sentence per curiam opinion did not set out the court's reasoning.[85]

On appeal after remand, a different panel of the Louisiana Third Circuit took an entirely different approach, incorporating and adopting as its own the trial judge's reasons for judgment.[86] The trial judge had reasoned that, because a judgment in favor of the principal is conclusive in favor of the surety, therefore, a judgment against the principal also is conclusive in favor of the surety to the extent that it limits the amount of any possible judgment against the surety.[87] The trial court then indicated that it deemed the surety to be entitled to assert not only personal or coverage defenses to the award, but to address the merits of the award itself, stating:

> Since this court cannot understand the underlying rationale for the award made by the arbitrators, the court will perform its own calculations and limit any award to $63,321.[88]

The language used by the trial court clearly leaves open the possibility that, had the arbitration award been comprehensible to the judge, he would have regarded it as conclusive as to the surety with respect to the principal's liability, preserving the surety's personal defenses, which would be consistent with the Supreme Court's remand.

However, the Court of Appeal, after completing its quotation of the trial judge's reasons, supplemented them in a way that increased the appearance that the surety might not be precluded in a meaningful manner by an arbitration award against its principal. Without mentioning the incomprehensibility of the arbitration award, the Court of Appeal stated:

> A surety is not liable for any judgments that may be rendered against the principal. *Wiemann v. Mainegra*, 36 So. 2d 358, 359 (La. 1904). A surety is liable only when the principal fails to faithfully discharge his duties or to respond in damages to its failure. A judgment in favor of the principal is necessarily conclusive in favor of the surety, since the liability of the principal is the basis for the liability of the surety. It follows that the judgment against the principal is conclusive for the surety, in that no greater judgment can be rendered against the surety than the amount due from the principal. *Id.*[89]

None of the *Town of Melville* cases mentions the case of *Louisiana Bank & Trust Company v. Murcambyr, Inc.*,[90] where the Court of Appeal found that guarantors of a debtor's obligation on a promissory note, who were sued in the same proceeding as the debtor, could not collaterally attack a default judgment against the debtor.[91]

---

84. 589 So. 2d at 627.
85. 593 So. 2d 376.
86. 651 So. 2d at 406.
87. 651 So. 2d at 407 [citing *Wiemann v. Mainegra*, 112 La. 305, 36 So. 358 (La. 1904)].
88. 651 So. 2d at 408.
89. 651 So. 2d at 408.
90. 419 So. 2d 106 (La. App. 2 Cir. 1982), *writ denied*, 423 So. 2d 1148 (La. 1982).
91. 419 So. 2d at 108.

The *Town of Melville* cases also are inconsistent with the more recent Louisiana case of *Hershell Corp. v. Fireman's Fund Insurance Co.*[92] In that case, after a notice of substantial completion had been filed and liens recorded, the liens were bonded off.[93] The court distinguished the *Town of Melville* cases as having involved only personal defenses of the surety,[94] a distinction that may not be accurate.[95] The Court of Appeal then gave the judgment against the principal full effect against the surety. Referring to the Louisiana Private Works Act,[96] the court stated:

> It would be counter-productive and defeat the purpose of the act to allow the surety to raise all of the defenses available to the owner and/or contractor in litigation by a contributor *after* judgment has been obtained against the owner and/or contractor who had the opportunity to raise all defenses available in that litigation.

(Emphasis added.)[97]

The *Hershell Corporation* case can be further distinguished from the *Town of Melville* cases in that *Hershell Corporation* involved a bond to remove a lien from the public record, which, obligating the surety to pay the claim if proven valid, had perhaps more in common with a judgment bond (that is, a bond that, by its terms, binds the surety to pay a judgment rendered against its principal)[98] than a typical performance bond. Accordingly, it can safely be said that in Louisiana, at least with respect to performance bonds that do not incorporate by reference arbitration agreements, an arbitration award against the principal is not preclusive against the surety with respect to the surety's personal defenses. It is problematic how much further that line of reasoning can be taken, although the second Court of Appeal opinion in the *Town of Melville* case would appear to immunize against charges of frivolity an argument that an arbitration award against the principal does no more than place a cap on the surety's liability.

The situation of the *Town of Melville* cases emphasizes the importance of current, state-specific knowledge of statutory and case law regarding performance bonds and arbitration.

III. *The Finality Of Arbitration*

As was alluded to at the beginning of this paper, the Federal Arbitration Act provides for only very limited judicial review of arbitration awards. An award may be modified only to correct clerical or mathematical error in the award itself, or if the award goes beyond the matter submitted for arbitration.[99] Very specific and limited grounds are set forth for the vacation of an award. Section 10 of the Act provides in pertinent part:

92. 98-1352 (La. App. 3 Cir. 6/2/99), 743 So. 2d 698, 1999 WL 346214.
93. 743 So. 2d at 699.
94. 743 So. 2d at 705.
95. See, Discussion, *supra*, at n.n. 87-88 and text.
96. La. R.S. 9:4813, 4823, 4835, and *passim*.
97. 743 So. 2d at 703.
98. See, *Ferrucci*, *supra*, n. 165.
99. 11 U.S.C. §11.

(a) In any of the following cases the United States court in and for the district wherein the award was made may make an order vacating the award upon the application of any party to the arbitration -

(1) Where the award was procured by corruption, fraud, or undue means.
(2) Where there was evident partiality or corruption in the arbitrators, or either of them.
(3) Where the arbitrators were guilty of misconduct in refusing to postpone the hearing, upon sufficient cause shown, or in refusing to hear evidence pertinent and material to the controversy; or any other misbehavior by which the rights of any party have been prejudiced.
(4) Where the arbitrators exceeded their powers, or so imperfectly executed them that a mutual, final, and definite award upon the subject matter submitted was not made.
(5) Where an award is vacated and the time within which the agreement required the award to be made has not expired the court may, in its discretion, direct a rehearing by the arbitrators.[100]

The courts generally have construed strictly each of the grounds for vacatur set forth in Section 10.[101]

Significantly greater judicial review of arbitration awards may be afforded by state arbitration acts. The Uniform Arbitration Act, which has been adopted in whole or in part by at least 35 states and the District of Columbia,[102] is in the process of being redrafted by the National Conference of Commissioners on uniform state laws. As of January 7, 2000, the draft under consideration treats vacation of an arbitration award in Section 20. Section 20, as currently being considered, is reproduced as follows:

SECTION 20. VACATING AN AWARD.

(a) Upon motion of a party, the court shall vacate an award if:

100. 9 U.S.C. §10.

101. For an excellent discussion of the construction of the grounds for vacatur, see Lawrence, Laird E. & Ward, Christopher R. *The Availability and Scope of Appeal of Arbitration Awards Under the Federal, Uniform and State Acts*, presented at the ABA Tort and Insurance Practice Session, 1999 Annual Meeting, (copyright 1999, American Bar Association).

102. Alaska, Alaska Stat. §09.43.010, *et seq.*; Arizona, Ariz. Rev. Stat. Ann. §12-1501, *et seq.*; Arkansas, Ark. Code Ann. §16-108-101, *et seq.*; Colorado, Col. Rev. Stat. §13-22-201, *et seq.*; Delaware, Del. Code Ann. tit. 10, §5701, *et seq.*; District of Columbia, D.C. Code Ann. §16-4301, *et seq.*; Florida, Fla. Stat. Ann. §682-01, *et seq.*; Idaho, Idaho Code §7-901, *et seq.*; Illinois, 710 Ill. Comp. Stat. 5/1; Indiana, Ind. Code Ann. §34-4-2-1, *et seq.*; Iowa, Iowa Code §679A.1, *et seq.*; Kansas, Kan. Stat. Ann. §5-401, *et seq.*; Kentucky, Ky. Rev. Stat. Ann. §417.045, *et seq.*; Maine, Me. Rev. Stat. Ann. tit. 14, §5927, *et seq.*; Maryland, Md. Cts. & Jud. Proc. Code Ann. §3-201, *et seq.*; Massachusetts, Mass. Ann. Laws ch. 251, §1, *et seq.*; Minnesota, Minn. Stat. Ann. §572.08, *et seq.*; Mississippi, Miss. Code Ann. §11-15-1, *et seq.*; Missouri, Mo. Ann. Stat. §435.350, *et seq.*; Montana, Mont. Code Ann. §27-5-111, *et seq.*; Nebraska, Neb. Rev. Stat. §25-2601, *et seq.*; Nevada, Nev. Rev. Stat. §38.015, *et seq.*; New Mexico, N.M. Stat. Ann. §44-7-1, *et seq.*; North Carolina, N.C. Gen. Stat. §1-567.1, *et seq.*; North Dakota, N.D. Cent. Code §32-29.1-01, *et seq.*; Oklahoma, Okla. Stat. Ann. tit. 15, §801, *et seq.*; Pennsylvania, Pa. Stat. Ann. tit. 42, §7301, *et seq.*; South Carolina, S.C. Code Ann. §15-48-10, *et seq.*; South Dakota, S.D. Codified Laws, §21-25A-1, *et seq.*; Tennessee, Tenn. Code Ann. §29-5-301, *et seq.*; Texas, Tex. Rev. Civ. Stat. Ann. Art. 224, *et seq.*; Utah, Utah Code Ann. §78-31a-1, *et seq.*; Vermont, Vt. Stat. Ann. tit. 12, §5651, *et seq.*; Virginia, Va. Code Ann. §8.01-577, *et seq.*; West Virginia, W. Va. Code §55-10-1, *et seq.*; Wyoming, Wyo. Stat. Ann. §6-36-101, *et seq.*

(1) the award was procured by corruption, fraud, or other undue means;
(2) there was evident partiality by an arbitrator appointed as a neutral or corruption or misconduct by any of the arbitrators prejudicing the right of a party;
(3) an arbitrator refused to postpone the hearing upon sufficient cause being shown for postponement, refused to consider evidence material to the controversy, or otherwise so conducted the hearing, contrary to the provisions of Section 12, as to prejudice substantially the rights of a party;
(4) an arbitrator exceeded the arbitrator's powers; or
(5) there was no arbitration agreement, unless the party participated in the arbitration proceeding without having raised the objection not later than the commencement of the arbitration hearing.

(b) One of the following alternatives:

Alternative I

In addition to the grounds to vacate an award set forth in subsection (a), the parties may contract in the arbitration agreement for judicial review of errors of law in the arbitration award. If they have so contracted, the court shall vacate an award made by an arbitrator if the arbitrator has committed an error of law substantially prejudicing the rights of a party.

Alternative II

In addition to the grounds to vacate an award set forth in subsection (a), the parties may contract for any other standard of review of the award not prohibited by applicable law. If they have so contracted, the court shall vacate an award made by an arbitrator if the arbitrator violates this standard of review.

Alternative IIIA

In addition to the grounds to vacate an award set forth in subsection (a), the parties may contract for appellate review of the arbitration award by another arbitrator or panel of arbitrators. If they have so contracted, the court shall vacate an award made by the original arbitrator if the appellate review by another arbitrator or panel of arbitrators overturns the award of the original arbitrator.

Alternative IIIB

In addition to the grounds to vacate an award set forth in subsection (a), the parties may contract for review of the arbitration award by an arbitral appeals panel. The appointment of such appellate arbitrators, the grounds for appeal, the standards for review, and other procedures for conducting the appeal shall be governed by the arbitration agreement. If the parties have so contracted, the court shall vacate an award made by the original arbitrator if the arbitral appeals panel overturns the award of the original arbitrator.

Alternative IV

No subsection (b).

(c) A motion under this section must be made within 90 days after delivery of a copy of the award to the movant unless the motion is predicated upon corruption, fraud, or other undue means, in which case it must be made within 90 days after those grounds are known or should have been known to the moving party.

(d) In vacating an award on a ground other than that stated in subsection (a)(5), a court may order a rehearing before new arbitrators, appointed in accordance with Section 8. If the award is vacated on grounds stated in subsection (a)(3) or (4), the court may order a rehearing before the arbitrator who made the award or the arbitrator's successor appointed in accordance with Section 8. The time within which the agreement requires the award to be made applies to the rehearing and commences after the date of the order.

(e) If a motion to vacate is denied and no motion to modify or correct the award is pending, the court shall confirm the award.[103]

Whether the proposed expanded appeal rights of the Uniform Arbitration Act (to the extent ultimately enacted by the States) will be available in a construction case involving interstate commerce must be considered in light of the preemptive effect of the Federal Arbitration Act, which creates "a body of federal substantive law of arbitrability, applicable to any arbitration agreement within the coverage of the Act."[104] A majority of federal circuits have recognized the existence of grounds for vacatur other than those specified in Section 10 of the FAA. So viewed, the proposed additional grounds in the Uniform Act revision draft would not be in conflict with the FAA.

The Third Circuit has recognized vacatur of an arbitration award on the ground that it lacked any factual support.[105] The Second, Eighth, Tenth and Eleventh Circuits have acknowledged that an award may be vacated if it violates public policy or requires a party to do so.[106] The Eleventh and Ninth Circuits have acknowledged that an award may be vacated if it is arbitrary and capricious.[107] At least the Sixth, Seventh, and Second Circuits appear to have acknowledged that an award may be vacated if the arbitrators committed manifest legal error.[108]

---

103. Draft Uniform Arbitration Act with preferatory note and reporters notes, copyright 1999 by National Conference of Commissioners on Uniform and State Laws, [http://www.law.upenn.edu/bll/ulc/uarba/arbam99.htm.]

104. *Moses H. Cone Memorial Hospital v. Mercury Construction Corporation*, 460 U.S. 1, 24, 103 S.Ct. 927, 941, (U.S.N.C. 1983).

105. *Mutual Fire, Marine & Inland Ins. Co. v. Norad Reinsurance Co., Ltd.*, 868 F.2d 52, 56 (3rd Cir. Pa. 1989); *Swift Indus. Inc. v. Botany Industries, Inc.*, 466 F.2d 1125, 1134-1135 (3rd Cir. (Pa.) 1972).

106. *Diapulse Corp. of America v. Carba, Ltd.*, 626 F.2d 1108 (2d Cir. (N.Y.) 1980); *PaineWebber, Inc. v. Argon*, 49 F.3d 347 (8th Cir. (Mo.) 1995); *Seymour v. Blue Cross/Blue Shield*, 988 F.2d 1020 (10th Cir. (Utah) 1993); *Brown v. Rauscher Pierce Refsnes, Inc.*, 994 F.2d 775 (11th Cir. (Fla.) 1993).

107. *Ainsworth v. Skurnick*, 960 F.2d 939 (11th Cir. 1992); *Todd Shipyards Corp. v. Cunard Line, Ltd.*, 943 F.2d 1056, 1060 (9th Cir. (Cal.) 1991) ["completely irrational", quoting from, *San Martine Compania De Navegacion v. Saguenay Terminals, Ltd.*, 293 F.2d 706, 800 (9th Cir. (Hawaii) 1961).

108. *Pontiac Trail Medical Clinic, P.C., v. PaineWebber, Inc.*, 1333 WL 288301 at 3, 1 F.3d 1241; *Health Services Management Corp. v. Hughes*, 975 F.2d 1253, 1257 (7th Cir. (Il.) 1992); *National R.R. Passenger Corp. v. Chesapeak & O.Ry.O.*, 551 F.2d 136, 141-42 (7th Cir. (Ind.) 1977); *Carte Blanch (Singapore) BPE, Ltd. v. Carte Blanch Intern. Ltd.*, 888 F.2d 260, 265 (2d Cir. (N.Y.) 1989).

These judicially constructed grounds for vacation are narrow. For example, manifest error of law is available only when:

> [T]he law alleged to have been disregarded is `well defined, explicit, and clearly applicable,' so that the error was `capable of being readily and instantly perceived by the average person qualified to serve as arbitrator.'[109]

These judicial remedies, however, by negating the exclusivity of the list of grounds for vacatur found in 9 U.S.C. §10, support the applicability of state-law created grounds for vacatur in cases involving commerce, on the theory that such remedies, not being in conflict with the Federal Arbitration Act, are not preempted by it.[110]

With respect to reliance on cases appearing to apply manifest error of law as a ground for vacation, however, a caveat is in order. Rejecting application of that remedy, a panel of the Seventh Circuit, in 1994 reviewed the prior cases (including prior Seventh Circuit authority) discussing vacation for manifest error of law, and characterized all of the language regarding manifest error as dictum, because, in the panel's view, the same result would have been obtained by application of statutory criteria.[111]

However, even without the enhanced authorization of the proposed revisions to the Uniform Act, judicial review of arbitration awards more generous than that provided in the Federal Arbitration Act already may be achieved contractually. The Tenth Circuit has recognized that the parties to an arbitration agreement may increase the scope of appellate review by including a choice of law provision selecting generally the law of a state with an arbitration act that affords greater review than does the federal act.[112] The Seventh Circuit in *Northern Illinois Gas Co. v. Airco Indus. Gases, A Division of Airco, Inc.*[113] however, has held that parties to a transaction in commerce cannot avoid the preemptive effect of the Federal Arbitration Act merely by including a choice of law provision calling generally for the application of a particular state's law.

In *Volt Information Services v. Board of Trustees*,[114] the Supreme Court held that the parties to an arbitration agreement were free to specify by contract the application of state arbitration procedures, including procedures for the stay of arbitration under certain circumstances not set out in the federal act.[115] The Supreme Court, however, declined to review, as outside its jurisdiction, the California Court of Appeal's determination, as a matter of state-law contract interpretation, that the contract's general choice of California law constituted a selection of California arbitration procedure.[116] Accordingly, consistent with the holding of *Northern Illinois Gas*, parties wishing to make their arbitration agreement subject to state arbitration provisions should do so specifically and explicitly rather than relying on a general choice of a state's law for the entire contract.

---

109. *Fine v. Bear, Stearns & Co., Inc.*, 765 F. Supp. 824, 827 (S.D.N.Y. 1991) [quoting from, *Merrill Lynch, Pierce, Fenner & Smith, Inc. v. Bobker*, 808 F.2d 930, 933-34 (2d Cir. (N.Y.) 1986)].

110. E.g., *Baravati v. Josephthal, Lyon & Ross, Inc.*, 834 F. Supp. 1023, 1029 (N. D. Ill. 1993) (discussing application of state arbitration law not in conflict with Federal Arbitration Act), *aff'd*, 28 F.3d 704 (7th Cir. (Ill.) 1994), and corrected 867 F. Supp. 648 (N.D. Ill. 1994).

111. *Baravati v. Josephthal, Lyon & Ross, Inc.*, 28 F.3d 704, 706 (7th Cir. (Ill.) 1994).

112. *Foster v. Turley*, 808 F.2d 38, 41 (10th Cir. 1980).

113. *Northern Illinois Gas Co. v. Airco. Indus. Gases, A Division of Airco, Inc.*, 676 F.2d 270, 274 (7th Cir. (Ill.) 1982).

114. 489 U.S. 468, 109 S.Ct. 1248, 103 L.Ed. 2d 488 (U.S. Ca. 1989).

115. 489 U.S. 476-478, 109 S.Ct. at 1254-1255.

116. 489 U.S. at 474-476, 109 S.Ct. at 1253-1254.

Further, the Fifth and Ninth Circuits have upheld the validity of arbitration clauses containing, not choice of law provisions, but specific provisions for enhanced appellate review.[117] As the Fifth Circuit stated with respect to an arbitration provision calling for judicial review of any legal error:

> Such a contractual modification is acceptable because, as the Supreme Court has emphasized, arbitration is a creature of contract and
>
> the FAA's pro-arbitration policy does not operate without regard to the wishes of the contracting parties . . . `[I]t does not follow that the FAA prevents the enforcement of agreements to arbitrate under different rules than those set forth in the Act itself. *Indeed, such a result would be quite inimical to the FAA's purpose of ensuring that private agreements to arbitrate are enforced according to their terms.* Arbitration under the Act is a matter of consent, not coercion, and parties are generally free to structure their arbitration agreements as they see fit. Just as they may limit by contract the issues which they will arbitrate, so too may they specify by contract the rules under which the arbitration will be conducted.'[118]

The extent that contractual freedom ***may*** reach in the arbitration context is highlighted by *dictum* contained in the Seventh Circuit's *Baravati* opinion:

> Indeed, short of authorizing trial by battle or ordeal, or more doubtfully, by a panel of three monkeys, parties can stipulate to whatever procedures they want to govern the arbitration of their disputes; parties are as free to specify idiosyncratic terms of arbitration as they are to specify any other terms in their contract.[119]

The question of appeal rights outside the provisions of 9 U.S.C. §10, when it is applicable, will not, however, be finally determined unless and until the United States Supreme Court decides whether the listing of reasons for vacation contained in Section 10 is exclusive.

Conclusion

The major question for the performance bond surety is the degree to which it will be affected by its principal's agreement to arbitrate. Aside from a few statutory anomalies, this is a question of case law. When the performance bond incorporates a construction contract containing an arbitration clause, the question becomes which breed of incorporation analysis the jurisdiction in question has adopted, or will adopt.

The treatment of an incorporated arbitration clause as an agreement by the surety to be bound by the outcome of the principal's arbitration as to the merits of the principal's defenses, and not as to the surety's defenses, seems the more realistic approach. This is so because the arbitration

---

117. *Gateway Technologies, Inc. v. MCI Telecommunications Corp.*, 64 F.3d 993 (5th Cir. 1995); *LaPine Technology Corp. v. Kyocera Corp.*, 130 F.2d 884 (9th Cir. (Cal.) 1997).

118. *Gateway Technologies*, 64 F.3d at 996 [quoting from *Mastrbuoro v. Shearson, Leaman, Hutton, Inc.*, 514 U.S. 52, 57, 115 S.Ct. 1212, 1216, 131 L. Ed. 2d 76 (1995), quoting in turn from *Volt International Sciences, Inc. v. Board of Trustees Lealand Stanford Junior University*, 489 U.S. 468, 479, 109 S.Ct. 1248, 1256, 103 L. Ed. 2d 488 (1989) (emphasis added by *Gateway* court)].

119. *Baravati v. Josephthal, Lyon & Ross, Inc.*, 28 F.3d 704, 709 (7th Cir. (Ill.) 1994).

clause in the construction contract typically calls for arbitration between the contractor and the owner of disputes arising out of the construction contract, without mentioning either the surety or disputes arising out of the bond. However, the expansive incorporation analysis, under which the surety is bound to arbitrate personal or coverage defense issues, is the majority view.

It is submitted that incorporation language could be devised eliminating or limiting the scope of the arbitration with respect to the surety. Such language should be given effect pursuant to the Federal Arbitration Act's requirement that arbitration be predicated on the agreement of the parties.

22

Extra-Contractual Damages

Thomas J. Casamassima
Mark E. Aronson
Frank E. Marchetti

Introduction

The vast majority of American jurisdictions recognize that the covenant of good faith and fair dealing is implied in every contract.[1] Under the covenant, parties to a contract agree that they will do nothing to injure the rights of the other parties to receive the benefits of the contract. Judges use the covenant to interpret, expand or clarify the language of contracts in order to effectuate the intentions and reasonable expectations of the parties to the contract.[2]

A surety bond is a contract, governed by general principles of contract law.[3] As with all other contracts, the covenant of good faith and fair dealing imposes upon each party to a surety bond a duty of good faith and fair dealing in interpreting, performing, and enforcing the terms of the bond agreement.

Because the covenant of good faith and fair dealing is a contract term, the remedy for its breach is generally limited to contract damages.[4] A narrow exception to this rule applies in the area of insurance contracts. Courts have held that an insurer has a "special relationship" with its insured. If an insurer breaches the covenant of good faith and fair dealing, extra-contractual damages may be recovered through a "bad faith" tort cause of action.

The "special relationship" which courts have found existing between insurers and their insureds arises out of the following characteristics which these courts believe to be inherent in insurance policies: unequal bargaining power, an insured who seeks protection from an unexpected calamity, and the insurance companies' exclusive control over how claims are evaluated.

Suretyship and insurance share many similar characteristics and they are often treated as one and the same in discussions of "bad faith." Suretyship agreements are distinct from insurance policies, however, and a reasoned analysis must keep these distinctions in mind. In determining whether to award extra-contractual damages when the covenant of good faith and fair dealing is breached in a suretyship context, courts should apply a "special relationship analysis."

A "special relationship analysis" would examine the characteristics inherent in suretyship agreements, compare those characteristics with the aforementioned characteristics which create a

---

1. *See* Restatement (Second) Contracts § 205 ("Every contract imposes upon each party a duty of good faith and fair dealing in its performance and its enforcement.")

2. *See Foley v. Interactive Data Corp.*, 47 Cal. 3d 654, 254 Cal. Rptr. 211, 765 P.2d 373 (Cal. 1988).

3. *See United State v. Figuerola*, 58 F.3d 502, 503 (9th Cir. 1995); *Continental Realty Corp. v. Andrew J. Crevolin*, 380 F. Supp. 246, 254 (S.D. W.Va. 1974).

4. Under the rule of *Hadley v. Baxendale*, 9 Ex. 341, 156 Eng. Rep. 145 (1854), contract damages are limited to those which were within the contemplation of the parties at the time the contract was made. Thus, special damages are not recoverable unless the defendant knew the particular risk at the time of contracting.

"special relationship" between insurers and insureds, and determine whether a comparable relationship exists between sureties and obligees or principals.

In only seven states have the highest appellate courts addressed a surety's common law liability for breach of the implied covenant of good faith and fair dealing.[5] In five of these states (Colorado, Arizona, Alaska, North Dakota, and Ohio), the courts held that a common law action is available to recover extra-contractual damages.[6] Only three of these five courts applied a "special relationship analysis" to determine whether extra-contractual damages are recoverable from a surety that acts in "bad faith."[7] The other two courts that have allowed causes of action in tort against sureties for "bad faith" failed to apply a "special relationship analysis."[8]

On the other hand, the highest appellate courts of two states (California and Texas) have held that there is no common law action for "bad faith" under which a surety can be held liable for extra-contractual damages.[9] Both of these courts applied a "special relationship analysis" and concluded that suretyship is distinct from insurance and therefore extra-contractual damages are not recoverable from a surety that commits "bad faith."

Courts have also determined that an award of extra-contractual damages for breach of the covenant in suretyship agreements may be based on a state's unfair insurance claims practice statute. Almost every state has enacted an unfair claims practice statute which authorizes the insurance commissioner to penalize insurance companies that commit the proscribed acts. Some unfair claims practice statutes are written broadly to regulate sureties as well as insurers. In states where the statute allows a private cause of action, extra-contractual damages may be available against sureties by way of a statutory cause of action.

In Part I, this chapter examines the "special relationship" between insurers and insureds that justifies an award of extra-contractual damages. This "special relationship" is then compared to the tripartite relationship inherent in all suretyship agreements.

Part II focuses on the decisions of the highest courts of California and Texas. As of the date of publication, the 1999 Supreme Court of California's decision in *Cates Construction, Inc. v. Talbot Partners*[10] is the most recent decision by a state's highest court to address this issue. The California and Texas courts carefully applied a "special relationship analysis" and concluded that a "special

---

5. *Cates Construction, Inc. v. Talbot Partners*, 21 Cal.4th 28, 86 Cal. Rptr. 2d 855, 980 P.2d 407 (Cal. 1999); *Transamerica Premier Ins. Co. v. Brighton School District*, 940 P.2d 348 (Col. 1997); *Great American Ins. Co. v. North Austin Municipal Utility*, 908 S.W.2d 415 (Tex. 1995); *Loyal Order of Moose, Lodge 1392 v. International Fidelity Insurance Co.*, 797 P.2d 622 (Alaska 1990); *Dodge v. Fidelity and Deposit Co. of Maryland*, 161 Ariz. 344, 778 P.2d 1240 (Ariz. 1989); *Szarkowski v. Reliance Ins. Co.*, 404 N.W.2d 502 (N.D. 1987); *Suver v. Personal Service Ins. Co.*, 11 Ohio St.3d 6, 462 N.E.2d 415 (Ohio 1984). Although some courts have included *Bd. of Dirs. of the Assoc. of Apt. Owners of the Discovery Bay Condominium v. United Pacific Ins. Co.*, 77 Haw. 358, 884 P.2d 1134 (Hawaii 1994), in this list of cases, the Hawaii Supreme Court expressly declined to address whether Hawaii recognizes a tort action against a surety for bad faith.

6. *Transamerica Premier Ins. Co. v. Brighton School District*, 940 P.2d 348 (Col. 1997); *Loyal Order of Moose, Lodge 1392 v. International Fidelity Insurance Co.*, 797 P.2d 622 (Alaska 1990); *Dodge v. Fidelity and Deposit Co. of Maryland*, 778 P.2d 1240 (Ariz. 1989); *Szarkowski v. Reliance Ins. Co.*, 404 N.W.2d 502 (N.D. 1987); *Suver v. Personal Service Ins. Co.*, 462 N.E.2d 415 (Ohio 1984).

7. *Transamerica Premier Ins. Co. v. Brighton School District*, 940 P.2d 348 (Col. 1997); *Dodge v. Fidelity and Deposit Co. of Maryland*, 778 P.2d 1240 (Ariz. 1989); *Suver v. Personal Service Ins. Co.*, 462 N.E.2d 415 (Ohio 1984).

8. *Loyal Order of Moose, Lodge 1392 v. International Fidelity Insurance Co.*, 797 P.2d 622 (Alaska 1990); *Szarkowski v. Reliance Ins. Co.*, 404 N.W.2d 502 (N.D. 1987).

9. *Cates Construction, Inc. v. Talbot Partners*, 980 P.2d 407 (Cal. 1999); *Great American Ins. Co. v. North Austin Municipal Utility*, 908 S.W.2d 415 (Tex. 1995).

10. 980 P.2d 407.

relationship" does not exist in the context of suretyship agreements which would justify an award of extra-contractual damages. Although these decisions reflect the minority view, they represent two of the last three decisions on this matter.

In Part III, this chapter reviews the decisions of the five state supreme courts that have allowed extra-contractual damages in actions against sureties for common law bad faith. In particular, this Part will focus on those decisions that applied a "special relationship analysis." The decisions of those courts that failed to give this issue sufficient analysis will be briefly examined because they still represent the current law in those states.

Part IV of this chapter reviews the statutorily created basis for extra-contractual liability, the Model Unfair Claims Settlement Practices Act and the widely varying state statutes which purport to implement the Model Act. This section also discusses those cases that have addressed whether the Miller Act preempts state law claims for bad faith.

I. *Extra-Contractual Damages and the Triparite Relationship of Suretyship Agreements*

Contracts of insurance are said to give rise to a special relationship which justifies awarding extra-contractual damages when the covenant of good faith and fair dealing is breached. Breach of the covenant, also referred to as the "bad faith" tort, gives the non-breaching party the ability to recover all proximately caused tort damages and, more importantly, punitive damages.

The special insurance relationship arises in large part because insureds purchase insurance policies to obtain peace of mind and protection from calamity, as opposed to securing a commercial advantage. The insured places trust in the insurer, and many times is completely dependant on the good faith performance of the insurance contract by the insurer. The insurer thus serves a public interest. Extra-contractual damages are awarded to encourage fair treatment of the public and avoid the routine denial of valid claims. The special relationship also arises out of the unequal bargaining power possessed by insurers and the adhesive nature of insurance policies.[11]

"Suretyship" is a contractual relationship "resulting from an agreement whereby one person, the surety, engages to be answerable for the debt, default, or miscarriage of another, the principal."[12] "The surety makes a direct promise to perform the obligation in the event the principal obligor fails to perform."[13] Thus, a *tripartite relationship* is formed between the surety, the principal, and the obligee.

The tripartite relationship that is formed by a suretyship agreement is in contrast to the bipartite relationship found in common insurance agreements. Pursuant to the terms of an insurance contract, the insurer agrees to indemnify the insured against loss, damage or liability resulting from a contingent or unknown event.

The business of compensated suretyship is the lending of security for a fee. For their part in insurance contracts, underwriters take the full risk of the hazard and charge a premium commensurate to the risk. Suretyship, on the other hand, is premised on the theory that the surety

---

11. *See* Hon. H. Walter Croskey, *Bad Faith in California: Its History, Development and Current Status*, 26 TORT & INS. L. J. 562 (1991); *see also Fletcher v. Western National Life Ins. Co.*, 10 Cal.App.3d 376, 403-04, 89 Cal. Rptr. 78 (1970).

12. 74 Am.Jur.2d, Suretyship, § 1, p. 12.

13. First Virginia Bank-Colonial v. Baker, 301 S.E.2d 8, 11 (Va. 1983).

takes little to no risk, but merely extends its credit to guarantee the principal's performance of the contract. The surety's premiums are thus theoretically "service fees" for providing the credit.

Courts generally do not impose fiduciary responsibilities upon the surety toward the obligee, but limit the surety's obligations to those of the principal, including the right of the surety to assert any defenses that the principal might assert against the obligee.

Essential to the existence of an insurance contract is the transfer or shifting of the risk insured against.[14] Unless specifically provided by contract, the insurer has no right of reimbursement or indemnity from the insured. Significantly, in suretyship, the principal is obligated, under the concepts of subrogation and indemnity, to reimburse the surety for any payments made by the surety on the bond.[15] Furthermore, a surety most likely has a written indemnity agreement from the principal and, perhaps, other parties as well.

Unlike an insurer, a surety has a duty of good faith and fair dealing to parties with separate and perhaps conflicting interests: the bond obligee and the principal. This dual duty can place the surety in an uncomfortable position. If the surety pays a claim, the principal may disagree with the decision; if the surety does not pay the claim, the obligee may disagree with the decision; and if the surety pays part but not all of the claim, both the principal and the obligee may be upset. The surety may find itself in litigation with one or both of the other parties regardless of its decision.[16]

In the case of construction performance and payment bonds, the surety enters into a commercial contract with the principal guaranteeing performance of the commercial contract entered into between the principal and the obligee. The principal and obligee enter into the commercial contract for the mutual purpose of achieving some commercial advantage. The principal and obligee should have evaluated the risks and benefits inherent in their commercial venture. Insurance, on the other hand, is obtained for protection from unforseen catastrophic events, be they medical problems, death in the family or exposure to a plaintiff in a lawsuit.

Typically, the principal and obligee on a construction surety bond are commercial entities, often financially strong and sophisticated in matters related to construction projects. In fact, the obligee may, by the very fact that he can demand a bond, be the stronger party in the negotiations. Consequently, the elements of unequal bargaining power and vulnerability which form the basis of the "adhesive nature" of insurance contracts are absent in the context of a construction surety bond. Furthermore, because the contract guaranteed is solely between the obligee and the principal, an

---

14. *See California Physicians' Serv. v. Garrison*, 172 P.2d 4 (Cal. 1946).

15. *See* A. Stearns, STEARN'S LAW OF SURETYSHIP § 11.35 at p. 505 (J. Elder 5th ed. 1951); *see also* Cal. Civ. Code § 2847 (Deering, 1998):

> If a surety satisfies the principal obligation, or any part thereof, whether with or without legal proceedings, the principal is bound to reimburse what he has disbursed, including necessary costs and expenses. . . .

> *See also* Cal. Civ. Code § 2848 (Deering 1998):
> A surety, upon satisfying the obligation of the principal, is entitled to enforce every remedy which the creditor then has against the principal to the extent of reimbursing what he has expended. . . .

16. *See* John J. Aromando, *The Surety's Liability For "Bad Faith" : Claims For Extra-Contractual Damages By An Obligee Under The Payment Bond*, 47 ME. L. REV. 389, 391 (1995); *see also Board of Dirs. of the Assoc. of Apt. Owners of the Discovery Bay Condo. v. United Pacific Ins. Co.*, 884 P.2d 1134, 1137-38 (Haw. 1994).

obligee would have a difficult time arguing that it entered into an "adhesive" contract dictated to it by the surety.

II. *California and Texas: Decisions Denying Extra-contractual Damages in the Suretyship Context*

The supreme courts of California and Texas are the only courts that have compared suretyship to insurance and held that sureties should not be subject to a cause of action in tort for bad faith breach of the covenant of good faith and fair dealing because there is no special relationship inherent in the context of suretyship. These decisions are important, not only because they applied a thorough analysis of the special relationship in the suretyship context, but also because they represent two of the three most recent decisions regarding this issue. These courts examined the decisions of the majority of states and expressly rejected them, holding that they applied the wrong standards or that they came to the wrong conclusion.

A. CATES CONSTRUCTION, INC. V. TALBOT PARTNERS

In 1999, the California Supreme Court held that a surety issuing a performance bond cannot be held liable for tort damages arising out of breach of the common law implied covenant of good faith and fair dealing. In *Cates Construction, Inc. v. Talbot Partners*,[17] the Court recognized that the unique, tripartite relationship inherent in suretyship agreements distinguishes the performance bond from insurance contracts. No special relationship exists between a bond obligee and the surety which is comparable to the relationship in the insurance context.[18]

---

17. 980 P.2d 407.

18. Over eight years before *Cates* was decided, the District Court for the Eastern District of California predicted that California would not recognize a common law cause of action for bad faith against a surety. In *United States ex rel. Ehmcke Sheet Metal Works v. Wausau Ins. Co.*, 755 F. Supp. 906 (E.D.Ca. 1991), a subcontractor on a federal construction project filed suit against the surety on its Miller Act bond. Subsequently, the subcontractor sought leave to amend the complaint to state a cause of action in tort for breach of the covenant of good faith and fair dealing. The surety argued that the court should not permit the amendment because California law did not recognize an obligee's right to sue a surety for "bad faith."

The Federal District Court, interpreting California law, held that a subcontractor could not sue a payment bond surety for tortious breach of the covenant of good faith and fair dealing. The *Ehmcke* court examined the factors enumerated by the California Supreme Court in *Moradi-Shalal v. Fireman's Fund Insurance Companies*, 758 P.2d 58 (Cal. 1985), in order to predict how the California Supreme Court would rule on whether a subcontractor could maintain a cause of action for "bad faith" on a payment bond. The court found that the *Moradi-Shalal* factors disfavoring a private cause of action for violating California's version of the Unfair Claims Settlement Practices Act could be equally applied to "bad faith" suits filed by obligees against sureties. *Ehmcke*, 755 F.Supp. at 910.

Initially, the *Ehmcke* court found that to permit such a cause of action might create multiple law suits. A subcontractor could sue first in federal court on the bond and then sue in state court for breach of the implied covenant of good faith and fair dealing. *Id.* at 910.

Secondly, the *Ehmcke* court stated that the threat of punitive damages, inherent in "bad faith" claims, could "induce litigants to assert unwarranted settlement demands, and ultimately to coerce inflated settlements." The *Ehmcke* court reasoned that this would result in higher bond costs for prime contractors on Miller Act projects, the cost of which would be passed on to the federal government. *Id.* at 910-911.

Thirdly, the *Ehmcke* court held that "permitting the subcontractor to sue the surety for bad faith would create an unresolvable conflict of interest for the surety." The *Ehmcke* court reasoned that the surety owed a duty of good

The *Cates* action arose from a construction performance bond issued by Transamerica Insurance Co. for its principal Cates Construction. Cates was a contractor on a condominium project under development by Talbot Partners. During construction, a dispute arose in which Cates claimed that Talbot owed it money. When Cates walked off the job, Talbot made a demand on Transamerica to perform on the performance bond.

The Supreme Court of California emphasized that the award of extra-contractual damages in insurance policy cases represents a major departure from traditional principles of contract law, and courts should take "great care" before extending liability in other contractual settings. The Court was not influenced by the fact that surety is listed in the California Insurance Code as a class of insurance for regulatory purposes. Instead, the Court focused on the elements of adhesion and unequal bargaining power, public interest and fiduciary responsibility that create a "special relationship" which justifies the imposition of tort damages in the insurance context.

The *Cates* court held that the elements of adhesion and unequal bargaining power which are inherent in the context of insurance policies are largely absent in the context of suretyship agreements.[19] The obligee determines the form of the bond it will accept from the principal, and thus it can require terms which provide the surety with an incentive to act in good faith. The performance bond typically incorporates the terms of the underlying construction contract; terms which the obligee and principal negotiated without any input from the surety. Finally, the Court noted that many bonds, such as the one before it, contain express waivers of certain suretyship defenses.

With regard to the public interest and fiduciary responsibility factors, the *Cates* court held that these also suggest that no special relationship exists between sureties and obligees.

---

faith and fair dealing to the principal that obtained the bond. Consequently, if the surety was also potentially liable to a third party obligee for "bad faith," it might be forced to "compromise" the duty to the principal to fulfill its duty to the obligee, thus creating another potential bad faith lawsuit by the principal. The court found that this potential conflict could "interfere with the progress of the primary lawsuit," creating uncertainty for the surety and disadvantaging the purchaser of the surety bond. *Id.* at 911.

The district court was of the view there was a regulatory scheme in place to sanction bad faith conduct by sureties under 31 C.F.R. §223.18. In the case of the Miller Act, the sureties were regulated by the United States Treasury Department. Therefore, there was no need to regulate them indirectly with a threat of "bad faith" litigation. *Id.* at 911.

Furthermore, the *Ehmcke* court found that California courts treat the surety relationship as a contract between the surety and the principal on the bond. In several cases, California courts stressed that the surety bond represents the full amount of the surety's liability on the contract. The court found considerable authority for the proposition that the surety is bound only by the express terms of the contract. The surety's liability must be found within the contract or not at all.

The Court found that to permit a cause of action in tort for breach of the covenant of good faith and fair dealing by the subcontractor would expand the surety's exposure beyond the bond, and more importantly, would subject the surety to suit by an entity not a party to the surety contract. This, the court found, was contrary to the law which stressed that the covenant of good faith and fair dealing arises from a contractual relationship and the only parties which may take advantage of the covenant are parties to the contractual relationship.

The *Ehmcke* court went on to examine prior California decisions where the Supreme Court did not allow causes of action for tortious breach of the implied covenant of good faith and fair dealing in settings other than "traditional" insurance contracts. These cases recognized the concept of a "special relationship" justifying extra-contractual damages in the context of insurance. The *Ehmcke* court pointed out that courts and commentators have long recognized that suretyship is different from liability insurance and has a distinct legal history. Consequently, the *Ehmcke* court was of the belief that Ehmcke's relationship to Wausau did not create a "special relationship."

For all of the above policy reasons, the *Ehmcke* court concluded that the California Supreme Court would not permit a cause of action by Ehmcke against Wausau for breach of the covenant of good faith and fair dealing or based on California common law. In *Cates*, the California Supreme Court affirmed the reasoning of the federal court.

19. 980 P.2d at 422.

While insurance is purchased in order to protect against calamities such as disability, fire, death, or flood, a construction bond is bargained for in order to protect the obligee against the possibility that it might not be able to collect from the principal should the principal fail to perform under the contract. The obligee is thus seeking to obtain the commercial advantage which is provided by possessing additional security. Unlike an insured, who typically is limited to looking to the insurer for recovery of a loss, the obligee has a right to recover from the principal, whose assets were already inspected by the surety before it wrote the performance bond.[20]

The *Cates* court specifically rejected the Colorado Supreme Court's holding in *Transamerica Premier Ins. Co. v. Brighton School Dist.*[21] that a bad faith tort claim is necessary to compensate the obligee and deter the surety. Obligees have "ample bargaining power," which they can use to negotiate terms that will ensure they are fully compensated if the surety breaches, such as providing for liquidated damages or attorneys fees and interest upon breach. These additional terms, along with the administrative sanctions available pursuant to the Insurance Code, serve to deter sureties from acting in bad faith.[22]

The California Supreme Court expressed its concern that tort remedies for breach of the covenant of good faith and fair dealing would lead obligees to abuse the tripartite relationship inherent in suretyship. The surety has separate and often conflicting legal duties to the principal and the obligee. The *Cates* court feared that if it made tort remedies available, obligees might more readily allege a principal's default because it would be easier to pressure the surety into paying questionable claims. The surety might be reluctant to risk disputing the claim if by doing so it risked liability for tort remedies. The surety might attempt to "find" bond coverage for obligees in an effort to avoid bad faith liability, and this would be charged to the principal.

B. GREAT AMERICAN INS. CO. V. NORTH AUSTIN MUNICIPAL UTILITY

The California Supreme Court was not the first court to hold that extra-contractual damages cannot be recovered from a surety for "bad faith." Four years before *Cates* was decided, the Supreme Court of Texas became the first court to apply a special relationship analysis and decide that sureties are not liable for extra-contractual damages in common law actions for "bad faith."

In *Great American Ins. Co. v. North Austin Municipal Utility Dist. No. 1*,[23] the Texas Supreme Court rejected the decisions of the Arizona[24] and North Dakota[25] supreme courts because those courts placed too much emphasis on the fact that suretyship is regulated under insurance laws, instead of considering the differences between suretyship and insurance. Despite the fact that Texas also regulates suretyship contracts in its Insurance Code, the *Great American* court concluded that the Texas Legislature did not intend to include suretyship as the "business of insurance" for all purposes. The Court further concluded that the common law of Texas did not recognize a cause of action for bad faith breach of the covenant of good faith and fair dealing against sureties.

---

20. *See id.* at 423.
21. 940 P.2d 348.
22. 980 P.2d at 425.
23. 908 S.W.2d 415.
24. *Dodge v. Fidelity and Deposit Co. of Maryland*, 778 P.2d 1240.
25. *Szarkowski v. Reliance Ins. Co.*, 404 N.W.2d 502.

Great American arose out of a construction project for a municipal wastewater lift station in which Great American issued payment, performance and maintenance bonds in North Austin's favor. One year after Underground Utilities Company installed a refurbished dry well, the metal sides of the dry well collapsed inward due to lateral earth pressure. Underground refused to correct the problem, claiming that it had performed the work according to the plans and specifications in the contract.

When North Austin demanded that Great American make payment on the bonds, Great American refused and requested evidence that Underground failed to conform to the contracted designs. North Austin sued, and a jury found that Great American had breached a common law duty of good faith and fair dealing. The court of appeals affirmed the judgment of the trial court. The Supreme Court of Texas reversed the court of appeals, holding that sureties had no common law duty of good faith and fair dealing.

The *Great American* court found that the factors which created a special relationship between a liability insurer and its insured and, thus, extra-contractual liability for breach of the duty of good faith and fair dealing, are absent in the suretyship setting. Factors which the Texas Supreme Court considered included unequal bargaining power, the nature of insurance contracts allowing insurers to take advantage of insured's misfortunes, and the insurance company's exclusive control over the claim evaluation process.[26]

The court determined that the parties possessed comparable bargaining positions when they entered into the suretyship agreement. Great American had no control over the form of the bonds used. State law mandated the form of the required bonds, and the bonds incorporated the terms of the contract between North Austin and Underground. North Austin did not dispute that it controlled the contract documents.

In considering the parties' control over the claim evaluation process, the Court held that the tripartite relationship between a surety, its principal and the bond obligee prevented Great American from exercising any control. The Court distinguished sureties from insurers, noting that a surety's obligations are secondary to those owed by the principal and sureties are entitled to rely upon all the defenses available to the principal as to the claim on the bond. Therefore, the Court held that Great American did not owe a common law duty of good faith and fair dealing to North Austin.

III. *The Majority View: Courts That Have Awarded Extra-contractual Damages in the Suretyship Context*

The majority of the state supreme courts that have addressed the issue have held that an action is available in tort against sureties for bad faith breach of the covenant of good faith and fair dealing. Only three of these courts, however, applied a "special relationship analysis." Of these three courts, only the Supreme Court of Colorado applied a "special relationship analysis" with the same degree of thoroughness as the supreme courts of Texas and California.

26. 908 S.W.2d at 418.

A. TRANSAMERICA PREMIER INSURANCE CO. V. BRIGHTON SCHOOL DISTRICT

In *Transamerica Premier Insurance Co. v. Brighton School District*,[27] the Supreme Court of Colorado held that commercial sureties could be liable for bad faith breach of the covenant of good faith and fair dealing. Adco Mechanical Contractors, Inc. contracted to perform the mechanical work on a construction project at Brighton High School. Pursuant to Colorado law, Adco provided Brighton with a performance bond on which Transamerica agreed to act as surety to guarantee Adco's performance.

Adco had been working on the project for almost one year when the Brighton School District removed Adco from the project. Brighton claimed that Adco's work was defective or incomplete and that Adco failed to comply with the architect's drawings and specifications. When Brighton contacted Transamerica to make a claim on the bond, Transamerica took the position that Adco had been wrongfully terminated. Transamerica demanded that Adco be returned to the project and refused to make progress payments for remedial work that was done on the project. Brighton brought a tort claim against Transamerica for bad faith denial of Brighton's claim on the bond, for which a jury subsequently awarded Brighton $10,000.00.

The Supreme Court of Colorado first concluded that the business of sureties is "in all essential particulars that of insurers."[28] The Court found support for this conclusion in the state legislature's intent to include sureties in the same regulatory scheme as insurance. Additional support for this conclusion came from the fact that other jurisdictions had recognized a cause of action in tort for a commercial surety's bad faith.[29]

The court was of the opinion that a special relationship existed between Transamerica and Brighton, similar to the relationship that exists in the insurance context, such that Brighton, as obligee under the bond, could bring a cause of action in tort for Transamerica's bad faith processing of Brighton's claim. The Court examined the factors which create a special relationship in the insurance context, and found that those factors also create a special relationship in the suretyship context.

According to the Supreme Court of Colorado, the obligee requests that the principal obtain a performance bond in order to insure itself from potentially catastrophic losses that would result should the principal default on the original contract. This is particularly true when the obligee is a public entity operating on a not-for-profit basis, constrained by a tight budget, and reliant on timely performance.

Unequal bargaining power also supported the finding of a special relationship in the suretyship context. Although the parties start out on equal footing when they enter the agreement, the surety gains a distinct advantage over the obligee because it controls performance under the bond. When the surety acts in bad faith, it defeats the core purpose of the suretyship agreement, i.e. to insulate the obligee from the risk of default.[30]

Finally, the *Transamerica* court held that permitting a cause of action in tort is necessary to encourage commercial sureties to handle claims responsibly. Contract damages do not compensate

---

27. 940 P.2d 348.

28. *See id.* at 352.

29. *See id.* at 352. The court cited *Loyal Order of Moose*, *Dodge*, *Szarkowski*, and *Suver*, discussed *supra*. In a string cite to these cases, the court included a "but see" cite to *Great American*. The court did not distinguish *Great American* or make any other reference to the decision of the Texas Supreme Court.

30. *See id.* at 353.

the obligee for the commercial surety's misconduct and have no deterrent effect on the surety to prevent it from acting in bad faith. A cause of action in tort thus serves to ensure that sureties handle claims responsibly and in good faith.

B. SUVER V. PERSONAL SERVICE INS. CO.

The Supreme Court of Ohio was the first state supreme court to impose tort liability on sureties for bad faith breach of the covenant of good faith and fair dealing. In 1984, the Court decided *Suver v. Personal Service Ins. Co.*,[31] in which the court held that an injured third party could state a claim for punitive damages against a surety that had issued a financial responsibility bond when the surety maliciously and willfully fails to pay the amount of the bond.[32]

The *Suver* court acknowledged that a financial responsibility bond, issued to protect the motoring public from damages caused by the principal driver, is not the same as an insurance policy. The primary difference was in who was protected and to whom the duty runs. The *Suver* court opined, however, that these differences were not so dramatic as to justify allowing a claim for bad faith in the insurance context but denying a claim in the bond context.

Although the court only briefly discussed its reasoning, its analysis resembles a modern application of the special relationship analysis. The court found that the relationship between an injured third party and a surety, in the context of a financial responsibility bond, is virtually identical to the relationship between a policy holder and an insurance company in the traditional insurance context. The court noted that both relationships were characterized by a great disparity in their financial resources and are affected with a public interest. The court concluded that in order to discourage sureties from routinely denying the payment of claims, a cause of action in tort must be available against the surety.[33]

C. DODGE V. FIDELITY AND DEPOSIT CO. OF MARYLAND

In 1989, the Arizona Supreme Court applied the special relationship analysis in the context of bad faith breach by a surety. Relying on insurance cases, the court in *Dodge v. Fidelity and Deposit Co. of Maryland*[34] found a basis for extending the tort of "bad faith" to performance bond sureties, based on factors creating a "relationship in which the law implies special duties not imposed on other contractual relationships."[35]

In *Dodge*, the plaintiffs had contracted with a construction company to build a residence. The contract required the contractor to obtain a performance bond in the amount of the contract. The bond provided that the surety would either promptly remedy any default of the contractor, complete the contract or obtain bids for completing the contract in the event of the contractor's default. Apparently, the surety did nothing when the contractor defaulted.

31. 462 N.E.2d 415.
32. *See id.* at 417.
33. *Id.*
34. 778 P.2d 1240.
35. *Id.* at 1242.

The Arizona Supreme Court held that homeowners who were the obligees on a performance bond issued in connection with the construction of a residence could maintain an action for bad faith against the surety for the surety's alleged refusal to investigate their claim. The Court held that statutory law, case law and public policy supported the plaintiff's simple position: "sureties are insurers; insurers are subject to bad faith tort liability; therefore, sureties are subject to bad faith tort liability."[36]

In concluding that sureties are subject to bad faith tort liability, the *Dodge* court first held that sureties should be considered to be insurers because Arizona statutes placed them in the same category. In *dicta*, the Court then identified the "two most important factors" creating a special relationship for which breach of contract will give rise to tort liability. These factors were (1) whether the plaintiff contracted for security or protection rather than for profit or commercial advantage, and (2) whether permitting tort damages would "provide a substantial deterrent against breach by the party who derives a commercial benefit from the relationship."[37] In finding these factors applicable to sureties, the court explained that an owner pays the premium on a performance bond not for commercial advantage but as protection from the "calamity" of the contractor's default. The court defined "calamity" as the "financial and personal hardship" experienced by a homeowner when a contractor defaults. The court stated that "[s]urety insurance is obtained with the hope of avoiding such hardships."[38]

Arguably, some of the policy concerns which have been relied upon to find a tort of bad faith in the insurance context may have some merit in the case of the individual homeowner who, compared with a contractor or surety, may be relatively unsophisticated in commercial matters. However, the facts of *Dodge* are not explicit in this regard. Nor is it apparent whether the homeowners were injured in any way by reason of the surety's conduct. It may reasonably be inferred that the homeowners were not left without means when the surety defaulted. The construction contract was in the amount of $205,903 for the construction of a home in 1978. Following arbitration on the contractor's default, the arbitrator awarded the plaintiffs only $9,714, which included $5,000 retained by the plaintiffs under the construction contract. As such, the facts do not suggest an unforeseen disaster or special vulnerability of the homeowners as a result of breach of trust by the surety. Nevertheless, the court concluded that the surety had breached its duty of good faith and fair dealing by refusing even to investigate the plaintiff's claim when the surety knew or had reason to know that defaults existed under the construction agreement.

---

36. In *Loyal Order of Moose Lodge v. International Fidelity Ins. Co.*, 797 P.2d 622 (1990), the Alaska Supreme Court relied on the rationale set forth in *Dodge* and held that a surety on a commercial construction contract may be liable in "bad faith" to the obligee for failure to investigate the reasonableness of the obligee's claim of contractor default.

The Alaska Supreme Court adopted the syllogism from *Dodge* that sureties are insurers; insurers are subject to "bad faith" tort liability; therefore, sureties are subject to "bad faith" tort liability. The court concluded that "the relationship of a surety to its obligee - an intended creditor third-party beneficiary - is more analogous to that of an insurer to its insured than to the relationship between an insurer and an incidental third-party beneficiary." The court thereby avoided the rule prohibiting common-law tort liability for bad faith between parties that did not have privity of contract. The Court concluded that an implied covenant of good faith and fair dealing exists between a surety and its obligee on payment and performance bonds.

37. 778 P.2d at 1242.

38. *Id.*

D. DECISIONS THAT ALLOWED TORT ACTIONS WITHOUT APPLYING A SPECIAL RELATIONSHIP ANALYSIS

In 1987, the Supreme Court of North Dakota held in *Szarkowski v. Reliance Ins. Co.*[39] that a common law cause of action for bad faith breach of the covenant of good faith and fair dealing could be brought against a surety. Instead of addressing the Ohio Supreme Court's *Suver* decision, which at the time was the only other state supreme court decision addressing this issue, the *Szarkowski* court relied primarily on *General Insurance Company of America v. Mammoth Vista Owner's Assoc.*,[40] a decision by a California Court of Appeals.[41] The North Dakota court reasoned without critical analysis that since sureties were regulated by the insurance code, sureties are engaged in the business of insurance and should therefore be liable for bad faith.

Although it has often been cited, the *Szarkowski* decision is severely flawed. First, it relies on *Mammoth Vista*, which itself is based on a decision which was reversed by the California Supreme Court three years after *Szarkowski* was decided. Additionally, *Szarkowski* failed to acknowledge that *Mammoth Vista* was expressly limited to an interpretation of the California Unfair Practices Act. *Mammoth Vista* did not stand for the proposition that sureties could be liable at common law for the tort of bad faith. Finally, the *Szarkowski* Court failed to properly analyze whether a special relationship exists in suretyship such that bad faith tort liability should be imposed.

In 1990, the Supreme Court of Alaska joined the majority of states with its decision in *Loyal Order of Moose, Lodge 1392 v. International Fidelity Insurance Co.*[42] Although the Alaskan decision was limited to claims by an obligee under a performance bond, the court stated in *dicta* that an implied covenant of good faith and fair dealing exists between a surety and its obligee on all payment and performance bonds.

Without analysis, the *Loyal Order* court concluded that "the relationship of a surety to its obligee - an intended creditor third-party beneficiary - is more analogous to that of an insurer to its insured than to the relationship between an insurer and an incidental third-party beneficiary."[43] The court relied on the decision of the Supreme Court of Arizona, quoting often from *Dodge*, before concluding that a surety could be liable in tort for breach of the implied covenant of good faith and fair dealing.

---

39. 404 N.W.2d 502.

40. 174 Cal.App.3d 810, 220 Cal. Rptr. 291 (3rd Dist., 1985).

41. In *Royal Globe Ins. Co. v. Superior Court*, 23 Cal.3d 880, 153 Cal.Rptr. 842, 592 P.2d 329 (Cal. 1979), the California Supreme Court held that section 790.03(h) of the California Unfair Practices Act impliedly created a private cause of action against insurers for bad faith. The California Court of Appeals in *Mammoth Vista* relied on *Royal Globe* when it held that a statutory cause of action for bad faith could be brought against sureties under section 790.03(h).

Three years later, the California Supreme Court cut the feet out from under *Mammoth Vista*. In *Moradi-Shalal v. Fireman's Fund Insurance Companies*, 46 Cal.3d 287, 250 Cal.Rptr. 116, 758 P.2d 58 (Cal. 1988), the Court overruled *Royal Globe*, noting that many adverse consequences flowed from *Royal Globe's* decision that a private cause of action exists. The Court noted that *Royal Globe* improperly promoted multiple litigation, encouraged claimants to coerce inflated settlement demands from insurers, and created serious conflicts of interests for insurers. Finally, the Court noted that the California Unfair Practices Act established a regulatory commission to enforce the law, making a private cause of action redundant.

42. 797 P.2d 622.

43. *Id.* at 628.

IV. *Statutorily Created Bases For Extra-contractual Liability*

Every state has a statutory scheme designed to regulate the insurance industry and protect insureds from unfair or deceptive acts by insurers. These statutes must be considered in order to gain a complete understanding of the extent to which a surety is potentially exposed to extra-contractual liabilities.

One of the primary goals of the National Association of Insurance Commissioners (NAIC) is to remedy the difficulties encountered by regulators and insurers relating to insurance claims practices, which is a continuing source of criticism and concern.[44] The genesis of the current state regulation of claims settlement practices is found in the NAIC's model Unfair Trade Practices Act (UTPA) and the model Unfair Claims Settlement Practices Act (UCSPA), which in various forms and versions are found in almost every state.

Initially, the NAIC adopted the UTPA to establish ground rules for regulating unfair trade practices and unfair claims settlement practices.[45] The UTPA regulates trade practices in the business of insurance by defining and prohibiting practices or acts which constitute unfair methods of competition or are otherwise unfair or deceptive.[46] The UTPA defines myriad unfair trade practices, including misrepresentations in advertising of insurance policies,[47] boycotts or collusion,[48] discrimination in premium charged[49] and paying illegal rebates.[50] Of significance to claims settlement practices are fourteen specifically defined claims settlement practices which are proscribed if committed or performed with such frequency as to indicate a general business practice.[51]

In June, 1990, the NAIC moved the unfair settlement practices section of the UTPA into a completely separate model act, entitled the Unfair Claims Settlement Practices Act (UCSPA), which deals solely with claim practices. The NAIC felt separate model acts were required to underscore the distinction between general unfair trade practices and more specific unfair claim settlement issues.[52] By doing so, the NAIC recommended that states modify, not repeal, existing acts to capture the substantive changes. States wishing to rewrite their approach to claims practices were advised to separate unfair claims practices from unfair trade practices.[53]

While it is not possible to consider the myriad details of each state's regulatory scheme, an analysis of extra-contractual damages must focus on three fundamental issues: (1) whether the state's version of the UTPA or UCSPA applies to suretyship; (2) whether a private cause of action is allowed by statute, as opposed to a regulatory scheme available for use by the insurance commissioner; and (3) the specific claim settlement acts or practices proscribed by the statute.

---

44. *See, e.g.*, Proceedings of the NAIC, *Laws, Legislation & Regulation (b) Committee; Unfair Trade Practices (B6) Subcommittee*, 1972-1 NAIC Proc. 490 (December 3, 1971).
45. *Id.* at 492.
46. Unfair Trade Practices Act, section 1.
47. Unfair Trade Practices Act, section 4(e).
48. Unfair Trade Practices Act, section 4(d).
49. Unfair Trade Practices Act, section 4(g).
50. Unfair Trade Practices Act, section 4(h).
51. Unfair Trade Practices Act, section 9.
52. *See* Unfair Trade Practices Act, Prefatory Note; Unfair Claims Settlement Practices Act, Prefatory Note.
53. *See* Unfair Trade Practices Act, Prefatory Note; Unfair Claims Settlement Practices Act, Prefatory Note.

A. APPLICATION OF THE MODEL ACTS TO SURETYSHIP

If each jurisdiction adopted the UCSPA in the form recommended by the National Association of Insurance Commissioners, the resulting state statute would not apply to suretyship. The UCSPA, however, was not enacted until 1990. For over twenty years the UTPA was used to guide the states in drafting their regulatory schemes including regulation of unfair claims settlement practices; and the UTPA did not exclude suretyship.

The UTPA's definitions, both before and after the separate UCSPA was created, clearly encompass suretyship within the scope of regulated contracts issued by the insurers. The term "policy" is used throughout the UTPA when dealing with specific conduct of the insurance industry. The UTPA defines "policy"[54] in connection with the prohibited trade practices as:

> any contract of insurance, indemnity, medical, health or hospital service, *suretyship*, or annuity issued, proposed for issuance, or intended for issuance by any insurer.[55]

Accordingly, a fair reading of the UTPA would include any contract of suretyship or bonds issued thereunder as subject to the provisions of the act.

The primary difference between the UTPA and the UCSPA is the specific exclusion of suretyship in the UCSPA. Perhaps cognizant of the inclusion of the surety in the UTPA, the NAIC took great pains to ensure the provisions of the UCSPA excluded suretyship. Section One of the UCSPA provides:

> The purpose of this Act is to set forth standards for the investigation and disposition of claims arising under policies or certificates of insurance issued to residents of [insert state]. It is not intended to cover claims involving workers' compensation, fidelity, suretyship or boiler and machinery insurance.[56]

Unlike the UTPA, the definition of "policy" or "certificate" in the UCSPA specifically excludes suretyship:

> 'Policy' or 'certificate,' for purposes of this Act, shall not mean contracts of workers' compensation, fidelity, suretyship or boiler and machinery insurance.[57]

Without question, the exclusion of suretyship from the UCSPA in 1990 should have significantly limited a surety's exposure to extra-contractual damages. However, the states have not followed the lead of the NAIC. Only twenty-seven states have generally implemented statutory schemes that resemble the UCSPA; and less that half of those states have additionally incorporated the language excluding suretyship. Consequently, the laws of each jurisdiction must be examined to determine whether that jurisdiction's statutory scheme applies to extend extra-contractual damages to suretyship.

---

54. *See* Unfair Trade Practices Act, section 4.
55. *See* Unfair Trade Practices Act, section 2(e).
56. *See* Unfair Claims Settlement Practices Act, section 1.
57. *See* Unfair Claims Settlement Practices Act, section 2(e).

The UCSPA anticipates implementing regulations. For example, in 1992, the California Department of Insurance promulgated regulations implementing the Unfair Claims Settlement Practices Statute. California Code of Regulations, Title 10, §§2695.1 through 2695.14 set forth guidelines for the claims handling practice. It must be noted that the California regulations recognize the unique nature of the surety relationship and make specific provisions for surety claims.

B. PRIVATE RIGHT OF ACTION

Although the UTPA[58] and the UCSPA[59] both state that the model acts are not meant to create a private cause of action, states have not uniformly incorporated this language into their statutes. As a consequence, state courts have differed on whether a private cause of action was implicitly created by adoption of the UCSPA or its predecessor sections in the UTPA.

The prohibition against creating a private cause of action is set forth in the claims practices regulations in some states,[60] while in others, courts have ruled that no private cause of action was created.[61] Of those states that have enacted trade practice statutes which model the UTPA, 15 do not provide for a private cause of action, although only three states make this clear in their statutes.[62] Of the remaining six states that have adopted statutes modeling the UTPA, the courts of five of these

58. *See* Unfair Trade Practices Act, section 1 ("Nothing herein shall be construed to create or imply a private cause of action for a violation of this Act.").

59. *See* Unfair Claims Settlement Practices Act, section 1, Drafting Note ("Any jurisdiction choosing to provide for a private cause of action should consider a different statutory scheme. This Act is inherently inconsistent with a private cause of action. This is merely a clarification of original intent and not indicative of any change of position.")

60. *See, e.g.*, Ga. Code § 33-6-37.

61. *See, e.g.*, *Earth Scientists v. U.S. Fidelity Ex. Guar.*, 619 F. Supp. 1465, 1468-69 (D.C. Kan. 1985) (all power under Act was vested in the insurance commissioner; no language is in the Act purporting to create a private cause of action); *Strack v. Westfield Co.*, 515 N.E.2d 1005 (Ohio, 1986) (Ohio Rev. Code §§ 3901.20, 3901.21 and 3901-1-07, which set forth prohibited unfair or deceptive trade practices in the insurance industry, do not create an implied private cause of action in favor of the insured).

62. Arkansas: Ark. Stat. Ann. § 23-66-202;
California: *Moradi-Shalal v. Fireman's Fund Ins. Cos.*, 758 P.2d 58 (Cal. 1988);
Colorado: *Schnacker v. State Farm Mut. Auto. Ins. Co.*, 843 P.2d 102 (Colo. App. 1992);
Delaware: *Yardley v. U.S. Healthcare, Inc.*, 698 A.2d 979 (Del. Super. Ct. 1996);
Florida: *Keehn v. Carolina Cas. Ins. Co.*, 758 F.2d 1522 (11th Cir. 1985);
Hawaii: *Wailva Assoc. v. Aetna Cas. & Sur. Co.*, 27 F. Supp.2d 1211 (D.Haw. 1998);
Iowa: *Terra Ind., Inc. v. Commonwealth Ins. Co. of America*, 990 F. Supp. 679 (D.Iowa 1997);
Kansas: *Spenser v. Aetna Life & Cas. Ins. Co.*, 611 P.2d 149 (Kan. 1980);
Minnesota: *Glass Service Co., Inc. v. State Farm Mut. Auto. Ins. Co.*, 530 N.W.2d 867 (Minn.App.1995);
New Hampshire: *Shaheen v. Preferred Mut. Ins. Co.*, 668 F. Supp. 716 (D.N.H. 1987);
New Jersey: *Picketts v. Lloyds'*, 621 A.2d 445 (NJ 1993);
North Carolina: N.C. Gen. Stat. § 58-63-15(11); *but see Horton v. New South Ins. Co.*, 468 S.E.2d 856 (N.C. App. 1996);
Ohio: *Strack v. Westfield Companies*, 515 N.E.2d 1005 (Ohio 1986);
Pennsylvania: *Hyde Athletic Ind., Inc. v. Continental Cas. Co.*, 969 F. Supp. 289 (E.D. Pa. 1997);
Tennessee: Tenn. Code Ann. § 56-8-104(8).

states have held that a private cause of action is available,[63] and the remaining state's courts have not addressed the issue.

Of those states that have enacted trade practices statutes that model the UCSPA, 18 do not provide a private cause of action, ten of which make this explicit in their statutes.[64] Four states have statutes that specifically provide for a cause of action,[65] the courts of three other states have determined that their legislators intended to provide a cause of action,[66] and the remaining two states have not addressed the issue.

Further reference to each jurisdiction's statutes and case law is necessary to ascertain whether the violation of the unfair trade practices legislation creates a private right of action or subjects the insurer to regulatory scrutiny.

C. UNFAIR OR DECEPTIVE ACTS DEFINED BY MODEL ACT LEGISLATION

In adopting either model act, states universally depart in varying degrees from the model language which defines prohibited acts or practices. Variation by the individual states from the model acts' language and definitions fails to reveal any discernable pattern, although many states have generally adopted the substance of definitions (a) through (g) concerning unfair claims settlement practices.

---

63. Connecticut: *National Semiconductor Corp. v. Allendale Mut. Ins. Co.*, 549 F.Supp. 1195 (D.C. Conn. 1982);
Louisiana: *Smith v. Midland Risk Ins. Co.*, 699 So.2d 1192 (La.App.2d 1997);
Massachusetts: *Harris v. Harvard Pilgrim Health Care, Inc.*, 20 F.Supp.2d 143 (D.Mass. 1998);
North Dakota: *Farmers' Union Cent. Exch., Inc. v. Reliance Ins. Co.*, 626 F.Supp. 583 (D.N.D. 1985);
West Virginia: *Maher v. Continental Cas. Co.*, 76 F.3d 535 (4th Cir. 1996).

64. Alaska: *O.K. Lumber Co. v. Providence Wash. Ins. Co.*, 759 P.2d 523 (Alaska 1988);
Arizona: Ariz. Rev. Stat. § 20-461(d);
Georgia: Ga. Code Ann. § 33-6-37;
Idaho: *Simper v. Farm Bureau Mut. Ins. Co. of Idaho*, 974 P.2d 1100 (Idaho 1999);
Illinois: *Purlee v. Liberty Mut. Fire Ins. Co.*, 631 N.E.2d 433 (Ill. 1994);
Indiana: Burns Ind. Code Ann. § 27-4-1-18;
Maine: 24-A Me. Rev. Stat. § 2164-D(8);
Maryland: Md. Ins. Code Ann. § 27-301(2);
Michigan: *Michigan State Univ. v. Continental Cas. Co.*, 730 F.Supp. 1408 (W.D. Mich. 1990);
Missouri: Mo. Rev. Stat. § 375.1000(2);
New York: *Kent Centre Assoc. v. Greater New York Mut. Ins. Co.*, 527 N.Y.S. 2d 269 (NY 2d Dept. 1988);
Oklahoma: *Walker v. Chouteau Lime Co., Inc.*, 849 P.2d 1085 (Okla. 1993);
Oregon: *Employers' Fire Ins. v. Love It Ice Cream*, 670 P.2d 160 (Or. 1983);
Rhode Island: R.I. Stat. § 27-9.1-1;
South Dakota: S.D. Code. Laws § 58-33-69;
Utah: Utah Code Ann. § 31A-26-303(5);
Virginia: Va. Code Ann. § 38.2-510(B);
Wyoming: *Herrig v. Herrig*, 844 P.2d 487 (Wyo. 1992).

65. Montana: Mont. Code Ann. § 33-18-242;
Nevada: Nev. Rev. Stat. Ann. § 686A.310(2);
New Mexico: N.M. Stat. Ann. § 59A-16-30;
Washington: Rev. Code Wash. § 284-30-400.

66. Kentucky: *Cummings v. Thomas Ind., Inc.*, 812 F.Supp. 99 (W.D.Ky. 1993);
South Carolina: *Robertson v. State Farm Mut. Auto. Ins. Co.*, 464 F.Supp. 876 (D.C.S.C. 1979);
Texas: *Higginbotham v. State Farm Mut. Auto. Ins. Co.*, 103 F.3d 456 (3d Cir. 1997).

Both the UTPA and the UCSPA have defined unfair settlement practices in substantially similar terms. The UCSPA proscribes the following practices:

A. Knowingly misrepresenting to claimants and insureds relevant facts or policy provisions relating to coverages at issue;

B. Failing to acknowledge with reasonable promptness pertinent communications with respect to claims arising under its policies;

C. Failing to adopt and implement reasonable standards for the prompt investigation and settlement of claims arising under its policies;

D. Not attempting in good faith to effectuate prompt, fair and equitable settlement of claims submitted in which liability has become reasonably clear;

E. Compelling insureds or beneficiaries to institute suits to recover amounts due under its policies by offering substantially less than the amounts ultimately recovered in suits brought by them;

F. Refusing to pay claims without conducting a reasonable investigation;

G. Failing to affirm or deny coverage of claims within a reasonable time after having completed its investigation related to such claim or claims;

H. Attempting to settle or settling claims for less than the amount that a reasonable person would believe the insured or beneficiary was entitled by reference to written or printed advertising material accompanying or made part of an application;

I. Attempting to settle or settling claims on the basis of an application that was materially altered without notice to, or knowledge or consent of, the insured;

J. Making claims payments to an insured or beneficiary without indicating the coverage under which each payment is being made;

K. Unreasonably delaying the investigation or payment of claims by requiring both a formal proof of loss form and subsequent verification that would result in duplication of information and verification appearing in the formal proof of loss form;

L. Failing in the case of claims denials or offers of compromise settlement to promptly provide a reasonable and accurate explanation of the basis for such actions;

M. Failing to provide forms necessary to present claims within fifteen (15) calendar days of a request with reasonable explanations regarding their use;

N. Failing to adopt and implement reasonable standards to assure that the repairs of a repairer owned by or required to be used by the insurer are performed in a workmanlike manner.[67]

D. INDIVIDUAL STATE VARIATIONS OF THE MODEL ACT

Each jurisdiction has made unique choices concerning the various components of the model acts to include in their own laws. This discussion focuses on each state's choice of regulating unfair trade practices through variations of the UTPA or the UCSPA.

Twenty-one states have enacted various forms of the old UTPA and have included within the statutory enactment a section relating to unfair claims settlement.[68] In all of these jurisdictions, the sections modeled after the UTPA do not state whether the statute applied to suretyship.

Reference to other definitions in the respective insurance codes of ten states indicates that a surety may be subject to these statutory provisions for its claims handling practices. For purposes of their claims settlement practices statute, each of these ten states define "insurance policy" or "insurance contract" as including suretyship agreements.[69] Courts in two of the UTPA states have

67. *See* Unfair Claims Settlement Practices Act, Unfair Claims Practices Defined, Section 4(a)-(n).

68. Arkansas: Ark. Stat. Ann. § 23-66-206(9);
California: Cal. Ins. Code § 790.03(h);
Colorado: CRS § 10-3-1104(1)(h);
Connecticut: Conn. Gen. Stat. § 38a-816(6);
Delaware: Del. Code Ann. Tit. 18, § 2304(16);
Florida: Fla. Stat. § 626.9541(i);
Hawaii: Haw. Rev. Stat. § 431-13-103(a)(10);
Iowa: Iowa Code § 507B.4(9);
Kansas: Kan. Stat. Ann. § 40-2404(9);
Louisiana: La. Rev. Stat. § 22:1214(14);
Massachusetts: Mass. Gen. Laws ch. 176D, § 3(9);
Minnesota: Minn. Stat. § 72A.201(4);
New Hampshire: N.H. Rev. Stat. Ann. § 417:4(xv);
New Jersey: N.J. Stat. § 17:29B-4(9);
North Carolina: N.C. Gen. Stat. § 58-63-15(11);
North Dakota: N.D. Cent. Code § 26.1-04-03(9);
Ohio: Ohio Ins. Reg. Rule § 3901.21(p);
Pennsylvania: Penn. Stat. Tit. 40, § 1171.5(a)(10);
Tennessee: Tenn. Code Ann. § 56-8-104(8);
Vermont: Vt. Code Tit. 8, § 4724(9);
West Virginia: W.Va. Code § 33-11-4(9).

69. Arkansas: Ark. Stat. Ann. § 23-66-203(3);
Colorado: CRS § 10-3-1102(2);
Delaware: Del. Code Ann. Tit. 18, § 2302;
Florida: Fla. Stat. § 624.03;
Iowa: Iowa Code § 507B.2(3);
Kansas: Kan. Stat. Ann. § 40-2402(c);
Louisiana: La. Rev. Stat. § 22:1212;
Pennsylvania: Penn. Stat. Tit. 40, § 1171.3;
Tennessee: Tenn. Code Ann. § 56-8-102(2);
Vermont: Vt. Code Tit. 8, § 4722.

determined that the statute does not apply to sureties.[70] The laws in the remaining nine states are unclear, however five of those states presumably would not apply their claims settlement laws to sureties because sureties are not included in the definition of "person" and suretyship agreements are not included in the definition of "insurance."[71]

Twenty-seven states have enacted a statutory scheme substantially similar to the UCSPA.[72] These states have apparently rewritten their approach to unfair claims practices and have separated the unfair claims from unfair trade practices as suggested by the NAIC. Notably absent, however, from the majority of these states adopting the UCSPA, in various forms, is language specifically excluding the suretyship from the Model Act's definitions. In fact, only seven states have specifically excluded suretyship.[73] Inexplicably, five of the states that have adopted the UCSPA

---

70. California: *Cates Construction, Inc. v. Talbot Partners,* 980 P.2d 407 (Cal. 1999);
Connecticut: *Blakeslee Arpaia Chapman, Inc. v. U.S. Fid. & Guar. Co.*, 1994 WL 76383 (Conn. Super. (March 3, 1994) (unreported decision).

71. Massachusetts: Mass. Gen. Laws ch. 176D, § 1;
Minnesota: Minn. Stat. § 72A.201(3)(9);
North Carolina: N.C. Gen. Stat. § 58-63-5;
North Dakota: N.D. Cent. Code § 26.1-04-03;
West Virginia: W.Va. Code § 33-11-2.

72. Alaska: Alaska Stat. § 21.36.125;
Arizona: Ariz. Rev. Stat. § 20-461;
Georgia: Ga. Code Ann. § 33-6-33;
Idaho: Idaho Code § 41-1329;
Illinois: 215 ILCS 5/154.6;
Indiana: Burns Ind. Code Ann. § 27-4-1-4.5;
Kentucky: Ky. Rev. Stat. § 304.12-230;
Maine: 24-A Me. Rev. Stat. Ann. § 2164-D;
Maryland: Md. Ins. Code Ann. § 27-304;
Michigan: Mich. Comp. Laws § 500.2026;
Missouri: Mo. Rev. Stat. § 375.1007;
Montana: Mont. Code Ann. § 33-18-201;
Nebraska: Neb. Rev. Stat. § 44-1540;
Nevada: Nev. Rev. Stat. Ann. § 686A.310;
New Mexico: N.M. Stat. Ann. § 59A-16-20;
New York: N.Y. Ins. § 2601;
Oklahoma: Okla. Stat. Tit. 36, § 1222;
Oregon: Or. Rev. Stat. § 746.230;
Rhode Island: R.I. Stat. § 27-9.1-4;
South Carolina: S.C. Code Ann. § 38-59-20;
South Dakota: S.D. Code Laws § 58-33-67;
Texas: Tex. Ins. Code § 21.21-2;
Utah: Utah Code Ann. § 31A-26-303;
Virginia: Va. Code Ann. § 38.2-510;
Washington: Rev. Code Wash. § 284-30-330;
Wisconsin: Wis. Admin. Code § 6.11;
Wyoming: Wyo. Stat. § 26-13-124.

73. Alaska: Alaska Stat. § 21.36.310;
Georgia: Ga. Code Ann. § 33-6-32;
Kentucky: Ky. Rev. Stat. § 304.12-013;
Maryland: Md. Ins. Code Ann. § 27-302(b)(3);
Missouri: Mo. Rev. Stat. § 375.1000(2);
Nebraska: Neb. Rev. Stat. § 44-1538(e);
Rhode Island: R.I. Stat. § 27-9.1-1.

have affirmatively *included* language by which sureties are regulated by the unfair claim practice statutes.[74]

The remaining fifteen states enacting various forms of the UCSPA are silent as to whether a surety's claims handling practices are subject to the unfair claims settlement practices as defined in these statutes. However, reference to other statutes in the respective states' insurance codes generally support the conclusion that the surety is subjected to exposure premised on the state's unfair claims handling act. The "purpose" statement in the various state enactments recite that they are to "regulate trade practices in the business of insurance." Many of these states define suretyship as a type of insurance.

Definitional inattention may provide a basis for subjecting the surety to liability under a state's version of the UCSPA. For example, the Idaho, Michigan, and Montana unfair claims statutes apply to any "person."[75] Person is defined as including any "insurer."[76] Idaho and Montana then go on to define "insurer" as including a "surety,"[77] and Michigan defines "insurer" as any entity engaged in the business of making surety contracts.[78]

In Arizona, it is not entirely clear whether the surety is properly excluded from its unfair claims settlement statute. Although the statute closely follows the model act in many respects, it fails to specifically exclude suretyship. However, the act requires the director of insurance "in prescribing rules to implement this section" to follow "to the extent appropriate" the NAIC's model act.[79] The surety can argue the specific exclusion of the surety in the NAIC model act necessarily mandates exclusion of the surety from the defined unfair acts or practices. However, reference to other statutory definitions may undercut the surety's argument and subject the surety to liability.[80]

Several states that have modeled their claims practices acts on the UCSPA have gone further then the UCSPA's list of prescribed acts. South Dakota, Washington and Wisconsin proscribe the usual unfair claims settlement practices, but also cloak their insurance commissioner with broad authority to subject any "person engaged in the business of insurance" to the unfair claims provisions if they are engaging in any undefined unfair or deceptive act.[81]

Alabama and Mississippi have declined to follow both the UTPA and the UCSPA and regulate unfair trade practices in a manner that merits separate discussion.

---

74. Michigan: Mich. Comp. Laws § 500.2003(3);
Oklahoma: Okla. Stat. Tit. 36, § 1250.2(5);
South Carolina: S.C. Code Ann. § 38-59-20;
Washington: Rev. Code Wash. § 284-30-320;
Wisconsin: Wis. Admin. Code § 6.75(2)(g).

75. Idaho Code § 41-1302; Mich. Comp. Laws § 500.2003; Mont. Code Ann. § 33-18-201.

76. Idaho Code § 41-104; Mich. Comp. Laws § 500.114; Mont. Code Ann. § 33-1-202(3).

77. Idaho Code § 41-103; Mont. Code Ann. § 33-1-201(6).

78. Mich. Comp. Laws § 500.106.

79. Ariz. Rev. Stat. Ann. § 20-461(c) provides:

> In prescribing rules to implement this section, the director shall follow, to the extent appropriate, the national association of insurance commissioners unfair claims settlement practices model regulation.

80. Section 20-461(a) of Arizona's statute states "a person shall not . . ." Ariz. Rev. Stat. Ann. § 20-105 defines "person" to include an "insurer." An "insurer" is defined in Ariz. Rev. Stat. Ann. § 20-104 as "every person engaged in the business of making contracts of insurance." Ariz. Rev. Stat. Ann. §§ 20-1531 and 20-1532 speak generally to surety in the context of insurance.

81. Wash. Rev. Code § 48.30.010(2); Wis. Stat. § 628.34(12); S.D. Code. Laws § 58-33-38.

Alabama provides that no insurer shall refuse to pay or settle claims arising under its policies with such frequency as to indicate a general business practice. This practice is evidenced by: (1) a substantial increase in the number of complaints against the insurer received by the insurance department; (2) a substantial increase in lawsuits against the insurer; and (3) other "relevant evidence."[82]

Mississippi's version of the UCSPA applies only to home warranty insurers;[83] however, the commissioner of insurance is empowered to investigate any person engaged in the business of insurance if that person is reasonably believed to be engaged in any unfair or deceptive act or practice not statutorily defined.[84]

To better understand the unique variations between states that have modeled their claims practices statutes on the different model acts, we will focus on the statutes of Florida and New York. In its version of the UTPA, Florida specifically provides a private cause of action against an insurer,[85] which by definition includes a surety.[86] Conversely, New York's version of the UCSPA does not permit a private right of action.[87]

In Florida, committing any number of defined acts or practices with such frequency as to evidence a general business practice will subject the surety to liability.[88] Other actions that expose the surety to liability regardless of their frequency include: (a) attempts to settle claims based on altered documents; (b) material misrepresentations made to effect settlements on more unfavorable terms than provided by policy or contract;[89] (c) failing to settle claims in good faith when it could have if it had acted fairly and honestly towards the insured; (d) making payments without accompanying a statement setting forth the coverages under which payment is made; or (e) failing to promptly settle claims when the obligation becomes reasonably clear under one portion of the policy in order to influence settlements under the other portions of the policy.[90]

In order to bring a private cause of action in Florida, the claimant must give written notice of the violation to both the department of insurance and the insurer which sets forth the statutory violation, the facts and circumstances of the case, names of individuals involved and reference to relevant policy language.[91] If the damages are paid or circumstances giving rise to the violation are

---

82. Ala. Stat. § 27-12-24.

83. Miss. Code. Ann. § 83-57-59.

84. Miss. Code. Ann. § 83-5-45(1).

85. Fla. Stat. § 624.155(1) provides: "Any person may bring a civil action against an insurer when such person is damaged: [¶] (a) By a violation of any of the following provisions by the insurer: [¶] (1) Section 626.9541(1)(i) . . ."

86. Fla. Stat. § 624.03 provides: "'insurer' includes every person engaged as indemnitor, surety, or contractor in the business of entering into contracts of insurance or of annuity."

87. Kent Centre Assoc. v. Greater New York Mut. Ins. Co., 527 N.Y.S.2d 269 (2d Dept. 1988) (Court properly dismissed insured's cause of action seeking compensatory and punitive damages for insurer's allegedly unfair claim settlement practices since section 2601 does not afford allegedly aggrieved parties any private right of action). However, the surety should be wary of a potential separate cause of action based on N.Y. Gen. Bus. Law § 349, which outlaws deceptive acts or practices in the conduct of any business, trade or commerce and provides a private cause of action to those injured by such violation.

88. Fla. Stat. § 626.9541(1)(i)(3). The specific acts or practices defined in Fla. Stat. § 626.9541(1)(i) are substantially similar to the acts defined in the UCSPA, Section 4(a)-(c), (g), (f) and (l). In addition, Florida proscribes failing to promptly notify the insured of any additional information necessary for claim processing together with an explanation of the nature of the requested information. Fla. Stat. § 626.9541(1)(i)(3)(g), (h).

89. Fla. Stat. § 626.9541(1)(i)(1), (2).

90. Fla. Stat. § 624.155(1)(b).

91. Fla. Stat. § 624.155(2)(a), (b).

corrected, no action will lie.[92] However, upon an adverse adjudication at trial or upon appeal, the insurer is liable for damages, together with court costs and reasonable attorney's fees incurred by the plaintiff.[93]

In Florida, no punitive damages are awarded unless the acts are shown to occur with such frequency as to indicate a general practice and are willful, wanton, malicious or in reckless disregard for the rights of any insured.[94] Any party seeking punitive damages, however, must post in advance the costs of discovery, which are awarded to the insurer if the trier awards no punitives to the plaintiff.[95] Recoverable damages under Florida's statute may exceed policy limits, so long as the damages are a reasonably foreseeable result of a specified violation of the statute.[96]

Under New York's version of the UCSPA, six acts by an insurer, if committed without cause and performed with such frequency as to indicate a general business practice, constitute unfair claims settlement practices.[97] This statute most likely applies to sureties.[98] Evidence as to the numbers and types of complaints to the insurance department and the department's experience with other insurers writing similar lines of insurance is admissible in evidence at any proceeding, but an insurer will not be deemed in violation solely by reason of the numbers and types of such complaints.[99]

The marked contrast between the statutory scheme in Florida and New York underscore the need to consult the jurisdiction to ascertain the exposure of the surety, the right to a private action, and defined unfair acts or practices.

E. JUDICIAL INTERPRETATIONS OF THE MODEL ACTS AND THE VIABILITY OF A PRIVATE CAUSE OF ACTION AGAINST SURETIES

How courts have interpreted each state's statute is significant in determining whether a private right of action is permitted under a state's version of its "bad faith" claim practices statute. The reader is advised to carefully review case law in the jurisdiction of concern. A sampling of some of these cases follows.

In *K-W Industries v. National Surety Corp.*,[100] the Montana Supreme Court, interpreting Montana's version of the Model Unfair Practices Act, held that sureties, designated as "insurers" under Montana Code, were therefore subject to Montana's Unfair Claims Settlement Practices Act and could be held liable in tort for damages beyond the express terms of their contract for violations of the Act.

92. Fla. Stat. § 624.155(2)(d).

93. Fla. Stat. § 624.155(3).

94. Fla. Stat. § 624.155(4).

95. Fla. Stat. § 624.155(4).

96. Fla. Stat. § 624.155(7).

97. *See* N.Y. Ins. Law § 2601(a). These actions are substantially similar to the prohibited acts defined in UCSPA Sections 4(a)-(e).

98. N.Y. Ins. Law § 2403 provides "[n]o person shall engage in any trade practice . . ." "Person" is defined in N.Y. Ins. Law § 2402(a) as "any legal entity subject to any provision of this chapter, engaged in the business of insurance in this state . . ." N.Y. Ins. Law § 1113(a)(16) defines the kinds of insurance authorized in the state as including "fidelity and surety insurance."

99. *See* N.Y. Ins. Law § 2601(b).

100. 231 Mont. 461, 754 P.2d 502 (Mont. 1988).

The surety argued that despite the inclusion of "surety" in Montana's statutory definition of "insurer," it was not subject to Montana's Unfair Claim Settlement Practices Act because the Act merely referred to the term "insurance" as a word which qualified the term "policies." The surety then pointed out critical distinctions between the nature of surety and insurance contracts. Most significantly, the surety argued that surety contracts are not indemnity contracts because the liability of the surety is not left up to chance. Unlike an insurance policy, a surety bond does not involve a spreading of risk. The nature, size and source of the possible loss to the creditor are known from the inception of the surety contract.

Relying on the language of Montana's statutes and the rationale set forth in the California Court of Appeals in *General Ins. Co. v. Mammoth Vista Owners' Assoc.*,[101] the *K-W* court reasoned that the surety was subject to the unfair claim practices provision of Montana's insurance code. Applying state common law principles that an insurer may be liable in tort for violation of the Act, the court held that a surety may also be liable for tort damages in a private action for "bad faith" under the statute.

In *Farmer's Union Cent. Exch. v. Reliance Ins. Co.*,[102] the plaintiffs, obligees on a construction payment bond, claimed they were entitled to tort damages for the surety's alleged violation of North Dakota's Unfair Insurance Practices Act and under common law.

The Federal District Court, in the absence of state law on the matter, examined the language of North Dakota's Unfair Insurance Practices Act and found it virtually identical to the language contained in the NAIC Model Unfair Trade Practices Act, which provides:

> No order of the commissioner under this Act or order of a court to enforce the same shall in any way relieve or absolve any person affected by such order from any liability under any other laws of this state.[103]

The Court noted that the majority of states had concluded that their version of the Model Unfair Trade Practices Act did not create a private cause of action under the statute. The court decided that North Dakota would follow the majority view. Furthermore, in adopting the Model Act, the court assumed that the North Dakota legislature intended to abide by the intent of the NAIC Model Act drafters who did not intend to create a new private right of action for claim practices prohibited by the Act.

The court in *Farmer's Union* found, however, that a common law action in tort for "bad faith" existed in North Dakota under the case *Szarkowski v. Reliance Ins. Co.*,[104] discussed above.

A few states have enacted legislation providing for recovery of extra-contractual damages without creating a private right of action for "bad faith." In *State Surety Co. v. Lamb Construction Co.*,[105] the Wyoming Supreme Court held that a provision of the state insurance code which provided that an "insurance company" is obligated to pay any judgment or defend any suit where coverage exists, applied to surety companies because other Wyoming insurance code sections established that surety contracts are subject to the state insurance code provisions.

---

101. 174 Cal. App. 3d 810, 220 Cal. Rptr. 291 (1985).
102. 675 F. Supp. 1534 (D. N.D. 1987).
103. *Id.* at 1537.
104. 404 N.W.2d 502 (N.D. 1987).
105. 625 P.2d 184 (Wyo. 1981).

The court in *Lamb Construction* rejected the surety's argument that the statute,[106] providing that "determin[ation] that the company has refused to pay the full amount of a loss . . . and that the refusal is unreasonable or without cause . . . [may result in the company's liability] for a reasonable sum as an attorney's fee and interest at ten percent per year," was a "penal statute" requiring narrow construction. The court stated that "the policy behind the statute [was] not to penalize insurance companies but to encourage claim . . . [settlements] . . . and to chill any tendencies on the part of insurance companies to unreasonably reject claims.[107]

F. PREEMPTION OF PRIVATE CAUSE OF ACTION DUE TO ADOPTION OF AN UNFAIR CLAIMS SETTLEMENT PRACTICE ACT

The existence of a statute regulating claim practices in the insurance industry can be a significant hindrance to any possible cause of action against a surety for "bad faith." A statutory scheme of regulation may very well be held to have preempted any private cause of action for "bad faith." The court in *Farmer's Union*, supra, as an additional rationale supporting its conclusion that the North Dakota Unfair Insurance Practices Act did not create a private cause of action, relied upon the concept of preemption as articulated by the United States Supreme Court in *Cort v. Ash.*

In *Cort v. Ash,*[108] the Supreme Court set forth a four part test to determine whether a statute preempts a private cause of action: (1) Is the plaintiff one of the class for whose special benefit the statute was enacted? (2) Was there a legislative intent to create or deny a remedy? (3) Is a private action consistent with the underlying purpose of the act? (4) Will the application of a private action intrude into an area over which the government has exclusive jurisdiction or which has been delegated to an administrative agency?

Without citation to *Cort v. Ash,*[109] the District Court for the Middle District of Pennsylvania rejected the obligee's suit against the surety for bad faith under a performance bond on a preemption theory.[110] In *Tudor Development Group, Inc. v. United States Fidelity and Guaranty Co.,*[111] the plaintiffs relied upon the rationale in *Mammoth Vista* to attempt to establish a cause of action for statutory bad faith against a surety based on the insurer's alleged breach of the Pennsylvania version of Unfair Claims Settlement Practices Act. However, the court disagreed with the plaintiffs on the grounds that the Pennsylvania Unfair Insurance Practices Act applied to suretyship agreements as well as insurance contracts and provided an adequate deterrent of "bad faith" conduct by insurance companies, thus preempting a private cause of action.

106. *See* Wis. Stat. § 26-15-126(c).
107. 625 P.2d at 188.
108. 422 U.S. 66 (1975).
109. 422 U.S. 66 (1975).
110. 692 F. Supp. 461 (M.D. Penn. 1988).
111. 692 F. Supp. 461 (M.D. Penn. 1988).

G. MILLER ACT PREEMPTION OF STATE LAW CLAIMS FOR BAD FAITH

Payment bonds are required by the Miller Act in order to protect those who supply labor or materials to a contractor on a federal project. The Miller Act supercedes the mechanic's lien which is normally available against improved property but which does not attach to federal property.

Several federal courts have considered whether state statutes permitting extra-contractual damages conflict with the Miller Act's objectives. Federal law preempts a state law under the following conditions: (1) when the federal law expressly preempts the state law; (2) when the federal law reflects Congressional intent to occupy the entire legal field in the area; or (3) when the state law conflicts with the federal law such that compliance with the state law would obstruct a federal objective.[112]

In *K-W Industries v. National Surety Corp.*,[113] the plaintiff sub-contractor's suit against the defendant contractor for compensatory and punitive damages under Montana's unfair insurance claims practices law was removed to federal court on the basis of diversity jurisdiction. The district court then dismissed the action *sua sponte*, reasoning that its removal jurisdiction was derivative of the jurisdiction of the state court, and the state court lacked subject matter jurisdiction because the Montana law was preempted by the Miller Act and federal courts have exclusive jurisdiction to hear Miller Act claims. The Ninth Circuit reversed, holding that the Montana law was not preempted by the Miller Act.

The *K-W* court found no conflict between Montana's law and the purposes of the Miller Act. The Court held that the Miller Act simply supplements the remedy offered by way of a mechanic's lien; it does not supplant any other remedies available under state law. The *K-W* court distinguished *F.D. Rich Co. v. U.S. ex rel. Industrial Lumber Company*,[114] in which the Supreme Court held that a successful plaintiff in a Miller Act case could not recover attorney's fees under a state law authorizing recovery of attorney's fees by prevailing plaintiffs, because unlike *F.D. Rich*, K-W's claims arose under Montana's unfair claims practices statute, not the Miller Act.[115]

In *U.S. for Pensacola Construction Co. v. St. Paul Fire and Marine Ins. Co.*,[116] the plaintiff amended its Miller Act suit to allege that the court could hear its state law claims for penalties and attorney's fees on the basis of diversity jurisdiction. The District Court for the Western District of Louisiana, however, dismissed the amended complaint on the grounds that the Miller Act preempted the state law claims. The Court specifically disagreed with *K-W*, stating that the Ninth Circuit "is wrong in its interpretation of the Miller Act." Relying heavily on *F.D. Rich*, the *Pensacola* court held that the Miller Act preempted Louisiana law and provided the sole remedies that could be recovered from the surety of a Miller Act bond.

In *U.S. ex rel. Cal's A/C & Electric v. The Famous Construction Corp.*,[117] the District Court for the Western District of Louisiana held that *F.D. Rich* and its progeny, including *Pensacola*, have been legislatively overruled by the 1988 amendments to the Prompt Payment Act. The learned district court thought that, as amended, 31 U.S.C.A. § 3905(j) expressly allows subcontractors on federal projects to sue a surety for penalties and attorney's fees when the surety is late or fails to pay

---

112. *See Michigan Canners & Freezers Ass'n, Inc. v. Agricultural Marketing and Bargaining Bd.*, 467 U.S. 461, 469 (1984); *Silkwood v. Kerr-McGee Corp.*, 464 U.S. 238, 248 (1984).

113. 855 F.2d 640 (9th Cir. 1988).

114. 417 U.S. 116 (1974).

115. 855 F.2d at 643.

116. 710 F.Supp. 638 (W.D. La. 1989).

117. 34 F.Supp.2d 1042.

on the bond, provided that state law allows for such a cause of action. The Court concluded that although Congress may have preempted all state law regarding contracting and subcontracting on federal projects, Congress left open an avenue through which extra-contractual damages could be recovered under state unfair claims practices laws. In fact, however, § 3905(j) merely says that § 3905 does not limit a contractor or subcontractor's other remedies. The court misinterpreted the statute.

Conclusion

It is clear that under the common law an insurer has a duty to deal fairly and in good faith when adjusting a claim of its insured. Sureties also have this duty, and in many states, their breach of this duty may result in liability for extra-contractual damages.

A majority of states recognize a common law cause of action for bad faith against sureties that fail to exercise the proper degree of care. However, the tide appears to be turning as more states address this issue and hold that sureties should not be liable for common law bad faith. The California Supreme Court's decision in *Cates* exemplifies this change in the courts.

A thorough understanding of the jurisdiction's statutes and case law pertaining to "bad faith" is essential in order to effectively defend or pursue a bond claim. Given appropriate circumstances, the prospect of extra-contractual liability for "bad faith" can be a potent weapon for the bond claimant. Sureties should therefore take greater care in reading their contracts and considering claims so as to meet the reasonable expectations of the parties.

23

The Surety's Subrogation Rights

George J. Bachrach
John V. Burch

I. *The Definition and Nature of the Surety's Subrogation Rights*

A. Definition and Theory of Subrogation in General

The doctrine of subrogation is deeply rooted in Anglo-American jurisprudence. Indeed, fewer doctrines are more firmly established than that "a surety who pays the debt of another is entitled to all the rights of the person he paid to enforce his right to be reimbursed."[1] As early as 1834, it was resolutely stated that "[t]he rule . . . is undoubted, and it is founded upon the plainest principles of natural reason and justice, that a surety paying off a debt shall stand in the place of the creditor, and have all the rights which he has, for the purpose of obtaining reimbursement."[2] So entrenched is this concept that when given the opportunity to alter it, the Supreme Court said it refused to repudiate a principle "so deeply imbedded in our commercial practices, our economy, and our law . . ."[3]

Historically, subrogation has been described as the substitution of one person (the surety) in place of another (the creditor) with respect to the other's lawful claim or right.[4] The substitution occurs when the surety discharges an obligation of the principal to the creditor. The surety then acquires the lawful claims or rights of the creditor.

It is said that the circumstances in which subrogation may apply are limitless.[5] However, in understanding the definition and theory of subrogation, it is necessary to know how the surety is subrogated to the creditor. The surety who completes the performance of its principal is

---

1. *Pearlman v. Reliance Insurance Company*, 371 U.S. 132, 137 (1962), citing *Hampton v. Phipps*, 108 U.S. 260, 263 (1883); *Lidderdale's Executors v. Robinson's Executor*, 12 Wheat. 594, 6 L. Ed. 740 (1827); *Duncan, Fox & Co. v. North and South Wales Bank*, 6 App. Cas. 1 (H.L. 1880). See generally Sheldon, SUBROGATION § 11 (1882).

2. *Hodgson v. Shaw*, 3 Mylne & K. 183, 190 (1834).

3. *Pearlman v. Reliance Insurance Company*, 371 U.S. 132, 140 (1962). Many cases concerning the surety's subrogation rights have been decided over the years. In order to provide a source with a listing of all of the cases describing the surety's subrogation rights and the fundamental principles and basis behind the surety's subrogation rights, the Fidelity and Surety Law Committee of the Tort and Insurance Practice Section of the American Bar Association has published a book entitled THE SUBROGATION DATABASE: CASES CONCERNING THE SUBROGATION RIGHTS OF THE CONTRACT BOND SURETY (George J. Bachrach ed., 1995) (hereinafter, "THE SUBROGATION DATABASE"). THE SUBROGATION DATABASE contains all of the cases concerning the subrogation rights of the surety organized in an Outline (Matrix) form. The Outline (Matrix) lists the significant issues concerning the subrogation rights of the surety, and provides a framework or structure to identify, organize and categorize all cases concerning the surety's subrogation rights.

4. 73 AM. JUR. 2D, *Subrogation* § 1 (1974). See also *Ammerman v. Miller*, 488 F.2d 1285, 1298-99 (D.C. Cir. 1973); *Belknap Hardware & Mfg. Co. v. Ohio River Contract Co.*, 271 F. 144, 146 (6th Cir. 1921); *Sundheim v. Philadelphia School District*, 311 Pa. 90, 101, 166 A. 365, 369-370 (Pa. 1933).

5. *Federal Land Bank v. Goodwin*, 107 Fla. 537, 145 So. 883, 885 (1933); *Fenley v. Revell*, 170 Kan 705, 228 P.2d 905, 908 (1951); *Wyoming Bldg. & L. Ass'n. v. Mills Constr. Co.*, 38 Wyo. 515, 269 P. 45, 49 (1928).

subrogated to the rights of the creditor and the principal.[6] The RESTATEMENT (THIRD) OF SURETYSHIP AND GUARANTY (1995), §28 provides that a surety who satisfies its principal's obligations to a creditor (in the RESTATEMENT, called the obligee) is subrogated, to the extent it contributed to that satisfaction, in the following way:

(a) To the rights of the obligee against the principal (in the RESTATEMENT, called the principal obligor);

(b) To the rights of the obligee against other sureties;

(c) To the interests of the obligee in property in which the obligee has no continuing interest; and

(d) To the rights of the obligee against other persons whose conduct has made them liable to the obligee.[7]

Comment *a.* to the RESTATEMENT (THIRD) OF SURETYSHIP AND GUARANTY (1995), § 27 states that when the property of one person is used to discharge the debt of another, the person whose debt is discharged is unjustly enriched by the retention of the benefit conferred. Consequently, the person who satisfied the debt is placed in the position of the obligee. Comment *a.* to § 27 goes on to say that although subrogation does not spring from contract, "it may be confirmed or qualified by contract [such as where the general indemnity agreement confirms the surety's rights]."[8] Comment *a.* to § 27 states that subrogation "is a rule that the law adopts to compel the eventual satisfaction of an obligation by the one who ought to pay it." Furthermore, in the suretyship context, subrogation provides a surety with all of the obligee's rights "with respect to the underlying obligation as though that obligation had not been satisfied."[9]

Under the common law, when the underlying debt was paid to the obligee, even if it was paid by the surety, the debt was treated as having been satisfied. Thus, when the surety satisfied the obligations owed, the debt was legally extinguished, and the original debtor had no further duties. The doctrine of equitable subrogation was developed to place the performing surety in the shoes of the obligee, and gave the surety all of the rights owed by the principal and the obligee under the original obligation as if they were never satisfied.

In the performance and payment bond context, Comment *a.* to § 27 of the RESTATEMENT (THIRD) OF SURETYSHIP AND GUARANTY (1995) means that the surety who performs the obligations of the principal under the bonded contract is subrogated to all of the rights of the obligee, including those rights which would arise if the principal's construction contract had not been completed. Obviously, if the obligee were an owner of a construction project, it would use the remaining contract funds to pay for the completion of the project. Thus, the surety who completes the project is entitled to use the remaining contract funds to reimburse itself for all of its costs in completing the project.

---

6. *Trinity Universal Insurance Company v. United States*, 382 F.2d 317, 320 (5th Cir. 1967); *Pearlman v. Reliance Ins. Co.*, 371 U.S. 132 (1962); *Continental Casualty Co. v. American Sec. Corp.*, 443 F.2d 649, 652 (D.C. Cir. 1970).

7. RESTATEMENT (THIRD) OF SURETYSHIP AND GUARANTY (1995), § 28. See also *Pearlman v. Reliance Insurance Company*, 371 U.S. 132, 138 (1962); *Aetna Life Ins. Co. v. Middleport*, 124 U.S. 534, 548; *Prairie State National Bank v. United States*, 164 U.S. 227, 17 S. Ct. 144 (1896). *See also* Patrick J. O'Connor, Jr., *The Surety's Rights of Restitution and Subrogation – Set-off Principles, in* THE IMPLICATIONS OF THE NEW RESTATEMENT OF THE LAW THIRD, SURETYSHIP AND GUARANTY, ON SURETY BONDS AND INDEMNITY AGREEMENTS (unpublished paper submitted at the ABA/TIPS Fidelity and Surety Law Committee program on April 18, 1996).

8. *Id.*

9. RESTATEMENT (THIRD) OF SURETYSHIP AND GUARANTY (1995), § 27, Comment *a.*

B. HISTORICAL UNDERPINNING OF SUBROGATION

Subrogation has its origins in the courts of equity, which first recognized and applied the right. The rights conferred upon the surety through subrogation are independent of contract rights and enforced solely to accomplish the ends of substantial justice.[10] In effect, subrogation is an equitable assignment where the surety is treated as the "assignee of the creditor, standing in his shoes to enforce the debt against the debtor together with any collateral held as security for the debt, entitled to all priorities and immunities enjoyed by the creditor."[11]

For the contract bond surety, the application of the right of subrogation is traced in part to several United States Supreme Court decisions. In *Prairie National Bank v. United States*,[12] the court recognized a performance bond surety's right of equitable subrogation and held that by exercising its subrogation rights, a performing surety could protect itself by resorting to the same securities and remedies that were available to the government obligee.

Shortly thereafter, in *Henningsen v. United States Fidelity & Guaranty Company*,[13] the court recognized that both payment and performance bond sureties had superior claims to unpaid contract funds over an assignee bank. In *United States v. Munsey Trust Co.*,[14] the court recognized a payment bond surety's subrogation rights, but held those rights were inferior to the government obligee's right to setoff its claims on an unrelated obligation owed by the principal to the government obligee. Finally, in *Pearlman v. Reliance Insurance Company*,[15] the court held that a payment bond surety was entitled to unpaid contract funds over a principal's trustee in bankruptcy.

After the surety is called upon to perform its obligations, subrogation operates as a vehicle for reimbursement to the surety to reduce or eliminate loss. In the construction context, the primary target of the surety's subrogation claim is the unpaid contract funds and retainage held by the obligee. The surety may not be the only party asserting rights to these funds. Competing claimants may be the obligee itself, the principal, third party beneficiary claimants under the

---

10. *Pearlman v. Reliance Insurance Company*, 371 U.S. 132, 138 (1962); *Memphis & L.R.R. Co. v. Dow*, 120 U.S. 287, 301-302, 7 S. Ct. 482, 488, 489 (1887); *Aetna Life Insurance Co. v. Middleport*, 124 U.S. 534, 548 (1887).

11. Simpson, SURETYSHIP § 47 (1950).

12. 164 U.S. 227 (1896). This case involved the competition between a bank and a surety to retainage held by the government obligee. The bank asserted its claim was superior to that of the surety because its lien arose prior to the date of the surety's performance. The surety argued its claim arose at the time of the contract of suretyship, which was prior in time to the bank's lien. The court held that as subrogee of the government obligee, the surety was subrogated to the rights the government obligee might have asserted against the retainage. Because the government obligee could clearly appropriate the retainage despite the claim of the bank, the surety as subrogee of the government obligee could also do so.

13. 208 U.S. 404 (1908). The surety was called upon to pay labor and material suppliers. The principal was indebted to a bank and assigned as further security the right to receive the contract balance. The court held the surety's subrogation rights arose from and related back to the date of the suretyship and were superior to the bank who, as a volunteer, had no right of subrogation.

14. 332 U.S. 234 (1947). The government obligee claimed a right to set off retainage over a surety who had paid laborers and found that the surety was subrogated to the rights of those it paid. Because the laborers and materialmen had no right to the retainage held by the government obligee, the surety could not defeat the government obligee's set off rights. Further, upon the surety's argument that it was also subrogated to the rights of the government obligee, the court was unwilling to hold that the retainage could only be applied to the project for which the surety provided its bonds.

15. 371 U.S. 132 (1962). The court held that the paying surety was subrogated to the rights of the government obligee, the unpaid labor and material suppliers, and the principal. Because the surety's loss exceeded the amount retained by the government obligee, it was entitled to all of the retainage.

surety's payment bond, the principal's lender, the trustee in bankruptcy, taxing authorities, and the general creditors of the principal, including judgment creditors.[16]

C. Essential Elements of Subrogation

Subrogation is dependent upon the equities and the particular facts and circumstances of each situation.[17] Yet, no matter how one defines subrogation, there are certain essential elements present in every context in which subrogation is asserted. These are:[18]

1. The existence of an obligation of the principal to the obligee;
2. The failure of the principal to perform that obligation;
3. Rights in the obligee arising from the principal's failure to perform; and
4. The performance by the surety, pursuant to the suretyship, of the obligation that the principal failed to perform.[19]

The first three elements are issues of contract law. The principal's obligations to the obligee arise from the contract between the parties. The principal's failure to perform, or default, is determined by the acts of the principal, the contract between the parties and the rules of contract interpretation. The rights of an obligee arising from the principal's failure to perform are governed by the contract and the law of contract damages. Finally, in order for the right of subrogation to exist, the surety, pursuant to the suretyship, must perform an obligation that the principal failed to perform. Each of these elements will be addressed more fully below.

II. *Subrogation as Distinguished From Assignment*

Assignment is the consensual creation by an agreement between the parties of rights in personal property in return for valuable consideration, and is governed by Article 9 of the Uniform Commercial Code (the "U.C.C."). The lien created is the creditor's security for the performance of the obligation incurred by the debtor. The rights created by assignment are distinct from those of subrogation. Subrogation arises by operation of law and is governed by equitable principles. It is important to understand the difference between these two concepts because the competition for the contract funds held by the obligee often involves the subrogated surety against the U.C.C.

---

16. See section V. of this chapter.

17. 73 Am Jur 2d, SUBROGATION § 11 (1974).

18. *District of Columbia v. Aetna Insurance Co.*, 462 A.2d 428, 430 (D.C. 1983); Daniel Mungall, Jr., *The Subrogation Rights of the Contract Bond Surety - Some Basics, in* SUBROGATION RIGHTS OF THE CONTRACT BOND SURETY (George J. Bachrach ed., 1990); Daniel Mungall, Jr., *The Subrogation Rights of the Contract Bond Surety – A Primer* (unpublished paper submitted at the ABA/TIPS Fidelity and Surety Law Committee annual midwinter meeting on January 31, 1986).

19. For an application of one or more of these elements, see *Prairie State National Bank v. United States*, 164 U.S. 227 (1896); *In re L. H. Duncan & Sons*, 127 F.2d 640 (3d Cir. 1942); *Continental Casualty Company v. United States*, 169 F. Supp. 945 (Ct. Cl. 1959); *Travelers Indemnity Co. v. West Georgia National Bank*, 387 F. Supp. 1090 (N.D. Ga. 1974); *National Union Fire Insurance Co. of Pittsburgh, Pa. v. United States*, 304 F.2d 465 (Ct. Cl. 1962). California recognizes the following prerequisites to the assertion of subrogation: (1) payment must have been made by the subrogee to protect his own interest, (2) the subrogee must not have acted as a volunteer, (3) the debt paid must be one for which the subrogee was not primarily liable, (4) the entire debt must have been paid, and (5) subrogation must not work any injustice to the rights of others. *Golden Eagle Ins. Co. v. First Nationwide Fin. Corp.*, 31 Cal.Rptr.2d 815 (Cal. App. 1 Dist. 1994).

secured creditor.[20] Additionally, the contract bond surety may also avail itself of the rights afforded by the U.C.C.

A. Elements of Assignment - Uniform Commercial Code

A valid assignment begins with an agreement creating the security interest and execution of a security agreement or some other act to meet the requirements of the Statute of Frauds. In addition, the creditor must give value for the interest, and the debtor must have rights or power to transfer rights in the collateral.[21] When these three requirements are satisfied, the security is said to have "attached."[22] Attachment has two general consequences: first, the security interest becomes "enforceable against the debtor;" and second, the security interest becomes "enforceable against...third parties."[23] It is important to note that Article 9 makes a distinction between "attachment" and "perfection," the latter of which helps to assure that a creditor will have superior rights to the collateral against the claims of other creditors upon the debtor's default.

The U.C.C. provides different ways a security interest may be perfected. With respect to accounts receivable and contract rights, the U.C.C. provides that a security interest is perfected by filing a financing statement.[24] With respect to certain kinds of collateral, such as negotiable documents, goods and money, possession may be used to perfect the security interest.[25] Finally, control is now recognized as a means of perfecting certain security interests such as deposit accounts and letter-of-credit rights.[26]

A new change under the 1998 Revised Article is to allow a security interest in instruments (which are defined as writings that evidence a right to the payment of a monetary obligation, e.g. promissory notes)[27] to be perfected by filing, as opposed to the former 1972 Article, which permitted instruments to be perfected only by possession. Commercial tort claims are also perfected by filing.[28] These provisions for assignment and perfection of commercial tort claims are new, and potentially could be of great interest to a surety. A commercial tort claim is defined as a tort claim which arises out of the debtor's business and is not a personal injury claim.[29] This means that a principal's tort claims against others such as design professionals, accountants and lenders can be assigned to and perfected by the surety in the general indemnity agreement.

In almost all instances, the surety's primary interest is in the remaining contract funds which, under the U.C.C., are called "accounts."[30] Rights to an account are perfected when the

---

20. See section V.B.4. of this chapter.

21. U.C.C. Rev. Art. 9-203 (1998). (U.C.C. 9-203 (1972)) Comment 6 to Rev. 9-203 (1998) explains that the phrase "or the power to transfer rights in the collateral to a secured party" recognizes that a debtor may have the power to transfer greater rights than the debtor has. Revised Article 9, which was adopted by the National Conference of Commissioners on Uniform State Laws in the summer of 1998, will be effective beginning July 1, 2001. As this chapter is being prepared, Revised Article 9 has been adopted by less than half of the states. However, because the authors anticipate that by the time this chapter is published Revised Article 9 will have been adopted by a number of more states, our discussion of Article 9 in this chapter will refer to the sections of Revised Article 9. Footnotes will refer the reader to the cited section of both the Revised Article 9 (1998) and Article 9 (1972).

22. U.C.C. Rev. Art. 9-203 (1998) (U.C.C. 9-203 (1972)).

23. *Id.*

24. U.C.C. Rev. Art. 9-310 (1998) (U.C.C. 9-302 (1972)).

25. U.C.C. Rev. Art. 9-313 (1998) (U.C.C. 9-304 (1972)).

26. U.C.C. Rev. Art. 9-314 (1998) (Substantially new; derived in part from U.C.C. 9-115(4) (1972)).

27. U.C.C. Rev. Art. 9-102(a)(47)(1998) (U.C.C. 9-105 (1972)).

28. U.C.C. Rev. Art. 9-308, 9-310 (1998).

29. U.C.C. Rev. Art. 9-102(a)(13)(1998).

30. U.C.C. Rev. Art. 9-102(a)(2) (1998) (U.C.C. 9-106 (1972)).

security agreement is signed[31] and a U.C.C. form-1 (a financing statement) is properly recorded.[32] A security interest in cash, such as money in the principal's bank account, is perfected by control.[33] Since most general indemnity agreements give the surety a secured interest in the contract proceeds, the surety's rights become enforceable when it records a U.C.C. form-1 incorporating the terms of the general indemnity agreement.

Once a valid security agreement exists and the interest is perfected, the secured creditor is poised to take possession of the collateral upon the debtor's default. However, two or more perfected secured creditors may claim an interest in the same collateral. In this situation, timing becomes an important element of perfection because the competition between perfected secured creditors is determined generally by which secured creditor perfected its interest first.[34] The U.C.C. recognizes the priorities of those security interests that are perfected and unperfected as well as those creditors with rights that arise outside of the U.C.C. These include lien creditors (which include the trustee in bankruptcy), bona fide purchasers for value, buyers of goods,[35] and the surety's subrogation rights.[36]

B. SURETY'S ASSIGNMENT RIGHTS

Sureties frequently take advantage of the assignment rights created by the U.C.C. by incorporating into their general indemnity agreement the transfer or assignment of the principal's rights to the contract funds upon the happening of an event such as a claim or the principal's default on a bonded project. The assignment may also include personal property of the principal such as tools, equipment, inventory of materials, and rights of action against subcontractors, suppliers and their sureties. If the general indemnity agreement acts as a security agreement and the principal defaults, then the surety who perfects its U.C.C. security interest may foreclose upon the collateral (the contract funds, the tools, equipment, and other personal property of the principal) in the same manner as any other secured creditor. The surety may also perfect a security interest in the principal's personal property through a separate security agreement against specific collateral as a result of a demand for exoneration made against the principal pursuant to the general indemnity agreement or an agreement by the surety to finance the principal's performance of the work covered by the bonded contracts.

The surety as assignee is empowered with the same rights as any other creditor with a security interest in the personal property. It is subject to the same rules for creation of the security interest, perfection and the priorities among competing creditors.

C. COMPARISON BETWEEN ASSIGNMENT RIGHTS AND THE SURETY'S SUBROGATION RIGHTS

31. U.C.C. Rev. Art. 9-203 (1998) (U.C.C. 9-203 (1972)) .

32. U.C.C. Rev. Art. 9-310 (1998) (U.C.C. 9-302 (1972)).

33. U.C.C. Rev. Art. 9-314 (1998) (Substantially new; derived in part from U.C.C. 9-115(4) (1972)).

34. U.C.C. Rev. Art. 9-322 (1998) (U.C.C. 9-312) (U.C.C. 9-312 (1972)).

35. See U.C.C. Rev. Art. 9-323 (1998) (U.C.C. 9-301 (1972)), Rev. Art. 9-331 (1998) (U.C.C. 9-309 (1972)), Rev. Art 9-320 (1998) (U.C.C. 9-307 (1972)).

36. *National Shawmut Bank of Boston v. New Amsterdam Casualty Co.*, 411 F.2d 843 (1st Cir. 1969); *Transamerica Ins. Co. v. Barnett Bank of Marion County, N.A.*, 540 So.2d 113 (Fla. 1989); *Finance Co. of America v. United States Fid. & Guar. Co.*, 277 Md. 177, 353 A.2d 249 (1976).

Subrogation is distinctly different from the assignment rights created by virtue of an agreement and governed in accordance with the U.C.C. Subrogation is governed by equity and arises by operation of law, not the provisions of an agreement.[37]

Subrogation is characterized as an "equitable" assignment to the surety of the rights, liens, security, causes of action and other advantages of the principal, creditor or obligee. In the language of the U.C.C., subrogation is an unrecorded interest. Despite being unrecorded, however, the subrogated surety has powerful rights to assert. Because the principal may often make a U.C.C. assignment of its accounts and contract funds to its lender who perfects its security interest long before a claim against the surety's bonds occurs, there often is competition for the contract funds between a secured creditor and a subrogated surety. In deciding this dispute, the surety's subrogation rights are not a "security interest" to be determined by the U.C.C.[38] Therefore, the U.C.C.'s priority rules are inapplicable. Under varying circumstances which will be explored in depth later in this chapter, the surety's subrogation rights defeat the rights asserted by the secured creditor perfected under the U.C.C.

III. *Factors Relating to the Maturity and Operation of the Surety's Subrogation Rights*

A. CONDITION PRECEDENT NO. 1 - THE NECESSITY OF DEFAULT BY THE PRINCIPAL

In most construction contracts, the principal's failure to perform is called a default. The principal's default is at the heart of the surety's subrogation rights because default triggers the surety's performance of its bonded obligations.[39] Without the principal's default, the surety performs as a "volunteer", and performance in that capacity does not provide the foundation necessary for subrogation.[40]

Before the surety can be compelled to perform, the principal must be in default.[41] In general terms, default is the principal's failure to do that which it is obligated to do. Default typically is a fact issue that often defies a bright line analysis and depends upon the particular circumstances of each case.

---

37. *In re J.V. Gleason Co.*, 452 F.2d 1219 (8th Cir. 1971); *National Shawmut Bank of Boston v. New Amsterdam Cas. Co.*, 411 F.2d 843 (1st Cir. 1969); *Transamerica Ins. Co. v. Barnett Bank of Marion Co., N.A.*, 540 So.2d 113, 116 (Fla. 1989); *United States Fid. & Guar. Co. v. First State Bank*, 208 Kan. 738, 494 P.2d 1149 (1972).

38. *Jacobs v. Northeastern Corp.*, 416 Pa. 417, 206 A.2d 49, 55 (1965); *National Shawmut Bank of Boston v. New Amsterdam Casualty Co.*, 411 F.2d 843, 847 (1st Cir. 1969); *Argonaut v. C&S Bank of Tifton*, 140 Ga. App. 807, 812-813, 232 S.E.2d 135 (1976); *Transamerica Ins. Co. v. Barnett Bank of Marion County*, 540 So.2d 113 (Fla. 1989). However, in *Transamerica Premier Ins. Co. v. United States*, 32 Fed. Cl. 308, 313 (1994), the court stated that "contract funds in the hands of the obligee are viewed as security or 'collateral' to which the surety can turn to cover any losses that may be incurred should the principal obligor (the contractor) default on the underlying obligation and the surety be required to pay out under its bond."

39. RESTATEMENT (THIRD) OF SURETYSHIP AND GUARANTY (1995), § 27, Comment *c*. William M. Dolan, III, *The Contractor's Default as a Condition Precedent to the Contract Bond Surety's Right of Subrogation ("Out of the Darkness and Into the Light"), in* SUBROGATION RIGHTS OF THE CONTRACT BOND Surety (George J. Bachrach ed., 1990).

40. *National Shawmut Bank of Boston v. New Amsterdam Casualty Co.*, 411 F.2d 843 (1st Cir. 1969); *Anderson v. United States*, 97 Ct. Cl. 545 (Ct. Cl. 1942).

41. *First Alabama Bank of Birmingham v. Hartford Accident & Indemnity Company*, 430 F. Supp. 907, 911-12 (N.D. Ala. 1977); *Fidelity & Deposit Co. of Maryland v. United States*, 393 F.2d 834, 837 (Ct. Cl. 1968); *In re Ram Construction Company, Inc.*, 32 B.R. 758, 760 (Bankr. W.D. Pa. 1983).

Default also takes many forms. There can be a formal default declaration, but this is not a necessity.[42] All that is required is that the principal be in default as a matter of fact. The construction contract can define the events of default. When the contract fails to define default, or there has been no formal declaration of default or termination, the material breach concept is often used to determine the existence of default.[43] A material breach is the failure to perform by one party to the contract that discharges the other party's duty to perform.[44] The material breach concept is important because it fleshes out varying degrees of non-performance and pinpoints when a failure to perform constitutes a default. Without a default, the right of subrogation cannot arise.[45]

In order to find default, one must look to the obligations of the principal. The principal's default may arise out of the underlying construction contract,[46] such as the principal's abandonment or repudiation of the construction contract with the obligee. Default may arise out of the performance bond.[47] This also may take the form of an abandonment or repudiation by the principal. Default may arise out of the payment bond by the principal's failure to pay subcontractors or suppliers.[48]

The effect of default is two-fold. First, it triggers the surety's performance of its obligations under the bonds. Second, it acts as the foundational support for the surety's assertion of its subrogation rights. Until default, the surety has no obligation to begin performance under its bonds and, therefore, cannot avail itself of any of the rights which subrogation provides.[49]

B. Condition Precedent No. 2 - The Necessity of Performance by the Surety

42. "It is not necessary that there be a formal declaration of the contractor's default. All that is necessary for the surety to prevail is that the contractor be in default as a matter of fact; and that as a result of such default, the surety has become obligated to pay under its payment or performance bond." *Fidelity and Deposit Co. of Md. v. United States*, 393 F.2d 834, 837 (Ct. Cl. 1968); *Royal Indemnity Company v. United States*, 371 F.2d 462 (Ct. Cl. 1967); *First Alabama Bank of Birmingham v. Hartford Accident & Indemnity Company*, 430 F. Supp. 907, 911-12 (N.D. Ala. 1977); *Travelers Indemnity Co. v. West Georgia National Bank*, 387 F. Supp. 1090, 1093 (N.D. Ga. 1974).

43. *Fidelity & Casualty Company v. Dykstra*, 208 F. Supp. 717, 722 (D. Minn. 1962); *Fidelity & Deposit Company of Maryland v. Scott Brothers Construction Co.*, 461 F.2d 640, 643 (5th Cir. 1972); *Atlantic Refining Company v. Continental Casualty Company*, 183 F. Supp. 478, 482 (W.D. Pa. 1960).

44. *Fidelity & Casualty Co. v. Dykstra*, 208 F. Supp. 717 (D. Minn. 1962), citing RESTATEMENT OF CONTRACTS §§ 274, 275.

45. *First Alabama Bank of Birmingham v. Hartford Accident & Indemnity Company*, 430 F. Supp. 907, 911-12 (N.D. Ala. 1977); *Fidelity & Deposit Co. of Maryland v. United States*, 393 F.2d 834, 837 (Ct. Cl. 1968); *In re Ram Construction Company, Inc.*, 32 B.R. 758, 760 (Bankr. W.D. Pa. 1983); *Lacy v. Maryland Casualty Co.*, 32 F.2d 48, 53 (4th Cir. 1929).

46. *In re Modular Structures, Inc.*, 27 F.3d 72 (3d Cir. 1994); *Atlantic Refining Co. v. Continental Casualty Co.*, 183 F. Supp. 478 (W.D. Pa. 1960); *Continental Casualty Company v. United States*, 169 F. Supp. 945 (Ct. Cl. 1959); *In re L. H. Duncan & Sons*, 127 F.2d 640 (3d Cir. 1942).

47. *Lambert v. Maryland Casualty Company*, 403 So.2d 739 (La. Ct. App. 1981).

48. *Fireman's Fund Insurance Co. v. United States*, 421 F.2d 706 (Ct. Cl. 1970); *City of Detroit v. Fidelity and Deposit Company of Maryland*, 240 Mich. 213, 215 N.W. 394 (1927).

49. *Cotton States Mutual Insurance Company v. Citizens & Southern Bank*, 168 Ga. App. 83, 86, 308 S.E..2d 199 (1983).

Once the principal defaults, performance by the surety to remedy the principal's default is also necessary to the surety's assertion of its subrogation rights.[50] The performance necessary by the surety varies according to the circumstances. The performance of the surety, however, is always dictated by the bond that it provided to the obligee on behalf of the principal. Typically, the bond will incorporate the construction contract. Therefore, the performance required by the surety is a question of the interpretation of the bond in relation to the construction contract.

Generally, the surety must fully satisfy the principal's failure to perform before its subrogation rights can be asserted.[51] This still begs the question of what must be performed or paid by the surety in order to assert these rights. Some cases hold that the surety's subrogation rights are not enforceable until the creditor's claim is paid in full.[52] This means that even if the surety pays the penal sum of its bond, which is inadequate to cover all claims, the surety may not assert its subrogation rights.[53] The rationale is that it is inequitable to allow subrogation in a way which would reduce the protection of the beneficiaries of the bonds.[54] This provides some harsh results for the surety. However, exceptions do exist. Some cases hold that the requirement of full performance and/or payment may only be asserted by the obligee.[55] Since subrogation is equitable in nature, some cases hold that the partially performing or paying surety may assert subrogation rights.[56]

As an example, one court allowed a surety to recover unpaid contract amounts, but only in excess of the amounts that the obligee had the right to pay for unpaid material and labor.[57] Another court found that the surety's subrogation rights to the remaining contract funds were superior to unpaid suppliers who failed to timely file claims against the payment bonds.[58] Still another court allowed subrogation where the surety was clearly solvent and unpaid laborers and materialmen had an adequate remedy by making a claim against the payment bond.[59] Finally, one court allowed a surety to assert its subrogation rights to the contract retainage by distinguishing between the surety as the subrogee of the obligee as opposed to the subrogee of the principal. As subrogee of the obligee, the surety's rights to the contract funds prevail over those rights of unpaid suppliers. The obligee has a right of set off that the surety can assert against the contract funds held by the obligee. As subrogee of the principal, however, the surety is obligated to pay the claims of laborers and materialmen. The court ultimately reasoned that the surety's completion

---

50. RESTATEMENT (THIRD) OF SURETYSHIP AND GUARANTY (1995), § 27, Comment *b*. David W. Slaughter, *The Contract Bond Surety's Performance as a Condition Precedent to its Rights of Subrogation ("Beyond a Twiddling of Thumbs"), in* SUBROGATION RIGHTS OF THE CONTRACT BOND SURETY (George J. Bachrach ed., 1990).

51. *Equilease Corp. v. United States Fidelity and Guaranty Co.*, 565 S.W.2d 125, 126 (Ark. 1978); *General Insurance Co. of America v. State Highway Commission*, 147 Mont. 450, 414 P.2d 526, 530 (1966).

52. *Fidelity & Deposit Co. of Maryland v. Hay*, 9 F.2d 749, 750 (3d Cir. 1926); *cert. denied*, 271 U.S. 663 (1926); *Martin v. National Surety Corporation*, 437 Pa. 159, 262 A.2d 672, 675 (1970); *see generally* 9 A.L.R. 1596, 32 A.L.R. 568, 46 A.L.R. 857, 53 A.L.R. 304, 91 A.L.R. 855.

53. *Covenant Mutual Insurance Company v. Able Concrete Pump*, 609 F. Supp. 27, 31 (N.D. Cal. 1984); *American Surety Co. v. Westinghouse Electric Mfg. Co.*, 296 U.S. 133, 137 (1935).

54. See section V.B.3 of this chapter.

55. *R.C. Mahon Co. v. R.S. Knapp Co.*, 268 Mich. 67, 255 N.W. 453 (1934).

56. *See generally Martin v. National Surety Corp.*, 437 Pa. 159, 262 A.2d 672 (1970); *United States Fidelity & Guaranty Co. v. Sweeney*, 80 F.2d 235 (8th Cir. 1935); *Corn Construction v. Aetna Casualty & Surety Co.*, 295 F.2d 685 (10th Cir. 1961); *United Pacific Insurance Co. v. United States*, 319 F.2d 893 (Ct. Cl. 1963).

57. *Fidelity & Deposit v. Hay*, 9 F.2d 749 (3d Cir. 1926), *cert. denied.*, 271 U.S. 663 (1926).

58. *General Acrylics v. United States Fidelity & Guaranty Co.*, 623 P.2d 839 (Ariz. Ct. App. 1980).

59. *United Pacific Insurance Company v. United States*, 319 F.2d 893 (Ct. Cl. 1963).

of the contract and full tender of its payment bond penalty satisfied all of the surety's obligations and entitled it to the retainage as the obligee's subrogee.[60]

Under similar equities, some courts have been willing to grant subrogation rights to the surety where the surety fully performs with respect to the performance bond, but only partially performs with respect to the payment bond.[61] For instance, despite the surety's failure to pay a subcontractor's entire claim, the court allowed reimbursement from the government obligee where recovery was conditioned upon the surety's payment of the remainder of the claim.[62] Further, even in the situation where there is no performance or payment by the surety, the equities of a situation may allow the surety to assert its subrogation rights.[63]

C. Performance by the Surety in Discharge of its Bond Obligations

Regardless of the performance undertaken by the surety, it is absolutely essential that the performance be in discharge of a legal obligation that the surety owes to the obligee or some other third party.[64] Put another way, the surety must perform "under compulsion of the surety bond."[65] The surety that performs outside of its bonded obligations is a volunteer for which no rights of subrogation are available.[66] Conversely, the surety that performs pursuant to its bond obligations is not a volunteer and is entitled to assert its subrogation rights.[67]

D. The Relation Back Concept

In the competition for the contract funds, the question arises as to when the surety's subrogation rights accrue and become enforceable against the claims of other parties. Many cases hold that the surety's subrogation rights arise at the time of the execution of the suretyship.[68] Although the surety's subrogation rights are not available and enforceable until all of the essential elements and conditions precedent are met, the right relates back to the time of the execution of

60. *Covenant Mutual Insurance Company v. Able Concrete Pump*, 609 F. Supp. 27 (N.D. Cal. 1984).

61. *Fidelity & Deposit Co. v. Hay*, 9 F.2d 749 (3d Cir. 1926); *American Fidelity Fire Ins. Co. v. United States*, 513 F.2d 1375 (Ct. Cl. 1975).

62. *American Fidelity Fire Ins. Co. v. United States*, 513 F.2d 1375 (Ct. Cl. 1975); *International Fidelity Ins. Co. v. United States*, 25 Cl. Ct. 469 (1992); *Fireman's Fund Ins. Co. v. United States*, 421 F.2d 706 (Ct. Cl. 1970).

63. *In re Ram Construction Company, Inc.*, 32 B.R. 758 (Bankr. W.D. Pa. 1983).

64. *National Shawmut Bank of Boston v. New Amsterdam Casualty Co.*, 411 F.2d 843, 848 (1st Cir. 1969); *United States Fidelity & Guaranty Co. v. N.J.B. Prime Investors*, 6 Mass. App. 455, 377 N.E.2d 440, 443 (1978); *Martin v. National Surety Corp.*, 437 Pa. 159, 262 A.2d 672, 675 (1970); *Maryland Casualty Co. v. City of Pittsburgh*, 51 F. Supp. 459 (W.D. Pa. 1943); *Lacy v. Maryland Casualty Co.*, 32 F.2d 48, 53 (4th Cir. 1929).

65. 4 Corbin, CONTRACTS § 901.

66. *U.S.F.&G. v. N.J.B. Prime Investors*, 377 N.E.2d 440, 443 (Mass. 1978); *Mass Bonding & Ins. Co. v. Fago Construction Corporation*, 82 F. Supp. 619, 622 (D. Md. 1949); *Cagle, Inc. v. Sammons*, 198 Neb. 595, 254 N.W.2d 398, 403 (1977).

67. *National Shawmut Bank of Boston v. New Amsterdam Casualty Co.*, 411 F.2d 843, 844 (1st Cir. 1969); *Mass. Bonding & Ins. Co. v. Fago Construction Corp.*, 82 F. Supp. 619, 621-22 (D. Md. 1949); *Henningsen v. United States Fidelity & Guaranty Co.*, 208 U.S. 404 (1908); *Prairie State National Bank v. United States, 164 U.S. 227 (1896); Morganthau v. Fidelity & Deposit Co. of Maryland*, 94 F.2d 632, 635 (D.C. Cir. 1937).

68. *In re Larbar Corp.*, 177 F.3d 439 (6th Cir. 1999); *Aetna Casualty & Surety Company v. Harvard Trust Company*, 344 Mass. 160, 181 N.E.2d 673, 678 (1962); *United States Fidelity & Guaranty Company v. Triborough Bridge Authority*, 297 N.Y. 31, 74 N.E.2d 226, 227 (1947); *Henningsen v. United States Fidelity & Guaranty Co.*, 208 U.S. 404 (1908); *Prairie State National Bank of Chicago v. United States*, 164 U.S. 227 (1896); *International Fidelity Ins. v. Ashland Lumber*, 463 S.E.2d 664 (Va. 1995).

the suretyship. The relation back concept allows the surety to assert all the rights that were available to the subrogor at the time of the suretyship. The relation back concept applies to both performance bond sureties[69] and payment bond sureties.[70]

The surety's reliance upon the relation back concept to defeat the claims of competing parties to the remaining contract funds has been criticized as being "wide of the mark."[71] As stated by Mr. Mungall:

> When the contractor defaults in the performance of its contract obligations, the owner, as a matter of contract law, has rights and remedies, the most obvious of which is the right to withhold his further performance until the contractor's default is cured. Thus, upon the occurrence of a major default, there is nothing due to the contractor and it follows inexorably that no one claiming through the contractor has any right to contract funds. This applies to a lending bank, an assignee, an attaching creditor and even tax claims.
>
> When the controversy over contract funds is with an adversary claiming rights derived through the contractor, the surety's first position should be that there is nothing due the contractor because of his default and thus there is nothing which the adversary's claim can reach. Courts indicate that the contractor has no property rights and no title in the contract balances; that there is no property and no debt due him; that he has no rights to or interest in the balances; and that he cannot assign what he does not have. If the contractor is not entitled to the unpaid contract funds, there is nothing which assignees and attaching creditors including United States tax liens may reach. (Citations omitted)[72]

In those jurisdictions which subscribe to the relation back concept, and hold that the surety's subrogation rights arise as of the time of the principal's default and relate back to the date of the suretyship, sureties may use the relation back concept to the extent that it provides "priority" over the claims of competing parties to the remaining contract funds. However, the real essence of the surety's subrogation rights lies in the simple concept that the surety has performed its obligations under its bonds when the principal has failed to perform, thus leaving "no debt" due to the principal from the obligee and nothing that any party taking through the principal, whether it is an assignee, attaching creditor or tax lienor, can reach. The surety obtains the remaining contract funds through its rights of subrogation to those who have rights to the remaining contract funds to the exclusion of the competing parties.

IV. *Rights of the Parties to Which the Surety Seeks Subrogation*

---

69. *Aetna Casualty & Surety Company v. Harvard Trust Company*, 344 Mass. 160, 181 N.E.2d 673 (1962); *First State Bank v. Reorganized School District R-3, Bunker*, 495 S.W.2d 471 (Mo. Ct. App. 1973); *First Alabama Bank of Birmingham v. Hartford Accident & Indemnity Company*, 430 F. Supp. 907 (N.D. Ala. 1977); *District of Columbia v. Aetna Casualty & Surety Company*, 462 A.2d 428 (D.C. 1983); *Prairie State National Bank of Chicago v. United States*, 164 U.S. 227 (1896).

70. *Fidelity & Deposit Company of Maryland v. United States*, 393 F.2d 834 (Ct. Cl. 1968); *Royal Indemnity Company v. United States*, 371 F.2d 462 (Ct. Cl. 1967); *United States Fidelity & Guaranty Company v. Triborough Bridge Authority*, 297 N.Y. 31, 74 N.E.2d 226 (1947); *First Alabama Bank of Birmingham v. Hartford Accident & Indemnity Company*, 430 F. Supp. 907 (N.D. Ala. 1977); *Henningsen v. United States Fidelity & Guaranty Company*, 208 U.S. 404 (1908).

71. Daniel Mungall, Jr., *The Subrogation Rights of the Contract Bond Surety - Some Basics, in* SUBROGATION RIGHTS OF THE CONTRACT BOND Surety (George J. Bachrach, ed., 1990) at 5.

72. *Id.*

The surety who pays under its performance bond or payment bond is subrogated to the rights of the obligee,[73] the rights of third party beneficiaries under the surety's payment bond (hereinafter the "claimants"),[74] and the rights of the principal.[75] Obligees, claimants and principals have many rights arising under contract, at law and in equity. Upon the failure of the principal to perform its obligations to the obligee, and the surety's performance of those obligations, the surety may step into the shoes of the obligee, the claimant and/or the principal[76] to enforce whatever rights they may have. The following are the kinds of rights to which the surety may be subrogated.

A. RIGHTS OF THE OBLIGEE

The obligee has rights against the principal to which the surety may be subrogated. Those rights include the obligee's rights to the remaining contract funds under the construction contract[77] as well as common law rights of setoff.[78] The obligee may have claims against third parties in contract and tort actions. For example, the obligee may have rights and claims against design professionals, including architects and engineers, to which the surety may be subrogated.[79] Such claims include contract claims,[80] the improper certification of payments,[81] the premature release of retainage,[82] negligent design,[83] negligent project administration,[84] and other claims.[85] The obligee may also have claims against accountants and assignees to which the surety may be subrogated.[86] Finally, the obligee may have claims against security provided by the principal in which the obligee no longer has a continuing interest.[87]

---

73. *Framingham Trust Co. v. Gould-National Batteries, Inc.*, 427 F.2d 856 (1st Cir. 1970).

74. *Pearlman v. Reliance Ins. Co.*, 371 U.S. 132, 83 S. Ct. 232 (1962).

75. *Henningsen v. United States Fid. & Guar. Co.*, 208 U.S. 404, 28 S. Ct. 389 (1908).

76. *National Shawmut Bank of Boston v. New Amsterdam Cas. Co.*, 411 F.2d 843 (1st Cir. 1969); *In re Alcon Demolition, Inc.*, 204 B.R. 440 (Bankr. D.N.J. 1997); *In re QC Piping Installations, Inc.*, 225 B.R. 553 (Bankr. E.D.N.Y. 1998); *In re John's Insulation, Inc.*, 221 B.R. 683 (Bankr. E.D.N.Y. 1998); *Transamerica Premier Ins. Co. v. United States*, 32 Fed. Cl. 308 (1994).

77. *In re Modular Structures, Inc.*, 27 F.3d 72 (3d Cir. 1994); *American Fire & Cas. Co. v. First Nat'l. City Bank*, 411 F.2d 755 (1st Cir. 1969); *Continental Cas. Co. v. United States*, 169 F. Supp. 945 (Cl. Ct. 1959).

78. *Merritt Commercial Sav. & Loan, Inc. v. Guinee*, 766 F.2d 850 (4th Cir. 1985).

79. James D. Ferrucci and Scott D. Baron, *The Surety's Claims Against Third Parties, in* SALVAGE BY THE SURETY (George J. Bachrach ed., 1998); Martha Crandall Coleman, *Design Professionals' Liability for Negligent Design and Project Management* (unpublished paper submitted at the ABA/TIPS Fidelity and Surety Law Committee annual midwinter meeting on January 24, 1997); Michael L. Chapman, *The Liability of Design Professionals to the Surety*, 20 FORUM 591 (1985); Martin J. Andrew, *Surety Recovery from the Architect or Engineer - Why Not?*, 8 FORUM 570 (1973).

80. *Aetna Ins. Co. v. Hellmuth, Obatta & Kassabaum, Inc.*, 392 F.2d 472 (8th Cir. 1968).

81. *Peerless Ins. Co. v. Cerny & Assocs., Inc.*, 199 F. Supp. 951 (D. Minn. 1961); *Westerhold v. Carroll*, 419 S.W.2d 73 (Mo. 1967).

82. *National Surety Corp. v. Malvaney*, 221 Miss. 190, 72 So.2d 424 (1954).

83. *Miller v. DeWitt*, 59 Ill. App. 2d 38, 208 N.E.2d 249 (1965).

84. *Unity Tel. Co. v. Design Serv. Co.*, 160 Me. 188, 201 A.2d 177 (1964).

85. *Id.*

86. Armen Shahinian and Scott D. Baron, *The Surety and Fidelity Insurers' Reliance Upon Accounting Professionals in Underwriting: Augmenting Salvage Prospects* (unpublished paper submitted at the Seventh Annual Northeast Surety and Fidelity Claims Conference on October 24, 1996); Michael R. Seidl, James L. Knoll and Thomas A. Joyce, *A Surety's Guide for Claims Against Providers of Inaccurate Information* (unpublished paper submitted at the ABA/TIPS Fidelity and Surety Law Committee annual midwinter meeting on January 28, 1994); Jerome M. Joseph, *Sureties' Claims for Negligence Against Accountants, Design Professionals and Lenders*, 24 THE BRIEF 16 (No. 2, 1995); *Insurance Co. of N. Am. v. Northampton Nat'l. Bank*, 708 F.2d 13 (1st Cir. 1983).

87. *Compare Allen v. See*, 196 F.2d 608 (10th Cir. 1952) with *Maryland Cas. Co. v. Mullett*, 295 F. Supp. 875 (W.D. Pa. 1969).

B. RIGHTS OF THE CLAIMANTS

Claimants may have direct claims against the obligee to which the surety may be subrogated. With respect to private and public contracts, there may be express provisions in the construction contract and the payment bond.[88] Claimants may also have mechanics' lien rights against the obligee[89] and statutory trust fund rights[90] or stop notice/withhold/direct payment rights under state law[91] to which the surety may be subrogated.

Claimants may have direct claims against the principal under an express contract,[92] the payment bond,[93] statutory trust fund rights,[94] and stop notice/withhold/direct payment rights under state law[95] to which the surety may be subrogated. Claimants may also have claims against third parties in contract and tort actions, such as claims against assignees[96] and others.[97]

C. RIGHTS OF THE PRINCIPAL

The surety is subrogated to the rights of its principal against the obligee under the construction contract,[98] mechanic's lien rights,[99] other statutory rights,[100] and common law rights.[101] To the extent that the principal has claims against third parties such as design professionals and others, the surety is subrogated to those rights.[102] The surety is also subrogated to the principal's claims against its subcontractors and the subcontractors' sureties.[103] Furthermore, the surety is subrogated to the principal's rights against the construction financing lender.[104]

As will be seen in section V below, the surety may utilize its subrogation to the rights of the obligee, the claimants and the principal in order to seek reimbursement from the remaining contract funds for losses incurred as a result of payments under the surety's performance and payment bonds. In many instances, the surety must compete with the conflicting claims of other claimants to the remaining contract funds.

---

88. *Active Fire Sprinkler Corp. v. United States Postal Serv.*, 811 F.2d 747 (2nd Cir. 1987); *In re L.H. Duncan & Sons*, 127 F.2d 640 (3rd Cir. 1942); *In re Comcraft, Inc.*, 206 B.R. 551 (Bankr. D. Or. 1997).

89. *Golden Eagle Ins. Co. v. First Nationwide Fin. Corp.*, 31 Cal. Rptr. 2d 815 (Cal. App. 1 Dist. 1994); *William Aupperle & Sons, Inc. v. American Indem. Co.*, 75 Ill. App. 3d 722, 394 N.E.2d 725 (1979).

90. *Universal Bonding Ins. Co. v. Gittens & Sprinkle Enters., Inc.*, 960 F.2d 366 (3rd Cir. 1992).

91. *Butler v. Pacific Nat'l. Ins. Co.*, 375 F.2d 518 (9th Cir. 1967); *In re Comcraft, Inc.*, 206 B.R. 551 (Bankr. D. Or. 1997).

92. *Segovia Dev. Corp. v. Constructora Maza, Inc.*, 628 F.2d 724 (1st Cir. 1980).

93. *Fidelity & Casualty Co. v. Dykstra*, 208 F. Supp. 717 (D. Minn. 1962).

94. *Montefusco Excavating & Contracting Co. v. County of Middlesex*, 82 N.J. 519, 414 A.2d 961 (1980).

95. *Ohio v. City of Greenfield*, 528 F. Supp. 955 (S.D. Ohio 1981).

96. *American Fidelity Co. v. National City Bank of Evansville*, 266 F.2d 910 (D.C. Cir. 1959).

97. *Van-Tex, Inc. v. Pierce*, 703 F.2d 891 (5th Cir. 1983); *Industrial Indem., Inc. v. Landrieu*, 615 F.2d 644 (5th Cir. 1980).

98. *Pearlman v. Reliance Ins. Co.*, 371 U.S. 132, 83 S. Ct. 232 (1962); *Continental Casualty Co. v. American Sec. Corp.*, 433 F.2d 649 (D.C. Cir. 1970); *In re Alcon Demolition, Inc.*, 204 B.R. 440 (Bankr. D.N.J. 1997); *National Surety Corp. v. United States*, 118 F.3d 1542 (Fed. Cir. 1997).

99. *Third Nat'l. Bank in Nashville v. Highlands Ins. Co.*, 603 S.W.2d 730 (Tenn. 1980).

100. *Dole Co. v. Aetna Casualty & Sur. Co.*, 269 F. Supp. 72 (D. Me. 1967).

101. *Federal Ins. Co. v. Constructora Maza, Inc.*, 500 F. Supp. 246 (D. P.R. 1979).

102. *Peerless Ins. Co. v. Cerny & Assoc., Inc.*, 199 F. Supp. 951 (1961).

103. *Menorah Nursing Home, Inc. v. Zukov*, 153 A.D.2d 13, 548 N.Y.S.2d 702 (1989).

104. *Twin City Constr. Co. v. ITT Indus. Co.*, 358 N.W.2d 719 (Minn. App. 1984); *Fred S. Conrad Constr. Co. v. Continental Assur. Co.*, 215 So.2d 45 (Fla. App. 1968), *cert. denied*, 222 So.2d 749 (1969).

V. *Conflicting Priorities and Claims to the Contract Funds: The Surety's Subrogation Rights v. the Rights of Other Claimants Against the Remaining Contract Funds*

A. DEFINITIONS AND DISTINCTIONS

1. Type of Surety

An essential element and condition precedent to the surety's exercise of its subrogation rights is the failure of the principal to perform an obligation to the obligee, thereby creating a default by the principal, whether in the underlying construction contract, the performance bond or the payment bond.[105] Many cases have found no distinction between the principal's default in its failure to perform the work under the contract as opposed to the principal's default in its failure to pay the claims of laborers and materialmen.[106] Some courts, however, attempt to define the role of the surety and distinguish the rights of the surety under its performance bond and the surety under its payment bond upon the default of the principal.[107]

A surety may perform under its performance bond in a number of ways. The surety may make payments to the obligee as a result of the default of its principal, may undertake the completion of the contract, or may finance its principal in order to complete the contract.[108] The surety may also be compelled by the obligee to keep the bonded project free and clear of all mechanics' liens.[109] Under any of these circumstances, the surety is performing under its performance bond obligations on behalf of the obligee.

A surety performing under its payment bond is normally paying claimants who have performed labor or supplied materials on the project bonded by the surety. Whether this is a valid distinction from the surety performing under its performance bond is questionable.[110]

2. Type of Remaining Contract Funds

The courts have also attempted to define the types of the remaining contract funds which may be in dispute. Frequently used terms are the following:

---

105. See section III.A. of this chapter.

106. *In re Modular Structures, Inc.*, 27 F.3d 72 (3d Cir. 1994); *In re Larbar Corp.*, 177 F.3d 439 (6th Cir. 1999); *Transamerica Premier Ins. Co. v. United States,* 32 Fed. Cl. 308 (1994); *United States v. Pennsylvania Dep't of Highways*, 349 F. Supp. 1370 (E.D. Pa. 1972); *Fid. and Cas. Co. of N.Y. v. Dykstra*, 208 F. Supp. 717 (D. Minn. 1962); *Atlantic Ref. Co. v. Continental Gas Co.*, 183 F. Supp. 478 (W.D. Pa. 1960); *United States Fid. & Guar. Co. v. Triborough Bridge Authority*, 74 N.E.2d 226 (N.Y. 1947).

107. See section V.B.1, footnotes 133 to 135 and section V.B.3, footnotes 143 and 146 of this chapter.

108. *Aetna Casualty & Sur. Co. v. United States*, 845 F.2d 971 (Fed. Cir. 1988); *Transamerica Ins. Co. v. United States,* 31 Fed. Cl. 532 (1994) (surety facilitated completion of the contract by tendering a completion contractor to the government and paying the completion contractor to complete the work).

109. *Third Nat'l Bank in Nashville v. Highlands Ins. Co.*, 603 S.W.2d 730 (Tenn. 1980).

110. *United States v. Munsey Trust Co.*, 332 U.S. 234, 67 S. Ct. 1599 (1947) is the leading case distinguishing the rights of the surety performing under its performance bond and paying under its payment bond. The distinction has been criticized. *See* Daniel Mungall, Jr., *The Subrogation Rights of the Contract Bond Surety - Some Basics, in* SUBROGATION RIGHTS OF THE CONTRACT BOND SURETY (George J. Bachrach ed., 1990). See also section V.B.1, footnotes 127 and 133 to 135 of this chapter.

- "Progress payments", which are those contract funds which the obligee periodically pays to the principal based upon satisfactory performance of the work.[111]
- "Earned but unpaid contract funds", which are those contract funds for work that has been performed by the principal which have not yet been paid by the obligee to the principal. Earned but unpaid contract funds include progress payments.
- "Retainage", which is that portion of each progress payment that is withheld by the obligee under the provisions of the construction contract to ensure completion of the contract and payment of outstanding obligations owed to the obligee.
- "Extras", "claims", and "bonuses", which are payments for amounts due for work performed by the principal beyond the scope of the original construction contract.

Generally, the priority of the surety pursuant to its subrogation rights against the claims of others to the remaining contract funds held by the obligee does not depend upon the type of contract funds involved.

> [T]here is no valid distinction between money held by the [obligee] which is a "retainage" and a "progress payment". In either case, the "total fund" remaining in the [obligee]'s possession, to the extent the surety has obligations arising under the contract, is available to the surety.[112]

For example, the surety has subrogation rights to current earned and unpaid estimates,[113] retainages,[114] claims,[115] amounts due under a changed conditions clause in the contract,[116] bonuses for early substantial completion of the contract,[117] rebates of liquidated damages assessed by the contract obligee,[118] and the proceeds of an arbitration award resulting from the obligee's wrongful termination of the principal's right to perform the contract.[119] As discussed below, there are instances where the courts have drawn distinctions between the various types of remaining contract funds. For the purposes of this chapter, all contract funds held by the obligee at the time the surety asserts its subrogation rights are referred to collectively as the "remaining contract funds".

B. Specific Conflicts Between the Surety and Other Claimants to the Remaining Contract Funds

Once the essential elements and conditions precedent to the surety's subrogation rights arise, the surety is subrogated to the rights of the obligee, third party beneficiaries under the payment bond, and the principal.[120] In competing with the claims of others to the remaining contract funds, the surety may utilize its subrogation rights to the rights of others to obtain priority in the payment of the remaining contract funds. The disputes and their resolution arise in

111. *In re Glover Constr. Co.*, 30 B.R. 873, 875 (Bankr. W.D. Ky. 1983).
112. *Balboa Ins. Co. v. United States*, 775 F.2d 1158, 1163 (Fed. Cir. 1985).
113. *Lacy v. Maryland Cas. Co.*, 32 F.2d 48 (4th Cir. 1929).
114. *Pearlman v. Reliance Ins. Co.*, 371 U.S. 132, 83 S. Ct. 232 (1962).
115. *In re Alliance Properties*, 104 B.R. 306 (Bkrtcy. S.D. Cal. 1989).
116. *In re Dutcher Constr. Corp.*, 378 F.2d 866 (2nd Cir. 1967).
117. *Aetna Cas. & Surety Co. v. Port of New York Authority*, 182 F. Supp. 671 (S.D.N.Y. 1960).
118. *Transamerica Ins. Co. v. United States*, 31 Fed. Cl. 532 (1994) (surety can assert claim to contract balance as of the time the surety notified the government of the principal's default, and challenge the government's subsequent assessment of liquidated damages); *In re Cummins Const. Corp.*, 81 F. Supp. 193 (D. Md. 1948).
119. *In re Alcon Demolition, Inc.*, 204 B.R. 440 (Bankr. D.N.J. 1997).
120. *Pearlman v. Reliance Ins. Co.*, 371 U.S. 132, 83 S. Ct. 232 (1962).

numerous circumstances. Described below are the kinds of claimants who seek to obtain the remaining contract funds in opposition to the surety performing under its performance bond or payment bond.

1. Surety v. Obligee[121]

Assuming there are no other competing claimants to the remaining contract funds, a surety may pursue the obligee for the remaining contract funds necessary to reimburse a surety for any losses paid under its performance bond or payment bond. A surety is subrogated to the rights of its principal under the original construction contract.[122] The obligee, however, may have contractual defenses to the payment of the remaining contract funds. For example, the obligee may contend that it has backcharges against the principal, there are liquidated damages or other delay claims as a result of late performance by the principal (or the surety as completing contractor[123]), or damages as a result of other breaches of the construction contract. Where the surety is pursuing the obligee pursuant to its subrogation rights to the rights of the principal, the resolution of the disputes with the obligee are straight contract law issues and not suretyship issues. The surety is standing in the shoes of its principal to enforce the terms of the construction contract, including the payment of the contract price represented by the remaining contract funds, and the obligee may or may not have good defenses to the payment of those remaining contract funds to the surety.

The surety's subrogation rights do come into play when the obligee admits owing the remaining contract funds on the bonded contract, but attempts to reduce the contract funds to be paid to the surety as a result of setoffs claimed by the obligee. Two examples frequently arise. The obligee may attempt to setoff against the remaining contract funds amounts owed to the obligee by the principal on other contracts or obligations between the obligee and the principal. Where the surety is a performance bond surety, the obligee may not exercise its setoff rights against the remaining contract funds.[124] Where the surety is a payment bond surety, the obligee has been able to exercise its setoff rights.[125]

A second example is the obligee that is also a government taxing authority attempting to setoff against the remaining contract funds certain taxes due and owing by the principal to the government obligee. Where the surety has acted to perform the contract and incurred losses under

---

121. THE SUBROGATION DATABASE, *supra* note 3 at B-18 to B-24 [Outline (Matrix) Nos. 0171-0242]; George J. Bachrach and Robert F. Carney, *The Surety and the United States Court of Federal Claims – Revisited* (unpublished paper submitted at the Tenth Annual Northeast Surety and Fidelity Claims Conference on October 21, 1999) updating George J. Bachrach and Robert F. Carney, *The Surety and the United States Court of Federal Claims* (unpublished paper submitted at the 1995 Surety Claims Institute annual meeting on June 22, 1995); Patrick J. O'Connor, Jr., *The Surety's Rights of Restitution and Subrogation – Set-off Principles, in* THE IMPLICATIONS OF THE NEW RESTATEMENT OF THE LAW THIRD, SURETYSHIP AND GUARANTY, ON SURETY BONDS AND INDEMNITY AGREEMENTS (unpublished paper submitted at the ABA/TIPS Fidelity and Surety Law Committee program in Chicago, Il. on April 18, 1996) (section 31 of the RESTATEMENT (THIRD) OF SURETYSHIP AND GUARANTY (1995) and its comments reject the doctrine articulated in *U.S. v. Munsey Trust Co.*, 332 U.S. 234 (1947); Daniel Mungall, Jr., *The Buffeting of the Subrogation Rights of the Construction Contract Bond Surety by U.S. v. Munsey Trust Co.*, 46 INS. COUNS. J. 607 (1979).

122. *Transamerica Ins. Co. v. Barnett Bank of Marion County, N.A.*, 540 So.2d 113 (Fla. 1989).

123. *Pacific Employers Ins. Co. v. City of Berkeley*, 204 Cal. Rptr. 387 (1984).

124. *Security Ins. Co. of Hartford v. United States*, 428 F.2d 838 (Ct. Cl. 1970); *United States Fid. & Guar. Co. v. Missouri Hwy. & Transp. Com'n.*, 783 S.W.2d 516 (Mo. App. 1990) (principal's obligation in an unrelated condemnation proceeding); *Miller-Stauch Construction Co. v. Williams-Bungart Electric, Inc.*, 959 S.W.2d 490 (Mo. App. 1998).

125. *Aetna Casualty & Sur. Co. v. United States*, 526 F.2d 1127 (Ct. Cl. 1975); *Guar. Co. of North America v. Tandy & Allen Constr. Co.*, 184 A.2d 426 (N.J. 1962). See also footnote 110 for commentary.

its performance bond, the government obligee has not been successful in setting off against the remaining contract funds the amounts of those taxes due from the principal.[126] However, in a case that has received a great deal of commentary, the government obligee has been able to setoff its tax claims against the remaining contract funds where the losses incurred by the surety are under its payment bond.[127]

The most frequent situation is where the obligee holds contract funds which it admits are due and owing to the principal, but refuses to pay them to the surety because it has received notice of the claims of others to the same contract funds. In this instance, the obligee is a mere stakeholder, having no independent interest in the contract funds. For its own protection, the obligee should hold onto the remaining contract funds pending a resolution of the disputes between the surety and the competing claimants, or the obligee may interplead the remaining contract funds into court, name all of the competing parties to the remaining contract funds as parties to the litigation, and receive a release and discharge from any further obligation with respect to the interpled contract funds.[128] Whether the surety or one or more of the competing claimants are ultimately entitled to the remaining contract funds depends upon the same arguments as discussed throughout this chapter with respect to the competition between the surety and one or more of the other competing claimants.

At times, the obligee <u>should</u> have been a stakeholder with respect to the remaining contract funds, having no interest in the remaining contract funds. Yet, despite receiving conflicting claims to the contract funds from the surety and other claimants, the obligee has paid the contract funds to the principal, assignees/lenders, and others. The surety has pursued the obligee as a result of the alleged wrongful payment, and has succeeded in having the obligee pay a second time, this time to the surety, as a result of its prior payment to the principal,[129] the assignee/lender[130] and taxing authorities other than the obligee.[131]

There is one final issue between the obligee and the surety seeking to enforce its

---

126. *Security Ins. Co. v. United States*, 428 F.2d 838 (Ct. Cl. 1970); *Trinity Universal Ins. Co. v. United States*, 382 F.2d 317 (5th Cir. 1967); *United States Fid. & Guar. Co. v. Missouri Hwy. & Transp. Com'n.*, 783 S.W.2d 516 (Mo. App. 1990) (surety financing principal).

127. *United States v. Munsey Trust Co.*, 332 U.S. 234, 67 S. Ct. 1599 (1947); *United States Fid. & Guar. Co. v. United States*, 475 F.2d 1377 (Ct. Cl. 1973); *Fireman's Fund Ins. Co. v. United States*, 362 F. Supp. 842 (D. Kan. 1973); Daniel Mungall, Jr., *The Buffeting of the Subrogation Rights of the Construction Contract Bond Surety by US v. Munsey Trust Co.*, 46 INS. COUNS. J. 607 (1979); Daniel Mungall, Jr., *The Subrogation Rights of the Contract Bond Surety - Some Basics, in* SUBROGATION RIGHTS OF THE CONTRACT BOND SURETY (George J. Bachrach, ed., 1990).

128. *Newark Ins. Co. v. United States*, 169 F. Supp. 955, 957 (Ct. Cl. 1959) ("Surely a stakeholder, caught in the middle between two competing claimants, cannot, in effect, decide the merits of their claims by the mere physical act of delivering the stake to one of them. If his position as stakeholder becomes uncomfortable, and the claimants do not take steps to get a judicial solution of the question, the law has provided him with an interpleader proceeding by which he can deposit the stake in court and walk out free of annoyance of being in the middle."). See also section V.B.1, footnotes 129 to 131 of this chapter.

129. *International Fidelity Ins. Co. v. United States,* 41 Fed. Cl. 706 (1998); *National Surety Corp. v. United States,* 118 F.3d 1542 (Fed. Cir. 1997); *Transamerica Premier Ins. Co. v. United States,* 32 Fed. Cl. 308 (1994); *American Fidelity Fire Ins. Co. v. United States*, 513 F.2d 1375 (Ct. Cl. 1975); *Fireman's Fund Ins. Co. v. United States*, 421 F.2d 706 (Ct. Cl. 1970); *Home Indem. Co. v. United States*, 376 F.2d 890, 893-94 (Ct. Cl. 1967); *National Sur. Corp. v. United States*, 319 F. Supp. 45 (N.D. Ala. 1970); *Home Indem. Co. v. United States*, 313 F. Supp. 212 (W.D. Mo. 1970); *Hanover Ins. Co. v. United States*, 279 F. Supp. 851, 853 (S.D.N.Y. 1967); *International Fidelity Ins. Co. v. United States*, 25 Cl. Ct. 469 (1992); *District of Columbia v. Aetna Ins. Co.*, 462 A.2d 428 (D.C. App. 1983). *But cf. United States Fidelity & Guar. Co. v. United States*, 475 F.2d 1377 (Ct. Cl. 1973).

130. *Great Am. Ins. Co. v. United States*, 492 F.2d 821, 824-25 (Ct. Cl. 1974); *Argonaut Ins. Co. v. United States*, 434 F.2d 1362 (Ct. Cl. 1970); *Reliance Ins. Co. v. Alaska State Housing Auth.*, 323 F. Supp. 1370 (Ak. 1971); *Newark Ins. Co. v. United States*, 169 F. Supp. 955, 957 (Ct. Cl. 1959).

131. *Home Indem. Co. v. United States*, 313 F. Supp. 212 (W.D. Mo. 1970).

subrogation rights. During the principal's performance of the construction contract, the surety may be placed on notice of various claims of laborers and materialmen who have provided work or materials on the bonded project. Whether or not the surety has paid the claims, the surety may place the obligee on notice of the claims and make demand for sufficient contract funds to pay the claims.[132] The obligee, however, may want the principal to receive the progress payments in order to continue the performance of the contract. The courts have found that the obligee has a vital interest in the timely and efficient completion of the work by the principal which allows the obligee broad discretion and flexibility in determining whether to withhold the progress payments for the benefit of the surety or to pay the progress payments to the principal to continue the performance of the contract.[133] However, despite this discretion, when the surety has provided notice to the obligee that the principal is in default, the obligee has an obligation to take reasonable steps to determine for itself that the principal has the capacity and intention to complete the project.[134] If the obligee pays the progress payments to the principal after notice to the obligee, the surety may hold the obligee liable again if the obligee has engaged in arbitrary or capricious action or abuse of discretion, or deliberate and fraudulent conduct (bad faith).[135]

2. Surety v. Principal[136]

On the rare occasion, the surety must compete for the remaining contract funds against its own principal. Both the surety and the principal may claim against the obligee for the remaining contract funds. The surety, who may have completed the work of the principal or paid bills of the laborers and materialmen on the bonded project, claims the remaining contract funds pursuant to its subrogation rights to the rights of the laborers and materialmen against the principal and to the

---

132. The issue of the surety's notice to the obligee is complex. *See* George J. Bachrach and Robert F. Carney, *The Surety and the United States Court of Federal Claims – Revisited* (unpublished paper submitted at the Tenth Annual Northeast Surety and Fidelity Claims Conference on October 21, 1999) updating George J. Bachrach and Robert F. Carney, *The Surety and the United States Court of Federal Claims* (unpublished paper submitted at the 1995 Surety Claims Institute annual meeting on June 22, 1995); Marilyn Klinger, *The Surety's Notice: What Does it Say and Does it Work?, in* SUBROGATION RIGHTS OF THE CONTRACT BOND SURETY (George J. Bachrach ed., 1990). In many instances, notice must be provided by the surety directly to the obligee, and notice from the principal's unpaid subcontractors and suppliers is insufficient. *Fireman's Fund Ins. Co. v. United States,* 909 F.2d 495 (Fed. Cir. 1990). When notice is given by the surety to the obligee, and the obligee's role is as a stakeholder of the contract funds, and the obligee pays an entity other than the surety, the obligee may have to pay a second time, this time to the surety. *See supra* notes 129 to 131. However, the surety does not need to give notice to the obligee when the obligee is in breach of its contract with the principal. *National Surety Corp. v. United States,* 118 F.3d 1542 (Fed. Cir. 1997) (obligee paid the retainage to the principal in breach of the terms of the contract).

133. *United States Fidelity & Guar. Co. v. United States*, 676 F.2d 622 (Ct. Cl. 1982); *United Bonding Ins. Co. v. Catalytic Constr. Co.*, 533 F.2d 469 (9th Cir. 1976); *United States Fidelity & Guar. Co. v. United States*, 475 F.2d 1377, 1384 (Ct. Cl. 1973); *Argonaut Ins. Co. v. United States*, 434 F.2d 1362 (Ct. Cl. 1970); *Fireman's Fund Ins. Co. v. United States*, 362 F. Supp. 842 (D. Kan. 1973).

134. *Royal Indem. Co. v. United States*, 529 F.2d 1312 (Ct. Cl. 1976); *Fireman's Fund Ins. Co. v. United States*, 362 F. Supp. 842 (D. Kan. 1973); *United States v. Continental Casualty Co.*, 346 F. Supp. 1239 (N.D. Ill. 1972).

135. *Balboa Ins. Co. v. United States*, 775 F.2d 1158, 1163 (Fed. Cir. 1985) (listing eight factors considered by the court to be important in determining whether the obligee has exercised reasonable discretion in distributing the funds to the principal); *Royal Indem. Co. v. United States*, 529 F.2d 1312 (Ct. Cl. 1976); *United Pacific Ins. Co. v. United States*, 16 Cl. Ct. 555 (1989) (surety entitled to judgment against government obligee as a result of abuse of discretion in releasing progress payment to principal).

136. THE SUBROGATION DATABASE, *supra* note 3 at B-24 to B-26 [Outline (Matrix) Nos. 0243-0270]; *In re Alcon Demolition, Inc.*, 204 B.R. 440 (Bankr. D.N.J. 1997); *In re FourStar Const. Co.*, 151 B.R. 817 (Bankr. N.D. Ohio 1993).

rights of the obligee holding the remaining contract funds.

Where the surety has paid labor and material claimants in excess of the remaining contract funds, it is entitled to the remaining contract funds ahead of the principal.[137] Where the surety makes advances to the principal to pay for labor and materials which the principal is unable to pay for, the surety does not become a "volunteer" as a result of the advances because it has a legal obligation to perform the contract and pay claims for labor and material on the bonded contract. As a result, the surety is entitled to the remaining contract funds.[138] However, if the bonded contract is completed at a profit, the principal may be entitled to that profit and not the surety.[139]

3. Surety v. Third Party Beneficiaries (subcontractors and suppliers of labor and material to the bonded project) (hereinafter the "claimants")[140]

In the normal course of business, claimants with valid claims against a surety's payment bond will be paid by the surety. Therefore, there will be no competing claims between the surety and the claimants for the remaining contract funds.[141] There are circumstances where potential claimants under a payment bond are not paid by the surety for various reasons, and the claimants compete with the surety for the remaining contract funds. In these instances, the claimants assert an equitable interest in the remaining contract funds in order to defeat the surety's claim under its subrogation rights.[142]

Where the surety both completed the performance of the contract at a cost greater than the remaining contract funds, and had deposited the full amount of the payment bond with the court, the surety was subrogated to the rights of the government obligee to the remaining contract funds even though the payment bond did not fully compensate all of the claimants.[143] Where a claimant failed to file a timely claim against the payment bond, and the payment bond was sufficient to pay the claimant's claim in full, the unpaid claimant lost any equitable interest it might have in the remaining contract funds. The claimant was reduced to the status of a general creditor of the principal, and as between the claimant and the surety, which had paid timely claims against the payment bond, the surety was entitled to the remaining contract funds.[144]

In other cases, however, a surety has been required to show that it fully paid the claims of the claimants arising out of the bonded contract before the surety can share in the remaining

---

137. *Continental Casualty Co. v. American Sec. Corp.*, 443 F.2d 649, 652 (D.C. Cir. 1970); *Home Indem. Co. v. United States*, 313 F. Supp. 212 (W.D. Mo. 1970); *Hanover Ins. Co. v. United States*, 279 F. Supp. 851 (S.D.N.Y. 1967); *In re Alcon Demolition, Inc.*, 204 B.R. 440 (Bankr. D.N.J. 1997); *In re Four Star Const. Co.*, 151 B.R. 817 (Bankr. N.D. Ohio 1993).

138. *Massachusetts Bonding & Ins. Co. v. Fago Constr. Corp.*, 82 F. Supp. 619 (D. Md. 1949).

139. *United States Fidelity & Guar. Co. v. Worthington & Co.*, 6 F.2d 502 (5th Cir. 1925).

140. THE SUBROGATION DATABASE, *supra* note 3 at B-26 to B-28 [Outline (Matrix) Nos. 0271-0301].

141. *United States v. TAC Construction Company, Inc.*, 760 F. Supp. 590, 594 (S.D. Miss. 1991).

142. Edward Graham Gallagher, *Unpaid Subcontractor's or Supplier's Right to Payment Out of Contract Funds,* 10 THE CONSTR. LAW. 9 (1990); Gordon S. Elkins, *Rights of Subcontractors, Laborers and Materialmen to Contract Balances*, 18 FORUM 695 (1983); Francisco Castro-Amy, *The Contest for Contract Retainage Between the Surety and Suppliers Without Resource Under the Bond*, 16 FORUM 1073 (1981); Kenneth M. Cushman, *Who Gets the Funds? Surety's Costs Exceed Retained Funds -- But Claimant Fails to Notify or Sue on Time*, 11 FORUM 1160 (1976); *Relative Rights, As Between Surety on Public Work Contractor's Bond and Unpaid Laborers or Materialmen, In Percentage Retained By Obligee*, 61 ALR2d 899 (1958).

143. *Covenant Mut. Ins. Co. v. Able Concrete Pump*, 609 F. Supp. 27, 31 (N.D. Cal. 1984).

144. *General Acrylics v. United States Fidelity & Guaranty Co.*, 623 P.2d 839, 844-45 (Ariz. App. 1980).

contract funds.[145] If the surety is not required to make any payments on the performance bond, and pays the full penal sum of the payment bond, if the payment bond was insufficient to cover all of the claims of the claimants, the claimants' rights to the remaining contract funds are superior to the surety.[146]

Finally, a surety who pays the claims of claimants up to the full penal sum of the payment bond, but did not pay all of the claims of the claimants covered by the payment bond, is subordinate to the rights of the claimants and may not share in an insolvent principal's assets by reason of the payments until the claimants covered by the payment bond are paid in full.[147]

4. Surety v. Assignees/Lenders (hereinafter the "bank")[148]

Conflicting claims to the remaining contract funds between the surety and the bank squarely pit the surety's subrogation rights to the rights of the principal,[149] the rights of labor and material claimants,[150] and the rights of the obligee[151] to the remaining contract funds against the bank's perfected security interest under the Uniform Commercial Code in all of the accounts receivable of the principal. The courts have uniformly held that the surety's subrogation right to the remaining contract funds is not a security interest requiring perfection under the Uniform Commercial Code.[152] As a result, the courts have held that the surety completing the contract under its performance bond[153] and the surety paying persons supplying labor and materials to the project under its payment bond[154] have priority to the remaining contract funds over the claims of the bank under its perfected security interest. The surety completing the contract under its performance

145. *United States v. TAC Construction Company, Inc.*, 760 F. Supp. 590, 593-94 (S.D. Miss. 1991); *Active Fire Sprinkler Corp. v. U.S. Postal Service*, 811 F.2d 747, 756 (2nd Cir. 1987); *North Denver Bank v. United States*, 432 F.2d 466 (Ct. Cl. 1970).

146. *United States Fidelity & Guaranty Co. v. United States*, 475 F.2d 1377, 1381, 201 Ct. Cl. 1 (1973).

147. *American Surety Co. v. Westinghouse Electric Mfg. Co.*, 296 U.S. 133, 137, 56 S. Ct. 9, 11 (1935); *American Surety Co. of New York v. Sampsell*, 148 F.2d 986, 987 (9th Cir. 1945).

148. THE SUBROGATION DATABASE, *supra* note 3 at B-29 to B-33 [Outline (Matrix) Nos. 0302-0357]; Sam H. Poteet, Jr. and J. Michael Franks, *Entitlement to Contract Funds Among Competing Surety, Lender, Contractor and the Internal Revenue Service,* 9 THE CONSTR. LAW. 11 (1989).

149. *Transamerica Ins. Co. v. Barnett Bank of Marion County, N.A.*, 540 So.2d 113, 115 (Fla. 1989).

150. *United States Fid. & Guar. Co. v. First State Bank of Salina*, 208 Kan. 738, 494 P.2d 1149, 1154 (1972).

151. *Pearlman v. Reliance Ins. Co.*, 371 U.S. 132, 137, 83 S. Ct. 232, 235 (1962); *Finance Co. of America v. United States Fid. & Guar. Co.*, 277 Md. 177, 353 A.2d 249, 252 (1976).

152. *In re Alcon Demolition, Inc.*, 204 B.R. 440 (Bankr. D.N.J. 1997); *In re Comcraft, Inc.*, 206 B.R. 551 (Bankr. D. Or. 1997); *Home Indem. Co. v. United States*, 433 F.2d 764, 765 (Ct. Cl. 1970); *National Shawmut Bank of Boston v. New Amsterdam Cas. Co.*, 411 F.2d 843, 845 (1st Cir. 1969); *Transamerica Ins. Co. v. Barnett Bank of Marion Co, N.A.*, 540 So.2d 113, 117 (Fla. 1989); *Finance Co. of America v. United States Fid. & Guar. Co.*, 277 Md. 177, 353 A.2d 249, 253 (1976); *Argonaut v. C&S Bank of Tifton*, 140 Ga. App. 807, 232 S.E.2d 135, 140 (1976); *Jacobs v. Northeastern Corp.*, 416 Pa. 417, 206 A.2d 49, 54-55 (1965). A different rule would apply if the surety attempts to use its subrogation rights to acquire priority in the principal's personal property other than the remaining contract funds (inventory, equipment, etc.) over a bank which has a perfected security interest under the Uniform Commercial Code in that personal property. *Aetna Cas. and Surety Co. v. J.F. Brunken & Son, Inc.*, 357 F. Supp. 290 (S.D. 1973); *State Bank & Trust Co. v. Ins. Co. of the West*, 132 F.3d 206 (5th Cir. 1997).

153. *Prairie State Nat. Bank v. United States*, 164 U.S. 227, 17 S. Ct. 142, 147 (1896); *Industrial Bank of Washington v. United States*, 424 F.2d 932, 934 (D.C. Cir. 1970); *Alaska State Bank v. General Ins. Co. of America*, 579 P.2d 1362, 1368 (Alaska 1978).

154. *Henningsen v. United States Fid. & Guar. Co.*, 208 U.S. 404, 28 S. Ct. 389, 391 (1908); *Riverview State Bank v. Wentz*, 34 F.2d 419, 421-22 (8th Cir. 1929); *Mid-Continent Cas. Co. v. First Nat'l Bank & Trust Co. of Chickasha*, 531 P.2d 1370, 1376-77 (Okl. 1975); *Federal Ins. Co. v. Community State Bank,* 905 F.2d 112 (5th Cir. 1990) (surety prevailed even though payment bond claimants did not perfect their mechanics' lien rights).

bond has rights to the remaining contract funds superior to those of the bank even though the proceeds of the bank's loan to the principal were used to pay suppliers of labor and materials to whom the surety would otherwise have been liable.[155] A surety does not waive its subrogation rights to the remaining contract funds even if it perfects a security interest in the contract funds because assignment rights are independent from subrogation rights.[156]

A surety is subrogated to the obligee's rights and can exercise those rights to apply the remaining contract funds to completing the construction contract and paying suppliers of labor and materials.[157] The obligee does not owe any contract funds to the principal until the obligations owed to the obligee and to the laborers and materialmen are satisfied.[158] The principal's bank, who takes the contract funds with the same rights as the principal, is therefore subject to the surety's superior rights.[159] Furthermore, the surety's subrogation rights relate back to the date that the bonds are executed to defeat the claims of the bank whose rights to the contract funds only arise through the principal and upon the completion of the work.[160]

The priority of the surety's subrogation rights over the remaining contract funds does not depend upon the type of the contract funds in the hands of the obligee.[161] Therefore, the courts have held that the surety's subrogation rights have priority over the bank with regard to earned but unpaid funds, including unpaid progress payments,[162] retainage held by the obligee during the principal's performance of the contract,[163] as well as all other funds held by the obligee, whether they are for extras, bonuses, claims or lease payments.[164]

The surety's rights to progress payments which have either been paid to its principal and then sent to the principal's bank or paid directly to the principal's bank depend on a number of factors. When the progress payments are earned and paid to the bank prior to the principal's default,[165] or if the bank receives payment from the principal without notice or knowledge that the principal has failed to pay suppliers of labor and material,[166] the surety has been unable to recover from the bank the payments received from the bonded contracts, despite losses incurred by the surety. The bank prevails over the surety even if the check from the principal was not collected

155. *National Shawmut*, 411 F.2d at 847; *Union Indemnity Co. v. New Smyrna*, 130 So. 453 (Sup. Ct. Fla. 1930); *State ex rel Southern Surety Co. v. Schlesinger*, 114 Ohio St. 323, 151 N.E. 177 (Sup. Ct. Ohio 1926).

156. *Old Kent Bank v. City of Detroit*, 444 N.W.2d 162, 165 (Mich. App. 1989).

157. *Finance Co. of America*, 353 A.2d at 252.

158. *In re Modular Structures, Inc.*, 27 F.3d 72 (3d Cir. 1994); *Centex-Simpson Constr. Co. v. Fidelity & Deposit Co. of Maryland*, 795 F. Supp. 35, 39 (D. Me. 1992).

159. *National Shawmut*, 411 F.2d at 848.

160. *Prairie State*, 164 U.S. 227, 17 S. Ct. at 147; *Pembroke State Bank v. Balboa Ins. Co.*, 144 Ga. App. 609, 241 S.E.2d 483, 484-85; *Interfirst Bank Dallas, N.A. v. United States Fid. & Guar. Co.*, 774 S.W.2d 391, 397-99 (Tex. App. 1989); *Third Nat'l Bank in Nashville v. Highlands Ins. Co.*, 603 S.W.2d 730, 734 (Tenn. 1980).

161. *American Fire & Cas. Co. v. First Nat'l City Bank*, 411 F.2d 755, 758 (1st Cir. 1969), *cert. denied*, 396 U.S. 1007, 90 S. Ct. 563 (1970); *Trinity Universal Ins. Co. v. United States*, 382 F.2d 317, 320 (5th Cir. 1967).

162. *National Shawmut*, 411 F.2d at 848; *Alaska State Bank*, 579 P.2d at 1368; *First Federal State Bank v. Town of Malvern*, 270 N.W.2d 818 (Iowa 1978); *First Hutchings-Sealy Nat'l Bank of Galveston v. Aetna Cas. & Sur. Co.*, 532 S.W.2d 114 (Tex. App. 1976).

163. *Prairie State*, 164 U.S. at 233, 17 S. Ct. at 145; *Trinity Universal*, 382 F.2d at 320-21; *Centex-Simpson*, 795 F. Supp. at 39-40; *Fidelity & Cas. Co. of N.Y. v. Indiana Nat'l Bank*, 216 N.E.2d 857, 860 (Ind. App. 1966); *Fidelity Nat'l Bank of Oklahoma City v. United States Cas. Co.*, 131 P.2d 75, 77-78 (Okl. 1942).

164. *London & Lanchshire Indem. Co. of America v. Endres*, 290 F. 98 (8th Cir. 1923); *In re Alliance Properties, Inc.*, 104 B.R. 306, 311-12 (Bankr. S.D. Cal. 1989); *Equilease*, 565 S.W.2d at 126-27.

165. *American Fire*, 411 F.2d at 758; *Reliance Ins. Co. v. U.S. Bank of Washington, N.A.*, 143 F.3d 502 (9th Cir. 1998). See section III.A. of this chapter.

166. *Reliance Ins. Co. v. U.S. Bank of Washington, N.A.*, 143 F.3d 502 (9th Cir. 1998); *Bank of Arizona v. National Sur. Corp.*, 237 F.2d 90, 93-94 (9th Cir. 1956).

from the drawee bank until after a declaration of default.[167] Generally, in the absence of knowledge or fraud on the part of the bank, progress payments paid to the bank cannot be collected by the surety from the bank pursuant to its subrogation rights.[168]

Banks have been held to be on notice of the surety's subrogation rights.[169] Where the principal is in default under the construction contract prior to the payment of the progress payment, and the bank is aware of the default, the surety is entitled to obtain from the bank the progress payment received by the bank.[170] Furthermore, where the bank received the contract funds with notice of the principal's default, the bank is not entitled to offset debts owed to it by the contractor which are unrelated to the construction contract.[171]

5. Surety v. Trustee in Bankruptcy/Debtor in Possession (hereinafter the "debtor")[172]

The conflicting claims for the bonded contract funds between the surety and the debtor or trustee in bankruptcy has begun anew since the enactment of the United States Bankruptcy Code[173] (hereinafter the "Code") in 1978 and the repeal of the old Bankruptcy Act. The seminal case under the Bankruptcy Act is *Pearlman v. Reliance Insurance Company*,[174] which was decided prior to the enactment of the Code. In finding that the surety who paid the claims of the bankrupt principal's laborers and materialmen has priority to the contract funds retained by the government obligee as against the claims of the bankrupt principal's trustee, the Supreme Court held that:

> the [obligee] had a right to use the retained fund to pay laborers and materialmen; that the laborers and materialmen had a right to be paid out of the fund; that the contractor, had he completed his job and paid his laborers and materialmen, would have become entitled to the fund; and that the surety, having paid the laborers and materialmen, is entitled to the benefit of all these rights to the extent necessary to reimburse it.[175]

Since the enactment of the Code, bankruptcy courts have had to address the issue of whether *Pearlman* is still good law under the Code.[176] In *Pearlman*, the Supreme Court held that the remaining contract funds were subject to the surety's equitable lien and not property of the estate under the Bankruptcy Act. Subsequently, section 541 of the Code was adopted which substantially expands the definition of property of the estate to include all legal and equitable

---

167. *Fidelity & Deposit Co. of Maryland v. Scott Brothers Constr. Co.*, 461 F.2d 640, 643 (5th Cir. 1972).

168. *American Fidelity Co. v. National City Bank of Evansville*, 266 F.2d 910, 915-17 (D.C. Cir. 1959).

169. *Standard Acc. Ins. Co. of Detroit v. Federal Nat'l Bank of Shawnee*, 112 F.2d 692, 695 (10th Cir. 1940); *National Surety Corp. v. United States*, 133 F. Supp. 381, 384-85 (Ct. Cl. 1955); *Royal Indem. Co. v. United States*, 93 F. Supp. 891, 894 (Ct. Cl. 1950).

170. *Insurance Co. of North Am. v. Northampton Nat'l Bank*, 708 F.2d 13, 15 (1st Cir. 1983); *Travelers Indem. Co. v. West Georgia Nat'l Bank*, 387 F. Supp. 1090, 1094 (N.D. Ga. 1974).

171. *Federal Ins. Co. v. Fifth Third Bank*, 867 F.2d 330, 334-36 (6th Cir. 1989); *Pacific Indem. Co. v. Grand Avenue State Bank of Dallas*, 223 F.2d 513, 518-19 (5th Cir. 1955); *Central National Ins. Co. v. Tri-County State Bank*, 823 F. Supp. 652 (D. Minn. 1993).

172. THE SUBROGATION DATABASE, *supra* note 3 at B-33 to B-35 [Outline (Matrix) Nos. 0358-0385]; George J. Bachrach and Cynthia E. Rodgers-Waire, *The Surety's Rights to the Contract Funds in the Principal's Chapter 11 Bankruptcy Case*, 35 TORT & INS. L. J. 1 (1999).

173. 11 U.S.C. § 101.

174. 371 U.S. 132, 83 S. Ct. 232 (1962).

175. 371 U.S. at 141-42, 83 S. Ct. at 237.

176. *In re Glover Constr. Co.*, 30 B.R. 873 (Bankr. W.D. Ky. 1983).

interests of the debtor.[177] With respect to the remaining contract funds, whether those contract funds consist of earned and unpaid progress payments,[178] retainage,[179] or the settlement of certain contract claims of the debtor,[180] the surety's equitable lien on the remaining contract funds as a result of the surety's performance of the work and payment of claimants supplying labor and materials relates back to the date of the bond[181] and gives the surety priority over the debtor to the remaining contract funds.[182]

Bankruptcy courts have utilized a number of theories in recognizing the surety's superior subrogation rights to the remaining contract funds. In several cases[183], the bankruptcy court determined that the debtor's failure to pay subcontractors and suppliers was equivalent to the debtor's failure to actually perform the contract. Therefore, the obligee did not owe the remaining contract funds to the debtor. Since the debtor had no legal or equitable interests in the remaining contract funds, the contract funds did not become property of the estate under section 541 of the Code.[184] Other cases recognize that the broad scope of section 541 of the Code would bring the remaining contract funds into the estate, subject to the equitable lien rights of the surety pursuant to the surety's subrogation rights and section 541(d) of the Code.[185]

Where the debtor continues the performance of the contract and looks to the progress payments to finance the performance of the work, the progress payments earned by the debtor have been found to be property of the estate.[186] However, bankruptcy courts have held that the surety has an interest in the progress payments pursuant to its subrogation rights which must be adequately protected under the Code.[187] As adequate protection, bankruptcy courts have given the surety the ability to control the debtor's payments to assure that the progress payments are dedicated to pay bona fide claims against the projects for which the surety would become liable under its bonds.[188] Furthermore, in those states that have either enacted trust fund statutes or recognized trust fund theories, all contract funds received by the debtor must be held in trust by the debtor for the benefit of the laborers and materialmen protected by the trust fund statute or trust fund theory, and the surety to the extent that the surety pays the laborers and materialmen, and

177. *In re Alliance Properties, Inc.*, 104 B.R. 306, 312 (Bankr. S.D. Cal. 1989).

178. *In re E.R. Fegert, Inc.*, 88 B.R. 258, 261 (Bankr. 9th Cir. 1988); *In re The Massart Co.*, 105 B.R. 610, 613 (W.D. Wash. 1989).

179. *In re Glover Constr. Co.*, 30 B.R. 873, 882 (Bankr. W.D. Ky. 1983); *In re QC Piping Installations, Inc.*, 225 B.R. 553 (Bankr. E.D.N.Y. 1998).

180. *In re Alliance Properties, Inc.*, 104 B.R. 306, 310 (Bankr. S.D. Cal. 1989).

181. *In re Ward Land Clearing and Drainage, Inc.*, 73 B.R. 313, 315 (Bankr. N.D. Fla. 1987).

182. *In re Glover Constr. Co.*, 30 B.R. 873, 882 (Bankr. W.D. Ky. 1983). In fact, the surety is subrogated to the debtor's rights to the remaining contract funds in the hands of the obligee, and may obtain the remaining contract funds ahead of the debtor. *In re Alcon Demolition, Inc.*, 204 B.R. 440 (Bankr. D.N.J. 1997); *In re Four Star Const. Co.*, 151 B.R. 817 (Bankr. N.D. Ohio 1993).

183. *In re Modular Structures, Inc.*, 27 F.3d 72 (3d Cir. 1994); *In re Pacific Marine Dredging and Constr.*, 79 B.R. 924, 929 (Bankr. D. Or. 1987).

184. *See also In re The Massart Company*, 105 B.R. 610, 613 (W.D. Wash. 1989); *In re Underground Storage Tank Technical Servs. Group, Inc.*, 212 B.R. 564 (Bankr. E.D. Mich. 1997); *In re Arnold*, 908 F.2d 52 (6th Cir. 1990).

185. *In re Glover Constr. Co.*, 30 B.R. 873, 881 (Bankr. W.D. Ky. 1983); *In re Alliance Properties, Inc.*, 104 B.R. 306, 312 (Bankr. S.D. Cal. 1989).

186. *In re Glover Constr. Co.*, 30 B.R. 873, 876 (Bankr. W.D. Ky. 1983).

187. *In re Glover Constr. Co.*, 30 B.R. 873, 882 (Bankr. W.D. Ky. 1983); *Cf. In re Universal Builders, Inc.*, 53 B.R. 183 (Bankr. M.D. Tenn. 1985). [The authors believe that *Universal Builders* may have been incorrectly decided by the court's failure to refer to applicable Tennessee law, *Third National Bank v. Highlands Ins. Co.*, 603 S.W.2d 730 (Tenn. 1980)].

188. *In re Glover Constr. Co.*, 30 B.R. 873, 882 (Bankr. W.D. Ky. 1983); *In re RAM Constr. Co.*, 32 B.R. 758, 759 (Bankr. W.D. Pa. 1983).

such contract funds may not be allocated or disbursed to general creditors or be used by the debtor in its efforts to reorganize.[189]

The surety's subrogation rights relate back to the date of the bonds.[190] Therefore, post-petition payments by the surety as a result of claims against its bonds executed pre-petition do not allow the debtor to intervene and claim the contract funds as a hypothetical lien creditor under section 544 of the Code.[191] Furthermore, the surety's payment of those claims post-petition is neither a violation of the automatic stay of section 362(a)(4) of the Code,[192] nor is it a preference under section 547 of the Code.[193] The surety has defeated the trustee's claims of preference under section 547 of the Code because of its equitable lien on the contract funds pursuant to its subrogation rights.[194] Finally, a performance bond surety completing multiple projects for the same obligee at a loss is subrogated to the obligee's common law setoff rights on those other projects completed at a "profit" because allowing setoff under section 553 of the Code serves as an incentive for sureties to complete their performance bond obligations.[195]

In summary, during an ongoing chapter 11 proceeding where debtor is performing the work and the obligee is paying progress payments, both the debtor and the surety have an interest in the contract funds. The debtor will normally be authorized to utilize the contract funds (progress payments) with the surety obtaining some fashion of adequate protection.[196] Where the work has been performed and the surety's payments exceed the remaining contract funds, whether they are progress payments, retainage or the settlement of certain contract claims, the surety maintains an equitable lien in the remaining contract funds pursuant to its subrogation rights to the extent of its losses.[197]

6. Surety v. Taxing Authorities Other Than the Obligee[198]

In a prior section of this chapter, we discussed the conflicting priorities and claims to the remaining contract funds between a surety performing under its performance bond or its payment bond and a government obligee attempting to setoff taxes owed to the obligee by the principal.[199] A surety, pursuant to its subrogation rights, may also compete for the remaining contract funds against a government tax lien from a taxing authority who is not the obligee, and against other governmental agencies making statutory claims against the remaining contract funds such as state

---

189. *Universal Bonding Insurance Co. v. Gittens and Sprinkle Enterprises, Inc.*, 960 F.2d 366, 371 (3rd Cir. 1992); *In re Marrs-Winn Company, Inc.*, 103 F.3d 584 (7th Cir. 1996).

190. *In re The Massart Company*, 105 B.R. 610, 612 (W.D. Wash. 1989); *In re Alliance Properties, Inc.*, 104 B.R. 306, 311 (Bankr. S.D. Cal. 1989); *In re Pacific Marine Dredging*, 79 B.R. 924, 929 (Bankr. D. Or. 1987). See section III.D. of this chapter.

191. *In re Pacific Marine Dredging*, 79 B.R. 924, 928 (Bankr. D. Or. 1987).

192. Section 362(a)(4) of the Code stays any act of a creditor of the debtor to create, perfect, or enforce any lien against property of the debtor's estate, i.e. the remaining contract funds.

193. *In re Pacific Marine Dredging*, 79 B.R. 924, 928-29 (Bankr. D. Or. 1987).

194. *In re E.R. Fegert, Inc.*, 88 B.R. 258, 260-61 (Bankr. 9th Cir. 1988). *See also Newbery Corporation v. Fireman's Fund Ins. Co.*, 106 B.R. 186 (D.Ariz. 1989).

195. *In re Larbar Corp.*, 177 F.3d 439 (6th Cir. 1999).

196. *In re Glover Constr. Co.*, 30 B.R. 873 (Bankr. W.D. Ky. 1983).

197. *In re Alliance Properties, Inc.*, 104 B.R. 306 (Bankr. S.D. Cal. 1989).

198. THE SUBROGATION DATABASE, *supra* note 3 at B-35 to B-37 [Outline (Matrix) Nos. 0386-0411]; Matthew M. Horowitz, *Evaluating Priority Disputes Between a Surety and the Internal Revenue Service* (unpublished paper submitted at the ABA annual meeting on August 8, 1995).

199. See section V.B.1 of this chapter.

labor departments. Whether the surety is a performance bond surety completing the contract of its principal[200] or the surety has paid the claims of laborers and materialmen under its payment bond,[201] the surety will prevail over the tax lien rights of the taxing authority to the remaining contract funds because the taxing authority can only claim those contract funds to which the principal is entitled to receive.[202] In addition, the surety's subrogation rights arise at the time that it gives its bond, and the rights become available to the surety when it suffers a loss.[203] Therefore, the surety's subrogation rights are superior to a government tax lien for unpaid taxes which arises after the date of the bond, but occurs prior to the date that the surety actually makes payment.[204]

Various state governmental agencies, such as state labor departments, may also compete with the surety's subrogation rights to the remaining contract funds, and some have found success depending upon the state statutes involved.[205]

One issue that may affect the priority between the surety and the taxing authority to the remaining contract funds is whether the principal is in default.[206] One court has held that the surety has priority over the taxing authority's tax liens which are filed after the principal is in default, but not as to any tax liens filed before the principal is in default.[207] However, all that is necessary for the surety's subrogation rights and equitable lien to attach to the remaining contract funds is for the principal to be in default as a matter of fact, and that the surety has become obligated to pay subcontractors, laborers and materialmen under its payment bond. In that instance, formal notice of default need not be given to the surety before its subrogation rights accrue against the remaining contract funds.[208]

7. Surety v. General Creditors of the Principal, Including Judgment Creditors (hereinafter the "general creditors")[209]

A surety may compete for the remaining contract funds on a contract bonded by the surety with general creditors of the principal who are not claimants under any contract bonded by the

200. *Central Surety & Ins. Corp. v. Martin Infante Co.*, 272 F.2d 231 (3rd Cir. 1959) (performing surety financed the principal); *Aetna Casualty and Surety Co. v. Port of New York Authority*, 182 F. Supp. 671, 673 (S.D.N.Y. 1960) (surety had priority against retainage and unpaid portion of a bonus for early substantial completion.)

201. *Fidelity and Deposit Company of Maryland v. New York City Housing Authority*, 241 F.2d 142 (2nd Cir. 1957); *Fid. and Cas. Co. of N.Y. v. Dykstra*, 208 F. Supp. 717 (D. Minn. 1962); *Atlantic Refining Company v. Continental Casualty Company*, 183 F. Supp. 478 (W.D. Pa. 1960); *United States Fidelity & Guaranty Co. v. Triborough Bridge Authority*, 74 N.E.2d 226 (N.Y. 1947).

202. *Amwest Sur. Ins. Co. v. United States,* 870 F. Supp. 432 (D. Conn. 1994). *But cf. Capitol Indem. Corp. v. United States,* 41 F.3d 320 (7th Cir. 1994); *In re Construction Alternatives, Inc.*, 2 F.3d 670 (6th Cir. 1993). *See* Matthew M. Horowitz, *Evaluating Priority Disputes Between a Surety and the Internal Revenue Service* (unpublished paper submitted at the ABA annual meeting on August 8, 1995).

203. *United States Fidelity & Guaranty Co. v. Triborough Bridge Authority*, 74 N.E.2d 226, 227 (N.Y. 1947). See section III.D. of this chapter.

204. *United States Fidelity & Guaranty Co. v. United States*, 201 F.2d 118, 121 (10th Cir. 1952).

205. *City of New York v. Cross Bay Contracting Corp.*, 709 N.E.2d 459, 686 N.Y.S.2d 750 (Ct. App. 1999); *Titan Indem. Co. v. Triborough Bridge and Tunnel Auth.*, 135 F.3d 831(2nd Cir. 1998). *See* Darryl Weissman and Scott D. Baron, *The Surety's Priority Battle With State Labor Departments Over Unpaid Contract Funds – Whatever Happened to Subrogation?* (unpublished paper submitted at the Ninth Annual Northeast Surety & Fidelity Claims Conference on October 22, 1998); John W. Morris, *The Labor Department Versus the Subrogated Surety, Who Wins?* (unpublished paper submitted at the 1999 National Bond Claims Association annual meeting on September 30, 1999).

206. See section III.A. of this chapter.

207. *International Fidelity Insurance Co. v. United States*, 949 F.2d 1042 (8th Cir. 1991).

208. *Kansas City, Missouri v. Tri-City Construction Company*, 666 F. Supp. 170, 172 (W.D. Mo. 1987).

209. THE SUBROGATION DATABASE, *supra* note 3 at B-37 to B-40 [Outline (Matrix) Nos. 0412-0437].

surety.[210] This situation is very similar to the surety competing for the remaining contract funds with a taxing authority other than the obligee which has a filed tax lien against the principal. The general creditor may have a judgment against the principal and may have executed or garnished the remaining contract funds, or it merely may be owed a general unsecured debt from the principal.

Whether the surety has performed under its performance bond or payment bond, the surety's subrogation rights to the remaining contract funds are superior to those of general creditors even where the remaining contract funds had been attached by general creditors first.[211] Where the surety completed the performance of the contract at a cost greater than the remaining contract funds, and had deposited the full amount of the payment bond with the court, the surety was subrogated to the rights of the government obligee to the remaining contract funds even though the payment bond did not fully compensate all of the payment bond claimants, who then became general creditors of the principal.[212]

In determining the priority rights to the remaining contract funds in a dispute involving a bank as the assignee of the principal, a surety who issued a contract surety bond, and general creditors, including a general creditor that had issued a writ of garnishment after the surety bond was executed, the court determined that the surety's subrogation rights, which relate back to the date of the execution of the surety bond, took priority over the claims of the principal's general, unsecured creditors.[213]

Where the principal has received progress payments from the obligee and paid general creditors on obligations not arising from the principal's performance of the bonded contract, courts have generally held that the general creditor may retain the payment received. Where the principal paid the general creditor prior to the principal's default on the bonded contract, the general creditor could retain the payment barring any allegation or proof by the surety that the payment was a fraudulent conveyance by the principal.[214] When the general creditor had no knowledge of the principal's default, the surety cannot, on a theory of subrogation, recover from the general creditor the amount paid in satisfaction of a just debt.[215]

In those states that have enacted trust fund statutes, all contract funds received by the principal must be held in trust for the benefit of the laborers and materialmen protected by the trust fund statute, <u>and</u> the surety to the extent that the surety pays the laborers and materialmen, and such contract funds may not be allocated or disbursed to general creditors of the principal.[216] Query: Can the surety recover from a general creditor contract funds received by the general creditor where the general creditor knew or had reason to know that the contract funds came from a contract subject to a statutory trust fund? The issue has not yet been addressed by any court.

---

210. A general creditor may also include a subcontractor claimant who has failed to file a timely claim against the surety's payment bond. *General Acrylics v. United States Fidelity & Guaranty Company*, 623 P.2d 839, 844-45 (Ariz. App. 1981). See also section V.B.3 of this chapter.

211. *International Fidelity Ins. Co. v. Ashland Lumber Company, Inc.*, 463 S.E.2d 664 (Va. 1995); *Segovia Development Corporation v. Constructora Maza, Inc.*, 628 F.2d 724 (1st Cir. 1980); *Stehle v. United Surety Co.*, 107 Md. 470, 68 Atl. 600 (Ct. App. Md. 1908).

212. *Covenant Mut. Ins. Co. v. Able Concrete Pump*, 609 F. Supp. 27 (N.D. Cal. 1984). See also section III.B. of this chapter.

213. *Kimberly-Clark Corp. v. Alpha Bldg. Co.*, 591 F. Supp. 198 (N.D. Miss. 1984).

214. *American Cas. Co. of Reading v. Line Materials Indus.*, 332 F.2d 393 (10th Cir. 1964).

215. *California Bank v. United States Fidelity & Guaranty Co.*, 129 F.2d 751 (9th Cir. 1942).

216. *Universal Bonding Insurance Company v. Gittens & Sprinkle Enterprises, Inc.*, 960 F.2d 366, 371 (3rd Cir. 1992).

C. Setoff Issues: The Surety's Subrogation Rights to the Obligee's Setoff Rights to Defeat the Claims of Other Claimants (Common Obligee Theory)

As discussed previously, the surety is subrogated to all of the rights and remedies of the obligee as a result of its performance of the work under the performance bond and payment of claimants under the payment bond.[217] The obligee may have one or more contracts with the principal, whether bonded by the surety or not, and the principal may owe the obligee money as a result of other obligations (debts for taxes due and owing, debts on other contracts). Under these circumstances, the obligee may attempt to exercise its setoff rights against funds the obligee owes the principal under the contract or contracts (funds in which the obligee has an interest) to reimburse itself for debts owed by the principal to the obligee.[218] The issue of whether a performance bond surety or payment bond surety may use its subrogation rights to the setoff rights of the obligee to obtain the proceeds owed by the obligee to the principal on one contract to reimburse the surety for losses it has incurred on another contract[219] is limited to those instances where the obligee is a mere stakeholder of the remaining contract funds and has no independent interest in them.

A surety that performs its obligations under its performance bond[220] or its payment bond[221] is subrogated to all of the rights and remedies of the obligee. As a result, several courts have held that where the only claimants to certain monies held by the obligee as a stakeholder are the surety and the principal, the surety who has performed under its performance bond to complete the bonded contract of its principal, upon full satisfaction of its obligations, is subrogated to all of the rights and remedies that the obligee may have had against the principal had the obligee been forced to complete the bonded contract itself. Among those remedies is the common law right of the obligee to setoff monies owed to the principal on one contract against debts owed by the principal to the obligee on another.[222] Courts have routinely affirmed that a surety should not be punished for completing a bonded contract as opposed to forcing the obligee to complete it and make a claim under the surety's performance bond for any resulting loss.[223] Similarly, another court allowed a payment bond surety to exercise the obligee's setoff rights to apply contract balances from one contract bonded by the surety to offset losses incurred by the surety on another bonded contract based upon the language in the two bonded contracts.[224] Furthermore, the surety has the right to compel an obligee to assert its setoff rights against an insolvent principal in order to reduce the surety's loss.[225]

Not all courts have supported the surety's subrogation rights to utilize the obligee's rights of setoff. In one case, the court did not allow a payment bond surety to exercise the obligee's rights

217. *Pearlman v. Reliance Ins. Co.*, 371 U.S. 132, 83 S. Ct. 232 (1962).

218. See section V.B.1. and the distinctions made by courts between a surety performing under its performance bond and paying under its payment bond.

219. Edward G. Gallagher, *Surety's Subrogation to Obligee's Right of Setoff,* 18 FORUM 73 (1982).

220. *Prairie State Nat. Bank v. United States*, 164 U.S. 227, 17 S. Ct. 142 (1896).

221. *Henningsen v. United States Fid. & Guar. Co.*, 208 U.S. 404, 28 S. Ct. 389 (1908).

222. *Transamerica Ins. Co. v. United States,* 989 F.2d 1188 (Fed. Cir. 1993); *In re Larbar Corp.*, 177 F.3d 439 (6th Cir. 1999); *District of Columbia v. Aetna Ins. Co.*, 462 A.2d 428 (D.C. App. 1983).

223. *United States v. Munsey Trust Company*, 332 U.S. 234, 67 S. Ct. 1599 (1947) ["A surety would rarely undertake to complete a job if it incurred the risk that by completing it might lose more than if it had allowed the government to proceed." 322 U.S. at 244.]

224. *United States Fidelity & Guaranty v. Housing Authority of Town of Berwick*, 557 F.2d 482, 483-85 (5th Cir. 1977).

225. *Merritt Commercial Sav. & Loan, Inc. v. Guinee*, 766 F.2d 850, 855 (4th Cir. 1985); *In re Yale Express System, Inc.*, 362 F.2d 111 (2nd Cir. 1966).

of setoff because the state statute which allowed unpaid subcontractors and suppliers to sue the obligee (the State of Ohio) only allowed such suit for the remaining contract funds due to the principal on each separate contract. The court rejected the surety's rights to apply excess contract funds from one job to setoff the surety's loss on another job because the obligee did not have the right under the statute to exercise such a setoff.[226] In another case, the surety sought to use its status as a performance bond surety on some contracts to obtain funds due to its principal on another contract in which the surety had only a payment bond loss. The competing claimants to the remaining contract funds were the surety and the government obligee, which was not a stakeholder but rather had its own claims as a taxing authority against the excess contract funds. The court found that the surety, as a payment bond surety, was not entitled to utilize its performance bond surety subrogation rights to require the obligee to setoff the remaining contract funds in favor of the surety and ahead of the obligee's own tax claims against the principal.[227]

In the bankruptcy area, a performance bond surety completing multiple projects for the same obligee at a loss is subrogated to the obligee's common law setoff rights on those other projects completed at a "profit."[228] However, another bankruptcy court found that the payment bond surety could not setoff profits created under a post-petition contract with the obligee against losses incurred under its payment bond on a pre-petition contract with the obligee, in part because the obligee had no such rights of setoff under the Bankruptcy Code.[229]

In summary, while some cases state that the surety's subrogation rights to the remaining contract funds are limited to the contract on which the surety's loss was incurred and do not give the surety rights in the excess contract funds from another contract,[230] other cases hold just the opposite.[231] The decision of the United States Court of Appeals for the Federal Circuit in *Transamerica*[232] has decided the issue as far as contracts with the United States government are concerned.

VI. *Jurisdiction of Equitable Subrogation Claims Against the Federal Government*

A. THE TUCKER ACT

The Tucker Act gives the Court of Federal Claims jurisdiction "to render judgment upon any claim against the United States founded either upon the Constitution, or any Act of Congress or any regulation of an executive department, or upon any express or implied contract with the United States, or for liquidated or unliquidated damages in cases not sounding in tort."[233]

While the Tucker Act is merely jurisdictional, and does not create any substantive rights, there are a legion of cases in which the federal courts have found that the Tucker Act provides a

226. *Western Casualty and Surety Company v. Brooks*, 362 F.2d 486 (4th Cir. 1966).

227. *Dependable Insurance Company, Inc. v. United States*, 846 F.2d 65, 67 (Fed. Cir. 1988).

228. *In re Larbar Corp.*, 177 F.3d 439 (6th Cir. 1999).

229. *RAM Construction Company, Inc. v. American States Insurance Company*, 749 F.2d 1049 (3rd Cir. 1984).

230. *Transamerica Ins. Co. v. Barnett Bank of Marion Co., N.A.*, 540 So.2d 113, 117 (Fla. 1989); *In re Eastern Marine*, 104 B.R. 421 (Bankr. N.D. Fla. 1989).

231. See footnotes 222, 224 and 225 of section V.C. above.

232. *Transamerica Ins. Co. v. United States*, 989 F.2d 1188 (Fed. Cir. 1993).

233. 28 U.S.C. § 1491(a)(1).

vehicle for the surety to assert its claims of equitable subrogation to the contract funds on federal government contracts.[234]

B. THE BLUE FOX DECISION

In the recent decision of *Dept. of Army v. Blue Fox, Inc.,*[235] the United States Supreme Court held that federal courts did not have jurisdiction over a claim by a subcontractor asserting an equitable lien on funds held by the Army. Federal government attorneys are now trying to stretch this opinion into an argument that the Tucker Act[236] does not give jurisdiction to the Court of Federal Claims over the surety's claim to the federal government construction contract funds based upon the surety's rights of equitable subrogation.

In *Blue Fox,* a subcontractor endeavored to assert an equitable lien on federal government contract funds, contending that the Administrative Procedure Act[237] waived immunity for equitable actions and that it could pursue a claim against the federal government for the contract funds. The Ninth Circuit, relying on several surety equitable subrogation cases, held that the federal courts had jurisdiction over a subcontractor's claims of an equitable lien on the contract funds held by the federal government. The Ninth Circuit cited *Prairie State Bank v. United States,*[238] *Henningsen v. United States Fidelity & Guaranty Co.,*[239] and *Pearlman v. Reliance Ins. Co.*[240] In reversing the Ninth Circuit, the Supreme Court held that there was no jurisdiction for the subcontractor's claims against the Department of Army.

Even though *Blue Fox* did not involve a surety and did not involve consideration of the Tucker Act's grant of jurisdiction for a surety's claim of equitable subrogation, federal government attorneys are now arguing that it stands for the proposition that federal government agencies have sovereign immunity from the surety's claim of equitable subrogation. They base this contention on the fact that the last paragraph of the *Blue Fox* decision states that none of the trilogy of older Supreme Court cases just cited involved a question of sovereign immunity.

In spite of the fact that *Blue Fox* was limited to the issue of whether district courts have jurisdiction over a subcontractor's claims for an equitable lien on contract funds held by the federal government, the question has arisen as to whether this somehow upsets the long standing recognition of jurisdiction in the Court of Federal Claims for actions brought by a surety seeking to enforce its right of equitable subrogation. In fact, there are many grounds upon which jurisdiction over the surety's right of equitable subrogation exists.

C. TUCKER ACT JURISDICTION OVER THE SURETY'S CLAIM OF EQUITABLE SUBROGATION

234. *Balboa Ins. Co. v. United States*, 775 F.2d 1158 (Fed. Cir. 1985); *Transamerica Ins. Co. v. United States*, 31 Fed. Cl. 532 (1994); *Transamerica Ins. Co. v. United States*, 31 Fed. Cl. 602 (1994); George J. Bachrach and Robert F. Carney, *The Surety and the United States Court of Federal Claims – Revisited* (unpublished paper submitted at the Tenth Annual Northeast Surety and Fidelity Claims Conference on October 21, 1999) updating George J. Bachrach and Robert F. Carney, *The Surety and the United States Court of Federal Claims* (unpublished paper submitted at the 1995 Surety Claims Institute annual meeting on June 22, 1995).

235. 525 U.S. 255, 119 S. Ct. 687, 142 L.Ed.2d 718 (1999)

236. 5 U.S.C. § 710

237. 5 U.S.C. § 710

238. 164 U.S. 227, 32 Ct. Cl. 614, 17 S. Ct. 142, 41 L. Ed. 412 (1896).

239. 208 U.S. 404, 28 S. Ct. 389, 52 L. Ed. 547 (1908).

240. 371 U.S. 132, 83 S.Ct. 232, 9 L.Ed.2d 190 (1962).

It is beyond the scope of this chapter to go into depth to describe the basis for the Court of Federal Claims' jurisdiction over cases involving the surety's right of equitable subrogation. The beginning point is obviously the long recognition of Tucker Act jurisdiction over these claims.[241] These cases and the ones they cite have held for a great many years that the United States can be sued by sureties on the theory of equitable subrogation.

The Tucker Act expressly grants jurisdiction over cases "upon any express or implied contract with the United States..."[242] There are several ways in which the surety is in contractual privity with the United States. The general contractor obviously is in privity with the United States and has the right to sue in the Court of Federal Claims on its contract. The surety fulfilling its obligations on its bonds is subrogated to the contractor's rights, and this of course includes being subrogated to the principal's rights on its contract with the government, putting the surety in privity with the government. As previously quoted from the Supreme Court's decision *in Pealman v. Reliance Ins. Co.*, the surety who performs is subrogated to all the rights available to enforce its rights of subrogation.[243]

Second, the surety has provided the federal government with its payment and performance bonds, and these bonds place it in privity of contract with the United Sates. The mere fact that the United States has not executed the bonds does not mean it is not in privity with the surety. The law recognizes a host of contractual relationships in which only one party signs the contract. Chief among these are promissory notes and deeds, signed by makers and grantors, respectively, and by no one else. One can hardly fathom an argument even being made that the payee on a promissory note or the guarantee of a deed is not in contractual privity with the maker or grantor.

Furthermore, there are many cases recognizing that suretyship is a three-party agreement, one by which the surety becomes liable for the principal's debt to the obligee, who is the third party to the agreement.[244] There are quite a number of cases and several treatises acknowledging that suretyship is a tri-parte relationship.[245]

Indeed, it has been recognized that as a result of this three party agreement, the surety is as much a party to a federal government contract as the contractor.[246] In addition, the Supreme Court has taken the view that terms of the contract are read into the bond,[247] thus again putting the surety in privity with the government.[248]

The Federal Court of Claims has jurisdiction under the Tucker Act over claims of third-party beneficiaries.[249] When the government entered into the general contract with the contractor, it obviously intended to pay the contract proceeds as consideration for completion of the construction project. The surety who fulfills obligations under its bonds is a beneficiary to the promise to pay the contract price. When the surety's role is analyzed under the rules set out in the

241. See, for example, those cases and articles cited *supra* note 234, such as *Balboa Ins. Co. v. United States*, 775 F.2d 1158 (Fed. Cir. 1985).

242. 28 U.S.C. § 1491.

243. 28 U.S.C. § 1491.

244. *Balboa Ins. Co. v. United States*, 775 F.2d 1158, 1160 (Fed. Cir. 1985) (citing *United States v. United States Fidelity & Guaranty Co.*, 236 U.S. 512, 35 S.Ct. 289, 59 L. Ed. 696 (1915)).

245. *Hanover Ins. Co. v. United States*, 279 F. Supp. 851 (S.D. N.Y. 1967) (citing Stearnes, LAW OF SURETYSHIP, (4th Ed. 1934), Sec. 5.).

246. *Federal Ins. Co. v. United States*, 29 Fed Cl. 302 (1993).

247. *Martin v. Nat'l. Surety Co.*, 300 U.S. 588, 57 S.Ct. 531 (1937).

248. There are, however, cases which, without any real analysis, suggest that at least for purposes of the Contract Disputes Act, 41 U.S.C. § 601 *et seq.*, there is no privity between the surety and the government. *Westech Corp. v. United States*, 20 Cl. Ct. 475 (1990); *Universal Surety Co. v. United States*, 10 Cl. Ct. 794 (1986).

249. *Chin v. U. S.*, 890 F.2d 1143 (Fed. Cir. 1989).

Restatement (Second) of Contracts[250] one sees that the surety is a third-party beneficiary to the general contract. In the context of Miller Act bonds, the promise of the government to pay money certainly is intended to benefit the surety in the event of a default and the surety's performance of its duties – those duties which were the principal's responsibility under the general contract.

Finally, it should be noted that the Tucker Act includes a grant of jurisdiction for claims arising under a federal statute. The surety's bond to the United States is of course provided under the Miller Act.[251] Although the Miller Act does not expressly set out a cause of action by the United States on a performance bond in the detail that it does for actions on a payment bond, it clearly puts in place relationships which impose duties and rights between the parties. When the Miller Act mandates a performance bond for the protection of the United States,[252] obviously the United States has a Miller Act cause of action in the event of a breach. The federal government's relation with the surety arises out of the Miller Act, and the inception of any claim by the federal government against the performance bond is under the Miller Act. The Miller Act creates the relationship, and claims both by and against the federal government are rightly stated to be under the Miller Act. The Miller Act, which creates the relationship in the first place, is the beginning point of the surety's right of equitable subrogation.

In the final analysis, *Blue Fox* does not say what some federal government attorneys hope it does. It does not hold that the federal courts have no jurisdiction over the surety's claim of equitable subrogation. As this chapter is going to publication, the jurisdictional issue is being presented to the Federal Circuit Court of Appeals, and, hopefully, this question will be answered with a sharp and succinct "yes," the Tucker Act does indeed provide a jurisdictional basis in the Court of Federal Claims for the surety's claim of equitable subrogation to the contract funds on federal government contracts.

250. Restatement (Second) of Contracts, § 302.
251. 40 U.S.C. § 270a.
252. 40 U.S.C. § 270a(a).

SELECTED BIBLIOGRAPHY - SUBROGATION

BOOKS

SALVAGE BY THE SURETY (George J. Bachrach ed., 1998)

RESTATEMENT (THIRD) OF SURETYSHIP AND GUARANTY (1995)

THE SUBROGATION DATABASE: CASES CONCERNING THE SUBROGATION RIGHTS OF THE CONTRACT BOND SURETY (George J. Bachrach ed., 1995)

SUBROGATION RIGHTS OF THE CONTRACT BOND SURETY (George J. Bachrach ed., 1990)
- Mungall, Daniel, Jr., *The Subrogation Rights of the Contract Bond Surety – Some Basics*
- Dolan, William M., III, *The Contractor's Default as a Condition Precedent to the Contract Bond Surety's Right of Subrogation ("Out of the Darkness and Into the Light")*
- Slaughter, David W., *The Contract Bond Surety's Performance as a Condition Precedent to its Rights of Subrogation ("Beyond a Twiddling of Thumbs")*
- Klinger, Marilyn, *The Surety's Notice: What Does it Say and Does it Work?*
- Reinert, Bernard A., *Elements of Proof in the Contract Bond Surety's Subrogation Action to Recover the Bonded Contract Funds*

ARTICLES AND PAPERS

Andrew, Martin J., *Surety Recovery from the Architect or Engineer - Why Not*? 8 FORUM 570 (1973)

Bachrach, George J. and Rodgers-Waire, Cynthia E., *The Surety's Rights to the Contract Funds in the Principal's Chapter 11 Bankruptcy Case,* 35 TORT & INS. L. J. (1999).

Bachrach, George J. and Carney, Robert F., *The Surety and the United States Court of Federal Claims -- Revisited* (unpublished paper submitted at the Tenth Annual Northeast Surety and Fidelity Claims Conference on October 21, 1999)

Bachrach, George J., *The Surety's Rights to Obtain Salvage – Exoneration, Reimbursement, Subrogation and Contribution, in* SALVAGE BY THE SURETY (George J. Bachrach ed., 1998)

Bachrach, George J. and Carney, Robert F., *The Surety and the United States Court of Federal Claims* (unpublished paper submitted at the 1995 Surety Claims Institute annual meeting on June 22, 1995)

Bachrach, George J. and Burch, John V., *The Surety's Subrogation Rights, in* THE LAW OF SURETYSHIP (Edward G. Gallagher ed., 1993)

Carney, Robert F., *Reimbursement and Subrogation Rights Under the Bankruptcy Code and the Surety's Proof of Claim* (unpublished paper submitted at the Seventh Annual Northeast Surety and Fidelity Claims Conference on October 24, 1996)

Carney, Robert F., *Subrogation Rights of the Surety Against its Principal's Insurer: Could the Principal Possibly Have a Deep Pocket*? (unpublished paper submitted at the Sixth Annual Northeast Surety and Fidelity Claims Conference on November 16, 1995)

Castro-Amy, Francisco, *The Contest for Contract Retainage Between the Surety and Suppliers Without Recourse Under the Bond*, 16 FORUM 1073 (1981)

Chapman, Michael L., *The Liability of Design Professionals to the Surety,* 20 FORUM 591 (1985)

Dolan, William M., III, *The Contractor's Default as a Condition Precedent to the Contract Bond Surety's Right of Subrogation ("Out of the Darkness and Into the Light"), in* SUBROGATION RIGHTS OF THE CONTRACT BOND SURETY (George J. Bachrach ed., 1990)

Elkins, S. Gordon, *Rights of Subcontractors, Laborers and Materialmen to Contract Balances* 18 FORUM 695 (1983)

Ferrucci, James D. and Baron, Scott D., *The Surety's Claims Against Third Parties, in* SALVAGE BY THE SURETY (George J. Bachrach ed., 1998)

Franks, J. Michael and Evans, Michael E., *A Defense of Established Landmarks: Claims of Construction Sureties to Contract Funds Under Chapter 11,* 25 TORT & INS. L. J. 28 (1989)

Gallagher, Edward Graham, *Entitlement to Contract Proceeds, in* THE LAW OF PERFORMANCE BONDS (Lawrence R. Moelmann and John T. Harris eds., 2000)

Gallagher, Edward Graham, *Entitlement to Contract Proceeds, in* THE LAW OF PAYMENT BONDS (Kevin L. Lybeck and H. Bruce Shreves eds., 1998)

Gallagher, Edward Graham, *Unpaid Subcontractor's or Supplier's Right to Payment Out of Contract Funds,* 10 THE CONSTR. LAW. 9 (1990)

Gallagher, Edward Graham, *Surety's Subrogation to Obligee's Right of Setoff,* 18 FORUM 73 (1982)

Haug, William F., *Bankruptcy 1984 v. the Surety's Right to Contract Proceeds,* 20 FORUM 725 (1985)

Hollabaugh, Lewis B., *Surety's Right to Equitable Subrogation: Overture for an Arrow,* 51 INS. COUNS. J. 547 (1984)

Horowitz, Matthew M., *Evaluating Priority Disputes Between a Surety and the Internal Revenue Service* (unpublished paper submitted at the ABA annual meeting on August 8, 1995)

Joseph, Jerome M., *Sureties' Claims for Negligence Against Accountants, Design Professionals and Lenders,* 24 THE BRIEF 16 (No. 2, 1995)

King, Bruce C., *Claims by Surety Against Architect-Engineer* (unpublished paper submitted at the Forum on the Construction Industry and the ABA/TIPS Fidelity and Surety Law Committee joint program on January 22, 1987)

Klinger, Marilyn, *The Surety's Notice: What Does it Say and Does it Work?, in* SUBROGATION RIGHTS OF THE CONTRACT BOND SURETY (George J. Bachrach ed., 1990)

Lerner, Lawrence and Witten, Keith, *Salvage/Subrogation Considerations, in* BOND DEFAULT MANUAL (Duncan L. Clore ed., 2d ed. 1995)

McNaughton, Kim, Jetton, Mary Paty Lynn and Franks, J. Michael, *Surety's Rights to Contract Funds Under Trust Fund Provisions in Indemnity Agreements and Trust Fund Statutes* (unpublished paper submitted at the 1999 Surety Claims Institute annual meeting on June 24-26, 1999)

Morris, John W., *The Labor Department Versus the Subrogated Surety, Who Wins?* (unpublished paper submitted at the 1999 National Bond Claims Association annual meeting on September 30, 1999)

Mungall, Daniel, Jr., *The Subrogation Rights of the Contract Bond Surety – Some Basics, in* SUBROGATION RIGHTS OF THE CONTRACT BOND SURETY (George J. Bachrach ed., 1990)

Mungall, Daniel, Jr., *The Subrogation Rights of the Contract Bond Surety - A Primer* (unpublished paper submitted at the ABA/TIPS Fidelity and Surety Law Committee annual midwinter meeting on January 31, 1986)

Mungall, Daniel, Jr., *The Buffeting of the Subrogation Rights of the Construction Contract Bond Surety by US v. Munsey Trust Co.,* 46 INS. COUNS. J. 607 (1979)

O'Connor, Patrick J., Jr., *The Surety's Rights of Restitution and Subrogation – Set-off Principles, in* THE IMPLICATIONS OF THE NEW RESTATEMENT OF THE LAW THIRD, SURETYSHIP AND GUARANTY, ON SURETY BONDS AND INDEMNITY AGREEMENTS (unpublished paper submitted at the ABA/TIPS Fidelity and Surety Law Committee program in Chicago, Il on April 18, 1996)

Palladino, Anthony N. and Clarke, Anna P., *The Recognition of Sureties' Rights Under Government Contracts,* 25 TORT & INS. L. J. 637 (1990)

Poteet, Sam. H., Jr., and Franks, J. Michael, *Entitlement to Contract Funds Among Completing Surety, Lender, Contractor and the Internal Revenue Service,* 9 THE CONSTR. LAW. 11 (1989)

Preaus, Eugene R. and Hootsell, S. Ault, III, *Bankruptcy Principal: Defining the Construction Surety's Interest in Contract Balances* (unpublished paper submitted at the 1990 Surety Claims Institute annual meeting on June 21, 1990)

Reinert, Bernard A., *Elements of Proof in the Contract Bond Surety's Subrogation Action to Recover the Bonded Contract Funds, in* SUBROGATION RIGHTS OF THE CONTRACT BOND SURETY (George J. Bachrach ed., 1990)

Ruck, Andrew J. and Bevan, John S., *Is the Surety's Right to Contract Balances Absolute?,* 56 DEF. COUNS. J. 306 (1989)

Ruprecht, G. Steven, *Surety's Rights and Remedies Against Principals and Against Indemnitors Under the General Indemnity Agreement, in* THE LAW OF PERFORMANCE BONDS (Lawrence R. Moelmann and John T. Harris eds., 2000)

Schexnayder, Chad L., *Bankruptcy, in* THE LAW OF PERFORMANCE BONDS (Lawrence R. Moelmann and John T. Harris eds., 2000)

Slaughter, David W., *The Contract Bond Surety's Performance as a Condition Precedent to its Rights of Subrogation ("Beyond a Twiddling of Thumbs"),in* SUBROGATION RIGHTS OF THE CONTRACT BOND SURETY (George J. Bachrach ed., 1990)

Smith, Richard W. and Covalt, Victor, E., III, *Should the Surety Stand on its Equitable Subrogation Rights or File its Indemnity Agreement Under the Uniform Commercial Code?* 69 NEB. L. REV. 664 (1990)

Wallach, Henry James, *The Owner's Right of Setoff and the Surety's Right of Subrogation to the Contract Balance: Who Gets What, When and Why* (unpublished paper submitted at the 1997 National Bond Claims Association annual meeting on September 26, 1997)

Weissman, Darryl and Baron, Scott D., *The Surety's Priority Battle With State Labor Departments Over Unpaid Contract Funds – Whatever Happened to Subrogation?* (unpublished paper submitted at the Ninth Annual Northeast Surety & Fidelity Claims Conference on October 22, 1998)

1252764v3

24

Exoneration and Quia Timet

Jay M. Mann

I. *Introduction*

This writing is an update of the author's writing which appeared as Chapter 28 in the first edition of the Law of Suretyship,[1] and a compilation of prior writings by the author on the topics of exoneration and *quia timet*.[2] The author has also borrowed citations and ideas liberally from other well-written articles regarding enforcement of the surety's collateral rights.[3]

According to Black's Law Dictionary, *"quia timet"* is a Latin phrase meaning "because he fears or apprehends."[4] In fact, *quia timet* is the technical name of an equitable remedy which can be extremely valuable to the surety practitioner. Although bills *quia timet* date back to ancient Common Law, until the 1990s their modern applications were not generally known or sufficiently used by the surety industry.

Quia timet has long been the subject of discussion by legal scholars.[5] From the modern surety's prospective, the landmark writing was a comprehensive study of *quia timet* prepared by Walter W. Downs, entitled *Quia Timet as a Preventor of Anticipated Mischief*, and presented to the 1956 Annual Convention of the American Bar Association.[6] But as recently as 1982, two separate articles were published in which the authors (Charles A. Meeker and John R. Baylor) bemoaned the rare use of *quia timet* by the surety industry.[7]

The decade of the 1990s witnessed a resurgence of exoneration and *quia timet* actions by the surety industry. The author believes this is primarily due to the special attention given to this area of surety law by the Second Circuit Court of Appeals in numerous reported cases,[8]

---

1. Gallagher, ed., *The Law of Suretyship* (1st ed. 1993). The author gratefully acknowledges the assistance of his associate, Gretchen B. Friedlander, in the preparation of this updated article.

2. Mann & Jennings, *Quia Timet: A Remedy for the Fearful Surety*, 20 Forum 685 (1985); Mann, *Enforcing the Surety's Rights Prior to Actual Payment of Claims*, in Moelmann, ed., *The Pursuit of Subrogation and Indemnity Claims* (Defense Research Institute 1991).

3. *See, e.g.*, Getz, *Collateral: What to Take, How to Take It, and What to Do With It Once You Have It* (Amer. Bar Assoc. 1999); Slaughter, *The Preliminary Injunction As a Tool for Preserving and Enforcing the Surety's Rights: Does It Work? (Dealing With the Sometimes Short Arm of the Law)* (Western States Surety Conference 1994); Franks, *Specific Performance of the Indemnity Agreement*, 12 Construction Lawyer 1 (April, 1992); Solan, *The General Indemnity Agreement Revisited – Traps for the Unwary in Obtaining Attorneys' Fees and Collateral Security*, 27 Tort & Ins. L. J. 127 (1991).

4. Black's Law Dictionary, 1122 (5th ed. 1979).

5. Story, Commentary on Equity Jurisprudence, Vol. 2, § 825; Snell's Principles of Equity, 27th ed., p. 454; McClintock on Equity, 2d ed., § 191, Clark, Principles of Equity, §§ 405-422.

6. 1956 Amer. Bar. Assoc., Section of Insurance, Negligence and Compensation Law Proceedings 173.

7. For a discussion of these two articles, *see* Franks, *supra* note 3 at 6.

8. *See, e.g.*, American Motorists Ins. Co. v. United Furnace Co., 876 F.2d 293 (2d Cir. 1989); Abish v. Northwestern Nat. Ins. Co., 924 F.2d 448 (2d Cir. 1991); Borey v. National Union Fire Ins. Co., 934 F.2d 30 (2d Cir. 1991).

this area of surety law by the Second Circuit Court of Appeals in numerous reported cases,[8] discussed below, and to the articulate opinion of the California Court of Appeals in a widely reported case known as *Escrow Agents' Fid. v. Superior Court (Abelman).*[9] With New York and California squarely on the *quia timet* bandwagon, the rest of the country will certainly follow this trend.

Also, it is very significant that the Restatement of the Law (Third) of Suretyship and Guaranty explicitly recognizes the surety's exoneration and *quia timet* remedies. Section 21 of the Restatement reads, in pertinent part, as follows:

> § 21. Principal Obligor's Duty of Performance
>
> (1) If the principal obligor is charged with notice of the secondary obligation (§ 20), the principal obligor has the duty to the second obligor
>
> (a) to perform the underlying obligation to the extent that failure to do so would leave the secondary obligor liable for performance that would entitle the secondary obligor to reimbursement by the principal obligor, and
>
> (b) to refrain from conduct that impairs the expectation of the secondary obligor that the principal obligor will honor its duty of performance.
>
> *(2) Upon breach by the principal obligor of a duty set forth in subsection (1), the secondary obligor is entitled to relief that will properly protect its rights with respect to the principal obligor's duty of performance.*[10]

Comments (i), (j) and (k) to Section 21(2) above specifically approve of exoneration and *quia timet* relief for the surety under appropriate circumstances ("Among the courses open to a court are to direct performance by the principal obligor, to require that a sum due the obligee by the principal obligor be paid into court for the obligee, or to require that the principal give the secondary obligor adequate security for its ultimate reimbursement." [11]).

II. *Historical Background*

A bill *quia timet* is a bill in equity to protect a party against the occurrence of some future injury which he fears he may suffer, and which he cannot avoid by a present action at law. It is a remedy of particular importance to the surety of a construction contractor because it may be utilized, under appropriate circumstances, prior to the time that the surety's liability has become fixed. *Quia timet* is not, however, restricted to use by sureties. For example, *quia timet*

---

8. *See, e.g.*, American Motorists Ins. Co. v. United Furnace Co., 876 F.2d 293 (2d Cir. 1989); Abish v. Northwestern Nat. Ins. Co., 924 F.2d 448 (2d Cir. 1991); Borey v. National Union Fire Ins. Co., 934 F.2d 30 (2d Cir. 1991).

9. 4 Cal.App.4th 491, 5 Cal.Rptr.2d 698 (Cal. App. 1992). California treatises which have cited Escrow Agents include Rutter, *California Practice Guide, Chapter 4-D* (1998) and 3 Witkin, *California Procedure*, Chapter IV (1996). *See also* 15A Am. Jur. 2d, *Common Law*, § 9 and 27A Am. Jur. 2d, *Equity*, § 93.

10. American Law Institute, Restatement of the Law (Third) of Suretyship and Guaranty § 21 (1995) (emphasis added). In the arcane language of the Restatement, the bond principal is referred to as the "principal obligor," the surety is referred to as the "secondary obligor" and the surety's obligation is referred to as the "secondary obligation."

11. *Id.*, Comment K thereto.

may properly be used to seek cancellation of a negotiable instrument which is voidable while in the hands of a present holder, but which may be enforced against the maker if it is transferred to a bona fide purchaser for value.[12]

Quia timet was originally enforced as a writ of prevention. There were six writs at ancient Common Law (all of which are now obsolete) that could be maintained *quia timet* before "molestation, distress or impleading." These were called *Brevia Anticipantia* – anticipatory relief to accomplish the ends of precautionary justice. The common thread underlying these six ancient writs was that *quia timet* should be applied so as to prevent wrongs or anticipated mischiefs, and not merely to redress wrongs after they were done."[13]

Many courts have taken the Latin phrase literally and applied bills *quia timet* in unexpected "fearful" contexts. These include the following:

(1) Suit to determine plaintiff's status as the wife of defendant;[14]
(2) Suit by wife to declare that Mexican divorce decree was invalid;[15]
(3) Suit for cancellation of execution upon judgment;[16]
(4) Suit to determine title to shares of stock;[17]
(5) Suit to determine liability insurer's duty to defend;[18]
(6) Suit to remove cloud on title;[19]
(7) Suit to establish easement upon real property;[20]
(8) Suit to quiet title to vessel;[21]
(9) Suit by property owner to determine that he had never been the owner of a supper club and therefore not liable for cabaret taxes;[22]
(10) Suit to determine patent infringement;[23]
(11) Suit to perpetuate testimony of severely injured person in action thereafter commenced;[24]
(12) Suit to set aside antenuptial agreement due to fraud and misrepresentation.[25]

These cases are representative of the many factual situations to which *quia timet* may be applicable. All of these cases involved an absence of actual present injury, a reasonable apprehension of future injury, and danger that irreparable harm would result if the relief prayed for was not granted. The combination of these essential elements made *quia timet* appropriate relief under the disparate factual circumstances of the above cases.

III. *Surety's Use of Exoneration and Quia Timet Remedies*

12. McClintock on Equity, 2d ed., § 191.
13. Story, Commentary on Equity Jurisprudence, Vol. 2, § 825.
14. Untermann v. Untermann, 19 N.J. 507, 117 A.2d 599 (1955).
15. Spindel v. Spindel, 283 F.Supp. 797 (E.D. N.Y. 1968).
16. Lenett v. Lutz, 215 Ga. 369, 110 S.E.2d 628 (1959).
17. Newman Mach. Co. v. Newman, 275 N.C. 189, 166 S.E.2d 63 (1969).
18. Porter v. Alabama Farm Bureau Mut. Cas. Ins. Co., 279 Ala. 499, 187 So.2d 254 (1966).
19. Roberts v. Cootrell, 559 S.W.2d 795 (Tenn. App. 1977).
20. Burdess v. United States, 553 F.Supp. 646 (D. Ark. 1982).
21. Kawa Leasing, Ltd. v. Yacht Sequoia, 544 F.Supp. 1050 (D. Md. 1982).
22. Floyd v. United States, 241 F.Supp. 996 (D. S.C. 1965), *aff'd*, 361 F.2d 312.
23. Broadview Chemical Corp. v. Loctite Corp., 474 F.2d 1391 (2d Cir. 1973).
24. Mosseller v. United States, 158 F.2d 380 (2d Cir. 1946).
25. Nathan v. Nathan, 166 Mass. 294, 44 N.E. 221 (1896).

It has been said that "no principle in equity is more familiar or more firmly established than that a surety, after the debt for which he is liable has become due, without paying or even being called on to pay a debt, may file a bill in equity in the nature of a bill *quia timet* to compel the principal to exonerate him by its payment, provided no rights of creditors are prejudiced thereby."[26] This oft-repeated statement demonstrates the importance of *quia timet* in surety law. Nevertheless, the courts and legal scholars have frequently confused exoneration and *quia timet* remedies of the surety. An understanding of the distinction between exoneration and *quia timet* is essential to proper representation of the surety.

Exoneration is an equitable remedy available only to a surety. The general definition of exoneration is "the removal of a burden, charge or duty-particularly the act of relieving a person or estate from a charge or liability by casting the same upon another person or estate."[27] In the context of a bonded construction contractor, exoneration is the surety's right to require that contract proceeds be used to pay contract obligations of its principal which, if unpaid, shall become the obligation of the surety. Also, exoneration includes the surety's right to require its principal to use his own funds to discharge the primary obligation for payment, even in the absence of the surety having made any payment itself in discharge of its secondary bond obligation.[28] The goal of exoneration is to compel the principal, after the debt has matured, to honor his debt and thereby discharge the surety's obligation.[29] To invoke the exoneration remedy, a surety must demonstrate that the liability is absolute and that the liability ultimately rests with the principal.[30]

Quia timet is much broader than exoneration. As stated above, the term *quia timet is* a Latin term meaning "because he fears or apprehends." A surety may seek *quia timet* relief when it has reasonable grounds for fearing that its rights are being jeopardized in a potential loss situation, particularly in the diversion of contract proceeds from bonded contract obligations or in the principal's failure to post collateral for probable bond liability. A *quia timet* suit by the surety is anticipatory and preventive, before the obligation to the obligee has become enforceable. A surety is under no obligation to file a *quia timet* suit, although the failure to promptly do so at the time of anticipated liability may result in substantially increased losses at a later date.

Thus, *quia timet* is more readily available to the surety than exoneration because *quia timet* may arise before the surety's obligation has matured.[31] *Quia timet* is also a more flexible remedy – it can be tailored to fit the particular circumstances facing the surety.[32] The importance of *quia timet* to the surety was best expressed by Downs in his 1956 presentation to the American Bar Association:

---

26. Fireman's Fund Ins. Co. v. S.E.K. Construction Co., 436 F.2d 1345, 1349 (10th Cir. 1971) (*quoting* 50 Am. Jur., *Suretyship*, § 225).

27. Black's Law Dictionary, 516 (5th ed. 1979).

28. Downs, *A Surety's Basic Rights and Remedies*, 15 Def. L. J. 139, 165-176 (1966).

29. Restatement of the Law (Third) of Suretyship and Guaranty § 21, *supra* note 10; Filner v. Shapiro, 633 F.2d 139 (2d Cir. 1980).

30. Admiral Oriental Line v. United States, 86 F.2d 201, 204 (2d Cir. 1936); Borey v. National Union Fire Ins. Co., 934 F.2d 30, 33 (2d Cir. 1991).

31. *See, e.g.*, Morley Const. v. Maryland Casualty Co., 90 F.2d 976 (8th Cir. 1937) (surety was denied exoneration but granted *quia timet* relief).

32. *See, e.g.*, Fidelity & Deposit Co. of Maryland v. McClintic-Marshall Corp., 115 N.J. Eq. 470,171 A. 382 (N.J. Ch. 1934), *aff'd*, 176 A. 341 (N.J. 1935) (the court appointed a receiver, established a joint control account and issued an injunction to prevent the diversion of bonded contract funds and directed the posting of collateral security for anticipated bond losses).

> The surety need no longer wait until it has paid claims and is subrogated or to wait until the "obligation has become due" in order to obtain exoneration, or to be limited to the security of the retained percentage before it has a right to protect itself against a diversion of the contract price by the contractor to purposes other than paying his contract creditors.
>
> From the inception of its obligation to the complete discharge of its obligation the surety now has a right to control the entire price through *quia timet,* including all additional compensation awarded the contractor in connection therewith, whenever it has reasonable cause to be apprehensive about the contractor's use of that money at the expense of the surety or his laborers and materialmen.[33]

This writing will explore how sureties, particularly sureties for construction contractors, may use exoneration and *quia timet* relief to prevent the diversion of contract funds and to require the posting of collateral to cover anticipated bond losses.[34] The author does not, however, intend to imply that these are the only kinds of relief that may be obtained by sureties in exoneration and *quia timet* actions. It is submitted that these equitable remedies may in future cases be used in a variety of other situations, depending upon the resourcefulness of surety practitioners and their ability to persuade courts of the sureties' need for equitable relief in particular "fearful" situations.

IV. *Preventing the Diversion of Bonded Contract Funds*

A. Legal Requirements to Protect Contract Funds

Upon the principal contractor's default of the bonded construction contract (including default in obligations to laborers and materialmen), the surety is entitled to have contract proceeds applied to contract obligations. Alternatively, the surety is entitled to be reimbursed from contract proceeds to the extent of payments made in discharge of bond obligations. In the early stages of a claim matter, the practical problem facing the surety is how to preserve the contract funds until its obligations are dearly defined.

The United States Supreme Court first recognized the surety's subrogation rights to bonded contract funds in the 1896 case known as *Prairie State Nat'l Bank of Chicago v. United States.*[35] The surety's rights were confirmed twelve years later by the Supreme Court in *Henningsen v. United States Fidelity & Guar. Company.*[36] The *Prairie State* and *Henningsen* cases were decided at the time of the Heard Act,[37] the predecessor of the Miller Act.[38] Any doubts as to the continuing validity of the surety's rights in unpaid contract proceeds under the Miller Act were resolved in the 1962 United States Supreme Court case of *Pearlman v. Reliance Insurance Company.*[39] In this contest between the surety (who had paid claims

33. Downs, *supra* note 6 at 183-184.

34. Actions to enforce collateral deposit clauses of indemnity agreements are frequently referred to as "specific performance" suits, rather than "*quia timet*" suits, in part to avoid the stigma of using an "antiquated" Common Law remedy in modern litigation.

35. 164 U.S. 227, 17 S.Ct. 142, 41 L.Ed. 412 (1896).

36. 208 U.S. 404, 28 S.Ct. 389, 52 L.Ed. 547 (1908).

37. 40 U.S.C. § 270 (repealed).

38. 40 U.S.C. § 270a *et seq.*

39. 371 U.S. 132, 83 S.Ct. 232, 9 L.Ed.2d 190 (1962).

pursuant to its Miller Act payment bond obligations) and the trustee for the bankrupt contractor, the Supreme Court ruled that the surety was entitled to the contract balances. Mr. Justice Black, writing for the majority, stated:

> We therefore hold in accord with the established legal principles stated above that the Government had a right to use the retained fund to pay laborers and materialmen; that the laborers and materialmen had a right to be paid out of the fund; that the contractor, had he completed his job and paid his laborers and materialmen, would have become entitled to the fund; *and that the surety having paid the laborers and materialmen, is entitled to the benefit of all these rights to the extent necessary to reimburse it.* Consequently, since the surety in this case has paid out more than the amount of the existing fund, it has a right to all of it.[40]

The right to have contract funds applied to contract obligations is meaningless unless the surety may take protective actions to prevent dissipation of the funds. Before actually making any bond payments, the surety does not technically have subrogation rights in the contract proceeds. If, however, it has a reasonable basis for fearing dissipation, the surety may bring a *quia timet* suit to compel exoneration by the principal contractor.

Cases which have granted *quia timet* relief to prevent the diversion of bonded contract proceeds include *Morley Constr. Co. v. Maryland Casualty Co.*[41] (contractor's insolvency provided the surety with a reasonable apprehension of diversion), *National Surety Corp. v. Barth*[42] (right of surety to have contract funds paid to payment bond claimants was held superior to right of contractor to such funds, and superior to right of United States to which contractor owed income taxes), *Western Casualty and Surety Co. v. Biggs*[43] (court seized contract funds due to contractor who had failed to pay subcontractors at the bonded project), and *Lambert v. Maryland Casualty Co.*[44] (surety of an insolvent contractor entitled to take action to "freeze" contract funds for subsequent payment of bond claims).

Frequently, *quia timet* requests are not readily accepted by judges who are unfamiliar with this doctrine of law. For example, in *Escrow Agents Fid. v. Superior Court (Abelman),*[45] the continuing viability of *quia timet* was questioned by a California trial court. Indeed, that court denied *quia timet* relief to the surety and ruled that *quia timet* is "a concept that pre-dates movable type, and has virtually no application in modern society."[46] The Court of Appeals strongly disagreed with the trial court's analysis and its reported opinion affirmed the modern case of *quia timet,* as follows:

> Although a surety may file an action at law to compel its principal to perform the obligation on a bond when due (Civ. Code, § 2846), the fact that it may eventually obtain a judgment against the principal is of little comfort to the surety if, in the interim, the principal has absconded with the very funds which could have been used to satisfy the bond. Quia timet allows the surety to prevent the principal from dissipating those funds if the surety knows it will be called upon to "pay the debt or perform the obligation" on the bond, suspects that the principal has some or all of the necessary funds to do so, and fears that the principal may abscond with those funds.[47]

---

40. *Id.* at 141, 83 S.Ct. at 237, 9 L.Ed.2d at 196. (Emphasis added.)
41. 90 F.2d 976 (8th Cir. 1937).
42. 20 N.J. Super. 100, 89 A.2d 104, *aff'd*, 11 N.J. 506, 95 A.2d 145 (N.J. 1953).
43. 217 F.2d 163 (7th Cir. 1954).
44. 403 So.2d 739 (La. App. 1982), *aff'd*, 418 So.2d 553 (La. 1982).
45. 4 Cal. App. 4th 491, 5 Cal. Rptr. 2d 698 (Cal. App. 1992).
46. 5 Cal. Rptr. 2d at 701.
47. *Id.*

Morley Constr. Co. v. Maryland Casualty Co.[48] is another case in which *quia timet* relief was originally denied but later granted following an appeal. In *Morley,* the Eighth Circuit originally ruled that the surety of an insolvent contractor was not entitled to exoneration because its bond liability had not matured. After reversal and remand by the Supreme Court, the Eighth Circuit then decided that the surety had made out a valid claim for *quia timet* relief. Although the record failed to disclose any indication that the contractor intended to voluntarily divert contract funds, the court ruled in the latter opinion that the contractor's insolvency provided the surety with a reasonable apprehension of diversion.

The remedy of *quia timet is* not unlimited, as shown by the Tenth Circuit's opinion in *Fireman's Fund Ins. Co. v. S.E.K. Constr. Co.*[49] This case involved a dispute between a surety and a contractor's assignee-bank to a progress payment owed on a bonded highway project. The contractor had admitted to the surety that it owed $140,000 in outstanding bills, many of which were past due, but maintained that it was not insolvent because credit arrangements had been made with its creditors. No claims had been made against bonds issued by the surety, and the contractor was not in default in its work at the bonded project. The court ruled that the surety should not have instructed the State Highway Department to withhold the progress payment which the contractor intended to endorse to the assignee-bank. The court's reasoning for refusing the surety's *quia timet* request was that the surety's rights to exoneration and subrogation could not be asserted unless and until a default by the contractor occurred; only when the contractor was in default under the bonded contract, according to the court, would the surety prevail over the contractor and the contractor's bank. The *Morley* case was distinguished as follows:

> The Morley case applied the identical rules we have heretofore set out, and reached the decision that a bill in the nature of *quia timet* permitted the surety's exoneration, only because of facts which do not exist in the instant suit. First, the construction company was insolvent when the bill of complaint was filed. Second, the creditors were demanding payment on past due bills. Third, an agreement had been entered into between surety and principal whereby the former loaned the latter large sums of money to keep the company operational, in exchange for which the principal agreed to first apply the construction contract proceeds to bills for labor and materials furnished.[50]

The *S.E.K. Construction* case illustrates the danger of a surety seeking to enforce its *quia timet* and exoneration rights without a sufficient showing of probable bond liability. While the *S.E.K. Construction* decision may be criticized for taking an overly restrictive view of when a contractor is in default, nevertheless the surety should definitely have waited to file suit until it had a better factual foundation upon which to seek relief.

B. PROCEDURAL CONSIDERATIONS

The common law right of a surety to control contract funds of its principal was first confirmed by the United States Supreme Court in *Martin v. National Surety Co.*[51] *Quia timet*

48. 90 F.2d 976 (8th Cir. 1937).
49. 436 F.2d 1345 (10th Cir. 1971).
50. *Id.* at 1349.
51. 300 U.S. 588, 575 S.Ct. 531, 81 L.Ed. 822 (1937).

relief, in the form of an injunction, was granted to prevent the diversion of contract proceeds before paying claims of laborers and materialmen. Actually, the court based its injunctive relief on two grounds. One, an assignment in the indemnity agreement with the surety, effective upon default by the contractor, to the extent needed to pay bond claimants. Two, under common law, the failure to pay laborers and materialmen was a sufficient default to require the contractor to turn over payments to the surety upon appropriate demand. The progress payments were deposited with the court for the benefit of unpaid laborers and materialmen.

The *Martin* decision required the deposit of contract funds into court for distribution to bond claimants, with the surplus (if any) distributed to the principal contractor, contractor's assignee-bank and others according to an established priority formula. Other courts have followed this approach, including *Fidelity & Deposit Co. of Maryland v. McClintic-Marshall Corp.*[52] and *Glades County, Florida v. Detroit Fidelity & Surety Co.*[53] These cases resemble interpleader suits in which the surety's superior right to the contested fund is recognized by the court.

The problem with this procedure is that it is too cumbersome for an ongoing construction project. Dynamics of keeping laborers and material suppliers paid and the work going forward according to schedule do not permit the time-consuming deliberation often required by the judicial process. It is suggested that a better approach is to establish a joint control trust account to which progress payments are deposited and, after verification by the surety, from which project bills are paid.

Court approval for establishment of a joint control trust account will be needed unless the principal will agree to share control of project receipts and payments with the surety. Even if the principal will so agree, court approval must be obtained if the principal is a debtor-in-possession in a pending Chapter 11 bankruptcy proceeding.[54]

Included in Appendix A to this chapter is a form trust account agreement, which is adapted from an actual agreement approved by a bankruptcy court for completion of a project by a debtor-in-possession principal. When this trust agreement was executed, the principal was behind in payments to project creditors, but the surety had not yet paid any claims and the extent of its bond obligations were not known. Court approval was obtained for the trust agreement on the basis of the surety's reasonable fear of bond losses, under the doctrine of *quia timet,* unless project funds were strictly applied to project expenses incurred by the debtor in the course of its bonded contract.

If the principal cannot or will not agree to a joint control account, the surety should file a suit for immediate relief. Among other things, the suit should request specific enforcement of the trust fund provision of the standard surety form of indemnity agreement. The trust fund provision typically provides that contract funds are held in trust "for the benefit and payment of all persons to whom the principal incurs obligations in the performance of such contract, for which the surety would be liable under the bond." There are no reported cases directly

---

52. 115 N.J. Eq. 470, 171 A. 382 (N.J. Ch. 1934), *aff'd*, 176 A. 341 (N.J. 1935).

53. 57 F.2d 449 (9th Cir. 1932).

54. In re Ram Construction Company, Inc., 32 B.R. 758 (Bankr. W. D. Pa. 1983); In re Glover Construction Co., Inc., 30 B.R. 873 (Bankr. W. Ky. 1983). Note that if the parties cannot agree upon administration of a joint control account ordered by the court, it may be advisable to have a trustee or receiver appointed to manage the account. *See* Glover, 30 B.R. at 882.

enforcing the trust fund provision, although there is no logical reason why the provision should not be so enforced.[55]

It is submitted that the best way for the surety to protect bonded contract funds, in the absence of cooperation from the principal, is to proceed expeditiously to court. A two-prong position should be taken by the surety in support of its request for relief (which may include an application for temporary restraining order and/or preliminary injunction), based upon common law exoneration and *quia timet* rights and further based upon a right to specific performance of the indemnity agreement. Precious time can slip away while the court considers the surety's pleadings. Accordingly, it is suggested that even before going to court, the surety should put the bond obligee on notice that contract funds may not be disbursed, thereby effectively freezing the contract funds until the court can enter an appropriate order compelling use of these funds for potential bond obligations of the surety.[56]

V. *Requiring Collateral for Anticipated Bond Losses*

A. Legal Requirements to Obtain Collateral From Indemnitors

In addition to the all-inclusive indemnification clause, the standard form indemnity agreement between surety, principal contractor and indemnitors (individuals or companies, including the principal, who have agreed to be responsible for obligations owed to the surety) provides that the indemnitors must post collateral, upon demand, to secure anticipated bond liabilities. The contractual right of the surety to be placed in funds or collateralized by its indemnitors is independent of, and in addition to, the common law. Under the doctrine of *quia timet* such common law right may be exercised, before the bond obligation becomes due, under appropriate circumstances of anticipated losses.

The leading common law case addressing the surety's *quia timet* right to be collateralized is a 1958 Alabama case called *Doster v. Continental Casualty Co.*[57] This case involved a contractor, Doster, who declared to his surety, Continental, upon completion of a school construction project, that he was unable to pay approximately $24,000 owed for materials used at the project. Doster had $21,000 on hand, the bulk of which consisted of progress payments received from the school, but refused to pay the material suppliers whose accounts were past due. The surety brought a *quia timet* suit, and prayed that the court order Doster to use all available funds to pay project bills and, if such funds were not sufficient, then that Doster "be required to protect and secure and indemnify Continental by a transfer of all his assets not subject to exemption over to Continental." The trial court granted the surety a temporary injunction consistent with its prayer for relief, which injunction was later made permanent.

Although Doster had signed a written indemnity agreement which included a provision for transferring assets to the surety as collateral, the court's affirmance of the trial court's injunctive relief was decided on common-law principles. In particular, the court rejected the

---

55. *See* Lawrence, *The Agreement of Indemnity, the Surety's Handling of Contract Bond Problems: Enforcement of the Surety's Rights Against the Principal and the Indemnitors Under the Agreement of Indemnity* (Amer. Bar Assoc. 1989).

56. *See* Lambert v. Maryland Casualty Co., 403 So.2d 739 (La. App. 1982), *aff'd*, 418 So.2d 553 (La. 1983).

57. 268 Ala. 123, 105 So.2d 83 (Ala. 1958); *see also* Ellis v. Phillips, 363 Mich. 587, 110 N.W.2d 772 (Mich. 1961); 72 C.J.S. Principal & Surety, § 303.

argument that fraudulent disposition of property, or any other special reason for fearing a loss, had to be shown before a surety could invoke its *quia timet* rights. The following essential elements were set forth in the *Doster* opinion for requiring a contractor to transfer assets as collateral to the surety:

> The requirements of our cases for a bill of exoneration are more than met in the bill in the instant case in that:
>
> (1) The relationship of surety and principal is alleged.
>
> (2) It is averred that the respondent had, in substance, declared himself in default under his bond by reason of his inability and failure to make payment of the bills of materialmen who had furnished material and supplies for the construction of the North Roebuck School on which the complainant was the contractor's surety.
>
> (3) It is averred that numerous of the materialmen who had furnished the project had made demand upon the complainant, Continental Casualty Company as surety, for payment under the terms of the performance and labor and material payment bond which the surety had executed on the respondent as principal pursuant to the provisions of § 16 of Title 50 of the Code of Alabama of 1940.
>
> (4) Averments are made concerning the financial status of the respondent, including his possession and control of substantial funds collected as earnings off of the construction of the job bonded by the complainant, and the refusal of the respondent to use the same for the payment of the material bills incurred on the project.
>
> (5) The Complainant in the bill offers to do equity and avers that it makes no effort to avoid its secondary liability to the materialmen for the reasonable value of materials and labor furnished for the construction of the North Roebuck School, for which the materialmen would be entitled to recover from the complainant as surety pursuant to the aforesaid public works statute, and further avers that equity, good conscience and simple honesty dictate and require that the respondent be made to fulfill his obligations to the extent that he is reasonably able, and that the complaint, as his surety, be permitted exoneration to the extent that the materialmen and obligee under the bond for the construction of the North Roebuck School will not be prejudiced on any valid and legitimate claims possessed by them.[58]

Doster is not the only case to rely upon common law rather than the indemnity agreement to provide quia *timet* relief to the surety. Due to a dispute as to the efficacy of a subsequent indemnity agreement, the New York district court in *Northwestern Nat'l Ins. Company of Milwaukee, Wis. v. Alberts*[59] also chose to base its decision upon common law principles. Also see a 1998 unpublished opinion of the United States Court of International Trade entitled *U.S. v. Almany,*[60] in which a contractual indemnity agreement did not exist but the surety was still granted exoneration on common law principles. Nevertheless, most courts

58. 268 Ala. at 126-127, 105 So.2d at 87.

59. 741 F.Supp. 424, 430 (S.D. N.Y. 1990), *rev'd on other grounds*, 937 F.2d 77 (2d Cir. 1991).

60. This 1998 unpublished opinion is to be found at 1998 WL 299345.

prefer to couch their decision in terms of specific performance of the written indemnity agreement, sometimes without reference to the equitable *quia timet* and exoneration remedies.[61]

No reported decision known to this author has outright rejected the argument that the surety is entitled to collateral under appropriate *quia timet* circumstances. There are, however, instances in which the requested *quia timet* relief has been rejected due to the particular factual situation presented to the court. One example is *Transamerica Premier Insurance Company v. Cavalry Constr., Inc.*, a 1989 decision from the Florida Court of Appeals.[62]

In the *Transamerica Premier* case, the surety moved for a temporary injunction and *quia timet* relief, essentially asking that a receiver be appointed to take over the assets of the principal Cavalry and the individual indemnitors. The surety had issued $1,187,000 performance and payment bonds on behalf of Cavalry in connection with an underground piping contract. Cavalry and the owner became embroiled in a dispute during the course of construction, and eventually Cavalry was defaulted and forcefully removed from the project. Cavalry admittedly owed approximately $250,000 to suppliers and subcontractors, but claimed to be owed in excess of $350,000 by the owner. The surety demanded that Cavalry and the indemnitors furnish it with collateral equal in value to the total amount of its obligations under the bonds, $1,187,000. When the demand for collateral was refused, the surety filed suit.

The problem with the surety's presentation in court was that, other than the bare claim from the project owner, no evidence was offered to show that the surety had a reasonable basis to apprehend bond liability. The evidence admitted at the injunction hearing totally supported Cavalry's position against the owner. Even the surety's own experts could not justify the surety's collateral demand, other than to note that Cavalry planned to auction its equipment in an upcoming liquidation sale. The trial court refused the surety's request for a receiver, but did grant partial *quia timet* relief by restricting the first $250,000 from Cavalry's liquidation sale to pay outstanding project debts covered by the payment bond. The appellate court affirmed, as follows:

> Transamerica asserts that under these circumstances it was entitled to enforcement of its collateral security clause. While we agree that such clauses are enforceable in equity, the party seeking *quia timet* relief must clearly establish a basis for it. As the trial court noted at the hearing, the issue was not whether Transamerica actually feared a $1,187,000 loss, but whether there was any rational basis for such a fear.
>
> We agree that Transamerica failed to flesh out the nature and approximate amount of the claims and liabilities it might reasonably anticipate under the bond from Timberleaf's claims. The claims of the unpaid subs, laborers and materialmen owed by Cavalry under the project were sufficiently established to permit the trial court to (in effect) grant *quia timet* relief, which was granted. However, without proof that the surety realistically faces loss under the performance bond and is in jeopardy, the trial court correctly determined that additional *quia timet* relief was not appropriate.[63]

Despite the fact that the surety lost in *Transamerica Premier,* the decision is extremely instructive for surety practitioners because it helps define the limits of a *quia timet* suit. The

---

61. *See, e.g.*, United Bonding Ins. Co. v. Stein, 273 F.Supp. 929 (E.D. Pa. 1967); American Motorists Ins. Co. v. United Furnace Co., Inc., 876 F.2d 293 (2d Cir. 1989); Safeco Ins. Co. of America v. Schwab, 739 F.2d 431 (9th Cir. 1984); Milwaukee Constr. Co. v. Glen Falls Ins. Co., 367 F.2d 964 (9th Cir. 1966).

62. 552 So.2d 225 (Fla. App. 1989).

63. *Id.* at 226-227.

court in *Transamerica Premier* explicitly recognized the cause of action, but denied the surety's *quia timet* request due to an inadequate evidentiary showing at the injunction hearing. The lesson to be learned from *Transamerica Premier is* that the surety must prove in court that its fear of bond liability is reasonably based on objective facts – in some jurisdictions, including Florida, it is simply not enough for the surety to merely show that a bond claim has been made and the principal is insolvent.

Transamerica Premier is similar to *Fireman's Fund Ins. Co. v. S.E.K. Constr. Company,*[64] discussed above, in that both cases involved sureties who were denied *quia timet* requests because they made an insufficient showing of anticipated bond liability. *In re Gas Reclamation, Inc. Securities Litigation,*[65] a 1990 decision from the Southern District of New York, is different because the surety's anticipated liability under a financial guarantee bond was well-founded. Nonetheless, the surety's *quia timet* request to have collateral posted by the indemnitors was rejected due to the indemnitors' affirmative claims against the surety for fraud, negligence and securities violations. It was important to the court that the surety's motion for summary judgment on the indemnitors' claims had previously been denied; thus, according to the court, the affirmative claims were proved to be more substantial than mere allegations. Three other cases involving similar facts, in which *quia timet* requests were granted by the courts, were distinguished because the investors in *In re Gas Reclamation* made "a more significant showing of the merits of their claims against [the surety]."[66] In other words, the surety made an insufficient showing of likelihood of success on the merits (which is discussed, in detail below, to be a requirement for *quia timet* injunctive relief).

Furthermore, the surety in *In re Gas Reclamation* waited too long to bring the *quia timet* request. The court commented that in the other three similar suits, the sureties had all moved at a earlier stage in the litigation proceedings. The litigants in *In re Gas Reclamation* had spent over three years in discovery matters, and the court had twice ruled favorably upon the merits of the investors' claims in pretrial motions. *Quia timet* is an extraordinary remedy that requires exigent circumstances to justify the drastic relief sought – lengthy delay such as in the *In re Gas Reclamation* case severely undermines the surety's contention that extraordinary measures are needed to preserve the *status quo* pending final resolution of the case. After all, the indemnitors argued against the surety, if the surety felt comfortable waiting three years before asking that the indemnitors post collateral, why should the surety feel less secure while the litigation proceeds to trial over the next several years? The *In re Gas Reclamation* surety could not answer this question, resulting in the surety's request for collateral security being denied by the court.[67]

Interestingly, most cases which have been decided since the 1989 *Transamerica Premier* case have disagreed with its holding. Several recent cases have determined that, if the collateral deposit clause in an indemnity agreement is properly drafted, the obligee's demand on the bond is sufficient to trigger the surety's right to have collateral deposited.[68] Of course, if the

---

64. 436 F.2d 1345 (10th Cir. 1971).

65. 741 F.Supp. 1094 (S.D. N.Y. 1990), *aff'd on other grounds*, Abish v. Northwestern Nat. Ins. Co., 924 F.2d 448 (2d Cir. 1991).

66. 741 F.Supp. at 1106.

67. Similar delay by sureties in seeking *quia timet* relief contributed to preliminary injunctive requests being denied in Borey v. National Union Fire Ins. Co., 934 F.2d 30, 35 (2d Cir. 1991)(three-year delay) and in Abish v. Northwestern Nat. Ins. Co., 924 F.2d 448, 454 (2d Cir. 1991)(four-year delay).

68. American Home Assur. Co. v. Peter Gun, Inc., ____ F.Supp. _____, 1999 WL 672569 (S.D. N.Y. Aug. 26, 1999); American Motorists Ins. v. Penn Beads Corp., 983 F.Supp. 437 (S.D. N.Y. 1977). *See also* Safeco Ins. Co. of America v. Schwab, 739 F.2d 431 (9th Cir. 1984).

collateral deposit clause is not properly drafted, the opposite result may occur. See, e.g., *Fidelity and Deposit Co. of Maryland v. Rosenmutter,*[69] in which the surety was denied collateral relief because the indemnity agreement provided that the indemnitors were required to post collateral "as soon as Fidelity shall be liable therefor" – which the court interpreted to mean when the surety's liability had become fixed and certain. As the triggering event had not occurred, according to the court, the surety was unable to obtain collateral to protect its interests.

Courts agree that if the surety is otherwise entitled to collateral from the bond principal and indemnitors, the fact that the liability is disputed by the bond principal does not adversely affect the surety's collateral rights. Otherwise, the surety would not have the collateral, for which it bargained at the time of issuance of the bonds for its principal, while the principal's defenses to bond liability are being litigated.[70]

Assuming that the surety is entitled to be collateralized, the issue then becomes the amount of collateral that must be provided to the surety. Some courts take the view that the amount of collateral should be equal to the amount of the bond claim against the surety.[71] Other courts permit the amount of collateral to exceed the bond claim, as long as the amount demanded is reasonable in the sole discretion of the surety.[72] To avoid possible problems associated with the surety having too much restriction, most indemnity agreements condition the right to collateral with the creation of a liability reserve.[73] As reserves serve a purpose unrelated to collateral issues – to cover anticipated claims in accordance with regulatory requirements – and are treated as liabilities on the surety's balance sheet, abuse by the surety in setting reserves for the purpose of demanding collateral is unlikely.[74]

Revenue Markets, Inc. v. Amwest Surety Ins. Co.[75] addressed what the surety may properly do with the collateral which it receives from indemnitors. In this interesting case, the bonded contractor eventually won its litigation against the bond obligee Dade County and was awarded approximately $3.5 million in damages. But previously when the project was outstanding, Dade County had submitted its claim on the surety's performance bond and the surety had liquidated a collateral letter of credit posted by the contractor in order to pay claims-related expenses. The Florida district court ruled that (notwithstanding the fact that contractor eventually won its dispute with Dade County) the contractor was in "default" under the surety's

69. 614 F.Supp. 348 (N.D. Ill. 1985).

70. American Motorists Ins. Co. v. Penn Beads Corp., *supra* note 68 (court ruled it was not contrary to public policy to require indemnitors to post collateral while their liability is pending in litigation); American Home Assur. Co. v. Peter Gun, Inc., *supra* note 68.

71. American Motorists Ins. Co. v. Penn Beads Corp., *supra* note 68.

72. BIB Constr. Co., Inc. v. Fireman's Ins. Co., 214 A.D.2d 521, 625 N.Y.S.2d 550 (1995). *See also* American Home Assur. Co. v. Peter Gun, Inc., *supra* note 68.

73. *See, e.g.*, the 1995 Model Agreement of Indemnity, Section I-B, which states as follows:

> The Undersigned will deposit with the Company as collateral security, immediately upon demand, a sum of money, at the option of the Company, equal to (1) the liability of the Company, if established; (2) the liability asserted against the Company; or (3) the reserve established by the Company, or any increase thereof, to cover any liability, loss, expense or possible liability for any loss or expense for which the Undersigned may be obligated to indemnify the Company under the terms of this Agreement.

Project Update 1995: Illustrative Provisions of a General Indemnity Agreement Taken in Connection With Contract Surety Bonds, 62 Defense Counsel J. 259 (April 1995).

74. For a more in-depth discussion of liability reserves, *see* Franks *supra* note 3.

75. 35 F.Supp.2d 899 (S.D. Fla. 1998).

indemnity agreement, and the surety's rights were triggered as soon as Dade County declared the contractor to be in default. The surety was explicitly authorized by the indemnity agreement to liquidate the collateral "for expenses incurred or expected without first having paid any amounts to Dade County."[76]

One additional case to consider herein, in which the surety was denied *quia timet* relief, is the Ninth Circuit's unpublished opinion in *United Pacific Ins. Co. v. Gregory Timber Resources, Inc.*[77] In this case, the obligee U.S. Forest Service made demand upon the surety's performance bond, but the court determined that the Forest Service's claim against the bond principal was barred by the federal statute of limitations. Although the surety's indemnity agreement provided for the posting of collateral should the surety set up a reserve "for any reason whatsoever," the court held that the surety's discretion was not unlimited – the surety's potential liability had to arise from the bond which is the subject of the indemnity agreement. Although the surety was being pressured with debarment from federal contracts unless it paid money that it did not owe, the court still characterized its status as a volunteer had it decided to make payment. Since the surety had no reason to fear liability on its bond, it was not entitled to *quia timet* relief in the form of collateral from its bond principal and indemnitors.

B. Procedural Considerations

Probably even more so than when trying to prevent dissipation of contract funds, there is a great need for the surety to take prompt action when seeking collateralization from indemnitors. Injunctive relief to prevent transfers of assets is required. However, to have any real benefit for the surety, the injunction must be entered at the commencement of the lawsuit against the indemnitors, and must be in effect during the pendency of the litigation. Otherwise, the assets may be gone by the time that the surety can have final judgment entered against the indemnitors.

The standards for preliminary injunctive relief in a *quia timet* and exoneration case are no different than in other injunction cases. These standards are:

1. Whether the movant will suffer irreparable injury unless the injunction issues, and a concomitant absence of an adequate remedy at law;
2. Whether there is (a) a substantial likelihood that the movant will ultimately prevail on the merits, or (b) sufficiently serious questions going to the merits of movant's claims to make them fair ground for litigation;
3. Whether the threatened injury to movant outweighs damage to the opposing party if the injunction is granted (i.e., a balancing of hardships in favor of the movant); and
4. Whether the injunction would be adverse to the public interest.[78]

No single factor on this list is dispositive. A balancing of all the elements in required, but frequently the balancing focuses upon the irreparable harm in the absence of injunctive relief and the harm to the opposing party as a result of the injunctive relief. Furthermore, as a

76. *Id.* at 905.

77. 129 F.3d 129 (9th Cir. 1997) (this unpublished opinion may be found at 1997 WL 686010).

78. Alliance Bond Fund v. Grupo Mexicano de Dessariollo, S.A., 143 F.3d 688 (2d Cir. 1998); Polymer Technology Corp. v. Mimran, 37 F.3d 74 (2d Cir. 1994); Wingsco Energy, Inc. v. Vangard Groups Resources 1984, Inc., 1989 WL 223756 (S.D. Tex. 1989); Blackwelder Furniture Co. v. Selig Mg. Co., Inc., 550 F.2d 189 (4th Cir. 1977).

practical matter, a strong showing of likelihood of success on the merits may diminish the proof required for the other three elements.[79]

Frequently the surety in a *quia timet* and exoneration case will request a "mandatory" injunction, i.e., an injunction which commands a positive act that alters, rather than preserves, the status quo. A mandatory injunction requires a higher standard of proof than ordinarily required for a preliminary injunction. The surety-movant must show a "clear" entitlement to relief or that "extreme or very serious damage" will result from denial of the requested injunction.[80]

Turning first to the requirement of irreparable injury and concomitant absence of an adequate remedy at law, the court in *United Bonding Ins. Co. v. Stein* stated, without further discussion, that a legal remedy for subsequent damages would not suffice when an indemnitor refuses to voluntarily comply with a surety's demand for collateral.[81] The Ninth Circuit in *Milwaukee Constr. Co. v. Glen Falls Ins. Co.* seemed inclined to rule that inadequacy of remedy and irreparable injury could be presumed in these circumstances; also in that case, there was evidence that one of the indemnitors had transferred assets out of the country to avoid creditors.[82] Also in *Safeco Ins. Co. of America v. Schwab,* the Ninth Circuit commented that "if a creditor is to have the security position for which he bargained, the promise to maintain the security must be specifically enforced."[83] In the *Doster* case discussed above, the court ruled that a showing of fraudulent disposition of property was not a prerequisite to *quia timet* relief against the indemnitors.[84] Finally, in *U.S. Fidelity & Guaranty Co. v. Feibus,* a 1998 Pennsylvania case, the district court had no difficulty with irreparable injury and granted specific performance of a collateral deposit clause upon the surety's showing that it had established a liability reserve, and the indemnitors had ignored its demands to be placed in funds for protection against future losses.[85]

On the other hand, surety practitioners need to be aware of a 1977 case from the Ninth Circuit called *Commercial Ins. Co. of Newark v. Pacific-Peru Constr. Corp.*[86] In that case, a surety was unable to require collateralization because the court believed it had an adequate remedy at law. The court was apparently impressed with the fact that the bond obligee's claim had been reduced to judgment, thereby removing any uncertainty about the surety's liability. The surety's remedy, according to the court, was for money damages rather than specific performance of the indemnity agreement.

More troubling for surety practitioners are certain Second Circuit cases which have distinguished between inadequacy of legal remedy for purposes of specific performance, and irreparable injury for purposes of preliminary injunctive relief, in collateralization situations. These cases, entitled *Northwestern Nat. Ins. v. Alberts,*[87] *Borey v. National Union Fire Ins.*

---

79. Wingsco, *supra* note 78. *See also,* Citibank N.A. v. Citytrust, 756 F.2d 273, 275 (2d Cir. 1985) (the showing of irreparable harm is "perhaps the single most important prerequisite for the issuance of a preliminary injunction.").

80. Phillips v. Fairfield Univ., 118 F.3d 131, 133 (2d Cir. 1997); U.S. Fidelity & Guar. v. J. United Elec. Contracting, 62 F.Supp.2d 915, 921 (E.D. N.Y. 1999).

81. 273 F.Supp. 929, 930 (E.D. Pa. 1967).

82. 367 F.2d 964, 966-967 (9th Cir. 1966).

83. 739 F.2d 431, 433 (9th Cir. 1984)(quoting Midland Trust Co. of New York v. Alleghany Corp., 28 F.Supp. 680, 683-684 (S.D. N.Y. 1939)).

84. 105 So.2d at 86.

85. 15 F.Supp.2d 579 (M.D. Pa. 1998).

86. 558 F.2d 948 (9th Cir. 1977).

87. 937 F.2d 77 (2d Cir. 1991).

Co.,[88] and *Abish v. Northwestern Nat. Ins. Co.*,[89] all involve similar facts in which limited partnership investor notes were backed by financial guarantee bonds in favor of financing banks. When the investors defaulted in their notes, the obligee banks made demand upon the sureties. The sureties then made demand upon indemnitors for collateral to secure their bond obligations. According to these cases, *quia timet* and exoneration are final remedies, and there is not an automatic linkage between preliminary injunctive relief and final relief.[90] In other words, the surety must demonstrate inadequacy of legal remedy to obtain collateral as the final outcome of the case, but must make an additional showing of irreparable injury to have a preliminary injunction entered during the pendency of the action.[91]

The showing of irreparable injury required by the Second Circuit for a preliminary injunction is very difficult for the surety to meet in most cases. As explained in *Abish v. Northwestern Nat. Ins. Co.:*

> In determining whether irreparable harm exists, the critical inquiry is not whether the surety's rights are lost, but whether the loss of those rights will cause serious or irreparable harm. Behind Northwestern's claim for *quia timet* and exoneration relief, it is evident that both rights merely contemplate money payments during the pendency of the action. The nature of the relief sought being monetary compensation, there is no reason why Northwestern cannot be made whole upon resolution of the merits. We have often held that irreparable injury means injury for which a monetary award cannot be adequate compensation.[92]

Abish and the other Second Circuit decisions do, however, recognize certain limited circumstances when irreparable injury may be shown by the surety. For example, irreparable injury may be shown when total bond losses and expenses exceed the indemnitor's ability to pay, and thus the indemnitor will likely be forced to file bankruptcy. Another example of irreparable injury is when the likelihood of an extra-jurisdictional transfer or dissipation of assets can be proven by the surety.[93] The key for the surety, according to the Second Circuit, is to present "evidence of damage that cannot be rectified by financial compensation."[94]

U.S. Fidelity & Guar. v. J. United Elec. Contracting,[95] a 1999 Eastern District of New York case, is instructive of how the surety may meet the Second Circuit's requirements for irreparable injury. In *United,* the surety sought to compel collateralization in a specific amount which was reasonable under the circumstances - $2,839,050, based upon $1,302,308 losses incurred to date, $73,323 expenses incurred to date, and $1,463,419 estimated to be the surety's

88. 934 F.2d 30 (2d Cir. 1991).

89. 924 F.2d 448 (2d Cir. 1991).

90. Borey v. National Union Fire Ins. Co., 934 F.2d at 33.

91. Fireman's Ins. Co. of Neward, N.J. v. Keating, 753 F.Supp. 1146, 1152 (S.D. N.Y. 1990).

92. 924 F.2d at 453. *See also* Borey v. National Union Fire Ins. Co., 934 F.2d at 34 ("But, when a party can be fully compensated for financial loss by a money judgment, there is simply no compelling reason why the extraordinary equitable remedy of a preliminary injunction should be granted") and Northwestern Nat. Ins. v. Alberts, 937 F.2d at 82 ("loss of surety's rights to *quia timet* and examination does not cause irreparable harm where surety can be made whole upon resolution of merits").

93. Abish v. Northwestern Nat. Ins. Co., 924 F.2d at 454.

94. Borey v. National Union Fire Ins. Co., 934 F.2d at 34.

95. 62 F.Supp.2d 915 (E.D. N.Y. 1999).

future net losses to meet its bond obligations.[96] It was shown that while the indemnitor had assets that he could deposit as collateral security, the anticipated total amount of bond losses were beyond his financial ability. It was further shown that the indemnitor had engaged in misconduct in forging his wife's signature on the indemnity agreement and then secretly transferring property to her. The Magistrate Judge, to whom this case was referred, found that the surety was in danger of irreparable injury and recommended a preliminary injunction (following issuance of a temporary restraining order) in favor of the surety. The Magistrate Judge's recommendation was adopted in its entirety by the reported decision of the District Judge.

It is significant that other reported financial guarantee bond cases, not emanating from the Second Circuit, have taken a different view of irreparable injury in exoneration and *quia timet* suits. These cases, *Northwestern Nat'l Ins. v. Barney*[97] and *Wingsco Energy One v. Vanguard Groups Resources 1984, Inc.,*[98] involve the same basic facts as did the Second Circuit cases. The *Barney* and *Wingsco* courts had no problem finding irreparable injury to support the surety's request for a preliminary injunction during the pendency of the action against indemnitors.

This author believes that the *Barney* and *Wingsco* courts have adopted the correct approach in collateralization suits. Inadequacy of remedy and irreparable injury should be presumed from the indemnitors' failure to voluntarily post collateral. When the issuance of bonds was first contemplated by the principal and surety, the indemnitors promised to provide collateral to the surety under appropriately described circumstances in the indemnity agreement. If such promise cannot be enforced at the inception of an equitable action for specific performance, but rather must await determination in a final judgment that will only be entered after adjudication on the merits, then the promise to collateralize is meaningless. It should be remembered that in another provision of the agreement, the indemnitors have already agreed to fully repay the surety for all bond losses and expenses. Unless the surety has recourse to obtain collateral while the lawsuit for damages is pending, then the promise to collateralize adds nothing to the surety's rights under the indemnity agreement.

The Second Circuit's position regarding irreparable injury led to a 1995 revision in the Model General Indemnity Agreement of the International Association of Defense Counsel, Fidelity & Surety Committee. The following was added to section I-B, the collateral deposit provision of the Model General Indemnity Agreement:

> The Undersigned acknowledge that the failure of the Undersigned to deposit with the Company, immediately upon demand, the sum demanded by the Company as collateral security shall cause irreparable harm to the Company for which the Company has no adequate remedy at law. The Undersigned agree that the Company shall be entitled to injunctive relief for specific performance of the obligation of Undersigned to deposit with the Company the sum demanded as collateral security and hereby waive any claims or defenses to the contrary.[99]

---

96. The court stated, in reaching its decision for the surety, that the burden was upon the defendant-indemnitor to refute the amount of the surety's demand by showing that the surety's stated losses and expenses were unreasonable or were incurred in bad faith. 62 F.Supp. 2d at 922. *See also* Taylor Woodrow v. Blitman, 603 F.Supp. 1152, 1155 (S.D. N.Y. 1985).

97. 886 F.2d 1316 (N.D. Ohio 1988)(this case is not published in a printed volume, but a full text of the opinion may be found at 1988 WL 215411).

98. This case is not published in a printed volume, but a full text of the opinion may be found at 1989 WL 223756 (S.D. Tex. 1989).

99. *Project Update 1995, supra* note 73.

To the best knowledge of the author, this change has not yet been widely implemented by the surety industry. No reported cases have been published which have interpreted this provision, and so it remains to be seen whether this provision will be helpful to the surety seeking to establish irreparable injury for preliminary injunctive relief.

Parenthetically, the Second Circuit's overly-technical interpretation of the irreparable injury requirement in collateralization suits may lead the surety to more traditional prejudgment remedies. If indemnitors have identifiable assets which are presumably available to reimburse the surety upon final judgment (thereby negating irreparable injury to the surety, according to the Second Circuit), then in many jurisdictions the surety may be able to invoke statutory prejudgment remedies to garnish or attach the indemnitors' assets. It has been held that these statutory remedies have not replaced *quia timet,* but rather are in addition to common law *quia timet* rights of the surety.[100] The problem for the surety is that statutory prejudgment remedies are typically less flexible – and therefore less useful – than *quia timet* to meet the surety's needs in a dynamic bond loss situation.

Regarding the remaining three requirements for a preliminary injunction, *Barney* and Wingsco are again instructive. These decisions applied the well-established standards to the surety's request for a preliminary injunction. As stated above, in both cases the surety was found to be facing irreparable injury unless the injunction was granted. The surety was further found to have a likelihood of success on the merits. As to the balance of hardships and public interest standards, the decisions were "balanced" by ordering that the indemnitors' assets be paid into court rather than to the sureties. The *Barney* court stated:

> To satisfy the fourth element, serving the public interest, NNIC states the public's interest surely is served when the issuance of a preliminary injunction preserves inviolate the rights accruing to parties that cannot be preserved by a mere action for damages and that are mooted otherwise.
>
> The shareholder-defendants counter that it is in the greater public interest that defendants in civil litigation not be stripped of money and assets before being given the full due process of a trial on the merits of their defenses.
>
> The principals expressly assumed the risk of payment in the Indemnity Agreement and agreed to hold NNIC harmless. To ignore the express terms of this Agreement and the bargained for risks would not be in the public interest. Moreover, the shareholder-defendants specifically, in paragraph (4) of the Indemnity Agreement expressly agreed to subject their assets to a demand of their surety, NNIC. Additionally, the court is not ordering defendants' obligated assets to be turned over to NNIC, but, rather that the assets be paid into court, subject to further court order. To do so will also protect NNIC against the possibility, as claimed, that if injunctive relief is not ordered defendants' assets may be dissipated by the time defendants' securities claims are fully litigated. Under the totality of the circumstances, the fourth element has been satisfied.[101]

100. Escrow Agents' Fidelity v. Superior Court (Abelman), *supra* note 9. *See also* U.S. Fidelity & Guar. v. J. United Elec. Contracting, *supra* note 95, in which the surety was granted an attachment under New York prejudgment procedures as an alternative to a portion of the preliminary injunctive relief which it requested.

101. 1988 W.L. 215411 at p. 9.

Another case which balanced interests and applied injunction standards to a collateral demand by a surety is *Safeco, Ins. Co. of America v. Criterion Inv. Corp.*[102] The surety's request for collateral was granted, but the court would not enjoin the indemnitors from transferring assets to other persons before satisfying their collateral obligations. The court explained:

> The Court will not award such injunctive relief, finding that the requisite showing of irreparable harm has not been made. The availability of means for the enforcement of judgments, such as the registration of judgments to create liens against judgment debtors' assets, provides the plaintiff in this case with adequate means by which to enforce the defendants' collateral security obligations.[103]

Although not expressly stated, the author believes the *Criteron* court would have granted all of the requested injunctive relief had the surety been able to show any concealment or transfer of assets or other acts of wrongdoing by the indemnitors. The value of this type of evidence, in these proceedings, cannot be overstated.

Included in Appendix B to this chapter is a set of pleadings which were used in a case to obtain a temporary restraining order, without notice, from a federal district court. The order specifically provided the surety with a lien upon all assets of indemnitors and prohibited the indemnitors from transferring assets during the pendency of the order. Diversity jurisdiction was invoked to enable the district court to hear the case. The surety preferred to have an order from the federal court, rather than from the state court, because there was the possibility that out-of-state assets were owned by the indemnitors. Enforcement of injunctions, particularly affecting disposition of real property, is more easily accomplished across state lines with orders of the federal court.

Rule 65 of the Federal Rules of Civil Procedure governs issuance of temporary restraining orders. It provides that a temporary restraining order may only be entered if it clearly appears from specific facts shown by affidavit or by verified complaint that immediate and irreparable injury will result before the adverse party can be heard in opposition, and that the applicant's attorney must certify in writing the reasons why notice to the adverse party should not be required. The order only remains in effect for ten days, unless extended by agreement of the parties or for good cause shown for an additional ten days. The hearing on applicant's motion for preliminary injunction, after notice to the adverse party, must be scheduled at the earliest possible time and take precedence over other matters before the court. The temporary restraining order must be supported by an injunction bond, in an amount to be determined by the court.

The pleadings included in Appendix B are a complaint for injunctive and other relief, and an application for temporary restraining order. In that case, a hearing on preliminary injunction was held four days after service of the temporary restraining order upon the indemnitors. The court sustained surety's request for *quia timet* relief, and a preliminary injunction was entered for the pendency of the litigation.

Obviously, these form pleadings must be adapted to the particular facts of the situation in which they are used. In particular, if the indemnitors are known to have transferred assets or done other things which give the surety special reason to be fearful, these facts should be specified in the pleadings. It is, however, noteworthy that in the case in which the pleadings

102. 732 F.Supp. 834 (E.D. Tenn. 1989).

103. *Id.* at 844.

were actually used, *quia timet* orders were entered by the court without such additional facts being shown – the surety's reasonable anticipation of losses and the indemnitors' refusal to collateralize the surety were held to be a sufficient basis for *quia timet* relief.

This author believes that sureties frequently wait too long before asking for exoneration and *quia timet* relief. At the inception of litigation, if warranted by the circumstances, the surety should seek a temporary restraining order to enjoin the transfer of assets by the indemnitors. If the TRO is granted, the assets will be preserved pending the preliminary injunction hearing that must be held shortly thereafter. The preliminary injunction, entered following an evidentiary hearing, will be a broader order that requires the posting of collateral to secure anticipated bond liability. It is not an exaggeration to say that these court orders, obtained at the earliest opportunity by the surety, can change the course of a bond loss matter. It may, indeed, be the difference between losses and full indemnification against losses for the surety.

VI. Conclusion

There is no question that extremely strict scrutiny is placed upon sureties requesting *quia timet* and exoneration relief. Because it is a drastic remedy, *quia timet* should only be used when the surety's apprehension of bond losses may be proved by objective evidence admissible in court. Furthermore, a surety should expect to receive only the minimal equitable relief needed under the circumstances to protect its rights. An overzealous surety who brings a *quia timet* and exoneration action without reasonable anticipation of liability, or an overreaching surety who seeks a wide-ranging injunction against its principal and indemnitors, faces an uphill battle in court.

On the other hand, the recent cases unanimously confirm the surety's right to *quia timet* and exoneration relief under appropriate circumstances. As a practical matter, prompt use of *quia timet* and exoneration remedies may be the surety's only hope to preserve contract funds or to obtain collateral to secure future bond losses. If the right situation is presented, the surety definitely should not wait until after payment of claims to bring suit against the principal and indemnitors. Rather, the surety should be aggressive and take appropriate action at the earliest possible time of anticipated bond liability.

APPENDIX A

TRUST AGREEMENT

THIS AGREEMENT made and entered into this ___ day of ________, 2000,by and between INSOLVENT CONSTRUCTION COMPANY, an Arizona corporation (hereinafter referred to as "Principal"), and JOHN OWNER and MARY OWNER, husband and wife (hereinafter said individuals are collectively referred to as the "Indemnitors"), and FEARFUL INSURANCE COMPANY, a Maryland corporation (hereinafter referred to as "Surety").

WITINESSETH:

WHEREAS, Surety has heretofore executed bonds from time to time on behalf of Principal at the request of Principal and Indemnitors on certain projects, including the following: ____(hereinafter referred to as the "Bonded Project");

WHEREAS, Principal and Indemnitors, to induce Surety to execute the aforesaid bonds on their behalf, agreed to indemnify and save Surety harmless from any claim, loss, cost, or expense by reason of executing said bonds;

WHEREAS, on __________, 2000, Principal and Indemnitors executed a General Indemnity Agreement in favor of Surety wherein and whereunder Principal and Indemnitors, jointly and severally, agreed to indemnify Surety against any loss or liability it might incur as a consequence of executing surety bonds on behalf of Principal;

WHEREAS, on __________, 2000, Principal filed a voluntary petition under Chapter 11 in the United States Bankruptcy Court for the District of ______________ *(In re Insolvent Construction Company,* Cause No. ___________). Principal remains in possession of its property and continues to operate its business as a debtor in possession;

WHEREAS, Principal is unable to meet obligations for both performance and payment covered under the above-described bonds for the Bonded Project; and

WHEREAS, Principal, Indemnitors and Surety agree that the execution of this Agreement and the performance of its terms, provisions and conditions will be to the mutual benefit of Principal, Indemnitors, Surety and the general creditors of principal, and in furtherance of the performance and completion of the work at the above-described Bonded Project.

NOW, THEREFORE, in consideration of the mutual promises and covenants hereinafter contained, the parties hereto agree as follows:

1. Principal and Indemnitors, and each of them, do hereby reaffirm their General Indemnity Agreement, dated ___________, 2000, in favor of Surety notwithstanding anything contained herein.

2. Surety shall have a first right of priority, superior to all other claims to the unpaid balance of the contract proceeds (including unpaid draws and retention sums) of the bonded contract, to the extent necessary to reimburse Surety for any and all losses, costs, expenses, including attorneys' fees, and interest on any advances that may be made by Surety at the rate of ten percent (10%) per annum, which it has incurred or may hereafter incur as a result of the execution of the above-described bonds for the Bonded Project.

3. There shall be a bank account established at the ____________________Bank. The account shall be known as the "Insolvent Construction Company Trust Account" (hereinafter referred to as "Trust Account").

A. With regard to the Trust Account:

(1) The Trust Account shall be a general operations account for the Bonded Project.

(2) The following monies, receipts or payments shall be deposited in said account: (a) all monies, presently in the possession of Principal, representing proceeds or payments received by Principal from the bonded contract; (b) all monies which may be received, after execution of this Agreement, representing proceeds or payments from the bonded contract; and (c) funds that may be advanced by Surety to pay expenses described in sub-paragraph (3) below.

(3) The Trust Account shall be used for the following purposes, for which uses and purposes a trust is hereby imposed upon said account: (a) to pay all necessary labor, materials, supplies, equipment, contracts and expenses for the continued performance of the bonded contract, for which Surety would be liable under its above-described bonds for the Bonded Project; and (b) to reimburse Surety to the extent of reimbursement described in paragraph 2 above.

(4) Withdrawals to be made from the Trust Account shall be only by checks signed either (a) by any two designated representatives of Surety, or M by any one designated representative of Surety and by any one designated representative of Principal. The designated representatives of Surety and Principal are set forth in paragraph (B) below.

(5) Nothing contained in this paragraph 3 shall obligate Surety to provide funding to Principal. Should the above-described Trust Account be depleted and funding be needed by Principal in connection with performance of the bonded contract, the decision to provide or not provide funding shall be at the sole discretion of Surety.

B. The designated representatives of Surety and Principal, for purposes of withdrawals from the trust account, are as follows:

(1) For Surety: ____ __________________________. Surety shall have the right at any time to name substitutions in place and instead of these individuals.

(2) For Principal: ____ __________________________. Principal shall have the right at

any time to name substitutions in place and instead of these individuals.

C. It is understood that the Trust Account shall remain the property of Surety at all times to the extent necessary for reimbursement described in paragraph 2 above. Surety may, at any time and without prior notice or consent of Principal or Indemnitors, withdraw all or any part of the balance of the Trust Account for the purpose and to the extent of said reimbursement.

D. Principal shall render periodic accountings, as requested by Surety, of all deposits into and withdrawals from the Trust Account, together with such payroll reports, invoices, billings and other supporting documents requested by Surety.

4. Principal shall execute an irrevocable Direction of Payment to ____________,owner of the Bonded Project. Such Direction of Payment shall require the owner to make all payments of the unpaid balance of the bonded contract proceeds (including unpaid draws and retention sums) by checks payable to the order of the "Insolvent Construction Company Trust Account," and shall further require delivery of such checks to counsel for Surety. Upon receipt, counsel for Surety shall promptly deposit each check into the Trust Account.

5. It is agreed that funds in the Trust Account shall be used to reimburse Surety as follows: First, to the payment of any advances that may be made directly by Surety, with regard to the bonded contract, to bond claimants or deposited into the Trust Account or otherwise. Second, to the payment of all other costs, expenses and attorneys' fees incurred by Surety as a result of execution of bonds on behalf of Principal for the Bonded Project.

6. Surety shall have the right, through its own employees or by outside auditors, to audit and inspect the books of Principal at such reasonable time or times as it may desire.

7. Principal and Indemnitors agree that Surety may at any time, in its sole discretion and with or without cause or notice, terminate this Agreement; provided, however, such termination shall not in any way lessen Surety's obligations under the above-described bonds for the project. Principal and Indemnitors agree and fully understand, and have had the advice of counsel, that this provision is for the protection of Surety.

8. Principal agrees to do all things necessary to affirm the bonded contract as soon as such affirmation can reasonably be accomplished.

9. The rights afforded Surety under this Agreement are in addition to any and all other rights which Surety has, may have or acquire against Principal and Indemnitors, whether under the terms of any indemnity agreements or otherwise. This Agreement shall not be deemed to modify or alter any existing indemnity or other agreement. In particular, Surety specifically reserves its right to demand collateral and to be placed in funds by Indemnitors, and further to take over or relet the bonded contract, and further to seek the appointment of a trustee or examiner in the above-described Chapter 11 proceeding.

10. Nothing contained in this Agreement or done pursuant thereto shall be construed to enlarge any obligation of Surety under any bond or undertaking executed on behalf of principal and it is further agreed that this Agreement is solely for the benefit of the parties hereto and shall not create any rights in or for any other persons, firms, or corporations.

11. Any waiver by Surety of any provisions of this Agreement or any failure on the part of Surety to act or take advantage of its provisions shall not in any way limit, vary, or discharge Principal or Indemnitors under this or any other agreement.

12. Principal and Indemnitors agree to reimburse Surety for any and all reasonable expenses, including any attorneys' fees which it may have, or may hereafter incur as a result of the execution of the above-described bonds or under the terms of this Agreement.

13. Principal and Indemnitors hereby agree to all of -the terms of this Agreement, and to comply therewith and to execute any and all instruments deemed by Surety as necessary or proper to effectuate this Agreement.

14. Time is of the essence of this Agreement.

15. This Agreement shall extend to and be binding upon and inure to the benefit of the parties and their respective successors, heirs and assigns.

16. This Agreement is expressly conditioned upon formal approval of the United States Bankruptcy Court, which approval Principal shall seek to obtain promptly upon execution of this Agreement.

17. To the extent that Surety is fully reimbursed for any and all losses, costs, expenses and attorneys' fees, then remaining proceeds received from the Bonded Project and any remaining balances in the Trust Account described in paragraph 3 above shall be promptly paid to Principal.

IN WITNESS WHEREOF, this Agreement has been duly executed by the parties hereto on the day and year first hereinabove written.

APPENDIX B

UNITED STATES DISTRICT COURT

DISTRICT OF ARIZONA

<table>
<tr><td>FEARFUL INSURANCE COMPANY,
a Maryland corporation,

Plaintiff,

vs.

INSOLVENT CONSTRUCTION
COMPANY, an Arizona corporation;
JOHN OWNER and MARY OWNER,
husband and wife,

Defendants.
______________________________</td><td>)
)
)
)
)
)
)
)
)
)
)
)
)
)</td><td>No.________________

COMPLAINT FOR INJUNCTIVE
AND OTHER RELIEF</td></tr>
</table>

For its complaint against defendants, plaintiff alleges as follows:

Count One

I

Plaintiff is a corporation incorporated under the laws of the State of Maryland and has its principal place of business in the State of Maryland. Defendant Insolvent Construction Company ("Insolvent") is a corporation incorporated under the laws of the State of Arizona. Defendants John Owner and Mary Owner, husband and wife, are citizens of the State of Arizona. The matter in controversy exceeds, exclusive of interest and costs, the sum of Fifty Thousand Dollars ($50,000.00). Accordingly, this Court has diversity jurisdiction over this action pursuant to 28 U.S.C. § 1332.

II

On or about ______________, 2000, Insolvent (as principal) and defendants John Owner and Mary Owner (as indemnitors) executed a General Indemnity Agreement with plaintiff. By the terms of such General Indemnity Agreement, defendants agreed, among other things, to exonerate, indemnify and keep indemnified the surety plaintiff from and against any and all liabilities, losses and expenses of whatsoever kind or nature (including but not limited to, interest, court costs and counsel fees) imposed upon, sustained, or incurred by surety plaintiff by reason of: (1) surety plaintiff having executed bonds in behalf of principal Insolvent, or (2) defendants' failure to perform or comply with any of the provisions of the General Indemnity Agreement. Further by the terms of the General Indemnity Agreement, defendants agreed that in order to exonerate or indemnify surety plaintiff, defendants shall upon demand of surety plaintiff place surety plaintiff in funds before surety plaintiff makes any payment; such funds to be, at the surety plaintiff's option, money or property, or liens or security interests in property, the amount of such money or property or the value of the property to become subject to liens or security interests as determined by the surety plaintiff. A copy of the said General Indemnity Agreement is attached hereto as Exhibit "A" and incorporated by reference herein.

III

At the request of defendants and pursuant to the terms of the said General Indemnity Agreement, plaintiff, as surety, and Insolvent, as principal, executed payment and performance bonds in connection with construction projects in which Insolvent had agreed to be the general contractor thereon. There are presently outstanding ______________ such payment and performance bonds issued by plaintiff for Insolvent, in the total sum of $________________.

IV

Defendant Insolvent does not have the financial resources to pay its obligations on the bonded construction projects and is, therefore, in default to its material suppliers and subcontractors at such projects. Further with regard to Insolvent's uncompleted construction contracts, defendant Insolvent does not have the resources to finance completion of same.

V

Plaintiff justifiably fears that it will sustain a loss in the completion of the bonded projects. Further, plaintiff justifiably fears that it will be required to pay claims of unpaid material suppliers and subcontractors at the bonded projects. To date, plaintiff has paid, pursuant to its bond obligations, the sum of $______________ to unpaid material suppliers and subcontractors of Insolvent. However, based upon a review of Insolvent's books and records, and further based upon numerous notices of claims received from material suppliers and subcontractors, it is estimated that the losses to plaintiff in connection with the bonds issued for Insolvent will actually exceed $__________________.

VI

In accordance with the General Indemnity Agreement, plaintiff made demand upon defendants to be placed in funds prior to making any payment, such funds to be money, property, or liens or security interests in property as determined by plaintiff. By virtue of the said General Indemnity Agreement and by virtue of the equitable doctrines of exoneration and quia timet, plaintiff is entitled to have defendants place funds or other security with plaintiff that is sufficient to cover the above-described bond losses.

VII

Defendants have failed and refused to meet their obligations under the General Indemnity Agreement. In particular, defendants have refused to place plaintiff in funds, both in the amount and according to the procedure set forth in the Agreement.

VIII

Upon information and belief, the assets of the defendant Insolvent are insufficient to adequately secure plaintiff for its obligations under the above-described payment and performance bonds. Unless the personal assets of the individual defendants, as well as the corporate assets of Insolvent, are collateralized, plaintiff will not be adequately secured for its obligations on the bonded projects.

IX

Plaintiff is entitled to be fully collateralized by defendants prior to making any further payments in discharge of its bond obligations. Unless the injunctive relief requested below is granted, plaintiff will not be adequately secured for its obligations prior to making such further payments. Further, unless the injunctive relief requested below is granted, defendants are likely to sell, transfer, dispose, lien, secure, or otherwise divert their assets from being used to discharge defendants' obligations to exonerate and indemnify plaintiff, all to plaintiff's irreparable harm.

X

Plaintiff is without a plain, speedy or adequate remedy at law, and will be irreparably and permanently injured unless this Court grants the injunctive and equitable relief as prayed herein.

XI

Plaintiff has been forced to retain legal counsel and incur other expenses in pursuit of its rightful interests in this matter, and is entitled to recompense therefor pursuant to the terms of the General Indemnity Agreement.

WHEREFORE, plaintiff demands judgment against defendants, jointly and severally, as follows:

A. For an order requiring defendants to render to plaintiff a full and complete accounting of all assets owned by them or in which they have an interest.

B. For an order requiring defendants to allow plaintiff full and complete access to all financial books, records and accounts maintained by them.

C. For an order requiring defendants to place plaintiff in funds by money, property, or liens or security interests in property, as determined by plaintiff to be ample security for its obligations on the bonded projects.

D. For an order permanently enjoining and restraining defendants from selling, transferring or disposing or liening their assets and property, and further enjoining and restraining defendants from allowing their assets and property to be liened, unless and until plaintiff shall be placed in funds as prayed for in paragraph (C) above.

E. For an order granting a lien upon all assets and property, including realty, personalty and mixed, owned by defendants and property in which defendants have an interest. Such lien shall secure plaintiff against any loss that it may sustain or incur by virtue of its having executed bonds for Insolvent. Such lien shall remain in effect unless and until plaintiff shall be placed in funds as prayed for in paragraph (C) above.

F. For an order requiring defendants to indemnify and exonerate plaintiff for all liabilities, losses and expenses incurred by plaintiff as a result of plaintiff having executed bonds for Insolvent.

G. For plaintiff's costs, including reasonable attorneys' fees, incurred herein.

H. For such other and further relief as this Court deems just and equitable.

Count Two

XII

By this reference, plaintiff incorporates the allegations contained in paragraphs I through XI, inclusive, of the complaint.

XIII

By the express provisions of the General Indemnity Agreement and by virtue of the equitable doctrines of exoneration and quia timet, plaintiff is entitled to be placed in funds, upon demand, prior to making further payments upon its bonds issued for Insolvent. Unless preliminary injunctive relief is granted, plaintiff will not be adequately secured for its obligations prior to making further payment thereon. Further unless the preliminary injunctive relief is granted, defendants are likely to sell, transfer, dispose, lien, secrete, or otherwise divert their assets from being used to discharge defendants' obligations to exonerate and indemnify plaintiff, all to plaintiff's irreparable harm.

WHEREFORE, plaintiff prays that the Court grant the following preliminary relief:

A. Issue its order to defendants to show cause at the earliest possible date why the relief demanded herein should not be granted.

B. Schedule a hearing at which evidence will be taken.

C. Thereafter issue a Preliminary Injunction which includes the following:

(1) Requires defendants to render to plaintiff a full and complete accounting of all assets owned by them or in which they have an interest.

(2) Requires defendants to allow plaintiff full and complete access to all financial books, records and accounts maintained by them.

(3) Requires defendants to place plaintiff in funds by money, property, or liens or security interests in property, as determined by plaintiff to be ample security for its obligations on the bonded projects.

(4) Enjoins and restrains defendants from selling, transferring or disposing or liening their assets and property, and further enjoins and restrains defendants from allowing their assets and property to be liened, unless and until plaintiff shall be placed in funds as prayed for in paragraph (3) above.

(5) Grants a lien upon all assets and property, including realty, personalty and mixed, owned by defendants and property in which defendants have an interest. Such lien shall secure plaintiff against any loss that it may sustain or incur by virtue of its having executed

bonds for Insolvent. Such lien shall remain in effect unless and until plaintiff shall be placed in funds as prayed for in paragraph (3) above.

(6) Requires defendants to indemnify and exonerate plaintiff for all liabilities, losses and expenses incurred by plaintiff as a result of plaintiff having executed bonds for Insolvent.

D. For plaintiff's costs, including reasonable attorneys' fees incurred herein.

E. For such other and further relief as this Court deems just and equitable.

RESPECTFULLY SUBMITTED this ____ day of ________________, 2000.

UNITED STATES DISTRICT COURT

DISTRICT OF ARIZONA

FEARFUL INSURANCE COMPANY, a Maryland corporation, Plaintiff, vs. INSOLVENT CONSTRUCTION COMPANY, an Arizona corporation; JOHN OWNER and MARY OWNER, husband and wife, Defendants.	)	No.____________________ APPLICATION FOR TEMPORARY RESTRAINING ORDER

Plaintiff hereby applies to this Court for a Temporary Restraining Order, and in support thereof alleges as follows:

I

By this reference, plaintiff hereby incorporates the allegations contained in its Complaint for Injunctive and Other Relief filed concurrently herewith.

II

To date, plaintiff has advanced, pursuant to its bond obligations, the sum of $ ________ to unpaid material suppliers and subcontractors of Insolvent Construction Company ("Insolvent"). Based upon a review of Insolvent's books and records, and further based upon numerous notices of claims received from material suppliers and subcontractors, plaintiff justifiably fears that further substantial advances will be required and, accordingly, estimates its losses, upon bonds issued for Insolvent, in the sum of $____________.

III

By virtue of the General Indemnity Agreement executed by plaintiff and defendants on or about __________________, 2000, a copy of which was attached to the complaint as Exhibit "A", and by virtue of the equitable doctrines of exoneration and quia timet, plaintiff is entitled to be fully collateralized by defendants prior to making further payments upon its bonds issued for Insolvent.

IV

Unless restrained and enjoined therefrom, defendants are likely to sell, transfer, dispose, lien, secrete or otherwise divert their assets from being used to discharge defendants' obligations to exonerate and indemnify plaintiff, all to plaintiff's irreparable harm.

V

Should notice of the pending issuance hereof be given to defendants, there exists a strong likelihood that they will commit one or more of the above acts before this order could be entered and served upon them, and immediate and irreparable loss, damage and harm would thereby result to plaintiff.

WHEREOF, plaintiff requests that this Court issue an ex parte temporary restraining order which includes the following:

A. Enjoins and restrains defendants from selling, transferring, disposing or liening their assets and property and further enjoins and restrains defendants from allowing their assets and property to be liened during the pendency of this order;

B. Grants a lien in favor of plaintiff upon all assets and property of defendants, including realty, personalty and mixed, owned by defendants and property in which defendants have an interest. Such lien shall secure plaintiff against any loss that it may sustain or incur by virtue of its having executed bonds for Insolvent. Such lien shall remain in effect during the pendency of this order; and

C. Requires defendants to appear within ten (10) days and show cause why said temporary restraining order should not remain in effect as a preliminary injunction pending disposition of this lawsuit.

RESPECTFULLY SUBMITTED this ____ day of ______________, 2000.

25

The General Agreement of Indemnity

Armen Shahinian[1]

Introduction

Surety bonds, issued by compensated sureties, are meant to function as credit accommodations in which the surety anticipates no loss. Before issuing its bond, the surety will have conducted an underwriting analysis to satisfy itself as to both the principal's capacity to perform the bonded obligation and its financial ability to fulfill its common law duties to indemnify and exonerate the surety against any loss sustained or threatened as a result of the issuance of the bond. The compensated surety will not rely solely upon its common law rights of indemnity and exoneration, however. A condition uniformly imposed by the surety is that its principal and usually the individuals who control it execute an agreement of indemnity to augment the surety's common law rights.

The specific terms of the General Indemnity Agreement will vary from surety to surety. The common objectives of such agreements, however, are to provide the surety with a contractual right of recovery against the principal and other named indemnitors, to facilitate the handling of bond claims, to require the deposit of collateral to secure the surety against losses once bond claims are asserted, to ease burdens of proof in actions to recover losses and expenses, and to provide a security interest in the principal's equipment, machinery and receivables. In furtherance of those objectives, the General Indemnity Agreement expressly establishes the surety's right to pay or otherwise settle its bond obligations, thereby enabling it to avoid unnecessary and costly litigation while protecting its rights of indemnity against the principal and the named indemnitors.

This paper will explore the rights and remedies of the surety under important provisions commonly found in the General Indemnity Agreement, as interpreted and applied by the courts.[2] It will also discuss the advantages to the surety of filing the General Indemnity Agreement as a financing statement to complement the surety's subrogation rights to the principal's contract receivables.

---

1. The author wishes to acknowledge the assistance contributed by Andrew S. Kent, an associate at Wolff & Samson.

2. It is beyond the scope of this paper to address all of the provisions found in typical General Indemnity Agreements. For an excellent model form of a General Indemnity Agreement, annotated on a provision by provision basis, the reader is referred to the materials prepared by the Fidelity and Surety Law Committee of the International Association of Defense Counsel which were published in *Project Update 1995: Illustrative Provisions of a General Indemnity Agreement Taken in Connection with Contract Surety*, 62 Defense Counsel Journal 259 (1995). (hereinafter IADC's Project Update 1995).

Agreement as a financing statement to complement the surety's subrogation rights to the principal's contract receivables.

I. *The Indemnity Clause*

Indemnity is the common law right which inures to one who has discharged a duty which is owed by him, but which, as between himself and another, should be discharged by the other. Thus, the equitable right of indemnification in favor of a surety arises when the surety, pursuant to its bond obligations, discharges an obligation for which the principal is liable. Where there is an express indemnification contract, however, the rights of the parties are governed by the terms of the contract.[3] The parties can, by contract, extend a principal's indemnification obligation beyond those obligations to third parties for which the principal is found to be liable. Most General Indemnity Agreements do just that by expressly requiring indemnification for all losses sustained by the surety in good faith as a result of its issuance of its bond on behalf of the principal whether or not the principal turns out to have been liable to the bond claimant causing the surety's loss. An example of a common indemnity provision is as follows:

> The Contractor and Indemnitors shall exonerate, indemnify, and keep indemnified the Surety from and against any and all liability for losses and/or expenses of whatsoever kind or nature (including, but not limited to, interest, court costs and counsel fees) and from and against any and all such losses and/or expenses which the surety may sustain and incur: (1) by reason of having executed or procured the execution of the bonds, (2) by reason of the failure of the Contractor or Indemnitors to perform or comply with the covenants and conditions of this agreement or (3) in enforcing any of the covenants and conditions of this agreement. Payment by reason of the aforesaid causes shall be made to the Surety by the Contractor and Indemnitors as soon as liability exists or is asserted against the Surety, whether or not the Surety shall have made any payment therefor. Such payment shall be equal to the amount of the reserve set by the Surety. In the event of any payment by the Surety the Contractor and Indemnitors further agree that in any accounting between the Surety and the Contractor, or between the Surety and the Indemnitors, or either or both of them, the Surety shall be entitled to charge for any and all disbursements made by it in good faith in and about the matters herein contemplated by this Agreement under the belief that it is or was liable for the sums and amounts so disbursed, or that it was necessary or expedient to make such disbursements, whether or not such liability, necessity or expediency existed; and that the vouchers or other evidence of any such payments made by the Surety shall be prima facie evidence of the fact and amount of the liability to the Surety.[4]

A. THE SURETY'S RIGHT TO INDEMNITY FOR ALL PAYMENTS

Association of Defense Counsel which were published in *Project Update 1995: Illustrative Provisions of a General Indemnity Agreement Taken in Connection with Contract Surety*, 62 Defense Counsel Journal 259 (1995). (hereinafter IADC's Project Update 1995).

3. *Fidelity and Deposit Company of Maryland v. Bristol Steel & Iron Works, Inc.*, 722 F.2d 1160, 1163 (4th Cir. 1983); *Commercial Ins. Co. of Newark, N.J. v. Pacific-Peru Const. Corp.*, 558 F.2d 948, 953 (9th Cir. 1977); *General Insurance Company of America v. Singleton*, 115 Cal.Rptr. 291, 293 (Cal. Ct. App. 1974); *Insurance Company of North America v. Bath*, 726 F. Supp. 1247, 1250 (D.Wy. 1989).

4. The quoted clause is contained as part of the General Indemnity Agreement drafted by a subcommittee of the Claims Advisory Committee of the Surety Association of America in 1965.

MADE IN GOOD FAITH

The impact of such indemnity clauses was recognized by the court in *Commercial Ins. Co. of Newark, N.J. v. Pacific-Peru Const. Corp.*[5] There the principal sought to defend against the surety's contractual indemnification claim by asserting that the surety should not have sustained any loss because a foreign judgment obtained against the surety and paid by it was invalid. The Court, upholding the surety's claim, noted:

> . . . equity generally implies a right to indemnification in favor of a surety only when the surety pays off a debt for which his principal is liable . . . However, resort to implied indemnity principles is improper when an express indemnification contract exists. There can be no question but that a surety is entitled to stand upon the letter of his contract . . .
>
> * * *
>
> The indemnity agreement does not limit [the principal's] liability for indemnification to losses incurred . . . based upon [an enforceable] judgment. The broad terms of the clause provide indemnification for any loss by [the surety] by 'reason . . . of having executed the performance bond'.[6]

Courts have repeatedly upheld such contractual indemnity provisions subject *only* to the condition that the payment by the surety is not the product of its fraud or bad faith.[7] The rationale underlying these decisions is that the expense, delay and risk of loss to the surety is a sufficient safeguard against an unwarranted payment by the surety.[8] It has also been suggested by at least one court that imposing any stricter duty on sureties would create reluctance on their part to satisfy valid claims under their bonds.[9] As one court explained:

> Sureties enjoy such discretion to settle claims because of the important function they serve in the construction industry, and because the economic incentives motivating them are a sufficient safeguard against payment of invalid claims. The many parties to a typical construction contract -- owners, general contractors, subcontractors and sub-subcontractors -- look to sureties to provide assurance that defaults by any of the myriad other parties involved will not result in a loss to them. Courts have recognized that as a practical matter the suppliers and small

---

5. 558 F.2d 948 (9th Cir. 1977).

6. *Id.*, at 953.

7. *See, e.g.*, *United States Fidelity & Guaranty Co. v. Feibus*, 15 F. Supp.2d 579, 585 (M.D.Pa. 1998), *aff'd* 185 F.3d 864 (3rd Cir. 1999); *General Accident Insurance Company of America v. Merritt-Meridian Construction Corp.*, 975 F. Supp. 511, 516 (S.D.N.Y. 1997); *Associated Indemnity Corporation v. CAT Contracting, Inc.*, 964 S.W.2d 276 (Tex. 1998); *Fidelity & Deposit Co. of Maryland v. Fleischer*, 772 S.W.2d 809, 815 (Mo. Ct. App. 1989); *Bristol Steel & Iron Works, Inc.*, 722 F.2d at 1163; *Pacific-Peru Const. Co.*, 558 F.2d at 953; *Transamerica Ins. Co. v. Bloomfield*, 401 F.2d 357, 362-363 (6th Cir. 1968); *Engbrock v. Federal Ins. Co.*, 370 F.2d 784, 786 (5th Cir. 1967); *Fireman's Fund Ins. Co. v. Nizdil*, 709 F. Supp. 975, 977 (D.Or. 1989); *Bath*, 726 F. Supp. at 1252.

8. *Merritt-Meridian Construction Corp.*, 975 F. Supp. at 516; *Feibus*, 15 F. Supp.2d at 585; *Engbrock v. Federal Ins. Co.*, 370 F.2d 784, 786 (5th Cir. 1967).

9. *See, e.g. CAT Contracting, Inc.*, 964 S.W.2d at 282.

contractors on large construction projects need reasonably prompt payment for their work and materials in order for them to remain solvent and stay in business.[10]

Thus, to recover under its General Indemnity Agreement, a surety need only have made payments in good faith. The surety need not prove the actual validity of the claims it paid. In *General Insurance Company of America v. Singleton*,[11] for example, an indemnitor challenged a surety's decision to settle a bond claim. The indemnitor argued that, in order to recover, the settling surety must prove that it was, in fact, liable for the amount paid. Rejecting that argument, the court noted as follows:

> To require plaintiff to establish a case against the defendants [the indemnitors] in the same manner that a claimant against the indemnitee would have been obligated to do, would defeat the purpose of the clauses of the indemnity agreement allowing the indemnitee to settle claims. 'The purpose of clauses in indemnity agreements of the type here involved is to facilitate the handling of settlements by sureties and obviate unnecessary and costly litigation.'[12]

Indeed, a number of courts have gone as far to observe that in enforcing a surety's right to indemnity for losses incurred in good faith, "it is *irrelevant* whether [the principal] was actually liable on the underlying debt[.]"[13]

---

10. *General Accident Insurance Company of America. v. Merritt-Meridian Construction Corp.*, 975 F. Supp. 511, 516 (S.D.N.Y. 1997).

11. 115 Cal.Rptr. 291 (Cal. Ct. App. 1974).

12. *Id.*, at 294, *quoting Transamerica Insurance Company v. Bloomfield*, 401 F.2d 357, 363 (6th Cir. 1968). *See, also, Fidelity & Deposit Co. of Maryland v. Fleischer*, 772 S.W.2d 809, 816 (Mo. Ct. App. 1989) ("F&D's right to reimbursement is not dependent on a determination that it was, in fact, liable for losses under the bonds.").

13. *International Fidelity Insurance Company v. Spadafina*, 596 N.Y.S.2d 453, 454 (N.Y.App.Div. 1993) (emphasis supplied). *Accord, Reliance Insurance Company v. Romine*, 707 F. Supp. 550, 553 (S.D.Ga. 1989) ("...the only material issue here is whether plaintiff exhibited bad faith or abuse of discretion in paying the claimant."); *United States ex rel. International Brotherhood of Electrical Workers Local #449 v. United Pacific Insurance Company*, 697 F. Supp. 378, 381 (D.Idaho 1988) ("Hence, under the express terms of the Agreement, the Indemnitors are liable to indemnify UPIC no matter what the legal defenses or other avenues of resolution may have been."); *Safeco Insurance Company of America v. Gaubert*, 829 S.W.2d 274, 282 (Tex. Ct. App. 1992) ("[W]hether Safeco was liable on the bond makes no difference.").

But see, General Insurance Company of America v. K. Capolino Construction Corp., 908 F. Supp. 197 (S.D.N.Y. 1995). In *Capolino*, the court, on reconsideration of its prior decision denying the surety's motion for summary judgment (reported at 903 F. Supp. 623), noted the case law holding that the principal could not defeat the surety's summary judgment motion by arguing that an issue of fact existed as to whether or not the principal was actually in default of the underlying agreement. *Id.*, at 199. Adhering to its prior decision, the court distinguished the case before it from other cases on the dubious basis that the principal was alleging a default by the bond obligee, as opposed to its non-liability. *Id.* In support of its ruling, the court also noted that the "indemnity agreement itself references the bonds," and therefore, the court reasoned, it was required to look to "the terms of the performance bonds in order to determine whether the surety's expenses were incurred because it executed the bonds." *Id.*, at 199-200. While the court recognized it was denying literal enforcement of the indemnity agreement, the court stated that it was "not convinced" that it should overlook "the equally specific terms of the performance bond," which was expressly effective only in the absence of any default by the bond obligee. *Id.*

The decision in *Capolino* can only be regarded as an aberration "which is contrary to the majority of jurisdictions." *United States Fidelity & Guaranty Co. v. Feibus*, 15 F. Supp.2d 579, 583, n.6 (M.D.Pa. 1998), *aff'd* 185 F.3d 864 (3rd Cir. 1999). Indeed, as noted in *Feibus*, *GeneralAccident Insurance Company of America v. Merritt-Meridian Construction Corp.*, 975 F. Supp. 511, 516 (S.D.N.Y. 1997), which cited *Capolino*, found it "irrelevant" whether a principal had actually defaulted, "so long as [the surety] acted in good faith in making the payments."

In *Continental Cas. Co. v. Guterman*,[14]for example, the district court refused to vacate a summary judgment order in favor of a surety, based upon the district court's adoption of the earlier recommendations of a magistrate judge. The district court acknowledged that the principal did not receive notice of the magistrate's recommendations until after the district court had granted summary judgment. The district court nevertheless declined to reconsider summary judgment because none of the indemnitor's substantive objections created any defense under the specific language of the indemnity agreement at issue in the case. The principal argued that the surety had failed to raise the principal's equitable defenses to the bonded claims and that those defenses would have absolved the surety of its obligation to pay the claims. The principal also claimed that the surety failed to mitigate damages. The court, however, rejected those objections as a matter of law, and held that, pursuant to the express terms of the indemnity agreement, the surety would be entitled to full reimbursement for all of the claims it paid, "even if [the surety] paid off debts for which [the principal] was not liable[.]"[15] The Court also found that the indemnitors had failed to establish that the surety had either a duty or opportunity to mitigate damages through the sale of collateral pledged to it by the principal.

B. WHAT IS BAD FAITH?

1. The Majority View – Bad Faith Requires Proof of an Improper Motive

The majority of courts are in agreement that "[g]ross negligence or bad judgment is insufficient to amount to bad faith."[16] In *Engbrock v. Federal Ins. Co.*,[17] the indemnitors attempted to escape liability from their obligations under the indemnity agreement by claiming that the surety "did not do what it should have done in order to limit or minimize the costs on [the project]."[18] Affirming the entry of judgment in favor of the surety, the Fifth Circuit found that:

> At most, the pleading alleges negligence by [the] Surety. But neither lack of diligence nor negligence is the equivalent of bad faith; and improper motive, which is not alleged, is an essential

---

14. 708 F. Supp. 953, 954 (N.D.Ill. 1989).

15. *Id.*

16. *Feibus*, 15 F. Supp.2d at 586. *See also, American Employers' Insurance Company v. Horton*, 622 N.E.2d 283, 285 (Mass.App.Ct. 1993), *quoting Hartford Acc. & Indem. Co. v. Millis Roofing and Sheet Metal, Inc.*, 418 N.E.2d 645, 647 (Mass.App.Ct. 1981)("Want of good faith involves more than bad judgment, negligence or insufficient zeal. It carries an implication of a dishonest purpose, conscious doing of wrong, or breach of duty through motive of self-interest or ill will."). *Accord, Associated Indemnity Corporation v. CAT Contracting, Inc.*, 964 S.W.2d 276, 285 (Tex. 1998) ("We hold that "good faith" in the surety agreement before us refers to conduct which is honest in fact, free of improper motive or wilful ignorance of the facts at hand."); *Safeco Ins. Co. of America v. Criterion Inv. Corp.*, 732 F. Supp. 834, 841 (E.D.Tenn. 1989) ("'Good faith' means honesty in fact in the conduct or transaction concerned."); *Fidelity & Deposit Co. of Maryland v. Wu*, 552 A.2d 1196, 1200 (Vt. 1988) ("At best, the jury could draw the conclusion that plaintiff was negligent in analyzing Atom's bills – there was no evidence of lack of good faith for the jury.").

17. 370 F.2d 784 (5th Cir. 1967).

18. *Id.*, at 787.

> element of bad faith . . . Hence, we conclude that it was not error for the trial judge to deny admission into evidence of the testimony of [the indemnitors] that the payments were excessive.[19]

In *Employers Ins. of Wausau v. Able Green, Inc.*,[20] the principal asserted that the surety had acted in bad faith by negligently failing to obtain complete copies of all construction agreements and improperly paying claims in order to forego litigation. Despite the fact that the surety's action may have been negligent, the court held that such acts do not rise to the level of deliberate malfeasance which is required to establish bad faith. The court went on to note that the surety's decision to avoid litigation indicated good faith rather than bad faith where the costs of litigation would far exceed the expense of settling the claim.

A surety does not engage in "bad faith" even when it settles questionable claims to protect its own best interests, as opposed to the interests of the indemnitors. In *Fidelity & Deposit Co. of Maryland v. Bristol Steel & Iron Works, Inc.*,[21] for example, the principal constructed a bridge, which the Pennsylvania Department of Transportation ("PennDOT") found inadequate and refused to accept. PennDOT brought a a performance bond claim, and both the principal and the sureties denied liability. An arbitration commenced between PennDOT and the principal. While the arbitration was pending, however, PennDOT, displeased with the sureties' refusal to pay, disqualified the sureties from bonding future PennDOT projects. In response, the sureties entered into an agreement with PennDOT, whereby the sureties made payment to the PennDOT in order to regain their qualified status.[22] The sureties then sought and were awarded indemnity under an indemnity agreement requiring reimbursement of all payments made by the sureties "in good faith … under the belief that [they were] liable for the sums or amount so disbursed, or that it was necessary or expedient to make such disbursements, whether or not such liability, necessity or expediency existed[.]"[23] Affirming, the Fourth Circuit noted that a principal under a surety contract is required to keep its surety "unmolested," that "there would have been no justification for a finding of fraud or bad faith simply because [the sureties] made the payment to secure their removal from PennDOT's blacklist."[24] Similarly, the court in *Banque Nationale de Paris S.A. v. Insurance Company of North America*,[25] analogized the surety's discretion in settling claims to the business judgment rule in corporate law, and noted that in the absence of self-interest or fraud, the surety's "decision ought to be regarded as presumptively correct." The court also observed that, in this context, "self interest" does not include the surety's interest in minimizing its losses through settlement.[26]

---

19. *Id.*

20. 749 F. Supp. 1100, 1103 (S.D.Fla. 1990).

21. 722 F.2d 1160 (4th Cir. 1983) (Applying Pennsylvania law).

22. The agreement also provided that PennDOT would refund the money, with interest, if the principal prevailed in its arbitration with PennDOT. *Bristol Steel*, at 1164.

23. *Id.*, at 1163, n. 5.

24. *Id.*, at 1165. *See also United States Fidelity Co. v. Sandoval*, 223 U.S. 227, 32 S.Ct. 298, 56 L.Ed. 415 (1912), cited in *Bristol Steel*, as well as the following cases citing *Bristol Steel* as controlling on this point: *Arntz Contracting Co. v. St. Paul Fire and Marine Insurance Company*, 54 Cal.Rptr.2d 888, 900-901 (Cal. Ct. App. 1996) and *United States Fidelity & Guaranty Co. v. Feibus*, 15 F. Supp.2d 579, 585-586 (M.D.Pa. 1998), *aff'd* 185 F.3d 864 (3rd Cir. 1999)

25. 896 F. Supp. 163, 166 (S.D.N.Y. 1995) (Applying New York law).

26. *Id.*, at 165, n. 2.

2. The Minority View – Objectively Unreasonable Conduct or Negligence May Constitute Bad Faith

Although a clear majority of courts to have considered the issue have defined surety "bad faith" as something akin to fraud,[27] there are a small number of cases in which courts have entertained the "bad faith" defense based upon surety conduct which, although honest, was nevertheless unreasonable or negligent.

An example is the case of *Arntz Contracting Co. v. St. Paul Fire and Marine Insurance Company*.[28] There, applying "the standard of good faith implied in every contract," the court held that a surety's bad faith could be demonstrated by proof of "objectively unreasonable conduct, regardless of the actor's motive."[29] Noting that the indemnity agreement authorized the surety to complete a project at the indemnitor's expense when "in its sole opinion, such action is desirable or necessary," the court observed that the "covenant of good faith finds particular application in situations where one party is invested with a discretionary power affecting the rights of another."[30] Although there was apparently no *direct evidence* of any evil intention on the part of the surety in incurring expenses, the court in *Arntz* nevertheless held that "substantial evidence" supported the finding that the surety, which incurred certain expenses despite having been provided with "overwhelming evidence" that those expenses were unwarranted, "did not in good faith believe it was either 'desirable or necessary'" to incur those expenses.[31]

The court in *The Hartford v. Tanner*,[32] for example, held that "good faith requires a surety seeking indemnification to show that its conduct was reasonable."[33] Applying that standard, the court affirmed summary judgment dismissing the surety's claims, observing that the surety "did not conduct a thorough investigation," had "simply paid the claims and sought indemnification," and had "made no attempt to mitigate the claims."[34] Despite that finding, the court appeared to accept the surety's argument that it was still entitled to recover what its

---

27. *See, e.g.*, *Reliance Insurance Company v. Romine*, 707 F.Supp. 550, 552 (S.D.Ga. 1989) (no evidence of bad faith; bad faith equated with the arbitrary or capricious standard for proving an abuse of discretion); *United States ex rel. International Brotherhood of Electrical Workers Local #449 v. United Pacific Insurance Company*, 697 F. Supp. 378, 381 (D. Idaho 1988) (no evidence of fraud or bad faith); *Associated Indemnity Corporation v. CAT Contracting, Inc.*, 964 S.W.2d 276, 284 (Tex. 1998) (bad faith defined as involving "wilful misconduct or improper motive."); *General Insurance Company of America v. Singleton*, 115 Cal.Rptr. 291 (Cal. Ct. App. 1974) (not bad faith to settle claim where there were differences of opinion on the chances of success in litigation and no dispute that litigation would be costly).

28. 54 Cal.Rptr.2d 888 (Cal. Ct. App. 1996) (Applying California law).

29. *Id.*, at 899.

30. *Id.*, at 898.

31. *Id.*, at 899. Other cases suggesting that "good faith" would not include payments made in objectively unreasonable amounts include *Ideal Electronic Security Co, Inc. v. International Fidelity Insurance Company*, 129 F.3d 143, 150 (D.C.Cir. 1997) (referencing a surety's right to recover its attorney's fees, and stating "any decisions to pay counsel must pass a test of reasonableness in order to be in good faith.") and *Acstar Insurance Company v. Teton Enterprises*, 670 N.Y.S.2d 588, 589 (N.Y. App. Div. 1998) ("...payments made by sureties under such provisions are scrutinized only for good faith and reasonableness as to amount paid.").

32. 910 P.2d 872 (Kan.Ct.App. 1996).

33. *Id.*, at 880.

34. *Id.*

losses would have been had its conduct been reasonable.[35] As the surety had offered no evidence of what its losses would have been, however, the court affirmed the dismissal of the case. Similarly, the court in *City of Portland v. George D. Ward & Associates, Inc.*,[36] held that to prove "bad faith," the indemnitors "need only prove that [the surety] failed to make a reasonable investigation of the validity of the claims against them or to consider reasonably the viability of their counterclaims and defenses, not that [the surety] acted for dishonest purposes or improper motives."[37] Applying that standard of proof, the *City of Portland* court affirmed the trial court's refusal to enter a directed verdict in favor of the surety against the indemnitors.[38]

The standard of "bad faith" applied in the *City of Portland* case, however, was not set forth as a general rule of law, but was limited to "an indemnity agreement which subjects the right to compromise a claim to the sole discretion of the surety[.]"[39] Under *those* terms, the court concluded that parties to such an agreement "must reasonably expect" that the surety would compromise claims only after a reasonable investigation, and the court gave force to those expectations by invoking the "implied obligation of good faith" in all contracts.[40] The same observation may be made concerning the decision in *Arntz Contracting Co.*, which noted the "particular application" of the implied covenant of good faith to an indemnity agreement which authorized the surety to determine in its "sole opinion" what claims should be compromised.[41] It can therefore be fairly argued that had the indemnity agreements in *City of Portland* and *Arntz Contracting Co.* not given the sureties *exclusive* authority over settlements, but had contained a provision permitting the indemnitors to "opt out" of the surety's right-to-settle clause by posting collateral,[42] the courts in those cases would have required a stronger showing of "bad faith" to support a defense to indemnity.[43]

---

35. An ironic element of the *Tanner* case is that the trial court apparently accepted the indemnitor's argument that the surety should have "protested" and "delayed payment" until statute of limitations had expired on the bond – the same kind of conduct which may cause bond claimants to cry "bad faith!" The reviewing court agreed with the surety that evidence of what would have happened had the surety protested the claims was "speculative." *Id.*, at 882. Nevertheless, the decision in *Tanner* noted, with apparent regret, that the surety's "payment of the claims, however, eliminated any chance that the statute of limitations might expire on the other bonds." *Id.*, at 881. It is unlikely that the court intended to suggest that a surety, acting in "good faith," should intentionally delay paying valid claims until they are time-barred. This, however, is exactly the message sent, and underscores why some courts have refused, on policy grounds, to impose stricter standards of surety "good faith" vis-à-vis indemnitors. *See, e.g. Associated Indemnity Corporation v. CAT Contracting, Inc.*, 964 S.W.2d 276, 282 (Tex. 1998) ("[I]f such a duty were imposed … a surety might be reluctant to satisfy an obligee's valid claims[.]").

36. 750 P.2d 171 (Or.Ct.App. 1988) (applying Oregon law).

37. *Id.*, at 175.

38. *Id.*, at 176.

39. *Id.* Indeed, *City of Portland* court distinguished the case before it from cases "based on contracts in which the language explicitly set a fraud standard" [for determining bad faith]. *Id.*, at 174.

40. *Id*, at 174. The court in *U. S. for Use of Trustees of Elec. Workers Local Pension Fund v. D Bar D Enterprises, Inc.*, 772 F. Supp. 1167, 1170 (D.Nev. 1991), for example, cited *City of Portland* for the proposition that "[w]here an indemnification agreement subjects the right to settle a claim to the *sole discretion* of the surety, the parties may expect that the surety will settle only after reasonable investigation of the claims, counterclaims, and possible defenses." (emphasis supplied).

41. *Arntz Contracting*, at 898.

42. Many modern General Indemnity Agreements include such a provision. *See* discussion *infra* in Point II.A.

43. *See* cases cited in footnote 27, *supra*.

The indemnity agreement in *Tanner* also gave the surety the "exclusive right" to determine settlements.[44] *Tanner*, however, appears to adopt a "reasonableness standard" as the test for a surety's good faith as a general rule of law, without reference to the specific terms of the indemnity agreement before it. This is surprising, in that the three surety cases with which the *Hartford* court purported to "agree"[45] on this point do not support the general application of such a standard. The first case, *City of Portland*, was limited to indemnity agreements giving the surety *exclusive* discretion over settlements. The second case cited by *Tanner*, *J.F. White Engineering Corporation v. General Insurance Company of America*,[46] approved a jury instruction which held a surety to a "reasonable diligence and precaution" standard in the context of whether the surety had failed to mitigate damages. The terms of the indemnity agreement in that case, however, were not set forth in the opinion, and the issue of "good faith" was nowhere mentioned. It therefore can only be assumed that that the indemnitors in *J.F. White* had not expressly contracted to use "good faith" as the measure for the surety's right to indemnity. The third case, *Rush Presbyterian St. Luke's Medical Center v. Safeco Insurance Company of America*,[47] no longer accurately reflected Illinois law, if it ever did, and should not have been cited as authoritative.[48]

Regardless of the flaws in the *Tanner* decision and the breadth of its language, the case is still easily distinguishable from cases arising under indemnity agreements affording the indemnitors the option of posting collateral and assuming the defense of claims. The *Tanner* court was unwilling to interpret or enforce the indemnity agreement in a manner which "leaves the indemnitor at the mercy of the surety's unreasonable conduct."[49] That concern, however,

44. *The Hartford v. Tanner*, 910 P.2d 872, 875 (Kan.Ct.App. 1996).

45. *Id.*, at 880.

46. 351 F.2d 231, 233 (10th Cir. 1965).

47. 712 F. Supp. 1344, 1345-1346 (N.D. Ill. 1989) (purporting to apply Illinois law).

48. *Rush Presbyterian*, citing a single insurance case which had nothing to do with suretyship or an indemnity agreement, held that Illinois law "requires only a showing of negligence in actions alleging a breach of a surety's duty towards its insured, where the insured is obligated to indemnify the surety." *Id.*, at 346. The full extent of the court's reasoning was set forth in an earlier opinion in the same case, which was subsequently reported. *Windowmaster v. Morse/Diesel, Inc.*, 722 F. Supp. 1532 (N.D. Ill. 1988). *Windowmaster* acknowledged that Illinois construed indemnity contracts in the same manner as any other contract. *Id.*, at 1534. The court, however, held that "this was no ordinary contract," but rather equated to "an insurance contract," under which "the insurer owes its insured a duty of fair treatment." *Id.* It should be noted that the decision in *Windowmaster* appears to have resulted largely from the court's concern that the indemnity agreement at issue, like those in *City of Portland*, *Arntz Contracting Co.* and *Tanner*, gave the surety the "exclusive right" to determine settlements. *Id.* Thereafter, however, an Illinois intermediate appellate court in *United States Fidelity and Guaranty Company v. Klein Corporation*, 558 N.E.2d 1047 (Ill.App. Ct. 1990), affirming summary judgment in favor of a surety against its indemnitors, confirmed that the courts of Illinois will indeed construe an indemnity agreement in favor of a compensated surety "as any other contract," and added further that "a surety is entitled to stand on the language of the contract." *Id.*, at 1049-1050, *citing Fidelity & Deposit Co. of Maryland v. Bristol Steel & Iron Works, Inc.*, 722 F.2d 1160 (4th Cir. 1983). *Klein Corporation* also noted the absence of Illinois precedent interpreting indemnity agreements permitting sureties to recover for payments made in "good faith." *Id.*, at 1050. The *Klein* court therefore chose to follow the interpretation of a similar indemnity agreement in *Hess v. American States Insurance Co.*, 589 S.W.2d 548 (Tex.Civ.App. 1979). *Hess*, for its part, held that such an indemnity agreement permits a surety to recover for all payments made by it in its discetion "limited only by the bounds of fraud." *Id.*, at 551.

49. *Tanner*, at 881.

would be of considerably less force under an indemnity agreement which gave the indemnitors the option of posting collateral and determining for themselves whether or not claims should be litigated.[50]

II. *The Right-to-Settle Provision*

The right-to-settle provision is another important component of the General Indemnity Agreement. Depending upon the particular form of General Indemnity Agreement in use, the right-to-settle clause may be found either within the specific language of the indemnity clause or set out separately.

The right-to-settle clause permits the surety to discharge the principal's obligations before suit[51] without endangering its indemnification rights. Thus, this provision allows the surety effectively and efficiently to resolve claims, seek immediate reimbursement from the principal and indemnitors and avoid unnecessary litigation.

A. THE INDEMNITORS' OPTION TO POST COLLATERAL AND REQUEST LITIGATION

As discussed previously, a right-to-settle clause may give the surety exclusive discretion to determine whether and upon what terms to settle bond claims.[52] More commonly, however, the right-to-settle provision presents the indemnitors with the option of posting collateral with the surety to protect it from bond claims in order to require the surety to litigate the claims. A typical right-to-settle clause including such an option may provide as follows:

> The Company shall have the exclusive right for itself and for the Undersigned to decide and determine whether any claim, demand, suit, or judgment shall, on the basis of liability, expediency or otherwise, be paid, settled, defended or appealed, and the Company's determination shall be final, conclusive and binding upon the Undersigned.
>
> If the Undersigned desire that the Company litigate such claim or demand, or defend such suit, or appeal from such judgment, they shall deposit with the Company, at the time of such request, cash or collateral satisfactory to the Company in kind and amount to be used in paying any judgment or judgments rendered, or which might be rendered, against Company together with interest, costs and attorneys' fees.[53]

Where, as in the above-quoted provision, the right-to-settle clause permits the indemnitors to require the defense of claims after posting collateral with the surety, but the indemnitors do not do so, the courts generally will not entertain the indemnitors' protestations

---

50. *See, e.g.*, *Fidelity & Deposit Co. of Maryland v. Fleischer*, 772 S.W.2d 809, 816 (Mo. Ct. App. 1989), noting the significance of the indemnitor's failure to take advantage of such an option.

51. *Transamerica Ins. Co. v. Bloomfield*, 401 F.2d 357, 362 (6th Cir. 1968); *National Sur. Corp. v. Peoples Milling Co.*, 57 F. Supp. 281 (W.D. Ky. 1944); *Commercial Union Ins. Co. v. Melikyan*, 430 So. 2d 1217 (La. Ct. App. 1983); *Hess v. American State Ins. Co.*, 589 S.W.2d 548 (Tex.Civ.App. 1979)

52. *See* discussion, *supra*, notes 39 - 49 and accompanying text.

53. *IADC'S Project Update 1995*, *supra* footnote 2, at 267.

over the surety's settlement determinations. Thus, the court in *Employers Insurance of Wausau v. Able Green, Inc.*,[54] observed as follows:

> Able Green did not request, in compliance with paragraph eight, that Wausau litigate these claims nor did Able Green post collateral to cover the litigation expenses. As stated in paragraph eight, unless Able Green meets these two criteria, Wausau has the exclusive right to determine whether bonds shall be paid. Although Able Green alleges that Wausau made bad faith payment of claims just to forego litigation, this allegation cannot withstand Able Green's own failure to comply with the terms of paragraph eight of the indemnity agreement.[55]

Such provisions, which permit the surety to compromise and settle claims and which may be coupled with clauses providing that vouchers and other evidence of payment of claims shall be *prima facie* evidence of the propriety thereof,[56] have been routinely upheld.[57] Courts have recognized that these provisions afford the surety broad discretion in determining which claims should be compromised and settled, and have held that the surety's decision will be binding on the principal and the indemnitors as long as the surety acted in good faith.

B. GOOD FAITH IN SETTLING CLAIMS

Good faith in the context of the right-to-settle clause raises the same issues as the good faith inquiry under the indemnity clause.[58] In both cases the focus is on the surety's handling of the claims. Among the factors considered by courts in evaluating the surety's good faith in settling a claim are: whether the surety exceeded the face amount of the bond;[59] whether the principal has cooperated with the surety and provided information and documentation supporting denial of the claim;[60] whether the surety was subjected to undue or unusual pressure from the obligee;[61] and whether the surety performed a reasonable investigation of the claim before settling it.[62] Courts have also noted that a finding of good faith is supported by the fact the surety makes payments when the prospect of recovering indemnity is in doubt;[63] or when

54. 749 F. Supp. 1100 (S.D.Fla. 1990).

55. *Id.*, at 1103. See *also Transamerica Ins. Co. v. Avenell*, 66 F.3d 715, 719-720 (5th Cir. 1995) (holding that the surety had "no obligation to hear, much less honor," an indemnitor's demand not to settle a case, unless that demand was accompanied by security, and that the posing of security and request for defense were "conditions precedent" to preventing the surety from settling.); *Accord, Fidelity & Deposit Company of Maryland v. Fleischer*, 772 S.W.2d 809, 816 (Mo.Ct. App. 1989).

56. *See* Section III, *infra*.

57. *See* cases cited in footnote 10, *supra*. *But see* discussion, *infra*, notes 79 - 85 and accompanying text.

58. *See* discussion *supra* Part I.

59. *Commercial Union Ins. Co. v. Melikyan*, 430 So. 2d 1217, 1222 (La. Ct. App. 1983).

60. *United States Fidelity & Guaranty Co. v. Feibus*, 15 F. Supp.2d 579, 586 (M.D.Pa. 1998), *aff'd* 185 F.3d 864 (3rd Cir. 1999). *See also Glens Falls Indem. Co. of Glens Falls v. Carobine*, 36 N.Y.S.2d 253 (City Ct. 1942).

61. *Fidelity & Deposit Co. of Maryland v. Bristol Steel & Iron Works, Inc.*, 722 F.2d 1160 (4th Cir. 1983). *See also* cases cited in footnote 24, *supra*.

62. *City of Portland v. George D. Ward & Associates, Inc.*, 750 P.2d 171, 175 (Or.Ct.App. 1988); *The Hartford v. Tanner*, 910 P.2d 872 (Kan.Ct.App. 1996).

63. *See Safeco Ins. Co. of America v. Criteron Inv. Corp.*, 732 F.Supp. 834, 841 (E.D. Tenn. 1989), in which the court was "unable to find a bad motive in the plaintiff's payment of these claims, particularly in light of

the indemnitors fail to post collateral;[64] or when the surety is facing claims from numerous parties;[65] or when it appears that defending the claim would be unjustifiably costly.[66]

Other courts, when addressing whether the surety has settled claims in "good faith" have also focused on whether the surety reasonably believed that the claim should be paid. In *United States ex rel. Trustees of Electrical Workers Local Pension Fund v. D Bar D Enterprises, Inc.*,[67] for example, the principal argued that the surety acted in bad faith when it settled claims apparently preempted by ERISA. Although noting that there was strong legal authority for finding preemption, the court found that because the surety reasonably considered the claims and its possible defenses to the claims, it had acted in good faith and should be indemnified.

III. *The Prima Facie Evidence Clause*

In conjunction with the surety's right to compromise and settle claims, and to recover for expenses incurred in good faith, courts have also upheld clauses which provide, in substance, as follows: "In the event of payments by the Surety, the Indemnitors agree to accept the voucher of the Surety or other evidence of such payments as prima facie evidence of the propriety thereof, and of the Indemnitor's liability therefor to the Surety."[68]

A. THE EFFECT OF THE PRIMA FACIE EVIDENCE CLAUSE

The purpose and effect of the prima facie evidence clause is to simplify the surety's task in proving its case for indemnity, and to shift to the indemnitors the burden of going forward with evidence that any of the surety's payments are improper or unrecoverable. Thus, under such clauses, "courts have routinely held that once a surety has submitted the required documentation of payments, the burden under Rule 56[69] shifts to the principal to prove the existence of a genuine issue of material fact for trial."[70] This means that, except in the rare case where the indemnitors are able to submit sufficient admissible evidence (as opposed to

the fact that the plaintiff expended its own money in circumstances in which the financial conditions of its indemnitors made recovery of the money spent less than completely certain." *See also Transamerica Insurance Co. v. H.V.A.C. Contractors, Inc.*, 857 F. Supp. 969, 974 (N.D.Ga. 1994) ("Plaintiff had nothing to gain by inflating payments. To the contrary, each payment required more work and risk on plaintiff's part that it might not recover from defendants under the Agreement of Indemnity.").

64. *Feibus*, 15 F. Supp.2d at 586; *Employers Insurance Company of Wausau v. Able Green, Inc.*, 749 F. Supp. 1101, 1103 (S.D.Fla. 1990).

65. *General Accident Insurance Company of America v. Merritt-Meridian Construction Corp.*, 975 F. Supp. 511, 519 (S.D.N.Y. 1997) (The surety was "faced with numerous subcontractor claims on Merritt projects, which would reasonably lead it to conclude that the owners' claims were valid and Merritt's complaints meritless.").

66. *Able Green, Inc.*, 749 F. Supp. at 1103; *General Insurance Company of America v. Singleton*, 115 Cal.Rptr. 291, 294 (Cal. Ct. App. 1974).

67. 772 F. Supp. 1167 (D.Nev. 1991).

68. *Acstar Insurance Company v. Teton Enterprises*, 670 N.Y.S.2d 588 (N.Y. App. Div. 1998) (enforcing prima facie evidence clause and finding that indemnitors had failed to produce evidence sufficient to overcome the surety's right to summary judgment).

69. Fed. R. Civ. Pr. 56, which applies to motions for Summary Judgment.

70. *United States Fidelity & Guaranty Co. v. Feibus*, 15 F. Supp.2d 579, 587 (M.D.Pa. 1998), *aff'd* 185 F.3d 864 (3rd Cir. 1999).

mere speculation or argument), to demonstrate an entitlement to go to trial on the issue of "bad faith" or to contest the amount of the surety's payments, the surety will be entitled to summary judgment.[71]

The prima facie evidence clause is also of significant utility in that, in conjunction with other clauses of the General Indemnity Agreement such as the Right-to-Settle provision, it relieves the surety of the initial evidentiary burden of justifying its payments. Illustrative of this point is *Hawaiian Insurance & Guaranty Company, Ltd. v. Higashi*,[72] a case which applied the "general rule" that an indemnitee bears the "burden of proving reasonableness and good faith[.]"[73] In so holding, the court noted the absence of a right-to-settle and prima facie evidence clause in the indemnity agreement before it and stated, in *dicta*, that "[o]bviously, where such a provision is in the agreement, the burden of proof on those issues shifts."[74]

The utility of the prima facie evidence clause, of course, has its limits. A surety relying on such a clause should still be prepared to put on evidence of the basis for its payments. As observed in *Ideal Electronic Security Co., Inc. v. International Fidelity Insurance Company*,[75] which concerned a surety's claim for attorney's fees: "[S]omething more than evidence of mere payment will be required if a charge is challenged. Thus, this provision is hardly conclusive with regard to the amount of a reasonable fee award, but rather shifts to [the indemnitors] the burden of proving that the fees claimed are excessive." Similarly, the court in *Associated Indemnity Corporation v. CAT Contracting, Inc.*,[76] referencing the prima facie evidence clause, stated: "This provision, however, only shifts the burden of production regarding good faith, not the burden of persuasion." While not necessarily required, it is certainly advisable that a surety moving for summary judgment, in addition to providing proof of the fact of its payments, also provide the court detailed affidavits and documentation of its losses and expenses.[77] It should also be noted that at least one court has refused to enforce a prima facie evidence clause where the surety's only proffered proof of payment, a copy of a draft check, did not satisfy standards for the document to be admitted as evidence.[78]

---

71. *See, e.g., Gundle Lining Construction Corporation v. Adams County Asphalt, Inc.*, 85 F.3d 201, 211 (5th Cir. 1996); *Safeco Insurance Company of America v. Guabert*, 829 S.W.2d 274, 282-283 (Tex.Ct.App. 1992); *General Insurance Company of America v. Singleton*, 115 Cal.Rptr. 291 (Cal. Ct. App. 1974); *United States Fidelity & Guaranty Company v. Lipsmeyer Construction Company, Inc.*, 754 F. Supp. 81 (M.D.La. 1990); *United States Fidelity & Guaranty Company v. Klein Corporation*, 558 N.E.2d 1047 (Ill. App. Ct. 1989). *See ,also, Continental Cas. Co. v. American Sur. Corp.*, 443 F.2d 649 (D.C. Cir. 1970), *cert. denied*, 402 U.S. 907, *reh'g denied*, 403 U.S. 912 (1971) (where the surety presents prima facie evidence of payment by way of affidavit and supporting documentation the case is ideally suited for summary judgment); *Buckeye Union Ins. Co. v. Boggs*, 109 F.R.D. 420, 423-424 (S.D.W.Va. 1986) (surety's affidavit as to expenses incurred was sufficient evidence on which to grant summary judgment).

72. 675 P.2d 767 (Hawaii 1984).

73. *Id.*, at 769.

74. *Id.*

75. 129 F.3d 143, 151 (D.C.Cir. 1997).

76. 964 S.W.2d 276, 283, n. 5 (Tex. 1998).

77. *See, e.g., Feibus*, 15 F.Supp.2d at 582; *Fidelity & Deposit Co. of Maryland v. Wu*, 552 A.2d 1196, 1198 (Vt. 1988).

78. *United States Fire Insurance Co. v. Twin City Concrete, Inc.*, 684 S.W.2d 171 (Tex. Ct. App. 1984).

B. THE CONCLUSIVE EVIDENCE CLAUSE

While courts have repeatedly upheld the prima facie as not being against public policy,[79] the courts are split on the validity of clauses in indemnity agreements which state that evidence of payment will be "conclusive" evidence rather than prima facie evidence of the indemnitors' liability to the surety. Several courts have enforced the conclusive evidence provision as long as the surety acted in good faith.[80] In *Home Indem. Co. v. Wachter*,[81] for example, a New York appellate court upheld a clause in the indemnity agreement which provided that vouchers for payment or a sworn statement by an officer of the surety would be conclusive evidence of the indemnitors' liability to the surety. The court stated that by signing the indemnity agreement which included that provision, the indemnitors were bound by its terms and liable to the surety when the surety settled claims in good faith.

Other courts have refused to enforce conclusive evidence provisions because they deprive indemnitors of the opportunity to introduce proofs to rebut the surety's evidence.[82] The court in *The Hartford v. Tanner*,[83] for example, held a conclusive evidence clause void as contrary to public policy because, were it to be enforced, it would hold the surety "to no standard other than its own expediency."[84] In *Sork v. United Benefit Fire Ins. Co.*,[85] the court rejected the conclusive effect of such a clause because it precluded the indemnitor from contesting the surety's legal bills on the ground that the attorneys' fees charged were unreasonable. Such a preclusion, the court held, violated public policy.

Because the courts have recognized the validity of prima facie evidence clauses, a surety which resolves claims under its right to settle clause will often be able to use vouchers and affidavits to obtain summary judgment enforcing its right under the General Indemnity Agreement to indemnification for the losses and expenses incurred in discharging its bond obligations. Even where summary judgment is not granted, the prima facie evidence clause effectively shifts to the indemnitors the burden of showing that the surety did not act in good faith in settling claims and incurring expenses. As sureties generally make payments only upon a reasonable belief that the expenditures are necessary or expedient, indemnitors should not be able to meet that burden in the usual case.

IV. *The Surety's Right to Compromise its Principal's Affirmative Claims*

---

79. *Singleton*, 115 Cal.Rptr. at 294; *Feibus*, 15 F.Supp.2d at 582; *Fidelity and Deposit Company of Maryland v. Bristol Steel & Iron Works, Inc.*, 722 F.2d 1160, 1163 (4th Cir. 1983); *Transamerica Insurance Company v. Bloomfield*, 401 F.2d 357, 362-363 (6th Cir. 1968).

80. *Engbrock v. Federal Ins. Co.*, 370 F.2d 784 (5th Cir. 1967); *U. S. Fidelity & Guar. Co. v. Jones*, 87 F.2d 346, 348 (5th Cir. 1937); *Home Indem. Co. v. Wachter*, 496 N.Y.S.2d 252 (N.Y. App. Div. 1985); *Standard Acc. & Ins. v. Higgins*, 170 N.Y.S.2d 73, 75 (N.Y. Sup. Ct. 1957). *See, also, National Surety Co. v. Fulton*, 183 N.Y.S. 237 (N.Y.App.Div. 1920), upholding a "conclusive evidence" conditioned only upon the surety acting in good faith, and citing earlier cases from various jurisdictions which held conclusive evidence clauses either valid or void.

81. 496 N.Y.S.2d 252 (N.Y.App.Div. 1985).

82. *The Hartford v. Tanner*, 910 P.2d 872, 879 (Kan. Ct. App. 1996); *Sork v. United Benefit Fire Ins. Co.*, 161 So. 2d 54, 56 (Fla. Dist. Ct. App. 1964); *Fidelity & Deposit Co. of Maryland v. Davis*, 284 P. 430 (Kan. 1930); *Fidelity & Cas. Co. of New York v. Eickhoff*, 65 N.W. 351 (Minn. 1895).

83. 910 P.2d 872 (Kan. Ct. App. 1996).

84. *Id.*, at 879.

85. 161 So. 2d 54, 56 (Fla. Dist. Ct. App. 1964).

The surety's contractual right to settle claims under its bond alone will often prove insufficient to extricate the surety from a dispute between the bond principal and the party making a claim under the bond. This situation commonly arises when the principal has interposed its own affirmative claim against the party alleging a breach of contract against the principal. A typical example is where a performance bond obligee terminates the principal's rights under its contract, allegedly "for cause," and the principal disputes the termination. If the termination was indeed wrongful, the bond obligee has breached its contract, has no valid claim under the performance bond, and may be liable for any losses suffered by the principal as a result of the wrongful termination. If, alternatively, the termination was proper, then the principal has no valid claim against the bond obligee. Often in these situations, the principal will bring a claim against the obligee, and the obligee will assert a claim against both the principal and the surety. In such cases, the obligee will often hesitate, if not outright refuse, to discuss any settlement with the surety which does not, in addition to settling the obligee's claim under the bond, also include a settlement of the principal's affirmative claim against the obligee. The obligee will often place considerable value on achieving finality and avoiding litigation expenses and will regard these as critical elements of the benefits of a compromise settlement with the surety. This value can effectively be obtained only if the dismissal of the principal's affirmative claims is made part of the surety's settlement.

A. THE SURETY'S AUTHORITY TO SETTLE ITS PRINCIPAL'S AFFIRMATIVE CLAIMS

The typical right-to-settle clause, however, does not by itself expressly authorize the surety to settle the principal's affirmative claims. Rather, the surety must look to other clauses of the General Indemnity Agreement, namely the assignment clause and attorney-in-fact provision.[86]

In *Hutton Const. Co., Inc. v. County of Rockland*,[87] the United States Court of Appeals for the Second Circuit affirmed an order of the District Court enforcing a settlement which included a surety's agreement to dismiss the affirmative claims of its objecting principal. Construing the relevant provisions of a typical General Indemnity Agreement, *Hutton* held as follows:

> The court concluded that Hutton's failure to make the demanded indemnity payments constituted a breach of Hutton's obligation to the Sureties and thus activated the Assignment

86. The assignment clause of the General Indemnity Agreement generally provides that, in the event of any default by the principal under any bond or under the General Indemnity Agreement itself, that the principal assigns to the surety, retroactive to the date of the bond, any and all rights arising out of bonded contracts, any subcontracts, as well as the principal's rights of ownership in its materials and equipment. The attorney-in-fact provision irrevocably appoints the surety as the principal's attorney-in-fact with the right, but not the obligation, to execute binding documents concerning the rights assigned to the surety by virtue of the assignment clause. This Point IV addresses the assignment clause as it pertains to the principal's assignment to the surety of the principal's affirmative claims against bond obligees and/or claimants. The assignment clause is discussed in more general terms in Section VII, *infra*.

87. 52 F.3d 1191 (2nd Cir. 1995).

Clause, causing assignment to the Sureties of all of Hutton's rights growing out of the construction contracts, as collateral securing its obligations to the Sureties, and giving the Sureties the right to settle not only the County's claims against Hutton, but also Hutton's affirmative claims against the County and CBA.

The court also noted that the Attorney in Fact Clause unambiguously appointed the Sureties as Hutton's attorneys in fact with the power to exercise all rights assigned to them under the Agreement.

We agree with the district court. The Agreement of Indemnity unambiguously provides that all of Hutton's rights "growing in any manner out of" the insured contracts were assigned to the Sureties when Hutton breached the Agreement by failing to indemnify the Sureties on demand. The Assignment Clause and the Attorney in Fact clause give the Sureties the authority to settle all claims on behalf of Hutton, including not only claims against the Sureties "upon the bonds," but also Hutton's affirmative claims growing out of its insured contracts.

* * *

Hutton is correct that the Settlements Clause does not furnish the Sureties with the power to settle Hutton's affirmative claims. Nonetheless, because that power is furnished by other provisions of the agreement, its absence from the Settlements Clause is of no moment.[88]

Case law prior to *Hutton* recognized the binding effect, after the fact, of a surety's settlement of its principal's affirmative claims under the assignment provisions of a General Indemnity Agreement.[89] *Hutton*, however, appears to be the first reported decision to expressly enforce a surety's right to settle its principal's affirmative claims over the contemporaneous objection of its principal.

B. STANDARDS BY WHICH COURTS WILL JUDGE THE SURETY'S DETERMINATION TO SETTLE ITS PRINCIPAL'S AFFIRMATIVE CLAIMS

While *Hutton* confirmed the surety's right to settle its defaulted principal's claim, *Hutton* was not an indemnity case. Thus *Hutton* offered no guidance as to whether or by what standards an indemnitor could contest the surety's settlement *after the fact* as a defense to indemnification.

1. The "Good Faith" Standard

In *General Accident Insurance Company of America v. Merrit-Meridian Construction Corp.*,[90] however, the Southern District of New York, citing *Hutton*, appears to have considered that issue and to have judged the surety's settlement of the principal's potential

---

88. *Id.*, at 1192-1193.

89. *See, James McKinney & Son, Inc. v. Lake Placid 1980 Olympic Games, Inc.*, 462 N.E.2d 137 (N.Y. 1984). *Compania DE Remorque Y Salvamento, S.A. v. Esperance, Inc.*, 187 F.2d 114 (2nd Cir. 1951).

90. 975 F. Supp. 511 (S.D.N.Y. 1997).

affirmative claims by the same good faith/bad faith standard applied to the settlement of bond claims:

> Defendants also contend that [the surety's] dealings with the owners evidence bad faith. They assert that [the surety's] decision to pay the owners on the performance bonds, despite [the surety's] awareness that Merrit considered two of those owners to have been in default, demonstrates bad faith. In essence, they contend that good faith required [the surety] to protect Merrit's interests as vigorously as it protected the interests of the owners. However, the performance bonds were entered into for the benefit of the owners, not to protect Merrit. [The surety] thus had no obligation under any of the agreements to which it was a party to act on Merrit's claims of default against the owners. ... In addition, *under the assignments clause and attorney in fact clause of the indemnity agreement* [the surety] *had the right to settle not only claims against Merritt, but Merritt's affirmative claims against the owners as well. The exercise of these rights after Merritt declined to post collateral or indemnify* [the surety] *is not evidence of bad faith.* [91]

Similarly, in *Compania De Remorque Y Salvamento, S.A. v. Esperance, Inc.*,[92] the United States Court of Appeals for the Second Circuit addressed a principal/indemnitor's claim that its surety had "wrongfully and unlawfully" disposed of the principal's claim against a bond obligee, when the surety dismissed its principal's claim as part of the surety's settlement with the obligee. Recognizing the validity of the assignment clause in the General Indemnity Agreement, the Second Circuit affirmed the dismissal of the principal's claim against the surety, noting uncontested evidence that the surety "made the settlement in good faith."[93]

2. The "Commercially Reasonable" Standard

Compania was decided before the adoption of the Uniform Commercial Code,[94] and *Merrit-Meridian* did not address an issue which the Court of Appeals in *Hutton* declined to consider because it was raised for the first time on appeal, i.e., whether a surety's settlement of its principal's affirmative claim is required to be "commercially reasonable" under UCC provisions governing the disposal of collateral by secured creditors. In a 1998 decision, *Associated Indemnity Corp. v. CAT Contracting, Inc.*,[95] however, the Supreme Court of Texas stated, in *dicta*, that "[e]xisting commercial law duties prohibit a surety from disposing of collateral – including causes of action – in a commercially unreasonable manner,"[96]

Cat Contracting, Inc. cited UCC § 9-504 as the source of the surety's duty to dispose of collateral in a commercially reasonable manner.[97] This is significant because UCC 9-504 requires two things which "good faith" under the right to settle provision of the General

91. *Merrit-Meridian*, at 519, emphasis supplied, citation omitted.
92. 187 F.2d 114 (2nd Cir. 1951).
93. *Id.*, at 117.
94. The Uniform Commercial Code is hereinafter referred to as the UCC.
95. 964 S.W.2d 276 (Tex. 1998).
96. *Id.*, at 282, *citing* UCC §§ 9-102, 9-106, 9-207 and 9-504.
97. *Id.*

Indemnity Agreement is generally held not to require: (i) that the creditor give reasonable notice to the debtor prior to disposing of any collateral, and (ii) that the collateral be disposed of in a "commercially reasonable" manner.

With respect to notice, UCC article 9-504(3) provides, in part, that "[u]nless collateral is perishable or threatens to decline in value, or is of a type customarily sold on a recognized market, reasonable notification of the time and place of any public sale or reasonable notification of the time after which any private sale or intended disposition is to be made shall be sent by the secured party to the debtor, if he has not signed *after default* a statement renouncing or modifying his right to notification of sale." (emphasis supplied) Since the General Indemnity Agreement would have been signed prior to default, if UCC § 9-504(3) is deemed to apply, any waiver of notice provision in the General Indemnity Agreement may be ineffective as against the principal/indemnitor's statutory right to "reasonable notification" of the "intended disposition" of the subject collateral, i.e., the principal's affirmative claim. Of course, the surety might be able to argue that the settlement "value" of the principal's affirmative claim is "perishable or threatens to decline" if a settlement is not quickly reached without notice to the defaulting principal, but the surety would probably bear the burden of proof on that issue. Where, in negotiating a settlement, time does not appear to be of the essence, prudence would dictate that a surety wishing to give maximum protection to its indemnity rights give the principal/indemnitor at least some prior notice of the contemplated settlement and an opportunity to present the surety with a better deal, even though the principal/indemnitor is already clearly in default of the General Indemnity Agreement.

The above discussion of notice, however, presupposes that the court in *Cat Contracting, Inc.*, which was speaking purely in *dicta*, was correct in citing UCC § 9-504 as the section of the UCC applicable to the disposition of collateral in the form of a debtor's causes of action assigned to a secured creditor. More likely, the citation to that section was an error. Indeed, in an earlier case, *Cullen Frost Bank v. Dallas Sportswear Company, Inc.*,[98] the Supreme Court of Texas itself expressly held UCC § 9-504 is inapplicable to security interests in accounts receivable, and that another section, UCC § 9-502 applies in such cases.[99] That section, which applies to a secured creditor's liquidation of "intangible collateral,"[100] like § 504, requires the secured creditor "to proceed in a commercially reasonable manner."[101] Section 502 does *not*, however, require a secured creditor to give notice to the debtor prior to

98. 730 S.W.2d 668 (Tex. 1987)

99. *Id.*, at 669. *Accord, Interchange State Bank v. Rinaldi*, 696 A.2d 744, 750 (N.J. Super. Ct. App. Div. 1997) (section 502, rather than 504, applies where the collateral consists of accounts receivable). *See also* 68A Am. Jur. 2d *Secured Transactions* § 584 (1993) ("Section 9-502 of the Uniform Commercial Code provides a procedure for liquidation of intangible collateral separate and apart from UCC § 9-505."). *But see* Richard C. Tinney, Annotation, *What is "Commercially Reasonable" Disposition of Collateral Required by UCC § 9-504(3)*, 7 A.L.R. 4th 308 (1981), at § 20, "Accounts" (collecting cases).

100. UCC § 9-106 makes UCC article 9 applicable to security interests in both "accounts" and "general intangibles ... including things in action[.]" *Cat Contracting, Inc.*, 964 S.W.2d at 282 also cited UCC § 9-106 on this point. Numerous other courts have similarly recognized that § 9-106 permits recorded security interests in lawsuits sounding in contract. *See Corcoran v. Land O'Lakes, Inc.*, 39 F. Supp.2d 1139, 1147-1148 (N.D. Iowa 1999) (collecting cases). *See also* 68A Am. Jur. 2d *Secured Transactions* § 584 (1993).

101. UCC § 9-502(2).

proceeding against the intangible collateral.[102] Nevertheless, a surety, acting out of caution, may eliminate any hypothetical "notice" issue by notifying its indemnitors in advance of any potential settlement of a principal's affirmative claim(s), and offering the indemnitors a brief but reasonable opportunity to offer the surety a better deal than the surety is able to negotiate with the obligee/claimant.[103]

The UCC requirement that collateral be disposed of in a commercial reasonable manner is not particularly difficult to meet. Nevertheless, commercial reasonableness requires more than the standards generally applied to assessing a surety's good faith (or absence of bad faith) in settling bond claims. Moreover, the prima facie evidence clause, as normally drafted, would not apply to whether a surety's settlement of its principal's affirmative claims is "commercially reasonable." Thus, if *CAT Contracting* is correct, and commercial reasonableness is indeed the standard, the surety may have the initial burden of proving that it acted in a commercially reasonable manner.

Perhaps because there are so many different kinds of collateral, the UCC does not attempt to define "commercially reasonable," and what is or is not commercially reasonable will therefore depend on the facts of each case and the nature of the collateral involved. Generally speaking, a secured creditor disposes of collateral in a commercially reasonable manner when it "acts in good faith, avoids loss, and makes effective realization."[104] This may be shown by demonstrating that the disposition of collateral (i.e., the settlement of the principal's affirmative claim) was "made in keeping with the prevailing trade practices among respectable and responsible business and commercial enterprises engaged in the same or similar business."[105] Since surety companies routinely evaluate the strengths and weaknesses of construction contract disputes in connection with the determination of whether to litigate or settle claims and on what terms, a surety should therefore be able to demonstrate its commercial reasonableness in settling its principal's affirmative claim by documenting that the surety followed the same kinds of procedures ordinarily followed by sureties in adjusting claims. These include gathering documentation from both sides of the dispute, consulting with experts, and performing some form of cost-benefit analysis of the resources which would be required to fully litigate the dispute. The principal's failure to post collateral may also be used as evidence of the commercial reasonableness of the surety's determination to settle its principal's affirmative claim, because it gives rise to a fair inference that either the principal placed little value on its claim, or that the principal lacked the financial resources to effectively litigate its claim.

It should also be noted that commercial reasonableness is measured by the procedures utilized in disposing of collateral and not by whether those procedures yield the maximum

102. *Cullen Frost Bank.*, 730 S.W.2d at 670 ("Notice to the debtor is not required when the secured party collects directly from the account debtor."); *Rinaldi*, 696 A.2d 744, 750 (UCC § 9-502 does not require any notice to the debtor). *See also* 68A Am. Jur. 2d *Secured Transactions* § 586 (1993).

103. The indemnitors' failure to present the surety with a better proposal than the obligee/claimant would also help illustrate the commercial reasonableness of the surety's determination to include the dismissal of its principal's affirmative claims as part of the surety's settlement with the obligee/claimant.

104. *In re Auer*, 103 B.R. 700, 703 (Bankr. W.D.Pa. 1989).

105. *Leasing Service Corp. v. First Tenn. Bank Nat. Ass'n*, 826 F.2d 434, 439 (6th Cir. 1987).

possible return.[106] Because of the multiplicity of variables involved, the valuation of a lawsuit prior to settlement is inherently speculative, and it would therefore be very difficult for a court to find as commercially unreasonable any thoughtful settlement determination reached by a surety. For example, in *Frank Briscoe Company, Inc. v. The Travelers Indemnity Company*,[107] a contractor sued its former surety for, among other things, having settled the contractor's lawsuits in an allegedly commercially unreasonable manner. The surety in that case relied upon an agreement (other than a General Indemnity Agreement) which expressly gave it "absolute discretion" to settle the contractor's affirmative claims. Also, because the contractor was the plaintiff, the contractor bore the burden of proof on the issue of commercial reasonableness – a burden usually borne by the creditor. Nevertheless, the court's holding is instructive:

> The speculative nature of the alleged possible recovery in conjunction with the anticipated legal fees for pursuit of the various claims leads this Court to conclude that Travelers, in the exercise of absolute discretion, reasonably decided that settlement was the most advantageous disposition of that collateral. Briscoe does not create a triable issue of fact by making the unsupported argument that it could have recovered more. Every settlement holds the possibility of greater or lesser recovery through litigation. Settlements, however, provide security against the possibility of recovering nothing through litigation, as well as incurring substantial additional legal fees.[108]

The failure of a principal to support its affirmative claims with hard facts and evidence will also help establish the commercial reasonableness of a surety's determination to settle those claims. Instructive on this point, by analogy, is the case *Western Decor & Furnishings Industries, Inc. v. Bank of America National Trust and Savings Association*.[109] That case concerned the commercial reasonableness of a bank's efforts to collect certain accounts receivable which were assigned to the bank as security for a line of credit. At the time of the debtor's default on its loan obligations, the debtor's books showed approximately $238,000 in accounts receivable.[110] Several of the account debtors, however, disclaimed knowledge of any open accounts with the debtor, while others claimed to have already paid or otherwise disputed the alleged accounts.[111] The bank, despite its efforts, was ultimately unsuccessful in collecting any of the subject accounts receivable. The debtor alleged that the bank's failure to collect the accounts was commercially unreasonable, but the court put the blame squarely on the debtor's failure to document its claims against the account debtors:

> Although it is Western Decor who asserts Bank of America failed to behave in a commercially reasonable manner by refusing to send to Western Decor responses from account debtors who disputed the debt, the converse seems to be more accurate. Western Decor's collection expert testified that in order to have a successful collection program, it is often necessary to have an invoice, delivery slip or other supporting records from the immediate debtor to establish that the account receivable is valid. On two separate occasions, Bank of

106. *Id.*, at 439.
107. 65 F.Supp.2d 285 (D.N.J. 1999).
108. *Id.*, at 300.
109. 154 Cal. Rptr. 287 (Cal. Ct. App. 1979).
110. *Id.*, at 293.
111. *Id.*

> America requested Western Decor to provide it with supporting records since several account debtors responded that unless they receive evidence of the debt, they would not pay. Western Decor failed to do so. *Bank of America was under no duty to keep Western Decor informed of its collection efforts. Rather, it was Western Decor's obligation to provide the necessary supporting records to Bank of America.*[112]

Whether or under what terms to settle a lawsuit is so inherently subjective that it may be fair to argue that except in extraordinary cases, any "good faith" settlement determination is, in fact, "commercially reasonable."[113] Clearly, a surety's settlement of its principal's affirmative claim is very different from the kinds of chattel sales generally covered by UCC 9-504. Unlike automobiles, equipment, or retail inventory, there is no market for lawsuits. They cannot be sold at auctions. Indeed, unless or until the lawsuit is brought to judgment or settled, the cash value of the lawsuit is not even in the surety's possession. On this point, it is worth noting that a 1993 Massachusetts case, *Arlington Trust Company v. Caimi*,[114] held that since "one cannot dispose of what one does not have," a creditor's compromise of a lawsuit in order to acquire funds it did not previously possess "does not constitute a disposition of collateral" under UCC § 9-504.

Assuming the applicability of the UCC's notice[115] or commercial reasonableness requirements, a surety's violation of either requirement will create difficulties for the surety, but not necessarily insurmountable ones. For example, the surety's settlement of the principal's affirmative claim should still be effective to bind the principal, so long as the *other* settling party, i.e., the bond claimant or obligee, acts "in good faith."[116] In this context, "good faith" means "honesty in fact in the conduct of the transaction concerned."[117] In other words, the settlement need not be "commercially reasonable" to result in the binding dismissal of the principal's affirmative claims as part of the surety's settlement with an obligee or claimant.

Failure to give notice prior to settling the principal's affirmative claim or making what is later determined to be a commercially unreasonable settlement, however, could still have a potentially deleterious effect on the surety's indemnity rights. In most jurisdictions, where a secured creditor fails to provide notice to a debtor prior to disposing of collateral or disposes of collateral in a commercially unreasonable manner, there arises a rebuttable presumption that the "value of the collateral equaled the indebtedness assumed, thereby extinguishing the

---

112. *Id.* (emphasis supplied). *See also In re Emergency Beacon Corp.*, 48 B.R. 341, 349 (Bankr. S.D.N.Y. 1985) (holding that the fact that a creditor realized a very low return in collecting "stale" and "distressed" accounts receivable did not demonstrate the creditor acted in a commercially unreasonable manner).

113. *See In re Emergency Beacon Corp.*, 48 B.R. at 349 ("The evidence in this case does not reveal imprudence or a lack of good faith ... which would warrant a finding of commercial unreasonableness.); *In re Nicsinger*, 136 B.R. 228, 235 (Bankr. W.D.Mo. 1992) (holding that a bank's "good faith effort" to collect assigned accounts receivable established that it had been commercially reasonable).

114. 610 N.E.2d 948, 952 (Mass. 1993).

115. There is compelling authority for the proposition that the UCC does not require notice in this context. *See* footnotes 98 - 102, *supra*, and accompanying text.

116. UCC § 9-504(4)(b).

117. UCC § 1-201(19).

indebtedness unless the secured party rebuts the presumption."[118] Thus, in such cases, to recover indemnity, the surety may be required to prove that it settled its principal's affirmative claim for fair value under the circumstances. Given the inherently speculative nature of assigning a value to a contested lawsuit however, as noted in *Frank Briscoe Co.*, a surety should be able to meet that burden by showing that the surety investigated the claim, consulted with experts, and that settlement was thoughtfully considered before being entered into, giving due weight to the risk and prospective attorney's fees which surety would have faced had it not settled the claim.

IV. *Recovery of Counsel Fees*

The indemnity provision also expands the surety's common law right of reimbursement to include recovery of attorneys' fees incurred by the surety both in handling claims under the bond and in enforcing the General Indemnity Agreement itself. Where the principal posts liquid collateral sufficient to cover the surety's exposure in any suit instituted against the surety and principal by a claimant under the bond, the surety's interest usually will be adequately protected and it may allow the principal's attorney, if he or she is willing, to assume its defense and thereby reduce expenses.

Where the principal does not post collateral, however, the conflicting interests of the surety and the principal often require that the surety retain its own independent legal counsel to protect its interests. The surety may have different defenses to assert than does the principal; but the surety will also have affirmative claims against the principal which the surety may have to assert against the principal in the same proceeding (depending upon the forum), or which the surety may find advantageous to assert in that proceeding. Because the surety is entitled to reimbursement from the principal and indemnitors for any loss it sustains in the litigation, the surety cannot rely upon the principal's counsel to protect its indemnification rights as such counsel has an inevitable conflict of interest.

The courts have adopted two basic approaches to dealing with the surety's right to recover counsel fees. One approach is to treat the surety's attorney's fees like any other of the surety's losses recoverable under the General Indemnity Agreement. Under this approach, courts will accept the fact and amount of the surety's payments as prima facie evidence of the indemnitors' liability therefore, absent evidence of bad faith. The second approach is to limit the surety's recovery of counsel fees to that which, in the view of the court, is "reasonable." Cases applying this second approach usually appear to involve abbreviated indemnity agreements or indemnity agreements which lack a prima facie evidence clause, or in which specific language permitting the surety to recover for all expenditures made in "good faith" is absent. There are, however, some courts which have imposed an extra-contractual "reasonableness" requirement on attorneys fees sought to be recovered by the surety, regardless of the language of the General Indemnity Agreement.

---

118. *Federal Deposit Ins. Corp. v. Rodenberg*, 571 F. Supp. 455, 461 (D. Md. 1983). *See, also, In re Wells*, 51 B.R. 563, 568 (Bankr. D.D.C. 1985) and *Ingersoll-Rand Financial Corp. v. Miller Min. Co.*, 817 F.2d 1424, 1428 (9th Cir. 1987).

Illustrative of enforcing the General Indemnity Agreement as written is *Fallon Electric Co, Inc. v. The Cincinnati Insurance Company*.[119] There, the United States Court of Appeals for the Third Circuit construed an indemnity agreement, which included a prima facie evidence clause, as well as an indemnity clause binding the indemnitors to reimburse payments made by the surety "in the reasonable belief that [the surety] was liable for the amount disbursed, or that that such payment or compromise was reasonable under the circumstances."[120] The district court, following cases from other jurisdictions, found that surety had failed to sustain its burden of proof as to the "reasonable necessity" of a portion of its attorneys fees. On appeal, the Third Circuit distinguished the cases relied upon by the district court, noting that the indemnity agreements in those cases did not contain the same "prima facie evidence" language as the indemnity agreement underlying the appeal. The appeals court then went on to hold as follows:

> We conclude that the Pennsylvania courts would hold that a "prima facie evidence" clause in an indemnity agreement shifts to the indemnitor the burden of proving that the costs incurred were not recoverable. We further conclude that *what an indemnitor must demonstrate to escape liability for attorney's fees depends upon the precise language used in the agreement.*
>
> * * *
>
> Here … the agreement provides that Ravin would be liable to indemnify CIC only for those payments "made … in the reasonable belief that [CIC] was liable for the amount disbursed, or that such payment or compromise was reasonable under all of the circumstances." Pursuant to the foregoing, the court should have placed on Ravin the burden of proving both that: CIC did not actually believe that it was liable for the attorney's fees disbursed, or that its belief in that respect was unreasonable; and CIC did not actually believe that the payment of such fees (as opposed to the incurrence of the fees) was reasonable under the circumstances, or that its belief in that respect was unreasonable. A showing that CIC did not actually believe it was liable for the fees or that CIC did not actually believe that the payment of such fees was reasonable under all the circumstances would be tantamount to a showing of bad faith of fraud.[121]

Since the record on appeal contained no evidence that the surety paid its attorneys fees in the belief that the fees were unnecessary or unreasonable, the Court of Appeals directed that the District Court enter judgment awarding the surety "attorney's fees in the amount it requested."[122]

The *Fallon Electric* court distinguished the language of the indemnity agreement before it from those found in such cases as *Perkins v. Thompson*[123] and *Sentry Insurance Co. v. Davidson Fuel & Dock Co.*,[124] which limited the surety's recovery of attorney's fees to those which the surety could demonstrate were reasonably incurred. In *Perkins*, for example, the

119. 121 F.3d 125 (3rd Cir. 1997).

120. *Id.*, at 126.

121. *Id.*, at 129, emphasis supplied, internal citations omitted.

122. *Id.*, at 130.

123. 551 So.2d 204 (Miss. 1989).

124. 396 N.E.2d 1071 (Ohio Ct. App. 1978).

indemnity agreement required the indemnitors "to completely indemnify the company from and against any liability, loss, cost, attorney's fees and expenses whatsoever which the company shall at any time sustain as surety or by reason of having been surety on this bond or any other bond issued for applicant, or for the enforcement of this agreement."[125] The language of the indemnity agreement in *Sentry Insurance Co.* was similar. Neither case noted the presence of a prima evidence clause, nor language by which the indemnitors agreed to be bound by the surety's "good faith" determination to pay expenses. The holding in *Perkins*, which limited the surety to the recovery of "reasonable" attorney's fees, does not appear to have been stated as a general rule of law, but was, rather, "under this indemnity agreement here[.]"[126] Likewise, the holding in *Sentry Insurance Co.* was based on the "language quoted" from the indemnity agreement at issue, which did not expressly require indemnity for all payments made in "good faith." The court, therefore, "rejected[ed] the surety's position that *the language of the indemnity agreement* would permit it to recover all fees and expenses incurred or paid by it in its sole discretion, limited only by its good faith."[127]

Another case distinguished by *Fallon Electric* was *Central Towers Apartments, Inc. v. Martin*.[128] While *Central Towers* made no mention of a prima facie evidence clause, the indemnity agreement did expressly require indemnity for all disbursement made by the surety in "good faith under the belief that it was liable for the amount so disbursed, or that it was necessary or expedient to make such disbursements, whether such liability, necessity or expediency existed or not."[129] Although the principal had the financial ability to satisfy any judgment entered against it and had retained competent counsel to defend itself and the surety, the surety retained independent counsel and sought to require that the principal reimburse it for its legal expenses. The court stated that:

> [W]hen the principal and his indemnified surety are sued by the obligee under the surety bond, and the surety exercises its right under the indemnity agreement of the principal to hire its own separate counsel and incur litigation expenses in defense of the action, the liability of the principal for attorney fees and expenses thus incurred by the surety depends on whether, under all the facts of the case, it was reasonably necessary for the surety to so act in its own defense, and whether the surety acted in good faith toward the principal.[130]

Attorneys fees was also at issue in *United Riggers & Erectors, Inc. v. Marathon Steel Co.*,[131] which quoted a "good faith" provision of an indemnity agreement similar to that found in *Central Towers* and, as in *Central Towers*, made no mention of any prima facie evidence clause. In *United Riggers*, the court reversed a district court order denying a surety's request for indemnification of counsel fees under its indemnity agreement. Below, the indemnitors had successfully argued that, because they had offered to defend the surety against the obligee's

---

125. *Perkins*, 551 So.2d at 209.

126. *Id.*, at 210.

127. *Sentry*, 396 N.E.2d at 1074, emphasis supplied.

128. 453 S.W.2d 789, 799 (Tenn. Ct. App. 1969).

129. *Id.*, at 794.

130. *Id.*, at 799. Applying that standard, the court concluded under the facts of that case that "the surety did not act in good faith and under a reasonable necessity in the hiring of separate attorneys so as to charge the contractor for these fees and expenses." *Id.*, at 800.

131. 725 F.2d 87 (10th Cir. 1984).

claim and had succeeded at trial in defeating such claim, the surety was not entitled to be reimbursed the fees it had incurred for its separate counsel. The Tenth Circuit rejected that argument, noting that the indemnitors had been unable to post the collateral requested by the surety in accordance with the indemnity agreement and that the surety had reason to doubt the principal's ability to satisfy an adverse judgment and even perhaps its ability to remain solvent during the pendency of the litigation. For this reason, the court held the surety's hiring of separate counsel was justified. The appeals court found further justification for the surety's determination to engage counsel in the fact that the surety had asserted separate defenses to the obligee's claims based upon material modification of the bonded contract without the surety's consent – defenses which were unavailable to the principal. Nevertheless, the case was remanded to the district court for a determination of the amount of attorney's fees "reasonably expended" by the surety, with the suggestion that fees for services by the surety's attorney which duplicated those of the principal's attorney would not be considered reasonable. That suggestion, of course, means that the surety would not be able to recover for attorney's fees which, while based on duplicative services, were nevertheless paid by the surety in "good faith."

A more extreme example of a court refusing to enforce, as written, an indemnity agreement calling for the reimbursement of attorneys fees incurred in "good faith" is *International Fidelity Insurance Company v. Jones*.[132] There, the court rejected "the view that under an indemnity agreement the obligor has no defense and that truly unreasonable [attorney's fees] payments must be reimbursed as long as they are made in good faith," observing that the "[f]ailure [of courts] to oversee the reasonableness of such awards could result in inequities if not corruption."[133] In support of this holding, *Jones* cited *Perkins v. Thompson*, which, of course, involved an indemnity agreement absent any provision making "good faith" the standard for the surety's right to indemnity. Also, left unexplained by *Jones* is why the application of a "good faith" standard would be an insufficient guard against "truly unreasonable" attorneys fees or "corruption." Presumably, "truly unreasonable" fees or fees paid as a result of corruption would not have been incurred in good faith.

The court in *Ideal Electronic Security Co, Inc. v. International Fidelity Insurance Company*,[134] saw no distinction between the good faith and reasonableness standards. "[D]ecisions to pay counsel must pass a test of reasonableness in order to be in good faith."[135] Otherwise, as observed by the court, the surety "would have no incentive to police its attorneys' activities and charges, since it could simply dump any and all charges billed onto the indemnitor."[136] *Ideal*, however, did note and give force to the prima facie evidence clause, which it held shifted to the indemnitor "the burden of proving that the fees claimed are excessive."[137] Practitioners should also take note of the fact that *Ideal* held that, in defense of indemnity, the indemnitor was entitled to unredacted copies of the subject attorney's billing

132. 682 A.2d 263 (N.J. Super. Ct. App. Div. 1996).
133. *Id.*, at 265.
134. 129 F.3d 143 (D.C.Cir. 1997).
135. *Id.*, at 151.
136. *Id.*
137. *Id.*, at 151.

statements, and that the surety, by offering redacted copies into evidence, had waived the attorney-client privilege as to those billing statements "and any other communication going to the reasonableness of the amount of the fee award."[138]

In *Transamerica Premier Insurance Company v. Nelson*,[139] in contrast, the Supreme Court of Nevada held as follows:

> Transamerica maintains that many district courts treat the award of attorney's fees to a surety pursuant to a GIA as a discretionary matter to be determined based upon the court's subjective analysis of the "reasonableness" of the fees under the circumstances. We conclude that such a standard is in contravention of the purpose of the GIA to hold the surety harmless for all expenses consequential to the issuance of the bond. Thus, we adopt a standard under which courts should consider only whether the attorney's fees were incurred in good faith as a result of or in consequence of the issuance of a bond. When the parties contractually agree that good faith is the standard, undertaking a determination of anything other than good faith is inappropriate.[140]

Transamerica Premier also enforced the prima facie evidence clause as written, and awarded the surety summary judgment for the full amount of its attorney's fees. *Id.*, at 318.

American Employers' Insurance Company v. Horton,[141] is another case in which both a contractually-agreed standard of "good faith" and a prima facie evidence clause were present. Although the court noted the absence of any evidence of bad faith and appears to have awarded the surety the full amount of attorney's fees sought, the court justified its ruling, in part, by the fact that the indemnitor had not contested the "reasonableness" of the amount of attorney's fees before the motion judge.[142] *Wilson and Company, Engineers and Architects v. Walsenburg Sand and Gravel Company, Inc.*,[143] a case quoting "good faith" language from the indemnity agreement, but making no mention of a prima facie evidence clause, affirmed an award of full attorneys fees to the surety, noting the absence of any bad faith, based on an uncontested affidavit of the surety's counsel providing "sufficient evidence ... to support the amount claimed."[144]

The case of *Estate of Burgess v. Peterson*,[145] should also be of interest to sureties seeking to establish the reasonableness of their attorney's fees. While the surety in that case was limited to "reasonable fees and expenses" under a trust agreement separate from its indemnity agreement, the opinion nevertheless observed that the expenses the surety was entitled to recover as a result of having issued the bonds "would reasonably include the amount the companies were required to expend to realize the financial protection the [indemnity] agreement was intended to afford them."[146] The court also acknowledged that it was

---

138. *Id.*, at 152.

139. 878 P.2d 314 (Nev. 1994).

140. *Id.*, at 317.

141. 622 N.E.2d 283 (Mass. App. Ct. 1993).

142. *Id.*, at 285.

143. 779 P.2d 1386 (Colo. Ct. App. 1989).

144. *Id.*, at 1387. See, *also*, *United States v. International Fidelity Insurance Company*, 999 F. Supp. 1420 (D. Kan. 1998) (attorney's fees found to have been incurred in good faith).

145. 571 N.W.2d 432 (Wis. Ct. App. 1997).

146. *Id.*, at 436.

"reasonable" for the surety to engage an experienced surety attorney who charged in excess of local insurance-defense rates:

> Furthermore, the court [below] did not err by finding the hourly attorney rate reasonable. The sureties' attorney charged $135 and $140 per hour. Although Eau Claire attorneys charge only $90 to $100 per hour, the trial court reasoned that a surety company differs significantly from an insurance company, that the issues involved were complex, and that the surety companies appropriately selected an attorney with whom they were comfortable. Further, we believe it was appropriate for the trial court to consider that there are few experienced surety attorneys in Wisconsin, none of whom live in Eau Claire. Unrebutted testimony demonstrated that experienced surety attorneys reside in Madison and Milwaukee, where hourly rates are higher, and that this particular surety's attorney's rates were low in comparison.[147]

In *T.P.K. Const. Corp. v. Southern American Ins. Co.*,[148] the Court went further and found that the language of the indemnity agreement was not limited to the surety's recovery of attorneys' fees in suits instituted by bond claimants and obligees, or even to actions commenced by the surety to enforce the indemnity agreement. Rather, the court recognized that the surety may also be entitled to reimbursement of its counsel fees even in cases brought against the surety by the principal itself. In that case, the surety had issued bid bonds to the principal on two public projects in New York. After it was later discovered that the surety was not legally authorized to write bonds in New York, the principal sued the surety for negligence and breach of contract. Because the principal had signed a General Indemnity Agreement, the surety counterclaimed against the principal and brought a third-party action against the indemnitors for the legal fees incurred by it in defending the action. Although the court dismissed the principal's negligence count and deferred ruling on the breach of contract count and the surety's affirmative claims, the court acknowledged that under the indemnity provision, the surety would be entitled to recover its attorneys' fees unless the principal showed that the surety had breached the covenant of good faith and fair dealing. Under the indemnity provision, therefore, the surety may recover the expenses it incurs both as a result of the execution of its bond and in enforcing its rights under the General Indemnity Agreement.

Indeed, the General Indemnity Agreement permits recovery of even post-judgment expenses. While the courts of many jurisdictions will interpret contractual attorney's fees provisions as not applying to post-judgment collection expenses,[149] General Indemnity Agreements usually contain language specifying that "separate suits may be brought" by the surety to enforce its rights. Under that language, the court in *Republic Insurance Company v. Culbertson*[150] held that a surety may bring a second lawsuit to collect its post-judgment collection costs, even though post-judgment expenses are not considered a separate cause of action from enforcing the indemnity agreement itself. The same case also notes that the

147. *Id.*
148. 752 F. Supp. 105, 112-113 (S.D.N.Y. 1990).
149. *See, e.g., Hatch v. T&L Associates*, 726 A.2d 308 (N.J. Super. Ct. App. Div. 1999).
150. 717 F. Supp. 415, 419-420 (E.D.Va. 1989).

majority of courts hold that express contractual provisions for attorney's fees cover attorney's fees incurred on appeal, and that the language of the General Indemnity Agreement is sufficiently broad to encompass fees for appellate work.

There is one additional issue concerning attorney's fees which should be of concern to sureties. Certain states have statutes which mandate that a contractual provision "which allows recovery of attorneys fees to only one party to the contract be construed to allow a reciprocal allowance of fees to the other party if it prevails."[151] Under such statutes, a party successfully defending a surety's indemnity action would be entitled to recover attorney's fees from the surety. Sureties litigating in unfamiliar jurisdictions, or in any jurisdiction where choice of law is at issue, should therefore consult the law of the applicable state(s) for the presence of such statutes.

VI. *The Collateral-Deposit Provision*

The collateral-deposit clause serves to force a protesting principal or indemnitor to provide to the surety a reserve of funds when the surety is faced with claims on its bonds. Under such a provision, once a surety receives a demand on its bond, the principal and/or indemnitors must deposit with the surety funds sufficient to secure it against the claim. If the claim must be paid, then the surety will do so out of the deposited funds. If the surety does not have to pay the claim, the remaining funds, net of expenses incurred, must then be returned.[152] A typical collateral security provision may provide as follows:

> The Undersigned will deposit with the Company as collateral security, immediately upon demand, a sum of money, at the option of the Company, equal to (1) the liability of the Company, if established; (2) the liability asserted against the Company; or (3) the reserve established by the Company, or any increase thereof, to cover any liability, loss, expense or possible liability for any loss or expense for which the Undersigned may be obligated to indemnify the Company under the terms of this Agreement.[153]

Generally, there is no requirement that the surety be liable to the obligee and/or claimant in order to demand that the principal post collateral. Instead, the only condition necessary to invoke the collateral reserve obligation is that there be a "claim" or "demand" upon the surety to perform under the bond.[154] The clause presumes the surety's right to be secured by the principal against the loss being reserved while the ultimate liability of the principal to the claimant is being resolved.

---

151. See, *e.g.*, City *of Portland v. George D. Ward & Associates, Inc.*, 750 P.2d 171, 176 (Or.Ct.App. 1988), *citing* ORS 20.096. *See, also*, *Arntz Contracting Co. v. St. Paul Fire and Marine Insurance Company*, 54 Cal.Rptr.2d 888, 905-906 (Cal. Ct. App. 1996), *citing* California Civil Code § 1717(a).

152. *United States Fidelity & Guaranty Co. v. Feibus*, 15 F. Supp.2d 579, 588 (M.D.Pa. 1998), *aff'd* 185 F.3d 864 (3rd Cir. 1999); *Safeco Ins. Co. of America v. Schwab*, 739 F.2d 431, 433 (9th Cir. 1984); *American Motorists Insurance Company v. United Furnace Co., Inc.*, 876 F.2d 293, 300 (2nd Cir. 1989).

153. IADC's Project Update 1995, *supra* footnote 2, at 260 (first of three paragraphs).

154. *American Motorists*, 876 F.2d at 301; *Feibus*, 15 F. Supp.2d at 588; *Safeco*, 739 F.2d at 434; *United Bonding Insurance Company v. Stein*, 273 F. Supp. 929, 929-930 (E.D.Pa. 1967).

Courts have recognized that "[s]ureties are ordinarily entitled to specific performance of collateral security clauses."[155] The surety, however, still must demonstrate its right to the equitable remedy of specific performance. In most jurisdictions that will require the surety to demonstrate (i) that it will suffer "irreparable harm" or that there is no adequate remedy at law and (ii) that the surety has a clear entitlement for relief.[156]

Courts have found that where the amount of the bond claims are indefinite, there is no adequate remedy at law available to the surety because its future damages are not ascertainable and it cannot yet institute an action for indemnification.[157] An example is the case of *Milwaukie Const. Co. Inc. v. Glens Falls Ins. Co.*[158] There, the principal defaulted on four construction projects and the surety instituted an action for specific performance of the collateral-deposit clause. At the time of trial, the surety's damages "still could not be definitely determined, but the estimate of ultimate liability had risen to approximately $83,000."[159] The trial court entered judgment directing the indemnitors to deposit $83,000 with the surety as security. The indemnitors appealed, arguing that the case did not justify equitable relief in that the surety had an adequate remedy at law. Affirming, the United States Court of Appeals for the Ninth Circuit stated that "[i]t is clear that where the [surety] knew it was going to have liability claims filed against it but did not know the amount of those claims, the legal remedy of money damages would not be adequate."[160]

On the other hand, as noted by the Ninth Circuit in *Commercial Ins. Co. of Newark, N.J. v. Pacific-Peru Const. Corp.*,[161] once the surety's debt becomes fixed, the surety will be deemed to have an adequate remedy at law by virtue of the fact that the surety can then institute an action for indemnification under the indemnity agreement. As a result, the courts will not grant specific performance of the collateral security provision where the surety is able to determine the amount of its losses.

Another rationale recognized by the courts for granting equitable relief enforcing collateral deposit provisions is that, absent specific performance, sureties would be deprived of their bargained-for secured position.[162] In *American Motorists Insurance Co. v. Pennsylvania Beads Corp*,[163] for example, the indemnitor argued that "public policy" required that the surety not be permitted to bankrupt the indemnitor by demanding collateral security for claims the

155. *Safeco*, 739 F.2d at 433; *Feibus*, 15 F. Supp.2d at 588 ("Thus, in order to protect the surety's bargain, courts have granted specific performance to enforce collateral security provisions."); *United States Fidelity and Guaranty Company v. J. United Electrical Contracting Corp.*, 62 F. Supp.2d 915, 922 (E.D.N.Y. 1999); *American Motorists Insurance Co. v. Pennsylvania Beads Corp.*, 983 F. Supp. 437 (S.D.N.Y. 1997); and *Safeco Insurance Company of America v. Criterion Investment Corporation*, 732 F. Supp. 834, 843 (E.D.Tenn. 1989).

156. *J. United Electrical Contracting Corp.*, 62 F. Supp.2d at 921.

157. *J. United Electrical Contracting Corp.*, 62 F. Supp.2d at 923; *American Motorists*, 876 F.2d at 300; *Stein*, 273 F. Supp. at 930; *Feibus*, 15 F. Supp.2d at 588; and *Standard Surety & Casualty Co. of New York v. Caravel Industries Corp.*, 15 A.2d 258, 260 (N.J. Ch. 1940).

158. 367 F.2d 964 (9th Cir. 1966).

159. *Id.*, at 966.

160. *Id.*

161. 558 F.2d 948, 955 (9th Cir. 1977).

162. *J. United Electrical Contracting Corp.*, 62 F. Supp.2d at 923; *Safeco*, 739 F.2d at 433; *Feibus*, 15 F. Supp.2d at 588; and *American Motorists.*, 983 F. Supp. at 441.

163. 983 F. Supp. 437 (S.D.N.Y. 1997).

indemnitor was in the process of disputing. Turning that argument back against the indemnitor, the court held as follows:

> The only remaining support for defendant's public policy argument is its unsubstantiated claim that the financial hardship which would result from enforcement of the Indemnity Agreement would bankrupt PB Co. "needlessly." While that possible outcome would indeed be unfortunate, it does not, standing alone, provide a valid justification for denying plaintiff access to the security it specifically bargained for. In fact, absent enforcement of the Indemnity Agreement's collateral security clause, plaintiff could – in the bankruptcy situation contemplated by defendant – be relegated to an unsecured claim and therefore be forced to share its debtor's property with other creditors. If anything, public policy considerations dictate against such a result, since it is that precise situation which AMICO sought to avoid in bargaining for the collateral security clause.[164]

Of course, the surety will have to establish a basis for the amount of collateral it seeks. Thus in *Transamerica Premier Insurance Company v. Cavalry Construction, Inc.*,[165] the court affirmed an order granting specific performance of a collateral deposit provision to the extent of $250,000 needed as security against "disputed and undisputed" potential payment bond claims.[166] The court, however, also affirmed the denial of specific performance respecting a collateral demand for the full $1,187,000 penal sum of the surety's performance bond, which was made in response to what the court clearly perceived to have been an inflated claim by the bond obligee. In support of its holding, the court observed that the surety had "failed to flesh out the nature and approximate amount" of its potential performance bond exposure.[167] Nevertheless, the court did note with approval the trial court's statement that "the issue was not whether Transamerica actually feared a $1,187,000 loss, but whether there was any rational basis for that fear."[168]

Among the obvious advantages of seeking specific performance of the collateral reserve provision is that it allows the surety to receive the benefit of the indemnity agreement while the principal may still have assets to post as collateral. Moreover, even if the principal is insolvent, there may still be indemnitors with assets against whom the surety may enforce this provision. Specific performance, therefore, can prevent uncooperative indemnitors from dissipating or hiding assets which would otherwise be available to offset the surety's losses.

When preventing dissipation is an objective, the specific performance action should be commenced by an order to show cause or an equivalent procedure seeking a temporary restraining order and a preliminary injunction. The standards for interlocutory relief in the collateral reserve case are the same as those in any other injunction case: (1) that there is no adequate remedy at law and that the movant will suffer irreparable injury; (2) that the movant will likely succeed on the merits; (3) that the threatened harm to the movant outweighs the

164. *Id.*, at 441.

165. 552 So.2d 225 (Fla. Dist. Ct. App. 1989).

166. *Id.*, at 226.

167. *Id.*, at 227.

168. *Id.*; *See also American Motorists.*, 983 F. Supp. at 440. That case concerned a collateral deposit provision requiring "sufficient funds to cover the liability." The court, noting that the bond obligee made demand upon the surety for $225,379..24, and that the bond's penal sum was $50,000 per year and that the bond had been in effect for two years, held that "$100,000 is the amount which must be deposited[.]" *Accord, Bib Construction Co., Inc. v. Fireman's Insurance Company of Newark*, 625 N.Y.S.2d 550, 552 (N.Y.App.Div. 1995), which noted that an indemnitor was required to abide by the collateral deposit provision "[s]o long as the sum demanded is reasonable[.]"

injury to be suffered by the opposing party if the injunction is granted; and (4) that the injunction will not offend the public interest. The legal authorities bearing upon the surety's effort to obtain preliminary injunctive relief are extensively analyzed in the following article in this publication: Jay M. Mann, Chapter 24: *Exoneration and Quia Timet*. The reader is referred to that article for a full consideration of that subject.

The General Indemnity Agreement also usually contains a provision which entitles the surety to demand that collateral be posted by the principal and indemnitors when either of them insist that the surety refrain from paying a claim.[169] In such situations, the surety should require that the indemnitors post collateral sufficient to cover the amount of the claim, estimated interest to the date of probable resolution, and the estimated expenses, including attorneys' fees, to be incurred by the surety in defense of the claim. In addition to securing the surety against an adverse determination of the bond claim, the surety's demand for collateral will discourage the principal and indemnitors from raising spurious defenses merely to delay payment because they must collateralize both the amount of the claim and the surety's cost of defending against it. As compliance with the demand for collateral is a condition to any objection which the principal may interpose to the surety's payment of a claim, the use of this provision can greatly assist in the resolution of claims without compromising indemnification rights. This provision may be particularly useful when there is reason to anticipate that the surety's good faith may be attacked by the principal or its indemnitors.[170]

VII. *The Assignment Clause*

Another useful clause of the General Indemnity Agreement is the assignment provision which operates to assign to the surety various rights in the principal's contracts, equipment and receivables conditioned upon the receipt of claims under the surety's bonds or defaults under the indemnity agreement. Generally, assignment provisions allow the surety to recover all of the funds owed to the principal under both bonded and unbonded contracts, as well as the principal's rights under any subcontracts, and are effective against the principal.[171] As against third parties laying claim to the principal's assets, however, the effectiveness of the assignment provision may depend upon whether or not the General Indemnity Agreement has been filed as a financing statement under the UCC.[172]

A typical assignment clause provides:

> The Contractor, the Indemnitors hereby consenting, will assign, transfer and set over, and does hereby assign, transfer and set over to the Surety, as collateral, to secure the

---

169. *See* Point II, *supra.*

170. *See* text accompanying footnotes 53 and 54, *supra.*

171. *In re John's Insulation, Inc.*, 221 B.R. 683, 690 (Bankr. E.D.N.Y. 1998); *James McKinney & Son, Inc. v. Lake Placid 1980 Olympic Games, Inc.*, 61 N.Y.2d 836, 462 N.E.2d 137, 473 N.Y.S.2d 960 (1984); *American Fidelity Fire Insurance Company v. General Railway Signal Company*, 540 N.E.2d 557 (Ill. App. Ct. 1989); *Hutton Const. Co., Inc. v. County of Rockland*, 52 F.3d 1191 (2nd Cir. 1995); and *General Accident Insurance Company of America v. Merrit-Meridian Construction Corp.*, 975 F. Supp. 511, 519 (S.D.N.Y. 1997).

172. *See* Point VIII, *infra.*

> obligations in any and all of the paragraphs of this Agreement and any other indebtedness and liabilities of the Contractor to the Surety, whether heretofore or hereafter incurred, the assignment in the case of each contract to become effective as of the date of the Bond covering such contract, but only in the event of (1) any abandonment, forfeiture or breach of any contracts referred to in the Bond or of any breach of any said Bonds; or (2) of any breach of the provisions of any of the paragraphs of this Agreement; or (3) of a default in discharging such other indebtedness or liabilities when due; or (4) of any assignment by the Contractor for the benefit of creditors, or of the appointment, or of any application for the appointment of a receiver or trustee for the Contractor whether insolvent or not; or (5) of any proceeding which deprives the Contractor of the use of any of the machinery, equipment, plant, tools or material referred to in section (b) of this paragraph; or (6) of the Contractor's dying, absconding, disappearing, incompetency, being convicted of a felony, or imprisoned if the Contractor be an individual: (a) All the rights of the Contractor in, and growing in any manner out of all contracts referred to in the Bonds, or in, or growing in any manner out of the Bonds; (b) All the rights, title and interest of the Contractor in and to all machinery, equipment, plant, tools and materials which are now or may hereafter be, about or upon the site or sites of any and all of the contractual work referred to in the Bonds or elsewhere, including materials purchased for or chargeable to any and all contracts referred to in the Bonds, materials which may be in process of construction, in storage elsewhere, or in transportation to any and all of said sites; (c) All the rights, title and interest of the Contractor in and to all subcontracts let or to be let in connection with any and all contracts referred to in the Bonds, and in and to all surety bonds supporting such subcontracts; (d) All actions, causes of actions, claims and demands whatsoever which the Contractor may have or acquire against any subcontractor, laborer or materialman, or any person furnishing or agreeing to furnish or supply labor, material, supplies, machinery, tools or other equipment in connection with or on account of any and all contracts referred to in the Bonds; and against any surety or sureties of any subcontractor, laborer or materialman; (e) Any and all percentages retained and any and all sums that may be due or hereafter become due on account of any and all contracts referred to in the Bonds and all other contracts whether bonded or not in which the Contractor has an interest.[173]

As reflected by the quoted language, a major purpose of the assignment clause is to assign to the surety the proceeds of all contracts on which the principal is working. The assignment is not limited only to those projects on which the principal has been declared to be "in default".[174] Once the principal is in default of any obligation on any bonded project, or has breached any of the provisions of the General Indemnity Agreement,[175] the surety has an enforceable assignment which extends to contract funds on projects which are not in default, and on projects which are in default, but where losses will be less than remaining contract proceeds. Those funds will offset the surety's losses on projects where contract proceeds fail to cover losses.

Because the surety's assignment rights can arise upon a declaration of default or the mere receipt of a payment claim, they may give the surety rights to contract funds which are superior to, and arise earlier than, those rights provided under the equitable doctrine of

---

173. The quoted clause is contained as part of the General Indemnity Agreement drafted by a subcommittee of the Claims Advisory Committee of the Surety Association of America in 1965.

174. *Gray v. Travelers Indemnity Co.*, 280 F.2d 549, 552 (9th Cir. 1960).

175. *Hutton*, 52 F.3d at 1192 (The "failure to make the demanded indemnity payments constituted a breach of Hutton's obligations to the Sureties and thus activated the Assignment Clause, causing assignment to the Sureties of all of Hutton's rights growing out of the construction projects[.]").

subrogation which requires that the surety actually pay a claim or even all claims before such rights arise. Moreover, while the surety's equitable right of subrogation will provide it with a priority claim to contract balances to the extent of its losses on a particular bonded contract, the surety's right to subrogation may not permit a surety to recover its costs and expenses in investigating and defending claims;[176] subrogation will not, by itself, permit the surety to reach its principal's tools, equipment and inventory;[177] and subrogation does not permit the surety to offset losses on one project against contract proceeds due from a different owner on another project.

The surety's rights under the assignment clause may provide critical protection to the surety where it has not yet paid any losses under the particular contract in which the principal has an account receivable. The assignment clause grants the surety the right to take immediate possession of contract funds due the principal. Further, in order to enable the surety to complete the work on the project as economically as possible, the assignment provision also assigns to the surety all rights, title and interest of the principal in all job-related supplies, tools, equipment and materials.[178] The materials and equipment assigned include all materials on or around the job site and additionally, all materials that already have been purchased or ordered for the job, whether the materials are in transit to the job site, in the process of being manufactured, or are being held in storage prior to delivery to the job.

As with the assignment of contract funds, the surety is authorized to execute any necessary instruments in the name of the principal[179] in order to provide itself with absolute and immediate title to the supplies, material and property assigned to it, and is further authorized to use this property in completing the bonded project. This is true whether the surety plans to exercise its option to complete performance itself or through another contractor. If the surety decides not to utilize the materials, the indemnity agreement may empower the surety to sell any property assigned to it.

The assignment clause also generally assigns to the surety the principal's interest in all project subcontracts as well as all surety bonds covering the subcontracts. The surety, therefore, has the alternative of utilizing some or all of the principal's subcontractors to complete the bonded contract.[180]

---

176. *Interfirst Bank of Dallas, N.A. v. United States Fidelity and Guaranty Company*, 774 S.W.2d 391, 399 (Tex. Ct. App. 1989).

177. *State Bank & Trust Company v. Insurance Company of the West*, 132 F.3d 203, 207 (5th Cir. 1997); *In re Merts Equipment Company*, 438 F. Supp. 295, 298 (M.D.Ga. 1977); *Aetna Casualty and Surety Company v. J.F. Brunken & Son, Inc.*, 357 F. Supp. 290 (D.S.D. 1973).

178. *Travelers Indem. Co. v. West Georgia National Bank*, 387 F. Supp. 1090 (N.D.Ga. 1974). Note that, as was not the case in *Travelers*, under current law, the assignment clause will not give the surety a priority position vis-à-vis other creditors with respect to equipment and materials unless the surety files its security interest pursuant to the U.C.C. *See In re Merts*, 438 F. Supp. at 299.

179. *See Hutton Const. Co., Inc. v. County of Rockland*, 52 F.3d 1191, 1192 (2nd Cir. 1995), recognizing the sureties' right, under the Attorney in Fact Clause in the subject indemnity agreement, to act on a principal's behalf in settling a principal's affirmative claims against a bond obligee.

180. *See American Fidelity Fire Insurance Company v. General Railway Signal Company*, 540 N.E.2d 557 (Ill. App. Ct. 1989).

The assignment clause also gives the surety the right to all claims, actions, or causes of action which the principal may have against the project subcontractors, laborers, or materialmen. This assignment right also includes the right of the surety to bring any claim or cause of action the principal may have against the surety of any such subcontractor, laborer or materialman.[181] These rights can be of substantial benefit to the surety and can create negotiating leverage in dealing with payment bond claims.

It should be noted, however, that the surety often will not wish to avail itself of its assignment rights with respect to subcontracts because acceptance of the assignment may create liability to subcontractors beyond the scope of the surety's liability under the payment bond. By way of example, a subcontractor may have suffered consequential damages such as damages resulting from delays caused by the principal's breach of the subcontract. Consequential damages are ordinarily not covered by the payment bond except to the extent they consist of additional material or labor furnished to the bonded project. Should the surety elect to avail itself of its assignment rights under the General Indemnity Agreement, however, it might also put itself in the position of having succeeded to the burdens as well as the benefits of such contract. Particular care must therefore be taken to assure that the surety's assignment rights are invoked only where it is clearly advantageous to do so and where the risk of assumption of subcontract obligations has been adequately assessed. Often, these concerns can be addressed by negotiating a ratification agreement with the subcontractor whereby the rights and obligations of the surety and the subcontractor are carefully defined and limited.

As an alternative to enforcement of its assignment rights, the surety may demand that the owner invoke its rights with respect to the job-related property of the principal. For example, the surety can demand that the owner mitigate its damages by exercising contractual rights which it may have over the material purchased for the project.[182]

VIII. *Filing the Indemnity Agreement*

The General Indemnity Agreement will often provide that the agreement, itself, is both a security agreement between the surety and the principal and its indemnitors and a financing statement under the UCC. A typical provision of this kind is as follows:

> This Agreement shall constitute a Security Agreement to [the Surety] and also a Financing Statement, both in accordance with the provisions of the Uniform Commercial Code of every jurisdiction wherein such Code is in effect, but the filing or recording of this Agreement shall be solely at the option of the [Surety], and the failure to do so shall not release or impair any of the

---

181. *Id.* In *General Railway Signal Company*, a surety, as assignee of its principal under an indemnity agreement, sued and recovered judgment against a company which breached a contract to perform certain of the principals' obligations on two bonded contracts. Note, however, that there is some authority that a surety could also succeed to its principal's affirmative rights against a subcontractor through the doctrine equitable subrogation, with or without a contractual assignment of rights. *National Surety Corp. v. Allen-Codell Co.*, 70 F. Supp. 189, 191 (E.D.Ky. 1947).

182. The owner, for example, may have already paid for, and thereby taken title to, the material stored on or about the project site. With respect to materials not yet paid for by the owner, however, the owner's rights would probably be inferior to a bank or other creditor with a perfected security interest in the materials. *See* cases cited in footnote 177, *supra*.

> obligations of the Undersigned under this Agreement or otherwise arising, nor shall such failure be in any manner in derogation of the rights of the [Surety] under this Agreement or otherwise.[183]

Such a provision enables the surety to file the General Indemnity Agreement and obtain a perfected security interest in contract funds and tangible property of the principal. Although the clause provides that the agreement itself constitutes a UCC financing statement, it may be a better practice for the surety to file a standard UCC-1 form which incorporates the assignment provision of the General Indemnity Agreement, and which annexes a copy of the General Indemnity Agreement itself. Frequently, the filing of a UCC-1 form will be required by the local filing clerk.

The surety's exercise of its assignment rights and right to utilize the General Indemnity Agreement as a financing statement under the UCC is facilitated by another typical clause in the General Indemnity Agreement under which the principal and indemnitors expressly and irrevocably appoint the surety as their attorney-in-fact. A typical attorney-in-fact clause states:

> The Undersigned hereby irrevocably nominate, constitute, appoint and designate the [Surety] or any person or persons designated by the [Surety] as their attorney-in-fact with the right to exercise all of the rights assigned, transferred or conveyed to the [Surety] by this Agreement, and in their name execute and deliver any and all additional or other assignments, instruments or documents deemed necessary or desirable by the [Surety] to vest in the [Surety] absolute title to any and all monies, property and rights hereby assigned, and to provide the protection and rights to the [Surety] contemplated by the provisions of this agreement.[184]

As attorney-in-fact for the principal and the indemnitors under such a provision, the surety has full authority not only to act in its discretion to handle claims and causes of action, but also to execute UCC-1 forms to provide record notice of its assignment rights. In this context, the power of attorney is invaluable because, at the claim stage, the principal may be uncooperative and unwilling to execute a UCC-1 form.[185]

When the surety is seeking to recover contract proceeds on unbonded projects or on bonded projects on which the surety has incurred no losses or is seeking to recover the principal's equipment, the surety must file the General Indemnity Agreement in order to establish priority over claims of third parties to the property of the principal. When a principal defaults on a project, there often will be competing claims to the unpaid contract funds and retainage. For example, a bank may have received an assignment to such contract funds from the principal and filed a UCC-1 statement perfecting a security interest in such proceeds which would give it priority over the surety's unperfected assignment. Similarly, an Internal Revenue Service ("IRS") lien may have been perfected against the contract funds prior to the filing of the General Indemnity Agreement, or a bankruptcy petition may be filed prior to the perfection

183. IADC's Project Update 1995, *supra* footnote 2, at 271.

184. IADC's Project Update 1995, *supra* footnote 2, at 271.

185. Annexing a copy of the General Indemnity Agreement, which was signed by the principal, to a UCC-1 financing statement, signed by the surety as the principal's attorney-in-fact, should be sufficient to satisfy the requirement that a financing statement be "signed by the debtor." *In re Waldick Aero-Spaces Devices, Inc.*, 71 B.R. 932 (Bankr. D.N.J. 1987).

of the surety's right to be assigned the contract funds or during the three-month preference period under the Bankruptcy Code. In each of these instances, the surety's rights pursuant to the indemnity agreement will be subordinate to those of the bank, the IRS or the trustee in bankruptcy.

There may be, however, one exception. Where a *performing* surety is seeking to recover surplus[186] contract funds on the contract which is being performed, which the surety may need to recoup expenses or losses on other projects, there is authority for the proposition that the surety may rely on the assignment provision of the General Indemnity Agreement to establish its priority to those funds, whether or not the surety has filed its indemnity agreement. Specifically, UCC § 9-104(f) states that the UCC does not apply to, *inter alia*, "a transfer of a right to payment under a contract to an assignee who is also to do the performance under the contract[.]" Construing this section, the Supreme Court of Florida in *Transamerica Insurance Company v. Barnett Bank of Marion County*,[187] noted as follows:

> [T]he U.C.C. itself suggests that a surety's assignment from a contractor, should be excluded from the U.C.C. [U.C.C. § 9-104(f)] excludes a transfer of a right to payment under a contract to an assignee who is also to do the performance under the contract. A surety's assignment is contingent on performance by the surety in the event the contractor defaults. This contingent assignment based on contractual performance contrasts sharply with the noncontingent assignment to a financier which does not call for performance and which is uncontrovertably a security interest.[188]

Nevertheless, while a performing surety may have priority as an assignee of contract proceeds (over and above its subrogation rights),[189] not all courts will necessarily agree,[190] and

186. A surety will generally be able to rely on the doctrine of equitable subrogation to establish its priority position over contract funds to the extent of the surety's actual expenses in performing and paying claims under that contract. With respect to any remaining contract funds, which the surety may wish to obtain and apply to offset other losses, subrogation theory will not give the surety priority over a creditor with a perfected security interest in the receivable. *Interfirst Bank Dallas, N.A. v. United States Fidelity and Guaranty Company*, 774 S.W.2d 391, 399 (Tex. Ct. App. 1989).

187. 540 So.2d 113 (Fla. 1989). *Transamerica* primarily concerned the surety's rights as subrogee, not as assignee. With respect to the former, *Transamerica* restated and followed the "overwhelming and essentially unanimous view" that no UCC filing is necessary to protect the surety's rights, and that the surety's subrogation rights are superior to those of an assignee bank. *Id.*, at 117.

188. *Id.*, at 116. *Accord*, *In re V. Pangori & Sons, Inc.*, 53 B.R. 711, 717 n. 2 (Bankr. E.D.Mich. 1985), which states that an assignment effected by a surety's indemnity agreement is "expressly excluded" by UCC § 9-104(f). In that decision, however, the court appears not to have fully understood the distinction between the surety's subrogation and assignment rights, and held that a surety's subrogation rights arising from having paid claimants after its principal's bankruptcy were subordinate to the bankruptcy trustee's status as a judicial lien creditor. *See also Canter v. Schlager*, 267 N.E.2d 492, 494 (Mass. 1971), which mentioned, but did not pass upon, the possibility that § 9-104(f) would except a performing surety's assignment of contract funds from UCC filing requirements. Note that *Cantor* holds that sureties need not file UCC financing statements to establish the superiority of their subrogation rights over the rights of secured lenders. *Cantor* is particularly weighty as authority on this issue because Justice Braucher, who wrote for the court, "was one of the principal drafters of the UCC[.]" *American Oil Company v. L. A. Davidson, Inc.*, 290 N.W.2d 144, 145 n. 6 (Mich. Ct. App. 1980) (holding that a surety's subrogation rights were not diminished by the enactment of the UCC, and that a surety does not waive its subrogation rights by filing a UCC financing statement to protect its assignment rights).

189. It has also been suggested that a performing surety can reach surplus contract funds, under the theory that where a contractor defaults prior to "substantial performance," the owner is entitled to take the benefit of any

therefore a surety desiring maximum protection of its rights should file its indemnity agreement.

Where the surety is seeking contract funds and tangible property of the principal on bonded contracts, the issue of recording the General Indemnity Agreement is juxtaposed with the doctrine of equitable subrogation. Because of the powerful rights afforded to the surety under the doctrine of subrogation, the surety is often lulled into a position of security believing that there is no need to file the agreement since it will have the same rights under the doctrine of subrogation regardless of whether it files the General Indemnity Agreement.

The Uniform Commercial Code protects only "contract rights" and does not have any effect on those rights which arise by operation of law. Because a surety's equitable subrogation rights arise by operation of law, the surety is not required to file a financing statement under the UCC to preserve such rights.[191]

The benefits of cross-collateralization to contract funds on unbonded jobs or on jobs on which there may be no losses and, therefore, no subrogation rights, justify filing the General Indemnity Agreement to augment the surety's recovery prospects upon receipt of claims. In addition, because the surety's subrogation rights arise only upon payment of claims, there may be substantial benefits to be derived from filing the General Agreement of Indemnity while claims are being investigated but have not yet been paid. As previously noted, the General Indemnity Agreement usually contains provisions requiring payment by the principal of the amount of the surety's reserves against future losses. Upon the principal's default in making such payment, the surety's assignment rights under the General Indemnity Agreement ripen entitling it to the receipt of progress payments and retainage due. Of course, the surety will stand behind any previously filed UCC-1, which may exist such as that of a financing bank, in which event the surety's only claim of priority to contract balances would be through

---

savings it realizes in completing performance itself. By subrogating to the rights of the owner/obligee, a performing surety may take the entire contract balance for itself, even if that results in a profit for the surety. *In re John's Insulation, Inc.*, 221 B.R. 683 (Bankr. E.D.N.Y. 1998).

190. The court in *In re Kuhn Construction Company, Inc.*, 11 B.R. 746, 749 (Bankr. S.D.W.Va. 1981) held that UCC § 9-104(f) does not apply to a performance bond surety because, the court reasoned, a surety generally has the option of tendering a new contractor to finish a defaulted project, in which case the new contractor, and not the surety, would be entitled to receive remaining progress payments.

191. It is well settled that a surety who makes payment to subcontractors, laborers and materialmen or who undertakes completion of its principal's obligations is entitled to be reimbursed out of and to the full extent of funds remaining in the hands of the obligee. *Pearlman v. Reliance Ins. Co.*, 371 U.S. 132, 141 (1962); *National Shawmut Bank v. New Amsterdam Cas. Co.*, 411 F.2d 843 (1st Cir. 1969). The surety's equitable right of subrogation is not a security interest as defined under the UCC, and a UCC filing is not required to perfect the surety's interest in bonded contract funds to the extent of its losses on such bonded contract. *Canter v. Schlager*, 267 N.E.2d 492 (Mass. 1971); *Transamerica Ins. Co. v. Barnett Bank of Marion County, N.A.*, 540 So.2d 113 (Fla. 1989); *American Oil Company v. L. A. Davidson, Inc.*, 290 N.W.2d 144 (Mich. Ct. App. 1980); *Alaska State Bank v. General Insurance Co. of America*, 579 P.2d 1362 (Alaska 1978); *Interfirst Bank Dallas, N.A. v. United States Fidelity and Guaranty Company*, 774 S.W.2d 391 (Tex. Ct. App. 1989); *First Alabama Bank of Birmingham v. Hartford Acc. & Indem. Co., Inc.*, 430 F. Supp. 907 (N.D.Ala. 1977); *Finance Company of North America v. U. S. Fidelity & Guar. Co.*, 353 A.2d 249 (Md. 1976); *Mid-Continent Cas. Co. v. First National Bank & Trust Co.*, 531 P.2d 1370 (Okl. 1975).

invocation of its subrogation rights or rights under any applicable construction trust fund statute.[192]

Finally, the potential advantages of filing the General Indemnity Agreement may be illustrated by court decisions which have limited or threatened to limit the surety's traditional subrogation rights. *In re Construction Alternatives, Inc.*,[193] for example, concerned a dispute between a surety and the IRS as to which enjoyed a priority to an unpaid final progress payment held by a school district under a construction contract. The surety, which had not filed its indemnity agreement, argued that it was subrogated to the contract funds by virtue of having paid claims under its payment bond. The court, however, found that the surety was not subrogated to the rights of the school district, which the court described as a mere "stakeholder."[194] In so holding, the court distinguished the case before it from *Pearlman*, on the ground that the school district's contract did not call for funds to be retained "to pay any unpaid suppliers or subcontractors."[195] The court further found that the surety could not achieve priority through subrogation to the rights of the subcontractors it had paid, as those subcontractors had not filed mechanic's liens.[196] Finally, the court held that the surety's failure to file a UCC financing statement meant that the surety did not possess a security interest sufficient to defeat the priority of the IRS under its notice of tax lien.[197]

In *In re Universal Builders*,[198] a bankruptcy court limited the surety's right of equitable subrogation to retainage and refused to apply the surety's subrogation claim to progress payments. In *In re V. Pangori & Sons Inc.*,[199] a bankruptcy court, while recognizing that the surety's equitable subrogation rights were outside the scope of the UCC, nonetheless held that the rights of the bankruptcy trustee and the assignee bank were superior to those of the surety. The basis for the court's decision was its holding that the surety's subrogation rights arise only when the surety becomes obligated to perform under its bonds; and in the case of payment bonds, the court found that this occurs only after the subcontractors or materialmen demand payment under the bond and does not relate back to the date of the execution of the bonds.[200]

While these cases clearly depart from the majority view and appear to be erroneously decided, they demonstrate that the surety's subrogation rights may not be as invincible as the surety would hope. Therefore, by filing the indemnity agreement under the UCC, the surety will not only establish priority over others who perfect their assignment at a later time, but will also enhance its priority rights against claims of third-parties.[201]

Notwithstanding the many advantages which may be gained through filing the General Indemnity Agreement, the surety should carefully consider that step because filing of the General Indemnity Agreement may dissipate other sources of financing for the principal which may result in the contractor's inability to fund the continued performance of its bonded

---

192. *See e.g.*, *Universal Bonding Ins. Co. v. Gittens & Sprinkle Enterprise, Inc.*, 960 F.2d 366 (3d Cir. 1992).
193. 2 F.3d 670 (6th Cir. 1993).
194. *Id.*, at 676.
195. *Id.*, at 675.
196. *Id.*, at 676.
197. *Id.*, at 678.
198. 53 B.R. 183, 186 (Bankr. M.D.Tenn 1985).
199. 53 B.R. 711, 717 (Bankr. E.D.Mich. 1985).
200. *Id.*, at 720-721.
201. *See* Friedberg, Ronald P., *Construction Sureties: Don't Put All Your Eggs in the Equitable Subrogation Basket*, 41 Cas. W. Res. L. Rev. 305 (1990), collecting cases.

obligations. Many sureties resolve those competing considerations by not filing the General Indemnity Agreement until they become concerned that the principal will be unable to meet its obligations. At that time, prompt filing may augment the surety's recovery prospects. The delayed filing of the General Indemnity Agreement has disadvantages, however, as the filing may be voided as a preferential transfer in the event of a bankruptcy within three months of the UCC-1 filing. In addition other creditors may receive and file assignments and obtain a priority in the interim.

Conclusion

The General Indemnity Agreement is a useful and powerful device enhancing the surety's prospects for avoiding losses in resolving claims under its bonds and maximizing salvage. It is important, therefore, that the surety recognize and utilize the advantages afforded it under the different provisions discussed above, and apply its various rights and remedies in order to achieve the maximum benefit of the General Indemnity Agreement in each particular circumstance.

26

The Surety's Right To Indemnity (Indemnitor's Defenses And Counterclaims)

Bruce C. King

The principal's defenses to an indemnity claim by his surety are not well documented in early caselaw. That is probably because few defenses, other than incapacity of the principal, illegality of the underlying obligation, release by the surety, or payment to the surety exist as to the principal. With the advent of the written indemnity agreement which added third party indemnitors, however, more contractual and equitable defenses to the surety's indemnity claim have emerged. This paper should be read in conjunction with the previous article written by Armen Shahinian.

The surety industry's intent in drafting the standard general indemnity agreement ("GIA") was to reduce to writing the surety's basic rights against the principal, expand them where possible, and provide a vehicle for securing the same rights against third party indemnitors. In light of the surety's experience with defenses traditionally raised by its principal, the GIA was also designed to address those defenses through contractual provisions which would reduce the burden of the surety in defending against them. Generally speaking, the surety is entitled to rely upon the terms of its indemnity contract and they should be strictly construed in the surety's favor.[1] Some courts construe indemnity agreements strictly in favor of the indemnitors, however.[2] In either event, the GIA supersedes any common law or statutory right to indemnity.[3] The following topics discuss the principal's and third party indemnitors' most common defenses and reference standard GIA provisions, as applicable, which relate to those defenses.[4]

I. *Lack of Consideration*

As long as a surety relationship exists, wherein the principal and indemnitors have both benefitted therefrom, consideration is clearly present. The lack of consideration defense is infrequently raised, but it does exist and can render the agreement of indemnity unenforceable. In cases where the bond and the GIA are executed simultaneously, there is consideration for the

---

1. For a good analysis of an indemnity agreement's broad scope and enforceability, see The Revenue Markets, Inc. v. Amwest Surety Insurance Co., 35 F. Supp.2d 899 (S.D. Fla. 1998), aff'd _____ F.2d _____ (11th Cir. 1999). See also, *United States v. United Pac. Ins. Co.*, 697 F. Supp. 378 (D. Idaho 1988); *Commercial Ins. Co. v. Pacific-Peru Const. Co.*, 558 F.2d 948 (9th Cir. 1977).

2. *United Pac. Ins. Co. v. Gregory Timber Resources, Inc.*, 129 F.3d 129 (9th Cir. 1997) (noting that under Oregon law indemnity agreement written by surety "will be construed most strongly against it"); *Safeco Ins. Co. of America v. Gaubert*, 829 S.W.2d 274 (Tex. Ct. App. 1992).

3. Fireman's Fund Ins. Co. v. Nizdil, 709 F. Supp. 975 (D. Or. 1989); *Union Pacific R.R. Co. v. Bridal Veil Lumber Co.*, 219 F.2d 825 (9th Cir. 1955), cert. denied, 350 U.S. 981 (1956).

4. *See*, Jeffrey W. Sachs and Harvey C. Koch, the Agreement of Indemnity and the Defenses of the Indemnitors (January 27, 1989) (unpublished manuscript, on file with the American Bar Association), for a thorough discussion of nine traditional and nine non-traditional defenses to the general indemnity agreement.

indemnity agreement. The language of the standard GIA supports this conclusion: "This Agreement of Indemnity is executed by the undersigned for the purpose of indemnifying (surety) in connection with any Bonds written on behalf of (principal)."

The doctrine of promissory estoppel can be used to enforce a subsequently delivered indemnity agreement.[5] One Court noted that the signing of a GIA four months after the bond was issued would fail for lack of consideration, but that an oral promise to indemnify made before the bond was issued constituted adequate consideration. Execution of the subsequently signed indemnity agreement was held to be in pursuance and in consummation of a prior arrangement.[6] The standard GIA also deals with a subsequently signed instrument: "This agreement applies to all Bonds executed or procured by the surety for the principal whether prior or subsequent to the execution and delivery of this Agreement."

In most instances, the language of the indemnity agreement preempts any defense based on a lack of consideration.

II. *Indemnitors' Failure to Sign, Understand or Deliver the Indemnity Agreement*

The Indemnitor's failure to understand the terms of a signed indemnity agreement is not a defense to the agreement if the indemnitor had an opportunity to read the document (even if he did not do so) before signing it, absent a showing of fraud.[7] Failure of the indemnitor to read the written indemnity agreement will not be sufficient grounds for an argument of mutual mistake to reform the agreement either.[8] The surety does not have a specific duty to inform the indemnitor that the indemnity agreement covers bonds that the principal applies for in the future.[9]

Failure to sign the bond is not a defense if the GIA has been signed by the indemnitor.[10] Failure of the indemnitor to designate that he was signing "individually" does not constitute a defense either.[11] An indemnitor may have a defense if he signed the indemnity agreement believing that the principal would sign the agreement as well, if such signature was never procured by the surety. [12] The language of the standard general indemnity agreement attempts to avoid this result, however:

> If any of the persons named herein as Principal and Indemnitor fail to execute this agreement or if the execution hereof by any of the undersigned shall be defective or invalid for any reason, such failure, defect or invalidity shall not in any manner diminish or otherwise affect the obligations or liability hereunder of any other of the undersigned.

---

5. *American Druggists' Ins. Co. v. Shoppe*, 448 N.W.2d 103 (Minn. Ct. App. 1989).

6. Engbrock v. Federal Ins. Co., 370 F.2d 784, 789 (5th Cir. 1967). *See also Jacobson v. American Fidelity Fire Ins. Co.*, 541 P.2d 2 (Nev. 1975) (holding indemnity agreement executed one month after issuance of surety bond enforceable where intention of parties is clear that agreement is to apply to surety bond).

7. *United States v. Thomas*, 938 F.2d 831 (8th Cir. 1991); *Insurance Co. of North America v. Bath*, 726 F. Supp. 1247 (D. Wyo. 1989); *Jackson v. Lambert*, 492 So. 2d 498 (La. Ct. App. 1986); *Trinity Universal Ins. Co. v. Good*, 202 So. 2d 379 (La. Ct. App. 1967).

8. Universal Sur. Co. v. JED Constr. Co., Inc., 265 N.W.2d 219 (Neb. 1978).

9. *United States. v. Thomas*, 938 F.2d 831 (8th Cir. 1991).

10. *United States v. United Pac. Ins. Co.*, 697 F. Supp. 378 (D. Idaho 1988).

11. *Owens v. Banks*, 202 F.2d 689 (5th Cir. 1953), *cert. denied*, 346 U.S. 813 (1953).

12. *Denton v. Fireman's Fund Indem. Co.*, 352 F.2d 95 (10th Cir. 1965).

In some states, the countersignature of a resident agent on the bond is necessary if the bond is issued by a non-resident agent.[13]

Failure to deliver the GIA to the surety (even if fully signed) can constitute a defense in those states where delivery is considered indispensable to a contract's effectiveness. Since an indemnity agreement usually must be in writing to circumvent the Statute of Frauds, proof that there is a written agreement may be necessary. Even without actual delivery of the signed agreement, many courts have held that constructive delivery has occurred when a contracting party has in some way evidenced an intention to make it an enforceable obligation against himself by surrendering control over it and intentionally placing it under the power of the other contracting party or some third person.[14]

III. *Surety's Failure to Adequately Pursue the Principal*

The agreement of indemnity permits the surety to pursue its indemnitors prior to exhausting its rights against the principal: "Surety is not required to exhaust its remedies or rights against the principal before asserting its rights under this agreement against the indemnitors." Moreover, since the obligation to the surety is joint and several, as discussed above, there is no established priority in execution or collection efforts by the surety.

IV. *Lack of Notice to the Indemnitors*

Notice questions between indemnitors and indemnitees usually arise when the agreement of indemnity is silent on the subject. The standard GIA specifically waives notice requirements:[15] "The undersigned hereby waive notice of the execution of any Bond and of any act, fact or information concerning or affecting the rights or liabilities of the surety or the rights or liabilities of the undersigned."[16]

Even in the absence of a contract governing the matter, the surety is not generally obligated to give the indemnitor notice that payment has been made in order to make a demand on him.[17] Nevertheless, some courts have held that notice to indemnitors is required.[18] Some jurisdictions have statutes requiring such notice.[19] Notice of a pending lawsuit against the surety to the indemnitors

---

13. *American Druggists Ins. Co. v. Brownlee*, 562 F. Supp. 898 (E.D. Ark. 1983); *American Fidelity Fire Ins. Co. v. Builders United Constr., Inc.*, 613 S.W.2d 379 (Ark. 1981).

14. *Charmglow Products, Inc. v. Mitchell State Street Bank*, 687 F. Supp. 448 (E.D. Wisc. 1988); *Lincoln National Bank & Trust Company v. Bank of Commerce*, 764 F.2d 392 (5th Cir. 1985).

15. *United States v. United Pac. Ins. Co.*, 697 F. Supp. 378 (D. Idaho 1988); *Safeco Ins. Co. of America v. Criterion Inv. Corp.*, 732 F. Supp. 834 (E.D. Tenn. 1989); *Hawaiian Ins. and Guar. Co. v. Higashi*, 672 P.2d 556 (Haw. Ct. App. 1983), *aff'd in part, rev'd in part*, 675 P.2d 767 (Haw. 1984).

16. *See The Revenue Markets, Inc., 35 F. Supp.2d at 901*; *Westchester Fire Insurance v.* Campbell, 55 F.3d 32 (1st Cir. 1995); Republic *Insurance Company v. Real Development*, 161 A.2d 189 (Sup. Ct. N.Y. 1990).

17. *Safeco Ins. Co. of America v. Gaubert*, 829 S.W.2d 274 (Tex. Ct. App. 1992); *Republic Ins. Co. v. Real Dev. Co.*, 161 A.2d 189 (N.Y. App. Div. 1990).

18. *United States v. D Bar D Enters., Inc.*, 772 F. Supp. 1167 (D. Nev. 1991); *Palevac v. Mid Century Non Auto*, 710 P.2d 1389 (Nev. 1985); *New Amsterdam Casualty Company v. Lundquist*, 198 N.W. 2d 543 (Minn. 1972).

19. *E.g.*, Louisiana Civ. Code 3052. *See, Jackson v. Lambert*, 492 So. 2d 498 (La. Ct. App. 1986).

constitutes notice by the surety even if the suit papers are not sent by the surety to the indemnitors.[20] Failure of the surety to add the indemnitors as third party defendants in a suit by a bond claimant does not constitute a lack of notice defense.[21]

V. *Waiver by Surety*

While it is possible for a surety to lose its basic rights by waiver or estoppel, there are few cases supporting this defense. Oral representations by a surety are not the basis of a waiver argument when a written indemnity agreement is involved.[22] A surety's written consent to the owner of a project to make payment to the contractor/principal in a case where the surety did not know that the contractor was in default or would fail to use the funds to pay the suppliers of materials and labor does not constitute a waiver of the surety's indemnity rights against the contractor/principal.[23]

The surety may also impose upon itself an obligation to finance the principal or issue additional bonds beyond the scope of the GIA when executing supplemental takeover agreements.[24]

VI. *Surety's Failure to Write Additional Bonds for the Principal*

The surety has no obligation to issue a bond to its principal simply because it has issued one to him previously. The standard GIA makes this clear: "The surety may decline to execute any bond applied for without incurring any liability whatever to the undersigned."

Similarly, by issuing a bid bond to the principal, the surety is not obligated to issue a final contract bond:[25]

> If the Surety shall execute a bid or proposal bond, or any similar undertaking, it may nevertheless decline to execute any and all Bonds that may be required in connection with any award made on the proposal for which the bond or undertaking is given, and the Principal shall have the right to procure from another surety any bonds that may be required in connection with any award under the proposal for which the bond or undertaking is given.

Some courts have relied on custom and usage, however, as a basis for finding that an implied agreement to issue performance and payment bonds existed between the parties.[26] The surety may

---

20. *Burke v. Ripp*, 619 F.2d 354 (5th Cir. 1980). *But see Atlantic Richfield Co. v. Interstate Oil Transport Co.*, 784 F. 2d 106, 112 (2d Cir. 1986) (holding that in indemnity action indemnitee can only recover from an indemnitor upon proof of the indemnitee's potential liability if (1) settlement is reasonable, and if (2) the indemnitor has sufficient notice in which to object to the terms and if the indemnitor objects to settlement and indemnitee fails to defend, indemnitee must prove actual liability against the indemnitor to recover).

21. *Trinity Universal Ins. Co. v. Good*, 202 So. 2d 379 (La. Ct. App. 1967).

22. *Home Indem. Co. v. Wachter*, 115 A.D.2d 590 (N.Y. App. Div. 1985).

23. *Travelers Indem. Co. v. Clark*, 254 So. 2d 741 (Miss. 1971).

24 *Arntz Contracting Company v. St. Paul Fire and Marine Insurance Company*, 47 Cal. App. 4th 464, 54 Cal. Rptr. 2d 888 (1996).

25. Kerr, "Does Issuance of a Bid Bond Constitute a Performance Commitment?" 15 Forum 465 (1980).

26. *L.F. Pace & Sons, Inc. v. Travelers Ins. Co.*, 514 A.2d 766 (Conn. App. Ct. 1986), *cert. denied*, 516 A.2d 886 (Conn. 1986). *But see Chas. H. Tompkins v. Lumbermens Mutual Cas. Co.*, 732 F. Supp. 1368, 1373 (E.D. Va. 1990) (distinguishing *L.F. Pace* and noting that it resulted in a "nonsensical" result for the surety); *L.G. Defelice, Inc. v.*

also obligate itself beyond the scope of the GIA to finance the principal or issue additional bonds when executing takeover agreements.[27]

VII. *Release of Indemnitors or Termination of Bond*

A contract of indemnity continues in force during such time as is expressly or impliedly provided for in the contract, and where no time is fixed, either party may end it at his pleasure if he acts in good faith.[28] The standard GIA requires that written notice be given by the indemnitor to the surety and usually there is both a waiting period and a mailing requirement.[29]

> [T]he Undersigned may notify the Surety at its Home Office of such Undersigned's withdrawal from this Agreement; such notice shall be sent by certified or registered mail and shall state when, not less than thirty days after receipt of such notice by the Surety, such withdrawal shall be effective. Such Undersigned will not be liable under this Agreement as to any Bonds executed by the Surety <u>after</u> the effective date of such notice (emphasis added).

Only if the contractual requirements have been complied with will the indemnitor be released or his indemnity obligation terminated. The defense by an indemnitor that it has been implicitly released by the surety is occasionally asserted, but the cases dealing with such defenses are infrequent. In one instance where surety and principal entered into special account in trustee bank to receive funds paid under bonded contracts to principal with principal and surety to exercise joint control over disbursements, it did not constitute a novation under a joint control theory which would serve to release the indemnitors.[30]

Release of one indemnitor does not operate as a release by the surety of any other indemnitor since the indemnity obligation is both joint and several. The language of the standard GIA supports this conclusion: "The undersigned shall continue to remain bound under this agreement even though the surety may, from time to time and with or without notice to or knowledge of the undersigned have heretofore accepted or released, or shall hereafter accept or release other agreements of indemnity or collateral in connection with the execution of the Bonds from the undersigned or from others."

At common law, parties who are jointly and severally liable on a judgment have no right of contribution; any right of indemnity claimed by them must arise from a surety relation established by contract or imposed by law.[31] If co-indemnitors have a right of contribution against each other, then the surety's release of one indemnitor could impair the contribution rights of the second indemnitor.[32] The language of the standard GIA attempts to deal with this problem: "The surety is hereby expressly authorized to settle any claim based upon this agreement with any one or more of

---

Fireman's Ins. Co., 41 F. Supp.2d 152, 160 n.13 (D. Conn. 1998) (disagreeing with *L.F. Pace's* rationale).

27. *Arntz Contracting Company v. St. Paul Fire and Marine Insurance Company*, 47 Cal. App. 4th 464, 54 Cal. Rptr. 2d 888 (1996).

28. *Western Sur. Co. v. Welty*, 134 N.W.2d 288 (Neb. 1965); 42 C.J.S. Indemnity ? 11.

29. *Insurance Co. of North America v. Lanseair Travel Agency, Inc.*, 617 P.2d 366 (Utah 1980).

30. *United Pac. Ins. Co. v. Johnson-Gillanders Co.*, 280 F. Supp. 90 (D. N.D. 1968).

31. *Economy Rentals, Inc. v. Garcia*, 819 P.2d 1306 (N.M. 1991).

32. *Massachusetts Bonding and Ins. Co. v. Osborne*, 43 Cal. Rptr. 761 (Cal. Ct. App. 1965).

the undersigned individually, and such settlement or compromise shall not affect the liability of any of the rest of the undersigned."

Liability under an indemnity agreement does not terminate upon the principal's death.[33]

VIII. *Lack of Venue for Bringing Suit, Lack of Service of Process, and Lack of Jurisdiction*

Lack of venue, lack of service of process, lack of jurisdiction and related procedural defenses are not unique to surety indemnity cases. The general indemnity agreement may include provisions that service of process on one indemnitor constitutes service on the others and that service on the Secretary of State is sufficient if personal service cannot be obtained, thus eliminating some technical defenses. The standard GIA provides:

> In the event of legal proceedings against the Surety, upon or on account of any said Bond or Bonds, the Surety may apply for a court order making any or all of the Undersigned parties defendants, and each Undersigned hereby consents to the granting of such application and agrees to become such a party defendant and to allow judgment to be rendered also against such Undersigned in like amount and in favor of the Surety.

Jurisdictional constraints may make it impossible to bring indemnitors into a lawsuit in a venue where they do not reside, however.[34]

IX. *The Improper Default Defense*

The surety must always fully investigate a default of the principal by the obligee to ascertain whether it is proper.[35] Even where the indemnity agreement leaves the right to settle a claim to the sole discretion of the surety, courts will impose a duty on the surety to reasonably investigate the claims, counterclaims and possible defenses before settling.[36] In the absence of a contractual provision to the contrary, when a surety settles a claim before the validity of that claim has been adjudicated, then the burden is upon the surety to prove a valid and legal liability in an action against its indemnitor.[37] Payment of a claim over a principal's objection may bar the surety's claim for indemnity if a good faith effort to protect the best interests of the principal is not made.[38] The standard written indemnity agreement gives the indemnitor the right to object to and direct a surety's

33. *In re Estate of Bierman*, 410 S.W.2d 342 (Mo. Ct. App. 1966); *Denton v. Fireman's Fund Indem. Co.*, 352 F.2d 95 (10th Cir. 1965).

34. *Gundle Lining Construction Corp. v. Adams County Asphalt, Inc.*, 85 F.3d 201 (5th Cir. 1996) (Pennsylvania resident indemnitors could not be sued in Texas where surety was named in payment bond litigation).

35. *Windowmaster Corp. v. Morse/Diesel*, 722 F.Supp. 1532 (N.D. Ill. 1988); Hartigan, "The Duty of an Indemnitee to An Indemnitor," 41 *Insurance Couns. J.* 229 (1974).

36. *City of Portland v. George D. Ward & Assocs.*, 750 P.2d 171 (Or. Ct. App. 1988). *But see Associated Indemnity Corp. v. CAT Contracting, Inc.*, 964 S.W.2d 276, 282 (Tex. 1998) (expressly holding that a bond surety does not owe a common law duty of good faith to its principal).

37. *Seaboard Sur. Co. v. Glenayre Estates, Inc.*, 252 N.E.2d 712 (Ill. App. Ct. 1969).

38. *Fireman's Fund Ins. Co. v. Clark*, 490 S.W.2d 447 (Ark. 1973); *Engbrock v. Federal Ins. Co.*, 370 F.2d 784 (5th Cir. 1967).

payment of a claim, if the indemnitor posts collateral with the surety for the amount of the surety's potential liability. Failure to post that collateral gives the surety an absolute right to settle claims as long as it is done in good faith.[39]

Significant litigation has focused on the surety's conduct leading to a default of the principal.[40] The surety does not have any obligation to the obligee until there is a declared default, but the surety should not prompt the default even if an earlier default will minimize the damages sustained by the surety. In a case where the surety refused to write additional performance bonds to the principal, failed to execute further release of lien bonds and failed to make additional cash advances knowing that such actions would put the principal in bankruptcy, the court nevertheless held that the surety did not precipitate a default of the principal.[41]

X. *Payments Improperly or Unnecessarily Made by the Surety*

The fact that the surety suffers a loss does not automatically render the principal or indemnitor liable either under the common law principle of reimbursement or the contractual obligation of indemnity. Generally speaking, the liability of the principal is the measure of the surety's liability, and should the surety pay where the principal has no actual liability it is not entitled to recover from the principal or the indemnitors because the payment is deemed to be voluntary. Therefore, before use of the written indemnity agreement, it was not uncommon for principals and indemnitors to take the position that the surety should not have made a payment because the principal had no liability or because the surety had overpaid a claim.[42]

Even in the face of comprehensive language in the standard GIA, indemnitors will argue against their liability to the surety for damages claimed. The defense that an indemnitor is not liable for payments made by the surety or for the damages claimed by the surety seldom prevails, however. The standard GIA provides that: "The undersigned agree to indemnify the surety against any and all losses and expenses which the surety may sustain or incur by reason of having executed or procured the execution of any Bond or Bonds." The agreement also gives the surety the exclusive right to determine whether a claim, demand, suit or judgment should be paid "on the basis of liability, expediency, or otherwise," and it also says that the surety's determination "shall be final, conclusive, and binding" upon the indemnitors. The standard GIA gives the surety almost carte blanche authority to pay a claim and seek reimbursement from the indemnitors.

The real controversy under this defense centers around the issue of the surety's good faith or absence thereof in incurring a loss.[43] If the surety acts in good faith when making payments or incurring losses, it should be entitled to full reimbursement from its principal and indemnitors. At least one court has held, however, that in order to recover attorneys' fees, the surety also had to show

39. *Fidelity and Deposit Co. of Maryland v. Fleischer*, 772 S.W.2d 809 (Mo. Ct. App. 1989).

40. *Lambert v. Maryland Casualty Co.*, 403 So. 2d 739 (La. Ct. App. 1981), *aff'd*, 418 So. 2d 553 (La. 1982); *Gerstner Elec. Inc. v. American Ins. Co.*, 520 F.2d 790 (8th Cir. 1975).

41. *Lambert v. Maryland Casualty Co.*, 403 So. 2d 739 (La. Ct. App. 1981), *aff'd*, 418 So. 2d 553 (La. 1982).

42. *See*, J. Hayes, The General Indemnity Agreement - The Beginning and the End (January 1986) (unpublished manuscript on file with the American Bar Association).

43. *United States Fidelity & Guar. Co. v. Napier Elec. & Constr. Co.*, 571 S.W.2d 644 (Ky. Ct. App. 1978). *See also Fallon Elec. Co, Inc. v. Cincinnati Ins. Co.*, 121 F.3d 125 (3d Cir. 1997) (finding "prima facie evidence" clause enforceable but determining that indemnitor's burden of proof is controlled by the express terms of the clause).

that the fees were reasonable.[44] Because the surety in most situations is simply acting to enforce its contractual rights, the surety will normally prevail on the good faith issue barring what would be termed, in some jurisdictions, a tortuous breach of contract. The defense of good faith is more fully explored in the next section.

In addition to payments made by a surety to claimants of the principal, the surety is also entitled to indemnification from the principal for funds advanced to the principal. Frequently in a performance bond situation the surety will advance funds to the principal rather than allowing the principal to be formally defaulted by the obligee. The surety has a right to assist its principal and will not be treated as a "volunteer" in this instance, thus barring its indemnity rights against the principal.[45] The standard agreement provides:

> The Surety is further authorized and empowered to advance money or to guarantee loans to the Contractor which the Surety may see fit to advance to said Contractor for the purpose of any contract referred to in or guaranteed by said Bond or Bonds; and all money so loaned or advanced shall be conclusively presumed to be a loss by the Surety for which each and all of undersigned shall be responsible.

Generally speaking, indemnification depends upon an interpretation of the indemnity contract and not on the validity or enforcement of the bond.[46]

XI. *The Breach of Good Faith Defense*

Most indemnity agreements permit the surety to pay claims and seek indemnity on the simple showing that payment was made. However, the principal can challenge the payment if it was not made in good faith by the surety.[47] Regardless of the terms of the indemnity agreement which establish a presumption that the surety has acted in good faith, courts have held that the duty to exercise good faith arises from an implied covenant of good faith and fair dealing inherent in any

---

44. *International Fidelity Insurance Company v. Jones*, 294 N.J. Super. 1, 682 A.2d 263 (1996); but see, *Fallon Electric Co. v. The Cincinnatti Insurance Co.*, 121 F.3d 125 3d Cir. 1997.

45. *Alaska Nat'l. Bank of the North v. Gwitchyaa Zhee Corp.*, 639 P.2d 984 (Alaska 1981); *Indemnity Ins. Co. v. Lane Contracting Corp.*, 227 F. Supp. 143 (D. Neb. 1964).

46. *Commercial Ins. Co. of Newark, N.J. v. Pacific-Peru Constr. Co.*, 558 F.2d 948 (9th Cir. 1977); *Fireman's Fund v. Nizdil*, 709 F. Supp. 975 (D. Or. 1989).

47. *The Hartford v. Tanner*, 910 P.2d 872 (Ct. App. Kan. 1996) (holding that surety's obligation of good faith and fair dealing is implied and "superimposed" on the entire surety contract); *General Accident Insurance Company of America v. Meritt-Meridian Constr. Corp.*, 975 F. Supp. 511 (S.D. N.Y. 1997); *Transamerica Insurance Company v. HVAC Contractors, Inc.*, 857 F. Supp. 969 (N.D. Ga. 1994); *Horton v. United States Fidelity & Guar. Co.*, 392 S.E.2d 25 (Ga. Ct. App. 1990); *Republic Ins. Co. v. Real Dev. Co.*, 161 A.D.2d 189 (N.Y. App. Div. 1990); *Reliance Ins. Co. v. Romine*, 707 F. Supp. 550 (S.D. Ga. 1989), *aff'd*, 888 F.2d 1844 (1989); *Hartford Accident and Indem. Co. v. Millis Roofing and Sheet Metal, Inc.*, 418 N.E.2d 645 (Mass. App. Ct. 1981); *United States Fidelity & Guar. Co. v. Napier Elec. & Constr. Co., Inc.*, 571 S.W.2d 644 (Ky. Ct. App. 1978); *Seaboard Sur. Co. v. Dale Constr. Co.*, 230 F.2d 625 (1st Cir. 1956). *But see Cates Construction, Inc. v. Talbot Partners*, 980 P.2d 407 (Cal. 1999) (holding that recovery for breach of surety's breach of the implied covenant of good faith and fair dealing is limited to contract damages while reversing punitive damage award against surety); *Great American Insurance Co. v. North Austin Municipal Utility District No. 1*, 908 S.W.2d 415 (Tex. 1995) (similar holding).

contract.[48] The concept of good faith and fair dealing underlies all aspects of the agreement of indemnity and can, therefore, be raised by the indemnitors in conjunction with any of the defenses.[49]

Some courts have held that where the insured is obligated to indemnify the surety, a negligent breach of the surety's duty of good faith is sufficient to establish a defense.[50] Other courts have held that lack of diligence or negligence is not the equivalent of bad faith, so a showing of bad motive is necessary to support a defense that a surety has not acted in good faith.[51] In either event, the surety's bad faith act which prejudices the indemnitor should only release the indemnitor to the extent of the prejudice. For instance, a surety's failure to settle a claim which results in an adverse judgment against the indemnitor and additional fees incurred by the surety will only release the indemnitor from payment over and above what the claim could have been settled for by the surety.[52] Some courts have refused to apply a duty of good faith unless required specifically by the bond.[53]

XII. *The Interference With Contract Claim or Defense*

This claim/defense frequently arises in cases where after a default the surety has notified the owner/obligee of its claim to all contract balances which remain on the job. The owner then refuses to pay the contractor which has the effect of cutting the contractor off from cash flow which is needed to fund on-going operations. Thereafter, the contractor defends an indemnity claim by the surety or brings a tort action for damages against the surety on the theory that the surety interfered with its contract with the owner. This claim/defense is often asserted along with the improper default defense.

In order to recover on such a claim, the plaintiff must prove that the surety maliciously, *i.e.*, with knowledge of the contract and without justifiable cause, induced its breach.[54] If the surety enters into a separate takeover agreement involving the principal, new duties may be imposed upon the surety beyond the scope of the GIA. In such instance of a second undertaking, the surety's liability to its principal and indemnitors may be expanded.[55]

---

48. *United States v. United Pac. Ins. Co.*, 697 F. Supp. 378 (D. Idaho 1988); *City of Portland v. George D. Ward & Assocs.*, 750 P.2d 1717 (Or. Ct. App. 1988); *Martin v. Lyons*, 558 P.2d 1063 (Idaho 1977); *Fidelity & Deposit Co. of Maryland v. Bristol Steel and Ironworks, Inc.*, 722 F.2d 1160 (4th Cir. 1983); *Windowmaster Corp. v. Morse/Diesel, Inc.*, 722 F. Supp. 1532 (N.D. Ill. 1988); *Rush Presbyterian St. Luke's Medical Center v. Safeco Ins. Co. of America*, 712 F. Supp. 1344 (N.D. Ill. 1989); *Transamerica Ins. Co. v. Bloomfield*, 401 F.2d 357 (6th Cir. 1968). *But see supra* note 48 and accompanying text.

49. *See*, Wilson, "Resisting Bad Faith Claims by Indemnitors," The Pursuit of Subrogation and Indemnity Claims, a special publication by the Defense Research Institute, Volume 1991, No. 3.

50. *Rush Presbyterian St. Luke's Medical Center v. Safeco Ins. Co.*, 722 F. Supp. 485 (N.D. Ill. 1989); *City of Portland v. George D. Ward & Assocs.*, 750 P.2d 171 (Or. Ct. App. 1988); *Barr/Nelson, Inc. v. Tonto's, Inc.*, 336 N.W. 2d 46 (Minn. 1983).

51. *Safeco Ins. Co. of America v. Criterion Inv. Corp.*, 732 F. Supp. 834 (E.D. Tenn. 1989); *Engbrock v. Federal Ins. Co.*, 370 F.2d 784 (5th Cir. 1967) (applying Texas law); *Lemoine v. American Fidelity Fire Ins. Co.*, 491 So. 2d 812 (La. Ct. App. 1986); *H.M. Ford v. Aetna Ins. Co.*, 394 S.W.2d 693 (Tex. Ct. App. 1965).

52. *Republic Ins. Co. v. Prince George's County*, 608 A.2d 1301 (Md. Ct. Spec. App. 1992), *cert. granted*, 615 A.2d 262 (Md. 1992).

53. *Associated Indemnity Corporation v. CAT Contracting*, 41 Tex. Sup. Ct. J. 389, 964 S.W. 2d 276 (1998); *United States Fidelity & Guaranty Co. v. Feibus*, 15 F. Supp. 2d 579 (M.D. Pa. 1998).

54. *Gerstner Elec. Inc. v. American Ins. Co.*, 520 F.2d 790 (8th Cir. 1975).

55. *Arntz Contracting Co. v. St. Paul Fire and Marine Insurance Company*, 47 Cal. App. 4th 464, 54 Cal. Rptr. 2d 888 (1996).

XIII. *The Abuse of Rights/Domination Claim or Defense*

The abuse of rights doctrine states that liability can be imposed upon a party who attempts to exercise a right legally given it if such right is exercised with the intention of harming or imposing a detriment upon another. If a person exercises his rights with a predominant intent to harm, as evidenced by the fact that he obtains little or no benefit from the exercise of his rights while, at the same time the other party or parties suffer damages thereby, courts have found the act abusive, thus imposing liability for damages upon the party who has improperly exercised its legal rights. The abuse of rights theory of claim or defense, which is frequently argued in conjunction with the interference with contract claim/defense, has also been characterized as a domination argument.

The surety has no obligation to support its principal by advancing additional funds to it or to forbear to exercise its legal rights as surety.[56] The surety will have no right of indemnification against its principal for damages incurred as a result of liability based upon the surety's independent tortuous conduct, however.[57]

XIV. *Mitigation of Damages*

Written indemnity agreements are similar to all other contracts in that there is always a duty to mitigate damages.[58] Some courts have held that sureties have a duty to take reasonable actions to avoid passing on unreasonable losses to the principal and indemnitors.[59] In the case of *The Hartford v. Tanner*, the surety sought indemnification from the principal on two bond contracts that the principal had signed as indemnitor.[60] The principal defended on the grounds that the surety failed to mitigate its damages because the surety did not conduct a thorough investigation and instead simply paid the bond claims when presented and sought indemnification. The court found for the principal, as it was persuaded by the principal's evidence that in other similar situations the surety had been able to mitigate the claims. In addition, the court rejected the surety's argument that it should have received at least a reasonable amount of what it paid, primarily because the surety presented no evidence on the amount that would have been assessed had the claims been protested, investigated and negotiated.

Other courts have found no duty for indemnitee to mitigate damages for their indemnitors.[61] In these cases, the courts ruled against the indemnitors' mitigation defense because either: (1) The indemnitors presented insufficient evidence that the surety paid an excessive sum to complete the

---

56. *Lambert v. Maryland Casualty Co.*, 403 So. 2d 739 (La. Ct. App. 1981), *aff'd*, 418 So. 2d 553 (La. 1982).

57. *Szarkowski v. Reliance Ins. Co.*, 404 N.W.2d 502 (N.D. 1987); *Barr/Nelson, Inc. v. Tonto's, Inc.*, 336 N.W.2d 46 (Minn. 1983).

58. *See* generally, *The Law of Payment Bonds*, §13 "The Surety's Common Law and Contractual Rights of Indemnity" (ABA 1998).

59. *See International Minerals & Chemical Corporation v. Avon Products, Inc.*, 817 S.W. 2d 903, 910 (Mo. 1991); *Federal Insurance Company v. Walker*, 422 N.E. 2d 548, 552 (N.Y. 1981); *Town Pump v. Diteman*, 622 P.2d 212, 216 (Mont. 1981). In these cases, summary judgment was denied the surety because the record contained evidence of unfair overreaching by the surety. Such overreaching resulted in the surety paying excessive sums to complete the principal's work.

60. 910 P.2d 872 (Kan. 1996).

61. See *American States Insurance Company v. Glover*, 960 F.2d 149 (6th Cir. 1992); *Four Seasons Environmental, Inc. v. Westfield Companies*, 638 N.E. 2d 91, 93 (Ohio 1994); *Moya v. Fidelity & Casualty Company of New York*, 406 P.2d 173, 176 (N.M. 1965).

principal's work; or (2) The surety was under no duty to mitigate by pursuing possible claims against the owners of the construction projects. In additional, it has been held that the language of the indemnity clause in the standard written indemnity agreement makes clear that the mitigation defense will fail unless there is convincing proof that the surety did not act in good faith.[62]

Preservation of collateral is not the duty of the surety unless the guarantor is relying upon the collateral and a surety's failure to perfect a security interest in accounts receivable assigned to the surety by the principal debtor will not act as a release or otherwise serve to discharge the indemnitor.[63] Failing to sell a principal's pledged collateral at a particularly profitable moment has also been held insufficient to support a mitigation defense. Likewise, a release of collateral to the indemnitors by the surety does not constitute a release of indemnity claims or failure to mitigate by the surety.[64] The standard indemnity agreement provides:

> The Surety may sell or realize upon any or all such collateral security, at public or private sale, with or without notice to the undersigned.

Failing to settle a creditor's claim, which resulted in a judgment far in excess of what the claim could have been settled for, will not constitute a mitigation defense where the principal objected to the settlement initially.[65]

XV. *Material/Cardinal Change*

If there is a material or cardinal change by the surety in the undertaking indemnified without the consent of the indemnitor that increases the risk to or prejudices the indemnitor, the indemnitor may be discharged from liability.[66] A party who indemnified the surety on a warehouseman's bond for an amount equal to the bond was not prejudiced by the surety increasing the amount of the bond during the indemnity period without the indemnitor's consent, however, where the surety seeking to enforce the indemnity agreement sought only the amount of the original bond from the indemnitor.[67]

The standard indemnity agreement attempts to avoid any argument regarding material changes to the underlying contract through the following language:

> The Surety is authorized, without notice to or knowledge of the Undersigned, to assent to any change whatsoever in any Bond and any contract covered by a Bond, including, but not limited to, any change in the time for the completion of the contract and for payments or advances thereunder, to assent to or to take any assignment or assignments, to execute or consent to the execution of any continuations, extensions, renewals, enlargements, modifications, changes or alterations of any Bond and to execute

62. See *Continental Casualty Company v. Guterman,* supra note 33.

63. *Fireman's Fund Ins. Co. v. Joseph J. Biafore, Inc.*, 526 F.2d 170 (3d Cir. 1975).

64. *Olympic Dev. Group, Inc. v. American Druggists' Ins. Co.*, 333 S.E.2d 622 (Ga. Ct. App. 1985); *Elk River Concrete Prods. Co. v. American Casualty Co.*, 129 N.W.2d 309 (Minn. 1964).

65. *Briggs v. Travelers Indem. Co.*, 289 So. 2d 762 (Fla. 3d DCA 1974), *cert. denied,* 302 So. 2d 413 (Fla. 1974).

66. *United States Fidelity & Guar. Co. v. Hathaway*, 394 S.E.2d 764 (W. Va. 1990); *Olympic Dev. Group, Inc. v. American Druggists Ins. Co.*, 333 S.E.2d 622 (Ga. Ct. App. 1985).

67. *United States v. Fireman's Fund Ins. Co.*, 191 F. Supp. 317 (D. Idaho 1961).

any substitute or substitutes therefor, with the same or different conditions, provisions and obligees and with the same or larger or smaller penalties,

and

the Undersigned shall remain bound under the terms of this Agreement even though any such assent by the Surety does or may substantially increase the liability of the Undersigned.

The material change defense is frequently asserted in conjunction with a lack of notice defense.

XVI. *Bankruptcy*

The indemnitor's best defense to a surety's indemnity claim may be insolvency or bankruptcy. *See*, Chad Schexnayder's article in this volume. The surety will be a secured creditor if it has recorded its GIA as a UCC-1 Financing Statement and will be in a preferred position as a completing surety to the extent of available contract balances. The indemnitor's obligation to the surety will otherwise be discharged in bankruptcy, however, unless some showing of fraud is made by the surety.

27

Contractor Default Insurance And Directed Suretyship

Lynn M. Schubert
Dean B. Thomson
Edward G. Gallagher

For over 100 years, contract performance and payment bonds have been the accepted means to protect against contractor or subcontractor default. For public works projects, the federal government[1] and every state[2] require the contractor to provide bonds. For private works, statutes, case law and well accepted forms[3] have lead to a reasonable ability of project participants to know the legal obligations of the bond.

A contractor or subcontractor required to furnish surety bonds has traditionally gone to its own bond producer[4] and surety. The surety considers the contractor or subcontractor's work program, experience and financial capability before deciding whether or not to issue the required bonds.[5]

In recent years, however, certain large brokers and insurers have attempted to cause changes in this traditional method of assuring contractor and subcontractor performance. These changes are usually urged as an extension of the scope of an owner's Owner Controlled Insurance Program.

I. *Directed Suretyship*

One such change sometimes urged by brokers is for the project owner or its representative to require that all contractors or subcontractors furnish bonds from a particular surety or through a particular producer. This practice, usually called Directed Suretyship, is illegal on federal public works projects[6] and state public projects in about half of the states.[7]

There are public policy arguments against directed suretyship. It encourages, or at least opens the door to, the type of cronyism or corruption which public bidding requirements are designed to avoid. Although the construction contract may be open to bids, the contract to furnish the bonds is not. There have been examples of states in which anyone who expected to succeed in public work would get his or her bonds from a particular agency or company with political

---

1. The Miller Act, 40 U.S.C. § 270a, et. seq.

2. See the Appendix to Gallagher, ed, *Payment Bond Manual, 2nd ed.* (American Bar Association, 1995) for the text of state bond statutes.

3. For example, the American Institute of Architects, the Associated General Contractors of America, and the Engineers Joint Construction Documents Committee (EJCDC) all publish performance and payment bond forms.

4. The term bond producer encompasses both insurance agents and brokers and connotes someone who specializes in surety obligations.

5. See Chapter 4 for a detailed discussion of how contract bonds are underwritten.

6. 31 U.S.C. § 9304(b).

7. See, for example, Cal. Govt. Code § 4420; N.Y. Ins. Law §§ 2404 and 2405; 30 ILCS 550/1; MGLA 268A § 8.

connections. Directed suretyship also reduces competition because only contractors acceptable to one company can compete. Suppose the selected surety has an existing contractor-client that wants a particular job, and it rejects potential competitors for the project? There will certainly be questions of how impartial it is and whether the owner should delegate its duty to determine who is a responsible bidder to a private entity. On the other hand, if the selected surety avoids such objections by agreeing to write bonds for anyone who is a low bidder, the owner is deprived of the prequlification services which are one of the primary benefits of requiring bonds in the first place.

Directed suretyship is anti-competitive and has been formally opposed by the Associated General Contractors of America[8] and The Surety Association of America.[9] The same public policies which have led Congress and many state legislatures to ban it should lead private owners and public entities to reject it on its merits.

II. *Contractor Default Insurance*

Contractor default insurance is an attempt to craft an insurance product to compete with surety bonds by providing indemnity for damages caused by contractor or subcontractor default. Unlike bonds, Contractor default insurance is a new product with no judicial precedent or standardized policies. An example of one such policy, however, is an appendix to this Chapter.

The relative merits of Contractor default insurance and traditional surety bonds vary depending on whether a public project or private project is involved, but there are also basic differences common to both. This discussion first focuses on the basic differences and then addresses the practical considerations on public and private projects. Finally, it address an actual project, the expansion of the Minneapolis Convention Center, on which contractor default insurance was carefully evaluated and rejected in favor of surety bonds.

A. THE BASIC DIFFERENCES

Default by a contractor or subcontractor on a construction project is not a fortuitous event. A surety examines the character, capacity and capital of the prospective principal to be sure it is able to perform both the job for which the bonds are requested and its other work on hand. If the surety's underwriters do not make any mistakes in such examinations, and other circumstances do not change, the surety should never have a loss. Naturally, mistakes do happen, and losses are paid. The surety industry recognizes, however, that the long term route to profitable operation is by quality underwriting to prevent losses. Sureties pay substantial expenses in this underwriting process precisely because they have learned that effort put into underwriting will save many times its cost later on in avoided losses.

Contractor default insurance, on the other hand, treats contractor or subcontractor default as a fortuitous event. Instead of using premium income to avoid default, the insurer uses the premiums to pay claims. This fundamental difference has several consequences for the insured.

---

8. Resolution of The Associated General Contractors of America at is 33rd annual convention, February 25 to 28, 1952.

9. Resolution of the Executive Committee of The Surety Association of America dated February 5, 1975.

First, the chance of default on the project is significantly increased. There is one less entity screening the potential contractors or subcontractors. The contractor default insurer attempts to shift this qualification obligation onto the insured through policy provisions "warrantying" certain standards and through deductibles, co-payments and sublimits of insurance, but the insured does not have the time or information to duplicate the surety's underwriting.

Second, whatever the default insurance policy form used, its does not have the history of legal precedent or the 100% coverage of performance and payment bonds. As an examination of the Appendix to this Chapter shows, it is not an easy task to write a new type of insurance policy without the background of understood terms derived from years of precedent.

Third, an insurance policy, unlike a bond, indemnifies only the insured. However that works when compared to a performance bond, it simply cannot provide coverage comparable to a payment bond. As a non-insured, the unpaid subcontractor or supplier has no recourse against the insurer. A payment bond provides a direct right of action by the claimant. A default insurances policy does not.

B. THE BEST PROTECTION FOR PUBLIC WORKS PROJECTS: A COMPARISON OF SURETY BONDS AND CONTRACTOR DEFAULT INSURANCE

1. Background

Virtually all public construction in the United States is performed under competitively bid, fixed price contracts. Bid bonds from all bidders and performance and payment bonds from the ultimate recipient of the contract are an integral part of this procurement system. The surety industry provides assurance that the low bidder will enter into the contract, that the work will be performed for the contract price, and that the contractor's debts for labor and material will be paid. The system of bid, performance and payment bonds also assures that the competing bidders are able to perform the contract work by forcing sureties to prequalify the bidders. The surety has to be satisfied that the prospective bidder has the capacity, capital and character to perform the work before it will agree to support the bid by issuing the required bonds.

In the past year, at least one company, with the help of several insurance brokers, has attempted to persuade owners on large public construction projects to use an insurance product, called contractor default insurance, in place of bid, performance and payment bonds. The proponents of this product concentrate on the performance bond portion of the surety's services and represent to the public owner that it can save money by using a program which offers indemnity insurance if the contractor defaults in performance of the work. There are three basic fallacies in using contractor default insurance for public or quasi-public projects, and two major fallacies with the proponents' marketing claims.

2. The Product

First, contractor default insurance provides less protection for the owner than the traditional bid, performance and payment bonds. A single insurer simply is unable to prequalify all prospective bidders. It does not have the long-standing relationship and access to confidential financial data, work in progress and personnel information that the prospective bidder's own surety has. If the public owner does attempt to have the single insurer decide who can bid, it invites the cronyism and corruption that the public bidding system is designed to prevent. If a surety makes a mistake and rejects a qualified bidder, the bidder has a number of other sureties to whom it can go to secure a bond. If every bidder has to be acceptable to the one insurer, there is no alternative. Suppose a long-standing client of the single insurer wants to obtain a particular contract or subcontract. There is nothing to stop the insurer from rejecting other potential competitors to help its client obtain the work.

Contractor default insurance also does not obligate the insurer to complete the work or to obtain another contractor. The owner has to relet the work, subject to whatever laws apply in terms of advertising and bidding, pay for the completion of the work, and then seek indemnity from the insurer for "qualifying losses." By contrast, a surety often will finance its principal to complete the work or tender a completion contractor and pay the owner up front for any cost overrun. Proponents of contractor default insurance talk about the owner's ability to "manage" claims, but in reality they mean the owner's obligation to arrange and pay for completion.

This new product also has deductibles, co-payment requirements, limits on the insurer's liability and sublimits for certain types of costs. By contrast, a performance bond pays from the first dollar of loss and guarantees performance of the contract with no limits or sublimits other than the penal sum of the bond which is 100% of the contract price.

Finally, the contractor default insurance product provides nothing comparable to the payment bond. The insurer undertakes no responsibility to anyone other than the insured. The insurer does not have to pay a defaulting contractor's bills, and it does not have to indemnify for such defaults unless the unpaid subcontractor or supplier can force the owner to pay. Because public works are not subject to liens, this would be a rare occurrence. By contrast, an unpaid subcontractor or supplier can make a claim directly against the surety. The owner can tell any such claimant to deal with the surety. The owner does not have to decide what is owed or make any payment.

The second fallacy of the attempt to sell contractor default insurance to public owners is the supposition that contractor default is a fortuitous event. An insurer expects losses and charges a sufficient premium to pay for them and still make a reasonable profit. The insurer uses premiums to pay losses rather than to prevent defaults. A surety, on the other hand, tries to avoid losses by prequalifying the contractor and, if cost effective, financing it to complete the work. Over 100 years of experience has taught sureties that the benefit from money spent to avoid loss is greater than from money used to pay losses after they happen. The delay and disruption from a contractor's default will often cost more than completion of the work. It always is better and less expensive to do something right the first time than to have to pay to do it over.

The third fallacy of contractor default insurance for public works is legal. Federal and state statutes require bonds on public works projects over a minimal size. This has forced the insurer to offer to provide both 100% performance and payment bonds and contractor default insurance. These two distinct products are offered with a "combining agreement" which attempts to rationalize away the overlap and contradictions. Since the contractor default insurance policy provides demonstrably less coverage, and the bonds are required by statute, it is logical to ask what benefit is being received from the insurance policy. How can a company provide bonds and insurance for less than the cost of the bonds alone? If the combining agreement takes away some of the bond coverage, the program no longer complies with the applicable statute. If it does not take away some of the bond coverage, there is a duplication for which the owner is paying.

3. Arguments advanced on behalf of Contractor Default Insurance

First, proponents of contractor default insurance on public projects argue that it will enable more small, disadvantaged and minority contractors to participate because they will not have to secure bonds. The surety industry, however, has numerous programs, both internally and in cooperation with state and federal agencies, to assure that such contractors can obtain bonds. Indeed, a public project with aggressive participation goals will do more long term good for disadvantaged contractors by helping them establish a relationship with a surety than it will by having them participate in a one-shot insurance or bond program. In today's market and with a number of sureties actively seeking small contractors, any contractor qualified to perform the work can obtain bonds with the help of a qualified bond agent or broker.

The adverse impact of the contractor default insurance program on small and minority contractors is most evident at the subcontractor level. Most emerging contractors start as sub or sub-sub contractors, not as bidders on multi-million dollar public prime contracts. The assurance of payment through the payment bond requirement, not provided with contractor default insurance, is a significant benefit to these contractors.

Second, proponents of contractor default insurance on public projects represent that it provides a cost saving compared to performance and payment bonds. In fact, it does not. Traditional bid, performance and payment bonds cost less than the insurance package. For example, on the Minneapolis Convention Center Expansion project discussed below, the insurer proposing contractor default insurance was going to charge a rate of $11.35 per thousand whereas 100% performance and payment bonds were available at an average rate of less than $7.00 per thousand. Even if the most optimistic assumptions are made as to losses, contractor default insurance simply is not cheaper than bonds.

C. A COMPARISON OF CONTRACTOR DEFAULT INSURANCE AND SURETY BONDS ON PRIVATE PROJECTS

Since 1994, large general contractors have been offered an insurance alternative to subcontractor performance and payments bonds. More recently, private project owners have been offered a similar alternative for bonding general contractors. Marketers of these contractor default insurance policies have represented these products as offering both reduced costs and simplified claims handling. In many instances, the purported benefits have been significant enough to cause some owners to seriously consider this alternative. However, a serious risk management analysis of these two options - bonds or default insurance - indicates that bonds are the best and most efficient method to prevent losses due to contractor default. The small number of default insurance policies that have actually been sold shows that contractors and owners have come to the same conclusion.

Marketers of contractor default insurance have described it as a pure risk transfer insurance product. Theoretically, a successful insurance program requires a detailed analysis of anticipated losses and future loss payout patterns based on a fortuitous event. In the case of contractor default insurance, the "event" being insured against is contractor default. However, contractor default is not a fortuitous event that occurs by chance; defaults can be prevented by a careful examination and pre-qualification of contractors and subcontractors. History has demonstrated clearly that default is a preventable risk, and that financial viability can be achieved through sound management practices, strategic decisions and technical expertise. Whereas contractor default insurance charges a premium to fund future losses due to contractor default, surety bonds focus on preventing defaults by evaluating contractors' operations and abilities before issuing the bond.

A second consideration in analyzing these two options is the optimum approach to damages caused by a default. Owners contract with general contractors to complete the work in accordance with the contract terms; general contractors, in turn, contract portions of the work to subcontractors. Ultimately, the owner wants timely performance of the contract. That is, the owner wants the various contractors to complete the work they were contracted to do, such as laying the foundation, erecting the structural steel, pouring the concrete, or installing the HVAC system.

On a bonded project, if a contractor fails to meet its contractual obligation, the surety may intercede to effect performance. In some instances, this involves providing cash flow assistance to the contractor, and in others it means hiring a replacement contractor to finish the work. In contrast, default insurers merely provide compensation for "damages." The owner is left to fund the default and obtain performance on its own. Further, the insurer's involvement is triggered only upon the occurrence of a default, whereas a surety may assist a troubled contractor before an actual default in order to mitigate the size of the loss.

1. Prequalification Services

Surety bonds take a better approach of focusing on preventing defaults. Pre-qualification of contractors is a significant service provided by the surety. Through prequalification, a surety seeks to prevent defaults up front rather than "waiting" to pay future losses. Prior to issuing a bond, the surety analyzes the contractor's financial position, management ability, and expertise in the type of work for which it is seeking a bond. Contractors who are not bondable (i.e., unqualified contractors) will not be awarded the contract. The owner thereby avoids a potential loss. Contractor default insurers do not provide pre-qualification services.

2. Handling a Default

Owners considering contractor default insurance should consider how they would rather spend their money. Surety bonds provide an assurance of performance in the event of default, which is ultimately what project owners want. Contractor default insurance provides no such assurance. Generally, these policies promise to indemnify the insured for a "qualified loss" after the application of the deductible and co-payment. (See the example later in this article for a discussion of how these features apply, as they are different than in most insurance policies). In addition, the owner is left with the responsibility of managing the defaulting contractor's obligations.

A surety bond, on the other hand, obligates the surety to assume the defaulting contractor's obligations. In the event of a default, the surety will ensure that the subcontractor's obligations are fulfilled. In fact, the surety may provide assistance to a troubled contractor before default occurs, a feature lacking in contractor default policies.

Even when a loss is significant enough to exceed a default insurance policy's deductible, the insured gets only a monetary settlement (assuming it has complied with the terms and conditions of the policy), but no assistance in completing the project.

3. Cost Comparison

Surety bonds make economic sense both in terms of the protection and services provided, and in terms of total out of pocket costs. The contractors and owners to whom default insurance is being marketed are of a size that would indicate an approximate bond cost of $5.50 - $6.50 per thousand of contract price. For some contractors with long standing surety relationships the cost could be even lower. Bonds have no deductible, no co-payment requirements and no "non-qualifying loss" provisions.

In contrast, default insurance carries an initial premium commensurate to bonds, yet it is subject to deductibles and co-payment requirements and only provides indemnity after the contractor has failed and the owner has paid its losses. For example, one general contractor paid $5.80 per thousand dollars of unbonded subcontracts for a default policy with an aggregate limit of $50,000,000, while the insured's total contract price was roughly $200,000,000. The Policy had a $2,000,000 aggregate deductible on qualifying losses, and a 20% co-payment above the deductible. Further, losses not exceeding $25,000 were "non-qualifying losses," which means that losses that do not exceed this threshold are not covered by the policy and must be paid separately by the general contractor.

Marketers of default insurance claim that this coverage offers owners and contractors the possibility of reduced costs versus bonds. Some policies indicate that part of the initial premium (which is the "maximum premium") is subject to refund if loss experience is good. However, any amounts paid out of the "experience premium" (the difference between the minimum premium and maximum premium) in the form of deductibles and co-pays for qualified losses reduce the amount the contractor will receive as a refund at the end of the coverage period.

Further, owners and contractors who purchase default insurance instead of bonds run the risk of exceeding the policy's aggregate limit because the limit is significantly less than the total value of covered contracts. The policy also contains a sublimit for indirect costs, which bonds do not contain. For example, the policy referenced above included a $5,000,000 sublimit for indirect costs associated with a qualifying loss.

For the many reasons cited above, surety bonds remain the most frequent choice for protecting against contractor and subcontractor defaults on private projects. In the five years default insurance coverage has been available, approximately 20 policies have been sold. Owners and contractors that take the time to investigate the merits of each option will agree that bonds offer the best value, as well as the best method for preventing defaults, assuring performance, and protecting against financial loss.

Corporate sureties have been providing protection against contractor default for over 100 years, and surety bonds are still the most effective means to provide protection against default. Insurance - which does not seek to prevent default or guarantee performance - is simply the wrong tool for the job.

D. A CASE HISTORY: SURETY BONDS OR DEFAULT INSURANCE ON THE MINNEAPOLIS CONVENTION CENTER ADDITION PROJECT

The following is a history of the debate before the Minneapolis City Council and Staff over whether to use traditional payment and performance bonds or a new "Subguard" insurance product on the new Minneapolis Convention Center Addition project.

The Minneapolis Convention Center Addition project has an estimated construction value of approximately $150,000,000 and the construction of the project has been divided into many bid packages. Minnesota Statutes § 574.26-.32 requires that municipalities such as Minneapolis obtain performance and payment bonds for the full value of any public project. Consistent with this law, the first several bid packages that were awarded required the successful bidder to post payment and performance bonds.

At this point in the project, Zurich Insurance Company ("Zurich") proposed that the City should use a new "Subguard" product that one of Zurich's subsidiaries had developed in lieu of surety bonds for all remaining bid packages. Under the Zurich proposal that was analyzed, an insurance company with multiple subsidiaries offered to issue the necessary performance and payment bonds, as required by state law, to multiple prime contractors for this project. The performance and payment bonds were to be managed by subsidiaries of the insurance company that issued the surety bonds.

The insurance company then offered to issue an insurance policy to the public owner, ". . . which shall provide an alternative to managing losses associated with prime contractor and subcontractor defaults, and will indemnify the public owner for costs resulting from defaults by prime contractors and subcontractors covered by the policy in performance of the project, and from any contractor's failures to pay subcontractors for supplies, materials, and labor performed for the project . . . ." A subsidiary of the insurance company, different from those managing the performance and payment bonds, would manage the project under the insurance policy. The program Zurich offered was "intended to combine and coordinate the [surety] bonds, the insurance policy, premiums, and 'recorded losses' on the project."

In its proposals to the City, Zurich claimed there were four main advantages to its new product: 1) Subguard was the equivalent of payment and performance bonds; 2) Subguard was cheaper than traditional bonds; 3) Subguard promoted the inclusion of more minority subcontractors in the project; and 4) Subguard allowed the City to engage in advantageous claim administration. The discussion below will trace the history of the debate of these issues as they were framed by Zurich and the surety industry.

1. Whether Subguard was the Equivalent of Performance and Payment Bonds

In one of its initial proposals, Zurich offered an insurance product that only insured against contractor performance and payment failures. The Minnesota Surety Association ("MSA") observed that whatever the merits of such an insurance program would be on a private construction project, Minn. Stat. § 574.26 requires payment and performance bonds for public projects. Accordingly, MSA argued that the Subguard product did not satisfy Minnesota law. In response to this criticism, Zurich offered the City the option of either surety bonds or the Subguard insurance product through what Zurich called a "combining agreement." Under the revised Zurich proposal, if a performance default occurred, the City could either call upon the performance or payment bond that Zurich had posted or it could choose to process the loss through the Subguard insurance policy. If the City chose the latter option, the City could submit a notice of loss to the insurance subsidiary. If the insurer deemed the loss to be a "qualified loss," under the terms and conditions of the policy, it would pay the loss as a claim under the policy, up to a certain predetermined amount.

The Minneapolis City Attorney was of the opinion that since the Zurich's "combining agreement" proposal now provided payment and performance bonds, the Subguard product complied with Minn. Stat. § 574.26. The MSA contended, however, that the legislature did not allow a municipality the *option* to use payment and performance bonds; instead, the law *required* that bonds be used. The MSA argued that the effective limits of the Subguard insurance option were less than the limits provided by surety bonds and that a municipality should not have the discretion to chose an option that left its citizens with less protection than what the legislature had prescribed. Ultimately, the legality of Zurich's "combining agreement" was never tested in court because the City chose not to utilize Zurich's proposal.

2. The Respective Costs of Traditional Surety Bonds Compared to Subguard

Zurich criticized the cost of traditional bonding and claimed that excessively large percentages of the bond premiums were used to cover underwriting expenses not losses. Zurich promised the City that the cost of the Subguard program would be far less than traditional surety bonds. In making this comparison, Zurich used $12.50 per thousand as an average cost of surety bonds and assumed that all prime contractors *and* the entire first tier of subcontractors would be bonded.

The MSA and Surety Association of America ("SAA") responded that the cost of traditional surety bonds as stated by Zurich was greatly inflated and that it would be more appropriate to use a figure of $6.00 per thousand in calculating the actual cost of surety bonds. The MSA also pointed out that it was unrealistic to assume that the entire first tier of subcontractors would be bonded because this does not reflect industry practice. Therefore, based on MSA's and SAA's calculations, it appeared that traditional bonding would cost less than the Subguard product.

3. Whether the Traditional Surety Bonds or the Subguard Product Promotes More Inclusion of Minority Contractors

The minority contracting community in Minneapolis wanted assurances that it would perform a large percentage of construction for the new project. Zurich alleged that the requirement of traditional surety bonds was antithetical to this goal because surety underwriting practices often excluded minority contractors from receiving bonding. Zurich claimed that its Subguard product was more inclusive of minority participation because all subcontractors would be covered under its Subguard policy irrespective of whether the subcontractors could obtain bonding. Perhaps more than any other, this claim by Zurich peaked the City's interest in the Subguard product throughout the debate.

The surety industry responded to this issue in a variety of ways. First, the MSA and SAA pointed out that the issue was largely illusory because the prime contractor's bidding on the major bid packages would likely not be minority contractors. Therefore, the requirement that prime contractors post surety bonds was not, in reality, preventing minority participation in the project at the subcontractor level.

Implicit in Zurich's comments was a charge that the surety industry was not interested in encouraging minority participation in the construction market. The surety industry, and the MSA in particular, took strong exception to these allegations. First, the MSA membership sent the City scores of letters explaining how many of their members devoted their entire practice to soliciting and developing minority contractors as clients. Second, the industry explained that minority contractors represented a new market for premium revenues and that it would be irrational (and therefore highly unlikely) for the surety industry to have been ignoring this vast, potential market. Third, even though the surety industry felt it was spending significant resources to develop the minority construction market, the MSA promised to do even more. Accordingly, the MSA established a surety outreach program which promised to team any minority contractor that had been denied surety credit with a seasoned surety agent who would assist the minority contractor through the underwriting process. In addition, the MSA promised to conduct several seminars for the minority community not only on how to obtain surety credit, but also on the basics of how to operate a successful construction company. Finally, the MSA established liaisons with various SBE groups and established a working relationship with the Minneapolis SBE department to devise other initiatives to encourage minority participation in public construction. The City found these efforts particularly significant in concluding that the requirement of surety bonding would not preclude minority participation on this particular project or, hopefully, on future projects.

Third, the surety industry argued that the Subguard product was not as "inclusive" as Zurich claimed. Initially, Zurich retained the right to decide which subcontractors qualified for the Subguard program. The surety industry pointed out that Zurich's ability to reject proposed subcontractors was the equivalent of surety underwriting and, therefore, no more inclusive. Moreover, the surety industry alleged that Zurich's right to decide who would qualify for the program amounted to directed suretyship which was legally and practically problematic.

As a result of these criticisms, Zurich later dropped its demand that it be allowed to prequalify subcontractor participants in the Subguard program. This decision, however, raised additional problems. The surety industry pointed out that with no prequalification procedure, the City was exposed to bids from irresponsible contractors. One of the benefits of traditional surety bonds was the underwriting or prequalification due diligence that the surety industry performed. Historically, public owners have typically depended on the surety industry to determine bidder responsibility. In contrast, the Zurich proposal would have required the City to undertake the responsibility of prequalifying bidders, which was a procedure the City was not well equipped to perform.

In addition, the Zurich program was now so inclusive that there was no assurance that minority contractors would receive any greater share of subcontracts. In other words, without any prequalification, subcontracts could be awarded to the lowest priced subcontractor irrespective of whether it was a minority contractor, and the Subguard policy would assume the risk of that subcontractor's performance failure. In this sense, Zurich's proposal was "over inclusive" in that it did not target minority contractors.

Finally, the debate over prequalification highlighted a significant difference between the Subguard product and traditional surety bonding. The surety industry contended that the underwriting and prequalification process was actually a benefit to minority contractors because it ensured that they had the systems in place to promote long term success after the Convention Center Addition project was over. The MSA pointed to history to prove its point. The first Convention Center project had a high level of minority contractor participation, but ten years later very few of those minority contractors were still in business. The MSA concluded that participation itself does not promote long-term success unless the participants put in place the systems and practices necessary for continued survival after the project was over. In contrast to Subguard, the surety industry argued that its agents seek to establish long-term relationships with contractors that focus on developing the systems, resources, and experience necessary to survive in a competitive marketplace. In its final decision to select surety bonding for the remainder of the Project, the City emphasized the benefit to the minority contracting community of establishing a surety relationship to better ensure its viability after the Project was concluded.

4. Whether There Were Advantages to More City Involvement in Loss Control Management

One advantage marketed by Zurich was a rebate of premium should the claims or losses on the Project be less than anticipated. This option of a premium rebate was only available if the City decided to manage its losses through the insurance part of the program rather than through the surety bonds that Zurich would provide. If the City decided to handle the claim through Subguard's insurance policy, the City would have to finance the loss, tender its claim for reimbursement to the insurance carrier, and then also subrogate its position to Zurich to allow Zurich to recover from the party responsible for the loss. Obviously, the prospect of a rebate is attractive to any municipality, and the City also debated the merits of this aspect of Zurich's proposal.

The surety industry countered Zurich's claim in two ways. First, the MSA and the SAA pointed out that the promised savings came at a considerable price. The terms of the Subguard insurance policy were untested and its scope of actual coverage unknown. In contrast, the terms of and the claims allowable pursuant to bonds have a long history of judicial interpretation upon which municipalities can rely with assurance. In addition, when there is a claim under a surety bond, the surety is responsible for resolving the claim. On the other hand, the Subguard insurance policy requires the City to resolve the claim using its own resources which requires an experienced staff which municipalities are often not equipped to provide.

Second, based on its analysis, the surety industry contended that even with the full rebate promised by Zurich, the Subguard policy was still more expensive than traditional surety bonds. The surety industry argued that this only made logical sense because the Subguard program was actually an insurance policy *and* surety bonds combined together, so the Subguard program should cost more than surety bonds standing alone. If the cost of the Subguard program even *with* a full rebate was more than the cost of traditional surety bonds, then there was no advantage to the City in allocating staff resources to managing claims under the Subguard program when they could avoid this expense through traditional surety bonds.

Because each side of the debate posited different cost assumptions, it was difficult for the City to conclude which option would truly have been less expensive. Although the City was intrigued by the potential cost savings promised by Zurich, the City appeared to rest its final decision on the effect that its selection would have on the City's minority contracting community. In this regard, the City concluded that encouraging the minority contracting community to establish long term surety relationships was in the community's best interest. Relying heavily on the MSA's promise to encourage and foster such long term relationships, the City Council voted to continue to use traditional surety bonds on the remainder of the project, but cautioned that it would revisit the issue should the City continue to hear complaints that the surety industry was not responsive to the needs of the minority community. Therefore, continued use of traditional surety bonds for public projects in Minneapolis and other major metropolitan areas will depend significantly on how responsive the surety industry is to the emerging minority construction community.

Conclusion

Directed suretyship and its cousin, contractor default insurance both restrict competition and are incompatible with open public bidding. On private projects, default insurance clearly provides less coverage and no prequalification without a counter balancing cost saving. Suretyship has evolved as the method to guard against contractor or subcontractor default because it is the most cost effective alternative available.

Renewal of: ______

Policy Number ______

SUBGUARD POLICY

DECLARATIONS

Item 1.

Named Insured: ______________________________

____

Mailing Address: ______________________________

____

Named Insured is:

☐ Individual ☐ Partnership ☐ Corporation

☐ Other -

Producer Name and Address:

Item 2. Policy Period:

From (effective date):

To (expiration date):

at 12:01 a.m. standard time at the above mailing address.

Producer Code:

IN RETURN FOR THE PAYMENT OF PREMIUM AND SUBJECT TO ALL THE TERMS OF THIS POLICY, WE AGREE WITH YOU TO PROVIDE THE INSURANCE AS STATED IN THIS POLICY.

Item 3. Limits Of Liability

$ ______________ Annual Aggregate Limit of Liability

$ ______________ Subcontractor/Supplier Limit of Liability

Item 4. Annual Indirect Costs Sublimit

$ ______________ Each Subcontractor/Supplier

Item 5. Non-Qualifying Loss Limit

$ ______________ Each Loss

Item 6. Deductible: $ ________ Each Qualifying Loss

Deductible Aggregate: $ __________ All Qualifying Losses (Including any Co-Payments Made by the Insured)

Item 7. Co-Payment Percentage: _____% Each Qualifying Loss up to $__________ in Excess of the Deductible.

Item 8. Advanced Percentage: _____%

Total Estimated Policy Premium $______________. This amount is Adjustable Annually at Audit at a Rate of $____________ per ______________ of Unbonded Subcontracts and Purchase Orders. (This premium does not include taxes and surcharges.)

Countersigned this _____ day of ______________________ ______________________.

Authorized Representative

Throughout this Policy the words "you" and "your" refer to the **Insured** shown in the Declarations and any other person or organization qualifying as an **Insured** under this Policy. The words "we", "us", and "our" refer to the company providing this insurance.

In consideration of the payment of premium, in reliance upon the statements in the Declarations, Application and **Qualification Procedures** made a part hereof, and subject to all terms of this Policy, we agree with you as follows:

I. INSURING AGREEMENT

We will indemnify you for **Loss** that exceeds the amount stated in item 5. of the Declarations after application of the deductible stated in item 6. of the Declarations and after application of your **Co-Payment Percentage** designated in item 7. of the Declarations, directly caused by the **Default of Performance** of the **Subcontractor/Supplier** under the terms of the **Subcontract or Purchase Order Agreement** executed during the **Policy Period.**

II. DEFINITIONS

A. **Balance of the Subcontractor/Supplier Price** means the total amount payable by you to the **Subcontractor/Supplier** under the terms of the **Subcontract or Purchase Order Agreement** and the amount the Subcontractor/Supplier would be entitled to after **Default of Performance** for additional work, less the amount actually paid by you to the **Subcontractor/Supplier.**

B. **Co-Payment Percentage** is the portion of **Qualifying Loss**, after application of the deductible, which is your responsibility and for which we will not indemnify you.

C. **Default of Performance** means failure of the Subcontractor/Supplier to fulfill the terms of the **Subcontract or Purchase Order Agreement.**

D. **Indirect Costs** mean costs and expenses paid by you as a result of a **Default of Performance** of a Subcontractor/Supplier and are not specifically included in Definition G, **Loss**, item 1. through 4. **Indirect Costs** and expenses include, but are not limited to, those paid by you because of liquidated damages, job acceleration, and extended overhead.

E. **Insolvency/Insolvent** means that any of the following steps, or equivalent steps, have been taken by or against a Subcontractor/Supplier by or in a court having jurisdiction over, the **Subcontractor/Supplier's** affairs or pursuant to a statute applicable to the Subcontractor/Supplier and its creditors:

1. Bankruptcy or insolvency is adjudicated against the **Subcontractor/Supplier.**
2. Voluntary or involuntary proceedings are initiated under Chapter 7 or Chapter 11 of the Federal Bankruptcy Code of the United States or any similar statute in another country.
3. A voluntary resolution is accepted by the **Subcontractor/Supplier** or a Court order is issued for the winding-up or liquidation of the **Subcontractor/Supplier's** affairs.

F. **Insured** means the person(s) or entity(ies) named or designated in item 1. of the Declarations or designated as an **Insured** by endorsement to this Policy.

G. **Loss** means the cost and expenses paid by you as a result of a **Default of Performance** of a **Subcontractor/Supplier** under the terms of a **Subcontract or Purchase Order Agreement** and includes:

1. Cost of completing **Subcontractor/Supplier's** obligations under the **Subcontract or Purchase Order Agreement.**
2. Cost of correcting defective or nonconforming work or materials.
3. Legal and other professional expenses incurred by you resulting directly from the **Subcontractor/Supplier Default of Performance.**
4. Costs, charges, and expenses incurred in the investigation, adjustment, and defense of disputes of such **Qualifying Loss.**
5. **Indirect Costs.**

Less the **Balance of the Subcontractor/Supplier Price.**

H. **Policy Period** means the period of time set forth in item 2. of the Declarations or any shorter period of time arising as a result of termination or cancellation of this Policy.

I. **Qualification Procedures** means the written criteria to which you adhere to assure that the **Subcontractor/Supplier** will be able to carry out the terms of the **Subcontract or Purchase Order Agreement.**

J. **Qualifying Loss** means the total amount of the **Losses** that exceed the amount stated in item 5. of the Declarations which are incurred and paid by you solely and directly as a result of a **Default of Performance**, subject to any applicable limits and sublimits.

K. **Subcontract or Purchase Order Agreement** means the signed, written agreement, order form, invoice, or other written document, customarily utilized by you, to evidence the agreement between you and your **Subcontractor/Suppliers**, as such may be amended from time to time.

L. **Subcontractor/Supplier** means:

1. A duly organized and legally existing entity which has entered into a **Subcontract or Purchase Order Agreement** with you, except for any subsidiary, subsidiary of a subsidiary whether direct or indirect, affiliated company or partnership, joint venture or corporation of any **Insured** or others not named herein, now existing or hereafter formed or acquired, and whether partially or wholly owned or controlled, which shall be excluded from coverage.

2. The receiver, trustee, liquidator, administrator, or similar representative of any **Subcontractor/Supplier** as described in **1.**, or its creditors, or the **Subcontractor/Supplier** as described in **1.** as debtor in possession under Chapter 11 of the Federal Bankruptcy Code or any similar statute in another country.

3. Any successor to such duly organized and legally existing corporation, proprietorship, receiver, trustee, liquidator, administrator, or similar representative referred to in **1.** and **2.**

4. Any corporation and other entity controlling, controlled by, or under common control of such duly organized and legally existing corporation, proprietorship, receiver, trustee, liquidator, administrator, or similar representative referred to in 1., 2., and 3.

III. EXCLUSIONS

This insurance does not apply to **Qualifying Loss**:

A. Arising from any **Subcontractor/Supplier** that is in **Default of Performance** by you on the first day of the **Policy Period**, unless this is a renewal of a Policy previously issued by us, in which case you must disclose such **Default of Performance** at the time the renewal Application is completed. Such disclosure will extend this insurance to the **Subcontractor/Supplier**, unless the **Subcontractor/Supplier** is specifically excluded by endorsement to this Policy. Failure to make such disclosure will exclude insurance for the **Subcontractor/Supplier** under this renewal Policy.

B. Arising from any **Subcontractor/Supplier** about which you provided us inaccurate information and which we would not have agreed to provide insurance coverage if such information had been accurate.

This paragraph does not apply if the inaccurate information was based on the representation or statements of third parties and were true to the best of your knowledge, after a reasonable investigation.

C. Arising from any **Subcontract or Purchase Order Agreement** that are purchased or otherwise acquired by you from any other person or entity, or sold or otherwise transferred by you to any other person or entity. However, this exclusion shall not apply to any **Subcontractor/Supplier** which you are required by the Owner to use at inception pursuant the contract between the project owner and the **Insured**.

D. Arising from any dishonest or fraudulent act or any dishonest or fraudulent omission committed by you or your agents.

E. Arising from any material breach of or inaccuracy regarding any **Warranty or Covenants** made herein or failure to perform or to fulfill any warranty, covenant, or agreement made by you.

F. Arising from nuclear reaction or nuclear radiation or radioactive contamination.

G. Arising from any consequence, whether direct or indirect, of war, invasion, act of foreign enemy, hostilities (whether war be declared or not), civil war, rebellion, revolution, insurrection or military or usurped power, riot, or civil commotion.

H. Arising out of the rendering of or the failure to render professional services by an **Insured**, including (a) the preparation or approval of maps, drawings, opinions, reports, surveys, designs, or specifications and (b) supervisory inspection or engineering services.

IV. TERRITORY

This insurance only applies to claims made or brought in the United States, its territories or possessions, Canada, or Puerto Rico.

V. DEDUCTIBLE AND INSURED CO-PAYMENT PERCENTAGE

The deductible is the amount of each **Qualifying Loss** which is to be borne by you with respect to each and every **Qualifying Loss** to which this Policy applies. The amount of the deductible is stated in item **6.** of the Declarations.

Your **Co-Payment Percentage** applies to each **Qualifying Loss** after application of the deductible, if applicable, as stated in item 7. of the Declarations.

Your total liability for all deductible and co-payment amounts for **Qualifying Loss** to which this insurance applies shall not exceed the deductible aggregate amount shown in item 6. of the Declarations.

Your rights and duties in the event of a **Default of Performance** apply irrespective of the application of the deductible amount and your **Co-Payment Percentage**.

VI. LIMITS OF LIABILITY

A. The limits of insurance shown in the Declarations and the rules below determine the most we will pay regardless of the number of:

1. Insureds, subcontractors, suppliers;
2. Claims or suits brought; or
3. Persons or organizations making claims or bringing suits.

B. Our total liability for all **Qualifying Losses** in excess of the deductible and co-payment amounts from all **Defaults of Performance** shall not exceed the limit of liability shown in the Declarations item 3., Annual Aggregate Limit of Liability.

Once the Aggregate Limit of Liability in any **Policy Period** has been completely eroded, we shall have no further obligation to indemnify you for **Qualifying Losses**.

C. Subject to B. above, the Limit of Liability shown in Declarations item 3., **Subcontractor/Supplier** Limit of Liability, is the most we will pay for **Qualifying Losses** in excess of the deductible and co-pay amounts from **Default of Performance** arising out of any one **Subcontractor/Supplier**.

D. Subject to **B.** and **C.** above, the Limit of Liability shown in the Declarations item 4., Annual Indirect Costs Sublimit is the most we will pay for **Qualifying Losses** in excess of the deductible and co-pay amounts for **Indirect** Costs arising out of the Default of Performance of any one **Subcontractor/Supplier**.

VII. PROOF OF PAYMENT OF CLAIMS AND RECOVERIES

You must submit to us a satisfactory written proof of loss which documents the Loss as a Qualifying Loss and quantifies the amount of the Loss.

Our indemnification of your Qualifying Loss shall be calculated as follows, subject to the provisions of this Policy:

1. Calculate the amount of the Qualifying Loss.
2. Subtract the deductible from the lesser of either the Qualifying Loss or the applicable Subcontractor/Supplier Limit of Liability.
3. Multiply the lesser of either the amount determined in 2. above or the amount shown in Declarations item 7. by the **Co-Payment Percentage**.
4. Subtract the amount determined in 3. above from the amount determined in 2. above.

The payment for a **Qualifying Loss** will be made within thirty (30) days after we accept a satisfactory proof of loss.

You are responsible for proving a **Qualifying Loss** under this Policy and evidencing compliance with all conditions, warranties, and covenants. You may submit interim proofs of Loss for Losses that occur over a period of time greater than thirty (30) days.

If an amount would constitute a **Qualifying Loss** except that the amount of the **Qualifying Loss** or the **Default of Performance of Subcontractor/Supplier** has not been finally determined, we will pay you the Advanced Percentage, as stated in item **8.** of the Declarations, of the **Loss** payment which would have been payable as calculated above, after we accept a satisfactory proof of loss. You must immediately return the advance payment to us if it is finally determined that the **Loss** is not a **Qualifying Loss**.

In the event you and we cannot agree that a claim is a **Qualifying Loss** or cannot agree on the amount of loss you have incurred and paid, arbitration proceedings will commence in accordance with Section IX, Paragraph M.

You must cooperate with us in the investigation, settlement, or defense of any claim or suit; and you must assist us, upon request, in the enforcement of any right against any person or organization which may be liable to you because of loss to which this insurance applies.

After payment of the **Qualifying** Loss, any such funds or salvage will be paid to us and shared between you and us as follows:

1. First, we will be fully reimbursed for our costs of recovery, and the insured percentage of all sums recovered. Then you shall receive the remaining percentage of such sums until the amount of our payment of the **Qualifying Loss** and our cost of recovery have been fully reimbursed.
2. All further sums recovered shall be retained by you.

The application of amounts recovered as described above apply regardless of any designation of amounts by the **Subcontractor/Supplier** or any other party.

VIII. WARRANTY AND COVENANTS

You warrant and agree:

A. To cease awarding contracts to any **Subcontractor/Supplier** that is in **Default of Performance** and for so long as the **Subcontractor/Supplier** is in **Default of Performance**, unless the aggregate sum of such defaulted obligations that have not been disputed by the **Subcontractor/Supplier** in writing does not exceed the amount stated in item 5. of the Declarations, or unless we otherwise consent.

B. That in the event of the **Insolvency** of the **Subcontractor/Supplier**, you shall immediately take all steps necessary to establish the debt owed by the **Subcontractor/Supplier** to you as a valid obligation of the **Subcontractor/Supplier** in accordance with any applicable statutes and procedures.

C. To use all reasonable measures to prevent and to minimize the **Loss** at all times including filing any claims and enforcing any liens or security interests against a **Subcontractor/Supplier** or its property.

D. To retain without recourse to any party the amount of the deductible and co-payment amounts.

X. CONDITIONS

A. INSPECTION AND AUDIT

We shall be permitted but not obligated to inspect, sample, and monitor on a continuous basis an **Insured's** property or operations at any time. We shall be permitted to examine or require to be produced copies of any corporate records or books, internal documents and correspondence, letters, or other documentation or records, in whatever form and wherever situated in your possession or control relating to or connected with this Policy or to any transaction between you and a **Subcontractor/Supplier.** At our request, you must take any and all reasonable steps to obtain such information in the possession of others relating to or connected with this Policy or any **Qualifying Loss.**

B. CANCELLATION

You are not permitted to cancel this Policy.

We are not permitted to cancel this Policy, except for nonpayment of premium, upon a **Change in the Composition of the Insured**, as provided in Section **IX**, Paragraph C, or upon repeated violations in the application of your **Qualification Procedures.** In the event of such cancellation, we must mail to you at the address shown in this Policy written notice stating not less than ten (10) days thereafter such cancellation shall be effective. The mailing of notice shall be sufficient proof of notice. If the Policy is canceled, a pro-rata return of premium shall be made.

The effective date of cancellation stated in the notice shall become the end of the **Policy Period.** Delivery or facsimile of such written notice shall be equivalent to mailing.

C. CHANGE IN THE COMPOSITION OF THE INSURED

You must notify us in writing if, during the **Policy Period**, you consolidate, merge with, or sell all or substantially all of your assets to any other person or entity, or if another person or entity should acquire beneficial ownership of shares having a majority of the ordinary voting power in the election of directors. Upon receipt of such notice, we may cancel this Policy effective with the date of such change in the composition or control of the **Insured.**

D. CHOICE OF LAW

In the event that you and we dispute the meaning, interpretation, or operation of any term, condition, definition, or provision of this Policy resulting in litigation, arbitration, or other form of dispute resolution, the law of the state of New York shall apply and all litigation, arbitration, or other form of dispute resolution shall take place in New York.

E. ASSIGNMENT

Assignment of interest under this Policy shall not bind us unless our consent is endorsed to the Policy.

F. OTHER INSURANCE

This insurance shall be excess over any other valid bond, insurance, or other indemnity available to you by the **Subcontractor/Supplier.** You must inform us of any bond, insurance, or other indemnity in place at the inception of the Policy, or as they may arise during the **Policy Period.**

Where this insurance is excess, we will pay only our share of the amount of **Loss**, if any, that exceeds the total amount that all such other insurance would pay for the **Loss** in the absence of this insurance.

G. ACTION AGAINST US

No claim, action or arbitration proceedings arising out of this Policy may be brought against us unless you have complied with all terms of the Policy and such action is commenced (a) within seven (7) years following the last day of completion of any **Subcontract or Purchase Order Agreement** entered into during the **Policy Period**, or (b) within six (6) months after our first disposition of a specific claim which is the cause of the action or proceeding, whichever event occurs later.

H. FALSE OR FRAUDULENT STATEMENTS, REPORT OR CLAIMS, CONCEALMENT

If you make any statement, report, or claim known to be false or fraudulent, or if you knowingly conceal any material fact, this Policy shall become void and all claims made and premium paid hereunder shall be forfeited, and all payment made by us shall be returned with interest by you upon demand.

I. REPORTING

You shall give written notice to us within ten (10) days after you are aware that any **Subcontractor/Supplier** may be in **Default of Performance** or is **Insolvent.**

You shall give written notice to us within ten (10) days after you determine that a **Loss** has reasonable potential to develop into an amount greater than that stated in item 5. of the Declarations.

J. CHANGES

Notice to any agent or by any other persons shall not effect a waiver or a change in any part of the Policy or stop us from asserting any right under the terms of this Policy; nor shall the terms of this Policy be waived or changed, except by endorsement issued to form a part of the Policy.

K. SOLE AGENT

The **Insured** named in item 1. of the Declarations shall act on behalf of all **Insureds** for all purposes, including but not limited to the payment or return of premium, receipt, and acceptance of any endorsement issued to form a part of this Policy, complying with all applicable notice provisions, giving and receiving notice of cancellation or nonrenewal.

L. DECLARATIONS

By acceptance of this Policy, you agree that the statements in the Declarations and Application are your agreements and representations, that this Policy is issued in reliance upon the truth of such representations, and that this Policy embodies all agreements existing between you and us or any of your agents relating to this insurance.

Furthermore, you warrant and represent that you have no knowledge at Policy inception of any circumstances that may reasonably result in a **Qualified Loss**, except for that which is specifically disclosed in the Application.

M. ARBITRATION

In the event you and we agree to resolve a dispute by arbitration, any such arbitration shall be in accordance with the Commercial Arbitration Rule of the American Arbitration Association.